Ancrene Wisse

Middle English Texts

The Middle English Texts Series is designed for classroom use. Its goal is to make available to teachers and students texts which occupy an important place in the literary and cultural canon but which have not been readily available in student editions. The series does not include those authors such as Chaucer, Langland, or Malory, whose English works are normally in print in good student editions. The focus is, instead, upon Middle English literature adjacent to those authors that teachers need in compiling the syllabuses they wish to teach. The editions maintain the linguistic integrity of the original work but within the parameters of modern reading conventions. The texts are printed in the modern alphabet and follow the practices of modern capitalization and punctuation. Manuscript abbreviations are silently expanded, and *u/v* and *j/i* spellings are regularized according to modern orthography. Hard words, difficult phrases, and unusual idioms are glossed on the page, either in the right margin or at the foot of the page. Explanatory and textual notes appear at the end of the text, along with a glossary. The editions include short introductions on the history of the work, its merits and points of topical interest, and also include briefly annotated bibliographies.

Ancrene Wisse

Edited by
Robert Hasenfratz

Published for TEAMS
(The Consortium for the Teaching of the Middle Ages)
in Association with the University of Rochester

by

Medieval Institute Publications

WESTERN MICHIGAN UNIVERSITY

Kalamazoo, Michigan — 2000

Library of Congress Cataloging-in-Publication Data

Ancren riwle.
    Ancrene wisse / edited by Robert Hasenfratz.
        p. cm. -- (Middle English texts)
    Includes bibliographical references and indexes.
    ISBN 1-58044-070-3 (alk. paper)
    1. Monasticism and religious orders for women--Rules--Early works to 1800. 2.
Spiritual life--Catholic Church--Early works to 1800. 3. Christian literature, English
(Middle) I. Hasenfratz, Robert J., 1957- II. Title. III. Middle English texts (Kalamazoo,
Mich.)

PR1806 .H37 2000
255'.901--dc21

                                                                                    00-045252

ISBN 1-58044-070-3

Cover design by Linda K. Judy

For my family

Contents

Preface

This project had its beginnings in a graduate seminar in Early Middle English I taught at the University of Connecticut in the spring of 1994. I am much indebted to the wonderful group of students in that seminar, especially Wendy Goldberg and Kathryn Laity, who helped me think about the overall shape of this edition and who also put in many hours helping to type in and proofread the preliminary text.

I have many more people to thank: Linda Georgianna gave some very helpful advice at the beginning of the project, while Nicholas Watson and Richard Dance offered valuable suggestions for the glossary. The sessions organized by Susannah Chewing on Anchoritic Spirituality at the International Congress on Medieval Studies in Kalamazoo have proved wonderfully helpful and inspiring. In a conversation at a recent session, Alexandra Barratt helped me to put Dobson's claims for *Moralities on the Gospels* in a more skeptical light, and Anne Savage's ideas about collaborative authorship have influenced several elements of the introduction.

Much of the glossary was composed while I was a visiting fellow at Clare Hall, Cambridge, and I wish to thank the Master and Fellows for their hospitality and stimulating lunch-time conversation. I am also grateful to Gill Cannell for making my visit to the Parker Library (Corpus Christi College) so pleasant and to Robert Edwards for helping me to slip more confidently into the role of editor.

My thanks go to the Research Foundation at the University of Connecticut for providing financial support for this edition. I am also grateful to Frederick Biggs for reading and providing valuable advice about the introduction; to Elizabeth Robertson, David Benson and Thomas Jambeck for their encouragement and enthusiasm; to Christine Cooper for reading and commenting on the introduction and explanatory notes; and to Rachel Bertoni for helping me to shape ideas of community.

I reserve special thanks to Russell Peck and the TEAMS editorial staff for their unflagging patience and incredible hard work. Jennifer Church and Ann Robinson put in literally hundreds of hours on this volume; Mara Amster and Dana Symons proofed portions of the manuscript and prepared the final camera-ready copy; and Alan Lupack read the entire text carefully. I also wish to thank the National Endowment for the Humanities for its generous support of the Middle English Texts Series.

Finally, I must thank my friends and especially my family for sustaining me through the long years of editing.

Ancrene Wisse

Introduction

Ancrene Wisse or the "Anchoresses' Guide" (Cambridge, Corpus Christi College, MS 402), written sometime roughly between 1225 and 1240, represents a revision of an earlier work, usually called the *Ancrene Riwle* or "Anchorites' Rule,"[1] a book of religious instruction for three lay women of noble birth, sisters, who had themselves enclosed as anchoresses somewhere in the West Midlands, perhaps somewhere between Worcester and Wales. The author was apparently either an Augustinian canon or a Dominican friar, and by the time of the revision, *Ancrene Wisse*'s readership had expanded to include a much wider community of anchoresses, over twenty in number according to the text,[2] scattered mainly in the west of England.

This edition provides a reading text of the entire Corpus version.

Ancrene Wisse's Place in Literary History

It may at first seem startling that such a vivid and sophisticated vernacular prose as one finds in *Ancrene Wisse* (henceforth *AW*) and its related texts sprang to life in the Welsh borders and at a time (the early thirteenth century) when English was not at all a prized medium for serious religious instruction. *AW*, however, was written in a vernacular literary culture which in some senses stretched back to the late Anglo-Saxon period. The homilies of Ælfric and Wulfstan continued to be copied well into the twelfth century in Worcester, where they were also annotated and studied in the thirteenth. As Thorlac Turville-Petre writes, "This suggests a tradition of respect for works in English that must have itself acted as a stimulus to writings throughout the thirteenth century. Indeed, the quality and diversity of the English texts composed or copied in this region is striking."[3] These texts include such important monuments of early Middle English as Layamon's *Brut* and *The Owl and the Nightingale* as well as MS Digby 86, which contains *Dame Sirith*, perhaps the earliest fabliau in English. The situation

---

[1] For a further discussion of the title, see Explanatory Note to Pref.1.

[2] See Explanatory Notes to 4.164 and 4.916 ff.

[3] *England the Nation*, p. 182. See the Select Bibliography for full reference.

must have been different in the East Midlands, which gave birth to the much rougher *Ormulum*.

Thus, in West Midlands English, the *AW* author found a language already adapted to literary uses. E. K. Chambers, in his classic study, *The Continuity of English Prose from Alfred to More and his School*, argued that the *AW* author carried on the work of late Old English writers such as Æthelwold and Ælfric, and that *AW* acted something like a linguistic Noah's arc, preserving English traditions in a time of Anglo-Norman and French deluge: "The *Ancren Riwle* therefore occupies a vital position in the history of English prose. Its popularity extends over the darkest period of our literature."[4] As Bella Millett has pointed out, however, this view of *AW* and its related texts as vessels of "Englishness" ignores the strong continental influence on the *AW*'s exegetical prose which was shaped in large part by twelfth-century Latin literature.[5] Though it has some important connections to late Old English, then, *AW*'s vernacular prose does not descend directly from it.

Why the Vernacular?

One question remains, however: Despite the fact that the *AW* author had a form of literary English at his disposal, it is not at first clear why he chose it as a vehicle for the rather advanced religious instruction of *AW* when, in the early thirteenth century, Latin or French would have been a more natural medium.[6] One answer to this question lies in the nature of *AW*'s audience, a group of quasi-lay women, some of high birth. Though they could apparently read French (see 1.340), the fact that almost all the Latin quotations are translated into English suggests that their literacy in Latin was limited and thus that they were not nuns. *AW* was composed in English, then, because it was written for lay people, though of a very special type (see the section on "Audience" below), because it was written for women (whose educational opportunities were much more restricted than those of men), and because it was composed in a region which valued English literary culture.

The Anchoritic Life

Medieval anchorites, as strange as it may seem to us, sought to withdraw so radically from the world that they had themselves sealed into cells for life. In fact, the word *anchorite* comes

---

[4] See p. xcvii.

[5] See "*Hali Meiðhad, Sawles Warde*, and the Continuity of English Prose," pp. 107–08.

[6] Indeed, *AW* was translated into both these languages within a hundred and fifty years of its composition — a curious reversal of the usual direction of translation.

ultimately from the Greek verb *ἀναχωρέ–ειν*, which means "to withdraw." Anchorites (both men and women) withdrew from the world not only to avoid physical temptation, but to engage in the kind of spiritual warfare practiced by desert saints like St. Anthony (the founder of Western monasticism), who around 285 A.D. wandered into the Egyptian desert searching for God through complete solitude and who attempted to tame the wickedness of the body with physical suffering and discipline.

Desert Spirituality

In the fourth and fifth centuries, a number of holy men and women like St. Anthony retired to the Egyptian desert to seek a severe life of solitude. In many senses they were something like spiritual athletes. In fact, the word *ascesis* (from which *asceticism* derives) referred originally to the regimen of exercise practiced by athletes. *AW* refers admiringly to some of the superstars of the desert: Anthony, Paul the Hermit, Macarius, Arsenius, Sarah, Synceltica, Hilarion, retelling their feats of perseverance and discipline from a text known as the *Vitas Patrum* (*The Lives of the [Desert] Fathers*).[7] Peter Brown manages to recapture some of the excitement of desert spirituality, and his remarks are worth quoting at some length:

> It is precisely the bleak and insistent physicality of ascetic anecdotes [in the *Lives of the Desert Fathers*] that shocks the modern reader. They have led scholars to speak of "Contempt for the human condition and hatred of the body" as the principal motive that led the monks to undergo so much physical privation. Far from confirming this view, the mood prevalent among the Desert Fathers implicitly contradicts it. The ascetics imposed severe restraints on their bodies because they were convinced that they could sweep the body into a desperate venture. For the average ascetics — ordinary, pious Christian men and women, squatting in cells within sight of the green fields of their villages . . . — the imagined transfiguration of the few great ascetics, on earth, spoke to them of the eventual transformation of their own bodies on the day of Resurrection.[8]

In a sense, the lure of desert spirituality lay in its promise of recapturing paradise and restoring fallen human bodies to their Edenic state. Brown continues,

> It takes some effort of the modern imagination to recapture this aspect of the ascetic life . . . The bodies of Adam and Eve . . . had acted like a finely tuned engine, capable of "idling" indefinitely. It was only the twisted will of fallen men that had crammed the body with unnecessary food, thereby generating in it the dire surplus of energy that showed itself in

---

[7] See Explanatory Notes to Pref.99–101 and 2.310.

[8] *Body and Society*, p. 222.

physical appetite, in anger, and in the sexual urge. In reducing the intake to which he had become accustomed, the ascetic slowly remade his body. He turned it into an exactly calibrated instrument. Its drastic physical changes, after years of ascetic discipline, registered . . . the long return of the human person, body and soul together, to an original, natural and uncorrupted state.[9]

To remake their fallen bodies, some desert ascetics were willing to undertake extreme physical disciplines. John the Hermit, for example, is said to have survived on nothing but the Eucharist for three years, while in the fifth century Symeon the Stylite lived for over forty years atop a column nearly fifty feet tall.[10] Others wore heavy chains or made their diets out of the sparest or most disgusting foods. In general, *AW* seems to admire such feats of physical mortification, and in Part Six mentions a man who is searching for new and more potent ways to subdue his body — heavy chains and hair shirts have little effect on him, so he prays for a severe illness, despairing that God will send him no real pain (see 6.417–28 ff.). The *AW* author, however, does not recommend such severe disciplines for his own charges, and in fact calls for moderation (see 3.221–22, 4.540–45, 8.27–29, and, especially, 8.101–09).

Another aspect of desert spirituality which profoundly influenced *AW* is its sense that the spiritual life requires an almost physical battle against the devil. The following anecdote is told about Helle, a desert saint:

> One of the brethren, desiring to be saved, asked him [Helle] if he might live with him in the desert. He replied that he would not be able to bear the temptations of the demons, but the brother contradicted him vehemently and promised to bear all things. And so the father accepted him and recommended that he should live in a neighbouring cave. The demons appeared at night and tried to strangle the brother, after first shaking him with obscene thoughts. He ran out of his cave and told Abba Helle all that had happened. The father drew a line around the place and commanded his disciple henceforth to remain in it without fear.[11]

It is no accident that two of the saints in the Katherine Group (see the section on "Related Texts" below), Margaret and Juliana, wrestle physically with demons, while Part Four of *AW* (on temptations) takes spiritual battle as its central metaphor. For many solitaries entering a dank anchorhold in England must have seemed like stepping into the parched landscape of the Egyptian desert.

---

[9] *Body and Society*, p. 223.

[10] For the account of John the Hermit, see Russell's translation of *The Lives of the Desert Fathers*, p. 23. An anecdote about Symeon the Stylite can be found in Ward's translation, *The Sayings of the Desert Fathers*, p. 47.

[11] Russell, *The Lives of the Desert Fathers*, p. 91.

Introduction

Becoming an Anchorite

To become an anchorite in England (from the twelfth century on) involved making an application of sorts to a bishop. As Ann K. Warren makes clear in her study *Anchorites and their Patrons in Medieval England*, bishops had the primary responsibility for investigating the claims of any would-be anchorites:

> Legal responsibility for recluses was vested in the bishop. It was a fivefold charge. The bishop, usually through a commission set up for this purpose, first ruled on the personal credentials of the candidate — on his [or her] fitness for such a life — sometimes ordering a probationary period before permanent enclosure. Second, the bishop determined if the financial support was adequate to sustain the recluse for his or her lifetime. Third, he aided in the finding of a suitable reclusorium. Fourth, he performed (or ordered performed) the rite of enclosure. And finally, he entered into an extended period of supervision that might bring in its wake the appointment of confessors, gifts of alms, grants of indulgences to others who supported the recluse, legislation to correct abuses, visitations, and a general paternal involvement.[12]

All in all, however, it must be said that *AW* does not lay particular stress on the authority of bishops. Though Part Two refers to the bishop's visits, they seem to have little to do with his role as supervisor of the anchoress' life:

> If the bishop comes to see you, hasten immediately toward him, but beg him sweetly, if he asks to see you, that you might with respect to that conduct yourself toward him as you have done and continue to do to all others. If he still wants to have a look, see to it that it is very short — with your veil down, and draw yourself well back [from the window]."[13]

Essentially, the bishop appears here as just another man, subject to the same temptations as other men are, not as an authority figure. In fact, the only call to obey the bishop's dictums comes in the Preface, where the anchoress is to vow that she will never leave her anchorhold, unless "for [absolute] necessity . . . force and fear of death, [or in] obedience to her bishop or his superior."[14]

---

[12] See p. 53.

[13] 2.185–88. I have used translations of the Middle English text in the Introduction to facilitate ease of reading. The translations here do not correspond word for word with the glosses at the foot of the text. Those glosses are designed to clarify the literal statement in the Middle English text and, if quoted without the original vocabulary, syntax, or immediate reference, are too clumsy for the context here.

[14] Pref.55–57.

Rites of Enclosure

As Warren notes, one of the duties of the bishop was to officiate personally or through a deputy at the enclosure of the anchoress, and several enclosure ceremonies survive in pontificals (i.e., handbooks for bishops, containing the texts of rites and sacraments which they must perform).[15] Though there are a number of variations, the enclosure ceremony usually includes the following elements: an anchorite receives last rites, has the Office of the Dead said over her, enters her cell, and is bricked in, accompanied at each stage by various prayers.

Attractions of the Anchoritic Life

For late twentieth-century readers, the inevitably macabre drama of enclosure fails to convey why more and more women in the course of the thirteenth, fourteenth, and fifteenth centuries were drawn to a life of perpetual enclosure. Warren charts the number of anchorites in England from the twelfth through sixteenth centuries and shows that women far outnumbered men, particularly in the thirteenth century:

Numbers of Anchorites: 1100–1539[16]

	Female	Male	Indeterminate	Totals
Twelfth cent.	48	30	18	96
Thirteenth cent.	123	37	38	198
Fourteenth cent.	96	41	77	214
Fifteenth cent.	110	66	28	204
Sixteenth cent.	37	27	4	68

What drew so many women to the anchorhold? One answer may be that, in a strange sense, many anchorites withdrew from the world only to find themselves squarely in the center of village life. We can perhaps glimpse this obliquely in a list of prohibited activities for anchoresses in Part Eight of the *AW*. There, the *AW* author advises anchoresses not to keep valuables in their anchorholds (8.89–92), run a school (8.162–65), or send, receive or write letters (8.166). Further, in Part Two, the author warns his readers that the anchorhold should

---

[15] See especially the chapter entitled "Enclosure and Rule," pp. 92–126. Clay gives the translation of an early sixteenth-century enclosure ceremony in Appendix A of her book *The Hermits and Anchorites of England*.

[16] See p. 20. Warren extrapolates this data from a variety of documents, though wills (with their frequent bequests to local anchorites) are often the richest sources. Appendix 1 breaks down the figures by county (pp. 292–93).

never become a source of news or gossip (2.486–88). These prohibitions offer a tantalizing glimpse into some of the social functions of the typical anchoress in her village setting. At least some anchorholds, it seems, became the center of town life, acting as sort of bank, post office, school house, shop, and newspaper — services which today are provided mainly by public and quasi-public institutions. The *AW* author, of course, advises against these activities mainly because they draw the heart of the anchoress outside her anchorhold, but that they must be prohibited points to the fact that many anchorites became something like spiritual celebrities — they became the focus for the communal religious life of the village. Warren suggests that the

> anchorite was part of the routine life of the community . . . . We can conjecture an England in which a village anchorite was a feature of religious life both commonplace and awe-inspiring; an England whose parish life was enhanced by the residence of one among them who had chosen this difficult way; an England in which the quality of daily life was enriched by the example of one so low who might become so high. Identification with the anchorite provided the villager with a private conduit to heaven and salvation. (p. 282)

In fact, Part Three likens the recluse to an architectural prop or buttress: she holds up the entire parish with her prayers (see 3.267 ff.).

Some anchoresses achieved enough celebrity that they were sought out as spiritual advisors. In the twelfth century, the anchoress Christina of Markyate became the confidant and advisor to Geoffrey, the powerful abbot of St. Albans, and in the fifteenth century, Margery Kempe consulted Julian in her anchorhold in Norwich.[17] *AW* assumes that the faithful will come to the anchoresses for advice — though such visits from men may not be entirely desirable — and suggests, "If any good man has come from afar, hear his speech and answer with a few words to his questionings" (2.270–71). A bit later, however, the *AW* author takes a somewhat sterner position: "[Do] not preach to any man . . . nor [should] a man ask you [for] counsel or tell [it] to you. Advise women only" (2.280–81).

Attraction of Anchoritic Community

Not only did an anchoress become part of a village community, but *AW* strongly suggests that she also entered into an anchoritic community as well. At first glance, this seems a rather absurd idea — that a woman would enter a cell and be bricked in by herself in order to find a communal religious life. But *AW* does spend a good deal of time discussing the joys of and impediments to communality. Part Eight reveals some details about how this community

---

[17] For Christina's life, see Furlong's *The Life of Christina of Markyate*. For Margery Kempe's description of her remarkable meeting with Julian of Norwich see Staley's edition of *The Book of Margery Kempe*, chapter 18, pp. 53–54.

functioned: anchoresses communicated with one another through a network of "maidens" or servants who carried verbal messages to other anchoresses (see the section on "Audience" below).

Daily Life of Anchoresses

What was daily life like for the anchoresses for whom *AW* was written? In their edition of Part One, Ackerman and Dahood offer a glimpse of the anchoresses' daily activities in the following itinerary, reconstructed from Part One's advice about liturgy and prayer:[18]

3–5 A.M.	Preliminary devotions and prayers
	Matins and Lauds of Our Lady (recited *seriatim*)
	Dirige (Matins and Lauds of the Office of the Dead)
	Suffrages and Commendations
	Litany of the Saints (daily except Sundays)
	Lauds of the Holy Ghost (optional)
5–6	Listen to the priest's celebration of the canonical hours when possible.
6–7	Prime of the Holy Ghost (optional)
	Prime of Our Lady
7–8	Preciosa
8–9	Terce of the Holy Ghost (optional)
	Terce of Our Lady
9–10	Prayers and supplications
	Devotions before the cross
10–11	Devotions to Our Lady
	The Seven Penitential Psalms
	The Fifteen Gradual Psalms
11–12	Mass (communion fifteen times annually)
12–1 P.M.	Sext of the Holy Ghost (optional)
	Sext of Our Lady
	Meal (first meal in summer; only meal on weekdays in winter)
1–2	None of the Holy Ghost (optional)
	None of Our Lady
2–3	Rest period
3–5	Private prayers and meditation
	Reading in the Psalter, *AR*, and other edifying books in English and French
	Instruction of maidservants
	Work: plain needlework on church vestments or clothing for the poor

---

[18] Ackerman and Dahood, pp. 37–38.

	Vespers of the Holy Ghost (optional)
	Vespers of Our Lady
	Placebo (Vespers of the Office of the Dead, omitted before a feast of nine lessons)
	Meal (second meal on Sundays; on weekdays in summer only)
5–7	Compline of the Holy Ghost (optional)
	Compline of Our Lady
	Bedtime prayers and devotions.

For further information on the liturgical forms presented in this table see the Explanatory Notes for Part One.

Architecture of Anchorholds

Very few anchorholds survive from the Middle Ages — after the death of the anchorite, they seem to have been demolished, converted to other uses, such as vestries, sacristries, or chapels, or obscured by further construction. In Chester-le-Street, near Durham, a surviving late medieval anchorhold consists of two large rooms, one on top of the other, built into the northwest side of the church. The upper room has a squint (i.e., a slit or small window) offering the anchorite a view of the side altar which was reserved for public use. Even in the case of Chester-le-Street, however, the surviving cell has been altered considerably (having been converted into an almshouse after the Middle Ages by the addition of two rooms), and part of what was the anchorite's lower room now houses the boiler for the church. It seems that anchorholds could range in size from a single small room to a set of apartments with an inner garden, some with servants' quarters and some without. Locating and identifying anchorholds, then, is a difficult business which involves a combination of archaeological investigation, documentary history, and guesswork. Surveying descriptions of anchorholds, Clay concludes that many were on the north side of the churches to which they were attached, perhaps to expose them to the cold northern winds.[19] Warren notes that though not typical, it was not unheard of for two anchorites to live in adjoining cells.[20]

Only Parts Two and Eight offer any substantial hints about the internal arrangements of the anchorhold. One suspects that the very specific details of Part Two may have applied more to the living conditions of the original three sisters than to those of the twenty-plus anchoresses, whose houses must have taken a variety of forms. And in fact, the prescriptions of Part Eight seem more vague.

---

[19] The anchorhold at Staindrop, though, had a fireplace (see Clay, pp. 79–84).

[20] See pp. 33–34.

The anchorhold described in Part Two could have had two or three rooms:

> Talk to no one through the church-window, but show honor to it for the holy sacrament that you see through it, and use the house-window for your women (i.e., servants) and for the others, the parlor. (2.259–61)

At the core of the anchorhold was of course the recluse's cell: it had three windows as well as a private altar, a bed, and a crucifix (see 1.348–49, 2.183–85, and 1.31 respectively). The church window commanded a view of the high altar in the church and must have been on the ground floor if it was possible to talk through it (in the Chester-le-Street anchorhold, where the church window looked out from the upper room, this would have been patently impossible). The "house" window looked into the servants' quarters (clearly a separate room) and was perhaps large enough to pass through food or a chamber pot. The "parlor" window, through which the anchoress spoke to visitors, faced either outside to the church courtyard or perhaps into a small room. The parlor window was to be the smallest of the three, since it provided dangerous contact with the outside world (see 2.16–17).

There is some question about what the world *parlur* may have meant. The following two definitions from the *Middle English Dictionary* seem most relevant: "(a) A chamber in a religious house used for consultation or conversation, esp. for conversation with persons outside the monastic community; (b) a grate or window through which the enclosed religious can make confession or communicate with persons outside the cloister." The evidence in *AW* tends to suggest that the *parlur* was a separate room: Part Two refers to "your parlor's window" (*ower parlurs thurl*, 2.203) and says that of all the windows, "the parlor's window be the least (i.e., smallest) and narrowest" (2.16–17). It seems unlikely that *parlur* could refer to a simple grate or window, since "the grate's window" makes for a difficult sense. Whether a separate room or merely a window, however, the parlor must have been visible from the servants' quarters since *AW* advises an anchoress to check with her maiden to see who is at the parlor window before deciding whether or not to open it (see 2.203–04).

The servants' quarters must have been reasonably large since anchoresses were encouraged to have guests entertained there ("If anyone has a cherished guest, [let her] have her maidens, as if in her place, entertain her fairly. And she will have permission to unblock her window once or twice and make signs toward her (i.e., the guest) of a fair welcoming," 2.263–65). Some anchorholds must have had a door between the servants' quarters and the cell proper since *AW* warns against dining with guests at the same table: "Some anchoress (i.e., sometime an anchoress) will sit to dinner (lit., make her board) outside with her guest (*ute-with*). That is too much friendship" (8.30–31). Further, anchoresses are advised to invite the visiting maidens of other anchoresses to spend the night, presumably in the servants' quarters (see 8.62–64).

Introduction

The following diagram attempts to account for as many of the preceding details as possible, though of course the positions of the rooms may have varied considerably.

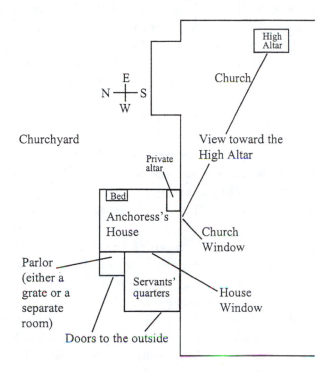

The Anchorhold as described in *AW*: A Conjectural Reconstruction

Authorship

Since Morton's 1853 edition of *AW*, scholars have attempted to attribute *AW* to the pen of a number of writers: Simon of Ghent, Richard Poor (Bishop of Salisbury, d. 1237), Gilbert of Sempringham (1089–1189), Robert Bacon, the hermit Godwine, and Brian of Lingen.[21] None of these attributions has proved ultimately very convincing, and perhaps the best we can hope for is to know what sort of person, but not exactly who, the author was.

So far, the detective work has focused on clues which might reveal the religious order to which the *AW* author belonged. The author refers to his order obliquely in his instructions for taking

---

[21] See the discussion of authorship in Millett's indispensible bibliography: *Ancrene Wisse, The Katherine Group, and The Wooing Group*, pp. 7–13.

communion in Part Eight: "Therefore you should not receive the Eucharist—*except as our brothers do*—fifteen times within a year" (8.9–10, italics mine).[22] The most promising evidence for such an approach is clearly to be found in the liturgical program described in Part One, in certain practices of the outer rule (such as instructions for diet, silence, hair trimming, and communion) described in Part Eight, and in scattered references to religious habits. For the most part, interpreting these clues successfully depends on an in-depth technical knowledge of early thirteenth-century religious rules.

The two most likely hypotheses identify the *AW* author as either an Augustinian canon or a Dominican friar. E. J. Dobson has made the strongest case for the Augustinian origins of *AW*, an idea first proposed seriously by Derek Brewer. In *The Origins of Ancrene Wisse*, Dobson carefully builds his case by comparing *AW*'s dictums about clothing, bloodletting, vows of silence, diet, and hair trimming (tonsuring) to the Augustinian statutes. He concludes that the handling of these practices is very similar to that of the Premonstratensian Statutes of 1236–38 (themselves derived from earlier rules) but that the author belonged rather to the Augustinian congregation of St. Victor (p. 113). Dobson goes on to identify Brian of Lingen, an Augustinian canon at St. James priory, Wigmore, as the author of *AW*.[23]

A word on the term *Augustinian canon* may be in order here. Originally, the title *canon* referred to any member of the official staff of a diocese but later narrowed to refer to the several ranks of clergy serving in a cathedral. These clergy came to be known as "secular canons" because they pursued their calling in the world. Nuns and monks, of course, were cloistered away from the world, but the prestige of the monastic orders inspired the canons in Southern France and Northern Italy to organize themselves into communities living under a quasi-monastic rule. These canons were known as "regular" canons since they lived under a rule. From the eleventh century on, most communities of regular canons adopted some form of the Rule of St. Augustine. In fact, at least four different texts circulated under this title, only two of which were arguably written by Augustine himself: the "Precept," a set of instructions written for men at Augustine's home monastery at Hippo, as well as a rule for women based on Augustine's *Letter* 211, but prefaced with other material. Until the end of the thirteenth century, individual houses of Augustinian canons such as St. Victor in Paris did not operate under strong centralized control and were relatively free to develop their own variations on the rule.[24] In general, the Rule of St. Augustine, in its various forms, looks to the early church for its view of an apostolic Christianity ministering to the sick and poor. In their collection of monastic, canonical, and mendicant rules, Douglas J. McMillan and Kathryn Smith Fladenmuller write that "Augustine essentially called for having all possessions in common,

---

[22] As Dobson points out, Nero reads "as our lay (*leawude*) brethren do" (*Origins*, p. 9).

[23] See *Origins*, pp. 322–27. Dobson's attribution, though a brilliant piece of detective work, rests on somewhat shaky foundations. See Explanatory Notes to Pref.20 and 8.289.

[24] For a concise history of the Augustinian canons, see the article "Canons Regular of St. Augustine" in the *New Catholic Encyclopedia*.

common times of communal prayer, no individual distinctive clothing, and strict obedience to the leader of the community" and that the "canonical life was thought of as one of compromise, halfway between that of the secular clergy and that of Benedictine monks."[25]

As Bella Millett and others have pointed out, some of the practices which Dobson assigned to the Augustinian canons have more exact parallels in the legislation of the Dominicans.[26] Dobson fended off this suggestion (advanced by McNabb and Kirchberger) by pointing out that Dominican customs evolved from the Augustinian rule and that any resemblances between the practices of *AW* and those of the Dominicans must be assigned to earlier, and in some cases, lost Augustinian statutes.[27]

Recently, Millett has made a strong case for reconsidering Dobson's reasoning. In reviewing the research since the seventies, Millett concludes that practices revolving around communion, tonsure, and the reciting of the Office of the Dead are in most cases closer to Dominican practice, though the first surviving record of some of these practices comes from a later document, the first Dominican *Ordinarium* of 1256. On other points, *AW* seems to stand in very close relationship to the Premonstratensian statutes of 1236–38. The Premonstratensian canons — named for the place of their foundation, Prémontré, near Laon — formed an independent congregation operating under an Augustinian Rule. Through his friendship with St. Bernard of Clairvaux, their founder St. Norbert brought the order under Cistercian influence. Millett suggests that practices in *AW* which most resemble those of the Premonstratensians "are of Dominican origin, but date from a transitional period, the two decades following 1216, when Premonstratensian and Dominican customs were running closely alongside each other and local Dominican practice was still far from uniform. Their links with Premonstratensian legislation could then be explained by the initial and continuing influence on Dominican practice of the Premonstratensian statutes."[28]

Implications

At first, it may seem that attributing *AW* to an Augustinian canon or a Dominican friar is a technical matter which makes little real difference to understanding the evolution of the text. However, placing *AW* in the sphere of the Augustinians or Dominicans does have a number of interpretative implications. By the early thirteenth century, the Premonstratensians had become almost indistinguishable from other monastic communities, and thus an Augustinian *AW* would best be understood as a representative of current monastic concerns (under the heavy influence of St. Bernard's theology).

---

[25] See *Regular Life*, pp. 11–12.

[26] Millett, "Origins," p. 217.

[27] Dobson, *Origins*, pp. 81–82.

[28] Millett, "Origins," p. 217.

A Dominican origin for *AW*, on the other hand, implies a program much more oriented towards lay spirituality, and would explain the heavy emphasis on penance and confession (Parts Four, Five, and Six), directed apparently at a general audience (see the section on "Audience" below). The Dominicans, as Millett points out, "were actively involved in the implementation of the programme of pastoral reform laid down by the Fourth Lateran Council in 1215; one of their main functions was to assist the bishops with their increased pastoral workload by preaching, the hearing of confessions, and the provision of spiritual advice."[29]

The order was founded around 1220 by St. Dominic, one of the great preachers of the age, to help combat the rising tide of heresies popular in southern Europe. To reach lay audiences, new emphasis was placed on such devices as *exempla* and comparisons (*similitudines*) drawn from the everyday world of the laity as well as references to phenomena in the natural world drawing on beast lore, lapidaries and herbals. In the course of the thirteenth century a whole new array of reference works and preacher's tools came into being, perhaps the most notable of which were alphabetized or indexed collections of sermon stories, many of them compiled by Dominicans.[30]

In many ways, this new interest in orthodoxy and pastoral care gave lay women fresh opportunities for organized religious life. Jacques de Vitry, one of the great preachers, played a hand as a confidante of Mary of Oignes, in the founding of the Beguine movement in the Netherlands,[31] and it is perhaps no coincidence that in England the *AW*'s community of twenty or so anchoresses were forming in the west country at about the same time, and that their spiritual director, like Jacques de Vitry, was also steeped in the new methods of preaching.

In the course of the thirteenth century, the Dominicans spent more and more time acting as spiritual advisors to women. In fact, Emicho of Colmar became the first Dominican to gather a group of recluses into a regular community in the early 1220s.[32] Some within the order, particularly Jordan of Saxony, however, began to have reservations about the wisdom of supervising women, since it was occupying more and more of the order's time and resources, and in 1228 the chapter attempted to stop any new relationships of this sort: "In virtue of the Holy Spirit and under pain of excommunication we strictly forbid any of our friars from striving or procuring, henceforth, that the care or supervision of nuns or any other women be committed to our brethren . . . we also forbid anyone henceforth to tonsure, clothe in a habit, or receive the profession of any woman."[33] This ruling did not put a halt to Dominican involvement in the Beguine movement, however.

---

[29] Millett, "Origins," p. 216.

[30] See D. L. d'Avray, *The Preaching of the Friars*, pp. 132–203.

[31] See Ernest W. McDonnell, *The Beguines and Beghards in Medieval Culture*, pp. 20–39.

[32] Hinnebusch, vol. 1, p. 388.

[33] Hinnebusch, vol. 1, p. 389.

Interestingly, the Premonstratensian canons had been similarly released from supervising women in 1198.[34]

Collaborative Authorship

The quest to identify the author of *AW* may have been hampered by a narrow conception of authorship which assumes a single, authoritative creator for a text. It is possible to imagine clusters of anchoresses copying and reading *AW* intensively, interpreting and responding to the text, sometimes prompting the author (their spiritual advisor or advisors) to clarify, expand, or revise the text. One could perhaps go further, to suggest that some of the revisions and additions to the text may have been made by the anchoresses themselves (since they acted as scribes), perhaps originally as marginal glosses which were incorporated into the main text at the next copying.[35]

First and foremost, it is important to realize that what Tolkien called the "AB language," the language in which the various versions of *AW* were composed (see the section on "Language" below), is a *communal* language, with its own distinctive vocabulary, syntax, and spelling system. The unusual degree of standardization implies a strong sense either of hierarchical control of texts or, alternatively, of community investment in a common language. Not only the original author but also the scribes and presumably readers were well versed in the dialect and its conventions, since it served as the major socio-linguistic glue for the community. In fact, the idea of a communal language may muddy the waters of authorship here — "style" is not so much a matter of individual personality as communal convention, and it may be difficult to distinguish between contributions by different members of the community.

Audience

The original audience of *AW* apparently consisted of three sisters of noble birth. The Nero version preserves a passage (omitted in Corpus and much abbreviated in Cleopatra and Titus[36]) which addresses the three sisters directly on the topic of external temptations and hardships:

---

[34] McDonnell, pp. 103–04.

[35] In a recent conference paper, Anne Savage has suggested that the anchoresses (particularly the three original sisters) collaborated with the male author in another way: the author may at times act as a biographer, recording the thoughts and meditations of the anchoresses themselves ("Writing and the Solitary Community: The Authorship of *Ancrene Wisse*," 34th International Congress on Medieval Studies, Kalamazoo, MI, May 1999. An article based on this paper is forthcoming).

[36] For a description of the various versions see the "List of Manuscripts" below.

You, my dear sisters, of all the anchoresses whom I know are the ones who have the least need of comfort for these temptations, except only for sickness. For I know of no anchoress who may have with more comfort and more honor all that she might need than you three have, our Lord be thanked. For you do not worry about food or about clothing, either for you or for your maidens. Each one of you has all that she needs from one friend, nor does your servant (lit., maiden) need to seek either bread or food further than at his hall. God knows, many others know little of this kind of abundance but are often afflicted with want, with shame, and with hardship. If this [book] comes into their hands, it may be a comfort to them. You must fear the soft more than the hard share of these temptations which is called outer. For happily would the devil beguile you if he might with flattery make you badly behaved, [and this might happen] if you were not cleverer. There is much talk of you, what noble women you are, sought after for your goodness and generosity, and sisters of one father and one mother. In the blossom of your youth you forsook all the world's joys and became anchoresses.[37]

This passage reveals several details about the sisters — that they have a male patron whose hall is near enough to their anchorholds to act as a source of provisions, that the sisters are of noble birth, and that they enclosed themselves at a young age.[38] Interestingly, the author already has an idea that *AW* may circulate more widely among anchoresses with less secure support: "If this [book] comes into their hands, it may be a comfort to them."

Expanded Audience

By the time of the Corpus revision, the audience had expanded to a group of twenty or more anchoresses spread in the west of England, as the following added passage shows:

You are the anchoresses of England, so many together, twenty now or more. May God multiply you in good, among whom there is the greatest peace, the greatest unity and single-mindedness and concord in your common life according to one rule, so that all pull as one, all are turned one way, and none away from the other, according to what I have heard. For this reason, you are going forward strongly and are prospering on your path, for each is proceeding along with the other in one way of life, as if you were a convent of London, and of Oxford, of Shrewsbury, or of Chester, where all are one, with one common custom, and without singularity — that is,

---

[37] For the ME version of this passage see Explanatory Note to 4.164. Wada suggests that this passage is not necessarily a survival from the original text of *AW* and compares it carefully to the other truncated versions, suggesting that the Nero passage may be an expansion (pp. lxxx–lxxxii).

[38] Scholars have attempted to identify these three sisters. Hope Emily Allen argued that *AW* was written for three sisters, Emma, Gunilda, and Christina, enclosed in an anchorhold at Kilburn, sometime between 1127 and 1135 ("The Origin"), while Dobson identified them as three women enclosed at Deerfold near Limebrook Priory (*Origins*, pp. 234 ff.; see also Explanatory Note 4.593 ff.).

individual contrariness — a base thing in religion, for it destroys unity and shared custom which there ought to be in an order. Now then, this is your high fame: that you are all as if you were in one convent. This is pleasing to God. This is widely known already so that your convent begins to spread to the end of England. You are like the mother-house from which they are born. You are like a wellspring: if the wellspring falters the streams falter as well. (4.916–29)

It is important to note that this group is to act *as if* it were a convent, since the anchoresses were probably not nuns.[39] Also notable is the idea that the movement was gaining even more momentum, spreading to the end of England, and that the anchoresses were marching, like a unified army, in a single direction.[40] Unity can only be a goal if the anchoresses formed some sort of community.

Community

The kind of community implied in the passage cited above is difficult to account for precisely. The anchorholds must have been far enough apart so that they would cover a territory reaching to the "end of England." On the other hand, they must have been close enough to each other for the servants or maidens of the anchoresses to travel easily between anchorholds. The following passage from Part Four implies a rather intimate connection between anchoresses in that it allows for complex communication between anchorholds via messengers:

Let each of you, nonetheless, warn the other through a very trustworthy messenger, sweetly and lovingly as if it were her dear sister, about anything that she takes wrong — if she knows it for a fact. And let whoever will carry the message repeat it often in her presence before she goes, so the anchoress can hear how she will say it, so that she not say it in any other way nor patch more onto it. (4.945–49)

In some sense, the idea of community which emerges here presents a paradox: it is a group which can never actually meet face to face but which must be held together with words and texts, under the authority of a single spiritual director, who may be the *AW* author himself:

When your sister's maidens come to you for comfort, come to them at the window in the late morning and early afternoon once or twice . . . . If any word is spoken which might hurt someone's heart, let it not be carried out nor brought to another anchoress who is sensitive (lit., easy to hurt). It should be reported to him who looks after them all. (8.264–69)

---

[39] See Explanatory Note to 1.49.

[40] Dobson believes that the "end of England" refers to the Welsh borders (see Explanatory Note to 4.916 ff.).

Mixed Audience

Part Five, the section on confession, seems in particular to be directed at a mixed audience including nuns, anchoresses, virgins, married women, and even men: the author clearly had an interest in instructing a variety of people, both religious and lay, about the new sacrament of confession, perhaps further evidence that he was a Dominican. In explaining the circumstances or "trappings" of sin, he provides a sort of fill-in-the-blank confession: "I am an anchoress, a nun, a wedded wife, a virgin, a woman that was trusted, a woman who has been burnt before by such things . . . . Let each person, according to what he is, describe his circumstances, a man as it applies to him, a woman what touches her" (5.216–18, 247–48).

Near the end of the section he explains that the sixteen attributes of confession have not been written specifically for the anchoresses:

> My dear sisters, this fifth part, which is about confession, applies to all men alike; therefore, do not be surprised that I have not spoken to you specifically in this part. Have, however, for your profit, this little last end. (5.486–88)

The section, for the benefit of the specific anchoresses, describes which sins an anchoress might confess herself and those which she must confess to a priest, adding that she must not describe her sins in much detail to avoid tempting the priest, advice which contradicts the earlier teaching that confession must be naked (i.e., must hide nothing). As Linda Georgianna has pointed out, the priest's role in the anchoresses' confession is a limited one.[41] In some ways, this attitude towards priests and bishops (see the section on "Becoming an Anchorite") creates a space in which male authority can be questioned and in some cases excluded, however temporarily or incompletely.

Part Six, I would argue, also has a dual audience, but of a different kind. Here, the author seems to be addressing both advanced anchoresses (perhaps the original three) as well as newcomers to the anchoritic life: "Everything that I have said about the mortification of the flesh is not for you, my dear sisters — who sometimes suffer more than I would want — but is for someone who may readily enough read this, but who handles herself too softly" (6.376–78). He goes on to describe this indulgent anchoress (or perhaps lay woman) as a young seedling which needs to be protected from the devil by a circle of thorns (i.e., pain), another image of enclosure. This same phenomenon may be at work in a passage discussed above which begins by addressing the entire group of twenty anchoresses, who are spreading to the end of England, but which seems to end with praise for the original anchoresses, who "are like the mother-house from which they are born" (4.927–28).

---

[41] See the headnote to Part Six in the Explanatory Notes.

Introduction

Date

Though none of the versions of *AW* can be dated with absolute certainty, the two references to the Franciscans and Dominicans in the Corpus manuscript (both lacking in the other versions) narrow the date of the Corpus revision to the period after the arrival of the Dominicans and the Franciscans in England (1221 and 1224 respectively):

> Our preaching friars (Dominicans) and friars minor (Franciscans) are of such an order that all people might be amazed if any of them "turned an eye towards the shelter of the wood" (i.e., thought about forbidden pleasures). Therefore, when any of them come to you out of charity to teach and comfort you in God — if he is a priest — say before he leaves "Mea Culpa!" (i.e., the beginning of the confession). (2.236–39)

> Let no one eat in your presence except by your director's permission, whether general (i.e., blanket permission) or special: general for preaching friars (Dominicans) and minors (Franciscans), special for all others. (8.65–66)

Further, Millett suggests that a list of place names in Part Four (occurring only in Corpus) — if they refer to Dominican foundations — must set the earliest possible date for Corpus around or somewhat before 1236. The passage in question urges the twenty or more anchoresses to live in unity, "as if you were a convent of London, and of Oxford, of Shrewsbury, or of Chester" (4.921–22). Millett points out that the Dominicans' earliest priories were established in Shrewsbury sometime before 1232 and in Chester sometime before 1236. She makes the strong case that we should view the early 1230s as an "anchor" which establishes the latest possible date for the first versions of *AW* and the earliest possible one for the Corpus revision (*AW* bibliography, p. 12).[42] To sum up, Corpus clearly cannot have been written much before 1225 because of its mention of the Dominicans (who arrived in England in 1224). Since it incorporates marginal revisions made to the Cleopatra manuscript (written between 1225 and 1230) it seems logical to push the earliest date for Corpus to around 1230. Further, if Corpus' list of place names refers to Dominican houses, the earliest possible date would move forward to the time of the latest Dominican foundation in the list, that of Chester, which is known to have existed by 1236. The latest possible date, on the other hand, is more difficult to fix: the language and handwriting of Corpus suggest a rough end date of 1250, though most scholars would probably not place it so late. Taking all the variables into account and allowing for the widest possible margin of error in theories of authorship, the dating of Cleopatra, etc., it is relatively safe to assume that Corpus was written sometime between 1225 and 1240.

---

[42] For a summary of dates based on linguistic and paleographical criteria, see Millett's introduction to her excellent annotated bibliography, pp. 9–13 and 49–59.

Localization

By a process of elimination, the language of *AW* can be localized to the West Midlands. We know that it did not come from the South since it lacks typical features of late West Saxon; it cannot come from the more northerly dialects because of its verb endings; and it cannot come from the Eastern Midlands because of the distinctive way it spells OE *y* and *eo* (see d'Ardenne, *Seinte Iuliene*, pp. 179–80). In addition, *AW* contains one, possibly two words of Welsh origin: *cader* "cradle" and perhaps *baban* "baby" (see glossary). This linguistic evidence, coupled with the inscription on the first folio of the Corpus version indicating that the manuscript was given to St. James priory in Wigmore, led Dobson to locate the author and thus the text in the vicinity of Wigmore, approximately forty kilometers to the northwest of Worcester and less than twenty kilometers east of Wales (Dobson, *Origins*, chapter 3). More recently Margaret Laing and Angus McIntosh have suggested that the original AB dialect should perhaps be placed further north. It should be noted, however, that the scant number of early texts which can be firmly located makes dialect mapping for this period very difficult. Nevertheless, the forthcoming *Linguistic Atlas of Early Middle English* may be able to add more precision to the general picture we already have.

Structure

The overall structure of *AW*, as the author outlines it in Pref.130–51, is relatively straightforward: it consists of eight parts, the first and last devoted exclusively to the outer rule, the middle sections to the inner rule. An extensive outline of each individual part appears in the Explanatory Notes, so I will characterize them only briefly here.

The Preface establishes the difference between the outer rule, which governs the external behavior of the anchoresses in matters of prayer, food, clothing, etc., and the inner rule of the heart, which is the far more important goal of the anchoritic life. In fact, the outer rule should be a mere servant to the lady of the inner rule.

Part One gives basic recommendations for daily prayer.

Part Two, though difficult to describe briefly, shows the anchoress how to regulate her five senses so that the outside world does not intrude into her anchorhold through the dangerous portals of eyes, ears, nose, mouth, or hands. To compensate for this loss, the anchoress will have delight in a set of inner senses: spiritual sight, taste, touch, etc.

Part Three stresses the importance of regulating the inner life (in distinction to Part Two which focuses on the external senses) by comparing anchoresses to birds with various allegorical properties.

Part Four catalogues various branches of external and internal temptations, organized around the concept of the seven deadly sins. This massive section also includes remedies against and comforts for each temptation.

Part Five turns to the subject of confession, listing the sixteen attributes of good confession, while *Part Six* explores the concept of penance and becomes in effect a general meditation on the value of suffering rather than a manual on sacramental penance.

Part Seven, the climactic chapter of *AW*, maintains that divine love, not pain and penance, is the highest goal of the anchoritic life, likening the love of Christ to that of a knight whose recalcitrant mistress refuses his advances. Part Seven also likens God's love to Greek fire, a kind of medieval napalm.

Part Eight returns to the concerns of the outer rule, giving various recommendations on such varied topics as clothing, diet, observing silence, manual labor, keeping pets, entertaining guests, and dealing with servants.

The author's concern for organization (seen in the summary of chapters at the end of the preface) also reveals itself in the physical layout of the book. As Dahood has observed, both Corpus and Cleopatra employ a system of capital letters of varying sizes to indicate different levels of subdivision within the text, a system which Dahood believes may have been put in place in the exemplar of Cleopatra. Though in Corpus the system begins to lose its consistency after a few folios, it is clear that, in Dahood's words, "Whoever first imposed the system of graduated initials was concerned that readers grasp the relationships between divisions and not just focus on discrete passages" ("Coloured Initials," p. 97).

Language

J. R. R. Tolkien first coined the term "AB language" in 1929 to describe the remarkable orthographic and linguistic consistency he noticed between the Corpus version of *Ancrene Wisse* (manuscript "A" in Hall's *Early Middle English*) and Oxford, Bodleian Library, MS Bodley 34, containing a complete selection of what is now called the Katherine Group (Hall's manuscript "B"). These remarkable similarities (despite the fact that the two manuscripts were written by different scribes) suggest that the original texts were written in roughly the same place and time (Tolkien, p. 111). The term "AB language" is now rather baffling — since few now refer to Corpus as "A" or Bodley 34 as "B," but it has stuck, for better or worse. What is remarkable about the AB language is not so much that it represents a distinctive regional dialect, but the fact that it is really a kind of standard *written* language, descended in part from late Old English, and such a standard implies a common literate community.

What are the characteristics of AB language? S. R. T. O. d'Ardenne undertook a thorough description of it in her edition of the life of St. Juliana (one of the Katherine Group texts) and reports the following features:

> 1) the vocabulary contains a roughly equal mixture of French and Norse loans, though they seem
> to have been completely naturalized in English. That is, the French words in *AW* seem to be in

common colloquial use. Further, the extent of French influence on the vocabulary is probably minimized because the scribes were "conservative clerks who loved the English language as they knew it" (p. 177). The strong Norse elements imply that the underlying local dialect was situated near the old centers of Danish influence, i.e., further north.

2) the spelling is conservative, resisting both the trends introduced by Anglo-Norman scribes as well as sound changes in the local dialect. In this sense, the spelling system may be consciously "English," drawing on literate traditions going back to late Anglo-Saxon England. Further, it is "a literary idiom — not a phonetic transcript from the mouths of peasants made by practical philologists" (p. 178).

3) though literate, the AB language has "its roots in living speech" and makes remarkable use of vigorous colloquial speech (p. 178).

4) it contains some of the archaic diction and alliterative flow of "ancient English" (p. 178).

The following guide is intended to provide readers with practical grammatical information for reading, not to give a full linguistic description of the AB language. Readers interested in a fuller treatment should see d'Ardenne's *Seinte Iuliene*, pp. 177–250.

Spelling

Since the AB language is conservative and resists some Norman conventions which modern English has inherited, the spelling system of *AW* often obscures a word which modern readers might otherwise recognize. The following chart lists a few of the most common or confusing spellings in *AW* along with their modern equivalents.

AW Spelling	Modern Equivalent	Examples	Comments
-h- or -h	gh	*niht* = "night," *thoht* = "thought," *boh* = "bough"	h either in the middle or at the end of a word (a Norman convention).
hw-	wh	*hwet* = "what," *hwer* = "where"	
v- or -v-	f	*va* = "foe," *vet* = "feet," *hwer-vore* = "wherefore," *vorth* = "forth," *bivoren* = "before"	f often changed to v (see modern English "wife-wives"). When this occurs at the beginning of a word it is typical of southern ME.
-a-	o	*rad* = "rode," *nane* = "none," *hali* = "holy," *clath* = "cloth," *stan* = "stone," *bat* = "boat," *hwa* = who	long a when it occurs in the middle or at the end of a word.
e, o	ee, oo	*breden* = "breed," *the* = "thee," *teth* = "teeth," *god* = "good," *boke* = "book"	long e and o are doubled in spelling to indicate length (a Norman convention).

-*u*-	*i*	*fulth* = "filth," *lutle* = "little," *sunne* = "sin," *suster* = "sister," *wule* = "will," *kun* = "kin"	short *u* when it occurs in the middle of a word (only in some cases).
u- or -*u*-	*ou, ow*	*ure* = "our," *hus* = "house," *uttre* = "outer," *thu* = "thou," *nu* = "now," *hu* = "how," *tun* = "town," *tur* = "tower"	long *u* at the beginning or in the middle of a word (a Norman convention).

Reduced Spellings

In a few cases early ME contractions and consonant reductions (as reflected in the spelling system) can make words difficult to recognize. Two of the most difficult involve the *th* sound. In the first, the *th*- at the start of any word is reduced to a simple *t* if the sound immediately before it (the last sound in the preceding word) is a *t* or *d*.

thu > *tu*	*art tu*: "art thou"
the > *te*	*thet te Hali Gast*: "that the Holy Spirit"
the > *te*	*mid te crune*: "with the crown"
thet > *tet*	*swa thet tet deorewurthe blod ron*: "so that that precious blood ran"

The second reduction occurs in verbs. If the verb root ends in a *d* or *t* and an -*eth* follows, the -*eth* collapses into the *d* or *t* (since the sounds are formed in a similar way) and is simplified to *t*.

Infinitive	Root	Normal Form	Reduced Form
beaten	*beat*-	*beateth*: "beats"	*beat*
haten	*hat*-	*hateth*: "commands"	*hat*
freten	*fret*-	*freteth*: "devours"	*fret*
breden	*bred*-	*bredeth*: "breeds"	*bret*
finden	*find*-	*findeth*: "finds"	*fint*
huden	*hud*-	*hudeth*: "hides"	*hut*

Nouns

The main difficulty in interpreting nouns comes in deciding their number (singular or plural) and whether or not they are possessive. As the following chart shows, the AB language had a number of different methods for signaling the plural (see the "summary" column) derived from a much more complicated gender-based system in OE. Though this system survives to a certain degree in the AB language, a majority of nouns form plurals with either *-es* or *-en*. The possessive singular is usually easy enough to identify in that it takes the *-es* familiar to speakers of modern English. More difficult is the possessive plural marker *-ene*, seen in the title of the work *Ancrene Wisse* "the anchoresses' guide."

Noun Endings

Nominative, Objective	"soul" (OE feminine)	"angel" (OE masculine)	"limb" (OE neuter)	"tooth"	SUMMARY
Sing.	*sawle*	*engel*	*lim*	*toth*	*-, -e*
Pl.	*sawles, sawlen*	*engles*	*lime, limen*	*teth*	*-es, -en, -e* vowel change
Possessive					
Sing.	*sawle, sawles*	*engles*	*limes*	*tothes*	*-es, -e*
Pl.	*sawle, sawlene*	*engle, englene*	*lime, limene*	*tothes*	*-ene, -e, -es*

The Definite Article

The normal definite article in *AW* is *the*, though very occasionally fragments of the much more complex OE definite article appear:

then, based on the OE masculine accusative singular *þone*.

> *ha ondswerde Gabriel then engel*: "she answered Gabriel the angel"
> *schrift schent then deovel*: "confession shames the devil"

ther, based on the OE feminine objective or possessive singular *þære*.

> *to ther eorthe*: "to the earth"

Who/Which and That

Besides representing the definite article, *the* often functions as the relative pronoun "who" or "which" or as a demonstrative "that." When it is a feminine or plural demonstrative it usually appears as *theo*.

> *to wummon the wilneth hit*: "to a woman who desires it"
> *ant theo the ow servith*: "and those who serve you"

Introduction

Personal Pronouns

Though *AW*'s personal pronouns are by and large similar to their modern counterparts, the third person can prove confusing for modern readers.

Personal Pronouns

	Singular		Plural	
1st Person	*ich*	"I"	*we*	"we"
	me	"me"	*us*	"us"
	mine	"my, mine"	*ure*	"our"
2nd Person	*þu*	"thou"(familiar)	*ye*	"you" (polite)
	þe	"thee"	*ow*	"you"
	þine	"thy, thine"	*ower*	"your"
3rd Person	*he; ha/heo; hit*	"he; she; it"	*ha/heo*	"they"
	him; hire; him	"him; her; it"	*ham*	"them"
	his; hire/hare; his	"his; hers; its"	*hare*	"their"

The main difficulty is that the pronouns for "she" and "they" are usually identical (*ha* or *heo*). To decide whether a *ha* or *heo* is a "she" or "they," readers must pay attention to the verb endings which in most, but not all, cases provide the pivotal information. For example, *ha is* must mean "she is" while *ha beoth* must translate as "they are" (see the verb chart below). Similarly, in the following two phrases, the verbs *schal* and *schulen* indicate singular feminine and plural respectively.

> *ha schal libben bi ealmesse*: "she must live on alms"
> *ha schulen habben heovenliche smealles*: "they will have heavenly aromas"

Some verbs, however, make no distinction between singular and plural third person: *ha leaveth* "she leaves" is identical to *ha leaveth* "they leave." In this and similar cases, context is the only guide to deciding between the two. *AW*, for the most part, distinguishes between *hire* "her" and *hare* "their," as well as *him* "him, its" and *ham* "them."

Another pitfall for readers is the second person singular objective form *the* "thee," since it is identical in form to the definite article *the* as well as the relative pronoun and demonstrative *the*. As indicated by its modern spelling "thee," the vowel in the second person pronoun *the* was long, while the relative and demonstrative forms of *the* had a short and unstressed vowel.

Adjective Endings

Besides endings signaling the comparative (*-er*, *-re*) and superlative (*-est*), the only normal ending possible for adjectives is an *-e*, and though it is possible to read *AW* without knowing the nuances of the ending, it will sometimes be useful to know what kind of information it gives. An *-e* might be added to an adjective for one of the following two reasons:

1) because a definite article (*the*) precedes the adjective. When this happens, whether the noun is singular or plural the adjective takes an *-e* ending (see the examples below). In most cases, possessives like "my," "our," "your," "their," "the woman's," etc., act as equivalents to *the*.

> *the alde lahe*: "the old law"
> *the alde ten heastes*: "the old ten commandments"
> *ure alde moder*: "our old mother"
>
> *the brihte sihthe*: "the bright sight"

2) because the noun is plural. When there is no preceding *the*, an adjective without an *-e* ending must be singular, and one with an *-e* must be plural. Note: the indefinite article *an* does not affect the ending the way *the* does.

> *alde ancres*: "old anchoresses"
> *an ald ancre*: "an old anchoress"
>
> *briht sihthe*: "bright sight"
> *a briht sihthe*: "a bright sight"

Occasionally, fragments of the far more robust OE adjective system survive, but these are exceptions. See, for example, the *-re* ending on *alre* of the phrase *swetest alre leafdi* "the sweetest of all ladies." Here the *-re* signals the possessive (i.e., genitive) plural.

Verbs

Though it is hardly possible to cover the myriad of developments and irregularities in the verb system of *AW*, it may be useful to mention some of the potential pitfalls. The main complications can be traced back to the OE verb system which had several classes of "weak" verbs (i.e., regular verbs like "walk-walked-walked") as well as seven classes of "strong" verbs (i.e., irregular verbs like "sing-sang-sung").

The following chart gives an overview of endings for the most important categories of verbs, though those familiar with Shakespearean or King James' English ("thou goest," "she goeth")

Introduction

should have few difficulties for the most part. Beyond the regular present and past tense endings, the chart also provides forms for the subjunctive (conditional or theoretical statements: "if I were you," "were she to come," etc.) as well as the imperative (commands: "come!" "look!").

Principal Verb Endings

		Irreg.	Weak Ia	Weak Ib	Weak IIa	Weak IIb	Strong	Summary
		"to be"	"to leave"	"to tell"	"to look"	"to love"	"to bear"	
infinitive		beon	leaven	tellen	lokin	luvien	beoren	-en, -in, -ien
PRESENT								
singular	1 *ich*	eom/beo	leave	telle	loki	luvie	beore	-e, -i, -ie
	2 *thu*	art/bist	leavest	telest	lokest	luvest	berest	-est
	3 *ha*	is/bith	leaveth	teleth	loketh	luveth	bereth	-eth
plural	1,2,3 *we/ye/ha*	beoth/aren	leaveth	telleth	lokith	luvieth	beoreth	-eth, -ith, -ieth
PAST								
singular	1 *ich*	wes	leafde	talde	lokede	luvede	ber	-(e)de
	2 *thu*	were	leafdest	taldest	lokedest	luvedest	bere	-dest, -e
	3 *ha*	wes	leafde	talde	lokede	luvede	ber	-(e)de
plural	1,2,3 *we/ye/ha*	weren	leafden	talden	lokeden	luveden	beren	-en
Subjunct.								
Present	sg.	beo	leave	talde	loki	luvie	beore	-e, -i, -ie
	pl.	beon	leaven	talden	lokin	luvien	beoren	-en, -in, -ien
Past	sg.	were	leafde	talde	lokede	luvede	ber	-e, -
plural	pl.	weren	leafden	talden	lokeden	luveden	beren	-en
Imperative	sg.	beo	leaf	tele	loke	luve	ber	-, -e
	pl.	beon	leafen	tellen	lokin	luvien	beoren	-en
pres. part.		*	leavinde	tellinde	lokinde	luviende	beorinde	-inde, -iende
past part.		*	i-leavet	i-tald	i-loket	i-luvet	i-boren	-et, -d, -en

Many verbs belong to the weak classes Ia and Ib and thus it is impossible to tell the difference between the third person singular (present tense) *-eth* and the plural (present tense) *-eth*.

> *yef we wel fehteth*: "if we fight well"
> *theo fehteth treowliche*: "she truly fights" or "they truly fight"

Weak class II, however, does distinguish between these two: while *-eth* still signals the third person singular, verbs with present plural subjects take the very distinctive *-ith* or *-ieth*.

> *ha druncnith*: "they drown"

> *Salome spealeth pes*: "Salome means 'peace'"
> *ba ha spealieth an*: "they both mean one [and the same thing]"

> *ne luveth ha me nawt*: "she does not love me"
> *ha luvieth the*: "they love you (lit., thee)"

Manuscripts

AW is preserved in whole or in fragments in seventeen manuscripts: nine in Middle English, four in French and four in Latin.[43] The consensus of scholarly opinion is now that the original language of the text was English and that the French and Latin versions represent later translations.[44] Dobson has attempted to work out the manuscript relationships as follows (note that *x* represents the author's original text while the Greek letters stand for manuscripts which did not survive but whose existence can be inferred. The dotted lines indicate cross-influence, where one manuscript has been collated and corrected with another, however partially).

The manuscript transmission of *AW* is obviously complex (in fact, Dobson's diagram looks a bit like higher calculus), but the following conjectural account will perhaps give a useful overview, subject to re-evaluation. What complicates the story is that in many cases our only evidence for earlier manuscripts exists in later copies which themselves have been compared and corrected with other versions. With many medieval texts, it is possible to sketch out much simpler tree diagrams (known as *stemmas*) which describe the genetic relationships of various families of manuscripts. In the case of *AW*, this process is particularly dodgy, given the intensive

---

[43] See Dahood's article in *Middle English Prose*, pp. 2–5, and Millett's *AW* bibliography, pp. 49–59, for convenient descriptions of each of the manuscripts.

[44] The case for the priority of French (put most forcefully by Macaulay) was laid to rest mainly by Dymes and by Käsmann. See Millett's *AW* bibliography for further references.

cross-fertilization (some would say "contamination") between branches. Dobson was the first to attempt to see through this thicket of relationships, but it should be emphasized that his conclusions have been challenged and that no one has yet undertaken a complete collation (i.e., a word-by-word comparison) of each of the versions. It is possible that our picture of the manuscript transmission (and thus the evolution of the text) may change, perhaps radically, when Millett's full critical edition appears. But for the moment, Dobson's account (with modifications) is the best explanation we have.

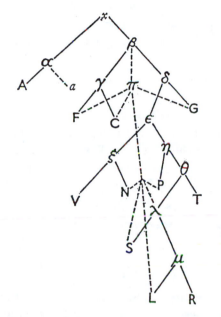

The Evolution of the Text

It seems that the author originally wrote his "guide" for three sisters who became anchoresses (perhaps near Wigmore in Worcestershire). This earliest version seems not to have survived, though the Nero MS contains several elements of it. As the community expanded, more copies were produced, perhaps one for each new anchoress and perhaps copied out by the anchoress herself,[46] each with incidental changes and additions. Thus, the text evolved. The anchoresses using these texts seem to have been in contact with each other and with the author; they

---

[46] Dobson writes that there "can be little doubt that the β group originated with manuscripts copied by the anchoresses themselves" ("Affiliations," p. 163), and the Corpus version states that each anchoress should say her hours "as she has written them" (1.75).

circulated some additions and sometimes collated their versions with others.[46] In fact, the messy manuscript evidence is the best testament to a thriving community in which these texts were shared, copied, revised, and compared. At some point, according to Dobson, a scribe, perhaps a cleric or anchoress, prepared a fresh copy (Cleopatra) which a second scribe, perhaps the author, corrected and expanded, often in the margins (see the description of the Cleopatra manuscript below). After working through the text in this way, a scribe produced Corpus (or its immediate ancestor) as a fair or clean copy of what had been worked through in Cleopatra, though Corpus itself has yet more substantial additions and a few deletions. Dobson calls Corpus "a close copy of the author's own final and definitive revision of his work" ("Affiliations," p. 163). After this, curiously, the Corpus "fair copy" does not seem to have been used to produce more authoritative copies. Instead, Cleopatra and the versions leading up to and derived from it continue to be copied.

List of Manuscripts[47]

The manuscripts listed below are in a rough chronological order, though the exact sequence is difficult to know — for example, whether Nero (or Titus) was copied before or after Corpus is difficult to say. The only relatively sure conjecture is that Cleopatra (with its many marginal additions) came before Corpus (which incorporates these additions into the main text). For more information about provenance and dialect, see Millett's *AW* bibliography, pp. 49–59. The letters in brackets provide a key to Dobson's tree diagram reproduced above.

English Versions:

Cleopatra [C]. London, British Library, Cotton Cleopatra C.vi. Eastern Worcestershire, c. 1225–30. Dobson identifies three scribes: Scribe A, who "was certainly clerically trained" (*Cleopatra*, pp. lv–lvi), made the original copy, while Scribe B, responsible for a number of marginal additions and corrections, may have been the *AW* author himself (*Cleopatra*, p. cxiv). A much later annotator, Scribe D, modernized the text. Some revisions and additions in the Preface and Part Eight are not carried over to Corpus (*Cleopatra*, pp. cxix–cxx).

Nero [N]. London, British Library, Cotton Nero A.xiv. Western Worcestershire, c. 1225–50. This version preserves elements of the earliest version of *AW* (see Explanatory Note to 4.164)

---

[46] For evidence that some additions circulated on slips of parchment, see Textual Note to 2.694.

[47] I have based the following descriptions of the manuscripts on Millett's useful summaries (*AW* bibliography, pp. 49–59), as well as on the lists of Dahood (in his article in *Middle English Prose*, pp. 2–5) and Wada (pp. xlvi–lxiv).

and also provides expanded versions of the prayers in Part One (Corpus tends to give only very brief tags). Dobson comments, somewhat crankily: "an innovating manuscript . . . written by a fussy and interfering scribe, constantly archaizing the accidence, attempting to improve the syntax, word-order, and sentence construction (almost invariably with unhappy results), and padding out the phrasing" ("Affiliations," p. 133). Since Morton chose Nero for his influential 1853 edition, it has, in Millett's words, "a special position in *AW* studies which it retained in some quarters long after its defects had been pointed out" (*AW* bibliography, p. 52).

Titus [T]. London, British Library, Cotton Titus D.xviii. Southern Cheshire, c. 1225–50. Lacks the preface and a significant portion of Part One. Occasional changes in pronouns suggest that it was adapted for a male audience.

Corpus [A]. Corpus Christi College Cambridge, MS 402, c. 1225–40. Dobson characterizes Corpus as "a close copy of the author's own final and definitive revision of his work" ("Affiliations," p. 163). It incorporates the majority of additions made in Cleopatra (to which it is closely related), along with many more expansions which are preserved in Corpus alone. Millett comments that its "linguistic consistency and generally high textual quality have made it increasingly the preferred base manuscript for editions, translations, and studies of *AW*" (*AW* bibliography, p. 49).

Lanhydrock Fragment. Oxford, Bodleian Library, MS Eng. th.c.70, c. 1300–50. Consists of a single parchment leaf (employed as a wrapper for another book), containing text which corresponds to 3.238–79. Dobson assigned it to the Nero type in his review of Mack and Zettersten's edition.

Pepys [P]. Cambridge, Magdalene College, Pepys 2498. Essex, last quarter of the fourteenth century. A fairly radical reshaping of *AW* for a readership of men and women, with a number of revisions, abridgments, and additions, by a compiler with Lollard sympathies. It contains some readings from Corpus or its near relative in Part Four. The text is titled "The Recluse" in the manuscript. See Colledge's article, "*The Recluse*: A Lollard Interpolated Version of the *Ancren Riwle*." The manuscript contains several other devotional texts in English and was once owned by the diarist Samuel Pepys.

Vernon [V]. The Vernon Manuscript. Oxford, Bodleian Library, MS Eng. Poet.a.1. West Midlands, late fourteenth century. A late, fairly reliable text of *AW* (closely related to Nero, but with corrections from Corpus or its near relative in Parts Two, Four, and Eight) with some missing folios and omissions. The Vernon Manuscript is a massive, deluxe volume of devotional texts, perhaps assembled for a lay audience.

Caius [G]. Cambridge, Gonville and Caius MS 234/120. Hereford?, c. 1350–1400 A series of excerpts from Parts Three, Four, Five, Six, Seven rearranged in "what seems a completely haphazard order" (Dobson, *Origins*, p. 296). Judging from spelling, the scribe was not trained in England (Wilson, *Gonville and Caius*, pp. x–xi). The manuscript also contains extracts from *The Lives of the Desert Fathers*. See Wilson's edition (p. xiv) for a table matching the Caius extracts to the text of Morton's edition.

Royal [R]. London, British Library, Royal 8 C.i. Fifteenth century. A reshaping of Parts Two and Three of *AW*. Attributed to the fifteenth-century preacher William Lichfield (see Baugh's edition).

French Versions

Vitellius [F]. London, British Library, Cotton Vitellius F.vii. Early fourteenth century. A translation into French from a manuscript very close to that of Cleopatra, but one which has some additions from Corpus — for this reason, Vitellius is very useful for restoring lost or mistaken readings in Corpus. Vitellius suffered severe damage in the 1731 fire at Ashburnham House, home to Robert Cotton's manuscript collection. The manuscript contains other devotional texts in French.

Trinity [S]. Cambridge, Trinity College, MS 883 (R.14.7). Late thirteenth/early fourteenth century. A translation and adaptation of *AW* into French, independent of Vitellius. The *AW* text is "broken up, rearranged, inflated, and embedded in a lengthy 'Compilation,' or series of treatises constituting a sort of handbook or manual of religious living" (Trethewey, p. ix). Two further copies, the second partial, are based on Trinity: Paris, Bibliothèque Nationale, MS. fonds français 6276 (early fourteenth century); and Oxford, Bodleian Library, Bodley 90 (late thirteenth/early fourteenth century).

Latin Versions

Latin [L]. Oxford, Merton College MS c.i.5 (Merton 44). C. 1300–50. A translation of *AW* into Latin; it breaks off after the beginning of Part Eight. Dobson comments that L, "though faithful to the gist of the original, tends to translate more freely than the different idiom of Latin would of itself require; its tendency is to omit and to compress, and in the process it often alters the phrasing at the very points where critical readings might be expected" ("Affiliations," p. 134). Though it related in some way to Titus, it also has corrected readings from Corpus or its near relative in Parts Four and Eight ("Affiliations," pp. 135–36). There are three other Latin versions based on or related to the Merton College MS: Oxford, Magdalen College MS Latin 67 (c. 1400), with Part Eight altogether missing; London, British Library, Cotton

Vitellius E.vii (early fourteenth century), which survives only in charred fragments; and London, British Library, Royal 7 C.x (beginning of sixteenth century), which has a significant omission, ending after the first 9 lines of Part Eight, as does Merton.

Related Texts

Two other groups of texts — the so-called Katherine and Wooing groups — are closely related to *AW* in language, date, and subject matter. It is likely that they were intended for the same audience of anchoresses, and that they came from the same author or school, though as Millett rightly cautions, "The linking of *AW,* KG, and WG as a larger group is . . . modern, and there is still no general agreement on whether we are dealing with a single, well-defined *oeuvre* or with a scattering of works by different authors and with ill-defined boundaries. Nevertheless, there are good reasons for treating these works at least provisionally as a single group with a common origin" (*AW* bibliography, p. 6), especially since they appear together in various combinations in thirteenth-century manuscripts.

The Katherine Group, preserved most fully in MS Oxford, Bodleian Library, Bodley 34, consists of five texts in prose: the lives of three virgin martyrs: 1) St. Katherine (in which Katherine defends herself against a group of pagan scholars), 2) St. Margaret (who does battle with the devil in the form of a dragon, specifically with the weapon of prayer), and 3) St. Juliana (who captures a demon and makes him explain the techniques he uses to tempt the faithful), along with two prose treatises: 4) "Hali Meiðhad" ("Holy Maidenhood," a vivid and often radical discussion of the value of virginity in comparison to that of marriage and widowhood — it paints an unpleasant picture of married life from a woman's point of view) and 5) "Sawles Warde" ("The Keeping of the Soul," an allegorical treatise in which the soul is represented as a house belonging to a husband called Wit and a housewife called Will: to prevent an impending robbery a variety of allegorical figures such as Caution, Fear, Justice, etc., advise the couple).

AW refers explicitly to "ower Englische boc of Seinte Margarete" (4.796), and various texts in the Katherine Group may well have been intended as devotional reading for the anchoresses,[48] who in Part One are urged to keep themselves occupied with reading in English or French (1.340) and who in Part Four are advised to read as a remedy for sloth, a remedy perhaps more potent than prayer itself:

---

[48] Savage and Watson note that the lives of Margaret and Katherine may be the earliest texts written for the anchoresses, though they both address themselves to a wider audience of married women, widows, and lay people in general (p. 285).

The remedy for sloth is the spiritual joy and the comfort of glad hope through reading, through holy meditation, or from man's mouth. Often, dear sisters, you should pray less in order to read more. Reading is itself good prayer. Reading teaches how and what one should pray for, and prayer acquires it afterwards. In the middle of reading, when the heart is pleased, a devotion (or, reverence) comes up which is worth many prayers. (4.1320–24)

The so-called "Wooing Group" consists of a series of monologues or prayers with the editorial titles, "The Wohunge of ure Lauerd" ("The Wooing of Our Lord," in which a female voice woos Christ and sets out reasons for loving him), "Ureisun of ure Louerde" ("Prayer of our Lord," another passionate love poem to Christ), "On Lofsong of ure Lefdi" ("A Song of Praise for our Lady," a litany or list-like prayer to the Virgin), and "On Lofsong of ure Louerde" ("A Song of Praise for our Lord," a prayer for mercy, also with a list-like structure). The "Wooing of Our Lord," though not found in any of the associated *AW* manuscripts, is clearly written in the language and style of Part Seven of *AW*, though here, Christ's beloved responds passionately (in *AW*, Christ woos an indifferent lady). "A Song of Praise for our Lady," the bulk of which is taken up with a series of prayers to the Virgin, has obvious points of contact with Part One of *AW*.

The following chart, adapted from Shepherd's introduction (p. xiv), shows the manuscripts in which some combination of these texts occur.

CCCC 402	Bodley 34	Royal 17 A.xxvii	Cotton Nero A.xiv	Cotton Titus D.xviii	Cotton Cleopatra c.vi
Ancrene Wisse			*Ancrene Riwle*	*Ancrene Riwle*	*Ancrene Riwle*
	Katherine	*Katherine*			
	Margaret	*Margaret*			
	Juliana	*Juliana*			
	Hali Meiðhad			*Hali Meiðhad*	
	Sawles Warde	*Sawles Warde*		*Sawles Warde*	
		On Lofsong of ure Leafdi	*On Lofsong of ure Leafdi*		
			Ureisun of ure Leafdi		
			Ureisun of ure Lauerd		
			On Lofsong of ure Louerd		
			Wooing of our Lord		

Later Influence of AW

AW exerted a strong influence on the devotional literature which followed it, particularly that of the fifteenth century. The following texts contain excerpts or adaptations from *AW*: *The Tretyse of Loue* (printed in 1493), the *Regula Reclusorum Dubliniensis* ("The Rule of the Recluses of Dublin," early fourteenth century), *The Chastising of God's Children* (early fifteenth century), *The Poor Caitif* (latter half of fourteenth century), the *Gratia Dei* (an English version of de Guilleville's *Péligrinage*), William of Lichfield's *Treatise of the Five Senses* (fifteenth century), the Vernon Manuscript's *The Life of Adam and Eve* (late fourteenth century),[49] as well as *The Pater Noster of Richard Ermyte* and a prose treatise on the Seven Deadly Sins (see Diekstra's "Some Fifteenth-Century Borrowings from the *Ancrene Wisse*").

Sources and Background

Though scholars have identified no single direct source for *AW*, they have identified a myriad of borrowings and influences from a vast range of texts including biblical commentaries, other religious rules, patristic writings (particularly those of Jerome, Gregory, Augustine, and Bernard), theological and preaching manuals, and various Latin treatises.[50]

Moralities on the Gospels

One proposed source deserves special attention and perhaps special scrutiny. The so-called *Moralities on the Gospels*, as Anne Hudson first discovered, shares a number of interpretations, images, and patristic quotations with *AW* (Dobson, *Moralities*, p. 1). In his study and partial edition, *Moralities on the Gospels: A New Source of Ancrene Wisse*, Dobson finds over one hundred parallels between the two texts, some rather loose, and concludes that *Moralities* is "a major source" of *AW*, "perhaps the most important single source yet discovered" (p. 21). Some of the most striking similarities include *Moralities'* comparison of the hypocrite to a flightless ostrich (*AW* Part Three), the sixteen attributes of confession (*AW* Part Five), the four loves (*AW* Part Seven), the idea of Christ's body as a shield (*AW* Part Seven), as well as a number of images: Greek fire, speech as mere wind, the cross-like shape of birds, the hidden hand of Moses, confession as the cleaning of a room, etc. Many of the reviewers of *Moralities*, however, have expressed scepticism about Dobson's conclusions. Joseph Wittig, for example, thinks that many

---

[49] For more details about these texts, see Wada's account (pp. xci–xcii), the basis for the list given here. Hope Emily Allen first discovered and reported on these parallels in a series of articles spanning the twenties and thirties (see Millett's bibliography for details).

[50] See the very useful index of biblical and patristic citations in *AW* (and related texts) at the end of Savage and Watson's *Anchoritic Spirituality*, pp. 435–71.

of the parallels Dobson saw in *Moralities* "are on the whole unpersuasive," since they also occur in other sources known to the *AW* author (p. 189). But the sheer number of parallels, however loose, is interesting, and the two texts may derive from a shared tradition of preaching and exegesis, or may draw on another, as yet undiscovered text.[51]

Other Religious Rules

The *AW* author clearly knew the anchoritic rule which Aelred of Rievaulx wrote for his sister between 1160 and 1162, *De Institutione Inclusarum* "Concerning the Instruction of Recluses" (lit., enclosed women), from which he seems to have borrowed the key concept of the inner and outer rules. Other borrowings from Aelred are clustered mainly in the Preface, Parts Two, Six, and Eight, and many of them concern the regulation of external behavior. See the Explanatory Notes for specific parallels. A strong case can be made that *AW* draws on some combination of the Augustinian Rule, the Augustinian Institutes of Prémontré, or the Domincan constitutions (see the section on "Authorship" above), and it is possible that the *AW* author knew other anchoritic rules, such as the tenth- or eleventh-century rule of Grimlac of Metz, the *Liber Confortatorius* by Goscelin (c. 1080), certain letters of Anselm (c. 1103–07) directed to anchoresses,[52] or the Carthusian *Consuitudines* of Guigo (Barratt, "Anchoritic Aspects," pp. 37 ff.).

The Bible and Bible Commentaries

As Shepherd writes in the excellent introduction to his partial edition of *AW*,

> The Bible provides most of the material of the Rule — the medieval Bible, a vast indivisible unity, but perceived only by glimpses. The author knows the Bible well (from a text usually recognizable as the Vulgate), but he appears to know it primarily as it was interpreted for moral and devotional purposes, and also in its use in the services of the Church . . . . Often his approach to the text is through the crust of traditional commentary, at times bizarre enough to the modern mind. On several occasions he refers to a gloss . . . . Often it is a gloss which leads him to the scriptural text, not an initial memory of Scripture[,] which prompts him to interpretation . . . .

---

[51] See Explanatory Notes to 2.801 ff., 3.50, 3.150, 3.153, 3.192 ff., 3.330, 3.504–05, 4.1382–83, 5.54 ff., 5.175 ff., 5.251, 7.53 ff., 7.86–89, 7.112 ff., 7.223, for parallels to *Moralities*.

[52] Warren describes a number of anchoritic rules from the Continent (p. 30n22) and in an appendix provides a description of all known English anchoritic rules (pp. 294–98). Earlier in the century, scholars like Hall suggested that *AW* was written by Gilbert of Sempringham (1083–1189), the founder of the Gilbertine order. Though this idea has been discarded, it is possible that *AW* took some inspiration from the Gilbertine order which founded a number of double monasteries (i.e., for both men and women) operating under the Augustinian Rule.

36

Often, of course, his use of Scripture depends on the use made of it by the author he is following. (pp. xxv–xxvi)

In interpreting biblical passages, the *AW* author often uses an encyclopedia of biblical names (wrongly attributed to St. Jerome), using the etymology of the names as a springboard into an allegorical interpretation. A good example of this method is the treatment of the Judith story, where Judith's (etymology: "confession") beheading of Holofernes (etymology: "stinking in hell") becomes an allegory for the stages of confession: (see 3.208–09 and 5.9–20). See also the allegorical treatment of Shimei in 3.583–606 as an anchoress who strays from her anchorhold.

Reference Works

AW may make use of a variety of biblical reference works which were coming into being at the time of its writing. Shepherd mentions the alphabetic handbooks known as *Distinctiones* (p. xxxviii), which listed alternative meanings for biblical words and concepts along with allegorical interpretations and etymologies,[53] and, in fact, *Moralities on the Gospels* is probably best viewed as a set of *Distinctiones*. The thirteenth-century passion for preaching gave rise to other kinds of reference works, particularly collections of exempla (sermon stories) as well as books called *Similitudines* (listing a variety of similes and metaphors to explain moral and biblical concepts). For example, the following comparison from an entry titled *intention* in the *Similitudinarium* of William de Montibus (1140–1213) explains with a colorful comparison how intentions can go wrong: "If you carry flour in the wind, the wind may scatter it."[54] *Similitudines* helped preachers to find instructive, startling, or entertaining comparisons for their sermons, and they often seem to be derived from the life-world of the laity. *AW* is fond of such startling comparisons — God's love as Greek fire (7.223 ff.), the spiritual life compared to rowing upstream (2.714 ff.), flatterers and backbiters as the devil's toilet attendants (2.433 ff.), Christ as a village wrestler (4.1240–51) — and it may be that the stimulus for some of them came from *Similitudines*. Unfortunately, the vast majority of surviving *Similitudines* have never been edited or translated.

The Lives of the Desert Fathers

AW cites several anecdotes from this collection, which it calls the *Vitas Patrum*. Written first in Greek and translated into Latin, *The Lives of the Desert Fathers* consists of several originally separate works, all offering accounts of the lives and sayings of the desert saints (both men and women).[55] Though these stories have a particular relevance to anchoresses (see the section on

---

[53] See Explanatory Note to Pref.130.

[54] *Farina si in uento portatur a uento dispergitur.* See Goering, p. 321.

[55] See Explanatory Note to 2.310.

Desert Spirituality above), it is important to realize that *The Lives of the Desert Fathers* was the forerunner of the exempla collections which multiplied in the thirteenth century, and its stories of heroism in the desert often made their way into popular preaching (see Welter's *L'Exemplum dans la littérature religieuse et didactique du moyen age*, pp. 28–42).

Patristic Sources

Among the most cited Latin authors in *AW* are Jerome, Augustine, and Gregory the Great, along with the later writers Anselm and Bernard. It is difficult to know whether the *AW* author knew these writers in full texts or whether he found the relevant quotations in collections or other handbooks. See the Explanatory Notes for remarks on specific sources.

Anglo-Latin Sources

At the moment, we know very little about how *AW* may have drawn on prominent twelfth- and thirteenth-century Anglo-Latin authors like Alexander Neckam (1157–1217), Archbishop of Canterbury Stephen Langton (died 1228), William de Montibus (1140–1213), and others. Some tentative attributions have been made (see the scattered references in Millett's *AW* bibliography), but Anglo-Latin writings from this age are a vast *terra incognita*: the majority have never been edited.[56]

Critical Reception

The Beginnings

Three projects have dominated nineteenth- and twentieth-century scholarship on *AW*. The first, the search for the identity of the anchoresses and the *AW* author, has already been discussed in the sections on *Authorship* and *Audience*, above. The second is easy to take for granted — that is, the search for the texts of *AW,* the subsequent editing of them, and the working out of the relationships between them. The third, the search for sources, continues (see the section on *Sources* above), along with some efforts at cultural assessment of the work.

---

[56] For identifications and descriptions of Neckam's many works, see Hunt's *The Schools and the Cloister*, appendix A. For Langton's sermons, see Roberts' *Studies in the Sermons of Stephen Langton*, and for William de Montibus' various handbooks and collections, see Goering's *William de Montibus: The Schools and the Literature of Pastoral Care*.

Introduction

EETS Project

The original aims of the Early English Text Society's plan to publish all the versions of *AW* are shrouded in some mystery, though it seems clear that they were intended in some way to provide the raw material from which a critical edition could be constructed. The first of the editions, that of the Latin versions, "was begun," as D'Evelyn explains, "some time ago as part of a joint undertaking to publish all surviving manuscripts of [*Ancrene Riwle*]. Once the extant texts are available the problems with which the *Ancrene Riwle* has been hedged about can be referred back at least to a common body of information and a common system of reference" (p. viii). The first phase of this monumental project is nearing completion: with Bernard Diensberg's edition of the Vernon manuscript of *AW* (forthcoming in 2000) all known manuscripts of *AW* will be represented.

The only criticism which one might voice about the EETS editions concerns their somewhat Spartan appointments — that is, they provide no glossaries, notes, or general introductions, and focus much energy on providing diplomatic texts of their manuscripts (i.e., they are essentially facsimiles in print), with no emendations or word division. As useful as they are, the EETS editions are almost impossible to use as reading texts. It is hoped that the current edition will provide a more accessible student's edition of the entire Corpus version. In turn, Bella Millett's forthcoming full critical edition will work out much more completely *AW*'s sources and manuscript relations and should bring to a close the nearly century-long search for a full scholarly text of *AW*.

Style

Many studies of *AW* in roughly the middle part of the twentieth century concentrate on issues of vocabulary and style. This focus was appropriate for the way *AW* once fit into literary history — as a representative of English style in a time when the language was threatened by the dominance of French and Latin (see the section on *Ancrene Wisse's Place in Literary History* above).

One important question revolved around the exact percentages of French, Norse, and native elements in the *AW* vocabulary. Cecily Clark showed that *AW* has a relatively high percentage of French loans (about 10% for Parts Six and Seven alone) compared to the percentage (2–6%) in the Katherine Group texts ("Lexical Divergence," p. 120). And in a remarkable series of detailed studies Arne Zettersten turned his attention to each of the components of *AW*'s vocabulary (French, Norse, and native), working out a number of etymologies and definitions (see *Middle English Word Studies*, *Studies in the Dialect*, and "French Loan-words"). Somewhat later, Diensberg compared the language of the fourteenth-century Vernon manuscript to that of the much earlier Corpus and Nero versions, concluding that Vernon modernized the language of *AW* in part by introducing more Romance loanwords (a total of 6–7%) compared with the overall proportion for Corpus (approximately 3% for the entire text ["Lexical Change," pp. 309–10]).

On general issues of style, Rygiel ("A Holistic Approach") proposed a formalistic approach to the *AW*'s style based on a modified kind of close reading, while two studies by Clark ("Wið Scharpe Sneateres") and Rygiel ("'Colloquial' Style") warned about the dangers of assuming an uncomplicated colloquial element in *AW*'s style.

The imagery of *AW* also captured the attention of many scholars. Perhaps the most important study is Janet Grayson's *Structure and Imagery in "Ancrene Wisse,"* which shows how images in *AW* tend to build into complex, cumulative patterns. See for example her analysis of various images of enclosure including the anchorhold, grave, body, womb, nest, etc. (chapters 2 and 3). Jocelyn Price also focuses on images and analogies, stressing the radical nature of metaphor and simile in *AW* (see Explanatory Note to 6.376).

Women's Spirituality

In the 1980s, *AW* began to find a new place in the literary history of early Middle English literature. More and more, scholars began to turn to *AW* as a witness of the lives and spirituality of medieval women. The turning point was Linda Georgianna's important book *The Solitary Self: Individuality in the Ancrene Wisse*. In this study, Georgianna finds in *AW* a concern for a conscious and reflective inner life and places it in the context of the twelfth-century Renaissance:

> The subtlety and specificity with which the *Wisse* author examines the inner life is ample evidence of his central interest in promoting individuality in the solitary life rather than the more traditional otherworldly goals usually set for solitaries. In this interest the author reflects the complex world of late twelfth-century and early thirteenth-century thought, a world in which various systems of thought first collided, then fused to produce a rather new set of values centering upon the individual rather than the community. In particular, the author writes at a time when the traditional distinction between an elite theology for monks and a theology for laymen collapses, resulting in a new moral theology, equally applicable to all Christians. (p. 141)

Georgianna almost single-handedly redirected scholarly attention away from the technical issues of vocabulary, sources, manuscript relations to the psychology of the anchorhold.

As the eighties and nineties progressed, feminist scholars began to broaden this picture by scrutinizing the construction of gender in *AW*, a central issue. Among the most important contributions on this topic is Elizabeth Robertson's study, *Early English Devotional Prose and the Female Audience*, which places the male author's conceptions of gender and sexuality in the foreground:

> Clearly the author's understanding of the anchoress's situation . . . was influenced by the contemporary views of female sexuality . . . . The style of *Ancrene Wisse* reflects its male

author's assumption that the spiritual potential of the women for whom he wrote was circumscribed and defined by their femininity. For example, the style of the work is accommodative, emphasizing the temporal and interactive rather than atemporal and static, focusing not on timeless Christian ideals but on the exfoliation of those ideals in daily life. The work also focuses on the personal and the contemporary rather than on the universal and the historical; it is nonteleological, concrete rather than abstract, and practical rather than theoretical. Such stylistic emphases . . . reflect the author's organization of his discussion around his underlying belief that female sexuality leads to the downfall of mankind and that a woman can achieve union with God only by recognizing that her body is responsible for that *poena damn*. (pp. 45–46)

Robertson goes on to suggest that the *AW*'s vigorous and vivid style may in itself be a reflection of these assumptions about gender.

Following the lead of Carolyn Walker Bynum in her two influential studies *Jesus as Mother* and *Holy Feast, Holy Fast*, a number of scholars emphasize that female spirituality as conceived in *AW* is linked not to the spirit but lived through the body. Jocelyn Wogan-Browne, for example, writes that much of *AW*'s "account of sense experience focuses on entry and impermeability, enclosure and leakage, sealing and opening . . . . The recluse's bodily experience in the cell is represented as a constant struggle for regulation of these permeabilities."[57] Karma Lochrie ("The Language of Transgression") and Robertson ("Medieval Medical Views") add to the discussion by looking at affective and medical assumptions about the female body.

One of the most important feminist projects has been the recovery of women's voices which in the Middle Ages were often lost, ignored, or suppressed. Robertson provides insight into this issue in "The Rule of the Body," where she stresses the fact that women's voices as they appear in *AW* are constructed by the author and tend to represent the female voice as querulous and wrong-headed. *AW* holds up silence and passivity as the highest ideals for women (p. 130). Anne Clark Bartlett's *Male Authors, Female Readers* makes a similar argument about Aelred's anchoritic rule, suggesting that Aelred makes an explicit link between female speech and sexual activity (p. 45).

The Question of Mysticism

Whether or to what extent the spirituality of *AW* is mystical remains a topic of debate. Sitwell, in his introduction to Salu's translation, was perhaps the first to suggest that the interests of the *AW* author centered more on moral or pastoral theology rather than the contemplative life (leading to mystical union with God) prized by Rolle, Hilton, and other fourteenth-century

---

[57] "Chaste Bodies: Frames and Experiences," *Framing Medieval Bodies*, ed. Sarah Kay and Miri Rubin (Manchester: Manchester University Press, 1994), p. 28.

mystics (Salu, pp. xvi–xxi). Shepherd endorsed this idea, writing that "[t]here is little point in speaking of *AW* as a mystical work" since the author "does not exalt the life of pure contemplation. It is a life of penitence he urges throughout" (pp. lvii, lviii). This view, as Watson points out, may be somewhat extreme, however. Though Watson suggests that *AW* does not see the spiritual life as a progressive path towards direct union with God in the way that later mystics did, nevertheless the intensity of emotions surrounding the inner life in *AW* for him approaches that of the English mystics of the next century ("Methods and Objectives," pp. 143 ff.).

Perhaps the most mystical passage in the entire *AW* appears in a seemingly unlikely place, in Part One's discussion of the anchoresses' prayers and liturgy (as part of the outer rule). Here, after the kiss of peace in the mass, the anchoress is to enter into a mystical union with God via the Eucharist: "After the kiss of peace, when the priest sanctifies [the Host] — forget there all the world, be there completely out of your body, embrace there in sparkling love your lover, who has descended into your bower from heaven, and hold him firmly until he has granted you all that you ever ask" (1.203–06). In the vast bulk of *AW*, on the other hand, the anchoress remains firmly rooted in a (gendered) body of pain, and the promise of spiritual embraces must, by and large, wait for the next life. It is curious that even Part Seven, which turns to spiritual love, defers the embrace of bride and bridegroom, knight and lady. Christ, in the guise of a romantic knight, makes the offer of love, but for most of Part Seven, the feminized soul refuses his embrace.

AW also differs from the writings of later English mystics like Julian of Norwich and Margery Kempe, especially in regard to devotional practices. While their books are built around the direct experience of mystical visions, the *AW* author encourages his charges to reject such sights as possibly infernal temptations: "Consider no sight that you see, either in sleep or while awake, anything but error, for it is nothing but his (i.e., the devil's) guile" (4.561–62). A bit later, "dreams" and "showings" are equated with the devil's witchcraft: "his deceitful witchcrafts and all his tricks, such as lying dreams and false visions" (4.1103–04). In this sense, *AW* may betray a male fear of women's spirituality.

In her book Margery Kempe describes meditations which seem to be in the mainstream of late medieval affective piety: she imagines biblical scenes in great detail, sometimes projecting herself in them, much as the Pseudo-Bonaventuran *Meditations on the Life of Christ* encouraged believers to do. Aelred includes a similar set of meditations at the end of his *De Institutione Inclusarum* ("Concerning the Instruction of Recluses"), where he encourages his sister and other anchoresses to imagine scenes from the past (Old and New Testament scenes), present (personal sins and gifts), and future (death, Last Judgment, heaven, and hell). In one early meditation, for example, the anchoress is to imagine herself in Bethlehem at the manger: "with all your devotion accompany the Mother as she makes her way to Bethlehem. Take shelter in the inn with her, be present and help her as she gives birth, and when the infant is laid in the manger break out into words of exultant joy. . . . Embrace that sweet crib, let love overcome your reluctance, affection drive out fear."[58]

By and large, *AW* encourages its readers to approach the spiritual life not through such meditative exercises, but through a relentlessly allegorical and exegetical way of reading. Even the meditations on the passion embedded in Part Two, though they have their affective side, are mainly tied into arguments about the body and how it is to be regulated.

Editorial Principles

This edition aims to provide a reading text of the Corpus version of *AW*, though it is *not* a full critical edition in one important sense: it is not based on a full collation (i.e., a painstaking comparison) of all the versions. Instead, other manuscripts are consulted only when Corpus has gone wrong in some way, either by recording a mistaken form or by omitting text inadvertently.

Though this method may seem close to "best text" editing, it is somewhat different in spirit. In "best text" editing, an editor decides which of the many versions is closest to the author's intended text and then reproduces it with a minimum of editorial intervention.[59] (Eclectic editions, by contrast, might take readings from any of the versions, provided these readings can be deemed authorial — though in practice such judgments are often very subjective.) The main difference between the editorial approach employed here and best text editing has to do with the attitude towards authorial intention. The Corpus version was not chosen as the basis of this edition because it represents, in Dobson's words, "a close copy of the author's own final and definitive revision of his work" ("Affiliations," p. 163). The Corpus version is simply one of the most interesting versions, since it incorporates a number of earlier additions as well as its own expansions. After surveying twentieth-century editorial theory, Millett suggests that *AW* changes and shifts so much that even such a revision as Corpus cannot be viewed as definitive or final ("*Mouvance*," p. 18). It seems best to view *AW* as an evolving text — each of the versions is worthy of study (and thanks to the far-sighted EETS project to edit all the versions separately, such study is possible).

One problem with placing too much emphasis on authorial intention is that such an attitude tends to make idiots of scribes, who in this textual model can do nothing but either preserve or (more likely) corrupt the author's original text, rendering "unauthoritative" versions unworthy of interest (see Dobson's description of the Nero manuscript above). Though scribes clearly

---

[58] All quotations from Aelred's treatise come from Sister Penelope's translation, *Treatises & Pastoral Prayer*.

[59] Speer describes the the evolution of best text editing in the hands of Joseph Bédier: "Bédier, reacting against composite texts with elaborate variant apparatus prepared by editors who viewed themselves as collaborators with the authors, emphasized his own restraint: . . . 'I offer the reader nothing but the text of a good manuscript, repaired only in the few cases enumerated above'" (p. 396).

make mistakes, it seems to me possible to view the production of *AW* texts as in some sense collaborative, involving not just the author's intentions but also the suggestions and additions of its female audience and its scribes. In this respect it may be a more useful cultural document than the original.

Textual Notes

Some effort has been given to make the textual notes accessible to ordinary readers and to avoid the nearly indecipherable calculus of variants found in some critical editions. Each variant is recorded separately and the reasoning behind each emendation is given. Any italics or brackets in the main text of *AW* indicate that Corpus has been changed in some way and that interested readers can find a textual note on the subject.

Regularization of Spelling

In accordance with the goal of this series I have regularized the spelling of the text: Þ/þ and ð have been transliterated as *th*, while yogh (3) almost always appears as *y*. In addition I have brought variations between *u/v* and *i/j* into line with modern practice. Since the goal of this edition is to provide a convenient reading text for students, I have hyphenated difficult compounds.

Same Page Glosses

The aim of the same-page glosses is not to give a fluid, running translation of the text (for this consult the excellent translations of White or Savage and Watson), but rather to provide the literal sense of the Middle English text as an aid for understanding it on its own terms. Sometimes the glosses themselves will be somewhat challenging to modern idiomatic sense, though they do provide guiding suggestions and supply words not in the Middle English (in parentheses) to complete the meaning. Since biblical quotations in *AW* are often loose, either because they are cited from memory or consciously simplified, they are translated freshly rather than taking them from modern English translation of the Vulgate.

Introduction

Select Bibliography

Concordance

Potts, Jennifer, Lorna Stevenson, and Jocelyn Wogan-Browne, eds. *Concordance to Ancrene Wisse, MS Corpus Christi College Cambridge 402*. Woodbridge, Suffolk: D. S. Brewer, 1993.

AW Bibliography

Millett, Bella. *Ancrene Wisse, The Katherine Group, and The Wooing Group*. Annotated Bibliographies of Old and Middle English Literature, no. 2. With the assistance of George B. Jack and Yoko Wada. Cambridge: D. S. Brewer, 1996.

EETS Editions of the Various Versions of *AW*

Baugh, A. C., ed. *The English Text of the Ancrene Riwle: Edited from British Museum MS Royal 8 C.i*. EETS o.s. 232. London: Oxford University Press, 1956.

Day, Mabel. *The English Text of the Ancrene Riwle: Edited from Cotton MS Nero A.xiv, on the Basis of a Transcript by J. A. Herbert*. EETS o.s. 225. London: Oxford University Press, 1952.

D'Evelyn, Charlotte, ed. *The Latin Text of the Ancrene Riwle: Edited from Merton College MS 44 and British Museum MS Cotton Vitellius E.vii*. EETS o.s. 216. London: Oxford University Press, 1944.

Diensberg, Bernard, ed. *The English Text of the Ancrene Riwle: MS. Bodleian Library Eng. Poet. a.1*. EETS. Forthcoming 2000. [See also *The Vernon Manuscript: A Facsimile of Bodleian Library, Oxford, MS. Eng. Poet. a.1*. With an introduction by A. I. Doyle. Cambridge: D. S. Brewer, 1987.]

Dobson, E. J., ed. *The English Text of the Ancrene Riwle: Edited from British Museum Cotton MS. Cleopatra C.vi*. EETS o.s. 267. London: Oxford University Press, 1972.

Herbert, J. A., ed. *The French Text of the Ancrene Riwle: Edited from MS. Cotton Vitellius F.vii*. EETS o.s. 219. London: Oxford University Press, 1944.

Mack, F. M., ed. *The English Text of the Ancrene Riwle: Edited from Cotton MS. Titus D.xviii. and Bodleian MS. Eng. th.c.70.* EETS o.s. 252. London: Oxford University Press, 1963

Tolkien, J. R. R., ed. *The English Text of the Ancrene Riwle: Ancrene Wisse: Edited from MS. Corpus Christi College, Cambridge 402.* Intro. by N. R. Ker. EETS o.s. 249. London: Oxford University Press, 1962.

Trethewey, W. H., ed. *The French Text of the Ancrene Riwle: Edited from Trinity College, Cambridge MS R.147.* EETS o.s. 240. London: Oxford University Press, 1958.

Wilson, R. M., ed. *The English Text of the Ancrene Riwle: Edited from Gonville and Caius College MS. 234/120.* Intro. by N. R. Ker. EETS o.s. 229. London: Oxford University Press, 1954.

Zettersten, Arne, ed. *The English Text of the Ancrene Riwle: Edited from Magdalene College, Cambridge MS. Pepys 2498.* EETS o.s. 274. London: Oxford University Press, 1976.

Full Editions

Morton, James, ed. *The Ancren Riwle: A Treatise on the Rules and Duties of Monastic Life, Edited and Translated from a Semi-Saxon MS. of the Thirteenth Century.* London: Camden Society, 1853. [Based on Nero.]

Partial Editions

Ackerman, Robert W., and Roger Dahood, eds. *Ancrene Riwle: Introduction and Part I.* Binghamton, NY: Medieval & Renaissance Texts & Studies, 1984.

Bennett, J. A. W., and G. V. Smithers, eds. *Early Middle English Verse and Prose.* Glossary by Norman Davis. Second ed. Oxford: Clarendon Press, 1968.

Hall, Joseph, ed. *Selections from Early Middle English, 1130–1250.* 2 vols. Oxford: Clarendon Press, 1920.

Millett, Bella, and Jocelyn Wogan-Browne, eds. *Medieval English Prose for Women from the Katherine Group and Ancrene Wisse.* Oxford: Clarendon Press, 1990.

Shepherd, Geoffrey, ed. *Ancrene Wisse: Parts Six and Seven*. London: Thomas Nelson & Sons, 1959. Rev. ed. Exeter: University of Exeter Press, 1991.

Wada, Yoko, ed. and trans. *"Temptations" from Ancrene Wisse*. Vol. 1. Suita, Osaka: Institute of Oriental and Occidental Studies, Kansai University, 1994.

Translations of *AW*

Salu, Mary, trans. *The Ancrene Riwle (The Corpus MS.: Ancrene Wisse)*. Preface by J. R. R. Tolkien. Intro. by Gerard Sitwell. London: Burns and Oaks, 1955/Exeter: University of Exeter Press, 1990.

Savage, Anne, and Nicholas Watson, trans. *Anchoritic Spirituality: Ancrene Wisse and Associated Works*. Pref. by Benedicta Ward. New York: Paulist Press, 1991.

White, Hugh, trans. *Ancrene Wisse: Guide for Anchoresses*. London: Penguin Books, 1993.

Primary Sources

Aelred of Rievaulx. *Treatises & Pastoral Prayer*. Trans. Sister Penelope. Intro. by David Knowles. Kalamazoo, MI: Cistercian Publications, 1971.

Anselm. *The Prayers and Meditations of Saint Anselm with the Proslogion*. Trans. Benedicta Ward. Foreword by R. W. Southern. Harmondsworth: Penguin Books, 1973.

Bernard of Clairvaux. *Sermons on Conversion and Lenten Sermons on the Psalm "He who Dwells."* Translated with Introduction by Marie-Bernard Saïd. Kalamazoo, MI: Cistercian Publications, 1981.

———. *The Steps of Humility and Pride*. Trans. M. Ambrose Conway. Intro. by M. Basil Pennington. Kalamazoo, MI: Cistercian Publications, 1989.

Brown, Carleton, ed. *English Lyrics of the XIIIth Century*. Oxford: Clarendon, 1932.

Bruce, J. D. "*De Ortu Waluuanii*: An Arthurian Romance now first edited from the Cottonian MS. Faustina B.vi., of the British Museum." *PMLA* 13 (1898), 365–456.

Colledge, Eric. "*The Recluse*: A Lollard Interpolated Version of the *Ancren Riwle*." *Review of English Studies* 15 (1939), 1–5, 129–45.

Curley, Michael J., trans. *Physiologus*. Austin: University of Texas Press, 1979.

d'Ardenne, S. R. T. O, ed. *Þe Liflade ant te Passiun of Seinte Iuliene*. EETS o.s. 248. London: Oxford University Press, 1961.

D'Evelyn, Charlotte, and Anna J. Mill, eds. *The South English Legendary*. EETS o.s. 236. London: Oxford University Press, 1956.

Furlong, Monica, trans. *The Life of Christina of Markyate*. Berkhamsted, Hertfordshire: Arthur James, 1997.

Isidore of Seville. *Isidori Hispalensis episcopi Etymologiarum sive Originum livri XX*. 2 vols. Ed. W. M. Lindsay. Oxford: Clarendon Press, 1911.

Jacobus de Voraigne. *The Golden Legend, Readings on the Saints*. 2 vols. Trans. William Granger Ryan. Princeton: Princeton University Press, 1993.

Kempe, Margery. *The Book of Margery Kempe*. Ed. Lynn Staley. Kalamazoo, MI: Medieval Institute Publications, 1996.

Mack, Frances M., ed. *Seinte Marherete þe Meiden ant Martyr: Re-edited from MS. Bodley 34, Oxford, and MS. Royal 17A xxvii, British Museum*. EETS o.s. 193. London: Oxford University Press, 1934.

McMillan, Douglas J., and Kathryn Smith Fladenmuller. *Regular Life: Monastic, Canonical, and Mendicant Rules*. Kalamazoo, MI: Medieval Institute Publications, 1997.

Millett, Bella, ed. *Hali Meiðhad*. EETS o.s. 284. London: Oxford University Press, 1982.

Rothwell, Harry, ed. *English Historical Documents, 1189–1327*. New York: Oxford University Press, 1975.

Russell, Norman, trans. *The Lives of the Desert Fathers*. Intro. by Benedicta Ward. Kalamazoo, MI: Cistercian Publications, 1980.

Thompson, W. Meredith, ed. *Þe Wohunge of Ure Lauerd. Edited from British Museum Ms. Cotton Titus D.XVIII, together with On Ureisun of Ure Louerde, On wel swuðe god Ureisun of God Almihti, On Lofsong of Ure Louerde, On Lofsong of Ure Lefdi [and] Þe Oreisun of Seinte Marie, from the Manuscripts in Which They Occur.* EETS o.s. 241. London: Oxford University Press. 1958.

Ward, Benedicta, trans. *The Sayings of the Desert Fathers: The Alphabetical Collection.* Kalamazoo, MI: Cistercian Publications, 1984.

White, T. H., trans. *The Book of Beasts: Being a Translation from a Latin Bestiary of the Twelfth Century.* New York: Putnam, 1954/New York: Dover, 1984.

Wilhelm, James J., ed. *The Romance of Arthur: An Anthology of Medieval Texts in Translation.* Second ed. New York: Garland, 1994.

Wright, Thomas, ed. *Alexandri Neckam De Naturis Rerum Libri Duo with the Poem of the Same Author, De Laudibus Divinae Sapientiae.* London: Longman, 1863.

Secondary Criticism

Abulafia, Anna Sapir. *Christians and Jews in the Twelfth Century Renaissance.* New York: Routledge, 1995.

Ackerman, Robert W. "The Liturgical Day in *Ancrene Riwle*." *Speculum* 53 (1978), 734–44.

Allen, Hope Emily. "The Origin of the *Ancren Riwle*." *PMLA* 33 (1918), 474–546.

———. "On the Author of the *Ancrene Riwle*." *PMLA* 44 (1929), 679–80.

Astell, Ann W. *The Song of Songs in the Middle Ages.* Ithaca: Cornell University Press, 1990.

Baldwin, Mary. "*Ancrene Wisse* and its Background in the Christian Tradition of Religious Instruction and Spirituality." Ph.D. Diss. University of Toronto, 1974.

———. "Some Difficult Words in the *Ancrene Riwle*." *Medieval Studies* 38 (1976), 268–90.

Barratt, Alexandra. "Anchoritic Aspects of *Ancrene Wisse*." *Medium Ævum* 49 (1980), 32–56.

————. "The Five Wits and Their Structural Significance in Part II of *Ancrene Wisse*." *Medium Ævum* 56 (1987), 12–24.

Bartlett, Anne Clark. *Male Authors, Female Readers: Representation and Subjectivity in Middle English Devotional Literature.* Ithaca: Cornell University Press, 1995.

Bennett, J. A. W. "Lefunge O Swefne, O Nore." *Review of English Studies* 9 (1958), 280–81.

Bishop, Ian. "Greek Fire in the 'Ancrene Wisse' and Contemporary Texts." *Notes and Queries* 26 (1979), 198–99.

Bloomfield, Morton W. *The Seven Deadly Sins: An Introduction to the History of a Religious Concept, with Special Reference to Medieval English Literature.* East Lansing, MI: Michigan State College Press, 1952.

Boyle, L. E. "Summa confessorum." *Les genres littéraires dans les sources théologiques et philosophiques médiévales. Définition, critique, et explotation.* Publications de l'Institute d'Études Médiévales, ser. 2/5. Louvain: Université Catholique de Louvain, 1982. Pp. 227–37.

Breeze, Andrew. "Welsh *Baban* 'Baby' and *Ancrene Wisse*." *Notes & Queries* 40 (1993), 12–13.

Brewer, Derek. "Two Notes on the Augustinian and Possibly West Midland Origin of the *Ancren Riwle*." *Notes and Queries* 3 (1956), 232–35.

Brook, G. L., ed. *The Harley Lyrics: The Middle English Lyrics of Ms. Harley 2253.* Manchester: Manchester University Press, 1956.

Brown, Peter. *The World of Late Antiquity.* New York: Harcourt Brace Jovanovich, 1979.

————. *The Body and Society: Men, Women, and Sexual Renunciation in Early Christianity.* New York: Columbia University Press, 1988.

Bynum, Caroline Walker. *Jesus as Mother: Studies in the Spirituality of the High Middle Ages.* Berkeley: University of California Press, 1982.

————. *Holy Feast, Holy Fast: The Religious Significance of Food to Medieval Women.* Berkeley: University of California Press, 1987.

Introduction

Chambers, E. K. *On the Continuity of English Prose from Alfred to More and his School: An Extract from the Introduction to Nicholas Harpsfield's Life of Sir Thomas More*. EETS o.s. 191A. London: Oxford University Press, 1957.

Clark, Cecily. "*Ancrene Wisse* and *Katherine Group*: A Lexical Divergence." *Neophilologus* 50 (1966), 117–24.

———. "As Seint Austin Seith." *Medium Ævum* 46 (1977), 212–18.

———. "'Wið Scharpe Sneateres': Some Aspects of Colloquialism in 'Ancrene Wisse.'" *Neuphilologische Mitteilungen* 79 (1978), 341–53.

Clay, R. M. *The Hermits and Anchorites of England*. London: Methuen, 1914.

Cooper, Sister Ethelbert. "Latin Elements of the *Ancrene Riwle*." Ph.D. Diss. Birmingham University, 1956.

Cross, F. L., and E. A. Livingstone, eds. *The Oxford Dictionary of the Christian Church*. Second corrected ed. Oxford: Oxford University Press, 1983.

Dahood, Roger. "A Lexical Puzzle in *Ancrene Wisse*." *Notes and Queries* 25 (1978), 1–2.

———. "*Ancrene Wisse*, the Katherine Group, and the Wohunge Group." In *Middle English Prose: A Guide to Major Authors and Genres*. Ed. A. S. G. Edwards. New Brunswick: Rutgers University Press, 1984. Pp. 1–34.

———. "Design in Part I of *Ancrene Riwle*." *Medium Ævum* 56 (1987), 1–11.

———. "The Use of Coloured Initials and Other Division Markers in Early Versions of *Ancrene Wisse*." In *Medieval English Studies Presented to George Kane*. Ed. Edward Donald Kennedy. Woodbridge: Brewer, 1988. Pp. 79–97.

d'Ardenne, S. R. T. O. "Two Words from *Ancrene Wisse* and the *Katherine Group*." *Notes and Queries* 29 (1982), 3.

———. "Two Notes on Early Middle English Texts." In *Five Hundred Years of Words and Sounds: A Festschrift for Eric Dobson*. Ed. E. G. Stanley and Douglas Gray. Cambridge: D. S. Brewer, 1983. Pp. 201–02.

d'Avray, D. L. *The Preaching of the Friars: Sermons diffused from Paris before 1300.* Oxford: Clarendon Press, 1985.

Delaney, John. *Dictionary of Saints.* Garden City, NY: Doubleday, 1980.

Diekstra, F. N. M. "Some Fifteenth-Century Borrowings from the *Ancrene Wisse.*" *English Studies* 7 (1990), 81–104.

Diensberg, Bernhard. "*Ancrene Wisse/Riwle,* 'Surquide,' 'Caue,' 'Creauant/Creaunt,' 'Trusse,' 'Bereget' and 'Babanliche.'" *Archiv* 215 (1978), 79–82.

———. "Lexical Change in the 'Ancrene Riwle,' with Special Consideration of the Romance and Scandinavian Loanwords." In *Symposium on Lexicography 5: Proceedings of the Fifth International Symposium on Lexicography, May 3–5, 1990, at the University of Copenhagen.* Ed. Karl Hyldgaard-Jensen and Arne Zettersten. Tübingen: Max Niemeyer, 1992. Pp. 295–313.

Dobson, E. J. "The Affiliations of the Manuscripts of *Ancrene Wisse.*" In *English and Medieval Studies Presented to J. R. R. Tolkien.* Ed. Norman Davis and C. L. Wrenn. London: George Allen and Unwin, 1962. Pp. 128–63.

———. Rev. of Mack and Zettersten. *Titus-Lanhydrock Fragment. Medium Ævum* 36 (1967), 187–91.

———. *Moralities on the Gospels: A New Source of Ancrene Wisse.* Oxford: Clarendon Press, 1975.

———. *The Origins of "Ancrene Wisse."* Oxford: Clarendon Press, 1976.

Dolan, T. P. "'Riote' in *Ancrene Wisse.*" *ELN* 16 (1979), 198–200.

Dymes, Dorothy M. E. "The Original Language of the *Ancren Riwle.*" *Essays and Studies* 9 (1924), 31–49.

Evans, Joan. *Magical Jewels of the Middle Ages and the Renaissance, particularly in England.* Oxford: Clarendon Press, 1922.

Fletcher, Alan J. "Black, White, and Grey in *Hali Meiðhad* and *Ancrene Wisse.*" *Medium Ævum* 62 (1993), 69–78.

Introduction

Georgianna, Linda. *The Solitary Self: Individuality in the Ancrene Wisse*. Cambridge, MA: Harvard University Press, 1981.

Goering, Joseph. *William de Montibus: The Schools and the Literature of Pastoral Care*. Toronto: Pontifical Institute, 1992.

Gow, Andrew Colin. *The Red Jews: Antisemitism in an Apocalyptic Age, 1200–1600*. Leiden: E. J. Brill, 1995.

Gray, J. H. "The Influence of Confessional Literature in the Composition of the 'Ancrene Riwle.'" Ph.D. Diss. University of London, 1961.

Grayson, Janet. "The Eschatalogical Adam's Kirtle." *Mystics Quarterly* 11 (1985): 153–60.

————. *Structure and Imagery in "Ancrene Wisse."* Hanover, NH: University Press of New England, 1974.

Hinnebusch, William. *The History of the Dominican Order*. 2 vols. New York: Alba House, 1966.

Hunt, R. W. *The Schools and the Cloister: The Life and Writings of Alexander Nequam*. Ed. and rev. by Margaret Gibson. Oxford: Clarendon, 1984.

Innes-Parker, Catherine. "The Lady and the King: *Ancrene Wisse*'s Parable of the Royal Wooing Re-Examined." *English Studies* 75 (1994), 509–22.

Jack, George B. "*Luste* in *Ancrene Wisse*." *Neuphilologische Mitteilungen* 78 (1977), 24–26.

Jung, C. J. *Mysterium Conjunctionis: An Inquiry into the Separation and Synthesis of Psychic Opposites in Alchemy*. Second ed. Trans. R. F. C. Hull. New York: Pantheon, 1963.

Kaske, R. E. "The Three Leaps of Eve." *Medium Aevum* 29 (1960), 22–24.

Käsmann, Hans. "Zur Frage der ursprünglichen Fassung der *Ancrene Riwle*." *Anglia* 75 (1957), 134–56.

Kirchberger, Clare. "Some Notes on the *Ancrene Riwle*." *Dominican Studies* 7 (1954), 215–38.

Laing, Margaret, and Angus McIntosh. "The Language of the *Ancrene Riwle*, The Katherine Group Texts and *Þe Wohunge of Ure Lauerd* in BL Cotton Titus D XVIII." *Neuphilologische Mitteilungen* 96 (1995), 235–63.

Latham, R. E., ed. *Revised Medieval Latin Word-List from British and Irish Sources*. London: British Academy, 1965.

Lochrie, Karma. "The Language of Transgression: Body, Flesh, and Word in Mystical Discourse." In *Speaking Two Languages: Traditional Disciplines and Contemporary Theory in Medieval Studies*. Ed. Allen J. Frantzen. Albany: State University of New York Press, 1991. Pp. 115–40, 253–59.

Macaulay, G. C. "The 'Ancren Riwle.'" *Modern Language Review* 9 (1914), 14–60, 63–78, 324–31, 463–74.

Magoun, Francis P. "*Ancrene Wisse* vs. *Ancrene Riwle*." *ELH* 4 (1937), 112–13.

Maybury, James. "On The Structure and Significance of Part III of the *Ancrene Riwle* With Some Comment on Sources." *American Benedictine Review* 28 (1977), 95–101.

Mayr-Harting, H. "Functions of a Twelfth-Century Recluse." *History* 60 (1975), 337–52.

McDonnell, Ernest W. *The Beguines and Beghards in Medieval Culture, With Special Emphasis on the Belgian Scene*. New York: Octagon Books, 1969.

McNabb, Vincent. "The Authorship of the Ancren Riwle." *Archivum Fratrum Praedicatorum* 4 (1934), 49–74.

Millett, Bella. *"Hali Meiðhad, Sawles Warde,* and the Continuity of English Prose." In *Five Hundred Years of Words and Sounds: A Festschrift For Eric Dobson*. Ed. E. G. Stanley and Douglas Gray. Cambridge: D. S. Brewer, 1983. Pp. 100–08.

———. "The Origins of the *Ancrene Wisse*: New Answers, New Questions." *Medium Ævum* 61 (1992), 206–28.

———. "*Mouvance* and the Medieval Author: Re-Editing *Ancrene Wisse*." In *Late-Medieval Religious Texts and their Transmission: Essay in Honour of A. I. Doyle*. Ed. A. J. Minnis. Woodbridge, Suffolk: D. S. Brewer, 1994. Pp. 9–20.

————. "*Peintunge* and *Schadewe* in *Ancrene Wisse* Part 4." *Notes and Queries* 43 (1996), 399–403.

————. "Women in No Man's Land: English Recluses and the Development of Vernacular Literature in the Twelfth and Thirteenth Centuries." In *Women and Literature in Britain, 1150–1500*. Ed. Carol M. Meale. Second ed. Cambridge: Cambridge University Press, 1996. Pp. 86–103.

Owst, G. R. *Literature and Pulpit in Medieval England: a Neglected Chapter in the History of English Letters & of the English People*. Cambridge: Cambridge University Press, 1933.

Partington, J. R. *A History of Greek Fire and Gunpowder*. Reprint with new intro. by Bert S. Hall. Baltimore: The Johns Hopkins University Press, 1999.

Price, Jocelyn. "Inner and Outer: Conceptualizing the Body in *Ancrene Wisse* and Aelred's *De Institutione Inclusarum*." In *Medieval English Religious and Ethical Literature: Essays in Honour of G. H. Russell*. Ed. Gregory James and James Simpson. Cambridge: Cambridge University Press, 1986. Pp. 192–208.

Roberts, Phyllis Barzillay. *Studies in the Sermons of Stephen Langton*. Toronto: Pontifical Institute, 1968.

Robertson, Elizabeth. "The Rule of the Body: The Feminine Spirituality of the *Ancrene Wisse*." In *Seeking the Woman in Late Medieval and Renaissance Writings: Essays in Feminist Contextual Criticism*. Ed. Janet E. Halley and Sheila Fisher. Knoxville: University of Tennessee Press, 1989. Pp. 109–34.

————. "An Anchorhold of her Own: Female Anchoritic Literature in Thirteenth-Century England." In *Equally in God's Image:Women in the Middle Ages*. Ed. Julia Bolton Holloway, Constance S. Wright, and Joan Bechtold. New York: P. Lang, 1990. Pp. 170–83.

————. *Early English Devotional Prose and the Female Audience*. Knoxville: University of Tennessee Press, 1990.

————. "Medieval Medical Views of Women and Female Spirituality in the *Ancrene Wisse* and Julian of Norwich's *Showings*." In *Feminist Approaches to the Body in Medieval Literature*. Ed. Linda Lomperis and Sarah Stanbury. Philadelphia: University of Pennsylvania Press, 1993. Pp. 143–67.

Rouse, Richard H., and Mary H. Rouse. "Biblical *Distinctiones* in the Thirteenth Century." *Archives d'histoire docrtrinale et littéraire du moyen âge* 41 (1974), 27–37.

Rouse, Richard H., and Siegfried Wenzel. Review of E. J. Dobson, *Moralities on the Gospels. Speculum* 52 (1977), 648–52.

Rousseau, Phillip. *Ascetics, Authority, and the Church in the Age of Jerome and Cassian.* New York: Oxford University Press, 1978.

Rumsey, Lucinda. "The Scorpion of Lechery and the *Ancrene Wisse.*" *Medium Ævum* 61 (1992), 48–58.

Russell-Smith, Joy. "Ridiculosae Sternutationes (*o nore* in *Ancrene Wisse*)." *Review of English Studies* 8 (1957), 266–69.

Rygiel, Dennis. "The Allegory of Christ the Lover-Knight in *Ancrene Wisse*: An Experiment in Stylistic Analysis." *Studies in Philology* 73 (1976), 343–64.

———. "Structure and Style in Part Seven of *Ancrene Wisse.*" *Neuphilologische Mitteilungen* 81 (1980), 47–56.

———. "*Ancrene Wisse* and 'Colloquial' Style — a Caveat." *Neophilologus* 65 (1981), 137–43.

———. "A Holistic Approach to the Style of *Ancrene Wisse.*" *Chaucer Review* 16 (1982), 270–81.

Savage, Anne. "The Translation of the Feminine: Untranslatable Dimensions of Anchoritic Works." In *The Medieval Translator 4*. Ed. Roger Ellis and Ruth Evans. Binghamton, NY: Medieval and Renaissance Texts and Studies, 1994. Pp. 181–99.

Shepherd, Geoffrey. "All the Wealth of Croesus . . . : A Topic in the 'Ancren Riwle.'" *Modern Language Review* 51 (1956), 161–67.

Smithers, G. V. "Two Typological Terms in the *Ancrene Riwle.*" *Medium Ævum* 34 (1965), 126–28.

Speer, Mary B. "Old French Literature." In *Scholarly Editing: A Guide to Research*. Ed. D. C. Greetham. New York: Modern Language Association, 1995. Pp. 394–416.

Introduction

Stanley, E. G. "*The Owl and the Nightingale* 1335: 'Thu Liest Iwis, Thu Fule Thing!'" *Notes and Queries* 38 (1991), 152.

Szittya, Penn. *The Antifraternal Tradition in Medieval Literature*. Princeton: Princeton University Press, 1986.

Thorndike, Lynn. *A History of Magic and Experimental Science*. 8 vols. New York: Macmillan, 1923–58.

Tolkien, J. R. R. "*Ancrene Wisse* and *Hali Meiðhad*." *Essays and Studies* 14 (1929), 104–26.

Turville-Petre, Joan. "Two Etymological Notes: Ancrene Wisse *Eskibah, hond þet ilke*." *Studia Neophilologica* 41 (1969), 156–61.

Turville-Petre, Thorlac. *England the Nation: Language, Literature, and National Identity, 1290–1340*. Oxford: Clarendon Press, 1996.

Waldron, R. A. "Enumeration in *Ancrene Wisse*." *Notes and Queries* 16 (1969), 86–87.

Warren, Ann K. *Anchorites and their Patrons in Medieval England*. Berkeley: University of California Press, 1985.

Watson, Nicholas. "The Methods and Objectives of Thirteenth-Century Anchoritic Devotion." In *The Medieval Mystical Tradition in England: Exeter Symposium IV*. Ed. Marion Glasscoe. Cambridge: Cambridge University Press, 1987. Pp. 132–54.

Welter, J. *L'Exemplum dans la littérature religieuse et didactique du moyen âge*. Paris: Occitania, 1927.

Wenzel, Siegfried. "The Three Enemies of Man." *Mediaeval Studies* 29 (1967), 47–66.

Whiting, B. J. *Proverbs, Sentences and Proverbial Phrases from English Writings Mainly before 1500*. Cambridge, MA: Belknap Press of Harvard University Press, 1968.

———. Rev. of Carleton Brown, *English Lyrics of the Thirteenth Century*. *Speculum* 9 (1934), 219–25.

Wilson, Edward. "The Four Loves in *Ancrene Wisse*." *RES* 19 (1968), 41–47.

Wittig, Joseph S. Rev. of E. J. Dobson, *Moralities on the Gospels*. *Anglia* 98 (1980), 185–90.

Woolf, Rosemary. "The Theme of Christ the Lover-Knight." *Review of English Studies* 13 (1962), 1–16.

Zettersten, Arne. *Middle English Word Studies*. Lund: C. W. K. Gleerup, 1964.

———. *Studies in the Dialect and Vocabulary of the Ancrene Riwle*. Copenhagen: C. W. K. Gleerup, 1965.

———. "French Loan-Words in the *Ancrene Riwle* and Their Frequency." *Mélanges de philologie offerts à Alf Lombard*. Lund: C. W. K. Gleerup, 1969. Pp. 227–50.

Ancrene Wisse

Author's Preface

I the Feaderes ant i the Sunes ant i the Hali Gastes nome her biginneth Ancrene Wisse.

Recti diligunt te (in Canticis, sponsa ad sponsum). Est rectum gramaticum, rectum geometricum, rectum theologicum. Et sunt differencie totidem regularum. De recto theologico sermo nobis est, cuius regule due sunt: una circa cordis directionem. Altera versatur circa exteriorum rectificationem. Recti diligunt te.

"Laverd," seith Godes spuse to hire deore-wurthe spus, "the rihte luvieth the." Theo beoth rihte the luvieth efter riwle. Ant ye, mine leove sustren, habbeth moni dei i-cravet on me efter riwle. Monie cunne riwlen beoth, ah twa beoth bimong alle thet ich chulle speoken of thurh ower bone, with Godes grace. The an riwleth the heorte ant maketh efne ant smethe, withute cnost ant dolc of woh in-wit ant of wreiyende, the segge "her

---

1 I, In; **nome**, name; **Ancrene Wisse**, Anchoresses' Guide. **2–6** *Recti diligunt te . . . te*, "The righteous love you" (in the *Song of Songs* [1:3], the bride to the bridegroom). There is a right grammar, a right geometry, a right theology. There are different rules for each discipline. Our topic is right theology, which has two rules: one concerning the direction of the heart. The other is occupied with the ordering or rectification of outer things. "The righteous love you." **7–9 "Laverd," seith Godes spuse . . . me efter riwle**, "Lord," says God's spouse (or, bride) to her precious spouse (or, bridegroom), "the righteous love you." They are righteous who love according to a rule. And you, my dear sisters, have many a day begged for a rule from me. **9–10 Monie cunne riwlen beoth . . . ower bone**, There are many kinds of rules, but [there] are two from among all [of them] that I will speak about at your request. **10–12 The an riwleth . . . hit ahte!** The one rules the heart and makes [it] even and smooth, without the lump and gash of a twisted conscience, and of an accusing [one], which [might] say, "here you sin!" or "this is not

59

thu sunegest!" other "this nis nawt i-bet yet ase wel as hit ahte!" Theos riwle is eaver
in-with ant rihteth the heorte. **Et hec est caritas, quam describit Apostulus: de corde
puro et consciencia bona et fide non ficta.** "Theos riwle is chearite of schir heorte

15   ant cleane in-wit ant treowe bileave." **Pretende, inquit Psalmista, misericoridam
tuam scientibus te per fidem non fictam, et justiciam tuam — id est, uite
rectitudinem — hiis qui recto sunt corde — qui sunt omnes voluntates suas
dirigunt ad regulam divine voluntatis. Isti dicuntur boni anto[no]masice.
Psalmista: Benefac, Domine, bonis et rectis corde. Istis dicitur ut glorientur**

20   **testimonio videlicet bone conscientie. Gloriamini omnes recti corde, quos scilicet rectificavit regula illa supprema, rectificans omnia. De qua Augustinus: Nichil
petendum preter regulam magisterii. Et Apostolus: Omnes in eadem regula
permaneamus.** The other riwle is al withuten ant riwleth the licome ant licomliche
deden, the teacheth al hu me schal beoren him withuten, hu eoten, drinken, werien,

25   singen, slepen, wakien. **Et hec est exercitio corporis que, juxta apostolum, modicum valet, et est quasi regula recti mechanici quod geometri[c]o recto continetur.**

atoned for as well as it ought [to be]!" **12–13 Theos riwle . . . heorte**, This rule is always
within and directs the heart. **13–14 *Et hec . . . ficta***, And this is the love which the Apostle
describes: "from pure heart and good conscience and unfeigned faith" (1 Timothy 1:5). **14–
15 chearite of schir . . . bileave**, the love of a clean heart and a pure conscience and true belief.
15–23 *Pretende, inquit Psalmista . . . permaneamus*, "Extend," says the Psalmist, "your
mercy to those who know you through a faith unfeigned, and through your justice — that is,
through rectitude of life — to those who are upright in heart" (Psalms 35:11) — all of those
who direct their wills by the rule of the divine will. Such ones are said antonomastically (i.e.,
by rhetorical substitution — see note) to be good. The Psalmist: "Bless, o Lord, the good and
right of heart" (Psalms 124:4). Concerning such ones it is said that they should glory mani-
festly in the testimony of a good conscience. "Glory, all those right in heart" (Psalms 31:11),
who are directed by the highest rule, which rectifies all things, concerning which Augustine
[writes], "Seeking nothing beyond the rule of the Master," and the Apostle, "Let all of us
remain in the same rule" (Philemon 3:16). **23–25 The other riwle . . . wakien**, The second rule
— which teaches thoroughly how a person must behave (lit., bear himself) externally, how
[one must] eat, drink, dress, sing, sleep, wake (or, hold vigils) — is completely without (i.e., on
the outside) and governs the body and bodily deeds. **25–26 *Et hec est exercitio . . . continetur***,
And this is the exercise of the body which, according to the Apostle, "avails little" (1 Timothy
4:8) and is like the rule of correct mechanics, which is contained within correct geometry.

Ant theos riwle nis nawt bute for-te servi the other: the other is as leafdi, theos as hire thuften. For al thet me eaver deth of the other withuten nis bute for-te riwlin the heorte withinnen.

30 Nu easki ye hwet riwle ye ancren schulen halden. Ye schulen alles weis, with alle mihte ant strengthe, wel witen the inre, ant te uttre for hire sake. The inre is eaver i-lich; the uttre is mislich, for euch schal halden the uttre efter thet ha mei best, with hire servi the inre. Nu thenne is hit swa thet alle ancren mahen wel halden an riwle, **quantum ad puritatem cordis, circa quam versatur tota religio.** Thet is, alle mahen ant ahen

35 halden a riwle "onont purte of heorte" — thet is, cleane ant schir in-wit (conscientia), withuten weote of sunne thet ne beo thurh schrift i-bet. This maketh the leafdi riwle, the riwleth ant rihteth ant smetheth the heorte ant te in-wit of sunne, for nawt ne maketh hire woh bute sunne ane. Rihten hire ant smethin hire is of euch religiun ant of euch ordre the go*d* ant al the strengthe. Theos riwle is i-maket nawt of monnes fundles, ah is

40 of Godes heaste; for-thi ha is eaver ant an withute changunge, ant alle ahen hire in an eaver to halden. Ah alle ne mahe nawt halden a riwle, ne ne thurve nawt, ne ne ahe nawt

---

27–28 nis nawt bute . . . thuften, does not exist (lit., is not) except to serve the other: the other is like a lady, this (i.e., the external rule) like her servant (or, handmaid). **28–29 For al thet me . . . withinnen,** For everything that a person ever does by the second [rule] without (i.e., the external rule) is only to rule the heart within. **30–31 Nu easki ye . . . hire sake,** Now, you ask what rule you anchoresses should hold. You should [in] every way, with all [your] might and strength, defend well the inner, and the outer (*te* = reduced form of *the* after preceding -*t*) for its sake. **33 is hit swa . . . riwle,** it is so that all anchoresses can well hold one rule. **33–34 *quantum . . . religio,*** with respect to purity of heart, about which all religion is concerned. **34–35 mahen ant ahen halden,** can and ought to keep. **35–36 onont purte . . . i-bet,** "with respect to purity of heart" — that is, pure and clean conscience, without the accusation of sin which is not atoned for through confession. **36–38 This maketh the leafdi . . . sunne ane,** This makes [up] the Lady Rule, which governs and directs (or, straightens) and smoothes the heart and the conscience of sin (*te* = reduced form of *the* after preceding -*t*), for nothing makes it crooked but sin alone. **38–39 Rihten hire ant . . . strengthe,** To straighten it (lit., her, the heart) and smooth it is the good and power of each religion (i.e., religious profession) and of each order (i.e., religious community). **39–42 i-maket nawt . . . uttre riwle,** not made by man's invention, but is by God's commandment; therefore, she is always the same (lit., and one) without changing, and everyone ought to keep her always the same (lit., in one). But all [people] cannot keep one rule, nor need not, nor ought not to keep the outer rule in

61

halden on a wise the uttre riwle, **quantum scilicet ad observantias corporales** — thet is, "onont licomliche locunges" efter the uttre riwle, thet ich thuften cleopede, ant is monnes fundles, for na thing elles i-stald bute to servi the inre, the maketh feasten, wakien, calde ant hearde werien — swucche othre heardschipes thet moni fles mei tholien, moni ne mei nawt. For-thi mot theos changin hire misliche efter euch-anes manere ant efter hire evene. For sum is strong, sum unstrong, ant mei ful wel beo cwite ant paie Godd mid leasse. Sum is clergesse, sum nawt, ant mot te mare wurchen ant on other wise seggen hire bonen. Sum is ald ant ethelich ant is the leasse dred of. Sum is yung ant luvelich ant is neod betere warde. For-thi schal euch ancre habben the uttre riwle efter hire schriftes read, ant hwet-se he bit ant hat hire in obedience, the cnaweth hire manere ant wat hire strengthe. He mei the uttre riwle changin efter wisdom as he sith, thet te inre mahe beo best i-halden.

Nan ancre, bi mi read, ne schal makien professiun — thet is, bihaten ase heast — bute threo thinges: thet beoth obedience, chastete, ant stude steathel-vestnesse, thet ha ne schal thet stude neaver mare changin bute for nede ane, as strengthe ant deathes

one [single] way. **42 *quantum scilicet ad observantias corporales***, "indeed, with respect to bodily observances." **43–46 "onont licomliche locunges" . . . mei nawt**, "with respect to bodily observances (lit., lookings)" according to the outer rule, which I called a servant, and is man's invention, established for nothing else but to serve the inner [rule], which causes [people] to fast, hold vigils, wear cold and rough [clothes] — [and to undertake] such other hardships which many [a person's] flesh (or, body) can suffer, many [a person's] cannot. **46–48 For-thi mot . . . mid leasse**, Therefore this [outer rule] must change herself variously according to each one's practice and according to her character. For one is strong, another weak, and can very well be excused and please God with less. **48–49 Sum is clergesse . . . dred of**, One is a learned woman (or, a woman in an order), another not, and must work the more (i.e., harder) and say her prayers in another way. Another is old and frail and is the less to fear for. **50–52 luvelich . . . hire strengthe**, lovely and is in need of better guarding. Therefore each anchoress will have (i.e., arrange) the outer rule according to her confessor's advice, and whatsoever he asks (*bit* = reduced form of *biddeth*) and commands her in obedience, who is familiar with her ways (lit., manner) and knows her strength. **53 sith**, sees [fit]; **thet te inre . . . i-halden**, [so] that the inner [rule] may be best kept. **54 bi mi read**, by my advice; **bihaten ase heast**, promise as a vow. **55–57 thet beoth . . . his herre**, those are obedience, chastity, and steadfastness (or, fixity) of place, that she will never more change that place except for necessity (or, emergency) alone, [such] as force and fear of death,

dred, obedience of hire bischop other of his herre. For hwa-se nimeth thing on hond ant bihat hit Godd as heast for-te don hit, ha bint hire ther-to, ant sunegeth deadliche i the bruche, yef ha hit breketh willes. Yef ha hit ne bihat nawt, ha hit mei do thah ant leaven

60   hwen ha wel wule, as of mete, of drunch, flesch forgan other fisch, alle other swucche thinges, of werunge, of liggunge, of ures, of othre beoden — segge swa monie other o swucche wise. Theos ant thulliche othre beoth alle i freo wil to don other to leten hwil me wule ant hwen me wule, bute ha beon bihaten. Ah chearite — thet is, luve — ant eadmodnesse ant tholemodnesse, treoweschipe ant haldunge of the alde ten heastes,

65   schrift ant penitence — theos ant thulliche othre, the beoth summe of the alde lahe, summe of the neowe, ne beoth nawt monnes fundles, ne riwle thet mon stalde, ah beoth Godes heastes. Ant for-thi euch mon mot ham nede halden, ant ye over alle, for theos riwleth the heorte. Of hire riwlunge is al meast thet ich write, bute i the frumthe of this boc ant i the leaste ende. The thinges thet ich write her of the uttre riwle, ye ham haldeth

70   alle, mine leove sustren — ure Laverd beo i-thonket! — ant schulen thurh his grace se lengre se betere. Ant thah nulle ich nawt thet ye bihaten ham as heaste to halden, for as

obedience to her bishop or to his superior (lit., higher). **57–59 For hwa-se nimeth . . . willes**, For whosoever takes a thing in hand and promises it to God as a vow to do it, she binds (*bint* = reduced form of *bindeth*) herself to it (lit., there-to) and sins mortally in the breach (or, violation) if she breaks it willingly. **59–62 Yef ha hit . . . swucche wise**, If she does not promise it, she can do it nevertheless and stop when she well wants, with (*as* not translated) food, with drink, to forgo (i.e., with going without) meat or fish, all other such things, with dressing, with sleeping (lit., lying), with [liturgical] hours, with other prayers — [she may] say as many or in such a way [as she wants]. **62 thulliche othre**, such others. **62–63 to leten . . . bihaten**, to stop while one wants and when one wants, unless they are promised. **63 Ah**, But. **64–67 eadmodnesse . . . Godes heastes**, humility and patience, loyalty and the keeping of the ancient ten commandments, confession and penitence — these and such others, some of which are from the old law, some from the new, are not man's invention, or a rule which man established, but are God's commandments. **67–68 mot ham . . . heorte**, must needs keep them, and you (pl.) above all, for these govern the heart. **68–69 Of hire riwlunge . . . leaste ende** About its (i.e., the heart's) governance is mostly all that I write, except in the beginning of this book and at the very (lit., last) end. **69–71 ye ham haldeth . . . betere**, you keep them (i.e., are keeping them) all, my dear sisters — our Lord be thanked! — and will [continue to keep them] through His grace, the longer the better. **71 Ant thah nulle ich nawt**, And nevertheless I do not want; **heaste**, command.

ofte as ye th'refter breken eni of ham, hit walde to swithe hurten ower heorte ant makien ow swa offearet, thet ye mahten sone — thet Godd forbeode ow! — fallen i desesperance — thet is, in an unhope ant an unbileave for-te beon i-borhen. For-thi thet
75   ich write ow, mine leove sustren, of uttre thinges i the earste dale of ower boc, of ower servise, ant nomeliche i the leaste, ye ne schule nawt bihaten hit, ah habbeth hit on heorte ant doth hit as thah ye hit hefden bihaten.

Yef ei unweote easketh ow of hwet ordre ye beon, as summe doth, *ye* telleth me — the siheth the gneat ant swolheth the flehe — ondswerieth "of Sein James," the wes
80   Godes Apostel ant for his muchele halinesse i-cleopet Godes brother. Yef him thuncheth wunder ant sullich of swuch ondswere, easkith him hwet beo ordre, ant hwer he funde in Hali Writ religiun openluk*er* descriv*et* ant i-sutelet then is i Sein James canonial epistel. He seith *hwe*t is religiun, hwuch is riht ordre. **Religio munda et immaculata apud Deum et Patrem hec est: visitare puppillos et viduas in necessitate sua et**
85   **immaculatum se custodire ab hoc seculo.** Thet is, "cleane religiun ant withute wem is i-seon ant helpen wyd*ewen* ant fe[der]lese children, ant from the world witen him

72–74 hit walde to swithe . . . beon i-borhen, it would too severely wound your heart and make you so afraid that you could soon — may God forbid that for you! — fall into despair — that is, into a hopelessness and a disbelief that you will be saved (lit., a disbelief to be saved). **74–75 thet ich write ow**, what I write you. **75–77 earste dale . . . bihaten**, first part of your book, concerning your service (i.e., divine service), and especially in the last [part], you must not promise it, but have it in heart and do it as though you had promised it. **78–80 Yef ei unweote . . . brother**, If any ignorant person asks you of which order (i.e., religious community) you are, as some do, you tell me — who strain the gnat and swallow the flea (or, fly) (see Matthew 23:24) — answer "of [the order of] Saint James," who was God's Apostle and for his great holiness called God's brother. **80–82 Yef him thuncheth . . . epistel**, If [it] seems strange and curious to him concerning such an answer, ask (imper.) him what an order is, and where he [might] find [it] more openly described and revealed in Holy Writ than [it] is in Saint James' canonical epistle. **83 hwuch**, which (or, what); **riht ordre**, a right, proper order. **83–85 *Religio munda . . . seculo***, "Clean and unspotted religion before God the Father is this: to visit orphans and widows in their need and to keep oneself unspotted from this world" (James 1:27). **85 withute wem**, without blemish. **86–87 i-seon ant helpen . . . unwemmet**, to see and help widows and fatherless children and to keep oneself pure and unspotted from the world. **87–89 The leatere dale . . . religiuse**, The latter part of his saying applies to recluses, for [in the saying] there are two parts [corresponding] to the two ways

cleane ant unwemmet." Thus Sein Jame descriveth religiun ant ordre. The leatere dale of his sahe limpeth to reclusen, for ther beoth twa dalen to twa manere the beoth of religiuse. To either limpeth his dale, as ye mahen i-heren: gode religiuse beoth i the world

90 summe, nomeliche prelaz ant treowe preachurs, the habbeth the earre dale of thet Sein Jame seide, thet beoth, as he seith, the gath to helpen wydewen ant feaderlese children. The sawle is widewe the haveth forloren hire spus — thet is, Jesu Crist — with eni heaved sunne. The is alswa federles the haveth thurh his sunne forloren the feader of heovene. Gan i-seon thulliche ant elnin ham ant helpen with fode of hali lare — this is

95 riht religiun, he seith, Sein Jame. The leatere dale of his sahe limpeth to ower religiun, as ich ear seide, the witeth ow from the worlt, over othre religiuse, cleane ant unwemmet. Thus the apostle Sein Jame, the descriveth religiun, nowther hwit ne blac ne nempneth he in his ordre. Ah moni siheth the gneat ant swolheth the flehe — thet is, maketh muche strengthe ther-as is the leaste. Pawel, the earste ancre, Antonie ant Arsenie,

100 Makarie ant te othre, neren ha religiuse ant of Sein James ordre? Alswa Seinte Sare ant Seinte Sinclerice, ant monie othre swucche, wepmen ba ant wummen, with hare greate matten ant hare hearde heren, neren ha of god ordre? "Ant hwether hwite other blake?"

of life which there are for religious [people] (i.e., those in religious professions). **89–91 To either limpeth . . . children,** To each applies its part, as you can hear: some good religious are in the world, especially prelates and true preachers, who have the first part of what Saint James said, who are, as he says, [those] who go to help widows and fatherless children. **92 forloren hire spus,** lost her spouse (or bridegroom). **92–93 eni heaved sunne,** any capital sin (lit., head sin). **93 The is alswa federles the,** He (or, the person) is also fatherless who. **94 Gan i-seon thulliche . . . lare,** To go to see such [people] and strengthen them and help [them] with the food of holy teaching. **95–96 The leatere dale . . . unwemmet,** The latter part of his saying applies to your profession, as I said before, [you] who keep yourselves from the world pure and unblemished. **98–99 Ah moni siheth . . . leaste,** But many strain out the gnat and swallow the flea (or, fly) — that is, [they] put great importance where there is the least (Matthew 23:24). **99–102 Pawel, the earste ancre . . . of god ordre?** Paul, the first anchorite, [Saint] Anthony and Arsenius, Macarius and the others, were they not professed and from Saint James' order? Also Saint Sarah and Saint Syncletica, and many such others, both men (lit., males — see glossary) and women, with their coarse beds (lit., mats) and their rough hairshirts, were they not from a good order? **102–03 Ant hwether hwite . . . curtel,** "And [were their habits] white or black (*hwether* not translated — see glossary)?" as unwise [people] ask you, who imagine that the

as unwise ow easkith, the weneth thet ordre sitte i the curtel. Godd wat, no-the-les ha weren wel bathe, nawt tah onont clathes, ah as Godes spuse singeth bi hire-seolven,

105 **Nigra sum set formosa.** "Ich am blac ant tah hwit," ha seith — unseowlich withuten, schene withinnen. O this wise ondswerieth to the easkeres of ower ordre, hwether hwite other blake — seggeth ye beoth ba twa, thurh the grace of Godd, ant of Sein James ordre, thet he wrat leatere: **Inmaculatum se custodire ab hoc seculo** — thet is thet ich seide ear, "from the worlt witen him cleane ant unwemmet." Her-in is religiun

110 — nawt i the wide hod, ne in the blake cape, ne i the hwite rochet, ne i the greie cuvel. Ther-as monie beoth i-gederet togederes, ther for anrednesse me schal makie strengthe of annesse of clathes, ant of other-hwet of uttre thinges, thet te annesse withuten bitacni the annesse of a luve ant of a wil thet ha alle habbeth i-meane withinnen. With hare habit, thet is an, thet euch haveth swuch as other, ant alswa of other-hwet, ha

115 yeiyeth thet ha habbeth alle togederes a luve ant a wil, euch alswuch as other. Loke thet ha ne lihen. Thus hit is i cuvent, ah hwer-se wummon liveth, other mon, bi him ane, hearmite other ancre, of thinges withuten hwer of scandle ne cume nis nawt muche strengthe. Hercne Michee: **Indicabo tibi, O homo, quid sit bonum et quid Deus**

order resides in the tunic (i.e., outer garment). **103–05 Godd wat . . . formosa,** God knows, indeed they were properly (lit., well) both, not though (*tah* = reduced form of *thah* after preceding *-t*) with respect to clothes, but as God's spouse (or, bride) sings about herself, "I am black, but beautiful" (Song of Songs 1:4). **105 tah,** nevertheless. **105–06 ha seith . . . withinnen,** she says — ugly on the outside, beautiful within. **106–07 this wise . . . seggeth,** In this way answer (imper.) [back] to the askers (i.e., those who ask) about your order, whether [it be] white or black — say (imper.). **108–09 thet he wrat . . . unwemmet,** which he wrote later (i.e., in the second half): "To keep oneself unblemished from this world" — that is what I said before, "to keep oneself from the world pure and unblemished." **110 hod,** hood; **cape,** cope (i.e., hooded garment); **hwite rochet,** white surplice; **greie cuvel,** gray cowl. **111–13 Ther-as monie . . . withinnen,** Where (*as* not translated) many are gathered together, there for constancy (or, single-mindedness) one must put importance on (or, make a strength of) unity of clothes, and on some other matters of external things, [so] that the unity (*te* = reduced form of *the* after preceding *-t*) on the outside may symbolize the unity of one love and of one will which they all have in common within. **113–15 With hare habit . . . as other,** With their habit, which is one, which each has such as the other, and also with other things, they cry out that they all have together one love and one will, each [one] just as the other. **118 Hercne Michee,** Hearken (i.e., listen to) Micah. **118–20 Indicabo tibi . . . tuo,** "I shall point out to you, O man,

requirat a te, utique facere judicium et justiciam et sollicite ambulare cum Domino
120   **Deo tuo.** "Ich chulle schawi the, mon," seith the hali Michee, Godes prophete — "Ich chulle schawi the sothliche hwet is go*d*, ant hwuch religiun, ant hwuch ordre, hwuch halinesse Godd easketh of the" — low, this, understond hit — do wel ant dem wac eaver the-seolven, ant with dred ant with luve ga mid Godd ti Laverd. Ther-as theose thinges beoth, ther is riht religiun, ther is soth ordre. Ant do al thet other, ant lete this nis 125   bute trichunge ant a fals gile. **Ve vobis, scribe et pharisei, ypocrite, qui mundatis quod deforis est calicis et parapsidis. Intus autem pleni estis omni spur*c*icia similes sepulcris dealbatis.** Al thet gode religiuse doth other werieth efter the uttre riwle, al togedere is her-vore, al nis bute ase tole to timbrin her-towart. Al nis bute as thuften to servi the leafdi to riwlin the heorte.

130   *This an boc is todealet in eahte leasse bokes.*

     Nu, mine leove sustren, this boc ich todeale on eahte destinctiuns thet ye cleopieth "dalen." Ant euch withute monglunge speketh al bi him-seolf of sunderliche thinges, ant thah euch-an riht falleth efter other, ant is the leatere eaver i-teiet to the earre.

     — The earste dale speketh al of ower servise.

what is good and what God requires from you, especially that you execute judgment and do justice and walk carefully with the Lord your God" (Micah 6:8). **120 "Ich chulle . . . mon,"** "I will show you, O man." **121 sothliche,** truly. **121–22 hwuch religiun . . . of the,** what kind of profession, and what kind of order, and what kind of holiness God requires of you. **122 low,** lo, behold. **122–23 dem wac . . . Laverd,** always judge yourself [to be] weak, and with fear and with love go with God, your Lord (*ti* = reduced form of *thi* 'thy' after preceding -*d*). **123–25 Ther-as theose thinges . . . gile,** Where these things are (*as* not translated), there is right religion (or, profession), there is true order. And to do all the other [things] and to omit this is [nothing] but treachery and false deceit. **125–27 Ve vobis . . . dealbatis,** "Woe unto you, scribes and pharisees, hypocrites, who wash what is on the outside of the cup and the dish. On the inside, however, you are full of all filth like whitewashed tombs" (Matthew 23:25, 27). **127 doth other werieth,** do or wear. **128 is her-vore . . . her-towart,** is to this end (lit. here-for), everything is [nothing] but as a tool to build toward this; **thuften,** handmaiden, servant. **130 This an boc . . . bokes,** This one book is divided into eight lesser books. **131–33 Nu, mine leove sustren . . . the earre,** Now, my dear sisters, I divide this book into eight divisions (lit., distinctions) which you call "parts." And each without mixing [will] speak all by itself of various things, and nevertheless each one comes (lit., falls) right after the other, and the later [section] is always tied to the earlier. **134 The earste dale,** The first part; **ower servise,** your [divine] service.

135 — The other is hu ye schulen thurh ower fif wittes witen ower heorte, thet ordre ant religiun ant sawle lif is inne. I this destinctiun aren chapitres five, as fif stuchen efter fif wittes, the witeth the heorte as wake-men, hwer-se ha beoth treowe, ant speketh of euch *wit* sunderlepes o rawe.

— The thridde dale is of anes cunnes fuheles the Davith i the Sawter eveneth him-seolf

140 to as he were ancre, ant hu the cunde of the ilke fuheles beoth ancren i-liche.

— The feorthe dale is of fleschliche fondunges ant gasteliche bathe, ant confort ayeines ham ant of hare salven.

—The fifte dale is of schrift.

—The seste dale is of penitence.

145 —The seovethe of schir heorte, hwi me ah, ant hwi me schal Jesu Crist luvien, ant hwet binimeth us his luve ant let us him to luvien.

—The eahtuthe dale is al of the uttre riwle, earst of mete ant of drunch, ant of othre thinges thet falleth ther-abuten, th'refter of the thinges the ye mahen undervon ant hwet thinges ye mahen witen other habben, th'refter of ower clathes ant of swucche thinges

150 as ther-abuten falleth, th'refter of ower werkes, of doddunge ant of blod-letunge, of ower meidnes riwle, aleast hu ye ham schulen leofliche learen.

135–36 The other is . . . is inne, The second is how you will through your five senses protect your heart, which order and profession and the soul's life is in. **136–38 as fif stuchen . . . o rawe**, as five pieces (i.e., sub-divisions) corresponding to the five senses which protect the heart as watchmen, wherever they be trustworthy, and speaks of each sense separately in a row. **139–40 of anes cunnes fuheles . . . i-liche**, about birds of a (or, one) kind which David in the Psalter compares himself to, as if he were an anchorite, and how the nature of the same birds are like anchorites. **141–42 fleschliche fondunges . . . hare salven**, fleshly (or, bodily) temptations and spiritual [ones] both, and comfort against them, and about their remedies. **143 schrift**, confession. **145–46 schir heorte . . . luvien**, clean heart, why one ought, and why one must love Jesus Christ and what takes away His love [from] us and prevents us from loving (lit., to love) Him. **147 eahtuthe**, eighth. **147–51 earst of mete . . . leofliche learen**, first about food and drink, and about other things which pertain to that (lit., there-about), after that about the things which you may receive and what things you may keep or have (i.e., own), after that about your clothes and about such things as pertain to that, after that of your actions, about the clipping [of your hair] and about bloodletting, about your maiden's (or, servant's) rule, lastly how you must teach them lovingly.

Part One

The Outer Rule (Hours and Prayers)

Her biginneth the earste boc of ures ant ureisuns the gode beoth to seggen.

H wen ye earst ariseth, blescith ow ant seggeth, **In nomine Patris et Filii et Spiritus sancti, Amen**. Ant biginneth anan, **Veni, Creator Spiritus**, with up ahevene ehnen ant honden toward heovene, buhinde o cneon forthward up-o the bedde, ant seggeth swa al the ymne ut with the verset, **Emitte spiritum tuum**, ant te ureisun, **Deus, qui corda fidelium**. Her-efter, scheoiende ow ant clathinde ow, seggeth **Pater noster** ant **Credo; Jesu Criste, fili Dei vivi, miserere nobis, qui de Virgine dignatus es nasci, miserere nobis**. This word seggeth eaver athet ye beon

---

1 Her biginneth . . . beoth to seggen, Here begins the first book [which is] about hours and prayers which are good to say. **2 Hwen ye earst ariseth . . . seggeth**, When you first arise, cross yourself and say. **2–3 In nomine Patris . . . Amen**, "In the name of the Father, and of the Son, and of the Holy Spirit, Amen" (monastic invocation to the Trinity). **3 biginneth anan**, begin (imper.) at once; **Veni, Creator Spiritus**, "Come, Creator Spirit" (hymn to the Holy Spirit, often attributed to Rabanus Maurus). **4–5 with up ahevene ehnen . . . with the verset**, with eyes and hands lifted up towards heaven, bowing on knees forward upon the bed, and say out thus (i.e., in this posture) all the hymn with the versicle. **5–6 Emitte spiritum tuum**, "Send forth your spirit" (versicle based on Psalm 103:30). **6 ant te ureisun**, and the prayer (*te* = reduced form of *the*); **Deus, qui corda fidelium**, "God, who [did teach] the hearts of the faithful" (prayer to the Holy Spirit). **6–7 Her-efter, scheoiende ow . . . seggeth**, After that, putting on your shoes and clothes (lit., shoeing yourself and clothing yourself), say. **7 Pater noster ant Credo**, "Our Father" (i.e., the Lord's Prayer) and "I believe" (i.e., the Apostles' Creed). **7–8 Jesu Criste, fili Dei . . . miserere nobis**, "Jesus Christ, Son of the living God, have mercy on us, you who thought it worthy (or, deigned) to be born of the Virgin, have mercy on us" (a prayer). **8–10 This word seggeth . . . sitten ye other stonden**, Say (imper.) this word (or,

al greithe. This word habbeth muchel on us ant i muth ofte, euch time thet ye mahen,

10   sitten ye other stonden.

Hwen ye beoth al greithe, sprengeth ow with hali-weater, thet ye schulen eaver habben, ant thenchen o Godes flesch ant on his deore-wurthe blod, thet is abuve the hehe weoved, ant falleth adun ther-towart with theose gretunges:

Ave, principium nostre creationis,

15   **Ave, precium nostre redemptionis,**

Ave, viaticum nostre peregrinationis,

Ave, premium nostre expectationis,

Ave, solamen nostre sustentationis.

Tu esto nostrum gaudium,

20   **Qui es futurus premium.**

Sit nostra in te gloria

Per cuncta semper secula.

Mane nobiscum, Domine.

Noctem obscuram remove;

25   **Omne delictum ablue;**

Piam medelam tribue.

speech) continually until you are completely ready. Have (imper.) this word much in use (i.e., use this prayer often) and in [your] mouth often, each time that you can, [whether] you sit or stand. **11–13 Hwen ye beoth . . . with theose gretunges**, When you are completely ready, sprinkle yourself with holy water, which you always ought to have [available], and think on God's flesh (or, body) and on his precious blood, which is above the high altar, and fall down towards it with these greetings. **14–29 *Ave, principium nostre creationis . . . Cum Patre, et cetera***, "Hail, beginning of our creation, / Hail, price of our redemption, / Hail, viaticum (i.e., allowance for a journey; or, Eucharist at the last rites) for our pilgrimage, / Hail, reward of our expectation, / Hail, comfort for our patient suffering. // Be our joy, / You who will be [our] reward. / May our glory [be] in You / through all [time], for ever and ever. // Stay with us, O Lord. / Take away the dark night; / Wash clean every wrong; / Grant a holy remedy. // Glory [be] to you, O Lord, / You who were born of the Virgin. / With the Father, etc." (a prayer, or hymn typically recited at the

70

Gloria tibi, Domine,
Qui natus es de virgine.
Cum Patre, et cetera.

30 Alswa ye schule don hwen the preost halt hit up ed te measse, ant bivore the **Confiteor** hwen ye schule beon i-huslet. Efter this falleth o cneon to ower crucifix with theose fif gretunges, ine munegunge of Godes fif wunden: **Adoramus te, Christe, et benedicimus tibi quia per sanctam crucem redemisti mundum. Tuam crucem adoramus, Domine. Tuam gloriosam recolimus passionem. Miserere nostri qui passus es pro nobis.**

35 **Salve, crux sancta,**
Arbor digna,
Cuius robur preciosum
Mundi tulit talentum.

Salve, crux, que in corpore Christi dedicata es, et ex membris eius tanquam
40 **margaritis ornata.**

O crux, lignum triumphale,
Mundi vera salus, vale.

elevation of the host). **30–31 Alswa ye schule . . . schule beon i-huslet**, You ought to do likewise when the priest holds it (i.e., the host) up at the mass, and before the "I confess" (i.e., the form of confession used in the mass) when you are given the Eucharist (lit., houseled). **31–32 Efter this falleth o cneon . . . Godes fif wunden**, After this, fall on [your] knees at your Crucifix with these five greetings, in remembrance of God's five wounds. **32–34 *Adoramus te, Christe . . . qui passus es pro nobis***, "We worship You, Christ, and bless You because You have, through the Holy Cross, redeemed the world. We worship Your Cross, O Lord. We contemplate Your glorious passion. Have mercy on us, You who have suffered for us" (antiphon and response for matins on the Feasts of the Invention and Exaltation of the Cross). **35–38 *Salve, crux sancta . . . Mundi tulit talentum***, "Hail, Holy Cross, / Worthy tree, / Whose precious strength / Bore the weight of the world" (hymn for the Mass of the Cross). **39–40 *Salve crux, que . . . margaritis ornata***, "Hail [O] Cross, [you] who are consecrated in the body of Christ, and by His limbs are decorated as with pearls" (antiphon for the Feast of St. Andrew). **41–46 *O crux, lignum triumphale . . . egras sana***, "O Cross,

Inter ligna nullum tale
Fronde, flore, germine.

45 **Medicina Christiana**
Salva sanas, egras sana.

Ant with this word beateth on ower breoste: **Quod non valet vis humana, sit in tuo nomine**.

Hwa-se ne con theos five, segge the earste **Adoramus te**, cneolinde, fif sithen ant
50 blescith ow with euch-an of theose gretunges. Ant with theose wordes, **Miserere nostri, qui passus es pro nobis**, beateth ower heorte ant cusseth the eorthe i-cruchet with the thume. Th'refter wendeth ow to ure Leafdi onlicnesse ant cneolith with fif **Avez**, aleast to the othre ymagnes, ant to ower relikes luteth other cneolith, nomeliche to the halhen the ye habbeth to thurh luve i-turnd ower weofdes, swa muche the reathere
55 yef ei is i-halhet.

Ther-efter anan-riht ure Leafdi uht-song — ant seggeth o this wise: yef hit is werc-dei, falleth to ther eorthe; yef hit is hali-dei, buhinde sum-deal dune-ward seggeth **Pa-**

victorious wood, / True safety of the world, hail. / Among wood (or, trees) [there is] no such [a one] / In leaf, flower, bud. // Christian medicine, / Save the healthy (fem.), heal the sick (fem.)" (stanzas from the hymn *Laudes crucis atollamus*). **47 beateth**, (imper.) beat. **47–48** *Quod non valet . . . in tuo nomine*, "What human strength is not strong [enough] for, [let it] be [done] in your name." **49–50 Hwa-se ne con theos five . . . gretunges**, Whosoever does not know these five say the first, "We worship you" (see gloss to 1.32–35 above) kneeling, five times and cross yourself with each one of these greetings. **50–51** *Miserere nostri . . . nobis*, "Have mercy on us, [you] who have suffered for us" (the end of the response in the *Adoramus te* — see gloss to 1.32–34 above). **51–52 beateth ower heorte . . . with the thume**, beat your heart (i.e., chest) and kiss the earth, crossed with the thumb. **52–55 Th'refter wendeth ow . . . yef ei is i-halhet**, After that (lit., thereafter), direct yourself to our Lady's likeness and kneel with five "Aves," and lastly to the other images, and bow to your relics or kneel, namely to the saints to which you have turned your altars, so much more readily if any [of them] is consecrated (lit., hallowed). **56–58 Ther-efter anan-riht . . . ba stille**, Immediately after that (lit., thereafter at once) [say] our Lady's matins (lit., morning song) — and say [it] in this way: if it is a work day, fall to the ground; if it is a holiday (i.e., feast day), bowing somewhat downward say, "Our Father" (i.e., the Lord's Prayer) and "I believe" (i.e.,

ternoster ant **Credo** ba stille. Rihteth ow up th'refter ant seggeth, **Domine, labia mea aperies**. Makieth on ower muth a creoiz with the thume. Ed **Deus in adiutorium**, a
60 large creoiz with the thume ant with the twa fingres, from buve the forheaved dun to the breoste, ant falleth to the eorthe — yef hit is werc-dei with **Gloria Patri**, other buheth dune-ward, yef hit [is] hali-dei athet **Sicut erat**. Thus ed euch **Gloria Patri** ant ed te biginnunge of the **Venite**, ant i the **Venite**, ed **Venite, adoremus**, ant ed te **Ave, Maria**, ant hwer-se ye eaver hereth Maries nome i-nempnet, ant ed euch **Pater noster**
65 thet falle to ower ures ant to the **Credo** ant to the collecte ed eaver-euch tide, ant ed te leate-meste vers of eaver-euch ymne, ant ed te leaste vers withuten an of the salm, **Benedicite, omnia opera Domini, Domino**. Ed alle thes ilke, yef hit is hali-dei, buheth sum-del dune-wart. Yef hit is werc-dei, falleth to ther eorthe. Ed te biginnunge of eaver-euch tide, with **Deus in adiutorium**, makieth rode-taken as ich ear tahte. Ed **Veni,**
70 **Creator** buheth other cneolith efter thet te dei is. With **Memento, salutis auctor**,

the Apostles' Creed). **58–59 Rihteth ow up . . . with the thume**, Straighten yourself up after that and say, "Lord, open my lips" (versicle based on Psalm 50:17). Make a cross on your mouth with the thumb. **59–62 Ed *Deus in adiutorium . . . Sicut erat***, At "God [come] to [my] aid" (Psalm 69:2 as a response, recited at the beginning of each of the canonical hours except compline), [make] a large cross with the thumb and with the two fingers, from above the forehead down to the chest, and fall to the ground — if it is a work day, with the "Glory [be] to the Father" (i.e., the lesser doxology) or bow down if it is a holiday (i.e., feast day) until the "As it was [in the beginning]" (i.e., the last verse of the *Gloria Patri*). **62–68 Thus ed euch *Gloria Patri* . . . to ther eorthe**, So (i.e., do the same — make the sign of the Cross) at the beginning (or, start) of the "Come" (i.e., the "invitation" to matins, Psalm 94) and in (i.e., during) the "Come," at "Come, let us adore" (Psalm 94:6) and at the "Hail Mary," and wheresoever you hear Mary's name named, and at each "Our Father" that belongs (lit., falls) to your hours and to the "I believe" (i.e., the Apostles' Creed), and to the collect at each and every canonical hour (lit., tide), and at the final verse of each and every (lit., every each) hymn, and at the last verse but one of the psalm, "Bless, Lord, all the works of the Lord" (the canticle of the three children — see Daniel 3:57). At all these very [things], if it is a holiday, bow somewhat downward. If it is a work day, fall to the ground. **68–69 Ed te biginnunge . . . as ich ear tahte**, At the beginning of each and every canonical hour, [start] with. **69 *Deus in adiutorium***, "God [come] to [my] aid" (Psalm 69, recited at the beginning of each canonical hour except compline). **69–70 makieth rode-taken . . . te dei is**, make the sign of the Cross (lit., Rood-token), as I taught [you] before. At "Come, Creator" (see gloss to 1.3) bow or kneel according to what the day is (i.e., which day it is). **70–73 With *Memento . . . Homo factus est***, At "Remember, Author of salvation" (from a Christmas hymn, *Christe redemptor omnium*), always fall down, and at this word —

falleth eaver adun, ant ed tis word, **Nascendo formam sumpseris**, cusseth the eorthe, ant alswa i the **Te Deum laudamus**, ed tis word: **Non horruisti virginis uterum**, ant ed te messe i the muchele **Credo**, ed **ex Maria Virgine** ant **Homo factus est**.

Euch-an segge hire ures as ha haveth i-writen ham, ant euch tide sunderliche, ase forth as ye mahen, seggeth in his time, ear to sone then to leate yef ye ne mahen eaver halde the time. Uht-song bi niht i winter, i sumer i the dahunge. This winter schal biginnen ed te Hali-Rode Dei ine hervest, ant leasten athet Easter. Prime in winter earliche, i sumer bi forth-marhen, **Pretiosa** th'refter. Yef ye habbeth neode for eani hihthe to speoken, ye muhe seggen hit bivoren ant efter uht-song anan yef hit swa neodeth. Non eaver efter mete — ant hwen ye slepeth, efter slep — hwil thet sumer leasteth bute hwen ye feasteth, i winter bivore mete hwen ye al veasteth, the Sunne-dei thah efter mete for ye eoteth twien. Ed te an salm ye schulen stonden yef ye beoth eise, ant ed te other sitten, ant eaver with **Gloria Patri** rungen up ant buhen. Hwa-se mei stonden al

"Once born, You took on [our] form" (a later verse in the same hymn) — kiss the earth and also in the "We praise You, God" (i.e., the "*Te Deum*," a famous hymn intregal to matins) at this word (or, phrase): "You did not shudder at [the thought of entering] the Virgin's womb" (a later verse in the "Te Deum") and at the mass in the great "I believe" (i.e., the Apostles' Creed) at "from the Virgin Mary," and "[He] was made man" (later verses in the Creed). **74–76 Euch-an segge . . . i the dahunge**, Let each one say her hours as she has written them [down], and each [canonical] hour separately, as far as you can, say in its [proper] time, rather too soon than too late if you cannot always keep the time. Matins by night in winter, in summer at the dawning (or, daybreak). **76–78 This winter schal biginnen . . . *Pretiosa* th'refter**, This winter will begin at the Holy Cross Day (i.e., September 14) in the fall, and last until Easter. Prime [will be] early in winter, in summer around morning, and "Precious [in the sight of the Lord]" after that (Psalm 115:15, opening to a quasi-office associated with prime). **78–79 Yef ye habbeth neode . . . swa neodeth**, If you have an urgent need to speak (lit., if you have need to speak because of any impetuosity, or haste), you may say it before and after matins immediately if it is thus necessary. **79–82 Non eaver efter mete . . . for ye eoteth twien**, As long as summer lasts, [let] None (i.e., the canonical hour at midday, originally the ninth) always [be] after the meal, except when you all are fasting, and, when you sleep (i.e., take midday nap), after sleep. In winter, [let None come] before the meal, when you are all fasting; on Sunday (lit., the Sunday), however, [let it come] after the meal since you eat twice. **82–83 Ed te an salm . . . ant buhen**, At the first (lit., one) psalm [of each canonical hour], you will stand if you are able, and at the second sit, and always with the "Glory to the Father" [you will] rise up and bow. **83–86 Hwa-se mei stonden . . . the *Pater noster***, Whosoever can stand, all for

on ure Leafdi wurthschipe, stonde o Godes halve. Ed alle the seove tiden singeth **Pater**
85 **noster** ant **Ave Maria** ba bivoren ant efter; **Fidelium anime** efter euch tide, bivore the
Pater noster. Ed threo tiden seggeth **Credo** with **Pater noster**: bivoren uht-song ant
efter prime ant eft[er complie]; from ower complie athet efter **Pretiosa** haldeth silence.

Efter even-song anan ower **Placebo** euche niht seggeth hwen ye beoth eise, bute hit
beo hali niht for feaste of nihe lesceuns the cume ine marhen, bivore cumplie other efter
90 uht-song. **Dirige** with threo salmes ant with threo lesceuns euche niht sundri. In
aniversaries of ower leoveste freond seggeth alle nihene. I stude of **Gloria** ed euch
psalmes ende, **Requiem eternam dona eis, Domine, et lux perpetua luceat eis.** Ed
Placebo sitteth athet **Magnificat**, alswa ed **Dirige** bute ed te lesceuns, ant ed te **Miserere**
ant from **Laudate** al ut. **Requiescant in pace** i stude of **Benedicamus** seggeth on
95 ende. Ine marhen other i niht efter the suffragies of uht-song seggeth commendaciun,

our Lady's honor, [let her] stand for God's sake (lit., side). At all of the seven [canonical] hours
sing (imper.) "Our Father," and "Hail, Mary" both before and after; [sing] "Souls of the faithful"
(versicle concluding prime) after each hour, before the "Our Father." **86–87 Ed threo tiden . . .
haldeth silence**, At [these] three hours, say "I believe" with "Our Father": 1) before matins and 2)
after prime, and 3) after compline; from your compline until after "Precious [in the Lord's sight]"
keep silence (Psalm 115:15 — see gloss to 1.76–78 above). **88–90 Efter even-song anan . . . efter
uht-song**, After vespers (lit., evensong) say at once your "I shall please [the Lord]" (an antiphon
from the Office of the Dead, based on Psalm 114:9) each night when you are at leisure (or, are
able), unless it be a holy night for a feast of nine lessons which comes in the morning, before
compline, or after vespers. **90 Dirige**, "Direct [my path]" (an antiphon from the Office of the
Dead, based on Psalm 5:8). **90–92 In aniversaries . . . lux perpetua luceat eis**, On anniversaries
[of the death] of your dearest friends say all nine [lessons]. In place of "Gloria" at the end of each
psalm, [say] "Give them eternal peace, Lord, and let perpetual light shine on them" (versicle and
response from the Office of the Dead). **92–94 Ed Placebo . . . Laudate al ut**, At "I shall please [the
Lord]" sit until "[My soul shall] magnify [the Lord]" (the "Magnificat," from the Office of the
Dead, based on Luke 1:46), likewise [sit] at "Direct [my path]," except at the lessons, at the "Have
mercy" (Psalm 50, used in the Office of the Dead) and from "Praise [the Lord]" (Psalm 150, used
in the Office of the Dead) completely to the end (lit., all out). **94 Requiescant in pace . . .
Benedicamus**, [Say] "May they rest in peace" (versicle from the Office of the Dead) in the place
of (or, instead of) "Let us bless [the Lord]" (versicle recited near the end of the day). **95–96 Ine
marhen . . . other stondinde**, In the morning or at night after the intercessory prayers (lit.,
suffrages) of matins say the Commendation (see glossary), [say] the psalms sitting, the prayers

sittinde the salmes, cneolinde the ureisuns other stondinde. Yef ye thus doth euche niht bute ane Sunne-niht, ye doth muche betere. In a-mel-dei we seggeth ba **Placebo** ant **Dirige** efter the mete-graces. I twi-mel-dei efter non, ant ye alswa mote don.

100

105

Seove psalmes seggeth sittinde other cneolinde with the letanie. Fiftene psalmes seggeth o this wise: the earste five for ow-seolf, ant for alle the ow god doth other unnen. The othre five for the peis of al Hali Chirche, the thridde five for alle Cristene sawles. Efter the forme five, **Kyrie eleison, Christe eleison, Kyrie eleison; Pater noster...et ne nos; Salvos fac servos tuos et ancillas tuas, Deus meus, sperantes in te; Oremus: Deus cui proprium est.** Efter the othre five alswa: **Kyrie eleison, Christe eleison, Kyrie eleison; Pater noster . . . et ne nos; Domine, fiat pax in virtute tua, et abundancia in turibus tuis; Oremus: Ecclesie tue quesumus, Domine, preces placatus.** Efter the thridde five, the ye schulen seggen — withuten **Gloria Patri — Kyrie eleison; iii Pater noster . . . et ne nos; A porta inferi, erue, Domine, animas eorum; Oremus: Fidelium Deus omnium.** Seove salmes ant thus

kneeling or standing. **96–98 Yef ye thus doth . . . the mete-graces,** If you do thus each night except Sunday night only, you do much better. On a one-meal-day we (i.e., members of our order) say both "I shall please [the Lord]" and "Direct [my path]" (see glosses to lines 88–90 above) after the prayers of thanks for food (lit., food-graces). **98 I twi-mel-dei . . . mote don,** On a two-meal-day [we say them] after None, and you may do likewise. **99 Seove psalmes** (i.e., the seven penitential psalms: 6, 31, 37, 50, 101, 129, and 142); **letanie,** Litany; **Fiftene psalmes** (i.e., the fifteen gradual psalms, often recited for private devotion: 119–33). **100 o this wise,** in this way. **100–02 the earste five . . . the forme five,** the first five for yourself and for all who do or wish good to you. The second five for the peace of all Holy Church, the third five for all Christians' souls. After the first five [say]. **102–04 *Kyrie eleison . . . cui proprium est,*** "Lord have mercy; Christ have mercy; Lord have mercy" (a prayer used in both the mass and the divine office); "Our Father" . . . "and [lead] us not [into temptation]"; "Save your servants and handmaidens, my God, [who] are hoping in you" (versicle and response based on Psalm 85:2, 16:7); Let us pray: "God, whose nature it is [always to forgive]" (prayer). **105–07 *Domine, fiat pax . . . placatus,*** "Lord, let there be peace in your strength and abundance in your towers" (Psalm 121:7 as versicle); Let us pray: "We beseech you to be pleased with the prayers of your church" (prayer). **107–09 Efter the thridde five . . . *Deus omnium,*** After the third five, without the "Glory be to the Father" you must say "Lord have mercy"; three [times] "Our Father" . . . "and [lead] us not [into temptation]"; "From the gate of hell, O Lord, deliver their souls" (versicle from the Office of the Dead); Let us pray: "God, [Creator and Redeemer] of all the faithful" (prayer).

110   theose fiftene seggeth abuten under, for abute swuch time as me singeth measse in alle religiuns ant ure Laverd tholede pine up-o the rode, ye ahen to beo nomeliche i beoden ant i bonen, ant alswa from prime athet mid-marhen hwen preostes of the worlt singeth hare meassen. Ye mahen, yef ye wulleth, seggen ower **Pater nostres** this wise:

    "Almihti Godd, Feader, Sune, Hali Gast, as ye beoth threo an Godd, alswa ye beoth
115   an mihte, an wisdom, ant an luve, ant thah is mihte i-turnd to the in Hali Writ, nomeliche, thu deore-wurthe Feader; to the wisdom, seli Sune; to the luve, Hali Gast. Yef me, an almihti Godd thrile i threo hades, thes ilke threo thinges: mihte for-te servi the, wisdom for-te cweme the, luve ant wil to don hit — mihte thet ich mahe don, wisdom thet ich cunne don, luve thet ich wulle don aa thet te is leovest. As thu art ful of euch god —
120   alswa nis na god wone ther-as theose threo beoth: mihte ant wisdom ant luve i-veiet togederes — thet tu yetti me ham, Hali Thrumnesse, i the wurthschipe of the." Threo **Pater nostres; Credo; Verset: Benedicamus Patrem et Filium, cum Spirito Sancto; Laudemus et superexaltemus eum in secula; Oremus: Omnipotens sempiterne Deus, qui dedisti famulis tuis in confessione vere fidei eternae gloriam [trinitatis]**
125   **agnoscere. Alpha et Omega,** hwa-se hit haveth, other [sum other] of the hali thrumnesse segge the wulle.

110–13 abuten under ... hare meassen, around Tierce (or, morning), for around such time as people sing mass in all religious orders and our Lord suffered pain upon the Cross, you ought to be especially in prayers and in petitions, and likewise from Prime until mid-morning, when priests of the world (i.e., secular priests) sing their masses. **114 an Godd,** one God. **115–19 ant thah is mihte ... leovest,** and nevertheless in Holy Writ power is directed to You, especially, You precious Father; wisdom to You, blessed Son; love to You, Holy Spirit. Give me, [O] one almighty God threefold in three persons (or, occupations), these very three things: power to serve You, wisdom to please You, love and desire to do it — power that I may do, wisdom that I can do, love that I want to do always what is most dear to You. **119–21 As thu art ful ... of the,** As you are full of every good — likewise, [there] is no lack of good where these three are: power and wisdom and love, joined together — [I pray] that You [may] grant them to me, Holy Trinity, in the worship of You. **122–26 *Verset: Benedicamus ... the wulle,*** Versicle: "Let us bless the Father and the Son along with the Holy Spirit; let us praise and exalt Him above all others forever" (versicle for Trinity Sunday); Let us pray: "Omnipotent, eternal God, You who have granted Your servants in the confession of the true faith to know the glory of the eternal Trinity" (prayer for Trinity Sunday). "Alpha and Omega" (a famous hymn to the Trinity by Hildebert of Lavardin [1056–1133] — see also Revelations 1:8, 21:6, and 22:13) — whoever has it (i.e., by heart), or whoever wants [may] say some other [prayer] about the Holy Trinity.

"A Jesu, thin are! Jesu, for mine sunnen ahonget o rode, for the ilke fif wunden the thu on hire bleddest, heal mi blodi sawle of alle the sunnen thet ha is with i-wundet thurh mine fif wittes. I the munegunge of ham thet hit swa mote beon, deore-wurthe Laverd:" Fif

130 **Pater nostres; verset: Omnis terra adoret te, et psalmum dicat nomini tuo; Oremus: Juste Judex** — yef thu const, other of the creoiz sum other — **Deus, qui unigeniti tui, Domini nostri Jesu Christi, pretioso sanguine vexillum sancte crucis** — this is an of the beste.

"For the seove yiftes of the Hali Gast, thet ich ham mote habben, ant for the seove tiden

135 thet Hali Chirche singeth, thet ich deale in ham, slepe ich other wakie, ant for the seove bonen i the **Pater noster** ayein the seoven heaved ant deadliche sunnen, thet tu wite me with ham ant alle hare brokes ant yeove me the seovene selie eadinesses the thu havest, Laverd, bihaten thine i-corene i thin eadi nome:" Seove **Pater nostres; verset: Emitte spiritum tuum; Oremus: Deus, cui cor omne patet; Ecclesie tue quesumus, Domine;**

140 **Exaudi quesumus, Domine, supplicum preces.**

127–29 "A Jesu . . . deore-wurthe Laverd," "Ah, Jesus, [grant me] Your grace! Jesus, hung on a Cross for my sins, by the very five wounds [from] which You bled on it, heal my bloody soul of all the sins which she is wounded with by my five senses. That it [may] be so, in the memory of them (i.e., the five wounds), precious Lord, [I will pray]." **129–32 Fif *Pater nostres . . . sancte crucis*,** [Say] five "Our Fathers"; versicle: "Let all the earth adore You, and recite a psalm to Your name"; Let us pray: "O righteous Judge" (hymn probably by Berengar of Tours [999–1088]) — if you can (or, know [it]), or [say] some other [prayer] about the Cross — "God, who by the precious blood of Your only begotten Son, our Lord Jesus Christ, [wanted to sanctify] the emblem (or, standard) of the Holy Cross." **134 yiftes,** gifts. **134–38 thet ich ham mote habben . . . eadi nome,** that I might have them, and for the seven hours (i.e., the liturgical hours) that Holy Church sings, that I [may] share in them, [whether] I sleep or wake, and for the seven prayers in the "Our Father" against the seven capital and mortal sins, that you protect me from them and all their branches (or, perhaps, miseries — see glossary) and give me the seven happy blessings (or, happinesses) which You have, Lord, promised Your elect in Your blessed name." **138–40 Seove *Pater nostres . . . preces*,** [Say] seven "Our Fathers"; versicle: "Send forth Your spirit" (versicle based on Psalm 103:30); Let us pray: "God, to whom every heart opens" (collect); We beg You, Lord, [to hear the prayers] of Your church; We beg You to hear, Lord, the prayers of the supplicants" (prayer from the Litany).

78

"For the ten heastes the ich i-broken habbe, summe other alle, ant me-seolven —
towart te hwet-se beo of other-hwet untreoweliche i-teohethet — i bote of theose bruchen
for-te sahtni me with the, deore-wurthe Laverd:" Ten **Pater nostres; verset: Ego dixi
Domine miserere mei; Sana animam meam, quia peccavi tibi; Oremus: Deus cui
proprium est misereri.** "[I] the wurthgunge, Jesu Crist, of thine tweof apostles, thet
ich mote over-al folhin hare lare, thet ich mote habben thurh hare bonen the tweolf
bohes the bloweth of chearite, as Seinte Pawel writeth, blisfule Laverd:" Tweolf **Pater
nostres; verset: Annuntiaverunt opera Dei, et facta eius intellexerunt; Oremus:
Exaudi nos, Deus salutaris noster, et apostolorum tuorum nos tuere presidiis.**

H[a]lhen the ye luvieth best — in heore wurthgunge seggeth other leas other ma, as
ow bereth on heorte, ant thet **verset** efter-ward with hare collecte: "[F]or alle theo the
habbeth eani god i-do me, i-seid me other i-unnen me, ant for alle the ilke the wurcheth
the six werkes of misericorde, mearciable Laverd:" Six **Pater nostres; verset: Dispersit,
dedit pauperibus. Justicia eius manet; Oremus: Retribuere dignare, Domine.**

145 (line marker)

150 (line marker)

141–43 "For the ten heastes . . . Laverd," "For the ten commandments which I have broken,
some or all, and for myself — for whatever of anything else which is tithed (i.e., which I have
tithed) unfaithfully to You — in repentance for these breaches (or, violations), in order to reconcile myself to You, precious Lord, [I will say]." **143–45 *verset: Ego dixi . . . misereri***, versicle: "I
said to the Lord, have mercy on me, heal my spirit, because I have sinned against You" (a
response); Let us pray: "God, whose nature it is [always to forgive]" (prayer). **145–47 "[I] the
wurthgunge . . . blisfule Laverd,"** "In honor, Jesus Christ, of Your twelve Apostles, that I might
everywhere follow their teaching, that I might have through their prayers the twelve branches
which blossom with love, as Saint Paul writes, blessed Lord [I will say]." **148–49 *verset:
Annuntiaverunt . . . presidiis***, versicle: "They made known the works of God; and understood
His deeds" (versicle and response for the Feast of the Apostles); Let us pray: "Hear us, God our
salvation, and watch over us with the protection of Your Apostles" (collect for the Feast of the
Apostles). **150–53 H[a]lhen the ye luvieth best . . . Laverd,** The saints which you love best — in
their honor say either more or less as your heart directs (lit., as [it] best weighs You in heart), and
[say] the versicle[s] afterwards with their collect: "For all those who have done any good to me,
said [it] to me, or wished [it] to me, and for all those who accomplish the six works of mercy, [O]
merciful Lord [I will say]." **153–54 *verset: Dispersit . . . Domine***, versicle: "He has bestowed, He
has given [to the poor]; His justice remains" (versicle and response for lauds); Let us pray:
"Condescend to reward, Lord" (prayer for after the meal).

155 Hwa-se wule, segge the salm **Ad te levavi** bivore the **Pater nostres** ant **Kyrie eleison, Christe eleison, Kyrie eleison.**

"For alle the sawlen the beoth forth-fearen i the bileave of the fowr Goddspelles, the haldeth al Cristendom up-o fowr halves, thet tu the fowr marhe-yeven yeove ham in heovene, milzfule Laverd:" Fowr **Pater** *nostres*. Yef ye seggeth nihene — as ther beoth
160 nihene englene weoredes — thet Godd thurh his mearci hihi ham ut of pine to hare feolah-redden — ye doth yet betere. Ant her, alswa ye wulleth, seggeth **De profundis** bivore the **Pater nostres,** ant **Kyrie eleison (iii); verset: A porta inferi; Oremus: Fidelium.**

Bi dei sum time, *oth*er bi niht, gederith in ower heorte alle seke ant sarie thet wa ant
165 poverte tholieth, the pinen the prisuns tholieth ant habbeth ther ha liggeth with irn hevie i-fetheret, nomeliche of the Cristene the beoth in heathenesse, summe i prisun, summe in ase muche theowdom as oxe is other asse. Habbeth reowthe of theo the beoth i stronge temptatiuns: alle hare sares setteth in ower heorte ant siketh to ure Laverd thet he neome reowthe of ham ant bihalde toward ham with the ehe of his are. Ant yef ye
170 habbeth hwile, seggeth the salm **Levavi oculos; Pater noster; verset: Convertere,**

155 Hwa-se wule . . . Pater nostres, Whoever wants [may] say the psalm "To You I have lifted up [my eyes]" (Psalm 122) before the "Our Fathers." **157–59 beoth forth-fearen . . . Laverd,** which have departed in the belief of the four Gospels which hold up all Christendom on four sides (i.e., corners), [I pray] that You [may] give them the four bridal-gifts in heaven, gracious Lord. **159–61 Yef ye seggeth nihene . . . betere,** If you say nine — as there are nine troops of angels — [so] that God through His mercy [may] hurry them (i.e., the departed souls) out of pain into their (i.e., the angels') fellowship — you do even better. **161 De profundis,** "From the Depths" (Psalm 129, one of the seven penitential Psalms). **162–63 Kyrie eleison . . . Fidelium,** "Lord have mercy" three [times]; versicle: "From the gate of hell [deliver their souls]" (antiphon from the Office of the Dead); Let us pray: "[O God, Creator and Savior] of all the faithful" (prayer from the Litany). **164–67 Bi dei sum time . . . other asse,** By day some time, or by night, gather in your heart all sick and sorrowful [people] who suffer distress and poverty, the pains which prisoners suffer and experience where they lie, weighed down heavily with iron, especially for the Christians who are in heathen lands, some in prison, some in as much servitude (or, slavery) as [an] ass is or ox. **167–69 Habbeth reowthe . . . are,** Have pity on those who are in severe temptations: set all their sorrows in your heart and sigh to our Lord that He [may] take pity on them and look at them with the eye of His grace. **170 hwile,** time. **170–72 Levavi oculos . . . famulabus,** "I have lifted [my] eyes [to the mountains]" (Psalm 120);

Domine — usquequo. Et deprecabilis esto super servos tuos; Oremus: Pretende, Domine, famulis et famulabus.

I the measse hwen the preost heveth up Godes licome, seggeth this vers stondinde: **Ecce salus mundi, verbum Patris, hostia vera, viva caro, deitas integra, verus**

175 **homo.** Ant thenne falleth adun with theose gretunges:

> **Ave, principium nostre creationis,**
> **Ave, pretium nostre redemptionis,**
> **Ave, viaticum nostre peregrinationis,**
> **Ave, premium nostre expectationis,**
180 > **Ave, solamen nostre sustentationis.**

> **Tu esto nostre gaudium,**
> **Qui es futurus premium.**
> **Sit nostra in te gloria**
> **Per cuncta semper secula. Amen.**

185 > **Mane nobiscum, Domine.**
> **Gloria tibi, Domine.**

Set quis est locus in me quo veniat in me Deus meus, quo Deus veniat aut maneat in me, Deus qui fecit celum et terram? Itane, Domine, Deus meus, est quicquam

"Our Father"; versicle: "Return, O Lord — How long [will you stay away]? And be receptive to your servants" (prayer for Ash Wednesday); Let us pray: "Stretch out, Lord, [your right hand] to your servants and handmaids" (collect in the Litany). **173 heveth up . . . stondinde**, lifts up God's body, say (imper.) this verse, standing. **174–75 *Ecce salus . . . verus homo***, "Behold the salvation of the world, the word of the Father, the true sacrifice (or, Host), living flesh, divinity complete, true man" (invocation in the consecration). **176–86 *Ave, principium . . . Gloria tibi, Domine***, "Hail, beginning of our creation, / Hail, price of our redemption, / Hail, viaticum (i.e., allowance for a journey; or, Eucharist at the last rites) for our pilgrimage, / Hail, reward of our expectation, / Hail, comfort for our patient suffering. // Be our joy, / You who will be [our] reward. / May our glory [be] in You / Through all [time]. Amen. // Stay with us, O Lord. // Glory [be] to You, O Lord" (see gloss to 1.14–29 above). **187–94 *Set quis est locus . . . famule tue***, But what place is there in me where my God may come into me, where God may come and remain

in me quod capiat te? Quis michi dabit ut venias in cor meum et inebries illud, et
190   unum bonum meum amplectar te? Quis michi es? Miserere ut loquar. Angusta
est tibi domus anime mee. Quo venias ad eam, dilatetur abs te. Ruinosa est:
refice eam. Habet que offendant oculos tuos, fateor et scio, set quis mundabit
eam? Aut cui alteri preter te clamabo? Ab ocultis meis munda me, Domine, et
ab alienis parce famule tue.

195   Miserere, miserere, miserere mei, Deus, secundum magnam — ant swa al the
salm ut with **Gloria Patri; Christe, audi nos** twien; **Kyrie eleison, Christe eleison,
Kyrie eleison; Pater noster; Credo carnis resurrectionem et vitam eternam.
Amen; Salvam fac famulam tuam, Deus meus, sperantem in te. Doce me facere
voluntatem tuam, quia Deus meus es tu. Domine, exaudi orationem meam, et**
200   **clamor meus ad te veniat. Oremus: Concede, quesumus, omnipotens Deus, ut
quem enigmatice et sub aliena spetie cernimus, quo sacramentaliter cibamur in
terris, fatie ad fatiem eum videamus, eo sicuti est veraciter et realiter frui
mereamur in celis, per eundum Dominum.** Efter the measse-cos, hwen the preost

in me, the God who created heaven and earth? Is it so, Lord, my God? Is [there] something in me which
captures (or, contains) You? Who will grant to me that You may come into my heart and make it drunk
and that I may embrace You, my one good? Who are You to me? Have mercy so I may speak. My spirit
is a narrow house for You. In order that You come to it, let it be enlarged by You. It is broken down:
restore it. It may have [things] which offend Your eyes, I confess and know, but who will clean it? Or to
whom else except You will I cry out? Cleanse me, Lord, from my hidden [sins], and spare Your servant
from others (i.e., other sins)" (Based on Augustine, *Confessions*, Book 1, chs. 2 and 5). **195** *Miserere
. . . magnam*, "Have mercy, have mercy, have mercy on me, God, according to [Your] great [compas-
sion]" (Psalm 50, used in the Office of the Dead). **195–96 ant swa al the salm . . . twien**, and so [say] the
psalm out with "Glory be to the Father" (the doxology) and "Christ, hear us" (an antiphon) twice. **196–
203** *Kyrie eleison . . . Dominum*, "Lord have mercy, Christ have mercy, Lord have mercy"; "Our
Father"; "I believe in the resurrection of the body and life everlasting. Amen." (the Apostles' Creed);
"Save Your servant, my God, who hopes in You" (versicle and response based on Psalm 85:2, 16:7);
"Teach me to do Your will, because You are my God" (from Psalm 142:10); "Lord, hear my prayer, and
may my cries reach You" (Psalm 101, one of the penitential Psalms); Let us pray: "Grant, we ask, all-
powerful God, that Him whom we see obscurely and in a strange form, on whom we dine sacramentally
on earth, we may see Him face to face, and that we may be worthy to delight in Him in heaven just as He
actually and truly is, through the same Lord" (prayer for the Lauds of Our Lady). **203–06 Efter the
measse-cos . . . easkith**, After the kiss of peace (lit., mass-kiss), when the priest consecrates [the

205 sacreth — ther foryeoteth al the world, ther beoth al ut of bodi, ther i sperclinde luve bicluppeth ower leofmon, the into ower breostes bur is i-liht of heovene, ant haldeth him hete-veste athet he habbe i-yettet ow al thet ye eaver easkith.

This ureisun bivore the muchele rode is of muche strengthe:

Abute mid-dei hwa-se mei — hwa-se ne mei thenne, o sum other time — thenche o Godes rode, ase muchel as ha eaver con mest, other mei, ant of his derve pine. Ant
210 biginne th'refter the ilke fif gretunges the beoth i-writen th'ruppe, ant alswa cneolin to euch an ant blescin, as hit seith ther, ant beate the breoste ant makie a thulli bone:

Adoramus te, Christe. Tuam crucem. [Salve, crux sancta.] Salve, crux que .... O, crux lignum. Aris thenne ant bigin the antefne **Salva nos, Christe salvator, per virtutem sancte crucis** with the rode-taken, ant segge stondinde the salm **Jubi-**
215 **late** with **Gloria Patri**. Ant thenne the antefne segge eaver thus: **Salva nos, Christe salvator, per virtutem sancte crucis** ant blescin with **Qui salvasti Petrum in mare, miserere nobis** ant beate the breoste ant tenne falle adun ant segge **Christe, audi nos.**

Eucharist] — there forget all the world, there be completely out of [your] body, there in sparkling (or, shining) love embrace your beloved (or, lover) who has lighted (or, descended) from heaven into the bower of your breast (or, heart), and hold Him firmly until He has granted you all that you ever ask. **207 This ureisun . . . strengthe,** This prayer, [recited] before the great Cross, is of great power. **208–09 hwa-se mei . . . derve pine,** whoever can — whoever cannot then, at some other time — [should] think on God's Cross and His cruel pain, as much as she ever most knows how or is able. **209–11 Ant biginne . . . bone,** And [let her] begin afterwards the same five greetings (or, salutations) which are written above, and also kneel at each one and make the sign of the Cross, as it says there (i.e., above), and beat your (lit., the) breast and make one such prayer [as this]. **212–13 Adoramus te . . . lignum,** "(1) We worship You, Christ. (2) [We worship] Your Cross. (3) Hail, Holy Cross. (4) Hail, O Cross, which. . . . (5) O, Cross, wood [victorious]" (i.e., the five greetings mentioned above). **213 antefne,** antiphon. **213–14 Salva nos . . . crucis,** "Save us, Christ [our] savior, by the power of the Holy Cross" (antiphon from the Feast of the Exaltation of the Cross). **214–20 rode-taken . . . sanctam crucem as ear,** sign of the Cross and say standing the psalm, "Rejoice [in the Lord]" (Psalm 99) with "Glory be to the Father" (the doxology). And then say the antiphon always in this way: "Save us, Christ [our] Savior, by the power of Your Holy Cross" (antiphon for the Feast of the Exaltation of the Cross) and make the sign of the Cross with "[You] who have saved Peter on the ocean, have mercy on us" (antiphon based on Matthew 14:28–31) and beat [your] breast and then fall down and say, "Christ, hear us. Jesus Christ, hear us" (an antiphon); "Lord have mercy, Christ have mercy, Lord have mercy"; "Our Father" . . .

Jesu Christe, audi nos; Kyrie eleison, Christe eleison, Kyrie eleison; Pater noster . . . et ne nos; Verset: Protector noster aspice, Deus, et respice in faciem Christi tui; Oremus: Deus, qui sanctam crucem as ear. Eft biginne **Adoramus** as ear, alle five; **Salva nos, Christe**, the antefne, as ear; the salm **Ad te levavi;** the antefne as ear al ut, ant tenne as ear to the eorthe; **Christe, audi nos** twien; **Kyrie eleison** iii; **Pater noster . . . et ne nos; Verset: Protector noster,** as ear; **Oremus: Adesto, quesumus, Domine, Deus noster, et quos sancte crucis letari facis** — thridde chearre riht alswa, ant feorthe chearre, ant fifte: na-wiht ne changeth bute the salmes ant te ureisuns. The forme salm **Jubilate**, the other **Ad te levavi**, the thridde **Qui confidunt**, the feorthe **Domine, non est exaltatum**, the fifte **Laudate Dominum in sanctis eius**. Ant in euch beoth fif vers. The fif ureisuns beoth: **Deus, qui sanctam crucem; Adesto, quesumus, Domine; Deus, qui pro nobis filium tuum; Deus, qui unigeniti; Juste Judex;** with **O beata et intemerata.** Ant hwa-se ne con theos fif ureisuns, segge eaver an. Ant hwa-se thuncheth to long, leave the salmes.

220

225

230

"and [lead] us not [into temptation]" (Lord's prayer); versicle: "Our protector, God, see and look into the face of Your Christ" (based on Psalm 83:10); Let us pray: "God, who [ascended] the Holy Cross" (antiphon for matins) as before. **220–27 Eft biginne . . . in sanctis eius,** Begin again "We worship" (see gloss to 1.32–34 above) as before, all five; "Save us, Christ," the antiphon as before, the psalm "To you [Lord] I have lifted up [my eyes]" (Psalm 122); [say] the antiphon as before completely out (i.e., to the end), and then as before [kneel] to the ground; "Christ, hear us" twice; "Lord have mercy" three [times]; "Our Father" . . . "and [lead] us not [into temptation]"; versicle: "Our Protector," as before; Let us pray: "Defend (lit., be present), we pray, O Lord our God, those whom You cause to rejoice in the Holy Cross" (prayer for after the Mass of the Holy Cross) — a third time [say these prayers] just so, and a fourth time, and a fifth: change nothing at all except the psalms and the prayers. The first psalm [is] "Rejoice [in the Lord]" (Psalm 99), the second, "To You I have lifted up [my eyes]" (Psalm 122), the third, "Those who trust [in the Lord]" (Psalm 124), the fourth, "Lord, [my heart] is not lifted up" (Psalm 130), the fifth, "Praise the Lord in His sanctuary" (Psalm 150). **228–30 Ant in euch beoth . . . intemerata,** And in each [there] are five verses. The five prayers are: "Lord, who [ascended] the Holy Cross" (collect); "Defend, Lord, we pray" (post-communion prayer); "God, who for us [consented that] Your Son should suffer" (collect); "God, who [with the precious blood] of Your only begotten Son" (mass prayer for Feast of the Exaltation of the Cross); "Upright Judge" (hymn); with "O blessed and unsullied" (variant of a prayer to the Virgin and St. John). **230–31 Ant hwa-se . . . salmes,** And whoever does not know these five prayers, may always say one. And whoever thinks [it] too long may leave out the psalms.

"Leafdi Seinte Marie, for the ilke muchele blisse thet tu hefdest in-with the i thet ilke time thet Jesu Godd, Godes sune, efter the engles gretunge nom flesch ant blod in the ant of the, underfeng mi gretunge with the ilke **Ave** ant make me telle lutel of euch blisse 235 ute-with, ah frovre me in-with ant ernde me theo of heovene. Ant ase wis as i the ilke flesch thet he toc of the nes neaver sunne, ne i thin — as me leveth efter the ilke tacunge, hwet-se bivore were — clense mi sawle of fleschliche sunnen." Biginne the **Ave** athet **Dominus tecum** as me biginneth antefne, ant tenne the salm, ant efter the salm al ut fif sithen, ant thus to euch salm **Ave, Maria, gratia plena, Dominus tecum;** 240 **Magnificat; Ave, Maria** al ut fif sithen.

"Leafdi Seinte Maria, for the ilke muchele blisse thet tu hefdest tha thu sehe the ilke blisfule bearn i-boren of thi cleane bodi to mon-cunne heale, withuten eaver-euch bruche, with i-hal meithhad ant meidenes menske, heal me thet am thurh wil tobroken, as ich drede, hwet-se beo of dede. Ant yef me in heovene seon thi blisfule leor, ant bihalde 245 lanhure meidenes menske, yef ich nam wurthe for-te beon i-blisset in hare ferredden." **Ave, Maria gratia plena, Dominus tecum; Ad Dominum cum tribularer; Ave** as ear five.

232–35 Leafdi Seinte Marie . . . of heovene, Lady, Saint Mary, for the same great joy which you had within you in the very time that Jesus God, God's son, after the angel's greeting, took flesh and blood in you and from you, receive my greeting with the same "Hail" [as the angel used] and make me think little of each external joy, but comfort me within and obtain for me those [joys] from heaven. **235–37 Ant ase wis . . . sunnen**, And as surely as in that same body which He took of you [there] was no sin, nor in yours — as people believe [that your body was sinless] after this same taking (i.e., the incarnation), whatever [it] might have been before — cleanse my soul of bodily sins. **238–40 *Ave* athet . . . sithen**, "Hail [Mary]" until "The Lord be with you" (i.e., end of the first verse of the "Ave") as one begins the antiphon, and then the psalm, and after the psalm, [said] out completely five times, and so at [the end of] each psalm [say] "Hail Mary, full of grace, the Lord be with you" (the "Ave," based on Luke 1:28). "[My soul] magnifies [the Lord]" (the "Magnificat," based on Luke 1:46); "Hail, Mary" out completely five times. **241–44 tha thu sehe . . . of dede**, when you saw the same joyful Son born from your pure body for mankind's healing (or, salvation), without ever any rupture, with intact virginity and virgin's honor, heal me who, I fear, am shattered by desire (or, by my will), whatever [the case may] be concerning [my] actions. **244–45 Ant yef me . . . ferredden**, And give (or, grant) me in heaven to see your joyful face, and at least to behold the virgins' honor, if I am not worthy to be blessed in their companionship. **246–47 *Ave, Maria* . . . ear five**, "Hail, Mary full of grace, [may] the Lord [be] with you"; "When I was in trouble [I cried out] to the Lord" (Psalm 119, first of 15 gradual psalms); "Hail" — five, as before.

"Leafdi Seinte Marie, for the ilke muchele blisse thet tu hefdest tha thu sehe thi deore deore-wurthe sune efter his derve death arisen to blisful lif, his bodi seve-valt brihtre then the sunne, yef me deien with him ant arisen in him — worltliche deien, gasteliche libben — dealen in his pinen feolahliche in eorthe, for-te beon i blisse his feolahe in heovene. For the ilke muchele blisse thet tu hefdest, Leafdi, of his blisful ariste efter thi muchele sorhe, efter mi sorhe thet ich am in her, lead me to thi blisse." **Ave, Maria gratia plena, Dominus tecum; Retribue servo tuo; Ave** fif sithen.

250

"Leafdi Seinte Marie, for the ilke muchele blisse thet tu hefdest tha thu sehe thi brihte blisfule Sune, thet te Giws wenden for-te athrusmin i thruh, se wurthliche ant se mihtliche on Hali Thursdei stihe to his blisse into his riche of heovene, yef me warpe with him al the worlt under fet ant stihen—nu heorteliche; hwen ich deie, gasteliche; o Domes-dei al licomliche to heovenliche blissen." **Ave, Maria gratia plena, Dominus tecum; In convertendo; Ave** fif sithen.

255

260

"Leafdi Seinte Marie, for the ilke muchele blisse thet fulde al the eorthe tha he underveng the into unimete blisse ant with his blisfule earmes sette the i trone ant cwene crune o*n* heaved, brihtre then the sunne, heh heovenliche cwen, underveng theos gretunges of me swa on eorthe thet ich mote blisfulliche grete the in heovene." **Ave, Maria gratia**

248–52 tha thu sehe . . . in heovene, when you saw your dear precious Son after His cruel death arise to joyful life, His body seven times brighter than the sun, give (or, grant) me to die with Him and arise in Him — to die worldly (i.e., with respect to the world), to live spiritually — to share in His pains as a comrade on earth, in order to be His comrade in joy in heaven. **252–53 of his blisful ariste . . . muchele sorhe,** from His joyful resurrection after your great sorrow. **253 ich am in her,** I am in here. **254** *Retribue servo tuo,* "Restore your servant" (Psalm 118:7). **255–59 tha thu sehe . . . blissen,** when you saw your bright, joyful Son, whom the Jews hoped to suffocate (or, kill) in the tomb, rise so worthily and so power-fully on Holy Thursday to His joy into His kingdom of heaven, grant me to throw all the world under foot (lit., feet) and climb with Him to heavenly joys — now, in heart (lit., heart-ily); when I die, spiritually; on Judgment Day, quite bodily. **259** *Ave, Maria . . . tecum,* "Hail, Mary, fully of grace, the Lord be with you" (first line of the "Ave"). **259–60** *In convertendo,* "[The Lord] in reversing [the captivity of Zion]" (Psalm 125, one of the 15 gradual psalms). **261–64 thet fulde al the eorthe . . . in heovene,** which filled all the earth when He received you into immeasurable (or, unimaginable) joy and with His joyful arms set you in the throne and [set] the queen's crown on [your] head, brighter than the sun, [O] high heavenly queen, receive these greetings from me in such a way on earth that I might greet you joyfully in heaven.

265 **plena, Dominus tecum; Ad te levavi; Ave** fif sithen, ant thenne thet **verset: Spiritus sanctus superveniet in te, et virtus altissimi obumbrabit tibi; Oremus: Gratiam tuam;** Antefne:

> **Ave, Regina celorum,**
> **Ave, Domina angelorum,**
270 > **Salve, Radix Sancta,**
> **Ex qua mundo lux,**
> **Vale, valde decora,**
> **Et pro nobis semper Christum exora.**

Verset: Egredietur virga de radice Jesse, et flos de radice eius ascendet. Oremus:
275 **Deus, qui virginalem aulam.** Antefne:

> **Gaude, Dei Genitrix, Virgo inmaculata,**
> **Gaude, que gaudium ab angelo suscepisti,**
> **Gaude, que genuisti eterni luminis claritatem,**
> **Gaude, Mater.**
280 > **Gaude, sancta Dei Genitrix Virgo,**

265 *Ad te levavi*, "To you I have lifted up [my eyes]" (Psalm 122, one of the 15 gradual psalms). **265–67 *verset: Spiritus sanctus . . . Gratiam tuam***, versicle: "The Holy Spirit will come over you and the strength of the Most High will overshadow you" (Luke 1:35 as versicle for the Feast of the Assumption); Let us pray: "[Pour out] your grace" (collect for Easter vespers of Our Lady). **267 Antefne**, [and say this] antiphon. **268–73 *Ave, Regina celorum . . . exora***, "Hail, Queen of heaven, / Hail, Ruler (lit., Lady) of angels, / Greetings, Sacred Root (or, source), / From whom light has arisen to the world, / Hail, O exceedingly beautiful [one], / And always pray to Christ for us" (antiphon for the Feast of the Nativity of Our Lady). **274–75 *Verset: Egredietur . . . aulam***, Versicle: "A shoot will spring out from the root of Jesse, and a flower will rise up from his root" (Isaiah 11:1 as a versicle and response). Let us pray: "God, who [lowered Himself to choose] the virginal palace (i.e., Mary's womb)" (collect for the Feast of the Assumption). **276–83 *Gaude, Dei Genitrix . . . Interventrix***, "Rejoice, Mother of God, unblemished Virgin, / Rejoice, [you] who have received joy from the angel, / Rejoice, [you] who have given birth to the splendor of eternal light, / Rejoice, Mother. / Rejoice, holy Virgin, Mother of God, / You alone are a virgin-Mother, / Every creature of your Son praises you, Mother of light, / Be for us a holy Intercessor (fem.)"

Tu sola Mater innupta,

Te laudat omnis filii tui creatura Genitricem lucis,

Sis pro nobis pia Interventrix.

Verset: Ecce, Virgo concipiet et pariet Filium, et vocabitur nomen euis Emmanuel;

285 **Oremus: Deus, qui de beate Marie Virginis utero.** Antefne:

Gaude, Virgo,

Gaude, Dei Genitrix,

Et gaude, gaudium, Maria, omnium fidelium.

Gaudeat ecclesia in tuis laudibus assidua,

290 **Et, pia Domina, gaudere fac nos tecum ante Dominum.**

Verset: Ecce, concipies in utero et paries filium, et vocabis nomen eius Jesum;

Oremus: Deus, qui salutis eterne beate Marie virginitate fecunda humano generi.

Antefne:

Alma Redemptoris Mater, que pervia celi

295 **Porta manes et stella maris, succurre cadenti**

Surgere qui curat populo; tu que genuisti —

Natura mirante — tuum sanctum Genitorem,

(antiphon for Tierce of Our Lady). **284–85** *Verset: Ecce, Virgo . . . utero,* versicle: "Behold, a Virgin will conceive and bear a Son, and His name will be called Emmanuel" (Isaiah 7:14, as a *capitulum*); Let us pray: "God, who from the womb of the blessed Virgin Mary" (prayer). **286–90** *Gaude, Virgo . . . Dominum,* "Rejoice, [O] Virgin, / Rejoice, Mother of God, / And rejoice, Mary, joy of all the faithful. / May the church, never ceasing, rejoice in your praises, / And, holy Lady, make us rejoice with you before the Lord" (untraced antiphon). **291–92** *Verset: Ecce, concipies . . . generi,* versicle: "Behold, you will conceive in your womb and will give birth to a Son, and you shall call His name Jesus" (based on Luke 1:31); Let us pray: "God, [You] who by the fruitful virginity of eternally blessed Mary [have obtained the reward] of salvation for the human race" (collect for the Tierce and Vespers of Our Lady). **294–99** *Alma Redemptoris . . . miserere,* "Gracious Mother of the Redeemer, who remains the accessible (or, open) gate of heaven / And star of the sea, help the falling people / To rise, who care to rise; you who have given birth to — / Nature was dumbfounded — your holy Father, / Virgin before and afterwards, from the mouth of Gabriel / Receiving that 'Hail,'

88

Virgo prius ac posterius, Gabrielis ab ore
Sumens illud "Ave," peccatorum miserere.

300   Her sitteth the **Avez**, fifti other hundret, other ma other leas efter thet me haveth hwile.
On ende thet **verset: Ecce, ancilla Domini. Fiat michi secundum verbum tuum;**
Oremus: O Sancta Virgo virginum. Hwa-se wule mei stutten th'ruppe anan-rihtes
efter the forme ureisun, **Gratiam tuam**, ant segge thenne hire tale of **Avez** efter the
leaste salm, **Ad te levavi.** Eaver bivore the salm biginnen an **Ave** athet **Dominus tecum**

305   ant segge stondinde the salm. The salmes beoth i-numene efter the fif leattres of ure
Leafdis nome — hwa-sa nimeth yeme — ant al this ilke ureisun efter hire fif heste
blisses eorneth bi five. Tele i the antefnes ant tu schalt finden in ham gretunges five. The
ureisuns thet ich nabbe buten ane i-mearket beoth i-writen over al withute the leaste.
Leoteth writen on a scrowe hwet-se ye ne kunnen. Thus ich biginne mine **Avez** other-

310   hwiles:

   "Leafdi, swete Leafdi, swetest alre leafdi, Leafdi, leovest Leafdi, lufsumest Leafdi. **O**
pulcherrima mulierum. Leafdi Seinte Marie, deore-wurthe Leafdi, Leafdi cwen of

have mercy on sinners" (an eleventh-century hymn sometimes used as an antiphon for the Feast
of the Nativity of the Virgin). **300 Her sitteth . . . hwile**, Sit here [to say] the "Aves," fifty or a
hundred, or more or less according to [whether] one has time. **301–02** *verset: Ecce, ancilla*
Domini . . . virginum, versicle: "Behold, the handmaid of the Lord. Let it be to me according to
your word" (Luke 1:38 as antiphon for the Feast of the Annunciation); Let us pray: "O holy
Virgin of virgins" (a collect by Marbod of Rennes). **302–03 Hwa-se wule . . . tale of** *Avez*,
Whoever wants may stop above right after the first prayer, "[Pour out] your grace" (collect
for Easter vespers of Our Lady), and [let her] say then her full count of "Aves." **304** *Ad te*
levavi, "To you I have lifted up [my eyes]" (Psalm 122). **304–07 Eaver bivore . . . bi five**,
Before the psalm, always begin (imper. pl.) [with] one "Hail" until "The Lord [be] with you"
and say the psalm standing. The psalms are chosen (lit., taken) according to the five letters
of our Lady's name — whoever pays (lit., takes) attention [will see] — and all this same
prayer runs by fives according to her five highest (or, most exalted) joys. **307 Tele i the**
antefnes, count (imper.) in the antiphons. **307–09 The ureisuns . . . kunnen**, The prayers,
which I have but (i.e., only) indicated, except the last [one], are written everywhere. Have
written on a scroll whatsoever you do not know. **309–10 other-hwiles**, sometimes. **311–12**
swetest alre leafdi . . . *mulierum*, sweetest of all ladies, Lady, most beloved Lady, loveliest
Lady. "O most beautiful of women" (Song of Songs 5:9, 17). **312 deore-wurthe**, precious.

heovene, Leafdi cwen of are, Leafdi, do me are. Leafdi meiden Moder, Meiden Godes Moder, Jesu Cristes Moder, Meiden of milce, Moder of grace.

315   **O Virgo virginum,**

    Maria Mater gratie,

    Mater misericordie,

    Tu nos ab hoste protege

    Et hora mortis suscipe.

320   **Per tuum, Virgo, Filium,**

    Per Patrem, Paraclitum,

    Assis presens ad obitum

    Nostrumque muni exitum.

    Gloria tibi, Domine,

325   **qui natu*s* es de Virgine, et cetera.**

Ant fallen to ther eorthe ant cussen hire with this leaste vers, hwa-se is hal i-heafdet, ant tenne **Avez** tene ant tene togederes, the teohethe eaver thus forth: **Ave, Maria gratia plena, Dominus tecum, benedicta tu in mulieribus, et benedictus fructus ventris tui; Spiritus sanctus superveniet in te, et virtus altissimi obumbrabit tibi. Ideoque**

330 **et quod nascetur ex te sanctum vocabitur Filius Dei. Ecce ancilla Domini, fiat**

313 cwen of are . . . are, queen of grace, Lady, have mercy on me (lit., do me grace). **314 milce**, mercy. **315–25 *O Virgo virginum . . . et cetera***, "O Virgin of virgins, / Mary Mother of grace, / Mother of mercy, / Protect us from the enemy / And receive [us] at the hour of death. / Through your Son, Virgin, / Through the Father, and the Paraclete (i.e., the Holy Spirit), / May you be present at [our] passing away, / And prepare a way for our departure. / Glory be to You, Lord, / [You] who were born from the Virgin, etc." (hymn). **326–27 Ant fallen . . . thus forth**, And fall (imper., pl.) to the ground and kiss it (lit., her) at this last verse, whoever is in good health (lit., healthy headed), and then ten "Hail [Mary]s," and [say those] ten together, the tenth always [say it] out this way. **327–29 *Ave, Maria . . . ventris tui***, "Hail Mary, full of grace, the Lord be with you; blessed are you among women, and blessed is the fruit of your womb" (the "Ave," based on Luke 1:28, 42). **329–30 *Spiritus sanctus . . . Filius Dei***, "The Holy Spirit will come over you and the power of the Most High will overshadow you. And therefore the holy one [who] will be born from you will be called the Son of God" (Luke 1:35 as versicle for the Feast of the Assumption). **330–31 *Ecce ancilla . . . verbum tuum***, "Behold the handmaid of the Lord, let it be to me

michi secundum verbum tuum — ant cusse the eorthe on ende, other degre, other bench, other sum-hwet herres, ant biginnen, "Leafdi, swete Leafdi," as ear. The forme tene the fifti cneolinde up ant dun; the othre cneolinde i-riht up stille, buten ed te **Ave, Marie** sum semblant with the other cneo a lutel; the thridde tene adun ant up-o the elbohen riht to ther eorthe; the feorthe, the elbohen o degre, other o bench, ant eaver to the **Ave** lute with the heaved; the fifte tene stondinde, ant eft biginne the turn as i the frumthe.

335

Al thet ye eaver seggeth of thulliche othre bonen, as **Pater nostres** ant **Aves** on ower ahne wise, salmes ant ureisuns, ich am wel i-paiet. Euch-an segge ase best bereth hire on heorte verseilunge of sawter, redunge of Englisc other of Frensch, halie meditatiuns, ower cneolunges hwen-se ye eaver mahen i-yemen, ear mete ant efter —eaver se ye mare doth, se Godd ow eche forthre his deore-wurthe grace. Ah lokith swa, ich bidde ow, thet ye ne beon neaver idel, ah wurchen other reden, other beon i bonen, ant swa don eaver sum-hwet, thet god mahe of awakenin. The ures of the Hali Gast —yef ye ham wulleth seggen, seggeth euch tide of ham bivoren ure Leafdi tide.

340

345

according to your word" (Luke 1:38 as antiphon for the Feast of the Annunciation). **331–32 ant cusse . . . as ear**, and kiss (imper.) the ground at the end, or a step, or a bench, or something higher, and begin, "Lady, sweet Lady," as before. **332–37 The forme tene . . . i the frumthe**, [Say] the first ten of the fifty kneeling [alternatively] up and down; the second [group of ten] kneeling upright and still, except at the "Hail Mary" [you should make] some show [of kneeling] with the other knee a little; [say] the third ten down and upon the elbows right to the ground; [say] the fourth, the elbows on a step, or on a bench, and always bow your head (lit., with the head) at the "Hail"; the fifth ten [say] standing, and begin the cycle (lit., turn) again as at the start. **338–42 Al thet ye eaver seggeth . . . grace**, All that you ever say of other prayers of this kind, [such] as "Our Fathers," and "Hail [Mary]s" in your own way, psalms and prayers, I am well pleased [with]. [Let] each one say as her heart best directs (lit., as [it] best weighs her in heart) the recitation of the Psalter, reading of English or French, holy meditations, your kneelings whenever (lit., whensoever) you can attend to [them], before meals (lit., food) and after — always as you do more, so [may] God further increase His precious grace [in] you. **342–44 Ah lokith swa . . . awakenin**, But so look [to it], I beg you, that you are never unoccupied, but work or read or be in prayers and thus always do something [from] which good may arise (lit., awake). **344–45 The ures of the Hali Gast . . . tide**, The hours of the Holy Spirit — if you want to say them, say each hour of them before our Lady's hour.

Toward te preostes tiden hercnith se forth as ye mahen, ah with him ne schule ye nowther verseilin ne singen thet he hit mahe i-heren. Ower graces stondinde bivore mete ant efter, as ha beoth i-writen ow. Ant with the **Miserere** gath bivoren ower weoved ant endith thear the graces. Bitweone mel, the drinken wule, segge **Benedicite.**

350 **Potum nostrum Filius Dei benedicat. In nomine Patris** — ant blesci efter-wart. **Adiutorium nostrum in nomine Domini, qui fecit celum et terram. Sit nomen Domini benedictum, ex hoc nunc et usque in seculum. Benedicamus Domino. Deo gratias.**

Hwen-se ye gath to ower bedd i niht other in even, falleth o cneon ant thencheth i

355 hwet ye habbeth i the dei i-wreathet ure Laverd, ant crieth him yeorne merci ant foryevenesse. Yef ye habbeth ei god i-don, thonkith him of his yeove, withute hwam we ne mahen ne wel don, ne wel thenchen, ant seggeth **Miserere** ant **Kyrie eleison, Christe eleison, Kyrie eleison; Pater noster . . . et ne nos; Verset: Salvas fac ancillas tuas, Deus meus, sperantes in te; Oremus: Deus cui proprium est;** ant

360 stondinde, **Visita, Domine, habitationem istam;** ant aleast thenne, **Christus vincit ✠,**

346–48 Toward te preostes . . . i-writen ow, Listen (imper.) to the priest's hours as far as you can, but [you] must not either recite or sing with him [so] that he might hear it. [Say] your graces (i.e., prayers of thanks at mealtimes) standing before meals (lit., food) and after, as they are written for you. **348–49 Ant with the *Miserere* . . . segge,** And with the "[Lord] have Mercy" go before your altar and end the graces there. Whoever wants to drink between meals [should] say. **349–53 *Benedicite . . . Deo gratias,*** "A blessing. The Son of God blesses our drink. In the name of the Father" (a monastic blessing) — and make the sign of the Cross afterwards. "Our help [is] in the name of the Lord, who made heaven and earth. Blessed be the name of the Lord from this time forth and forevermore. Let us bless the Lord. Thanks be to God" (a versicle). **354 even,** evening, night. **354–55 thencheth i hwet . . . Laverd,** think in what you have angered our Lord during the day. **355 yeorne,** eagerly, earnestly. **356–57 Yef ye habbeth . . . thenchen,** If you have done any good, thank Him for His gift, without whom we cannot do well (i.e., any good), or think well. **357–65 *Miserere* . . . efter-warde clauses,** "[Lord] have mercy" and "Lord have mercy, Christ have mercy, Lord have Mercy"; "Our Father" . . . "and [lead] us not [into temptation]"; versicle: "My God, Save your handmaidens [who are] hoping in you"; Let us pray: "God, whose nature it is [always to have mercy]" (prayer); and standing [say] "Visit, O Lord, this house" (prayer for Compline of Our Lady); and then lastly, "Christ conquers, Christ reigns, Christ rules" (antiphon for Easter) with three [signs of the] Cross with the thumb on the forehead, and then "Behold the Cross of the Lord; flee enemy; the lion of the tribe of Judah, the

Christus regnat ✠, Christus imperat ✠, with threo creoiz with the thume up-o the forheaved, ant thenne **Ecce crucem Domini; fugite partes adverse; vicit leo de tribu Juda, radix Davith. Alleluia.** A large creoiz as ed **Deus in adiutorium** with **Ecce crucem Domini,** ant tenne fowr creoiz o fowr half with theose fowre efter-warde clauses:

365

Crux ✠ fugat omne malum.
Crux ✠ est reparatio rerum.
Per crucis hoc signum ✠
Fugiat procul omne malignum.
370 **Et per idem signum ✠,**
Salvetur quodque benignum.

On ende, [on] ow-seolf ant o the bedd bathe, **In nomine Patris et Filii.** I bedd se vorth se ye mahen, ne do ye, ne ne thenchen na thing bute slepen.

The ne con other uht-song, other ne mei hit seggen, segge for uht-song thritti **Pater**
375 **nostres** ant **Ave, Maria** efter euch **Pater noster,** ant **Gloria Patri** efter euch **Ave,** aleast **Oremus** (hwa-se con): **Deus cui proprium est; Benedicamus Domino; Anime fidelium.** For even-song twenti, for euch other tide segge fiftene o this ilke wise, bute

root of David, has conquered. Alleluia" (antiphon for the Feast of the Exaltation of the Cross). [Make] a large [sign of the] Cross as [you did] at "God, [come] to my aid" with "Behold the Cross of the Lord," and then [make] four [signs of the] Cross on four sides (i.e., in each of the four directions) with these four following clauses. **366–71 Crux ✠ fugat . . . benignum,** "The Cross puts to flight all evil. / The Cross is the restorer of things. / By this sign of the Cross / May all evil flee far away. / And by this very symbol, / May whatever is good be saved" (an untraced hymn). **372–73 On ende . . . slepen,** At last, [make the sign of the Cross] over yourself and over the bed as well, "In the name of the Father and of the Son" (monastic invocation to the Trinity). In bed, as far as you can, do not do or think of anything but sleeping (lit., to sleep). **374–80 The ne con . . . adiutorium,** Whoever either does not know matins (lit., morning song) or cannot say it, [let her] say in place of matins thirty "Our Fathers" and [thirty] "Hail, Marys" after each "Our Father," and "Glory be to the Father" after each "Hail," and finally, "Let us pray," — whoever knows [it] — "God, whose nature it is [always to forgive]" (prayer); "Let us bless the Lord" (versicle recited near the end of the day); "The souls of the faithful" (versicle concluding prime). For vespers (lit., evensong) [say] twenty, for every other [canonical] hour say fifteen in this way, except that at

thet ed uht-song schal seggen earst hwa-se con, **Domine, labia mea aperies, et os meum; Deus in adiutorium,** ant ed Complie, **Converte nos, Deus salutaris; Deus**
380 **in adiutorium.** Ed alle the othre tiden, **Deus in adiutorium.**

Hwa-se is unheite forkeorve of uht-song tene, of euch of the othre five — the halven-dal of euch-an, yef ha is seccre. Hwa-se is ful meoseise, of al beo ha cwite. Neome hire secnesse nawt ane tholemodliche, ah do swithe gleadliche; ant al is hiren thet Hali Chirche ret other singeth. Thah ye ahen of Godd thenchen in euch time, meast
385 thah in ower tiden, thet ower thohtes ne beon fleotinde thenne. Yef ye thurh yemeles gluffeth of wordes, other misneometh vers, neometh owe[r] **Venie** dun ed ter eorthe with the hond ane — al fallen adun for muche misneomunge, ant schawith ofte i schrift ower yemeles her-abuten.

This is nu the forme dale, the haveth i-speken hider-to of ower servise. Hwet-se beo
390 u ther-of, theose riwlen her-efter ich walde ha weren of alle — as ha beoth of ow, thurh Godes grace — i-halden.

matins whosoever knows [it] will say first, "Lord, open my lips, and my mouth" (monastic prayer recited before beginning the divine office); "God, [come] to my aid" (Psalm 69:2 as a response, recited at the beginning of each of the canonical hours except compline), and at Compline, "Convert us, beneficent God" (versicle) and "God, [come] to my aid." At all the other hours, "God, [come] to my aid." **381–84 Hwa-se is unheite . . . singeth,** Whosoever is unwell [may] cut out from matins ten and from each of the other [hours] five — [she may cut out] half of each one (i.e., each hour), if she is sicker. Whosoever is full of discomfort (i.e., terribly sick), [let her] be released from all. [Let her] take her sickness not only patiently but do [so] very gladly; and everything is hers that Holy Church reads or sings. **384–88 Thah ye ahen . . . her-abuten,** Although you ought to think of God at all times (lit., in each time), most [of all], though, in your hours, [so] that your thoughts are not wandering then. If you, through carelessness, skip over words, or mistake a verse, make (lit., take) your "Pardon" with only your (lit., the) hand down on the ground — fall down completely (i.e., kneel with your body fully bowed forward) for serious mistakes, and reveal often in confession your careless-ness in this (lit., hereabout). **389–91 This is nu . . . i-halden,** This is now the first part (i.e., the first part is now finished), which has spoken up to now about your [divine] service (or, devotional duties). Whatever may now be concerning that (i.e., as the case may be concern-ing your divine service), these following rules (i.e., those concerning the inner rule) — I would they were kept by all, as they are by you, through God's grace.

Part Two

The Five Senses

§ *Her biginneth the other dale of the heorte warde thurh the fif wittes.*

Omni custodia serva cor tuum quia ex ipso vita procedit. "With alles cunnes warde," dohter, seith Salomon, "wite wel thin heorte, for sawle lif is in hire" — yef ha is wel i-loket. The heorte wardeins beoth the fif wittes: sihthe, ant herunge, smechunge, ant smeallunge, ant euch limes felunge. Ant we schulen speoken of alle, for hwa-se wit theose wel, he deth Salomones bode: he wit wel his heorte ant his sawle heale. The heorte is a ful wilde beast ant maketh moni liht lupe. As Seint Gregoire seith, **Nichil corde fugatius.** "Na thing ne etflith mon sonre then his ahne heorte." Davith, Godes prophete, meande i sum time thet ha wes etsteart him: **Cor meum**

5

---

1 Her biginneth . . . the fif wittes, Here begins the second part, concerning the heart's guarding (i.e., protecting the heart) through the five senses (lit., wits). **2 *Omni custodia . . . procedit***, "With all watchfulness preserve your heart, for from it life comes forth" (Proverbs 4:23). **2–4 With alles cunnes . . . wel i-loket**, "With all watchfulness (lit., watchfulness of every kind), protect well your heart, for the soul's life is in her (i.e., the heart)" — if she is well looked after. **4–5 The heorte wardeins . . . euch limes felunge**, The heart's guardians are the five senses: sight, and hearing, tasting, and smelling, and each limb's feeling (i.e., touch). **5–7 Ant we schulen . . . his sawle heale**, And we shall speak of all [of them], for whosoever guards (*wit* = reduced form of *witeth*) these well, he does Solomon's commandment: he guards well his heart and his soul's well-being (or, salvation). **7 The heorte is a . . . moni liht lupe**, The heart is a very wild beast and makes many a wanton leap. **8 *Nichil corde fugatius***, "Nothing is more fleeting than the heart" (Gregory, *Pastoral Care*, 3.14); **"Na thing ne etflith . . . heorte,"** "Nothing flees from a person sooner than his own heart." **9 Davith** (spelled *Davið* in Corpus), **Godes prophete . . . etsteart him**, David, God's prophet, complained at a certain time that she (i.e., the heart) had started away from him. **9–10 *Cor meum dereliquit***

10 **dereliquit me.** Thet is, "min heorte is edflohe me." Ant eft he blisseth him ant seith thet ha wes i-cumen ham: **Invenit servus tuus cor suum**. "Laverd," he seith, "min heorte is i-cumen ayein eft. Ich hire habbe i-funden." Hwen-se hali mon ant se wis ant se war lette hire edstearten sare mei an-other of hire fluht carien. Ant hwer edbrec ha ut from Davith the hali king, Godes prophete? Hwer? Godd wat, ed his eh-thurl, thurh a sihthe

15 thet he seh thurh a bihaldunge, as ye schulen efter i-heren.

For-thi mine leove sustren, the leaste thet ye eaver mahen luvieth ower thurles. Alle beon ha lutle, the parlurs least ant nearewest. The clath in ham beo twa-fald: blac thet clath, the cros hwit withinnen ant withuten. Thet blake clath bitacneth thet ye beoth blake ant unwurth to the world withuten, thet te sothe sunne haveth ute-with forculet

20 ow, ant swa with*u*ten as ye beoth, unseowlich i-maket ow thurh gleames of his grace. The hwite cros limpeth to ow, for threo crosses beoth: read ant blac ant hwit. The reade limpeth to theo the beoth for Godes luve with hare blod-schedunge i-rudet ant i-readet,

---

me, "My heart has abandoned me" (Psalm 39:13). **10 is edflohe me**, has escaped (lit., fled away from) me. **10–11 eft he blisseth him . . . i-cumen ham**, again he rejoices (reflex.) and says that she had come home. **11 *Invenit . . . suum***, "Your servant has found his heart" (2 Samuel 7:27). **11–12 "Laverd . . . habbe i-funden,"** "Lord," he says, "my heart has come back again. I have found her." **12–13 Hwen-se . . . carien**, When a man so holy, so wise, and so vigilant allowed her to escape, another (i.e., an average person) may worry intensely about her (i.e., the heart's) flight. **13–14 Ant hwer edbrec ha ut . . . Hwer?** And where did she break out from David the holy king, God's prophet? Where? **14–15 Godd wat . . . as ye schulen efter i-heren**, God knows, at his eye-hole (i.e., the window of his eye), through a sight that he saw through an [act of] beholding, as you will hear after[wards] (i.e., in a moment). **16 For-thi mine leove sustren . . . ower thurles**, Therefore, my dear sisters love your windows (lit., holes) as little as you possibly can, (lit., the least that you ever may). **16–17 Alle beon . . . nearewest**, [Let them] all be small, [and let] the parlor's [window be the] least (i.e., smallest) and narrowest. **17–20 The clath in ham . . . gleames of his grace**, Let the cloth in them be of two kinds (lit., twofold): the cloth black, the cross white within and without (i.e., inside and outside). The black cloth symbolizes that you are black and worthless to the world outside (lit., without), that the (*te* = reduced form of *the*) true sun has charred you on the outside and has thus made you unlovely on the outside as you are, through the gleams of His grace. **21 The hwite cros limpeth to ow . . . blac ant hwit**, The white cross relates to you, for [there] are three crosses: red and black and white. **21–23 The reade limpeth . . . the martirs weren**, The red [cross] relates to those who are, for God's love, made ruddy and reddened with the shedding of their blood (lit., with

96

as the martirs weren. The blake cros limpeth to theo the makieth i the worlt hare penitence for ladliche sunnen. The hwite limpeth ariht to hwit meidenhad ant to cleannesse,
25   thet is muche pine wel for-te halden. Pine is i-hwer thurh cros i-don to understonden.
Thus bitacneth hwit cros the warde of hwit chastete, thet is muche pine wel to biwitene.
The blake clath alswa, teke the bitacnunge, deth leasse eil to the ehnen ant is thiccre
ayein the wind ant wurse to seon thurh ant halt his heow betere for wind ant for other-
hwet. Lokith thet te parlures [clath] beo on eaver-euch half feaste ant wel i-tachet, ant
30   witeth ther ower ehnen leaste the heorte edfleo ant wende ut, as of Davith, ant ower
sawle seccli sone se heo is ute. Ich write muchel for othre thet na-wiht ne rineth ow,
mine leove sustren, for nabbe ye nawt te nome — ne ne schulen habben, thurh the
grace of Godd — of totilde ancres, ne of tollinde locunges, ne lates thet summe other-
hwiles — wei-la-wei! — uncundeliche makieth. For ayein cunde hit is ant unmeath sulli
35   wunder thet te deade dotie ant with cwike worlt-men wede thurh sunne.

their bloodshedding), as the martyrs were. **23–24 The blake cros . . . for ladliche sunnen,** The
black cross relates to those who make in the world their penance for loathsome sins. **24–25
The hwite limpeth . . . to understonden,** The white [cross] relates rightly to white virginity (lit.,
maidenhead) and to chastity, which is much pain (or, trouble) to hold well. Pain (i.e., hardship)
is everywhere through [the symbol of the] cross to be understood (lit., made to be understood
[passive inf.]). **26 Thus bitacneth hwit cros . . . to biwitene,** Thus the white cross symbolizes
the protection of white chastity, which is a great pain (or, hardship) to protect well. **27–29 The
blake clath alswa . . . for other-hwet,** The black cloth also, besides [its] symbolism, does less
harm to the eyes and is thicker against the wind and harder (lit., worse) to see through and
holds (*halt* = reduced form of *haldeth*) its color better against (lit., before) wind and against
other things (lit., other what). **29–31 Lokith thet . . . se heo is ute,** Look that the curtain (lit.,
cloth) in the parlor be always on both sides secured and well attached, and defend there your
eyes lest the heart escape and go out, as with David, and [lest] your soul sicken as soon as
she (i.e., the heart) is out (i.e., gone). **31–34 Ich write muchel . . . uncundeliche makieth,** I
write much for others that not at all touches you, my dear sisters, for you do not have the
name (or, reputation) — nor will [you] have, through the grace of God! — of peeper-
anchoresses, nor of [making] enticing looks, or expressions which some at times make — alas!
— unnaturally. **34–35 For ayein cunde . . . thurh sunne,** For it is against nature and an
incredibly strange wonder (lit., immeasurably marvelous wonder), that the dead [should] dote
(or, become silly) and go mad with living world-men (i.e., men living in the world) through sin.

"Me leove sire," seith sum, "ant is hit nu se over-uvel for-te totin ut-wart?" Ye hit, leove suster, for uvel the ther kimeth of, hit is uvel ant over-uvel to eaver-euch ancre, nomeliche to the yunge, ant to the alde for-thi, thet ha to the yungre yeoveth uvel forbisne ant scheld to werien ham with. For yef ei edwit ham, thenne seggeth ha anan:

40 "Me sire, theo deth alswa, thet is betere then ich am ant wat betere then ich hwet ha haveth to donne." Leove yunge ancre, ofte a ful haher smith smeotheth a ful wac cnif! The wise folhe i wisdom, ant nawt i folie. An ald ancre mei do wel thet te thu dest uvele. Ah totin ut withuten uvel ne mei ower nowther. Nim nu yeme hwet uvel beo i-cumen of totunge. Nawt an uvel, ne twa, ah al the wa thet nu is ant eaver yete wes, ant eaver

45 schal i-wurthen — al com of sihthe. Thet hit beo soth, lo her preove:

Lucifer, thurh thet he seh ant biheold on him-seolf his ahne feiernesse, leop into prude ant bicom of engel eatelich deovel. Of Eve, ure alde moder, is i-writen, on alre earst in hire sunne in-yong of hire eh-sihthe. **Vidit igitur mulier quod bonum esset**

36 "Me leove sire . . . ut-wart?" "But dear sir," says some[ne] "and is it so over (i.e., completely, excessively) evil to gaze outward?" **36–39 Ye hit, leove suster . . . to werien ham with**, Yes it [is], dear sister, for the evil which comes from it (lit., there-of), it is evil and excessively evil to each [and] every anchoress, namely to the young, and to the old for the reason that they give to the younger [ones] a bad example and a shield (i.e., an excuse) to defend themselves with. **39–41 For yef ei edwit ham . . . hwet ha haveth to donne**, For if anyone criticize them, then they say at once (lit., anon), "But sir, she does [it] also, who is better than I am and knows better than I what she has (i.e., ought) to do." **41 Leove yunge ancre . . . ful wac cnif!** My dear young anchoress, often a very expert smith forges (lit., smiths) a very shoddy (lit., weak) knife! **42 The wise folhe . . . i folie**, Follow (imper.) the wise in wisdom, and not in folly. **42–43 An ald ancre . . . ne mei ower nowther**, An old anchoress may do well that which you do inappropriately (lit., evilly). But to gaze out without evil can neither of you do. **43–44 Nim nu yeme . . . of totunge**, Pay (lit., take) attention now what evil has come from gazing (or, looking). **44–45 Nawt an uvel . . . lo her preove**, Not one evil, nor two, but all the woe that now is and ever yet was, and ever shall be — all [of it] came from sight. That it be true, lo, here [is the] proof. **46–47 Lucifer, thurh thet he seh . . . eatelich deovel**, Lucifer, because he saw and beheld in himself his own fairness (or, beauty), leapt into pride and from an angel became a horrible devil. **47–48 Of Eve, ure alde moder . . . of hire eh-sihthe**, Of Eve, our ancient mother, [it] is written, [that] first of all sin entered into her from her eyesight. **48–50 Vidit igitur . . . viro suo**, "The woman, therefore, saw that the tree was good for eating and appealing to the eyes, delicious in aspect, and took of its fruit and

lignum ad vescendum, et pulcrum oculis, aspectuque delectabile, et tulit de fructu
50   **ejus et comedit, deditque viro suo.** Thet is, "Eve biheold o the forboden eappel ant
seh hine feier ant feng to delitin i the bihaldunge, ant toc hire lust ther-toward, ant nom
ant et th'rof, ant yef hire laverd." Low, hu Hali Writ speketh ant hu inwardliche hit teleth
hu sunne bigon. Thus eode s*ihthe* bivoren ant makede wei to uvel lust, ant com the dede
th'refter thet al mon-cun i-feleth.

55   Thes eappel, leove suster, bitacneth alle the thing thet lust falleth to ant delit of sunne.
Hwen thu bihaldest te mon, thu art in Eve point — thu lokest o the eappel. Hwa-se hefde
i-seid to Eve, tha ha weorp earst hire ehe th'ron, "A, Eve! Went te awei. Thu warpest
ehe o thi death!" Hwet hefde ha i-ondsweret? "Me leove sire, thu havest woh. Hwer-of
chalengest tu me? The eappel thet ich loki on is forbode me to eotene, ant nawt to
60   bihalden." Thus walde Eve inoh-reathe habben i-ondsweret. O mine leove sustren, as
Eve haveth monie dehtren the folhith hare moder, the ondswerieth o thisse wise: "Me
wenest tu," seith sum, "thet ich wulle leapen on him thah ich loki on him?" Godd wat,

ate it, and gave it to her husband" (Genesis 3:6). **50–52 "Eve biheold . . . yef hire laverd,"**
"Eve looked on the forbidden apple and saw it (lit., him; *hine* = old accusative form) [to be]
fair and began to delight in the beholding (i.e., looking), and took her delight in it (lit., there
toward), and took and ate of it, and gave [it] to her lord (i.e., husband). **52–53 Low, hu Hali
Writ . . . hu sunne bigon,** Look how Holy Writ speaks and how inwardly (i.e., insightfully) it
tells how sin began. **53–54 Thus eode sihthe . . . al mon-cun i-feleth,** So sight went before
(i.e., ahead) and made way to evil desire, and [then] the deed came thereafter which all
mankind [still] feels. **55 Thes eappel . . . ant delit of sunne,** This apple, dear sister, symbolizes
all the things which belong to (lit., fall to) desire and delight in sin. **56 Hwen thu bihaldest
. . . o the eappel,** When you look [on] a man (lit., the man) you are in Eve's state (or, situation)
— you look on the apple. **56–58 Hwa-se hefde i-seid to Eve . . . o thi death!** Whosoever had
said to Eve, when she first cast her eye on it (lit., there-on), "O, Eve! Turn away (reflex.)! You
cast an eye (i.e., you are looking on) your death!" **58–60 Hwet hefde ha i-ondsweret . . . nawt
to bihalden,** What [would] she have (lit., had) answered? "But dear sir, you are wrong (lit.,
have wrong). Of what do you accuse me? The apple that I look on is forbidden for me to eat,
and not to behold (i.e., look on)." **60 Thus walde Eve . . . i-ondsweret,** Thus would Eve readily
enough have answered. **60–62 O mine leove sustren . . . thah ich loki on him?** O my dear
sisters, Eve (*as* not translated) has many daughters who follow their mother, who answer in
this way: "But do you expect," says some[one], "that I will leap on him [even] though I
[simply] look on him?" **62–63 Godd wat . . . wunder i-lomp,** God knows, dear sister, stranger

99

leove suster, mare wunder i-lomp. Eve, thi moder, leop efter hire ehnen — from the ehe to the eappel, from the eappel i parais, dun to ther eorthe, from the eorthe to helle, ther

65 ha lei i prisun fowr thusent yer ant mare, heo ant hire were ba, ant demde al hire ofsprung to leapen al efter hire to death withuten ende. Biginnunge ant rote of al this ilke reowthe wes a liht sihthe. Thus ofte, as me seith, of lutel muchel waxeth. Habbe thenne muche dred, euch feble wummon, hwen theo the wes riht ta i-wraht with Godes honden wes thurh a sihthe biswiken ant i-broht into brad sunne thet al the world overspreadde.

70 **Egressa est Dyna, filia Jacob, ut videret mulieres alienigenas, et cetera.** "A meiden, Dyna het, Jacobes dohter," as hit teleth i Genesy, "eode ut to bihalden uncuthe wummen" — yet ne seith hit nawt thet ha biheold wepmen. Ant hwet come, wenest tu, of thet bihaldunge? Ha leas hire meidenhad ant wes i-maket hore. Th'refter of thet ilke, weren trowthen tobrokene of hehe patriarches, ant a muchel burh forbearnd, ant te

75 king ant his sune ant te burh-men i-slein, the wummen i-lead forth, hire feader ant hire

things have happened (lit., a greater wonder happened). **63–66 Eve, thi moder, leop . . . to death withuten ende,** Eve, your mother, leapt after (i.e., according to) her eyes — from the eye to the apple in paradise, down to the earth, from the earth to hell, where she lay in prison four thousand years and more, she and her man (i.e., husband) both, and judged (i.e., condemned) all her offspring to leap all [together] after her to death without end. **66–67 Biginnunge ant rote . . . liht sihthe,** The beginning and root of all this same sorrow was a careless (or, wanton) look. **67 Thus ofte . . . muchel waxeth,** Thus, often, as is said (lit., as one says), from little grows much (i.e., great things come from small). **67–69 Habbe thenne muche dred . . . al the world overspreadde,** Let each feeble woman, then, have much dread, when she who was right there (i.e., immediately, directly) wrought (i.e., made) with God's hands was deceived through a look and brought into broad (i.e., boundless) sin which spread over all the world. **70 *Egressa est Dyna . . . cetera,*** "Dinah, the daughter of Jacob, went out that she might see the foreign women, and so on" (adapted from Genesis 34:1). **70–72 A meiden, Dyna het . . . biheold wepmen,** "A maiden, named Dinah, Jacob's daughter," as it tells in Genesis, "went out to behold (or, look upon) unknown women" — yet it does not say that she beheld men (lit., males). **72–73 Ant hwet come . . . wes i-maket hore,** What came, do you expect, of that beholding (i.e., looking)? She lost her maidenhead (i.e., virginity) and was made a whore. **73–76 Th'refter of thet ilke . . . utlahen i-makede,** Afterwards from that same [act], oaths were broken by high patriarchs, and a great city burned down, and the king and his son, and the citizens (lit., burg-men) slain, the women led away [into captivity], her father and her brothers,

brethren, se noble princes as ha weren, utlahen i-makede. Thus eode ut hire sihthe. Al thullich the Hali Gast lette writen o boc for-te warni wummen of hare fol ehnen. Ant nim ther-of yeme, thet tis uvel of Dyna com — nawt of thet ha seh Sichen, Emores sune, thet ha sunegede with, ah dude of thet ha lette him leggen ehnen on hire, for thet
80 tet he dude hire wes i the frumthe sare hire unthonkes.

Alswa Bersabee, thurh thet ha unwreah hire i Davithes sihthe, ha dude him sunegin on hire, se hali king as he wes ant Godes prophete. Nu kimeth forth a feble mon, halt him thah ahelich yef he haveth a wid hod ant a loke cape, ant wule i-seon yunge ancres, ant loki nede ase stan hu hire wlite him liki, the naveth nawt hire leor forbearnd i the
85 sunne, ant seith, ha mei baldeliche i-seon hali men — ye, swucche as he is, for his wide sleven. Me surquide sire, ne herest tu thet Davith, Godes ahne deorling, bi hwam he seolf seide, **Inveni virum secundum cor meum** — "Ich habbe i-funden," quoth he, "mon efter min heorte" — thes the Godd seolf seide bi this deore-wurthe sahe king ant prophete i-curet of alle, thes thurh an ehe-wurp to a wummon as ha wesch hire, lette ut

as noble princes as they were, made outlaws. **76 Thus eode ut hire sihthe,** Thus [it] went out from her sight (i.e., all this happened because of her looking). **76–77 Al thullich . . . of hare fol ehnen,** All such [things] the Holy Ghost had (i.e., caused to be) written in the book in order to (lit., for to) warn women of their foolish eyes. **77–80 Ant nim ther-of yeme . . . sare hire unthonkes,** Pay (lit., take) attention to this (lit., thereof), that this evil came from Dinah — not because (lit., of that) she saw Sichem, Hamor's son, whom she sinned with, but [it] happened (lit., did) because she let him lay eyes on her, for that which he did to her was in the beginning very much against her will (see *unthonkes* in glossary). **81–82 Alswa Bersabee . . . Godes prophete,** Likewise Bathsheba, because she uncovered herself in David's sight, she made him sin with her, as holy a king as he was and God's prophet. **82–86 Nu kimeth forth a feble mon . . . for his wide sleven,** Now comes forth a feeble man, thinks (lit., holds; *halt* = reduced form of *haldeth*) himself nevertheless substantial if he has a wide hood and a clasped cowl (i.e., is a friar), and wants to see young anchoresses, and [must] needs stare as a stone [to see] how her beauty pleases him, who has not burnt up her face in the sun, and says, she may boldly see holy men — indeed, such as he is, for his wide sleeves. **86–91 Me surquide sire . . . deadliche sunnen,** But proud sir, have you not heard (lit., hear you not) that David, God's own darling, of whom he himself said "I have found a man according to my heart" (Acts 13:22) — "I have found," said he, "a man after my heart" — [have you not heard that] this [man] whom God himself declared (lit., said) with this precious pronouncement king and prophet, chosen over all, this [man] through a glance (lit., eye-throw) at a woman as she washed herself let out his

90 his heorte ant foryet him-seolven, swa thet he dude threo ut-nume heaved ant deadliche
sunnen: o Bersabees, spus-bruche, the leafdi thet he lokede on; treisun ant mon-slaht on
his treowe cniht, Urie, hire laverd. Ant tu, a sunful mon, art se swithe hardi to keasten
cang ehnen up-o yung wummon! Ye, mine leove sustren, yef ei is ane-wil to seon ow,
ne wene ye ther neaver god, ah leveth him the leasse. Nulle ich thet nan i-seo ow, bute

95 he habbe of ower meistre spetiale leave. For alle the threo sunnen thet ich spec of least,
ant al thet uvel of Dina thet ich spec of herre, al com nawt for-thi thet te wummen
lokeden cangliche o wepmen, ah *for heo unwriyen heom in monnes ech-siththe ant
duden hwar-thurch ha machten fallen in sunne.*

For-thi wes i-haten on Godes laye thet put were i-wriyen eaver, ant yef ani were
100 *unwriyen ant beast feolle ther-in, he the unwreah the put hit schulde yelden. This is a
swithe dredful word to wummon thet schaweth hire to wepmones echne. Heo is bitacned
bi theo thet unwrith the put — the put is hire feire neb, hire hwite swire, hire lichte
echnen, hond, yef ha halt forth in his echye-sihthe. Yet beoth hire word put, bute ha*

heart and forgot himself, so that he committed (lit., did) three especially cardinal and deadly
sins. **91–92 o Bersabees . . . Urie, hire laverd**, 1) with (lit., on) Bathsheba, adultery — the lady
that he looked on; 2) treason and 3) manslaughter on his loyal knight, Uriah, her lord (or,
husband). **92–93 Ant tu, a sunful mon . . . up-o yung wummon!** And you, a sinful man, are so
very brave (lit., hardy) to cast foolish eyes upon young women! **93–94 Ye, mine leove sustren
. . . leveth him the leasse**, Indeed (lit., yea), my dear sisters, if any[one] is insistent to see you,
never expect good of it (lit., there), but trust him the less. **94–95 Nulle ich . . . spetiale leave**,
I do not want any[one] to see you, unless he have from your director (or, teacher) special
permission. **95–98 For alle the threo . . . fallen in sunne**, For all the three sins which I spoke
of last, and all the evil of Dinah that I spoke of above (lit., higher), all [of it] came not because
the women looked foolishly on men (i.e., males), but // because they uncovered themselves in
man's eye-sight and did (i.e., acted) whereby they might fall into sin. **99–100 For-thi wes i-
haten . . . hit schulde yelden**, Therefore, [it] was commanded in God's law that a pit was always
[to be] covered, and if any were uncovered and a beast fell into it, he who uncovered the pit
should pay for it (i.e., the beast). **101 swithe dredful word**, a very terrifying word; **thet schaweth
hire to wepmones echne**, who reveals herself to a man's eye. **101–03 Heo is bitacned . . . in his
echye-sihthe**, She is symbolized by the one (fem.) who uncovers the pit — the pit is her fair
face, her white neck, her bright (or, wanton) eyes, [her] hand, if she holds [it] out in his eye-
sight. **103–04 Yet beoth . . . the bet i-set**, Even (lit., yet) her words are a pit, unless they are the

Part Two

beon the bet i-set. Al yet the feayeth hire, hwet-se hit eaver beo, thurch hwat machte
105   sonre fol luve awacnin, al ure Laverd "put" cleopeth — this put he hat thet beo i-lided,
thet beast th'rin ne falle ant druncni in sunne.

Best is the beastlich mon thet ne thenchet naut on God, ne ne noteth naut his wit as
mon ach to donne, ach secheth for to fallen in this put thet ich spec of, yef he hit open
fint. Ach the dom is ful strong to theo the the put unlideth. For heo schal yelde the best
110   thet th'rin bith i-fallen: ha is witi of his death biforen ure Laverd ant schal for his saule
ondsweren an Domes-dei, ant yelde the bestes lure hwenne ha navet other yeld thenne
hire-seolven. Strong yeld is her mid alle! Ant Godes dom is ant his heste thet heo hit
yelde allegate for heo unlidede the put thet hit adrong inne.

Thu thet unwrisd this put, thu thet dest ani thing thurch hwet mon is of the fleschliche
115   i-fonded — thach thu hit nute naut — dred this dom swithe. Ant yef he is i-fonded swa
thet he sunege deadliche on ani wise — thach hit ne beo naut with the bute with wil
toward the, other yef he secheth to fullen ed sum other the fondunge thet of the, thurch

better (i.e., very carefully) composed. **104–06 Al yet the feayeth hire . . . druncni in sunne,**
Still, everything to which she allies (lit., joins) herself, whatsoever it be, through which
foolish love might the sooner awaken, all [of this] our Lord calls a "pit" — this pit, he
commands that [it] be covered, [so] that a beast not fall in it and drown in sin. **107–09 Best
is the beastlich mon . . . yef he hit open fint,** The beast is the beastly man who does not think
about God, nor [does he] use his mind (or, reason) as a person ought to do, but tries to fall in this
pit that I spoke of, if he finds (*fint* = reduced form of *findeth*) it open. **109 Ach the dom . . .
unlideth,** But the judgment is very severe (lit., strong) for her who uncovers (lit., unlids) the
pit. **109–12 For heo schal yelde . . . other yeld thenne hire-seolven,** For she must pay for the
beast which has fallen in it: she is guilty of his death before our Lord and must answer for his
soul on Doomsday, and pay for the beast's loss when she does not have [any] other payment
than herself. **112 Strong yeld is her mid alle!** Here is a severe payment indeed! **112–13 Godes
dom is . . . thet hit adrong inne,** God's judgment and His command is that she pay for it always
(i.e., forever) because she uncovered the pit which it drowned in. **114–15 Thu . . . swithe,** You
(sing.) who uncover this pit, you who do any thing through which a man is by you bodily (i.e.,
carnally) tempted — though you do not know it — dread (imper.) this judgment very much.
115–18 Ant yef he is i-fonded . . . beo al siker of the dom, And if he is tempted so that he sin
mortally in any way — though it is not with you but with desire toward you, or if he seeks to
fulfill on some other [woman] the temptation which arose (lit., awoke) from you, through your

thi dede, awacnede — beo al siker of the dom. Thu schalt yelde the best for the puttes openunge, ant buten thu beo i-scrive ther-of, acorien his sunne. Hund wule in bluthelich
120 *hwar-se he fint open.*

Inpudicus oculus inpudici cordis est nuncius (Augustinus). *"Thet the muth ne mei for scheome, the licht echye speketh hit, ant is as erende-beorere of the lichte heorte." Ach nu is sum wummon the nalde for nan thing wilni fulthe to mon, ant thach ne rochte ha neaver thach he thochte toward hire ant were of hire i-fondet. Ant nu deth Sein*
125 *Austin ba twa theos in a cuple: "wilnin ant habbe wil for-to beon i-wilned."* **Non solum appetere, sed et appeti velle criminosum.** *"Yirni mon, other habbe wil for-to beon i-yirned of mon, ba is haved sunne."* **Oculi prima tela sunt adultere.** *"The echnen beoth the forme arewen of lecheries prickes." Alswa ase men worreth mid threo cunes wepnes (with scheotung ant with speres ord ant with sweordes egge), al richt with thilke*
130 *wepnen (thet is, with schute of eche, with spere [of] wundinde word, with sweord of*

deed — be (imper.) completely sure (i.e., you can be sure) of the judgment. **118–19 Thu schalt yelde the best . . . acorien his sunne,** You must pay for the beast because of the opening of the pit (lit., pit's opening), and unless you are confessed of that (lit., thereof), [you must] pay for his sin. **119–20 Hund wule in . . . fint open,** A dog will [blunder] happily into whatever he finds open (lit., A dog will [go] in blithely wheresoever he finds [it] open) (*fint* = reduced form of *findeth*). **121 Inpudicus . . . est nuncius (Augustinus),** "A lewd eye is the messenger of a lewd heart" (from the *Augustinian Rule,* based on a letter of Augustine, *Letters,* 211). **121–22 "Thet the muth . . . heorte,"** "What the mouth cannot [speak] for shame, the wanton eye speaks it, and is as a message bearer of the wanton heart." **123–24 Ach nu is sum wummon . . . of hire i-fondet,** But now [here] is some woman who would not for any thing desire filth with a man, and nevertheless she might not be concerned (*rochte* = past subj.) though he thought about her and would be (lit., were) tempted by her. **124–25 Ant nu deth Sein Austin . . . beon i-wilned,** And now St. Augustine makes (lit., does) both these two into a couple: "to desire and to have the urge (lit., will) to be desired." **125–26 Non solum . . . criminosum,** "Not only to desire but to want to be desired [is] criminal" (from the *Augustinian Rule,* based on a letter of Augustine, *Letters,* 211). **126–27 "Yirni mon . . . is haved sunne,"** "To yearn [for a] man or to have the desire to be yearned for by a man, both are (lit., is) a capital sin." **127 Oculi . . . adultere,** "The eyes are the first darts of the adulteress" (Hugh of Folieto, *Concerning the Enclosed Spirit* 1.4). **127–28 "The echnen . . . of lecheries prickes,"** "The eyes are the first arrows of lechery's pricks." **128–32 Alswa ase men worreth . . . thet is, Godes spuse,** Just as men war (i.e., make war) with three kinds of weapons (with shooting, and with spear's point,

deadlich hond) werreth lecherie, the stinkinde hore, upon the lavedi chastete — thet is, Godes spuse. Earest scheot the arewen of the licht echnen, the fleoth lichtliche forth ase flaa thet is i-vithered ant stiketh i there heorte, ther-efter schaketh hire spere ant neolachet upon hire, ant mid schakinde word yeveth speres wunde.

135   *Sweordes dunt [is] dun-richt — thet is, the hondlunge — for sweord smit of nech ant yeveth deathes dunt, ant hit is wei-la-wei nech i-do with ham the cumeth swa nech togederes, thet outher hondli other other i-fele other. Hwa-se is wis ant seli, with the schute wite hire — thet is, wite hire echnen. For al thet uvel ther-efter kimeth of th'echne arewen. Ant nis ha muche chang other to fol-hardi the hald hire heved baltliche ut of*

140   *the opene carnel, hwil me with quarreus ute-with assailleth the castel? Sikerliche ure fa, the werreur of helle, he scheot, as ich wene, ma quarreus to an ancre thenne to seovene ant fifti lavedis i the worlde: the carneus of the castel beoth hire hus-thurles.*

and with sword's edge), just so with those weapons (that is, with shot of eye, with spear of wounding word, with sword of deadly hand) lechery, the stinking whore, wars (i.e., makes war) upon the lady's chastity, who is God's spouse (or, bride). **132–34 Earest scheot the arewen . . . yeveth speres wunde,** First [lechery] shoots (*scheot* = reduced form of *scheoteth*) the arrows from the wanton eyes, which fly lightly forth as a shaft which is feathered and sticks in the heart (*ther* = inflected def. art.); afterwards, [she] shakes her spear and closes in (lit., approaches) upon her, and with an agitating (lit., shaking) word, gives the wound of the spear. **135–37 Sweordes dunt [is] . . . other i-fele other,** A sword's blow — that is, [human] touching — comes straight down (lit., is downright), for a sword smites from near-by and gives death's blow; and it is, alas, nearly finished (lit., done) for those who come so close together, who either handle [each] other or touch (lit., feel) each other. **137–38 Hwa-se is wis . . . wite hire echnen,** Whosoever is wise and innocent, [should] protect herself against the shot (or, blow) — that is, protect her eyes. **138–39 For al thet uvel . . . of th'echne arewen,** For all that evil comes afterwards from the eye's arrows. **139–40 Ant nis ha muche chang . . . assailleth the castel?** And is not she very crazy or too foolhardy who holds (*hald* = reduced form of *haldeth*) her head boldly out of the open battlement while people assail the castle from the outside with blunt-headed arrows? **140–42 Sikerliche ure fa . . . beoth hire hus-thurles,** Surely our foe, the warrior of hell, he shoots (*scheot* = reduced form of *scheoteth*), as I expect, more bolts at an anchoress than at fifty-seven ladies in the world: the battlements of the castle are her house-windows (lit., -holes).

Bernardus: sicut mors per peccatum in orbem, ita per has fenestras intrat in mentem. "As deth com," seith Sein Bernard, "into the world thorch sunne, asswa
145   death thurch theos ech-thurles haveth in-yong to the saule." Laverd Crist, as men walden steoke feste uh thurl [of hire hus], for hwon thet heo machten bisteoken death th'rute, ant an ancre nule naut tunen hire eil-thurl ayein the death of saule! Ant mid good richt muyen ha beon i-haten "eil-thurles" for ha habbeth i-don muchel eil to moni ancre.

    [Al holi writ is ful of warningge of eie.] *David: averte oculos meos, ne videant*
150   *vanitatem.* "Laverd," he seith, David, "went awei min echnen from the worldes dweole."

    Job: pepigi fedus cum oculis meis, ne cogitarem de virgine. "Ich'abbe i-festned foreward," seith Job, "mid min echnen thet ich ne misthenche." Hu dele! Thencheth me mid echye? God hit wat, he seith wel, for efter the echye kimeth the thocht ant ther-efter the dede. Thet wiste wel Jeremie thet mende thus: "Wei-la-wei!" he seith, "min eche
155   haveth i-robbed al min saule." Hwenne Godes prophete makede thulli mon of eche,

---

143–44 *Bernardus: sicut mors . . . in mentem*, Bernard: "As death [entered] through sin into the world, so through these windows (i.e., the eyes) it enters into the mind" (Bernard, *The Steps of Humility and Pride* 10.28). **144 com**, came; **thorch sunne**, through sin. **144–45 asswa death . . . saule**, just so death through these eye-holes (i.e., windows or, eyes) has entrance into the soul. **145 Laverd**, Lord. **145–47 men walden . . . death of saule!** men would block up securely each window (lit., hole) in their house provided they could shut out death from there (lit., there-out), and an anchoress does not [even] want to shut her window "pane" (lit., *eil-thurl* "pain-hole," a pun on *ei-thurl* "eye-hole or window" — approximated here by a pun on *pane/pain*) against the death of the soul! **147–48 Ant mid good richt . . . to moni ancre**, And with good right they may be called "panes" (lit., pain-holes) for they have done much pain to many an anchoress. **149 [Al holi writ . . . of eie]**, All Holy Writ is full of warning[s] about the eye. **149–50 *David: averte oculos . . . vanitatem***, David: "Turn away my eyes, lest they see vanity" (Psalm 118:37). **150 "Laverd . . . from the worldes dweole,"** "Lord," he says, David, "turn away my eyes from the world's error (or, folly)." **151 *Job: pepigi fedus . . . de virgine***, Job: "I have made a pact with my eyes, lest I think of a maiden" (Job 31:1). **151–52 "Ich'abbe . . . misthenche,"** "I have made an agreement," says Job, "with my eyes that I not misthink (i.e., think wrongly)." **152–53 Hu dele! . . . mid echye?** Hey, look! Does one think with the eye? **153–54 God hit wat . . . ther-efter the dede**, God knows (lit., God knows it), he says well, for after the eye comes the thought and after that the deed. **154–55 Thet wiste wel Jeremie . . . i-robbed al min saule**, Jeremiah knew that well, who lamented (lit., moaned): "Alas!" he says, "my eye has robbed all my soul" (Lamentations 3:51). **155–57 Hwenne Godes prophete . . . sorege of heore echye?** When God's prophet made such a lament (lit.,

hwic man, wenest thu, thet beo i-cumen to moni mon, ant [to moni wumman] — sorege of heore echye? The wise askith hwether ani thing harmi mare wimmon thenne deth hire echye: **Oculo quid nequius? totam faciem lacrimare faciet quoniam vidit.** *"Al the leor," he seith, "schal floyen of teres, for the ehe-sichthe ane." This is nu of this wit i-*

160 *noch i-seid to warni the seli. [We schulen thauh sone her-efter speken her-of more.]*

Ore pur ceo, toutes les overtures de toutes voz fenestres, ausi come ci devant a la vewe de touz hommes unt este closes, ausi soient ca en apres. Et si plus fermement poient, plus fermement soient closes. Generale reule est, toutes celes qe bien les closent, Dieu bien les garde. Et toutes celes qe . . . issi qil pecche . . . funt ensement . . . pecchier

165 *ou od fol oil, ou od bouche, ou od main et . . . cel od plus et multes tieles choses desavenantes et desnatureles a recluse sur toutes. Les queux ne fuissent james avant venues, si ele eust sa fenestre ferm estoppee. Et si nule contredit ceste, jeo treis a testmoigne sa conscience demeyne encontre lui, qele parmi sa fenestre demeine ad oil, ou bouche, ou main receu et fole parole oveqe, tout fut ele adubbe et od feinte seintete*

170 *falsement coloree. A, tricheour traitre!* "*Dieu, jeo nel faz a vous pur nul mal, ne pur*

moan) about the eye, what kind of lament [is it], do you expect, that has come to many a man and woman — sorrow from their eyes? **157–58 The wise askith . . . deth hire echye**, The wise ask (i.e., Solomon, here believed to be the writer of Ecclesiasticus) whether any thing harms a woman more than does her eye. **158 *Oculo quid nequius . . . faciet quoniam vidit***, "What is more evil than the eye? It will cause the entire face to weep since it has seen [something]" (Ecclesiasticus 31:15). **158–59 "Al the leor . . . the ehe-sichthe ane,"** "All the face," he says, "will (or, must) flow with tears, because of the eyesight alone." **159–60 This is nu of this wit . . . her-of more**, This is now enough said about this sense to warn the innocent. We shall nevertheless soon hereafter speak more of this (lit., here of). **161–72 Ore pur ceo . . . qi regarde la . . .** , Now therefore, all the openings of all your windows, just as they have been closed to the view of men before, so they should be closed hereafter. And if they can be the more securely [closed], [then let them] be the more securely closed. The general rule is, all those who close them well, God [will] protect them well. And all those who . . . so that they sin . . . fall likewise . . . to sin either with the foolish eye, or with the mouth, or with the hand and . . . these with more and many such things, disgraceful and unnatural for an anchoress above all. They never would have happened, if she had firmly blocked her window. And if anyone contradicts this, I call her conscience itself in testimony against her, that [should] she linger at her window with eye, or mouth, or [should she] receive a hand or a foolish word, she is falsely bedecked and painted with false holiness. Oh, treacherous traitor! "God, I would not

nule ordure," dit il ou ele. Et od cel meismes se soillent, et coroucent les oilz dampne Dieu, qi regarde la . . . traisun in-with the gale heorte. Nawt ane euch fleschlich hondlunge, ah yetten euch gal word is ladlich vilainie, ant Godes grome wurthe, thah hit ne weoxe forthre bitweone mon ant ancre. Nu, thurh riht Godes wrake, geath hit forthre

175   ant forthre ant bikimeth ofte ant ear me least wene, into thet fule sunne. We hit habbeth, wei-la-wei, i-herd of inohe. Ne leve na-mon ancre the let in monnes ehe to schawin hire-seolven. Over al thet ye habbeth i-writen in ower riwle of thinges withuten, this point — this article of wel to beo bitunde — ich wulle beo best i-halden. To wummon the wilneth hit, openith ow, o Godes half. Yef ha ne speketh nawt th'rof, leoteth swa i-

180   wurthen, bute yef ye dreden thet heo th'refter beo i-scandlet. Of hire ahne suster haveth sum i-beon i-temptet. In toward ower weoved ne beode ye na mon for-te bihalden. Ah yef his devotiun bit hit ant haveth grant, draheth ow wel in-ward ant te veil adun toward

do it to you for any evil, nor for any filthiness," says he or she [as an excuse]. But these very people dirty themselves, and their accursed eyes enrage God, who sees the . . . **172 traisun in-with the gale heorte**, treason (or, betrayal) within the bitter heart. **172–74 Nawt ane euch fleschlich hondlunge . . . bitweone mon ant ancre**, Not only each carnal touching, but also each bitter word is loathsome (or, hateful) villainy and worthy of God's wrath, [even] though it does not grow (i.e., proceed) [any] further between man and anchoress. **174–75 Nu, thurh riht . . . into thet fule sunne**, Now, by God's just vengeance, it goes further and further and often turns (lit., becomes) — and before one least expects — into that foul sin (or: Now, by right, God's vengeance [will come], [should] it go further and further . . .). **175–76 We hit habbeth . . . inohe**, We have, alas, heard of it [often] enough. **176–77 Ne leve na-mon . . . hire-seolven**, [Let] no one trust an anchoress who lets in man's eye to reveal herself. **177–78 Over al thet ye habbeth . . . best i-halden**, Above all that you have written in your rule of external things, this point — this clause (i.e., item in a rule) of being well enclosed — I wish to be best kept. **178–79 To wummon . . . o Godes half**, To a woman who desires it, reveal (lit., open) yourself, for God's sake (i.e., by all means). **179–80 Yef ha ne speketh nawt th'rof . . . beo i-scandlet**, If she does not speak of it (i.e., ask you to open up), let it be, unless you fear that she be scandalized (see glossary) afterwards. **180–81 Of hire ahne suster . . . i-temptet**, By her own sister has an anchoress (lit., some) [sometimes] been tempted. **181 In toward ower weoved . . . bihalden**, Do not offer (i.e., invite) any man to look in toward your altar. **181–83 Ah yef his devotiun . . . hete-veste**, But if his devotion asks it (*bit* = reduced form of *biddeth*) and gains permission (i.e., you allow it), draw yourself well inward and [draw] the veil down toward your breast, and immediately [afterwards] replace (lit., do) the cloth (i.e., curtain) again

ower breoste, ant sone doth the clath ayein ant festnith hete-veste. Yef he loketh toward bed other easketh hwer ye liggeth, ondswerieth lihtliche, "Sire, ther-of wel mei duhen,"

185 ant haldeth ow stille. Yef bisch[o]p kimeth to seon ow, hihith sone towart him, ah sweteliche bisecheth him, yef he bit to seon ow, thet ye moten ther-onont halden ow towart him as ye habbeth i-don ant doth to alle othre. Yef he wule allegate habben a sihthe, lokith thet hit beo ful scheort — the veil anan adun, ant draheth ow bihinden. An ancre wearnde eadmodliche Sein Martin hire sihthe, ant he ther-vore dude hire the

190 menske thet he neaver ne dude to nan other. Ant her-vore hire word is athet cume this dei i-boren in Hali Chirche. For as we redeth of hire, "hwa-se wule hire windowes witen wel with the uvele, ha mot ec with the gode." Hwen-se ye moten to eani mon ea-wiht biteachen, the hond ne cume nawt ut — ne ower ut, ne his in. Ant yef hit mot cumen in, ne rine nowther other. "Heo is siker," seith Hali Writ, "the feor from grunen draheth

195 hire, ant theo the luveth peril, i peril ha schal fallen." **Qui caret laqueis securus est, et**

and fasten [it] quickly. **183–85 Yef he loketh toward bed . . . haldeth ow stille**, If he looks toward [your] bed or asks where you lie [down], answer quickly (lit., lightly), "Sir, I am fortunate with respect to that" (lit., "[it] may prosper well with respect to that"; White: "I am well provided for in that"), and hold (or, keep) yourself still. **185–87 Yef bisch[o]p kimeth . . . ant doth to alle othre**, If the bishop comes to see you, hasten (lit., hie) immediately towards him, but sweetly beseech him, if he asks to see you, that you may, with respect to that, hold yourself (i.e., behave) towards him as you have done and [continue to] do to all others. **187–88 Yef he wule allegate . . . draheth ow bihinden,** If he wants nevertheless to have a look, see that it be very short — [pull] the veil down soon, and draw yourself behind (i.e., well back), **188–90 An ancre wearnde . . . to nan other,** An anchoress humbly denied St. Martin the sight of her (lit., her sight), and he therefore did her the honor that he never did to any other. **190–91 Ant her-vore . . . Hali Chirche,** And for this reason (lit., here-for), her word (or, reputation) is up to the present day (lit., until come this day) preserved in Holy Church. **191–92 For as we redeth of hire . . . with the gode,** For as we read of her, "whosoever wishes to protect her windows well against evil (lit., the evil), she must also [protect it] against the good" (Sulpicius Severus, *Dialogues* II.12). **192–93 Hwen-se ye moten . . . ne his in,** Whenever (lit., when so) you must give (lit., entrust) anything to any man, [do not let] the hand come out [of the window] — neither yours out nor his in. **193–94 Ant yef hit mot cumen in . . . nowther other,** And if it must come in, [let] neither touch the other. **194–95 "Heo is siker . . . schal fallen,"** "She is safe," says Holy Writ, "who draws herself far [away] from snares, and (i.e., but) she who loves peril, in[to] peril she will fall." **195–96 Qui caret laqueis . . . in illud,** "Whoever watches out for snares is safe," (Proverbs 11:5, paraphrased) "and whoever loves danger

qui amat periculum incidet in illud. The deofles grune is ofte i-tild ther me least weneth. Nis nan thet nis dredful thet ha nis i-lecchet, for Godd nule wite nan thet is se fol-hardi, thet ha ne wit wearliche with him hire-seolven. This is nu of this wit inoh i-seid ed tis chearre to warnin then seli. We schulen thah sone her-efter speoken her-of mare.

200   Spellunge ant smechunge beoth i muth bathe as sihthe is i the ehe, ah we schulen leten smechunge athet we speoken of ower mete, ant speoken nu of spellunge ant th'refter of herunge, of ba i-meane sum-chearre, as ha gath togederes.

On alre earst hwen ye schulen to ower parlurs thurl, witeth ed ower meiden hwa hit beo thet beo i-cumen. For swuch hit mei beon thet ye schule essinien ow. Hwen ye alles
205   moten forth, crossith ful yeorne muth, ehnen, ant earen ant te breoste mid al, ant gath forth mid Godes dred. To preost on earst **Confiteor**, ant th'refter **Benedicite** — thet he ah to seggen. Hercnith hise wordes ant haldeth ow al stille, thet hwen he parteth from ow thet he ne cunne ower god ne ower uvel nowther, ne ne cunne ow nowther

shall fall into it" (Ecclesiasticus 3:27). **196–97 The deofles grune . . . least weneth**, The devil's snare is often spread (i.e., set) where one least expects. **197–98 Nis nan thet nis dredful . . . with him hire-seolven**, There is not anyone (lit., none) who is not fearful that will not be caught (i.e., whoever feels safe will be caught), for God does not want to protect anyone (lit., none) who is so foolhardy that she does not warily protect herself against him (i.e., the devil, or his snare). **198–99 This is nu of this wit . . . then seli**, This is now enough said about this sense at this time to warn the innocent. **199 We schulen thah . . . her-of mare**, We will nevertheless soon hereafter speak of this (lit., hereof) more. **200–02 Spellunge ant smechunge . . . togederes**, Talking and tasting are both in the mouth as sight is in the eye, but we shall leave taste until we speak of your food, and speak now about talking, and thereafter about hearing, about both together at a certain time (White: in due course), since they go together. **203–04 On alre earst . . . thet beo i-cumen**, First of all, when you must [go] to your parlor's window find out (lit., know; imper.) from your servant (lit., maiden) who it is that has come. **204 For swuch hit mei beon . . . essinien ow**, For it may be such [a person] that you must excuse yourself. **204–06 Hwen ye alles moten forth . . . mid Godes dred**, When you must [come] forth (i.e., appear) at all, cross very carefully mouth, eyes and ears, and the breast as well, and go forth with God's dread (i.e., the fear of God). **206–07 To preost on earst . . . ah to seggen**, To the priest [say] at first "I confess," and after that [comes] "Let us bless [the Lord]" — which he ought to say. **207–09 Hercnith hise wordes . . . lastin ne preisin**, Listen to his words and keep yourself completely still, so that when he parts from you he does not know of your good or of your evil either, nor does [he] know [enough] to

210 lastin ne preisin. Sum is se wel i-learet other se wis i-wordet, thet ha walde he wiste hit the sit ant speketh toward hire, ant yelt him word ayein word, ant forwurtheth meistre the schulde beon ancre, ant leareth him thet is i-cumen hire for-te learen, walde bi hire tale beon sone with wise i-cuththet ant i-cnawen. I-cnawen ha is, for thurh thet ilke thet ha weneth to beo wis i-halden, he understont thet ha is sot, for ha hunteth efter pris, ant kecheth lastunge. For ed te alre leaste hwen he is awei i-went, theos ancre, he wule

215 seggen, is of muche speche. Eve heold i parais long tale with the neddre, talde him al the lesceun thet Godd hefde i-red hire ant Adam of the eappel, ant swa the feond thurh hire word understod anan-riht hire wacnesse ant i-fond wei toward hire of hire forlorenesse. Ure Leafdi, Seinte Marie, dude al on other wise. Ne talde ha then engel na tale, ah easkede him scheortliche thing thet ha ne cuthe. Ye, mine leove sustren, folhith ure

220 Leafdi, ant nawt te cakele Eve. For-thi, ancre hwet-se ha beo, hu muchel se ha eaver cunne, halde hire stille, nabbe ha nawt henne cunde. The hen, hwen ha haveth i-leid, ne

either blame or praise you. **209–12 Sum is se wel i-learet . . . with wise i-cuththet ant i-cnawen,** A certain one (lit., some) is so well taught or so gifted with words (lit., so wisely worded), that she would [that] he knew it, who sits (*sit* = contracted form of *sitteth*) and speaks to her, and pays him word for word, and is deformed (or, transformed) into a teacher (or, scholar) who should be an anchoress, and teaches him who has come to (lit., for to) teach her, would by her speech be immediately acknowledged and known [to be] among the wise. **212–14 I-cnawen ha is . . . kecheth lastunge,** Known she is, for by that very [behavior for] which she expects to be held wise, he (i.e., the priest) understands (*understont* = reduced form of *understondeth*) that she is foolish, for she hunts after respect and catches blame. **214–15 For ed te alre leaste . . . muche speche,** For in the end (lit., at the last of all), when he has gone away, this anchoress, he will say, is a great talker (lit., of much speech). **215–17 Eve heold i parais . . . of hire forlorenesse,** Eve held in paradise a long tale (or, conversation) with the serpent, told him all the lesson which God had read to her and Adam about the apple, and so the fiend through her words understood immediately her weakness and found a way to her for her damnation. **218 Ure Leafdi . . . wise,** Our Lady acted (lit., did) in a completely other way. **218–19 Ne talde ha then engel . . . thet ha ne cuthe,** She held no conversation with the angel (lit., told no tale), but asked him shortly the things which she did not know. **219–20 Ye, mine leove sustren . . . te cakele Eve,** Indeed, my dear sisters, follow our Lady and not the cackling Eve. **220–21 For-thi, ancre . . . henne cunde,** Therefore, an anchoress, whatsoever she be, as (lit., how) much as ever she can, [should] keep herself still, and [should] not have a hen's nature. **221–22 The hen, hwen ha haveth i-leid . . . biyet ha th'rof?** The hen, when she has laid, can [do nothing] but cackle, but what does she profit from that (lit.,

con bute cakelin, ah hwet biyet ha th'rof? Kimeth the kaue anan-riht ant reaveth hire hire eairen ant fret of thet schulde forth bringe cwike briddes. Al riht alswa, the cave deovel bereth awei from cakelinde ancres ant forswolheth al the god thet ha i-streonet habbeth, thet schulde as briddes beoren ham up towart heovene, yef hit nere i-cakelet. The wrecche povre peoddere — mare nurth he maketh to yeien his sape then the riche mercer al his deore-wurthe ware, as is i-seid her-efter. To sum gastelich mon thet ye beoth trusti upon, as ye mahe beon o lut, god is thet ye easki read ant salve thet he teache ow toyeines fondunges. Ant i schrift schawith him, yef he wule i-heren, ower greaste ant ower ladlukeste sunnen, for-thi thet him areowe ow ant thurh the areownesse inwardluker crie Crist mearci for ow ant habbe ow in his bonen. **Set multi veniunt ad vos in vestimentis ovium, intrinsecus autem sunt lupi rapaces.** "Ah witeth ow ant beoth warre," he seith, ure Laverd, "for monie cumeth to ow i-schrud mid lombes fleos, ant beoth wedde wulves." Worltliche leveth lut, religiuse yet leas, ne wilni ye nawt to muchel hare cuththunge. Eve withute dred spec with the neddre. Ure Leafdi

225

230

235

thereof)? **222–23 Kimeth the kaue . . . briddes,** Immediately the crow (or, jackdaw — see glossary) comes and steals from her her eggs and gobbles from what should bring forth living birds. **223–25 Al riht alswa . . . nere i-cakelet,** Exactly so, the fierce (or nimble — see note) devil steals (lit., bears away) from cackling anchoresses and swallows up all the good which they have brought forth, which should, like birds, bear them up towards heaven, if it were not cackled away. **226–27 The wrecche povre peoddere . . . i-seid her-efter,** The wretched poor peddler — more racket he makes to cry up (i.e., advertise) his soap than the rich cloth merchant all his expensive (lit., precious) wares, as is said hereafter. **227–29 To sum gastelich mon . . . toyeines fondunges,** From some spiritual (lit., ghostly) man whom you trust (lit., who you are trusty upon), since you may [trust] few, [it] is good that you ask (i.e., seek) advice and remedies which he [might] teach you against temptations. **229–31 Ant i schrift . . . ow in his bonen,** And in confession show (imper.) him, if he wants to hear, your greatest (or, most wicked) and most hateful sins, to the end that he may pity you (lit., that [it may] grieve him for you) and through the pity inwardly cry to Christ for mercy for you and have you in his prayers. **231–32 *Set multi veniunt . . . lupi rapaces*,** "For many shall come to you in sheep's clothing. Inside, however, they are ravening wolves" (Matthew 7:15). **232–34 "Ah witeth ow . . . wulves,"** "But protect yourselves]and be wary," he says, our Lord, "for many will come to you dressed with lambs' fleece and are maddened wolves." **234–35 Worltliche leveth . . . hare cuththunge,** Trust (imper.) the worldly (i.e., secular) little, the religious still less, nor desire (imper.) too much their acquaintance. **235 neddre,** serpent. **235–36 Ure Leafdi wes**

wes offearet of Gabrieles speche. Ure freres prechurs ant ure freres meonurs beoth of swuch ordre thet al folc mahte wundrin yef ei of ham "wende ehe towart te wude lehe." For-thi, ed euch time thet eani of ham thurh chearite kimeth ow to learen ant to frovrin i Godd, yef he is preost, seggeth ear then he parti **Mea culpa**. "Ich schrive me to Godd almihti ant to the, thet ich, as ich drede, riht repentant neaver nes of mine greaste sunnen thet ich habbe i-schawet to mine schrift-feaderes. Ant tah min entente beo to beten ham her-inne, ich hit do se povreliche, ant sunegi in othre dei-hwamliche seoththen ich wes nest i-schriven, ant thet wes thenne, ant of the" — ant nempnin. "Ich habbe thus i-sunget." Ant segge o hwucche wise, as hit is i-writen ow in ower schriftes boc, towart te ende th'rof. Ant aleast seggeth "This ant muche mare, **Confiteor**." Ant bide him undervo the spetiale in his god, ant thonke him of his in-turn ant bisech him aleast greten the ant te, ant thet ha bidden for the.

    Withuten witnesse of wummon other of wepmon the ow mahe i-heren, ne speoke ye with na mon ofte ne longe, ant tah hit beo of schrift. Allegate i the ilke hus, other ther he

offearet, Our Lady was frightened. **236–37 Ure freres prechurs . . . towart te wude lehe**, Our preaching friars (i.e., the Dominicans) and friars minor (i.e., the Franciscans) are of such an order that all people might be amazed if any of them "turned an eye to the shelter of the wood" (an allusion to popular song — see explanatory note to 2.569–70). **238–39 For-thi . . . he parti *Mea culpa***, Therefore, at each time that any of them in charity comes to teach you and to comfort [you] in God, if he is a priest, say before he [de]parts, "The fault is mine" (formula of confession). **239–41 Ich schrive me . . . to mine schrift-feaderes**, "I confess myself to you (lit., thee), that I, as I fear, never was completely repentant for my greatest sins that I have shown to my confessors (lit., confession-fathers)." **241–43 Ant tah min entente . . . ant nempnin**, "And though my intent is to atone for them in this, I do it so poorly and sin in other [matters] daily since I was last confessed, and that was then, and with that [person]" — and name (i.e., give the name). **243–45 Ich habbe thus . . . th'rof**, "I have sinned thus." And say in what way, as it is written for you in your book of confession, toward the end of it. **245 aleast**, at last, at the end; **"This ant muche mare, *Confiteor*,"** "This and much more, 'I confess.'" **245–46 bide him undervo . . . his god**, and ask him to accept you specially into his good [will]. **246–47 ant thonke him . . . for the**, and thank him for his stopping by (lit., turning in) and beseech him in the end to greet this [person] and that, and that they [should] pray for you. **248 other of wepmon . . . i-heren**, or of a man who can hear you. **248–49 ne speoke ye . . . schrift**, do not speak with any man (or, anyone) often or long, even though it is concerning confession. **249–50 Allegate i the ilke hus . . . trukie**, Always in the same house, or where he can look toward you, let the third [one] sit, except if another place is

250 mahe i-seon toward ow, sitte the thridde, bute yef the ilke thridde other stude trukie. This nis nawt for ow, leove sustren, i-seid, ne for othre swucche; nawt-for-thi, the treowe is ofte mistrowet, ant te saclese bilohen, as Josep i Genesy of the gale leafdi, for wone of witnesse. Me leveth the uvele sone, ant te unwreaste blitheliche liheth o the gode. Sum unseli haveth, hwen ha seide ha schraf hire, i-schriven hire al to wundre.
255 For-thi ahen the gode habben eaver witnesse — for twa acheisuns nomeliche. The an is thet te ondfule ne mahe lihen on ham, swa thet te witnesse ne pruvie ham false. The other is for-te yeoven the othre forbisne ant reavi the uvele ancre the ilke unseli gile thet ich of seide.

Ut thurh the chirche-thurl ne halde ye tale with na-mon, ah beoreth ther-to wurthmunt
260 for the hali sacrement thet ye seoth ther-thurh, ant neometh other-hwile to ower wummen the huses thurl, to othre the parlur. Speoken ne ahe ye bute ed tes twa thurles.

Silence eaver ed te mete. Yef othre religiuse, as ye witen, doth hit, ye ahen over alle. Yef ei haveth deore geast, do hire meidnes as in hire stude to gleadien hire feire. Ant heo

lacking for this aforementioned third [person]. **251–53 This nis nawt . . . witnesse,** This is not said for you, dear sisters, nor for others such [as you are]; nevertheless, the faithful [person] is often mistrusted and the faultless lied about, as Joseph [was] in Genesis by the bitter lady, for lack of witness. **253–54 Me leveth . . . gode,** People believe the bad immediately (or, evil is believed immediately), and the wicked happily lie about the good. **254–55 Sum unseli haveth . . . nomeliche,** A certain unhappy one has, when she said she confessed herself, confessed herself in a very strange way indeed. Therefore, the good ought to have a witness always — for two reasons particularly. **255–58 The an is . . . seide,** The first (lit., one) is that the envious cannot lie about them without the witness proving them false (lit., so that the witness would not prove them false). The second is to give the others an example and to deprive the evil anchoress of that same unholy guile that I spoke of (see gloss to 2.36–39 above). **259–61 Ut thurh . . . twa thurles,** Out through the church window (i.e., the window facing into the church) hold no conversation with anyone (or, any man), but show honor to it for the holy sacrament which you see through it, and use (lit., take) sometimes the house's window for your women, and for other [people] the parlor [window]. You ought not to speak except at these two windows. **262 Silence eaver . . . over alle,** Silence always at meals (lit., at the food). If other religious (i.e., those in orders) do it, as you know, you ought to above all. **263 Yef ei haveth . . . feire,** If anyone has a cherished guest, let her have her maidens, as if in her place, entertain her fairly. **263–65 Ant heo schal . . . chere,** And she will have permission to unblock her window once or twice and make signs toward her (i.e., the guest) of a fair

schal habbe leave for-te unsperren hire thurl eanes other twien, ant makie sines toward
hire of a glead chere. Summes curteisie is i-turnt hire to uvel. Under semblant of god is
ofte i-hulet sunne. Ancre ant huses leafdi ah muchel to beon bitweonen. Euche Fridei of
the yer haldeth silence bute hit beo duble feaste, ant tenne haldeth hit sum other dei i the
wike. I the Advenz ant i the Umbri-wiken, Weodnesdei ant Fridei, i the lenten, threo
dahes, ant al the swiing-wike athet non *on Easter* even. To ower wummen ye mahen
thah seggen with lut word hwet-se ye wulleth. Yef eani god mon is of feorren i-cumen,
hercnith his speche ant ondswerieth with lut word to his easkunges.

   Muche fol were the mahte to his bihove, hwether se he walde, grinden greot other
hweate, yef he grunde the greot ant lette the hweate. Hweate is hali speche, as Seint
Anselme seith. Heo grint greot the chafleth. The twa cheken beoth the twa grindel-
stanes. The tunge is the cleappe. Lokith, leove sustren, thet ower cheken ne grinden
neaver bute sawle fode, ne ower eare ne drinke neaver bute sawle heale, ant nawt ane
ower eare, ah ower eh-thur[l] sperreth to ayeines idel speche. To ow ne cume na tale,
ne tidinge of the worlde.

   Ye ne schule for na thing wearien ne swerien, bute yef ye seggen "witerliche" other
"sikerliche," other o sum swuch wise. Ne preachi ye to na mon, ne mon ne easki ow

265

270

275

280

welcoming. **265–66 Summes curteisie . . . bitweonen,** The courtesy of an anchoress (lit., some) is
[sometimes] turned to evil for her. Under the semblance of good is a sin often covered. There ought to
be much [difference] between an anchoress and a lady of a house. **267 bute hit beo duble feaste,** unless
it be a double feast; **tenne,** then (= reduced form of *thenne* after preceding -*t*). **268 Advenz,** Advent
[time]; **Umbri-wiken,** Ember weeks; **lenten,** Lent. **268–69 threo dahes,** three days. **269 swiing-wike,**
holy week (i.e., the week before Easter — lit., silence week); **athet non . . . even,** until Nones on Easter
evening. **269–71 To ower . . . easkunges,** To your women you may nevertheless tell with a few words
whatever you want. If any good man has come from afar, hear his speech and answer with a few words
to his questionings. **272–73 Muche fol . . . the hweate,** He would be a great fool [indeed] who might for
his good grind [either] chaff or wheat, whichever he wanted, if he would grind the chaff and leave the
wheat. **274–75 Heo grint . . . cleappe,** She who chatters grinds chaff (*grint* = reduced form of *grindeth*).
The two cheeks are the two grindstones. The tongue is the clapper. **275–77 Lokith, leove . . . speche,**
Look [to it], dear sisters, that your cheeks never grind [anything] but soul's food, nor your ear ever drink
[anything] but the soul's health, and not only your ear, but close [also] your eye-window (i.e., the
window of your eye) against idle speech. **277–78 To ow . . . worlde,** Let no tale come to you, nor news
of the world. **279–80 Ye ne schule . . . wise,** You should not for any reason curse or swear, unless you
say "certainly" or "surely," or [speak] in some other such way. **280–81 Ne preachi . . . preachin,** Do not

cunsail ne ne telle ow. Readeth wummen ane. Seint Pawel forbeot wummen to preachin. **Mulieres non permitto docere**. Na wepmon ne chastie ye, ne edwiten him his untheaw, bute he beo the over-cuthre. Halie alde ancres hit mahe don summes weis, ah hit nis nawt siker thing, ne ne limpeth nawt to yunge. Hit is hare meoster, the beoth over othre

285   i-set ant habbeth ham to witene as Hali Chirche larewes. Ancre naveth for-te loken bute hire ant hire meidnes. Halde euch hire ahne meoster, ant nawt ne reavi othres. Moni weneth to do wel the deth al to wundre, for as ich seide ear, under semblant of god is ofte i-hulet sunne. Thurh swuch chastiement haveth sum ancre arearet bitweonen hire ant hire preost other a falsinde luve other a muche weorre.

290   **Seneca: ad summam volo vos esse rariloquas tuncque pauciloquas**. "Thet is the ende of the tale," seith Seneke the wise, "ich chulle thet ye speoken seldene ant thenne lutel." Moni punt hire word for-te leote ma ut, as me deth weater ed mulne. Swa duden Jobes freond the weren i-cumen to frovrin him, seten stille seove-niht, ah tha ha hefden alles bigunnen to speokene, tha ne cuthen ha neaver stutten hare cleappe. **Gregorius:**

preach to any man (or, anyone), nor [should] a man ask you for]counsel or tell [it] to you. Advise women only. St. Paul forbade women to preach. **282 Mulieres non ... docere**, "I do not allow women to teach" (1 Timothy 2:12). **282–83 Na wepmon ... over-cuthre**, Do not chastise any man nor reproach him for his fault unless he be to you entirely more familiar (lit, more over-known). **283–84 Halie alde ancres ... yunge**, Holy old anchoresses may do [it] in some way, but it is not a certain thing, nor does it belong to the young. **284–85 Hit is hare meoster ... larewes**, It is their job who are set over others and have [the duty] to guard them as Holy Church's teachers. **285–86 Ancre naveth ... othres**, An anchoress has nothing [to do] but to watch out for herself and her servants. Let each keep her own job and not steal it from others. **286–89 Moni weneth to do wel ... muche weorre**, Many [a person] thinks to do well who does everything marvelously wrong, for as I said before, under the semblant of good, sin is often hidden. By such correction (i.e., of men) many an anchoress (lit., some anchoress) has [sometimes] raised up between herself and her priest either a deceptive (or, treacherous) love or a great war. **290 Seneca ... pauciloquas**, Seneca: "Foremost I want you to be seldom of speech, and [even] then of few words" (untraced). **291 ich chulle**, I wish, desire. **292–94 Moni punt ... hare cleappe**, Many dam up their words (*punt* = reduced form of *pundeth*) to let more out [later], as one does water at a mill. So did Job's friends who had come to comfort him, sat still [for a] week (lit., seven nights), but when they had began to speak everything, then they could never shut their traps (lit., stop their clapper[s]). **294–95 Gregorius: Censura ... verbi**, Gregory: "The severity of silence is a nourisher of words"

295 **Censura silencii nutritura est verbi**. Swa hit is of monie as Sein Gregoire seith: "Silence is wordes fostrilt ant bringeth forth chaffle." On other half, as he seith, **Juge silentium cogit celestia meditari**. "Long silence ant wel i-wist nedeth the thohtes up towart heovene." Alswa as ye mahe seon weater hwen me punt hit ant stoppeth hit bivore wel, thet hit ne mahe dune-ward, thenne is hit i-nedd ayein for-te climben uppart

300 — ant ye, al thisses weis pundeth ower wordes, forstoppith ower thohtes, as ye wulleth thet ha climben ant hehin toward heovene, ant nawt ne fallen dune-ward ant tofleoten yont te worlt as deth muchel chaffle. Hwen ye nede moten, a lute wiht lowsith up ower muthes flod-yeten, as me deth ed mulne, ant leoteth adun sone.

Ma sleath word then sweord. **Mors et vita in manibus lingue**. "Lif ant death," seith

305 Salomon, "is i tunge honden." **Qui custodit os suum, custodit animam suam**. "Hwa-se witeth wel his muth, he witeth," he seith, "his sawle." **Sicut urbs patens et absque murorum ambitu, sic, et cetera. Qui murum silencii non habet, patet inimici jaculis civitas mentis**. "Hwa-se ne withhalt his wordes," seith Salomon the wise, "he

(Gregory, *Homilies on Ezechiel* 1.11 —commenting on Ezechiel 3:16 [*PL* 76.907]). **295–96 Swa hit is . . . chaffle**, So it is with many, as St. Gregory says, "Silence is the fosterer (or, nurse) of words and brings forth chattering." **296 On other half**, On the other side. **296–97** *Juge silentium . . . meditari*, "Perpetual silence compels one to meditate on celestial things" (Gregory, *Letters* 28.3). **297–98 "Long silence . . . heovene,"** "Long and well-directed silence forces thoughts up towards heaven." **298–302 Alswa as ye mahe seon . . . chaffle**, Just as you can see water when one dams it (*punt* = reduced form of *pundeth*) and stops it in front of the well[head], so that it cannot [go] downward, then is it forced to climb again upwards — so (lit., and) you, completely this way dam up (imper.) your words, stop up your thoughts, as you wish that they may climb and rise towards heaven, and not fall downward and float away through the world as much chattering does. **302–03 Hwen ye nede moten . . . adun sone**, When you needs must, loosen up your mouth's flood-gates a little bit, as one does at the mill, and let [it] down immediately. **304 Ma sleath . . . sweord**, The word slays more than the sword; *Mors . . . lingue*, "Death and life [are] in the hands of the tongue" (Proverbs 18:21). **305 i tunge honden**, in the tongue's hands; *Qui custodit os suum . . . suam*, "He who guards his mouth, guards his soul" (Proverbs 13:3). **305–06 Hwa-se witeth**, Whoever protects. **306–08** *Sicut urbs patens . . . mentis*, "As a city open and lacking a circuit of walls, in this way, so . . . ," etc. (Proverbs 25:28); "Whoever does not have the wall of silence, opens the city of his mind to the darts of the enemy" (Gregory, *Pastoral Care* 3.14). **308–09 Hwa-se ne withhalt . . . over al**, "Whosoever does not withhold his words," says Solomon the wise, "he is as the castle without a wall which

310 is as the burh withute wal thet ferde mei in over al. The feond of helle mid his ferd wend thurh-ut te tutel the is eaver open, into the heorte." I *Vitas Patrum* hit teleth thet an hali mon seide tha me preisede ane brethren thet he hefde i-herd of muche speche: **Boni utique sunt set habitatio eorum non habet januam, quicumque vult intrat et asinum solvit.** "Gode," quoth he, "ha beoth, ah hare wununge naveth na yete. Hare muth meatheleth eaver. Hwa-se eaver wule, mei gan in ant leaden forth hare asse" —

315 thet is, hare unwise sawle. For-thi seith Sein Jame, **Si quis putat se religiosum esse non refrenans linguam suam set seducens cor suum, huius vana est religio.** Thet is, "yef eni weneth thet he beo religius ant ne bridli nawt his tunge, his religiun is fals — he gileth his heorte." He seith swithe wel, "ne bridleth nawt his tunge." Bridel nis nawt ane i the horses muth, ah sit sum up-o the ehnen, ant geath abute the earen. For alle

320 threo is muche neod thet ha beon i-bridlet. Ah i the muth sit tet irn, ant o the lihte tunge, for thear is meast neod hald hwen the tunge is o rune ant i-fole to eornen.

Ofte we thencheth, hwen we foth on to speoken, for-te speoke lutel ant wel i-sette wordes, ah the tunge is slubbri, for ha wadeth i wete ant slit lihtliche forth from lut

an army may [enter] from any side (lit., over all)." **309 feond**, enemy, fiend; **mid his ferd**, with his army; **wend**, goes (reduced form of *wendeth*); **310 thurh-ut te tutel . . . open**, throughout the gate which is always open; *Vitas Patrum, The Lives of the [Desert] Fathers*; **hit teleth thet**, it tells what. **311 tha me preisede . . . speche**, when one praised a group of brothers whom he had heard [to be] of much talk (i.e., very talkative). **311–13** *Boni utique sunt . . . solvit*, "They are by all means good, but their lodging has no door; whoever wants to goes in and unties the ass" (*The Lives of the Desert Fathers* 5.4). **313 ha beoth**, they are. **313–14 ah hare wununge . . . asse**, but their dwelling does not have any gate. Their mouths chatter continuously. Whosoever wants to, may go in and lead away their ass. **315 hare**, their. **315–16** *Si quis putat . . . religio*, "If someone believes himself to be religious (or, professed), not restraining his tongue but leading his heart astray, his religion is empty" (James 1:26). **317 yef eni weneth**, if anyone thinks; **ne bridli nawt his tunge**, does not bridle his tongue. **318 gileth**, beguiles, tricks; **swithe**, very, exceedingly. **318–19 Bridel nis nawt ane**, A bridle is not only. **319 ah sit sum . . . earen**, but sits (*sit* = reduced form of *sitteth*) some up on [top of] the eyes, and goes around the ears. **319–20 For alle threo . . . i-bridlet**, For all three there is great need that they be bridled. **320–21 Ah i the muth . . . eornen**, But the iron [bit] sits in the mouth (*sit* = reduced form of *sitteth*) and on the loose tongue, for there is greatest need for restraint when the tongue is in a trot (lit., run) and is about to (lit., has fallen into) run [wild]. **322 thencheth**, think, intend; **hwen we foth on**, when we begin (compare German *anfangen*). **322–24 for-te speoke . . . into monie**, to speak few and well-framed words, but the

word into monie. Ant tenne, as Salomon seith, **In multiloquio non deerit peccatum**.

325 "Ne mei nawt muche speche" — ne ginne hit neaver se wel — "beo withute sunne." For from soth hit slit to fals, ut of god into sum uvel, from meosure into unimete, ant of a drope waxeth into a muche flod, the adrencheth the sawle. For with the fleotinde word tofleoteth the heorte, swa thet longe th'refter ne mei ha beon riht i-gederet togederes. **Et os nostrum tanto est Deo longinqum, quanto mundo proximum,**

330 **tantoque minus exauditur in prece, quanto amplius coinquinatur in locutione**. This beoth Seint Gregoires word in his *Dyaloge*: "Ase neh as ure muth is to worldlich speche, ase feor he is Godd hwen he speketh toward him ant bit him eani bone." For-thi is thet we yeiyeth upon him ofte, ant he firseth him awei frommard ure stevene, ne nule nawt i-heren hire, for ha stinketh to him al of the worldes meathelunge ant of hire

335 chafle. Hwa-se wule thenne thet Godes eare beo neh hire tunge, firsi hire from the world, elles ha mei longe yeiyen ear Godd hire i-here, ant seith thurh Ysaie: **Cum extenderitis manus vestras, avertam oculos meos a vobis, et cum multiplicaveritis**

tongue is slippery, because she wades in wetness and slides (*slit* = reduced form of *slideth*) carelessly away from few words into many. **324 Ant tenne**, And then (= reduced form of *thenne* after preceding -*t*); *In multiloquio . . . peccatum*, "In talkativeness sin is not lacking" (Proverbs 10:19). **325 "Ne mei nawt muche speche . . . sunne,"** "Much speech may not" — [even if] it begins ever so well — "be without sin." **326 from soth . . . unimete**, from truth it slides (*slit* = reduced form of *slideth*) to falsehood, out of good into some evil, from moderation (lit., measure) into excess (i.e., immoderation). **327 waxeth**, grows; **muche flod . . . sawle**, a great flood which drowns the soul. **327–28 fleotinde word . . . heorte**, wandering (lit., floating) word the heart floats away. **328–29 swa thet longe . . . togederes**, so that long thereafter it (lit., she, the heart) cannot be rightly gathered together. **329–30 *Et os nostrum . . . locutione***, "And our mouth is further from God, the closer [it is] to the world; it is heard the less in prayer the more fully it is defiled in speech" (Gregory, *Dialogues* 3.15). **331 This beoth . . . *Dyaloge***, These are St. Gregory's words in his *Dialogue*. **331 neh**, nigh, near; **worldlich**, worldly. **332 ase feor he is . . . eani bone**, just as far as it (lit., he, the mouth) is to God, when it speaks toward Him and asks (*bit* = reduced form of *biddeth*) Him any request. **332–35 For-thi is . . . chafle**, Therefore [it] is that we cry out to Him often and He withdraws Himself away from our voice, does not want to hear her, for she stinks to Him of the world's chatter and of her prattle. **335–36 Hwa-se wule thenne . . . hire i-here**, Whosoever wants then that God's ear be near to her tongue, [should] withdraw herself from the world, else she may long cry out before God hear her. **336 ant seith**, and [God] says. **336–38 *Cum extenderitis manus vestras . . . vos***, "When you (pl.) extend your hands, I shall turn

orationes, non exaudiam vos. Thet is, "thah ye makien moni-falde ower bonen to-ward me, ye the pleieth with the world, nule ich ow nawt i-heren, ah ich wulle turne me 340 awei hwen ye heoveth toward me hehe ower honden."

Ure deore-wurthe Leafdi, Seinte Marie, the ah to alle wummen to beo forbisne, wes of se lutel speche, thet no-hwer in Hali Writ ne finde we thet ha spec bute fowr sithen, ah for se selt speche, hire wordes weren hevie ant hefden muche mihte. **Bernardus ad Mariam: In sempiterno Dei verbo facti sumus omnes et ecce morimur. In tuo** 345 **brevi responso refitiendi sumus ut ad vitam revocemur. Responde verbum et suscipe verbum; profer tuum et concipe divinum**. Hire forme wordes thet we redeth of weren tha ha ondswerede Gabriel then engel, ant teo weren se mihtie, thet with thet ha seide, **Ecce, ancilla Domini; fiat michi secundum verbum tuum** — ed tis word — Godes sune ant soth Godd bicom mon, ant te Laverd thet al the world ne mahte nawt 350 bifon, bitunde him in-with hire meidnes wombe. Hire othre wordes weren tha ha com ant grette Elyzabeth hire mehe. Ant hwet mihte wes i-cud ed theose wordes? Hwet? — thet a child bigon to pleien toyeines ham: thet wes Sein Juhan in his moder wombe.

My eyes from you, and when you multiply your prayers, I shall not hear you" (Isaiah 1:15). **338–40 makien moni-falde . . . honden**, though you make manifold (i.e., numerous) your requests towards Me, you who play with the world, I will not hear you, but I will turn Myself away when you lift up your hands high toward Me. **341 Ure deore-wurthe Leafdi**, Our dear Lady. **341–43 the ah . . . mihte**, who ought to all women to be an example, was of so little speech, that nowhere in Holy Writ do we find that she spoke but four times, but for such (lit., so) seldom speech, her words were heavy (i.e., weighty) and had much power. **343–46 *Bernardus ad Mariam . . . divinum***, Bernard to Mary: "In the eternal word of God we all are made and indeed we are dying. In your short answer we are to be remade so that we may be recalled to life. Give a word and receive a word; give yours and bring forth the divine" (Bernard, *Concerning the Praises of the Virgin Mother* 4.8). **346–47 Hire forme wordes . . . engel**, Her first words that we read about were those [which] she answered to Gabriel the angel. **347–49 ant teo weren se mihtie . . . bicom mon**, and they were so mighty, that when (lit., with that) she said, "Behold, [I am] the handservant of the Lord; let it be done to me according to your word" (Luke 1:38) — at this word — God's son and true God became man (i.e., human). **349–50 ant te Laverd . . . meidnes wombe**, and the Lord which all the world could not grasp (or, seize), enclosed himself inside her virgin's womb (or, belly). **350–51 Hire othre wordes . . . mehe**, Her second words were when she came and greeted Elizabeth, her kinswoman. **351 Ant hwet mihte . . . wordes?** And what power was made known by these words? **352 thet a child . . . moder wombe**, that a child began to play (or, move around) in answer to (lit., towards) them: that was St. John in his mother's womb.

Part Two

Idem: Vox eius Johannem exultare fecit in utero. Th*e* thridde time thet *ha spec*, thet wes ed te neoces, ant ter thurh hire bisocne wes weater i-went to wine. The feorthe

355 time wes tha ha hefde i-mist hire sune, ant eft him i-funde. Ant hu muche wunder folhede theose wordes! Thet Godd almihti beah to mon, to Marie ant to Joseph, to a smith ant to a wummon, ant folhede ham ase heoren, hwider se ha walden. Neometh nu her yeme ant leornith yeorne her-bi hu seltsene speche haveth muche strengthe.

Vir linguosus non dirigetur in terra. "Feole i-wordet mon," seith the Salm-wruhte,

360 "ne schal neaver leaden riht lif on eorthe." For-thi he seith elles-hwer, **Dixi custodiam vias meas ut non delinquam in lingua mea**. Y*p*allage: ant is as thah he seide, "Ich chulle wite mine weies with mi tunge warde. Wite ich wel mi tunge, ich mei wel halden the wei toward heovene." For as Ysaie seith, **Cultus justicie, silentium**. "The tilunge of rihtwisnesse, thet is silence." Silence tileth hire, ant heo i-tilet bringeth forth sawles

---

353 *Idem: Vox eius . . . in utero*, The same [chapter]: "Her voice made John jump for joy in the womb" (loose rendering of Luke 1:44). **353–54 The thridde time . . . wine,** The third time that she spoke, that was at the wedding [at Cana] and there (*ter* = reduced form of *ther*) through her request water was turned into wine. **355 tha ha hefde i-mist hire sune . . . i-funde**, when she had missed her son and [had] found him again. **355–56 hu muche wunder . . . theose wordes!** and how great a wonder followed these words! **356–57 Thet Godd almihti . . . ha walden**, [It happened] that God almighty bowed to man, to Mary and Joseph, to a handworker (lit., smith) and to a woman, and followed them as theirs (i.e., as if He were theirs), wherever they wanted. **357–58 Neometh nu her yeme . . . muche strengthe**, Now pay (lit., take) attention here and learn eagerly from this how infrequent (lit., seldom) speech has much strength. **359** *Vir linguosus . . . terra*, "A wordy man will not be set straight in this world" (Psalm 139:12). **359–60 "Feole i-wordet mon . . . eorthe,"** "A many worded man," says the Psalmist (lit., Psalm-wright), "will never lead an upright life on earth." **360–61** *Dixi custodiam . . . lingua mea*, "I said I shall keep my ways so that I shall not let down [my guard] with my tongue" (Psalm 38:2). **361 Ypallage**, a rhetorical figure in which the attributes of one element are exchanged with those of another. **361–62 Ich chulle . . . warde**, I will protect my ways with the guarding of the tongue. **362–63 Wite ich wel . . . heovene**, [If] I protect my tongue well, I can hold well the way toward heaven. **363** *Cultus justicie, silentium*, "Silence is the cultivation of justice" (Isaiah 32:17). **363–64 tilunge of rihtwisnesse**, cultivation (lit., tilling) of righteousness. **364 tileth hire**, cultivates it (lit., her justice). **364–65 ant heo i-tilet . . . witneth**, and she (i.e., justice), cultivated, brings forth the soul's eternal food,

365   eche fode, for ha is undeadlich, as Salomon witneth: **Justicia inmortalis est**. For-thi feieth Ysaie hope ant silence bathe togederes ant seith in ham schal stonden gastelich strengthe: **In silentio et spe erit fortitudo vestra**. Thet is, "i silence ant in hope schal beon ower strengthe." Neometh yeme hu wel he seith, for hwa-se is muche stille, ant halt silence longe, ha mei hopien sikerliche thet hwen ha speketh toward Godd thet he

370   hire i-here. Ha mei ec hopien thet ha schal singen thurh hire silence sweteliche in heovene. This is nu the reisun of the veiunge, hwi Ysaie veieth hope ant silence ant cupleth ba togederes. Teke thet, he seith i the ilke auctorite, thet i silence ant in hope schal beon ure strengthe i Godes *servise* toyein the deofles turnes ant his fondunges. Ah lokith thurh hwet reisun: hope is a swete spice in-with the heorte thet sweteth al thet bitter thet te

375   bodi drinketh. Ah hwa-se cheoweth spice, ha schal tunen hire muth, thet te swote breath ant te strengthe th'rof leave withinnen. Ah heo the openeth hire muth with muche meathelunge ant breketh silence, ha spit hope al ut, ant te swotnesse th'rof mid worltliche wordes, ant leoseth ayein the feond gastelich strengthe. For hwet maketh us stronge i Godes servise ant ine fondunges for-te drehe derf, to wreastli steale-wurthliche toyein

for she is immortal, as Solomon witnesses. **365 *Justicia inmortalis est*,** "Justice is immortal" (Wisdom 1:15). **365–67 For-thi feieth Ysaie . . . strengthe,** Therefore Isaiah joins hope and silence both together and says [that] in them will stand spiritual (lit., ghostly) strength. **367 *In silentio . . . fortitudo vestra*,** "In silence and hope will be your strength" (Isaiah 30:15). **368–70 Neometh yeme . . . hire i-here,** Pay (lit., take) attention how well he says [this], for whoever is very still and keeps silence for a long time, she may hope securely that when she speaks to God that He [will] hear her. **370 Ha mei ec hopien,** She may also hope; **sweteliche,** sweetly. **371–72 This is nu . . . togederes,** This is now the reason of the joining, why Isaiah joins hope and silence and couples both together. **372 Teke thet, he seith . . . auctorite,** Besides that, he says in the same authority (i.e., book); **ure,** our. **373 toyein the deofles turnes ant his fondunges,** against the devil's tricks and his temptations. **373–75 Ah lokith . . . drinketh,** But look for what reason: hope is a sweet spice inside the heart which sweetens all the bitterness which the body drinks. **375 Ah hwa-se,** But whoever. **375–78 ha schal tunen . . . strengthe,** she must close her mouth, [so] that the sweet breath and strength of it remain within. But she who opens her mouth with much chattering and breaks [her] silence, she spits (*spit* = reduced form of *spiteth*) hope out entirely and the sweetness of it with worldly words, and loses spiritual strength against the fiend. **379–80 ant ine fondunges . . . mede,** in [the midst of] temptations to endure pain, to wrestle stalwartly against the devil's

122

380 the deofles swenges, bute hope of heh mede? Hope halt te heorte hal, hwet-se the flesch
drehe — as me seith "yef hope nere, heorte tobreke." A, Jesu, thin are! Hu stont ham
the beoth ther-as alle wa ant weane is withuten hope of ut-cume, ant heorte ne mei
bersten? For-thi as ye wulleth halden in-with ow hope ant te swete breath of hire the
yeveth sawle mihte, with muth i-tunet cheoweth hire in-with ower heorte, ne blawe ye

385 hire nawt ut with meathelinde muthes, with yeoniende tuteles. **Non habeatis linguam
vel aures prurientes**. "Lokith," seith Sein Jerome, "thet ye nabben yicchinde nowther
tunge ne earen." Thet is to seggen, thet ow ne luste nowther speoken, ne hercni worltlich
speche. Hider-to is i-seid of ower silence, ant hu ower speche schal beo seltsene.
Contrariorum eadem est disciplina. Of silence ant of speche nis bute a lare, ant for-

390 thi i writunge ha eorneth ba togederes. Nu we schulen sum-hwet speoken of ower
herunge ayein uvel speche, thet ye ther-togeines tunen ower earen, ant yef ned is,
spearren ower thurles.

blows, but hope of high reward? **380 halt te heorte hal**, keeps the heart whole (or
healthy). **380–81 hwet-se the flesch drehe . . . tobreke**, whatever the body may suffer —
as they say, "if there were not hope, the heart would break apart." **381 A, Jesu, thin are!**
Ah, Jesus, [give me] Thy mercy! **381–83 Hu stont ham . . . bersten?** How does it go with
them (lit., how stands [it to] them) who are where all woe and misery is without hope of
escape (lit., out-com[ing]), and [whose] hearts cannot burst? **383–85 For-thi as ye
wulleth halden . . . yeoniende tuteles**, For this reason, as you want to hold within you
hope and the sweet breath of that (lit., her hope) which gives power to the soul, chew
her (i.e., hope) with mouth shut inside your heart, do not blow her out with chattering
mouths, with yawning chops. **385–86 *Non habeatis . . . prurientes***, "Do not have itching tongue or ears" (Jerome, *Letters* 52.14). **386–88 nabben yicchinde . . . worltlich
speche**, do not have either an itching tongue or ears. That is to say, that you [should]
not want either to speak, nor hear worldly speech. **388 Hider-to is i-seid . . . seltsene**,
Hitherto [up to this point] the topic has been (lit., is said) of your silence and how your
speech must be seldom. **389 *Contrariorum eadem est disciplina***, "The same teaching is
[made] of opposites." **389–90 Of silence ant of speche . . . togederes**, Concerning
silence and concerning speech [there] is but one teaching, and therefore in writing they
run both together. **390–92 Nu we schulen sum-hwet speoken . . . ower thurles**, Now we
shall speak somewhat of your hearing of (i.e., listening to) evil speech, so that you shut
your ears against it (lit., there against), and if need be, block your windows.

For al uvel speche, mine leove sustren, stoppith ower earen, ant habbeth wleatunge of the muth the speoweth ut atter. **De omni verbo otioso, et cetera**. Uvel speche is
395 threo-fald: attri, ful, ant idel. Idel speche is uvel, ful speche is wurse, attri is the wurste. Idel is ant unnet al thet god ne kimeth of, ant of thulli speche, seith ure Laverd, schal euch word beon i-rikenet, ant i-yeve reisun hwi the an hit seide, ant te other hit lustnede. Ant this is thah thet leaste uvel of the threo uveles. Hwet, hu thenne schal me yelde reisun of the wurse? Hwet, hu of the wurste? Thet is, of attri ant of ful speche? Nawt
400 ane thet hit speketh, ah thet hit hercneth. Ful speche is as of leccherie, ant of othre fulthen thet unweschene muthes speoketh other-hwiles. Theose beoth alle i-schrapede ut of ancre riwle. The swuch fulthe spit ut in eani ancre earen, me schulde dutten his mu*th*, nawt with scharpe sneateres, ah with hearde fustes.

Attri speche is heresie: thweart-over leasunge, bac-bitunge, ant fikelunge — theos
405 beoth the wurste. Heresie, Godd have thonc, ne rixleth nawt in Englelond. Leasunge is se uvel thing thet Seint Austin seith thet for-te schilde thi feader from death, ne schuldest

---

393 For al uvel speche, Before (i.e., in the presence of) all evil speech. **393–94 stoppith ower earen . . . atter**, stop your ears and have disgust for the mouth that spews (or, vomits) out poison. **394 *De omni verbo otioso, et cetera***, "For every idle word, etc." (condensed reference to Matthew 12:36: "Every idle word which they may say, men will give an account of it on the Day of Judgment"); **Uvel**, Evil. **395 threo-fald**, threefold; **attri, ful, ant idel**, venomous, foul, and idle (or, vain). **396–97 Idel is ant unnet . . . lustnede**, Idle and useless is everything from which no good comes, and of such speech, says our Lord, each word will be reckoned, and justified (lit., given a reason), why the one said it and the other listened to it. **398 thah thet leaste . . . uveles**, nevertheless the least evil of the three evils. **398–399 Hwet, hu thenne . . . wurste?** What, how then will one give a reason for (or, justify) the worse? What, how for the worst? **399–400 Nawt ane thet . . . hercneth**, Not only who speaks it, but who listens (lit., hearkens) to it. **400–01 Ful speche is . . . other-hwiles**, Foul speech is for example about lechery and other filths that unwashed mouths speak sometimes. **401–02 Theose beoth . . . ancre riwle**, Let all these be scraped out (i.e., erased) of the anchorite's rule. **402–03 The swuch fulthe . . . fustes**, Whoever spits out such filth (*spit* = reduced form of *spiteth*) into any anchorite's ear, they should shut his mouth, not with sharp murmurings (i.e., useless words), but with hard fists. **404 Attri**, Venomous; **thweart-over . . . fikelunge**, perverse (or, antagonistic) lying, backbiting and flattery. **405 thonc**, thanks; **ne rixleth nawt**, does not reign, have sway. **405–07 Leasunge is se uvel thing . . . lihen**, Lying is so evil a thing that St. Augustine says that [even] to shield your father from death, you

tu nawt lihen. Godd seolf seith thet he is soth, ant hwet is mare ayein soth then is leas? **Diabolus mendax est et pater ejus.** "The deovel is leas ant leasunge feader." The ilke thenne the stureth hire tunge i leasunge, ha maketh of hire tunge cradel to the deofles

410   bearn ant rocketh hit yeornliche as his nurrice.

Bac-bitunge ant fikelunge ant eggunge to don uvel ne beoth nawt monnes speche, ah beoth the deofles bleas ant his ahne stevene. Yef ha ahen to beo feor alle worltliche men, hwet, hu ahen ancren heatien ham ant schunien, thet ha ham ne i-heren? I-heren, ich segge, for hwa-se speketh ham, nis ha nawt ancre. **Salomon: Si mordet serpens in**

415   **silentio, nichil minus eo habet qui detrahit in occulto.** "The neddre," seith Salomon, "stingeth al stille, ant theo the speketh bihinden thet ha nalde bivoren nis na-wiht betere. Herst tu hu Salomon eveneth bac-bitere to stinginde neddre? Swa hit is witerliche ha is neddre cundel ant bereth theo the uvel speketh atter i the tunge.

"The fikelere blent mon ant put him preon i the ehe thet he with fikeleth." **Gregorius:**

420   **Adulator ei cum quo sermonem conserit, quasi clavum in oculo figit.** The bac-

---

should not lie. **407 Godd seolf . . . leas?** God Himself says that He is truth, and what is more against the truth than a lie? **408 Diabolus mendax . . . ejus,** "The devil is lying and the father of lies" (condensed from John 8:44). **408–10 The ilke thenne . . . nurrice,** The same [one] then who stirs her tongue in lying, she makes of her tongue a cradle to the devil's child and rocks it attentively as its nurse. **411 fikelunge ant eggunge to don uvel,** flattery and egging on (i.e., incitement) to do evil. **411–12 ne beoth nawt . . . stevene,** are not a man's speech, but are the devil's blowings (i.e., breath) and his own voice. **412–13 Yef ha ahen . . . i-heren?** If they ought to be far from all worldly men, what, how ought anchoresses to hate and shun them, [so] that they do not hear (or, listen to) them? **413–14 I-heren, ich segge . . . nawt ancre,** I say "hear," for whoever speaks them, she is no anchoress. **414–15 Salomon: Si mordet . . . occulto,** "If the serpent bites in silence, [he is] nothing less who tears down [a person] in secret" (Ecclesiastes 10:11). **415 neddre,** serpent. **416 ant theo the speketh . . . betere,** and she who speaks behind (i.e., in secret) what she does not wish [to speak] before (i.e., in the open) is not at all the better. **417 Herst tu . . . neddre?** Do you hear how Solomon compares the backbiter to a stinging serpent? **417–18 Swa hit is . . . the tunge,** So it is indeed she is the serpent's offspring, and she who speaks evil bears venom in the tongue. **419 "The fikelere . . . fikeleth,"** "The flatterer blinds a person whom he flatters against and puts a spike in his eye (*him . . . i the ehe* = "in his eye")." **419–20 Gregorius: Adulator . . . figit,** Gregory: "A flatterer of someone when he has a word with him, [it is] as if he puts a pin (or, spike) in his eye" (Gregory, *Moral Discourses on Job* 14.52.61 [*PL* 75.1071]).

bitere cheoweth ofte monnes flesch i Fridei ant beaketh with his blake bile o cwike charoines as the thet is thes deofles corbin of helle. **Salomon: Noli esse in conviviis eorum, et ceterea, qui conferunt carnes ad vescendum, et cetera**. Yef he walde pilewin ant toteoren with his bile rotet stinkinde flesch, as is reavenes cunde — thet is,

425 walde he seggen uvel bi nan other, bute bi theo the rotieth ant stinketh al i fulthe of hare sunne — hit were leasse wunder, ah lihteth up-o cwic flesch, tolimeth ant toluketh hit — thet is, misseith bi swuch thet is cwic ine Godd. He is to yiver reven ant to bald mid alle. On other half, neometh nu yeme of hwucche twa meosters thes twa menestraws servith hare laverd, the deovel of helle. Ful hit is to seggen, ah fulre for-te beon hit, ant

430 swa hit is allegate. **Ne videatur hec moralitas minus decens. Recolat in Esdra quod Melchia hedificavit portam stercoris. Melchia enim Corus Domino interpretatur filius Rechab, id est, mollis patris. Nam ventus aquilo dissipat pluvias, et faties tristis linguam detrahentem**. Ha beoth thes deofles gong-men ant beoth aa in his gong-hus. The fikeleres meoster is to hulie the gong-thurl. Thet he deth as ofte as he

421 i Fridei, (i.e., when one ought to abstain from meat). **421–22 beaketh with his blake . . . helle**, pecks with his black bill on living corpses as one that is the raven of the devil of hell. **422–23** *Salomon: Noli esse . . . et cetera*, Solomon: "Do not be at their banquets, etc., who gather meat to eat, etc." (Proverbs 23:20). **423–27 Yef he walde pilewin . . . ine Godd**, If he wanted to strip and tear apart with his bill [only] rotted, stinking flesh, as is the raven's nature, that is, [if] he would say evil about no other but about those who utterly rot and stink in the filth of their sin, it would be less strange, but [he] lights upon living flesh, dismembers (lit., delimbs) and rips it apart — that is, speaks falsely about such [a one] who is alive in God. **427–28 He is to yiver . . . mid alle**, He is too gluttonous a raven and too bold besides. **428–29 On other half . . . deovel of helle**, On the other side (i.e., at the same time), pay attention to what two kinds of jobs (i.e., the two occupations with which) these two ministers (i.e., the flatterer and backbiter) serve their lord, the devil of hell. **429–30 Ful hit is . . . allegate**, It is nasty to talk about, but nastier to be it, and so it [will] always be. **430–33** *Ne videatur . . . detrahentem*, Lest this moralization seem less decent [than it ought], one should recall that in Esdra (i.e., the book of the Bible also known as Nehemiah), Melchias, [the son of Rechab,] builds a gate [out] of shit (see 2 Esdras — i.e., Nehemiah — 3:14). But "Melchias" is interpreted [to mean] "North-west wind to the Lord"; "son of Rechab," that is (or, means) "of a gentle father." "For the north wind disperses the rains, and the sad face [disperses] the disparaging tongue" (Proverbs 25:23). **433–34 Ha beoth . . . gong-hus**, They are this devil's toilet-men (lit., "going"-men) and are ever in his toilet house. **434 The fikeleres meoster . . . gong-thurl**, The flatterer's job is to cover the toilet hole. **434–36 Thet he deth . . . ne**

435 with his fikelunge ant with his preisunge writh mon his sunne, thet stinketh na thing fulre. Ant he hit huleth ant lideth, swa thet he hit nawt ne stinketh. The bac-bitere unlideth hit ant openeth swa thet fulthe, thet hit stinketh wide. Thus ha beoth aa bisie i this fule meoster, ant either with other striveth her-abuten. Thulliche men stinketh of hare stinkinde meoster, ant bringeth euch stude o stench thet ha to nahith. Ure Laverd

440 schilde, thet te breath of hare stinkinde throte ne nahi ow neaver. Other spechen fuleth, ah theose attrith bathe the earen ant te heorte. Thet ye bet i-cnawen ham, yef ei kimeth toward ow, low, her hare molden. Fikeleres beoth threo cunnes: the forme beoth uvele inoh, the othre thah beoth wurse, the thridde thah beoth wurst. **Ve illis qui ponunt pulvillos, et cetera. Ve illis qui dant bonum malum, et malum bonum, ponentes**

445 **lucem tenebras, et tenebras lucem. Hoc scilicet detractatoribus et adulatoribus pervenit**. The forme, yef a mon is god, preiseth him bivoren him-seolf ant maketh him inoh-reathe yet betere then he beo. Ant yef he seith wel other deth wel, heveth hit to hehe up with over-herunge. The other, yef a mon is uvel, ant seith ant deth se muche

stinketh, That he does as often as he with his flattery and praising hides [from a] man [his] sin, which nothing stinks nastier [than]. And he hides it and covers [it], so that he (i.e., the person flattered) does not smell it. **436–38 The bac-bitere unlideth . . . her-abuten**, The backbiter uncovers it and opens that filth in such a way that it stinks widely (i.e., far and wide). Thus they are always employed (lit., busy) in this nasty occupation, and the one strives (or, competes) with the other in this (lit., here about). **438–39 Thulliche men stinketh . . . nahith**, Such men stink of their stinking occupation and bring each place into a stink that they near (or, come near) to. **439–40 Ure Laverd schilde . . . ow neaver**, [May] our Lord defend [you] (or, God forbid), [so] that the breath (*te* = reduced form of *the*) of their stinking throats [may] never come near you. **440–41 Other spechen fuleth . . . te heorte**, Other [kinds of] speech corrupt, but these poison (or, envenom) both the ears and the heart. **441–43 Thet ye bet i-cnawen ham . . . beoth wurst**, So that you know them better, if any [of them] comes toward you, look, here [are] their types (lit., molds). Flatters are of three kinds: the first are evil enough, the second are yet worse, the third though are the worst. **443–46 *Ve illis qui . . . pervenit***, "Woe unto those who place pillows [under the elbow and pillows under the head]," etc. (Ezekiel 13:18). "Woe unto those who call good evil and evil good, regarding light [as] darkness, and darkness light" (Isaiah 5:20). This of course holds true for backbiters and flatterers. **446–47 The forme . . . he beo**, The first [kind of flatterer], if a man is good, praises him before himself (i.e., in his presence) and quickly makes him [out to be] even better than he is. **447–48 Ant yef . . . over-herunge**, And if he speaks well or acts well, [he] exalts it too high up with over-praise. **448– 50 The other . . . uvel leasse**, The second [kind of flatterer], if a man is evil, and says and does so much wrong that it is so (i.e., such) an open sin that he cannot in any way deny it completely, he nevertheless

450 mis thet hit beo se open sunne, thet he hit ne mahe nanes weis allunge withseggen, he thah bivore the mon seolf maketh his uvel leasse. "Nis hit nawt nu," he seith, "se over-uvel as me hit maketh. Nart tu *nawt i this* thing the forme ne the leaste — thu havest monie feren. Let i-wurthe, god mon, ne geast tu nawt te ane — moni deth muche wurse." The thridde cunne of fikelere is wurst, as ich seide, for he preiseth the uvele ant his uvele dede, as the the seith to the cniht the robbeth his povre men: "A, Sire, as

455 thu dest wel, for eaver me schal thene cheorl peolkin ant pilien, for he is as the within the spruteth ut the betere thet me hine croppeth ofte." **Laudatur peccator in desideriis anime sue et iniquus benedicitur. Augustinus: Adulantium lingue alligant hominem in peccatis.** Thus thes false fikeleres ablendeth the ham her[c]nith, as ich ear seide, ant wriheth hare fulthe, thet ha hit ne mahe stinken, ant thet is hare muchel

460 unselhthe. For yef ha hit stunken, ham walde wleatie ther-with, ant eornen to schrift ant speowen hit ut ther, ant schunien hit th'refter. **Clemens: Homicidarum tria esse genera dixit Beatus Petrus, et eorum parem penam esse voluit, qui corporaliter occidit, et qui detrahit fratri, et qui invidet.**

in front of the man himself makes his evil [seem] less. **450–52 Nis hit nawt nu . . . feren,** "Now, it is not," he says, "so excessively (lit., over) evil as people make it. You are not (*nart = ne art*) the first in this thing nor the last — you have many comrades." **452–53 Let i-wurthe . . . wurse,** Let it be (i.e., do not worry), good man, you do not walk alone — many [a one] does much worse. **453–56 The thridde cunne . . . croppeth ofte,** The third kind of flatterer is the worst, as I said, for he praises the evil [person] and his evil deed, just as [he] who says to the knight who robs his poor men, "Ah, Sir, (*as* untranslated) you do well (i.e., you are doing right), for one must rob (lit., pluck) and strip the peasant (*thene* = declined def. art.), for he is like the willow which sprouts out the better because (lit., that) one crops it often." **456–58 *Laudatur peccator . . . in peccatis*,** "A sinner is praised in the desires of his spirit and an evil [one] is blessed" (Psalm 9:24). Augustine: "The tongue of flattering binds a man in sin" (Augustine, *Commentaries on the Psalms* 9.21 [*PL* 36.126]). **458–60 Thus thes false fikeleres . . . unselhthe,** Thus these false flatterers blind [those] who listen to them, as I said before, and cover their filth, so that they cannot smell it, and that is to their great misery. **460–61 For yef ha hit stunken . . . th'refter,** For if they smelled it, [it] would disgust them on that account (lit., there-with), and [they would] run to confession and vomit (lit., spew) it out there, and shun (or, avoid) it after that. **461–63 *Clemens: Homicidarum tria . . . qui invidet*,** Clement: "[There are] three kinds of murderers, said Blessed Peter, and he wanted their punishment to be equal, [he] who kills bodily, and [he] who slanders a brother, and [he] who envies" (Pseudo-Clement, *Decretal Letters* 1 [*PG* 1.480]).

Part Two

465 Bac-biteres, the biteth bihinde bac othre, beoth of twa maneres, ah the leatere is wurse. The earre kimeth al openliche ant seith uvel bi an-other, ant speoweth ut his atter, se muchel se him eaver to muth kimeth, ant culcheth al ut somet thet te attri heorte sent up to the tunge. Ah the leatere kimeth forth al on other wise — wurse feond then the other is — ant under freondes huckel warpeth adun thet heaved, feth on for-te siken ear he eawt segge, ant maketh drupi chere, bisampleth longe abuten, for-te beo bet i-

470 levet. Hwen hit alles kimeth forth, thenne is hit yeolow atter. "Weila," ha seith, "wa is me, thet he other heo habbeth swuch word i-caht. Inoh ich wes abuten, ah ne healp me nawt to don her-of bote. Yare is thet ich wiste th'rof, ah thah thurh me ne schulde hit beon neaver mare i-uppet. Ah nu hit is thurh othre swa wide i-broht forth, thet ich ne mei hit nawt withsaken. Uvel me seith thet hit is, ant yet hit is wurse. Sorhful ich am ant

475 sari thet ich hit schal seggen, ah for sothe swa hit is, ant thet is muchel sorhe, for i feole other thing he other heo is swithe to herien, ah onont this thing — wa is me — ther-vore

464–65 Bac-biteres . . . wurse, Backbiters, who bite others behind the back, are of two kinds, but the latter is worse. **465–67 The earre kimeth . . . the tunge,** The former (lit., earlier) comes all openly and says evil about another, and vomits out his venom, as much as ever comes to his mouth (lit., comes him to the mouth), and spits out everything together that the venemous heart sends up to the tongue (*sent* = reduced form of *sendeth*). **467–70 Ah the leatere . . . i-levet,** But the latter comes forward completely in another way — a worse fiend (or, enemy) than the other is — and under a friend's cloak (i.e., under the cover of friendship) casts down the head, begins (see German *fängt an*) to sigh before he says anything (lit., aught), and makes a droopy (i.e., down-cast) face, offers excuses about it [for a] long [time], [in order] to be better believed. **470 Hwen hit alles . . . yeolow atter,** When it finally (lit., in all) comes out, then it is yellow venom (or, bile); **"Weila," ha seith,** "Alas (or, too bad)," she says. **471 other heo habbeth swuch word i-caht,** or she has caught such a reputation. **471–72 Inoh ich wes abuten . . . bote,** I was trying hard enough (lit., I was enough about [it]), but [it] did me no good (lit., did not help me) to try to fix things (lit., to make a remedy of that). **472–73 Yare is . . . i-uppet,** [It] is a long time (lit., yore) that I knew about it, but still it would not ever [have been] mentioned by me. **473–74 Ah nu hit is . . . withsaken,** But it is now so widely spread about (lit., brought forth) by others, that I cannot fight against (or, counter) it. **474 Uvel me seith . . . wurse,** They say (lit., one says) that it is bad, but yet it is worse; **Sorhful,** Sorrowful, sad. **475 thet ich hit schal seggen,** that I have to say it. **475–77 ah for sothe swa hit is . . . werien,** but truly (lit., forsooth) that is the way it is (lit., so it is), and that is a great pity (lit., sorrow), for in many other things he or she is much to [be] praised (passive inf.), but in this thing — woe is me (i.e., I am afraid) — no one can protect them from it (lit., there

ne mei ham na-mon werien." This beoth the deofles neddren, the Salomon speketh of. Ure Laverd thurh his grace halde ower earen feor hare attrie tungen, ne leve ow neaver stinken thet fule put thet ha unwreoth as the fikeleres wreoth, ant hulieth, as ich seide.

480 Unwreon hit to ham-seolven, theo the hit tolimpeth, ant hulien hit to othre — thet is a muche theaw, nawt to theo the hit schulden smeallen ant heatien thet fulthe.

Nu, mine leove sustren, from al uvel speche thet is thus threo-vald — idel, ful, ant attri — haldeth feor ower eare. Me seith upon ancren, thet euch meast haveth an ald cwene to feden hire earen, a meathelilt the meatheleth hire alle the talen of the lond, a

485 rikelot the cakeleth al thet ha sith ant hereth, swa thet me seith i bisahe: "From mulne ant from chepinge, from smiththe ant from ancre-hus me tidinge bringeth." Wat Crist, this is a sari sahe, thet ancre-hus, thet schulde beon anlukest stude of alle, schal beon i-feiet to the ilke threo studen, thet meast is in of chaffle. Ah ase cwite as ye beoth of thullich, leove sustren, weren alle othre, ure Laverd hit uthe.

before). **477 This beoth**, These are; **neddren**, serpents, vipers; **the**, which, that. **478–79 Ure Laverd . . . as ich seide**, [May] our Lord through His grace keep (lit., hold) your ears far [from] their venemous tongues, nor allow you ever to smell that nasty (lit., foul) pit which they uncover, which (lit., as) the flatterers cover and hide, as I said. **480–81 Unwreon hit to ham-seolven . . . thet fulthe**, To uncover it to [the people] themselves, those to whom it applies, and to hide it from others, that is a great virtue, not [to uncover it] to those who would smell and hate that filth (i.e., third parties). **482–83 thet is thus threo-vald . . . eare**, which is threefold thus — idle, nasty (lit., foul), and venemous — keep (imper.) your ear far away. **483–85 Me seith upon ancren . . . bisahe**, They say (lit., one says) against anchoresses that most every one has an old crone (lit., quean) to feed her ears, a gossip (or, blabberer) who chatters to her all the tales of the land, a magpie who cackles all that she sees and hears, so that they say in a proverb. **485–86 "From mulne . . . bringeth,"** "News comes (lit., people bring tidings) from mill, from market (lit., bargaining), from smithy and from anchor-house." **486 Wat Crist**, Christ knows (an exclamation). **486–88 this is a sari sahe . . . chaffle**, this is a sorry saying, that the anchor-house, which should be the most solitary place of all, must be linked to the very three places which there is the most jawing (lit., most of jawing) in. **488–89 Ah ase cwite . . . hit uthe**, But [may] our Lord grant that all others were as free (lit., acquitted) as you are of such [things], dear sisters.

490   Nu ich habbe sunder-lepes i-speken of thes threo limen — of ehe, of muth, of eare. Of eare is al this leaste to ancre bihove, for leflich thing nis hit nawt thet ancre beore swuch muth, ah muchel me mei dreden to swucche muthes sum-cheare thet ha beie hire eare. Of sihthe, of speche, of hercnunge is i-seid sunder-lepes of euch-an o rawe. Cume we nu eft ayein ant speoken of alle i-meane.

495   **Zelatus sum Syon zelo magno (in propheta Zacharia).** Understond, ancre, hwas spuse thu art ant hu he is gelus of alle thine lates. **Ego sum Deus zelotes (in Exodo).** "Ich am," he seith bi him-seolf, "the geluse Godd." **Zelatus sum, et cetera.** "Ich am gelus of the, Syon, mi leofmon, with muche gelusie." Thuhte him nawt inoh i-seid, thet he is gelus of the, bute he seide ther-to "with muche gelusie." **Auris zeli audit omnia,**
500   seith Salomon the wise. **Ubi amor, ibi oculus.** Wite the nu ful wel — his eare is eaver toward te ant he hereth al. His ehe aa bihalt te yef thu makest ei semblant, eani luve-lates toward untheawes. **Zelatus sum Syon.** Syon, thet is "schawere." He cleopeth the his schawere, swa his thet nan othres, for-thi he seith in Canticis, **Ostende michi fatiem**

490 **Nu ich habbe . . . threo limen**, Now I have spoken separately of these three limbs. 491–93 **Of eare is al this leaste . . . hire eare,** All this last [section] is about the ear, for the profit of anchoresses, for it is not an attractive (lit., lovely) thing that an anchoress [should] have (lit., bear) such a mouth, but one may much fear that that she [might] sometimes bend her ear (i.e., listen) to such mouths. 493–94 **Of sihthe . . . i-meane,** Of sight, of speech, of hearing [something] is said (i.e., has now been said) separately about each one in a row (i.e., one after the other). [Let us] come now back again and speak of [them] all together. 495 *Zelatus sum . . . Zacharia,* "I am jealous of Zion with great jealousy" (in the prophet Zachariah [8:2]). 495–96 **Understond, ancre . . . lates** Understand (imper.), anchoress, whose spouse (or, bride) you are and how He is jealous of all your ways. 496 *Ego sum . . . Exodo,* "I am a jealous God" (in Exodus [simplified rendition of 20:5]). 497 **bi him-seolf,** about, concerning Himself. 498 **of the, Syon, mi leofman,** of you, Zion, my leman (or, lover). 498–499 **Thuhte him . . . ther-to,** [It] seemed to Him not enough said that He is jealous of you, but He said in addition (lit., there-to). 499 *Auris zeli audit omnia,* "The ear of the jealous one hears all things" (Wisdom 1:10). 500 *Ubi amor, ibi oculus,* "Where [there is] love, there [is the] eye (i.e., love is vigilant)" (a proverb); **Wite the nu ful wel,** Protect yourself (i.e., look after yourself) now very well. 501–02 **His ehe aa bihalt te . . . untheawes,** His eye always beholds you [to see] if you make any expression, any love-looks at vices (lit., un-virtues). 502 **Syon, thet is "schawere,"** Zion, that is (i.e., means) "mirror." 502–03 **He cleopeth the . . . in Canticis,** He calls you his mirror, as his which is [the property] of no other (i.e., belongs to no one else), therefore he says in the Canticles (i.e., Song of Songs). 503–04 *Ostende michi fatiem tuam,* "Show your face

131

tuam. "Schaw thi neb to me," he seith, "ant to nan other. Bihald me yef thu wult habbe
505 briht sihthe with thine heorte ehnen. Bihald in-ward ther ich am ant ne sech thu me nawt
withute thin heorte. Ich am wohere scheomeful, ne nule ich no-hwer bicluppe mi leofmon
bute i stude dearne." O thulli wise ure Laverd speketh to his spuse. Ne thunche hire
neaver wunder yef ha nis muchel ane, thah he hire schunie, ant swa ane thet ha putte
euch worldlich thrung, ant euch nurth eorthlich ut of hire heorte, for heo is Godes
510 chambre. Nurth ne kimeth in heorte bute of sum thing thet me haveth other i-sehen
other i-herd, i-smaht other i-smeallet, ant ute-with i-felet. Ant thet witeth to sothe, thet
eaver se thes wittes beoth mare i-sprengde ut-ward, se ha leasse wendeth in-ward.
Eaver se recluse toteth mare ut-ward, se ha haveth leasse leome of ure Laverd in-ward
ant alswa of the othre. **Qui exteriori oculo negligenter utitur, justo Dei judicio**
515 **interiori cecatur.** Lo, hwet Sein Gregoire seith: "Hwa-se yemelesliche wit hire uttre
ehnen thurh Godes rihtwise dom, ha ablindeth i the inre," thet ha ne mei i-seo Godd mid
gastelich sihthe, ne thurh swuch sihthe i-cnawen, ant thurh the cnawleachunge over

to me" (Song of Songs 2:14). **504 neb**, face. **504–05 yef thu wult . . . ehnen**, if you want to have
bright sight with your heart's eyes. **505–06 Bihald in-ward . . . thin heorte**, Look inward where
I am and do not seek me outside your heart. **506–07 Ich am wohere scheomeful . . . dearne**, I am
a bashful wooer, and I will not embrace my beloved anywhere (lit., nowhere) but in a secret place.
507 O thulli wise ure Laverd, In such a way our Lord. **507–10 Ne thunche hire neaver . . . Godes
chambre**, [It should not] ever seem to her strange if she is (lit., is not) much alone, though he
avoids her, and thus [she is] alone [so] that she [might] put each worldly commotion, and each
earthly noise (or, racket) out of her heart, for she (i.e., the heart or the anchoress) is God's chamber
(or private room). **510–11 Nurth ne kimeth . . . i-felet**, Noise does not come into the heart except
from something which one has either seen or heard, tasted or smelled, and felt from the outside.
511–12 Ant thet witeth to sothe . . . wendeth in-ward, And know this for a truth, that always as
(lit., as ever) these senses (lit., wits) are scattered (or, dispersed) outward more, so they turn
inward the less. **513–14 Eaver se recluse toteth . . . of the othre**, Always as the recluse gazes
more outward, so she has less light from our Lord inside and also [less] from the other [senses].
514–15 *Qui exteriori oculo . . . cecatur*, "The person who negligently uses the outer eye, is
blinded in the inner eye by the just judgment of God" (Gregory, *Moral Discourses on Job*
21.8, 13 [*PL* 76.197]). **515–18 Hwa-se yemelesliche wit hire uttre ehnen . . . alle thing luvien**,
Whosoever carelessly damages (*wit* = reduced form of *witeth*) her outer eyes, through God's
righteous judgment she goes blind in the inner [eyes], so that she cannot see God with
spiritual (lit., ghostly) sight, nor through such sight know [Him], and through the knowing

alle thing luvien. For efter thet me cnaweth his muchele godnesse, ant efter thet me feleth his swote swetnesse, efter thet me luveth him mare other lesse.

520   For-thi, mine leove sustren, beoth withute blinde, as wes the hali Jacob ant Tobie the gode, ant Godd wule, as he yef ham, yeoven ow liht withinnen, him to seon ant cnawen, ant thurh the cnawlechunge over alle thing him luvien. Thenne schule ye i-seon hu al the world is nawt, hu hire frovre is fals. Thurh thet sihthe ye schule seon alle the deofles wiheles, hu he biwrencheth wrecches. Ye schulen i-seon in ow-seolf hwet beo yet to

525 beten of ower ahne sunnen. Ye schulen bihalde sum-cheare toward te pine of helle, thet ow uggi with ham, ant fleo the swithere ham frommard. Ye schulen gasteliche i-seon the blissen of heovene, the ontenden ower heorte to hihin ham toward. Ye schulen as i schawere i-seon ure Leafdi with hire meidnes, al the englene weoret, al the halhene hird, ant him over ham alle the blisseth ham alle, ant is hare alre crune. This sihthe, leove

530 sustren, schal frovrin ow mare then mahte ei worltlich sihthe. Hali men witen wel, the habbeth hit i-fondet, thet euch eorthlich gleadunge is unwurth her-toyeines. **Manna**

(lit., knowledging) love [Him] over all things. **518–19 For efter thet me cnaweth . . . mare other leasse,** For according as one knows His great goodness, and according as one feels His sweet sweetness, [so] according to these (lit., that) one loves Him more or less. **520–22 For-thi, mine leove . . . him luvien,** Therefore, my dear sisters, be (imper.) blind without (i.e., to things on the outside), as was the holy Jacob and Tobias the good, and God will, as He gave them, give you light within, to see and know Him and through the knowledge love Him over all things. **522–23 Thenne schule ye i-seon . . . fals,** Then you will see how all the world is nothing, how her (i.e., the world's) comfort is false. **523–24 Thurh thet sihthe . . . wrecches,** Through that sight you will see all the devil's wiles, how he fools [miserable] wretches. **524–25 Ye schulen i-seon . . . sunnen,** You will see in yourself what still is (i.e., remains) to atone (or, be atoned) for your own sins. **525–26 Ye schulen bihalde . . . ham frommard,** You must look (lit., behold) sometimes towards the pain of hell, [so] that [it may] horrify you with them (i.e., so that they may horrify you) and [you may] flee the more quickly from them. **526 gasteliche i-seon,** spiritually (lit., ghostly) see. **527 the ontenden ower heorte . . . toward,** which [will] kindle your heart to hasten (lit., hie) toward them. **527–29 Ye schulen . . . hare alre crune,** You will see as in a mirror our Lady with her maidens, all the host of angels, all the retinue of saints (lit., holy [ones]), and Him over all of them who gladdens them all, and is the crown of them all. **529 sihthe,** sight. **530 schal frovrin . . . wortlich sihthe,** will comfort you more than any worldly sight could (lit., might). **530–31 Hali men witen wel . . . her-toyeines,** Holy men who have experienced it know well that each earthly gladness is worthless in comparison to it (lit., there-against). **531–32 *Manna absconditum est . . . accipit,*** "It is hidden manna,"

absconditum est, et cetera. Nomen novum quod nemo scit, nisi qui accipit. "Hit is a dearne healewi," seith Seint Juhan Ewangeliste i the Apocalipse — "Hit is a dearne healewi, thet na-mon ne cnaweth thet naveth hit i-smecchet." This smech ant tis cnawunge

535 kimeth of gastelich sihthe, of gastelich herunge, of gastelich speche, thet ha schulen habben the forgath for Godes luve worldliche herunges, eorthliche spechen, fleschliche sihthen. **Videamus enim quasi per speculum in enigmate.** Ant efter thet sihthe thet is nu dosc her, ye schulen habbe th'ruppe the brihte sihthe of Godes neb thet alle gleadunge is of i the blisse of heovene muche bivore the othre. For the rihtwise Godd hit

540 haveth swa i-demet, thet euch-anes mede ther ondswerie ayein the swinc, ant ayeines the ennu, thet ha her for his luve eadmodliche tholieth. For-thi hit is semlich thet ancren theos twa marhe-yeoven habben bivoren othre: swiftnesse, ant leome of a briht sihthe. Swiftnes ayeines thet ha beoth nu swa bipinnet. Leome of briht sihthe, ayeines thet ha her theostrith nu ham-seolven, ne nulleth nowther i-seo mon, ne of mon beon i-sehene.

545 Alle theo in heovene schule beon ase swifte, as is nu monnes thoht, as is the sunne

etc. "A new name which no one knows unless he receives [it]" (adapted from Revelation 2:17). **532–34 "Hit is a dearne healewi . . . i-smecchet,"** "It is a secret medicine which no one knows who has not tasted it." **534–37 This smech . . . fleschliche sihthen,** This taste and this knowing comes from spiritual (lit., ghostly) sight, from spiritual hearing, from spiritual speech, which they will have who for God's love forgo worldly hearings (i.e., listenings), earthly speech, bodily sights. **537 *Videamus enim quasi per speculum in enigmate*,** "However we see as if through a mirror in mystery (or, obscurity)" (1 Corinthians 13:12). **537–39 Ant efter thet sihthe . . . bivore the othre,** And after that sight which is now dusky (i.e., dark, obscure) here, you will have up there the bright sight of God's face which is of all the gladness in the bliss of heaven much above the others (i.e., is the greatest joy of heaven). **539–41 For the rihtwise Godd . . . eadmodliche tholieth,** For the righteous God has judged it so that each one's reward there (i.e., in heaven) [will] correspond to the labor, and to the aggravation which they humbly suffer here for His love. **541–42 For-thi hit is semlich . . . of a briht sihthe,** Therefore it is seemly that anchoresses have these two morning gifts (i.e., bridal gifts given the morning after the wedding, dowries) before others do: swiftness, and the light of a bright sight. **543–44 Swiftnes ayeines thet ha beoth nu swa bipinnet . . . beon i-sehene,** Swiftness in compensation for the fact that (lit., against that, or, for that) they are now so penned in. Light of bright sight, in compensation for the fact that they now darken themselves here, nor [do they] want to see a man nor be seen by a man. **545–46 Alle theo in heovene . . . the ehe openeth,** All those will be in heaven as swift as is now man's thought, as is the sun beam

gleam the smit from est into west, as the ehe openeth. Ah ancres, bisperret her, schulen beo ther, yef ei mei, lihtre ba ant swiftre, ant i se wide schakeles — as me seith — pleien in heovene large lesewen, thet te bodi schal beon hwer-se-eaver the gast wule in an hond-hwile. This is nu the an marhe-yeove thet ich seide ancren schulden habben bivoren othre. The other is of sihthe. **Gregorius: enim quod nesciunt ubi scientem omnia sciunt**. Alle theo in heovene seoth i Godd alle thing, ant ancren schule brihtluker, for hare blind-fellunge her, i-seon ant understonde ther Godes dearne runes ant his derve domes, the ne kepeth nu to witen of thinges withuten, with eare ne with ehe.

For-thi, mine leove sustren, yef ei mon bit to seon ow, easkith him hwet god ther-of mahte lihten. For moni uvel ich i-seo th'rin, ant nane biheve. Yef he is meadles, leveth him the wurse. Yef ei wurtheth swa awed thet he warpe hond forth toward te thurl-clath, swiftliche anan-riht schutteth al thet thurl to, ant leoteth him i-wurthen. Alswa, sone se eaver eani feleth into ei luther speche thet falle toward ful luve, sperreth the thurl anan-riht, ne ondswerie ye him na-wiht, ah wendeth awei with this vers, thet he hit

550

555

which smites from east to west, as the eye opens (i.e., in the twinkling of an eye). **546–49 Ah ancres, bisperret her . . . in an hond-hwile,** But anchoresses, locked in here will be there, if any may, both lighter and swifter, and [will] play (or, dance) in such "roomy shackles" — as they say — in heaven's large pastures, that the body will be wheresoever the spirit wishes in an instant (lit., hand-while). **549 an marhe-yeove,** the one (or, first) morning gift. **550 The other is of sihthe,** The second [gift] is of sight. **550–51 Gregorius . . . omnia sciunt,** Gregory: "For what do they not know, where they know Him who knows all things" (Gregory, *Moral Discourses on Job* 2.3.3 [*PL* 75.556]). **551–53 Alle theo in heovene seoth . . . ne with ehe,** All those in heaven see in God all things, and anchoresses will see more brightly, for (i.e., because of) their falling blind here, and [will] understand there God's secret whispers and His fierce judgments, who now does not care to know of things without (i.e., external things), with ear nor with eye. **554–55 yef ei mon bit to seon ow . . . mahte lihten,** if any man asks (*bit* = reduced form of *biddeth*) to see you, ask him what good may come (lit., light, descend) from that. **555 For moni uvel . . . nane biheve,** For I see many evils in that, and no advantage; **Yef,** If; **meadles,** persistent (or, immoderate). **555–56 leveth him the wurse,** believe him [to be] the worse (or, trust him the less). **556–57 Yef ei wurtheth . . . i-wurthen,** If anyone is (or, becomes) so mad that he throw[s] [his] hand out towards the window cloth (or, curtain), right then swiftly shut that window completely up, and let him be. **557–60 Alswa, sone se eaver . . . mahe i-heren,** Also, [as] soon as any[one] ever falls into any wicked speech that tends (lit., falls) toward love, bar the window right away, nor answer him at all, but turn away with this verse, so that he may

560 mahe i-heren: **Declinate a me, maligni, et scrutabor mandata Dei mei. Narraverunt michi iniqui fabulationes, Domine, sed non ut lex tua.** Ant gath bivoren ower weoved with the **Miserere.** Ne chastie ye na swuch mon neaver on other wise, for in-with the chastiement he mahte ondswerie swa, ant blawen se litheliche, thet sum sperke mahte acwikien. Na wohlech nis se culvert as o pleinte wise, as hwa-se thus seide, "ich

565 nalde, for-te tholie death, thenche fulthe toward te" — ant swereth deope athes — "ah thah ich hefde i-sworen hit, luvien ich mot te. Hwa is wurse then me? Moni slep hit binimeth me. Nu me is wa thet tu hit wast, ah foryef me nu thet ich habbe hit i-tald te. Thah ich schule wurthe wod, ne schalt tu neaver mare witen hu me stonde." Ha hit foryeveth him, for he speketh se feire, speoketh thenne of other-hwet. Ah "eaver is the

570 ehe to the wude lehe." Eaver is the heorte i the earre speche. Yet, hwen he is forthe, ha went in hire thoht ofte swucche wordes, hwen ha schulde other-hwet yeornliche yemen. He eft secheth his point for-te breoke foreward, swereth he mot nede, ant swa waxeth

hear it. **560–61 *Declinate a me . . . lex tua*,** "Depart from me, cursed [ones], and I shall examine the commands of my God" (Psalm 118:115). "The wicked have told me fables, Lord, but [that is] not as your law" (Psalm 118:85). **561–62 Ant gath bivoren . . . *Miserere*,** And go before your altar with the "Miserere" ([Lord] have mercy — Psalm 50). **562–64 Ne chastie ye . . . acwikien,** Do not chastise such a man ever in [any] other way, for during the chastisement he may so answer, and blow so lightly, that some spark may spring to life. **564–66 Na wohlech nis se culvert . . . mot te,** No wooing is so treacherous as [that which is] in the manner of a complaint, as if someone said the following: "I would not, to suffer death, think filth about you" — and [he] swears deep oaths — "but [even] though I had sworn [against] it, I must love you." **566 Hwa is wurse then me?** For whom is it worse than for me? **566–68 Moni slep hit binimeth me . . . stonde,** Much (lit., many) sleep it deprives me of. Now woe is me (i.e., I am sorry) that you know it, but forgive me now that I have told it to you. Though I will go (lit., become) mad, you will never more know how [it] stands [with] me (i.e., I will not burden you with knowledge of me.) **568–70 Ha hit foryeveth him . . . i the earre speche,** She forgives him for it (lit., forgives it him), for he speaks so graciously, [then they] speak of other things. But the eye is always [directed] "to the shelter of the wood" (see note). The heart is always [dwelling] on the earlier speech. **570–71 Yet, hwen he is forthe . . . yeornliche yemen,** Yet when he is gone, she often turns [over] (*went* = reduced form of *wendeth*) in her thought[s] such words, when she should eagerly mind (or, attend to) something else (lit., other-what). **572–73 He eft secheth . . . se wurse,** He again seeks his opportunity to break his agreement, swears he must needs [do so], and so, that woe grows the longer so the worse (i.e., grows the

thet wa se lengre se wurse. For na feondschipe nis se uvel, as is fals freondschipe.
Feond the thuncheth freond is sweoke over alle. For-thi, mine leove sustren, ne yeove
575   ye to swuch mon nan in-yong to speokene. For as Hali Writ seith, "hare speche spreat
ase cancre." Ah for alle ondsweres wendeth ow frommard him, alswa as ich seide
th'ruppe. Sawvin ow-seolven — ne maten him betere ne mahe ye o nane wise.

   Lokith nu hu propreliche the leafdi i Canticis, Godes deore spuse, leareth ow bi hire
sahe hu ye schule seggen: **En dilectus meus loquitur michi: Surge propera amica**
580   **mea, et cetera**. "Low," ha seith, "hercne, ich i-here mi leof speoken. He cleopeth me;
ich mot gan." Ant ye gan anan-riht to ower deore leofmon, ant meaneth ow to his earen,
the luveliche cleopeth ow to him with thes wordes: **Surge propera amica mea, columba**
mea, formosa mea, et veni. Ostende mihi fatiem tuam. Sonet vox tua in auribus
meis. Thet is, "aris up! hihe the heone-wart, ant cum to me mi leofmon, mi culvre, mi
585   feire ant mi schene spuse." **Ostende michi fatiem tuam**. "Schaw to me thi leove neb,
ant ti lufsume leor, went te from othre." **Sonet vox tua in auribus meis**. "Sei hwa

worse, the longer it goes on). **573 For na feondschipe . . . fals freondschipe,** For no hostility is so
evil as is false friendship. **574–76 Feond the thuncheth . . . ase cancre,** An enemy who seems [to
be] a friend is a traitor over all [others]. Therefore, my dear sisters, do not give to such a man any
entry to speak. For as Holy Writ says, "their speech spreads as a cancer" (2 Titus 2:17). **576–77**
Ah for alle ondsweres . . . o nane wise, But before all (i.e., any of his) answers, turn yourself away
from him, just as I said above (lit., there-up). Save yourself— you cannot defeat him (lit., mate him
— chess term) better in any other way. **578–79 Lokith nu hu propreliche . . . seggen,** Look now
how properly the lady, God's dear spouse, in the Canticles (i.e., the Song of Songs) teaches you
by her saying how you should speak (lit., say). **579–80 *En dilectus meus***
   . . . *amica mea, et cetera*, "Behold, my beloved speaks to me: 'Arise, my own friend,'" etc. (Song
of Songs 2:10). **580–82 "Low," ha seith . . . with thes wordes,** "Lo," she says, "listen, I hear my
beloved speak. He calls me; I must go." And do you go right away to your dear lover (lit., leman),
and complain (reflex.) in his ears, who lovingly calls you to him with these words. **582–84 *Surge***
***propera amica mea . . . in auribus meis*,** "Arise my own friend, my dove, my beautiful [one], and
come" (Song of Songs 2:10). "Show to me your face. Let your voice sound in my ears" (Song of
Songs 2:13–14). **584–85 hihe the heone-wart . . . mi schene spuse,** hasten yourself here (lit.,
hence-ward) and come to me, my lover, my dove, my fair and my beautiful spouse. **585 thi leove**
neb, your (lit., thy) beloved face. **586 ant ti lufsume leor . . . from othre,** and your lovely
countenance, turn yourself from others. **586–88 Sei hwa haveth i-do the . . . ne speoke bute to me,**
Say who has done [anything to] you, who has hurt my dear — sing in my ears. Because you do not

haveth i-do the, hwa haveth i-hurt mi deore — sing i mine earen. For-thi thet tu ne wilnest bute to seo mi wlite, ne speoke bute to me. Thi stevene is me swete, ant ti wlite schene." **Unde et subditur vox tua dulcis et facies tua decora**. This beoth nu twa things the beoth i-luvet swithe: swete speche ant schene wlite. Hwa-se ham haveth togederes, swucche cheoseth Jesu Crist to leofmon ant to spuse. Yef thu wult swuch beon, ne schaw thu na mon thi wlite, ne ne leote blitheliche here thi speche, ah turn ham ba to Jesu Crist, to thi deore-wurthe spus, as he bit th'ruppe, as thu wult thet ti speche thunche him swete, ant ti wlite schene, ant habben him to leofmon thet is thusent-fald schenre then the sunne.

Hercnith nu yeornliche, mine leove sustren, al an-other speche ant frommard tis earre. Hercnith nu hu Jesu Crist speketh as o wreaththe, ant seith as o grim hoker ant o scarn to the ancre the schulde beon his leofmon, ant secheth thah gealunge ut-ward ant frovre, with ehe other with tunge. **In Canticis: Si ignoras te o pulcra inter mulieres, egredere et abi post vestigia gregum tuorum et pasce edos tuos juxta tabernacula pastorum**. This beoth the wordes: "yef thu ne cnawest te-seolf, thu feier bimong

590

595

600

---

wish [anything] but to see my beauty, do not speak [to anyone] but me. **588–89 Thi stevene is me swete . . . schene**, Your voice is sweet to me and your beauty shining (lit., beautiful). **589 *Unde et subditur vox tua . . . decora***, At this point is added: "your sweet voice and your face seemly" (Song of Songs 2:14). **589–90 This beoth nu twa thinges . . . schene wlite**, These are now two things which are loved powerfully: sweet speech and shining beauty. **590–91 Hwa-se ham haveth togederes . . . to spuse**, Whosoever has them together, such [a one] Jesus Christ chooses for [His] lover and for [His] spouse (or, bride). **591–95 Yef thu wult swuch beon . . . schenre then the sunne**, If you want to be such [a one], do not show any man (or, anyone) your beauty, nor let [him] happily hear your speech, but turn them both to Jesus Christ, to your dear spouse, as he bids you above (i.e., in the text), since you desire that your speech may seem sweet to Him, and your beauty shining (lit., beautiful), and [that you may] have Him as a lover who is thousand-fold brighter (lit., more beautiful) than the sun. **596–99 Hercnith nu yeornliche . . . with tunge**, Hear now carefully, my dear sisters, a completely different speech (lit., a completely other speech), and contrary to this earlier [one]. Listen now how Jesus Christ speaks as in wrath, and speaks as if in grim spite and scorn to the anchoress who ought to be His lover and seeks nevertheless pleasure and comfort outside, with eye or with tongue. **599–601 *In Canticis: Si ignoras te . . . juxta tabernacula pastorum***, In the Canticles: "If you do not know yourself, O beautiful among women, go out and depart to the remnants of your flocks and feed your kids by the dwellings of the shepherds" (Song of Songs 1:7). **601–03 This beoth the wordes . . . ant of leaves**, These are

wummen, wend ut ant ga efter gate-heorden, ant lesewe thine tichnes bi heorde-menne hulen of ris ant of leaves." This is a cruel word, a grim word mid alle thet ure Laverd seith as o grome ant o scarn to totinde, ant to herc-wile, ant to speokele ancres. Hit is
605 bileppet ant i-hud, ah ich hit wulle unvalden. "Yef thu ne cnawest te-seolf," he seith, ure Laverd — neometh nu gode yeme — thet is, "yef thu nast hwas spuse thu art, thet tu art cwen of heovene yef thu art me treowe as spuse ah to beonne, yef thu this havest foryeten ant telest her[-of] to lutel, wend ut ant ga!" he seith. Hwider? Ut of this hehschipe, of this muchele menske "ant folhe heorde of geat," he seith. Hwet beoth heorde of geat?
610 Thet beoth flesches lustes, the stinketh ase geat doth bivoren ure Laverd. "Yef thu havest foryete nu thi wurthfule leafdischipe, ga ant folhe theos geat — folhe flesches lustes." Nu kimeth th'refter, "ant lesewe thine tichnes" — thet is, as *he* seide, "fed tine ehnen with ut-totunge, thi tunge with chaflunge, thine earen with spellunge, thi nease with smeallunge, thi flesch with softe felunge." Theos fif wittes he cleopeth tichnes, for
615 alswa as of a ticchen, thet haveth swete flesch, kimeth a stinkinde gat other a ful bucke, al riht alswa of a yung swete locunge, other of a swote herunge, other of a softe felunge

the words: "if you do not know yourself, you fair among women, depart (lit., turn out) and go after the goatherds, and pasture your kids by the herd-men's (i.e., shepherds') shelters [made] of branches and leaves. **603 mid alle**, as well, in addition. **604 as o grome . . . speokele ancres**, as in anger and in scorn to peering, and to curious (lit., desiring-to-hear), and to gabbing anchoresses. **604–05 Hit is bileppet . . . unvalden**, It is swaddled (or, wrapped) and hidden, but I will unfold (i.e., reveal) it. **606 neometh nu gode yeme**, now pay (lit., take) good attention. **606–08 yef thu nast hwas spuse thu art . . . he seith**, "if you do not know (*nast = ne wast*) whose spouse you are, that you are queen, provided that you are true to me as a spouse ought to be, if you have forgotten this and [if you] care too little for this (lit., hereof), depart and go!" he says. **608–09 Hwider? . . . heorde of geat?** Where to (lit., whither)? Out of the high place of this great honor, "and follow herds of goats," he says. What are "herds of goats"? **610 Thet beoth flesches lustes . . . ure Laverd**, Those are the lusts of the flesh, which stink as goats do before our Lord. **610–12 "Yef thu havest foryete . . . flesches lustes,"** "If you have forgotten now your worthy ladyship, go and follow these goats — follow the flesh's lusts." **612–14 Nu kimeth th'refter . . . with softe felunge**, Now comes after that, "and pasture your kids" — that is, as he said, "feed your eyes with gazing out, your tongue with chattering, your ears with tales (or, gossip, news), your nose with smelling, your flesh (or, body) with soft feeling." **614–17 Theos fif wittes . . . a ful sunne**, These five senses (lit., wits) he calls "kids," for just as from a kid, which has sweet flesh, comes a stinking goat or a foul buck, in the same way (lit., completely just so) from a young, sweet

waxeth a stincinde lust ant a ful sunne. Hwether ei totilde ancre fondede eaver this, the beaketh eaver ut-ward as untohe brid i cage? Hwether the cat of helle cahte eaver towart hire, ant lahte with his cleavres hire heorte heved? Ye, sothes, ant droh ut al the
620 bodi efter, with clokes of crokede ant kene fondunges, ant makede hire to leosen bathe Godd ant mon with brad scheome ant sunne, ant bireafde hire ed an cleap the eorthe ant ec the heovene. Inoh sari lure! To wrather heale beakede eaver swa ut ancre. **Egredere**, he seith o grome: "ga ut, as dude Dyne, Jacobes dohter, to himmere heile, hire to wrather heale," thet is to seggen, "leaf me ant mi cunfort thet is in-with thi breoste, ant
625 ga sech withuten the worldes frakele frovre, the schal endin eaver i sar ant i sorhe. Tac ther-to, ant leaf me hwen the swa is leovere, for ne schalt tu nanes-weis thes ilke twa cunforz — min ant te worldes, the joie of the Hali Gast ant ec flesches frovre, habbe togederes. Cheos nu an of thes twa, for the other thu most leten." **O pulcra inter mulieres**. "Yef thu ne cnawest te-seolf, thu feier bimong wummen," seith ure Laverd,
630 "thu feier bimong wummen, ye, nu her do ther-to thet schalt, ant tu wel wulle elles-

glance (lit., looking) or from a sweet hearing, or from a soft feeling grows a stinking lust and a foul sin. **617–18 Hwether ei totilde ancre . . . brid i cage?** Has any prying anchoress who is always sticking her beak out like an untame bird in a cage ever experienced this (i.e., the following)? **618–22 Hwether the cat of helle . . . ec the heovene**, Has the cat of hell ever snatched at her, and snatched with sharp claws (lit., cleavers) her heart's head (i.e., the head, the most important part of her heart)? Yes indeed, and drew (or, enticed) the entire body out afterwards with clutches of treacherous and sharp temptations, and made her lose both God and man with broad (i.e., immense) shame and sin, and robbed her at one clap (i.e., stroke) of the earth and also of heaven. **622 Inoh sari lure!** A sad enough loss!; **To wrather heale . . . ancre**, To [her] destruction an anchoress always poked her beak out in this way. **622–25 Egredere . . . i sar ant i sorhe**, "Go out," he says in anger: "go out, as did Dinah, Jacob's daughter, with miserable luck (?), to her destruction," that is to say, "leave me and my comfort that is within your breast, and go seek without (i.e., outside) the world's fragile comfort, which will always end in pain and sorrow. **625–28 Tac ther-to, ant leaf me . . . habbe togederes**, Take to it (i.e., go on), and leave me, if (lit., when) it is so preferable to you, for you will [in] no way have these same two comforts together — mine and the world's, the joy of the Holy Spirit and also the comfort of the flesh (or, body). **628 Cheos nu an**, Now choose one; **leten**, leave, give up. **628–29 O pulcra inter mulieres**, "O beautiful among women" (Song of Songs 1:7). **629–31 Yef thu ne . . . bimong engles**, "If you do not know yourself, you beautiful among women," says our Lord, "You beautiful among women, yes, now do here what must [be done] for this

hwer beo feier, nawt ane bimong wummen, ah bimong engles. Thu, mi wurthli spuse," seith ure Laverd, "schalt tu folhin geat o feld?" — thet beoth flesches lustes. Feld is willes breade. "Schalt tu o this wise folhi geat yont te feld, the schuldest i thin heorte bur biseche me cosses, as mi leofmon thet seith to me i thet luve-boc: **Osculetur me**

635 **osculo oris sui.**" Thet is, "cusse me, mi leofmon, with the coss of his muth, muthene swetest." This coss, leove sustren, is a swetnesse ant a delit of heorte swa unimete swete, thet euch worldes savur is bitter ther-toyeines. Ah ure Laverd with this coss ne cusseth na sawle the luveth ei thing buten him ant te ilke thinges for him the helpeth him to habben. Ant tu, thenne, Godes spuse, thet maht heren her-bivoren hu sweteliche thi

640 spus speketh ant cleopeth the to him se luveliche, th'refter hu he went te lof, ant speketh swithe grimliche yef thu ut wendest. Hald te i thi chambre. Ne fed tu nawt withuten thine gate tichnes, ah hald withinnen thin hercnunge, thi speche, ant ti sihthe, ant tun feaste hare yeten — muth ant ehe ant eare. For nawt ha beoth bilokene in-with wah

(lit., there-to) (i.e., behave here on earth as you ought to), and you will be very beautiful elsewhere, not only among women but among angels." **631–32 Thu, mi wurthli spuse . . . flesches lustes,** "You, my worthy spouse," says our Lord, "will you follow in this way goats in the field?" — which are the flesh's lusts. **632–35 Feld is willes breade . . . oris sui,** The "field" is [the full] extent (lit., breadth) of the will (or, one's desires). "Will you follow in this way goats in the field, who ought in your heart's bower beseech (i.e., beg) me for kisses, as my lover who says to me in that love-book: 'Let him kiss me with the kiss of his mouth'?" (Song of Songs 1:1). **635 leofmon,** lover (lit., leman); **coss,** kiss. **635–36 muthene swetest,** the sweetest of mouths (*muthene* = genitive pl.; compare *ancrene*). **636–37 swa unimete swete . . . ther-toyeines,** so immeasurably sweet, that each savor (or, taste) of the world is bitter in comparison to it (lit., there-against). **638 cusseth,** kisses. **638–39 na sawle the luveth . . . to habben,** any soul which loves anything but Him, and those same things for Him (i.e., for His sake), which help to have Him (i.e., no soul which loves anything but Him, and loves things in this world only because of Him, in order to gain Him). **639–41 Ant tu, thenne . . . yef thu ut wendest,** And you, then, God's spouse (or, bride), who could hear up above (i.e., in the text), how sweetly your spouse (or, bridegroom) speaks and calls you to Him so lovingly, [and could hear] after that how He changes course (lit., turns the spar; see *lof* in the glossary), and speaks very grimly if you go (lit., wend) out[wards] (or, leave). **641–43 Hald te i thi chambre . . . ehe ant eare,** Keep (lit., hold) yourself in your private room. Do not feed kids outside your gate, but keep your hearing within [on the inside], your speech and your sight, and shut fast (i.e., securely) their gates — mouth and eye and ear. **643–44 For nawt ha beoth bilokene . . . liveneth of sawle,** For nothing they are locked inside the wall who open these

other wal the thes yeten openith, bute ayein Godes sonde, ant liveneth of sawle. **Omni**
645   **custodia custodi cor tuum.** "Over alle thing thenne," as Salomon the leareth, ant ich
seide feor bivoren i the frumthe of this dale, mine leove sustren, "witeth ower heorte."
The heorte is wel i-loket yef muth ant ehe ant eare wisliche beon i-lokene. For heo, as
ich seide ther, beoth the heorte wardeins, ant yef the wardeins wendeth ut, the ham bith
biwist uvele. This beoth nu the threo wittes thet ich habbe i-speken of. Speoke we nu
650   scheortliche of the twa othre. Thah nis nawt speche the muthes wit, ah is smechunge,
thah ba beon i muthe.

    Smeal of nease is the feorthe of the fif wittes. Of this wit seith Seint Austin, **De**
odoribus non satago nimis. Cum assunt non respuo, cum absunt non requiro.
"Of smealles," he seith, "ne fondi ich nawt mucheles. Yef ha beoth neh — o Godes half
655   — yef feor, me ne recche." Ure Laverd thah thurh Ysaie threateth ham with helle stench
the habbeth delit her i fleschliche smealles: **Erit pro suavi odore fetor.** Ther-toyeines
ha schulen habben heovenliche smealles, the habbeth her of irnes swat, other of heren

gates, unless [they open them] for God's message, and for the sustenance of the soul. **644–
45** *Omni custodia custodi cor tuum*, "With all care guard your heart" (Proverbs 4:23). **645
thing**, things (pl.). **the leareth**, teaches you. **645–46 ant ich seide . . . this dale**, and I said far
before in the beginning of this part (or, section). **646 "witeth ower heorte,"** "protect your
hearts." **647 i-loket**, looked after; **ehe**, eye; **wisliche beon i-lokene**, are wisely locked. **647–
49 For heo, as ich seide ther . . . uvele**, For they, as I said there, are the heart's guardians (lit.,
wardens), and if the guardians go out (or, leave), the home is badly (lit., evilly) looked after.
649 This beoth nu . . . i-speken of, These are now three senses which I have spoken of. **649–
51 Speoke we nu scheortliche . . . beon i muthe**, Let us speak now briefly of the other two.
However, speech is not the mouth's sense, but taste is, [even] though both are in the mouth.
652 Smeal of nease, Smell[ing] of the nose. **652–53** *De odoribus . . . non requiro*, "Concerning smells I do not trouble myself exceedingly. When they are present I do not spit them out
(or, reject them). When they are absent I do not need (i.e., have to have) [them]" (Augustine,
Confessions 10.32 [*PL* 32.799]). **654 ne fondi ich nawt mucheles**, I do not trouble [myself]
much at all. **654–55 Yef ha beoth neh . . . me ne recche**, "If they are near (lit., nigh) — for God's
sake — [or] if far [away], [it does] not concern me." **655–56 Ure Laverd thah . . . fleschliche
smealles**, Our Lord though through Isaiah threatens them with hell's stench who have delight here in carnal smells. **656** *Erit pro suavi odore fetor*, "There will be a stench instead of
a sweet smell" (Isaiah 3:24). **656–59 Ther-toyeines ha schulen habben . . . i nease**, In compensation for that (lit., there-against), they will have heavenly smells who have here [tasted] from

thet ha beoreth, other of swati hettren, other of thicke eir in hire hus, ant muhlinde thinges, stench other-hwiles ant strong breath i nease.

660   Ther-of beoth i-warnet, mine leove sustren, thet other-hwile the feond maketh sum thing to stinken thet ye schulden notien, for-thi thet he walde thet ye hit schulden schunien. Other-hwile the wiheleare of sum dearne thing thet ye ne mahe nawt i-seon, as dust of dearne sedes, maketh a swote smeal cumen, as thah hit were of heovene, for ye schulden wenen thet Godd for ower hali lif sende ow his elne, ant leote wel to ow-
665   seolf, ant leapen into prude. Smeal the kimeth o Godes half frovreth the heorte mare then the nease. Theos ant othre truiles, thet he bitruileth monie, schulen beon i-broht to nawt with hali-weater ant with the hali rode-taken. Hwa-se thohte hu Godd seolf wes i this wit i-dervet, ha walde the derf th'rof thuldeliche tholien.

    I the munt of Calvarie, ther ure Laverd hongede, wes the cwalm-stowe, ther leien
670   ofte licomes i-rotet buven eorthe ant stunken swithe stronge. He, as he hongede, mahte habben hare breath with al his other wa, riht amidden his nease.

---

iron's sweat (i.e., from mailshirts worn as penance), or from hairs (i.e., hair shirts) that they wear, or from sweaty clothes or from close air in their house, and molding things, smells sometimes and strong stench (lit., breath) in [their] nose. **660–65 Ther-of beoth i-warnet . . . leapen into prude**, Be warned of that, my dear sisters, that at times the enemy (lit., fiend) makes something stink which you should use (or, make use of), because he [would] want you to shun it. At other times, the sorcerer (i.e., the devil) makes a sweet smell come from some secret thing that you cannot see, [such] as powder from secret seeds, as though it were from heaven, for you should (i.e., are supposed to) think that God because of your holy [way of] life sends you His strength, and [then you are supposed to] think [too] well of yourself and leap into pride. **665–66 Smeal the kimeth . . . the nease**, The smell which comes from God's side comforts the heart more than [it comforts] the nose. **666–67 Theos ant othre truiles . . . the hali rode-taken**, This and other tricks [with] which he tricks many will be brought to nothing with holy water and with the Holy Rood-token (i.e., the sign of the Holy Cross, or, perhaps, a Crucifix). **667– 68 Hwa-se thohte . . . thuldeliche tholien**, Whoever would think how God Himself was tortured in this sense, she would suffer the torture in that [sense] patiently. **669–70 I the munt . . . stunken swithe stronge**, On the mount of Calvary, where our Lord hung, was the death-place (i.e., place of execution) where often rotted corpses lay above the earth and stank exceedingly strong. **670–71 mahte habben hare breath . . . his nease**, could have their stench (lit., breath) with all His other suffering, right under (lit., amid) His nose.

Alswa as he wes i-dervet in alle his othre wittes — in his sihthe, tha he seh his deore-wurthe moder teares ant Sein Juhanes Ewangeliste ant te othre Maries, ant tha he biheold hu his deore deciples fluhen alle from him ant leafden him ane. He weop him-
675 seolve thrien with his feire ehnen. He tholede al thuldeliche thet me him blindfeallede, hwen his ehnen weren thus i schendlac i-blintfeallet, for-te yeove the ancre the brihte sihthe of heovene. Thah thu thine ehnen for his luve, ant i munegunge th'rof, blintfealli on eorthe to beoren him feolah-readden nis na muche wunder.

Amid the muth me gurde him, sum-cheare inoh-reathe as me tobeot his cheken, ant
680 spitte him o scarne, ant an ancre is for a word ut of hire witte! Hwen he tholede thuldeliche thet te Giws dutten, as ha buffeteden him, his deore-wurthe muth, with hare dreori fustes, ant tu for the luve of him, ant for thin ahne muchele biheve, thi tutelinde muth dute with thine lippen. Teke thet he smahte galle on his tunge, for-te learen ancre thet ha ne grucchi neaver mare for na mete ne for na drunch, ne beo hit swa unorne.
685 Yef ha hit mei eoten, eote ant thonki Godd yeorne. Yef ha ne mei nawt, beo sari thet ha mot sechen estfulre. Ah ear then thet biddunge areare eani scandle, ear deie martir in

672–74 **Alswa as he wes i-dervet . . . leafden him ane**, Just as He was tortured in His other senses — in His sight, when He saw His dear mother's tears and St. John's, the evangelist, and the other Marys' [tears], and when He saw how His dear disciples all fled from Him and left Him alone. 674–77 **He weop him-seolve . . . brihte sihthe of heovene**, He wept Himself three times with His fair eyes. When His eyes were thus shamefully (lit., in shame, humiliation) blindfolded, He allowed quite patiently that they blindfolded Him, in order to (lit., for to) give the anchoress the bright sight of heaven. 677–78 **Thah thu thine ehnen . . . na muche wunder**, Though you blindfold your eyes for His love and in remembrance of that, on earth to bear Him fellowship (or, company), [it] is no great wonder. 679–80 **Amid the muth . . . ut of hire witte!** They (lit., one) struck (or, pummeled) Him on the mouth at times readily enough as they beat His cheeks and spat [on] Him in scorn, and an anchoress is out of her wits because of a word! 680–83 **Hwen he tholede . . . dute with thine lippen**, Since (lit., when) He patiently allowed the Jews to shut, as they buffeted Him, His precious mouth with their cruel (perhaps, bloody) fists, then (lit., and) you for the love of Him, and for your own great good (lit., behoove), [should] shut your jabbering mouth with your lips. 683–84 **Teke thet he smahte galle . . . swa unorne**, Besides that, He tasted gall on His tongue, in order to teach the anchoress that she [should] not complain (lit., grouch) ever more about any food or about any drink, be it [ever] so poor. 685–86 **Yef ha hit mei eoten . . . sechen estfulre**, If she can eat it, let her eat and thank God eagerly. If she cannot, [let her] be sorry that she must seek more delicate [food]. 686–87 **Ah ear then . . . in hire meoseise**, But before that

144

hire meoseise. Death me ah for-te fleon ase forth as me mei withute sunne, ah me schal ear deien then me do eani heaved sunne. Ant nis hit muche sunne to makien thet me segge, "Estful is theos ancre. Muchel is thet ha bid." Yet is wurse yef me seith thet ha

690 is grucchilit ant ful-itohe, dangerus, ant erveth for-te paien. Were ha i-mid te world, ha moste beo sum-chearre i-paiet inoh-reathe mid leasse ant mid wurse. Muchel hofles hit is, cumen into ancre-hus, into Godes prisun willes ant waldes to stude of meoseise, for-te sechen eise th'rin ant meistrie ant leafdischipe, mare then ha mahte habben inoh-reathe i-haved *i* the worlde. Thenc, ancre, hwet tu sohtest tha thu forsoke the world i

695 thi biclusunge. Biwepen thine ahne ant othres sunnen, ant forleosen alle the blissen of this lif, for-te cluppen blisfulliche thi blisfule leofmon i the eche lif of heovene. "O," seith Sein Jer*emie*, **Quomodo obscuratum est aurum optimum, et cetera**. "O wei-la-wei, wei-la-wei, hu is gold i-theostret! Hu is feherest heow biturnd ant forweolewet!" The Apostle speketh to swucche grimliche as o wreaththe, **Quis vos fascinavit et**

request (lit., bidding) raise up any scandal (see glossary) — before [that], [let her] die a martyr in her discomfort (lit., mis-ease). **687–88 Death me ah for-te fleon . . . heaved sunne**, One ought to flee death as far as one can without sin, but one must sooner die than do any capital sin (lit., head sin). **688–90 Ant nis hit muche sunne . . . erveth for-te paien**, And is it not a great sin to make that they say (i.e., make them say), "Picky (or, pleasure-seeking) is this anchoress. Much [it] is that she asks for." Yet [it] is worse if they say that she is a grouchy woman and ill mannered, standoff-ish, and difficult to please. **690–91 Were ha i-mid te world . . . mid wurse**, Were she (or, [if] she were) in the world, she [would] sometimes have to be pleased readily enough with less, and [with] worse. **691–94 Muchel hofles hit is . . . i the worlde**, It is a great folly (i.e., it is very unreasonable) to come into an anchor-house, into God's prison, ready and willing (lit., willing and wanting — *willes ant waldes* is a set phrase like *willy nilly*), to a place of discomfort (lit., mis-ease), in order to seek ease there and authority (lit., mastery) and ladyship, more than she might have had readily enough in the world. **694–95 Thenc, ancre . . . i thi biclusunge**, Think, anchoress, what you sought when you forsook the world in your enclosure. **695–96 Biwepen thine ahne ant othres sunnen . . . eche lif of heovene**, Cry for (lit., beweep) your own and others' sins, and abandon all the joys of this life, in order to embrace joyfully your joyful lover (lit., leman) in the eternal life of heaven. **697 Jeremie**, Jeremiah; *Quomodo obscuratum . . . et cetera*, "How dull has the best gold become," etc. (Lamentations 4:1). **697–98 "O wei-la-wei . . . forweolewet!"** "O alas, alas, how gold has darkened! How has the fairest color turned and faded (lit., withered)!" **699 to swucche grimliche as o wreaththe**, to such [ones] grimly as if in anger. **699–700 *Quis vos fascinavit . . . consummamini?*** "Who has bewitched you? etc., that you began with the spirit

700 **cetera, ut cum spiritu ceperitis, carne consummamini?** "Me hwuch unseli gast
haveth swa bimalscret ow, thet ye i gast bigunnen, ant i flesch wulleth endin?" The
gastelich lif bigunnen i the Hali Gast beoth bicumene al fleschliche, al fleschliche i-
wurthen: lahinde, lihte i-latet, ane hwile lihte i-wordet, an-other luthere i-wordet, estfule
ant sarcurne ant grucchildes, meanildes ant — yet thet wurse is — cursildes ant chidildes,

705 bittre ant attrie with heorte tobollen. Bihofde nawt thet swuch were leafdi of castel.
Hoker ant hofles thing is, thet a smiret ancre ant ancre biburiet — for hwet is ancre-hus
bute hire burinesse? — ant heo schal beo greattre i-bollen, leafdiluker leoten of, then a
leafdi of hames! Yef ha maketh hire wrath ayeines gult of sunne, *ha* [shulde] sette*n* hire
wordes swa efne thet ha ne thunche over-sturet, ne nawt i-lead over skile, ah inwardliche

710 ant sothliche withuten hihthe ant hehschipe in a softe stevene. **Filia fatua in
deminoratione erit** — this is Salomones sahe. Thet hit limpe to ei of ow, Godd ne leve
neaver. "Cang dohter i-wurth as mone i wonunge" — thriveth as the cangun, se lengre

[but] have ended in the flesh?" (Galatians 3:1, 3). **700–01 "Me hwuch unseli gast . . . endin?"**
"But which unholy spirit has so bewitched you that you began in the spirit and will (or, want
to) end in the flesh?" **702 gastelich**, spiritual (lit., ghostly). **702–05 beoth bicumene al
fleschliche . . . tobollen**, has become completely carnal, turned completely carnal: laughing,
loosely behaved, [at] one time loosely worded (i.e., given to frivolous talk), [at] another
wickedly worded (i.e., given to evil talk), pleasure seeking (or, luxurious), and touchy, grouchy,
complaining and — what is still worse — cursing and scolding, bitter and venemous, with a
heart swollen up [in pride]. **705–08 Bihofde nawt . . . leafdi of hames!** [It would] not behoove
(i.e., it would not be fitting) that such [a one] were lady of a castle. A mockery and an
unreasonable thing [it] is, that an anointed (lit., smeared) anchoress and an anchoress buried
— for what is the anchor-house but her burial? — that (lit., and) she will be more greatly
swollen up, thought of as more a lady, than a lady of homes (i.e., a lady of the manor)! **708–
10 Yef ha maketh hire wrath . . . stevene**, If she makes her wrath against (i.e., gets angry
about) the guilt of sin, she should arrange her words so evenly that they do not seem overly
emotional (lit., over-stirred), nor pushed beyond reason (lit., led beyond 'skill'), but [that they
seem] inwardly and truly without haste and exaltation (or, arrogance) in a soft voice. **710–11
*Filia fatua in deminoratione erit***, "The foolish daughter will be made smaller (lit., in lessen-
ing)" (adapted from Ecclesiaticus 22:3). **711 sahe**, saying (lit., saw). **711–12 Thet hit limpe . . . ne
leve neaver**, That it [should] apply to any of you, may God never allow. **712–13 Cang dohter
. . . se wurse**, "A foolish daughter is like the moon in [its] waning" — [she] thrives like the fool,

se wurse. Ye, as ye wulleth waxen ant nawt wenden hind-ward, sikerliche ye moten rowen ayein stream, with muchel swinc breoken forth, ant gasteliche earm*es*
715 stealewurthliche sturien — ant swa ye moten alle. For alle we beoth i this stream, i the worldes wode weater the bereth adun monie. Sone se we eaver wergith ant resteth us i slawthe, ure bat geath hind-ward ant we beoth the cang dohter the gath woniende, the wlecche the Godd speoweth — as is i-writen her-efter — the bigunnen i gast, ant i flesch endith. Nai, nai, ah as Job seith, "the delveth efter golt-hord, eaver se he mare
720 nahheth hit, se his heortes gleadschipe maketh him mare lusti, ant mare fersch to diggin ant delven deoppre ant deoppre, athet he hit finde. Ower heorte nis nawt on eorthe; for-thi ne thurve ye nawt delven dune-wardes, ah heoven uppart the heorte, for thet is the up-rowunge ayein this worldes stream, driven hire ayein-ward to delven the golt-hord thet up is in heovene. Ant hwet is thet delvunge? Yeornful sechinde thoht, hwer hit beo,
725 hwuch hit beo, hu me hit mahe i-finden — this is the delvunge. Beon bisiliche ant yeornfulliche eaver her-abuten, with ane-wil yirnunge, with heate of hungri heorte, waden up of untheawes, creopen ut of flesch, breoken up over hire, astihen up on ow-

the longer the worse. **713–15 Ye, as ye wulleth waxen . . . swa ye moten alle**, You, as you want to grow and not regress (lit., turn backward, hind[er]ward), surely you must row against the stream, with much work break away, and stir your spiritual arms stalwartly — and so must you all. **715–16 For alle we beoth . . . bereth adun monie**, For we are all in this stream, in the world's mad (i.e., raging) water which bears many down (i.e., pulls many under). **716–19 Sone se we eaver . . . i flesch endith**, As soon as we ever weary (or, grow weary) and rest ourselves in sloth, our boat goes backwards, and we are the foolish daughter who goes waning (i.e., like the moon), the lukewarm [one] whom God spews out — as is written hereafter — who began in the spirit, and ends in the flesh. **719 Nai, nai**, No, no; **ah**, but. **719–21 the delveth efter golt-hord . . . athet he hit finde**, whoever digs for a gold-hoard, always the more he nears it, so his heart's gladness makes him more lusty (i.e., energetic), and fresher to dig and delve deeper and deeper, until he find[s] it. **721–24 Ower heorte nis nawt on eorthe . . . is in heovene**, Your heart is not on earth; therefore you need not dig downward, but [you need to] lift the heart upward, for that is the rowing up against this world's stream, [you need to] drive her (i.e., the boat/heart) against it (i.e., against the current) to dig the gold-hoard that is up in heaven. **724 delvunge**, digging. **724–25 Yeornful sechinde thoht . . . the delvunge**, An eager mind (lit., thought) seeking where it [might] be, what it [might] be, how one [might] find it — this is digging. **725–29 Beon bisiliche ant yeornfulliche . . . tholien**, Be (imper.) always busily and eagerly about (i.e., occupied with) this, with single-minded yearning, with the heat of a hun-

seolf with heh thoht toward heovene — swa muchel the neodeluker thet ower feble, tendre flesch heardes ne mei tholien. Nu thenne, ther-ayein yeoveth Godd ower heorte,
730 i softnesse, i swetnesse, in alles cunnes meoknesse, ant softest eadmodnesse — nawt nu granin ant peonsin, th'refter hehi stevene, wreathen hire unweneliche, sinetin hire wordes, wrenchen awei-ward, wenden the schuldre, keaste the heaved, swa thet Godd heateth hire ant mon hire scarneth. Nai, nai! Ripe wordes, lates ripe ant werkes bilimpeth to ancre. Hwen wordes beoth eadmodliche ant sothfestliche i-seide, nawt ful-itoheliche
735 ne babanliche, thenne habbeth ha burtherne to beo riht understonden. Nu is this al i-seid thet ye — efter Jesu Crist the me gurde ine muth ant galle yef to drinken — with muthes sunne witen ow, ant tholieth sum derf i thet wit as he wes th'rin i-dervet.

In his eare, he hefde, the heovenliche Laverd, al the edwit ant te upbrud, al the scarn ant al the scheome thet eare mahte i-heren, ant he seith bi him-seolf, us for-te learen: **Et**
740 **factus sum sicut homo non audiens et non habens in ore suo redargutiones**. "Ich heold me," he seith, "stille as dumbe ant deaf deth thet naveth nan ondswere, thah me

gry heart, wade up from vices, crawl (lit., creep) out of [your] body, break out over her (i.e., the body), climb upon (or, up over) yourself with high thought towards heaven — [which is] so much the more needful that (i.e., since) your feeble, tender body cannot suffer [anything] hard. **729–33 Nu thenne, ther-ayein . . . scarneth,** Now then, in return (lit., there-again[st]) give God your heart, in softness, in sweetness, in meekness of every kind, and softest humility — [she must] not, groan and fret now, raise [her] voice afterwards, enrage herself unbecomingly, punctuate her words with gestures, wrench (i.e., turn violently) away, turn [her] shoulder (i.e., shrug her shoulders), toss [her] head, so that God hates her and man scorns her. **733–34 Nai, nai! Ripe wordes . . . to ancre,** No, no! Ripe (i.e., mature) words, ripe behavior and actions belong to (or, are fitting for) an anchoress. **734–35 Hwen wordes beoth eadmodliche . . . riht understonden,** When words are said humbly and fixed in truth, not ill-mannerly or childishly (lit., babyishly), then they have the importance (lit., burden, weight) to be correctly understood. **735–37 Nu is this al i-seid . . . as he wes th'rin i-dervet,** Now all this is said [so] that you may — after (i.e., imitating) Jesus Christ, whom they struck in the mouth and gave gall to drink — guard yourself against the sin of the mouth, and suffer some torture in that sense as He was tortured in it. **738–39 In his eare . . . us for-te learen,** In His ear, He, the heavenly Lord, had all the insult and upbraiding, all the scorn and all the shame that ear may hear, and in order to to teach us He says [the following] about Himself. **739–40 Et factus sum . . . suo redargutiones,** "And I was made as a man not hearing (i.e., a deaf man) and not having insults in his mouth" (Psalm 37:15). **740–42 "Ich heold me . . . missegge,"** "I kept myself" He said, "quiet as a dumb and deaf [person] does who has no

148

him misdo other missegge." This is thi leofmonnes sahe, ant tu, seli ancre, the art his leove spuse, leorne hit yeorne of him thet tu hit cunne ant mahe sothliche seggen.

745 Nu ich habbe i-speken of ower fowre wittes, ant of Godes fowre, hu he thurh hise frovreth ow as ofte as ye in ower feleth eani weane. Nu hercnith of the fifte thet is meast neod elne, for the pine is meast th'rin — thet is, i felunge — ant te licunge alswa, yef hit swa turneth.

The fifte wit is felunge. This ilke an wit is in alle the othre, ant yont al the licome, ant for-thi hit is neod to habben best warde. Ure Laverd wiste hit wel, ant for-thi he walde

750 meast i thet wit tholien, al for-te frovrin us yef we tholieth wa th'rin, ant for-te wenden us frommard te licunge thet flesches lust easketh, nomeliche i felunge mare then in othre.

Ure Laverd i this wit nefde nawt in a stude, ah hefde over al pine, nawt ane yond al his bodi, ah hefde yet in-with in his seli sawle. In hire he felde the stiche of sari sorhe ant

755 sorhful thet dude him sike sare. This stiche wes threo-vald, the ase threo speren smat him to the heorte. The an wes his modres wop ant te othre Maries, the flowen o teares.

answer, though they mistreat (lit., mis-do) or slander (lit., mis-say) Him." **742–43 This is thi leofmonnes sahe . . . seggen,** This is your lover's saying (lit., saw), and you, happy anchoress, who are His beloved bride, learn it eagerly from Him [so] that you know it and can say [it] truly (i.e., by heart). **744–45 Nu ich habbe i-speken . . . eani weane,** Now I have spoken of your four senses, and of God's comfort, how He through His [senses] comforts you as often as you feel in yours any woes (lit., any of woes, *weane* = genitive). **745–47 Nu hercnith . . . yef hit swa turneth,** Now hear about the fifth [sense] which is in greatest need of strength, for the pain is greatest in it — that is, in [the sense of] feeling — and the pleasure too, if it turns [out] that way. **748–49 This ilke an wit . . . to habben best warde,** This same one sense is in all the others, and throughout all the body, and therefore it is need (i.e., there is need) to have best vigilance. **749–52 Ure Laverd wiste hit wel . . . mare then in othre,** Our Lord knew it well, and therefore He wanted to suffer most in that sense, in order to comfort us completely if we suffer pain in it (lit., therein), and in order to turn us away from the pleasure that the desire of the body demands, especially in [the sense of] feeling more than in the others. **753–54 Ure Laverd i this wit . . . his seli sawle,** Our Lord in this sense did not have in one place, but had pain overall (i.e., everywhere), not only throughout all His body, but had [it] even in His blessed soul. **754–56 In hire he felde . . . to the heorte,** In her (i.e., the soul) He felt the sting (compare German *Stich*) of painful and sorrowful sadness that made Him sigh sorely. The sting was threefold, which like three spears smote (or, struck) Him to the heart. **756–59 The an wes his modres wop . . . leafden him as fremede,** The one (or, first) was

149

The other, thet his ahne deore deciples ne lefden him na mare, ne ne heolden for Godd, for-thi thet he ne healp him-seolf in his muchele pine, ant fluhen alle from him ant leafden him as fremede. The thridde wes thet muchele sar ant te of-thunchunge thet he

760   hefde in-with him of hare forlorenesse, the drohen him to deathe, thet he seh onont ham al his swinc forloren thet he swonc on eorthe. Theos ilke threo stichen weren in his sawle. In his licome, euch lim, as Seint Austin seith, tholede sundri pine, ant deide yond al his bodi, as he ear yond al his bodi deathes swat sweatte. Ant her seith Sein Beornard thet "he ne weop nawt ane with ehnen, ah dude as with alle his limen": **Quasi inquit**

765   **membris omnibus flevisse videtur.** For se ful of ango*i*sse wes thet ilke ned-swat thet lihte of his licome ayein the angoisuse death thet he schulde tholien, thet hit thuhte read blod. **Factus est sudor ejus quasi gutte sanguinis decurrentis in terram.** On other half, "swa largeliche, ant swa swithe fleaw thet ilke blodi swat of his blisfule bodi, thet te streames urnen dun to ther eorthe." Swuch grure hefde his monliche flesch ayein the

His mother's weeping and [that of] the other Marys, who flowed in tears. The second [sting was], that His own dear disciples did not believe Him any more, nor did [they] hold [Him] for God, because He did not help Himself in His great pain, and everyone fled from Him and left Him as [one would a] stranger. **759–61 The thridde wes . . . he swonc on eorthe,** The third [sting] was the great pain and the grief that He had within Himself [because] of their perdition (i.e., because they were lost) who put (lit., drew) Him to death, that He saw with respect to them all His labor lost that He labored on earth. **761–63 Theos ilke threo stichen . . . deathes swat sweatte,** These very three stings were in His soul. In His body, each limb, as St. Augustine says, suffered separate pains, and [each limb] throughout His whole body died, and He, before, throughout His whole body sweated death's blood (lit., sweat; compare OE *sāwt* 'blood, fluid'). **763–64 Ant her seith Sein Beornard . . . alle his limen,** And here says St. Bernard that "He did not weep only with His eyes, but did so with all His limbs." **764–65 Quasi inquit . . . videtur,** "It seems," he says, "as if He had wept with all His members" (Bernard, *Sermon for Palm Sunday* 3 [*PL* 183.262]). **765–67 For se ful of angoisse . . . thuhte read blod,** For so full of anguish was that same sweat of distress (lit., distress-sweat) which dropped (lit., lighted) from His body in anticipation of (lit., against) the anguishing death that He would suffer, so that it seemed red blood. **767 Factus est sudor . . . in terram,** "His sweat was made like drops of blood running down into the ground" (Luke 22:44). **767–69 On other half . . . to ther eorthe,** On the other side (i.e., at the same time), "so freely, and so rapidly that some bloody fluid (lit., sweat) flowed from His blissful body, that the streams ran down to the ground" (*ther* = an inflected def. art., fem.). **769–70 Swuch grure hefde . . . hit schulde drehen,** Such horror His manly (or, human) flesh had in anticipation of (lit., against) the

770 derve pinen thet hit schulde drehen. Thet nes na feorlich wunder, for eaver se flesch is cwickre, se the reopunge th'rof ant te hurt is sarre. A lutel hurt i the ehe derveth mare then deth a muchel i the hele, for the flesch is deaddre. Euch monnes flesch is dead flesch — ayein thet wes Godes flesch as thet te wes i-numen of the tendre meiden ant na thing neaver nes th'rin thet hit adeadede, ah eaver wes i-liche cwic of thet cwike

775 Goddhead the wunede th'rinne. For-thi ın his flesch wes the pine sarre, then eaver eani mon in his flesch tholede. Thet his flesch wes cwic over alle flesches — lo, hwuc an essample: A mon for uvel thet he haveth, ne let him nawt blod o the seke halve, ah deth o the hale, to heale the seke. Ah in al the world the wes o the fevre, nes bimong al mon-cun an hal dale i-funden the mahte beon i-lete blod, bute Godes bodi ane the lette him

780 blod o rode, nawt o the earm ane, ah dude o fif halve for-te healen mon-cun of the secnesse thet te fif wittes hefden awakenet. Thus, lo, the hale half ant te cwike dale

torturous pains that it would suffer. **770–71 Thet nes na feorlich wunder . . . te hurt is sarre**, That is no great wonder (lit., strange miracle), for always as the flesh is more alive, so the sensation (i.e., sense of feeling) of it and the pain is more excruciating (lit., sorer). **771–72 A lutel hurt i the ehe . . . is deaddre**, A little wound in the eye tortures more than does a great [one] in the heel, for the flesh [of the heel] is deader. **772–75 Euch monnes flesch . . . th'rinne**, Each man's flesh is dead flesh — against that (i.e., in contrast to that), God's flesh was like that which was taken from the tender maiden (i.e., His mother), and [there] was never anything in it (lit., therein) which deadened it, but always [it] was constantly (lit., alike) alive from (i.e., because of) the living Godhead which dwelled therein. **775–76 For-thi in his flesch . . . tholede**, Therefore in His flesh was the pain sorer (i.e., more excruciating) than ever any man suffered in his flesh. **776–78 Thet his flesch wes cwic . . . the seke**, [To prove] that His flesh was alive above all flesh (lit., over all of flesh) — look what kind of example [follows]: A man because of the evil (i.e., malady) which he has, does]not let blood (i.e., have blood let) [from] himself on the sick side (lit., half), but does so on the healthy (lit., whole) [side], to heal the sick [side]. **778 Ah**, But. **778–81 the wes o the fevre . . . wittes hefden awakenet**, which was on the fever (i.e., had the fever), [there] was not among all mankind one healthy part found [from] which blood might be let, except for God's body alone, who let His own blood (lit., let blood from Himself, dat. of possession) on the Cross, not in the arm alone, but did [so] in five places (lit., sides) in order to heal mankind of the sickness that the five senses had spread (lit., awakened). **781–82 Thus, lo, the hale half . . . swa the seke**, Thus, indeed, the healthy side and the living part drew that evil (or, diseased) blood out away from the unhealthy [part], and thus

droh thet uvele blod ut frommard te unhale, ant healde swa the seke. Thurh blod is in
Hali Writ sunne bitacnet. The reisuns hwi beoth efter sutelliche i-schawet. Ah ther-of
neometh yeme, mine leove sustren, thet ower deore-wurthe spus, the luve-wurthe Laverd,
785   the Healent of heovene, Jesu Godd, Godes sune, the wealdent of al the world, tha he
wes thus i-lete blod, understondeth thet dei hwuch wes his diete. I the ilke blodletunge
se baleful ant se bitter, the ilke thet he bledde fore ne brohten ha him to present ne win,
ne ale, ne weater, yet tha he seide, **sicio,** ant meande as he bledde of thurst o the rode,
ah duden bitter galle. Hwer wes eaver i-yeven to eani blod-leten se povre pitance? Ant
790   tah ne gruchede he nawt, ah underveng hit eadmodliche for-te learen hise. Ant yet he
dude mare us to forbisne, dude his deore muth ther-to ant smahte th'rof, thah he hit
notie ne mahte. Hwa is thenne efter this, ant ancre hure ant hure, the gruccheth yef ha
naveth nawt other mete other drunch efter hire eise? Ant siker hwa-se gruccheth, ha
offreth yet ure Laverd his luthere pitance, as duden tha the Giws, ant is Giwes fere to
795   beoden him in his thurst drunch of sur galle. His thurst nis bute yirnunge of ure sawle

healed the sick [part]. **782–83 Thurh blod is in Hali Writ . . . sutelliche i-schawet,** Sin is
symbolized in Holy Writ through (or, by) blood. The reasons why are after[wards] clearly revealed. **783–86 Ah ther-of neometh yeme . . . hwuch wes his diete,** But pay (lit., take) attention,
my dear sisters, that your precious bridegroom, the loveworthy Lord, the Savior of heaven, Jesus
God, God's son, the wielder of all the world, when He was thus let blood (i.e., had His blood let),
understand that day what His diet was. **786–89 I the ilke blodletunge . . . ah duden bitter galle,**
In the same bloodletting so baleful and bitter, these same [people] that He bled for did not bring
to Him as a offering (i.e., did not offer him) either wine, or ale, or water, even when He said, "I
thirst" (John 19:28) and complained (lit., moaned), as He bled, of thirst on the Cross, then [they]
brought (lit., did) bitter gall. **789 Hwer wes eaver i-yeven . . . povre pitance?** Where was so poor
a pittance (or, ration) ever given to any [one] blood-let (i.e., who has had blood let)? **789–92 Ant
tah ne gruchede he nawt . . . he hit notie ne mahte,** And nevertheless He did not complain, but
received it humbly in order to (lit., for to) teach His [own]. And yet He did [so] more as an example
to us, put (lit., did) His mouth to it and tasted of it (lit., thereof), though He could not make use of
it (or, did not need it). **792–93 Hwa is thenne efter this . . . efter hire eise?** Who is [there] then,
after this, and which anchoress especially (lit., indeed and indeed!) who [dares to] complain if she
does not have anything, either food or drink, according to her liking (lit., ease)? **793–95 Ant
siker hwa-se gruccheth . . . of sur galle,** And surely whosoever complains, she offers again to
our Lord His wretched ration, as the Jews did then, and [she] is the Jews' companion to offer Him
in His thirst a drink of sour gall. **795–97 His thurst nis bute yirnunge . . . wes tha the galle,** His

heale, ant grucchunge of bitter ant of sur heorte is him surre ant bittrure nu then wes tha the galle. Ant tu, his deore spuse, ne beo thu nawt Giwes make for-te birlin him swa, ah ber him feolah-readden, ant drinc with him blitheliche al thet ti flesch thuncheth sur other bitter — thet is, pine ant wone ant alle meoseises — ant he hit wule the yelden as 800 his treowe fere with healewi of heovene.

Thus wes Jesu Crist, the almihti Godd, in alle his fif wittes derfliche i-pinet, ant nomeliche i this leaste — thet is, i felunge, for his flesch wes al cwic as is the tendre ehe. Ant ye witen this wit, thet is, flesches felunge, over alle the othre. Godes honden weren i-neilet o rode. Thurh the ilke neiles ich halsi ow ancres — nawt ow, ah do othre, 805 for hit nis na neod, mine leove sustren — haldeth ower honden in-with ower thurles. Hondlunge other ei felunge bitweone mon ant ancre is thing swa uncumelich, ant dede se scheomelich ant se naket sunne, to al the world se eatelich ant se muche scandle, thet nis na neod to speoken ne writen ther-toyeines, for al withute writunge thet ful is to etscene. Godd hit wat, as me were muche deale leovere thet ich i-sehe ow alle threo, 810 mine leove sustren, wummen me leovest, hongin on a gibet, for-te withbuhe sunne,

thirst is [nothing] but yearning for our soul's salvation (lit., healing), and the complaint of a bitter and sour heart is to Him sourer and bitterer now than the gall was then. **797–800 Ant tu, his deore spuse . . . with healewi of heovene**, And you, His dear spouse, do not be (lit., be thou not) the Jew's mate in order to serve Him a drink in this way, but bear Him fellowship, and drink with Him happily (lit., blithely) everything that seems sour or bitter to your flesh — that is, pain and woes and all discomforts — and He will repay it to you as His true companion with the balm (i.e., healing liquid) of heaven. **801–03 Thus wes Jesu Crist . . . othre**, Thus was Jesus Christ, the almighty God, cruelly pained in all His five senses, and especially in this last [sense] — that is, in feeling — because His flesh was completely alive as is the tender eye. And you, protect (imper.) this sense — that is, the flesh's feeling — over (or, better than) all the others. **804 i-neilet**, nailed. **804–05 Thurh the ilke neiles . . . in-with ower thurles**, Through (or, by) these nails I implore you anchoresses — not you, but [I] do [implore] others, for it is no need (i.e., there is no need), my dear sisters [to implore you] — keep your hands inside your windows. **806–09 Hondlunge other ei felunge . . . thet ful is to etscene**, Holding (or, touching) or any feeling between man and anchoress is a thing so uncomely (i.e., unseemly), and a deed so shameful and so naked a sin, to all the world so horrific and so great a scandal, that [there] is no need to speak or write against it (lit., there-against), for [even] without writing that foulness (or, nastiness) is [all] too evident. **809–11 Godd hit wat . . . swa as ich meane**, God knows it (i.e., God knows!), [it] were (or, would be) to me preferable (*as* not

then ich sehe an of ow yeoven anlepi cos eani mon on eorthe swa as ich meane. Ich am stille of thet mare. Nawt ane monglin honden, ah putten hond ut-ward bute hit beo for nede, is wohunge efter Godes grome ant tollunge of his eorre. Hire-seolf bihalden hire ahne hwite honden deth hearm moni ancre, the haveth ham to feire as theo the beoth 815 for-idlet. Ha schulden schrapien euche dei the eorthe up of hare put thet ha schu*l*en rotien in. Godd hit wat, thet put deth muche god moni ancre. For as Salomon seith, **Memorare novissima tua et in eternum non peccabis**. Theo the haveth eaver hire death as bivoren hire ehnen thet te put munegeth, yef thet ha thencheth wel o the dom of Domes-dei, ther the engles schule cwakien, ant te eche ant te eateliche pinen of helle, 820 ant over al ant al o Jesu Cristes passiun, hu he wes i-pinet — as is sum-deal i-seid — in alle his fif wittes, lihtliche nule ha nawt folhi flesches licunge efter willes lust, ne drahen in toward hire nan heaved sunne with hire fif wittes. This is nu inoh i-seid of the fif

translated) that I see you all three, my dear sisters, women to me most dear, hung on a gibbet, to escape (lit., bow away from) sin, than [that] I might see one of you give a single kiss to any man on earth so as (i.e., in the way) I mean. **811–12 Ich am stille of thet mare**, I am silent about any more. **812–13 Nawt ane monglin honden . . . of his eorre**, Not only to intertwine (i.e., hold or touch) hands, but to put the hand outward, unless it be for necessity, is wooing of God's fury and courting of His ire (or, anger). **813–15 Hire-seolf bihalden hire ahne . . . the beoth for-idlet**, For herself to behold (i.e., look at) her own white hands does harm to many an anchoress, who has (or, keeps) them too fair, as those [hands] which are ruined by idleness (lit., idled away; i.e., lack of activity). **815–16 Ha schulden schrapien . . . rotien in**, They (i.e., the hands) should scrape each day the earth up from their grave (lit., pit) that they will rot in. **816 Godd hit wat . . . moni ancre**, God knows, the grave does much good for many an anchoress. **817 *Memorare novissima . . . peccabis***, "Remember your last [end] in eternity (i.e., your death) and you will not sin" (Ecclesiasticus 7:40). **817–22 Theo the haveth eaver . . . with hire fif wittes**, She who always has her death, which the pit reminds of, before her eyes, if she thinks well on the judgment of Judgment Day (lit., doom of Doomsday), where the angels will quake, and [on] the eternal and the horrible pains of hell, and over all and [above] all on Jesus Christ's passion, how He was tortured — as has been discussed a great deal (lit., as is said some deal) — in all His five senses, she will not lightly follow the pleasure of the flesh after the desire of [her] will, nor [will she] draw in towards her (i.e., embrace) any deadly sin with her five senses. **822–23 This is nu inoh i-seid . . . sawle lif is inne**, This is now enough said of the five senses, which are as an external guard (lit., warden) of the heart, in

154

wittes, the beoth ase wardein withuten of the heorte, thet sawle lif is inne. As we seiden th'ruppe on earst thet Salomon seide, **Omni custodia custodi cor tuum quoniam ex ipso vita procedit**. Nu beoth, Crist have thonc, the twa dalen overcumen. Ga we nu with his help up-o *the* thridde.

825

which the life of the soul is. **823–24 As we seiden th'ruppe . . . Salomon seide**, As we said above (i.e., earlier in this book — see 2.2–4) at first what Salomon said. **824–25 *Omni custodia custodi . . . ex ipso vita procedit***, "With all watchfulness preserve your heart, for from it life comes forth" (Proverbs 4:23). **825–26 Nu beoth . . . up-o the thridde**, Now are, Christ have thanks, two parts (i.e., books) gotten through (or, accomplished). Let us go (lit., go we) now with His help into the third.

Part Three

Lessons from Nature

Mine leove sustren, alswa as ye witeth wel ower wittes ute-with, alswa over alle thing lokith thet ye beon in-with softe ant milde ant eadmode, swete ant swote i-heortet ant tholemode ayein woh of word thet me seith ow, ant werc thet me misdeth ow, leste ye al leosen. Ayein bittre ancres Davith seith this vers: **Similis factus sum pellicano solitudinis, et cetera**. "Ich am," he seith, "as pellican the wuneth bi him ane." Pellican is a fuhel se wea-mod ant se wreathful thet hit sleath ofte o grome his ahne briddes hwen ha doth him teone, ant thenne sone th'refter hit wurth swithe sari, ant maketh swithe muche man, ant smit him-seolf with his bile thet he sloh ear his briddes with, ant draheth blod of his breoste, ant with thet blod acwiketh eft his briddes i-sleine. This fuhel, pellican, is the wea-mode ancre. Hire briddes beoth hire gode werkes

5

10

1–4 **Mine leove sustren . . . leste ye al leosen**, My dear sisters, just as you protect well your senses on the outside, also above all things see (lit., look) that you be inside soft and mild and humble, sweet and sweetly hearted, and patient against injury of words which people (lit., one) say to you, and deeds which they perpetrate (lit., misdo) on you, lest you lose everything (lit., all). 4 **Ayein bittre ancres**, Against bitter anchoresses. 4– 5 *Similis factus sum pellicano . . . et cetera*, "I am made (or, have become) like a pelican of the wasteland," etc. (Psalm 101:7). 5–6 **"Ich am . . . bi him ane**," "I am," he says, "as a pelican which lives by itself alone." 6–10 **Pellican is a fuhel . . . his briddes i-sleine**, The pelican is a bird (lit., fowl) so petulant (lit., malice-minded) and so wrathful that it slays often in anger its own chicks (lit., birds) when they do it some harm, and then soon thereafter it becomes very sorry and makes a very great moan (or, complaint), and smites itself with its bill that it slew earlier its chicks with, and draws blood from its breast, and with that blood brings to life (or, revives) again its slain chicks. 10–11 **This fuhel, pellican . . . of scharp wreththe**, This bird, the pelican, is the petulant anchoress. Her chicks (lit., birds) are her good works which she slays often with the bill of sharp wrath

156

thet ha sleath ofte with bile of scharp wreththe. Ah hwen ha swa haveth i-don, do as deth the pellican: ofthunche hit swithe sone, ant with hire ahne bile beaki hire breoste — thet is, with schrift of hire muth, thet ha sunegede with ant sloh hire gode werkes — drahe thet blod of sunne ut of hire breoste — thet is, of the heorte thet sawle lif is inne

15 — ant swa schulen eft acwikien hire i-sleine briddes, thet beoth hire gode werkes. Blod bitacneth sunne, for alswa as a mon bibled is grislich ant eatelich i monnes ehe, alswa is the sunfule bivore Godes ehe. On other half, na-mon ne mei juggi wel blod ear hit beo i-colet. Alswa is of sunne. Hwil the heorte walleth in-with of wreaththe nis ther na riht dom, other hwil the lust is hat toward eani sunne, ne maht tu nawt te hwiles deme wel

20 hwet hit is, ne hwet ter wule cumen of. Ah let lust overgan, ant hit te wule likin. Let thet hate acolin as deth the wule iuggi blod, ant tu schalt demen ariht the sunne ful ant ladlich thet te thuhte feier, ant uvel se muchel cumen th'rof, yef thu hit hefdest i-don hwil thet hate leaste, thet tu schalt deme wod te-seolf tha thu ther-toward thohtest. This is of

(or, anger). **11–15 Ah hwen ha swa haveth i-don . . . beoth hire gode werkes**, But when she has done so, [let her] do as does the pelican: regret it very soon, and with her own bill [let her] peck her breast — that is, with confession of her mouth, which she sinned with and slew her good works — draw the blood of sin out of her breast — that is, from the heart which the soul's life is in — and thus will [she] again bring to life (lit., quicken) her slain chicks, which are her good works. **15–17 Blod bitacneth sunne . . . bivore Godes ehe**, Blood symbolizes sin, for just as a bloody (lit., beblooded) man is grisly and horrific in man's eye, just so is the sinful [person] before God's eye. **17–18 On other half . . . of sunne**, On the other side (i.e., at the same time), no one can judge (or, diagnose) blood well before it be cooled. Just [so it] is with sin. **18–20 Hwil the heorte walleth . . . wule cumen of**, While (or, as long as) the heart wells (or, surges) inwardly with wrath there is no right judgment, or while the desire is hot toward any sin, you cannot judge well for a while (lit., whiles) what it is, or what will come of that (lit., thereof ; *ter* = reduced form of *ther* after preceding -*t*). **20 Ah let lust overgan . . . wule likin**, But let desire pass over (lit., go over, i.e., subside), and it will please you (i.e., you will be pleased). **20–23 Let thet hate acolin . . . ther-toward thohtest**, Let the heat cool as does [the person] who wants to judge (or, diagnose) blood, and you will judge rightly the sin [to be] foul and loathsome which seemed to you fair, and [you will judge] so much evil to come from that (lit., thereof), if you had done it while the heat lasted, that you will judge yourself [to have been] mad (i.e., insane) when you thought about it (lit., there-toward). **23–24 This is of euch sunne . . . nomeliche of wreaththe**, This is true for each sin — why blood

euch sunne soth — hwi blod hit bitacneth — ant nomeliche of wreaththe. **Impedit ira**
animum ne possit cernere verum. "Wreaththe," hit seith, "hwil hit least, ablindeth
swa the heorte thet ha ne mei soth i-cnawen." **Maga quedam est transformans**
naturam humanam. Wreaththe is a forschuppilt, as me teleth i spelles, for ha reaveth
mon his wit ant changeth al his chere, ant forschuppeth him from mon into beastes
cunde. Wummon wrath is wulvene; mon, wulf other liun other unicorne. Hwil thet
eaver wreaththe is i wummone heorte, versaili, segge hire ures, **Avez**, **Paternostres**, ne
deth ha bute theoteth. Naveth ha bute — as theo thet is i-went to wulvene i Godes ehnen
— wulvene stevene in his lihte earen. **Ira furor brevis est**. Wreaththe is a wodschipe.
Wrath mon — nis he wod? Hu loketh he? Hu speketh he? Hu feareth his heorte in-with?
Hwucche beoth ute-with alle hise lates? He ne cnaweth na-mon. Hu is he mon thenne?
Est enim homo animal mansuetum natura. "Mon cundelich is milde." Sone se he

symbolizes it — and namely (or, particularly) for wrath. **24–25** *Impedit ira animum . . . cernere*
verum, "Wrath impedes the spirit so that it cannot discern truth" (*Distichs of Cato* 2.4). **25–26**
"hwil hit least . . . soth i-cnawen," "as long as it lasts (*least* = reduced form of *leasteth*) blinds the
heart so that she (i.e., the heart) cannot know truth." **26–27** *Maga quedam est . . . naturam*
humanam, "She is a kind of sorceress transforming human nature" (source unidentified). **27–29**
Wreaththe is a forschuppilt . . . into beastes cunde (a loose translation of the Latin), Wrath is an
enchanter (lit., transformer or misshaper), as they (lit., one) tell in tales, for she robs man [of] his
wit and completely changes his expression (i.e., deforms his face, which is contorted in anger),
and transforms him from a man into a kind of beast. **29 Wummon wrath . . . liun other unicorne**,
A woman, angry, is a she-wolf; man, a wolf or lion or unicorn. **29–31 Hwil thet eaver wreaththe**
. . . ne deth ha bute theoteth, As long as (lit., while that ever) wrath is in a woman's heart, [if she]
recites the divine office (lit., verses), says her [canonical] hours, "Aves," "Our Fathers," she does
[nothing] but howl. **31–32 Naveth ha bute . . . in his lihte earen**, She does not have [anything] but
a she-wolf's voice — as she who is changed into a she-wolf in God's eyes — in His quick (i.e.,
discerning) ears. **32** *Ira furor brevis est*, "Wrath is a brief madness (or, temporary insanity)"
(Horace, *Epistles* 1.2.62, but proverbial). **32–34 Wreaththe is a wodschipe . . . Hu is he mon**
thenne? Wrath is insanity. A wrathful man — is he not insane? How does he look? How does he
speak? How does his heart fare within? Which (i.e., what) are his expressions (or, behaviors) on
the outside? He does not know anyone. How is he a man then? **35** *Est enim homo . . . natura*,
"For man is an animal gentle by nature" (Alexander Neckham, *On the Natures of Things* 156);
"Mon cundelich is milde," Man is naturally mild. **35–37 Sone se he leoseth . . . as ich ear seide**,
[As] soon as he loses mildheartedness, he loses man's nature, and wrath, the enchanter (or,

leoseth mildheortnesse, he leoseth monnes cunde, ant wreaththe, the forschuppilt, forschuppeth him into beast, as ich ear seide. Ant hwet yef eni ancre, Jesu Cristes spuse, is forschuppet into wulvene? Nis thet muche sorhe? Nis ther bute sone forwarpe thet ruhe fel abute the heorte, ant with softe sahtnesse makien hire smethe ant softe, as

40 is cundeliche wummone hude, for with thet wulvene fel na thing thet ha deth nis Gode lic-wurthe.

Lo, her, ayeines wreaththe, monie remedies, frovren a muche floc ant misliche boten. Yef me misseith the, thench thet tu art eorthe. Ne totret me eorthe? Ne bispit me eorthe? Thah me dude swa bi the, me dude the eorthe rihte. Yef thu berkest ayein, thu art

45 hundes cunnes. Yef thu stingest ayein, thu art neddre cundel, ant nawt Cristes spuse. Thench — dude he swa? **Qui tanquam ovis ad occisionem ductus est et non aperuit os suum**. Efter alle the schendfule pinen thet he tholede o the longe Fri-niht, me leadde him ine marhen to hongin o weari-treo, ant driven thurh his fowr limen irnene neiles, ah "na mare then a schep," as the Hali Writ seith, "cwich ne cweth he neaver."

transformer), transforms him into a beast, as I said before. **37–38 Ant hwet yef eni ancre . . . Nis thet muche sorhe?** And what if any anchoress, Jesus Christ's spouse, is transformed into a she-wolf? Is that not a great sorrow? **38–41 Nis ther bute sone . . . nis Gode lic-wurthe**, There is not [any remedy] except [she] soon shed that rough hide about the heart, and with soft peace (or, reconciliation) make her (i.e., the heart) smooth and soft as is natural to woman's skin, for with that wolfish hide nothing that she does is pleasing (lit., like-worthy) to God. **42 Lo, her, ayeines . . . misliche boten**, Lo, here, against wrath, [are] many remedies, a great flock of comforts and various remedies. **43 Yef me misseith the . . . bispit me eorthe?** If one slanders (lit., missays) you, think (imper.) that you are [made of] earth. Does not one trample the earth? Does not one spit upon the earth? **44 Thah me dude swa bi the . . . the eorthe rihte**, Even though people did so by you (i.e., mistreated you in this way), they have done the earth right (i.e., have done the right thing to [something made of] earth). **44–46 Yef thu berkest ayein . . . dude he swa?** If you bark back, you are of a dog's nature. If you sting back, you are a serpent's offspring, and not Christ's spouse. Think — did He do so? **46–47 *Qui tanquam ovis . . . non aperuit os suum***, "Who was just like a lamb which is led to the slaughter and did not open his mouth" (Isaiah 53:7, Acts 8:32). **47–49 Efter alle the schendfule pinen . . . ne cweth he neaver**, After all the shameful pains that He suffered in the long night of good Friday (see glossary), they (lit., one) led Him in the morning to hang [Him] on a gallows (lit., punishment-tree), and drove through His four limbs iron nails, but "no more than a sheep," as Holy Writ says, "did He ever flinch or speak."

50   Thench yet, on other half, hwet is word bute wind? To wac ha is i-strengthet thet a
windes puf, a word, mei afellen ant warpen into sunne, ant hwa nule thunche wunder of
ancre wind-feallet? On other half yetten, ne schaweth ha thet ha is dust ant unstable
thing, the with a lute wordes wind is anan toblawen? The ilke puf of his muth, yef thu
hit wurpe under the, hit schulde beore the uppart toward te blisse of heovene, ah nu is
55   muche wunder of ure muchele meadschipe. Understondeth this word. Seint Andrew
mahte tholien thet te hearde rode heve him toward heovene, ant luveliche biclupte hire.
Sein Lorenz alswa tholede thet te gridil heve him uppardes with bearninde gleden. Seinte
Stefne th*olede th*e stanes thet me sende him ant underveng ham gleadliche ant bed for
ham the ham senden him, with hommen i-falden — ant we ne mahe nawt tholien thet te
60   wind of a word beore us towart heovene, ah beoth wode ayeines ham the we schulden
thonkin as the ilke the servith us of muche servise, thah hit beo hare unthonkes. **Impius
vivit pio velit nolit.** Al thet te unwreaste ant te uvele deth for uvel, al is the gode to god:

50 Thench yet . . . bute wind? Think still, on the other side (i.e., at the same time), what is a word
but wind? **50–52 To wac ha is . . . ancre wind-feallet?** Too weak she is fortified (lit., strengthened)
that a wind's puff, a word, may fell [her] and throw [her] into sin, and who will not think [that]
strange (i.e., be astonished) at an anchoress wind-felled (i.e., felled by a wind)? **52–53 On other
half yetten . . . is anan toblawen?** On the other side (i.e., at the same time) again, does she not show
that she is dust and an unstable thing, who with a little word's wind is immediately blown over?
53–55 The ilke puf . . . ure muchele meadschipe, The same puff of His mouth, if you cast it under
you, it should (i.e., ought to) bear you upwards toward the bliss of heaven, but now [there] is
great wonder (i.e., astonishment) about your great foolishness. **55–56 Seint Andrew mahte
tholien . . . biclupte hire,** St. Andrew was able to endure that the hard cross [should] heave (or,
lift) him toward heaven, and lovingly embraced her (i.e., the cross). **57 Sein Lorenz alswa tholede
. . . bearninde gleden,** St. Laurence also endured that the griddle [should] lift him upwards with
burning flames. **57–61 Seinte Stefne tholede . . . thah hit beo hare unthonkes,** St. Stephen
endured the stones which they (lit., one) threw at him and received them gladly and prayed for
them who threw them at him, on bent (lit., folded) knees — and we cannot endure that the wind
of a word bear us toward heaven, but are mad (or, insane) against them who[m] we should thank
as the very ones (lit., same) who serve us with much service, though it be unintentional on their
part (see glossary, *un-thonckes*). **61–62 *Impius vivit pio velit nolit*,** "The evil person lives [for
the benefit of] the pious, whether he wants to or not (lit., will he, will he not)" (Gregory, *Moral
Discourses on Job* 5.45.79 [*PL* 76.168–69). **62–63 Al thet te unwreaste . . . timbrunge toward
blisse,** All that the wicked and the evil do because of evil, all is to the good (i.e., profit) of the

al is his biheve ant timbrunge toward blisse. Let him — ant thet gleadliche! — breide thi crune. Thench hu the hali mon i **Vitas Patrum** custe ant blescede the othres hond the

65   hefde him i-hearmet, ant seide se inwardliche cussinde hire yeorne, "i-blescet beo eaver theos hond, for ha haveth i-timbret me the blissen of heovene." Ant tu segge alswa bi hond the misdeth the, ant bi the muth alswa the ewt misseith the, "i-blescet beo thi muth" — sei, "for thu makest lome th'rof to timbri mi crune. Wel me is for mi god ant wa thah for thin uvel, for thu dest me freame ant hearmest te-seolven." Yef ei mon

70   other wummon misseide other misdude ow, mine leove sustren, swa ye schulden seggen. Ah nu is muche wunder, yef we wel bihaldeth, hu Godes halhen tholeden wunden on hare bodi, ant we beoth wode yef a wind blawe a lutel toward us! Ant te wind ne wundeth nawt bute the eir ane, for nowther ne mei the wind — thet is, thet word thet me seith — ne wundi the i thi flesch, ne fule thi sawle, thah hit puffe up-o the, bute the-

75   seolf hit makie. **Bernardus: Quid irritaris quid inflammaris ad verbi flatum, qui**

good: all is his advantage and edification toward bliss (i.e., happiness). **63–64 Let him . . . breide thi crune**, Let him (i.e., the evil person) — and that gladly (i.e., and be glad about it)! — weave (lit., braid) your crown. **64–66 Thench hu the hali mon . . . the blissen of heovene**, Think how the holy man in *The Lives of the [Desert] Fathers* kissed and blessed the other's hand who had harmed him, and [he] said on the inside (or, to himself) kissing her (i.e., it, the hand) eagerly, thus: "blessed be this hand always, for she has built for me the joys of heaven." **66–68 Ant tu segge . . . to timbri mi crune**, And you [ought to] say also concerning the hand which mistreats (lit., misdoes) you, and about the mouth also which slanders (lit., missays) you at all, "blessed be your mouth," — say (imper.), "for you make (i.e., are making) a tool of it (i.e., the mouth), to construct my crown." **68–69 Wel me is . . . hearmest te-seolven**, "Well is me (i.e., I am happy) for my good, but woe [is me] (i.e., I am sad) however for your evil, for you do me benefit and harm yourself." **69–70 Yef ei mon other wummon . . . ye schulden seggen**, If any man or woman slandered or mistreated you, my dear sisters, so you ought to say. **71–72 Ah nu is muche wunder . . . a lutel toward us!** But now [it] is a great wonder, if we behold well (i.e., if we look at it rightly), how God's saints (lit., holy [ones]) endured wounds on their bodies, and we are insane (or, mad) if a wind blow[s] a little toward us! **72–75 Ant te wind ne wundeth . . . bute the-seolf hit makie**, And the wind does not wound [anything] but the air alone, for neither can (lit., may) the wind — that is, the word which one says — either wound you in your flesh, nor contaminate (lit., befoul) your soul, though it puff upon you, unless [you] yourself make it. **75–76 *Bernardus: Quid irritaris . . . nec inquinat mentem?*** Bernard: "Why are you irritated, why are you inflamed at the gust of a word, which neither harms the flesh nor stains the mind?" (from Geoffrey of

nec carnem vulnerat, nec inquinat mentem? Wel thu maht underyeoten thet ter wes lute fur of chearite, thet leiteth al of ure Laverdes luve, lute fur wes ther thet a puf acwencte, for thear as muche fur is, hit waxeth with winde.

Ayein mis-dede other mis-sahe, lo her on ende the beste remedie — ant cunneth this 80 essample. A mon the leie i prisun other ahte muche rancun ne o nane wise ne schulde ut, bute hit were to hongin, ear he hefde his rancun fulleliche i-paiet — nalde he cunne god thonc a mon the duste uppon him of peonehes a bigurdel for-te reimin him with ant lesen him of pine, thah he wurpe hit ful hearde ayeines his heorte? Al the hurd were foryeten for the gleadnesse. O this ilke wise we beoth alle i prisun her, ant ahen Godd 85 greate deattes of sunne; for-thi we yeiyeth to him i the **Paternoster**: **et dimitte nobis debita nostra**. "Laverd," we seggeth, "foryef us ure deattes, alswa as we foryeoveth ure deatturs," woh thet me deth us, other of word other of werc. Thet is ure rancun thet we schule reimin us with ant cwitin ure deattes toward ure Laverd — thet beoth ure sunnen. For withute cwitance up of this prisun nis nan i-numen thet nis anan ahonget,

Auxerre, *Declamations on the Debate between Simon and Jesus from the Collected Sermons of St. Bernard* 36.43 [*PL* 184.461]). **76–78 Wel thu maht underyeoten . . . hit waxeth with winde**, Well you can perceive that there was [only a] little fire of charity (or, love), which blazes completely (lit., all) with our Lord's love, little fire was there that a [mere] puff quenched [it], for where there is a great fire, it grows with the wind (i.e., you ought to see that if your little fire of love can be puffed out with a word, there was not much fire there to begin with). **79–80 Ayein mis-dede other mis-sahe . . . essample**, Against misdeed or missaying (i.e., slander), lo here in the end [is] the best remedy — and learn this example. **80–83 A mon the leie i prisun . . . ayeines his heorte?** A man who lay in prison or owed a great ransom, nor in any way would he [come, get] out, unless it were to hang, before he had fully paid his ransom — would he not be grateful to a man (lit., know thanks to a man) who threw at him a purse of pennies to ransom himself with and release himself from pain, [even] though he threw it very hard against his heart? All the hurt were (i.e., would be) forgotten for the gladness. **84–87 O this ilke wise we beoth . . . of word other of werc**, In this same way, we are all in prison here, and owe God great debts of sin, therefore we cry to him in the "Our Father": "and forgive us our debts" (Matthew 6:12). "Lord," we say, "forgive us our debts, just as we forgive our debtors," [just as we forgive] wrong that people do to us, either by word or by work (i.e., deed). **87–89 Thet is ure rancun . . . thet beoth ure sunnen**, That is our ransom that we will ransom ourselves with and pay our debts toward our Lord — which are our sins. **89–90 For withute cwitance . . . the pine of helle**, For without payment none is taken up (i.e., out) from this prison who is not immediately hanged, either in purgatory or

90   other i purgatoire other i the pine of helle. Ant ure Laverd seolf seith, **dimittite et dimittetur vobis**. "Foryef, ant ich foryeove the," as thah he seide, "thu art endeattet toward me swithe with sunnen, ah wult tu god foreward? Al thet eaver ei mon misseith the other misdeth the, ich wulle neomen on-ward the deatte the thu ahest me." Nu thenne, thah a word culle the ful hearde up-o the breoste ant, as the thuncheth, on earst

95   hurte thin heorte, thench as the prisun walde the the other hurte sare with the bigurdel, ant underveng hit gleadliche for-te acwiti the with, ant thonke the the the hit sent te, thah Godd ne cunne him neaver thonc of his sonde. He hearmeth him ant freameth the, yef thu hit const tholien. For as Davith seith swithe wel with alle, "Godd deth in his tresor the unwreaste ant te uvele, for-te hure with ham as me deth with gersum theo the wel

100   fehteth." **Ponens in thesauris abyssos. Glosa: crudeles quibus donat milites suos**.

    Eft upon other half, pellican, this fuhel, haveth an-other cunde, thet hit is aa leane. For-thi, as ich seide, Davith eveneth him ther-to in ancre persone, in ancre stevene: **Similis factus sum pellicano solitudinis**. "Ich am pellican i-lich, the wuneth bi him

in the pain of hell. **90–91 Ant ure Laverd seolf . . . *dimittetur vobis*,** And our Lord Himself says, "forgive and [it] will be forgiven you" (Luke 6:37). **91–93 "Foryef, ant ich foryeove the . . . deatte the thu ahest me,"** "Forgive, and I forgive you," as if (lit., though) He said, "you are indebted to me greatly for sins, but do you want a good agreement (i.e., deal)? Everything that ever any man says against you (lit., missays) or does against you (lit., misdoes) — I will accept it toward the debt which you owe Me." **93–97 Nu thenne, thah a word . . . thonc of his sonde,** Now then, though a word strike you very hard upon the breast and, as [it] seems to you, at first hurt your heart, think as the prisoner would whom the other hurt sorely with the purse, and receive it gladly in order to (lit., for to) acquit yourself with, and thank him who sent it to you, though God will never give him thanks for his message (lit., sending; i.e., giving you the blow). **97–98 He hearmeth him . . . const tholien,** He harms himself and strengthens you, if you can endure it. **98–100 For as Davith seith . . . the wel fehteth,** For as David says exceedingly well moreover (lit., withal), "God puts (lit., does) the wicked and the evil in His treasury in order to (lit., for to) hire with them, as one does with treasure (i.e., money), those who fight well. **100 *Ponens in thesauris abyssos . . . milites suos*,** "Putting (i.e., He puts) the depths in His treasury" (Psalm 32:7). Gloss: "the cruel ones, with which He pays His soldiers." **101–02 Eft upon other half . . . in ancre stevene,** Again on the other side (i.e., at the same time), a pelican, this bird, has another characteristic (lit., nature), that it is always lean. Therefore, as I said, David compares himself to it (lit., thereto) in the persona of anchoress, in an anchoress' voice. **103 *Similis factus . . . solitudinis*,** (see gloss to 3.4–5). **103–04 Ich am pellican i-lich . . . hit is leane,** "I am like the pelican which lives by itself alone."

ane." Ant ancre ah thus to seggen, ant beon i-lich pellican onond thet hit is leane. **Judith**
105 **clausa in cubiculo jejunabat omnibus diebus vite sue, et cetera**. Judith bitund inne,
as hit teleth in hire boc, leadde swithe heard lif — feaste ant werede here. Judith bitund
inne bitacneth bitund ancre the ah to leaden heard lif as dude the leafdi Judith, efter hire
evene — nawt ase swin i-pund i sti to feattin ant to greatin ayein the cul of the axe.

Twa cunnes ancren beoth thet ure Laverd speketh of ant seith i the Godspel: of false
110 ant of treowe. **Vulpes foveas habent et volucres celi nidos**. Thet is, "foxes habbeth
hare holen ant briddes of heovene habbeth hare nestes." The foxes beoth false ancres,
ase fox is beast falsest. Theose habbeth, he seith, holen the holieth in-ward eorthe with
eorthliche untheawes ant draheth into hare hole al thet ha mahen reopen ant rinnen.
Thus beoth gederinde ancres of Godd i the Godspel to voxes i-evenet. Fox ec is a frech
115 beast ant freote-wil mid alle, ant te false ancre draheth into hire hole ant fret, ase fox
deth, bathe ges ant hennen. Habbeth efter the vox a simple semblant sum-chearre, ant
beoth thah ful of gile. Makieth ham othre then ha beoth, ase vox, the is ypocrite. Weneth

And an anchoress ought to say thus (i.e., like this) and be like the pelican in the sense that it is lean. **104–05** *Judith clausa in cubiculo . . . vite sue, et cetera*, "Judith enclosed in [her] cell fasted every day of her life," etc. (condensed from Judith 8:5–6). **105–06 Judith bitund inne . . . werede here**, Judith enclosed inside, as it tells in her book, led a very hard life — fasted and wore a hair[shirt]. **106–08 Judith bitund inne bitacneth . . . cul of the axe**, Judith enclosed inside symbolizes the enclosed anchoress who ought to lead a hard life as did the lady Judith, according to [her] capacity (or, character) — not as pigs penned up in a sty, to fatten and to enlarge [them] against (i.e., in preparation for) the blow of the axe. **109–10 Twa cunnes ancren beoth . . . false ant of treowe**, There are two kinds of anchoresses that our Lord speaks of and talks [about] in the Gospel: of false and of true. **110** *Vulpes foveas . . . celi nidos*, "Foxes have [their] lairs and birds of the heaven [have their] nests" (Luke 9:58, Matthew 8:20). **111 hare holen**, their holes. **112–13 Theose habbeth . . . reopen ant rinnen**, These have, he says, holes who burrow into the earth with earthly vices (lit., unvirtues) and drag into their holes all that they may steal and seize. **114 Thus beoth gederinde ancres . . . to voxes i-evenet**, Thus are gathering (i.e., grasping) anchoresses compared by God in the Gospel to foxes. **114–16 Fox ec is a frech beast . . . bathe ges ant hennen**, A fox also is an impudent (compare German *frech* "rude") beast and ravenous (lit., desiring to gobble) besides (lit., withal), and the false anchoress drags into her hole and gobbles up, as the fox does, both geese and hens. **116–17 Habbeth efter the vox . . . the is ypocrite**, [False anchoresses] have after (i.e., in imitation of) the fox an innocent (lit., simple) expression (or, appearance) sometimes, and are nevertheless full of guile. [They] make themselves other than they are, as a fox, who is a hypocrite. **117–18 Weneth for-te gili Godd . . .**

for-te gili Godd as ha bidweolieth simple men, ant gilith meast ham-seolven. Gealstrith as the vox deth, ant yelpeth of hare god hwer-se ha durren ant mahen, chafflith of idel, ant se swithe worltliche i-wurtheth thet on ende hare nome stinketh as fox ther he geath forth. For yef ha doth uvele, me seith bi ham wurse.

120

Theos eoden into ancre-hus as dude Saul into hole, nawt as Davith the gode. Ba ha wenden into hole, Saul ant Davith, as hit teleth i Regum, ah Saul wende thider in for-te don his fulthe th'rin, as deth bimong monie sum unseli ancre—went into hole of ancre-hus to bifule thet stude, ant don dearnluker th'rin fleschliche fulthen then ha mahten yef ha weren amidde the worlde. For hwa haveth mare eise to don hire cweadschipes then the false ancre? Thus wende Saul into hole to bidon thet stude, ah Davith wende thider in, ane for-te huden him from Saul thet him heatede ant sohte to sleanne. Swa deth the gode ancre, the Saul — thet is, the feond — heateth ant hunteth efter. Ha deth hire in to huden hire from hise kene clokes. Ha hud hire in hire hole, ba from worltliche men ant

125

130

gilith meast ham-seolven, They expect to beguile (i.e., trick, fool) God as they confuse (or, lead into error) simple (or, honest) men, and (i.e., but) mostly beguile themselves. **118–21 Gealstrith as the vox deth . . . ther he geath forth,** [They] bark (or, howl) as the fox does, and boast about their good (i.e., advantages) wheresoever they dare and can, chatter about idle (i.e., trivial) [things], and become so very worldly that in the end their reputation (lit., name) stinks as the fox where he goes forth (i.e., wherever he goes about). **121–22 For yef ha doth uvele . . . Davith the gode,** For if they do evil, they (lit., one) say worse about them. These went into the anchor-house as did Saul into the hole, not as David the good. **122–26 Ba ha wenden into hole . . . ha weren amidde the worlde,** They both, Saul and David, went (lit., wended, turned) into a hole, as it tells in Kings, but Saul went in there (lit., thither) in order to do (or, put) his filth in there (i.e., relieve himself), as does some miserable anchoress among many [good anchoresses] — goes into the hole of the anchor-house to befoul that place, and to do (i.e., perform) more secretly in there (lit., therein) fleshly filths than she might if she were amidst the world. **126–27 For hwa haveth mare . . . false ancre?** For who has more leisure (lit., ease) to do her wickedness than the false anchoress? **127–28 Thus wende Saul . . . sohte to sleanne,** Thus Saul made his way (lit., wended) into the hole to befoul (i.e., relieve) himself, but David went in there (lit., thither), only in order to hide himself from Saul who hated [him] and sought to slay [him]. **128–30 Swa deth the gode . . . from hise kene clokes,** So does the good anchoress, whom Saul — that is, the devil (lit., fiend, enemy) — hates and hunts after. She puts herself in [the hole] to hide herself from his sharp clutches. **130–33 Ha hud hire in hire hole . . . Ebreische ledene,** She hides (*hud* = reduced form of *hudeth*) herself in her hole,

worltliche sunnen. Ant for-thi ha is gasteliche Davith — thet is, strong toyein the feond — ant hire leor lufsum to ure Laverdes ehnen — for swa muchel seith this word "Davith" on Ebreische ledene. The false ancre is "Saul," efter thet his nome seith. **Saul: abutens sive abusio.** For Saul on Ebreisch is "mis-notunge" on Englisch, ant te false

135 ancre mis-noteth ancre nome ant al thet ha wurcheth. The gode ancre is Judith, as we ear seiden, thet is, bitund as heo wes, ant alswa as heo dude, feasteth, waketh, swinketh ant wereth hearde. Ha is of the briddes thet ure Laverd speketh of efter the voxes, the with hare lustes ne holieth nawt dune-ward ase doth the voxes — thet beoth false ancres — ah habbeth on heh ase brid of heovene i-set hare nestes — thet is, hare reste.

140 Treowe ancres beoth briddes i-cleopede, for ha leaveth the eorthe—thet is, the luve of alle worltliche thinges — ant thurh yirnunge of heorte to heovenliche thinges fleoth uppart toward heovene. Ant tah ha fleon hehe with heh lif ant hali, haldeth thah the heaved lah thurh milde eadmodnesse, as brid fleonninde buheth thet heaved, leoteth al noht wurth thet ha wel wurcheth, ant seggeth as ure Laverd learde alle hise: **Cum**

both from worldly men and worldly sins. And therefore she is spiritually David — that is, strong against the devil (lit., fiend, enemy) — and her face [is] lovely to our Lord's eyes — for as much says (i.e., means) this word "David" in the Hebrew language. **133 efter thet his nome seith**, according to what his name says (i.e., means). **133–34 *Saul: abutens sive abusio***, "Saul: misusing or abuse." **134–35 For Saul on Ebreisch ... al thet ha wurcheth**, For Saul in Hebrew is (i.e., means) "misuse" in English, and the false anchoress misuses the name of anchoress and everything that she does (lit., works). **135–37 as we ear seiden ... ant wereth hearde**, as we said earlier, that is, enclosed as she was, and does also as she did: fasts, holds vigils (lit., wakes), works and wears a hair[shirt]. **137–39 Ha is of the briddes ... thet is, hare reste**, She is among the birds which our Lord speaks of after the foxes, who with their desires do not burrow (lit., hole) downward as do the foxes — those are the false anchoresses — but [they] have set their nests — that is, their rest — on high (i.e., up high) like a bird of heaven. **140–42 Treowe ancres beoth ... uppart toward heovene**, True anchoresses are called birds, for they leave the earth (or, ground) — that is, the love of worldly things — and through yearning of heart for heavenly things fly upwards to heaven. **142–44 Ant tah ha fleon hehe ... learde alle hise**, And though (*tah* = reduced form of *thah*) they fly high with high and holy life, [they] hold nevertheless the head low through mild humility, as a bird flying bows the head, considers everything worth nothing that she does well (i.e., discounts her good works), and says as our Lord taught all His [people]. **144–45 *Cum omnia benefeceritis ... sumus***, When you (pl.) have done all [things] well, say: "We

145   **omnia benefeceritis, dicite: "Servi inutiles sumus."** "Hwen ye al habbeth wel i-
don," he seith, ure Laverd, "seggeth thet ye beoth unnete threalles." Fleoth hehe ant
haldeth thah thet heaved eaver lahe. The wengen the uppard beoreth ham — thet beoth
gode theawes thet ha moten sturien into gode werkes, as brid hwen hit fleo wule stureth
hise wengen. The treowe ancres yetten, the we to briddes evenith — nawt we, thah, ah

150   deth Godd — ha spreadeth hare wengen ant makieth creoiz of ham-seolf as brid deth
hwen hit flith — thet is, i thoht of heorte ant i bitternesse of flesch beoreth Godes rode.

Theo briddes fleoth wel the habbeth lutel flesch, as the pellican haveth, ant feole
fitheren. The struc*i*on, for his muchele flesch, ant othre swucche fuheles, makieth a
semblant to fleon, ant beateth the wengen, ah the vet eaver draheth to ther eorthe.

155   Alswa fleschlich ancre the liveth i flesches lustes ant folheth hire eise — the hevinesse
of hire flesch ant flesches untheawes bineometh hire hire fluht, ant tah ha makie semblant
ant muche nurth with wengen — othres, nawt hiren — thet is, leote of as thah ha fluhe,
ant were an hali ancre. Hwa-se yeorne bihalt, lahheth hire to bismere, for hire vet eaver

are useless servants" (Luke 17:10). **145 Hwen**, When. **146 ure Laverd**, our Lord. **146 thet ye
beoth unnete threalles**, say (imper.) that you are useless thralls. **146–47 Fleoth hehe . . .
eaver lahe**, Fly high and hold nevertheless the (i.e., your) head always low. **147–49 The
wengen the uppard beoreth ham . . . stureth hise wengen**, The wings which bear them
upwards — those are good habits (or, virtues) which they may stir (i.e., set into motion) into
good works, as a bird when it flies will stir its wings. **149–51 The treowe ancres . . . beoreth
Godes rode**, The true anchoresses again which we compare to birds — not we, though, but
God does — they spread their wings and make a cross of themselves as a bird does when it
flies — that is, in thought of heart and in bitterness of flesh [the true anchoress] bears God's
Cross. **152–53 Theo briddes fleoth wel . . . feole fitheren**, Those birds fly well which have
little flesh, as the pelican has, and many feathers. **153–54 The strucion . . . to ther eorthe**,
The ostrich, because of (lit., for) his great flesh (i.e., big body), and other such birds (lit.,
fowls), make a show to fly (i.e., a pretense of flying), and beat the wings, but the feet always
pull (lit., draw) to the earth (or, ground). **155–58 Alswa fleschlich ancre . . . ant were an hali
ancre**, Also the fleshly anchoress who lives in the flesh's desires and follows (i.e., pursues)
her comfort (lit., ease) — the heaviness of her flesh and [her] flesh's vices (lit., unvirtues)
deprive her of her flight, and though she make a show and much noise with wings — with
others, not hers (i.e., with others' good works) — that is, lets on as though she [were] flying,
and [as if she] were a holy anchoress. **158–59 Hwa-se yeorne bihalt . . . draheth to ther
eorthe**, Whosoever carefully observes (lit., beholds — *bihalt* = reduced form of *bihaldeth*)

as doth the struc*io*ns — thet beoth hire lustes — draheth to ther eorthe. Theos ne beoth
160   nawt i-li*ch* the leane fuhel pellican, ne ne fleoth nawt on heh, ah beoth eorth-briddes, ant
nisteth on eorthe. Ah Godd cleopeth the gode ancres "briddes of heovene," as ich ear
seide. **Vulpes foveas habent, et volucres celi nidos**. "Foxes habbeth hare holen, ant
briddes of heovene habbeth hare nestes." Treowe ancres beoth ariht briddes of heovene,
the fleoth on heh ant sitteth singinde murie o the grene bohes — thet is, thencheth
165   uppart of the blisse of heovene the neaver ne faleweth, ah is aa grene — ant sitteth o this
grene singinde murie — thet is, resteth ham i thulli thoht, ant ase theo the singeth,
habbeth murhthe of heorte. Brid, tah, other-hwile for-te sechen his mete, for the flesches
neode, lihteth to ther eorthe. Ah hwil hit sit on eorthe, hit nis neaver siker, ah biwent him
ofte ant biloketh him aa yeornliche abuten, alswa the gode ancre. Ne fleo ha neaver se
170   hehe, ha mot lihten other-hwiles dun to ther eorthe of hire bodi: eoten, drinken, slepen,
wurchen, speoken, heren of thet hire neodeth to of eorthliche thinges. Ah thenne, as the
brid deth, ha mot wel biseon hire, bilokin hire on euch half thet ha no-hwer ne misneome

[her], laughs her to scorn, for her feet always, as do the ostriches' — those are their
desires — pull (lit., draw) to the earth. **159–61 Theos ne beoth . . . on eorthe**, These are
not like the lean bird, the pelican, nor [do they] fly up high (lit., on high), but are earth-
birds and nest on the earth (or, ground). **161–62 Ah Godd cleopeth . . . as ich ear seide**,
But God calls the good anchoresses "birds of heaven," as I said earlier. **162** *Vulpes*
foveas habent . . . nidos, (see gloss to 3.110). **163–67 Treowe ancres . . . habbeth**
murhthe of heorte, True anchoresses are rightly [thought of as] birds of heaven, which
fly on high and sit singing merrily on the green boughs — that is, they think upwards of
the bliss of heaven which never fades (or, withers), but is always green — and they sit
in this green singing merrily — that is, rest themselves in such a thought, and as those
who sing, have mirth of heart. **167–68 Brid, tah, other-hwile . . . to ther eorthe**, A bird,
though, (*tah* = reduced form of *thah* after preceding -*d*) sometimes in order to (lit., for to)
seek its food, for the need of the body (lit., flesh), lights to the earth. **168–69 Ah hwil hit**
sit on eorthe . . . the gode ancre, But while it sits on the ground (*sit* = reduced form of
sitteth), it is never safe, but turns itself often and looks about him always carefully, as
does the good anchoress. **169–71 Ne fleo ha neaver se hehe . . . of eorthliche thinges**,
Fly she ever so high (i.e., no matter how high she might fly), she must light sometime
down to the ground of her body, to eat, drink, sleep, work, speak, [and to] hear about
what is necessary for her of earthly things (i.e., what earthly things she must attend to).
171–74 Ah thenne . . . the hwil ha sit se lahe, But then, as the bird does, she must see

leste ha beo i-caht thurh sum of the deofles grunen, other i-hurt summes-weis, the hwil ha sit se lahe.

175   "Theos briddes habbeth nestes," he seith, ure Laverd. **Volucres celi nidos**. Nest is heard ute-with of prikinde thornes, in-with nesche ant softe — swa schal ancre ute-with tholien heard on hire flesch ant prikiende pinen, swa wisliche thah ha schal swenche thet flesch, thet ha mahe seggen with the Psalm-wruhte, **fortitudinem meam ad te custodiam,** thet is, "ich chulle wite mi strengthe, Laverd, to thine bihove." For-thi beo

180   flesches pine efter euch-anes evene. Thet nest beo heard withuten, ant softe ant swete the heorte withinnen. Theo the beoth of bitter other of heard heorte, ant nesche to hare flesch, ha makieth frommard hare nest, softe withuten, ant thorni withinnen. This beoth the wea-mode ant te estfule ancres — bittre withinnen, as thet swete schulde beon, ant estfule withuten, as thet hearde schulde beon. Theos i thulli nest mahen habben uvel

185   rest hwen ha ham wel bithencheth, for leate ha schulen bringe forth briddes of swuch nest — thet beoth gode werkes the fleon toward heovene. Job cleopeth nest the ancre-

to herself well, look about her on each side so that she nowhere mistakes (i.e., makes a mistake), lest she be caught by some of the devil's snares, or [is] hurt [in] some way, while she sits so low. **175** *Volucres celi nidos*, (see gloss to 3.110). **175–79 Nest is heard ute-with . . . to thine bihove,** A nest is hard on the outside (lit., without) with pricking thorns, [but] on the inside delicate and soft — so must an anchoress suffer outwardly in her flesh hard [things] and pricking pains, so wisely though that she will harass (or, mortify) the flesh, [so] that she may say with the Psalm-wright (i.e., Psalmist), "I shall guard my strength for You" (Psalm 58:10) — that is, "I will protect my strength, Lord, to Your advantage." **179–81 For-thi beo flesches . . . the heorte withinnen,** Therefore [let] the pain of the flesh be according to each one's ability. [Let] the nest be hard without (i.e., on the outside), and the heart soft and sweet within. **181–82 Theo the beoth . . . ant thorni withinnen,** Those who are of bitter or of hard heart, and soft to their flesh, they make their nest inside out (lit., fromward) — soft on the outside, and thorny on the inside. **182–84 This beoth the wea-mode . . . hearde schulde beon,** These are the petulant and indulgent anchoresses — bitter within, who (*as* not translated) should be sweet, and pleasure-seeking on the outside, who should be hard. **184–86 Theos i thulli nest . . . fleon toward heovene,** These in such a nest can have bad (lit., evil) rest when they well bethink themselves (i.e., when they consider it well), for they will bring forth chicks late from such a nest — those are good works which fly toward heaven. **186–87 Job cleopeth . . . as he were ancre,** Job calls the anchor-house a nest, and says as [if] he

hus, ant seith as he were ancre: **In nidulo meo moriar**. Thet is, "ich chulle deien i mi nest, beon ase dead th'rin — for thet is ancres rihte — ant wunien athet death th'rin, thet ich nulle neaver slakien, hwil the sawle is i the buc, to drehen heard withuten — alswa as nest is — ant softe beo withinnen."

190 Of dumbe beastes leorne wisdom ant lare. The earn deth in his nest a deore-wurthe yim-stan, "achate" hatte, for nan attri thing ne mei the stan nahhin, ne hwil he is i the nest hearmin his briddes. This deore-wurthe stan, thet is Jesu Crist, ase stan treowe ant ful of alle mihtes over alle yim-stanes — he is the achate thet atter of sunne ne nahhede

195 neaver. Do him i thi nest — thet is, i thin heorte. Thench hwuch pine he tholede on his flesch withuten, hu swote he wes i-heortet, hu softe withinnen, ant swa thu schalt driven ut euch atter of thin heorte ant bitternesse of thi bodi. For i thulli thoht — ne beo hit neaver se bitter pine thet tu tholie for the luve of him the droh mare for the — schal thunche the swote. Thes stan, as ich seide, afleieth attrie thinges. Habbe thu thes stan

200 in-with thi breoste, ther Godes nest is. Ne thearf thu noht dreden the attri neddre of helle. Thine briddes — thet beoth thine gode werkes — beoth al sker of his atter.

were an anchoress. **187 *In nidulo meo moriar***, "I shall die in my nest" (Job 29:18). **187–90 Thet is, "ich chulle . . . softe beo withinnen,"** That is, "I will die in my nest, be as [if] dead in it (lit., therein) — for that is right for an anchoress (lit., that is an anchoress' right) — and [I shall] dwell until death in there, [so] that I will never stop (lit., slack), while the soul is in the body, to suffer hard [things] without — just as the nest is — and to be soft within." **191–95 Of dumbe beastes . . . nahhede neaver**, From dumb beasts learn (imper.) wisdom and teaching (lit., lore). The eagle puts (lit., does) into its nest a precious gemstone, called an "agate," for no venemous thing can near the stone, nor while he (i.e., the stone) is in the nest [can it] harm his chicks. This precious stone, that is Jesus Christ, true as a stone (i.e., rock) and full of all powers above (i.e., beyond) all gemstones — He is the agate which the venom of sin never neared (i.e., approached). **195 Do**, Put (imper.). **195–97 Thench hwuch pine . . . of thi bodi**, Think (imper.) what (lit., which) pain He suffered on His flesh without, how sweet hearted He was, how soft within, and so you will drive out each venom from your heart and bitterness from your body. **197–99 For i thulli thoht . . . schal thunche the swote**, For in such a thought — be it ever so bitter pain that you suffer for the love of Him who suffered more for you — [it] will seem sweet to you. **199–200 Thes stan . . . ther Godes nest is**, This stone, as I said, puts venemous things to flight. Keep (imper.; lit., Have thou) this stone within your breast, where God's nest is. **200–01 Ne thearf thu noht . . . al sker of his atter**, You need not dread the venemous serpent of hell. Your chicks — which are your good works — are all safe from his poison.

170

Part Three

Hwa-se ne mei thes yim-stan habben ne halden i the nest of hire heorte, lanhure i the nest of hire ancre-hus habbe his i-liche — thet is, the crucifix. Bihalde ofte th'ron ant cusse the wunde-studen i swote munegunge of the sothe wunden the he o the sothe
205   rode thuldeliche tholede. Se vorth se ha mei, beo Judith — thet is, libben hearde, beon i-cnawen ofte to Godd his muchele godlec toward hire, ant hire fawtes toward him, thet ha him yelt hit uvele. Crie him yeorne th'rof mearci ant are, ant schrive hire i-lome. Thenne is ha Judith, the sloh Oloferne. For Judith on Ebreisch is "schrift" on Englisch, thet sleath gasteliche then deovel of helle. **Judith: Confessio**. For-thi seith ancre to
210   euch preost, **Confiteor** on alre earst ant schriveth hire ofte, for-te beo Judith ant slean Oloferne — thet is, the deofles strengthe. For ase muchel seith this nome Oloferne as "stinkinde in helle." **Secundum nominis ethimologiam Olofernus "olens in inferno," secundum interpretationem "infirmans vitulum saginatum."** On Ebreische ledene Oloferne is "the feond the maketh feble ant unstrong feat kealf" ant to wilde — thet is,

202–03 Hwa-se ne mei . . . thet is, the crucifix, Whosoever cannot have or hold this gem-stone in the nest of her heart, [should] at least have in the nest of her anchor-house His like (i.e., likeness) — that is, the Crucifix. **203–05 Bihalde ofte th'ron . . . thuldeliche tholede**, Look (lit., behold) often on it (lit., thereon) and kiss the wound-places in sweet remembrance of the true wounds which He suffered patiently on the true Cross. **205–07 Se vorth se ha mei . . . yelt hit uvele**, As far (lit., forth) as she can, [let her] be Judith — that is, live hard (i.e., a hard life), acknowledge (lit., be known) often to God His great goodness toward her, and her faults against Him, that she repays Him for it badly. **207 Crie him yeorne . . . schrive hire i-lome**, [Let her] cry to Him for mercy and grace for that (lit., thereof), and confess herself often. **208–09 Thenne is ha Judith . . . deovel of helle**, Then she is Judith, who slew Holofernes. For Judith in Hebrew is (i.e., means) "confession" in English, which slays spiritually the devil of hell (*then* = inflected def. art.). **209 *Judith: Confessio***, "Judith is Confession" (Pseudo-Jerome, *Book of Hebrew Names* [PL 23.1286]). **209–11 For-thi seith ancre . . . the deofles strengthe**, Therefore the anchoress says to each priest "I confess" first of all and confesses herself often, in order to (lit., for to) be Judith and slay Holofernes — that is, the devil's strength. **211–12 For ase muchel seith . . . in helle**, For this name Holofernes says so much as "stinking in hell." **212–13 *Secundum nominis ethimologiam . . . vitulum saginatum***, According to the etymology of the name, Holofernes [means] "stinking in hell," according to the interpretation, "weakening the fattened calf" (See Dobson, *Moralities*, pp. 136–37). **213–15 On Ebreische ledene . . . thurh eise ant thurh este**, In the Hebrew language Holofernes is the fiend (or, enemy) "who makes feeble and unstrong a calf [which is] fatted" and too wild — that is, the flesh

215   thet flesch the awildgeth sone se hit eaver featteth thurh eise ant thurh este. **Incrassatus est dilectus et recalcitravit.** "Mi leof is i-featte*d*," he seith, ure Laverd, "ant smit me with his hele." Sone se flesch haveth his wil, hit regibeth anan ase feat meare ant idel. This featte kealf haveth the feond strengthe to unstrengen ant buhen toward sunne, for swa muche seith this nome "Oloferne." Ah ancre schal beo Judith thurh heard lif ant

220   thurh soth schrift, ant slean as dude Judith thes uvele Oloferne, temie ful wel hire flesch, sone se ha i-feleth thet hit awilgeth to swithe, mid feasten, mid wecchen, with here, with heard swinc, with hearde disciplines — wisliche thah ant wearliche. **Habete, inquit, sal in vobis. Item: In omni sacrifitio offeretis michi sal.** Thet is, "in euch sacrefise," he seith, ure Laverd, "offrith me salt eaver. Veaste, wecche ant othre swucche,

225   as ich nempnede nu, beoth mi sacrefises." Salt bitacneth wisdom, for salt yeveth mete smech, ant wisdom yeveth savur al thet we wel wurcheth. Withute salt of wisdom thuncheth Godd smechles alle ure deden. On other half, withute salt flesch gedereth

which grows wild as soon as it ever grows fat through ease and through pleasure. **215–16** *Incrassatus est . . . recalcitravit,* "My love has grown fat and has kicked" (Deuteronomy 32:15). **216–17 "Mi leof is i-featted . . . with his hele,"** "My love is fattened," He says, our Lord, "and smites me with its heel." **217 Sone se flesch . . . feat meare ant idel,** [As] soon as flesh has his (i.e., its) will (or, desire), it kicks as does a fat and idle mare. **218–19 This featte kealf . . . this nome "Oloferne,"** (inverted syntax) The fiend has the strength to unstrengthen (i.e., weaken) this fat calf and bow (or, bend) [it] toward sin, for so much says (i.e., means) this name, "Holofernes." **219–22 Ah ancre schal beo Judith . . . wisliche thah ant wearliche,** But an anchoress ought to be Judith through a hard life and through true confession, and [she ought to] slay as did Judith this evil Holofernes, [and] tame very well her flesh, [as] soon as she feels that it goes wild too much, with fasts, with vigils, with hair[shirts], with hard toil, with hard disciplines — prudently though and warily (or, carefully). **222–23** *Habete, inquit, sal in vobis . . . offeretis michi sal,* "Have," he says, "salt in you." The same [verse]: "In every sacrifice you (pl.) ought to offer me salt" (adapted from Leviticus 2:13). **224 offrith,** offer (imper.); **eaver,** always. **224–25 Veaste, wecche . . . beoth mi sacrefises,** To fast, wake (i.e., hold vigils), and other such [things] as I named [just] now, are my sacrifices. **225 bitacneth,** symbolizes. **225–27 for salt yeveth . . . alle ure deden,** for salt gives food taste, and wisdom gives savor to all that we do (lit., work) well. Without the salt of wisdom all our deeds seem tasteless to God. **227–28 On other half . . . ant forroteth sone,** On the other side (i.e., at the same time), without salt, flesh (or, meat) gathers

172

wurmes, stinketh swithe fule ant forroteth sone. Alswa withute wisdom flesch, as
wurm, forfret hire ant wasteth hire-seolven, forfeareth as thing the forroteth ant sleath
230   hire on ende. Ah thulli sacrefise stinketh ure Laverd.

    Thah the flesch beo ure fa, hit is us i-haten thet we halden hit up. Wa we moten don
hit as hit is wel ofte wurthe, ah nawt fordon mid alle. For hu wac se hit eaver beo,
thenne is hit swa i-cuplet, ant se feste i-feiet to ure deore-wurthe gast, Godes ahne
furme, thet we mahten sone slean thet an with thet other. **Augustinus: Natura mentis**
235   **humane que ad ymaginem Dei creata est, et sine peccato est, solus Deus major**
est. Ant tis is an of the measte wundres on eorthe, thet te heste thing under Godd —
thet is, monnes sawle, as Seint Austin witneth — schal beo se feste i-feiet to flesch, thet
nis bute fen ant a ful eorthe, ant thurh thet ilke limunge luvien hit se swithe, thet ha for-
te cwemen hit in his fule cunde, geath ut of hire hehe heovenliche cunde, ant for-te
240   paien hire, wreatheth hire Schuppere, the scheop hire efter him-seolf thet is king ant
keiser of eorthe ant of heovene. Wunder over wunder ant hokerlich wunder! thet se

worms, stinks very badly and rots away soon. **228–30 Alswa withute wisdom . . . stinketh ure
Laverd**, Likewise without wisdom, the flesh, as [does a] worm, gobbles herself (i.e., itself, the
flesh) and wastes herself, degenerates (lit., fares badly) like a thing which rots away, and slays
(i.e., kills) herself in the end. But such sacrifice stinks to our Lord. **231–32 Thah the flesch
. . . nawt fordon mid alle**, Though the flesh be (i.e., is) our foe, it is commanded us that we hold
it up. We may do it woe (i.e., cause it pain), as it is very often worthy of, but [we may not]
destroy [it] as well. **232–34 For hu wac . . . with thet other**, For howsoever weak it be, still, it
is so coupled (i.e., joined) and so firmly connected to our precious spirit (lit., ghost), God's
own creation, that we could soon slay (i.e., kill) the one with the other. **234–36 *Augustinus:
Natura mentis . . . solus Deus major est***, Augustine: "Than the nature of the human mind
which is created in the image of God, and is without sin, God alone is greater" (Augustine,
Against Maximus 2.25 [*PL* 42.803]). **236–41 Ant tis is an of the measte wundres . . . ant of
heovene**, And this is one of the greatest wonders on earth, that the highest thing below God
— that is, man's soul, as St. Augustine witnesses — must be so firmly joined to the flesh,
which is but fen (i.e., mud) and a foul earth (i.e., dirt), and through that same joining [the soul
must] love it so much, that she, in order to please (or, comfort) it in its foul nature, goes out (i.e.,
departs) from her high heavenly nature, and in order to please her [the flesh], angers her Maker,
who made her after (i.e., according to, in imitation of) himself who is king and emperor (lit., caesar)
of earth and of heaven. **241–44 Wunder over wunder . . . withute Godd**, Marvel beyond marvels
and a shameful marvel! that so immeasurably low a thing — "almost nothing" "for nearly noth-

unimete lah thing — **fere nichil** "for neh nawt," seith Seint Austin — schal drahen into
sunne se unimete heh thing ase sawle is, thet Seint Awstin cleopeth **fere summum** —
thet is, "for neh hest thing," withute Godd. Ah Godd nalde nawt thet ha lupe i prude, ne
245   wilnede to climben ant feolle as dude Lucifer, for he wes bute charge, ant teide for-thi
a clot of hevi eorthe to hire as me deth the cubbel to the ku, other to the other beast thet
is to recchinde ant renginde abuten. This is thet Job seide: **Qui fecisti ventis — id est,
spiritibus — pondus.** "Laverd," he seith, "thu havest i-maket fother to fetherin with
the sawlen" — thet is thet hevie flesch thet draheth hire dune-ward. Ah thurh the
250   hehschipe of hire, hit schal wurthe ful liht, lihtre then the wind is, ant brihtre then the
sunne, yef hit folheth hire her, ne ne draheth hire to swithe into hire lahe cunde. Leove
sustren, for his luve thet ha is i-lich to, beoreth hire menske, ne leote ye nawt the lahe
flesch meistrin hire to swithe. Ha is her in uncuththe i-put in a prisun, bitund in a
cwalm-hus, ne nis nawt edscene of hwuch dignete ha is, hu heh is hire cunde, ne
255   hwuch ha schal thunche yet in hire ahne riche. Thet flesch is her ed hame, as eorthe the

ing," says St. Augustine — will (i.e., can) draw into sin so immeasurably high a thing as the
soul is, that St. Augustine calls "almost the highest" — that is, "nearly the highest (lit., next)
thing," except God. **244–47 Ah Godd nalde nawt . . . renginde abuten,** But God did not want
that she [should] leap into pride, nor [did He] want [her] to climb [in pride] and fall as did
Lucifer, for he was without burden (i.e., hardship; lit., weight), and therefore [He] tied a clod
of heavy earth to her as one does the hobble to the cow, or to the other animal that is too
straying and roaming about. **247 thet,** what. **247–48 Qui fecisti ventis . . . pondus,** "[You]
who have made a weight for the winds" — that is, for souls (Job 28:25). **248 Laverd,** Lord.
248–49 thu havest . . . hire dune-ward, you have made a heavy weight (lit., cart-load) to load
the souls with" — that is, the heavy flesh which draws her downward. **249–51 Ah thurh the
. . . into hire lahe cunde,** But through the loftiness of her (i.e., the soul) it (i.e., the flesh) shall
be very light, lighter than is the wind, and brighter than the sun, if it (i.e., the flesh) follows
(i.e., obeys) her here, nor draws her too powerfully into her low nature. **251–53 Leove
sustren . . . hire to swithe,** Dear sisters, for His love, whom she (i.e., the soul) is like to (i.e.,
whom the soul resembles), bear (imper.) her honor, nor let (imper. — lit., nor let you) the low
flesch master her too powerfully. **253–55 Ha is her in uncuththe . . . in hire ahne riche,** She
(i.e., the soul) is put here in a strange land, in a prison, enclosed in a death-house, nor is [it]
apparent of what kind of dignity she is, how high her birth (or, nature) is, nor what (lit.,
which) she will seem (or, appear as) however in her own kingdom. **255–57 Thet flesch . . . on
his ahne mixne,** The flesh is here at home, like earth which is in earth (i.e., dirt which is in the

is in eorthe, ant is for-thi cointe ant cover. As me seith, thet curre is kene on his ahne mixne. Ha haveth to much meistrie, wei-la-wei, o monie. Ah ancre, as ich habbe i-seid, ah to beon al gastelich yef ha wule wel fleon as brid thet haveth lutel flesch ant feole fitheren. Nawt ane yet tis, ah teke thet ha temeth wel hire ful-itohe flesch ant strengeth

260   ant deth menske the wurthfule sawle — teke this, ha mot yet thurh hire forbisne ant thurh hire hali beoden yeoven strengthe othre, ant uphalden ham, thet ha ne fallen i the dunge of sunne. Ant for-thi Davith anan efter thet he haveth i-evenet ancre to pellican, he eveneth hire to niht-fuhel the is under evesunges. **Simlis factus sum pellicano solitudinis; factus sum sicut nicticorax in domicilio.**

265   The niht-fuhel i the evesunges bitacneth recluses the wunieth for-thi under chirche evesunges, thet ha understonden thet ha ahen to beon of se hali lif, thet al Hali Chirche— thet is, Cristene folc — leonie ant wreothie upon ham, ant heo halden hire up, with hare lif halinesse ant hare eadie bonen. For-thi is ancre "ancre" i-cleopet, ant under chirche i-ancret as ancre under schipes bord, for-te halden thet schip, thet uthen ant stormes hit

ground), and is therefore cunning and villainous. As they say (lit., one says), the cur (i.e., dog) is fierce on his own dunghill. **257–59 Ha haveth to . . . ant feole fitheren**, She (i.e., the flesh) has too much mastery (or, power), alas, over many. But an anchoress, as I have said, ought to be completely spiritual (lit., ghostly) if she will fly well as a bird which has little flesh and many feathers. **259–62 Nawt ane yet . . . the dunge of sunne**, Not only this, though, but besides [the fact] that she tames her ill-mannered flesh well and strengthens and does honor to the worthy soul — besides this, she must still through her example and through her holy prayers give strength to others, and hold them up, so that they do not fall into the dung of sin. **262–63 Ant for-thi . . . under evesunges**, And therefore David soon after he has compared an anchoress to the pelican, he compares her to a night-bird (lit., night-fowl) which is under the eaves. **263–64 Simlis factus . . . in domicilio**, "I am made (or, have become) like the pelican of the wasteland; I am made as the night bird in the cottage." (Psalm 101:7). (The Vulgate reads *bubo* 'owl' instead of *nicticorax*.) **265–68 The niht-fuhel . . . eadie bonen**, The night-bird in the eaves symbolizes (lit., betokens) recluses who live for this reason under the church's eaves, [so] that they understand that they ought to be of so holy a life, that all Holy Church — that is, Christian folk — [ought to] lean and support [itself] upon them (i.e., the recluses), and they hold her (i.e., the church) up, with their life's holiness and their blessed prayers. **268–70 For-thi is ancre "ancre" . . . hit ne overwarpen**, Therefore (i.e., for this reason) is an anchoress called an "anchor," and anchored under the church like an anchor under a ship's side, in order to (lit., for to) hold the ship, so that waves and storms do not

270   ne overwarpen. Alswa al Hali Chirche, thet is schip i-cleopet, schal ancrin o the ancre, thet heo hit swa halde thet te deofles puffes—thet beoth temptatiuns — ne hit overwarpen. Euch ancre haveth this o foreward, ba thurh nome of ancre ant thurh thet ha wuneth under the chirche: to understiprin hire yef ha walde fallen. Yef ha breketh foreward, loki hwam ha lihe, ant hu continuelement, for ha ne stureth neaver. Ancre wununge ant hire

275   nome yeieth eaver this foreward, yet hwen ha slepeth.

     On other half, the niht-fuhel flith bi niht ant biyet i theosternesse his fode. Alswa schal ancre fleon with contemplatiun — thet is, with heh thoht, ant with hali bonen bi niht toward heovene — ant biyeote bi niht hire sawle fode. Bi niht ah ancre to beon waker ant bisiliche abuten gastelich biyete. For-thi kimeth anan th'refter, **Vigilavi et**

280   **factus sum sicut passer solitarius in tecto. Vigilavi,** "Ich wes waker," seith Davith in ancre persone, "ant i-lich spearewe under rof ane." **Vigilavi,** "ich wes waker" — for thet is ancre rihte muchel for-te wakien. **Ecclesiasticus: Vigilia honestatis tabefatiet**

overturn it. **270–71 Alswa al Hali . . . ne hit overwarpen,** Likewise (lit., also) the entire Holy Church, which is called a ship, must anchor onto the anchoress, so that she may hold (i.e., stabilize) it so that the devil's blasts — those are temptations — do not overturn it. **272–73 Euch ancre haveth . . . ha walde fallen,** Each anchoress has this in covenant (i.e., as part of her agreement), both through the name of "anchoress" and because (lit., through that) she lives under the church: to prop her [up] if she was about (lit., wanted) to fall. **273–74 Yef ha breketh . . . ne stureth neaver,** If she breaks [her] agreement, look whom she cheats (or, is lying to), and how continually, for she never stirs (i.e., moves). **274–75 Ancre wununge . . . hwen ha slepeth,** An anchoress' dwelling and her name cry (i.e., declare) constantly this agreement, even when she sleeps. **276 On other half . . . theosternesse his fode,** On the other side (i.e., at the same time), the night-bird flies by night and gets (or, obtains) its food in darkness. **276–78 Alswa schal ancre . . . hire sawle fode,** Likewise the anchoress must fly with contemplation — that is, with high thought, and with holy prayers by night toward heaven — and get by night her soul's food. **278–79 Bi niht ah . . . anan th'refter,** By night an anchoress ought to be vigilant and busily about (i.e., striving for) spiritual profit. For this reason immediately after comes [this verse]. **279–80 *Vigilavi et factus sum . . . in tecto,*** "I was awake and am made (or, have become) like a lonely sparrow on the roof" (Psalm 101:8). **280–81 *Vigilavi* . . . under rof ane,** "I was awake," "I was vigilant," says David in an anchoress' persona, "and like a sparrow under the roof alone." **281–82 for thet is . . . for-te wakien,** for it is right [for the] anchoress to wake (i.e., hold vigils, stay awake) often (lit., much). **282–83 *Ecclesiasticus . . . tabefatiet carnes,*** Ecclesiasticus: "The vigil of honesty

carnes. Na thing ne awealdeth wilde flesch, ne ne maketh hit tomre, then muche wecche. Wecche is in Hali Writ i feole studen i-preiset. **Vigilate et orate ne intretis in**
285 **temptationem**. "Alswa as ye nulleth nawt fallen into fondunge," he seith, ure Laverd, "wakieth ant i-biddeth ow" — thet schal don ow stonden. Eft he seith, **Beatus quem invenerit vigilantem**. "Eadi is the ilke, thet hwen ure Laverd kimeth i-fint wakiende." Ant he him-seolf sum-chearre **pernoctavit in oratione,** "wakede i beoden al niht." Ant swa he tahte us wecche, nawt ane with his lare, ah dude with his dede.
290 Eahte thinges nomeliche leathieth us to wakien eaver i sum god ant beo wurchinde: this scheorte lif; this stronge wei; ure god, thet is se thunne; ure sunnen, the beoth se monie; death, thet we beoth siker of, ant unsiker hwenne; thet sterke dom of Domes-dei ant se nearow mid alle, thet euch idel word bith ther i-broht forth, ant idele thohtes the neren ear her i-bette. **Dominus in Ewangelio: de omni verbo otioso, et cetera.**

(or, virtue) consumes the flesh" (Ecclesiasticus 31:1). **283–84 Na thing ne . . . studen i-preiset,** Nothing controls wild flesh, nor makes it tamer than many a (lit., much) vigil. The vigil is praised in Holy Writ in many places. **284–85 *Vigilate et orate . . . temptationem,*** "Wake and pray lest you enter into temptation" (Mark 14:38, Matthew 26:41). **285–86 Alswa as ye . . . don ow stonden,** "Just as you do not want to fall into temptation," He says, our Lord, "wake and pray (imper.; lit., pray you)" — that will make you stand. **286 Eft,** Again. **286–87 *Beatus quem invenerit vigilantem,*** "Blessed [is he] whom [God] will find waking" (adapted from Luke 12:37). **287–88 "Eadi is the . . . i beoden al niht,"** "Blessed is the same [one], who when our Lord comes [He] finds waking (*i-fint* = reduced form of *i-findeth*)." And He Himself sometimes (or, formerly) "spent the night in prayer" (adapted from Luke 6:12), "stayed awake in prayers all night." **288–89 Ant swa he . . . with his dede,** And so He taught us to wake (i.e., hold a vigil), not only with His teaching (lit., lore), but did [it] with His deed (or, action). **290–94 Eahte thinges nomeliche . . . ear her i-bette,** Eight things especially invite us to wake continually (lit., ever) in some good [action] and to be working: 1) this short life; 2) this formidable path; 3) our goodness, which is so trifling (lit., thin); 4) our sins, which are so many; 5) death, which we are sure of, and (i.e., but) unsure of when [it will come]; 6) the stern judgment — and so exacting as well — of Judgment Day, so that each idle (or, trivial) word is (i.e., will be) brought forward there, and idle thoughts [as well] which were not atoned for here beforehand. **294–95 *Dominus in Ewangelio . . . non evadet inpunita,*** The Lord in the Gospel: "of every careless word," etc. (adapted from Matthew 12:36.) Likewise: "and the hairs of the head shall not perish" (adapted from Luke 21:18) — that is, thought (does) not escape unpunished. (The full text of Matthew 12:36: "but I say to you therefore,

295 **Item: et capilli de capite non peribunt — id est, cogitatio non evadet inpunita. Anselmus: Quid faties in illa die quando exigetur a te omne tempus inpensum qualiter sit a te expensum, et usque ad minimam cogitationem**. Loke nu hwet beo of unwreaste willes ant sunfule werkes. Yet the seovethe thing the munegeth us to wakien, thet is the sorhe of helle. Ther bihald threo thing: the untaleliche pinen, the

300 echnesse of euch-an, the unimete bitternesse. The eahtuthe thing: hu muchel is the mede i the blisse of heovene, world buten ende. Hwa-se waketh her wel ane hond-hwile, hwa-se haveth theos eahte thing ofte in hire heorte, ha wule schaken of hire slep of uvel slawthe. I the stille niht hwen me ne sith na-wiht, nowther ne ne hereth thet lette the bone, the heorte is ofte se schir, for na thing nis witnesse of thing thet me thenne

305 deth, bute Godes engel, the is i swuch time bisiliche abuten to eggin us to gode. For ther nis nawt forloren as is bi dei ofte. Hercnith nu, leove sustren, hu hit is uvel to uppin, ant hu god thing hit is to heolen god-dede, ant fleo bi niht as niht-fuhel, ant gederin bi theostre — thet is, i privite, ant dearnliche — sawle fode.

every careless word which will have been spoken — men will give a reason [or, account] of it in the Day of Judgment.") **296–97** *Anselmus: Quid faties . . . ad minimam cogitationem*, Anselm: "What will you do on that day when each moment spent by you will be examined, how it was spent by you, and up to (i.e., including) the most trivial thought" (Anselm, *Meditations* 1 [*PL* 158.723]). **297–98 Loke nu hwet . . . sunfule werkes**, See (lit., look) now what is (i.e., comes) from wicked wills (or, desires) and sinful works. **298–99 Yet the seovethe . . . sorhe of helle**, Still [there is] the seventh thing which reminds us to wake (i.e., hold vigil), that is 7) the sorrow of hell. **299– 300 Ther bihald threo . . . unimete bitternesse**, There behold (or, consider) three things: the innumerable pains, the eternity of each one, the immeasurable bitterness. **300–01 The eahtuthe thing . . . world buten ende**, The eighth thing: 8) how great the reward in the bliss of heaven is, world without end (i.e., forever and ever). **301–03 Hwa-se waketh . . . of uvel slawthe**, Whoso-ever wakes here well for a moment (lit., a hand-while), whosoever has these eight things often in her heart, she will shake off [from] her the sleep of evil sloth (or, laziness). **303–05 I the stille . . . us to gode**, In the still night when one sees not a whit, or hears what [might] hinder the prayer, the heart is often so free, for nothing is witness of the things which one then does, except God's angel, who is in such a time busily about inciting us to good (lit., to incite, egg us on). **305–08 For ther nis nawt forloren . . . ant dearnliche — sawle fode**, For there is nothing lost, as [there] is often by day. Hear (i.e., pay attention) now, dear sisters, how it is evil to mention, and how good a thing it is to cover up a good deed, and fly by night as a night bird does and gather by darkness — that is, in privacy (or, in secret), and secretly — the soul's food.

Part Three

Oratio Hester placuit regi Assuero — thet is, "Hesteres bone, the cwen, wes the

310 King Assuer lic-wurthe ant i-cweme." "Hester" on Ebreisch, thet is "i-hud" on Englisch, ant is to understonden thet bone ant other god-dede thet is i-don on hudles is Assuer i-cweme — thet is, the king of heovene. For "Assuer" on Ebreisch is "eadi" on Englisch — thet is, ure Laverd the is eadi over alle. Davith speketh to ancre the wes i-wunet in hudles wel for-te wurchen, ant seoththen o sum wise uppeth hit ant schaweth: **Ut quid**

315 **avertis manum tuam et dexteram tuam de medio sinu tuo in finem** — thet is, "hwi drahest tu ut thin hond, ant yet ti riht hond, of midde thi bosum?" **In finem** — "on ende." Riht hond is god werc. Bosum is privite, ant is as thah he seide, "the riht hond thet tu heolde, ancre, i thi bosum" — thet is, thi gode werc thet tu hefdest i-don privement, as thing is dearne i bosum — "hwi drahest tu hit ut **in finem**—on ende?" — thet is, thet

320 ti mede endi se sone, thi mede thet were endeles yef thi god-dede i-hole were. Hwi openest tu hit ant nimest se scheort mede, hure thet is agan in an hond-hwile? **Amen**

309 *Oratio Hester . . . Assuero,* "The prayer (or, request) of Esther pleased Ahasuerus the king" (adapted from Esther 5:4). **309–10 thet is . . . lic-wurthe ant i-cweme,** that is, "Esther's prayer, the queen, was pleasing and agreeable to King Ahasuerus." **310–12 "Hester" on Ebreisch . . . the king of heovene,** "Esther" in Hebrew, that is (i.e., means), "hidden" in English, and is to [be] understood (passive inf.) that prayer and [any] other good deed which is done in hiding is agreeable to Ahasuerus — that is, to the King of heaven. **312–13 For "Assuer" on Ebreisch . . . eadi over alle,** For "Ahasuerus" in Hebrew is "blessed" (or, happy) in English — that is, our Lord who is blessed over all [others]. **313–14 Davith speketh to . . . hit ant schaweth,** David speaks to the anchoress who had lived in hiding in order to (lit., for to) work well, and afterwards in some way [she] mentions and shows (i.e., displays) it. **314–15** *Ut quid avertis manum . . . in finem,* "Why do you turn away (i.e., withdraw) your hand, your right hand, from the middle of your bosom for ever?" (Psalm 73:11). **315–16 thet is . . . midde thi bosum?** that is, "why do you draw out your hand, and yet (i.e., especially) your right hand from the midst [of] your bosom?" **317–20 Bosum is privite . . . god dede i-hole were,** The bosom is (or, represents) secrecy, and [it] is as though he said, "the right hand which you held, anchoress, in your bosom — that is, your good works which you had done privately (i.e., secretly), since (lit., as) a thing in the bosom (or, heart) is secret — why do you draw it out in the end?" — that is, so that your reward ends so soon, your reward that would have been (lit., were) endless if your good deed were covered (i.e., hidden). **320–21 Hwi openest tu . . . in an hond-hwile?** Why do you reveal it and take so short (i.e., skimpy) a reward, pay that is lost in an instant (lit., a hand-while)? **321–22** *Amen dico vobis . . . mercedem suam,* "Indeed, I say to you they have their reward"

dico vobis receperunt mercedem suam. "Thu havest i-uppet thi god," he seith, ure Laverd, "witerliche thu havest undervo thi mede." Sein Gregoire awundreth him ant seith thet men beoth wode the trochith swa uvele: **Magna verecundia est grandia**
325 **agere et laudibus inhiare. Unde celum mereri potest, nummum transitorii favoris querit**. "Muchel meadschipe hit is," he seith, "don wel ant wilni word th'rof, don hwer-thurh he buth the kinedom of heovene, ant sullen hit for a windes puf of wordes here-word of monnes herunge." For-thi, mine leove sustren, haldeth ower riht hond in-with ower bosum, leste mede endeles neome scheort ende. We redeth in Hali Writ thet
330 Moyseses hond, Godes prophete, sone se he hefde i-drahen hire ut of his bosum, bisemde o the spitel-uvel ant thuhte lepruse, thurh hwet is bitacnet thet god-dede i-drahe forth nis nawt ane forloren thurh thet uppinge, ah thuncheth yet eatelich bivore Godes ehe, as spitel-uvel is eatelich bivore monnes sihthe. Lo, a feorli god word thet te hali Job seith: **Reposita est hec spes mea in sinu meo**. "I mi bosum," he seith, "is al min hope i-
335 halden," as thah he seide, "hwet god se ich do, were hit ut of bosum i-uppet ant i-drahe forth, al min hope were edslopen. Ah for-thi thet ich hit heole ant hude as i bosum, ich

(Matthew 6:2). **322–23 "Thu havest i-uppet . . . undervo thi mede,"** "You have mentioned (i.e., spoken of) your good," He says, our Lord, "truly you have received your reward." **323–24 Sein Gregoire awundreth . . . swa uvele**, St. Gregory is amazed (lit., wonders himself, reflex.) and says that men are mad who fall short so badly. **324–26 *Magna verecundia est . . . transitorii favoris querit*,** "[It] is a great shame to do grand [things] and to covet (or, gape at) praises. Instead of that by which heaven can be won (or, merited), he seeks the coin of transitory applause" (Gregory, *Moral Discourses on Job* 8.43.70 [*PL* 75.844]). **326 Muchel meadschipe**, Great madness. **326–28 "don wel . . . of monnes herunge,"** "to do well and desire a reputation for it (lit., thereof), to do [something] with which (lit., where-through) he buys the kingdom of heaven and to sell it for a wind's puff of a word's praise, [for a puff] of man's praising." **328–29 For-thi, mine leove sustren . . . neome scheort ende**, Therefore, my dear sisters, hold your right hand inside your bosom, lest endless reward take a short end. **329–33 We redeth in Hali Writ . . . bivore monnes sihthe**, We read in Holy Writ that the hand of Moses, God's prophet, [as] soon as he had drawn her (i.e., the hand) out of his bosom, seemed [to be suffering] from leprosy (lit., hospice-sickness) and seemed leprous, through which (lit., what) [it] is symbolized that a good deed drawn forth (i.e., called attention to) is not only lost through that mentioning, but seems also horrific before God's eye, as leprosy is horrible before man's sight. **333 Lo, a feorli god word . . . Job seith**, Lo, a marvelously good word which the holy Job says. **334 *Reposita est hec spes mea in sinu meo*,** "This hope of mine is stored in my breast" (Job 19:27). **334–35 i-halden**, held. **335–37 as thah he seide . . . hopie**

hopie to mede." For-thi yef ei deth eani god, ne drahe ha hit nawt ut-ward ne yelpe na-wiht th'rof, for with a lutel puf, with a wordes wind hit mei beon al toweavet.

Ure Laverd i Johel meaneth him swithe of theo the forleoseth ant spilleth al hare god
340 thurh wilnunge of here-word ant seith theos wordes: **Decorticavit ficum meam nudans spoliavit eam et projecit. Albi facti sunt rami ejus**. "Allas," seith ure Laverd, "theos the schaweth hire god haveth bipilet mi fier, i-rend al the rinde of, despuilet hire steort-naket, ant i-warpen awei, ant te grene bohes beoth fordruhede ant forwurthen to drue, hwite rondes." This word is dosc, ah neometh nu yeme hu ich hit wulle brihtin. Fier is
345 a cunnes treo the bereth swete frut thet me cleopeth "figes." Thenne is the fier bipilet ant te rinde i-rend of hwen god-dede is i-uppet. Thenne is the lif ut; thenne adeadeth the treo hwen the rinde is awei; ne nowther ne bereth hit frut, ne greneth th'refter i lufsume leaves, ah druhieth the bohes, ant wurtheth hwite rondes — to na thing betere then to fures fode. The boh, hwen hit adeadeth, hit hwiteth ute-with ant adruheth in-with ant

to mede, as though he said, "whatsoever good I do, if it were revealed from the heart and drawn out of my bosom, all my hope would have (lit., were) slipped away. But because I cover and hide it as [if] in the heart, I hope for reward." **337–38 For-thi yef ei . . . beon al toweavet**, Therefore if any[one] does any good [deed], [let him] not draw it outward nor boast at all of it (lit., thereof) for with a little puff, with a word's wind it may be completely wafted away. **339–40 Ure Laverd i Johel . . . seith theos wordes**, Our Lord in Joel complains (reflex.) grievously of those who lose and destroy all their good through desiring of praise-word (i.e., desire for praise) and says these words. **340–41 *Decorticavit ficum meam . . . rami ejus***, "[A nation] has stripped my fig tree and, uncovering [it], has despoiled it and thrown [it] down. Its branches are made white" (Joel 1:7). **341–44 "theos the schaweth . . . to drue, hwite rondes,"** "those who show their good [deeds] have stripped (lit., peeled) my fig tree, torn (lit., rent) all the bark off, despoiled (i.e., stripped) her stark naked, and thrown [her] away, and the green boughs are dried out and deformed (or, transformed) into dry, white sticks (or, logs)." **344 This word is dosc . . . hit wulle brihtin**, This word is dark (i.e., obscure), but pay (lit., take) attention how I will brighten it. **344–46 Fier is a cunnes . . . is i-uppet**, A fig tree is a tree of the kind which bears sweet fruit which they (lit., one) call "figs." Then the fig tree is peeled and the bark is ripped (lit., rent) off when a good deed is revealed (or, mentioned). **346–49 Thenne is the lif . . . to fures fode**, Then the (i.e., its) life is out, then the tree deadens, when the bark is gone (lit., away), neither does it bear fruit, nor green (i.e., become green) thereafter with (lit., in) lovely leaves, but the boughs dry out, and become white sticks (or, logs) — for nothing better than as fire's food (i.e., to feed the fire). **349–50 The boh . . .**

350　warpeth his rinde. Alswa god-dede the wule adeadin forwarpeth his rinde — thet is, unhuleth him. The rinde the writh hit is the treoes warde, ant wit hit i strengthe ant i cwicnesse. Alswa the hulunge is the god-dedes lif, ant halt hit i strengthe. Ah hwen the rinde is offe, thenne as the boh deth hwiteth hit ute-with thurh worltlich here-word, ant adruheth in-with ant leoseth the swetnesse of Godes grace, the makede hit grene ant lic-

355　wurthe Godd to bihalden. (For grene, over alle heowes, frovreth meast ehnen.) Hwen hit is swa adruhet, thenne nis hit to nawt se god, as to the fur of helle, for the earste bipilunge, hwer-of al this uvel is, nis bute of prude. Ant nis this muche reowthe thet te fier the schulde with hire swete frut — thet is, god-dede — fede Godd gasteliche, the Laverd of heovene, schal adruhien rindeles thurh thet hit is unhulet ant wurthen buten

360　ende helle fures fode? Ant nis ha to unseli the with the wurth of heovene buth hire helle? Ure Laverd i the Godspel seolf eveneth heove-riche to gold-hord, the "hwa-se hit fint," as he seith, "hudeth hit." **Quem qui invenit homo abscondit.** Golt-hord is god-dede,

warpeth his rinde, The bough, when it deadens, it grows white on the outside and dries out on the inside and throws off its bark. **350–51 Alswa god-dede . . . unhuleth him**, Likewise (lit., also) a good deed which is about to (lit, wants to) die (lit., deaden) throws off its bark — that is, uncovers itself. **351–52 The rinde the writh . . . i cwicnesse**, The bark which covers it is the tree's defense, and protects (*wit* = reduced form of *witeth*) it in [its] strength and vigor. **352 Alswa the hulunge . . . i strengthe**, Likewise the covering is the life of the good deed, and keeps (lit., holds) it in strength. **352–55 Ah hwen the rinde . . . Godd to bihalden**, But when the bark is off, then, as the bough does it whitens outside through (or, by) worldly praise-word (i.e., words of praise) and dries out inside and loses the sweetness of God's grace, which made it green and pleasant (lit., like-worthy) for God to behold. **355–56 For grene . . . fur of helle**, (For green, more than [lit., over] all colors, comforts the eyes most.) When it is dried out thus, then it is good for nothing so [much] as for the fire of hell. **356–57 for the earste bipilunge . . . of prude**, for the first peeling (or, stripping), from which (lit., whereof) all this evil is (i.e., comes), is nothing but from pride. **357–60 Ant nis this . . . helle fures fode?** And is this not a great pity that the fig tree which ought to with her sweet fruit — that is, the good deed — feed God spiritually, the Lord of heaven, must dry out barkless because (lit., through that) it is uncovered and [has] become without end (i.e., forever) the food of hell's fire? **360 Ant nis ha . . . hire helle?** And is she not (*nis* = *ne is*) too wretched who buys hell for herself with the price of heaven? **361–62 Ure Laverd i the Godspel . . . "hudeth hit,"** Our Lord Himself in the Gospel compares the heavenly kingdom to a gold-hoard, which "whoso-ever finds it," as He says, "hides it." **362 *Quem qui invenit homo abscondit*,** "[A treasure] which a man found he hid" (Matthew 13:44). **362–64 Golt-hord is god-dede . . . hit is forlore sone,**

182

the is to heovene i-evenet, for me hit buth ther-with, ant this golt-hord, bute hit beo the betere i-hud ant i-holen, hit is forlore sone. For as Sein Gregoire seith, **Depredari**
365 **desiderat qui thesaurum puplice portat in via**. "The bereth tresor openliche i wei thet is al ful of reaveres ant of theoves, him luste leosen hit ant beon i-robbet." This world nis bute a wei to heovene other to helle, ant is al biset of hellene mucheres the robbith alle the golt-hordes thet ha mahen underyeoten thet mon other wummon i this wei openeth. For ase muchel wurth is as hwa-se seide ant yeide as he eode, "Ich beore
370 golt-hord! Ich beore golt-hord! Lowr hit her read gold, hwit seolver inoh ant deore-wurthe stanes!" A sapere the ne bereth bute sape ant nelden yeiyeth hehe thet he bereth. A riche mercer geath forth al stille. Freinith hwet i-tidde of Ezechie the gode king, for-thi thet he schawde the celles of his aromaz, his muchele thinges, his deore-wurthe tresor. Nis hit nawt for nawt i-writen i the hali Godspel of the threo kinges the comen to
375 offrin Jesu Crist the deore threo lakes, **procidentes adoraverunt eum, et apertis thesauris suis obtulerunt, et cetera,** thet tet ha walden offrin him, ha heolden eaver

The gold hoard is a good deed which is compared to heaven, for one buys it (i.e., heaven) with that (lit., therewith, i.e., the good deed), and this gold hoard, unless it be hidden and covered the better, it is (i.e., will be) lost soon. **364–65 *Depredari desiderat . . . portat in via*,** "Who-ever carries a treasure openly (lit., publicly) on the road wants to be robbed" (Gregory, *Homilies on the Gospels* 1.12). **365–66 "The bereth tresor . . . beon i-robbet,"** "Whoever bears treasure openly in the way (or, path) which is completely full of robbers and of thieves, [it] pleases him (i.e., he would like) to lose it and be robbed." **366–69 This world nis . . . i this wei openeth,** This world is [nothing] but a path to heaven or to hell, and is beset with hell's pilferers (or, petty thieves) who rob all the gold-hoards which they may find out that man or woman reveals (lit., opens) on this path. **369 For ase muchel . . . as he eode,** For [that] is as much good (lit., is worth as much) as if someone said and cried as he went. **369–71 "Ich beore golt-hort! . . . deore-wurthe stanes!"** "I am carrying a gold hoard! I am carrying a gold hoard! See it here red gold, white silver enough, and precious stones!" **371 A sapere the . . . thet he bereth,** A soapmaker (or, peddler; lit., soaper) who [does not] carry (lit., bear) [anything] but soap and needles cries up loudly (lit., highly) what he carries. **372–74 A riche mercer . . . deore-wurthe tresor,** A rich cloth merchant goes out completely still (i.e., quiet). Ask (imper.) what bitided (i.e., happened) to Hezekiah the good king because he showed the store-rooms [full] of his spices, his many things (i.e., possessions), his precious treasure. **374–77 Nis hit nawt for . . . thet ha beren,** It is not written for nothing in the holy Gospel about (lit., of) the three kings who came to offer to Jesus Christ the priceless (lit., dear) three gifts, "falling down,

i-hud athet ha comen bivoren him, tha earst ha unduden the presenz thet ha beren. For-thi, mine leove sustren, bi niht as the niht-fuhel, thet ancre is to i-evenet, beoth yeorne sturiende. Niht ich cleopie privite. This niht ye mahen habben euch time of the dei, thet
380   al the god thet ye eaver doth, beo i-don as bi niht ant bi theosternesse, ut of monnes ehe, ut of monnes eare. Thus i niht beoth fleonninde, ant sechinde ower sawle heovenliche fode: thenne ne beo ye nawt ane, **pellicanus solitudinis**, ah beoth ec **nicticorax in domicilio**.

    Vigilavi et factus sum sicut passer solitarius in tecto. Yet is ancre i-evenet her to
385   spearewe thet is ane under rof as ancre. Spearewe is a chiterinde brid, chitereth aa, ant chirmeth. Ah for-thi thet moni ancre haveth thet ilke untheaw, Davith ne eveneth hire nawt to spearewe the haveth fere, ah deth to spearewe ane. **Sicut passer solitarius**. "Ich am," he seith bi ancre, "as spearewe thet is ane." For swa ah ancre hire ane in anlich stude as ha is chirmin ant chiterin eaver hire bonen. Ant understondeth leofliche,
390   mine leove sustren, thet ich write of anlich lif for-te frovrin ancren, ant ow over alle.

they worshiped him, and having opened up their treasures, offered [them to him]" (Matthew 2:11), [so] that what they wished to offer him, they held always hidden until they came before him, when they first opened (lit., undid) the presents that they carried. **377–79 For-thi, mine leove . . . beoth yeorne sturiende**, Therefore, my dear sisters, be (imper.) stirring diligently by night, as the night bird, to which the anchoress is compared. **379–81 Niht ich cleopie . . . of monnes eare**, I call night "privacy" (or, secrecy). This "night" you can have each time of the day, [so] that all the good that you ever do is done as if by night and by darkness, out of man's eye, out of man's ear. **381–83 Thus i niht . . . *nicticorax in domicilio***, Thus be (imper.) flying at night, and seeking your soul's heavenly food: then you are not alone, "pelican in the wastelands," but are also the "night-raven in the cottage" (i.e., under the cottage-eaves). **384 *Vigilavi et factus sum . . . in tecto***, "I have held a watch (or, stayed awake) and am made like a solitary sparrow on (lit., in) the roof" (Psalm 101:8). **384–85 Yet is ancre . . . rof as ancre**, Still (i.e., once more) the anchoress is compared here to a sparrow that is alone under the roof, as an anchoress [is]. **385–87 Spearewe is a . . . to spearewe ane**, A sparrow is a chattering bird, chatters forever, and chirps. But because many an anchoress has that very vice, David does not compare her to a sparrow which has a companion, but does [so] to a sparrow alone. **387–88 *Sicut passer solitarius . . . thet is ane***, "As a solitary sparrow." "I am," he says about the anchoress, "as a sparrow that is alone." **388–90 For swa ah ancre . . . ow over alle**, For so ought an anchoress, alone [and] in a solitary place as she is, to chirp and chatter her prayers continually. And understand lovingly my dear sisters, that I write about the solitary life in order to (lit., for to) comfort anchors, and you above all.

Hu god is to beon ane, is ba i the alde lahe ant i the neowe i-sutelet. For i bathe me i-fint thet Godd his dearne runes ant heovenliche privitez schawde his leoveste freond — nawt i monne floc, ah dude ther ha weren ane bi ham-seolven. Ant heo ham-seolf alswa as ofte as ha walden thenchen schirliche of Godd ant makien cleane bonen ant beon in
395   heorte gasteliche i-hehet toward heovene — aa me i-fint thet ha fluhen monne sturbunge, ant wenden bi ham ane, ant ther Godd edeawde ham ant schawde him-seolf to ham ant yef ham hare bonen. For-thi thet ich seide thet me i-fint tis ba i the alde testament ant ec i the neowe, ich chulle of ba twa schawin forbisne.

Egressus est Ysaac in agrum ad meditandum — quod ei fuisse creditur
400   **consuetudinarium**. Ysaac the patriarche, for-te thenche deopliche, sohte anlich stude ant wende bi him ane, as Genesys teleth. Ant swa he i-mette with the eadi Rebecca — thet is, with Godes grace. **Rebecca enim interpretatur, "multum dedit et quicquid habet meriti preventrix gratia donat."** Alswa the eadi Jacob, tha ure Laverd schawde him his deore-wurthe nebscheft ant yef him his blesceunge ant wende his nome betere,
405   he wes i-flohe men ant wes him al ane. Neaver yete i monne floc ne cahte he swuch

---

391 Hu god is . . . neowe i-sutelet, How good [it] is to be alone is revealed both in the old law and in the new. **391–95 For i bathe me . . . toward heovene**, For in both one finds (*i-fint* = reduced form of *i-findeth*) that God showed His secret mysteries and heavenly secrets to His dearest friends — not in a crowd (lit., flock) of men, but [He] did [so] where they were alone by themselves, and they themselves also as often as they wanted to think clearly of God and make pure prayers and be at heart spiritually (lit., ghostly) raised toward heaven. **395–97 aa me i-fint . . . ham hare bonen**, One always finds that they fled the chaos (lit., disturbance) of man and went by themselves alone, and there God revealed to them and showed Himself to them and gave (i.e., granted) them their prayers. **397–98 For-thi thet ich . . . schawin forbisne**, Because I said that one finds this both in the Old Testament and also in the New, I will from both (lit., both two) reveal an example (or, illustration). **399–400 *Egressus est Yssac . . . consuetudinarium***, "And Issac had gone out into the field" — which is believed to have been a custom of his (Genesis 24:63). **400–01 Ysaac the patriarche . . . as Genesys teleth**, Isaac the patriarch, in order to think deeply, sought a solitary place and went by himself alone, as Genesis tells. **402–03 *Rebecca enim interpretatur . . . gratia donat***, "Rebecca in fact is interpreted as '[she] gave much and whatever merit she has, prevenient grace gives it to her'" (based on Pseudo-Jerome, *Book of Hebrew Names* [see *PL* 23.1208]). **403–05 Alswa the eadi Jacob . . . wes him al ane**, Also the blessed Jacob, when our Lord showed him His precious face and gave him His blessing, turned his name better (i.e., into a better name, Israel; see Genesis 32:28 ff.), he had fled men and was by himself all alone. **405–06 Neaver yete i . . .**

185

biyete. Bi Moysen ant bi Helye, Godes deore-wurthe freond, is sutel ant edscene hwuch baret ant hu dredful lif is eaver i-mong thrung, ant hu Godd his privitez schaweth to theo the beoth privement ham ane. Me schal, leove sustren, theose estoires tellen ow, for ha weren to longe to writen ham here, ant thenne schule ye al this brihte understonden.

410 **Set et Jeremias solus sedet**. The eadi Jeremie seith he sit ane ant seith the reisun forhwi. **Quia comminatione tua replesti me**. Ure Laverd hefde i-fullet him of his threatunge. Godes threatunge is wontreathe ant weane i licome ant i sawle, worlt buten ende. The were of this threatunge, as he wes, wel i-fullet, nere ther nan empti stude i the heorte to underfon fleschliche lahtren. For-thi he bed wealle of teares. **Quis dabit**
415 **michi fontem lacrimarum**? Thet ha ne adruhede neaver na mare then wealle for-te biwepe slei folc — thet is, meast al the world thet is gasteliche i-slein mid deadliche sunnen. **Ut lugeant interfectos populi mei**. Ant to this wop, lokith nu, he bit anlich

swuch biyete, Never yet in man's flock (i.e., in a crowd of people) did he catch (or, receive) such a benefit. **406–08 Bi Moysen ant bi Helye . . . privement ham ane**, Through Moses and Elijah, God's precious freinds, [it] is revealed and evident which (i.e., what kind of) strife and how dreadful a life [there] is always among the throng (or, crowd) and how God shows His secrets to those who are intimate [with] Him alone. **408–09 Me schal, leove . . . this brihte understonden**, One must, dear sisters, tell you these histories, for they were (i.e., would be) too long to write them here, and then you will understand all this clearly. **410** *Set et Jeremias solus sedet*, "But also Jeremiah sits alone" (adapted from Jeremiah 15:17). **410–11 The eadi Jeremie . . . the reisun forhwi**, The blessed Jeremiah says he sits (*sit* = reduced from of *sitteth*) alone and says the reason why. **411** *Quia comminatione tua replesti me*, "Because you have filled me with your threat" (Jeremiah 15:17). **411–12 Ure Laverd hefde . . . of his threatunge**, Our Lord had filled him with His threatening. **412–13 Godes threatunge . . . worlt buten ende**, God's threatening is hardship and suffering in body and in soul, world without end (i.e., forever and ever). **413–14 The were of this . . . underfon fleschliche lahtren**, Whoever would be (lit., were) well filled with His threatening as he (i.e., Jeremiah) was — there would be no empty place in the heart to receive carnal laughter (lit., fleshly laughters). **414 For-thi he bed wealle of teares**, Therefore he prayed for a well of tears. **414–15** *Quis dabit michi fontem lacrimarum?* "Who will give me a fountain of tears?" (adapted from Jeremiah 9:1). **415–17 Thet ha ne adruhede . . . mid deadliche sunne**, So that she (i.e., the anchoress) [would] not ever dry up, any more than a well, in order to weep over the slain folk — that is, [al]most all the world, which is spiritually slain with deadly sins. **417** *Ut lugeant interfectos populi mei*, "So that they may lament the slain of my people" (adapted from Jeremiah 9:1). **417–22 Ant to this wop . . . to beon ane**, And for this weeping, look now, he (the holy prophet) asks for

stude: **Quis michi dabit diversorium viatorum in solitudine ut, et cetera**, the hali prophete, for-te schawi witerliche thet hwa-se wule biwepen hire ahne ant othres sunnen,

420 as ancre ah to donne, ant hwa-se wule i-finden ed te nearewe domes-mon mearci ant are, a thing thet let him meast is beowiste — thet is, wununge bimong men — ant thet swithest furthreth hit, thet is anlich stude, mon other wummon either to beon ane. Yet speketh Jeremie of anlich stude mare. **Sedebit solitarius et tacebit**. "Me schal sitten," he seith, "him ane ant beo stille." Of this stilnesse he speketh ther-bivoren lutel: **Bonum**

425 **est prestolari cum silentio salutare Dei. Beatus qui portaverit jugum Domini ab adholescencia sua**. "God hit is i silence i-kepen Godes grace, ant thet me beore Godes yeoc anan from his yuhethe," ant thenne kimeth th'refter: **Sedebit solitarius et tacebit, quia levabit se supra se**. Hwa-se swa wule don, "ha schal sitten ane ant halden hire stille, ant swa heoven hire-seolf buven hire-seolven" — thet is, with heh lif hehi toward

430 heovene over hire cunde. Teke this, hwet other god cume of this anlich sittunge thet Jeremie speketh of, ant of this seli stilthe, kimeth anan efter: **Dabit percuscienti se**

---

a solitary place, "Who will give me [a dwelling] in the desert (or, solitude) of many wayfarers, so that . . . ," etc. (Jeremiah 9:2), in order to to show plainly that for whosoever will weep for her own and others' sins, as an anchoress ought to do, and for whosoever will find (or, obtain) from the strict judge (lit., man of judgments) mercy and grace, the one thing that hinders him most is dwelling — that is, living among men — and what most powerfully furthers it, that is a solitary place, [for a] man or a women too to be alone. **422 Yet**, Still. **423 mare**, more; *Sedebit solitarius et tacebit*, "He will sit alone and be silent" (Lamentations 3:28). **423–24 "Me schal sitten . . . beo stille,"** "One must sit," he says, "[by] himself alone and be still." **424 Of this stilnesse . . . ther-bivoren lutel**, Concerning this stillness, he speaks a little before that. **424–26** *Bonum est prestolari . . . ab adholescencia sua*, "[It] is good to wait in silence for the salvation of God. Blessed [is he] who has borne the yoke of the Lord from his youth" (Lamentations 3:26–27). **426 God**, Good; **i-kepen**, to expect (or, receive — see glossary). **426–27 ant thet me beore Godes yeoc . . . kimeth th'refter**, and [it is good] that one bear God's yoke immediately from his youth, and then comes after that [the following verse]. **427–28** *Sedebit solitarius . . . levabit se supra se*, "He shall sit alone and be quiet, for he will raise himself above himself" (Lamentations 3:28). **428–30 Hwa-se swa wule . . . over hire cunde**, Whosoever wants to do so, "she must sit alone and hold herself still, and so lift herself above herself" — that is, with high life rise toward heaven over her nature. **430–31 Teke this . . . kimeth anan efter**, Besides this, what other good may come from this solitary sitting which Jeremiah speaks of, and from this blessed stillness, comes immediately after (i.e., in the text). **431–32** *Dabit percuscienti se . . . saturabitur obprobriis*, "He shall give his

maxillam et saturabitur obprobriis. "Ha wule," he seith, "the swa liveth, ayeines the smitere beode forth the cheke ant beo thurh-fullet with schentfule wordes." Her beoth i theos word twa eadi theawes to noti swithe yeorne, the limpeth ariht to ancre:

435 tholemodnesse i the earre half, i the leatere, eadmodnesse of milde ant meoke heorte. For tholemod is, the thuldeliche abereth woh thet me him deth. Eadmod is, the tholie mei thet me him mis-segge. Theos the ich habbe i-nempnet her weren of the alde testament. Cume we nu to the neowe.

Sein Juhan Baptiste — bi hwam ure Laverd seide, **Inter natos mulierum non**

440 **surrexit major Johanne baptista,** thet "bimong wives sunen ne aras neaver herre" — he kenneth us openliche bi his ahne dede thet anlich stude is bathe *siker* ant biheve. For thah the engel Gabriel hefde his burde i-bocket, al were he i-fullet of the Hali Gast anan in-with his moder wombe, al were he thurh miracle of b*araigne* i-boren ant in his i-borenesse unspende his feader tunge into prophecie — for al this, ne durste he yet

445 wunie bimong men, se dredful lif he seh th'rin, thah hit nere of nawt elles bute of

cheek to [him who is] persecuting him, and he will be filled with reproaches" (Lamentations 3:30). **432–33 "Ha wule," he seith . . . with schentfule wordes,"** "She will," he says, "whoever lives thus, offer up the cheek to the smiter and be filled through [and through] with disparaging words." **433–35 Her beoth i theos word . . . ant meoke heorte**, Here are in these words two blessed virtues to note very carefully, which pertain rightly to an anchoress: patience in the first case (lit., on the earlier side), in the latter, humility of a mild and meek heart. **436–37 For tholemod is . . . mis-segge**, For the patient [person] is whoever patiently bears the wrong people do to him. The humble [person] is whoever can suffer what people say wrongly [against] him. **437–38 Theos the ich . . . to the neowe**, These which I have named here were from the Old Testament. Let us come now to the New. **439–41 Sein Juhan Baptiste . . . bathe siker ant biheve**, St. John the Baptist — about whom our Lord said, "Among the sons of women no greater one has risen up than John the Baptist" (Matthew 11:11), that "among the sons of women a higher [one] never rose" — he makes known to us openly by his own deed that a solitary place is both secure and beneficial. **441–46 For thah the engel . . . of speche ane**, For [even] though the angel Gabriel had prophesied his birth (lit., registered it in a book), even though (lit., all were) he was filled with the Holy Spirit at once in his mother's womb, even though he was born through a miracle from a barren [woman] and at his birth unlocked his father's tongue in prophecy — for all this, he still dared not live among men, so dreadful (i.e., frightening) a life he saw in it (lit., therein), even if (lit., though) it was (i.e., consisted) of nothing else than of speech alone (i.e., even if life among men meant

speche ane. Ant for-thi hwet dude he? Yung of yeres, fleh awei into wildernesse, leste he with speche sulde his cleane lif, for swa is in his ymne:

> **Antra deserti teneris sub annis**
> **civium turmas fugiens petisti,**
> **450   ne levi saltem maculare vitam**
> **famine posses.**

He hefde, as hit thuncheth, i-herd Ysaie, the meande him ant seide, **Ve michi quia homo pollutis labiis ego sum**. "Wumme, wa is me," he seith, the hali prophete, "for ich am a mon of sulede lippen," ant seith the acheisun hwer-vore: **Quia in medio 455 populi polluta labia habentis ego habito**. "Ant thet is for-thi," he seith, "thet ich wunie bimong men the suleth hare lippen mid misliche spechen." Lo, hu Godes prophete seith he wes i-sulet thurh beowiste bimong monne. Swa hit is sikerliche: beo neaver se briht or, metal, gold, seolver, irn, stel, thet hit ne schal drahe rust of an-other thet is i-rustet, for-hwon thet ha longe liggen togedere. For-thi fleh Sein Juhan the feolahschipe

merely speaking to them, let alone interacting with them). **446–47 Ant for-thi hwet . . . in his ymne**, And therefore what did he do? Young of years, [he] fled away into the wilderness, lest he sully with speech his clean (or, pure) life, for thus [it] is in his hymn. **448–51 *Antra deserti . . . famine posses***, "You occupied caves of the desert in your early years (lit., under, before [your] years), / fleeing the towers of cities you sought [them] (i.e., the caves) out, / so that you could not stain [your] life / even with trivial talk" (Paul the Deacon, hymn for the Feast of St. John the Baptist). **452–53 He hefde, as hit . . . *ego sum***, He had, as it seems, heard Isaiah, who lamented (lit., moaned him, [reflex.]) and said, "Woe [is] me because I am a man with unclean lips" (adapted from Isaiah 6:5). **453 Wumme**, Alas. **454 sulede lippen**, sullied lips; **ant seith the acheisun hwer-vore**, and says the reason why (lit., wherefore). **454–55 *Quia in medio populi . . . ego habito***, "Because I live in the midst of the people who have defiled their lips" (Isaiah 6:5). **455–56 "Ant thet is . . . mid misliche spechen,"** "And that is because," he says, "I live among men who sully their lips with various speeches (i.e., much talking)." **456 hu**, how. **457 i-sulet thurh beowiste bimong monne**, sullied by living among man. **457–59 Swa hit is sikerliche . . . longe liggen togedere**, So it is surely: neither ore, metal, gold, silver, iron [or] steel will ever be so bright that it will not draw rust from another [metal] that is rusted, as long as they lie long together. **459–60 For-thi fleh Sein Juhan . . . he were i-fulet**, Therefore, St. John fled the fellowship of foul men, lest he be befouled (i.e.,

460 of fule men, leste he were i-fulet. Ah yet for-te schawin us thet me ne mei the uvele fleon bute me fleo the gode, he fleh his hali cun, i-coren of ure Laverd, ant wende into anli stude ant wunede i the wildernesse. Ant hwet biyet he ther? He biyet thet he wes Godes baptiste. O, the muchele hehnesse thet he heold i fulluht under hise honden, the Laverd of heovene, the halt up al the world with his anes mihte! Ther the Hali Trinite —

465 "thrumnesse" on Englisch — schawde hire al to him: the Feader in his stevene, the Hali Gast i culvre heow, the Sune in his honden. In anlich lif he biyet threo preminences: privilegie of preachur, merite of martirdom, meidenes mede. Theos threo manere men habbeth in heovene, with overfullet mede, crune up-o crune. Ant te eadi Juhan, in anlich stude as he wes, alle theose threo estaz ofearnede him ane.

470 Ure leove Leafdi, ne leadde ha anlich lif? Ne fond te engel hire in anli stude al ane? Nes ha no-wher ute, ah wes biloken feste, for swa we i-findeth: **Ingressus angelus ad eam dixit. Ave Maria, gratia plene, Dominus tecum; benedicta tu in mulieribus.** Thet is, "the engel wende into hire." Thenne wes heo inne in anli stude hire ane. Engel

so that he would not be sullied). **460–62 Ah yet for-te schawin . . . i the wildernesse,** And yet in order to show us that one cannot flee the evil unless one [also] flees the good, he (i.e., John) fled his holy kin (or, family), chosen by our Lord, and departed into a lonely place and lived in the wilderness. **462–63 Ant hwet biyet . . . Godes baptiste,** And what did he profit (or, gain) there? He profited [in] that he was the baptizer of God. **463–64 O, the muchele hehnesse . . . his anes mihte!** Oh, the great glory, that he (i.e., John) held in baptism with his hands, the Lord of heaven, who holds up all the world (*halt* = reduced form of *haldeth*) with his single might! **464–66 Ther the Hali Trinite . . . in his honden,** There the Holy Trinity — "threeness" in English — showed herself completely to him: the Father in his voice, the Holy Spirit in the dove's shape, the Son in his hands. **466–67 In anlich lif . . . meidenes mede,** In the solitary life he gained three distinctions (or, special honors): the special rights of a preacher, merit of martyrdom, [and the] virgin's reward. **467–69 Theos threo manere . . . ofearnede him ane,** These three kinds [of] men [will] have in heaven, with overflowing (lit., overfilled) reward, crown upon crown. And the blessed John, in a solitary place as he was, earned all these three estates (i.e., statuses) by himself alone. **470–71 Ure leove Leafdi . . . i-findeth,** Our dear Lady, did she not lead a solitary (or, lonely) life? Did not the angel find her in a solitary place all alone? She was nowhere outside, but was locked up securely, for so we find. **471–72 *Ingressus angelus . . . in mulieribus*,** "The angel entered and spoke to her. 'Hail Mary full of grace, the Lord [be] with you; O blessed are you among women'" (Luke 1:28). **473 wende,** went. **473–74 Thenne wes heo inne . . . ne eadeawede neaver ofte,** Then (i.e., at that time) was she inside in

to mon i thrung ne edeawede neaver ofte. On other half, thurh thet no-wher in Hali Writ
475 nis i-writen of hire speche bute fowr sithen, as is i-seid th'ruppe, sutel prufunge hit is
thet ha wes muchel ane, the heold swa silence.

Hwet seche ich other? Of Godd ane were inoh forbisne to alle, the wende him-seolf
into anli stude, ant feaste ther-as he wes ane i wildernesse for-te schawin ther-bi thet
bimong monne thrung ne mei nan makien riht penitence. "Ther in anli stude him
480 hungrede," hit seith, ancre to frovre thet is meoseise. Ther he tholede thet te feond
fondede him feole-weis, ah he overcom him, alswa for-te schawin thet te feond fondeth
muchel theo the leadeth anlich lif, for onde thet he haveth to ham. Ah he is ther overcumen,
for ure Laverd seolf ther stont bi ham i fehte ant bealdeth ham hu ha schulen stonden
strongliche ayein, ant yeveth ham of his strengthe. He, as Hali Writ seith, thet na nurth
485 ne thrung of folc ne mahte letten him of his beoden, ne desturbin his god, he thah no-
the-leatere, hwen he walde beon i beoden, he fleh nawt ane othre men, ah dude yet his
halie deore-wurthe apostles, ant wende ane upon hulles, us to forbisne thet we schule

a solitary place by herself alone. An angel [has] never appeared often to a man in a throng (or,
crowd). **474–76 On other half . . . the heold swa silence,** On the other side (i.e., at the same
time), since (lit., through that) nowhere in Holy Writ is [anything] written about her speech
(i.e., talking) but four times, as is said above, it is a clear proof that she was much alone, who
kept silence thus. **477–79 Hwet seche ich other? . . . makien riht penitence,** Why (lit., what)
do I seek another [example]? From God alone [there] would be enough of an example to all,
who betook Himself (i.e., went) into a solitary place, and fasted while he was alone in the
wilderness in order to show thereby that among the throng of man no one (lit., none) can make
right penitence. **479–80 Ther in anli stude . . . thet is meoseise,** "There in a solitary place he
hungered" (reflex.) (Matthew 4:2) it says, as a comfort [to the] anchoress who is distressed
(or, suffering discomfort). **480–82 Ther he tholede . . . to ham,** There He allowed that the fiend
tempted Him in a variety of ways (lit., many-ways), but He overcame him, also in order to show
that the fiend tempts much those who lead a solitary life, for the envy which he has of them.
482–84 Ah he is ther . . . his strengthe, But he is there overcome, because our Lord Himself
stands there by them in the fight and emboldens (i.e., instructs) them how they must stand
strongly in opposition (lit., against), and gives them [something] from His strength. **484–89
He, as Hali Writ . . . we beoth i bonen,** He, as Holy Writ says, whom no noise or crowd of
people might hinder (*Him* omitted in translation) from His prayers, or disturb His good, He still
nonetheless, when He wanted to be in prayer, He fled not only other [ordinary] people, but
did even [flee from] His precious holy Apostles and went alone upon the hills as an example

turne bi us-seolf ant climben with him on hulles — thet is, thenchen hehe ant leaven lahe under us alle eorthliche thohtes hwiles we beoth i bonen. Pawel ant Antonie, Hylariu*n*
490 ant Benedict, Sincletice ant Sare, ant othre swucche, monie men ant wummen bathe, fondeden witerliche ant underyeten sothliche the biyete of anlich lif, as theo the duden with Godd al thet ha walden. Sein Jerome nu leate seith bi him-seolven: **Quotiens inter homines fui, minor homo recessi**. "As ofte as ich eaver wes," he seith, "bimong men, ich wende from ham leasse mon then ich ear wes." For-thi, seith the wise
495 Ecclesiasticus, **Ne oblecteris in turbis; assidua est enim commissio** — thet is, "ne thunche the neaver god i-mong monne floc, for ther is eaver sunne." Ne seide the stevene — to Arsenie — of heovene, **Arseni, fuge homines et salvaberis?** "Arseni, flih men ant tu schalt beon i-borhen." Ant eft hit com ant seide, **Arseni, fuge, tace, quiesce** — thet is, "Arseni, flih, beo stille, ant wune stude-vestliche i sum stude ut of monne."
500 Nu ye habbeth i-herd, mine leove sustren, forbisne of the alde lahe ant ek of the neowe hwi ye ahen anlich lif swithe to luvien. Efter the forbisnes, hereth nu reisuns hwi

to us that we should turn by ourselves and climb with Him on the hills — that is, to think high (or, loftily) and leave low under us all earthly thoughts while we are in prayer. **489–92 Pawel ant Antonie . . . al thet ha walden,** Paul and Anthony, Hilarion and Benedict, Syncletica and Sarah, and other such [ones], many men and women both, found out surely and understood truly the advantage of a solitary life, as those who did with God all that they wanted. **492–93 Sein Jerome . . . *minor homo recessi*,** Now St. Jerome let it be said (lit., let say) about himself: "As often as I was among men, I departed a lesser man" (cited as Jerome by Peter the Cantor, *Abbreviated Discourse*, 69 [*PL* 205.206]). **493 bimong,** among. **494 leasse mon then ich ear wes,** less a man (or, person) than I was before. **495 *Ne oblecteris . . . est enim commissio*,** "You should not delight in crowds, for their commotion is continual" (adapted from Wisdom 18:32). **495–96 "ne thunche the neaver . . . eaver sunne,"** "[let it] never seem good to you among the flock (or, press) of men, for there is sin always." **496–97 Ne seide the stevene . . . of heovene,** Did not the voice of heaven say to Arsenius (lit., said not the voice . . .). **497 *Arseni, fuge homines et salvaberis?*** "Arsenius, flee men and you will be saved"? (*The Lives of the Desert Fathers* 190). **498 i-borhen,** saved; **Ant eft hit com ant seide . . . *quiesce*,** And again it (i.e., the voice) came and said, "Arsenius, flee, be quiet, [and] be at peace" (*The Lives of the Desert Fathers* 190). **499 ant wune stude-vestliche . . . ut of monne,** and dwell fixedly in some place away from (lit., out of) men. **500–01 Nu ye habbeth i-herd . . . luvien,** Now you have heard, my dear sisters, an example from the old law and also from the new why you ought to love very much the solitary life. **501–02 Efter the forbisnes . . . eahte ed te leaste,** After the

192

me ah to fleo the world, eahte ed te leaste. Ich ham segge scheortliche — neometh the betere yeme.

The forme is sikernesse. Yef a wod liun urne yont te strete, nalde the wise bitunen
505   hire sone? Ant Seinte Peter seith thet helle liun rengeth ant reccheth eaver abuten for-tc sechen in-yong sawle to forswolhen, ant bid us beo wakere ant bisie in hali beoden leste he us lecche: **Sobrii estote et vigilate in orationibus, quia adversarius vester diabolus tanquam leo rugiens circuit querens quem devoret.** This is Seinte Petres word thet ich ear seide. For-thi beoth ancren wise the habbeth wel bitund ham ayein helle liun for-
510   te beo the sikerure.

The other reisun is — the bere a deore licur, a deore-wurthe wet as basme is, in a feble vetles, healewi i bruchel gles, nalde ha gan ut of thrung bute ha fol were? **Habemus thesaurum istum in vasis fictilibus dicit apostolus.** This bruchele vetles, thet is wummone flesch, thah no-the-leatere the basme, the healewi is meidenhad thet is th'rin
515   — other eft[er] meith-lure, chaste cleannesse. This bruchele vetles [is] bruchel as is

examples, hear now the reasons why one ought to flee the world, eight [reasons] at the [very] least. **502–03 Ich ham segge . . . betere yeme,** I [shall] say them shortly (i.e., briefly) — pay the better attention (i.e., pay closer attention since I describe them briefly). **504 The forme is sikernesse,** The first is safety. **504–05 Yef a wod liun . . . bitunen hire sone?** If a mad lion ran through the street, would not the prudent enclose herself quickly? **505–07 helle liun rengeth . . . leste he us lecche,** the lion of hell always ranges and strays about to seek an opportunity to swallow up the soul, and bids us to be vigilant and busy in holy prayers, lest he (i.e., the lion) catch us (i.e., so that he will not be able to catch us). **507–08 *Sobrii estote et vigilate . . . querens quem devoret*,** "Be sober and be vigilant in [your] prayers, because your enemy the devil, as a raging lion, circles about seeking whom he may devour" (1 Peter 5:8). **508–09 thet ich ear seide,** which I said (or, mentioned) before. **509–10 For-thi beoth ancren wise . . . beo the sikerure,** Therefore [those] anchors are wise who have enclosed themselves well against hell's lion in order to be the safer. **511 other,** second. **511–12 the bere a deore . . . bute ha fol were?** whoever would carry (lit., bear) an expensive liquid, a precious fluid as balsam in a breakable container (lit., feeble vessel), a healing potion in brittle glass, would she not go out of the throng (i.e., get out of the crowd), unless she were a fool? **512–13 *Habemus thesaurum istum . . . dicit apostolus*,** "We have this treasure in clay vessels" says the Apostle (2 Corinthians 4:7). **513–16 This bruchele vetles . . . as is eani gles,** This fragile vessel, it is women's flesh, while (lit., still nonetheless) the balsam, the healing liquid, is the virginity which is in it (lit., therein) — or after loss of virginity, chaste purity. This fragile

eani gles. For beo hit eanes tobroken, i-bet ne bith hit neaver, i-bet ne hal as hit wes ear, na mare thene gles. Ah yet hit breketh mid leasse then bruchel gles do. For gles ne tobreketh nawt bute sum thing hit rine, ant hit, onont meith-lure, mei leosen his halnesse with a stinkinde wil, swa vorth hit mei gan ant leaste se longe. Ah this manere bruche

520 mei beon i-bet eft ase hal allunge as hit wes eaver, halest thurh medecine of schrift ant bireowsunge. Nu the preove her-of: Sein Juhan Ewangeliste — nefde he brud i-broht ham? Nefde he i-thoht tha — yef Godd nefde i-let him — meithhad to forleosen? Seoththen thah, nes he meiden neaver the unhalre, ah "wes meiden bitaht meiden to witene." **Virginem virgini commendavit.** Nu as ich segge, this deore-wurthe healewi

525 i bruchel vetles is meithhad ant cleannesse in ower bruchele flesch, bruchelure then eani gles, thet yef ye weren i worldes thrung, with a lutel hurlunge ye mahten al leosen as the wrecches i the world the hurlith togederes ant breoketh hare vetles ant cleannesse schedeth. For-thi ure Laverd cleopeth thus: **In mundo pressuram in me autem pacem**

vessel is [as] breakable as is any glass. **516–17 For beo hit eanes tobroken . . . na mare thene gles,** For be it once broken (i.e., if it is ever broken), it [will] never be repaired, [never] repaired nor whole as it was before, any more than glass. **517 Ah yet hit breketh . . . bruchel gles do,** But it breaks with even less [cause] than brittle glass may do. **517–19 For gles ne tobreketh . . . ant leaste se longe,** For glass does not break unless something touch[es] it, and as concerns loss of virginity, it may lose its wholeness with a stinking desire, so far can it go and last so long. **519–21 Ah this manere bruche . . . schrift ant bireowsunge,** But this kind of break may be repaired again as completely intact (lit., whole) as it ever was, most whole (see glossary) through the medicine of confession and repentance. **521–24 Nu the preove . . . meiden to witene,** Now the proof for that (lit., hereof): St. John the Evangelist — had he not brought a bride home? Had he thought (i.e., did he not intend) then — if God had not hindered him — to lose [his] virginity? Afterwards though, was he not a virgin nevertheless complete (lit., the more unwhole), and "was not the Virgin entrusted to a virgin (i.e., John) to protect?" **524 Virginem virgini commendavit,** "The Virgin was commended to a virgin" (source unidentified). **524–28 Nu as ich segge . . . ant cleannesse schedeth,** Now as I say, this precious medicine in the brittle vessel is virginity and chastity in your brittle flesh, brittler than any glass, so that if you were in the world's throng (or, tumult), with a little collision (or, jostling) you might lose everything (lit., all) as the unfortunates in the world who collide together and break their vessels and spill [their] purity. **528 For-thi ure Laverd cleopeth thus,** Therefore, our Lord cries [out] thus. **528–29 In mundo pressuram . . . pacem habebitis,** "In the world you will have tribulation, but in Me [you will have] peace" (John

habebitis. "Leaveth the world ant cumeth to me, for ther ye schulen beon i thrung, ah
530 reste ant peis is in me."

The thridde reisun of the worldes fluht is the biyete of heovene. The heovene is
swithe heh. Hwa-se wule biyeoten hit ant areachen ther-to, hire is lutel inoh for-te
warpen al the world under hire fotes. For-thi alle the halhen makeden of al the world as
a scheomel to hare vet to areache the heovene. **Apocalypsis: Vidi mulierem amictam**
535 **sole et luna sub pedibus ejus**. This is Sein Juhanes word, Ewangeliste, i the Apocalipse:
"Ich i-seh a wummon i-schrud mid te sunne ant under hire vet the mone." The mone
woneth ant waxeth, ne nis neaver stude-vest, ant bitacneth for-thi worltliche thinges
the beoth as the mone eaver i change. Thes mone mot te wummon halden under hire
vet — thet is, worldliche thinges totreoden ant forhohien — the wule heovene areachen
540 ant beo ther i-schrud mi*d* te sothe sunne.

The feorthe reisun is preove of noblesce ant of largesce. Noble men ant gentile ne
beoreth nan*e* packes, ne ne feareth i-trusset with trussews, ne with purses. Hit is
beggilde riht to beore bagge on bac, burgeise to beore purse — nawt Godes spuse, the

---

16:33). **529 Leaveth**, Leave (imper. pl.). **529–30 ther ye schulen . . . peis is in me**, there you
will be in tumult (lit., in the throng), but rest and peace is in me. **531 of the worldes fluht is the
biyete of heovene**, for the flight of the world (i.e., to flee the world) is the gaining of heaven.
532 swithe heh, very high. **532–33 Hwa-se wule biyeoten . . . under hire fotes**, Whosoever
wants to acquire it and reach up to it (lit., thereto), for her [it] is little enough (i.e., a small
enough thing) to throw all the world under her feet. **533–34 For-thi alle the halhen . . .
areache the heovene**, Therefore all the saints made of all the world a footstool (or, platform)
for their feet [in order to] to reach up to the heaven. **534–35 *Apocalypsis: Vidi mulierem
. . . sub pedibus ejus***, Apocalypse: "I saw a woman clothed in the sun and the moon under
her feet" (adapted from Revelation 12:1). **536 i-seh**, saw; **i-schrud**, clothed. **536–38 The
mone woneth . . . eaver i change**, The moon wanes and waxes, nor is [it] ever steadfast, and
betokens (i.e., symbolizes) therefore worldly things which are, as the moon, always in change
(or, flux). **538–40 Thes mone mot te . . . te sothe sunne**, The woman must hold this moon
under her feet — that is, tread down (or, trample) and reject worldly things — whoever wants
to reach heaven and be clothed there with the true sun. **541–42 preove of noblesce . . . ne
with purses**, proof of nobility and of largess (or, generosity). Noble and gentle men do not
carry any packs, nor [do they] travel (lit., fare) loaded down with bundles or with purses.
542–44 Hit is beggilde . . . leafdi of heovene, It is right [for the] beggar woman to carry a bag
on [her] back, right [for a] burgess (or, townswoman) to carry a purse — [but it is] not [right

195

is leafdi of heovene. Trussen ant purses, baggen ant packes beoth worltliche thinges:
545   alle eorthliche weolen ant worltliche rentes.

The fifte resiun is, noble men ant wummen makieth large relef, ah hwa mei makie largere then the other theo the seith with Seinte Peter, **Ecce nos reliquimus omnia et secuti sumus te**. "Laverd, for-te folhi the, we habbeth al forleavet." Nis this large relef? Nis this muche lave? Mine leove sustren, kinge[s] ant keisers habbeth hare liveneth
550   of ower large relef thet ye i-leavet habbeth. "Laverd, for-te folhi the," seith Seinte Peter, "we habbeth al forleavet," as thah he seide, "we wulleth folhi the i the muchele genterise of thi largesce. Thu leafdest to othre men alle richesces ant makedest of al relef ant lave se large. We wulleth folhi the. We wulleth don alswa, leaven al, as thu dudest, folhi the on eorthe i thet ant in other-hwet — for-te folhi [the] ec into the blisse of heovene, ant
555   yet tear over al folhi the hwider-ward se thu eaver wendest, as nane ne mahen bute ane meidnes: **Hii secuntur agnum quocumque ierit, utroque scilicet pede, id est, integritate cordis et corporis.**

for] God's spouse, who is a lady of heaven. **544–45 Trussen ant purses . . . ant worltliche rentes,** Bundles and purses, bags and packs are worldly things: [as are] all earthly riches and worldly revenues. **546–47 makieth large relef . . . with Seinte Peter,** make generous donations, but who can make more generous [ones] than he or she who says with St. Peter. **547–48 *Ecce nos reliquimus . . . sumus te*,** "Behold we have left everything behind and have followed you" (Matthew 19:27). **548 for-te folhi the,** to follow you; **forleavet,** abandoned. **548–49 Nis this large relef? . . . lave?** Is this not a generous donation? Is this not a great legacy? **549 keisers,** emperors. **549–50 hare liveneth . . . habbeth,** their livelihood from your generous donation which you have left (i.e., willed to them). **551–52 we wulleth folhi the . . . of thi largesce,** we will follow you in the great graciousness of your largess (or, generosity). **552–53 Thu leafdest to othre men . . . lave se large,** You left to other men all [your] riches and made of everything so generous a donation and legacy. **553–56 We wulleth folhi the . . . bute ane meidnes,** We will follow you. We will do likewise, leave everything, as you did, follow you on earth in that and in other things — in order to (lit., for to) follow you also into the bliss of heaven, and still to follow you there (*tear* = reduced form of *thear* "there") above all follow you in whatever direction (lit., whitherward) you ever go, as none can but virgins alone. **556–57 *Hii secuntur agnum . . . integritate cordis et corporis*,** "These follow the lamb wherever it may go," indeed with both feet, that is, with the wholeness of heart and body (adapted from Revelation 14:4, with gloss).

The seste reisun is hwi ye habbeth the world i-flohen — familiarite, muche cun-redden, for-te beo prive with ure Laverd. For thus he seith bi Osee: **Ducam te in**
560 **solitudinem et ibi loquar ad cor tuum**. "Ich chulle leade the," he seith to his leofmon, "into anli stude, ant ter ich chulle luveliche speoke to thin heorte, for me is lath preasse." **Ego Dominus, et civitatem non ingredior.**

The seovethe reisun is for-te beo the brihtre ant brihtluker seon in heovene Godes brihte nebscheft, for ye beoth i-flohe the world ant hudeth ow for hire her. Yet ter-teken
565 thet ye beon swifte as the sunne gleam, for ye beoth with Jesu Crist bitund as i sepulcre, bibarret as he wes o the deore rode, as is i-seid th'ruppe.

The eahtuthe reisun is to habben cwic bone — ant lokith yeorne hwer-vore. The eadmode cwen Hester bitacneth ancre, for hire nome seith "i-hud" on Englische ledene. As me ret in hire boc, ha wes the King Assuer over al i-cweme, ant thurh hire bone
570 arudde of death al hire folc, the wes to death i-demet. This nome Assuer is i-spealet "eadi," as is ear i-seid, ant bitacneth Godd eadi over alle. He yetteth Hester the cwen —

558 **seste**, sixth. **558–59 is hwi ye habbeth . . . with ure Laverd**, is why you have fled the world — intimacy (or, acquaintance), great kinship, to be privy (or, intimate) with our Lord. **559 bi**, through, by means of; **Osee**, Hosea. **559–60** *Ducam te in solitudinem . . . ad cor tuum*, "I shall lead you into solitude and there I shall speak to your heart" (Hosea 2:14). **560 Ich chulle**, I shall; **leofmon**, sweetheart (or, leman). **561 ant ter ich chulle . . . lath preasse**, and there I will speak lovingly to your heart, for to me a crowd (lit., press) is loathsome. **562** *Ego Dominus . . . non ingredior*, "I am the Lord, and I will not enter the city" (adapted from Hosea 11:9). **563 seovethe**, seventh. **563–64 for-te beo the brihtre . . . ow for hire her**, in order to be the brighter and see the more brightly in heaven God's bright face, for you have fled the world and [you] hide yourself from her (lit., before her) here. **564–66 Yet ter-teken thet . . . i-seid th'ruppe**, Yet besides that you are swift as the sun beam, because you are enclosed with Jesus Christ as [if] in a sepulchre, restrained (lit., barred) as He was on the dear Cross, as is said above. **567 eahtuthe**, eighth; **to habben cwic . . . yeorne hwer-vore**, to have living prayer — and look carefully why (lit., wherefore). **567–68 The eadmode cwen . . . on Englische ledene**, The humble Queen Esther betokens (or, symbolizes) the anchoress, for her name says (i.e., means) "hidden" in the English language. **569–70 As me ret in hire . . . to death i-demet**, As one reads (*ret* = reduced form of *redeth*) in her book, she was pleasing to King Ahasuerus over all [others], and through her prayer (or, request) saved from death all her people, who were (lit., was) judged to death. **570–71 This nome Assuer . . . eadi over alle**, This name Ahasuerus is interpreted [as] "happy, blessed," as is said before, and symbolizes God, blessed over all [creation]. **571–73 He yetteth Hester . . . ham muche folc**, He grants to Esther the queen

thet is, the treowe ancre, thet is riht Hester, thet is riht "i-hud" — he hereth ant yetteth hire alle hire benen, ant sawveth thurh ham muche folc. Monie schulde beo forloren the beoth thurh the ancre benen i-borhen, as weren thurh Hesteres, for-hwon thet ha beo

575 Hester ant halde hire as heo dude, Mardochees dohter. "Mardoche" is i-spealet **amare conterens inpudentem** — thet is, "bitterliche totreodinde thene scheomelese." Scheomeles is the mon the seith eani untu other deth bivoren ancre. Yef eani thah swa do, ant heo breoke bitterliche his untohe word other his fol dede, totreod*e* ham anan-riht with unwurth tellunge, thenne is ha Hester, Mardochees dohter, bitterliche breokinde

580 thene scheomelese. Bitterluker ne betere ne mei ha him neaver breoken then is i-taht th'ruppe with **narraverunt michi**, other mid tis vers: **Declinate a me maligni et scrutabor mandata Dei mei**, ant wende in-ward anan toward hire weovede ant halde hire ed hame, as Hester, the "i-hudde." Semei i Regum hefde death ofservet, ah he criede mearci ant Salomon foryef hit him, thah thurh swuch a foreward: thet he ed

— that is, the true anchoress, who is a proper Esther, who is properly "hidden" — He hears and grants her all her prayers, and saves through them many (lit., much) people. **573–75 Monie schulde beo . . . Mardochees dohter**, Many would be lost who are saved through the anchorite's prayers, as were through Esther's, provided that she (i.e., the anchoress) be Esther and holds herself (i.e., behaves) as she (i.e., Esther) did, Mordecai's daughter. **575–76 "Mardoche" is i-spealet . . . totreodinde thene scheomelese**, "Mordecai" is interpreted [as] "bitterly grinding (or, trampling) the shameless" (source unidentified) — that is, "bitterly treading down (or, trampling) the shameless" (*thene* = inflected def. art.). **577 the seith eani untu . . . bivoren ancre**, who says or does any ill-mannered [thing] before (i.e., in the presence of) an anchoress. **577–80 Yef eani thah . . . breokinde thene scheomelese**, If anyone nevertheless does so, and [then] she break[s] (i.e., condemns) bitterly his ill-mannered word[s] or his foul deed, [if she] trample[s] them at once by counting [them] worthless, then she is Esther, Mordecai's daughter, harshly crushing (or, defeating) the shameless. **580–81 Bitterluker ne betere . . . mid tis vers**, She cannot ever crush (or, defeat) him more harshly nor better than is taught above with "[evil ones] have told me [lying fables]" (Psalm 118:85), or with this verse. **581–82 Declinate a me . . . Dei mei**, "Depart from me cursed [ones] and I shall search the commands of my God" (Psalm 118:115 — see 2.560 above). **582–83 ant wende in-ward . . . as Hester, the "i-hudde,"** and [let her] turn inward at once toward her altar and hold (or, keep) herself at home, as Esther did, the "hidden" [one]. **583–86 Semei i Regum . . . to death i-demet**, Shimei in Kings (1 Kings 2:36–46) had deserved death but he cried "mercy" and Solomon forgave it him, though with such an agreement: that he [should] keep himself at home in Jerusalem where he lived and [should] hide himself in his house, [and] if he

585　hame heolde him i Jerusalem as he wunede ant hudde him in his huse, yef he o-hwider wende ut — swuch wes the foreward — thet he were eft al ful ant to death i-demet. He thah brec foreward thurh his unselhthe. His threalles edfluhen him ant edbreken him ut, ant he folhede ham ant wende ut efter ham — hwet wult tu mare? — wes sone forwreiet to the king, Salomon, ant for the foreward tobroken wes, fordemet to deathe.

590　Understondeth yeorne this, mine leove sustren. Semey bitacneth the ut-warde ancre, nawt Hester, the "i-hudde." For Semey seith **audiens,** thet is "herinde" on ure ledene — thet is the recluse the haveth asse earen, longe to here feor, thet is hercninde efter ut-runes. Semeis stude wes Jerusalem, thet he schulde in huden him yef he walde libben. This word "Jerusalem" spealeth "sihthe of peis" ant bitacneth ancre-hus. For th'rinne

595　ne thearf ha seon bute peis ane. Ne beo neaver Semei — thet is, the recluse swa swithe forgult toward te sothe Salomon — thet is, ure Laverd. Halde hire ed hame i Jerusalem thet ha na-wiht nute of the worldes baret. Salomon yetteth hire blitheliche his are, ah yef ha entremeateth hire of thinges withuten mare then ha thurfte, ant hire heorte beo ute-

went out anywhere — such was the agreement — that he was again offending (lit., foul) and condemned (lit., judged) to death. **586–87 He thah brec foreward ... his unselhthe,** He nevertheless broke the agreement through his wretchedness. **587–89 His threalles edfluhen ... fordemet to deathe,** His servants (lit., thralls) fled [from] him and broke out [away from] him, and he followed them and went out after them — what more do you want (i.e., and what do you expect)? — [and] was accused [or, betrayed] to king, Solomon, and, since the agreement was broken, condemned to death. **590–91 Semey bitacneth ... the "i-hudde,"** Shimei symbolizes the external (lit., outward) anchoress, not Esther, the "hidden" [one]. **591–93 For Semey seith** *audiens* **... hercninde efter ut-runes,** For Shimei says (i.e., means) "hearing" which is "listening" in our language — that is, the recluse who has ass' ears, long [in order] to hear far, [and] who is listening for news (or, rumors). **593 Semeis stude wes Jerusalem ... he walde libben,** Shimei's place was Jerusalem which he should (i.e., was supposed to) hide himself in if he wanted to live. **594 spealeth,** means; **"sihthe of peis" ant bitacneth ancre-hus,** "sight of peace" and symbolizes the anchor-house. **594–96 For th'rinne ne thearf ... te sothe Salomon,** For in there (i.e., the anchor-house) she need not see [anything] but peace alone. Let her never be Shimei — that is, the recluse so very guilty toward the true Solomon. **596–97 thet is, ure Laverd ... the worldes baret,** that is, our Lord. [Let her] keep herself at home in Jerusalem [so] that she [might] know nothing (*nute = ne wite*) at all of the world's strife. **597–600 Salomon yetteth hire ... efter his threalles,** Solomon grants her happily his grace, but if she interferes (reflex.) with things outside (i.e., external things) more than she need, and her heart is [focused on the] outside, [even] though her (lit., a) clod of earth — that

with, thah a clot of eorthe — thet is, hire licome — beo in-with the fowr wahes, ha is
i-wend with Semei ut of Jerusalem alswa as he dude efter his threalles. Theos threalles
beoth the ethele fif wittes, the schulden beon et hame ant servin hare leafdi. Thenne ha
servith wel the ancre, hare leafdi — hwen ha notieth ham wel in hare sawle neode: hwen
the ehe is o the boc, other o sum other god, the eare to Godes word, the muth in hali bonen.
Yef ha wit ham uvele ant let ham thurh yemeles etfleon hire servise ant folhi ham ut-wart
with hire heorte — as hit bitimeth eaver meast thet gan the wittes ut, the heorte geath ut
efter — ha breketh Salomon foreward with the unseli Semey ant is to death i-demet.

For-thi mine leove sustren, ne beo ye nawt Semey, ah beoth Hester, the "i-hudde,"
ant ye schule beon i-hehet i the blisse of heovene. For the nome of Hester ne seith nawt
ane **abscondita** — thet is, nawt ane "i-hud" — ah deth ther-teken, **elevata in populis**
— thet is, "i folc i-hehet." Ant swa wes Hester, as hire nome cwiddeth, i-hehet to cwen
of a povre meiden. I this word "Hester" beoth "hudunge" ant "hehnesse" i-feiet togederes,
ant nawt ane "hehnesse," ah "hehnesse over folc" for-te schawin witerliche thet teo the

is, her body — is within the four walls, she has gone with Shimei out of Jerusalem just as he
did after his servants. **600–01 Theos threalles beoth . . . servin hare leafdi,** These servants
(lit., thralls) are the in-born (or, native) five senses, which should be at home and serve their
lady. **601–03 Thenne ha servith . . . in hali bonen,** They serve well the anchoress, their lady
— then when they put themselves to good use in her soul's need: when the eye is on the
book or on some other good [thing], the ear to God's word, the mouth in holy prayers. **604–
06 Yef ha wit ham . . . to death i-demet,** If she guards them badly (*wit* = reduced form of
witeth) and lets them through carelessness escape her service and [if she] follows them
outward with her heart — it happens most often (lit., ever most) that [if] the senses go out,
the heart goes out after [them] — she breaks Solomon's agreement with the unfortunate
Shimei and is judged (or, condemned) to death. **607–08 ne beo ye nawt . . . blisse of heovene,**
do not be (imper.) Shimei, but be Esther, the "hidden" [one], and you will be exalted (or, lifted
up) into the bliss of heaven. **608–10 For the nome of Hester . . . "i folc i-hehet,"** For the
name of Esther does not say (i.e., mean) "hidden" only — that is, not only "hidden" — but
does (i.e., means) besides that "raised among the people" — that is, "exalted among the
people." **610 swa,** so (or, thus). **610–11 as hire nome cwiddeth . . . a povre meiden,** as her
name says, raised (i.e., promoted) into a queen from a poor virgin. **611–14 I this word
"Hester" . . . wurthliche i-hehet,** In this word "Esther" are [the words] "hiding" and "highness" (or, loftiness) joined together, and not only "highness," but "highness over people,"
in order to show clearly that those who hide themselves rightly in their anchor-house, in

hudeth ham ariht in hare ancre-hus — ha schulen beon in heovene over othres cunnes folc wurthliche i-hehet. Ba Hesteres nome ant hire hehunge pruvieth thet ich segge. On other half understondeth: ye beoth i Jerusalem. Ye beoth i-flohe to chirche grith. For n*is* ower nan thet nere sum-chearre Godes theof. Me weiteth ow — thet wite ye ful yeorne — withuten, as me deth theoves the beoth i-broke to chirche. Haldeth ow feaste inne. Nawt te bodi ane, for thet is the unwurthest, ah ower fif wittes ant te heorte over al, ant al ther the sawle lif is. For beo ha bitrept ute-with, nis ther bute leade forth toward te geal-forke — thet is, the weari-treo of helle. Beoth ofdred of euch mon alswa as the theof is, leste he drahe ow ut-wart — thet is, biswike with sunne — ant weiti for-te warpen upon ow his cleches. Bisecheth yeornliche Godd as theof i-broke to chirche, thet he wite ant wardi ow with alle the ow weitith. Chiterith ower beoden aa as spearewe deth [thet is] ane, for this an word is i-seid of anlich lif, of anlich stude, ther me mei

615

620

heaven, they will be raised worthily (i.e., in honor) above other kinds of people (lit., over folk of other kind). **614–15 Ba Hesteres nome . . . i Jerusalem**, Both Esther's name and her raising prove what I say (i.e., have been saying). On the other side (i.e., at the same time), understand (imper.): you are in Jerusalem. **615 Ye beoth i-flohe . . . grith**, You have fled to the church's sanctuary (or, peace). **615–16 For nis ower nan . . . Godes theof**, For [there] is not (*nis = ne is*) one of you that was not [at] some time [or another] God's thief. **616–17 Me weiteth ow . . . i-broke to chirche**, People wait (i.e., are waiting) for you outside — you know that very well — as [they do for] thieves who have escaped to a church. **617 Haldeth ow feaste inne**, Keep (lit., hold) yourself fast (i.e., firmly) inside. **618–19 Nawt te bodi . . . sawle lif is**, Not the body (i.e., your body) alone, for that is the most worthless, but your five senses and the heart above all, and all [things] where (or, in which) the life of the soul is. **619–20 For beo ha bitrept . . . weari-treo of helle**, For [if] she (i.e., the heart) is trapped outside, there is [nothing to do] but [to be] led up to the gallows (passive inf.) — that is, the punishment-tree (i.e., gibbet) of hell. **620–22 Beoth ofdred of . . . ow his cleches**, Be afraid of each man just as the thief is, lest he draw (i.e., tempt) you out — that is, deceive [you] with sin — and lie in wait to get (lit., throw) his clutches on you. **622–23 Bisecheth yeornliche Godd . . . the ow weitith**, Beseech (or, beg) God eagerly as a thief [who has] escaped to the church, that He protect and guard you against all who lie in wait for you. **623–25 Chiterith ower beoden . . . euch gastelich biyete**, Chirp your prayers continually as the sparrow does which is "alone," for this one word is said of the solitary life, of the solitary place, where one can be Esther, hidden away from the world, and [where one can] do (or, undertake) better than in the crowd (lit.,

625   beon Hester, i-hud ut of the world, ant do betere then i thrung euch gastelich biyete. For-thi eveneth Davith ancre to pellican thet leat anlich lif, ant to spearewe ane.

    Spearewe haveth yet a cunde thet is biheve ancre, thah me hit heatie — thet is, the fallinde uvel. For muche neod is, thet ancre of hali lif ant of heh habbe fallinde uvel. Thet uvel ne segge ich nawt thet me swa nempneth, ah fallinde uvel ich cleopie licomes

630   secnesse other temptatiuns of flesches fondunges hwer-thurh hire thunche thet ha falle dune-ward of hali hehnesse. Ha walde awilgin elles other to wel leoten of [hire-seolven], ant swa to noht i-wurthen; the flesch walde awilgin ant bicumen to ful-itohen toward hire leafdi — yef hit nere i-beaten — ant makie sec the sawle — yef secnesse hit ne temede with uvel other with sunne.

635   The licome ne the gast — yef hare nowther nere sec, as hit timeth seldene, orhel walde awakenin, thet is the measte dredfule secnesse of alle. Yef Godd fondeth ancre with ei uvel ute-with, other the feonde in-with with gasteliche untheawes, ase prude, wreaththe, onde, other with flesches lustes, ha haveth thet fallinde uvel, thet me seith is

throng) each spiritual profit. **626 For-thi eveneth Davith . . . to spearewe ane,** For this reason David compares the anchoress to a pelican which leads (*leat* = reduced form of *leadeth*) a solitary life, and to a solitary sparrow. **627–28 Spearewe haveth yet . . . fallinde uvel,** A sparrow has nevertheless a nature (or, characteristic) that is an advantage [to an] anchoress, though one [might] hate it — that is, the falling sickness (i.e., epilepsy). **628 For muche neod is . . . habbe fallinde uvel,** For [there] is a great need that an anchoress of holy and of high life have the falling sickness. **628–31 Thet uvel ne segge . . . of hali hehnesse,** I do not mean (lit., say) that sickness which they name thus, but I call a "falling sickness" sickness of the body or trials of the temptation of the flesh, by which [it] seems to her that she falls downward from a holy height. **631–34 Ha walde awilgin elles . . . with sunne,** She would grow wild or else think too well of herself, and so come (lit., be) to nothing; the flesh would grow wild and become too badly behaved toward her lady — if it were not beaten — and make the soul sick — if sickness did not tame it with evil or with sin. **635–36 The licome ne the gast . . . secnesse of alle,** If neither of them, the body or the spirit, were sick, as it seldom happens, pride would awaken which is the most dreadful sickness of all. **636–39 Yef Godd fondeth ancre . . . is spearewe uvel,** If God tests (or, tempts) the anchoress with any sickness on the outside (i.e., external sickness), or the fiend (i.e., devil) inside [tempts her] with spiritual vices, [such] as pride, wrath, envy, or with the flesh's desires, she has the falling sickness,

640 spearewe uvel. Godd hit wule for-thi thet ha beo eaver eadmod ant with lah haldunge of hire-seolven falle to ther eorthe, leste ha falle i prude.

Nu we hurteth, leove sustren, to the feorthe dale, thet ich seide schulde beon of feole fondunges, for ther beoth uttre ant inre, ant either moni-valde. Salve ich bihet to teachen toyeines ham ant bote, ant hu hwa-se haveth ham mei gederin of this dale cunfort ant frovre toyeines ham alle. Thet ich thurh the lare of the Hali Gast mote halden foreward,

645 he hit yetti me thurh ower bonen.

which they say (lit., one says) is the sparrow's sickness. **639–40 Godd hit wule . . . falle i prude**, God desires (lit., wants it) therefore that she always be humble and with low opinion (lit., holding) of herself [He wants her to] fall to the earth (or, ground), lest she fall in[to] pride. **641–42 Nu we hurteth . . . ant either moni-valde**, Now we dash on, dear sisters, to the fourth part, which I said should be about many temptations, for there are outer and inner [temptations], and many of each (lit., manifold of either). **642–44 Salve ich bihet to teachen . . . toyeines ham alle**, I promised to teach you a salve (i.e., medicine) against them and a remedy, and how whoever has them (i.e., temptations) can gather from this part comfort and consolation against them all. **644–45 Thet ich thurh the lare . . . thurh ower bonen**, That I, by the teaching of the Holy Spirit, keep the agreement, may He grant it to me through your prayers.

Part Four

Temptations

Ne wene nan of heh lif thet ha ne beo i-temptet: mare beoth the gode, the beoth i-clumben hehe, i-temptet then the wake — ant thet is reisun. For se the hul is herre, se the wind is mare th'ron. Se the hul is herre of hali lif ant of heh, se the feondes puffes — the windes of fondunges — beoth strengre th'ron ant mare. Yef ei ancre is the ne veleth nane fondunges, swithe drede i thet puint thet ha beo over-muchel ant over-swithe i-fondet. For swa Sein Gregoire seith: **Tunc maxime inpugnaris cum te inpugnari non sentis.** Sec mon haveth twa estaz swithe dredfule: thet an is hwen he ne feleth nawt his ahne secnesse, ant for-thi ne secheth nawt leche ne lechecreft, ne easketh na-mon read, ant asteorveth ferliche ear me least wene. This is the ancre the nat nawt hwet is fondunge. To

5

10

1–2 Ne wene nan of heh lif . . . thet is reisun, Let no one (lit., none) of high life expect that she [will] not be tempted: the good, who have climbed high, are more tempted than the weak — and that is reasonable. **2–5 For se the hul is herre . . . strengre th'ron ant mare,** For the higher the hill (lit., as the hill is higher), so the wind is greater on it. The higher the hill of holy and high life (lit., as the hill of holy and high life is higher), so the enemy's blasts — the winds of temptations — are stronger on it (lit., thereon) and greater. **5–6 Yef ei ancre is . . . over-swithe i-fondet,** If there is any anchoress who does not feel any temptations, let her very much dread in that point (or, case) that she is excessively (lit., over-much) and very powerfully tempted. **6 For swa,** For as. **7 Tunc maxime inpugnaris . . . non sentis,** "You are then precisely attacked (or, under attack) when you do not feel yourself to be attacked" (cited in Jerome, *Letter to Heliodorus* 4 [*PL* 22.349]). **7–10 Sec mon haveth twa estaz . . . ear me least wene,** A sick man has two conditions, [both] very frightful: the first is when he does not feel his own sickness, and for that reason does not seek a doctor (lit., leech) or healing arts, nor asks advice from anyone, and dies suddenly before one least expect[s]. **10–11 the nat nawt . . . i the Apocalipse,** who does not know what temptation is. To her the angel speaks in the Apoca-

theos speketh the engel i the Apocalipse: **Dicis quia dives sum et nullius egeo, et nescis quia miser es et nudus, et pauper et cecus**. "Thu seist the nis neod na medecine, ah thu art blind i-heortet, ne ne sist nawt hu thu art povre ant naket of halinesse ant gastelich wrecche." Thet other dredfule estat thet te seke haveth is al

15 frommard this. Thet is hwen he feleth se muchel angoise thet he ne mei tholien thet me hondli his sar ne thet me him heale. This is sum ancre the feleth se swithe hire fondunges ant is se sare ofdred thet na gastelich cunfort ne mei hire gleadien ne makien to understonden thet ha mah*e* ant schul*e* thurh ham the betere beon i-borhen. Ne teleth hit i the Godspel thet te Hali Gast leadde ure Laverd seolf into

20 anlich stude, to leaden anlich lif for-te beon i-temptet of the unwine of helle? **Ductus est Jesus in desertum a spiritu ut temptaretur a diabolo**. Ah his temptatiun — the ne mahte sunegin — wes ane withuten.

Understondeth thenne on alre earst, leove sustren, thet twa cunne temptatiuns, twa cunne fondunges beoth — uttre ant inre, ant ba beoth feole-valde. Uttre

---

lypse. **11–12 *Dicis quia dives sum . . . et pauper et cecus***, "You say 'because I am rich I am in no way in need,' and you do not know that for that reason you are pitiful and naked and poor and blind" (Revelation 3:17). **12–14 "Thu seist the nis neod . . . gastelich wrecche,"** "You say [that] for you there is no need of medicine, but you are blind hearted, nor do [you] see how you are poor and naked of holiness and spiritually wretched." **14–16 Thet other dredfule estat . . . thet me him heale,** The second fearful condition that the sick has is quite opposite [from] this. That is when he feels so much anguish that he cannot bear that one [should] handle (or, touch) his sore or that one should heal him. **16–19 This is sum ancre . . . the betere beon i-borhen,** This is the anchoress who [sometimes] feels her temptations so very much and is so sorely afraid that no spiritual comfort can gladden her or make [her] understand that she can and will be the better saved (or, rescued) through them. **19–20 Ne teleth hit . . . the unwine of helle?** Does it not say (lit., tell) in the Gospel that the Holy Spirit led our Lord Himself into a solitary place, to lead a solitary life in order to be tempted by the enemy of hell? **21 *Ductus est Jesus . . . a diabolo***, "Jesus was led into the desert by the spirit so that He might be tempted by the devil" (Matthew 4:1). **21 Ah,** But. **22 the ne mahte sunegin . . . withuten,** for [him] who could not sin — was external only. **23–24 Understondeth thenne . . . beoth feole-valde,** Understand then (imper.) first of all, dear sisters, that [there] are two kinds of temptations, two kinds of tests — the author glosses *temptatiuns*, a French word, with the native *fondunges*) — outer and inner, and both are manifold (i.e., numerous). **24–27 Uttre fondunge is hwer-of kimeth . . . te flesch eileth,** Outer (i.e., external) temptation is [that] from which (lit., whereof)

25   fondunge is hwer-of kimeth licunge other mislicunge withuten other withinnen. Mislicunge withuten: ase secnesse, meoseise, scheome, unhap, ant euch licomlich derf thet te flesch eileth. Withinnen: heorte sar, grome — ant wreaththe *a*lswa, onont thet ha is pine. Licunge withuten: licomes heale, mete, drunch, clath inoh ant euch flesches eise onont swucche thinges. Licunge withinnen: as sum fals
30   gleadschipe other of monne here-word, other yef me is i-luvet mare then an-other, mare i-olhnet, mare i-don god other menske. This dale of this temptatiun thet is uttre i-cleopet, is swikelure then the other half. Ba beoth a temptatiun ant, either withinnen ant withuten, bathe of hire twa dalen. Ah ha is uttre i-cleopet, for ha is eaver other i thing withuten other of thing withuten, ant te uttre thing is the
35   fondunge. Theos fondunge kimeth other-hwile of Godd, of mon other-hwiles. Of Godd: as of freondes death, secnesse other on ham other o the-seolven, poverte, mishapnunge, ant othre swucche, heale alswa ant eise.

pleasure or displeasure comes inside or outside (lit., without or within). [Displeasure] outside: [such] as sickness, discomfort, shame (or, humiliation), bad fortune, and each bodily suffering which ails (or, tortures) the flesh. **27–28 Withinnen . . . is pine,** [Displeasure] inside: the heart's sorrow, grief — and wrath also, in the sense that she (i.e., wrath) is pain. **28–29 Licunge withuten . . . onont swucche thinges,** Pleasure outside: the body's health, food, drink, enough clothes and each comfort (lit., ease) of the flesh regarding such things. **29–31 Licunge withinnen . . . mare i-don god other menske,** Pleasure inside: [such] as some false rejoicing either at men's praise (lit., praise word) or if one is loved more than another, more flattered, better treated or honored (lit., more good or honor done [to her]). **31–32 This dale of this temptatiun . . . the other half,** This part (or, section) of this temptation which is called "outer" is more treacherous (or, deceptive) than the other side (or, part). **32–33 Ba beoth a temptatiun . . . twa dalen,** Both are one temptation and, whether inside or outside, both [are] two parts of her (i.e., temptation). **33–35 Ah ha is uttre i-cleopet . . . te uttre thing is the fondunge,** But she (i.e., this kind of temptation) is called "outer" because she is always either in the things without or from things without, and the outer thing is (i.e., brings) the temptation. **35–37 Theos fondunge . . . heale alswa ant eise,** This temptation comes sometimes from God, other times from man. From God: such as a friend's death, sickness — either in them (i.e., the friends) or in yourself — poverty, accident, and other such [things], prosperity also and comfort.

Of mon: as mislich woh — other of word other of werc, o the other, o thine —
alswa here-word other god-dede. Theos cumeth alswa of Godd, ah nawt as doth
40 the othre, withuten euch middel. Ah with alle he fondeth mon hu he him drede ant
luvie. Inre fondunges beoth misliche untheawes, other lust towart ham other thohtes
swikele, the thuncheth thah gode. Theos inre fondunge kimeth of the feond, of the
world, of ure flesch other-hwile. To the uttre temptatiun is neod patience — thet
is, tholemodnesse. To the inre is neod wisdom ant gastelich strengthe. We schulen
45 nu speoken of the uttre ant teachen theo the habbeth hire, hu ha mahen with Godes
grace i-finde remedie — thet is, elne ayeines hire to frovrin ham-seolven.

Beatus vir, qui suffert temptationem, quoniam cum probatus fuerit, accipiet
coronam vite quam repromisit Deus diligentibus se. "Eadi is ant seli the haveth
i temptatiun tholemodnesse, for hwen ha is i-pruvet," hit seith, "ha schal beon i-
50 crunet mid te crune of lif the Godd haveth bihaten his leove i-corene." "Hwen ha

38–39 Of mon . . . god-dede, From man: such as various injuries — either of word or of
deed, toward others, [or] toward yours (i.e., you and yours) — also praise (lit., praise-
word) or good deeds. **40 middel,** go-between (i.e., human agent). **40–41 Ah with alle he**
fondeth . . . ant luvie, But with everything He tests a man, how (or, to what extent) he
fears and loves Him. **41–42 Inre fondunges beoth misliche . . . the thuncheth thah gode,**
Inner temptations are various vices, either desire towards them or deceptive thoughts, which
seem nevertheless good. **42–43 Theos inre fondunge . . . of ure flesch other-hwile,** This
inner temptation comes from the devil (lit., enemy), from the world, from our flesh sometimes. **43–44 To the uttre temptatiun . . . gastelich strengthe,** For (or, in the face of)
outer temptation [there] is need for patience — that is, long-suffering (see glossary — the
author glosses *patience*, a French word, with the native *tholemodnesse*). In the face of the
inner [there] is need for wisdom and spiritual strength. **44–46 We schulen nu speoken . . . to**
frovrin ham-seolven, We shall now speak of the outer [temptation] and teach those who
have it (lit., her), how they can with God's grace find a remedy — that is, strength against
it (lit., her, outer temptation) to comfort themselves. **47–48 Beatus vir . . . Deus diligentibus**
se, "Blessed [is the] man who endures temptation, for when he has been proved, he will receive
the crown of life which God has promised to those who love him" (James 1:12). **48–50 "Eadi**
is ant seli . . . leove i-corene," "[She] is favored and blessed who has patience in temptation,
for when she is proven," it says, "she will be crowned with the crown of life (*te* = reduced form
of *the* after preceding *-t*) which God has promised to His beloved chosen."

is i-pru[v]et," hit seith. Wel is hit i-seid, for alswa pruveth Godd his leove i-corene, as the golt-smith fondeth thet gold i the fure. Thet false gold forwurtheth th'rin; thet gode kimeth ut brihtre. Secnesse is a brune hat for-te tholien, ah na thing ne clenseth gold as hit deth the sawle.

55 Secnesse thet Godd send — nawt thet sum lecheth thurh hire ahne dusi-schipe — deth theose six thinges: (i) wescheth the sunnen the beoth ear i-wrahte, (ii) wardeth toyein theo the weren towardes, (iii) pruveth pacience, (iiii) halt in eadmodnesse, (v) muchleth the mede, [vi] eveneth to martir thene tholemode. Thus is secnesse sawlene heale, salve of hire wunden, scheld, thet ha ne kecche 60 ma, as Godd sith thet ha schulde, yef secnesse hit ne lette. Secnesse maketh mon to understonden hwet he is, to cnawen him-seolven — ant, as god meister, beat for-te leorni wel hu mihti is Godd, hu frakel is the worldes blisse. Secnesse is thi gold-smith the i the blisse of heovene overguldeth thi crune. Se the secnesse is mare, se the golt-smith is bisgre, ant se hit lengre least, se he brihteth hire swithere

51–52 Wel is hit i-seid . . . i the fure, It is said well, for God so proves (or, tests) His beloved chosen, as the goldsmith tests gold in the fire. **52–54 Thet false gold forwurtheth . . . as hit deth the sawle,** False gold perishes in there (lit., therein); the good [gold] comes out brighter. Sickness is a burning (or, flame) hot to suffer, but nothing cleanses gold as [well as] it does the soul. **55–58 Secnesse thet Godd send . . . eveneth to martir thene tholemode,** A sickness which God sends (*send* = reduced form of *sendeth*) — not [one] that someone catches through her own stupidity — does these six things: 1) washes [away] the sins which are committed before, 2) guards against those which were tending (or, coming), 3) proves (or, tests) patience, 4) keeps [one] in humility, 5) increases the reward, 6) makes the patient [one] equal to the martyr. **59–60 Thus is secnesse . . . yef secnesse hit ne lette,** Thus sickness is the healing of souls, salve (or, ointment) for her wounds, a shield, so that she catch (or, receive) no more, as God sees that she would, if sickness did not prevent it. **60 mon,** a man (or, one, a person). **61–62 hwet he is . . . the worldes blisse,** what he is, to know himself — and, like a good teacher, [sickness] beats (*beat* = reduced form of *beateth*) in order to teach well (or, effectively) how mighty God is, [and] how vile the world's joy is. **62 thi,** your. **63 the i the blisse . . . thi crune,** who (or, which) in the joy of heaven [will] gild your crown. **63–65 Se the secnesse is mare . . . thurh a hwilinde wa,** The greater the sickness (lit., as the sickness is more), the busier is the goldsmith — and the longer it (i.e., the sickness) lasts, the more quickly he brightens (or, shines) her to be a martyr's equal through a temporary

65 to beo martirs evening thurh a hwilinde wa. Hwet is mare grace to theo the hefde
ofearnet the pinen of helle, world abuten ende? Nalde me tellen him alre monne
dusegest, the forseke a buffet for a speres wunde? a nelde pricchunge for an
bihefdunge? a beatunge for an hongunge on helle weari-treo, aa on ecnesse? Godd
hit wat, leove sustren, al the wa of this world is i-evenet to helle alre leaste pine.

70 Al nis bute bal-plohe. Al nis nawt swa muchel as is a lutel deawes drope toyeines
the brade sea ant alle worldes weattres. The mei thenne edstearten thet ilke grisliche
wa, the eateliche pinen thurh secnesse thet agea*th*, thurh ei uvel thet her is, seliliche
mei ha seggen.

On other half leornith moni-valde frovren ayein the uttre fondunge the kimeth
75 of monnes uvel, for theos, the ich habbe i-seid of, is of Godes sonde. Hwa-se
eaver misseith the other misdeth the — nim yeme ant understond thet he is thi vile
the lorimers habbeth ant fileth al thi rust awei ant ti ruhe of sunne. For he fret
him-seolven, weilawei, as the file deth, ah he maketh smethe ant brihteth thi sawle.

suffering. **65–68 Hwet is mare grace . . . aa on ecnesse?** What is a greater grace to those who
had deserved the pains of hell, world without end? Would not one account him the stupidest of
all men who would refuse a buffet (or, blow) for a spear's wound? a needle's prick for a
beheading? a beating for a hanging on the gallows (lit., accursed tree) of hell, forever in eternity? **68–69 Godd hit wat . . . leaste pine**, God knows (lit., God knows it), dear sisters, all the
suffering of this world is compared to the least of all of hell's pain. **70–71 Al nis bute bal-
plohe . . . alle worldes weattres**, All [suffering in the world] is [nothing] but ball-play (i.e., a
very easy and pleasant thing). All [of it] is not so much as a little drop of dew against (i.e., in
comparison to) the broad sea and all the world's waters. **71–73 The mei thenne edstearten . . .
seliliche mei ha seggen**, Whoever can then escape that same grisly suffering, the horrific
pains, through a sickness which passes, through any disease that is here [in the world] — she
can call [herself] fortunate. **74–75 On other half . . . is of Godes sonde**, On the other side (i.e.,
at the same time), learn manifold (i.e., many) comforts against the outer temptation which
comes from man's evil (or, malice), for this, which I have spoken of (i.e., sickness), is of God's
sending. **75–77 Hwa-se eaver misseith . . . ti ruhe of sunne**, Whosoever slanders or mistreats
you — pay (lit., take) attention and understand that he is your file which metal smiths (or,
tinkers) have and [he] files all the rust away and your roughness of sin (*ti* = reduced form of *thi*
after preceding -*t*). **77–78 For he fret him-seolven . . . brihteth thi sawle**, For he eats himself
up (or, wears himself away; *fret* = reduced form of *fretteth*), alas, as a file does, but he smoothes
and brightens (or, shines) your soul.

On other wise thench hwa-se-eaver hearmeth the other eni wa deth the, scheome,
grome, teone — he is Godes yerde. For swa he seith thurh Sein Juhanes muth i the
Apocalipse: **Ego quos amo arguo et castigo.** "Ne beat he nan bute hwam-se he
luveth ant halt for his dohter," na-mare then thu waldest beaten a fremede child
thah hit al gulte. Ah nawt ne leote he wel of thet is Godes yerde, for as the feader
hwen he haveth inoh i-beaten his child ant haveth hit i-tuht wel, warpeth the
yerde i the fur, for ha nis noht na-mare, alswa the Feder of heovene hwen he
haveth i-beaten with an unwreast mon other an unwrest wummon his leove child
for his god, he warpeth the yerde — thet is, the unwreste — into the fur of helle.
For-thi he seith elles-hwer, **Michi vindictam; ego retribuam** — thet is, "min is
the wrake: ich chulle yelden," as thah he seide, "ne wreoke ye nawt ow-seolven,
ne grucchi ye ne wearien hwen me gulteth with ow, ah thencheth anan thet he is
ower feadres yerde ant thet he wule yelden him yerde servise." Ant nis thet child
ful-itohen thet scratleth ayein ant bit up-o the yerde? Thet deboneire child hwen

79–80 On other wise . . . Godes yerde, In another way, think [that] whosoever harms you or
does you any woe (i.e., inflicts any suffering on you), shame, anger, aggravation — he is God's
rod (or, stick). **80 swa,** so; **muth,** mouth. **81 *Ego quos amo arguo et castigo,*** "I denounce (or,
accuse) and chastise those whom I love" (Revelation 3:19). **81–83 Ne beat he nan . . . thah hit
al gulte,** "He does not beat any [one] but [her] whom he loves and holds (*halt* = reduced form
of *haldeth*) for his daughter" (adapted from Proverbs 3:11–12 or Hebrews 12:6), no more than
you would beat a strange child though it completely did wrong. **83–85 Ah nawt ne leote he
wel of . . . i the fur,** But [let] him who is God's rod (i.e., scourge) not think highly of [himself],
for [just] as when he has beaten his child enough and has disciplined it well throws the stick in
the fire, for it (lit., she, the stick) is nothing (i.e., of no use) any more, just so the Father of
heaven, when he has beaten His beloved child for his [own] good with a wicked man or a
wicked woman, He throws the stick — that is, the wicked [one] — into the fire of hell. **88 For-
thi,** For this reason; **elles-hwer,** elsewhere; *Michi vindictam; ego retribuam,* "Let vengeance
be Mine; I shall repay" (Romans 12:19, see Hebrews 10:30). **88–91 "min is the wrake . . .
yerde servise,"** "vengeance is Mine: I will repay," as though (or, if) He said, "do not avenge
yourselves, nor complain or curse when [some]one does wrongs against you, but think (or,
consider) at once that He is your Father's stick (or, rod) and that He will pay him for a stick's
service (i.e., treat him like a stick)." **91–93 Ant nis thet child ful-itohen . . . don alswa,** And
is not the child ill-mannered (or, badly disciplined) who scratches against and bites on the
stick? The meek (i.e., well-behaved) child, when it is beaten, if the father commands it [to do

hit is i-beaten, yef the feader hat hit, hit cusseth the yerde — ant ye don alswa, mine leove sustren. For swa hat ower feader thet ye cussen naw*t* with muth, ah
95   with luve of heorte theo the he ow with beateth. **Diligite inimicos vestros. Benefacite hiis qui oderunt vos et orate pro persequentibus et calumpniantibus vos**. This is Godes heste, thet him is muchel leovre then thet tu eote gruttene bred other weredest hearde here: "luvieth ower va-men," he seith, "ant doth god yef ye mahen to theo thet ow weorrith." Yef ye elles ne mahen, biddeth yeorne for theo
100   thet ow eni eil doth other misseggeth. Ant te Apostle leareth, "ne yelde ye neaver uvel for uvel, ah doth god eaver ayein uvel" as dude ure Laverd seolf ant alle his hali halhen. Yef ye thus haldeth Godes heaste, thenne beo ye his hende child ant cusseth the yerde the he haveth ow with i-thorschen. Nu seith other-h[w]ile sum, "his sawle — other hiren — ich chulle wel luvien, his bodi o nane wise." Ah thet
105   nis nawt to seggen. The sawle ant te licome nis bute a mon ant ba ham tit a dom.

so], it kisses the stick, and you [should] do likewise, my dear sisters. **94–95 For swa hat ower feader . . . beateth**, For your Father thus commands (*hat* = reduced form of *hateth*) that you [ought to] kiss, not with [your] mouth, but with love of [your] heart, those whom He thrashes you with. **95–97 *Diligite inimicos vestros . . . et calumpniantibus vos***, "Love your enemies. Bless those who hate you and pray for those who persecute and slander you" (Matthew 5:44 and Luke 6:27–28). **97–99 This is Godes heste . . . thet ow weorrith**, This is God's command, which is much dearer (or, more preferable) to Him than that you [would] eat bran (i.e., coarse) bread or wear a rough hair[shirt]: "love your foe-men (i.e., enemy)," he says, "and do good if you can to those that attack you." **99–102 Yef ye elles ne mahen . . . his hali halhen**, "If you cannot do otherwise (lit., else), pray earnestly for those who do you any injury or [who] slander (lit., missay) [you]." And the Apostle teaches, "do not ever pay evil for evil, but always do good [in return] for evil as did our Lord Himself and all His holy saints" (1 Thessalonians 5:15, see 1 Peter 3:9). **102–03 Yef ye thus haldeth Godes heaste . . . with i-thorschen**, If you thus keep (lit., hold) God's command, then you are His gracious child and [you] kiss the stick which He has thrashed you with. **103–04 Nu seith other-h[w]ile sum . . . o nane wise**, Now sometimes some[one] says, "I will love his soul — or hers — [but] his body in no way (or, on no account)." **104–05 Ah thet nis nawt to seggen**, But that is not to [be] said (i.e., ought not to be mentioned). **105–06 The sawle ant te licome . . . to an i-sompnet?** The soul and the body is but one man (or, person) and one judgment will befall both [of] them (*tit* = reduced form of *tideth*). Will you divide into two [that] which God has joined

211

Wult tu dealen o twa, the Godd haveth to an i-sompnet? He forbeot hit ant seith, **Quod Deus conjunxit homo non separet**. Ne wurthe nan se wod thet he to-deale the thing the Godd haveth i-veiet.

Thencheth yet thisses weis: thet child, yef hit spurneth o sum thing other hurteth, me beat thet hit hurte on, ant thet child is wel i-paiet, foryeteth al his hurt ant stilleth hise teares. For-thi frovrith ow-seolven: **Letabitur justus cum viderit vindictam**. Godd schal o Domes-dei don as thah he seide, "Dohter, hurte thes the? Dude he the spurnen i wreaththe other in heorte sar, i scheome other in eani teone? Loke, dohter, loke," he seith, "hu he hit schal abuggen." Ant ther ye schule seon bunkin him with thes deofles betles, thet wa bith him thes lives. Ye schulen beo wel i-paiet th'rof, for ower wil ant Godes wil schal swa beon i-veiet thet ye schulen wullen al thet he eaver wule, ant he al thet ye wulleth.

Over alle othre thohtes in alle ower passiuns, thencheth eaver inwardliche up-o Godes pinen, thet te worldes wealdent walde for his threalles tholien swucche

into one? **106 forbeot**, forbids (*forbeot* = reduced form of *forbeoteth*). **107 *Quod Deus conjunxit homo non separet***, "What God has joined [let] no man put asunder (lit., separate)" (Matthew 19:6). **107–08 Ne wurthe nan se wod . . . the Godd haveth i-veiet**, Let no one (lit., none) be so mad that he separate the thing which God has joined. **109–11 Thencheth yet thisses weis . . . stilleth hise teares**, Think yet in this way: the child, if it trips on something or strikes against [it], one beats what it struck against, and the child is well pleased, forgets completely its hurt (or, knock) and stops its tears. **111 For-thi frovrith ow-seolven**, For this reason, comfort yourselves. **111–12 *Letabitur justus cum viderit vindictam***, "The just [one] shall rejoice when he shall see vengeance (or, punishment)" (Psalm 57:11). **112–14 Godd schal o Domes-dei . . . he hit schal abuggen**, God will on Doomsday do as though (or, if) He said, "Daughter, did this [one] hurt you (or, strike you)? Did he make you stumble in anger or in heart's sorrow (or, pain), in shame or in any hardship? Look, daughter, look," He says, "how he will pay for (lit., buy) it." **114–15 Ant ther ye schule seon . . . thes lives**, And there you will see him bonked (*bunkin* = passive inf.: lit., you will see him [to be] beaten) with the devil's (*thes* = inflected def. art.) sledgehammers [so] that he will despair of his life (lit., woe is him of life). **115–17 Ye schulen beo wel i-paiet . . . al thet ye wulleth**, You will be well pleased with that (lit., thereof), for your will and God's will will be so joined that you will desire all [things] that He ever desires, and He all [things] that you desire. **118–25 Over alle othre thohtes . . . helpeth him-seolven!** Beyond all other thoughts in all your sufferings, think always to yourself (lit., inwardly) on God's pains, that the world's wielder (or, lord) wanted to suffer for His

212

120 schendlakes, hokeres, buffez, spatlunge, blindfeallunge, thornene crununge thet
set him i the heaved swa thet te blodi strundes striken adun ant leaveden dun to
ther eorthe; his swete bodi i-bunden naket to the hearde piler ant i-beate swa thet
tet deore-wurthe blod ron on euche halve; thet attri drunch thet me him yef, tha
him thurste o rode; hare heafde sturunge upon him, tha heo on hokerunge gredden
125 se lude, "Lo, her the healde othre! Lo, hu he healeth nu ant helpeth him-seolven!"
Turneth th'ruppe ther ich spec hu he wes i-pinet in alle his fif wittes ant eveneth al
ower wa, secnesse ant other-hwet, woh of word other of werc, ant al thet mon mei
tholien to thet tet he tholede, ant ye schulen lihtliche i-seon hu lutel hit reacheth,
nomeliche yef ye thencheth thet he wes al ladles ant thet he droh al this nawt for
130 him-seolven, for he ne agulte neaver. Yef ye tholieth wa, ye habbeth wurse ofservet,
ant al thet ye tholieth al is for ow-seolven.

Gath nu thenne gleadluker bi strong wei ant bi swincful toward te muchele
feaste of heovene, ther-as ower gleade freond ower cume i-kepeth, thenne dusie

thralls (or, servants) such humiliations, mockings, buffets, spitting, blindfolding, crowning of
thorns, which sunk into His head (lit., set Him in the head) so that the bloody streams flowed
downwards and washed down to the earth; His sweet body bound naked to the hard pillar and
beaten so that that precious blood ran (or, flowed) on every side; [think on] the poisonous
drink that they (lit., one) gave Him, when He was thirsty (lit., when [it] thirsted to Him) on the
Cross; [think on] the wagging of their heads (in derision) up at Him, when they in mockery
cried so loud, "Look, here [is the one] who healed others! Look, [let us see] how He now heals
and helps Himself!" (see Matthew 27:39–43). **126–30 Turneth th'ruppe ther ich spec . . . he
ne agulte neaver,** Turn [to the page] above (lit., up there) where I spoke [about] how he was
tortured in all his five senses (see gloss to 2.667 ff.) and compare (imper.) all your woe (or,
pain), sickness and anything else, insult of word or of deed, and everything that man may
suffer to that which He suffered, and you will easily see how little it extends (i.e., how little
man's suffering compares with His), especially if you consider that He was completely innocent, and that He suffered all this not for Himself (i.e., on his own account), for He never did
wrong (or, sinned). **130–31 Yef ye tholieth wa . . . for ow-seolven,** If you suffer pain, you
have deserved worse, and everything that you suffer, all [of it] is for yourself (i.e., because of
your own guilt). **132–34 Gath nu thenne gleadluker . . . death of helle,** Go then more gladly
along the difficult and laborious path toward the great feast of heaven, where your glad friend
expects (lit., keeps) your coming, [go more gladly] than foolish (lit., dizzy) men of the world

135 worldes men gath bi grene wei toward te weari-treo ant te death of helle. Betere is
ga sec to heovene then hal to helle, to murhthe with meoseise then to wa with eise.
**Salomon: Via impiorum complantata est lapidibus — id est, duris
afflictionibus**. Nawt for-thi witerliche wrecche worltliche men buggeth deorre
helle then ye doth the heovene. A thing to sothe wite ye — a misword thet ye
tholieth, a deies longunge, a secnesse of a stunde, yef me chapede ed ow an of
140 theos o Domes-dei — thet is, the mede the ariseth th'rof — ye hit nalden sullen
for al the world of golde. For thet schal beon ower song bivoren ure Laverd:
Letati sumus pro diebus quibus nos humiliasti, annis quibus vidimus mala —
thet is, "wel is us for the dahes thet tu lahedest us with other monne wohes, ant
wel is us nu Laverd for the ilke yeres thet we weren seke in, ant sehen sar ant
145 sorhe." Euch worltlich wa — hit is Godes sonde. Heh monnes messager me schal
hehliche undervon ant makien him glead chere — nomeliche yef he is prive with

go by the green path toward the gallows (lit., criminal tree) and the death of hell. **134–35
Betere is ga sec to heovene . . . to wa with eise**, [It] is better to go sick to heaven than whole
(or, healthy) to hell; [it is better to go] to mirth with discomfort than to suffering with comfort.
136–37 *Salomon: Via impiorum . . . duris afflictionibus*, Solomon: "The path of the wicked is
planted with stones" — that is, with hard sufferings (based on Ecclesiaticus 21:11). **137–38
Nawt for-thi witerliche . . . the heovene**, Nonetheless (lit., not for that reason) certainly miserable worldly men [will] buy (or, pay for) hell more dearly (or, expensively) than you do
heaven. **138–41 A thing to sothe wite ye . . . the world of golde**, Know (imper.; lit., know
you) one thing for certain (lit., as truth): an insult (lit., mis-word) that you suffer, a day's
anxiety, a sickness of an hour, if one bargained (or, wanted to exchange) with you for one of
these on Doomsday — that is, the reward which arises from it (lit., thereof) — you would
not sell it for the (i.e., a) world of gold. **141 For thet schal beon . . . ure Laverd**, For this
will be your song before our Lord. **142 *Letati sumus pro diebus . . . vidimus mala***, "We
have rejoiced for the days on which you humbled us, for the years in which we have seen
evil [things]" (Psalm 89:15). **143 wel is us**, [it] is well for us (i.e., we rejoice); **dahes**,
days; **lahedest us with other monne wohes**, humbled (lit., lowered) us with other men's
insults. **144–45 nu Laverd for the ilke yeres . . . sar ant sorhe**, now Lord for the same
years that we were sick in, and saw pain and sorrow. **145–47 Euch worltlich wa . . . with
his laverd**, Each earthly woe — it is God's message-bearer. A high (or, noble) man's
messenger one must receive highly (or, lavishly) and [one must] welcome him (lit., make

his laverd. Ant hwa wes mare prive with the king of heovene hwil he her wunede then wes thes sondes-mon — thet is, worldes weane, the ne com neaver from him athet his lives ende? Thes messager — hwet teleth he ow? He frovreth ow o this

150 wise: "Godd, as he luvede me, he send me to his leove freond. Mi cume ant mi wununge, thah hit thunche attri, hit is halwende. Nere thet thing grislich, hwas schadewe ye ne mahte nawt withute*n* hurt felen? Hwet walde ye seggen bi thet eisfule wiht thet hit of come? Wite ye to sothe thet al the wa of this world nis bute schadewe of the wa of helle. Ich am the schadewe," seith thes messager — thet is,

155 worldes weane — "nedlunge ye moten other undervo me other thet grisliche wa thet ich am of schadewe. Hwa-se underveth me gleadliche ant maketh me feier chere, mi laverd send hire word thet ha is cwite of thet thing thet ich am of schadewe." — Thus speketh Godes messager. For-thi seith Sein Jame: **Omne gaudium existimate, fratres, cum in temptationes varias incideritis**. "Alle blisse

160 haldeth hit to fallen i misliche of theose fondunges," the uttre beoth i-haten. Ant

---

him glad cheer) — especially if he is intimate with his lord. **147–49 Ant hwa wes mare prive . . . athet his lives ende?** And who was more intimate with the King of heaven while He lived here than was this message-bearer — that is, the world's misery, which did not come from (i.e., leave) Him until his life's end? **149 hwet teleth he ow?** what does he tell you? **149– 51 He frovreth ow . . . hit is halwende**, He comforts you in this way: "God, since he loved me, He sent me to His dear friend. My coming and my stay (or, dwelling), though it seem poisonous (or, pestilential), it is healing. **151–53 Nere thet thing grislich . . . thet hit of come?** Would that not be a grisly thing whose [mere] shadow you could not feel without pain? What would you say about the horrible creature [itself] that it (i.e., the shadow) came from? **153–54 Wite ye to sothe . . . the wa of helle**, Know (imper.) for a truth that all the woe of this world is but a shadow of the woe of hell. **154 Ich**, I. **155 worldes weane**, the world's misery. **155–56 nedlunge ye moten other undervo . . . of schadewe**, You must by necessity receive either me or the grisly suffering of which I am the shadow. **156–58 Hwa-se underveth me . . . ich am of schadewe**, Whosoever receives me gladly and welcomes me (lit., makes me fair cheer), my lord sends her word that she is quit (or, free) of that thing which I am the shadow of. **158 For-thi**, For this reason. **158–59 *Omne gaudium . . . temptationes varias incideritis***, "Consider [it] all joy, brothers, when you meet with (or, fall into) various temptations" (James 1:2). **159–60 Alle blisse haldeth hit . . . the uttre beoth i-haten**, "Hold (i.e., consider) it all bliss to fall into various of these temptations," which are called outer (i.e., external).

Seint Pawel: **Omnis disciplina in presenti videtur esse non gaudii set meroris; postmodum vero fructum, et cetera**. "Alle the ilke fondunges the we beoth nu i-beaten with thuncheth wop, nawt wunne, ah ha wendeth efter-ward to weole ant to eche blisse."

165   The inre fondunge is twa-valt, alswa as is the uttre. For the uttre is [adversite ant prosperte ant theos cundleth the inre: mislicunge] in adversite ant i prosperite licunge the limpeth to sunne. This ich segge for-thi thet sum licunge is ant sum mislicunge the ofearneth muche mede, as licunge i Godes luve ant mislicunge for sunne. Nu as ich segge, the inre fondunge is twa-vald: fleschlich ant gastelich.

170   Fleschlich — as of leccherie, of glutunie, of slawthe. Gastelich — as of prude, of onde, ant of wreaththe, alswa of yiscunge. Thus beoth the inre fondunges the seoven heaved sunnen ant hare fule cundles. Flesches fondunge mei beon i-evenet to fot-wunde. Gastelich fondunge, thet is mare dred of, mei beon for the peril i-cleopet breost-wunde. Ah us thuncheth greattre flesliche temptatiuns for-thi thet

161–62 *Omnis disciplina . . . vero fructum, et cetera*, "Every discipline for the present seems to be not joyful, but mournful; afterwards truly [it will yield the most peaceful] fruit, etc." (slightly altered from Hebrews 12:11). **162–64 "Alle the ilke fondunges . . . to eche blisse,"** "All the very temptations which we are now beaten with seem [to be] weeping not joy, but they turn afterwards into happiness (lit., weal) and into eternal joy." **165–67 The inre fondunge is twa-valt . . . limpeth to sunne,** The inner temptation is twofold, just as the outer is. For the outer is (i.e., consists of) adversity and prosperity and these kindle the inner [temptations]: displeasure in adversity and in prosperity the pleasure which belongs to sin. **167–69 This ich segge . . . mislicunge for sunne,** I say this because [there] is some pleasure and some displeasure which deserves much reward, [such] as pleasure in God's love and displeasure towards sin. **169–70 Nu as ich segge . . . slawthe,** Now as I say, the inner temptation is two-fold: bodily (lit., fleshly) and spiritual. Bodily [temptations] — [such] as from lechery, from gluttony, from sloth. Spiritual [temptations] — [such] as from pride, from envy, and from wrath, also from covetousness. **171–73 Thus beoth the inre fondunges . . . to fot-wunde,** Thus the inner temptations are the seven deadly (lit., head, or chief) sins and their foul progenies (or, offspring). The temptation of the flesh can be compared to a foot wound. **173–74 Gastelich fondunge . . . breost-wunde,** A spiritual temptation, concerning which there is more fear (i.e., which is more frightening), can, because of the danger, be called a chest wound. **174–75 Ah us thuncheth . . . heo beoth eth-fele,** But bodily temptations seem to us greater (or, more severe) because they

175 heo beoth eth-fele. The othre, thah we habben ham, ofte nute we hit nawt ant beoth thah greate ant grisliche i Godes ehe ant beoth muchel for-thi to drede the mare. For the othre the me feleth wel secheth leche ant salve. The gasteliche hurtes ne thuncheth nawt sare, ne ne salvith ham with schrift ne with penitence ant draheth to eche death ear me least wene.

180 Hali men ant wummen beoth of alle fondunges swithest ofte i-temptet, ant ham to goder heale. For thurh the feht toyeines ham, ha biyeoteth the blisfule kempene crune. Lo, thah hu ha meaneth ham i Jeremie: **Persecutores nostri velociores aquilis celi, super montes persecuti sunt nos; in deserto insidiati sunt nobis**. Thet is, "Ure wither-iwines swiftre then earnes up-o the hulles ha clumben efter

185 us, ant ther fuhten with us, ant yet i the wildernesse ha spieden us to sleanne. Ure wither-iwines beoth threo: the feond, the worlt, ure ahne flesch, as ich ear seide. Lihtliche ne mei me nawt other-hwile i-cnawen hwuch of theos threo him weorreth,

are easy to feel. **175–77 The othre, thah we habben ham . . . drede the mare**, The others (i.e., spiritual temptations), though we have them, often we do not know it, and [they] are nevertheless dangerous and horrific (lit., grisly) in God's eye and [they] are for that reason to be dreaded much the more. **177–79 For the othre the me feleth . . . ear me least wene**, For the others which one feels well (or, clearly), seek (imper.) a doctor and medicine (lit., salve). The spiritual wounds do not seem severe (lit., sore), or do not heal themselves with confession or with penitence, and [so] lead to eternal death before one least expect[s]. **180–81 Hali men ant wummen . . . to goder heale**, Holy men and women are tempted by all temptations most strongly, and to their good (or, benefit — see *heale* in glossary). **181–82 For thurh the feht . . . i Jeremie**, For through the fight (or, struggle) against them, they gain the joyful champions' crown. Lo (or, see), though, how they complain (reflex.) in Jeremiah. **182–83 *Persecutores nostri . . . insidiati sunt nobis***, "Our persecutors, swifter than eagles of the sky, have pursued us over the mountains; they have lain in wait for us in the desert" (Lamentations 4:19). **184–85 Ure wither-iwines swiftre then earnes . . . us to sleanne**, Our enemies swifter than eagles on the hills have climbed after us, and there fought with us, and still they plotted (lit., spied) to slay us in the wilderness. **185–90 Ure wither-iwines beoth threo . . . the her-efter beoth i-nempnet**, Our enemies are three: the devil (lit., fiend), the world, [and] our own flesh, as I said before. Sometimes one cannot easily know which of these three [is] attacking him, for each [one] helps the other, though the devil naturally (or, characteristically) incites to malice (lit., venomousness), [such] as to pride, to disdain, to envy and to wrath, and to their poisonous

for euch helpeth other, thah the feond proprement eggeth to atternesse, as to prude,
to over-hohe, to onde ant to wreaththe, ant to hare attri cundles the her-efter beoth
190   i-nempnet. The flesch sput proprement toward swetnesse, eise, ant softnesse. The
world bit mon yiscin worldes weole ant wurthschipe, ant othre swucche give-
gaven the bidweolieth cang men to luvien a schadewe. "Theos wither-iwines," hit
seith, "folhith us on hulles, ant weitith i wildernesse hu ha us mahen hearmin."
Hul — thet is heh lif, ther the deofles asawz ofte beoth strengest. Wildernesse is
195   anlich lif of ancre wununge. For alswa as i wildernes beoth alle wilde beastes ant
nulleth nawt tholien monne nahunge, ah fleoth hwen ha heom i-hereth, alswa
schulen ancres over alle othre wummen beo wilde o thisse wise, ant thenne beoth
ha over othre leove to ure Laverd, ant swetest him thuncheth ham. For of all flesches
is wilde deores fle*sch* leovest ant swetest.

200   Bi this wildernesse wende ure Laverdes folc, as Exode teleth, toward te eadi
lond of Jerusalem, thet he ham hefde bihaten. Ant ye, mine leove sustren, wendeth

progenies (or, offspring) which are named hereafter. **190–92 The flesch sput proprement
. . . luvien a schadewe,** The flesh urges (*sput* = reduced form of *sputteth*) naturally toward
sweetness, pleasure, and softness. The world asks one to covet the world's wealth and
honor, and other such gewgaws (or, baubles) which deceive foolish men to love (i.e., into
loving) a shadow. **192–93 "Theos wither-iwines . . . us mahen hearmin,"** "These enemies," it says, "follow us onto hills, and lie in wait (i.e., plot) in the wilderness how they
can harm us." **194–95 Hul — thet is, heh lif . . . ancre wununge,** A hill — that is, the high
(or, spiritual) life, where the devil's assaults often are the strongest. The wilderness is the
solitary life of the anchoress' dwelling (or, cell). **195–98 For alswa as i wildernes . . .
thuncheth ham,** For just as [there] are wild beasts in the wilderness, and [they] will not
allow men's approach (or, nearing), but flee when they hear them, just so ought anchoresses
above all other women to be wild in this way, and then are they over [all] others dear to
our Lord, and seem sweetest to Him (lit., [He] thinks them [to be] sweetest to Him). **198–
99 For of all flesches . . . leovest ant swetest,** For of all meat (lit., flesh), wild animal's
meat is the most beloved (i.e., sought after) and sweetest. **200–01 Bi this wildernesse
wende ure Laverdes folc . . . hefde bihaten,** Along this wilderness our Lord's people
went, as Exodus tells, towards the blessed (or, rich) land of Jerusalem, which He had
promised them. **201–03 Ant ye, mine leove sustren . . . his i-corene,** And you, my dear
sisters, go (or, walk) along the same path (lit., way) toward the high Jerusalem, the king-

bi the ilke wei toward te hehe Jerusalem, the kinedom thet he haveth bihaten his i-corene. Gath, thah, ful warliche, for i this wildernesse beoth uvele beastes monie: liun of prude, neddre of attri onde, unicorne of wreaththe, beore of dead slawthe, 205 vox of yisceunge, suhe of yivernesse, scorpiun with the teil of stinginde leccherie — thet is, galnesse. Her beoth nu o rawe i-tald the seoven heaved sunnen:

The Liun of prude haveth swithe monie hwelpes, ant ich chulle nempni summe: **vana gloria** — thet is, hwa-se let wel of ei thing thet ha deth other seith, other haveth: wlite other wit, god acointance other word mare then an-other, cun other 210 meistrie, ant hire wil forthre. Ant hwet is wlite wurth her? Gold ring i suhe nease — acointance i religiun. Wa deth hit ofte. Al is **vana gloria**, the let ea-wiht wel of, ant walde habben word th'rof, ant is wel i-paiet yef ha is i-preiset, mispaiet yef ha nis i-tald swuch as ha walde. An-other is **indignatio** — thet is, the thuncheth hokerlich of ei thing thet ha sith bi other other hereth, ant forhoheth chastiement,

dom which He has promised His chosen [ones]. **203–06 Gath, thah, ful warliche . . . heaved-sunnen,** Go, however, very carefully (lit., warily), for in this wilderness there are many evil beasts: the lion of pride, serpent of venomous envy, unicorn of wrath, bear of dead[ly] sloth, fox of covetousness, sow of gluttony, scorpion with his (lit., the) tail of stinging lechery — that is, lechery (the author glosses French *lecherie* with the native *galnesse*). Here now the seven deadly sins (lit., head sins) are described (or, counted up) in a row (or, one by one). **207 The Liun of prude . . . nempni summe,** The Lion of pride has very many whelps, and I will name some. **208–10 *vana gloria* . . . hire wil forthre,** "vainglory" — that is, whosoever thinks well of anything that she does or says or has: beauty or knowledge, good acquaintance (i.e., connections) or a reputation better (lit., word more) than another, lineage or mastery (i.e., power), and [having] her wishes [advanced] further (i.e., getting her way; Savage/Watson: "more willpower"). **210 Ant hwet is wlite wurth her?** And what good (lit., worth) is beauty to her? **210–11 Gold ring . . . hit ofte,** Acquaintance (i.e., connections) in religion — [it is a] gold ring in a sow's nose. It does mischief (lit., woe) often. **211–13 Al is *vana gloria* . . . as ha walde,** All is vainglory (see Ecclesiastes 1:2), which (or, who) thinks at all well of [herself], and would have a reputation for that (lit., thereof), and is well-pleased if she is praised, displeased if she is not described such as she would [be]. **213–15 An-other is *indignatio* . . . ei lahres lare,** Another [whelp of pride] is "indigna-tion" — that is, whoever thinks disdainfully of anything that she sees or hears concerning another, and despises (or, rejects) chastisement (i.e., correction), or the teaching of any

215   other ei lahres lare. The thridde hwelp is **ypocresis**, the maketh hire betere then ha is. The feorthe is **presumtio**, the nimeth mare on hond then ha mei overcumen, other entremeteth hire of thing thet to hire ne falleth, other is to overtrusti up-o Godes grace other on hire-seolven, to bald upon ei mon, thet is fleschlich as heo is, ant mei beon i-temptet. The fifte hwelp hatte inobedience — nawt ane the ne

220   buheth, [ah the] other grucchinde deth, other targeth to longe: thet child the ne buheth ealdren, underling his prelat, paroschien his preost, meiden hire dame — euch lahre his herre. The seste is loquacite: the fedeth this hwelp the is of muche speche, yelpeth, demeth othre, liheth other-hwile, gabbeth, upbreideth, chideth, fikeleth, stureth lahtre. The seovethe is blasphemie. This hwelpes nurrice is, the

225   swereth greate athes other bitterliche curseth, other misseith bi Godd other bi his halhen for ei thing thet he tholeth, sith other hereth. The eahtuthe is inpatience. This hwelp fet, the nis tholemod ayein alle wohes ant in alle uveles. The nihethe

---

lower [person]. **215–16** *ypocresis . . . ha is*, "hypocrisy," whoever makes herself [out to be] better than she is. **216–19 The feorthe is *presumtio* . . . mei beon i-temptet**, The fourth is "presumption," which (or, whoever) takes more in hand than she can overcome (i.e., manage), or inserts herself (i.e., meddles) in a thing which does not concern her (lit., fall to her), or is too over-confident of God's grace or of herself, too bold towards any man, who is fleshly (or, physical) as she is, and can be tempted. **219–22 The fifte hwelp hatte inobedience . . . euch lahre his herre**, The fifth whelp is named "disobedience" — not only whoever does not obey (lit., bow), but whoever either does [so] grumbling, or delays too long: the child who does not obey [its] elders, an underling his superior (lit., prelate), a parishioner his priest, a maid her lady — each lower [one] his higher (or, superior). **222–24 The seste is loquacite . . . stureth lahtre**, The sixth is loquacity (or, talkativeness): the person (lit., who) feeds this whelp who is of much talk, boasts, condemns others, lies sometimes, mocks, upbraids, chides, flatters (or, deceives by flattery), [or] stirs up laughter. **224 seovethe**, seventh; **nurrice**, nurse. **224–26 the swereth greate athes . . . sith other hereth**, whoever swears great oaths or curses bitterly, or blasphemes (i.e., says something amiss) about God or about His saints because of anything that he (i.e., the swearer) suffers, sees or hears. **226 eahtuthe**, eighth. **227 This hwelp fet . . . in alle uveles**, [She] feeds (*fet* = reduced form of *fedeth*) this whelp who is not patient in response to (lit., against) all insults and in all evils (or, illnesses). **227–30 The nihethe is contumace . . . ut of hire riote**, The ninth is contumacy (i.e., stubbornness), and [she] feeds this, whosoever is stubborn in a thing which she has undertaken to do — be it good, be it evil

is contumace, ant this fet hwa-se is ane-wil i thing thet ha haveth undernume to donne — beo hit god, beo hit uvel — thet na wisure read ne mei bringen hire ut of hire riote. The teohethe is **contentio** — thet is, strif to overcumen, thet te other thunche underneothen awarpen ant cravant, ant heo me*i*stre of the mot, ant crenge ase champiun the haveth biyete the place. I this untheaw is upbrud, ant edwitunge of al thet uvel thet ha mei bi the other ofthenchen — ant eaver se hit biteth bittrure, se hire liketh betere, thah hit were of thing the wes bivore yare amendet. Her-imong beoth other-hwiles nawt ane bittre wordes, ah beoth fule stinkinde scheomelese ant schentfule, sum-chearre mid great sware, monie ant prude wordes with warinesses ant bileasunges. Her-to falleth evenunge of ham-seolf, of hare cun, of sahe other of dede. This is among nunnen, ant gath with swuch muth seoththen, ear schrift ham habbe i-weschen, to herie Godd with loft-song, other biddeth him privee bonen! Me, thinges amansede, nuten ha thet hare song ant hare bonen to Godd stinketh fulre to him ant to alle his halhen, then ei rotet dogge?

— so that no wiser advice can bring her out of her extravagance (or, draw her off the wrong scent — see *riote* in glossary). **230–32 The teohethe is** *contentio* **. . . biyete the place,** The tenth is "contention" — that is, the striving to overcome (i.e., come out ahead), so that the other may seem [to be] thrown underneath and defeated, and she [may seem the] master of the meeting (or, encounter, debate) and strut as the champion who has won the place (or, field). **232–34 I this untheaw . . . bivore yare amendet,** In (or, along with) this vice is upbraiding and blame for all the evil that she can think of concerning the other — and the bitterer it bites, so [much the] better [it] pleases her, even though it were concerning a thing which was amended a long time before (lit., before yore). **234–37 Her-imong beoth other-hwiles . . . warinesses ant bileasunges,** Along with this (lit., here-among) [there] are sometimes not only bitter words, but [there] are foul, stinking, shameless and disgraceful [ones], sometimes with great swearing, many and proud words with cursings and lies (or, slanders). **237–38 Her-to falleth evenunge of ham-seolf . . . of dede,** To this (lit., here-to) belongs comparison of themselves, of their family (or, lineage), of their talk or of their deed (i.e., actions). **238–40 This is among nunnen . . . privee bonen!** This is (i.e., sometimes happens) among nuns, and [they] go with such mouths afterwards, before confession has washed them, to praise God with praise-song, or pray intimate prayers to Him! **240–41 Me, thinges amansede . . . then ei rotet dogge?** But, cursed things, do they [not] know that their songs and their prayers to God stink fouler to Him and to all His saints, than any rotted (or, decomposing) dog?

221

The ealleofte hwelp is i-fed with supersticiuns, with semblanz ant with sines, as beoren on heh thet heaved, crenge with swire, lokin o siden, bihalden on hokere, winche mid ehe, binde seode mid te muth, with hond other with heaved makie scuter signe, warpe schonke over schench, sitten other gan stif as ha i-staket were, luve lokin o mon, speoken as an innocent, ant wlispin for then anes. Her-to falleth of veil, of heaved clath, of euch other clath to ove[r]gart acemunge other in heowunge other i pinchunge, gurdles ant gurdunge o dameiseles wise, scleaterunge mid smirles, fule fluthrunges, heowin her, litien leor, pinchen bruhen other bencin ham uppart with wete fingres. Monie othre ther beoth the cumeth of weole, of wunne, of heh cun, of feier clath, of wit, of wlite, of strengthe. Of heh *lif* waxeth prude, ant of hali theawes. Monie ma hwelpes then ich habbe i-nempnet haveth the liun of prude. Ah abute theose studieth wel swithe, for ich ga lihtliche over, ne do bute nempni ham. Ah ye eaver i-hwer se ich ga swithere vorth, leaveth ther

242–46 The ealleofte hwelp is i-fed . . . for then anes, The eleventh whelp is fed (or, nourished) with fancy airs, with appearances and with signs (or, gestures), [such ones] as bear [their] head[s] on high, proudly arch their necks (lit., swagger with the neck), look to the side (lit., sides), behold (or, look around) in disdain, purse the lips (lit., bind a purse with the mouth), with hand or with head make a taunting gesture (lit., sign), throw [one] leg over [the other] leg, sit or walk, stiff as if they were staked (i.e., tied to a stake, or impaled), love to look at a man, speak as an innocent, and lisp for the purpose (*for then anes = for the nanes* "for the nonce" — see *nanes* in glossary). **246–50 Her-to falleth of veil . . . with wete fingres**, To this belongs (lit., here-to falls) too overwrought an adornment of the veil, of the head-cloth, of any other cloth (or, piece of clothing) either in coloring (or, ornamenting) or in pleating, belts and belting (or, wearing of belts) in a young lady's style (lit., way), plastering with ointments (i.e., makeup), foul flirtings, coloring the hair, painting [her] face, pinching (or, plucking) the brows or arching them upwards with wet fingers. **250–52 Monie othre ther beoth . . . of hali theawes**, There are many others (i.e., signs of pride) which come from wealth, from joy, from high lineage, from beautiful clothing, from knowledge, from beauty, from strength. From a high (or, spiritual) life pride grows (i.e., can grow), and from holy virtues [as well]. **252–53 Monie ma hwelpes . . . liun of prude**, The lion of pride has many more whelps than I have named. **253–54 Ah abute theose . . . bute nempni ham**, But concerning these, study (or, pay attention) very carefully, for I go lightly over [them], and do but name them (i.e., and merely list them). **254–55 Ah ye eaver i-hwer . . . tene other tweolve**, But you always, wheresoever I go more quickly forward, linger there the longest, for there I load into one word ten or twelve

255   lengest, for ther ich fetheri on a word tene other tweolve. Hwa-se-eaver haveth
eani untheaw of theo the ich her nempnede, other ham iliche — ha haveth prude
sikerliche hu-se-eaver hire curtel beo i-schapet other i-heowet. Heo is the liunes
make thet ich habbe i-speken of, ant fet hire wode hwelpes in-with hire breoste.

      The Neddre of attri onde haveth seove hwelpes: **ingratitudo** — this cundel

260   bret hwa-se nis i-cnawen god-dede, ah teleth lutel th'rof other foryet mid alle.
God-dede — ich segge nawt ane thet mon deth him, ah thet Godd deth him, other
haveth i-don him — other him other hire — mare then ha understont yef ha hire
wel bithohte. Of this untheaw me nimeth to lutel yeme, ant is thah of alle an
lathest Godd ant meast ayein his grace. The other cundel is **rancor sive odium** —

265   thet is, heatunge other great heorte. The bret hit i breoste, al is attri to Godd thet
he eaver wurcheth. The thridde cundel is ofthunchunge of othres god; the feorthe,
gleadschipe of his uvel; the fifte, wreiunge; the seste, bac-bitunge; the seovethe,

(i.e., I pack one word with the meaning of ten or twelve). **255–57 Hwa-se-eaver haveth eani untheaw . . . i-schapet other i-heowet,** Whosoever has any vice of those which I named here, or [vices] like them — she has pride surely, howsoever her gown is shaped or colored. **257–58 Heo is the liunes make . . . in-with hire breoste,** She is the lion's mate which I have spoken of, and feeds (*fet* = reduced form of *fedeth*) her mad (or, raging) whelps within her breast (or, heart). **259–60 The Neddre of attri onde . . . foryet mid alle,** The Serpent of venemous envy has seven whelps (or, offspring): "ingratitude" — [the person] breeds this offspring who does not acknowledge good deeds, but thinks little of them (lit., thereof) or forgets [them] as well. **261–63 God-dede . . . bithohte,** Good deeds — I do not mean (lit., say) only that [which] someone does for him (i.e., the ungrateful person), but what God is doing for him, or has done for him — either him or her — more than she understands if she had considered (reflex.) well. **263–64 Of this untheaw . . . ayein his grace,** People pay (lit., take) little attention to this vice, but [it] is nevertheless of all [vices] one [of] the most hateful to God and [the one] most against His grace. **264–65 The other cundel is *rancor sive odium* . . . great heorte,** The second offspring is "rancor or hatred" — that is, hating a big (i.e., swollen) heart. **265–66 The bret hit i breoste . . . of othres god,** To whomever breeds (*bret* = reduced form of *bredeth*) it in [his] heart everything that he ever does (lit., works) is venemous to God. The third offspring is grief (or, regret) at another's good. **266–68 the feorthe, gleadschipe . . . other scarnunge,** The fourth, happiness for his evil (or, harming); the fifth, betrayal (or, denunciation); the sixth, backbiting; the seventh, upbraiding

up-brud other scarnunge. The eahtuthe is **suspitio** — thet is, misortrowunge bi mon other bi wummon withuten witer tacne, thenchen, "this semblant ha maketh.

270 This ha seith other deth, me for-te gremien, hokerin other hearmin" — ant thet hwen the other neaver thide[r]-ward ne thencheth. Her-to falleth falsdom, thet Godd forbeot swithe, as thenchen other seggen, "ye, ne luveth ha me nawt. Her-of ha wreide me. Lo, nu ha speoketh of me the twa — the threo, other the ma the sitteth togederes. Swuch ha is ant swuch, ant for uvel ha hit dude." I thulli thoht

275 we beoth ofte bichearret, for ofte is god thet thuncheth uvel, ant for-thi beoth al dei monnes domes false. Her-to limpeth alswa luthere neowe fundles ant leasunges ladliche thurh nith ant thurh onde. The nihethe cundel is sawunge of unsibsumnesse, of wreaththe, ant of descorde. Theo the saweth this deofles sed — ha is of Godd amanset. The teohethe is luther stilthe, the deofles silence, thet te an nule for onde

280 speoken o the other, ant this spece is alswa cundel of wreaththe, for hare teames beoth i-mengt ofte togederes. Hwer as ei of theos wes, ther wes the cundel — other the alde moder — of the attri neddre of onde.

or scorning. **268–71 The eahtuthe is *suspitio* . . . ne thencheth,** The eighth is "suspicion" — that is, false suspicion of a man or of a woman without sure evidence, to think, "she is making this face. She does or says this in order to anger, spite, or harm me" — and that [thought], when the other never thinks in that direction (lit., thitherward) [at all]. **271–74 Her-to falleth falsdom . . . ha hit dude,** To this belongs falsehood, which God forbids strongly (*forbeot* = reduced form of *forbeodeth*), as to think or say, "indeed, she does not love me. In this (lit., here-of) she betrayed (or, accused) me. Look, now they [are] talking about me, the two, the three, or more [of them] who sit together. She is a such and such, and she did it for evil (i.e., to cause harm)." **274– 76 I thulli thoht . . . monnes domes false,** In such a thought we are often misled, for often what seems evil is good, and for this reason men's judgments are false every day (i.e., constantly). **276–77 Her-to limpeth alswa . . . thurh onde,** To this (lit., hereto) pertains also wicked new inventions (or, fabrications), and lies [made] loathsome by malice and by envy. **277–79 The nihethe cundel . . . Godd amanset,** The ninth offspring is the sowing (or, planting) of strife, of wrath, and of discord. She who sows this devil's seed — she is cursed by God. **279–81 The teohethe is luther stilthe . . . ofte togederes,** The tenth is wicked stillness (or, silence), the devil's silence, that (i.e., when) the one will not, for envy, speak about the other, and this type is also an offspring of wrath, for their progeny are often mixed together. **281–82 Hwer as ei of theos wes . . . of onde,** Where any of these [characteristics] has been (lit., was), there has been the brood of the poisonous serpent of envy, or the original (lit., old) mother [herself].

The Unicorne of wreaththe, the bereth on his nease the thorn thet he asneaseth with al thet he areacheth, haveth six hwelpes. The earste is chast other strif. The

285 other is wodschipe. Bihald te ehnen ant te neb hwen wod wreaththe is i-munt. Bihald hire contenemenz, loke on hire lates, hercne hu the muth geath, ant tu maht demen hire wel ut of hire witte. The thridde is schentful up-brud. The feorthe is wariunge. The fifte is dunt. The seste is wil thet him uvel tidde, other on him- seolf, other on his freond, other on his ahte. The seovethe hwelp is, don for

290 wreaththe mis, other leaven wel to don, forgan mete other drunch, wreoken hire with teares yef ha elles ne mei, ant with weariunges hire heaved spillen o grome, other on other wise hearmin hire i sawle ant i bodi bathe. Theos is homicide ant morthre of hire-seolven.

The Beore of hevi slawthe haveth theose hwelpes: **torpor** is the forme: thet is,

295 wlech heorte — unlust to eni thing — the schulde leitin al o lei i luve of ure Laverd. The other is **pusillanimitas** — thet is, to povre heorte ant to earh mid alle ei heh thing to underneomen in hope of Godes help, ant i trust on his grace, nawt

---

283–84 The Unicorne of wreaththe . . . six hwelpes, The Unicorn of wrath, which bears on its nose the spine (or, horn — see note) with which he gores everything he can get at, has six whelps (or, colts). **284–87 The earste is chast other strif . . . ut of hire witte**, The first is quarreling or strife. The second is madness (or, rage). Behold (i.e., look at) the eyes and the face when mad wrath has mounted up. Look at her behavior, look at her expressions (or, bear- ing, appearance), listen how the (i.e., her) mouth goes, and you might judge her [to be] well out of her wits. **287–89 The thridde is schentful up-brud . . . other on his ahte**, The third is humiliating invective. The fourth is cursing. The fifth is violence (or, striking). The sixth is the desire that [something] evil may happen to him, either to himself or to his friend, or to his possessions. **289–92 The seovethe hwelp is . . . i bodi bathe**, The seventh offspring is to do wrong because of wrath, or omit to do well, to go without food or drink, to avenge herself with tears if she cannot [do anything] else, and to damn her [own] head with cursings [uttered] in a rage, or in any way to harm herself both in soul and in body. **293 morthre**, murder. **294–96 The Beore of hevi slawthe . . . luve of ure Laverd**, The Bear of sluggish sloth has these whelps (or, cubs): "torpor" is the first: that is, a lukewarm heart — lack of desire (or, disincli- nation) for anything — which should blaze completely in flame for love of our Lord. **296–98 The other is *pusillanimitas* . . . of hire strengthe**, The second is "pusillanimity" (or, faint- heartedness) — that is, a heart too poor and cowardly as well to undertake any high (or, spiri-

225

of hire strengthe. The thridde is **cordis gravitas**. This haveth hwa-se wurcheth god ant deth hit tah mid a dead ant mid an hevi heorte. The feorthe is ydelnesse, hwa-se stut mid alle. The fifte is heorte grucchunge. The seste is a dead sorhe for lure of ei worltlich thing other for eni unthonc, bute for sunne ane. The seovethe is yemelesschipe other to seggen other to don, other to biseon bivoren, other to thenchen efter, other to miswiten eni thing thet ha haveth to yemen. The eahtuthe is unhope. This leaste beore hwelp is grimmest of alle, for hit tocheoweth ant tofret Godes milde milce ant his muchele mearci ant his unimete grace.

The Vox of yisceunge haveth theose hwelpes: triccherie ant gile, theofthe, reaflac, wite, ant herrure strengthe, false witnesse other ath, dearne symonie, gavel, oker, festschipe, prinschipe of yeove other of lane — this is i-cluht heorte, untheaw Gode lathest the yef us al him-seolven — mon-slaht other-hwile. This untheaw is to vox for moni reisun i-evenet. Twa ich chulle seggen. Muche gile is i vox ant swa is i yisceunge of worltlich biyete. An-other: the vox awurieth al a floc thah he

300

305

310

tual) thing in hope of God's help, and in trust of His grace, not in her [own] strength. **298–99 The thridde is *cordis gravitas* . . . mid an hevi heorte**, The third is "heaviness of heart." [She] has this, whosoever does good and does it, however, with a dead and with a heavy heart. **300 hwa-se stut mid alle**, whoever stops (or, quits) with everything (*stut* = reduced form of *stutteth*). **300–01 The fifte is heorte grucchunge . . . for sunne ane**, The fifth is the heart's complaining (or, grumbling). The sixth is a dead[ly] sorrow for the loss of any worldly thing or for any offense, except for sin alone. **301–03 The seovethe is yemelesschipe . . . haveth to yemen**, The seventh is inattentiveness either to say or to do (i.e., in saying or doing [something]), either watching out before[hand], or thinking afterwards, or neglecting anything that she has (or, ought) to pay attention to. **303–05 The eahtuthe is unhope . . . his unimete grace**, The eighth is despair. This last bear's cub is the grimmest of all, for it chews apart and gobbles up God's mild forgiveness and His great mercy and His immeasurable grace. **306–09 The Vox of yisceunge . . . mon-slaht other-hwile**, The Fox of covetousness has these whelps: treachery and guile, thievery, plundering, fining (or, extortion) and superior force, false witness or oath, secret simony, lending at interest (lit., tribute), usury (or, interest), stinginess, parsimony of gift or of loan (i.e., reluctance to either give or loan) — this is a tight-fisted heart, a vice most hateful to God who gives us all of Himself — manslaughter (or, killing) sometimes. **309–11 This untheaw is to vox . . . of worltlich biyete**, This vice is compared to a fox for many reasons. I will mention (lit., say) two. Much guile is in the fox and so [also] in covetousness of worldly gain. **311–12 An-other: the vox awurieth . . . an frechliche swolhen**, A second (i.e.,

ne mahe buten an frechliche swolhen. Alswa yisceth a yiscere thet tet moni thusent mahten bi flutten, ah thah his heorte berste ne mei he bruken on him-seolf bute a monnes dale. Al thet mon wilneth mare — other wummon — then ha mei rihtliche
315 leade thet lif bi — euch efter thet ha is — al is yisceunge ant rote of deadlich sunne. Thet is riht religiun, thet euch efter his stat borhi ed tis frakele world se lutel se ha least mei of mete, of clath, of ahte, of alle hire thinges. Notith thet ich segge "euch efter his stat," for thet word is i-fetheret. Ye mote makien — thet wite ye — i moni word muche strengthe, thenchen longe ther-abuten, ant bi thet
320 ilke an word understonden monie the limpeth ther-to. For yef ich schulde writen al, hwenne come ich to ende?

The Suhe of yivernesse haveth gris thus i-nempnet: "to earliche" hatte thet an, thet other "to esteliche," thet thridde "to frechliche." Thet feorthe hatte "to muche," thet fifte "to ofte." I drunch mare then i mete beoth theos gris i-ferhet. Ich speoke
325 scheortliche of ham, for nam ich nawt ofdred, mine leove sustren, leste ye ham feden.

the second reason): the fox strangles (i.e., rips the throats of) an entire flock though he can swallow but one [sheep] greedily. **312–14 Alswa yisceth a yiscere . . . a monnes dale,** Just so a coveter covets that which many thousand could live on, but though his heart burst he cannot use (or, consume) by himself but one person's portion. **314–16 Al thet mon wilneth mare . . . deadlich sunne,** Everything that a man — or woman — desires more than she can properly lead life (i.e., live) by — each according to what [rank or type of person] she is — all is covetousness and the root of deadly sin. **316–17 Thet is riht religiun . . . of alle hire thinges,** This is right religion, that each borrow according to his state from this wicked world as little as she ever (lit., least) can of food, of clothing, of possessions, of all her (i.e., the world's) things. **317–18 Notith thet ich segge . . . is i-fetheret,** Note that I say "each according to his state," for that word [i.e., "state"] is loaded [with meaning]. **318–20 Ye mote makien . . . the limpeth ther-to,** You must place (lit., make) great importance — you know this [very well] — on many a word, think long about [it], and by that same one word understand many [more] which pertain to it. **320–21 For yef ich schulde writen al . . . to ende?** For if I should write everything, when would I come to an end? **322–23 The Suhe of yivernesse . . . "to frechliche,"** The Sow of gluttony has piglets named thus: the first is called "too early," the second "too pickily," the third, "too greedily." **323 hatte,** is called. **324 I drunch mare then i mete . . . gris i-ferhet,** In drink more than in food these piglets are farrowed (or, littered). **324–26 Ich speoke scheortliche . . . leste ye ham feden,** I speak briefly (lit., shortly) about them, for I am not afraid, my dear sisters, that (lit., lest) you [will] feed (or, nurture, suckle) them.

The Scorpiun of leccherie — thet is, of galnesse — haveth swucche cundles thet in a wel i-tohe muth, hare summes nome ne sit nawt for-te nempnin, for the nome ane mahte hurten alle wel i-tohene earen ant sulen cleane heorten. Theo
330 thah me mei nempnin wel, hwas nomen me i-cnaweth wel, ant beoth — mare hearm is — to monie al to cuthe: horedom, eaw-bruche, meith-lure, ant incest — thet is bituhe sibbe fleschliche other gasteliche. Thet is o feole i-dealet: ful wil to thet fulthe with skiles yettunge, helpen othre thider-ward, beo weote ant witnesse th'rof, hunti th'refter with wohunge, with toggunge, other with eni tollunge, with
335 gigge lahtre, hore ehe, eanie lihte lates, with yeove, with tollinde word, other with luve-speche, cos, unhende grapunge, thet mei beon heaved sunne, luvie tide other stude for-te cumen i swuch keast, ant othre foreridles the me mot nede forbuhen, the i the muchele fulthe nule fenniliche fallen. As Seint Austin seith, **Omissis occasionibus que solent aditum aperire peccatis, potest consciencia esse**
340 **incolumis**. Thet is, "hwa-se wule hire in-wit witen hal ant fere, ha mot fleon the

327–29 The Scorpiun of leccherie . . . sulen cleane heorten, The Scorpion of lechery — that is, of lust — has such offspring that the name of some of them [is] not proper to name in a well-disciplined mouth, for the name alone could harm all well-trained ears and sully pure hearts. **329–32 Theo thah me mei nempnin wel . . . fleschliche other gasteliche**, Nevertheless, one may well mention those whose names one knows well and are — more is the harm — all too known (or, familiar) to many: whoredom, adultery, loss of virginity (or, fornication), and incest — which is between natural (lit., fleshly) or spiritual kin (i.e., relatives). **332–38 Thet is o feole i-dealet . . . nule fenniliche fallen**, That is divided into many [parts]: a foul desire for that filth with the reason's consent, helping (lit., to help) another [person] in that direction (lit., thitherward), to be spectator and witness to it, to hunt after it with wooing, with flirting, or with any enticement, with flirtatious (or, flighty — see *gigge* in glossary) laughter, whorish eye, any loose gestures (or, behavior), with gifts, with enticing words, or with love-talk, a kiss, indecent touching (or, caressing) which may be a capital (lit., head) sin, to love the time or place to come into such an encounter, and other forerunners (or, preliminaries) which one must needs avoid — who[ever does] not want to fall into the great filth muckily (or, vilely). **338–40** *Omissis occasionibus . . . incolumis*, "Having avoided occasions which usually open the entrance into sins, the conscience can be safe (or, unharmed)" (source unidentified). **340–41 "hwa-se wule hire in-wit witen . . . in sunne,"** "whosoever wants to keep (lit., protect) her conscience whole (or, healthy) and strong, she must flee the occasions which were wont often

foreridles the weren i-wunet ofte to openin the in-yong ant leoten in sunne." Ich
ne dear nempnin the uncundeliche cundles of this deofles scorpiun, attri i-teilet.
Ah sari mei ha beon the bute fere, other with, haveth swa i-fed cundel of hire
galnesse — thet ich ne mei speoken of for scheome ne ne dear for drede, leste sum

345   leorni mare uvel then ha con ant beo th'rof i-temptet. Ah thenche on hire ahne
aweariede fundles in hire galnesse: for hu se hit eaver is i-cwenct, wakinde ant
willes, with flesches licunge, bute ane i wedlac, hit geath to deadlich sunne. I
yuhethe me deth wundres. Culche hit i schrift ut utterliche, as ha hit dude, the
feleth hire schuldi, other ha is i-demet thurh thet fule brune cwench to thet eche

350   brune of helle. The scorpiunes cundel the ha bret in hire bosum — schake hit ut
with schrift, ant slea with deadbote. Ye, the of swucches nute nawt, ne thurve ye
nawt wundrin ow, ne thenchen hwet ich meane, ah yeldeth graces Godd thet ye
swuch uncleannesse nabbeth i-fondet, ant habbeth reowthe of ham the i swuch
beoth i-fallen.

---

to open the entrance and let in sin." **341–45 Ich ne dear nempnin . . . th'rof i-temptet,** I
dare not name the unnatural progenies of this devil's scorpion, venomously tailed (i.e.,
with a poisonous tail). But she may be sorry who without a companion, or with [one], has
thus fed (or, nursed) the progeny of her lust — I cannot speak about that for shame nor [do
I] dare for fear, lest someone learn more evil than she knows [already] and is (lit., be)
tempted by it (lit., thereof). **345–47 Ah thenche on hire ahne aweariede fundles . . . to
deadlich sunne,** But [let her] think of (or, consider) her own cursed invention in her lust:
for howsoever it is satisfied, [while she is] waking (or, awake) and willing, with the body's
pleasure, except only in wedlock, it goes (i.e., leads) to deadly sin. **347–50 I yuhethe me
deth wundres . . . eche brune of helle,** In youth people do wonders (i.e., astonishing
things). Let her who feels herself [to be] guilty vomit it out in confession utterly, [pre-
cisely] as she did it, or she is (i.e., will be) condemned for the satisfaction of that foul
burning to the eternal flame of hell. **350–51 The scorpiunes cundel . . . with deadbote,**
The scorpion's brood which she breeds (*bret* = reduced from of *bredeth*) in her bosom —
let her shake it out with confession, and kill [it] with penance. **351–54 Ye, the of swucches
nute nawt . . . i swuch beoth i-fallen,** You who do not know anything of such [things] —
you need not be amazed (reflex.), nor ponder what I mean, but give thanks to God that you
have not experienced such impurity, and have pity on them who have fallen into such
[things].

355   Inoh is etscene hwi ich habbe i-evenet prude to liun, onde to neddre, ant of theo
alle the othre, withute this leaste — thet is, hwi galnesse beo to scorpiun i-evenet.
Ah lo, her the skile th'rof, sutel ant etscene: scorpiun is a cunnes wurm the haveth
neb — as me seith — sum-deal i-lich wummon, ant neddre is bihinden, maketh
feier semblant, ant fiketh mid te heave*d*, ant stingeth mid te teile. This is leccherie.
360   This is the deofles beast thet he leat to chepinge, ant to euch gederunge, ant chepeth
for-te sullen ant biswiketh monie, thurh thet ha ne bihaldeth nawt bute the feire
neb other thet feire heaved. Thet heaved is the biginnunge of galnesse sunne, ant
te licunge — hwil hit least — the thuncheth swithe swote. The teil thet is the ende
th'rof is sar ofthunchunge ant stingeth her with atter of bitter bireowsunge, ant of
365   deadbote. Ant seliliche mahen ha seggen, the the teil swuch i-findeth, for thet
atter ageath, ah yef hit ne suheth her, the teil ant te attri ende is the eche pine of
helle. Ant nis he fol chapmon the hwen he wule buggen hors other oxe, yef he
nule bihalden bute thet heaved ane? For-thi, hwen the deovel beodeth forth this

355–56 Inoh is etscene . . . to scorpiun i-evenet, [It] is sufficiently clear why I have likened
pride to a lion, envy to a serpent, and all the others to those, except this last [one] — that is,
why lust is likened to a scorpion. **357–58 Ah lo, her the skile th'rof . . . neddre is bihinden,**
But look (lit., lo!) here [is] the reason for it (lit., thereof), evident and clear: the scorpion is a
kind of snake (lit., worm) which has a face — as they say — quite a bit (lit., some deal) like a
woman's, and is a serpent behind, makes (or, presents) a fair appearance, and flatters with the
head, and (or, but) stings with the tail. **360 deofles,** devil's. **360–62 thet he leat to chepinge
. . . thet feire heaved,** which he leads (*leat* = reduced form of *leadeth*) to market, and to each
gathering, and bargains to sell and deceives many, because they do not behold (i.e., look at)
anything but the fair face or the fair head. **362–63 Thet heaved is the biginnunge . . . swithe
swote,** The head is the beginning of the sin of lust and [of] the pleasure — while it lasts —
which seems very sweet. **363–65 The teil thet is the ende th'rof . . . of deadbote,** The tail,
which is the end of it, is painful regret and [it] stings her with the venom of bitter remorse (or,
contrition), and of penance. **365–67 Ant seliliche mahen ha seggen . . . eche pine of helle,**
And they may be said (passive inf.) [to be] fortunate, who find the tail so (i.e., with remorse
and repentance), for that venom goes away, but if it does not inflict pain here, the tail and the
venomous end is the eternal pain of hell. **367–68 Ant nis he fol chapmon . . . thet heaved
ane?** And is he not a foolish tradesman (or, bargainer) who when he wants to buy a horse or an
ox, if he does not want to look at [anything] but the head alone? **368–70 For-thi, hwen the
deovel beodeth forth . . . schaweth forth the heaved,** For this reason, when the devil offers

370 beast — beot hit to sullen ant bit ti sawle ther-vore — he hut eaver the teil ant schaweth forth the heaved. Ah thu, ga al abuten ant schaw the ende forth mid al — hu the teil stingeth — ant swithe flih ther-frommard ear thu beo i-attret.

Thus, mine leove sustren, i the wildernesse ther ye gath in with Godes folc toward Jerusalemes lond — thet is, the riche of heovene — beoth thulliche beastes, thulliche wurmes. Ne nat ich na sunne thet ne mei beon i-lead other to an of ham 375 seovene other to hare streones. Unsteathelvest bileave ayein Godes lare — nis hit te spece of prude inobedience? Her-to falleth sygaldren, false teolunges, lefunge o swefne, o nore, ant on alle wicchecreftes. Neomunge of husel in eani heaved sunne, other ei other sacrement — nis hit te spece of prude thet ich cleopede **presumptio** — yef me wat hwuch sunne hit is? Yef me hit nat nawt, thenne is hit 380 yemeles under accidie, thet ich "slawthe" cleopede. The ne warneth other of his uvel other of his biyete — nis hit slaw yemeles other attri onde? Teohethi mis,

---

up this animal — offers (*beot* = reduced form of *beodeth*) to sell it and asks (*bit* = reduced form of *biddeth*) your soul for it (i.e., in exchange) — he always hides (*hut* = reduced form of *hudeth*) the tail and shows off the head. **370–71 Ah thu, ga al abuten . . . i-attret,** But you, go (imper.) all around and bring the end into view (lit., reveal the end) as well — how the tail stings — and swiftly flee away from there before you are poisoned. **372–74 i the wildernesse . . . thulliche wurmes,** in the wilderness where you go in with God's people towards the land of Jerusalem — that is, the kingdom of heaven — there are such beasts, such serpents. **374–75 Ne nat ich na sunne . . . to hare streones,** I do not know any sin which cannot be led (or, traced) either to one of these seven (lit., them seven) or to their progeny. **375–77 Unsteathelvest bileave . . . on alle wicchecreftes,** Unsteadfast (or, wavering) belief in response to God's teaching — is it not a (lit., the) species of proud disobedience? Under this heading (lit., Hereto) fall incantations, false (or, deceptive) sorcery, belief in dreams, in sneezing, and in all witchcrafts. **377–79 Neomunge of husel . . . hwuch sunne hit is?** The taking of the Eucharist [while] in any capital sin, or [taking] any other sacrament — is it not the species of pride which I called "presumption" — if one knows what kind of sin it is (i.e., if one knows one's sin)? **379–80 Yef me hit nat nawt . . . thet ich "slawthe" cleopede,** If one does not know it, then it is carelessness under [the heading of] idleness which I called "sloth." **380–81 The ne warneth other . . . other attri onde?** Whoever is not on his guard either about his evil or about his profit — is it not sluggish (lit., slow) carelessness or venomous envy? **381–83 Teohethi mis . . . anes cunnes theofthe?** To tithe falsely (or, improperly), withhold a legacy, a windfall (or, a trea-

edhalden cwide, fundles other lane, other ther-with misfearen — nis hit spece of yisceunge, ant anes cunnes theofthe? Edhalden othres hure over his rihte terme — nis hit strong reaflac — hwa-se yelden hit mei, the is under yisceunge? Yef me

385 yemeth wurse ei thing i-leanet, other bitaht to witene, then he wene the ah hit — nis hit other triccherie other yemeles of slawthe? Alswa is dusi heast other folliche i-pliht trowthe, longe beon unbischpet, falsliche gan to schrift, other to longe abiden, ne teache **Pater noster** god-child ne **Credo** — theos ant alle thulliche beoth i-lead to slawthe — thet is, the feorthe moder of the seove sunnen. The

390 dronc drunch other ei thing dude hwer-thurh na child ne schulde beon on hire i-streonet, other thet i-streonede schulde forwurthen — nis this strong mon-slaht of galnesse awakenet? Alle sunnen sunderliche bi hare nomeliche nomen ne mahte na-mon rikenin, ah i theo the ich habbe i-seid, alle othre beoth bilokene. Ant nis, ich wene, na-mon the ne mei understonden him of his sunne nomeliche under sum

395 of the ilke i-meane the beoth her i-writene. Of theose seove beastes ant of hare

sure-trove; lit., something found), or loan, or do wrongly with them (lit., therewith) — is it not a species of covetousness, and theft of a kind? To withhold another's pay beyond its rightful term (i.e., time limit) — is it not blatant robbery [on the part of] whosoever can pay it, [but] who is [acting] under covetousness? **384–86 Yef me yemeth wurse . . . yemeles of slawthe?** If one looks after anything loaned, or entrusted [to him/her] to protect, worse than he who owns it expects [him to] — is it not either treachery or carelessness [arising] from sloth? **386–89 Alswa is dusi heast . . . moder of the seove sunnen**, Likewise (or, just so) is a foolish promise or foolishly plighted troth (i.e., faithfulness foolishly promised), to be unconfirmed for a long time, to go dishonestly (lit., falsely) to confession, or to wait too long, not to teach the Lord's prayer or the Creed [to a] godchild — these and all such [things] are traced to sloth — that is, the fourth mother of the seven [deadly] sins. **389–92 The dronc drunch . . . of galnesse awakenet?** Whoever drank a drink (i.e., a potion) or did anything through which any child should not be conceived in her, or the conceived [child] should be destroyed (i.e., aborted) — is this not blatant murder, awakened (i.e., having arisen) from lechery? **392–93 Alle sunnen sunderliche . . . alle othre beoth bilokene**, No one can reckon (or, count up) all the various sins by their particular names, but in those which I have mentioned (lit., said), all others are locked up. **393– 95 Ant nis, ich wene . . . the beoth her i-writene**, And [there] is not, I expect, anyone who cannot understand himself concerning his particular sin (i.e., identify his sins by name) under some of those same common [sins] which are written [down] here. **395–97 Of theose seove beastes . . . to fordonne**, [It] has been (lit., is) mentioned up to this point (lit., hereto — i.e., the

streones i wildernesse of anlich lif is i-seid her-to, the alle the for[th]-fearinde
fondith to fordonne. The liun of prude sleath alle the prude, alle the beoth hehe
ant over-hohe i-heortet; the attri neddre, the ontfule ant te luthere i-thonket;
wreathfule, the unicorne; alswa of the othre o rawe. To Godd ha beoth i-sleine, ah

400   ha libbeth to the feond ant beoth alle in his hond ant servith him in his curt, euch
of the meoster the him to falleth.

The prude beoth his bemeres, draheth wind in-ward with worltlich here-word,
ant eft with idel yelp puffeth hit ut-ward as the bemeres doth, makieth noise ant
lud dream to schawin hare orhel. Ah yef ha wel thohten of Godes bemeres, of the

405   englene bemen, the schulen o fowr half the world bivore the grurefule dom grisliche
blawen, "Ariseth, deade! Ariseth! Cumeth to Drihtines dom for-te beon i-demet!"
thear na prud bemere ne schal beon i-borhen — yef ha thohten this wel, ha walden
inoh-reathe i the deofles servise dimluker bemin. Of theose bemeres seith Jeremie,
Onager solitarius in desiderio anime sue attraxit ventum amoris sui. Of the

410   wind "drahinde in for luve of here-word," seith [Jeremie] as ich seide.

topic up to this point has been) concerning these seven beasts and their broods in the wilderness of
the solitary life, [beasts] which attempt to destroy all wayfaring (or, forward-traveling) [people].
397–99 The liun of prude . . . alswa of the othre o rawe, The lion of pride slays all the proud
[people], all [those] who are haughtily and disdainfully hearted (i.e., have haughty and disdainful
hearts); the venomous serpent [slays] the envious and the evil thoughted (or, wicked minded); the
unicorn [slays the] wrathful; likewise with the others in order. **399–401 To Godd ha beoth i-sleine
. . . the him to falleth,** They are slain (i.e., dead) to God, but they live to the fiend and are completely in his hand[s] and serve him in his court, each with the skill (or, job) that falls (or, belongs)
to him. **402–04 The prude beoth . . . to schawin hare orhel,** The proud are his trumpeters, [they]
draw wind inward with worldly praise (lit., praise-words), and puff it back out (lit., outward) with
empty boasting as trumpeters do, make noise and loud sound to display their pride. **404–08 Ah yef
ha wel thohten . . . dimluker bemin,** But if they thought (or, considered) well about God's trumpeters, about the trumpets of angels, which will in the four corners (lit., sides) of the world blow
terrifyingly (lit., grisily) before the horrific judgment, "Arise, [you] dead! Arise! Come to the Lord's
judgment to be judged!" where no proud trumpeter will be saved — if they considered this well,
they would readily enough trumpet more dimly (or, faintly) in the devil's service. **409 *Onager
solitarius . . . ventum amoris sui*,** "A wild ass alone in the desire of his heart drew in (or, snuffed)
the wind of love" (Jeremiah 2:24). **409–10 Of the wind . . . as ich seide,** Concerning the wind,
"drawing [it] in for love of praise," [Jeremiah] says just as I have said.

Part Four

Summe juglurs beoth the ne cunnen servin of nan other gleo bute makien cheres, wrenche the muth mis, schulen with ehnen. Of this meoster servith the unseli ontfule i the deofles curt, to bringen o lahtre hare ondfule laverd. Yef ei seith wel other deth wel, ne mahen ha nanes weis lokin thider with riht ehe of god heorte, ah winkith o thet half ant bihaldeth o luft yef ther is eawt to edwiten, other ladliche thider-ward schuleth mi*d* either. Hwen ha i-hereth thet god, skleatteth the earen adun, ah the lust ayein thet uvel is eaver wid open. Thenne he wrencheth the muth, hwen he turneth god to uvel, ant yef hit is sum-del uvel, thurh mare lastunge wrencheth hit to wurse. Theos beoth forecwidderes, hare ahne prophetes. Theos bodieth bivoren hu the eateliche deoflen schulen yet ageasten ham with hare grennunge, ant hu ha schulen ham-seolf grennin ant nivelin ant makien sur semblant for the muchele angoise i the pine of helle. Ah for-thi ha beoth the leasse to meanen thet ha bivoren-hond leornith hare meoster to makien grim chere.

411–12 Summe juglurs beoth . . . with ehnen, [There] are certain jugglers (or, entertainers) who can perform no other entertainment but to make faces, wrench their mouths askew, squint (or, look askance) with [their] eyes. **412–13 Of this meoster . . . ondfule laverd**, In this capacity (or, skill, job) the wretched envious [people] serve in the devil's court, to bring to laughter their envious lord. **413–16 Yef ei seith wel . . . schuleth mid either**, If any[one] speaks well or does well, they (i.e., the envious) cannot in any way look in that direction (lit., thither) with the right eye of a good heart, but wink (i.e., close the eye) on that side and look to the left [to see] if there is anything (lit., aught) to blame, or [they] look askance in that direction with both [eyes] fiercely (or, disgustingly). **416–17 Hwen ha i-hereth . . . eaver wid open**, When they hear the good (i.e., something good), [they] clap [their] ears down (i.e., shut), but the hearing (MS: "left ear" — see textual note) is always wide open towards evil. **417–19 Thenne he wrencheth the muth . . . to wurse**, Then he twists [his] mouth when he turns good into evil, and if it is [already] somewhat evil, through more blame [he] twists it to [something] worse. **419–22 Theos beoth forecwidderes . . . i the pine of helle**, These [people] are foretellers, their own prophets. These [people] prophesy before[hand] how the gruesome devils will ultimately terrify (lit., aghast) them with their grinning (or, grimacing), and how they will themselves grin and wrinkle up their noses, and make a sour face because of [their] great anguish in the torment of hell. **422–23 Ah for-thi ha beoth . . . makien grim chere**, But for this reason they are the less to be lamented (passive inf.), that (or, since) they learn their occupation of making (lit., to make) grim face[s] beforehand.

The wreathfule bivore the feond skirmeth mid cnives ant is his cnif warpere,
425   ant pleieth mid sweordes, bereth ham bi the scharp ord upon his tunge. Sweord
ant cnif either beoth scharpe ant keorvinde word thet he warpeth from him ant
skirmeth toward othre, ant he bodeth hu the deoflen schulen pleien with him mid
hare scharpe eawles, skirmi with him abuten ant dusten ase pilche-clut euch toward other, ant with helle sweordes asneasen him thurh-ut — thet beoth kene ant
430   eateliche ant keorvinde pinen.

The slawe lith ant slepeth o the deofles bearm as his deore deorling, ant te
deovel leith his tutel dun to his eare ant tuteleth him al thet he wule. For swa hit is
sikerliche to hwam-se is idel of god: meatheleth the feond yeorne, ant te idele
underveth luveliche his lare. Idel ant yemeles is thes deofles bearnes slep, ah he
435   schal o Domes-dei grimliche abreiden with the dredfule dream of the englene
bemen, ant in helle wontreathe echeliche wakien. **Surgite! — aiunt — Mortui,
surgite! et venite ad judicium Salvatoris.**

424–25 The wreathfule bivore the feond . . . upon his tunge, The wrathful [one] juggles
(or, fences) with knives before the fiend and is his knife-thrower, and plays (or, performs)
with swords, carries them on his tongue by the sharp point. **425–30 Sweord ant cnif . . .
keorvinde pinen,** Sword and knife are (i.e., represent) both sharp and cutting words that
he throws from himself and juggles (or, tosses) toward others, and he (i.e., the thrower)
prophesies (i.e., foretells) how the devils will sport with him with their sharp awls, juggle
(or, throw) about with him, and toss [him] like a ragged cloak each to the other, and gore
him throughout [his body] with hell's swords — those are the sharp and horrific and cutting tortures. **431–32 The slawe lith ant slepeth . . . al thet he wule,** The slow (i.e., lazy)
[one] lies and sleeps in the devil's lap as his dear darling, and the devil lays his pursed lips
down to his ear and whispers to him all that he wants. **432–34 For swa hit is . . . underveth
luveliche his lare,** For, certainly, so it is for whomsoever is idle for good (or, useless for
good): the fiend talks eagerly [to him, her], and the idle (or, useless) receive lovingly his
teaching. **434–36 Idel ant yemeles . . . echeliche wakien,** Idle and careless is the sleep of
this devil's child, but he will get up (i.e., start out of his sleep) grimly on Doomsday with
the dreadful blast (or, din) of the angels' trumpets, and wake (or, stay awake) eternally in
hell's misery. **436–37 *Surgite! . . . ad judicium Salvatoris,*** "Arise!" they say, "O [you]
dead, arise and come to the Judgment of the Savior" (see Ephesians 5:14 and Pseudo-
Jerome, *Monks' Rule* 30 [*PL* 30.417]).

The yiscere is his eskibah, feareth abuten esken ant bisiliche stureth him to rukelin togederes muchele ant monie ruken, blaweth th'rin ant blent him-seolf,

440 peathereth ant maketh th'rin figures of augrim, as thes rikeneres doth the habbeth muche to rikenin. This is al the canges blisse ant te feond bihalt tis gomen ant laheth thet he bersteth. Wel understont, euch wis mon, thet gold ba ant seolver, ant euch eorthlich ahte, nis bute eorthe ant *esken* the ablendeth euch mon the ham in blaweth — thet is, the bolheth him thurh ham in heorte prude. Ant al thet he

445 rukeleth ant gedereth togederes ant ethalt of ei thing thet nis bute esken mare then hit neodeth, schal in helle wurthen him tadden ant neddren. Ant ba, as Ysaie seith, schulen beon of wurmes — his cuvertur ant his hwitel — the nalde ther-with neodfule feden ne schruden. **Subter te sternetur tinea et operimentum tuum vermis**.

450 The yivere glutun is the feondes manciple, ah he stiketh eaver i celer other i cuchene. His heorte is i the dissches, his thoht al i the neppes, his lif i the tunne,

438–41 The yiscere is his eskibah . . . muche to rikenin, The covetous [person] is his hearth-tender (lit., ash-stirrer — see glossary), [who] lives (lit., fares) amidst ashes and busily bestirs himself to heap together many and huge piles; [he] blows into them (lit., therein) and blinds himself, pokes them and makes figures of calculations (i.e., scratchings which look like calculations — see note) in them, as these account-keepers (lit., reckoners) do who have much to reckon (or, calculate). **441–42 This is al the canges blisse . . . thet he bersteth,** This is all the fool's joy, and the fiend (or, enemy) looks at this entertainment and laughs [so] that (i.e., until) he bursts. **442–44 Wel understont . . . in heorte prude,** Each wise man understands well that both gold and silver, and each earthly possession is [nothing] but earth and ashes which blind each person who blows into them — that is, who puffs himself [up] through them in heart's pride. **444–46 Ant al thet he rukeleth . . . tadden ant neddren,** And everything that he piles up (or, amasses) and gathers together and holds back (or, saves) of anything which is but ashes more than is necessary (lit., it needs) — [all these things] will in hell change into toads and serpents for him. **446–48 Ant ba, as Ysaie seith . . . ne schruden,** And "both his blanket and his sheet," as Isaiah says, "will be [made] of worms (or, serpents)," who[ever did] not want to sustain (see *feden* in glossary) or clothe the needy with them (i.e., his coverings). **448–49 Subter te sternetur . . . tuum vermis,** "Beneath you the moth will be spread, and your covering (or, blanket) will be of worm[s]" (Isaiah 14:11, slightly altered). **450–52 The yivere glutun . . . the crohhe,** The voracious glutton is the fiend's manciple (or, food procurer), but he always hangs around in (or, sticks to) the cellar or in the kitchen. His heart is in the dishes, his thought completely in the mugs, his life in the barrel, his soul in the pot

236

his sawle i the crohhe. Kimeth bivoren his laverd bismuddet ant bismulret, a disch in his an hond, a scale in his other. Meatheleth mis wordes, wigleth as fordrunke mon the haveth i-munt to fallen, bihalt his greate wombe — ant te deovel lahheth.

455 Theose threatith thus Godd thurh Ysaie: **Servi mei comedent et vos esurietis, et cetera**. "Mine men schulen eoten, ant ow schal eaver hungrin, ant ye schule beon feo[ndes fod]e world buten ende." **Quantum glorificavit se et in deliciis fuit, tantum date illi tormentum et luctum. In Apocalipsi: Contra unum poculum quod miscuit miscete ei duo.** Yef the kealche-cuppe wallinde bres to drinken,

460 yeot in his wide throte thet he swelte in-with. "Ayein an, yef him twa." Thullich is Godes dom ayein yivere ant drunc-wile i the Apocalipse.

The lecchurs i the deofles curt habbeth riht hare ahne nome, for i thes muchele curz, theo me cleopeth lecchurs the habbeth swa forlore scheome thet heom nis na-wiht of scheome, ah secheth hu ha mahen meast vilainie wurchen. The lecchur

(lit., crock). **452–53 Kimeth bivoren his laverd . . . in his other**, [He] comes before his lord besmutted (lit., stained) and besmeared, a dish in his one hand, a drinking cup in his other. **453–54 Meatheleth mis wordes . . . ant te deovel lahheth**, [He] says his words amiss (i.e., slurs his words), staggers (lit., wiggles) like a drunk man who is about to fall, looks at (*bihalt* = reduced form of *bihaldeth*) his huge stomach — and the devil laughs (or, perhaps, [the devil] looks at his huge stomach and he laughs). **455 Theose threatith . . . Ysaie**, God warns these [gluttons] through Isaiah, thus. **455–56 *Servi mei comedent . . . et cetera***, "My servants will eat and you will be hungry, etc." (Isaiah 65:13). **456–57 schulen eoten . . . buten ende**, will eat, and you will always be hungry (lit., [it] will always hunger, be hungry for you), and you will be the fiend's food world without end (i.e., forever and ever). **457–58 *Quantum glorificavit . . . luctum***, "As much as [she] has glorified herself and has been (i.e., lived) in delights (or, pleasure), so much give (imper.) her torment and mourning" (Revelation 18:7). **458–59 *In Apocalipsi . . . miscete ei duo***, "In the Apocalypse: Against (i.e., In return for) one cup which she mixed (or, prepared), mix her two" (Revelation 18:6). **459–60 Yef the kealche-cuppe . . . he swelte in-with**, Give the tosspot (or, drunkard) boiling brass to drink; pour [it] into his wide throat, [so] that he [might] die inside. **460 "Ayein an, yef him twa**," "For one, give him two." **460–61 Thullich is Godes dom . . . i the Apocalipse**, Such is God's judgment in the Apocalypse against gluttons and drunkards (lit., [people] desirous of drink). **462–64 habbeth riht hare ahne nome . . . vilainie wurchen**, have, rightly, their own name (i.e., they keep their own name), for in this great court, one calls those [people] lechers who have so lost [their] shame that [there] is no whit of shame [in] them, but [on the contrary they] seek how they may carry out (lit., work) the greatest villainy (or, shameful wrongs). **464–67 The lecchur . . . eani swote**

237

465 i the deofles curt bifuleth him-seolven fulliche ant his feolahes alle, stinketh of thet fulthe ant paieth wel his laverd with thet stinkinde breath betere then he schulde with eani swote rechles. Hu he stinke to Godd, i **Vitas Patrum** the engel hit schawde, the heold his nease tha ther com the prude lecchur ridinde, ant nawt for thet rotede lich thet he healp the hali earmite to biburien! Of alle othre thenne
470 habbeth theos the fuleste meoster i the feondes curt, the swa bidoth ham-seolven. Ant he schal bidon ham, pinin ham with eche stench i the put of helle.

Nu ye habbeth ane dale i-herd, mine leove sustren: of theo the me cleopeth the seove moder-sunnen, ant of hare teames, ant of hwucche meosters thes ilke men servith i the feondes curt, the habbeth i-wivet o theose seoven haggen, ant hwi ha
475 beoth swithe to heatien ant to schunien. Ye beoth ful feor from ham, ure Laverd beo i-thoncket! Ah thet fule breath of this leaste untheaw — thet is, of leccherie — stinketh se swithe feor, for the feond hit saweth ant toblaweth over al, thet ich am sum-del ofdred leste hit leape sum-chearre into ower heortes nease. Stench stiheth uppart, ant ye beoth hehe i-clumben ther the wind is muchel of stronge
480 temptatiuns. Ure Laverd yeove ow strengthe wel to withstonden.

rechles, The lecher in the devil's court befouls (i.e., dirties) himself disgustingly and all his comrades, stinks from that filth and pleases well his lord better with that stinking breath (or, stench) than he would with any sweet incense. **467–69 Hu he stinke to Godd . . . to biburien!** How he might stink to God the angel in *The Lives of the [Desert] Fathers* showed, who held his nose when the proud lecher came riding and not (i.e., but did not hold his nose) because of the rotted corpse that he helped the holy hermit to bury! **470–71 fuleste meoster . . . i the put of helle**, the foulest (or, most disgusting) occupation in the fiend's court, who thus befoul themselves. And he will befoul them, torture them with eternal stench in the pit of hell. **472–75 Nu ye habbeth ane dale i-herd . . . to heatien ant to schunien**, Now you have heard one section [of this book], my dear sisters: [the section] on those which people call the seven mother sins, and about their broods, and in which occupations these same men serve in the devil's court who have had sex with (or, married) these seven hags, and why they are [to be] intensely hated and avoided (passive inf.). **475–76 Ye beoth ful feor from ham . . . i-thoncket!** You are very far from them, our Lord be thanked! **476–78 Ah thet fule breath . . . ower heortes nease**, But the foul stench (lit., breath) of this last vice — that is, of lechery — stinks so very far, for the fiend scatters it and blows [it] around everywhere (lit., over all), that I am somewhat (lit., some deal) afraid lest it leap sometime into your heart's nose. **478–80 Stench stiheth uppart . . . temptatiuns**, A stench climbs upwards, and you have climbed high where the wind is great (or, powerful) with strong temptations.

Sum weneth thet ha schule stronglukest beon i-fondet i the forme tweof-moneth thet ha bigon ancre lif, ant i the other th'refter. Ant hwen ha efter feole yer feleth ham stronge, wundreth hire swithe, ant is ofdred leste Godd habbe hire al forwarpen. Nai, nawt nis hit swa! I the forme yeres nis bute bal-plohe to monie

485 men of ordre. Ah neometh yeme hu hit feareth bi a forbisne: Hwen a wis mon neowliche haveth wif i-lead ham, he nimeth yeme al softeliche of hire maneres. Thah he seo bi hire thet him mispaieth, he let yet i-wurthen, maketh hire feire chere, ant is umben euches weis thet ha him luvie inwardliche in hire heorte. Hwen he understont wel thet hire luve is treoweliche toward him i-festnet, thenne

490 mei he sikerliche chastien hire openliche of hire untheawes, thet he ear forber as he ham nawt nuste. Maketh him swithe sturne, ant went te grimme toth to, for-te fondin yetten yef he mahte hire luve toward him unfestnin. Alest hwen he understont thet ha is al wel i-tuht, ne for thing thet he deth hire ne luveth him the leasse, ah mare ant mare — yef ha mei — from deie to deie, thenne schaweth he

481–82 Sum weneth thet . . . i the other th'refter, Some [anchoress] expects that she will be most strongly tempted in the first year that she began the anchoress' life, and in the second [year] after that. **482–84 Ant hwen ha efter feole yer . . . habbe hire al forwarpen,** And when she after many years feels them strongly, [she] is very surprised (reflex.) and is frightened lest God might have thrown her over (i.e., abandoned her) completely. **484 Nai, nawt nis hit swa!** No, it is not so! **484– 85 I the forme yeres . . . bi a forbisne,** In the first years [it] is [nothing] but ballplay to many men in [holy] order[s]. But pay (lit., take) attention how it goes (lit., fares) with an example (i.e., exemplum). **485–86 Hwen a wis mon neowliche . . . of hire maneres,** When a wise man has recently led [his] wife home (i.e., married), he pays attention very quietly (lit., all softly) to her manners (or, way of behaving). **487–88 Thah he seo bi hire . . . in hire heorte,** Though he see in her [something] that displeases him, he lets [it] be for the time being (lit., yet), is very kind to her (lit., makes her fair cheer — see glossary under *chere*), and is [aiming in] every way that she [should] love him in- wardly in her heart. **489–91 Hwen he understont wel . . . as he ham nawt nuste,** When he under- stands well that her love is truly fastened on him, then he can confidently chastise her openly about her faults (or, vices), which he tolerated before, as though he did not know them. **491–92 Maketh him swithe sturne . . . toward him unfestnin,** [He] makes himself very stern, and turns (*went* = reduced form of *wendeth*) the grim tooth towards [her] (i.e., snarls, grimaces at her), in order to test further if he [might] be able to unfasten (or, shake) her love towards him. **492–96 Alest hwen he understont . . . thet he wel i-cnaweth,** At last, when he understands that she is well trained, nor for anything that he does to her [does she] love him the less, but [loves him] more and more — if she

495 hire thet he hire luveth sweteliche, ant deth al thet ha wule, as theo thet he wel i-
cnaweth. Thenne is al thet wa i-wurthe to wunne. Yef Jesu Crist, ower spus, deth
alswa bi ow, mine leove sustren, ne thunche ow neaver wunder. I the frumthe nis
ther buten olhnunge for-te drahen in luve. Ah sone se he eaver understont thet he
beo wel acointet, he wule forbeoren ow leasse. Efter the spreove, on ende thenne

500 is the muchele joie. Al o this ilke wise tha he walde his folc leaden ut of theowdom,
ut of Pharaones hond, ut of Egypte, he dude for ham al thet ha walden: miracles
feole ant feire, druhede the Reade Sea, ant makede ham freo wei thurh hire, ant
ther ha eoden dru-fot, adrencte Pharaon ant hare fan alle. I the desert forthre tha
he hefde i-lead ham feor i the wildernesse, he lette ham tholien wa inoh, hunger,

505 thurst, ant muche swinc, ant weorren muchele ant monie. On ende, he yef ham
reste, ant alle weole ant wunne, al hare heorte wil, ant flesches eise ant este.
Terram fluentem lacte et melle. Thus ure Laverd speareth on earst the yunge ant
te feble, ant draheth ham ut of this world, swoteliche ant with liste. Sone se he

can (i.e., if such a thing is possible) — then he shows her that he loves her sweetly, and does everything that she wants, as for her whom he knows well. **496–97 Thenne is al thet wa . . . ow neaver wunder**, Then all that suffering (lit., woe) has turned (lit., has become) into joy. If Jesus Christ, your spouse, does also (i.e., the same) with you, my dear sisters, never let it seem strange to you. **497–99 I the frumthe . . . forbeoren ow leasse**, In the beginning there is [nothing] but flattery (or, blandishments) in order to draw [one] into love. But [as] soon as he ever understands that he is quite informed (lit., acquainted) he will forbear (i.e., show patience toward) you less. **499–500 Efter the spreove . . . the muchele joie**, After the testing, at the end then is great joy. **500–03 Al o this ilke wise . . . ant hare fan alle**, Exactly in this same way, when He wanted to lead His people out of servitude, out of Pharaoh's hand, out of Egypt, He did for them all that they wanted, miracles many and splendid, dried up the Red Sea, and made them a free path through it (lit., her, the Red Sea), and there they went dry-footed, [and He] drowned Pharaoh and all their foes. **503–05 I the desert forthre . . . weorren muchele ant monie**, Later in the desert when He had led them far into the wilderness, He let them experience suffering (lit., woe) enough: hunger, thirst, and great travail, and wars great and many. **506 ant alle weole . . . eise ant este**, and all prosperity and joy, all their heart's desire, and the comfort and delight of the flesh (i.e., physical comforts). **507 *Terram fluentem lacte et melle***, "A land flowing with milk and honey" (Exodus 3:17, 13:5, 33:3, etc. — a common Old Testament phrase). **507–10 Thus ure Laverd speareth . . . weane to tholien**, In this way our Lord spares at first the young and the feeble and draws them out of this world, sweetly and with skill (or, cunning). [As] soon as He sees them harden (or, toughen), He lets (*let* = reduced form

240

510 sith ham heardin, he let weorre awakenin ant teacheth ham to fehten ant weane to tholien. On ende efter long swinc, he yeveth ham swote reste — her, ich segge, i this world, ear ha cumen to heovene. Ant thuncheth thenne swa god, the reste efter the swinc; the muchele eise efter the muchele meoseise thuncheth se swote!

Nu beoth i the Sawter under the twa temptatiuns thet ich ear seide — thet beoth the uttre ant te inre, the temeth alle the othre — fowr dalen todealet thus: fondunge

515 liht ant dearne, fondunge liht ant openlich, fondunge strong ant dearne, fondunge strong ant openlich, as is ther understonden: **Non timebis a timore nocturno, a sagitta volante in die, a negotio perambulante in tenebris, ab incursu et demonio meridiano.** Of fondunge liht ant dearne seith Job theose wordes: **Lapides excavant aque, et all*u*vione paulatim terra consumitur.** Lutle dropen thurlith

520 the flint the ofte falleth th'ron, ant lihte, dearne fondunges the me nis war of falsith a treowe heorte. Of the lihte, openliche bi hwam he seith alswa, **Lucebit post eum semita**, nis nawt se muche dute. Of strong temptatiun, thet is thah dearne,

of *leoteth*) war awaken and [He] teaches them to fight and to endure misery. **510 swinc**, travail, struggle. **511 ear ha**, before they. **511–12 Ant thuncheth thenne swa god . . . thuncheth se swote!** And then [it] seems so good, rest after the struggle; great comfort after the great discomfort (or, suffering) seems so sweet! **513–16 Nu beoth i the Sawter . . . as is ther understonden,** Now, in the Psalter [there] are under [the heading of] the two temptations that I mentioned before — those are the outer and the inner, which give birth to all the others — four parts (or, categories), divided thus: minor (lit., light) and hidden (lit., secret) temptation, minor and obvious (lit., open) temptation, severe (lit., strong) and hidden temptation, severe and obvious temptation, as is [to be] understood (passive inf.) here. **516–18 Non timebis a timore nocturno . . . demonio meridiano,** "You will not be afraid of night-time terror, of an arrow flying during the day, of trouble (or, business) walking in darkness, [nor] of an attack, or of the mid-day demon" (Psalm 90:5–6). **518 Of fondunge liht ant dearne . . . theose wordes,** Concerning minor and hidden temptation, Job says these words. **518–19 Lapides excavant aque . . . terra consumitur,** "Waters hollow out rocks, and the earth (or, ground) is little by little eaten up by the ebb and flow [of water]" (Job 14:19). **519–21 Lutle dropen . . . a treowe heorte,** Little drops which often fall thereon pierce the flint, and minor, hidden temptations of which one is not aware falsify (or, deceive) a true heart. **521 Of the lihte, openliche . . . he seith alswa,** Concerning the minor, obvious [temptations] about which he says also. **521–22 Lucebit post eum semita,** "The path will be clear (or, shining) after him (i.e., the Leviathan)" (Job 41:23). **522–23 nis nawt se muche dute . . . thet Job meaneth,** there is not so much doubt

is ec thet Job meaneth: **Insidiati sunt michi et prevaluerunt, et non erat qui adjuvaret.** Thet is, "mine fan weitith me with triccherie ant with treisun, ant ha
525 strengden up-o me ant nes hwa me hulpe." **Ysaias: Veniet malum super te et nescies ortum ejus.** "Wa schal cumen on the, ant tu ne schalt witen hweonne." Of the feorthe fondunge — thet is, strong ant openlich — he maketh his man of his fan, the hali Job, ant seith: **Quasi rupto muro et aperta janua irruerunt super me.** Thet is, "ha threasten in up-o me as thah the wal were tobroken ant te yeten
530 opene." The forme ant te thridde fondunge of theose fowre beoth al meast under the inre. The other ant te feorthe falleth under the uttre, ant beoth al meast fleschliche ant eth for-thi to felen. The othre twa beoth gasteliche, of gasteliche untheawes, ant beoth i-hud ofte ant dearne hwen ha derveth meast, ant beoth muche for-thi the mare to dreden. Moni thet ne weneth nawt, bret in hire breoste sum
535 liunes hwelp, sum neddre cundel the forfret the sawle, of hwucche Osee seith:

(or, fear). Concerning severe temptation which is nevertheless hidden is also what Job bemoans. **523–24 *Insidiati sunt michi . . . qui adjuvaret***, "They have lain in wait against me and have grown strong (or, prevailed), and there was not [anyone] who would help" (adapted from Job 30:13). **524–25 "mine fan weitith me . . . nes hwa me hulpe,"** "my foes lie in wait (lit., wait) for me with treachery and treason, and they prevailed (i.e., used force) upon me and there was not [anyone] who [would] help me." **525–26 *Ysaias: Veniet malum super te . . . ortum ejus***, Isaiah: "Evil will come over you, and you will not know its source (or, rising)" (Isaiah 47:11). **526 "Wa schal cumen on the . . . hweonne,"** Woe (or, suffering) will come [up]on you, and you will not know from where (lit., whence). **526–28 Of the feorthe fondunge . . . ant seith,** Concerning the fourth temptation — that is, severe and obvious — he, the holy Job, makes his moan (or, complaint) about his foes and says. **528–29 *Quasi rupto muro . . . super me***, "As if through a breached wall and an open door, they rushed in on me" (Job 30:14). **529–30 "ha threasten in up-o me . . . te yeten opene,"** "they rushed (or, poured) in upon me as though the wall were broken down and the gates open." **530–32 The forme ant te thridde fondunge . . . for-thi to felen,** The first and the third temptation of these four are all mostly under [the heading of] the inner [temptations]. The second and the fourth fall under the outer [temptations] and are all mostly physical (lit., fleshly) and easy to feel. **532–34 The othre twa . . . mare to dreden,** The other two are spiritual, from spiritual vices (or, faults), and are often hidden and secret when they harm the most, and are therefore to be feared (passive inf.) much more. **534–35 Moni thet ne weneth nawt . . . of hwucche Osee seith,** Many [a person] who does not imagine it, breeds (*bret* = reduced form of *bredeth*) in her breast some lion's cub, some serpent's brood, which gobbles up (or, devours) the soul, concerning which Hosea says.

242

Alieni comederunt robur ejus et ipse nesciuit. Thet is, "Unholde forfreten the strengthe of his sawle ant he hit nawt nuste." Yet is meast dred of hwen the sweoke of helle eggeth to a thing thet thuncheth swithe god mid alle, ant is thah sawle bone, ant wei to deadlich sunne. Swa he deth as ofte as he ne mei with open uvel

540   cuthen his strengthe. "Na," he seith, "ne mei ich nawt makien theos to sungin thurh yivernesse, ant ich chulle, as the wreastleare, wrenchen hire thider-ward as ha meast dreaieth, ant warpen hire o thet half ant breiden ferliche adun, ear ha least wene," ant eggeth hire toward se muchel abstinence thet ha is the unstrengre i Godes servise, ant to leaden se heard lif, ant pinin swa thet licome, thet te sawle

545   asteorve. He bihalt an-other thet he ne mei nanes-weis makien luthere i-thoncket, se luveful, ant se reowthful is hire heorte: "Ich chulle makien hire," he seith, "to reowthful mid alle. Ich schal don hire se muchel thet ha schal luvien ahte, thenchen lesse of Godd, ant leosen hire fame," ant put thenne a thulli thonc in hire softe heorte: "Seinte Marie! naveth the mon, other the wummon, meoseise ant na mon

---

536 *Alieni comederunt . . . ipse nesciuit,* "Strangers ate up his strength and he himself did not know" (Hosea 7:9). **536–37 "Unholde forfreten the strengthe . . . nawt nuste,"** "Unfriendly [ones] gobbled up the strength of his soul and he did not know it." **537–39 Yet is meast dred of . . . to deadlich sunne,** Yet there is most to fear for when the traitor (or, deceiver) of hell incites to a thing that seems very good perhaps, and is nevertheless the soul's murderer (or, slayer), and the path to deadly sin. **539–40 Swa he deth as ofte . . . his strengthe,** So he does as often as he cannot make known his strength with obvious (or, evident) evil. **540–45 "Na," he seith . . . thet te sawle asteorve,** "No," he says, "I cannot make this [woman] sin through gluttony, and (i.e., but) I will, like the wrestler, wrench (or, twist) her in the direction to which (lit., as) she most tends to (lit., pulls), and throw her on that side and fling [her] suddenly down, before she least expects," and [he] incites her to so much abstinence that she is the weaker (lit., unstronger) in God's service, and [incites her] to lead so hard a life, and to so mortify (lit., pain) the body, that the soul [may] die. **545–46 He bihalt an-other . . . is hire heorte,** He beholds (or, observes — *bihalt* = reduced form of *bihaldeth*) another whom he cannot in any way make evil minded (lit., thoughted), so loving and compassionate is her heart. **546–49 "Ich chulle makien hire" . . . hire softe heorte,** "I will make her," he says, "entirely too compassionate. I will do so much to her that she will love possessions, think less about God, and lose her fame (or, good reputation)," and then [he] puts some such thought in her soft heart. **549–53 Seinte Marie! . . . to huse-wif of halle,** "St. Mary! [does not] this (lit., the) man or this woman have discomfort (i.e., a hard life), and no one wants to do anything for them. People would

243

550 nule don ham nawt. Me walde me yef ich bede, ant swa ich mahte helpen ham ant don on ham ealmesse" — bringeth hire on to gederin, ant yeoven al earst to povre, forthre to other freond, aleast makien feaste ant wurthen al worldlich, forschuppet of ancre to huse-wif of halle. Godd wat, swuch feaste maketh sum hore. Weneth thet ha wel do, as dusie ant adotede doth hire to understonden, flatrith hire of

555 freolec, herieth ant heoveth up the ealmesse thet ha deth, hu wide ha is i-cnawen. Ant heo let wel of ant leapeth in orhel. Sum seith inoh-reathe thet ha gedereth hord — swa thet hire hus mei, ant heo ba, beon i-robbet. Reowthe over reowthe! Thus the traitre of helle maketh him treowe reades-mon! Ne leve ye him neaver. Davith cleopeth him **demonium meridianum**, "briht, schininde deovel," ant Seinte

560 Pawel, **angelum lucis** — thet is, "engel of liht." For swuch ofte he maketh him ant schaweth him to monie. Na sihthe thet ye seoth, ne i swefne ne waken, ne telle ye bute dweole, for nis hit bute his gile. He haveth wise men of hali ant of heh lif ofte swa bichearret, as the thet he com to i wummone liche i the wildernesse,

[help] me if I asked, and so I could help them and bestow (lit., do) alms on them" — [the devil] leads (lit., brings) her on to gather (or, save), and give all, first to the poor, later to other friends, finally to make feasts and become completely worldly, transformed (or, degenerated) from an anchoress [in]to a housewife (i.e., lady) of a hall. **553–56 Godd wat . . . leapeth in orhel**, God knows, such feasting makes some a whore (or, makes a whore of some). [She] imagines that she does well, as stupid and silly [people] make her understand, flatter her for [her] generosity, praise and raise up (or, exalt) the charity that she does, how widely she is known. And she thinks well of [this] and leaps into pride. **556–57 Sum seith inoh-reathe . . . beon i-robbet**, Some[one will] say readily enough that she [is] gathering a hoard — so that (i.e., and the result will be that) her house and she too (lit., both) may be robbed. **557–58 Reowthe over reowthe! . . . leve ye him neaver**, Pity beyond pity! Thus the traitor of hell makes himself a true advisor (note the heavy irony)! Do not believe him ever. **559–60 Davith cleopeth him . . . angelum lucis**, David calls him "mid-day demon," "bright, shining devil" (Psalm 90:6), and St. Paul, [calls him the] "angel of light" (2 Corinthians 11:14). **560–62 For swuch ofte he maketh him . . . bute his gile**, For he often makes himself such and shows himself to many. No marvel (or, vision) that you see, either in a dream or waking, consider (imper.) [anything] but deception, for it is [nothing] but his guile. **562–64 He haveth wise men . . . efter herbearhe**, He has misled wise men of holy and high (or, exalted) life often thus, like him whom he came to in woman's likeness in the wilderness, said she had gone in error (i.e., astray, was lost) and wept like a destitute thing (or, wretched creature) for lodging.

seide ha wes i-gan o dweole, [ant weop] as meoseise thing, efter herbearhe. Ant te
565   other hali mon thet he makede i-leven thet he wes engel, bi his feader, thet he wes
the deovel, ant makede him to slean his feader — swa ofte ther-bivoren he heafde
i-seid him eaver soth, for-te biswiken him sariliche on ende. Alswa of the hali
mon thet he makede cumen ham for-te dealen his feader feh to neodfule ant to
povre, se longe, thet he deadliche sunegede o wummon, ant swa feol into unhope,
570   ant deide in heaved sunne. Of mon the speketh with ow thulliche talen, hereth hu
ye schulen witen ow with thes deofles wiltes, thet he ow ne bichearre.

    Sum of ow sum-chearre he makede to leven thet hit were fikelunge yef ha speke
feire, ant yef ha eadmodliche meande hire neode, yef ha thonckede mon of his
god-dede — ant wes mare over-hohe for-te acwenchen chearite, then rihtwisnesse.
575   Sum he is umben to makien se swithe fleon monne frovre, thet ha falleth i deadlich
sar — thet is, accidie — other into deop thoht swa thet ha dotie. Sum heateth swa
sunne, thet ha haveth over-hohe of othre the falleth, the schulde wepen for hire,

564–67 Ant te other hali mon . . . on ende, And the other holy man whom he made (i.e.,
caused to) believe that he was an angel, and concerning his father, that he was the devil, and
made him slay his father — so often before this he (i.e., the devil) had always told him the
truth, in order to deceive him pitifully in the end. **567–70 Alswa of the hali mon thet he
makede cumen . . . in heaved sunne,** Likewise [there is the story] of the holy man that he
made (or, forced to) come home in order to distribute his father's money to the needy and to
the poor, so long (i.e., he stayed at home so long), that he sinned mortally with (lit., on) a
woman, and so fell into despair, and died in capital sin. **570–71 Of mon the speketh with ow
. . . ne bichearre,** From the person who recites to you such tales (i.e., the author?), hear
(imper.) how you ought to protect yourselves against this devil's wiles, so that he does not
deceive you. **572–74 Sum of ow sum-chearre . . . then rihtwisnesse,** He made some of you
sometimes believe that it were (i.e., would be) flattery if she spoke politely, and if she humbly
complained of her needs, if she thanked a person (or, man) for his good deed — and [yet this]
was more disdain (lit., over-highness) to extinguish love, than [it was] righteousness. **575–76
Sum he is umben to makien . . . thet ha dotie,** He is after another (lit., some) to make [her] so
quickly flee men's comfort that she [will] fall into deadly sorrow — that is, despair — or into
deep thought so that she goes out of her wits (or, does foolish things — see *dotie* in glossary).
576–79 Sum heateth swa sunne . . . of his brethren, A certain [one] hates sin so [much] that
she has disdain towards another who falls — [she] who should weep for her, and should sorely
dread for such a [thing] with respect to herself, and [who ought to] say as the holy man who

580 ant sare dreden for a swuch onont hire-seolven, ant seggen as the hali mon the seac ant weop ant seide, tha me him talde the fal of an of his brethren, **"Ille hodie, ego cras."** "Wei-la-wei, strongliche wes he i-temptet ear he swa feolle. As he feol to-dei, ich mei," quoth he, "alswa fallen to-marhen."

Nu, mine leove sustren, monie temptatiuns ich habbe ow i-nempnet under the seove sunnen — nawt, thah, the thusent-fald thet me is with i-temptet. Ne mahte — ich wene — ham na-mon nomeliche nempnin. Ah i theo the beoth i-seid, alle
585 beoth bilokene. Lut beoth i this world, other nan mid alle, thet ne beo with hare sum other-hwile i-temptet. He haveth se monie buistes ful of his letuaires, the luthere leche of helle — the forsaketh an, he beot an-other forth anan-riht, the thridde, the feorthe, ant swa eaver forth athet he cume o swuch thet me on ende undervo. Ant he thenne with thet birleth him i-lome — thencheth her of the tale of
590 his ampoiles! Hereth nu, as ich bihet, ayein alle fondunges moni cunne frovre, ant with Godes grace, th'refter the salve.

sighed and wept and said, when they told him [about] the fall of one of his brothers. **579–80 *Ille hodie, ego cras,*** "He today, I tomorrow" (*The Lives of the Desert Fathers* 7.16). **580–81 "Wei-la-wei . . . fallen to-marhen,"** "He was severely tempted before he fell so. As he fell today, I may," he said, "also fall tomorrow." **582–83 ow i-nempnet . . . with i-temptet,** named for you under [the headings of] the seven sins — not, though, the thousand-fold [ones] that one is tempted with. **583–84 Ne mahte — ich wene . . . nempnin,** No one — I expect — could name them specifically (lit., namely). **584–86 Ah i theo the beoth i-seid . . . other-hwile i-temptet,** But in those which are mentioned (lit., said), all are locked (i.e., contained). There are few in this world, or none perhaps, who are not tempted by some of them sometime (*hare* = genitive pl., dependent on *sum*). **586–89 He haveth se monie . . . on ende undervo,** He has so many boxes full of his medicines, the wicked doctor (lit., leech) of hell — whoever refuses one, he offers another up straight-away, the third, the fourth, and so on (lit., ever further) until he comes upon such [a medicine] that is accepted in the end (lit., which one accepts). **589–91 Ant he thenne with thet birleth . . . th'refter the salve,** And he then plies him often with that — think (imper.) here of the number of his ampoules (or, phials)! Hear now, as I promised, [about] the many kinds of comfort against all temptations, and with God's grace (i.e., and if God gives me the ability), after that the remedy.

Siker beo of fondunge hwa-se eaver stont in heh lif — ant this is the earste frovre. For eaver se herre tur, se haveth mare windes. Ye beoth tur ow-seolven, mine leove sustren, ah ne drede ye nawt hwil ye beoth se treoweliche ant se feste 595 i-limet with lim of an-red luve, euch of ow to other. For na deofles puf ne thurve ye dreden bute thet lim falsi — thet is to seggen, bute luve bitweonen ow thurh the feond wursi. Sone se ei unlimeth hire, ha bith sone i-swipt forth; bute yef the othre halden hire, ha bith sone i-keast adun as the lowse stan is from the tures cop into the deope dich of sum suti sunne.

600 Nu an-other elne muchel ah to frovrin ow hwen ye beoth i-temptet: the tur nis nawt asailit, ne castel ne cite, hwen ha beoth i-wunnen. Alswa the helle weorrur ne asaileth nan with fondunge the he haveth in his hond, ah deth theo the he naveth nawt. For-thi, leove sustren, hwa-se nis nawt asailet, ha mei sare beon ofdred leste ha beo biwunnen.

592–93 Siker beo of fondunge . . . mare windes, Let her be sure of temptation (i.e., sure that she will be tempted), whoever stands (*stont* = reduced form of *stondeth*) in the high life — and this is the first comfort. For the higher the tower, the more winds [it] has (lit., for ever so higher the tower, so [it] has more winds). **593–95 Ye beoth tur ow-seolven . . . of ow to other**, You are tower[s] yourselves, my dear sisters, but do not fear (lit., dread) while you are so securely and firmly cemented with the lime (i.e., mortar) of resolute love, each of you to the other. **595–97 For na deofles puf . . . thurh the feond wursi**, For you need fear no devil's puff (or, blast) unless the mortar fails — that is to say, unless love between you worsens because of the enemy (or, fiend). **597–99 Sone se ei unlimeth hire . . . sum suti sunne**, As soon as anyone uncements (or, unsticks) herself, she is (or, will be) immediately swept away; unless (lit., but if) the others hold her, she will be immediately cast down as is the loose stone from the tower's summit (or, crown — see *tur* in glossary) into the deep ditch of some sooty (or, filthy) sin. **600–01 Nu an-other elne . . . ha beoth i-wunnen**, Now another strength ought to comfort you much when you are tempted: the tower is not attacked (lit., assailed), nor castle nor city, when (i.e., after) they are won. **601–03 Alswa the helle weorrur . . . he naveth nawt**, Likewise, the warrior of hell does not assail any[one] with temptation whom he has in his hand (i.e., power), but does [so to] those whom he does not have [in his power]. **603–04 For-thi, leove sustren . . . beo biwunnen**, For this reason, dear sisters, whosoever is not attacked, she may be sorely afraid lest (i.e., in case) she be conquered.

605   The thridde cunfort is thet ure Laverd seolf i the **Pater noster** teacheth us to
bidden, **Et ne nos inducas in temptationem** — thet is, "Laverd Feader, ne suffre
thu nawt the feond thet he leade us allunge into fondunge." Lo, neometh yeme!
He nule nawt thet we bidden thet we ne beon nawt i-fondet, for thet is ure
purgatoire, ure cleansing fur, ah thet we ne beon nawt allunge i-broht th'rin with
610   consens of heorte, with skiles yettunge.

The feorthe frovre is sikernesse of Godes help i the fehtunge ayein, as Seinte
Pawel witneth: **Fidelis est Deus, qui non sinit nos temptari ultra quam pati
possumus, set et cetera**. "Godd," he seith, "is treowe. Nule he neaver suffrin thet
te deovel tempti us over thet he sith wel thet we mahen tholien." Ah i the temptatiun
615   he haveth i-set to the feond a mearke, as thah he seide, "Tempte hire swa feor, ah
ne schalt tu gan na forthre!" Ant swa feor he yeveth hire strengthe to withstonden;
the feond ne mei nawt forthre gan a pricke.

Ant this is the fifte frovre, thet he ne mei na thing don us, bute bi Godes leave.
Thet wes wel i-schawet as the Godspel teleth, tha the deoflen thet ure Laverd

605–07 The thridde cunfort is . . . into fondunge, The third comfort is that our
Lord Himself in the Paternoster (i.e., Lord's prayer) teaches us to pray, "And lead us
not into temptation" (Matthew 6:13, Luke 11:4) — that is, "Lord Father, do not allow the fiend to lead us (lit., that he lead us) entirely into temptation." **607–10 Lo,
neometh yeme! . . . with skiles yettunge**, Look, pay (lit., take) attention! He does
not want that we pray that we not be tempted, for that (i.e., temptation) is our purgatory, our cleansing fire, but [he wants us to pray] that we not be completely brought
into it (lit., therein) with the consent of [our] heart, [or] with the reason's permission. **611 The feorthe frovre . . . ayein**, The fourth comfort is confidence of God's help
in the fighting against (i.e., resistance). **612–13 *Fidelis est Deus . . . quam pati possumus, set et cetera***, "God is faithful, who does not allow us to be tempted more than we can
bear, but" etc. (adapted freely from 1 Corinthians 10:13). **613–14 Nule he neaver suffrin
. . . we mahen tholien**, He will never allow that the devil tempt us over that [which] he
sees well that we can bear. **615 he haveth i-set . . . mearke**, He has set the devil a limit.
616–17 Ant swa feor he yeveth . . . gan a pricke, And so far (i.e., up to this point) He
gives her strength to withstand; the enemy cannot go one prick (or, jot) further. **618 frovre**,
comfort; **don**, do to. **619–20 Thet wes wel i-schawet . . . ant seiden**, That was well revealed
(lit., shown) as the Gospel tells, when the devils which our Lord cast out of a man begged and

620 weorp ut of a mon bisohten ant seiden, **Si eicitis nos hinc, mittite nos in porcos**. "'Yef thu heonne drivest us, do us i theos swin her,' the eoden ther an heorde. Ant he yettede ham." Lo, hu ha ne mahten nawt fule swin swenchen withuten his leave. Ant te swin anan-riht urnen an urn to the sea to adrenchen ham-seolven. Seinte Marie! swa he stonc to the swin, thet ham wes leovre to adrenchen ham-
625 seolven then for-te beoren him, ant an unseli sunful, Godes i-licnesse, bereth him in his breoste, ant ne nimeth neaver yeme! Al thet he dude Job eaver he nom leve th'rof ed ure Laverd. The tale i *Dyaloge* lokith thet ye cunnen, hu the hali mon wes i-wunet to seggen to the deofles neddre, **Si licenciam accepisti, ego non prohibeo**. "Yef thu havest leave, do sting yef thu maht" — ant bead forth his
630 cheke. Ah he nefde tha nan bute to offearen him, yef bileave him trukede. Ant hwen Godd yeveth him leave on his leove children, hwi is hit bute for hare muchele biheve thah hit ham grevi sare?

said. **620 *Si eicitis nos hinc . . . in porcos***, "If you drive us out from here, send us into the pigs" (adapted from Matthew 8:31, see also Mark 5:12 and Luke 8:33). **621–22 "Yef thu heonne drivest us . . . yettede ham,"** "'If you drive us away from here (lit., hence), put us in these swine here,' who were wandering (lit., went) there as one herd. And he granted [it] to them." **622–23 Lo, hu ha ne mahten nawt . . . adrenchen ham-seolven**, Look, how they could not harass [even] filthy pigs without His permission. And the pigs immediately ran a gallop (or, ran violently) to the sea to drown themselves. **624–26 Seinte Marie! . . . nimeth neaver yeme!** St. Mary! he (i.e., this demon) stank so to the pigs that [it] was preferable to them to drown themselves than to bear (or, carry) him, and a wretched sinful [person], bears God's likeness in his breast (or, heart) and never pays [the least] attention! **626–28 Al thet he dude . . . deofles neddre**, For everything that he (i.e., the devil) did to Job, he always got permission for it from our Lord. See (i.e., Make sure) that you know the story in [Gregory's] *Dialogues*, how the holy man was wont (i.e., accustomed) to speak to the devil's serpent. **628–29 *Si licenciam accepisti, ego non prohibeo***, "If you have received permission, I do not forbid you" (Gregory, *Dialogues* 3.16 [PL 77.257]). **629–30 do sting yef thu maht . . . yef bileave him trukede**, "make a sting (i.e., sting — imper.) if you can" — and [he] offered up his cheek. But he (i.e., the serpent) did not then have any (i.e., any permission) except to frighten him, [to see] if [his] belief would fail him. **630–32 Ant hwen Godd yeveth him leave . . . grevi sare?** And when God gives him (i.e., the devil) permission [to perpetrate temptations] on his beloved children, why is it except for their great benefit, [even] though it grieves (or, agonizes) them sorely?

The seste confort is thet ure Laverd, hwen he tholeth thet we beon i-temptet, he pleieth with us as the moder with hire yunge deorling, flith from him ant hut hire, ant let him sitten ane ant lokin yeorne abuten, cleopien, "Dame! Dame!" ant wepen ane hwile — ant thenne with spredde earmes leapeth lahhinde forth, cluppeth ant cusseth ant wipeth his ehnen. Swa ure Laverd let us ane i-wurthen other-hwile, ant withdraheth his grace, his cunfort ant his elne, thet we ne findeth swetnesse i na thing thet we wel doth, ne savur of heorte, ant thah i thet ilke point ne luveth us ure Laverd neaver the leasse, ah deth hit for muche luve. Ant thet understod wel Davith, tha he seide, **Non me derelinquas usquequaque.** "Allunge," quoth he, "Laverd, ne leaf thu me nawt." Lo, hu he walde thet he leafde him, ah nawt allunge. Ant six acheisuns notith hwi Godd for ure god withdraheth him other-hwiles. An is thet we ne pruden; an-other, thet we cnawen ure ahne feblesce, ure muchele unstrengthe ant ure wacnesse. Ant this is a swithe muche god, as Seint Gregoire seith: **Magna perfectio est sue inperfectionis cognitio** — thet is, "muche godnesse hit is to cnawen wel his wrecchehead ant his wacnesse." **Ecclesiasticus:**

635

640

645

633 tholeth, allows. **634–37 flith from him ant hut hire . . . ehnen**, flies away from him (or, it) and hides (*hut* = reduced form of *hudeth*) herself, and lets him sit alone and look longingly (or, yearningly) about, lets him cry, "Mother! Mother!" and [lets him] weep a while — and then with arms spread [wide she] leaps out laughing, hugs and kisses [him] and wipes his eyes. **637–40 Swa ure Laverd let us ane i-wurthen . . . for muche luve**, Just so, our Lord lets us be alone sometimes, and withdraws His grace, His comfort, and His strength, so that we [can] find sweetness in nothing that we do well, nor savor (i.e., relish) of heart, and nevertheless in that very situation our Lord does not love us any the less, but does it because of great love. **641 tha**, when; *Non me derelinquas usquequaque*, "Do not forsake me utterly" (Psalm 118:8). **641–42 "Allunge . . . leaf thu me nawt,"** "Completely," he said, "[O] Lord, do not leave me." **642–43 Lo, hu he walde . . . other-hwiles**, Look (lit., lo!) how he wanted Him to leave him (lit., that He [should] leave him), but not completely. And note six reasons why God withdraws himself for our good sometimes. **643–45 An is thet we ne pruden . . . ure wacnesse**, The first (lit., one) is so that we not become proud; a second [reason], that we know our own feebleness, our great lack of strength and our weakness. **645 swithe muche god**, a very great good. **646 *Magna perfectio . . . inperfectionis cognitio***, "Great perfection is the recognition of one's imperfection" (not found in Gregory's known works). **647 to cnawen wel his wrecchehead ant his wacnesse**, to know well his wretchedness and his weakness. **647–48 *Ecclesiasticus: Intemptatus qualia scit?*** Ecclesiasticus: "What kind of things does the untempted (or, untested) person

Intemptatus qualia scit? "Hwet wat he," seith Salomon, "the thet is unfondet?"
Ant Seint Austin bereth Seint Gregoire witnesse with theose wordes: **Melior est**
650 **animus cui propria est infirmitas nota, quam qui scrutatur celorum fastigia
et terrarum fundamenta.** "Betere is the the truddeth ant ofsecheth wel ut his
ahne feblesce, then the the meteth hu heh is the heovene, ant hu deop the eorthe."
Hwen twa beoreth a burtherne, ant te other leaveth hit, thenne mei the the up
haldeth hit felen hu hit weieth. Alswa, leove suster, hwil thet Godd with the bereth
655 thi temptatiun, nast tu neaver hu hevi hit is, ant for-thi ed sum-chearre he leaveth
the ane, thet tu understonde thin ahne feblesce ant his help cleopie, ant yeie lude
efter him yef he is to longe. Hald hit wel the hwile up, ne derve hit te se sare.
Hwa-se is siker of sucurs thet him schal cume sone, ant yelt tah up his castel to his
wither-iwines — swithe he is to edwiten. Thencheth her of the tale hu the hali
660 mon in his fondunge seh bi west toyeines him se muche ferd of deoflen ant forleas,
for muche dred, the strengthe of his bileave, athet te othre sei*de* him: "Bihald,"

know?" (adapted from Ecclesiasticus 34:9). **648 "Hwet wat he . . . the thet is unfondet?"**
"What does he know, says Solomon, he who (lit., who that) is untempted?" **649–51 *Melior est**
animus . . . et terrarum fundamenta*, "The spirit to which its own weakness is known (i.e.,
which knows its own weakness) is better than [the spirit] which examines the heights of the
heavens and the foundations of the earth" (Augustine, *Concerning the Trinity* 4.1 [*PL* 42.885,
887]). **651–52 "Betere is the the truddeth . . . hu deop the eorthe,"** "Better is he who tracks
down and seeks out his own feebleness effectively, than he who measures how high heaven is
and how deep the earth." **653–54 Hwen twa beoreth a burtherne . . . hu hit weieth**, When
two [people] carry a burden, and the second [one] leaves it (i.e., lets it go), then he who holds
it up can feel how [much] it weighs. **654–57 Alswa, leove suster . . . yef he is to longe**, Just so,
dear sister, while (or, as long as) God carries your temptation with you, you never know how
heavy it is, and for this reason sometimes He leaves you alone, so that you may understand
your own feebleness and call for His help, and cry loudly for Him if He is [away] too long.
657–59 Hald hit wel the hwile up . . . he is to edwiten, Hold it (i.e., the burden of temptation)
up well in the meantime, [even though] it torment you [ever] so sorely (i.e., however badly it
taxes you). Whosoever is sure (or, confident) of help, which will come soon to him (i.e., whoever is confident that help will come soon to him), and yields up (*yelt* = reduced form of
yeldeth) nevertheless his castle to his enemies — he is very much to blame (or, be blamed). **660**
fondunge, temptation. **660–62 seh bi west . . . bi esten!** saw in the west so great an army of
devils [coming] against him, and lost, because of [his] great fear, the strength of his belief,

quoth he, "bi esten!" **Plures nobiscum sunt quam cum illis** — "we habbeth ma then heo beoth to help on ure halve." For the thridde thing is thet tu neaver ne beo al siker, for sikernesse streoneth yemeles ant over-hohe, ant ba theose streonith

665 inobedience. The feorthe acheisun is hwi ure Laverd hut him — thet tu seche him yeornluker, ant cleopie ant wepe efter him as deth the lutel baban efter his moder. Th'refter is the fifte — thet tu his yein-cume undervo the gleadluker. The seste — thet tu th'refter the wisluker wite him hwen thu havest i-caht him ant festluker halde, ant segge with his leofmon, **Tenui eum nec dimittam.** Theose six reisuns

670 beoth under the seste frovre the ye mahen habben, mine leove sustren, ayeines fondunge.

The seovethe confort is thet alle the hali halhen weren wodeliche i-temptet. Nim of the heste on alre earst: to Seinte Peter seide ure Laverd: **Ecce, Sathan expetivit vos, ut cribraret sicut triticum, et cetera.** "Lo!" quoth he, "Sathan is

675 yeorne abuten for-te ridli the ut of mine i-corene. Ah ich habbe for the bisoht thet

until the other [one] said to him, "Look," he said, "to the east!" **662** *Plures nobiscum sunt quam cum illis*, "There are many more with us than with them" (*The Lives of the Desert Fathers* 5.18). **662–63 "we habbeth ma . . . on ure halve,"** "we have more than they are (i.e., have) to help on our side." **663–65 ne beo al siker . . . streonith inobedience**, [should] never be completely confident, for confidence breeds carelessness and arrogance, and both these breed disobedience. **665–66 The feorthe acheisun . . . efter his moder**, There is a fourth reason why our Lord hides (*hut* = reduced form of *hudeth*) Himself — so that that you should seek Him more eagerly and call and weep for Him as the little baby does for its (or, his) mother. **667–69 thet tu his yein-cume . . . his leofmon**, that you receive His return (lit., again-coming) the more gladly. The sixth — that you afterwards may guard (or, keep) Him the more wisely when you have caught Him, hold [Him] the more firmly, and say with His leman (i.e., lover). **669** *Tenui eum nec dimittam*, "I have held Him fast, nor will I give [Him] up (or, let Him go)" (Song of Songs 3:4). **670–71 beoth under the seste frovre . . . ayeines fondunge**, are under [the heading of] the sixth comfort which you can have, my dear sisters, against temptation. **672–73 alle the hali halhen . . . ure Laverd**, all the holy saints were furiously tempted. Take one of the highest [saints] first of all (*alre* = genitive pl.): our Lord said to St. Peter. **673–74** *Ecce, Sathan expetivit vos . . . sicut triticum, et cetera*, "Lo, Satan desires [to have] you so that he may sift you like wheat," etc. (Luke 22:31). **675–76 yeorne abuten for-te ridli the . . . allunge ne trukie**, eagerly about [his work] to sift you out from my chosen [ones]. But I have

ti bileave allunge ne trukie." Seint Pawel hefde, as he teleth him-seolf, flesches pricunge: **Datus est michi stimulus carnis mee** — ant bed ure Laverd yeorne thet he dude hit from him, ant he nalde, ah seide, **Sufficit tibi gratia mea: virtus in infirmitate perficitur** — thet is, "mi grace schal wite the, thet tu ne beo overcumen.

680 Beo strong in unstrengthe: thet is muche mihte." Alle the othre beoth i-crunet thurh feht of fondunge. Seinte Sare — nes ha fulle threottene yer i-temptet of hire flesch? Ah for-thi thet ha wiste thet i the muchele angoise aras the muchele mede, nalde ha neaver eanes bisechen ure Laverd thet he allunge delivrede hire th'rof, ah this wes hire bone: **Domine, da michi virtutem resistendi.** "Laverd, yef me

685 strengthe for-te withstonden." Efter threottene yer com the acursede gast the hefde hire i-temptet, blac ase bla-mon, ant bigon to greden, "Sare, thu havest me overcumen!" Ant heo him ondswerede, "thu lihest," quoth ha, "ful thing! Nawt ich, ah haveth Jesu Crist, mi Laverd." Lo, the sweoke, hu he walde makien hire aleast to leapen into prude. Ah ha wes wel war th'rof ant turnde al the meistrie to

besought (i.e., interceded, prayed) for you so that your belief may not completely fail. **676–77 Seint Pawel hefde . . . pricunge**, St. Paul had, as he says himself, a pricking of [his] flesh (i.e., a thorn in his flesh). **677 *Datus est michi stimulus carnis mee***, "A goad (or, sting) in my flesh was given to me" (2 Corinthians 12:7). **677–78 ant bed ure Laverd . . . ah seide**, and [he] asked our Lord eagerly that He [might] take it from him, and He would not, but said. **678–79 *Sufficit tibi gratia mea: virtus in infirmitate perficitur***, "My grace is sufficient for you: strength is perfected in weakness" (2 Corinthians 12:9). **679 wite the . . . overcumen**, protect you [so] that you [will] not be overcome. **680 mihte**, might (or, power). **680–81 Alle the othre beoth i-crunet . . . feht of fondunge**, All the other [saints] are crowned through (or, by means of) the struggle against temptation (lit., fight of temptation). **681–84 Seinte Sare . . . ah this wes hire bone**, St. Sarah — was she not tempted for fully thirteen years in her flesh (or, body)? But because she knew that in great anguish, great reward would arise (lit., arose), she did not want ever once to beseech our Lord that He would completely deliver her of it (lit., thereof), but this was her prayer. **684 *Domine, da michi virtutem resistendi***, "Lord, give me strength of resisting (i.e., to resist)" (see *The Lives of the Desert Fathers* 5.10–11); **yef**, give. **685–88 Efter threottene yer . . . mi Laverd**, After thirteen years the accursed spirit which had tempted her came, black as a Moor (lit., black man), and began to wail, "Sarah, you have overcome me!" And she answered him, "you lie," she said, "foul thing! Not I, but Jesus Christ my Lord has [overcome you]." **688–90 Lo, the sweoke . . . to Godes strengthe**, Look, the traitor (or, deceiver), how he wanted to make her leap into pride at last (or, in the end). But she was well aware of that (lit.,

690   Godes strengthe. Sein Beneit, Seint Antonie, ant te othre — wel ye witen hu ha weren i-temptet, ant thurh the temptatiuns i-pruvede to treowe champiuns, ant swa with rihte ofserveden kempene crune.

    Ant this is the eahtuthe elne — thet alswa as the golt-smith cleanseth thet gold i the fur, alswa deth Godd te sawle i fur of fondunge.

695   The nihethe confort is thet yef the feond with fondunge greveth the sare, thu grevest him hwen thu edstondest hundret sithe sarre, for threo reisuns nomeliche. The an is thet he forleoseth, as Origene seith, his strengthe for-te temptin eaver mare ther-onuven of swuch manere sunne. The other is thet he forthluker echeth his pine. The thridde fret his heorte of sar grome ant of teone thet he, unthonc hise

700 teth, i the temptatiun thet tu stondest ayein, muchleth thi mede, ant for pine thet he wende for-te drahe the toward, breideth the crune of blisse — ant nawt ane an ne twa, ah ase feole sithen as thu overkimest him, ase feole crunen — thet is to seggen, ase feole mensken of misliche murhthen. For swa Sein Beornard seith, **Quotiens vincis, totiens coronaberis.** The tale i **Vitas Patrum** witneth this ilke,

thereof) and turned (i.e., assigned) all the triumph (lit., mastery) to God's strength. **690 witen,** know. **691–92 i-pruvede to treowe champiuns . . . crune,** tried (or, proven) as true champions, and so by right [they] deserved the crown of champions. **693–94 Ant this is the eahtuthe elne . . . fur of fondunge,** And this is the eighth strength (or, comfort) — that just as the goldsmith purifies gold in the fire, just so does God [purify] the soul in the fire of temptation. **695–98 greveth the sare . . . sunne,** tortures you grievously, you torture him a hundred times more grievously (lit., sorely) when you stand against [him], for three reasons particularly. The first is that he loses, as Origen says, his strength to tempt thereafter ever again with such manner [of] sin. **698–703 The other is thet . . . murhthen,** The second is that he further increases his punishment (or, pain). The third gnaws at his heart with terrible anger and vexation that he, damn his teeth (i.e., despite himself), increases your reward in the temptation which you stand against, and instead of (lit., for) the punishment that he expected to draw you toward, [he] weaves (lit., braids) you a crown of bliss — and not only one or two, but as many times as you overcome him, [he weaves] as many crowns — that is to say, so many honors of various joys. **703 swa,** thus, so. **704 *Quotiens vincis, totiens coronaberis*,** "As often as you conquer, so often you will be crowned" (Bernard, *Sermons for Quadragesima* 5.3 [*PL* 183.179]). **704–07 The tale i *Vitas Patrum* . . . slep swithe!** The story in *The Lives of the [Desert] Fathers* witnesses (or, confirms) the same [thing], [the story] of the disciple who sat before his master and his master fell (lit., became) asleep while he taught him and slept until

705   of the deciple the set bivoren his meistre, ant his meistre warth o slepe hwil thet he
learde him ant slepte athet mid-niht, tha he awakede: "Art tu," quoth he, "yet her?
Ga ant slep swithe!" The hali mon, his meistre, warth eft o slep sone as the the
hefde ther-bivoren i-beon i muche wecche, ant seh a swithe feier stude, ant i-set
forth a trone, ant th'ron seove crunen, ant com a stevene ant seide: "this sege ant

710   theose crunen haveth thin deciple this ilke niht ofsarvet." Ant te hali mon abreaid
ant cleopede him to him. "Sei," quoth he, "hu stod te hwil thu, as ich slepte, sete
bivore me?" "Ich thohte," quoth he, "ofte thet ich walde awakenin the, ant for thu
sleptest swote, ne mah[te] ich for reowthe. Ant thenne thohte ich gan awei to
slepen for me luste, ant nalde bute leave." "Hu ofte," quoth his meister, "over-

715   come thu thi thoht thus?" "Seove sithen," seide he. Tha understond his meister
wel hwet weren the seove crunen — seove cunne blissen thet his deciple hefde in
euch a chearre ofservet, thet he withseide the feond, ant overcom him-seolven.

     Al thus, leove sustren, i wreastlunge of temptatiun ariseth the biyete. **Nemo
coronabitur nisi qui legittime certaverit.** "Ne schal nan beon i-crunet," seith

midnight when he awoke: "Are you," he said, "still here? Go and sleep at once (lit., quickly)!"
707–10 The hali mon, his meistre . . . this ilke niht ofsarvet, The holy man, his master, fell
back asleep at once like a person who had been before that (lit., there-before) on a great vigil
(i.e., one who had been awake for a long time), and [he] saw a very beautiful place and [saw] a
throne set out, and on it seven crowns, and [there] came a voice and said: "your disciple has
earned this seat and these crowns this very night." **710–12 Ant te hali mon abreaid . . . sete
bivore me?** And the holy man started [out of his sleep] and called him to him. "Tell [me]," he
said, "how it went (lit., stood) [with] you while you sat before me as I slept?" **712–14 "Ich
thohte," . . . nalde bute leave,"** "I often thought," he said," that I would wake you up, but (lit.,
and) because you slept [so] sweetly, I could not [wake you] for pity. And then I thought to go
away to sleep, for [it] pleased me (or, I wanted to), but (lit., and) did not want to without
permission." **714–15 "Hu ofte," . . . seide he,** "How often," said his master, "did you thus
overcome your thought (or, intention)?" "Seven times," he said. **715 Tha,** Then. **716–17 seove
cunne blissen . . . him-seolven,** seven kinds of joy that his disciple had earned on each single
occasion that he opposed (or, contradicted) the fiend, and overcame (or, mastered) himself.
718 Al thus, leove sustren . . . the biyete, Exactly in this way (lit., completely thus), dear
sisters, in wrestling (or, struggling) with temptation, a benefit mounts up for you. **718–19
*Nemo coronabitur . . . certaverit,*** "No one will be crowned unless he has properly struggled"
(slightly altered from 2 Timothy 2:5). **719–21 "Ne schal nan . . . the feond of helle,"** "None

Part Four

720   Seinte Pawel, "bute hwa-se strongliche ant treoweliche fehteth ayein the world, ayein him-seolf, ayein the feond of helle." Theo fehteth treoweliche, the hu se ha eaver beoth i-weorret with theos threo wither-iwines — nomeliche of the flesch — hwuch se eaver the lust beo, se hit meadluker is, wrinnith ayein festluker, ant withseggeth the grant th'rof with ane-wile heorte, ne prokie hit se swithe. Theo

725   the thus doth beoth Jesu Cristes feolahes, for ha doth as he dude honginde o rode. **Cum gustasset acetum, noluit bibere** — thet is, "he smahte thet bittre drunch, ant withdroh him anan, ant nalde hit nawt drinken thah he ofthurst were." Heo is, the swa deth, with Godd on his rode, thah hire thurste i the lust, ant te deovel beot hire his healewi to drinken. Understonde ant thenche thah thet ter is galle under.

730   Ant tah hit beo a pine, betere is for-te tholien thurst then to beon i-attret. Let lust overgan, ant hit te wule eft likin. Hwil the yicchunge least hit thuncheth god to gnuddin, ah th'refter me feleth hit bitterliche smeorten. Wei-la-wei! Ant moni an is for muchel heate se swithe ofthurst mid alle, thet hwil ha drinketh thet drunch,

will be crowned," says St. Paul, "except whoever strongly and truly (or, faithfully) fights against the world, against himself, [and] against the fiend (lit., enemy) of hell." **721–24 Theo fehteth treoweliche . . . ne prokie hit se swithe**, They fight faithfully who, howsoever they are attacked with these three adversaries — especially by the flesh — whatever the desire [may] be, the more furious it is (lit., so it is more furious), the more firmly [they] struggle against [it], and deny the granting of (or, giving in to) it with a resolute heart, [even if] it goad [them] ever so powerfully. **724–25 Theo the thus doth . . . honginde o rode**, Those who do (or, act) thus are Jesus Christ's comrades, for they do as He did [while He was] hanging on the Cross. **726 *Cum gustasset acetum, noluit bibere***, "When he had tasted the vinegar, he did not want to drink" (based on Matthew 27:34). **726–27 "he smahte thet bittre drunch . . . ofthurst were,"** "He tasted that bitter drink and drew Himself back immediately, and did]not want to drink it though he was very thirsty." **727–29 Heo is, the swa deth . . . his healewi to drinken**, She, who does so (i.e., acts like this), is with God on His Cross, [even] though she thirst in desire (lit., [it] thirsts to her in the desire), and the devil offers her his sweet medicine to drink. **729–30 Understonde ant thenche . . . to beon i-attret**, Understand and think nevertheless that there is gall under[neath] (i.e., hidden in with the sweet medicine). And though it is (lit., be) a torture, [it] is better to suffer thirst than to be poisoned. **730–32 Let lust overgan . . . bitterliche smeorten**, Let desire pass over, and it will please you (i.e., you will be satisfied) afterwards. While the itching lasts it seems good to rub (i.e., scratch), though afterwards (lit., thereafter) one feels it smarting (lit., to smart) bitterly. **732–35 Wei-la-wei! . . . ne nimeth neaver yeme**, Alas! And many a one is so very, very thirsty because of the great heat,

256

ne beo hit ne se bitter, ne feleth ha hit neaver, ah gluccheth in yiverliche, ne nimeth
735   neaver yeme. Hwen hit is al over, spit ant schaketh thet heaved, feth on for-te
nivelin, ant makien grim chere — ah to leate thenne [naut-for-thi! For efter uvel,
god is penitence. Thet is the best thenne.] Speowen hit anan ut with schrift to the
preoste. For leave hit in-with, hit wule death breden. For-thi, mine leove sustren,
beoth bivoren warre, ant efter the frovren the beoth her i-writene ayein alle
740   fondunges secheth theose salven:

Ayein alle temptatiuns — ant nomeliche ayein fleschliche — salven beoth ant
bote under Godes grace: halie meditatiuns in-warde ant meadlese, ant angoisuse
bonen, hardi bileave, redunge, veasten, wecchen, ant licomliche swinkes, othres
frovre for-te speoke toward i the ilke stunde thet hire stont stronge. Eadmodnesse,
745   freolec of heorte, ant alle gode theawes beoth armes i this feht, ant anrednesse of
luve over alle the othre. The his wepnen warpeth awei, him luste beon i-wundet.

Hali meditatiuns beoth bicluppet in a vers thet wes yare i-taht ow, mine leove
sustren,

moreover, that while she drinks that drink, be it ever so bitter (i.e., no matter how bitter it may be),
she does not ever detect it, but gulps [it] in greedily (lit., gluttonously), nor [does she] ever notice it
(lit., take care, notice). **735–37 Hwen hit is al over . . . beste thenne,** When it is all gone (lit., over),
[she] spits (*spit* = reduced form of *spitteth*) and shakes [her] head, starts to wrinkle her nose and
make a terrible face — but [it is] too late then! Nevertheless, after evil, penitence is good. It is the
best [thing] then. **737–38 Speowen hit anan ut . . . wule death breden,** Spew (or, vomit — imper.)
it out immediately in confession to the priest. For, [if you] leave it within, it will breed death. **738–
40 For-thi, mine leove sustren . . . secheth theose salven,** For this reason, my dear sisters, be aware
(or, wary) before[hand], and after the comforts for all temptations which are written (or, described)
here seek (imper. — i.e., you will find) these remedies (or, medicines). **741–44 ant nomeliche
ayein fleschliche . . . thet hire stont stronge,** and especially against fleshly (or, carnal) [tempta-
tions] — [there are] cures and remedies under God's grace: holy meditations, heartfelt (lit., inward)
and continual, and anguished prayers, strong belief, reading, fasts, vigils, and physical toil (lit.,
bodily toils), the comfort of another [person] to talk to in the very moment that things are going
badly (lit., [it] stands strongly or severely to her). **744–46 Eadmodnesse . . . beon i-wundet,** Humility, generosity of heart, and all good virtues are arms (or, weapons) in this fight, and constancy of
love above all the others. Whoever throws his weapons away wants to be wounded (lit., [it] pleases
him to be wounded). **747–48 Hali meditatiuns . . . mine leove sustren,** Holy meditations are
contained (or, embraced) in a verse that was taught to you a long time ago, my dear sisters.

Mors tua, mors Christi, nota culpe, gaudia celi,
750   **Judicii terror, figantur mente fideli.**

Thet is,
    Thench ofte with sar of thine sunnen,
    Thench of helle wa, of heove-riches wunnen,
    Thench of thin ahne death, of Godes death o rode —
755   The grimme dom of Domes-dei munneth *ofte* i mode.
    Thench hu fals is the worlt, hwucche beoth hire meden,
    Thench hwet tua hest Godd for his god deden.
Euch-an of theose word walde a long hwile for-te beo wel i-openet.

    Ah yef ich hihi forth-ward, demeori ye the lengre. A word ich segge: efter
760   ower sunnen, hwen-se ye thencheth of helle wa ant of heove-riches wunnen,
understondeth thet Godd walde o sum wise schawin ham to men i this world bi
worltliche pinen ant worltliche wunnen, ant schaweth ham forth as schadewe.
For na lickre ne beoth ha to the wunne of heovene, ne to the wa of helle then is

749–50 Mors tua, mors . . . figantur mente fideli, "[May] your death, the death of
Christ, the disgrace of sin, the joys of heaven, / The terror of judgment be fixed in the
[your] faithful mind" (source unidentified). **752–57 Thench ofte with sar . . . his
god deden**, Think often with sorrow on your sins, / Think of hell's misery, of heaven-
kingdom's joys, / Think of your own death, of God's death on the Cross — / Remember (or, call to mind) often the grim judgment of Doomsday. / Think how false the
world is, what sort are her (i.e., the world's) rewards, / Think what you owe God for
His good deeds. **758 Euch-an of theose word . . . wel i-openet**, Each one of these words
would want (i.e., require) a long time to be well opened (i.e., explained). **759–62 Ah yef
ich hihi forth-ward . . . schaweth ham forth as schadewe**, But if I rush (lit., hie) forward, you [should] pause the longer. I [will] say one word (i.e., thing): after your sins,
whensoever you think of hell's misery, and of heaven-kingdom's joys, understand that
God wanted in some way to show them to men in this world by [means of] worldly pains
and worldly joys, and [He] shows them forth (i.e., reveals them) as a shadow. **763–64 For
na lickre ne beoth . . . hit is of schadewe**, For they are no more like (lit., liker unto) the
joy of heaven, or to the misery of hell than is a shadow like the thing of which it is a

schadewe to thet thing thet hit is of schadewe. Ye beoth over this worldes sea, up-
765 o the brugge of heovene — lokith thet ye ne beon nawt the hors eschif i-liche the
schuncheth for a schadewe, ant falleth adun i the weater of the hehe brugge. To
childene ha beoth the fleoth a peinture the thuncheth ham grislich ant grureful to
bihalden. Wa ant wunne i this world — al nis bute peintunge, al nis bute schadewe.

Nawt ane hali meditatiuns — as of ure Laverd, ant of alle his werkes, ant of alle
770 his wordes, of the deore Leafdi ant of alle hali halhen — ah othre thohtes sum-
chearre i meadlese fondunges habbeth i-holpen, fowr cunne nomeliche, to theo
the beoth of flesches fondunges meadlese asailet: dredfule, wunderfule, gleadfule,
ant sorhfule — willes withute neod arearet i the heorte. As thenchen hwet tu waldest
don yef thu sehe openliche stonde bivore the, ant yeoniende wide up-o the, then
775 deovel of helle — as he deth dearnliche i the fondunge. Yef me yeide, "Fur! Fur!"
thet te chirche bearnde. Yef thu herdest burgurs breoke thine wahes — theos ant
othre thulliche dredfule thohtes. Wunderfule ant gleadfule: as yef thu sehe Jesu

shadow. **764–66 Ye beoth over this worldes sea . . . the hehe brugge,** You are over the sea of
this world, upon the bridge of heaven — look [to it] that you be not like the skittish horse
which is terrified (or, shies) because of a shadow, and falls down into the water from the high
bridge. **766–68 To childene ha beoth . . . bute schadewe,** They are too childish who flee
[from] a painting which seems to them grisly and horrific to look at. Misery and joy in this
world — all is [nothing] but painting, all is [nothing] but shadow. **769–73 Nawt ane hali
meditatiuns . . . arearet i the heorte,** Not only holy meditations — such as [those] on our
Lord, and on all His works, and on all His words, on the dear Lady and on all holy saints — but
other thoughts have helped sometimes in continual temptations; four kinds especially, [are
helpful] to those who are assailed by the temptations of the flesh continually: 1) fearful, 2)
wonderful (or, astounding), 3) joyful, and 4) sorrowful [thoughts] — [thoughts] voluntarily
raised up in the heart without compulsion. **773–75 As thenchen hwet tu waldest don . . . i the
fondunge,** Think (*as* not translated) what you would do if you saw the devil of hell (*then* =
declined def. art. — see glossary) stand openly before you and gaping wide upon you, as he
does secretly (or, in a concealed way) in the temptation. **775–77 Yef me yeide . . . dredfule
thohtes,** [What would you do] if [some]one yelled, "Fire! Fire!" that the church was burning
(lit., burned). [What would you do] if you heard burglars break [down] your walls — these and
other such dreadful thoughts. **777–79 Wunderfule ant gleadfule . . . thet tu withstode,** Wonderful (or, astounding) and joyful [thoughts]: as if you saw Jesus Christ and heard Him ask you
what would be most desirable to you — after your salvation and [that of] your dearest friend —

259

Crist, ant herdest him easki the hwet te were leovest efter thi salvatiun, ant thine leoveste freond, of thing o thisse live, ant beode the cheosen with thet tu withstode.

780 Yef thu sehe al witerliche heovene ware ant helle ware i the temptatiun bihalde the ane. Yef me come ant talde the thet mon thet te is leovest, thurh sum miracle, as thurh stevene of heovene, were i-coren to Pape — ant alle othre swucche. Wunderfule ant sorhfule: as yef thu herdest seggen thet mon thet te is leovest were ferliche adrenct, i-slein other i-murthret, thet tine sustren weren in hare hus

785 forbearnde. Thulliche thohtes ofte i fleschliche sawlen wrencheth ut sonre fleschliche temptatiuns then sum of the othre earre. In-warde, ant meadlese, ant ancrefule bonen biwinneth sone sucurs ant help ed ure Laverd ayeines flesches fondunges — ne beon ha neaver se ancrefule ne se ful-itohene, the deovel of helle duteth ham swithe. For teke thet ha draheth adun sucurs ayein him, ant

790 Godes hond of heovene — ha doth him twa hearmes: bindeth him ant bearneth. Lo, her preove of bathe: Publius, an hali mon, wes in his bonen ant com the feond

of things in this life, and [heard Him] offer you to choose provided that you withstood. **780–81 Yef thu sehe al witerliche . . . bihalde the ane**, If you saw quite plainly the inhabitants of heaven and the inhabitants of hell watching you alone in [your] temptation. **781–82 Yef me come ant talde the . . . alle othre swucche**, If they (lit., one) came and told you that the man that is dearest to you (*te* = reduced form of *the*), by some miracle, [such] as by the voice of heaven, were elected to Pope — and all other such [thoughts]. **783–85 Wunderfule ant sorhfule . . . in hare hus forbearnde**, Astounding and sorrowful [thoughts]: as if you heard tell that the man who is most dear to you were suddenly drowned, killed, or murdered, that your sisters were burned up in their house. **785–86 Thulliche thohtes ofte . . . of the othre earre**, Such thoughts often wrench out (or, drive away) fleshly (or, carnal) temptations in fleshly souls sooner than some of the other earlier [thoughts do]. **786–89 In-warde, ant meadlese, ant ancrefule . . . duteth ham swithe**, Deeply felt (lit., Inward) and continuous and anchor-like prayers soon win succor (i.e., aid) and help from our Lord against the flesh's temptations — be they ever so (i.e., no matter if the prayers are) anguished or [on the other hand] so badly executed, the devil of hell is afraid of them very much. **789–90 For teke thet ha draheth adun sucurs . . . bindeth him ant bearneth**, For besides [the fact] that they draw down aid against him, and God's [helping] hand from heaven — they do him two injuries: bind and burn him. **791–95 Lo, her preove . . . thider ten dahes fulle**, Look, here [is the] proof of both: Publius, a holy man, was in his prayers and the fiend came flying through the air and was supposed to (lit., should) [go] toward the extreme western part of the world, by Julian's [the

260

fleonninde bi the lufte, ant schulde al on toward te west half of the worlt, thurh Julienes heast (the empereur), ant warth i-bunden hete-veste with the hali monne bonen, the oftoken him as ha fluhen uppard toward heovene, thet he ne mahte

795 hider ne thider ten dahes fulle. Nabbe ye alswa of Ruffin the deovel, Beliales brother, in ower Englische boc of Seinte Margarete? Of thet other me redeth thet he gredde lude to Sein Bartholomew the muchel wes i benen: **Incendunt me orationes tue!** "Bartholomew, wa me! Thine beoden forbearneth me!" Hwa-se mei thurh Godes yeove i beoden habbe teares, ha mei don with Godd al thet ha

800 eaver wule, for swa we redeth: **Oratio lenit, lacrima cogit; hec ungit, illa pungit.** "Eadi bone softeth ant paieth ure Laverd, ah teares doth him strengthe. Beoden smirieth him with softe olhnunge, ah teares prikieth him," ne ne yeoveth him neaver pes ear then he yetti ham al thet ha easkith. Hwen me asa[i]leth burhes other castel, theo withinnen healdeth scaldinde weater ut, ant werieth swa the walles. Ant ye

805 don alswa as ofte as the feond asaileth ower castel ant te sawle burh: with in- warde bonen warpeth ut upon him scaldinde teares, thet Davith segge bi the,

emperor's] command, and (i.e., but) was bound tightly by the holy man's prayers, which over- took him as they flew upwards toward heaven, [so] that he could not [go] hither or thither (i.e., to or fro) for fully ten days. **795–97 Nabbe ye alswa of Ruffin . . . wes i benen,** Do not you also have [the story] of Ruffin the devil, Belial's brother, in your English book of St. Margaret? Concerning the second [devil] (i.e., Belial), one reads that he cried out loudly to St. Bartholomew who was much in prayers. **797–98** *Incendunt me orationes tue!* "Your prayers are burning me!" (see Pseudo-Bede, "Concerning St. Bartholomew," *Homilies* 2.90 [*PL* 94.490–91]). **798 wa me!** woe [is] me!; **Thine beoden forbearneth me!** Your prayers are burning me up! **798– 800 Hwa-se mei thurh Godes yeove . . . for swa we redeth,** Whosoever can by God's gift have tears in [her] prayers, she can do with God all that she ever wants, for so we read. **800** *Oratio lenit . . . illa pungit,* "Prayer softens, tears (lit., a tear) compel; the former soothes (lit., anoints), the latter stings" (source unidentified). **801–03 Eadi bone softeth . . . al thet ha easkith,** "A holy prayer softens and pleases our Lord, but tears do Him violence. Prayers anoint (or, soothe) Him with soft flattery (or, persuasion), but tears prick Him," nor do [they] ever give Him peace before He grants them all that they ask. **803–06 Hwen me asa[i]leth burhes . . . thet Davith segge bi the,** When one assails (or, attacks) towns or a castle, those within pour out scalding water, and thus protect the walls. And you do likewise (imper.) as often as the fiend assails your castle and your soul's town (or, city): with inward (i.e., heartfelt) prayers cast out upon him scalding tears, [so] that David may say concerning you.

Contribulasti capita draconum in aquis — "thu havest forscaldet te drake heave*d* with wallinde weater" — thet is, with hate teares. Thear as this weater is, sikerliche the feond flith leste he beo forscaldet. Eft an-other: castel the haveth dich abuten,

810 ant weater beo i the dich — the castel is wel carles ayeines his unwines. Castel is euch god mon thet te deovel weorreth. Ah habbe ye deop dich of deop eadmodnesse, ant wete teares ther-to, ye beoth strong castel. The weorrur of helle mei longe asailin ow ant leosen his hwile. Eft me seith, ant soth hit is, thet a muche wind alith with a lute rein, ant te sunne th'refter schineth the schenre. Alswa a muche

815 temptatiun — thet is, the feondes bleas — afealleth with a softe rein of ane lut wordes teares, ant [te] sothe sunne schineth th'refter schenre to the sawle. Thus beoth teares gode with in-warde bonen, ant yef ye understondeth, ich habbe i-seid of ham her fowr muchele efficaces for-hwi ha beoth to luvien. In alle ower neoden, sendeth cwicliche anan thes sonde toward h[e]ovene. For as Salomon seith, **Oratio**

807 *Contribulasti capita draconum in aquis*, "You have crushed the heads of dragons in the waters" (Psalm 73:13). **807–08 thu havest forscaldet . . . hate teares**, "You have scalded the dragon's head badly with boiling water" — that is, with hot tears. **808–09 Thear as this weater is . . . he beo forscaldet**, Wherever (*as* not translated) this water is, surely the fiend flees lest (or, for fear that) he be badly scalded. **809–10 Eft an-other . . . ayeines his unwines**, Yet another [example]: the castle which has a ditch around [it], and water is in the ditch — the castle is quite without fear (lit., careless) against its enemies (lit., unfriends). **810–12 Castel is euch god mon . . . ye beoth strong castel**, Every good man that the devil attacks (lit., wars against) is a castle. But [if] you have a deep ditch of deep humility and wet tears besides (lit., thereto), you are a strong castle. **812–14 The weorrur of helle . . . schineth the schenre**, The warrior of hell may assail you long and lose his time (or, effort). Again one says (i.e., they say), and it is true, that a great wind subsides (lit., lies down) with a little rain, and the sun shines afterwards (lit., thereafter) the brighter. **814–16 Alswa a muche temptatiun . . . to the sawle**, Likewise, a great temptation — that is, the fiend's gust (or, blast) — falls down (or, dies down) with one soft rain from the tears of one little word (i.e., prayer), and the true sun shines afterwards more brightly to the soul. **816–18 Thus beoth teares gode . . . ha beoth to luvien**, Thus tears with deeply felt (lit., inward) prayers are good, and if you understand (i.e., have been paying attention), I have spoken concerning them here four great efficacies (or, powers), for which reason they are to [be] loved (passive inf.). **818–19 In alle ower neoden . . . toward h[e]ovene**, In all your difficulties, send quickly at once this messenger (i.e., tearful prayers) toward heaven. **819–20 Oratio humiliantis se penetrat nubes, et cetera**, "The prayer of one

820 **humiliantis se penetrat nubes, et cetera** — thet is, "the eadmodies bone thurleth the weolcne." Ant ter seith Seint Austin, **Magna est virtus pure conscientie, que ad Deum intrat et mandata peragit, ubi caro pervenire nequit**. "O muchel is the mihte of schir ant cleane bone, the flith up ant kimeth in bivoren almihti Godd" — ant deth the ernde se wel, thet Godd haveth o lives boc i-writen al thet ha seith,

825 as Sein Beornard witneth, edhalt hire with him-seolf, ant sent adun his engel to don al thet ha easketh. Nule ich her of bone segge na mare.

Hardi bileave bringeth the deovel o fluht anan-rihtes — thet witneth Sein Jame: **Resistite diabolo et fugiet a vobis**. "Edstont ane the feond, ant he deth him o fluhte." Edstond — thurh hwet strengthe? Seinte Peter teacheth, **Cui resistite**

830 **fortes in fide**. "Stondeth ayein him with stronge bileave," beoth hardi of Godes help, ant witeth hu he is wac, the na strengthe naveth on us bute of us-seolven. Ne mei he bute schawin forth sum-hwet of his eape-ware, ant olhnin other threatin

humbling himself pierces the clouds," etc. (adapted from Ecclesiasticus 35:21). **820–21 "the eadmodies bone thurleth the weolcne,"** "the humble [person]'s prayer pierces the clouds (lit., the welkin)." **821 Ant ter**, And here (*ter* = reduced form of *ther* after preceding -*t*). **821– 22 *Magna est virtus . . . ubi caro pervenire nequit***, "Great is the power of a pure conscience, which enters to God and carries through [her] commands (or, errands) where the flesh cannot come" (source unidentified). **822–26 O muchel is the mihte . . . al thet ha easketh**, "Oh, great is the might of bright and pure prayer, which flies up and comes in before almighty God" — and does the errand so well that God has written all that she says into the book of life, as St. Bernard bears witness, [and He] keeps her with Himself, and sends (*sent* = reduced form of *sendeth*) down His angel to do all that she asks. **826 Nule ich her of bone segge na mare**, Here I do not want to say any more about prayer. **827 Hardi bileave . . . witneth Sein Jame**, Stout belief puts (lit., brings) the devil to flight immediately — St. James bears witness to that. **828 *Resistite diabolo et fugiet a vobis***, "Resist the devil and he will flee from you" (James 4:7). **828–29 Edstont ane the feond . . . thurh hwet strengthe?** "Only withstand the fiend, and he [will] put himself in flight (i.e., will flee)." Withstand — with what strength? **829–30 *Cui resistite fortes in fide***, "Resist him, firm in faith" (1 Peter 5:9). **830–31 beoth hardi of Godes help . . . bute of us-seolven**, be sure (lit., hardy) of God's help and know how he (i.e., the devil) is weak, who has no power over us except from ourselves (i.e., unless we ourselves grant it to him). **831–33 Ne mei he bute schawin forth . . . bugge th'rof**, Nor can he [do anything] but show forth (i.e., display) a certain amount of his ape wares, and cajole (or, flatter) or threaten

thet me bugge th'rof. Hwether se he deth, scarnith him, lahheth the alde eape lude
to bismere thurh treowe bileave, ant he halt him i-schent ant deth him o fluht

835   swithe. **Sancti per fidem vicerunt regna** — thet is, "the hali *halhen alle* overcomen
thurh bileave the deofles rixlunge" thet nis bute sunne, for ne rixleth he i nan,
bute thurh sunne ane. Neometh nu gode yeme hu alle the seovene deadliche sunnen
muhen beon afleiet thurh treowe bileave. On earst nu of prude.

    Hwa halt him muchel, as the prude deth, hwen he bihalt hu lutel the muchele

840   Laverd makede him in-with a povre meidenes breoste? Hwa is ontful, the bihalt
with ehnen of bileave hu Jesu Godd — nawt for his god, ah for othres god —
dude, ant seide, ant tholede al thet he tholede? The ontfule ne kepte nawt thet eani
dealde of his god. Ant Godd almihti yet, efter al thet other, lihte dun to helle for-
te sechen feolahes ant to deale with ham the god thet he hefde. Lo, nu hu frommard

845   beoth ontfule ure Laverd. The ancre the wearnde an-other a cwaer to lane —
f[e]or ha hefde heone-ward hire bileave ehe.

[so] that people may buy from them (lit., thereof). **833–35 Hwether se he deth . . . o fluht
swithe**, Whichever he does, scorn him, laugh the old ape loudly to scorn through true faith, and
he [will] hold (or, count) himself disgraced and [will] put himself to flight (lit., will flee)
quickly. **835 *Sancti per fidem vicerunt regna***, "The saints conquered [entire] kingdoms through
faith" (adapted from Hebrews 11:33). **835–37 the hali halhen . . . thurh sunne ane**, "all the
holy saints overcame through belief the devil's rule (or, sway)," which is [nothing] but sin, for
he rules in no one except by sin alone. **837–38 Neometh nu gode yeme . . . On earst nu of
prude**, Pay (lit., take) good attention now how all the seven deadly sins may be put to flight
through true belief. At first now, [let us say something] about pride. **839–40 Hwa halt him
muchel . . . a povre meidenes breoste?** Who holds (or, considers) himself great, as the proud
[person] does, when he sees how small the great Lord made Himself inside a poor virgin's
breast? **840–43 Hwa is ontful . . . dealde of his god**, Who is envious who sees with eyes of
belief how Jesus God — not for His good, but for others' good — acted and spoke, and suffered all that He suffered? The envious [person would] not desire that any[one should] share in
his good (or, good things). **843–44 Ant Godd almihti yet . . . the god thet he hefde**, And
almighty God still, after all the other [acts], descended down to hell to seek out comrades and
to share with them the good (or, good things) that He had. **844–46 Lo, nu hu frommard . . .
hire bileave ehe**, Look, now, how opposite (or, different) the envious are [from] our Lord. The
anchoress who [would] deny a quire (i.e., a small, unbound book) to another as a loan — she
[would] have the eye of her belief far away from here.

Hwa halt wreaththe, the bihalt thet God lihte on eorthe to makien thr[e]o-fald sahte: bitweone mon ant mon, bitweone Godd ant mon, bitweone mon ant engel? Ant efter his ariste tha he com ant schawde him, this wes his gretunge to his deore

850 deciples: **Pax vobis.** "Sahtnesse beo bitweonen ow." Neometh nu yeorne yeme. Hwen leof freond went from other, the leaste wordes thet he seith, theo schulen beo best edhalden. Ure Laverdes leaste wordes, tha he steah to heovene ant leafde his leove freond in uncuthe theode, weren of swote luve ant of sahtnesse: **Pacem relinquo vobis; pacem meam do vobis.** Thet is — "Sahtnesse ich do i-mong ow.

855 Sahtnesse ich leave with ow." This wes his druerie thet he leafde ant yef ham in his departunge. **In hoc cognoscetis quo*d* dicipuli mei sitis, si dilectionem adinvicem habueritis.** Lokith nu yeorne, for his deore-wurthe luve, hwuch a mearke he leide upon his i-corene tha he steah to heovene. **In hoc cognoscetis quo*d*, et cetera.** "Bi thet ye schulen i-cnawen," quoth he, "thet ye beoth mine

860 deciples: yef swete luve ant sahtnesse is eaver ow bitweonen." Godd hit wite —

847–48 Hwa halt wreaththe . . . mon ant engel? Who keeps (or, harbors — *halt* = reduced form of *haldeth*) wrath, who sees that God descended to earth to make a threefold reconciliation (or, peace): between man and man, between God and man, between man and angel? **849–50 Ant efter his ariste . . . to his deore deciples,** And after His rising (i.e., resurrection) when He came and showed Himself, this was His greeting to His dear disciples. **850 *Pax vobis*,** "Peace [be] to you" (John 20:19, 21, 26); **Sahtnesse,** Reconciliation (or, Peace). **850–53 Neometh nu yeorne yeme . . . ant of sahtnesse,** Pay (lit., Take) attention now carefully. When a beloved friend departs from the other, the last words that he says, they should be best paid attention to (lit., kept). Our Lord's last words, when He climbed to heaven and left His beloved friends in a strange country, were of sweet love and of peace. **853–54 *Pacem relinquo vobis . . . do vobis*,** "Peace I leave to you; my peace I give to you" (John 14:27). **854 Sahtnesse ich do i-mong ow,** Peace I put among you. **855–56 This wes his druerie . . . in his departunge,** This was His love-token that He left and gave them in His departing. **856–57 *In hoc cognoscetis . . . adinvicem habueritis*,** "By this you will recognize that you are My disciples: if you have love towards each other" (adapted from John 13:35). **857–58 Lokith nu yeorne . . . steah to heovene,** Look now carefully, what kind of (lit., which) a mark, for His precious love, He laid upon His chosen when He climbed (i.e., rose) to heaven. **859–60 "Bi thet ye schulen i-cnawen . . . ow bitweonen,"** "By that you will know," He said, "that you are My disciples: if sweet love and peace is always between you." **860–62 Godd hit wite . . . i-heortet,** May God know it — and He does know it ant he hit wat — me were leovere thet ye weren alle o the spitel-uvel then ye weren ontfule other feol i-heortet. For Jesu is al luve, ant i luve he resteth him ant haveth his wununge. **In pace factus est locus ejus. Ibi confregit potencias arcum, scutum, gladium, et bellum** — thet is, "i sahtnesse is Godes stude." Ant hwer-se sahte is ant luve, thear he bringeth to nawt al thes deofles strengthe. "Ther he breketh his bohe," hit seith — thet beoth dearne fondunges thet he scheot of feor — "ant his sweord bathe" — thet beoth temptatiuns keorvinde of neh ant kene.

865

Neometh nu yeorne yeme bi moni forbisne hu god is an-rednesse of luve, ant an-nesse of heorte. For nis thing under sunne thet me is leovere, ne se leof, thet ye habben. Nute ye ther men fehteth i thes stronge ferdes, the ilke the haldeth ham feaste togederes ne muhe beo descumfit o neaver nane wise? Alswa hit is in gastelich feht ayeines the deovel: al his entente is for-te tweamen heorten, for-te bineomen luve thet halt men togederes. For hwen luve alith, thenne beoth ha i-sundret, ant te deovel deth him bitweonen anan-riht ant sleath on euche halve.

870

— [it] would be preferable to me that you were all [suffering] with leprosy (lit., hospital-sickness) than [that] you were envious or cruel-hearted. **862 resteth him**, rests Himself. **863 wununge**, dwelling. **863–64 *In pace factus est locus ejus . . . et bellum***, "His place is made in peace. There [He] has shattered the powers of bows, the shield, the sword, and war" (adapted from Psalm 75:3–4). **864 sahtnesse**, peace (or, reconciliation); **stude**, place. **864–67 Ant hwer-se sahte is ant luve . . . neh ant kene**, And wheresoever [there] is peace and love, there He brings to naught all the devil's strength (*thes* = declined def. art.). "There he breaks his bow," it says — those are secret temptations that he shoots (*scheot* = reduced form of *scheoteth*) from afar — "and his sword as well (lit., both)" — those are sharp temptations which cut (lit., cutting) from close by. **868–70 Neometh nu yeorne yeme . . . thet ye habben**, Pay (lit., take) attention now carefully by many examples (or, exempla) how good constancy of love is, and oneness (or, unity) of heart. For [there] is nothing under the sun which is more preferable to me (lit., is more beloved to me), nor so dear, that you [should] have. **870–71 Nute ye ther men fehteth . . . o neaver nane wise?** Do you not know [that] where men fight in these powerful armies, the very [ones] who hold themselves firmly together cannot ever be defeated in any way? **871–73 Alswa hit is in gastelich feht . . . halt men togederes**, Just so it is in the spiritual fight against the devil: all his purpose is to split (or, divide) hearts, in order to (lit., for to) take away love that holds men (or, people) together (*halt* = reduced form of *haldeth*). **873–74 For hwen luve alith . . . on euche halve**, For when love subsides (lit., lies down), then they are parted (lit., sundered), and the devil puts himself between immediately and slays (i.e., kills) on both sides (lit., on each side).

875 Dumbe beastes habbeth this ilke warschipe, thet hwen ha beoth asailet of wulf
other of liun, ha thrungeth togederes al the floc feste, ant makieth scheld of ham-
seolf, euch of heom to other, ant beoth the hwile sikere. Yef eani unseli went ut,
hit is sone awuriet. The thridde: ther an geath him ane in a slubbri wei, he slit ant
falleth sone; ther monie gath togederes, ant euch halt othres hond, yef eani feth to

880 sliden, the other hine breid up ear he ful falle; yef ha wergith euch-an halt him bi
other. Fondunge is sliddrunge. Thurh wergunge beoth bitacnet the untheawes under slawthe, the beoth i-*nempnet* th'ruppe. This is thet Sein Gregoire seith, **Cum
nos nobis per orationis opem conjungimus, per lubricum incedentes, quasi
adinvicem manus teneamus, ut tanto quisque amplius roboretur quanto alteri**

885 **innititur.** Alswa i strong wind ant swifte weattres the me mot overwaden, of monie
euch halt other; the i-sundrede is i-swipt forth ant forfeareth eaver. To wel we
witen hu the wei of this world is slubbri, hu the wind ant te stream of fondunge

875–77 Dumbe beastes habbeth this ilke warschipe . . . ant beoth the hwile sikere, Dumb
beasts have (i.e., show) this same wariness (or, caution), that when they are assailed by wolf or
by lion, they throng (or, band) the flock together firmly, and make a shield of themselves, each
of them for the other, and are safer for the time. **877–78 Yef eani unseli went ut . . . sone
awuriet,** If any unfortunate [beast] goes out (*went* = reduced form of *wendeth*) [from the flock],
it is immediately strangled (or, has its throat ripped out). **878–81 The thridde . . . halt him bi
other,** The third [exemplum]: where one walks (reflex.) alone on a slippery path, he slides (*slit*
= reduced form of *slideth*) and falls quickly; where many walk together, and each [one] holds
(*halt* = reduced form of *haldeth*) the other's hand, if any starts to slide, the other pulls him up
before he falls fully; if they grow weary, each one holds himself [up] by the other. **881–82
Fondunge is sliddrunge . . . beoth i-nempnet th'ruppe,** Temptation is sliding (or, slipping).
By weariness (lit., wearying) is symbolized the vices [grouped] under sloth, which are named
above (lit., up there — see 4.294–305). **882 thet,** what. **882–85 Cum nos nobis per orationis
. . . quanto alteri innititur,** "When we unite ourselves through the power of prayer, [we are]
walking through a slippery (or, dangerous) place as if we held each other's hand, so that each
[of us] is more greatly strengthened to the extent that he leans on the other" (Gregory, *Letters*
1.25 [*PL* 77.478]). **885–86 Alswa i strong wind . . . forfeareth eaver,** Likewise, in a strong
wind and swift waters which one must wade through, each of many (i.e., each one in the group)
holds up the other; [but] the sundered (or, person who is separated) is swept away and always
perishes. **886–89 To wel we witen . . . with luve othres honden,** We know too well how the
path of this world is slippery, how the wind and the stream of temptation are strong. [There] is

890 aren stronge. Muche neod is thet euch halde with bisie bonen ant with luve othres honden, for as Salomon seith, **Ve soli! quia cum ceciderit, non habet sublevantem.** "Wa eaver the ane! for hwen he falleth, naveth he hwa him areare." Nan nis ane the haveth Godd to fere, ant thet is euch thet soth luve haveth in his heorte. The seovethe forbisne is this, yef ye riht telleth: dust ant greot, as ye seoth, for hit is i-sundret ant nan ne halt to other, a lutel windes puf todriveth hit al to nawt. Thear hit is in a clot i-limet togederes, hit lith al stille. An hondful of

895 yerden beoth earveth to breoken hwil ha beoth togederes — euch-an i-tweamet lihtliche bersteth. A treo the wule fallen — undersete hit with an-other, ant hit stont feste; tweam ham, ant ba falleth. Nu ye habbeth nihene. Thus i thinges ute-with neometh forbisne hu god is an-nesse of luve ant somet-readnesse thet halt the gode somet, thet nan ne mei forwurthen! Ant this wule i-wiss habben the rihte

900 bileave. Bihald yeorne ant understont Jesu Cristes deore-wurthe wordes ant werkes,

great need that each [one] hold with diligent prayers and with love the others' hands. **889–90 *Ve soli! . . . non habet sublevantem*,** "Woe unto the one alone! Because when he falls, he has [no one] lifting him up (i.e., he does not have anyone to lift him up)" (adapted from Ecclesiastes 4:10). **890 Wa eaver the ane!** Woe be always to the solitary [person]!; **naveth,** [he does] not have; **hwa,** anyone (lit., who); **areare,** raise up. **891–92 Nan nis ane the haveth Godd . . . in his heorte,** No one is alone who has God as a companion, and that is each [person] who has true love in his heart (i.e., no one who has true love in his heart is alone, for he has God as a companion). **892–94 The seovethe forbisne . . . lith al stille,** The seventh exemplum is this, if you are counting correctly: dust and sand, as you can see, because it is separate and none [of it] holds (i.e., sticks) to the other, a little puff of wind scatters it [in]to nothing. Where it is cemented together in a clump it lies (or, stays) completely still. **894–96 An hondful of yerden . . . lihtliche bersteth,** A handful of sticks are difficult to break while they are together — separated, each one easily breaks (lit., bursts). **896–97 A treo the wule fallen . . . nihene,** A tree which wants to (or, is about to) fall — support (or, underpin) it with another, and it [will] stand firmly (*stont* = reduced form of *stondeth*); separate them, and both [will] fall. Now you have nine [exempla]. **897–900 Thus i thinges ute-with . . . the rihte bileave,** Thus take a lesson (i.e., learn) from external things how good unity is and concord of love which holds the good together, [so] that none can perish! And certainly, right faith (lit., the right belief) wants this (i.e., unity). **900–02 Bihald yeorne ant understont . . . lesceunes lare,** Look carefully and understand Jesus Christ's precious words and deeds, which were all [performed] in love and in sweetness. Above all things, I [would] wish that anchoresses learned well the teaching of

905

910

the i luve weren alle ant i swetnesse. Over alle thing ich walde thet ancren leorneden wel this lesceunes lare. For monie — mare hearm is! — beoth Samsones foxes, the hefden the neb euch-an i-wend frommard other, ant weren bi the teiles i-teiet togederes, as **Judicum** teleth, ant in euch-anes teil a blease bearninde. Of theose foxes ich spec feor th'ruppe, ah nawt o thisse wise. Neometh gode yeme hwet this beo to seggen: me turneth the neb blitheliche towart thing thet me luveth, ant frommard thing thet me heateth. Theo thenne habbeth the nebbes wrong-wende euch frommard other, hwen nan ne luveth other, ah bi the teiles ha beoth somet, ant beoreth thes deofles bleasen — the brune of galnesse. On an-other wise, teil bitacneth ende. In hare ende ha schulen beon i-bunden togederes as weren Samsones foxes bi the teiles ant i-set bleasen th'rin — thet is, thet fur of helle.

915

Al this is i-seid, mine leove sustren, thet ower leove nebbes beon eaver i-went somet with luveful semblant ant with swote chere, thet ye beon aa with an-nesse of an heorte ant of a wil i-limet togederes, as hit i-writen is bi ure Laverdes deore deciples: **Multitudinis credentium erat cor unum et anima una. Pax vobis:**

this lesson (or, reading). **902–04 For monie . . . a blease bearninde**, For many — more is the harm! — are Samson's foxes, which had [their] faces each one turned away from the other, and were tied together by [their] tails, as Judges tells, and in each one's tail [there was] a firebrand burning. **904–07 Of theose foxes ich spec . . . thet me heateth**, I spoke about these foxes far above this (i.e., several pages back), but not in this way. Pay (lit., Take) good attention to what this is (i.e., has) to say: one turns [his] face happily toward the thing that one loves, and away from the thing that one hates. **907–09 Theo thenne habbeth the nebbes . . . the brune of galnesse**, Those [people] then have [their] faces turned away each from the other, when no one loves the other, but they are joined by [their] tails, and carry the devil's firebrands (*thes* = declined def. art.) — the burning of lechery. **909–11 On an-other wise . . . thet fur of helle**, In another way, the tail symbolizes the end. At their end (i.e., death) they will be bound together as were Samson's foxes by the tails and they will [have] firebrands set amongst them (lit., therein) — that is, the fire of hell. **912–15 thet ower leove nebbes . . . deciples**, [so] that your dear faces [will] be always turned together with a loving expression and with a sweet appearance, [so] that you [will] be always be cemented together with unity of one heart and of one will, as it is written concerning our Lord's disciples. **915 *Multitudinis credentium . . . anima una***, "Among the multitudes of believers (lit., those believing) there was one heart and one spirit" (Acts 4:32). **915–16 *Pax vobis* . . . Grith beo bimong ow**, "Peace [be] to you" (John

this wes Godes gretunge to his deore deciples: "Grith beo bimong ow." Ye beoth the ancren of Englond, swa feole togederes, twenti nuthe other ma. Godd i god ow multi, thet meast grith is among, meast an-nesse ant an-rednesse ant somet-readnesse of an-red lif efter a riwle, swa thet alle teoth an, alle i-turnt anes-weis,

920 ant nan frommard other, efter thet word is. For-thi, ye gath wel forth ant spedeth in ower wei, for euch is with-ward other in an manere of lif-lade, as thah ye weren an cuvent of Lundene ant of Oxnefort, of Schreobsburi, other of Chester, thear as alle beoth an, with an i-meane manere, ant withuten singularite — thet is, an-ful frommardschipe — lah thing i religiun, for hit towarpeth an-nesse ant manere i-

925 meane, thet ah to beon in ordre. This nu thenne — thet ye beoth alle as an cuvent — is ower hehe fame. This is Godd i-cweme. This is nunan wide cuth, swa thet ower cuvent biginneth to spreaden toward Englondes ende. Ye beoth as the moder-hus thet heo beoth of i-streonet. Ye beoth ase wealle: yef the wealle woreth, the strunden woreth alswa. A, wei la, yef ye worith! — ne bide ich hit neaver! Yef ei

930 is i-mong ow the geath i singularite, ant ne folheth nawt the cuvent, ah went ut of

20:19, 21): this was God's greeting to His dear disciples, "Peace be among you." **916–20 Ye beoth the ancren of Englond . . . efter thet word is,** You are the anchoresses of England, so many together, twenty now or more. May God multiply you in good [things], among whom [there] is the greatest peace, the greatest oneness and single-mindedness and concord in [your] unified life according to one rule, so that all pull [as] one, all are turned one way, and none away from the other, according to what the report (lit., word) is (i.e., as I have heard). **920–25 For-thi, ye gath wel forth . . . to beon in ordre,** For this reason, you are going forward strongly (lit., well) and are prospering on your path, for each is [proceeding] along with the other in one way of life, as if you were a convent of London, and of Oxford, of Shrewsbury, or of Chester, where all are one, with one common custom (lit., manner), and without singularity — that is, individual contrariness (or, turning away) — a base thing in religion, for it destroys (or, smashes) unity and shared custom which [there] ought to be in an order. **925–26 This nu thenne . . . wide cuth,** Now then, this is your high fame: that you are all as [if you were in] one convent. This is pleasing to God. This is widely known already. **927–29 Ye beoth as the moder-hus . . . the strunden woreth alswa,** You are like the mother-house from which they are born. You are like a wellspring: if the wellspring falters (or, dries up) the streams falter as well. **929–35 A, wei la . . . of heovene,** O, alas, if you [were to] falter — I [would] never endure that! If [there] is any among you who walks in singularity (i.e., willful individuality), and does not follow the convent, but departs (*went* = reduced form of *wendeth*) out from the flock which

the floc, thet is as in a cloistre thet Jesu is heh priur over, went ut as a teowi schep ant meapeth hire ane into breres teilac, into wulves muth, toward te throte of helle — yef ei swuch is i-mong ow, Godd turne hire into floc, wende hire into cuvent, ant leve ow the beoth th'rin, swa halden ow th'rin, thet Godd the hehe priur neome

935   ow on ende theonne up into the cloistre of heovene. Hwil ye haldeth ow in an, offearen ow mei the feond — yef he haveth leave — ah hearmin nawt mid alle. Thet he wat ful wel, ant is for-thi umben deies ant nihtes to unlimin ow with wreaththe other with luther onde, ant sent mon other wummon, the telle the an bi the other sum suhinde sahe thet suster ne schulde nawt segge bi suster. Ower nan

940   — ich forbeode ow — ne leve the deofles sondes-mon, ah lokith thet euch of ow i-cnawe wel hwen he speketh i the uvele monnes tunge, ant segge anan-rihtes: "Ure meistre haveth i-writen us, as in heast to halden, thet we tellen him al thet euch of other hereth, ant for-thi loke the thet tu na thing ne telle me thet ich ne muhe him tellen, the mei don the amendement, ant con swa-liches don hit, thet ich ant tu

945   bathe, yef we beoth i the soth, schule beon unblamet." Euch, no-the-le[s], warni

---

is as in a cloister that Jesus is high prior over, goes out like an erring (? — see *teowi* in glossary) sheep and blunders herself alone into a tangle of briar[s], into the wolf's mouth, toward the throat of hell — if [there] is any such [one] among you, may God turn (or, guide) her into the flock, turn her into the convent, and [may He] grant you who are in it (i.e., the flock), so to keep yourself in it, that God, the high prior, [may] take you in the end from there up into the cloister of heaven. **935–36 Hwil ye haldeth ow in an . . . nawt mid alle**, While (or, as long as) you keep yourselves in one (i.e., in unity), the fiend may frighten you — if he has permission — but [he can]not harm you at all. **937–39 Thet he wat ful wel . . . segge bi suster**, He knows this very well, and is for that reason [busy] about [it] day and night (adverbial genitive) to detach (lit., un-cement) you with wrath or with wicked envy, and sends (*sent* = reduced form of *sendeth*) man or woman, who [may] tell the one some distressing tale (lit., saying) about the other that sister should not say about sister. **939–41 Ower nan . . . ant segge anan-rihtes**, [Let] none of you — I forbid you — believe the devil's messenger, but look (or, see to it) that each of you recognize well when he (i.e., the devil) speaks in the evil man's tongue, and say (imper.) immediately. **942–45 "Ure meistre haveth i-writen us . . . schule beon unblamet,"** "Our master has written us, to keep by command (*as* not translated), that we tell him everything that [we] hear from each other, and therefore look to yourself that you tell me nothing that I cannot tell him, who might correct you (lit., do you an amendment) but knows to do it in such a way that both you and I, if we are in the truth (or, in the right), will be unblamed." **945–47 Euch, no-the-le[s] . . . wat to**

other thurh ful siker sondes-mon sweteliche ant luveliche, as hire leove suster, of thing thet ha misnimeth — yef ha hit wat to sothe. Ant makie hwa-se bereth thet word recordin hit ofte bivoren hire, ear ha ga — hu ha wule seggen, thet ha ne segge hit other-weis, ne cluti ther-to mare. For a lute clut mei ladlechin swithe a

950 muchel hal pece. Theo the ed hire suster this luve-salve underveth, thoncki hire yeorne, ant segge with the Salm-wruhte, **Corripiet me justus in misericordia, et increpabit me, oleum autem peccatoris non inpinguet caput meum.** Ant th'refter with Salomon, **Meliora sunt vulnera corripientis quam oscula blandientis.** "Yef ha ne luvede me, nalde ha nawt warni me i misericorde." "Leovere me beoth hire

955 wunden then fikiende cosses" — thus ondswerie eaver. Ant yef hit is other-weis then the other understont, sende hire word ayein th'rof, luveliche ant softe, ant te other leve anan-riht, for thet ich chulle alswa, thet euch of ow luvie other as hire-seolven. Yef the feond bitweonen ow toblaweth eani wreaththe, other great heorte — thet Jesu Crist forbeode! — ear ha beo i-set wel, nawt ane to neomen Godes

960 flesch ant his blod, ne wurthe nan se witles, ah yet thet is leasse, thet ha eanes ne

sothe, [Let] each [of you], nonetheless, warn the other through a very trustworthy messenger, sweetly and lovingly, as if it were her dear sister, about anything that she does wrong (lit., mistakes) — if she knows it for a truth (i.e., fact). **947–49 Ant makie hwa-se ... ne cluti ther-to mare**, And let (imper.) whosoever bears that message (lit., word) repeat it often in front of her, before she go, in the way she will say [it], [so] that she not say it otherwise (i.e., in any other way), nor patch (i.e., add) more onto it. **949–51 For a lute clut ... with the Salm-wruhte**, For a little patch may disfigure a large, whole (or, uncut) piece [of cloth]. She who receives from her sister this love-cure, should thank her eagerly and say with the Psalm-wright. **951–52** *Corripiet me justus in misericordia ... caput meum*, "The just will accuse me in mercy, and will rebuke me, but [let] the oil of the sinner not fatten my head" (Psalm 140:5). **953** *Meliora sunt vulnera corripientis quam oscula blandientis*, "The wounds of an accuser are better than the kisses of a flatterer" (based loosely on Proverbs 27:6). **953–55 Yef ha ne luvede me ... thus ondswerie eaver**, "If she did not love me, she would not warn me in mercy." "Her wounds (i.e., the wounds she gives me) are more desirable to me than flattering kisses" — always answer thus (i.e., in this way). **955–58 Ant yef hit is other-weis ... as hire-seolven**, And if it is otherwise than the other [one] understands, let her send her word about it again, lovingly and softly, and [let] the other believe [it] immediately, because I wish also that each of you love the other as herself. **958–62 Yef the feond bitweonen ... as is i-seid th'ruppe**, If the fiend blows up any wrath between you, or [any] haughty heart (i.e., spirit) — which Jesus Christ forbid! — before she (i.e., wrath)

bihalde ther-on, ne loki i ful wreaththe toward him the lihte to mon in eorthe of heovene to makien threo-vald sahte, as is i-seid th'ruppe. Sende either thenne other word, thet ha haveth i-maket hire — as thah ha were bivoren hire — eadmodliche **Venie**. Ant theo the ear ofdraheth thus luve of hire suster, ant ofgeath

965   sahte, ant nimeth the gult toward hire, thah the other hit habbe mare, ha schal beo mi deore-wurthe ant mi deore dohter, for ha is Godes dohter. He him-seolf hit seith, **Beati pacifici, quoniam filii Dei vocabuntur.** Thus prude, ant onde, ant wreaththe beoth i-hwer afleiet hwer-se soth luve is ant treowe bileave to Godes milde werkes ant luvefule wordes. Ga we nu forthre to the othre on a reawe.

970   Hwa mei beo for scheome slummi, sloggi, ant slaw, the bihalt hu swithe bisi ure Laverd wes on eorthe? **Pertransiit benefatiendo et sanando omnes.** Efter al thet other, bihaldeth hu he i the even of his lif swong o the hearde rode. Othre habbeth reste, fleoth liht i chambre, hudeth ham hwen ha beoth i-lete blod on an earm ethre. — Ant he, o munt Calvaire, steah yet o rode herre, ne ne swong neaver

975   mon se swithe ne se sare as he dude thet ilke dei thet he bledde o fif half brokes of

is truly resolved (lit., well settled), [let] none be so witless [as] not only to take God's flesh and His blood, but moreover [let her not do] what is less [objectionable], that she once look on it (i.e., the host), or look in full wrath at Him who descended as a man to earth from heaven to make a threefold peace, as is described (lit., said) above (see 4.847–48). **962–64 Sende either thenne ... eadmodliche Venie,** Let then each [one] send word [to the] other that she has made her humble "Pardon," as though she were before her (i.e., in her presence). **964–66 Ant theo the ear ... ha is Godes dohter,** And she who first wins the love of her sister thus, and gains peace, and takes the guilt (or, fault) on herself, though the other has it more, she will be my precious and my dear daughter, for she is God's daughter. **967 *Beati pacifici, quoniam filii Dei vocabuntur,*** "Blessed are the peacemakers, for they will be called sons of God" (Matthew 5:9). **967–69 Thus prude ... to the othre on a reawe,** Thus, pride and envy and wrath are everywhere put to flight wherever there is true love and true belief in God's mild works and loving words. Let us go on now further to the others (i.e., the other deadly sins) in a row (i.e., one by one). **970–71 Hwa mei beo for ... on eorthe?** Who can, for the shame [of it], be drowsy, sluggish, and slow, who sees how very busy our Lord was on earth? **971 *Pertransiit benefatiendo et sanando omnes,*** "He went about, blessing and healing everyone" (Acts 10:38). **971–74 Efter al thet other ... earm ethre,** After all the other [things], look how He, in the evening of His life, toiled on the cruel (lit., hard) Cross. Others have rest, flee the light, in [their] room[s], conceal themselves when they have (lit., are) blood let from the vein of one arm. **974–78 Ant he, o munt ... ane o the**

ful brade wunden ant deope, withuten the ethren capitale the bledden on his heaved
under the kene thornene crune, ant withuten the ilke reowfule garces of the luthere
scurgunge yont al his leofliche lich, nawt ane o the schonken. Toyeines slawe ant
sleperes is swithe openliche his earliche ariste from deathe to live.

980   Ayeines yisceunge is his muchele poverte, the weox eaver upon him se lengre
se mare. For tha he wes i-boren earst, the thet wrahte the eorthe, ne fond nawt on
eorthe swa muche place as his lutle licome mahte beon i-leid upon. Swa nearow
wes thet stude, thet unneathe his moder ant Josep seten th'rin. Ant swa ha leiden
him on heh, up in a crecche with clutes biwrabbet, as thet Godspel seith, **Pannis**
985   **eum involuit.** Thus feire he wes i-schrud, the heovenliche Schuppent, the schrudeth
the sunne! Her-efter the povre meiden of heovene fostrede him ant fedde with
hire lutle milc as meiden deh to habben. This wes muche poverte, ah mare com
th'refter. For lanhure the yet, he hefde fode as feol to him, ant i stude of in, his
cradel herbearhede him. Seoththen, as he meande him, nefde he hwer he mahte

schonken, And He, on Mount Calvary, climbed still higher on the Cross, nor [did a] man ever
toil so sorely (or, heavily) as He did that very day [on] which in five places He bled streams
from very wide and deep wounds, without (i.e., not to mention) the capital veins (i.e., the veins
of the head) which bled on His head under the sharp crown of thorns, and not to mention the
same piteous gashes from the severe scourging over all His lovely body, not only on the legs.
978–79 Toyeines slawe ant sleperes . . . from deathe to live, Against (or, in opposition to)
the sluggish and the sleepers is very clearly (lit., openly) His early rising from death to life.
980–82 Ayeines yisceunge . . . beon i-leid upon, Against covetousness is His great poverty,
which always grew upon Him the longer the greater (i.e., more and more). For when He was
first born, [He] who made the earth did not find on earth so much space as His little body could
be laid upon. **982–84 Swa nearow wes thet stude . . . with clutes biwrabbet**, So narrow was
that place that [only] with difficulty His mother and Joseph sat in it (lit., therein). And so they
laid Him on high, up in a crèche (i.e., cradle) wrapped with rags. **984–85** *Pannis eum involuit*,
"She wrapped him in rags" (Luke 2:7). **985–87 Thus feire he wes i-schrud . . . as meiden deh
to habben**, Thus excellently (lit., fairly) He was dressed, the heavenly Creator, who clothes
the sun! After this, the poor maiden of heaven nursed Him and fed Him with her little milk (i.e.,
scarce supply of milk), as is fitting for a maiden (i.e., virgin) to have. **988–89 For lanhure the
yet . . . herbearhede him**, For at least as yet (lit., the yet), He had [such] food as fell to Him
(i.e., was fitting for Him), and in place of an inn, a cradle lodged Him. **989–90 Seoththen, as**

990   his heaved huden: **Filius hominis non habet ubi capud suum reclinet.** Thus
povre he wes of in; of mete he wes se neodful thet tha he hefde i Jerusalem o
Palm-sunnedei al dei i-preachet, ant hit neolechede niht, he lokede abuten, hit
seith i the Godspel, yef ei walde cleopien him to mete other to herbearhe, ah nes
ther nan. Ant swa he wende ut of the muchele burh into Bethanie, to Marie hus ant

995   to Marthen, ther-as he eode mid his deciples sum-chearre. Ha breken the eares bi
the wei, ant gnud.deden the curnles ut bitweonen hare honden ant eten for hunger,
ant weren ther-vore swithe i-calenget. Ah alre meast poverte com yet her-efter:
for steort-naket he wes despuilet o the rode. Tha he meande him of thurst, weater
ne mahte he habben. Yet thet meast wunder is of al the brade eorthe ne moste he

1000   habben a grot for-te deien upon. The rode hefde a fot other lute mare, ant thet wes
to his pine. Hwen the worldes Wealdent walde beo thus povre, unbilevet he is the
luveth to muchel ant yisceth worldes weole ant wunne.

he meande him . . . his heaved huden, Afterwards, as He complained (reflex.), He did not
have [any place] where He might hide His head. **991** *Filius hominis . . . capud suum reclinet*,
"The Son of man does not have [any place] where he might lay His head" (Matthew 8:20, Luke
9:58). **990–94 Thus povre he wes . . . ah nes ther nan**, He was thus poor of (i.e., with respect
to) lodging; with respect to food He was so needy that when He had preached all day in Jerusalem on Palm Sunday, and it neared night (i.e., night neared), He looked about, it says in the
Gospel, [to see] if anyone would invite Him to a meal or to lodging, but there was none (i.e., no
one). **994–95 Ant swa he wende ut . . . sum-chearre**, And so He went out of the great city into
Bethany, to Mary and Martha's house, where (*as* not translated) He went with his disciples
sometimes. **995–97 Ha breken the eares . . . i-calenget**, They broke [off] ears [of grain] along
the road, and rubbed the kernels between their hands and ate [them] for hunger, and were for
that reason swiftly challenged (or, accused). **997–99 Ah alre meast poverte . . . ne mahte he
habben**, But the greatest of all poverty came at length after that (lit., hereafter): for He was
stripped stark naked on the Cross. When He complained (reflex.) of thirst, He could not have
water. **999–1000 Yet thet meast wunder is . . . deien upon**, Yet the greatest marvel (lit.,
wonder) is, of all the wide earth He must not (i.e., was not allowed to) have one particle [of
land] to die on. **1000–02 The rode hefde a fot . . . worldes weole ant wunne**, The Cross had
(i.e., took up) a foot or a little more, and that was for His pain (or, suffering). When the world's
ruler wanted to be poor in this way, he is unbelieving who loves too much and covets the
world's riches and joy.

Ayein glutunie is his povre pitance thet he hefde o rode. Twa manere men habbeth neode to eote wel: swinkinde ant blod-letene. The dei thet he wes bathe i 1005 sar swinc ant i-lete blod, as ich nest seide — nes his pitance o rode bute a spunge of galle? Loke nu, hwa gruccheth — yef ha thencheth wel her-on — mistrum mel of unsavuree metes, of povre pitance? Of na mon ne of na wummon ne schule ye makie na man, ne pleainin ow of na wone, bute to sum treowe freond thet hit mei amendin, ant godin ham other ow. Ant thet beo priveiliche i-seid as under seel of 1010 schrift, thet ye ne beon i-blamet. Yef ye of ei thing habbeth wone, ant sum freond yeorne freini ow yef ye ei wone habbeth, yef ye hopieth god of him, ondswerieth o this wise: "Laverd Godd foryelde the! Ich drede mare ich habbe then ich were wurthe, ant leasse wone ich tholie then me neod were." Yef he easketh yeornluker, thonkith him yeorne ant seggeth, "Ich ne dear nawt lihen o me-seolven: wone ich 1015 habbe — ase riht is. Hwuch ancre kimeth into ancre-hus to habben hire eise? Ah nu thu wult hit alles witen. Ure Laverd te foryelde. This is nu an thing thet ich

1003 Ayein glutunie . . . o rode, Against gluttony is His poor pittance (or, ration) which He had on the Cross. **1003–06 Twa manere men habbeth neode . . . spunge of galle?** Two manner [of] men have need to eat well: working people and blood-let people (i.e., people who have had their blood let). The day that he was both at severe labor and was let blood, as I just said — was not his pittance [nothing] but a sponge of gall? **1006–07 Loke nu, hwa gruccheth . . . of povre pitance?** Look now, who — if she thinks carefully about it (lit., thinks well on it) — grumbles about a poor meal of unsavory (i.e., unappetizing) foods, [or who complains] about a poor pittance? **1007–09 Of na mon ne of na wummon . . . ant godin ham other ow**, You will (i.e., ought) not make any moan (or, complaint) about any man or about any woman, nor complain (reflex.) about any want, except to some true friend who may remedy (lit., amend) it, and do good to them or you. **1009–12 Ant thet beo priveiliche i-seid . . . o this wise**, And let that be said privately (or, in confidence) as if under seal of the confession, so that you be not blamed. If you have a lack of anything, and some friend asks you earnestly if you have any lack, if you expect good from him (i.e., trust him), answer in this way. **1012–13 "Laverd Godd foryelde the! . . . then me neod were,"** "Lord God repay you! I fear that I have more than I am (lit., would be) worth (i.e., I have more than I am worthy of), and I suffer less want than is (lit., would be) needful for me. **1013–17 Yef he easketh yeornluker . . . thet ich hefde neode to,** If he asks more earnestly, thank him earnestly and say, "I dare not lie about myself: I have a lack — as is right. What anchoress comes into the anchor-house to have her ease (i.e., to be comfortable)? But now you want to know it completely. Our Lord repay you. This now is

hefde neode to." Ant thus bid ure riwle thet we schawin to gode freond, as othre Godes povre doth hare meoseise, with milde eadmodnesse. Ne nawt ne schule we forsaken the grace of Godes sonde, ah thonkin him yeorne leste he wreathe him with us ant withdrahe his large hond ant th'refter with to muche wone abeate ure prude. Ant nis hit muchel hofles hwen Godd beot his hond forth, puttinde hire ayein, segge, "Ne kepe ich hit nawt — have the-seolf. Ich wulle fondin yef ich mei libben her-buten." Thurh this ich habbe i-herd *of* swuch thet nom uvel ende.

Ayein leccherie is his i-borenesse of thet cleane meiden ant al his cleane lif thet he leadde on eorthe, ant alle the hine fuleden. Thus, lo, the articles — thet beoth as thah me seide, "the lithes of ure bileave onont Godes monhead" — hwa-se inwardliche bihalt ham fehteth toyein the feond the fondeth us with theose deadliche sunnen. For-thi seith Seinte Peter, **Christo in carne passo et vos eadem cogitatione armemini.** "Armith ow," he seith, "with thoht up-o Jesu Crist, the in ure flesch wes i-pinet." Ant Seinte Pawel, **Recogitate qualem aput semet ipsum**

---

one thing that I had need of." **1017–18 Ant thus bid . . . with milde eadmodnesse,** And thus our rule directs that we show [our discomfort] to a good friend, as others of God's poor do (i.e., show) their discomfort, with mild humility. **1018–21 Ne nawt ne schule we . . . abeate ure prude,** We should not refuse the grace of God's sending (i.e., what God sends), but thank Him eagerly for fear that (lit., lest) He grow angry (reflex.) with us and withdraw His generous hand and after that with too much want beat down our pride. **1021–23 Ant nis hit muchel hofles . . . thet nom uvel ende,** And is it not very senseless (or, irrational) when God offers (*beot* = reduced form of *beodeth*) up his hand, to say, thrusting it back, "I do not care for it — keep [it] yourself. I will see (or, try) if I can live without it (lit., here-without)." By this [means], I have heard of such [ones] who took (i.e., had) an evil end. **1024–25 Ayein leccherie is his i-borenesse . . . the hine fuleden,** Against lechery is His birth (i.e., being born) from that pure virgin and all His pure life that He led on earth, and all [those] who followed Him. **1025–28 Thus, lo, the articles . . . deadliche sunnen,** So, indeed, the articles [of our faith] — which are as if one said (i.e., which can be defined as) "the joints of our belief concerning God's humanity" — whosoever considers them deeply fights against the fiend who tempts us with these deadly sins. **1028–29 Christo in carne . . . cogitatione armemini,** "Christ suffered in the flesh, and with this very thought you should arm yourselves" (1 Peter 4:1). **1029–30 "Armith ow . . . wes i-pinet,"** "Arm yourselves," he says, "with thought (i.e., by thinking) upon Jesus Christ, who was tormented in our flesh." **1030–31 Recogitate . . . ut non fatiget[is],** "Think what kind of

sustinuit contradictionem ut non fatiget[is]. "Thencheth, thencheth," seith Seinte Pawel, "hwen ye wergith i feht ayeines the deovel, hu ure Laverd seolf withseide his fleschliche wil, ant withseggeth ower." **Nondum enim usque ad sanguinem restitistis.** "Yet nabbe ye nawt withstonden athet te schedunge

1035 of ower blod," [as he dude of his for ow — ayeines him-seolven, anont he mon wes of ure cunde. Yet ye habbeth thet ilke blod], the[t] ilke blisfule bodi thet com of the meiden ant deide o the rode niht ant dei bi ow — nis bute a wah bitweonen. Ant euche dei he kimeth forth ant schaweth him to ow fleschliche ant licomliche in-with the measse — biwrixlet, thah, on othres

1040 lite under breades furme. For in his ahne, ure ehnen ne mahten nawt the brihte sihthe tholien. Ah swa he schaweth him ow, as thah he seide, "Lowr, ich her. Hwet wulle ye? Seggeth me hwet were ow leof. Hwer-to neodeth ow? Meaneth ower neode." Yef the feondes ferd — thet beoth his temptatiuns — asailith ow swithe, ondswerieth him ant seggeth, **Metati sumus castra juxta lapidem**

opposition He endured in Himself, that you may not grow weary" (adapted from Hebrews 12:3). **1032–33 "hwen ye wergith i feht . . . withseggeth ower,"** "when you grow weary in the fight against the devil, how our Lord Himself denied His carnal desire, and deny your own. **1033–34** *Nondum enim usque ad sanguinem restitistis,* "Truly, you have not yet resisted to the point of [the shedding of] blood" (Hebrews 12:4). **1034 Yet,** Up to now; **athet te schedunge,** to (or, to the point of) the shedding. **1035–38 as he dude of his for ow . . . nis bute a wah bitweonen,** as He did of His for you — against Himself (or, to his own detriment), in the sense that He was a man of our kind (or, with our nature — i.e., with vulnerable flesh). Even now you have by you (or, near you), night and day, that same blood, that same blissful body which came from the virgin and died on the Cross — there is [nothing] but a wall between (i.e., between you and the host). **1038–40 Ant euche dei he kimeth . . . under breades furme,** And each day He comes out and shows Himself to you physically and bodily within the mass — transformed, though, into the appearance (lit., color) of another [thing] in the form of bread. **1040–41 For in his ahne . . . tholien,** For in His own [form], our eyes could not bear the bright sight [of Him]. **1041–43 Ah swa he schaweth him ow . . . ower neode,** But in this way He shows Himself to you: as though He said, "Look, I [am] here. What do you want? Tell me what you would like (lit., what would be dear to you). What do you need (lit., to what [is it] needful for you)? Cry out your need." **1043–44 Yef the feondes ferd . . . ant seggeth,** If the fiend's army — which are his temptations — assail you mightily, answer him and say. **1044–45** *Metati sumus . . .*

1045 **adjutorii. Porro Philistiini venerunt in Afech.** "Ye, Laverd, wunder is: we beoth
i-loget her bi the thet art stan of help, tur of treowe sucurs, castel of strengthe, ant
te deofles ferd is woddre upon us then upon eani othre." This ich neome of **Regum**,
for ther hit teleth al thus thet Israel, Godes folc, com ant logede him bi the stan of
help, ant te Philistews comen into Afech. "Philistews" beoth unwihtes. "Afech"

1050 on Ebreisch spealeth "neowe wodschipe." Swa hit is witerliche, hwen mon logeth
him bi ure Laverd: thenne on earst biginneth the deovel to weden. Ah ther hit
teleth thet Israel wende sone the rug, ant weren fowr thusent i the fluht sariliche i-
sleine. Ne wende ye nawt te rug, mine leove sustren, ah withstondeth the feondes
ferd amidde the forheaved — as is i-seid th'ruppe — with stronge bileave. Ant

1055 with the gode Josaphath sendeth beode sondes-mon sone efter sucurs to the prince
of heovene.

In Para*lipomen*is: **In nobis quidem non est tanta fortitudo ut possimus huic
multitudini resistere que irruit super nos. Set cum ignoremus quid agere
debeamus, hoc solum habemus residui, ut oculos nostros dirigamus ad te.**

venerunt in Afech, "We have pitched tents near the stone of help. Then, the Philistines came to
Aphec" (based on 1 Samuel 4:1). **1045–47 "Ye, Laverd ... upon eani othre,"** "Yes, Lord, [it]
is wondrous: we are lodged here by You who are the stone of help, the tower of true aid, castle
of strength, and the devil's army is more enraged against us than against any other." **1047–50
This ich neome of *Regum* ... "neowe wodschipe,"** I take this from Kings, for there it tells
exactly in this way that Israel, God's people, came and lodged themselves by the stone of help
and the Philistines came into Aphec. "Philistines" are monsters (or, devils). "Aphec," in Hebrew means, "new madness (or, rage)." **1050–51 Swa hit is witerliche ... to weden,** So it is
certainly when one lodges himself by our Lord: then at first the devil begins to rage (or, go
mad). **1051–53 Ah ther hit teleth ... sariliche i-sleine,** But there it tells that Israel soon
turned [its] back and four thousand were pitifully slain in the flight. **1053–54 Ne wende ye
nawt te rug ... with stronge bileave,** Do not turn [your] back (i.e., flee), my dear sisters, but
withstand the fiend's army headfirst (or, in the forefront — lit., amidst the forehead) — as is
described above (see 4.827–38) — with strong faith (or, belief). **1054–56 Ant with the gode
Josaphath ... the prince of heovene,** And along with the good Jehosaphat send the messenger of prayer immediately for help to the Prince of heaven. **1057–63 *In Paralipomenis* ...
securi eritis,** In Chronicles: "In fact there is not such strength in us that we can resist that host
which rushes in over us. But when we do not know what we ought to do, this alone is left to us

1060 **Sequitur — Hec dicit Dominus vobis: Nolite timere et ne paveatis hanc
multitudinem. Non enim est vestra pugna set Dei. Tantummodo confidenter
state et videbitis auxilium Domini super vos. Credite in Domino Deo vestro,
et securi eritis.** This is thet Englisch: "In us nis nawt, deore-wurthe Laverd, swa
muchel strengthe thet we mahen withstonden the deofles ferd, the is se strong

1065 upon us. Ah hwen we swa beoth bisteathet, swa stronge bistonden, thet we mid
alle na read ne cunnen bi us-seolven, this an we mahe don: heoven ehnen up to the
mildfule Laverd. Thu send us sucurs. Thu todreaf ure fan, for to the we lokith."
Thus with the gode Josaphath — hwen Godd kimeth bivoren ow ant freineth hwet
ye wulleth, ant in euch time hwen ye neode habbeth — schawith hit swa sweteliche

1070 to his swote earen. Yef he sone ne hereth ow, yeieth luddre ant meadlesluker, ant
threatith thet ye wulleth yelden up the castel bute he sende ow sonre help, ant hihi
the swithere. Ah wite ye hu he ondswerede Josaphath the gode? Thus, o thisse
wise: **Nolite timere, et cetera.** Thus he onswereth ow hwen ye help cleopieth:
"Ne beo ye nawt offearede, ne drede ye ham na-wiht thah ha beon stronge ant

(lit., we have of a remnant), that we direct our eyes to you." It follows — Our Lord says these
things to you: "Do not fear and do not be afraid of this host. For it is not your fight, but God's.
Stand so much the more confidently and you will see the help of the Lord over you. Believe in
the Lord your God and you will be safe" (2 Chronicles 20:12, 15, 17, 20). **1063–67 This is thet
Englisch . . . to the mildfule Laverd,** This is the English: "There is not so much strength in us,
precious Lord, that we can withstand the devil's army, which is so strong (or, fierce) upon us.
But when we are hard pressed, so fiercely harassed that we know no remedy by ourselves at all
(translating *mid alle*), this one [thing] we can do: cast up [our] eyes to the gentle Lord." **1067
Thu send us sucurs . . . to the we lokith,** Send us help (*thu send* = imper.). Drive away our
foes, for we look to You. **1068–70 Thus with the gode Josaphath . . . to his swote earen,**
Thus with the good Jehosaphat — when God comes before you and asks what you will (or,
desire), and each time when you have a need — show (or, reveal) it thus sweetly to His sweet
ears. **1070–72 Yef he sone ne hereth ow . . . hihi the swithere,** If He does not hear you
immediately, cry louder and with less restraint (lit., more limitlessly), and threaten that you
will yield up the castle unless He send[s] you help sooner, and hurries the faster. **1072–73 Ah
wite ye hu he ondswerede . . . et cetera,** But do you know how he answered Jehosaphat the
good? Thus, in this way: "Do not fear," etc. **1073–76 Thus he onswereth . . . ant ye beoth al
sikere,** In this way He [will] answer you when you cry for help: "Do not be afraid, nor dread
them at all though they are strong and many. The fight is mine, not yours. Only stand confi-

1075 monie. The feht is min, nawt ower. Sulement stondeth sikerliche ant ye schulen
[seon] mi sucurs; habbeth ane to me trusti bileave, ant ye beoth al sikere." Lokith
nu hwuch help is hardi bileave, for al thet help the Godd bihat, the strengthe to
stonde wel, al is in hire ane. Hardi bileave maketh stonden up-riht, ant te unwiht
nis nawt lathre. For-thi this is his word in Ysaie: **Incurvare ut transeamus.** "Buh
1080 the," he seith, "dune-ward thet ich mahe over the." Theo buheth hire the to hise
fondunges buheth hire heorte, for hwil ha stont up-riht, ne mei he nowther upon
hire rukin ne riden. Lo, the treitre, hu he seith: **Incurvare ut transeamus.** "Buh
the, let me leapen up! — nule ich the nawt longe riden, ah ich chulle wenden
over." He liheth, seith Sein Beornard, ne lef thu nawt then traitre. **Non vult tran-**
1085 **sire, set residere.** "Nule he nawt wenden over, ah wule ful feaste sitten." Sum
wes thet lefde him, thohte he schulde sone adun as he bihat eaver. "Do," he seith,
"this en-chearre, ant schrif the th'rof to-marhen. Buh thin heorte — let me up.

---

dently and you will see My help; only have secure belief in Me, and you [will] be completely safe." **1076–79 Lokith nu hwuch help . . . nis nawt lathre**, See now what help
stout (lit., hardy) belief is, for all the help which God promises, the strength to stand (or,
persevere) well, all is [contained] in it (lit., her, belief) alone. Stout belief makes [one]
stand up straight (lit., upright), and [there] is nothing more loathsome to the devil (lit.,
monster). **1079 Ysaie**, Isaiah; *Incurvare ut transeamus*, "Bend down that we may go over"
(Isaiah 51:23). **1079–80 "Buh the . . . over the,"** "Bend yourself," he says, "downward
[so] that I can [walk] over you." **1080–82 Theo buheth hire . . . rukin ne riden**, She
bends herself who bends her heart to his temptations, for while she stands upright (*stont* =
reduced form of *stondeth*), he cannot either squat (i.e., mount) or ride on her. **1082 treitre**,
traitor. **1083–84 let me leapen up! . . . wenden over**, let me leap up! — I do not want to
ride long, but I [just] want to cross over. **1084 He liheth, seith Sein Beornard . . . then
traitre**, He lies, says St. Bernard, do not believe the traitor (*then* = declined def. art.).
1084–85 *Non vult transire, set residere*, "He does not want to cross over, but [instead he
wants to] sit down (i.e., remain)" (source unidentified). **1085 "Nule he nawt wenden over
. . . feaste sitten,"** "He does not want to cross over, but wants to sit quite firmly (or,
unmovably)." **1085–86 Sum wes thet lefde him . . . he bihat eaver**, There was someone
who believed him, thought he would soon [come] down, as he always promises. **1086–88
"Do . . . ride the longe,"** "Do [it]," he says, "this one time, and confess yourself of it
tomorrow. Bend your heart — let me up [on you]. Shake me down with confession if I

Schec me with schrift adun, yef ich alles walde ride the longe." Sum, as ich seide, lefde him ant beah him, ant he leop up ant rad hire bathe dei ant niht twenti yer
1090   fulle! Thet is, ha dude a sunne i the il[ke] niht thurh his procunge, ant thohte thet ha walde hire schriven ine marhen, ant dude hit eft ant eft ant fealh swa i uvel wune, thet ha lei ant rotede th'rin swa longe as ich seide. Ant yef a miracle nere, the pufte adun then deovel the set on hire se feaste, ha hefde i-turplet with him, bathe hors ant lade, dun into helle grunde. For-thi, mine leove sustren, haldeth ow
1095   efne up-riht i treowe bileave. Hardiliche i-leveth, thet al the deofles strengthe mealteth thurh the grace of thet hali sacrament, hest over othre, thet ye seoth as ofte as the preost measseth: the meidene bearn, Jesu Godd, Godes sune, the licomliche lihteth other-hwiles to ower in, ant in-with ow eadmodliche nimeth his herbearhe. Deu-le-set, ha beoth to wake ant to unwreaste i-heortet, the with swilli
1100   gest hardiliche ne fehteth. Ye schulen bileave habben, thet al Hali Chirche deth, red, other singeth, ant alle hire sacremenz strengeth ow gasteliche — ah nan ase forth ase this, for hit bringeth to noht al thes deofles wiheles, nawt ane his

would ride you at all [too] long." **1088–92 Sum, as ich seide . . . swa longe as ich seide**, Someone, as I said, believed him and bowed himself and he (i.e., the devil) leapt up and rode her both day and night fully twenty years! That is, she did (or, committed) one sin in that very night through his goading, and thought that she would confess herself in the morning, and committed it (i.e., the sin) again and again and thus got into an evil habit, so that she lay and rotted in it as long as I said. **1092–94 Ant yef a miracle nere . . . helle grunde**, And if there had not been (lit., were not) a miracle which blew down the devil who sat on her so firmly, she [would] have tumbled. **1094–99 For-thi, mine leove sustren . . . his herbearhe**, For that reason, my dear sisters, hold yourselves steadily upright in true belief. Believe (imper.) stalwartly that all the devil's strength melts through the grace of the holy sacrament, [which is] highest above the others, which you see as often as the priest says mass: the Virgin's child, Jesus God, God's son, who physically descends sometimes to your dwelling, and humbly takes His lodging within you. **1099–1100 Deu-le-set, ha beoth . . . hardiliche ne fehteth**, God knows, they are too weak and too wickedly hearted (i.e., evil-hearted), who, with such a guest, do not fight valiantly. **1100–06 Ye schulen bileave habben . . . ant god for-te donne**, You must have faith, that all [which] the Holy Church does, reads (or, explains; *red* = reduced form of *redeth*), or sings, and all her sacraments strengthen you spiritually — but none as much (lit., as far) as this, for it brings to nothing all the devil's wiles (*thes* = declined def. art.), not only his [acts of]

strengthes, ant his stronge turnes, ah deth his wiltfule crokes, his wrenchfule wicche-creftes, ant alle his yulunges, ase lease swefnes, false schawunges, dredfule
1105 offearunges, fikele ant sweokele reades, *as* thah hit were o Godes half ant god for- te donne. For thet is his unwrench, as ich ear seide, thet hali men meast dredeth, *thet haveth* moni hali mon grimliche biyulet. Hwen he ne mei nawt bringen to nan open uvel, he sput to a thing thet thuncheth god. "Thu schuldest," he seith, "beo mildre, ant leoten i-wurthe thi chast, nawt trubli thin heorte ant sturien into
1110 wreaththe." This he seith for-thi thet tu ne schuldest nawt chastien for hire gult ne tuhte wel thi meiden, ant bringe the into yemeles i stude of eadmodnesse. Eft riht ther-toyeines: "Ne let tu hire na gult toyeves," he seith. "Yef thu wult thet ha drede the, hald hire nearowe." "Riht-wisnesse," he seith, "mot beo nede sturne," ant thus he liteth cruelte with heow of riht-wisnesse. Me mei beon al to riht-wis.
1115 **Noli esse justus nimis (In Ecclesiaste).** Betere is wis liste then luther strengthe. Hwen thu havest longe i-waket ant schuldest gan to slepen — "nu is vertu," he

violence, and his powerful throws (or, tricks), but [it also] makes (lit., does) his wily trickery, his deceitful sorceries (lit., witchcrafts), and all his ruses, [such] as lying dreams, false visions, dreadful terrors, treacherous and deceitful advice (lit., advices), as though it were on God's behalf and good to do. **1106–08 For thet is his unwrench . . . thet thuncheth god,** For that is his evil device, as I said before, that holy men most fear, which has horribly deceived (or, bewitched) many a holy man. When he cannot bring [a person] to any open evil, he incites (*sput* = reduced form of *sputteth*) to a thing which seems good. **1108–10 "Thu schuldest . . . into wreaththe,"** "You should," he says, "be milder and let your quarreling (or, dispute) be, not trouble your heart and stir [it up] to wrath." **1110–11 This he seith . . . i stude of eadmodnesse,** He says this in order that you should not chastise your maiden for her fault[s] nor train [her] well, and [that you should] bring yourself into carelessness instead of humility. **1111–14 Eft riht ther-toyeines . . . with heow of riht-wisnesse,** [He says] afterwards exactly the opposite: "Do not allow her any fault freely (i.e., to get away easily with any fault)," he says. "If you want that she [should] fear you, hold her narrowly (i.e., keep her strictly). Righteousness," he says, "must needs be stern," and thus he colors cruelty with the appearance (or, hue) of righteousness. **1114 Me mei beon al to riht-wis,** One can be all too righteous. **1115 *Noli esse justus nimis*,** "Do not be excessively just" (Ecclesiastes 7:17). **1115–17 Betere is wis liste . . . Sei yet a nocturne,** Wise skill (or, cunning) is better than deceitful (or, severe) strength. When you have watched (or, stayed awake) long and ought to go to sleep — "Now, [it] is a virtue," he says, "to

seith, "wakien hwen hit greveth the. Sei yet a nocturne." For-hwi deth he swa?
For thet tu schuldest slepen eft hwen time were to wakien. Eft riht ther-toyeines:
yef thet [tu] maht wakien wel, he leith on the an hevinesse, other deth i thi thoht,
1120 "Wisdom is thinge best: Ich chulle ga nu to slepen, ant arise nunan ant don
cwicluker thene nu, thet ich don nuthe schulde" — ant swa ofte inoh-reathe ne
dest tu hit i nowther time. Of this ilke materie ich spec muchel th'ruppe. I thulliche
temptatiuns nis nan se wis, ne se war — bute Godd him warni — thet nis bigilet
ofte. Ah this hehe sacrement, in hardi bileave, over alle othre thing unwrith hise
1125 wrenches, ant breketh hise strengthes. I-wis, leove sustren, hwen ye neh ow feleth
him, for-hwon thet ye habben hardi bileave, nulle ye bute lahhen him lude to
bismere thet he is se muchel ald cang, the kimeth his pine to echen, ant breiden
ow crune? Sone se he sith ow hardi ant bald i Godes grace, his mihte mealteth ant
he flith sone. Ah yef he mei underyeoten thet ower bileave falsi, swa thet ow
1130 thunche thet ye mahten beon allunge i-lead forth over yef ye weren swithe i the
ilke stude i-temptet, ther-with ye unstrengeth ant his mihte waxeth.

stay awake when it vexes you. Say another nocturn." **1117–18 For-hwi deth he swa? . . . to
wakien**, Why does he [say] so? For the reason that you should sleep again when [it] would be time
to stay awake. **1118–22 Eft riht ther-toyeines . . . i nowther time**, Afterwards exactly the opposite:
if you can stay awake well (i.e., easily) he lays on you a heaviness or puts into your thought[s],
"Wisdom is the best of things (i.e., it is better to be wise): I will now go to sleep and rise right away
and do more quickly than now what I now ought to do" — and as often readily enough you do not
do it on either occasion. **1122–24 Of this ilke materie . . . bigilet ofte**, I spoke much of this same
matter above (lit., up there — see 3.284 and ff.). In such temptations there is none so wise, or so
vigilant — unless God put him on his guard — who is not often beguiled. **1124–25 Ah this hehe
sacrement . . . hise strengthes**, But this high sacrament, in strong belief, unravels his tricks (i.e.,
unbends his turns) over (i.e., better than) all other things, and breaks his powers (or, violent acts).
1125–28 I-wis, leove sustren . . . breiden ow crune? Certainly, dear sisters, when you feel him
near you, provided that you have a strong belief (or, faith), will you not laugh him loudly to scorn
that he is such (lit., so) a great old fool who comes to increase his own pain and to weave (lit., braid)
you a crown? **1128–29 Sone se he sith ow . . . he flith sone**, [As] soon as he sees you hardy and
bold in God's grace, his might melts and he flees straight away. **1129–31 Ah yef he mei underyeoten
. . . his mihte waxeth**, But if he can observe that your faith fails (or, is weakening) so that it seems
to you that you could be entirely led away (or, led astray) if you were tempted mightily in the same
place (i.e., on the same point), by that you weaken and his power grows.

We redeth i **Regum** thet Ysboset lei ant slepte, ant sette a wummon yete-ward the windwede hweate, ant come*n* Recabes sunen, Remon ant Banaa, ant funden the wummon i-stunt of hire windwunge ant i-folen o slepe, ant wenden in ant

1135 slohen Ysboset the unseli, thet lokede him se uvele. The bitacnunge her-of is muche neod to understonden. "Ysboset" on Ebrew is "mon bimeaset" on Englisch — ant nis he witerliche ameaset, ant ut of his witte, the amidden his unwines leith him to slepen? The yete-ward is wittes skile, thet ah to windwin hweate, schaden the eilen *ant te* chef from the cleane cornes — thet is, thurh bisi warschipe, sundri

1140 god from uvel, don the hweate i gerner, ant puffen eaver awei the deofles chef thet nis noht bute to helle smorthre. Ah the bimeasede Ysboset — lo, hu measeliche he dude! Sette a wummon to yete-ward — thet is feble warde. Wei-la, as feole doth thus. Wummon is the reisun — thet is, wittes skile — hwen hit unstrengeth, the schulde beo monlich, steale-wurthe ant kene in treowe bileave. This yete-

1145 ward lith to slepen, sone se me biginneth consenti to sunne, leoten lust gan in-

---

1132–35 We redeth i *Regum* . . . lokede him se uvele, We read in Kings (2 Samuel 4:1 ff.) that Isboseth lay and slept and set (i.e., appointed) a woman who winnowed (or, who was winnowing) wheat [as] gate-warden (i.e., guard), and Rechab's sons Remmon and Baana came, and found the woman stopped (or, exhausted) from her winnowing and fallen asleep, and [they] went in and slew the unfortunate Isboseth, who looked to himself so badly. **1135–36 The bitacnunge her-of . . . to understonden,** There is a great need to understand the meaning of this. **1136–38 "Ysboset" on Ebrew . . . leith him to slepen?** "Isboseth," in Hebrew, is (or, means) "a confused man" in English — and is he not surely confused and out of his wits, who lays himself [down] to sleep amidst his enemies? **1138–41 The yete-ward is wittes skile . . . to helle smorthre,** The gate-warden (or, guard) is reason's discernment which ought to winnow wheat, separate the bristles (or, awn) and the chaff from the pure grains — that is, through diligent vigilance, divide good from evil, put the wheat in the garner (or, bin), and always blow away the devil's chaff which is [good for] nothing but hell's stifling smoke. **1141–42 Ah the bimeasede Ysboset . . . feble warde,** But the confused Isboseth — look, how stupidly he did (or, acted)! He set (or, appointed) a woman as gate-warden — which is a feeble (or, weak) guardian. **1142–44 Wei-la, as feole doth thus . . . in treowe bileave,** Alas, many do thus (*as* not translated). Reason — that is, the mind's discernment — is a woman when it grows weak, [reason] which should be manly (or, virile), stalwart and bold in true faith. **1144–46 This yete-ward lith to slepen . . . te delit waxen,** This gate-warden lies down to sleep, as soon as one

ward, ant te delit waxen. Hwen Recabes sunen — thet beoth helle bearnes — i-findeth swa unwaker, ant swa nesche yete-ward, ha gath in ant sleath Ysboset — thet is, the bimeasede gast the in a slepi yemeles foryemeth him-seolven. Thet nis nawt to foryeoten, thet as Hali Writ seith, ha thurh-stichden him dun into the schere. Her seith Sein Gregoire, **In i[n]guine ferire est vitam mentis carnis delectatione perforare.** "The feond thurh-sticheth the schere, hwen delit of leccherie thurleth the heorte" — ant this nis bute i slep of yemeles ant of slawthe, as Sein Gregoire witneth: **Antiquus hostis, mox ut mentem otiosam invenerit, ad eam sub quibusdam occasionibus locuturus venit, et quedam ei de gestis preteritis ad memoriam reducit. — Et infra: — "Putruerunt et deteriorate sunt cicatrices mee!" Cicatrix quidem est figura vulneris, set sanati. Cicatrix ergo ad putredinem redit, quando peccati vulnus, quod per penitentiam sanatum est, in delectationem sui animum concutit.** This is thet Englisch: Hwen the alde unwine sith slepi ure skile, he draheth him anan toward hire ant feleth with hire i speche: "Thenchest tu," he seith, "hu the spec — other theo — of

1150

1155

1160

begins to consent to sin, to let pleasure go within and delight to grow. **1146–48 Hwen Recabes sunen ... foryemeth him-seolven**, When Rechab's sons — which are the children of hell — find so unwatchful, and so soft a gate-warden, they go in and slay Isboseth — that is, the confused spirit which in a sleepy carelessness neglects itself. **1148–50 Thet nis nawt to foryeoten ... into the schere**, This is not to be forgotten (passive inf.), that, as Holy Writ says, they pierced him down into the groin. **1150–51 In i[n]guine ferire est ... perforare**, "To strike into (or, stab) the groin is to pierce the life of the spirit with the delight of the flesh" (Gregory, *Moral Discourses on Job* 1.35.49 [*PL* 75.549]). **1151–53 The feond thurh-sticheth ... witneth**, "The fiend stabs the groin when delight of lechery pierces through the heart" — and this is only in the sleep of carelessness and sloth, as St. Gregory bears witness. **1153–58 Antiquus hostis ... sui animum concutit**, "The ancient enemy, as soon as he comes across an idle mind, comes talking to it at various opportune moments, and brings to memory a certain deed of the past. — And later: — 'My scars have festered and become worse!' (Psalm 37:6). Indeed a scar is a mark of a wound, but of a healed one. Therefore a scar begins to fester again when the wound of sin, which is healed through penitence, agitates the mind in pleasure of itself (i.e., remembering the pleasure of a sin already confessed)" (Gregory, *Letters* 9.2.52 [*PL* 77.984]). **1158–63 Hwen the alde unwine ... ha sum-hwile wrahte**, When the old enemy sees our reason [to be] sleepy, he draws himself immediately up to her and enters into speech with her: "Do you remember," he says,

286

flesches galnesse?" Ant speketh thus the alde sweoke toward hire heorte wordes thet ha yare herde fulliche i-seide, other sihthe thet ha seh, other hire ahne fulthen thet ha sum-hwile wrahte. Al this he put forth bivore the heorte ehnen, for-te bifulen hire with thoht of alde sunnen, hwen he ne mei with neowe, ant swa he

1165 bringeth ofte ayein into the adotede sawle thurh licunge the ilke sunnen, the thurh reowthful sar weren i-bet yare, swa thet heo mei wepen ant meanen sari man with the Salm-wruhte: **Putruerunt, et cetera.** "Wei-la-wei, mine wunden, the weren feire i-healet, gederith neowe wursum ant foth on eft to rotien." I-healet wunde thenne biginneth to rotien, hwen sunne the wes i-bet kimeth eft with licunge into

1170 munegunge, ant sleath the unwarre sawle. **Gregorius: Ysboset inopinate morti nequaquam succumberet, nisi ad ingressum mentis mulierem — id est, mollem custodiam — deputasset.** Al this unlimp i-warth thurh the yete-wardes slep thet nes war ant waker, ne nes nawt monlich, ah wes wummonlich: eth to overkeasten.

"how he — or she — spoke about lechery of the flesh?" And thus the old traitor speaks words toward her heart which she heard long ago said filthily, or a sight that she saw, or her own immoralities (lit., filths) which she committed (lit., wrought) once. **1163–67 Al this he put forth . . . with the Salm-wruhte,** All this he puts forward before [her] heart's eyes, [in order] to befoul her with the thought (or, memory) of old sins, when he cannot [do so] with new [sins], and so he often brings the same sin into the foolish soul through pleasure, [the sins] which were atoned for a long time ago through regretful sorrow, so that she can weep and make a grievous moan (lit., moan a sorry moan) with the Psalmist (lit., Psalm-maker). **1167 *Putruerunt, et cetera*,** "[My scars] have festered," etc. (Psalm 37:6). **1167–68 "Wei-la-wei, mine wunden . . . eft to rotien,"** "Alas! My wounds, which were properly (or, completely) healed, gather (i.e., are gathering) new pus and begin to fester again." **1168–70 I-healet wunde thenne . . . unwarre sawle,** A healed wound, then, begins to fester when sin which was atoned for comes again with [illicit] pleasure into [one's] memory, and slays the more unprepared (or, less wary) soul. **1170–72 *Gregorius: Ysboset inopinate . . . deputasset*,** Gregory: "Isboseth would in no way have succumbed to an unexpected death had he not placed a woman — that is, a soft (or, yielding) guardian — at the entrance of [his] mind" (Gregory, *Moral Discourses on Job* 1.35.49 [*PL* 75.549]). **1172–73 Al this unlimp i-warth . . . to overkeasten,** All this calamity happened through (i.e., because of) the sleep of the gate-warden, who was not watchful and vigilant, nor was she manly, but was womanly: easy to overthrow (or, defeat).

Beo hit wummon beo hit mon, thenne, is al the strengthe efter the bileave, ant
1175 efter thet me haveth trust to Godes help, thet is neh — bute bileave trukie, as ich
ear buven seide. Heo unstrengeth the unwiht ant deth him fleon anan-riht. For-thi,
beoth eaver ayein him hardi ase liun i treowe bileave, nomeliche i the fondunge
thet Ysboset deide on — thet is, galnesse. Lo, hu ye mahe cnawen thet he is earh
ant unwreast hwen he smit thider-ward: Nis he earh champiun the skirmeth to-
1180 ward te vet, the secheth se lahe on his kempe-ifere? Flesches lust is fotes wunde
— as wes feor i-seid th'ruppe — ant this is the reisun: As ure fet beoreth us, alswa
ure lustes beoreth us ofte to thing thet us luste efter. Nu thenne thah thi va hurte
the o the vet — thet is to seggen, fondeth with flesches lustes — for se lah wunde
ne dred tu nawt to sare, bute hit to swithe swelle thurh skiles yettunge with to
1185 muchel delit up toward te heorte, ah drinc thenne atter-lathe ant drif thet swealm
ayein-ward frommard te heorte — thet is to seggen, thench o the attri pine thet
Godd dronc o the rode, ant te swealm schal setten. Prude, ant onde, ant wreaththe,

1174–76 Beo hit wummon . . . deth him fleon anan-riht, Be it woman [or] be it man, then, all
the strength [to withstand] is according to [one's] faith, and according to [the extent] that one
has trust in God's help which is close by (lit., nigh) — unless faith should fail, as I said before
above. She (i.e., faith) weakens the devil (lit., monster) and makes him flee immediately. **1176–
78 For-thi, beoth eaver ayein him . . . thet is, galnesse**, For this reason, always be as stout-
hearted as a lion in true faith against him, especially in the temptation which Isboseth died from
— that is, lechery. **1178–80 Lo, hu ye mahe cnawen . . . on his kempe-ifere?** Look how you
can know that he is cowardly and pitiful (or, wicked) when he lashes out (lit., smites; *smit* =
reduced form of *smiteth*) in that direction: is he not a cowardly combatant who thrusts (or,
slashes) at the feet, who attacks (lit., seeks) so low on his fellow fighter? **1180–82 Flesches lust
is fotes wunde . . . thet us luste efter**, The desire of the flesh is the foot's wound (i.e., a foot
wound), as was said far above (see 4.172–73), and this is the reason: just as our feet carry us,
also our desires carry us often to a thing which we desire for (lit., which pleases us for). **1182–87
Nu thenne thah thi va . . . ant te swealm schal setten**, Now then, even though your foe hurt
you on the feet — that is to say, tempt [you] with desires of the flesh — do not fret too greatly
about so low a wound, unless it swell too terribly up toward the heart through the consent of
reason with too much delight (i.e., when your reason wrongly consents to lust), but drink then
the antidote and drive the inflammation back away from the heart — that is to say, think on the
poisonous pain that God drank on the Cross (see textual note for an alternative reading), and the
inflammation will subside. **1187–90 Prude, ant onde, ant wreaththe . . . beon i-salvet**, Pride

288

heorte sar for worltlich thing, dreori oflongunge, ant yisceunge of ahte — theose beoth heorte wunden, ant al thet of ham floweth, ant yeoveth deathes dunt anan,

1190 buten ha beon i-salvet. Hwen the feond smit thider-ward, thenne is i-wis to dreden — ant nawt for fot-wunden.

Prude salve is eadmodnesse; ondes, feolahlich luve; wreaththes, tholemodnesse; accidies, redunge, misliche werkes, gastelich frovre; yisceunges, over-hohe of eorthliche thinges; festschipes, freo heorte. Thet is to seggen nu of the earste on

1195 alre earst — yef thu wult beon eadmod, thench eaver hwet te wonteth of halinesse ant of gasteliche theawes. Thench hwet tu havest of the-seolf. Thu art of twa dalen: of licome ant of sawle. In either beoth twa thinges the mahen muchel meokin the, yef thu ham wel bihaldest. I the licome is fulthe ant unstrengthe. Ne kimeth of thet vetles swuch thing as ther is in? Of thi flesches fetles kimeth ther smeal of

1200 aromaz other of swote basme? Deale! Drue spritlen beoreth win-berien? Breres, rose blostmen? Thi flesch — hwet frut bereth hit in all his openunges? Amid te

and envy and wrath, the heart's pain for worldly things, the miserable longing, and coveting of possessions — these and everything that flows from them are wounds of the heart, and [they] deal out a death-blow (lit., give death's blow) immediately, unless they are healed (or, anointed with salve). **1190–91 Hwen the feond smit . . . for fot-wunden,** When the fiend strikes (or, attacks) in that direction, then [it] is certainly to fear (or, be feared — passive inf.) — and not because of [mere] foot wounds. **1192–94 Prude salve is eadmodnesse . . . freo heorte,** The remedy for pride (lit., pride's remedy) is humility; for envy, comradely (or, "brotherly") love; for wrath, patience; of sloth, reading, various works, spiritual comfort; for covetousness, contempt for earthly things; for stinginess (i.e., avarice), a generous heart. **1194–96 Thet is to seggen nu . . . of gasteliche theawes,** The first [of these remedies] is to be discussed first of all (lit., this is to be said concerning the first first of all) — if you will be humble, think always what is lacking [in] you with respect to (lit., of) holiness, and with respect to spiritual virtues. **1196–98 Thench hwet tu havest . . . yef thu ham wel bihaldest,** Think what you have from yourself. You are (i.e., consist) of two parts: of body and of soul. In both there are two things which can humble you (lit., make you meek) much, if you consider them well. **1198 licome,** body. **1198–1200 Ne kimeth . . . of swote basme?** Does not the kind of thing come from the vessel as there is in [it]? From your body's vessel, does there come a smell of spices or of sweet balm? **1200–01 Deale! Drue spritlen . . . blostmen?** What! Do dry (i.e., dead) twigs bear wine grapes? Do briars [bear] rose blossoms? **1201 openunges,** openings (i.e., orifices). **1201–04 Amid te menske of thi neb . . . wurme fode?** Amidst the beauty of your fair face — which is the fairest part [of the body] — what with (lit., between) the taste of the mouth and

menske of thi neb — thet is the fehereste deal — bitweonen muthes smech ant neases smeal, ne berest tu as twa prive thurles? "Nart tu i-cumen of ful slim? Nart tu fulthe fette. Ne bist tu wurme fode?" **Philosophus: Sperma es fluidum, vas**

1205 **stercorum, esca vermium.** Nu, a flehe mei eili the, makie the to blenchen — eathe maht tu pruden! Bihald hali men the weren sum-hwile, hu ha feasten, hu ha wakeden, i hwuch passiun, i hwuch swinc ha weren, ant swa thu maht i-cnawen thin ahne wake unstrengthe. Ah wast tu hwet awildgeth monnes feble ehnen, thet is hehe i-clumben? — thet he bihalt dune-ward. Alswa hwa-se bihalt to theo the

1210 beoth of lah lif, thet maketh him thunchen thet he is of heh lif. Ah bihald aa uppart toward heovenliche men the clumben se hehe, ant thenne schalt tu seon hu lahe thu stondest. **Augustinus: Sicut incentivum est elationis respectus inferioris, sic cautela est humilitatis consideratio superioris.** Feasten a seove-niht to weater ant to breade, threo niht togederes wakien — hu walde hit unstrengen thi fleschliche

1215 strenge? Thus theos twa thinges bihald i thi licome: fulthe ant unstrengthe; i thi sawle other twa: sunne ant ignorance — thet is, unwisdom ant unweotenesse. For

the smell of the nose, do you not bear [something] like two privy holes (i.e., toilet holes)? "Have you not come from foul slime? Are you not a vat of filth? Are you not worm's food?" **1204–05** *Philosophus: Sperma es fluidum. . . esca vermium,* The Philosopher: "You are liquid sperm, a vat of excrement (lit., pl.), the food of worms." **1205–08 Nu, a flehe mei eili the . . . thin ahne wake unstrengthe,** Now, a fly can afflict you, make you flinch — you may easily be proud! Consider holy men who were (i.e., lived) in a former time, how they fasted, how they held vigils, in what kind of suffering, in what kind of toil they were (or, lived), and so you might recognize your own weak frailty. **1208–09 Ah wast tu hwet awildgeth . . . bihalt dune-ward,** But do you know what dazzles the feeble eyes of a man (or, person), who has climbed high (i.e., in the spiritual life)? — when (lit., that) he looks downward (*bihalt* = reduced form of *bihaldeth*). **1209–12 Alswa hwa-sa bihalt . . . hu lahe thu stondest,** Likewise whosoever looks to those who are of low life, that makes him think (or, makes [it] seem to him) that he is of high life. But always look (imper.) upwards towards heavenly men who climbed so high, and then you will see how low you stand. **1212–13** *Augustinus: Sicut incentivum . . . consideratio superioris,* Augustine: "Just as the sight of an inferior is an incentive to pride, so the consideration of a superior is a warning of humility (i.e., to be humble)" (source unidentified). **1213–15 Feasten a seove-niht . . . strenge?** To fast a week on water and on bread, to watch (i.e., stay awake) three nights altogether — how would it weaken your physical strength? **1215 bihald i thi licome,** consider in your body. **1216 unweotenesse,** unawareness, lack of awareness. **1216–18 For ofte thet tu wenest god . . . thine scheome sunnen,** For often what you

ofte thet tu wenest go*d* is uvel ant sawle morthre. Bihald with wet ehe thine scheome sunnen. Dred yet thi wake cunde thet is eth-warpe, ant sei with the hali mon the bigon to wepen, ant seide tha me talde him thet an of his feren wes with a wummon

1220 i flesches fulthe i-fallen: **Ille hodie, ego cras** — thet is, "he to-dei, ant ich to-marhen," as thah he seide, "Of as unstrong cunde ich am as he wes, ant al swuch mei me i-limpen bute yef Godd me halde." Thus, lo, the hali mon — nefde he of the othres fal na wunderlich overhohe, ant biweop his unhap ant dredde thet him a swuch mahte bitiden. O this wise eadmodieth ant meokith ow-seolven. **Bernardus:**

1225 **Superbia est appetitus proprie excellencie; humilitas, contemptus ejusdem** — thet [is], "Alswa as prude is wilnunge of wurthschipe, riht alswa ther-toyeines, eadmodnesse is forkeastunge of wurthschipe," ant luve of lutel here-word ant of lahnesse. This theaw is alre theawene moder, ant streoneth ham alle. The is umben withuten hire to gederin gode theawes, he bereth dust i the wind, as Sein Gregoire

1230 seith, **Qui sine humilitate virtutes congregat, quasi qui in vento pulverem**

consider good is evil and the soul's murder (i.e., the death, or, torment of the soul). Look on your shameful sins with a wet eye. **1218–20 Dred yet thi wake cunde . . . i flesches fulthe i-fallen,** Fear (imper.) continually your weak nature which is easy to overthrow, and say with the holy man who began to weep and said when they (lit., one) told him that one of his comrades had fallen into the filth (or, corruption) of the flesh with a woman. **1220 *Ille hodie, ego cras*,** "He today, I tomorrow" (*The Lives of the Desert Fathers* 7.16). **1220–21 to-marhen,** tomorrow. **1221–22 "Of as unstrong cunde . . . Godd me halde,"** "I am of as weak a nature as he was, and exactly such [a thing] may happen to me unless God keep me." **1222–24 Thus, lo, the hali mon . . . meokith ow-seolven,** Thus, see, the holy man — he did not have any remarkable disdain for the other's fall, but (lit., and) wept for his misfortune and feared (*dredde* = past tense of *dreden*) that such a [misfortune] might befall him. In this way humble and make yourselves meek. **1224– 25 *Bernardus: Superbia est appetitus . . . contemptus ejusdem*,** Bernard: "Pride is an appetite for one's own supremacy; humility, contempt for it" (Bernard, *The Steps of Humility and Pride*, 4.14 [*PL* 182.949]). **1226–28 Alswa as prude is wilnunge . . . ant of lahnesse,** "Just as pride is the desire for honor, just so, by contrast, humility is the casting down (or, rejection) of honor," and the love of little praise (lit., praise-words) and of lowliness. **1228–29 This theaw is alre theawene moder . . . gode theawes,** This virtue is the mother of all virtues, and gives birth to them all. Whoever is aiming to acquire (lit., gather) good virtues without her (i.e., humility). **1230–31 *Qui sine humilitate . . . pulverem portat*,** "Whoever gathers virtues without humility,

portat. Theos ane bith i-borhen; theos ane withbuheth the deofles grunen of helle, as ure Laverd schawde to Seint Antonie, the seh al the world ful of the deofles tildunge. "A, Laverd!" quoth he, "hwa mei with theose witen him thet he ne beo with sum i-laht?" "Ane the tholemode," quoth he, ure Laverd. Swa sutil thing is

1235 eadmodnesse, ant swa gentilliche smeal ant se smuhel, thet na grune ne mei hire edhalden — ant, lo, muche wunder: thah ha hire makie swa smeal ant se meoke, ha is thinge strengest, swa thet of hire is euch gastelich strengthe. Seint Cassio*d*re hit witneth: **Omnis fortitudo ex humilitate.** Ah Salomon seith the reisun hwi: **Ubi humilitas, *ibi* sapientia.** "Ther-as eadmodnesse is, ther," he seith, "is Jesu

1240 Crist" — thet is, his feader wisdom ant his feader strengthe. Nis na wunder thenne thah strengthe beo ther-as he is thurh his in-wuniende grace: thurh the strengthe of eadmodnesse he weorp the thurs of helle. The yape wreastlere nimeth yeme hwet turn his fere ne kunne nawt, thet he with wreastleth, for with thet turn he mei him unmundlunge warpen. Alswa dude ure Laverd, ant seh hu feole the grimme

is like [someone] who carries dust in the wind" (Gregory, *Homilies on the Gospels* 7.4 [PL 76.1103]). **1231–33 Theos ane bith i-borhen . . . the deofles tildunge,** She alone is saved (i.e., will be saved); she alone [will] escape the snares of the devil of hell, as our Lord revealed to St. Anthony, who saw all the world full of the devil's snare-setting (or, spreading of nets). **1233–34 "A, Laverd! . . . with sum i-laht?"** "Oh Lord!" he says, "who can protect himself against these [snares so] that he not be caught by one [of them]?" **1234–37 Ane the tholemode . . . is euch gastelich strengthe,** "Only the patient," He, our Lord, says. So elusive (or, slender, cunning, etc. — see glossary) a thing is humility and so exquisitely small and so stealthy that no snare can hold her — and, look, a great marvel: though she (i.e., humility) make herself so small and so meek, she is the strongest of things, so that from her is (i.e., comes) each spiritual strength. **1237–38 Seint Cassiodre hit witneth,** St. Cassiodorus bears witnesses to it. **1238 *Omnis fortitudo ex humilitate*,** "All strength [comes] from humility" (Augustine, *Expositions in the Psalms*, commentary for Psalm 91 [PL 37.1184]); **Ah,** But. **1239 *Ubi humilitas, ibi sapientia*,** "Where [there is] humility, there [is] wisdom" (Proverbs 11:2). **1239 Ther-as eadmodnesse is,** Where [there] is humility (*as* not translated). **1240 his feader wisdom . . . strengthe,** His Father's wisdom and His Father's strength. **1240–42 Nis na wunder thenne . . . the thurs of helle,** [It] is no wonder then though (i.e., if) strength is where He is through His indwelling grace: through the strength of humility He overthrew the giant of hell. **1242–44 The yape wreastlere . . . unmundlunge warpen,** The astute wrestler pays (lit., takes) attention what throw (or, move) his opponent (lit., companion) whom he wrestles with does not know, for with that move he can throw him unexpectedly. **1244–47 Alswa dude ure Laverd . . . into helle grunde,**

1245 wreastlere of helle breid upon his hupe ant weorp with the hanche-turn into galnesse
— the rixleth i the lenden — hef on heh monie ant wende abuten with ham ant
swong ham thurh prude dun into helle grunde. Thohte ure Laverd the biheold al
this, "Ich schal do the a turn thet tu ne cuthest neaver, ne ne maht neaver cunnen:
the turn of eadmodnesse" — thet is, the fallinde turn — ant feol from heovene to
1250 eorthe, ant strahte him swa bi the eorthe, thet te feond wende thet he were al
eorthlich, ant wes bilurd with thet turn — ant is yet euche dei of eadmode men ant
wummen the hine wel cunnen. On other half, as Job seith, "he ne mei for prude
yet bute bihalden hehe." **Omne sublime vident oculi ejus.** Hali men the haldeth
ham lutle ant of lah lif beoth ut of his sihthe. The wilde bar ne mei nawt buhen
1255 him to smiten: hwa-se falleth adun ant thurh meoke eadmodnesse strecheth him bi
ther eorthe, he is carles of his tuskes. This nis nawt toyeines thet thet ich habbe i-
seid ear — thet me schal stonden eaver toyeines the deovel — for thet stondinge
is treowe trust of hardi bileave up-o Godes strengthe. This fallunge is eadmod

Our Lord did likewise, and saw how many [people] the grim (or, fierce) wrestler of hell flung up on
his hip and threw with the hip-throw into lechery — which rules in the loins — [He saw how the
devil] heaved many on high (i.e., up high) and went around with them [over his head] and hurled
them by pride down to the ground (or, bottom) of hell. **1247–49 Thohte ure Laverd . . . the turn
of eadmodnesse,** Our Lord, who beheld all this, thought, "I will use a throw on you (lit., do you a
turn) that you never knew how [to do] nor can ever know: the throw of humility." **1249 fallinde
turn,** falling throw. **1249–52 ant feol from heovene . . . the hine wel cunnen,** and [He] fell from
heaven to earth and stretched Himself out so close to the ground that the fiend thought that He was
completely earthly (i.e., made of earth) and was tricked (lit., lured) by that throw — and is still
[tricked] every day by humble men and women who know it (or, him: the devil) well. **1252–53 On
other half . . . bihalden hehe,** On the other side (i.e., furthermore), as Job says, "he (i.e., the devil)
cannot for pride [do anything] but continually gaze [up] high." **1253 Omne sublime vident oculi
ejus,** "His eyes see every high thing" (based on Job 41:25). **1253–56 Hali men the haldeth ham
. . . of his tuskes,** Holy men who keep themselves small (lit., little) and of lowly life are out of his
sight. The wild boar cannot bend himself [down] to strike (i.e., gore): whosoever falls down and
through meek humility stretches himself close to the ground (*ther* = inflected form of def. art.), he is
free of worry (i.e., need not worry) about his tusks. **1256–58 This nis nawt toyeines thet . . . up-o
Godes strengthe,** This is not against (or, contradicting) that which I have said before — that one
must always stand against the devil — for that standing is the true trust of steadfast faith in God's
strength. **1258–59 This fallunge is eadmod . . . thin unstrengthe,** This falling is a humble know-

cnawunge of thin ahne wacnesse, ant of thin unstrengthe. Ne nan ne mei stonde
1260 swa bute he thus falle — thet is, leote lutel tale ant unwurth ant ethelich eaver of
him-seolven, bihalde his blac ant nawt his hwit, for hwit awilgeth the ehe.
Eadmodnesse ne mei beon neaver ful preiset, for thet wes the lesceun thet ure
Laverd inwardlukest learde his i-corene, with werc ba ant with worde: **Discite a
me, quia mitis sum et humilis corde.** In hire he healdeth nawt ane drope-mel, ah
1265 flowinde yeotteth weallen of his graces, as seith the Salmiste: **Qui emittis fontes
in convallibus.** "I the dealen, thu makest" — he seith — "weallen to springen."
Heorte tobollen ant i-hoven ase hul ne edhalt na wete of grace. A bleddre i-bollen
of wind ne deveth nawt into theose halwende weattres. Ah a nelde prichunge
warpeth al the wind ut — an ethelich stiche other eche maketh to understonden hu
1270 lutel prude is wurth, hu egede is orhel.

Ondes salve, ich seide, wes feolahlich luve ant god unnunge ant god wil, ther
mihte of dede wonteth. Swa muchel strengthe haveth luve ant god wil, thet hit
maketh othres god ure god ase wel as his thet hit wurcheth. Sulement luve [h]is

ing (i.e., acknowledgment) of your own weakness and of your lack of strength. **1259–61 Ne nan
ne mei stonde . . . awilgeth the ehe,** None (i.e., no one) can so stand unless he falls in this way
— that is, [unless he] consider himself of little account and unworthy and insignificant, [unless
he] look at his black and not his white, for white dazzles the eye. **1262–63 Eadmodnesse ne mei
beon . . . with worde,** Humility can never be fully praised (i.e., praised too much), for that was
the lesson that our Lord most fervently taught His chosen [ones], with both deed and word.
1263–64 *Discite a me . . . humilis corde*, "Learn from me, for I am mild and humble of heart"
(Matthew 11:29). **1264–65 In hire he healdeth nawt . . . the Salmiste,** In her (i.e., humility) He
pours not only drop by drop, but, flowing, pours out streams of His grace (or, streams of His
grace gush forth flowing), as the Psalmist says. **1265–66 *Qui emittis fontes in convallibus*,**
"[You] who send out wellsprings in the valleys" (Psalm 103:10). **1266 I the dealen,** In the dales
(i.e., valleys). **1267–70 Heorte tobollen ant i-hoven . . . egede is orhel,** A heart swollen up and
raised up like a hill does not retain any moisture of grace (i.e., it runs off). A bladder swollen
with wind does not dive (i.e., cannot submerge) into these healing waters. But the pricking of a
needle casts (i.e., ejects) all the wind out — an insignificant stitch (or, pricking) or ache makes
[one] understand how little pride is worth, how foolish haughtiness is. **1271–72 Ondes salve
. . . of dede wonteth,** Envy's remedy, I said, was comradely (or, "brotherly") love and good
granting (i.e., well-wishing) and good will, where the power of action is lacking (i.e., where one
cannot do good in deed). **1273–74 Sulement luve [h]is god . . . th'rof,** Only love his (i.e., the

god, beo wil-cweme ant glead th'rof. Thus thu turnest hit to the, ant makest hit

1275   thin ahne. Sein Gregoire hit witneth, **Aliena bona si diligis, tua facis**. Yef thu havest onde of othres god, thu attrest te with healewi, ant wundest te with salve. Thi salve hit is — yef thu hit luvest — ayein sawle hurtes. Ant ti strengthe ayein the feond is al the god thet other deth, yef thu hit wel unnest. Witerliche, ich leve ne schulen flesches fondunges, na-mare then gasteliche, meistrin the neavere, yef

1280   thu art swote i-heortet, eadmod ant milde, ant luvest se inwardliche alle men ant wummen, ant nomeliche ancres, thine leove sustren, thet tu art sari of hare uvel, ant of hare god glead as of thin ahne. Unnen thet al the luveth the, luvede ham ase the ant dude ham frovre as the. Yef thu havest cnif other clath, other mete other drunch, scrowe other cwaer, hali monne frovre, other ei other thing thet ham walde

1285   freamien, unnen thet tu hefdest wonte the-seolf th'rof, with thon thet heo hit hefden. Yef eani is, the naveth nawt the heorte thus afeitet, with sorhfule sikes ba bi dei

---

other's) good, be pleased and glad of it. **1274 to the**, to yourself. **1275** *Aliena bona si diligis, tua facis*, "If you love another's good [deeds], you make [them] yours" (Gregory, *Pastoral Care* 3.10 [*PL* 77.63]). **1275–76 Yef thu havest onde . . . with salve**, If you have envy of another's good, you poison yourself with antidote (see *healewt* in glossary) and wound yourself with medicine (or, ointment). **1277–78 Thi salve hit is . . . yef thu hit wel unnest**, If you love it, it is your medicine for the soul's injuries. And your strength against the fiend (*ti* = reduced form of *thi* after preceding -*t*) is all the good which the other does, if you wish it well (i.e., if you desire the other person's good). **1278–82 Witerliche, ich leve ne schulen . . . of thin ahne**, Certainly, I believe [that] neither the temptations of the flesh any more than spiritual [temptations] will ever master you if you are sweet-hearted, humble and mild and [if you] love so deeply (lit., inwardly) all men and women and especially anchoresses, your dear sisters, that you are sorry for their evil (or, harm) and glad for their good as [if you were glad] for your own [good]. **1282– 83 Unnen thet al . . . frovre as the**, Wish (imper.) that all who love you would love them (i.e., the anchoresses) as [they love] you and would comfort (lit., would do comfort to) them as [they do] you. **1283–85 Yef thu havest cnif . . . thet heo hit hefden**, If you have a knife or [some] clothing, or food or drink, a scroll or quire (i.e., small book), the comfort of a holy man, or any other thing that would help them, desire that you yourself had the lack of these things (lit., thereof), in order that they [could] have it. **1286–88 Yef eani is . . . habbe hire swuch aturnet**, If there is anyone who does not have the heart thus disposed, [let her] cry to our Lord with sorrowful sighs both by day and by night, and never give Him peace until He has transformed

ant bi niht grede on ure Laverd, ne neaver grith ne yeove him athet he thurh his grace habbe hire swuch aturnet.

1290 Salve of wreaththe, ich seide, is tholemodnesse. Thet haveth threo steiren: heh, ant herre ant alre hest ant nest te hehe heovene. Heh is the steire yef thu tholest for thi gult, herre yef thu navest gult, alre hest yef thu tholest for thi god-dede. "Nai!" seith sum ameaset thing, "yef ich hefde gult ther-to, nalde ich neaver meanen." Art tu, thet swa seist, ut of the-seolven? Is the leovere to beon Judase feolahe then Jesu Cristes fere? Ba weren ahonget — ah Judas for his gult. Jesu withute gult for

1295 his muchele godlec wes ahon o rode. Hwetheres fere wult tu beon? With hwether wult tu tholien? Of this is th'ruppe i-writen muchel, hu he is thi file the misseith other misdeth the. "Lime" is the Frensch of "file." Nis hit or acurset, the i-wurtheth swartre ant ruhre se hit is i-filet mare, ant rusteth the swithere thet me hit scureth hearde? Gold, seolver, stel, irn — al is or. Gold ant seolver cleansith ham of hare

1300 dros i the fur: yef thu gederest dros th'rin, thet is ayein cunde. The chaliz the wes

her so through His grace. **1289–90 Salve of wreaththe . . . hehe heovene,** The remedy for wrath, I said, is patience (or, long-suffering). That has three stairs (or, steps): high and higher and highest of all and nearest (lit., next) to high heaven. **1290–91 Heh is the steire . . . for thi god-dede,** The stair is high if you suffer for your offense, higher if you do not have offense (or, guilt), highest of all if you suffer for your good deed. **1291–92 "Nai! . . . neaver meanen,"** "No!" says some confused thing (i.e., creature), "if I had guilt for it (lit., thereto) I would not ever complain." **1293 ut of the-seolven,** out of yourself (i.e., out of your wits). **1293–94 Is the leovere . . . Cristes fere?** Is [it] preferable to you to be Judas' comrade (or, accomplice? — see *feolahe* in glossary) rather than Jesus Christ's companion? **1294–95 Ba weren ahonget . . . ahon o rode,** Both were hanged, but Judas for his offense (or, crime). Jesus, without offense, was hung up on a Cross for His great goodness. **1295 Hwetheres fere,** Whose companion (or, the companion of which of these two). **1295–97 With hwether . . . misdeth the,** With which of these two do you want to suffer? Concerning this, much is written above, how he who slanders or wrongs you is a file (see 4.75–78). **1297–99 Nis hit or acurset . . . scureth hearde?** Is it not an accursed ore (i.e., execrable metal) which becomes darker and rougher the more it is filed, and rusts the quicker (or, more severely) because one polishes (lit., scours) it hard? **1299 irn,** iron; **ham,** themselves; **hare,** their. **1300 fur,** fire; **yef thu gederest . . . ayein cunde,** if you gather (or, accumulate) dross in it (lit., therein), that is against nature. **1300–03 The chaliz the wes ther-in i-mealt . . . his wruhte honden?** The chalice (or, drinking cup) which was melted in it (i.e., the fire) and vigorously boiled and [which was] afterwards by so many a [hammer] blow and polishing (or, working) so very beautifully made into

ther-in i-mealt ant strongliche i-weallet, ant seoththen thurh se moni dunt ant frotunge to Godes nep se swithe feire afeitet — walde he, yef he cuthe speoken, awearien his cleansing fur, ant his wruhte honden? **Argentum reprobum vocate eos.**

1305   Al this world is Godes smith to smeothien his i-corene. Wult tu thet Godd nabbe na fur in his smiththe, ne bealies ne homeres? Fur is scheome ant pine; thine bealies beoth the the misseggeth; thine homeres, the the hearmith. Thench of this essample: Hwen dei of riht is i-set, ne deth he scheome the deme, the a this half the i-sette dei breketh the triws ant wreketh him o the other on him-seolven?

1310   **Augustinus: Quid gloriatur impius, si de ipso flagellum fatiat Pater meus?** Ant hwa nat thet Domes-dei nis the dei i-set to don riht alle men? Hald the triws the hwiles, hwet woh se me deth the: [the richtwise deme haveth i-set t*e* dei to loki richt bitwenen ow.] Ne do thu nawt him scheome, forhohie wrake of his dom, ant neomen to thin ahne. Twa thinges beoth thet Godd haveth edhalden to him-seolven:

1315   thet beoth wurthschipe ant wrake, as Hali Writ witneth: **Gloriam meam alteri non dabo. Item: Michi vindictam. Ego retribuam.** Hwa-se eaver on him-seolf

God's drinking cup — would he (i.e., the cup), if he could speak, curse his (or, its) cleansing fire and the hands of his maker? **1303–04** *Argentum reprobum vocate eos*, "Call them rejected (or, false) silver" (Jeremiah 6:30). **1305 smith**, [black]smith; **to smeothien his i-corene**, to forge (lit., to smith) His chosen [ones]. **1305–07 Wult tu thet Godd . . . the the hearmith**, Do you wish that God [should] have no fire in His smithy, nor bellows or hammers? Fire is shame and punishment; your bellows are [those] who slander you; your hammers, [those] who harm you. **1308–09 Hwen dei of riht is i-set . . . on him-seolven?** When a day is set for judgment, does not he do the judge an insult who breaks the truce on this side of (i.e., before) the set day and avenges himself on the other by himself (or, perhaps, on his own authority)? **1310** *Augustinus: Quid gloriatur impius . . . Pater meus?* Augustine: "Why does the evil [man] rejoice proudly if my Father makes a scourge of him?" (Augustine, *Expositions in the Psalms*, commentary for *Psalm* 36:17, 61:6 [*PL* 36.738]). **1311–13 Ant hwa nat . . . bitwenen ow**, And who does not know that Doomsday is the day set to do justice to all men? Keep the truce until that time, whatever insult they do to you: the righteous judge has set the day to see justice between you. **1313–14 Ne do thu nawt him scheome . . . thin ahne**, Do not do him (i.e., the judge) an insult, despise (or, think little of) the vengeance of his judgment, and take on your own [vengeance]. **1314 Twa thinges beoth**, There are two things; **edhalden**, reserved. **1315–16** *Gloriam meam . . . Ego retribuam*, "I will give my glory to no other" (Isaiah 42:8). Again: "Vengeance is mine. I will repay" (Romans 12:19, Hebrews 10:30, based on Deuteronomy 32:35).

taketh owther of theos twa, he robbeth Godd ant reaveth. Deale! Art tu se wrath with mon other with wummon thet tu wult, for-te wreoke the, reavin Godd mid strengthe?

1320 Accidies salve is gastelich gleadschipe ant frovre of gleadful hope thurh redunge, thurh hali thoht, other of monnes muthe. Ofte, leove sustren, ye schulen uri leasse, for-te reden mare. Redunge is god bone. Redunge teacheth hu ant hwet me bidde, ant beode biyet hit efter. Amidde the redunge, hwen the heorte liketh, kimeth up a devotiun thet is wurth monie benen. For-thi seith Sein Jerome, **Jeronimus: Sem-**

1325 **per in manu tua sacra sit lectio; tenenti tibi librum sompnus subripiat, et cadentem faciem pagina sancta suscipiat.** "Hali redunge beo eaver i thine honden. Slep ga up-o the as thu lokest th'ron, ant te hali pagne i-kepe thi fallinde neb" — swa thu schalt reden yeornliche ant longe. Euch thing, thah, me mei overdon: best is eaver mete.

1330 Ayeines yisceunge ich walde thet othre schuneden, as ye doth, gederunge. To muche freolec cundleth hire ofte. Freo i-heortet ye schule beon. Ancre of other freolec haveth i-beon other-hwiles to freo of hire-seolven.

1317 owther, either; **reaveth**, steals [from him]. **1317–19 Deale! . . . mid strengthe?** What! Are you so angry with man or with woman that you want, in order to avenge yourself, to steal [from] God with strength (i.e., violence)? **1320–21 Accidies salve . . . monnes muthe**, The remedy of sloth is spiritual gladness and the comfort of glad hope through reading, through holy thought (i.e., meditation), or from man's mouth. **1321–23 Ofte, leove sustren . . . biyet hit efter**, Often, dear sisters, you should pray less in order to read more. Reading is [in itself] good prayer. Reading teaches how and what one should pray for, and prayer acquires it afterwards. **1323–24 Amidde the redunge . . . wurth monie benen**, In the middle of reading, when the heart is pleased, a devotion (or, reverence) comes up which is worth many prayers. **1324–26 *Jeronimus: Semper in manu tua . . . pagina sancta suscipiat***, Jerome: "Let there always be holy reading in your hand; may sleep steal upon you holding a book, and may holy pages receive your nodding (lit., falling) face" (Jerome, *Letters* 22 [*PL* 22.411]). **1327 Slep ga up-o the**, "Let sleep go (i.e., come) upon you." **1327–29 ant te hali pagne . . . eaver mete**, "and let the holy page receive your falling face" — thus, you must read eagerly and long. Each thing, though, one can overdo (i.e., can be overdone): moderation is always best. **1330 Ayeines yisceunge . . . gederunge**, Against covetousness I would that others, as you do, avoided saving (lit., gathering). **1330–32 To muche freolec . . . of hire-seolven**, Too much generosity often kindles (or, breeds — see *cundleth* in glossary) her (i.e., covetousness). You should be generously hearted, [but an] anchoress, with another [kind of] generosity, has sometimes been too generous with herself.

Galnesse kimeth of yivernesse ant of flesches eise, for *as* Sein Gregoire seith, "Mete ant drunch over riht temeth threo teames: lihte wordes, lihte werkes, ant

1335 leccheries lustes." Ure Laverd beo i-thonket, the haveth of yivernesse i-healet ow mid alle! Ah galnesse ne bith neaver allunge cleane acwenct of flesches fondunge. Ah thet understondeth wel, thet threo degrez beoth th'rin as Seint Beornard witneth. The forme is cogitatiun. The other is affectiun. The thridde is cunsence. Cogitatiuns beoth fleonninde thohtes the ne leasteth nawt, ant teo, as Sein Beornard seith, ne

1340 hurteth nawt te sawle. Ah thah ha bispottith hire with hare blake speckes swa thet nis ha nawt wurthe thet Jesu, hire leofmon, thet is al feier, bicluppe hire ne cusse hire ear ha beo i-wesschen. Swuch fulthe, as hit kimeth lihtliche, lihtliche geath awei with **Venies**, with **Confiteor**, with alle god-deden. Affectiun is hwen the thoht geath in-ward, ant delit kimeth up, ant te lust waxeth. Thenne, as wes spot

1345 ear up-o the hwite hude, ther waxeth wunde ant deopeth in toward te sawle efter thet te lust geath ant te delit th'rin forthre. Ant forthre thenne is neod to yeiyen,

1333–35 Galnesse . . . leccheries lustes, Lechery comes from gluttony and from enjoyment of the flesh, for as St. Gregory says, "Food and drink wrongly (lit., beyond [what is] right) give birth to three broods: frivolous words, frivolous deeds, and lechery's desire" (Gregory, *Pastoral Care* 3.19 [PL 77.82]). **1335–36 Ure Laverd beo i-thonket . . . of flesches fondunge,** Our Lord be thanked, who has healed you of gluttony entirely! But lechery is not ever completely (lit., entirely purely) quenched (i.e., eliminated) from the temptation of the flesh. **1337 understondeth,** understand (imper.); **thet threo degrez beoth th'rin,** that there are three stages (lit., steps) in it (lit., therein). **1338 forme,** first; **cogitatiun,** cogitation (i.e., thinking about it); **other,** second; **affectiun,** emotion; **cunsence,** consent. **1339 fleonninde,** fleeting (lit., flying); **teo,** they (*teo* = reduced form of *theo* after preceding -*t*). **1340–42 Ah thah ha bispottith hire . . . ha beo i-wesschen,** But nevertheless they (i.e., cogitations) stain (lit., bespot) her (i.e., the soul) with their black specks so (or, to such an extent) that she is not worthy that Jesus, her lover, who is completely fair (or, beautiful), should embrace her or kiss her before she be washed. **1342–43 Swuch fulthe . . . alle god-deden,** Such filth (or, vileness), since it comes lightly (or, easily), [it] goes away easily with pardons (or, kneeling — see glossary), with "I confess" (i.e., confession), with all good deeds. **1343 Affectiun,** Feeling (or, emotion). **1344 te lust waxeth,** and desire grows (lit., the desire). **1344–46 Thenne, as wes spot . . . delit th'rin forthre,** Then [where there] was a spot before on the white hood, there grows a wound and (i.e., which) goes deep in towards the soul after desire, and delight in it (lit., therein) goes further. **1346–47 Ant forthre . . . ich am i-wundet,** And then there is further need to cry out, "Heal me, Lord!" (Psalm 6:3,

Sana me, Domine! "A, Laverd, heal me! for ich am i-wundet." **Ruben, primogenitus meus, ne crescas!** "Ruben, thu reade thoht, thu blodi delit, ne waxe thu neaver!" Cunsense, thet is skiles yettunge, hwen the delit i the lust is i-gan se

1350 overforth thet ter nere nan withseggunge yef ther were eise to fulle the dede. This is hwen the heorte draheth to hire unlust, as thing the were amainet, ant feth on as to winkin, to leote the feond i-wurthen, ant leith hire-seolf dune-ward, buheth him as he bit, ant yeieth, "Cravant! Cravant!" ase softe swohninde. Thenne is he kene, the wes ear curre. Thenne leapeth he to, the stod ear feorren to, ant bit deathes bite

1355 o Godes deore spuse — i-wiss deathes bite, for his teth beoth attrie as of a wed dogge. Davith i the Sawter cleopeth hine dogge: **Erue a framea, Deus, animam meam et de manu canis unicam meam**.

For-thi, mi leove suster, sone se thu eaver underyetest thet tes dogge of helle cume snakerinde with his blodi flehen of stinkinde thohtes, ne li thu nawt stille,

1360 ne ne site nowther to lokin hwet he wule don, ne hu feor he wule gan, ne sei thu

Jeremiah 17:14). "Ah, Lord, heal me! for I am wounded." **1347–48** *Ruben, primogenitus meus, ne crescas!* "Ruben, my firstborn, do not grow!" (condensed from Genesis 49:3–4). **1348–49** **"Ruben, thu reade thoht ... neaver!"** "Ruben, you red thought, you bloody delight, may you never grow!" **1349–50 Cunsense, thet is skiles yettunge ... to fulle the dede**, Consent, which is the reason's permission, when the delight in the desire has gone so over-far that there (*ter* = reduced form of *ther*) would be no refusing if there were opportunity (or, leisure) to fulfill the deed. **1350–53 This is hwen the heorte ... ase softe swohninde**, This (i.e., consent) is when the heart, like a thing which was maimed (or, severely wounded), draws evil desire to herself and begins to shut [her] eyes, to let the fiend be (i.e., to stop fighting against him), and lays herself down, submits to him as he asks (*bit* = reduced form of *biddeth*) and cries, "I give up! I give up!" as if swooning (i.e., fainting) compliantly. **1353–54 Thenne is he kene ... ear curre**, Then he is ferocious who before was a [mere] cur (or, a harmless, growling dog — see *cur(re)* in glossary). **1354–56 Thenne leapeth he to ... a wed dogge**, Then he leaps near who before stood far off, and bites (*bit* = reduced form of *biteth*) the bite of death on God's dear spouse — certainly the bite of death, for his teeth are [as] venomous as [those] of a mad (or, rabid) dog. **1356 cleopeth hine dogge**, calls him a dog (*hine* = old accusative of *he*). **1356–57** *Erue a framea ... unicam meam*, "God, deliver my spirit from the sword and my one and only [spirit] from the clutches (lit., hand) of the dog" (Psalm 21:21). **1358–61 sone se thu eaver underyetest ... ne sei thu nawt slepinde**, as soon as you ever perceive that this dog of hell (*tes* = reduced form of *thes*) comes sneaking with his bloody flies (perhaps, fleas) of stinking thoughts, do not lie still or sit either to see what he will do, or how far he will go, or do not say, sleeping (i.e.,

nawt slepinde, "Ame, dogge! Ga her ut! Hwet wult tu nu her inne?" This tolleth him in-ward. Ah nim anan the rode-steaf mid nempnunge i thi muth, mid te mearke i thin hond, mid thoht i thin heorte, ant hat him ut heterliche, the fule cur-dogge, ant lithere to him lutherliche mid te hali rode-steaf stronge bac-duntes — thet is,

1365 rung up, sture the, hald up ehnen on heh ant honden toward heovene. Gred efter sucurs: **Deus, in adjutorium meum intende. Domine, ad adjuvandum. Veni Creator spiritus. Exurgat Deus et dissipentur inimici ejus. Deus, in nomine tuo salvum me fac. Domine, quid multiplicati sunt. Ad te, Domine, levavi animam meam. Ad te levavi oculos meos. Levavi oculos meos in montes.** Yef

1370 the ne kimeth sone help, gred luddre with hat heorte: **Usquequo, Domine, oblivisceris me in finem? Usquequo averteris faciem tuam a me?** — ant swa al the Salm over, **Pater noster**, **Credo**, **Ave Maria**, with halsinde bonen o thin ahne ledene. Smit smeortliche adun the cneon to ther eorthe, ant breid up the rode-

sleepily). **1361 "Ame, dogge! . . . nu her inne?"** "Hey, dog! Get out of here! What are you doing in here? (lit., go out of here! What do you want in here?)" **1361–65 This tolleth him . . . honden toward heovene**, This attracts him inside. But (i.e., instead) take straightaway the Rood-staff with the naming [of it] in your mouth (i.e., speak the name of the Cross), with the sign (lit., mark) in your hand, with thought in your heart, and order him out sternly, the foul cur-dog, and let loose on him viciously strong back-blows (i.e., blows to the back) with the holy Rood-staff — that is, get up, stir yourself, hold up [your] eyes on high and [hold your] hands towards heaven. **1365–66 Gred efter sucurs**, Cry out for help. **1366 Deus, in adjutorium . . . adjuvandum**, "God, come to my aid. Lord, [rush] to help [me]" (Psalm 69). **1366–67 Veni Creator spiritus**, "Come, Creator Spirit" (hymn). **1367 Exurgat Deus . . . inimici ejus**, "God rises up and His enemies scatter" (Psalm 67). **1367–68 Deus, in nomine tuo salvum me fac**, "Lord, in Your name save me" (Psalm 53). **1368 Domine, quid multiplicati sunt**, "Lord, how they are multiplied [who rise up against me]" (Psalm 3). **1368–69 Ad te, Domine, levavi animam meam**, "To You, Lord, I have lifted up my spirit" (Psalm 24). **1369 Ad te levavi oculos meos**, "To You I have lifted up my eyes" (Psalm 122); **Levavi oculos meos in montes**, "I have lifted up my eyes to the mountains" (Psalm 120). **1369–70 Yef the ne kimeth . . . hat heorte**, If help does not come soon to you, cry out louder with a hot (or, ardent) heart. **1370–71 Usquequo, Domine . . . faciem tuam a me?** "How long, Lord, will You forget me utterly? How long will You turn Your face away from me?" (Psalm 12). **1371–72 al the Salm over**, the whole Psalm (i.e., Psalm 12) through. **1372–73 with halsinde bonen . . . ahne ledene**, with pleading prayers in your own language. **1373–75 Smit smeortliche . . . eadi rode-taken**, Smite (i.e., drop) your knees down sharply to the ground and seize (or, brandish) the Rood-staff (i.e.,

steaf, ant sweng him o fowr half ayein helle dogge — thet nis nawt elles bute
1375   blesce the al abuten with the eadi rode-taken. Spite him amid te beard to hoker ant
to scarne, the flikereth swa with the ant fiketh dogge fahenunge. Hwen he for se
liht wurth — for the licunge of a lust ane hwile stucche — chapeth thi sawle —
Godes deore bune, thet he bohte mid his blod ant mid his deore-wurthe death o
the deore rode — aa bihald hire wurth thet he paide for hire, ant dem th'refter hire
1380   pris ant beo on hire the deorre. Ne sule thu neaver se etheliche his fa, ant thin
either, his deore-wurthe spuse thet costnede him se deore. Makie deofles hore of
hire is reowthe over reowthe. To unwreast mid alle ha is, the mei with toheoven
up hire threo fingres overcumen hire fa, ant ne luste for slawthe. Hef for-thi with
treowe ant hardi bileave up thine threo fingres, ant with the hali rode-steaf, thet
1385   him is lathest cuggel, lei o the dogge-deovel, nempne ofte Jesu, cleope his passiunes
help, halse bi his pine, bi his deore-wurthe blod, bi his death o rode, flih to his
wunden. Muchel he luvede us the lette makien swucche thurles in him for-te huden

Crucifix) and swing it in the four directions (i.e., north, south, east, and west) against hell's dog —
that is not anything else but bless yourself all about (i.e., in every direction) with the holy sign of the
Cross. **1375–76 Spite him amid te beard . . . dogge fahenunge,** Spit in his beard (dat. of possession) for contempt and for scorn [of him], who so toys with you and flatters [you] with a dog's
fawning. **1376–80 Hwen he for se liht wurth . . . ant beo on hire the deorre,** When he for so
cheap a price — for the pleasure of desire [which lasts only] for a short time — bargains for your
soul — God's dear (or, expensive) purchase which He bought with His blood and with His precious
death on the dear Cross — always consider (imper.) the price that He paid for her (i.e., your soul)
and judge according to that (lit., thereafter) her price and be (i.e., think) on her the dearer. **1380–82
Ne sule thu . . . reowthe over reowthe,** Do not ever sell so readily to His foe, and yours as well, His
precious spouse who cost Him so dearly. To make the devil's whore of her is the pity of pities (lit.,
pity beyond pity). **1382–83 To unwreast mid alle . . . for slawthe,** She is entirely too wicked who
can with [the mere] lifting up of three of her fingers overcome her foe and does not want to because
of laziness (lit., sloth). **1383–87 Hef for-thi with treowe . . . flih to his wunden,** Lift up (imper.)
therefore with true and courageous faith your three fingers, and with the holy Rood-staff (i.e.,
Crucifix), which is the most loathsome (or, hateful) cudgel to him (i.e., the devil), lay on the dog-
devil, name (i.e., call out the name of) Jesus often, cry out [for the] help of His sufferings, plead by
His pain, by His precious blood, by His death on the Cross, flee to His wounds. **1387–88 Muchel
he luvede us . . . ne beoth ha al opene?** He loved us much who let such holes be made (*makien* =
passive inf.) in Himself in order to hide us in. Creep (or, crawl) into them in your thought — are

us in. Creop in ham with thi thoht — ne beoth ha al opene? Ant with his deore-wurthe blod biblodge thin heorte. **Ingredere in petram, abscondere fossa humo.**

1390 "Ga into the stan," seith the prophete, "ant hud te i the dolven eorthe" — thet is, i the wunden of ure Laverdes flesch, the wes as i-dolven with the dulle neiles, as he i the Sawter longe vore seide: **Foderunt manus meas et pedes meos** — thet is, "ha dulven me bathe the vet ant te honden." Ne seide he nawt "thurleden," for efter this leattre — as ure meistres seggeth — swa weren the neiles dulle, thet ha

1395 dulven his flesch ant tobreken the ban mare then thurleden, to pinin him sarre. He him-seolf cleopeth the toward teose wunden: **Columba mea, in foraminibus petre, in cavernis macerie.** "Mi culvre," he seith, "cum, hud te i mine limen thurles, i the hole of mi side." Muche luve he cudde to his leove culvre, thet he swuch hudles makede. Loke nu thet tu, the he cleopeth culvre, habbe culvre cunde —

1400 thet is, withute galle — ant cum to him baldeliche, ant make scheld of his passiun, ant sei with Jeremie: **Dabis scutum cordis laborem tuum** — thet is, "thu schalt

they not completely open? **1388–89 Ant with his deore-wurthe blod . . . thin heorte,** And with His precious blood bloody your heart (or, make your heart all bloody). **1389** *Ingredere in petram . . . humo,* "Enter into the rock, hide in the hollowed-out earth" (Isaiah 2:10). **1390 "ant hud te i the dolven eorthe,"** "and hide yourself in the dug (i.e., hollowed-out) earth." **1391–92 the wes as i-dolven . . . vore seide,** who was as [if] dug into (or, gouged) with the dull (or, blunt) nails, as he said long before in the Psalter. **1392** *Foderunt manus meas et pedes meos,* "They [have] dug (or, gouged) my hands and my feet" (Psalm 21:17). **1393 "ha dulven me bathe the vet ant te honden,"** "they gouged both my feet and the hands" (*me* = dat. of possession). **1393–95 Ne seide he nawt "thurleden," . . . to pinin him sarre,** He did not say "pierced," for according to this letter (i.e., literal meaning) — as our teachers say — the nails were so dull that they dug into his flesh and broke up the bone more than pierced [it], to torture him the more sorely (or, painfully). **1396 cleopeth the toward teose wunden,** calls you towards these wounds (*teose* = reduced form of *theose* after preceding -*d*). **1396–97** *Columba mea . . . in cavernis macerie,* "My dove, in the openings of the rock, in the hollowed-out places of the garden wall [show your face to me]" (Song of Songs 2:14). **1397 culvre,** dove. **1397–98 "cum, hud te . . . mi side,"** "come, hide yourself in the piercings (or, openings) of my limbs, in the hollow (or, cave) in my side." **1398–1401 Muche luve he cudde . . . with Jeremie,** He revealed great love to his beloved dove that he made such a hiding place. See now that you, whom He calls "dove," have a dove's nature — that is, [be] without bitterness — and come to Him boldly, and make a shield of His Passion, and say with Jeremiah. **1401** *Dabis scutum cordis laborem tuum,* "You will give [them] the shield of the heart, your suffering" (adapted from Lamentations 3:65).

yeove me, Laverd, heorte scheld ayein the feond, thi swincfule pine." Thet hit swincful wes, he schawde hit witerliche inoh, tha he sweatte, ase blodes swat, dropen the runnen to ther eorthe. Me schal halden scheld i feht up abuven heaved, 1405 other ayein the breoste, nawt ne drahen hit bihinden. Al riht swa, yef thu wult thet te rode-scheld ant Godes stronge passiun falsi the deofles wepnen, ne dragse thu hit nawt efter the, ah hef hit on heh buve thin heorte heaved i thine breoste ehnen. Hald hit up toyein the feond, schaw hit him witerliche. The sihthe th'rof ane bringeth him o fluhte, for ba him scheometh ther-with ant griseth ut of witte efter 1410 the ilke time thet ure Laverd ther-with brohte swa to grunde his cointe coverschipe, ant his prude strengthe. Yef thu thurh thi yemeles werest te earst wacliche, ant yevest to the feond in-yong to forth i the frumthe, swa thet tu ne mahe nawt reculin him ayein-ward, for thi muchele unstrengthe, ah art i-broht se over-forth thet tu ne maht this scheld halden o thin heorte, ne wrenchen hire ther-under frommard te 1415 deofles earowen, nim the aleast forth Sein Beneites salve, thah ne thearf hit nawt beon se over-strong as his wes, the, of the walewunge, rug, ant side, ant wombe,

1402 heorte scheld, the heart's shield; **thi swincfule pine**, your toilsome pain. **1402–04 Thet hit swincful wes . . . to ther eorthe**, That it was toilsome, he showed it plainly enough when he sweat, as if sweat of blood, drops which ran to the ground (*ther* = declined def. art.). **1404–05 Me schal halden . . . hit bihinden**, In a fight, one must hold a shield up above the head or against the chest, not drag it behind. **1405–07 Al riht swa . . . i thine breoste ehnen**, Just so, if you desire that the Rood-shield and God's powerful Passion [should] falsify (or, cause to fail) the devil's weapons, do not drag hit after (or, behind) you, but lift it on high above your heart's head in your breast's eyes. **1408 toyein**, against, opposite; **schaw hit him witerliche**, show it to him clearly. **1408–11 The sihthe th'rof ane . . . his prude strengthe**, The sight of it alone brings (i.e., puts) him to flight, for [he] both shames himself (i.e., is ashamed) with it and shudders (or, is frightened) out of his mind after the same time (i.e., ever since) our Lord with it (lit., therewith) brought his clever treachery and his proud strength to ground (i.e., overthrew). **1411– 17 Yef thu thurh thi yemeles . . . o gure-blode**, If you through your carelessness [at] first defend yourself weakly and give to the fiend an entrance too far advanced in the beginning, so that you cannot beat him back again, because of your great lack of strength, but are brought so exceedingly far (lit., over far) that you cannot hold this shield on your heart, nor pull her (i.e., the heart) under it (i.e., the shield) away from the devil's arrows, [— if all this is the case, then] take out for yourself at last St. Benedict's remedy, though it need not be so excessively severe as his was, whose back and side and belly in the rolling [in thorns] ran completely in gory blood (lit.,

ron al o gure-blode. Ah lanhure yef the-seolf hwen the strongest stont a smeort discepline, ant drif as he dude thet swete licunge into smeortunge. Yef thu thus ne dest nawt, [ah] slepinde werest te, he wule gan to feor on the, ear thu least wene, ant bringe the of ful thoht into delit of ful lust, ant swa he bringeth the al over to skiles yettunge, thet is deadlich sunne withuten the dede, ant swa is ec the delit of thet stinkinde lust withute grant of the werc, se longe hit mei leasten. **Nunquam enim judicanda est delectatio esse morosa, dum ratio reluctatur et negat assensum.** "Thenne hit least to longe, hwen the skile ne fehteth na lengre ther-toyeines." For-thi, leove suster, as ure Laverd leareth, totred te neddre heaved — thet is, the biginnung of his fondunge. **Beatus qui tenebit et allidet parvulos suos ad petram.** "Eadi is," seith Davith, "the withhalt hire on earst, ant tobreketh [to] the stan the earste *sturunges, hwen* the flesch ariseth, hwil thet ha beoth yunge. Ure Laverd is i-cleopet stan for his treownesse. **Et in Canticis: Capite nobis**

1420

1425

in gore-blood) from rolling [in thorns]. **1417–18 Ah lanhure . . . into smeortunge,** But at least give yourself a sharp discipline when to you it stands most severe (i.e., when things are going their worst), and as he (i.e., St. Benedict) did, drive that sweet pleasure into a smarting (i.e., a smarting pain). **1418–22 Yef thu thus ne dest nawt . . . se longe hit mei leasten,** If you do not do thus, but defend yourself sleeping (i.e., sluggishly), he will go too far with you, before you least expect [it], and bring you from foul thought into pleasure of foul desire, and so he [will] bring you completely over to the consent of the reason, which is mortal sin without the deed, and so also is the delight in that stinking desire [a sin], [even] without granting of the act, as long as it may last. **1422–24 *Nunquam enim . . . negat assensum*,** "But (lit., For) pleasure is never to be judged as wayward, as long as the reason struggles against [it] and denies [its] consent" (source unidentified). **1424–26 Thenne hit least to longe . . . of his fondunge,** "It lasts then too long (*least* = reduced form of *leasteth*), when the reason does not fight any longer against it (lit., there-against)." Therefore, dear sister, as our Lord teaches, stomp on (lit., tread down) the serpent's head — that is, the beginning of his temptation. **1426–27 *Beatus qui tenebit . . . ad petram*,** "Blessed [is the person] who shall seize and dash her (i.e., the Queen of Babylon's) young on a rock" (adapted from Psalm 136:9). **1427 Eadi,** Blessed. **1427–28 the withhalt hire on earst . . . ha beoth yunge,** who restrains herself at first (*withhalt* = reduced form of *withhaldeth*), and shatters on the rock the first stirrings, when the flesh (i.e., carnal desire) arises, while they are young. **1429 Ure Laverd . . . his treownesse,** Our Lord is called a rock for His loyalty. **1429–30 *Et in Canticis . . . que destruunt vineas*,** And in the Song of Songs: "Catch for us the young foxes which pull down our vines" (adapted from Song of

1430 **vulpes parvulas que destruunt vineas.** "Nim ant keche us, leofmon, anan the
yunge foxes" — he seith, ure Laverd — "the strueth the win-yardes" — thet beoth
the earste procunges the strueth ure sawlen, the mot muche tilunge to, to beoren
win-berien. The deovel is beore cunnes, ant haveth asse cunde, for he is bihinden
strong, ant i the heaved feble, swa is beore ant asse — thet is, i the frumthe. Ne
1435 yef thu him neaver in-yong, ah tep him o the sculle, for he is earh as beore th'ron,
ant hihe him swa theone-ward, ant askur him se scheomeliche sone se thu
underyetest him, thet him grise with the stude thet tu wunest inne. For he is thinge
prudest, ant him is scheome lathest.

Alswa, leove suster, sone se thu eaver felest thet tin heorte with luve falle to
1440 eani thing eawt over mete, anan-rihtes beo war of the neddre atter, ant totred his
heaved. The cwene seide ful soth, the with a strea ontende alle hire wanes, thet
muchel kimeth of lutel. Ant nim nu yeme hu hit feareth: the sperke the wint up ne
bringeth nawt anan-riht the hus al o leie, ah lith ant kecheth mare fur, ant fostreth

Songs 2:15). **1430 leofmon**, beloved (or, sweetheart). **1431 "the strueth the win-yardes,"**
"which destroy the vineyards." **1432–33 the earste procunges . . . win-berien**, the first
proddings which destroy our souls, which need (lit., must [have]) much tending to, to bear
wineberries (i.e., grapes). **1433–34 The deovel is . . . i the frumthe**, The devil is of a bear's
character and has an ass' nature, for he is strong behind and feeble in the head, as is a bear and
an ass — that is, in the beginning. **1434–37 Ne yef thu him neaver in-yong . . . wunest inne**,
Do not ever give him an entrance, but rap him on the skull, for he is cowardly like a bear in that
part (lit., thereon), and hurry (imper.) him thus away from there, and chase him shamefully
(i.e., in a humiliating way) as soon as you perceive him, so that he may be afraid of (reflex.) the
place which you live in. **1438 him is scheome lathest**, and shame is [a thing] most loathsome
to him. **1439–41 Alswa, leove suster . . . totred his heaved**, Likewise, dear sister, as soon as
you ever feel that your heart (*tin* = reduced form of *thin* after preceding *-t*) falls in love (lit.,
with love) with any thing at all over [what is] appropriate, immediately be wary of the serpent's
venom and trample on his head. **1441–42 The cwene seide ful soth . . . of lutel**, The old
woman (lit., quean) who ignited her house with a straw said the absolute truth, that much
comes from little. **1442–45 Ant nim nu yeme . . . ear me least wene**, And now pay (lit., take)
attention how it happens (lit., fares): the spark which flies up (*wint* = reduced form of *windeth*)
does not immediately bring the house completely in flame, but lies and catches more fire and
nurses [it] further, and grows from less to more, until the entire house blazes up before one

forth, ant waxeth from leasse to mare, athet al the hus bleasie forth ear me least
1445   wene. Ant te deovel blaweth to, from thet hit earst cundleth ant mutleth his beali-
bleas eaver as hit waxeth. Understond tis bi the-seolf: a sihthe thet tu sist, other
anlepi word thet tu misherest — yef hit eawt stureth the, cwench hit with teares
weater ant mid Jesu Cristes blod, hwil hit nis bute a sperke, ear then hit waxe ant
ontende the swa, thet tu hit ne mahe cwenchen. For swa hit timeth ofte, ant hit is
1450   riht Godes dom, thet hwa ne deth hwen ha mei, ne schal ha hwen ha walde.
Ecclesiasticus: A scintilla una augetur ignis.

Moni cunnes fondunge is i this feorthe dale, misliche frovren ant moni-falde
salven. Ure Laverd yeove ow grace thet ha ow moten helpen. Of alle the othre
thenne is schrift the biheveste. Of hit schal beon the fifte dale as ich bihet th'ruppe.
1455   Ant neometh yeme hu euch-an dale falleth into other, as ich thear seide.

least expects. **1445–46 Ant te deovel blaweth . . . as hit waxeth**, And the devil blows towards
[it], from [the time] that it (i.e., the fire) first kindles, and [he] increases his bellow-blasts
continually as it grows. **1446–49 Understond tis . . . ne mahe cwenchen**, Understand this by
yourself: a sight that you see, or a single word that you mishear — if it stir (or, move) you at all,
quench it with the water of tears and with Jesus Christ's blood while it is [nothing] but a spark,
before it may grow and ignite you so (i.e., to such an extent) that you cannot quench it. **1449–
50 For swa hit timeth ofte . . . hwen ha walde**, For thus it happens often, and it is God's just
judgment, that who[ever does] not act when she can, may not when she would. **1451
*Ecclesiasticus . . . augetur ignis***, Ecclesiasticus: "From a single spark grows a fire"
(Ecclesiasticus 11:34). **1452–53 Moni cunnes fondunge . . . moten helpen**, Many kinds of
temptation are (lit., temptation of many a kind is) in this fourth part, various comforts and
manifold (or, a variety of) remedies. May our Lord give you grace [so] that they may help you.
1453–55 Of alle the othre . . . as ich thear seide, Of all the others (i.e., other remedies) then,
is confession the most beneficial. The fifth part will be about this as I promised above (lit.,
there-up). And take (i.e., pay) attention how each single part falls into (i.e., leads to) the other,
as I said there (see Pref.130–51).

Part Five

Confession

Twa thinges neome*th* yeme of schrift i the biginnunge: the earre, of hwuch mihte hit beo; the other, hwuch hit schule beon. This beoth nu as twa limen ant either is todealet, the earre o sixe, the other o sixtene stucchen. Nu is this of the earre:

5   Schrift haveth monie mihtes, ah nulle ich of alle seggen bute sixe: threo ayein the deovel ant threo on us-seolven. Schrift schent then deovel, hacketh of his heaved, ant todreaveth his ferd. Schrift wescheth us of alle ure fulthen, yelt us alle ure luren, maketh us Godes children. Ei*th*er haveth hise threo. Pruvie we nu alle. The earste threo beoth alle i-schawde i Judithe deden. Judith — thet is, schrift, as wes yare i-seid

10 — sloh Oloferne — thet is, the feond of helle. Turn th'ruppe ther we speken of

---

1–4 Twa thinges neometh yeme . . . the earre, Pay (lit., Take) attention to two things concerning confession in the beginning: the first (lit., earlier), concerning what power it has; the second, what kind it ought to be. These are now like two limbs (or, branches) and each one is divided, the former into six, the second into sixteen parts. Now this [following section] is concerning the former. **5 mihtes,** powers. **5–6 ah nulle ich . . . on us-seolven,** but I do not want to say any but six: three against the devil and three in ourselves. **6–7 schent then deovel . . . ure luren,** destroys (or, shames) the devil (*then* = declined def. art.; *schent* = reduced form of *schendeth*), hacks off his head, and scatters his army. Confession washes us of all our stains (lit., filths), repays us all our losses. **8–10 Either haveth hise threo . . . sloh Oloferne,** each [of the two subdivisions] has its three. We will now prove (i.e., illustrate) all [of them]. The first three are all shown in Judith's deeds. Judith — that is, confession, as was said before — slew Holofernes. **10–11 Turn th'ruppe . . . i-evenet to ancre,** Turn [to the section] above (lit., there-up) where we spoke about the kinds of birds which are compared to anchoresses

fuhelene cunde the beoth i-evenet to ancre. Ha hackede of his heaved ant seoththen com ant schawde hit to the burh-preostes. Thenne is the feond i-schend, hwen me schaweth alle hise cweadschipes: his heaved is i-hacket of, ant he i-slein i the mon, sone se he eaver is riht sari for his sunnen ant haveth schrift on heorte. Ah he nis nawt

15 the yet i-schend hwil his heaved is i-hulet, as dude on earst Judith, ear hit beo i-schawet — thet is, ear the muth i schrift do ut the heaved sunne — nawt te sunne ane, ah al the biginnunge th'rof, ant te fore-ridles the brohten in the sunne — thet is, the deofles heaved, thet me schal totreoden anan, as ich ear seide. Thenne fli[t]h his ferd anan as dude Olofernes: his wiheles ant his wrenches thet he us with asaileth, doth ham

20 alle o fluhte ant te burh is arud thet ha hefden biset. Thet is to seggen, the sunfule is delifret. Judas Macabeu — hwa stod ayein him? Alswa i **Judicum,** thet folc tha hit easkede efter Josues death, hwa schulde beon hare dug ant leaden ham i ferde: **Quis erit dux noster?** Ure Laverd ham ondswerede: Judas schal gan bivoren ow, ant ich chulle ower faes lond biteachen in his honden. Lokith nu ful yeorne hwet tis beo to

(see Part Three). **11–14 Ha hackede of his heaved . . . schrift on heorte,** She hacked off his head and afterwards came and showed it to the town-priests. Then is the fiend destroyed (or, shamed) when one reveals all his wicked deeds [in confession]: his head is hacked off, and he [is] slain in the man (or, person), as soon as he (i.e., the penitent) is ever very sorry for his sins and has confession in [his] heart. **14–18 Ah he nis nawt . . . totreoden anan,** But he is not yet destroyed as long as his [severed] head is concealed, as Judith did (i.e., concealed it) at first, before it is shown — that is, before the mouth in confession puts (or, casts) out the deadly sin — [and] not only the sin, but all the beginning of it (lit., thereof), and the forerunners which led into the sin — that is, the devil's head, which one must trample at once. **18– 20 Thenne fli[t]h his ferd . . . ha hefden biset,** Then his army flees at once as did Holofernes' [army]: his wiles and his tricks that he assails us with put themselves to flight (i.e., flee), and the town which they had besieged is rescued. **20 seggen,** say. **21 delifret,** delivered, set free. **21–22 Judas Macabeu . . . i ferde,** Judas Maccabeus — who stood against him? (see 1 Maccabees 4 ff.). Likewise, in Judges, the people when after Joshua's death they (lit., it) asked for [someone] who would be their leader and lead them in an army (perhaps, into battle). **22–23 *Quis erit dux noster?*** "Who will be our leader?" (adapted from Judges 1:1). **23 ham ondswerede,** answered them; **Judas,** Judah. **23–25 ant ich chulle ower faes . . . as Judith,** and I will deliver your foes' land into his hands. Look now very carefully what this is to say (i.e., what this means): Joshua means "health" (or, salvation) and Judah [means]

25 seggen: Josue spealeth "heale," ant Judas "schrift" — as Judith. Thenne is Josue dead hwen sawle heale is forloren thurh eani deadlich sunne. The sunfule seolf is the unwihtes lond, the is ure deadliche fa, ah this lond ure Laverd bihat to biteachen i Judase honden, for-hwon thet he ga bivoren. Schrift, lo, is gunfanuner, ant bereth the banere bivoren al Godes ferd — thet beoth gode theawes. Schrift reaveth the feond his lond — thet is,

30 the sunfule mon — ant al todriveth Chanaan the feondes ferd of helle. Judas hit dude licomliche, ant schrift thet hit bitacneth deth gasteliche thet ilke. This beoth nuthe threo thing [thet schrift deth o the deovel. The other threo thing] thet hit deth us-seolven — thet beoth theose her-efter.

Schrift wescheth us of alle ure fulthen, for swa hit is i-writen: **Omnia in confessione**

35 **lavantur. Glosa super: Confitebimur tibi, Deus, confitebimur.** Ant thet wes bitacnet tha Judith wesch hire ant despulede hire of widewene schrud, thet wes merke of sorhe — ant sorhe nis bute of sunne: **Lavit corpus suum et exuit se vestimentis sue viduitatis.** Schrift eft al thet god thet we hefden forloren thurh heaved-sunne bringeth al ayein ant yelt al togederes. **Joel: Reddam vobis annos quos comedit locusta,**

"confession" — as does Judith. **25–28 Thenne is Josue dead . . . he ga bivoren**, Then is Joshua dead when the soul's health is lost through any deadly sin. The sinful self is the devil's country (lit., the monster's land), who is our mortal enemy, but our Lord promised to deliver this land into Judah's hands, for which reason he goes before (i.e., is the leader). **28 gunfanuner**, the standard-bearer. **29 ferd . . . gode theawes**, army — which is (lit., are) good virtues. **29–31 Schrift reaveth . . . gasteliche thet ilke**, Confession steals from the devil his land — that is, the sinful man — and scatters (or, destroys) Canaan, the fiend of hell's army. Judah did it physically, and confession which it symbolizes does the same [thing] spiritually. **31–33 This beoth nuthe . . . her-efter**, These are now the three things which it (i.e., confession) does to the devil. The second (or, other) three things which it does to ourselves — that are these [which follow] hereafter. **34 wescheth**, washes. **34–35 Omnia in confessione lavantur . . . confitebimur**, "All things are washed [away] in confession." The gloss concerning [this verse]: "We shall confess to You, God, we shall confess" (Psalm 74:2; with gloss from Peter Lombard, *On the Psalms* [*PL* 191.698]). **35–37 Ant thet wes . . . bute of sunne**, And that was symbolized when Judith washed herself and stripped herself of [her] widow's clothing, which was a mark of sorrow — and there is no sorrow except from sin. **37–38 Lavit corpus suum . . . viduitatis**, "She washed her body and stripped herself of the clothes of her widowhood" (Judith 10:3). **38–39 Schrift eft al . . . togederes**, Confession brings back all the good that we had lost through deadly sin (lit., head, capital sin) completely again and restores [it] all together. **39–40 Joel: Reddam vobis . . . et erugo**, Joel: "I

310

40   **brucus, rubigo et erugo.** This wes bitacnet thurh thet *Jud*ith schrudde hire mid hali-
dahne weden ant feahede hire ute-with as schrift deth us in-with: with alle the feire
urnemenz the blisse bitacnith. Ant ure Laverd seith thurh Zacharie, **Erunt sicut fuerant
antequam projeceram eos.** Thet is, "schrift schal makie the mon al-swuch as he wes
bivore thet he sunegede," ase cleane ant ase feier, ant ase riche of alle god the limpeth
45   to sawle. The thridde thing is thet schrift deth us-seolven the frut of thes othre twa ant
endeth ham bathe — thet is, maketh us Godes children. This is bitacnet ther-bi thet
Judas i Genesy biwon of Jacob Benjamin. Benjamin seith ase muchel ase "sune of riht
half." Judas — thet is "schrift," alswa as is Judith, for ba ha spealieth an on Ebreische
ledene. Thes gasteliche Judas biyet of Jacob, his feader — thet is, ure Laverd — to
50   beon his riht-hondes sune, ant bruken buten ende the eritage of heovene. Nu we habbeth
i-seid of hwuch mihte schrift is, hwucc efficaces hit haveth, ant i-nempnet sixe. Loki
we nu yeornliche hwuch schrift schule beon, the beo of swuch strengthe. Ant for-te
schawin hit bet, deale we nu this lim o sixtene stucchen.

shall restore to you the years which the locust, the brucus (i.e., a kind of wingless locust),
mildew and the caterpillar have consumed" (Joel 2:25). **40–42 This wes bitacnet . . . the blisse
bitacnith,** This was symbolized by the fact that (lit., through that) Judith clothed herself with
holiday clothes and adorned herself externally as confession does (i.e., adorns) us internally:
with all the fair ornaments which joy symbolizes. **42 thurh Zacharie,** through Zacharias. **42–
43 *Erunt sicut . . . projeceram eos,*** "They will be as they were before I drove them away"
(adapted from Zacharias 10:6). **43–45 schal makie . . . to sawle,** will make the man just as he
was before he sinned, as pure and as fair, and as rich with all good which belongs to the soul.
45–46 The thridde thing . . . ham bathe, The third thing that confession does for ourselves
(i.e., us) is the fruit of these other two and completes (lit., ends) them both. **46–49 This is
bitacnet . . . on Ebreische ledene,** That is symbolized by the fact that (lit., thereby) Judah in
Genesis won Benjamin from Jacob (see Genesis 43). Benjamin says (or, means) as much as
"son from the right side." Judah — that is (or, means), "confession," as Judith is also, for
they both mean one [thing] in the Hebrew language. **49–50 Thes gasteliche Judas . . . of
heovene,** This spiritual Judah got from Jacob, his father — that is, our Lord — [the right] to
be his right-hand son, and enjoy without end the inheritance of heaven. **50–53 Nu we
habbeth i-seid . . . o sixtene stucchen,** Now we have said (i.e., spoken) of what kind of power
confession is (or, consists), which efficacies (or, powers) it has, and [have] named six. Let us
look now carefully at what confession must be, which is of (i.e., has) such strength. And in
order to show (or, reveal) it better, let us divide this limb into sixteen parts.

Schrift schal beo wreiful, bitter mid sorhe, i-hal, naket, ofte i-maket, hihful, eadmod,
55 scheomeful, [dredful], hopeful, wis, soth, ant willes, ahne, ant stude-vest, bithoht
bivore longe. Her beoth nu as thah hit weren sixtene stuchen the beoth i-feiet to schrift,
ant we [schulen] of euch-an sum word sunderliche seggen:

Schrift schal beo wreiful. Mon schal wreien him i schrift, nawt werien him, ne
seggen, "Ich hit dude thurh othre. Ich wes i-ned ther-to. The feond hit makede me
60 don." Thus Eve ant Adam wereden ham — Adam thurh Eve, ant Eve thurh the neddre.
The feond ne mei neden na-mon to na sunne, thah he eggi ther-to, ah ful wel he let of
hwen ei seith thet he makede him to sunegin, as thah he hefde strengthe the naveth nan
mid alle bute of us-seolven. Ah me ah to seggen, "Min ahne unwrestlec hit dude, ant
willes ant waldes ich beah to the deovel." Yef thu witest ei thing thi sunne bute the-
65 seolven, thu ne schrivest te nawt; yef thu seist thet tin unstrengthe ne mahte nawt elles,
thu wrenchest thi sunne up-o Godd the makede the swuch, thet tu, bi thin tale, withstonde
ne mahtest. Wreie we thenne us-seolven, for, lo, hwet Seinte Pawel seith, **Si nos ipsos**

54–57 Schrift schal beo wreiful . . . sunderliche seggen, Confession must be accusing, bitter with sorrow, whole (or, complete), naked, made often, quick, humble, full of shame, fearful, hopeful, wise, true, and voluntary, one's own, and steadfast, thought out long before. Here now are as it were sixteen parts which are connected to (or, associated with) confession, and we [will] say some words about each one separately. **58–60 Mon schal wreien him . . . makede me don,** One must accuse himself in confession, not protect himself, or say "I did it because of another [person]. I was forced to it. The fiend made me do it." **60 wereden ham,** protected themselves; **neddre,** serpent. **61–63 The feond ne mei neden . . . bute of us-seolven,** The fiend cannot force anyone into any sin, though he incite (lit., egg on) to it, but he thinks very well of [it] (i.e., the devil is very pleased) when anyone says that he made him sin, as though he (i.e., the devil) had power, who has none at all except from ourselves. **63–64 Ah me ah to seggen . . . the deovel,** But one ought to say, "My own wickedness did it, and willing and ready I bowed to (i.e., obeyed) the devil." **64–67 Yef thu witest ei thing . . . withstonde ne mahtest,** If you blame your sin on anything but yourself, you do not confess yourself; if you say that your lack of strength could not do anything else, you turn your sin upon God who made you thus, so that you, by your claim, cannot withstand (or, persevere). **67 Wreie we thenne us-seolven,** [Let us] accuse ourselves then. **67–68 *Si nos ipsos . . . judicaremur,*** "If we would judge ourselves, we would then not be judged" (1 Corinthians

dijudicaremus, non utique judicaremur — thet is, "yef we wreieth wel her ant demeth her us-seolven, we schule beo cwite of wreiunge ed te muchele dome," thear

70 as Seint Anselme seith theos dredfule wordes: **Hinc erunt accusancia peccata; illinc, ter[r]ens justicia; supra, iratus judex; subtra, patens horridum chaos inferni; intus, urens consciencia; foris, ardens mundus. Peccator sic deprehensus in quam partem se premet?** "O the an half o Domes[-dei] schulen ure swarte sunnen strongliche bicleopien us of ure sawle morthre. O the other half stont rihtwisnesse,

75 thet na reowthe nis with, dredful ant grislich, ant grureful to bihalden; buven us, the eorre deme" — for ase softe as he is her, ase heard he bith ther; ase milde as he is nu, ase sturne thenne; lomb her, liun ther, as the prophete witneth: **leo rugiet: quis non timebit?** "The liun schal greden," he seith. "Hwa ne mei beon offearet?" Her we cleopieth him lomb as ofte as we singeth **Agnus Dei, qui tollis peccata mundi.** — Nu

80 as ich seide, schule we seon buven us the ilke eorre deme thet is ec witnesse ant wat alle ure gultes; bineothen us, yeoniende the wide throte of helle; in-with us-seolven, ure ahne conscience — thet is, ure in-wit — forculiende hire-seolven, with the fur of

11:31). **68–69 ant demeth her us-seolven**, and judge ourselves here. **69 cwite of wreiunge . . . dome**, free of accusation at the great Judgment. **69–70 thear as**, where (i.e., concerning which place). **70–73 *Hinc erunt accusancia peccata . . . se premet?*** "On this side there will be accusing sins; on that side, terrifying justice; above, an angry judge; below, the horrible gaping netherworld of hell; inside, a burning conscience; outside, a blazing world. In what part of the earth can a sinner thus caught conceal himself?" (Anselm, *Meditation* 1 [*PL* 158.709 ff.]). **73–77 O the an half . . . the prophete witneth**, "On the one side on Judgment Day our black sins will violently accuse us of the murder of our soul. On the other side stands righteousness, with (or, in) which there is no pity, dreadful and grisly, and horrific to behold; above us, the angry judge" — for as soft as he is here, he [will] be hard there; as mild as he is now, [he will be] stern then; a lamb here, a lion there, as the prophet bears witness. **77–78 *leo rugiet: quis non timebit?*** "the lion will roar: who will not be afraid?" (Amos 3:8). **78 greden**, wail (i.e., roar); **offearet**, afraid. **79 cleopieth him lomb**, call Him lamb. **79 *Agnus Dei . . . mundi*,** "Lamb of God, [You] who take away the sins of the world" (from the Mass). **80 seon**, see. **80–83 the ilke eorre deme . . . to the skiwes**, the same angry judge who is also a witness and knows all our crimes; beneath us, yawning, [is] the wide throat of hell; inside ourselves, our own conscience — that is, our interior knowledge — charring itself, with the fire of sin; outside of us, all

sunne; withuten us, al the world leitinde o swart lei up into the skiwes. The sari sunfule
thus biset — hu schal him stonde thenne? To hwuch of thes fowre mei he him biwenden?

85 Nis ther buten heren thet hearde word, thet wa word, thet grisliche word, grureful
over alle: **Ite, maledicti, in ignem eternum qui paratus est diabolo et angelis ejus.**
"Gath ye, aweariede, ut of min eh-sihthe, into thet eche fur thet wes i-greithet to the
feond ant to his engles. Ye forbuhe monne dom thet ich demde mon to — thet wes to
libben i swinc, ant i sar on eorthe — ant ye schulen nu, for-thi, habben deofles dom,

90 bearne with him echeliche i the fur of helle." With this, schulen the forlorene warpen a
swuch yur, thet heovene ant eorthe mahen ba grimliche agrisen. For-thi, Seint Austin
leofliche us leareth, **Ascendat homo tribunal mentis sue, si illud cogitat, quod
oportet eum exiberi ante tribunal Christi. Assit accusatrix cogitatio; testis,
consciencia; carnifex, timor** — thet is, thenche mon o Domes-dei ant deme her him-

95 seolven thus o thisse wise. Skile sitte as domes-mon up-o the dom-seotel. Cume th'refter

the world blazing in dark flame up into the skies. **83–84 The sari sunfule thus biset . . .
thenne?** The sad sinful [person] thus surrounded — how will it go with him then (lit., how
will [it] stand for him then)? **84–86 To hwuch of thes fowre . . . grureful over alle,** To which
of these four (i.e., justice, conscience, the judge, or hell) can he turn to (reflex.)? There is
[nothing for him] but to hear the hard word (i.e., speech, sentence), the woeful word, the
grisly word, gruesome above all [other words]. **86 *Ite, maledicti . . . angelis ejus*,** "Go,
cursed ones, into eternal fire which is prepared for the devil and his angels" (based on
Matthew 25:41). **87 aweariede,** cursed ones. **87–88 ut of min eh-sihthe . . . to his engles,** out
of my eye-sight into the eternal fire that was prepared for the fiend and for his angels. **88–
90 Ye forbuhe monne dom . . . fur of helle,** You avoided men's punishment (or, judgment)
that I condemned man to — which was to live in travail and in pain on earth — and you will
now, for that reason, have the devil's judgment (i.e., punishment), [you will] burn with him
eternally in the fire of hell. **90–91 schulen the forlorene . . . agrisen,** the lost [souls] will
throw up such a howl that heaven and earth will (lit., may) both shudder grimly (or, horribly). **92 leofliche us leareth,** teaches us lovingly. **92–94 *Ascendat homo . . . carnifex,
timor*,** "A man ought to arise before the tribunal of his own mind, if he considers this, that
he must produce himself before the tribunal of Christ. The accuser Thought should be
present; [as well as] the witness, Conscience; [and] the hangman, Fear" (Augustine, *Sermons* 351.4.7 [*PL* 38.1429]). **94–95 thenche mon . . . thisse wise,** let a man think about
Doomsday and judge himself here thus in this way. **95–96 Skile sitte as domes-mon . . .
misliche sunnen,** Reason should sit as a judge upon the judgment seat. After that let his

forth his thohtes munegunge, wreie him ant bicleopie him of misliche sunnen: "Beal
ami, this thu dudest thear! ant tis thear! ant tis thear! ant o thisse wise." His in-wit beo
i-cnawes th'rof ant beore witnesse: "Soth hit is! Soth hit is! This, ant muchele mare."
Cume forth th'refter fearlac thurh the deme heast the heterliche hate: "Tac, bind him
100   hete-veste, for he is deathes wurthe. Bind him swa euch lim thet he haveth with i-
suneget thet he ne mahe with ham sunegi na mare." Fearlac haveth i-bunden him,
hwen he ne dear for fearlac sturie toward sunne. Yet nis nawt the deme — thet is, skile
— i-paiet, thah he beo i-bunden ant halde him with sunne, bute yef he abugge the sunne
thet he wrahte, ant cleopeth forth pine ant sorhe, ant hat thet sorhe thersche in-with the
105   heorte with sar bireowsunge, swa, thet hire suhie, ant pini the flesch ute-with mi*d*
feasten ant with othre fleschliche sares. Hwa-se o thisse wise, bivoren the muchele
dom, demeth her him-seolven, eadi he is ant seli. For as the prophete seith, **Non judicabit
Deus bis in id ipsum.** "Nule nawt ure Laverd thet a mon for a thing beo twien i-
demet." Hit nis nawt i Godes curt as i the schire, ther-as the thet nicketh wel mei beon

thought's memory come forward, accuse him and arraign him of various sins. **96–97 Beal
ami . . . dudest thear!** [My] fine fellow, you did this there! **97–98 His in-wit beo i-cnawes
. . . Soth hit is!** Let his conscience admit to this (lit., thereto) and bear witness: "It is true!"
99–101 Cume forth th'refter . . . na mare, Let fear come forward after that by the judge's
command who sternly commands: "Take [him], bind him tightly, for he is worthy of death.
Bind each of his limbs (lit., to him each limb) that he has sinned with in such a way (lit., so)
that he cannot sin with them anymore." **101–06 Fearlac haveth i-bunden him . . . othre
fleschliche sares,** Fear has bound him, when he does not dare stir towards sin for fear. Yet
the judge — that is, reason — is not pleased, though he be bound and [though he] keep
himself from sin, unless he atone for the sin that he committed (lit., wrought), and [Reason]
calls forth pain and sorrow, and commands that sorrow thrash the heart within with painful
contrition (or, remorse), in such a way, that it may afflict her (i.e., the heart), and torture the
flesh on the outside with fasts and with other physical pains. **106–07 Hwa-se o thisse wise
. . . seli,** Whosoever judges himself here in this way, before the great Judgment, he is happy
and blessed. **107–08** *Non judicabit Deus bis in id ipsum,* "God will not judge twice in the
same [case]" (a loose paraphrase of Nahum 1:9). **108–09 "Nule nawt . . . twien i-demet,"**
"Our Lord does not wish that a man be judged twice for one [and the same] thing." **109–10
i Godes curt . . . is i-cnawen,** in God's court as [it is] in the shire [court], where [he] who
denies well (i.e., makes effective denials) may be saved, and the person may be convicted

315

110 i-borhen, ant te ful the is i-cnawen. Bivore Godd is other-weis. **Si tu accusas, Deus excusat, et vice versa.** "Yef thu wreiest te her, Godd wule werie the thear," ant skerin mid alle ed te nearewe dome, for-hwon thet tu deme the as ich i-taht habbe.

Schrift schal beo bitter, ayein thet te sunne thuhte sum-chearre swete. Judith, the spealeth "schrift," as ich ofte habbe i-seid, wes Merarihtes dohter. Ant Judas — thet is
115 ec "schrift" — wivede o Thamar. "Merariht" ant "Thamar" ba ha spealieth an on Ebreische ledene. Neometh nu yeorne yeme of the bitacnunge; ich hit segge scheortliche. Bitter sar ant schrift — thet an mot cumen of the other, as Judith dude of Merariht. Ant ba beon somet i-feiet, as Judas ant Thamar. For nowther withuten other nis noht wurth, other lutel — Phares ant Zaram, ne temith ha neavre. Judas streonede of Thamar
120 Phares ant Zaram. **Phares divisio, Zaram oriens interpretatur**, the gasteliche bitacnith tweamunge from sunne, ant i the heorte th'refter arisinde grace. Fowr thinges, yef mon thencheth thet heaved sunne dude him, mahen makien him to sorhin ant bittrin his heorte. Lo, this the forme: yef a mon hefde i-losed in a time of the dei his feader ant his

who confesses. **110–11 Si tu accusas . . . vice versa**, "If you accuse, God will excuse, and vice versa." **111–12 Yef thu wreiest te her . . . i-taht habbe**, "If you accuse yourself here, God will defend you there," and clear [you] completely at the strict Judgment, provided that you judge yourself as I have taught. **113 ayein thet . . . swete**, in compensation for [the fact] that the sin seemed sometimes sweet. **113–14 the spealeth "schrift,"** who/which means "confession." **114 Merarihtes**, Merari's (Judith 8:1); **Judas**, Judah (Genesis 38:12 ff.). **115 ec**, also; **wivede o Thamar**, had sex with Thamar (Genesis 38:12 ff.). **115–16 ba ha spealieth . . . ledene**, they both mean one [and the same thing] in the Hebrew language (i.e., "bitterness"). **116–17 Neometh nu yeorne yeme . . . dude of Merariht**, Pay (lit., Take) now careful attention to the significance (or, meaning); I [will] say it briefly. Bitter pain and confession — the one must come from the other, as Judith did from Merari. **117–20 Ant ba beon somet i-feiet . . . ant Zaram**, And both are joined together, as Judah and Thamar [were]. For neither is worth anything without the other, or [very] little — [without the other] they never give birth to Phares and Zara. [On the contrary,] Judah begot Phares and Zara *on* Thamar (i.e., both together brought them forth). **120 Phares divisio . . . interpretatur**, "Phares is interpreted as 'division,' Zara as 'rising.'" **120–21 the gasteliche bitacnith . . . arisinde grace**, which symbolizes spiritually separation from sin and after that, rising grace in the heart. **121–23 Fowr thinges . . . bittrin his heorte**, Four things, if one considers that deadly sin caused them, may make him sorry for and embitter his heart. **123–26 Lo, this the forme . . . as he eathe mahte?** Look, this [is] the first: if a man had lost in the space of a day his father

moder, his sustren ant his brethren, ant al his cun, ant alle his freond thet he eaver
125 hefde weren astorven ferliche, nalde he over alle men sorhful beon ant sari, as he eathe
mahte? Godd wat, he mei beon muche deale sorhfulre thet haveth with deadlich sunne
gasteliche i-slein Godd in-with his sawle, nawt ane forloren the swete feader of heovene,
ant Seinte Marie, his deore-wurthe moder, other Hali Chirche — hwen he of hire
naveth ne leasse ne mare — ant te engles of heovene, ant alle hali halhen, the weren him
130 ear for freond, for brethren ant for sustren. As to him ha beoth deade. As onont him is,
he haveth i-slein ham alle, ant haveth, thear as ha livieth aa, leaththe of ham alle, as
Jeremie witneth: **Omnes amici ejus spreverunt eam; facti sunt ei inimici** — thet
is, "al thet him luvede yeieth spi him on, ant heatieth him alle." Yet mare, his children
sone se he sunegede deadliche deiden alle clane — thet beoth his gode werkes, the
135 beoth forloren alle. Yet upon al this ilke he is him-seolf biwrixlet ant bicumen of Godes
child the deofles bearn of helle, eatelich to seonne as Godd seolf i the Godspel seith:
Vos ex patre diabolo estis. Thenche euch of his estat, thet he is other wes in, ant he

and his mother, his sisters and his brothers, and all his kin, and all his friends that he ever
had were killed suddenly, would he not be sorrowful and sad above (i.e., more than) all
[other] men, as he easily (i.e., understandably) might? **126–30 Godd wat . . . ha beoth deade**,
God knows, he may be a great deal more sorrowful who has spiritually slain God within his
soul with mortal sin, [and has] lost not only the sweet Father of heaven and St. Mary, his
precious Mother, or Holy Church — when he [will] not have [anything] from her either less
nor more — and the angels of heaven, and all holy saints who were to him formerly as
friends, as brothers and as sisters. With respect to him they are dead. **130–31 As onont him
is . . . of ham alle**, As far as it concerns him (lit., as [it] is concerning him), he has slain them
all, and has the hatred of them all, where they live forever. **132 *Omnes amici . . . ei inimici***,
"All her friends have despised her; they have been made her enemies" (Lamentations 1:2).
133 "al thet him luvede . . . him alle," "everyone who loved him cry shame on him (i.e.,
shout at him in disgust)." **133–34 Yet mare . . . alle clane**, Still more, as soon as he sinned
mortally his children died quite completely (i.e., outright). **135–36 Yet upon al this ilke . . .
of helle**, Yet in all this same thing (or, matter) he himself is transformed from [being] God's
child and [has] become the devil's child of hell (or, the devil of hell's child). **136 eatelich,**
hideous. **137 *Vos ex patre diabolo estis***, "You are of [your] father the devil" (John 8:44).
137–38 Thenche euch of his estat . . . siken sare, Let each one think of his condition,
that he is or was in, and he may see the reason why (lit., wherefore) he ought to sigh

317

mei seon hwer-vore he ah to siken sare. For-thi seith Jeremie, **Luctum unigeniti fac tibi, planctum amarum.** "Make bitter man, as wif deth for hire child the nefde bute

140   him ane" ant sith hit bivoren hire fearliche asteorven. Nu the other thet ich bihet: A mon the were i-demet for a luther morthre to beo forbearnd al cwic, other scheomeliche ahonget — hu walde his heorte stonden? Me thu, unseli sunful, tha thu thurh deadlich sunne murthredest Godes spuse — thet is, thi sawle — tha thu were i-demet for-te beon ahonget o bearninde weari-tre i the eche lei of helle.

145   Ther thu makedest foreward mid te deovel of thi death, ant seidest in Ysaie with the forlorene, **Pepigimus cum morte fedus, et cum inferno inivimus pactum** — thet is, "we habbeth treowthe i-pliht death, foreward i-feast mid helle." For this is the feondes chaffere: he yeove the sunne, ant tu him thi sawle, ant ti bodi mid al, to weane ant to wontreathe, world abuten ende. Nu the thridde scheortliche: Thench — a mon

150   the hefde al the world o walde, ant hefde for his cweadschipe forloren al on a stunde — hu he walde murnin ant sari i-wurthen. Thenne ahest tu to beon hundret sithe

heavily. **138–39** *Luctum unigeniti . . . amarum,* "Make for yourself a lamentation [as] for an only child, a bitter complaint" (Jeremiah 6:26). **139 man,** moan, complaint. **139–40 as wif deth . . . asteorven,** as a woman does for her only child (lit., for her child which she had none but him alone) and sees it killed suddenly before her. **140 other,** second [example]; **bihet,** promised. **140–42 A mon the were i-demet . . . heorte stonden?** [Take the case of] a man who was condemned for a wicked murder to be burned alive, or shamefully hanged — how would his heart stand (i.e., what would be the condition of his heart)? **142–44 Me thu . . . lei of helle,** But you, wretched sinful [person], when you murdered by mortal sin God's spouse — that is, your soul — then you were condemned to be hanged on the burning gallows (lit., accursed-tree) in the eternal flame of hell. **145–46 Ther thu makedest . . . with the forlorene,** There you made a pact with the devil for your death, and said with the lost in Isaiah. **146** *Pepigimus cum morte fedus . . . pactum,* "We have concluded an agreement with death, and have entered into a pact with hell" (based on Isaiah 28:15). **147 habbeth treowthe . . . mid helle,** have plighted [our] troth to death, established an agreement with hell. **147–49 For this is the feondes chaffere . . . abuten ende,** For this is the fiend's bargain: he would give you sin, and you [would give] him your soul, and your body as well, in woe and misery, world without end (i.e., forever). **149 scheortliche,** briefly. **149–51 Thench — a mon the hefde . . . sari i-wurthen,** Consider [the following case] — a man who had all the world in [his] power, and had lost everything in a moment because of his wickedness — how he would mourn and be sorry (i.e., full of regrets). **151–54 Thenne ahest tu . . . ant heovene,**

318

sarure, the thurh an heaved sunne forlure the riche of heovene — forlure ure Laverd, thet is hundret sithen, ye, thusent thusent sithen betere then is al the world, eorthe ba ant heovene. **Que enim conventio Christi ad Belial.** Nu yet the feorthe: yef the king

155   hefde bitaht his deore sune to his an cniht to lokin, ant untheode leadde forth this child in his warde swa thet tet child seolf weorrede upon his feader with thet untheode, nalde the cniht beo sari ant scheomien ful sare? We beoth alle Godes sunen — the kinges of heovene — the haveth bitaht ure euch an engel i warde. Sari is he on his wise hwen untheode leat us forth — hwen we ure gode feader wreatheth with sunne. Beo we sari

160   thet we eaver schulen wreathen swuch feader ant sweamen swuch wardein, the wit ant wereth us eaver with the unseli gastes, for elles uvele us stode. Ah we schuhteth him awei hwen we doth deadlich sunne, ant heo leapeth thenne to, sone se he us firseth. Halde we him neh us with smeal of gode werkes, ant us in his warde. Wat Crist, ure euch-an to se g[ent]il wardein bereth to lutel menske, ant kunnen him to lutel

Then ought you to be a hundred times sorrier, [you] who by means of a mortal sin may lose the kingdom of heaven — may lose our Lord, who is a hundred times, indeed, a thousand thousand times better than is all the world, both earth and heaven. **154** *Que enim conventio Christi ad Belial*, "What [sort of] agreement [can there be] between Christ and Belial" (2 Corinthians 6:15). **154–57 yef the king hefde bitaht . . . scheomien ful sare?** if the king had entrusted his dear son to his one knight (i.e., to one of his knights) to look after, and a foreign people led forth this child in his ward (or, guardianship) so that the child himself warred (or, made war) upon his father with the foreign people, would not this knight be sorry and be very painfully ashamed? **157 sunen**, sons; **kinges**, (a possessive form, parallel to *Godes*). **158–59 the haveth bitaht . . . with sunne**, who has entrusted each of us in guardianship to an angel. He is sorry (or, regretful) in His [own] way when a foreign people leads us away (*leat* = reduced form of *leadeth*) — when we anger our good Father with sin. **159–61 Beo we sari . . . uvele us stode**, Let us be sorry that we ever must anger such a father and give pain to such a guardian, who defends (*wit* = reduced form of *witeth*) and protects us always against unhappy (i.e., cursed) spirits, for otherwise it would stand evil to us (i.e., it would go badly for us). **161–63 Ah we schuhteth him awei . . . us firseth**, But we drive Him away when we do [any] deadly sin, and they (i.e., the wicked spirits) leap then up, as soon as He withdraws [from] us. **163–65 Halde we him neh us . . . of his servise**, May we (i.e., let us) keep Him near us with the aroma of good works and [keep] ourselves in his guardianship. Christ knows, each one of us (*ure* = genitive form of *we*) bears too little honor to so gentle a guardian, and are not grateful enough (lit., know too little thanks to him) for His

165 thonc of his servise. Theos ant monie reisuns beoth hwi mon mei beo bitterliche sari
for his sunnen ant wepen ful sare. Ant wel is him the swa mei, for wop is sawle heale.
Ure Laverd deth toward us as me deth to uvel deattur: nimeth leasse then we ahen him,
ant is thah wel i-paiet. We ahen him blod for blod, ant ure blod, thah, ayein his blod thet
he schedde for us were ful unefne change. Ah wast tu hu me yeddeth: "me nimeth ed
170 uvel dettur aten for hweate," ant ure Laverd nimeth ed us teares ayein his blod, ant is
wil-cweme. He weop o the rode, o Lazre, o Jerusalem — for other monne sunnen. Yef
we wepeth for ure ahne, nis na muche wunder. "Wepe we," quoth the hali mon i **Vitas
Patrum**, tha me hefde longe on him i-yeiet efter sarmun. "Leote we," quoth he, "teares
leste ure ahne teares forseothen us in helle."

175   Schrift schal beon i-hal — thet is, i-seid al to a mon, ut of childhade. The povre
widewe, hwen ha wule hire hus cleansin, ha gedereth al the greaste on an heap on alre
earst, ant schuveth hit ut thenne. Th'refter kimeth eft ayein ant heapeth eft togederes
thet wes ear i-leavet ant schuveth hit ut efter. Th'refter o the smeale dust, yef hit

service. **165–66 hwi mon mei beo . . . sawle heale**, why one may be bitterly sorry for his sins
and weep very heavily. And well is him (i.e., opposite of "*woe* is him": he is happy) who may
do so, for weeping is the soul's salvation (or, health). **167–68 me deth . . . i-paiet**, one does
to a bad debtor: [he] takes less than we owe him, and is nevertheless well pleased. **168 ahen
him**, owe Him. **168–69 ayein his blod . . . unefne change**, against (i.e., in compensation for)
His blood that He shed for us would be a completely uneven (or, unfair) exchange. **169–71
Ah wast tu hu . . . ant is wil-cweme**, But you know how they say (lit., one says): "from a bad
debtor one takes oats for wheat" (i.e., you take what you can get), and our Lord takes from
us tears for (or, in compensation for) His blood, and is satisfied. **171–72 He weop o the rode
. . . na muche wunder**, He wept on the Cross, for Lazarus, for Jerusalem — for other men's
sins. If we weep for our own, it is no great wonder. **172–74 "Wepe we . . . in helle,"** "May
we weep (i.e., let us weep)," said the holy man in *The Lives of the [Desert] Fathers*, when
people (lit., one) had long cried out to him for a sermon. "May we shed," he said, "tears lest
(i.e., for fear that) our own tears scald us in hell." **175 i-hal**, whole, complete; **i-seid al . . .
childhade**, said completely to one man (i.e., the confessor), [all sins] from childhood [on].
175–77 The povre widewe . . . ut thenne, The poor widow, when she wants to clean her
house, she gathers all the coarsest (or, largest) things in one pile first of all, and then thrusts
(i.e., sweeps) it out. **177–79 Th'refter kimeth eft . . . al thet other**, After that [she] comes
back again and piles together again what was left before and thrusts it out after [the first].
After that, if it is very dusty (lit., if it dusts very much), she sprinkles water on the small dust

dusteth swithe, ha flasketh weater ant swopeth ut efter al thet other. Alswa schal the

180 schriveth him efter the greate schuven ut the smealre. Yef dust of lihte thohtes windeth
to swithe up, flaski teares on ham, ne schulen ha nawt thenne ablende the heorte
ehnen. Hwa-se heleth ea-wiht, he naveth i-seid na-wiht for-hwon he beo the skerre, a*h*
is i-lich the mon the haveth on him monie deadliche wunden ant schaweth the leche alle
ant let healen, buten an, thet he deieth upon as he schulde on alle. He is ase men in a

185 schip the haveth monie thurles ther the weater threasteth in, ant heo dutteth alle buten
an thurh hwam ha druncnith alle clane. Me teleth of the hali mon the lei on his death-
uvel ant wes lath to seggen a sunne of his childhad, ant his abbat bed him allegate
seggen. Ant he ondswerede thet hit nere na neod, for-thi thet he wes lute child tha he
hit wrahte. O least thah, unneathe thurh the abbates ropunge, thet he hit seide ant deide

190 th'refter sone. Efter his death, com a niht ant schawde him to his abbat i snaw-hwite
schrudes, as the thet was i-borhen, ant seide thet sikerliche, yef he nefde thet ilke thing
thet he dude i childhad i schrift utterliche i-seid, he were i-demet bimong the forlorene.
Alswa of an-other thet wes for neh fordemet for-thi thet he hefde en-chearre i-ned a

and sweeps [it] out after all the other [sweepings]. **179–82 Alswa schal the schriveth him . . . the heorte ehnen**, Likewise must [the person] who confesses himself thrust out the smaller [sins] after the great [ones]. If the dust of light (or, wanton) thoughts flies up too thickly, let her sprinkle tears on them, then they will not blind the heart's eyes. **182–84 Hwa-se heleth ea-wiht . . . schulde on alle**, Whosoever hides anything, he has not said anything for which he is the more blameless, but is like the man who has on him (i.e., on his body) many mortal wounds and shows the physician all [of them] and has [them] healed (passive inf.), except for one, which he dies from as he would have from all. **185–86 the haveth monie thurles . . . alle clane**, which has many holes where the water rushes in, and they plug all but one [hole] through which (lit., whom) they all drowned utterly. **186–88 Me teleth of the hali mon . . . allegate seggen**, One tells (i.e., they tell) of the holy man who lay in his mortal illness and was loath (or, reluctant) to say (i.e., confess) a sin from his childhood, and his abbot begged him to say it nevertheless. **188–90 thet hit nere na neod . . . th'refter sone**, that there was not any need, because he was a little child when he did it. At last though, [it was] with difficulty by the abbot's loud pleading, that he said (or, declared) it and died quickly thereafter (see textual note to line 189). **190–92 com a niht . . . the forlorene**, [he] came one night and revealed himself to his abbot in snow-white garments, like [a person] who was saved, and said that certainly, if he had not completely said (or, declared) in confession that very thing that he did in childhood, he would have been condemned among the lost. **193–94 Alswa of an-other . . .**

195 mon to drinken ant deide th'rof unschriven. Alswa of the leafdi, for-thi thet ha hefde i-leanet to a wake a wummon an of hire weden. Ah hwa-se haveth yeorne i-soht alle the hurnen of his heorte, ne ne con rungi mare ut, yef ther ea-wiht edluteth, hit is, ich hopie, i the schrift i-schuven ut mid tet other, hwen ther ne lith na yemeles, ant he walde fein mare yef he cuthe seggen.

200   Schrift schal beo naket — thet is, naketliche i-maket, nawt bisamplet feire, ne hendeliche i-smaket, ah schulen the wordes beon i-schawet efter the werkes. Thet is tacne of heatunge, thet me tuketh to wundre thing thet me heateth swithe. Yef thu heatest ti sunne, hwi spekest tu menskeliche th'rof? Hwi hudest tu his fulthe? Spec hit scheome schendfulliche, ant tuk hit al to wundre, alswa as thu wel wult schende then schucke. "Sire," ha seith, the wummon, "ich habbe i-haved leofmon," other "ich habbe 205 i-beon," ha seith, "fol of me-seolven." This nis nawt naket schrift. Biclute thu hit nawt. Do awei the totagges. Unwrih the ant sei, "Sire — Godes are! — ich am a ful stod-meare, a stinkinde hore." Yef thi fa a ful nome ant cleope thi sunne fule. Make hit i

th'rof unschriven, Likewise [they tell] of another [man] who was nearly condemned (or, damned) because he had one time forced a man to drink and he died of it unconfessed. **194–98 the leafdi . . . yef he cuthe seggen,** [it was] likewise with the lady because she had loaned one of her garments to a woman for a celebration (lit., wake; see glossary). But whosoever has diligently searched all the corners of his heart, and cannot wring [any] more out, if anything lurks there, it is (i.e., will be), I hope, swept out in confession with the rest, when no negligence lies (i.e., is) there, and he would willingly (lit., fain) say more if he could. **199 schal beo naket,** must be naked. **199–200 naketliche i-maket . . . the werkes,** made nakedly (i.e., completely), not explained away pleasantly, nor graciously adorned, but the words must be shown (i.e., revealed in confession) according to the acts. **200–01 Thet is tacne of heatunge . . . heateth swithe,** It is a token of hatred, that one horribly torments (or, scorns — see *tuk* in glossary) the thing that one hates exceedingly. **201–02 Yef thu heatest . . . his fulthe?** If you hate your sin (*ti* = reduced form of *thi*), why do you speak honorably about it (lit., thereof)? Why do you hide its filth? **202–04 Spec hit scheome schendfulliche . . . then schucke,** Revile it (lit., speak shame to it) with disgrace, and scorn it terribly, just as you [very] well want to disgrace the devil (*then* = inflected def. art.). **204–05 "ich habbe i-haved leofmon . . . me-seolven,"** "I have had a lover," or "I have been," she says, "sinful (or, foolish) with myself." **205 Biclute,** Dress up, prettify (imper.). **206–07 Do awei the totagges . . . stinkinde hore,** Cast off (lit., Put away) the trimmings (or, ornaments). Unmask yourself and say, "Sir — God's grace! — I am a foul stud-mare (or, breeder), a stinking whore." **207–09 Yef thi fa . . .**

schrift steort-naket — thet is, ne hel thu na-wiht of al thet lith ther-abuten, thah to fule me mei seggen. Me ne thearf nawt nempnin thet fule dede bi his ahne fule nome, ne the

210 schendfule limes bi hare ahne nome — inoh is to seggen swa thet te hali schrift-feader witerliche understonde hweat tu wulle meanen. Abute sunne liggeth six thing thet hit hulieth, o Latin "circumstances," on Englisch "totagges" mahe beon i-cleopede: persone, stude, time, manere, tale, cause. Persone the dude the sunne, other with hwam me hit dude, unwreo ant segge, "Sire, ich am a wummon ant schulde bi rihte beo mare

215 scheomeful to habben i-speken as ich spec, other i-don as ich dude, for-thi mi sunne is mare then of a wepmon, for hit bicom me wurse. Ich am "an ancre," "a nunne," "a wif i-weddet," "a meiden," "a wummon thet me lefde se wel," "a wummon the habbe ear i-beon i-bearnd with swuch thing, ant ahte the betere for-te beon i-warnet." Sire, hit wes with swuch mon" — ant nempni thenne — "munek," "preost," "other clearc," ant

220 of thet ordre, "a weddet mon," "a ladles thing," "a wummon as ich am." This is nu of persone. Alswa of the stude, "Sire, thus ich pleide other spec i chirche," "eode o ring

mei seggen, Give your foe a foul name and call your sin foul (*fule* is perhaps an adverb: "insultingly"). Make it stark-naked in confession — that is, do not conceal any bit of all (i.e., anything) which lies near it (lit., thereabout), though one can speak too foully (i.e., obscenely). **209–11 Me ne thearf nawt nempnin ... wulle meanen,** But it is not necessary (lit., it needs not) to name that foul deed by its own foul name, nor the shameful limbs by their own name[s] — it is enough to speak so that the holy confessor may understand clearly what you want to bemoan. **211–13 Abute sunne ... cause,** Six things lie around (i.e., are near to) sin [and] which conceal it, in Latin [these] may be called "circumstances," in English "trimmings" (or, trappings): person, place, time, manner, number [of occasions], cause. **213–16 Persone the dude the sunne ... bicom me wurse,** Uncover (i.e., reveal) the person who did the sin, or with whom one did it, and say, "Sir, I am a woman and should by right be more ashamed (i.e., modest) to have spoken as I spoke, or [to have] done as I did, therefore my sin is greater (lit., more) than [that] of a man, for it became (or, befit) me worse." **217–18 "a wummon thet me lefde ... i-warnet,"** "a woman whom one (i.e., they) trusted so well," "a woman who has (lit., have; first person) before been burned with such a thing, and ought to be the better warned." **219 swuch mon,** such [and such a] man; **nempni,** name [him] (imper.). **219–20 ant of thet ordre ... as ich am,** and of what order, "a wedded man," "an innocent thing," [or] "a woman as I am." **220–24 This is nu of persone ... hali thing,** This is now concerning person (i.e., the discussion of person is now ended). Likewise [speak] about the place, "Sir, I played thus or spoke in church," "went in the ring [dance] in

i chirch-yard," "biheold hit other wreastlunge, ant othre fol gomenes," "spec thus other pleide bivoren worltliche men, bivoren recluse in ancre-hus, ed other thurl then ich schulde, neh hali thing." "Ich custe him ther," "hondlede him i swuch stude, other

225 me-seolven." "I chirche ich thohte thus," "biheold him ed te weovede." Of the time alswa, "Sire, ich wes of swuch ealde thet ich ahte wel to habben wisluker i-wite me." "Sire, ich hit dude in lenten, i feasten dahes, in hali dahes, hwen othre weren ed chirche." "Sire, ich wes sone overcumen, ant is the sunne mare then yef ich hefde i-beon akeast with strengthe ant feole swenges." "Sire, ich wes the biginnunge hwi swuch thing

230 hefde forth-gong, thurh thet ich com i swuch stude ant i swuch time. Ich bithohte me ful wel ear then ich hit eaver dude, hu uvele hit were i-don ant dude hit no-the-leatere." The manere alswa seggen — thet is the feorthe totagge. "Sire, this sunne ich dude thus ant o thisse wise." "Thus ich leornede hit earst." "Thus ich com earst th'rin." "Thus ich dude hit forth-ward o thus feole wisen, thus fulliche, thus scheomeliche." "Thus

235 ich sohte delit, hu ich meast mahte paien mi lustes brune," ant seggen al the wise. Tale is the *fifte* totagge — [hu ofte hit is i-don tellen al: "Sire, ich habbe this thus ofte i-don,

the churchyard," "watched it or wrestling, and other foolish (or, evil) games," "spoke thus or played before (i.e., in the presence of) worldly men, before a recluse in an anchor-house, [or] at another window than I should have, near a holy thing." **224–25 "Ich custe him . . . ed te weovede,"** "I kissed him there," "touched him in such a place, or myself." "In church I thought thus (i.e., such and such)," "watched him at the altar." **226–27 ich wes of swuch ealde . . . ed chirche**, I was of such an age that I ought well to have protected myself more wisely. "Sir, I did in Lent, on feast days, on holy days, when others were at church." **228–30 ant is the sunne mare . . . i swuch time**, and the sin is greater than if I had been knocked down with force and many blows. "Sir, I was the beginning (i.e., instigator) why such a thing went forward (lit., had a forth-going), because I went to such [and such a] place and at such [and such] a time." **230–31 Ich bithohte me . . . no-the-leatere**, I considered [it] (reflex.) very well before I ever did it, [I considered] how evil it would be to do and did it nevertheless. **232–35 The manere . . . al the wise**, Say (or, describe) the manner also — that is, the fourth circumstance (or, trimming — see glossary). "Sir, I did this sin thus and in this way." "I learned it first thusly." "I first came into it (lit., therein) thusly." "Thusly I did it from that time on in thus many ways, thus foully, thus shamefully." "Thusly I sought pleasure, how I might most please the burning of my desire," and say completely the way (or, manner). **235–38 Tale is the fifte totagge . . . neode asketh**, Number [of occurrences] is the fifth circumstance — tell completely how often it is done: "Sir, I have done this thus often, [I

i-wonet for to speoke thus, hercni thullich speche, thenchen hwiche thochtes, foryeme thing ant foryeoten, lachyen, eoten, drinken, lasse other mare thenne neode asketh." "Ich habbe i-beon thus ofte wrath seoththen ich wes i-schriven nest, ant for thulli

240 thing, ant thus longe hit leste, thus ofte i-seid les, thus ofte this ant this." "Ich habbe i-don this to thus feole, ant thus feole sithen." Cause is the seste totagge.] Cause is hwi thu hit dudest, other hulpe othre ther-to, other thurh hwet hit bigon. "Sire, ich hit dude for delit, for uvel luve, for biyete, for fearlac, for flatrunge." "Sire, ich hit dude for uvel, thah ther ne come nan of." "Sire, mi lihte ondswere other mine lihte lates tulden

245 him earst up-o me." "Sire, of this word com other, of this dede wreaththe ant uvele wordes." "Sire, the acheisun is this hwi thet uvel leasteth yet." "Thus wac wes min heorte." Euch, efter thet he is, segge his totagges: mon as limpeth to him, wummon thet hire rineth. For her nabbe ich nan i-seid bute for-te munegin mon other wummon of theo the to ham falleth thurh theo the beoth her i-seide as on urn. Thus of theose six

250 wriheles despoile thi sunne ant make hit naket i thi schrift, as Jeremie leareth: **Effunde**

have been] wont to speak thus, to listen to such talk, to think such kinds of thought, to neglect things and forget [them], laugh, eat, drink, less or more than need requires (lit., asks)." **239–40 "Ich habbe i-beon . . . this ant this,"** "I have thus often been angry since I was last confessed, and for such [and such a] thing, and thus long it lasted, thus often [I have] said a lie, thus often [I have said] this and that." **240–41 "Ich habbe i-don this . . . feole sithen,"** "I have done this (i.e., such and such a thing) to thus many [people], and thus many times." **241 seste totagge**, sixth circumstance. **241–43 Cause is hwi thu hit dudest . . . for flatrunge**, Cause is why you did it, or helped others to it (lit., thereto), or by what [means] it began. "Sir, I did it for pleasure, for evil love, for [personal] gain, for fear, for flattery." **244–47 thah ther ne come nan of . . . min heorte**, even though no [evil] came of [it] there. "Sir, my light (or, wanton) answer or my light expressions (or, behavior) attracted him first to me." "Sir, from this word came another, from this deed [came] wrath and evil words." "Sir, this is the reason why that evil lasts (i.e., persists) still." "My heart was weak thus (i.e., in this way)." **247–49 Euch, efter thet he is . . . as on urn**, [Let] each, according to what he is, say his circumstances, a man as pertains to him, a woman whatever touches her. For here I have not said anything except to remind man or woman of those [circumstances] which fall to (i.e., are applicable to) them by means of those which are mentioned here as if in a gallop (i.e., in passing). **249–50 Thus of theose six . . . leareth**, Thus strip your sin of these six veils (or, cloaks) and make it naked in your confession, as Jeremiah teaches. **250–51 *Effunde***

sicut aquam cor tuum. "Sched ut ase weater thin heorte." Yef eoile schet of a feat, yet ter wule leaven in sum-hwet of the licur; yef milc schet, the heow leaveth. Yef win sched, the smeal leaveth. Ah weater geath al somet ut: alswa sched thin heorte — thet is, al thet uvel thet is i thin heorte. Yef thu ne dest nawt, lo, hu grurefulliche Godd seolf

255   threateth the thurh Naum the prophete: **Ostendam gentibus nuditatem tuam et regnis ignominiam tuam et proitiam super te abhominationes tuas.** "Thu naldest nawt unwreo the to the preost i schrifte, ant ich schal schawin al naket to al folc thi cweadschipe, ant to alle kinedomes thine scheome sunnen, to the kinedom of eorthe, to the kinedom of helle, to the kinedom of heovene, ant trussin al thi schendfulnesse o

260   thin ahne necke, as me deth o the theof the me leat to demen, ant swa with al the schendlac thu schalt trusse ant al torplin into helle." **O**, seith Sein Beornard, **quid confusionis, quid ignominie erit, quando dissipatis foliis et dispersis universa nudabitur turpitudo. Sanies apparebit.** "O," seith Sein Beornard, "hwuch schendlac, ant hwuch sorhe bith ther ed te dome, hwen alle the leaves schule beon towarplet, ant

sicut aquam cor tuum, "Pour out your heart like water" (Lamentations 2:19). **251 Sched,** Pour. **251–54 Yef eoile schet . . . i thin heorte,** If oil pours (or, is poured) out of a vat (*schet* = reduced form of *schedeth*), some of the liquid will remain. If milk is poured out, the color remains. If wine is poured out, the smell remains. But water goes out all together (i.e., leaves no traces): likewise pour out your heart — that is, [pour out] all the evil that is in your heart. **254–55 Yef thu ne dest nawt . . . Naum,** If you do not do that, look, how horribly God Himself threatens you through Nahum. **255–56 Ostendam gentibus . . . abhominationes tuas,** "I will reveal to the nations your nakedness and to kingdoms your shame and I shall throw down your abominations over you" (Nahum 3:5–6). **256–58 Thu naldest nawt unwreo . . . scheome sunnen,** You did not want to uncover (i.e., reveal) yourself to the priest in confession, and I will show your wickedness completely naked, to all people, and to all kingdoms [I will show] your shameful sins. **259–61 ant trussin . . . torplin into helle,** and [I will] load (or, tie — see *trusse, trussin* in glossary) all your disgraces on your own neck, as one does to the thief whom one leads (*leat* = reduced form of *leadeth*) to be judged (passive inf.), and so with all this (lit., the) shame you will pack off (i.e., depart — see *trussen* in glossary) and tumble into hell. **261–63 O . . . Sanies apparebit,** "Oh," says St. Bernard, "what confusion, what disgrace [there] will be, when the leaves having been scattered and dispersed all wickedness will be stripped naked. The pus (or, corruption) will be revealed" (Geoffrey of Auxerre, *Declamations from the Dialogue between Simon and Jesus Collected from the Sermons of St. Bernard* 50.61 [*PL* 184.469]). **263–67 hwuch schendlac . . . i-bet her,** what

265 al thet fulthe schaweth him, ant wringeth ut thet wursum bivoren al the wide worlt, eorth ware ant heovenes, nawt ane of werkes, ah of idelnesses, of wordes ant of thohtes the ne beoth i-bet her, as Seint Anselme witneth: **Omne tempus impensum requiretur a vobis, qualiter sit expensum.** "Euc tide ant time schal beo ther i-rikenet, hu hit wes her i-spenet." **Quando dissipatis foliis, et cetera.** "Hwen alle the

270 leaves," he seith, Sein Beornard, "schulen beo towarplet" — he biheold hu Adam ant Eve, tha ha hefden i the frumthe i-suneget, gedereden leaves ant makeden wriheles of ham to hare schentfule limen. Thus doth monie efter ham. **Declinantes cor suum in verba malicie ad excusandas excusationes in peccatis.**

Schrift schal beon ofte i-maket, for-thi is i the Sawter, **Confitebimur tibi, Deus,**

275 **confitebimur.** Ant ure Laverd seolf seith to his deciples, **Eamus iterum in Judeam.** "Ga we eft," seide he, "into Judee" — "Judee" spealeth "schrift," ant swa we i-findeth thet he wende ofte ut of Galilee into Judee. "Galilee" spealeth "hweol," for-te learen us thet we of the worldes turpelnesse ant of sunne hweol ofte gan to schrifte. For this is

shame, and what sorrow [will] be there at the Judgment, when all the leaves will be flung down, and all the filth [will] reveal itself, and [will] wring (or, force) out the pus before all the wide world, [before] the inhabitants of earth and of heaven, not only [the pus] of deeds, but of idleness (i.e., things not done), of words and of thoughts which are not atoned for here. **267–68** *Omne tempus . . . sit expensum,* "All time spent will be demanded of you, how it was expended" (Anselm, *Meditation* 1 [*PL* 158.709 ff.]). **268–69 "Euc tide ant time . . . i-spenet,"** "Each time and occasion will be reckoned (or, counted up) there, how it was spent here." **269** *Quando dissipatis foliis, et cetera,* "When the leaves having been scattered," etc. (St. Bernard, see above). **270 "schulen beo towarplet,"** "will be pulled down." **270–72 he biheold . . . efter ham,** he saw (lit., beheld) how Adam and Eve, when they had sinned in the beginning, gathered leaves and made coverings (or, clothes) out of them for their shameful members (lit., limbs). Many do thus in imitation of them (i.e., many behave just as they do). **272–73** *Declinates cor suum . . . in peccatis,* "Inclining their heart[s] to words of wickedness (or, cunning) to plead excuses in [their] sins" (adapted from Psalm 140:4). **274 ofte i-maket,** made often; **Sawter,** Psalter. **274–75** *Confitebimur . . . confitebimur,* "We shall confess to You, Lord, we shall confess" (Psalm 74:2). **275** *Eamus iterum in Judeam,* "Let us go again into Judea" (based on John 11:7). **276 "Ga we eft,"** "Let us go again." **276–78 spealeth "schrift" . . . gan to schrifte,** means "confession," and so we find that he went often out of Galilee into Judea. "Galilee" means "wheel," in order to teach us that we [should] often go from the world's turmoil and the wheel of sin to confession.

Part Five *Part Five*

the sacrement efter the weofdes sacrement, ant efter fulluht, thet te feond is lathest, as
280 he haveth to hali men him-seolf — sare his unthonckes i-beon hit — i-cnawen. Wule a
web beon ed en-chearre with a weater wel i-bleachet? A sol clath wel i-weschen? Thu
weschest thine honden in anlepi dei twien other thrien, ant nult nawt the sawle, Jesu
Cristes spuse — the eaver se ha is hwittre, se fulthe is senre upon hire, bute ha beo i-
wesschen — nult nawt to Godes cluppunge ofte umbe seove-niht wesschen hire eanes!
285 **Confiteor**, hali weater, beoden, hali thohtes, blesceunges, cneolunges, euch god word,
euch god werc wesscheth smeale sunnen the me ne mei alle seggen. Ah eaver is schrift
the heaved.

Schrift schal beon on hihthe i-maket: yef sunne timeth bi niht, anan other ine marhen.
Yef hit timeth bi dei, ear then me slepe. Hwa durste slepen hwil his deadliche fa heolde
290 an i-tohe sweord upon his heaved? The neappith upon helle breord, ha torplith ofte al
in, ear ha least wenen. Hwa-se is i-fallen amid te bearninde fur — nis he mare then

279 **sacrement**, (i.e., confession); **weofdes sacrement**, the sacrament of the altar (i.e.,
the Eucharist); **fulluht**, baptism. **279–80 thet te feond is lathest . . . i-cnawen**, which is
the most loathsome to the fiend (lit., enemy), as he himself has admitted to holy men —
be it very much against his will (i.e., very unwillingly). **280–81 Wule a web . . . i-
weschen?** Will a woven fabric be well bleached (i.e., whitened) with one washing (lit.,
water) at one time? [Will] a soiled cloth [be] well washed? **281–84 Thu weschest thine
honden . . . wesschen hire eanes!** You wash your hands twice or three times in a single
day, and you do not want [to wash] the soul, Jesus Christ's spouse — who the whiter
she ever is, the more filth is visible upon her, unless she be washed — often you do not
want to wash it [even] once in a week for God's embrace (i.e., to embrace God at the
Eucharist)! **285 *Confiteor***, Prayer of confession (lit., "I confess"). **285–87 beoden . . .
heaved**, prayers, holy thoughts, blessings, kneelings, every good word, every good work
wash [away] small sins all of which one cannot declare. But confession is always the head
(i.e., the chief thing). **288 on hihthe i-maket**, made in haste. **288–89 yef sunne timeth . . . me
slepe**, if sin happens at night, [make your confession] at once or in the morning. If it
happens by day, [make your confession] before you sleep (lit., earlier than one may sleep).
289–91 Hwa durste slepen . . . least wenen, Who would dare sleep while his mortal enemy
held a drawn sword over his head? Those who nap on the brink of hell, they often tumble
right in, before they least expect. **291–92 Hwa-se is i-fallen . . . arisen?** Whosoever has
fallen amidst the burning fire — is he not more than demented if he lies down, considers (lit.,

328

amead yef he lith, bithencheth him hwenne he wule arisen? A wummon the haveth i-losed hire nelde, other a sutere his eal, secheth hit anan-riht ant towent euch strea athet hit beo i-funden — ant Godd, thurh sunne forloren, schal liggen unsoht seove dahes

295   fulle! Nihe things beoth thet ahten hihin to schrift: the pine thet okereth, for sunne is the deofles feh thet he yeveth to okere ant to gavel of pine, ant eaver se mon lith lengre in his sunne, se the gavel waxeth of pine i purgatoire other her other in helle: **Ex usuris et iniquitate, et cetera.** The other thing is the muchele ant te reowthfule lure thet he leoseth, thet na thing thet he deth nis Gode lic-wurthe. **Alieni comederunt robur**

300   **ejus.** The thridde is death, thet he nat hwether he schule thet ilke dei ferliche asteorven. **Fili, ne tardes, et cetera.** The feorthe is secnesse, thet he ne mei thenche wel bute ane of his uvel, ne speoken as he schulde, bute granin for his eche, ant grunte, mare for his stiche then for his sunne. **Sanus confiteberis et vivens.** The fifte thing is

bethinks himself) when he will get up? **292–95 A wummon the haveth i-losed . . . seove dahes fulle!** A woman who has lost her needle, or a cobbler his awl, seeks it immediately and turns (*towent* = reduced form of *towendeth*) each straw upside down until it is found — and God, lost through sin, will lie unsought fully seven days! **295–97 Nihe things beoth . . . other in helle**, There are nine things which ought to rush [a person] to confession: the punishment (or, pain) which accrues interest, for sin is the devil's money which he gives out for usury and for the interest of punishment, and the longer one lies in his sin, the [more] the interest grows of pain in purgatory or here or in hell (lit., ever as one lies longer . . . so the interest grows). **297–98 Ex usuris et iniquitate, et cetera,** "[He will redeem the poor and needy] from usuries and iniquity," etc. (Psalm 71:14). **298–99 The other thing . . . lic-wurthe,** The second thing is the great and sorrowful loss that he (i.e., the sinner) suffers (lit., loses), that nothing that he does is pleasing to God. **299–300 Alieni comederunt robur ejus,** "Strangers have consumed His strength" (Hosea 7:9). **300 thet he nat . . . asteorven,** so that he does not know whether he will die suddenly that very day [or not]. **301 Fili, ne tardes,** "Son, do not delay [being converted to God]" (based on Ecclesiasticus 5:8). **301–03 The feorthe is secnesse . . . for his sunne,** The fourth is sickness, so that he cannot think rightly, except about his malady alone, nor [can he] speak as he should, but [can only] groan for his ache, and grunt, more for his sudden pain (lit., stitch) than for his sin. **303 Sanus confiteberis et vivens,** "[While] healthy and living you will confess (i.e., ought to confess)" (Ecclesiasticus 17:27). **303–05 The fifte thing . . . to healen,** The fifth thing is the great shame that it is, after a fall to lie down so long, and particularly under the devil. The sixth is the wound that always worsens as time goes on (lit., in hand — see *hond* in glossary), and is more difficult

305 muche scheome thet hit is, efter val to liggen se longe, ant hure under the schucke. The seste is the wunde thet eaver wurseth on hond, ant strengre is to healen. **Principiis obsta. [Sero] medicina paratur cum mala per longas.** The seovethe thing is uvel wune, thet Lazre bitacneth, the stonc — se longe he hefde i-lein i ther eorthe — o hwam ure Laverd weop, as the Godspel teleth, ant risede ant mengde him-seolven, ant yeide lude upon him ear he him arearde, for-te schawin hu strong hit is to arisen of uvel

310 wune, the roteth in his sunne. Seinte Marie! Lazre stonc of fowr dahes. Hu stinketh the sunfule of fowr yer other of five! **Quam difficile surgit quem moles male consuetudinis premit.** "O," seith Seint Austin, "hu earmliche he ariseth, the under wune of sunne haveth i-lein longe." **Circumdederunt me canes multi.** "Monie hundes," seith Davith, "habbeth biset me." Hwen gredi hundes stondeth bivore the

315 bord, nis hit neod yerde? As ofte as eani lecheth toward te ant reaveth the of thi mete, nult tu as ofte smiten? Elles ha walden kecchen of the al thet tu hefdest. Ant tu alswa thenne nim the yerde of thi tunge, ant as ofte as the dogge of helle kecheth ei god from

(lit., stronger) to heal. **305–06 Principiis obsta . . . per longas,** "Resist beginnings. A medicine is prepared too late when maladies [have gained strength] by long [delays]" (Ovid, *Remedies for Love*, 91–92). **306–10 uvel wune . . . in his sunne,** evil habit, which Lazarus symbolizes, who stank — so long he had lain in the earth (*ther* = declined def. art.) — over whom our Lord wept, as the Gospel tells, and trembled and was stirred up (lit., stirred Himself), and cried loudly over him before He raised him, in order to show how difficult it is to rise up from an evil habit, [for the person] who rots in his sin. **310–11 Lazre stonc . . . of five!** Lazarus stank after four days. How the sinful person stinks after four years or five! **311–12 Quam difficile . . . premit,** "With what difficulty does he get up whom a mass of bad habit presses down" (Augustine, *On the Gospel of John* 49.10.24 [*PL* 36.1756]). **312–13 "hu earmliche . . . i-lein longe,"** "how poorly he arises, who has lain long under the habit of sin." **313 Circumdederunt me canes multi,** "Many dogs have surrounded me" (Psalm 21:7). **314–16 Hwen gredi hundes . . . ofte smiten?** When voracious dogs stand before the table, is there not a need for the cudgel (i.e., to beat the dogs)? As often as anyone of them snatches at you and robs you of your food, will you not strike as often? **316 Elles ha walden . . . hefdest,** Otherwise they would seize (lit., catch) from you all that you had. **316–19 Ant tu alswa thenne . . . toward te,** And you just so then take (imper.) the cudgel of your tongue, and as often as the hound of hell snatches any good [thing] from you, beat (imper.) him immediately with the cudgel of your tongue in confession, and beat

330

the, smit him anan-riht mid te yerde of thi tunge i schrift, ant smit him se lutherliche thet him lathi ant drede to snecchen eft toward te. Thet dunt, of alle duntes, is him

320 dunte lathest. The hund the fret lether other awuri[e]th ahte — me hit beat anan-riht thet he understonde for-hwi he is i-beaten; thenne ne dear he nawt eft do thet ilke. Beat alswa mid ti tunge [i] schrift the hund of helle anan-riht, ant he wule beon ofdred to do the eft swuch thucke. Hwa is se fol thet he seith bi the hund thet fret lether, "Abid athet to-marhen! Ne beat tu him nawt yetten!" Ah, "anan-riht beat! Beat, beat anan-riht!"

325 Nis thing i the world thet smeorteth him sarre then deth swuch beatunge. Se me deoppre wadeth i the feondes lei-ven, se me kimeth up leatere. The eahtuthe thing is thet Seint Gregoire seith: **Peccatum quod per penitentiam non diluitur, mox suo pondere ad aliud trahit** — thet is, "sunne thet nis sone i-bet, draheth anan an-other," ant thet eft the thridde, ant swa euch-an cundleth mare ant wurse cundel then the

330 seolve moder. The nihethe reisun is — se he ear biginneth her to don his penitence, se

him so viciously that it is hateful to him and [he] may dread (i.e., be afraid) to snap at you again. **319–21 Thet dunt . . . do thet ilke**, That blow, of all blows, is to him the most hateful of blows. The dog which chews up (*fret* = reduced form of *freteth*) leather or kills (lit., worries — see *a-wurieth* in glossary) cattle — one beats (*beat* = reduced form of *beateth*) it immediately so that it may understand why it is beaten; then it does not dare to do the same again. **321–23 Beat alswa mid ti tunge . . . thucke**, Beat (imper.) likewise with your tongue in confession the hound of hell immediately, and he will be afraid to do you such a trick. **323–24 Hwa is se fol . . . nawt yetten!** Who is so foolish that he says concerning the dog that chews up leather, "Wait until tomorrow! Do not beat him yet!" **324 Ah**, On the contrary [one should say]; **anan-riht**, immediately. **325–26 Nis thing i the world . . . up leatere**, There is not anything in the world that smarts him (i.e., makes him smart) more painfully than does such a beating. As one wades deeper into the devil's marshy fen (i.e., swamp), so one comes out later (i.e., the deeper one wades into the devil's swamp, the longer it takes to come out again). **326 eahtuthe**, eighth. **327 thet**, what. **327–28** *Peccatum quod per penitentiam . . . trahit*, "A sin which has not been washed away by penitence, soon pulls by its weight in the direction of another [sin]" (Gregory, *Moral Discourses on Job* 25.9.22 [*PL* 76.334]). **328–30 thet nis sone i-bet . . . seolve moder**, "which is not atoned for soon straightway draws (or, attracts) another," and that [sin] in turn [draws] the third, and so each one breeds more and worse offspring than the mother herself. **330 nihethe**, ninth. **330–31 se he ear biginneth . . . purgatoire**, the sooner he begins (lit., so he begins before) to do his penance here, the less (lit., so . . . the less) he has to atone for in the pain (or, punishment)

he haveth to beten leasse i pine of purgatoire. This beoth nu nihe reisuns, ant monie ma ther beoth, hwi schrift ah to beon i-maket aa on hihthe.

    Schrift ah to beon eadmod, as the puplicanes wes, nawt as the phariseus wes, the talde his god-deden ant schawde thet hale forth, tha he schulde habben unw[r]ihen hise

335   wunden. For-thi, he wende unhealet — as ure Laverd seolf teleth — ut of the temple. Eadmodnesse is i-lich theose cointe hearloz, hare gute-feastre, hare flowinde cweise thet ha putteth eaver forth. Ant yef hit is eatelich, ha schawith hit yet eateluker i riche monnes ehnen, thet ha habben reowthe of ham ant yeoven ham god the reathere. Hudeth hare hale clath, ant doth on alre uvemest fite-rokes al totorene. O this ilke wise,

340   eadmodnesse eadmodliche bigileth ure Laverd ant biyet of his god with seli truandise: hudeth eaver hire god, schaweth forth hire poverte, put forth hire cancre, wepinde ant graninde bivore Godes ehnen, halseth meadlesliche on his derve passiun, on his deore-wurthe blod, on his fif wunden, on his moder teares, o the ilke tittes thet he seac, the milc thet hine fedde, on alle his halhene luve, o the deore druerie thet he haveth to his

345   deore spuse — thet is, to cleane sawle, other to Hali Chirche — on his death o rode, for

of purgatory. **331–32 This beoth nu . . . on hihthe,** These are now the nine reasons, and there are many more, why confession ought to be made always in haste. **333–35 ah to beon eadmod . . . hise wunden,** ought to be humble, as the publican's was, not as the pharisee's was, who reckoned his good deeds and showed into view the healthy [part], when he should have uncovered his wounds (see Luke 18:9–14). **335 he wende unhealet,** he departed (lit., turned) unhealed. **336–37 Eadmodnesse is i-lich . . . eaver forth,** Humility is like these clever beggars (or, layabouts), [like] their festering sores (lit., sore), their running boils (lit., boil) which they always put into view. **337–38 eatelich . . . the reathere,** hideous, they show it as still more hideous to rich men's eyes, so that they [will] have pity on them and give them goods (lit., good) the quicker. **339 Hudeth hare hale clath . . . totorene,** They hide their whole (i.e., undamaged) clothe[s], and on the topmost [layer] of all put on over-garments completely torn up. **339–46 this ilke wise . . . for hire to biyeotene,** just so, humility humbly (perhaps, happily — see textual note to line 340) fools our Lord and takes from His goods with blessed swindling: [humility] always hides her good, shows forth her poverty, puts forth her spreading sore, weeping and groaning before God's eyes, [humility] pleads continuously by His cruel suffering, by His precious blood, by His five wounds, by His mother's tears, by the very breasts that He sucked, the milk that nourished Him, by the love of all His saints, by the dear dalliance (or, love-token) which He has for His dear spouse — that is, for the pure soul, or for Holy Church — by His death on the Cross, [humility pleads

hire to biyeotene. With thus ane-wil ropunge, halseth efter sum help to the wrecche meoseise, to lechni with the seke, to healen hire cancre. Ant ure Laverd, i-halset swa, ne mei for reowthe wearnen hire ne sweamen hire with warne — nomeliche swa as he is se unimete large, thet him nis na thing leovere then thet he mahe i-finden acheisun 350 for-te yeovene. Ah hwa-se yelpeth of his god, as doth i schrift theos prude, hwet neod is ham to helpe? Moni haveth a swuch manere to seggen hire sunnen thet hit is wurth a dearne yelp, ant hunteth efter here-word of mare halinesse.

Schrift ah to beon scheomeful: bi thet te folc of Israel wende ut thurh the Reade Sea, thet wes read ant bitter, is bitacnet thet we moten thurh rudi scheome — thet is, i soth 355 schrift ant thurh bitter penitence — passin to heovene. God riht is, wat Crist, thet us scheomie bivore mon, the foryeten scheome tha we duden the sunne bivore Godes sihthe. **Nam omnia nuda sunt et aperta oculis ejus, ad quem nobis sermo.** "For al thet is, al is naket," seith Seinte Pawel, "ant open to his ehnen, with hwam we schulen rikenin alle ure deden." Scheome is the measte deal, as Seint Austin seith, of ure

by all these things] for her benefit (lit., for her to receive). **346–47 With thus ane-wil ropunge . . . hire cancre,** With such stubborn (or, persistent) crying-out, [humility] pleads for some help for the wretch's hardship to administer medicine against the sickness, to heal her sore[s]. **347–50 Ant ure Laverd . . . for-te yeovene,** And our Lord, entreated thus, cannot for pity refuse her or cause her pain with a refusal — particularly so as He is so inordinately generous, that nothing is more preferable (or, dearer) to Him than that He may find a reason to give. **350–52 Ah hwa-se yelpeth . . . mare halinesse,** But whosoever boasts of his goodness, as do these proud people in confession, what need is there to help them? Many a one has such a way to declare (lit., say) her sins that it is equal to a secret boast and [many a one] hunts after the reputation (lit., praise-word) of greater holiness. **353 scheomeful,** full of shame. **353–55 bi thet te folc . . . passin to heovene,** by the fact that the people of Israel departed out through the Red Sea, which was red and bitter, is symbolized that we must pass to heaven through red-faced (lit., ruddy) shame — that is, in true confession and through bitter penitence. **355–57 God riht is . . . Godes sihthe,** Christ knows, it is quite right that we be ashamed (lit., that [it] shame us) before man, [we] who forgot shame when we did the sin before God's sight. **357 Nam omnia nuda sunt . . . sermo,** "For all things are naked and open to His eyes, to whom our declaration (lit., speech) [must be made]" (Hebrews 4:13). **358 ehnen,** eyes. **358–59 with hwam . . . ure deden,** with whom we must reckon all our deeds. **359 measte deal,** greatest part.

360   penitence: **Verecundia pars est magna penetentie.** Ant Sein Bernard seith thet na
deore-wurthe yim-stan ne deliteth swa muchel mon to bihalden as deth Godes ehe the
rude of monnes neb the riht seith hise sunnen. Understond wel this word. Schrift is a
sacrement, ant euch sacrament haveth an i-licnesse ute-with of thet hit wurcheth in-
with — as hit is i fulluht: the wesschunge withuten bitacneth the wesschunge of sawle

365   withinnen. Alswa i schrift: the cwike rude of the neb deth to understonden thet te
sawle, the wes bla ant nefde bute dead heow, haveth i-caht cwic heow ant is i-rudet
feire. **Interior tamen penitentia non dicitur sacramentum, set exterior vel puplica
vel solempnis.**

     Schrift schal beo dredful, thet tu segge with Jerome, **Quociens confessus sum,**

370   **videor michi non esse confessus.** "As ofte as ich am i-schriven, eaver me thuncheth
me unschriven," for eaver is sum foryeten of the totagges. For-thi, seith Seint Austin,
Ve laudabili hominum vite, si remota misericordia discutias eam — thet is, "the
beste mon of al the world, yef ure Laverd demde him al efter rihtwisnesse, ant nawt

360 Verecundia pars . . . penetentie, "Shame (or, modesty) is the great part of penitence"
(Pseudo-Augustine, *Concerning True and False Penitence* 10.25 [*PL* 40.1122]). **360–62 na
deore-wurthe yim-stan . . . hise sunnen,** no precious gemstone delights man so much to
behold as the ruddiness of the face of a man who declares his sins rightly does (i.e.,
delights) God's eye. **363–65 haveth an i-licnesse . . . sawle withinnen,** has a similarity
outside to what it effects inside — as it is in baptism: the washing without (i.e., on the
outside) betokens the washing of the soul within. **365–67 the cwike rude . . . i-rudet feire,**
the living red (or, complexion) of the face makes [us] to understand that the soul, which was
gray (or, blackish blue) and had nothing but a dead color, has caught a living color and
is reddened beautifully. **367–68 Interior tamen penitentia . . . solempnis,** "Nevertheless interior penitence is not called a sacrament, but external or public or solemn [peni-
tence is]" (source unidentified). **369 dredful,** fearful; **thet tu segge,** so that you may
say. **369–70 Quociens confessus sum . . . confessus,** "As often as I have confessed, I
seem to myself not to have confessed" (source unidentified). **370 i-schriven,** confessed. **370–71 eaver me thuncheth . . . totagges,** I always consider (lit., it seems to me)
myself unconfessed," for something of the circumstances is always forgotten. **372 Ve
laudabili . . . discutias eam,** "Woe to the praiseworthy life of men, if mercy being taken
away, You [O Lord] rigorously examine it (i.e., the praiseworthy life of men)" (Augustine, *Confessions* 9.13 [*PL* 32.778]). **373–74 yef ure Laverd . . . i-wurthen,** if our Lord
judged him completely according to justice, and not according to mercy, woe would be

efter mearci, wa schulde him i-wurthen." **Set misericordia superexaltat judicium.**
375   "Ah his mearci toward us weieth eaver mare then the rihte nearewe."

    Schrift schal beon hopeful. Hwa-se seith as he con, ant deth al thet he mei, Godd ne bit na mare. Ah hope ant dred schulen aa beon i-mengt togederes. This for-te bitacnin wes i the alde lahe i-haten thet te twa grindel-stanes ne schulde na-mon twinnin. The neothere, the lith stille ant bereth hevi charge, bitacneth fearlac, the teieth mon from
380   sunne, ant is i-heveget her with heard for-te beo quite of heardre. The uvere stan bitacneth hope, the eorneth ant stureth hire i gode werkes eaver with trust of muche mede. Theos twa na-mon ne parti from other, for as Sein Gregoire seith, **Spes sine timore luxuriat in presumptionem. Timor sine spe degenerat in desperationem.** "Dred withuten hope maketh mon untrusten, ant hope withute dred maketh over-
385   trusten." Theos twa untheawes, untrust ant over-trust, beoth the deofles tristen, ther thet wrecche beast seldene edstearteth. Triste is ther me sit mid te grea-hunz for-te kepe the heare, other tildeth the nettes ayein him. Toward an of theos twa is al thet he

to him. **374** *Set misericordia superexaltat judicium,* "But mercy rises above justice" (based on James 2:13). **375 weieth . . . rihte nearewe,** always weighs more than narrow (i.e., strict) justice. **376–77 Hwa-se seith as he con . . . bit na mare,** Whosoever declares as he is able, and does all that he can, God asks no more (*bit* = reduced form of *biddeth*). **377 aa beon i-mengt,** always be mixed. **377–78 This for-te bitacnin . . . twinnin,** In order to symbolize this it was commanded in the old law that no one should separate the two grindstones. **378–80 The neothere . . . heardre,** The lower [stone], which lies still and carries the heavy burden, symbolizes fear, which restrains (lit., ties, binds) one from sin, and is weighed down here with a hard thing in order to be free of [something] harder. **380–82 The uvere stan . . . muche mede,** The upper stone symbolizes hope, which runs and busies itself (lit., herself) in good works always with the assurance of great reward. **382 Theos twa na-mon ne parti from other,** Let no one separate these two from the other. **382–83** *Spes sine timore . . . desperationem,* "Hope without fear is rank in presumption (or, audacity). Fear without hope degenerates into desperation" (Pseudo-Gregory, *Expositions in First Kings* 5.20.11 [*PL* 79.332]). **384 maketh mon untrusten,** makes one despair (or, lose trust). **384–85 maketh over-trusten,** makes [one] become overly confident. **385–86 twa untheawes . . . edstearteth,** two faults, lack of confidence and over-confidence, are the devil's traps (lit., hunting stations — see explanatory note), from which (lit., where) the wretched beast seldom escapes. **386–87 Triste is ther . . . ayein him,** A hunting station is where one sits (i.e., lies in wait) with the greyhounds in order to try to catch the hare, or [where one] spreads the nets for it. **387–88 Toward an of**

sleateth, for ther beoth his grea-hunz, ther beoth his nettes. Untrust ant over-trust beoth, of alle sunnen, nest te yete of helle. With dred, withuten hope — thet is, with
390   untrust — wes Caymes schrift ant Judasen, for-hwi ha forferden. With hope, withute dred — thet is, with over-trust — is the unselies sahe, the seith i the Sawter, **Secundum multitudinem ire sue non queret.** "Nis nawt Godd," quoth ha, "se grim as ye him fore makieth." "Na?" he seith, Davith. "Yeoi he," ant seith thenne, **Propter quid irritavit impius Deum? Dixit enim in corde suo non requiret.** On alre earst he
395   cleopeth the over-trusti unbilevet. "The unbilevet, with hwon gremeth he Godd almihti? With thon thet he seith, 'Nule he nawt se nearowliche demen as ye seggeth.'" Yeoi, siker ah he wule. Thus theos twa untheawes beoth to grimme robberes i-evenet. For the an — thet is, over-trust — reaveth Godd his rihte dom ant his rihtwisnesse. The other — thet is, untrust — reaveth him his milce. Ant swa ha beoth umben to fordon
400   Godd seolf, for Godd ne muhte nawt beon withuten rihtwisnesse, ne withuten milce. Nu thenne, hwucche untheawes beoth evening to theose the wulleth Godd acwellen on hare fule wise? Yef thu art to trusti ant haldest Godd to nessche for-te wreoke sunne,

theos twa . . . his nettes, Everything that he drives (or, hunts) is toward one of these two, for where are his greyhounds, there are his nets. **389 nest te yete of helle**, nearest to (lit., next) the gate of hell. **390 wes Caymes schrift . . . forferden**, was Cain's confession and Judas', for which reason they were destroyed. **391 unselies sahe . . . Sawter**, the wicked person's saying, who says in the Psalter. **391–92 *Secundum . . . queret***, "[God] will not judge (or, examine) according to the multitude of His anger" (Psalm 9:25). **392–93 "Nis nawt Godd . . . Yeoi he,"** "God is not," she says, "so grim as you make him out [to be]." "No?" he says, David. "Yes he [is]." **393–94 *Propter quid irritavit . . . requiret***, "For what reason has the evil man angered God? For he has said in his heart, "He will not demand [it]" (Psalm 9:34). **394–96 On alre earst . . . as ye seggeth**, First of all he calls the overconfident unbelieving (lit., unbelieved). "The unbelieving person, why does he provoke God almighty? For the reason that he says, "He will not judge as strictly as you say." **396–97 Yeoi, siker . . . i-evenet**, Yes, surely but He will. Thus these two faults are compared to grim robbers. **398 reaveth Godd . . . rihtwisnesse**, steals [from] God His right judgment and His righteousness. **399 milce**, mercy. **399–400 Ant swa ha beoth . . . withuten milce**, And so they (i.e., insecurity and presumption) are about it (or, are aiming) to destroy God Himself, for God could not be (or, exist) without righteousness, nor without mercy. **401–02 Nu thenne . . . fule wise?** Now then, which faults are comparable (lit., a comparison) to these which seek (lit., want) to kill God in their foul way? **402–03 Yef thu art to trusti . . . thin tale**, If you are too trusting

sunne liketh him, bi thin tale. Ah bihald hu he wrec in his heh engel the thohte of a prude, hu he wrec in Adam the bite of an eappel, hu he bisencte Sodome ant Gommorre,

405 were ant wif ant wenchel, the nome-cuthe burhes, al a muche schire, dun into helle grunde — ther-as is nu the Deade Sea thet na-wiht cwikes nis inne — , hu he i Noes flod al the world adrencte, bute eahte i the arche, hu he in his ahne folc Israel, his deorling, grimliche awrec him ase ofte as ha gulten: Dathan, ant Abyron, Chore ant his feren, the othre alswa the he sloh bi feole thusendes, ofte for hare gruchunge ane. On

410 other half loke, yef thu havest untrust of his unimete milce, hu lihtliche ant hu sone Seinte Peter, efter thet he hefde forsaken him, ant thet for a cwene wor*d*, wes with him i-sahtnet, *hu* the theof o rode, the hefde aa i-lived uvele, in a stert-hwile hefde ed him milce with a feier speche. For-thi, bitweone theos twa, untrust ant over-trust, hope ant dred beon aa i-feiet togederes.

415   Schrift yet schal beo wis, ant to wis mon i-maket — of uncuthe sunnen, nawt to yunge preostes — yunge, ich segge, of wit — ne to sotte alde. Bigin earst ed prude, ant

and hold (or, believe) God [to be] too soft to avenge sin, [then] sin pleases Him, by your account. **403–09 Ah bihald hu . . . hare gruchunge ane,** But look how He avenged in His high angel (i.e., Lucifer) the thought of a proud one, how He avenged in Adam the bite of an apple, how He sunk Sodom and Gomorrah, man and woman and child, the famous cities, all [together] a great county, down into the bottom of hell — where the Dead Sea is now in which there is nothing living — [look] how He in Noah's flood drowned all the world, except eight [people] in the ark, how He on His own people of Israel, His darling, grimly (or, fiercely) avenged Himself as often as they misbehaved: [for example,] Dathan (see Numbers 16:12), and Abiron (see Numbers 16:1), Core (see Numbers 16:1) and his companions, the others also that He slew by many thousands, often for their grumbling alone. **409–13 On other half loke . . . feier speche,** On the other side (lit., half) look, if you have any doubt of His immeasurable mercy, how easily and how soon St. Peter, after he had forsaken Him, and that for a strumpet's word, was reconciled with Him, how the thief on the cross, who had always lived wickedly, in a twinkling had from Him mercy with a pleasant speech. **413–14 For-thi, bitweone theos twa . . . togederes,** Therefore, with these two, lack of confidence (or, despair) and over-confidence, let hope and fear be always connected together. **415–16 to wis mon i-maket . . . sotte alde,** made to a wise man — concerning unknown (or, unusual) sins, [confession ought] not [to be] to young priests — young, I say, of knowledge — nor to foolish old [priests]. **416–17 Bigin earst . . . to the,** Begin first at pride, and seek out all

sech alle the bohes th'rof as ha beoth th'ruppe i-writene, hwuch falle to the. Th'refter alswa of onde, ant ga we swa dune-ward, rawe bi rawe, athet to the leaste. Ant drah togedere al the team under the moder.

420   Schrift ah to beo soth: ne lih thu nawt o the-seolf. For as Seint Austin seith, **Qui causa humilitatis de se mentitur, fit quod prius ipse non fuit, id est, peccator.** "The seith leas on him-seolf thurh to muchel eadmodnesse, he is i-maket sunful, thah he ear nere." Sein Gregoire seith thah, **Bonarum mentium est culpam agnoscere ubi culpa non est.** "Cunde of god heorte is to beon offearet of sunne ther-as nan nis

425   ofte," other weie swithre his sunne sum-chearre then he thurfte. Weien hit to lutel is ase uvel other wurse. The middel wei of meosure is eaver guldene. Drede we us eavre, for ofte we weneth for-te don a lutel uvel ant doth a great sunne; ofte wel to donne, ant doth al to cweade. Segge we eaver thenne with Seinte Anselme, **Etiam bonum nostrum est aliquo modo corruptum, ut possit non placere, aut certe displicere Deo.**

430   **Paulus: Scio quod non est in me, hoc est in carne mea, bonum.** Na god in us nis

the branches of it as they are written above, [those] which fall (or, apply to) you. **417–19 Th'refter alswa of onde . . . moder,** After that also of envy, and let us go thus downward, in order (lit., row by row), until [we come] to the last. And draw (or, gather) together all the brood [of sins] under the mother (i.e., the main sin). **420 soth . . . the-seolf,** true: do not lie about yourself. **420–21** *Qui causa humilitatis . . . peccator,* "Whoever lies about oneself because of humility, is himself changed into (lit., made) what he was not before, that is, a sinner" (Augustine, *Sermons* 181.4.5 [*PL* 38.981]). **422–23 "The seith leas . . . ear nere,"** "Whoever tells a lie about himself through too much humility, he is made sinful, though he was not before." **423–24** *Bonarum mentium . . . non est,* "[It is the sign] of good minds to perceive fault where there is no fault" (Gregory, *Letters* 11.4.64 [*PL* 77.1195]). **424–25 Cunde of god heorte . . . he thurfte,** It is the nature of a good heart to be afraid of sin where often none is," or to judge (lit., weigh) his sin sometimes more severely than he needed [to do]. **425–26 Weien hit to lutel . . . guldene,** To weigh it too little is as bad or worse. The middle way of moderation is always golden. **426–28 Drede we us eavre . . . to cweade,** Let us always be afraid, for often we expect to do a little evil and do a great sin; often [we expect] to do well, and do all too wickedly. **428 Segge we eaver,** Let us always say. **428–30** *Etiam bonum nostrum . . . bonum,* "Even our good is corrupt in a certain way, so that it cannot please, but on the contrary certainly can displease God" (Anselm, *Meditation* 1 [PL 158.709 ff.]). Paul: "I know that no good is in me, that is in my flesh" (based on Romans 7:18). **430–31 nis of us,** of us: ure god is Godes. Ah sunne is of us ant ure ahne. "Godes god, hwen ich hit do," quoth he, Seint Anselme, "swa o summe wise min uvel hit forgneaieth: other ich hit do ungleadliche, other to ear, other to leate, other leote wel th'rof, thah na-mon hit nute, other walde thet ei hit wiste, other yemelesliche do hit, other to unwisliche, to muchel

435 other to lutel. Thus eaver sum uvel mongleth him with mi god thet Godes grace yeveth me, thet hit mei lutel likin Godd, ant mislikin ofte." Seinte Marie! Hwen the hali mon seide thus bi him-seolf, hu mahe we hit witerliche seggen bi us wrecches?

Schrift ah to beon willes — thet is, willeliche, unfreinet, nawt i-drahen of the as thin unthonkes. Hwil thu const seggen eawt, sei al uneasket. Me ne schal easki nan, but for

440 neode ane, for of the easkunge mei uvel fallen bute hit beo the wisre. On other half, moni mon abit for-te schriven him athet te nede tippe. Ah ofte him liheth the wrench thet he ne mei hwen he wule, the nalde tha he mahte. Na mare cangschipe nis then setten Godd tearme, as thah grace were his as he bere hire in his purs to neomen up-o grace th'rin i the tearme as he him-seolf sette. Nai, beal ami, nai. The tearme is i Godes

---

is from us (double negative). **431 ure ahne**, our own. **431–35 Godes god . . . to lutel**, When I do God's good," he, St. Anselm, says, "in some way my evil thus gnaws it up: either I do it ungladly, or too early, or too late, or think too highly of it, though no one knows about it, or [I] would want that someone knew about it, or [I] do it carelessly, or too unwisely, too much or too little." **435–36 Thus eaver sum uvel . . . mislikin ofte**, Thus some evil always mingles itself with my good which God's grace gives me, so that it can please God [very] little, and displease [Him] often. **436–37 Hwen the hali mon seide . . . wrecches?** When that holy man said such a thing about himself, indeed how should we wretches say it about ourselves? **438 ah to beon willes**, ought to be voluntary (or, willing). **438–39 willeliche, unfreinet . . . uneasket**, [given] willingly, unasked for, not drawn from you as if against your will (see *un-thonckes* in glossary). While you can say anything [you want], say everything unasked. **439–40 Me ne schal easki . . . the wisre**, One must not ask anything, except for necessity alone, for evil may fall (i.e., occur) from the asking unless it be the wiser (i.e., is managed very carefully). **441 moni mon . . . te nede tippe**, many a man waits (*abit* = reduced form of *abideth*) to confess himself until calamity (lit., need) strike[s]. **441–44 him liheth the wrench . . . him-seolf sette**, the trick deceives him so that he cannot [confess] when he wants, who did not want to when he could. There is no greater foolishness than to set God a deadline, as though grace were his (i.e., already in his possession) as though he would carry it (i.e., grace) in his purse to take out the grace inside (lit., therein) at the deadline which he himself set. **444–46 Nai, beal ami . . . th'refter lokin**, No, good friend, no. The

339

445 hond, nawt i thi bandun. Hwen Godd beot hit te, reach to ba the honden, for withdrahe
he his hond, thu maht th'refter lokin. Yef uvel other other-hwet ned te to schrifte — lo,
hwet seith Seint Austin: **Coacta servicia Deo non placent.** "Servises i-nedde ne
cwemeth nawt ure Laverd," thah no-the-leatere, betere is o thene no. **Nunquam sera
penitentia si tamen vera.** "Nis neaver to leate penitence thet is sothliche i-maket," he
450 seith eft him-seolven. Ah betere is, as Davith seith, **Refloruit caro mea et ex voluntate
mea confitebor ei** — thet is, "mi flesch is i-fluret, bicumen al neowe, for ich chulle
schrive me ant herie Godd willes." Wel seith he "i-fluret," to bitacnin wil-schrift, for
the eorthe al unnet ant te treon alswa openith ham ant bringeth forth misliche flures. **In
Canticis: flores apparuerunt in terra nostra.** Eadmodnesse, abstinence, culvres
455 unlathnesse, ant othre swucche vertuz beoth feire i Godes ehnen, ant swote i Godes
nease, smeallinde flures. Of ham make his herbearhe in-with the-seolven, for his delices,
he seith, beoth ther for-te wunien: **Et delicie mee esse cum filiis hominum — in
libro Proverbiorum.**

deadline is in God's hand, not in your control. When God offers it to you, reach out both hands,
for [should He] withdraw His hand, you might look (or, search) afterwards [and never find it!].
446 other other-hwet ned te to schrifte, or something else (lit., other-what) compels (*ned =
reduced form of *nedeth*) you to confession. **447** *Coacta servicia Deo non placent*, "Forced
services do not please God" (see Pseudo-Augustine, *Sermons to Brothers in the Desert* 30 [*PL*
40.1289]). **447–48 Servises i-nedde ne cwemeth nawt**, Services compelled do not please. **448
thah no-the-leatere . . . no**, though nonetheless, one is better than none. **448–49** *Nunquam sera
penitentia si tamen vera*, "Penance [is] never too late if [it is] true for all that" (exact source
unidentified). **449 sothliche i-maket**, made truly (or, in truth). **450–51** *Refloruit caro mea . . .
confitebor ei*, "My flesh has flowered (or, flourished) again and by my [own free] will I confess
to him" (Psalm 27:7). **451–52 is i-fluret . . . Godd willes**, has flowered, become completely new,
for I will confess myself and praise God willingly. **452–53 to bitacnin wil-schrift . . . flures**, to
symbolize willing confession, for the earth quite unforced and the trees also open themselves
and bring forth various flowers. **453–54** *In Canticis . . . terra nostra*, In Canticles: "flowers have
appeared in our land" (condensed from Song of Songs 2:12). **454–56 Eadmodnesse, abstinence
. . . smeallinde flures**, Humility, abstinence, a dove's peacefulness, and other such virtues are
fair in God's eyes, and sweet in God's nose, fragrant flowers (see textual note). **456–57 Of ham
make his herbearhe . . . wunien**, Make (imper.) His lodging out of them within yourself, for His
delight, He says, is to dwell there. **457–58** *Et delicie mee . . . Proverbiorum,* "And My joy [is]
to be with the sons of men" — in the book of Proverbs (Proverbs 8:31).

Schrift ah to beon ahne. Na-mon ne schal i schrift wreien bute him-seolven, ase
460   forth as he mei. This ich segge for-thi thet swuch aventure bitimeth to sum mon other
to sum wummon thet ha ne mei nawt fulleliche wreien hire-seolven, bute ha wreie
othre. Ah bi nome, no-the-leatere, ne nempni ha nawt the ilke, thah the schrift-feader
wite wel toward hwam hit turne — ah "a munk," other "a preost," nawt "Wilyam" ne
"Water," thah ther ne beo nan other.

465   Schrift schal beo stude-vest to halde the penitence ant leave the sunne, thet tu segge
to the preost: "Ich habbe stude-festliche i thonc ant in heorte this sunne to forleten ant
do the penitence." The preost ne schal nawt easki the yef thu wult theonne-vorth
forhate thi sunne; inoh is thet tu segge thet tu hit havest on heorte treoweliche to donne
thurh Godes grace, ant yef thu fallest eft th'rin, thet tu wult anan-riht arisen thurh
470   Godes help ant cumen ayein to schrifte. **Vade et amplius noli peccare.** "Ga," quoth
ure Laverd to a sunful wummon, "ant have wil thet tu nult sungi na mare." Thus ne
easkede he nan other sikernesse.

Schrift ah to beon bithoht bivore longe. Of fif thinges with thi wit gedere thine
sunnen of alle thine ealdes — of childhad, of yuhethehad gedere al togederes. Th'refter

459 ahne, one's own. **459–60 Na-mon ne schal . . . he mei**, No one should accuse in
confession anyone but himself, as far as he can. **460–62 This ich segge . . . ha wreie othre**,
I say this because such an accident happens (or, will happen) to some man or some woman
so that she cannot fully accuse herself, unless she accuse the other. **462–64 Ah bi nome
. . . nan other**, But let her not call the same person by name, nonetheless, though the
confessor may know [very] well towards whom it turns (i.e., about whom it is) — but
[rather] "a monk," or "a priest," not "William" or "Walter," though there be no other [priest
or monk]. **465–67 stude-vest to halde the penitence . . . do the penitence**, steadfast to keep
to the penitence and leave the sin so that you may say to the priest: "I have [it] steadfastly
in thought and in heart to abandon this sin and to do the penitence." **467–70 The preost ne
schal . . . ayein to schrifte**, The priest must not ask you if you will from then on (lit.,
thenceforth) renounce your sin; [it] is enough that you say that you have it in heart to do
[so] faithfully through God's grace, and if you fall back into it (lit., therein), that you will
immediately rise up through God's help and come again to confession. **470 Vade et amplius
noli peccare**, "Go and sin no more" (John 8:11). **471 have wil thet tu nult sungi**, have the
desire that you will not sin. **471–72 Thus ne easkede he nan other sikernesse**, In this way,
he did not ask for any other pledge (or, assurance). **473 bithoht bivore longe**, considered a
long [time] before. **473–76 gedere thine sunnen . . . in euch ealde**, gather the sins of all your

475 gedere the studen thet tu in wunedest, ant thench yeorne hwet tu dudest in euch stude
sunderliche ant in euch ealde. Th'refter sech al ut ant trude thine sunnen bi thine fif
wittes, th'refter bi alle thine limen i hwuch thu havest i-suneget meast other oftest.
Aleast, sunderliche bi dahes ant bi tiden.

Nu ye habbeth alle i-haved, as ich understonde, the sixtene stucchen the ich bihet to
480 dealen, ant alle ich habbe tobroken ham ow, mine leove sustren, as me deth to children,
the mahten with unbroke bread deien on hunger. Ah me is — thet wite ye! — moni
crome edfallen. Secheth ham ant gederith, for ha beoth sawle fode.

Thulli schrift, thet haveth thus thes sixtene stucchen, haveth the ilke muchele mihten
thet ich earst seide: threo ayein the deovel, threo on us-seolven, ant threo ayeines the
485 world — deore-wurthe over gold or, ant yimmes of Ynde.

Mine leove sustren, this fifte dale, the is of schrift, limpeth to alle men i-liche; for-thi
ne wundri ye ow nawt thet ich toward ow nomeliche nabbe nawt i-speken i this dale.
Habbeth thah to ower bihove this lutle leaste ende. Of alle cuthe sunnen, as of prude, of
great other of heh heorte, of onde, of wreaththe, of slawthe, of yemeles, of idel word,

ages — from childhood, from youth gather everything together. After that gather the
places that you lived in, and think carefully what you did in each place separately and in
each age. **476–78 Th'refter sech al ut . . . bi tiden**, After that seek out everything and track
down your sins according to your five senses, after that by all the [bodily] members in
which you have sinned most or most often. Finally, [track down your sins] separately by
days and by times. **479–81 Nu ye habbeth alle i-haved . . . on hunger**, Now you have had, as
I understand, the sixteen pieces (or, sections) which I promised to divide, and I have broken
apart each of them for you, my dear sisters, as one does for children, who might die of
hunger on unbroken bread. **481–82 Ah me is . . . edfallen**, But many a crumb has fallen from
me — that you know (or, as you know)! **482 ha beoth sawle fode**, they are the soul's food.
483 Thulli schrift, Such confession; **stucchen**, parts; **the ilke muchele mihten**, the same
great powers. **485 deore-wurthe over gold . . . Ynde**, [such powers are] precious beyond
(i.e., more precious than) gold ore, and gems from India. **486–87 this fifte dale . . . i this dale**,
this fifth part, which is about confession, applies to all men (or, people) alike; therefore, do
not wonder (lit., do not wonder yourselves) that I have not spoken to you specifically in
this part. **488 Habbeth thah to ower bihove**, Have (imper.) however for your profit. **488–99
Of alle cuthe sunnen . . . enbrevet on his rolle**, [Let her confess herself] of all well-known
(or, common) sins, such as of pride, of a haughty or a high (i.e., arrogant) heart, of envy, of
wrath, of sloth, of carelessness, of idle words, of undisciplined thoughts, of some idle

490   of untohene thohtes, of sum idel herunge, of sum fals gleadunge, other of hevi murnunge, of ypocresie, of mete, of drunch to muchel other to lutel, of gruchunge, of grim chere, of silences i-brokene, of sitten longe ed thurl, of ures mis i-seide withute yeme of heorte, other in untime, of sum fals word, of sware, of plohe, of i-schake lahtre, of schede cromen other ale, of leote thinges muhelin, rustin other rotien, clathes unseowet,

495   bireinet, unwesschen, breoke nep other disch, other biseo yemelesliche ei thing thet me with feareth other ahte to yemen, of keorfunge, of hurtunge, thurh unbisehenesse — of alle the thinges the beoth i this riwle the beoth misnumene, of alle thulliche thing schrive hire euche wike eanes ed te leaste, for nan se lutel nis of theos thet te deovel naveth enbrevet on his rolle. Ah schrift hit schrapeth of, ant maketh him to leosen

500   muchel of his hwile. Ah al thet schrift ne schrapeth of, al he wule o Domes-dei rede ful witerliche for-te bicleopie the with: a word ne schal ther wontin. Nu thenne, ich reade, yeoveth him to writen thet leaste thet ye eaver mahen, for na meoster nis him leovere, ant hwet-se he writ, beoth umben to schrapien hit of cleanliche. With na thing ne mahe ye matin him betere. To euch preost mei ancre schriven hire of swucche utterliche

505   sunnen the to alle bifalleth. Ah ful trusti ha schal beon o the preostes god-lec thet ha

listening, of some false gladness, or of heavy mourning, of hypocrisy, of too much or too little food or drink, of grumbling, of fierce looks, of broken silences, of sitting (lit., to sit) for a long time at the window, of [canonical] hours said wrongly without attention of heart, or in the wrong time, of some false words, of swearing, of playing, of violent (lit., shaken) laughter, of spilling crumbs or ale, of letting things spoil, rust or rot, [of leaving] clothes unsewn, rained on, unwashed, breaking a cup or dish, or attending carelessly to anything which one handles (lit., fares with) or [which one] ought to pay attention to, of cutting (or, gashing), of hurting, through inattention — of all the things in this rule which are done wrong, of all such things let her confess herself each week once at the least, for none of these [sins] is so small that the devil has not recorded on his roll. **499–501 Ah schrift hit schrapeth of . . . wontin**, But confession scrapes it off (i.e., erases it), and makes him lose much of his time. But everything that confession does not scrape off, everything he will most certainly read on Judgment Day in order to accuse you with [it]: not one word will be missing there. **501–03 Nu thenne, ich reade . . . cleanliche**, Now then, I advise, give him the least to write that you ever can, for no occupation is more preferable to him, and whatsoever he write[s], be busy to scrape it off clean. **504 matin**, to checkmate, defeat. **504–05 of swucche . . . bifalleth**, of such external (or, venial) sins which happen to everyone. **505–07 Ah ful trusti ha schal beon . . . deathes dute**, But she must be very secure in the priest's goodness to whom she reveals

allunge schaweth to, hu hire stonde abute flesches temptatiuns, yef ha is swa i-fondet — bute i deathes dute. Thus, thah, me thuncheth thet ha mei seggen: "Sire, flesches fondunge thet ich habbe — other habbe i-haved — geath to vorth up-o me thurh mi theafunge. Ich am ofdred leste ich ga drivinde other-hwiles to swithe forth-ward mine

510   fol thohtes, ant fule umbe-stunde, as thah ich huntede efter licunge. Ich mihte thurh Godes strengthe schaken ham ofte of me yef ich were cwicliche ant steale-wurthliche umben. Ich am offearet sare thet te delit i the thoht leaste to longe ofte, swa thet hit cume neh skiles yettunge." Ne dear ich thet ha deopluker ne witerluker schrive hire to yung preost her-abuten, ant yet of this inoh-reathe him walde thunche wunder. Ah to

515   hire ahne schrift-feader, other to sum lif-hali mon, yef ha mei him habben, culle al the pot ut, ther speowe ut al thet wunder, ther with fule wordes, thet fulthe, efter thet hit is, tuki al to wundre, swa thet ha drede thet ha hurte his earen thet hercneth hire sunnen. Yef ei ancre nat nawt of thulliche thinges, thonki yeorne Jesu Crist, ant halde hire i drede. The deovel nis nawt dead, thet wite ha, thah he slepe.

[everything] completely, how she fares (i.e., how it is with her) concerning the flesh's temptations, if she is so tempted — except in fear of death. **507–09 Thus, thah, me thuncheth . . . theafunge,** However, it seems to me that she may speak in this way: "Sir, the temptation of the flesh that I have — or have had — comes too far on me (i.e., goes to far with me) by my own consent. **509–10 Ich am ofdred . . . efter licunge,** I am afraid lest (or, for fear that) I go driving my foolish thoughts, foul at times, too quickly forward sometimes, as though I hunted after pleasure. **511–12 schaken ham ofte of me . . . umben,** shake them often from me if I were quickly and stalwartly about [it]. **512–13 Ich am offearet sare . . . skiles yettunge,** I am sorely afraid that the delight in the thought [may] often last too long, so that it may come close (lit., nigh) to the reason's consent. **513–14 Ne dear ich . . . thunche wunder,** I would not dare [to advise] that she confess herself more deeply or openly to a young priest in this matter (lit., hereabout), and even concerning this (i.e., as much as I have suggested above) it would seem strange (or, monstrous). **514–18 Ah to hire ahne schrift-feader . . . hercneth hire sunnen,** But let her to her own confessor, or to some man of holy life, if she can have [access to] him, empty out the whole pot, let her spew (or, vomit) out there (i.e., in confession) all that monstrosity, let her there upbraid (or, mistreat) that filth, according to what it is, with foul words, quite horribly, so that she might fear that she hurt[s] his ears who listens to her sins. **518–19 Yef ei ancre nat nawt . . . he slepe,** If any anchoress does not know of such things, let her thank Jesus Christ earnestly, and keep herself in fear. The devil is not dead, that she should know (i.e., let her know that), though he may sleep.

520   Lihte gultes beteth thus anan bi ow-seolven, ant thah seggeth ham i schrift hwen ye thencheth ham on as ye speoketh mid preoste. For the leaste of alle, sone se ye underyeoteth hit, falleth bivoren ower weoved o cros to ther eorthe, ant seggeth **Mea culpa!** "Ich gulte! Mearci, Laverd!" The preost ne thearf for na gult, bute hit beo the greattre, leggen other schrift on ow then thet lif thet ye leadeth efter theos riwle. Ah

525   efter the absolutiun, he schal thus seggen: "Al thet god thet tu eaver dest, ant al thet uvel thet tu eaver tholest for the luve of Jesu Crist in-with thine ancre-wahes, al ich engoini the, al ich legge up-o the i remissiun of theose, ant foryevenesse of alle thine sunnen." Ant thenne sum lutles i-hweat he mei leggen upon ow, as a Salm other twa, **Pater nostres, Aves**, tene other tweolve. Disceplines echi to, yef him swa thuncheth.

530   Efter the totagges the beoth i-writen th'ruppe, he schal the sunne demen mare other leasse. A sunne ful foryevelich mei wurthe ful deadlich thurh sum uvel totagge the lith ther-bisiden. Efter schrift falleth to speoken of penitence — thet is, deadbote — ant swa we habbeth in-yong ut of this fifte dale into the seste.

520–21 Lihte gultes . . . mid preoste, Atone for small offenses (lit., light guilts) immediately in this way by yourself, and nevertheless declare them in confession when you think of them as you speak with the priest. **521–22 For the leaste of alle . . . eorthe**, For the least of all [offenses], as soon as you perceive it, fall (imper.) to the ground before your altar in [the shape of a] cross (*ther* = declined def. art.). **522–23** *Mea culpa!* "My fault" (from the prayer of confession). **523 Ich gulte!** I am at fault! **523–24 The preost ne thearf . . . theos riwle**, The priest need not on account of any offense, unless it be the greater, lay other penance on you than the life which you lead according to this rule. **525–28 dest, ant al thet uvel . . . thine sunnen**, do, and all the evil that you ever suffered for the love of Jesus Christ within your anchor-walls, I enjoin (or, charge) everything on you, I lay everything upon you in the remission, of these and forgiveness of all your sins. **528–31 Ant thenne sum lutles i-hweat . . . other leasse**, And then he can lay upon you some little something (i.e., a small penance), such as a Psalm or two, "Our Fathers," "Aves" (i.e., Hail Marys), ten or twelve. Let him add disciplines (i.e., physical mortifications) to [them], if it seems [appropriate] to him. According to the trappings (or, circumstances) which are described above, he must judge the sin [to be] greater or less. **531–33 A sunne ful foryevelich . . . into the seste**, A very forgivable sin can become quite mortal through some evil trapping (or, circumstance) which lies beside it (lit., there-beside). After confession it is fitting (lit., falls) to speak of penance — that is, amends — and so we have an entrance into the sixth from this fifth part.

Part Six

Penance

Al is penitence, ant strong penitence, thet ye eaver dreheth, mine leove sustren. Al thet ye eaver doth of god, al thet ye tholieth is ow martirdom i se derf ordre. For ye beoth niht ant dei up-o Godes rode — blithe mahe ye beon th'rof. For as Seinte Pawel seith, **Si compatimur, conregnabimus.** "As ye scottith with him of his pine on eorthe, ye schule scotti with him of his blisse in heovene." For-thi, seith Seinte Pawel, **Michi absit gloriari, nisi in cruce Domini mei, Jesu Christi.** Ant Hali Chirche singeth, **Nos opportet gloriari in cruce Domini nostri, Jesu Christi.** "Al ure blisse mot beon i Jesu Cristes rode." This word nomeliche limpeth to recluses, hwas blisse ah to beon allunge i Godes rode. Ich chulle biginnen herre, ant lihten swa her-to. Neometh nu gode yeme, for al meast is Sein Beornardes sentence.

---

1 strong, severe; **dreheth**, endure. **2–3 Al thet ye eaver doth . . . derf ordre**, All good things that you ever do (lit., all of good), all that you suffer is a martyrdom for you in so difficult (or, cruel) an order. **4 *Si compatimur, conregnabimus***, "If we suffer with [Him], we shall reign with [Him]" (2 Timothy 2:12, Romans 8:17). **4–5 As ye scottith with him of his pine on eorthe**, As you share with Him in His pain on earth. **6–7 *Michi absit gloriari . . . Christi***, "Far be it from me to boast (or, glory), except in the Cross of my Lord, Jesus Christ" (Galatians 6:14). **7–8 *Nos opportet gloriari . . . Christi***, "It is necessary for us to glory in the Cross of our Lord, Jesus Christ" (the Introit for the Feast of the Invention of the Holy Cross). **8 mot beon**, must be. **8–9 This word nomeliche . . . rode**, This word (i.e., statement) applies especially to recluses, whose joy ought to be completely in God's Cross. **10–11 Ich chulle biginnin herre . . . sentence**, I will begin higher (see explanatory note) and descend thus [back] to this point (lit., here to). Now pay good attention, for most all [of the following] is St. Bernard's opinion.

Threo manere men of Godes i-corene livieth on eorthe: the ane mahe beon to gode pilegrimes i-evenet; the othre, to deade; the thridde, to i-hongede with hare gode wil o Jesuse rode. The forme beoth gode; the othre beoth betere; the thridde best of alle.

To the forme gredeth Seinte Peter inwardliche, **Obsecro vos, tanquam advenas et peregrinos, ut abstineatis vos a carnalibus desideriis, que militant adversus animam.** "Ich halsi ow," he seith, "as el-theodie ant pilegrimes, thet ye withhalden ow from fleschliche lustes the weorrith ayein the sawle." The gode pilegrim halt eaver his rihte wei forth-ward. Thah he seo other here idele gomenes ant wundres bi the weie, he ne edstont nawt as foles doth, ah halt forth his rute ant hiheth toward his giste. He ne bereth na gersum bute his speonse gnedeliche, ne clathes bute ane theo thet him to neodeth. This beoth hali men the, thah ha beon i the world, ha beoth th'rin as pilegrimes ant gath with god lif-lade toward te riche of heovene, ant seggeth with the Apostle, **Non habemus hic manentem civitatem, set futuram inquirimus** — thet is, "nabbe we na wununge her, ah we secheth other." Beoth bi the leaste thet ha mahen, ne ne haldeth na tale of na worltlich

15

20

25

12–14 the ane mahe beon . . . Jesuse rode, the first may be compared to good pilgrims; the second, to the dead; the third, to those hanged with their good will (i.e., willingly) on Jesus' Cross. **14 forme**, first; **othre**, second. **16 gredeth**, cries out. **16–18** *Obsecro vos . . . adversus animam*, "I implore you, as foreigners and pilgrims, that you hold yourselves back from carnal desires which war against the spirit" (1 Peter 2:11). **18 "Ich halsi ow,"** "I implore you"; **el-theodie**, foreign ones, foreigners. **19 weorrith**, make war, attack. **20 halt**, holds, keeps to (*halt* = reduced form of *haldeth*). **20–22 Thah he seo other here . . . his giste**, Though he [may] see or hear idle games (or, entertainments) and marvels (i.e., amazing things) by the way, he does not stand still (*edstont* = reduced form of *edstondeth*) as fools do, but holds his route (or, course) forward and hurries toward his lodgings. **22– 23 He ne bereth na gersum . . . neodeth**, He does not carry any possessions (or, treasure) but barely money [enough] for his expenses, nor [does he carry any] clothes except only those that are necessary to him. **23 hali men the**, holy men who. **24–25 with god lif-lade . . . of heovene**, with a good way of life toward the kingdom of heaven. **25–26** *Non habemus . . . inquirimus*, "We do not have here (i.e., in this life) an enduring city, but we seek [a city which is] to come" (Hebrews 13:14). **26 wununge**, dwelling. **27–28 Beoth bi the leaste thet ha mahen . . . of pilegrim**, [Holy men] exist (lit., are) on the least that they

frovre, thah ha beon i worltlich wei — as ich seide — of pilegrim, ah habbeth hare heorte eaver toward heovene. Ant ahen wel to habben, for other pilegrimes gath

30 [i] muche swinc to sechen ane sontes banes, as Sein James other Sein Giles. Ah theo pilegrimes the gath toward heovene, ha gath to beon i-sontet, ant to finden Godd seolf ant alle his hali halhen, liviende i blisse, ant schulen livien with him i wunne buten ende. Ha i-findeth i-wis Sein Julienes in, the wei-fearinde men yeornliche bisecheth.

35 Nu beoth theose gode, ah yet beoth the othre betere, for allegate pilegrimes, as ich ear seide, al gan ha eaver forth-ward, ne bicumen burh-men i the worldes burh, ham thuncheth sum-chearre god of thet ha seoth bi weie, ant edstuteth sum-deal, thah ha ne don mid alle, ant moni thing ham falleth to hwer-thurh ha beoth i-lette, swa thet — mare hearm is! — sum kimeth leate ham, sum neaver mare. Hwa

40 is thenne skerre, ant mare ut of the world then pilegrimes? — thet is to seggen, then theo men the habbeth worltlich thing ant ne luvieth hit nawt, ah yeoveth hit as hit kimeth ham, ant gath untrusset, lihte as pilegrimes doth toward heovene? Hwa beoth betere thene theos? Godd wat, theo beoth betere the the Apostle speketh

can, nor do they hold worldly comfort of any value, though they be on the worldly path — as I said — of the pilgrim. **29–30 Ant ahen wel to habben . . . Giles,** And ought well to have, for other pilgrims go (or, proceed) in great difficulty (or, toil) to seek out one [single] saint's bones, such as St. James or St. Giles. **30–31 Ah theo pilegrimes the gath,** But those pilgrims who go. **31 i-sontet,** sainted, made saints. **32 hali halhen,** holy saints. **32–33 i wunne buten ende,** in joy without end. **33–34 Ha i-findeth i-wis . . . bisecheth,** They [will] certainly find St. Julian's inn, which wayfaring men eagerly seek out. **35 Nu beoth theose gode,** Now these are good. **35–39 for allegate pilegrimes . . . sum neaver mare,** for pilgrims nevertheless, as I said before, even though they all go continually forward, and do not become citizens (lit., town-men) in the world's city, [some] of [the things] that they see by the way seem good to them sometimes, and [they] linger a bit, though they do not do [so] completely, and many a thing happens to them whereby they are delayed (or, hindered), so that — more is the harm! — some come home late, some nevermore. **40 skerre,** freer, purer (see glossary). **41–42 then theo men . . . toward heovene?** than those men who have worldly property (lit., things) and do not love it, but give it as it comes to them, and go unburdened, light (or, easily) as pilgrims do toward heaven? **43 Hwa,** Who. **43–44 Godd wat . . . ant seith,** God knows, those [people] are better to whom the Apostle

to, ant seith in his epistle, **Mortui estis et vita vestra abscondita est cum Christo**

45   **in Deo. Cum autem apparuerit vita vestra, tunc et vos apparebitis cum ipso in gloria.** "Ye beoth deade ant ower lif is i-hud mid Criste. Hwen he thet is ower lif eadeaweth ant springeth as the dahunge efter nihtes theosternesse, ant ye schulen with him springen schenre then the sunne into eche blisse." The nu beoth thus deade, hare lif-lade is herre, for pilgrim eileth moni-hwet. The deade nis noht of,

50   thah he ligge unburiet ant rotie buven eorthe. Preise him, laste him, do him scheome, sei him scheome — al him is i-liche leof. This is a seli death thet maketh cwic mon thus, other cwic wummon, ut of the worlde. Ah sikerliche hwa-se is thus dead in hire-seolven, Godd liveth in hire heorte. For this is thet te Apostle seith, **Vivo ego iam non ego. Vivit autem in me Christus.** "Ich livie — nawt ich, ah

55   Crist liveth in me" thurh his in-wuniende grace, ant is as thah he seide, "worltlich speche, worltlich sihthe, ant euch worltlich thing i-findeth me deade. Ah thet te limpeth to Crist, thet ich seo ant here, ant wurche i cwicnesse." Thus riht is euch religius dead to the worlde ant cwic thah to Criste. This is an heh steire, ah yet is

speaks and declares. **44–46 Mortui estis . . . cum ipso in gloria**, "You have died and your life is hidden with Christ in God. When, however, your life (i.e., Christ) will have appeared, then you too will appear with Him (lit., the same) in glory" (Colossians 3:3–4). **46 i-hud mid Criste**, hidden with Christ. **47–48 eadeaweth ant springeth . . . blisse**, appears and springs (or, rises) like the dawning after night's darkness, and you will rise with Him more beautiful (or, brighter) than the sun into eternal joy. **48–49 The nu beoth thus deade . . . moni-hwet**, Whoever are now dead in this way, their way of life is higher, for many a thing afflicts (or, annoys) the pilgrim. **49–50 The deade nis noht of . . . buven eorthe**, To the dead it is of little importance (lit., it is of nothing), though he lie unburied and [though he] rot above ground. **50–51 Preise him . . . i-liche leof**, Praise him, blame him, do him shame, slander him (lit., say him shame) — all is equally pleasing to him. **51–52 This is a seli death . . . worlde**, This is a blessed death which thus puts a living man, or living woman, out of the world. **52 sikerliche hwa-se**, certainly whosoever. **53 this is thet**, this is what. **54 Vivo ego . . . Christus**, "I live, [but] indeed not I. On the contrary — Christ lives in me" (adapted from Galatians 2:20). **55 thurh his in-wuniende grace**, through His indwelling grace. **56 sihthe**, sight. **56–57 Ah thet te limpeth to Crist . . . cwicnesse**, But that which relates to Christ — that I see and hear, and do in vitality (lit., aliveness). **57–58 Thus riht . . . dead**, Thus, [quite] rightly, is each religious [person] (i.e., person who has taken religious vows) dead. **58–59 This is an heh steire . . . the seide**, This is a high stair, but [there] is still, nevertheless, a higher [one]. And who ever stood

thah an herre. Ant hwa stod eaver th'rin? Godd wat, the the seide, **Michi absit**
60   **gloriari nisi in cruce Domini mei, Jesu Christi, per quam michi mundus**
crucifixus est et ego mundo. This is thet ich seide th'ruppe: "Crist me schilde
for-te habben eani blisse i this world bute i Jesu Cristes rode, mi Laverd, thurh
hwam the world is me unwurth, ant ich am unwurth hire, as weari the is ahonget."
A, Laverd, hehe stod he the spec o thisse wise. Ant this is ancre steire thet ha thus
65   segge, **Michi autem absit gloriari, et cetera.** "I na thing ne blissi ich me bute i
Godes rode, thet ich tholie nu wa ant am i-tald unwurth as Godd wes o rode."
Lokith, leove sustren, hu this steire is herre then eani beo of the othre. The pilegrim
i the wor[l]des wei, thah he ga forth-ward toward te ham of heovene, he sith ant
hereth unnet, ant speketh umbe-hwile, wreatheth him for weohes, ant moni thing
70   mei letten him of his jurnee. The deade nis na mare of scheome then of menske, of
heard then of nesche, for he ne feleth nowther, ant for-thi ne ofearneth he nowther
wa ne wunne. Ah the the is o rode ant haveth blisse th'rof, he wendeth scheome to
menske ant wa into wunne, ant ofearneth for-thi hure over hure. This beoth theo

on it (lit., there-in)? God knows, he (i.e., the person) who said. **59–61 *Michi absit gloriari . . .***
ego mundo, "Far be it from me to glory unless in the Cross of my Lord, Jesus Christ, through
which the world is crucified to me and I [am crucified] to the world" (Galatians 6:14). **61 thet**
ich seide th'ruppe, what I said above (lit., up there). **61–63 "Crist me schilde . . . the is**
ahonget," "Christ shield me from having (lit., to have) any joy in this world except in the
Cross of Jesus Christ, my Lord, through whom the world is worthless to me and I am worthless
to her, as an criminal who is hanged." **64 hehe stod he the**, high stood he who; **ancre steire**, an
anchoress' stair. **65 *Michi autem absit . . . et cetera***, see gloss to 6.6–7; **ne blissi ich me**, not
take joy (reflex.). **66 thet ich tholie . . . o rode**, that I now suffer woe and am reckoned worthless as God was on the Cross. **67 herre**, higher. **68–70 ham of heovene . . . of his jurnee**,
home of heaven, he sees and hears vanity, and speaks [it] for a time, becomes angry (lit.,
enrages himself) because of wrongs, and many a thing may hinder him from his journey. **70–**
72 The deade nis na mare . . . ne wunne, To the dead there is no more of shame than of honor,
of harsh things than of soft, for he feels neither, and therefore he does not deserve (or, earn)
either woe or joy. **72–73 Ah the the is o rode . . . over hure**, But he who is on the Cross and
has joy in it (lit., thereof), he turns shame to honor and woe to joy, and earns reward over
reward. **73–76 This beoth theo . . . ant teone**, These (lit., This) are those who are never glad-
hearted except when they suffer (i.e., are suffering) some woe or some shame with Jesus on His
Cross. For this is happiness on earth, whoever (i.e., when a person) may have shame and

75 the neaver ne beoth gleade i-heortet bute hwen ha tholieth sum wa other sum scheome with Jesu on his rode. For this is the selhthe on eorthe, hwa-se mei for Godes luve habben scheome ant teone. Thus, lo, rihte ancres ne beoth nawt ane pilegrimes, ne yet nawt ane deade, ah beoth of theos thridde. For al hare blisse is for-te beon ahonget sariliche ant scheomeliche with Jesu on his rode. Theos mahe blithe with Hali Chirche singen, **Nos opportet gloriari, et cetera** — thet is as ich

80 seide ear. Hwet-se beo of *oth*re, the habbeth hare blisse summe i flesches licunge, summe i worldes dweole, summe in othres uvel, we mote nede blissin us i Jesu Cristes rode — thet is, i scheome ant i wa thet he droh o rode. Moni walde summes weis tholien flesches heardschipe, ah beon i-tald unwurth, ne scheome ne mahte he tholien. Ah he nis bute halflunge up-o Godes rode, yef he nis i-greithet to

85 tholien ham bathe.

　　Vilitas et asperitas, vilte ant asprete, theos twa, scheome ant pine, as Sein Beornard seith, beoth the twa leaddre-steolen the beoth up i-riht to heovene. Ant bitweone theose steolen beoth of alle gode theawes the tindes i-festnet, bi hwucche me climbeth to the blisse of heovene. For-thi thet Davith hefde the twa steolen of

90 this leaddre, thah he king were, he clomb uppard ant seide baldeliche to ure Laverd,

hardship for God's love. **76–77 Thus, lo, rihte ancres . . . theos thridde,** Thus, look, rightful anchoresses are not only pilgrims, nor yet only dead, but are of this third [group]. **78 sariliche,** sorrowfully (or, painfully). **78–79 Theos mahe blithe . . . singen,** These may joyfully sing with Holy Church. **79** *Nos opportet gloriari,* (see gloss to 6.7–8). **80 ear,** before. **80–82 Hwet-se beo of othre . . . droh o rode,** Whatever may be the case with (lit., is of) the others who have their joy, some in the pleasure of the flesh, some in the world's trickery (or, error), some in others' harm, we must needs rejoice (reflex.) in Jesus Christ's Cross — that is, in the shame and in the woe which He suffered on the Cross. **82–85 Moni walde summes weis . . . ham bathe,** Many [a person might] want to experience in some way the hardship of the flesh, but to be counted worthless or shameful he could not bear. But he is not but (i.e., is only) halfway upon God's Cross if he is not prepared to experience (or, suffer) them both. **86–89** *Vilitas et asperitas . . .* **blisse of heovene,** "Debasement and severity," these two, shame and pain, as St. Bernard says, are the uprights of the ladder which is directed to (i.e., leads to) heaven. And between these uprights the rungs of all good virtues are fastened, by which one climbs to the joy of heaven. **89 For-thi thet,** Because. **90 baldeliche,** boldly.

Vide humilitatem meam et laborem meum et dimitte universa delicta mea.
"Bihald," quoth he, "ant sih min eadmodnesse ant mi swinc, ant foryef me mine
sunnen alle togederes." Notith wel thes twa word the Davith feieth somet: "swinc"
ant "eadmodnesse" — swinc i pine ant i wa, i sar ant i sorhe; eadmodnesse ayein
95   woh of scheome thet mon dreheth, the is i-tald unwurth. "Ba theos bihald in me,"
quoth Davith, Godes deorling. "Ich habbe theos twa leaddre-steolen." **Dimitte
universa delicta mea.** "Leaf," quoth he, "bihinde me ant warp awei from me alle
mine gultes thet ich, i-lihtet of hare hevinesse, lihtliche stihe up to heovene bi
theos leaddre."

100   Theose twa thinges — thet is, wa ant scheome i-feiet togederes — beoth Helyes
hweoles the weren furene, hit teleth, ant beren him up to parais, ther he liveth
yetten. Fur is hat ant read. I the heate is understonden euch wa thet eileth flesch;
scheome bi the reade. Ah wel mei duhen, ha beoth her hweolinde ase hweoles,
overturneth sone, ne leasteth nane hwile. This ilke is ec bitacnet bi cherubines
105   sweord bivore paraise yeten, the wes of lei ant hweolinde, ant turninde abuten. Ne
kimeth nan into parais bute thurh this leitinde sweord, the wes hat ant read, ant in

91 *Vide humilitatem meam . . . delicta mea*, "See my humility and my toil and dismiss all
my faults" (Psalm 24:18). 92 **eadmodnesse ant mi swinc**, humility and my toil. 93–95
Notith wel . . . i-tald unwurth, Note well (imper.) these two words which David joins
together: "toil" and "humility" — toil in pain and woe, in sorrow, and in sadness; humility
in response to the injury of shame which a person (lit., one) suffers who is counted worthless. 95 **Ba theos**, Both these. 96–97 *Dimitte universa . . . mea*, see gloss to 6.91. 97–99
"Leaf . . . bi theos leaddre," "Put (lit., Leave)," he said, "behind me and cast away from
me all my faults [so] that I, lightened of their heaviness, may lightly climb up to heaven by
this ladder." 100–02 **i-feiet togederes . . . yetten**, joined together — are Elijah's wheels
which were burning, it says, and bore him up to paradise, where he lives still (see 2 Kings
2:1–18). 102 **is understonden**, is to be understood; **eileth**, afflicts, troubles. 103 **Ah wel
mei duhen . . . ase hweoles**, But it is very fitting (lit., may well be appropriate) [that] they
here are rotating like wheels, [and] revolve (lit., turn over) quickly, [and do] not pause any
while. 104–05 **This ilke is ec bitacnet . . . abuten**, This same [thing] is also symbolized
by the cherubim's sword before the gates of paradise (see Genesis 3:24), which was [made]
of flame and wheeling, turning about. 105–08 **Ne kimeth nan . . . agath sone**, None (i.e.,
no one) comes into paradise except through this blazing sword, which was hot and red,
and on Elijah's fiery wheels — that is, through sorrow (or, pain) and through shame, which

Helyes furene hweoles — thet is, thurh sar ant thurh scheome, the overturneth tidliche, ant agath sone. Ant nes Godes rode with his deore-wurthe blod i-rudet ant i-readet, for-te schawin on him-seolf thet pine, ant sorhe, ant sar schulden
110   with scheome beon i-heowet? Nis hit i-writen bi him, **Factus est obediens patri usque ad mortem, mortem autem crucis** — thet is, "he wes buhsum his feader, nawt ane to death, ah to death o rode"? Thurh thet he seide earst "death" is pine understonden. Thurh thet he th'refter seith "death o the rode" is schendlac bitacnet, for swuch wes Godes death o the deore rode pinful ant schentful over alle othre.
115   Hwa-se eaver deieth ine Godd, ant o Godes rode, theos twa ha mot tholien: scheome for him ant pine. Scheome ich cleopie eaver her beon i-tald unwurth, ant beggin as an hearlot, yef neod is, hire liveneth, ant beon othres beodes-mon — as ye beoth, leove sustren — ant tholieth ofte danger of swuch other-hwile the mahte beon ower threal. This is thet eadi scheome thet ich of talie. Pine ne truketh ow
120   nawt. I theos ilke twa thing, thet al penitence is in, blissith ow ant gleadieth, for ayein theos twa ow beoth twa-fald blissen i-yarket: ayein scheome, menske; ayein

turns over (or, revolves) quickly, and goes away soon. **108–10 Ant nes Godes rode . . . i-heowet?** And is God's Cross not ruddied and reddened with His precious blood in order to show in Himself that pain, and care, and sorrow should be colored (or, stained) with shame? **110 Nis hit i-writen bi him,** Is it not written concerning Him. **110–11 *Factus est obediens . . . crucis*,** "He was obedient (lit., made obedient) to the father to death, even death on a Cross" (based on Phillipians 2:8). **111 buhsum his feader,** obedient (ModE *buxom* — see glossary) to His father. **112–14 Thurh thet he seide . . . alle othre,** By the fact that He first said "death" is pain to be understood. By the fact that afterwards He says "death on the Cross," shame is symbolized, for thus God's death on the dear Cross was painful and shameful over all other [deaths]. **115 theos twa ha mot tholien,** she must suffer these two things. **116–19 Scheome ich cleopie eaver her . . . ower threal,** I always call shame here (i.e., in this section) to be counted worthless, and to beg like a vagabond, if there is need, for her food, and to be given charity to pray for others (lit., to be others' beadsman — see *beodes-mon* in glossary) — as you are, dear sisters — and to endure often the dominion (or, arrogance) of such [a person] sometimes who might be your thrall. **119–20 thet eadi scheome . . . ow nawt,** that blessed (or, fortunate) shame which I tell of. Pain [will] not deceive you. **120–22 I theos ilke twa thing . . . buten ende,** In these same two things, in which all penitence is (or, consists), rejoice and be glad (reflex.), for in compensation for these, two-fold (i.e., double) blessings are prepared for you: in compensation for shame,

pine, delit ant reste buten ende. **Ysa[ias]: In terra inquit sua duplicia possidebunt.** "Ha schulen," seith Ysaie, "in hare ahne lond wealden twa-vald blisse ayein twa-vald wa thet ha her dreheth." "In hare ahne lond," seith Ysaie,

125 for alswa as the uvele nabbeth na lot in heovene, ne *the* gode nabbeth na lot in eorthe. **Super epistolam Jacobi: Mali nichil habent in celo; boni vero nichil in terra.** In hare ahne lond ha schulen wealden blisse, twa-fald cunne mede, ayein twa-vald sorhe, as thah he seide, "Ne thunche ham na feorlich, thah ha her tholien as in uncuth lond, ant in uncuth eard, bituhhen untheode, scheome ba ant sorhe,

130 for swa deth moni gentil mon the is uncuth in uncuththe." Me mot ute swinken: ed hame me schal resten, ant nis he a cang cniht the secheth reste i the feht ant eise i the place? **Milicia est vita hominis super terram.** "Al this lif is a feht," as Job witneth. Ah efter this feht her, yef we wel fehteth, menske ant reste abit us ed hame in ure ahne lond — thet is, heove-riche. Lokith nu hu witerliche ure Laverd

135 seolf hit witneth: **Cum sederit Filius hominis in sede majestatis sue, sedebitis**

---

there is honor; in compensation for pain, delight and rest without end. **122–23** *Ysa[ias]: In terra . . . possidebunt*, Isaiah: "'In their land,' he says, 'they will possess double'" (Isaiah 61:7). **123–24 hare ahne lond . . . her dreheth**, their own land possess a two-fold (or, double) joy, in compensation for the double woe which they suffer here. **125–26 for alswa as the uvele . . . eorthe**, for just as the evil have no part in heaven, neither do the good have any part in earth. **126–27** *Super epistolam Jacobi . . . in terra*, Concerning the epistle of James: "The evil have (or, possess) nothing in heaven; the good indeed nothing on earth" (*Glossa Ordinaria* commentary on James 1:2 [*PL* 114.671]). **127–30 In hare ahne lond . . . in uncuththe**, In their own land they will possess joy, a double kind of reward, in compensation for [their] double sorrow, as though he said, "Let it not seem to them a strange thing, though they suffer here as in a strange land, and in a strange country, among strange people, both shame and sorrow, for so (i.e., in this way) many a gentle (or, well-born) man does (or, acts), who is a stranger in a strange land." **130–32 Me mot ute swinken . . . i the place?** Outside (or, away from home) one must work: at home one wants to rest, and is he not a foolish knight who looks for rest in the battle and ease in the field? **132** *Milicia est vita . . . terram*, "The life of man is warfare on earth" (Job 7:1). **133–35 menske ant reste . . . hit witneth**, honor and rest await us at home in our own land — that is, the kingdom of heaven. See now how clearly our Lord Himself bears witness to it. **135–37** *Cum sederit Filius hominis . . . commendatur*, "When the Son of man will sit in the seat of His majesty, you will sit judging," etc. (Matthew 19:28). Bernard: "In seats (or, thrones), peace undisturbed is commended; [and] in judging, the pinnacle of honor"

et vos judicantes, et cetera. Bernardus: In sedibus, quies inperturbata; in judicio, honoris eminencia commendatur. "Hwen ich sitte for-te demen," seith ure Laverd, "ye schulen sitten with me ant deme with me al the world thet schal beon i-demet: kinges, ant keisers, cnihtes, ant clearkes." I the sete is reste ant eise

140 bitacnet, ayein the swinc thet her is. I the menske of the dom thet ha schulen demen is hehschipe menskeful over alle understonden, ayein scheome ant lahschipe thet ha her for Godes luve mildeliche tholeden.

Nis ther nu thenne bute tholien gleadliche, for bi Godd seolf is i-writen, **Quod per penam ignominiose passionis, pervenit ad gloriam resurrectionis** — thet

145 is, "thurh schentful pine he com to gloire of blisful ariste." Nis na sel-cuth, thenne, yef we wrecche sunfule tholien her pine, yef we wulleth o Domes-dei blisfule arisen Ant thet we mahen thurh his grace, yef we us-seolf wulleth. **Quoniam si complantati fuerimus similitudini mortis eius, simul et resurrectionis erimus** — Seinte Paweles sahe the seith se wel eaver: "yef we beoth i-impet to the i-

150 licnesse of Godes death, we schulen of his ariste" — thet is to seggen, yef we libbeth i scheome ant i pine for his luve — i hwucche twa he deide — we schulen beon i-liche his blisful ariste, ure bodi briht as his is, world buten ende, as Seinte

(Geoffrey of Auxerre, *Declamations from the Dialogue between Simon and Jesus Collected from the Sermons of St. Bernard* 40.49 [*PL* 184.463]). **137 demen**, to judge. **138–39 thet schal beon i-demet**, which will be judged. **139–42 I the sete . . . mildeliche tholeden**, By the seat, rest and ease is symbolized, in compensation for the travail that is here. By the honor of judgment what they will judge (i.e., render), honorable majesty (or, loftiness) above all [other honors] is to be understood, in compensation for the shame and lowliness which they meekly suffered here for God's love. **143 tholien**, to suffer; **bi Godd seolf**, about God Himself. **143–44 Quod per penam . . . resurrectionis**, "Because through the pain of His shameful passion, He arrived at the glory of the resurrection" (source unidentified). **145 blisful ariste**, joyful resurrection (or, arising). **145–47 Nis na sel-cuth . . . us-seolf wulleth**, [It] is no wonder, then, if we sinful wretches suffer pain here, if we want to arise joyfully on Judgment Day. And we can do that through His grace, if we ourselves want to. **147–48 Quoniam si complantati . . . erimus**, "For if we will have been planted together (i.e., united) in the likeness of His death, we will likewise be [united in the likeness] of [His] resurrection" (Romans 6:5). **149–50 Seinte Paweles sahe . . . of his ariste**, [This is the] saying of St. Paul, who always speaks so well: "if we are grafted to the likeness of God's death, we shall [be] of His resurrection." **151 i hwucche twa he deide**, in which two He died. **152 i-liche**, like; **world buten ende**, world without end.

Pawel witneth: **Salvatorem expectamus, qui reformabit corpus humilitatis nostre configuratum corpori claritatis sue.** Let othre acemin hare bodi the eorneth bivoren-hond. Abide we ure Healent, the schal acemin ure efter his ahne. **Si compatimur, conregnabimus.** "Yef we tholieth with him, we schule blissin with him." Nis this god foreward? Wat Crist, nis he nawt god feolahe ne treowe, the nule scottin i the lure, as eft i the biyete. **Glosa: Illis solis prodest sanguis Christi, qui voluptates deserunt et corpus affligunt.** "Godd schedde his blod for alle, ah heom ane hit is wurth, the fleoth flesches licunge ant pinith ham-seolven." Ant is thet eani wunder? Nis Godd ure heaved ant we his limen alle? Ah nis euch lim sar with sorhe of the heaved? His lim thenne nis he nawt, the naveth eche under se sar akinde heaved. Hwen the heaved sweat wel, thet lim the ne swet nawt — nis hit uvel tacne? He the is ure heaved sweatte blodes swat for ure secnesse, to turnen us of thet lond-uvel thet alle londes leien on, ant liggeth yette monie. The lim the ne sweat nawt i swincful pine for his luve, deu-le-set, hit leaveth in his secnesse, ant

155

160

165

153–54 *Salvatorem expectamus . . . claritatis sue*, "We look for a Savior who will reshape the body of our lowliness, conforming [it] to the body of His brightness" (Phillipians 3:20–21). **154–55 Let othre acemin . . . his ahne,** Let others who run ahead adorn their bodies. Let us wait for our Savior, who will adorn our [bodies], according to His own. **155–56** *Si compatimur, conregnabimus*, "If we suffer with [Him], we shall reign with [Him]" (2 Timothy 2:12, Romans 8:17). **156–58 tholieth with him . . . i the biyete,** "suffer with Him, we shall rejoice with Him." Is this not a good agreement? Christ knows, he is not a good or true (i.e., loyal) friend who will not share in the loss, as in turn (i.e., as well as) in the profit. **158–59** *Glosa: Illis solis . . . affligunt,* Gloss: "The blood of Christ can help only those who abandon pleasures and [who] afflict [their] body" (source unidentified). **159–60 ah heom ane hit is wurth . . . ham-seolven,** but to them only is it good, who flee the pleasure of the flesh and [who] torment themselves. **161–63 Nis Godd ure heaved . . . akinde heaved?** Is God not our head and we all his limbs? But is each limb not sore with the pain of the head (i.e., when the head is in pain)? He is not his limb (i.e., God's limb), who does not have an ache under (or, beneath) so sore an aching head. **163–65 Hwen the heaved sweat . . . yette monie,** When the head sweats profusely (lit., well), that limb which does not sweat — is it not a bad sign? He who is our head sweat a sweat of blood for our sickness, to turn (i.e., cure) us of that pestilence (lit., land-disease) which all lands lay under (i.e., have lain under, suffered from), and many still lie. **165–67 The lim the ne sweat nawt . . . sar Godd,** The limb which does not sweat in laborious pain for His love — God knows, it remains in its sickness, and there is nothing [to do] but cut it off

nis ther bute forkeorven hit — thah hit thunche sar Godd. For betere is finger offe, then he ake eaver. Cwemeth he nu wel Godd, the thus bilimeth him of him-seolf, thurh thet he nule sweaten? **Oportebat Christum pati et sic intrare in gloriam**

170   **suam**. Seinte Marie, mearci! — "Hit moste swa beon," hit seith, "Crist tholie pine ant passiun, ant swa habben in-yong into his riche." Lo, deale, hwet he seith, "swa habben in-yong into his riche" — swa, ant nan other-weis. Ant we wrecches sunfule wulleth with eise stihen to heovene thet is se hehe buven us ant se swithe muchel wurth! Ant me ne mei nawt withuten swinc a lutel cote arearen, ne twa thwongede

175   scheos habbe withute bune! Other theo beoth canges, the weneth with liht leapes buggen eche blisse, other the hali halhen the bohten hit se deore. Nes Seinte Peter ant Seinte Andrew there-vore i-straht o rode? Sein Lorenz o the gridil, ant lathlese meidnes the tittes i-toren of, tohwitheret o hweoles, heafdes bicorven? Ah ure sotschipe is sutel. Ant heo weren i-lich theose yape children the habbeth *riche*

180   *feaderes*, the willes ant waldes toteoreth hare clathes, for-te habbe neowe. Ure

— though that seems sad to God. **168 then he ake eaver**, than [that] it always ache. **168–69 Cwemeth he nu wel ... sweaten?** Now does he please God well who thus cuts off a limb (*him* = reflex.) from himself, because he does not want to sweat? **169–70 *Oportebat Christum ... gloriam suam*,** "It was necessary for Christ to suffer and so enter into His glory" (based on Luke 24:26, see also Luke 24:46). **170 moste swa beon,** had to be so. **170–71 "Crist tholie ... his riche,"** "Christ [had to] suffer pain and passion, and so have entry into His kingdom." **171 Lo, deale, hwet he seith,** Look! See what he says. **172–75 swa, ant nan ... withute bune!** thus, and in no other way. And we sinful wretches want to climb with ease to heaven which is so high above us and worth so very much! And one cannot without toil raise up (i.e., build) a little cottage, or have two thonged shoes (i.e., shoes with leather laces) without the buying (i.e., without paying for them)! **175 Other theo beoth canges,** Either they are fools who expect to buy eternal joy on the cheap (see textual note), or the holy saints who bought it so dearly (i.e., expensively). **176–78 Nes Seinte Peter ... bicorven?** Were not St. Peter and St. Andrew stretched out on a cross for this? [And] St. Lawrence on the griddle? And [did not] innocent virgins [have] their breasts torn off, [were they not] shattered on wheels, [did they not have their] heads cut off? **178–80 Ah ure sotschipe is sutel ... habbe neowe,** Our foolishness is evident. And they (i.e., the saints) were like these shrewd children who have rich fathers, [children] who willingly and intentionally tear their clothes up in order to have new ones. **180–84 Ure alde curtel ... ant with weane,** Our old coat is the flesh which we have from Adam,

357

alde curtel is the flesch thet we of Adam ure alde feader habbeth; the neowe we schulen undervon of Godd, ure riche feader, i the ariste of Domes-dei, hwen ure flesch schal blikien schenre then the sunne, yef hit is totoren her with wontreathe ant with weane. Of theo the hare curtles toteoreth o thisse wise, seith Ysaie,

185 **Deferetur munus Domino exercituum a populo divulso et dilacerato, a populo terribili.** "A folc tolaimet ant totoren, a folc," he seith, "fearlich schal makien to ure Laverd present of him-seolven." Folc tolaimet ant totoren with strong lif-lade, ant with heard, he cleopeth "folc fear*l*ich," for the feond is of swucche offruht ant offearet. For-thi thet Job wes thullich, he meande him ant seide, **Pellem pro pelle**

190 **et uni[versa], et cetera** — thet is, "he wulle yeoven fel for fel," the alde for the neowe, as thah he seide, "Ne geineth me nawt to asailin him: he is of thet totore folc. He tereth his alde curtel ant torendeth the alde pilche of his deadliche fel." For the fel is undeadlich thet i the neowe ariste schal schine seove-vald brihtre then the sunne. Eise ant flesches este beoth thes deofles mearken. Hwen he sith

195 theos mearken i mon other i wummon, he wat the castel is his ant geath baldeliche

our original (lit., old) father; the new we must receive from God, our rich father, in the resurrection of Judgment Day, when our flesh will shine brighter than the sun, if it is torn apart here with misery and with woe. **184 theo the . . . thisse wise**, those who tear apart their coats in this way. **185–86 *Deferetur munus . . . populo terribili***, "A gift will be brought to the Lord of hosts by a people ripped and torn apart, by a frightful people" (Isaiah 18:7). **186–87 "A folc tolaimet . . . of him-seolven,"** "A people dismembered and torn apart, a fearful people," he says, "will make a present of themselves to our Lord." **187–89 Folc tolaimet . . . ant seide**, A people dismembered and torn apart with a severe and hard way of life he calls "a fearsome people," because the fiend is frightened and afraid of such [people]. Because Job was such [a person], he (i.e., the devil) complained (reflex.) and said. **189–90 *Pellem pro pelle . . . et cetera***, "Skin for skin and all [that a man has, he will give for his life]," etc. (Job 2:4). **190–92 yeoven fel for fel . . . deadliche fel**, "give skin for skin," the old for the new, as though he said, "[It] gains me nothing to attack him: he is from that torn-apart people. He tears his old coat and rips apart the old leather robe of his mortal skin." **193–94 For the fel is undeadlich . . . the sunne**, For that skin is immortal which in the new resurrection will shine sevenfold (i.e., seven times) brighter than the sun. **194–96 Eise ant flesches este . . . deth i castel**, Pleasure and the gratification of the flesh (or, body) are the devil's marks. When he sees these marks in a man or in a woman, he knows the castle is his and goes boldly in where he sees such banners raised up, as one does in

in ther he sith i-riht up swucche baneres, as me deth i castel. I thet totore folc he misseth his merken, ant sith in ham i-riht up Godes banere — thet is, heardschipe of lif — ant haveth muche dred th'rof, as Ysaie witneth.

"Me leove sire," seith sum, "ant is hit nu wisdom to don se wa him-seolven?"
200 Ant tu yeld me ondswere of tweie men hwether is wisre. Ha beoth ba seke: the an forgeath al thet he luveth of metes ant of drunches ant drinketh bitter sabraz for-te acovrin heale. The other folheth al his wil ant for*th*eth his lustes ayein his secnesse ant leoseth his lif sone. Hwether is wisre of thes twa? Hwether is betere his ahne freond? Hwether luveth him-seolf mare? Ant hwa nis sec of sunne? Godd for ure
205 secnesse dronc attri drunch o rode — ant we nulleth nawt bittres biten for us-seolven! Nis ther na-wiht th'rof. Sikerliche his folhere mot with pine of his flesch folhin his pine. Ne wene nan with este stihen to heovene.

"Me, sire," seith sum eft, "wule Godd se wracfulliche wreoken up-o sunne?"
Ye, mon! For loke nu hu he hit heateth swithe. Hu walde nu the mon beate thet
210 thing seolf, hwer-se he hit i-funde, the for muchel heatunge beote th'rof the

a castle (or, as is done in a castle). **197–98 misseth his merken . . . dred th'rof**, misses (i.e., does not find) his marks, and sees in them God's banner raised up — that is, hardship of life — and has much dread of that. **199–200 "Me leove sire" . . . wisre**, "But dear sir," some[one] says, "and is it now wisdom (i.e., a wise thing) to do such harm to oneself?" And you give me an answer (i.e., tell me) which of two men is wiser. **200–02 Ha beoth ba seke . . . acovrin heale**, They are both sick: the one forgoes all that he loves of foods and drinks and drinks a bitter elixir in order to recover [his] health. **202–03 The other folheth al his wil . . . thes twa?** The other (or, second, man) follows his pleasure completely and furthers (or, encourages) his desires despite his sickness and soon loses his life. Which is the wiser of these two? **203 ahne**, own. **204 nis sec of sunne**, is not sick with sin. **205–06 dronc attri drunch . . . us-seolven!** drank a poisonous drink on the Cross — and we do not want to taste (lit., bite — see *biten* in glossary) anything bitter for ourselves! **206–07 Nis ther na-wiht . . . his pine**, There is nothing for it. Surely His follower must with pain of his flesh follow His pain. **207 Ne wene nan . . . heovene**, Let no one expect to climb to heaven with pleasure. **208 "Me, sire . . . up-o sunne?"** "But, sir," someone again says, "will God take revenge so vengefully for sin?" **209–11 Ye, mon! . . . eani licnesse?** Yes, sir! For look now how very much he hates it. Now, how would that man beat the thing itself, wheresoever he might find it, who for great hatred would beat the shadow of it and

schadewe ant al thet hefde ther-to eani licnesse? Godd, feader almihti — hu beot he bitterliche his deore-wurthe sune, Jesu ure Laverd, thet neaver nefde sunne, bute ane thet he ber flesch i-lich ure, thet is ful of sunne? Ant we schulden beon i-spearet, the beoreth on us his sune death? The wepne thet sloh him — thet wes ure sunne, ant he the nefde nawt of sunne bute schadewe ane wes i the ilke schadewe se scheomeliche i-tuket, se sorhfulliche i-pinet, thet ear hit come ther-to, for the threatunge ane th'rof, swa him agras ther-ayein — thet he bed his feader are: **Tristis est anima mea usque ad mortem. Pater mi, si possibile est, transeat a me calix iste.** "Sare," quoth he, "me grulleth ayein mi muchele pine. Mi feader, yef hit mei beon, speare me ed tis time. Thi wil thah, ant nawt min eaver beo i-vorthet." His deore-wurthe feader for-thi ne forber him nawt, ah leide on him se lutherliche thet he bigon to greden with reowthfule stevene: **Heloy! Heloy! Lama zabatani?** "Mi Godd, mi Godd, mi deore-wurthe feader, havest tu al forwarpe me, thin an-lepi sune, the beatest me se hearde?" For al this ne lette he nawt, ah

215

220

everything that had any likeness (or, resemblance) to it? **211–13 hu beot he . . . of sunne?** how bitterly did He beat His precious Son, Jesus our Lord, who never had [any] sin, except only that He bore flesh like ours, which is full of sin? **213–14 Ant we schulden . . . sune death?** And should we be spared, [we] who bear on us (i.e., are responsible for) His Son's death? **214–17 The wepne thet sloh him . . . his feader are,** The weapon that slew Him — that was our sin, and He who did not have any sin (lit., any[thing] of sin) except the shadow alone was so shamefully abused in that same shadow, so painfully (or, sorrowfully) tormented, that before it came to that (i.e., before the crucifixion), because of the threat of it (i.e., crucifixion) alone, He was so terrified (lit., [it] terrified him) in anticipation of it that He asked for His father's mercy. **218–19 Tristis est anima mea . . . calix iste,** "My spirit is sad to the point of death. My father, if it is possible, let this cup pass from me" (Matthew 26:38–39). **219–21 "Sare . . . i-vorthet,"** "I am terribly afraid (lit., it frightens me sorely — see glossary)," He said, "of (or, in anticipation of) my great pain. My father, if it may be, spare Me at this time. Let Your will, though, and not mine, always be furthered." **221–22 His deore-wurthe feader . . . stevene,** His precious Father did not excuse Him for [all] that, but laid into Him so violently (or, viciously) that He began to wail with a pitiful voice. **222–23 Heloy! . . . Lama zabatani?** "My God! My God! Why have You forsaken Me?" (Matthew 27:46, Mark 15:34). **223–24 havest tu al forwarpe me . . . se hearde?** have You cast me off completely, Your only Son, [You] who beat Me so hard? **224–25 ne lette he nawt . . . o rode,** He did not stop, but beat [Him] so very long and so

225 beot se swithe longe ant se swithe grimliche, thet he stearf o rode. **Disciplina pacis nostre super eum**, seith Ysaie. Thus ure beatunge feol on him, for he dude him-seolven bitweonen us ant his feader, the threatte us for-te smiten, ase moder thet is reowthful deth hire bitweonen hire child ant te wrathe sturne feader hwen he hit wule beaten. Thus dude ure Laverd Jesu Crist, i-kepte on him deathes dunt
230 for-te schilden us ther-with. I-gracet beo his milce! Hwer-se muchel dunt is, hit bulteth ayein up-o theo the ther neh stondeth. Sothliche hwa-se is neh him the i-kepte se hevi dunt, hit wule bulten on him, ne nule he him neaver meanen, for thet is the preove thet he stont neh him. Ant liht is the bultunge to tholien for his luve the underveng se hevi dunt, us for-te burhen from the deofles botte i the pine of
235 helle.

"Yet," seith moni mon, "hweat is Godd the betere thah ich pini me for his luve?" Leove mon ant wummon, Godd thuncheth god of ure god. Ure god is yef we doth thet tet we ahen. Nim yeme of this essample: A mon the were feor i-fearen ant me

very grimly (or, horribly), that He died on the Cross. **225–26** *Disciplina pacis nostre super eum*, "The disciplining of our peace [was] upon Him" (Isaiah 53:5). **226–29 he dude him-seolven . . . beaten**, He put Himself between us and His Father, who threatened to hit (lit., smite) us, just as the mother who is compassionate puts herself between her child and the angry, stern father when he wants to (or, is about to) beat it. **229–30 i-kepte on him . . . his milce!** took on Himself death's blow in order to shield us against it (or, with it). Blessed (lit., thanked) be His mercy! **230–33 Hwer-se muchel dunt is . . . stont neh him**, Wherever there is a great blow (or, hit), it recoils back upon those who stand near there. Truly, whosoever is near Him who received so heavy a blow, it will recoil on him, nor will he ever complain (reflex.), because that is the proof that he stands (*stont* = reduced form of *stondeth*) near Him. **233–34 Ant liht is the bultunge . . . deofles botte**, And the recoiling (or, blow) is easy to suffer (or, tolerate) for the love of Him who received so heavy a blow in order to save us from the devil's cudgel. **236 hweat is Godd the betere . . . pini me**, how is God the better [pleased], though (i.e., if) I torment myself. **237 Leove**, Dear (or, Beloved). **237–38 Godd thuncheth god . . . we ahen**, God thinks well of (or, cares for) our good. Our good is if we do that which we ought. **238 Nim yeme**, Pay (lit., Take) attention. **238–42 A mon the were feor i-fearen . . . i delices?** [If there were] a man who had traveled far and someone came and told him that his dear spouse mourned so intensely for him that she had delight in nothing without him, but was lean and pale for thought of his love — would [that] not please him better than if (lit., that) one said to

240 come ant talde him thet his deore spuse se swithe murnede efter him thet heo withuten him delit nefde i na thing, ah were for thoht of his luve leane ant elheowet — nalde him betere likin, then thet me seide him thet ha gleowde ant gomnede ant wedde with othre men, ant livede i delices? Alswa ure Laverd, thet is the sawle spus, thet sith al thet ha deth, thah he hehe sitte — he is ful wel i-paiet thet ha murneth efter him, ant wule hihin toward hire mucheles the swithere with

245 yeove of his grace other fecchen hire allunge to him to gloire ant to blisse thurh-wuniende.

Ne grapi hire nan to softeliche, hire-seolven to bichearren. Ne schal ha, for hire lif, witen hire al cleane, ne halden riht hire chastete withuten twa thinges, as Seint Ailred the abbat wrat to his suster: thet an is pinsunge i flesch with feasten, with

250 wecchen, with disceplines, with heard werunge, heard leohe, with uvel, with muchele swinkes. The other is heorte theawes: devotiun, reowfulnesse, riht luve, eadmodnesse — ant vertuz othre swucche. "Me, sire," thu ondswerest me, "suleth Godd his grace? Nis grace wil-yeove?" Mine leove sustren, thah cleannesse of chastete ne beo nawt bune ed Godd ah beo yeove of grace, ungraciuse stondeth

255 ther-toyeines ant makieth ham unwurthe to halden se heh thing, the nulleth swinc

---

him that she made merry and played (or, enjoyed herself) and went mad with other men, and lived in delight? **242–46 Alswa ure Laverd . . . blisse thurh-wuniende,** Likewise our Lord, who is the soul's spouse, who sees everything that she does, though He sit on high — He is very well pleased that she mourns for Him, and [He] will hurry towards her much the faster with the gift of His grace or fetch her completely to Him to glory (i.e., heaven) and to perpetual bliss. **247 Ne grapi hire nan . . . bichearren,** Let no one handle (or, treat) herself too softly as to delude herself. **247–51 Ne schal ha . . . muchele swinkes,** Nor will she, for her life, keep herself completely pure, nor [will she] keep her chastity rightly without two things, as St. Aelred, the abbot, wrote to his sister: the one (or, first) is subduing (or, torture) of the flesh with fasts, with vigils, with [physical] discipline (see *discepline* in glossary), with rough clothing, rough shelter, with difficult [and] with great labors (or, physical exertions). **251–52 The other is . . . swucche,** The second thing is the good habits of the heart: devotion, compassion, right love, humility — and other such virtues. **252–53 "Me sire . . . wil-yeove?"** "But, sir," you answer me, "does God sell His grace? Is grace not a free gift?" **254–56 ne beo nawt bune . . . blitheliche tholien,** is not a purchase from God but is a gift of grace, unthankful [people] resist it (lit., stand there-against) and make themselves unworthy to hold so high a thing, who do not

ther-vore blitheliche tholien. Bitweonen delices, ant eise, ant flesches este, hwa wes eaver chaste? Hwa bredde eaver in-with hire fur thet ha ne bearnde? Pot the walleth swithe — nule he beon overleden, other cald weater i-warpe th'rin, ant brondes withdrahene? The wombe-pot the walleth of metes ant of drunches is se

260 neh nehbur to thet ful-itohe lim thet ha dealeth ther-with the brune of hire heate. Ah monie — mare hearm is — beoth se flesch-wise, ant swa over-swithe ofdred leste hare heaved ake, leste hare licome febli to swithe, ant witeth swa hare heale, thet te gast unstrengeth ant secleth i sunne. Ant theo the schulden ane lechnin hare sawle with heorte bireowsunge ant flesches pinsunge forwurtheth fisitiens ant

265 licomes leche. Dude swa Seinte Agace, the ondswerede ant seide to ure Laverdes sonde the brohte salve o Godes half to healen hire tittes, **Medicinam carnalem corpori meo nunquam adhibui** — thet is, "fleschlich medecine ne dude ich me neavre"? Nabbe ye i-herd tellen of the threo hali men? Bute the an wes i-wunet for his calde mahe to nutten hate speces, ant wes ornre of mete ant of drunch then

want to suffer happily any toil for it (lit., there-for). **256–57 Bitweonen delices . . . bearnde?** Who was ever chaste amidst pleasure, and comfort, and the gratification of the flesh (i.e., the body)? Who ever engendered (or, fostered) a fire within herself [in such a way] that she was not burned? **257–59 Pot the walleth swithe . . . withdrahene?** The pot which boils furiously — will it not be ladled out, or cold water thrown in it and the brands taken away? (Shepherd reads: "will it not spill over unless cold water be thrown . . . " — see *overleden* in glossary). **259–60 The wombe-pot . . . hire heate,** The belly-pot which boils with foods and with drinks is so near a neighbor to that badly disciplined limb (i.e., the genitals) that it (lit., she) shares with it the burning of its heat. **261–63 Ah monie . . . secleth i sunne,** But many — more is the harm — are so fleshly (i.e., concerned with the body), and so overly afraid lest their head ache, lest their body weaken too much, and thus [they] protect their health (or, well-being) [so] that the spirit weakens and sickens in sin. **263–65 Ant theo the schulden . . . licomes leche,** And those who should only heal their soul with contrition of heart and subduing of the flesh degenerate into physicians and doctor[s] of the body. **265–66 Dude swa Seinte Agace . . . hire tittes,** Did St. Agatha do so, who answered and said to our Lord's messenger who brought medicine (or, a remedy) on God's behalf to heal her breasts. **266–67 *Medicinam carnalem . . . adhibui,*** "I have never applied fleshly medicine to my body" (antiphon for the Feast of St. Agatha). **267–68 ne dude ich me neavre,** I never did (i.e., applied) to myself. **268 Nabbe ye i-herd tellen,** Have you not heard tell. **268–73 Bute the an . . . clowes de gilofre,** Only the first (or, the one) was used, because of his cold stomach, to take (or, use) hot spices and was pickier

270   the tweien othre [the], thah ha weren seke, ne nomen neaver yeme hweat wes hal, hwet unhal to eoten ne to drinken, ah nomen eaver forth-riht hwet-se Godd ham sende, ne makeden neaver strengthe of gingivre ne of zedual, ne of clowes de gilofre. A dei, as ha threo weren i-folen o slepe, ant lei bitweone thes twa the thridde thet ich seide, com the cwen of heovene ant twa meidnes with hire. The

275   an, as thah hit were, ber a letuaire, the other of gold a sticcke. Ure Leafdi with the sticke nom ant dude i the anes muth of the letuaire, ant te meidnes eoden forthre to the midleste. "Nai," quoth ure Leafdi, "he is his ahne leche. Ga over to the thridde." Stod an hali mon of feor, biheold al this ilke. Hwen sec mon haveth ed hond thing thet wule don him god, he hit mei wel notien. Ah beon th'refter se ancreful,

280   nomeliche religius, nis nawt Godd i-cweme. Godd ant his desciples speken of sawle leche-creft; Ypocras ant Galien, of licomes heale. The an the wes best i-learet of Jesu Cristes leche-creft seith, "flesches wisdom is death to the sawle": **Prudencia carnis, mors. / Procul odoramus bellum**, as Job seith. Swa we dredeth flesches uvel ofte ear then hit cume, thet sawle uvel kimeth up. Ant we tholieth

about food and about drink than the two others who, though they were sick, never took heed (or, paid attention to) what was wholesome, what unwholesome to eat or to drink, but always took immediately whatsoever God sent them, nor [did they] ever put store in (lit., make strength of) ginger or setwall or clove. **273–74 A dei, as ha threo . . . with hire**, One day, when they three had fallen asleep and the third whom I described (lit., said) lay between these two, the queen of heaven came and two maidens with her. **274–77 The an . . . the midleste**, The first [maiden] bore, as it were, a medicine (or, syrup), the second a spoon of gold. Our Lady took [some] of the medicine with the spoon and put [it] in the mouth of the first [sleeper], and the maidens went on (lit., further) to the middle-most [man]. **277 leche**, leech, doctor. **278 Stod**, There stood; **of feor**, some distance away; **ed hond**, at hand. **279 he hit mei wel notien**, he may well partake (or, make use) of it. **279–80 Ah beon th'refter . . . i-cweme**, But to be so anxious about it (i.e., the body), especially for religious people (i.e., living as monks or nuns according to a rule), is not pleasing to God. **281 sawle leche-creft . . . heale**, the soul's medicine (i.e., art of healing); Hippocrates and Galen, of the health of the body. **281–82 The an . . . seith**, The one who was best instructed in Jesus Christ's medicine says [that]. **283 *Prudencia carnis . . . bellum***, "The wisdom of the flesh [is] death" (Romans 8:6). / "We smell war from far away" (adapted from Job 39:25). **283–84 Swa we dredeth . . . kimeth up**, So we fear the disease of the body often before it may come, so that the disease of the soul arises (or, develops). **284–86 Ant we tholieth . . . mistohe wombe**, And we endure the disease of the soul in

285 sawle uvel for-te edstearten flesches uvel, as thah hit were betere to tholien
galnesses brune, then heaved-eche other grucchunge of a mistohe wombe. Ant
hwether is betere: i secnesse to beo Godes freo child, then i flesches heale to beo
threal under sunne? Ant this ne segge ich nawt swa thet wisdom ant meosure ne
beon over-al i-loket, the moder is ant nurrice of alle gode theawes. Ah we cleopieth

290 ofte wisdom thet nis nan. For soth wisdom is don eaver sawle heale bivore flesches
heale. Ant hwen he ne mei nawt ba somet halden, cheose ear licomes hurt then
thurh to strong fondunge sawle throwunge. Nichodemus brohte to smirien ure
Laverd an hundret weies — hit seith — of mirre ant of aloes — thet beoth bittre
speces ant bitacnith bittre swinkes ant flesches pinsunges. Hundret is ful tale ant

295 noteth perfectiun — thet is, ful dede — for-te schawin thet me schal ful do flesches
pine, ase forth as eaver evene mei tholien. I the weie is bitacnet meosure ant wisdom, thet euch mon with wisdom weie hwet he mahe don, ne beo nawt se over-
swithe i gast thet he foryeme the bodi, ne eft se tendre of his flesch thet hit i-

order to escape the disease of the flesh (i.e., body), as though it were better to endure the burning of lust than a headache or the grumbling of an unruly stomach. **286–88 Ant hwether is betere . . . under sunne?** And which [of these two] is better: to be God's free (or, noble) child in sickness or (lit., than) to be a slave under sin in [the full] health of the body? (or, Is to be God's free child in sickness better than to be a slave under sin in the health of the body?). **288–89 Ant this ne segge ich nawt . . . gode theawes,** And I do not say this so that prudence and moderation, which is the mother and nurse (or, fosterer) of all good virtues, [will] be completely disregarded (lit., not looked to). **289 cleopieth,** call. **290–92 For soth wisdom . . . sawle throwunge,** For it is true wisdom (or, prudence) always to put the soul's health before the body's health and, when he (i.e., a person; or, wisdom) cannot keep (or, maintain) both together, to choose rather injury of the body than the suffering of the soul through too difficult a temptation. **292–94 Nichodemus brohte to smirien . . . pinsunges,** Nicodemus brought to anoint our Lord a hundred weights — it says — of myrrh and of aloes — those are bitter spices and symbolize bitter toils and subduings (or, tortures) of the body. **294–96 Hundret is ful tale . . . mei tholien,** A hundred is a complete number and signifies perfection — that is, a complete action — in order to show that one must fully undertake the punishment (or, pain) of the body, as far as ever [one's] capacity can allow (or, powers can endure). **296 I the weie,** In (or, by) the weight (see above); **meosure,** moderation. **297–99 weie hwet he mah don . . . gast theowe,** should weigh (or, consider) what he can do, nor be not so excessively in the spirit that he

300 wurthe untohen ant makie the gast theowe. Nu is al this meast i-seid of bitternesse
ute-with. Of bitternesse in-with segge we nu sum-hweat, for of thes twa bitternesses
awakeneth swetnesse — her yet i this world, nawt ane in heovene.

As ich seide riht nu, thet Nichodemus brohte smirles to ure Laverd, alswa the
threo Maries bohten deore-wurthe aromaz, his bodi for-te smirien. Neometh nu
gode yeme, mine leove sustren. Theos threo Maries bitacnith threo bitternesses,
305 for this nome, "Marie," as "Meraht" ant "Merariht," thet ich spec th'ruppe of,
spealeth "bitternesse." The earste bitternesse is i sunne bireowsunge ant i deadbote,
hwen the sunfule is i-turnd earst to ure Laverd. Ant theos is understonden bi the
earste Marie, Marie Magdaleine — ant bi god rihte, for ha with muche bireowsunge
ant bitternesse of heorte leafde hire sunnen ant turnde to ure Laverd. Ah for-thi
310 thet sum mahte thurh to muche bitternesse fallen into unhope, "Magdaleine," the
spealeth "tures hehnesse," is to "Marie" i-feiet, thurh hwet is bitacnet hope of heh
mearci ant of heovene blisse. The other bitternesse is i wreastlunge ant i wragelunge
ayeines fondunges. Ant theos is bitacnet bi the other Marie, Marie Jacobi, for
"Jacob" spealeth "wreastlere." This wreastlunge is ful bitter to monie the beoth
315 ful forth i the wei toward heovene, for the[o] yet i fondunges — thet beoth the

neglect the body, nor conversely [be] so soft in his body that it become[s] unruly and make the
spirit into a slave. **299 meast**, mostly. **300 ute-with**, external (or, outer). **300–01 Of bitternesse
in-with . . . in heovene**, Concerning biterness inside let us now say something (lit., somewhat),
for from these two bitternesses sweetness arises (lit., awakens) — even here in this world, not
only in heaven. **302 smirles**, ointments. **303 bohten . . . smirien**, bought precious spices in
order to anoint His body. **303–04 Neometh nu gode yeme**, Now pay (lit., take) good attention.
304 bitacnith, symbolize. **305 nome**, name. **305–06 as "Meraht" . . . "bitternesse,"** [just] as
[the names] "Meraht" and "Merari," which I spoke of above, mean "bitterness." **306 i sunne
. . . deadbote**, in the remorse and penance of sin. **307 earst**, first. **308 with muche bireowsunge**,
with great remorse. **309 leafde**, left. **309–10 for-thi thet**, because. **310 to muche**, too much;
unhope, despair. **310–12 "Magdaleine," the spealeth . . . heovene blisse**, [the name]
"Magdalene," which means "the tower's height," is joined with [the name] "Mary," through
which hope of high mercy and heaven's joy is symbolized. **312 other bitternesse**, second
bitterness; **wreastlunge ant i wragelunge**, wrestling and resistance (or, struggling). **314–15
the beoth ful forth**, who are well advanced. **315–17 for the[o] yet . . . strong wraglunge**, for
they [who are well advanced] still stagger (or, totter) sometimes under temptations — which

deofles swenges — waggith other-hwiles ant moten wreastlin ayein with strong wraglunge. For as Seint Austin seith, **Pharao contemptus surgit in scandalum.** Hwil eaver Israeles folc wes in Egypte under *Ph*arones hond, ne leadde he neaver ferd th'ron; ah tha hit fleah from him, tha with al his strengthe wende he th'refter. For-thi is eaver bitter feht neod ayein Pharaon — thet is, ayein the deovel. For ase seith Ezechiel, **Sanguinem fugies, et sanguis persequetur te** — "Flih sunne, ant sunne wule folhin eaver efter." Inoh is i-seid th'ruppe hwi the gode nis neaver sker of alle fondunges. Sone se he haveth the an overcumen, i-kepe anan an-other. The thridde bitternesse is i longunge toward heovene, ant i the ennu of this world, hwen ei is se hehe thet he haveth heorte reste onont untheawes weorre, ant is as in heovene yeten, ant thuncheth bitter alle worltliche thinges. Ant tis thridde bitternesse is understonden bi Marie Salomee, the thridde Marie, for "Salome" spealeth "pes." Ant theo yet the habbeth pes ant reste of cleane in-wit habbeth in hare heorte bitternesse of this lif thet edhalt ham from blisse thet ham longeth to, from Godd thet ha luvieth. Thus lo, in euch stat rixleth bitternesse: earst i the

320

325

330

---

are the devil's blows (or, throws — see *sweng* in glossary) — and must wrestle back with strong resistance. **317** *Pharao contemptus surgit in scandalum*, "Pharaoh ridiculed rises up at the offense" (source unidentified). **318–19 ne leadde he neaver . . . th'refter**, he never led an army (i.e., made an attack) on them (lit., thereon), but when it (i.e., the people of Israel) fled from him, then with all his might he went after them (lit., thereafter). **320 feht**, fighting (or, battle); **neod**, necessary. **321** *Sanguinem fugies . . . te*, "You will flee blood, and blood will follow you" (adapted from Ezekiel 35:6); **Flih sunne**, Flee sin. **322 folhin**, follow. **322–23 Inoh is i-seid . . . fondunges**, Enough is said above why the good (i.e., good person) is never free from all temptations. **323 Sone se**, As soon as; **i-kepe anan an-other**, let him expect immediately another [temptation]. **324 ennu**, vexation. **325–26 hwen ei is se hehe . . . worltliche thinges**, when anyone is so high (i.e., spiritually advanced) that he has peace of heart with respect to the attack of vice (or, with respect to the war against vice), and is as at heaven's gates, and all worldly things seem bitter. **328 spealeth "pes,"** means "peace"; **Ant theo yet . . . cleane in-wit**, And even those who have peace and rest [which comes] from a pure conscience. **329 hare**, their. **329–30 thet edhalt ham . . . luvieth**, which keeps them from the joy which they long for (lit., which longs to them), from God whom they love. **330–32 in euch stat rixleth bitternesse . . . leaste ende**, in each state (or, condition) bitterness reigns: first in the beginning when one makes

biginnunge, hwen me sahtneth with Godd, i the forth-yong of god lif, ant i the leaste ende. Hwa is thenne, o Godes half, the wilneth i this world eise other este?

Ah neometh nu yeme, mine leove sustren, hu efter bitternesse kimeth swetnesse: bitternesse buth hit. For as thet Godspel teleth, theose threo Maries bohten swote 335 smeallinde aromaz to smirien ure Laverd. Thurh aromaz, the beoth swote, is understonden swotnesse of devot heorte. Theos Maries hit buggeth — thet is, thurh bitternesse me kimeth to swotnesse. Bi this nome "Marie" nim eaver "bitternesse." Thurh Maries bone wes, ed te neoces, weater i-went to wine — thet is to understonden, thurh bone of bitternesse thet me dreheth for Godd, the heorte 340 the wes weattri, smechles, ne ne felde na savur of Godd na-mare then i weater, schal beon i-went to wine — thet is, i-finden smech in him swete over alle wines. For-thi seith the wise, **Usque in tempus sustinebit paciens, et postea redditio jocunditatis.** "The tholemode tholie bitter ane hwile: he schal sone th'refter habben yeld of blisse." Ant Anna i Tobie seith bi ure Laverd, **Qui post tempestatem** 345 **tranquillum facit, et post lacrimationem et fletum exultationem infundit** — thet is, "i-blescet *b*eo thu, Laverd, the makest stille efter storm, ant efter wopi

peace with God, [then] in the progress (or, course) of a good life, and [also] in the final end. **332 Hwa is thenne . . . este?** Then who is [there], for God's sake, who desires comfort or pleasure in this world? **333 Ah neometh nu yeme,** But now pay (lit., take) attention. **334 buth hit,** buys it. **334–35 swote smeallinde . . . Laverd,** sweet smelling spices to anoint our Lord. **335 the beoth swote,** which are sweet. **336 Theos Maries hit buggeth,** These Marys buy it. **337 me kimeth,** one comes; **nim,** take, understand (imper.). **338 Thurh Maries bone . . . to wine,** At Mary's request (or, prayer) water was, at the wedding [of Cana], turned to wine. **339 dreheth,** suffers, experiences. **339–41 the heorte the wes weattri . . . alle wines,** the heart which was watery, tasteless, and experienced no savor in God any more than in water, will be turned to wine — that is, [will] find taste in Him sweet over all wines. **342–43 *Usque in tempus . . . jocunditatis,*** "The patient person will persevere for a time, and afterwards [there will be] a return of joyfulness" (Ecclesiasticus 1:29). **343–44 "The tholemode . . . of blisse,"** "The patient person may suffer a bitter [thing] for a time: he will have a reward of joy soon afterwards." **344 bi ure Laverd,** concerning our Lord. **344–45 *Qui post tempestatem . . . infundit,*** "[The Lord,] who brings about calm after a storm, and after tears and weeping pours in celebration" (Tobias 3:22). **346–47 "i-blescet beo thu . . . murhthes,"** "blessed are You, Lord, who makes a calm after storm, and after

weattres yeldest blithe murhthes." **Salomon: Esuriens etiam amarum, pro dulci sumet** — "yef thu art ofhungret efter thet swete, thu most earst witerliche biten o the bittre." **In Canticis: Ibo michi ad montem myrre, et ad colles turis**. "Ich

350   chulle," ha seith, Godes deore spuse, "gan to rechleses hul, bi the dun of myrre." Lo, hwuch is the wei to rechleses swotnesse: bi myrre of bitternesse. Ant eft i thet ilke luve-boc: **Que est ista, que ascendit per desertum sicut virgula fumi ex aromatibus myrre et thuris?** Aromaz me maketh of myrre ant of rechles, ah myrre he set bivoren, ant rechles kimeth efter. **Ex aromatibus myrre et thuris.**

355   Nu meaneth hire sum thet ha ne mei habben na swotnesse of Godd, ne swetnesse withinnen. Ne wundri ha hire na-wiht, yef ha nis Marie, for ha hit mot buggen with bitternesse withuten — nawt with euch bitternesse, for sum geath frommard Godd, as euch worltlich sar thet nis for sawle heale. For-thi i the Godspel of the threo Maries is i-writen thisses weis, **Ut venientes ungerent Jesum — non autem**

360   **recedentes.** "Theos Maries," hit seith — theose biternesses — "weren cuminde to

floods of tears (lit., weepy waters) You repay [with] happy joys (lit., mirths)." **347–48** *Salomon: Esuriens . . . dulci sumet*, Solomon: "The starving [soul] will take even bitter for sweet" (Proverbs 27:7). **348–49 "yef thu art ofhungret . . . bittre,"** "if you are famished for the sweet, you must first certainly bite into (or, taste from) the bitter." **349** *In Canticis: Ibo michi . . . colles turis*, In Canticles: "I will go to the mountain of myrrh, and to the hills of frankincense (or, incense)" (Song of Songs 4:6). **349–50 "Ich chulle," ha seith**, "I will," she says. **350 rechleses hul**, hill of incense; **dun**, mountain, hill. **351 Lo, hwuch is the wei . . . myrre of bitternesse**, Look, what the way is to the sweetness of incense: through the myrrh of bitterness; **eft**, again. **352 ilke**, same (or, very same). **352–53** *Que est ista . . . thuris?* "Who is she who goes up through the desert like a column (lit., branch or twig) of smoke [made] out of fragrant spices, myrrh and incense?" (Song of Songs 3:6). **353 Aromaz me maketh**, One makes perfume (or, perfume is made). **354 set bivoren**, put before, in front. **355–56 Nu meaneth hire sum . . . withinnen**, Now some [anchoress] complains (reflex.) that she cannot have any sweetness from God, or sweetness within. **356–58 Ne wundri ha hire . . . sawle heale**, Let her not wonder (or, be surprised — reflex.) at all, if she is not Mary (i.e., like Mary), for she must buy it (i.e., sweetness) with outward bitterness — not with every bitterness, for some go (or, lead) away from God, such as every worldly sorrow that is not for the soul's well-being (or, salvation). **359 thisses weis**, in this way, in the following way. **359–60** *Ut venientes . . . recedentes*, "[It is written that they were] coming so that they might anoint Jesus" — [it is not written] however that they left" (based on Mark 16:1). **360–61 weren cuminde to smirien,**

smirien ure Laverd." Theo beoth cuminde to smirien ure Laverd, the me tholeth for his luve, the strecheth him toward us as thing thet i-smired is, ant maketh him nesche ant softe to hondlin. Ant nes he him-seolf reclus i Maries wombe? Theos twa thing limpeth to ancre: nearowthe ant bitternesse, for wombe is nearow

365 wununge ther ure Laverd wes reclus, ant tis word "Marie," as ich ofte habbe i-seid, spealeth "bitternesse." Yef ye thenne i nearow stude tholieth bitternesse, ye beoth his feolahes, reclus as he wes i Marie wombe. Beo ye i-bunden in-with fowr large wahes? — ant he in a nearow cader, i-neilet o rode, i stanene thruh bicluset hete-feste! Marie wombe ant this thruh weren his ancre-huses. I nowther nes he

370 worltlich mon, ah [wes] as ut of the world for-te schawin ancren thet ha ne schulen with the world na thing habben i-meane. "Ye," thu ondswerest me, "ah he wende ut of ba!" Ye, went tu alswa of ba thine ancre-huses, as he dude, withute bruche, ant leaf ham ba i-hale — thet schal beon hwen the gast went ut on ende withuten bruche ant wem of his twa huses: thet an is the licome. Thet other is the uttre hus,

375 thet is as the uttre wah abute the castel.

were coming to anoint. **361–63 Theo beoth cuminde . . . to hondlin,** Those [things] which one suffers for His love are coming to anoint our Lord, who stretches Himself [out] toward us as a thing which is [being] anointed, and makes Himself tender and soft to touch. **363 Ant nes he him-seolf,** And was He not Himself. **363–66 Theos twa thing limpeth . . . spealeth "bitternesse,"** These two things apply to the anchoress: narrowness and bitterness, for the womb is a narrow dwelling where our Lord was a recluse, and this word "Mary," as I have often said, means "bitterness." **366–67 i nearow stude . . . i Marie wombe,** in a narrow place suffer bitterness, you are his fellows (or, companions), recluse as He was in Mary's womb. **367–69 Beo ye i-bunden . . . hete-feste!** Are you bound within four large (or, wide) walls? — and He [was bound] in a narrow cradle, nailed on the Cross, enclosed tightly (see *hete-veste, hete-feste* in glossary) in a stone tomb (or, coffin)! **369 Marie wombe,** Mary's womb; **ancre-huses,** anchor-houses. **369–71 I nowther nes he . . . i-meane,** In neither was he a worldly man, but was as if out of the world in order to show anchoresses that that they must not have anything in common with the world. **371 Ye,** Indeed (or, Yes). **371–72 "ah he wende ut of ba!"** "but He went out of both!" **372–74 Ye, went tu alswa . . . the licome,** Yes, you [will] go out (*went* = reduced form of *wendeth*) likewise from both your anchor-houses, as He did, without a rift (or, opening), and leave them both intact (lit., whole) — that will be when the spirit goes out goes out at the end without rift and injury from His two houses: the first is the body. **374–75 Thet other . . . castel,** The second is the outer house, which is like the outer wall around the castle.

Al thet ich habbe i-seid of flesches pinsunge nis nawt for ow, mine leove sustren — the other-hwile tholieth mare then ich walde — ah is for sum thet schal rede this inoh-reathe, the grapeth hire to softe. No-the-les, yunge impen me bigurd with thornes leste beastes freoten ham hwil ha beoth mearewe. Ye beoth yunge

380 impen i-set i Godes orchard; thornes beoth the heardschipes thet ich habbe i-speken of. Ant ow is neod thet ye beon biset with ham abuten, thet te beast of helle, hwen he snakereth toward ow for-te biten on ow, hurte him o the scharpschipe ant schunche ayein-wardes. With alle theose heardschipes beoth gleade ant wel i-paiet yef lutel word is of ow, yef ye beoth unwurthe, for thorn is scharp ant unwurth.

385 With theose twa beoth bigurde. Ye ne ahen nawt to unnen thet uvel word beo of ow. Scandle is heaved-sunne — thet is, thing swa i-seid other i-don thet me mei rihtliche turnen hit to uvele, ant sunegin th'refter ther-thurh with misthoht, with uvel word, on hire, on othre, ant sungin ec with dede. Ah ye ahen unnen thet na word ne beo of ow, na mare then of deade, ant beon blithe i-heortet yef ye tholieth

390 danger of Sluri the cokes cneave, the wescheth ant wipeth disches i cuchene — thenne beo ye dunes i-hehet toward heovene. For, lo, hu speketh the leafdi i thet

376 flesches pinsunge, the mortification of the flesh (or, subduing of the body). **377–78 the other-hwile ... to softe**, [you] who sometimes suffer more than I would want — but it is for some [anchoress] who may read this readily enough, [but] who handles (or, treats) herself too softly. **378–79 No-the-les, yunge impen ... mearewe**, Nonetheless, one encircles young saplings with thorns lest (or, for fear that) beasts may eat them up while they are tender. **380 i-set**, placed. **381–83 Ant ow is neod ... ayein-wardes**, And it is necessary for you that you be surrounded about with them, so that the beast of hell, when he sneaks (or, creeps) toward you to bite into you, [may] hurt himself on the sharpness [of the thorns] and be frightened back. **383–84 wel i-paiet ... unwurth**, be well pleased if there is little word (or, talk) of you, if you are [held to be] of no account, for a thorn is sharp and of no account. **385 bigurde**, encircled. **385–86 Ye ne ahen nawt ... of ow**, You ought not to allow (or, wish) that [there] be bad talk about you. **386–88 Scandle is heaved-sunne ... with dede**, Scandal (see glossary) is a capital sin — that is, a thing said or done so that one can rightly (or, directly) turn it to evil, and sin afterwards through it (lit., there-through), with bad thought, with evil talk, about her, about another, and sin also in deed. **388–91 Ah ye ahen unnen ... heovene**, But you ought to allow (or, wish) that there be no talk about you, any more than [there is talk] of the dead, and be joyful in heart (lit., joyfully hearted) if you suffer the bad mood of Slurry the cook's boy, who washes and dries dishes in the kitchen — then you are hills raised towards heaven.

371

swete luve-boc, **Venit dilectus meus saliens in montibus, transiliens colles.** "Mi leof kimeth leapinde," ha seith, "o the dunes, [overleapinde hulles." Dunes bitacneth theo the leadeth hechhest lif; hulles beoth the lachhere. Nu seith ha thet hire leof

395 leapeth o the dunes] — thet is, totret ham, tofuleth ham, tholeth thet me totreode ham, tuki ham al to wundre, schaweth in ham his ahne troden, thet me trudde him in ham, i-find*e* hu he wes totreden, as his trode schaweth. This beoth the hehe dunes — as munt of Muntgiw, dunes of Armenie. The hulles the beoth lahre, theo — as the leafdi seith hire-seolf — he overleapeth, ne trust nawt se wel on ham, for

400 hare feblesce *ne* mahte nawt tholien swuch totreodunge, ant he leapeth over ham, forbereth ham, ant forbuheth athet ha waxen herre, from hulles to dunes. His schadewe lanhure overgeath ant writh ham hwil he leapeth over ham — thet is, sum i-licnesse he leith on ham of his lif on eorthe, as thah hit were his schadewe. Ah the dunes undervoth the troden of him-seolven, ant schaweth in hare lif, hwuch

405 his lif-lade wes, hu ant hwer he eode, i hwuch vilte, i hwuch wa he leadde his lif on eorthe. Thulliche dunes the gode Pawel spek of, ant eadmodliche seide,

392 *Venit dilectus meus . . . colles*, "My beloved comes leaping on the mountains, springing over the hills" (adapted from Song of Songs 2:8). **393 dunes**, hills (or, mountains); **overleapinde**, leaping over. **393–97 bitacneth theo the . . . trode schaweth**, symbolize those who lead the highest life; hills are the lower [people]. Now she says that her beloved leaps on the mountains — that is, he tramples them (*totret* = reduced form of *totredeth*), soils (lit., fouls) them thoroughly, permits that people trample on them, mistreat them terribly, points out on them his own footprints, so that people may step (reflex.) in them, and discover how He [Himself] was trampled, as His track shows. **398 as munt . . . Armenie**, as (or, like) the Mount of Jove (or, perhaps, the Alps — see *Munt-giw* in Proper Names Index), [like the] hills of Armenia; **lahre**, lower. **398–401 theo . . . hulles to dunes**, these — as the lady says herself — he leaps over, [and] does not trust (*trust* = reduced form of *trusteth*) so well in them, because their feebleness (or, weakness) could not bear such a trampling, and he leaps over them, shuns them, and avoids [them] until they grow higher, from hills into mountains. **401–03 His schadewe lanhure . . . his schadewe**, His shadow at least passes over and covers them while he leaps over them — that is, some likeness he lays (or, imprints) on them of his life on earth, as though it were his shadow. **404–06 Ah the dunes . . . eadmodliche seide**, But the mountains receive the footprints of [Christ] Himself, and show in their life what His way of life was, how and where He went (or, walked), in what meanness, in what pain (or, woe) He lead His life on earth. Such mountains the good [St.] Paul spoke about, and humbly said.

Deicimur set non perimus. Mortificationem Jesu in corpore nostro circumferentes, ut et vita Jesu in corporibus nostris manifestetur. "Alle wa," quoth he, "ant alle scheome we tholieth; ah thet is ure selhthe, thet we beoren on 410 ure bodi Jesu Cristes deadlicnesse, thet hit suteli in us hwuch wes his lif on eorthe." Godd hit wat, the thus doth, ha pruvieth us hare luve toward ure Laverd. "Luvest tu me? Cuth hit!" For luve wule schawin him with uttre werkes. **Gregorius: Probatio dilectionis exhibitio est operis.** Ne beo neaver thing se heard, soth luve lihteth hit ant softeth ant sweteth. **Amor omnia fatilia reddit.** Hweat tholieth 415 men ant wummen for fals luve ant for ful luve — ant mare walden tholien? Ant hweat is mare wunder, thet siker luve, ant treowe, ant over alle othre swete, ne mei meistrin us se forth as deth the luve of sunne? Nawt for-thi, ich wat swuch thet bereth ba togederes hevi brunie ant here, i-bunden hearde with irn — middel, theh, ant earmes — mid brade thicke bondes, swa thet tet swat th'rof is passiun to 420 tholien. Feasteth, waketh, swinketh, ant, Crist hit wat, meaneth him thet hit ne

407–08 *Deicimur set non perimus . . . manifestetur,* "We are thrown down, but we do not perish. We are carrying around the dying (or, mortification) of Jesus in our body, so that also the life of Jesus may be revealed in our bodies" (2 Corinthians 4:9–10). **409 tholieth,** suffer (or, endure). **409–10 ah thet is ure selhthe . . . on eorthe,** but it is our happiness that we bear in our body Jesus Christ's mortality (or, dying), so that it may reveal in us what kind of life was his on earth. **411 Godd hit wat . . . ure Laverd,** God knows, those who do thus (or, act in this way), they prove to us their love towards our Lord. **412 Cuth hit!** Show it!; **schawin him,** reveal itself (reflex.). **412–13 *Gregorius . . . est operis,*** Gregory: "The demonstration of action is the proof of love" (Gregory, *Homilies on the Gospels* 3.30.1 [*PL* 76.1220]). **413–14 Ne beo neaver thing . . . sweteth,** Be a thing ever so hard (i.e., even if a thing is ever so hard), true love [will] lighten it and soften and sweeten [it]. **414 *Amor omnia fatilia reddit,*** "Love renders all things easy" (see Augustine, *Sermons* 70.3 [*PL* 38.444]); **tholieth,** suffer, endure. **415 ful luve,** foul, evil love; **ant mare walden tholien?** and would want to (or, would be willing to) suffer more? **416–17 thet siker luve . . . luve of sunne?** that sure love, and true, and [love] sweet beyond all others, cannot master us so far as (i.e., as much as) the love of sin does? **417–20 Nawt for-thi . . . to tholien,** In spite of that, I know such [a person] who wears (lit., bears) a heavy mail shirt and a hair shirt both together, bound heavily (or, cruelly) with iron — [on his] torso, thigh, and arms — with wide, thick bonds (or, bands), so that the sweat from it (lit., thereof) is a martyrdom to endure. **420–22 Feasteth, waketh . . . licome derven,** He fasts,

greveth him nawt, ant bit me ofte teachen him sum-hwet with hwet he mahte his licome derven. Al thet is bitter, for ure Laverdes luve, al him thuncheth swete. Deu-le-set, yet he wepeth to me, [as] wivene sarest, ant seith Godd foryet him for-thi thet he ne sent him na muchel secnesse. Godd hit wat, thet maketh luve.

425 For as he seith me ofte, for na thing thet Godd mahte don uvele bi him, thah he with the forlorene wurpe him into helle, ne mahte he neaver, him thuncheth, luvien him the leasse. Yef ei mon eani swuch thing ortrowi bi him, he is mare mat then theof i-nume with theofthe. Ich wat ec swuch wummon thet tholeth lutel leasse: ah nis ther bute thoncki Godd i strengthe thet he yeveth ham, ant i-cnawen

430 eadmodliche ure wacnesse. Luvie we hare god, ant swa hit is ure ahne. For as Sein Gregoire seith, of swa muchel strengthe is luve thet hit maketh othres god, withute swinc, ure ahne, as is i-seid th'ruppe. Nu me thuncheth we beoth i-cumen into the seovethe dale, thet is al of luve the maketh schir heorte.

holds vigils, works, and, Christ knows, complains (reflex.) that it does not harm (or, discomfort) him, and asks (*bit* = reduced form of *bideth*) me often to teach him something with which he might torment his body. **422 al him thuncheth swete**, all [this] seems sweet to him. **423–24 Deu-le-set . . . secnesse**, God knows, he cries to me still, like the most sorrowful of women, and says God forgets (*foryet* = reduced form of *foryeteth*) him because He does not send him (*sent* = reduced form of *sendeth*) any great sickness. **424 thet maketh luve**, love does that. **425–27 for na thing . . . the leasse**, for nothing bad that God might do to him, [even] though He might throw him into hell, he could never, it seems to him, love Him the less. **427–28 Yef ei mon . . . theofthe**, If anyone suspects such a thing about him (i.e., that he will love God the less), he is (or, will be) more confounded (or, overcome) than a thief caught with [his] theft[s]. **428–30 Ich wat ec . . . ure wacnesse**, I also know such a woman who suffers little less: but there is [nothing to do] but to thank God for (lit., in) the strength that He gives them, and acknowledge humbly our weakness. **430–32 Luvie we hare god . . . th'ruppe**, Let us love their good, and so it is (or, will be) our own. For as St. Gregory says, love is of so much power that it makes another's good, without work, our own, as is said above. **432–33 Nu me thuncheth . . . schir heorte**, Now it seems to me that we have come to the seventh part, which is all about love which makes the heart pure.

Part Seven

Love

Seinte Pawel witneth thet alle uttre heardschipes, alle flesches pinsunges, ant licomliche swinkes — al is ase nawt ayeines luve, the schireth ant brihteth the heorte. **Exercitio corporis ad modicum valet; pietas autem valet ad omnia**. Thet is, "licomlich bisischipe is to lutel wurth, ah swote ant schir heorte is god to alle thinges. **Si linguis hominum loquar et angelorum, et cetera. Si tradidero corpus meum ita ut ardeam, et cetera. Si distribuero omnes facultates meas in cibos pauperum, caritatem autem non habeam, nichil michi prodest**. "Thah ich cuthe," he seith, "monne ledene ant englene, thah ich dude o mi bodi alle pine ant passiun thet bodi mahte tholien, thah ich yeve povre al thet ich hefde, yef ich nefde luve ther-with, to Godd ant to alle men in him ant for him, al were i-spillet. For as the hali abbat Moyses seide, al thet wa ant al thet heard thet we tholieth o flesch, ant al thet god thet we eaver doth, alle swucche thinges

---

1–3 flesches pinsunges . . . the heorte, all mortifications of the body (lit., flesh) and bodily toils — all is as if nothing against (or, in comparison to) love, which purifies and brightens the heart. **3–4 *Exercitio corporis . . . ad omnia***, "The exercise of the body is good for little; godliness however is good in all things" (adapted from 1 Timothy 4:8). **4 licomlich bisischipe**, physical activity. **5–8 *Si linguis hominum loquar . . . prodest***, "If I speak (lit., will have spoken) with the tongues of men and angels," etc. "If I give over my body thus that I may burn (i.e., be burnt)," etc. "If I give away all my means for food for the poor, if however I do not have love, it profits me nothing" (1 Corinthians 13:1–3). **8 Thah ich cuthe . . . englene**, "Though I knew," he says, "the language of men and of angels." **9 tholien**, suffer, endure. **10 nefde luve ther-with**, did not have love along with it. **11 al were i-spillet**, everything would be destroyed; **abbat**, abbot. **11–13 al thet heard . . . the heorte**, all the hardship which we suffer in the flesh, and all the good which we ever do, all such things are nothing but tools to

375

ne beoth nawt bute as lomen to tilie with the heorte. Yef the axe ne kurve, ne
spitel-steaf ne dulve, ne the sulh ne erede, hwa kepte ham to halden? Alswa as na
15 mon ne luveth lomen for ham-seolf, ah deth for the thinges thet me wurcheth with
ham, alswa na flesches derf nis to luvien bute for-thi, thet Godd te reathere thider-
ward loki mid his grace ant mak*ie* the heorte schir ant of briht sihthe, thet nan ne
mei habben with monglunge of untheawes, ne with eorthlich luve of worltliche
thinges. For this mong woreth swa the ehnen of the heorte, thet ha ne mei cnawen
20 Godd, ne gleadien of his sihthe. Schir heorte, as Seint Bernard seith, makieth twa
thinges, thet tu al thet tu dest do hit other for luve ane of Godd, other for othres
god ant for his biheve. Have in al thet tu dest an of þes twa ententes, other ba
togederes, for the leatere falleth into the earre. Have eaver schir heorte thus ant
do al thet tu wult; have wori heorte, al the sit uvele. **Omnia munda mundis;**
25 **coinquinatis vero nichil est mundum (Apostolus). Item, Augustinus: Habe**
caritatem, et fac quicquid vis — voluntate videlicet rationis. For-thi, mine

work with the heart (or, with which to cultivate the heart). **13 ne kurve**, did not cut. **13–14 ne
spitel-steaf . . . to halden?** or [if] the shovel did not dig, or [if] the plowshare did not plow,
who would care to keep them? **14–19 Alswa as na mon . . . worltliche thinges**, Just as no one
loves tools for themselves, but does [so] for the things people make with them, just so no
suffering of the flesh (or, body) is to be loved (*luvien* = passive inf.) except for the reason that
God may look the more readily in that direction (lit., thitherward) with His grace and make the
heart pure and of bright sight, which no one can have (or, possess) with a mixing (i.e., contamination) of faults, nor with earthly love of worldly things. **19–20 For this mong . . . sihthe**, For
this mixture so confuses the eyes of the heart, that they cannot know God, nor be glad in His
sight. **20–22 Schir heorte . . . his biheve**, As St. Bernard says, two things make a pure heart,
that you, [in] all that you do, may do it either 1) for the love of God alone, or 2) for another's
good and for his benefit. **22–24 Have in al thet tu dest . . . sit uvele**, In everything that you do
have one of these two intents, or both together, for the latter falls (or, leads) into the former.
Always have a pure heart and so do everything that you want; have a confused heart, [and]
everything [will] suit (lit., sit) you badly. **24–25 *Omnia munda mundis . . . (Apostolus)***, "To
the clean all things are clean; truly to the polluted nothing is clean" (the Apostle) (Titus 1:15).
25–26 *Item, Augustinus . . . videlicet rationis*, Again, Augustine: "Have love, and do whatever you will — of course, according to the inclination of reason" (Augustine, *On the Epistle
of John* 7 [*PL* 35.2033] and *Confessions* 10.29 [*PL* 32.796]).

leove sustren, over alle thing beoth bisie to habben schir heorte. Hwet is schir heorte? Ich hit habbe i-seid ear, thet is thet ye na thing ne wilnin ne ne luvien, bute Godd ane ant te ilke thinges for Godd, the helpeth ow toward him — for

30 Godd, ich segge, luvien ham, ant nawt for ham-seolven, as is mete other clath, mon other wummon, the ye beoth of i-godet. For ase seith Seint Austin ant speketh thus to ure Laverd: **Minus te amat qui preter te aliquid amat, quod non propter te amat.** Thet is, "Laverd, leasse ha luvieth the, the luvieth eawt bute the, bute ha luvien hit for the." Schirnesse of heorte is Godes luve ane. I this is al the strengthe

35 of alle religiuns, the ende of alle ordres. **Plenitudo legis est dilectio.** "Luve fulleth the lahe," seith Seinte Pawel. **Quicquid precipitur, in sola caritate solidatur.** "Alle Godes heastes," as Sein Gregoire seith, "beoth i luve i-rotet." Luve ane schal beon i-leid i Seinte Mihales weie. Theo the meast luvieth, schulen beo meast i-blisset, nawt theo the leadeth heardest lif: for luve hit overweieth. Luve is heovene

40 stiward for hire muchele freolec, for heo ne edhalt na thing, ah yeveth al thet ha haveth ant ec hire-seolven — elles ne kepte Godd nawt of thet hiren were.

27 bisie, diligent (or, busy). **28–31 Ich hit habbe i-seid ear . . . of i-godet,** I have said it earlier, that is that you neither desire nor love anything except God alone and [that you love] for God the very things which help you towards Him — I say to love them for God, and not for themselves: for example (lit., as is) food or clothing, a man or woman through whom you are done good (or, have benefited). **32–33 *Minus te amat . . . te amat*,** "He loves You less who loves something before (i.e., more than) You, because he does not love [You] for Yourself" (Augustine, *Confessions* 10.29 [*PL* 32.796]). **33–34 leasse ha luvieth the . . . for the,** they love you less who love anything but You, unless they love it for You. **34 Schirnesse of heorte . . . ane,** Purity of heart is the love of God alone (i.e., loving God only). **35 religiuns,** religious professions; *Plenitudo . . . dilectio*, "Love is the fulfillment of the law" (Romans 13:10). **35–36 fulleth the lahe,** fulfills the law. **36 *Quicquid precipitur . . . solidatur*,** "Whatever is commanded, is made firm in love alone" (Gregory, *Homilies on the Gospels* 2.27 [*PL* 76.1205]). **37 heastes,** hests (or, commands); **i-rotet,** rooted. **38 i-leid Seinte Mihales weie,** laid in St. Michael's scales (or, balance). **38–39 Theo the meast luvieth . . . overweieth,** Those who love most will be most blessed, not those who lead the hardest life: for love outweighs it. **39–41 heovene stiward . . . hiren were,** heaven's steward because of her great generosity, because she does not withhold anything, but gives everything which she has and also [gives] herself — otherwise God would not care (or, have regard for) what might be hers (Shepherd [p. 54n20 ff.]: God would not set any store in her offices).

Godd haveth ofgan ure luve on alle cunne wise. He haveth muchel i-don us, ant mare bihaten. Muchel yeove ofdraheth luve. Me al the world he yef us in Adam, ure alde feader, ant al thet is i the world he weorp under ure fet, beastes ant fuheles,

45 ear we weren forgulte. **Omnia subjecisti sub pedibus ejus, oves et boves universas insuper et pecora campi, volucres celi, et pisces maris, qui perambulant semitas maris.** Ant yet al thet is, as is th'ruppe i-seid, serveth the gode to sawle biheve, yet te uvele servith eorthe, sea, ant sunne. He dude yet mare, yef us nawt ane of his, ah dude al him-seolven. Se heh yeove nes neaver i-

50 yeven to se lahe wrecch*e*s. **Apostolus: Christus dilexit ecclesiam et dedit semet ipsum pro ea.** "Crist," seith Seinte Pawel, "luvede swa his leofmon thet he yef for hire the pris of him-seolven." Neometh nu gode yeme, mine leove sustren, for-hwi me ah him to luvien. Earst as a mon the woheth, as a king thet luvede a gentil povre leafdi of feorrene londe, he sende his sonden bivoren — thet weren the

55 patriarches ant te proph[et]es of the alde testament — with leattres i-sealet. On ende he

42–43 Godd haveth ofgan . . . mare bihaten, God has gained our love in every kind of way. He has done much for us, and has promised more. **43–45 Muchel yeove . . . weren forgulte**, A large gift wins (lit., draws forth) love. But He gave us all the world in Adam, our original father, and everything that is in the world He cast under our feet, beasts and birds, before we had become guilty. **45–47 *Omnia subjecisti . . . semitas maris***, "You have subjected all things under his feet, all sheep and cattle, and in addition the beasts of the field, the birds of the heaven, and the fish of the sea, which wander about the paths of the sea" (Psalm 8:8–9; see Genesis 1:28). **47–48 as is th'ruppe i-seid . . . sunne**, as is said above (see 3.62–64), serves the good for [their] soul's benefit, yet (or, even so) the earth, sea, and sun serve the evil. **49 yef us nawt ane . . . him-seolven**, gave us not only from [what is] His, but gave (lit., did) all of Himself. **49–50 Se heh yeove . . . wrecches**, So high a gift was never given to such low wretches. **50–51 *Apostolus: Christus dilexit . . . pro ea***, The Apostle: "Christ loved the Church and gave himself for her" (based on Ephesians 5:25). **51 leofmon**, leman (or, lover); **yef**, gave. **52 pris**, price. **52–53 Neometh nu gode yeme . . . luvien**, Pay (lit., Take) good attention, my dear sisters, why one ought to love Him. **53–55 Earst as a mon . . . i-sealet**, At first, like a man who woos, like a king who loved a noble, poor lady from a faraway land, he sent his messengers before (or, in ad-vance) — they were the patriarchs and the prophets of the Old Testament — with sealed letters. **55–58 On ende he com . . . luve wealden**, Finally He came Himself and brought

com him-seolven ant brohte the Godspel as leattres i-openet ant wrat with his ahne blod saluz to his leofmon, luve-gretunge, for-te wohin hire with ant hire luve wealden. Her-to falleth a tale, a wrihe forbisne.

60

A leafdi wes mid hire fan biset al abuten, hire lond al destruet, ant heo al povre in-with an eorthene castel. A mihti kinges luve wes thah biturnd upon hire swa unimete swithe, thet he for wohlech sende hire his sonden, an efter other, ofte somet monie, sende hire beawbelez bathe feole ant feire, sucurs of liveneth, help of his hehe hird to halden hire castel. Heo underfeng al as on unrecheles, ant swa wes heard i-heortet, thet hire luve ne mahte he neaver beo the neorre. Hwet wult

65

tu mare? He com him-seolf on ende, schawde hire his feire neb, as the the wes of alle men feherest to bihalden, spec se swithe swoteliche, ant wordes se murie, thet ha mahten deade arearen to live, wrahte feole wundres ant dude muchele meistries bivoren hire eh-sihthe, schawde hire his mihte, talde hire of his kinedom, bead to makien hire cwen of al thet he ahte. Al this ne heold nawt — nes this

70

hoker wunder? For heo nes neaver wurthe for-te beon his thuften, ah swa thurh

---

the Gospel like letters patent (i.e., public letters confirming a grant) and wrote a salutation with His own blood to His lover, a greeting of love to woo her with and to possess her love. **58 Her-to falleth . . . forbisne**, Thereby hangs a tale (lit., concerning this [there] falls a tale), a hidden parable (or, an exemplum with a hidden meaning). **59–60 A leafdi wes . . . castel**, There was a lady besieged by her enemies on every side (lit., all about), her land completely destroyed, and she completely poor inside an earthen castle. **60–63 thah biturnd upon hire . . . hire castel**, nevertheless directed towards her, so immeasurably strongly, that he for wooing (i.e., in his wooing) sent her his messengers, one after the other, often many together, sent her jewels both many and fair, supplies of food, the help of his splendid army to hold her castle. **63–65 Heo underfeng al . . . tu mare?** She received everything as if in indifference, and was so hard-hearted that he could never be the nearer to her love. What more do you want? **65–69 He com him-seolf . . . al thet he ahte**, He came himself in the end, showed her his fair face, as he who was the fairest of all men to look on, spoke so very sweetly, and [with] words so delightful that they might raise the dead to life, performed many miracles and did great deeds before her eyes (lit., eye-sight), showed her his power, told her of his kingdom, offered to make her queen of all that he owned. **69–71 Al this ne heold . . . on ende**, All this did no good — was this disdain not strange? For she was never worthy to be his servant (or, handmaid), but because of his

his deboneirte luve hefde overcumen him, thet he seide on ende, "Dame, thu art i-weorret ant thine van beoth se stronge thet tu ne maht nanes-weis withute mi sucurs edfleon hare honden, thet ha ne don the to scheome death efter al thi weane. Ich chulle for the luve of the neome thet feht up-o me ant arudde the of ham the thi

75 death secheth. Ich wat thah to sothe thet ich schal bituhen ham neomen deathes wunde, ant ich hit wulle heorteliche for-te ofgan thin heorte. Nu thenne biseche ich the, for the luve thet ich cuthe the, thet tu luvie me lanhure efter the ilke dede dead, hwen thu naldest lives." Thes king dude al thus: arudde hire of alle hire van, ant wes him-seolf to wundre i-tuket ant i-slein on ende — thurh miracle aras thah

80 from deathe to live. Nere theos ilke leafdi of uveles cunnes cunde, yef ha over alle thing ne luvede him her-efter?

Thes king is Jesu, Godes sune, thet al o thisse wise wohede ure sawle, the deoflen hefden biset. Ant he as noble wohere efter monie messagers ant feole god-deden com to pruvien his luve ant schawde thurh cnihtschipe thet he wes luve-wurthe, as

85 weren sum-hwile cnihtes i-wunet to donne — dude him i turneiment ant hefde for

kindness love had so overcome him that he said in the end. **71–75 Dame, thu art i-weorret . . . secheth,** Madam, you are attacked and your enemies (lit. foes) are so strong that you cannot without my help in any way escape their hands [so] that they [will] not put you to a shameful death after all your suffering. I will for [my] love of you take the fight upon me and save you from them who seek your death. **75–78 Ich wat thah . . . naldest lives,** I know, though, truly (i.e., for a fact) that I will receive (lit., take) death's wound among them, and I will do it gladly (lit., heartily) in order to win your heart. Now then I beg you, for the love that I reveal to you, that you at least love me after the deed (lit., this same deed), [when I am] dead, since you would not [while I was] living. **78–80 Thes king . . . to live,** This king did everything just so: saved her from all her foes, and was himself horribly tormented and slain (i.e., put to death) in the end — though by a miracle [he] arose from death to life. **80–81 Nere theos ilke leafdi . . . her-efter?** Would not this same lady be of an evil sort of character (or, nature) if she did not love him after that (lit., hereafter) above all things? **82–83 wohede ure sawle . . . biset,** wooed our soul, which devils had besieged. **83–89 as noble wohere . . . up-o the other,** like a noble wooer after many messengers and many good deeds came to prove His love and showed through chivalry that He was worthy of her love, as knights sometimes were used to do — put Himself in the tournament and for the love of His beloved as a bold knight in the fight had His shield pierced on every side. His shield, which covered His Godhead (or, divinity), was His beloved body which

his leoves luve his scheld i feht as kene cniht on euche half i-thurlet. His scheld, the wreah his Godd-head, wes his leove licome thet wes i-spread o rode, brad as scheld buven in his i-strahte earmes, nearow bineothen as the an fot — efter monies wene — set up-o the other. Thet this scheld naveth siden is for bitacnunge thet

90 his deciples the schulden stonden bi him ant habben i-beon his siden fluhen alle from him ant leafden him as fremede, as the Godspel seith: **Relicto eo omnes fugerunt**. This scheld is i-yeven us ayein alle temptatiuns, as Jeremie witneth: **Dabis scutum cordis laborem tuum**. Nawt ane this scheld ne schilt us from alle uveles, ah deth yet mare, cruneth us in heovene. **Scuto bone voluntatis**. "Laverd,"

95 he seith, Davith, "with the scheld of thi gode wil thu havest us i-crunet." "Scheld" he seith "of god wil," for willes he tholede al thet he tholede. **Ysaias: Oblatus est quia voluit**.

"Me, Laverd," thu seist, "hwer-to ne mahte he with leasse gref habben arud us?" Yeoi, i-wiss, ful lihtliche, ah he nalde. For-hwi? For-te bineomen us euch

100 bitellunge ayein him of ure luve thet he se deore bohte. Me buth lihtliche thing thet me luveth lutel. He bohte us with his heorte blod — deorre pris nes neaver —

was stretched on the Cross, broad as a shield above (or, at the top) with His outstretched arms, narrow beneath since the one foot — according to the opinion of many — sat (i.e., was placed) upon the other. **89–91 Thet this scheld . . . Godspel seith,** The fact that this shield does not have sides is to symbolize (lit., for the symbolizing) that His disciples, who should have stood by Him and should have been His sides all fled from Him and left Him like a stranger, as the Gospel says. **91–92 *Relicto eo omnes fugerunt*,** "He having been abandoned, they all fled" (based on Matthew 26:56). **92 i-yeven,** given. **93 *Dabis scutum cordis laborem tuum*,** "You will give [them] a shield of heart, your labor" (Lamentations 3:65). **93–94 Nawt ane this scheld . . . in heovene,** Not only does this shield us from all evils, but [it] does still more, [it] crowns us in heaven. **94 *Scuto bone voluntatis*,** "With the shield of good will [you have crowned us]" (Psalm 5:13). **96 for willes he tholede . . . tholede,** for willingly He suffered all that He suffered. **96–97 *Oblatus est quia voluit*,** "He was offered up because He wished [it]" (Isaiah 53:7). **98–100 "Me, Laverd" . . . deore bohte,** "But, Lord," you say, "could He not have saved us with less suffering (lit., grief)?" Yes, certainly, [He could have] very easily, but He did not want to. Why? To deprive us of each excuse [we might give] to Him for [not giving] our love which He bought so dearly (or, expensively). **100–02 Me buth . . . se sare,** One buys cheaply a thing which one loves little. He bought us with His heart's blood — there was never a dearer (or,

381

for-te ofdrahen of us ure luve toward him, thet costnede him se sare. I scheld
beoth threo thinges: the treo, ant te lether, ant te litunge. Alswa wes i this scheld
the treo of the rode, thet lether of Godes licome, the litunge of the reade blod thet
105   heowede hire se feire. Eft the thridde reisun: efter kene cnihtes death, me hongeth
hehe i chirche his scheld on his mungunge. Alswa is this scheld — thet is, the
crucifix — i chirche i-set i swuch stude ther me hit sonest seo, for-te thenchen
ther-bi o Jesu Cristes cnihtschipe, thet he dude o rode. His leofmon bihalde th'ron
hu he bohte hire luve, lette thurlin his scheld, openin his side, to schawin hire his
110   heorte, to schawin hire openliche hu inwardliche he luvede hire, ant to ofdrahen
hire heorte.

    Fowr heaved luven me i-find i this world: bitweone gode i-feren, bitweone mon
ant wummon, bi[tweone] wif ant hire child, bitweone licome ant sawle. The luve
thet Jesu Crist haveth to his deore leofmon overgeath theos fowre, passeth ham
115   alle. Ne teleth me him god fere the leith his wed i Giwerie to acwitin ut his fere?
Godd almihti leide him-seolf for us i Giwerie ant dude his deore-wurthe bodi to

more expensive) price — in order to win (lit., draw forth) from us our love for Him, which
cost Him so heavily. **103 treo**, wood; **litunge**, coloring, painting. **104 thet**, the (old neuter
def. art.); **licome**, body. **105 heowede hire se feire**, colored it (lit., her, the cross/shield)
so fairly (or, beautifully); **Eft**, In turn. **105–06 efter kene cnihtes death ... his mungunge**,
after a brave knight's death, the people hang his shield high in the church in his memory.
107–08 i swuch stude ... o rode, in such a place where one [may] see it soonest (i.e.,
most easily), in order to think, through it (lit., thereby), of Jesus Christ's chivalry which
He did on the Cross. **108–09 His leofmon ... openin his side**, Let His lover see in it (lit.,
thereon) how He bought her love, [how He] let His shield be pierced, His side be opened.
110 inwardliche, deeply (or, sincerely); **to ofdrahen**, to draw forth (or, win). **112–13
Fowr heaved luven ... ant sawle**, Four main (or, chief) loves one finds (*i-find* = reduced
form of *i-findeth*) in this world: between good companions, between man and woman,
between a woman and her child, between body and soul. **114 leofmon**, leman (or, lover);
overgeath, surpasses. **115–17 Ne teleth me him ... of Giwene honden**, Does one not
account him (i.e., that person) a good companion who lays his pledge (i.e., collateral) in
Jewry (i.e., among Jewish moneylenders) to acquit his companion out [of debt]? God almighty laid Himself for us in Jewry (i.e., in the hands of the Jews) and put His precious
body up [as a pledge] to acquit (or, release) His beloved out of the hands of the Jews

acwitin ut his leofmon of Giwene honden. Neaver fere ne dude swuch fordede for his fere.

    Muche luve is ofte bitweone mon ant wummon, ah thah ha were i-weddet him,
120   ha mahte i-wurthen se unwreast, ant swa longe ha mahte forhorin hire with othre men thet thah ha walde ayein cumen, he ne kepte hire nawt. For-thi Crist luveth mare, for thah the sawle his spuse forhori hire with the feond under heaved-sunne, feole yeres ant dahes, his mearci is hire eaver yarow hwen ha wule cumen ham ant leten then deovel. Al this he seith him-seolf thurh Jeremie: **Si dimiserit vir ux-**
125   **orem suam, et cetera. Tu autem fornicata es cum multis amatoribus; tamen revertere ad me, dicit Dominus**. Yet he yeiyeth al dei, "thu thet havest se unwreaste i-don, biturn the ant cum ayein — welcume schalt tu beo me." **Immo et occurrit prodigo venienti**. "Yet he eorneth," hit seith, "ayein hire yein-cume ant warpeth earmes anan abuten hire swire." Hweat is mare milce? Yet her gleadfulre
130   wunder: ne beo neaver his leof forhoret mid se monie deadliche sunnen, sone se ha kimeth to him ayein he maketh hire neowe meiden. For as Seint Austin seith,

(*Giwene* = genitive pl.). **117–18 Neaver fere . . . his fere**, Never did a friend do such a service for his friend. **119–21 ah thah ha were i-weddet him . . . kepte hire nawt**, but even though she were wedded to him, she might become so worthless and she might prostitute herself with other men so long that even though she would want to come back [to him], he would not care for her. **122–24 for thah the sawle his spuse . . . then deovel**, for even though the soul his spouse might prostitute herself with the devil in mortal sin, for many years and days, His mercy is always ready for (or, available to) her when she wants to come home and leave the devil (*then* = old masc. accusative def. art.). **124–26 *Si dimiserit vir . . . dicit Dominus***, "If a man has sent his wife away", etc. "But you have prostituted [yourself] with many lovers; even so, return to Me, says the Lord" (Jeremiah 3:1). **126–27 Yet he yeiyeth . . . beo me**, Continually He cries all day, "you who have acted so wickedly, turn (reflex.) and come back — you will be welcome to Me." **127–28 *Immo et occurrit prodigo venienti***, "Yes, and he runs to meet the prodigal [as he is] approaching" (based loosely on Luke 15:20). **128–29 "Yet he eorneth . . . swire,"** "Still he runs," it says, "at her return (lit, again-coming) and throws [his] arms immediately around her neck." **129–31 Hweat is mare milce? . . . neowe meiden**, What is greater forgiveness (i.e., is there any greater forgiveness)? Yet here [is an even] more joyful marvel: be His beloved (i.e., even if His beloved is) ever so prostituted with so many deadly sins, as soon as she comes to Him again He makes her a new virgin.

swa muchel is *bitweonen* Godes neoleachunge ant monnes to wummon, thet monnes
neoleachunge maketh of meiden wif, ant Godd maketh of wif meiden. **Restituit,
inquit Job, in integrum**. Gode werkes ant treowe bileave — theose twa thinges

135 beoth meithhad i sawle.

Nu of the thridde luve. Child thet hefde swuch uvel thet him bihofde beath of
blod ear hit were i-healet — muchel the moder luvede hit, the walde this beath him
makien. This dude ure Laverd us the weren se seke of sunne ant swa i-sulet ther-
with thet na thing ne mahte healen us ne cleansin us bute his blod ane, for swa he

140 hit walde. His luve maketh us beath th'rof. I-blescet beo he eavre! Threo beathes
he greithede to his deore leofmon for-te weschen hire in ham se hwit ant se feier
thet ha were wurthe to his cleane cluppunges. The earste beath is fulluht. The
other beoth teares inre other uttre, efter the forme beath, yef ha hire suleth. The
thridde is Jesu Cristes blod thet halheth ba the othre, as Sein Juhan seith i the

145 Apocalipse: **Qui dilexit nos et lavit nos in sanguine suo**. Thet he luveth us mare
then eani moder hire child — he hit seith him-seolven thurh Ysaie: **Nunquid potest
mater oblivisci filii uteri sui? Et si illa obliviscatur, ego non obliviscar tui.**

132–33 swa muchel is bitweonen . . . wif meiden, there is so much [difference] between
God's approach and man's approach to woman, that man's approach makes a wife of a
virgin, and God makes a virgin of a wife. **133–34 *Restituit, inquit Job, in integrum***, "He
restores," says Job, "to its former condition (lit., in whole)" (Job 12:23). **134 Gode**, Good.
135 meithhad i sawle, virginity in the soul. **136–38 Child thet hefde . . . him makien**,
[Imagine a] child that had such a disease that it needed (lit., it behooved him) a bath of
blood before it would be healed — the mother [would] greatly love it, who would want to
make it this bath. **138–39 the weren se seke . . . ther-with**, who were so sick with sin and
so polluted (lit., sullied) with it. **140 His luve maketh us beath th'rof**, His love makes us
a bath of it (i.e., of His blood). **141–42 he greithede . . . cleane cluppunges**, He prepared
for His dear lover (or, beloved) in order to wash her (or, to wash herself) in them so white
and so fair that she would be worthy for His chaste embraces. **142–44 The earste beath
. . . the othre**, The first bath is baptism. Tears are the second, inner or outer, after the first
bath, if she pollutes herself. The third is Jesus Christ's blood which hallows both the
others. **145 *Qui dilexit nos . . . sanguine suo***, "[He] who loved us washed us in His blood"
(Revelation 1:5). **146–47 *Nunquid potest mater . . . obliviscar tui***, "Can a mother ever
forget the son of her womb? And if she should forget, I will not forget you" (adapted from
Isaiah 49:15).

"Mei moder," he seith, "foryeoten hire child? Ant thah heo do, ich ne mei the foryeoten neaver" — ant seith the resun efter: **In manibus meis descripsi te**. "Ich
150 habbe," he seith, "depeint te i mine honden" — swa he dude mid read blod up-o the rode. Me cnut his gurdel to habben thoht of a thing, ah ure Laverd, for he nalde neaver foryeoten us, dude mearke of thurlunge, in ure munegunge, i ba twa his honden.

Nu the feorthe luve: the sawle luveth the licome swithe mid alle, ant thet is
155 etscene i the twinnunge — for leove freond beoth sari hwen ha schulen twinnin — ah ure Laverd willeliche totweamde his sawle from his bodi for-te veien ure bathe togederes, world buten ende i the blisse of heovene. Thus, lo, Jesu Cristes luve toward his deore spuse — thet is, Hali Chirche other cleane sawle — passeth alle ant overkimeth the fowr measte luven thet me i-find on eorthe. With al this luve
160 yetten he woheth hire o this wise:

"Thi luve," he seith, " — other hit is for-te yeoven allunge, other hit is to sullen, other hit is to reavin ant to neomen with strengthe. Yef hit is for-te yeoven, hwer maht tu biteon hit betere then up-o me? Nam ich thinge feherest? Nam ich kinge richest? Nam ich hest i-cunnet? Nam ich weolie wisest? Nam ich monne hendest?

148–49 ich ne mei the foryeoten, I cannot forget you. **149** *In manibus meis descripsi te*, "I have depicted (or, carved) you in my hands" (Isaiah 49:16). **150 depeint**, painted; **swa he dude mid read blod**, so he did with red blood. **151–53 Me cnut his gurdel . . . his honden**, A person knots (i.e., puts a knot; *cnut* = reduced form of *cnutteth*) in his belt to have thought of (i.e., remember) a thing, but our Lord, because He did not want ever to forget us, made a mark of piercing, in our memory (i.e., as a reminder of us), in both of His two hands. **154–57 luveth the licome . . . of heovene**, loves the body very much, moreover, and that is evident in the parting (or, separation) — for dear friends are sorry when they must part — but our Lord willingly separated His soul from His body to join both of ours together, world without end (i.e., forever and ever) in the joy of heaven. **158 other cleane sawle**, or the chaste soul. **159 overkimeth the fowr measte luven . . . eorthe**, surpasses (lit., overcomes) the four greatest loves that one finds (*i-find* = reduced form of *i-findeth*) on earth. **160 yetten he woheth hire**, continually He woos her. **162 other hit is . . . with strengthe**, either it is to be given completely, or it is to be sold, or it is to be plundered and to be taken by force. **163 biteon**, bestow; **Nam ich thinge feherest?** Am I not the fairest (or, most beautiful) of things? **163–64 kinge richest**, the most powerful of kings. **164 hest i-cunnet**, the highest born; **weolie wisest**, the wisest of the wealthy; **monne hendest**, most courteous of men.

165   Nam ich thinge freoest? For swa me seith bi large mon the ne con nawt edhalden, thet he haveth the honden, as mine beoth, i-thurlet. Nam ich alre thinge swotest ant swetest? Thus alle the reisuns hwi me ah to yeove luve thu maht i-finden in me, nomeliche yef thu luvest chaste cleannesse. For nan ne mei luvie me bute ha hire halde. Ah ha is threo-vald: i widewehad, i spushad, i meidenhad, the heste.

170   Yef thi luve nis nawt to yeovene, ah wult thet me bugge hire — buggen hire? [Hu?] Other with other luve other with sum-hweat elles. Me suleth wel luve [for luve] ant swa me ah to sulle luve, ant for na thing elles. Yef thin is swa to sullen ich habbe i-boht hire with luve over alle othre. For of the fowr measte luven, ich habbe i-cud toward te the measte of ham alle. Yef thu seist thu nult nawt leote

175   th'ron se liht chap, ah wult yette mare, nempne hweat hit schule beon. Sete feor o thi luve. Thu ne schalt seggen se muchel thet ich nule yeove mare. Wult tu castles, kinedomes? Wult tu wealden al the world? Ich chulle do the betere, makie the, with al this, cwen of heove-riche. Thu schalt te-seolf beo seove-vald brihtre then the sunne. Nan uvel ne schal nahhi the. Na wunne ne schal wonti the. Al thi wil

165 thinge freoest, the most generous of things. **165–66 For swa me seith . . . i-thurlet**, For so people say about a generous man who cannot hold back that he has holes in his hands, as I do (lit., that he has the hands pierced, as mine are). **166 alre thinge**, of all creatures (or, things). **167 hwi me ah to yeove**, why one ought to give. **168 nomeliche**, especially. **168–69 bute ha hire halde**, unless she keep her (i.e., chastity). **169 ha is threo-vald . . . heste**, she (i.e., chastity) is threefold: in widowhood, in marriage (lit., spouse-hood), in virginity, the highest. **170–72 Yef thi luve . . . na thing elles**, If your love is not to be given (passive inf.), but you wish that one should buy her (i.e., love) — Buy her? How? Either with another love or with something else. One fittingly sells love [in exchange] for love and so (i.e., in this way) one ought to sell love, and for nothing else. **172–73 Yef thin is swa . . . othre**, If yours is thus to be sold I have bought it with a love beyond all others. **173–74 For of the fowr . . . ham alle**, For of the four greatest loves, I have shown towards you the greatest of them all. **174–76 Yef thu seist . . . thi luve**, If you say you will not allow so cheap a bargain for it (lit., thereon), but want still more, name what it will be. Set a price on your love. **176 Thu ne schalt seggen . . . mare**, You will not say so much that I will not give more. **177 Wult tu**, Do you want; **wealden**, to rule, possess. **177–78 Ich chulle do the betere . . . heove-riche**, I will do you [one] better, make you, in addition to all this, queen of the kingdom of heaven. **178 seove-vald**, sevenfold, seven times. **179 Nan uvel . . . wonti the**, No evil (or, disease) will come near you. No joy will be lacking to you. **179 wil**, will (or, desire).

180   schal beon i-wraht in heovene ant ec in eorthe — ye, ant yet in helle. Ne schal
neaver heorte thenchen hwuch selhthe thet ich nule yeoven for thi luve unmeteliche,
unevenliche, unendeliche mare. Al Creasuse weole, the wes kinge richest.
Absalones schene wlite, the as ofte as me evesede him, salde his evesunge, the her
thet he kearf of for twa hundret sicles of seolver i-weiet. Asaeles swiftschipe, the

185   straf with heortes of urn. Samsones strengthe, the sloh a thusent of his fan al ed a
time, ant ane, bute fere. Cesares freolec. Alixandres here-word. Moysese heale.
Nalde a mon for an of theos yeoven al thet he ahte? Ant alle somet, ayein mi bodi,
ne beoth nawt wurth a nelde. Yef thu art se swithe ane-wil ant swa ut of thi wit
thet tu, thurh nawt to leosen, forsakest swuch biyete, with alles cunnes selhthe, lo,

190   ich halde her heatel sweord up-o thin heaved to dealen lif ant sawle, ant bisenchen
ham ba into the fur of helle, to beon deofles hore schentfulliche ant sorhfulliche
world abuten ende. Ondswere nu ant were the, yef thu const, ayein me, other yette

---

180 i-wraht, wrought, performed. **180–82 Ne schal neaver heorte . . . mare**, Never will
the heart imagine such happiness that I will not give for your love immeasurably, incomparably, infinitely more. **182 Al Creasuse weole**, All [of] Croesus' wealth. **183–84
Absalones schene wlite . . . seolver i-weiet**, Absalom's shining beauty, who, as often as his
hair was cut, the clippings were sold (lit., as one cut his hair, [one] sold the clippings), the hair
that he cut off, for two hundred shekels of weighed silver (see 2 Kings 15:25–26). **184–85
Asaeles swiftschipe . . . of urn**, Asael's speed, who strove (or, competed) with the stag in
running (or, with the stag's speedy running: *of-urn*) (see 2 Kings 2:18 ff.). **185–86 the sloh a
thusent . . . bute fere**, who slew a thousand of his foes all at one time, and alone, without a
companion (see Judges 16). **186 Cesares freolec . . . heale**, Caesar's generosity. Alexander's
reputation (lit., praise-word). Moses's vigor (see Deuteronomy 34:7). **187 Nalde a mon . . . he
ahte?** Would a man not give all that he owned for one of these [things]? **187–92 Ant alle
somet . . . world abuten ende**, And all together, against (i.e., in comparison to) my body,
[these things] are not worth a needle. If you are so very stubborn and so out of your mind that
you, to lose by nothing (i.e., in fear of losing any of these blessings), refuse such a benefit,
along with happiness of every kind, look, I hold here a fierce sword at your head to separate
life and soul, and sink them both into the fire of hell, to be the devil's whore, in shame and in
sorrow (lit., shamefully and sorrowfully), world without end (i.e., for ever and ever). **192–94
Ondswere nu . . . muchele biheve**, Answer now (imper.) and protect yourself, if you can,
against me, or grant me your love which I yearn for so powerfully — not for mine, but for your

me thi luve the ich yirne se swithe — nawt for min ah for thin ahne muchele biheve."

195 Lo, thus ure Laverd woheth. Nis ha to heard i-heortet thet a thulli wohere ne mei to his luve turnen, yef ha wel thencheth theose threo thinges: hwet he is ant hwet heo is, ant hu muchel is the luve of se heh as he is toward se lah as heo is? For-thi seith the Salm-wruhte: **Non est qui se abscondat a calore ejus**. "Nis nan thet mahe edlutien thet ha ne mot him luvien." The sothe sunne i the under-tid wes 200 for-thi i-stihen on heh, o the hehe rode, for-te spreaden over-al hate luve-gleames. Thus neodful he wes ant is athet tes dei to ontenden his luve *i* his leoves heorte, ant seith i the Godspel: **Ignem veni mittere in terram, et quid volo nisi ut ardeat?** "Ich com to bringen," he seith, "fur into eorthe" — thet is, bearninde luve into eorthlich heorte — "ant hwet yirne ich elles bute thet hit bleasie?" Wlech luve is 205 him lath, as he seith thurh Sein Juhan i the Apocalipse: **Utinam frigidus esses aut calidus! Set quia tepidus es, incipiam te evomere de ore meo**. "Ich walde," he seith to his leofmon, "thet tu were i mi luve other allunge cald, other hat mid alle, ah for-thi thet tu art ase wlech bitweone twa, nowther hat ne cald, thu makest me to wleatien, ant ich wulle speowe the ut bute thu wurthe hattre."

own great benefit. **195–97 Nis ha to heard . . . as heo is?** Is she not too hard hearted whom such a wooer cannot turn (or, convert) to His love, [especially] if she considers these three things well: what He is and what she is, and how great is the love of so high a person as He is toward so low a person as she is? **198 Salm-wruhte**, Psalmist (lit., Psalm-maker); *Non est qui se abscondat a calore ejus*, "There is no one who can conceal himself from His flaming heat" (Psalm 18:7). **199 mahe edlutien . . . luvien**, can hide so that she does not have to love Him. **199–201 The sothe sunne . . . leoves heorte**, The true sun had for this reason climbed on high at the third hour (see Mark 15:25), onto the high Cross, in order to spread everywhere [His] hot love-rays. Thus, He was eager, and is to this day, to kindle His love in His beloved's heart. **202 *Ignem veni . . . ut ardeat?*** "I have come to send fire on the earth, and what do I want except that it may burn?" (Luke 12:49). **203 bearninde**, burning. **204–05 ant hwet yirne ich . . . him lath**, and what do I desire (lit., yearn) but that it blaze? Lukewarm love is hateful to Him. **205–06 *Utinam frigidus esses . . . ore meo***, "Would that you were either cold or hot! But because you are lukewarm, I am about to (lit., will begin to) vomit you out of My mouth" (Revelation 3:15–16). **206 Ich walde**, I would wish. **207 other**, either; **allunge**, completely; **mid alle**, completely. **208–09 ah for-thi thet tu art ase wlech . . . wurthe hattre**, but because you are as if lukewarm, between [these] two, neither hot nor cold, you make Me gag (or, feel disgusted), and I will spew you out unless you become hotter.

210   Nu ye habbeth i-herd, mine leove sustren, hu ant for-hwi Godd is swithe to luvien. For-te ontenden ow wel, gederith wude ther-to with the povre wummon of Sarepte, the burh the spealeth "ontendunge." **En inquit colligo duo ligna (Regum iii).** "Laverd," quoth ha to Helye the hali prophete, "lo, ich gederi twa treon." Theos twa treon bitacnith — thet a treo thet stod upriht, ant thet other the eode

215   thwert-over — o the deore rode. Of theos twa treon ye schulen ontende fur of luve in-with ower heorte. Biseoth ofte towart ham. Thencheth yef ye ne ahen eathe to luvien the king of blisse, the tospreat swa his earmes toward ow, ant buheth, as to beoden cos, dune-ward his heaved. Sikerliche ich segge hit: yef the sothe Helye — thet is, Godd almihti — i-fint ow theose twa treon bisiliche gederin,

220   he wule gestnin with ow ant moni-falden in ow his deore-wurthe grace, as Helie dude hire liveneth ant gestnede with hire thet he i-fond the twa treon gederin i Sarepte.

     Grickisch fur is i-maket of reades monnes blod, ant thet ne mei na thing bute migge ant sond ant eisil — as me seith — acwenchen. This Grickisch fur is the

210–11 Nu ye habbeth i-herd . . . to luvien, Now you have heard, my dear sisters, how and why God is very much to be loved (passive inf.). **211–12 For-te ontenden . . . spealeth "ontendunge,"** In order to ignite yourself well, gather (imper.) wood for that [purpose] (lit., thereto) with the poor woman of Sarephta, the town which (i.e., whose name) means "igniting." **212–13 *En inquit colligo duo ligna (Regum iii)*,** "Look!" she said, "I am gathering two sticks [that I may go in and prepare it for me and my son, that we may eat it, and die]" (3 Kings [17:12]). **213 Helye,** Elias; **gederi twa treon,** gather two pieces of wood (lit., two woods). **214–15 Theos twa treon . . . deore rode,** These two pieces of wood — the one piece which stood upright and the other which went crosswise — make the symbol of (lit., symbolize) the dear Cross. **215–16 Of theos twa treon . . . towart ham,** With these two pieces of wood you should kindle the fire of love within your heart. Look often towards them. **216–18 Thencheth yef ye ne ahen . . . his heaved,** Consider whether you should not easily love the King of joy, who so spreads out His arms towards you, and bends His head downward as if to offer a kiss. **218–22 Sikerliche ich segge hit . . . Sarepte,** I say it confidently: if the true Elijah — that is, almighty God — finds (*i-fint* = reduced form of *i-findeth*) you gathering these two pieces of wood (lit., finds you to gather), He will lodge (or, be a guest) with you and multiply in you His precious grace, as Elijah did her food and lodged with her whom he found gathering (lit., to gather) the two pieces of wood in Sarephta. **223–24 Grickisch fur . . . acwenchen,** Greek fire (i.e., burning pitch used as a weapon) is made from a red man's blood, and nothing but urine, and sand, and vinegar, as people say, can quench it.

225 luve of Jesu ure Laverd, ant ye hit schule makien of reade monnes blod — thet is,
Jesu Crist i-readet with his ahne blod o the deore rode — ant wes inread cundeliche
alswa, as me weneth. This blod, for ow i-sched up-o the earre twa treon, schal
makien ow Sareptiens — thet is, ontende mid tis Grickisch fur, thet as Salomon
seith, nane weattres — thet beoth worldliche tribulatiuns, nane temptatiuns, nowther
230 inre ne uttre — ne mahen this luve acwenchen. Nu nis thenne on ende bute witen
ow warliche with al thet hit acwencheth — thet beoth migge, ant sond, ant eisil, as
ich ear seide. Migge is stench of sunne. O sond ne groweth na god ant bitacneth
idel. Idel akeldeth ant acwencheth this fur. Sturieth ow cwicliche aa i gode werkes
ant thet schal heaten ow ant ontenden this fur ayein the brune of sunne. For alswa
235 as the an neil driveth ut then other, alswa the brune of Godes luve driveth brune of
ful luve ut of the heorte. The thridde thing is eisil — thet is, sur heorte of nith
other of onde. Understondeth this word: tha the nithfule Giws offreden ure Laverd
this sure present up-o the rode, tha seide he thet reowthfule word, **Consumatum
est.** "Neaver," quoth he, "ear nu nes ich ful pinet," nawt thurh thet eisil, ah thurh
240 hare ondfule nith thet tet eisil bitacnede thet heo him duden drinken, ant is i-lich

226 i-readet, reddened; **ahne**, own. **226–27 wes inread . . . weneth**, was very ruddy (or, red)
by nature also, as people believe. **227–30 for ow i-sched . . . luve acwenchen**, shed for you
upon the earlier (i.e., previously mentioned) two pieces of wood, will make you Sarephtans —
that is, ignite [you] with this Greek fire, which as Solomon says, no waters — those are worldly
tribulations, no temptations either inner or outer — can quench this love. **230–31 Nu nis thenne
. . . acwencheth**, Now there is not anything [to do] in the end but protect yourself cautiously
against everything that quenches it. **232–33 O sond . . . this fur**, In sand no good thing grows
and [it thus] symbolizes idleness. Idleness cools and quenches this fire. **233 Sturieth ow
cwicliche**, Always stir (or, busy) yourself quickly (or, vigorously). **234 heaten**, heat (verb);
ant ontenden this fur . . . sunne, and ignite this fire against the burning of sin. **234–36 For
alswa as the an neil . . . heorte**, For just as the one nail drives out the other, just so the burning
of God's love drives out the burning of foul love from the heart. **236 eisil**, vinegar. **236–37 sur
heorte . . . onde**, a sour heart of spite or of envy. **237–39 tha the nithfule Giws . . . *Consumatum
est***, when the spiteful Jews offered our Lord this sour present (i.e., vinegar) upon the Cross,
then He said the sorrowful words, "It is finished" (John 19:30). **239–42 "Neaver," . . . of his
hure**, "Never," He said, "before now was I fully tortured," not by the vinegar, but by their
envious spite which the vinegar symbolized which they made Him drink, and is just (lit., like)
as though a man who had long toiled and [who] came short of (or, failed to get) his pay after

as thah a mon thet hefde longe i-swunken, ant failede efter long swinc on ende of his hure. Alswa ure Laverd mare then twa ant thritti yer tilede efter hare luve, ant for al his sare swinc ne wilnede na thing bute luve to hure. Ah i the ende of his lif, thet wes as i the even-tid hwen me yelt werc-men hare deies hure, loke hu ha

245 yulden him: for piment of huni luve, eisil of sur nith ant galle of bitter onde! "O," quoth ure Laverd tha, **Consumatum est**. "Al mi swinc on eorthe, al mi pine o rode ne sweameth ne ne derveth me na-wiht ayein this — thet ich thus biteo al thet ich i-don habbe. This eisil thet ye beodeth me, this sure hure thurhfulleth mi pine." This eisil of sur heorte ant of bitter thonc over alle othre thing acwencheth Grickisch

250 fur — thet is, the luve of ure Laverd — ant hwa-se hit bereth i breoste toward wummon other mon, ha is Giwes make. Ha offreth Godd this eisil ant thurhfulleth onont hire Jesues pine o rode. Me warpeth Grickisch fur upon his fa-men ant swa me overkimeth ham. Ye schule don alswa hwen Godd areareth ow of ei va eani weorre. Hu ye hit schule warpen Salomon teacheth: **Si esurierit inimicus tuus,**

255 **ciba illum; si sitierit, potum da illi. Sic enim carbones ardentes congeres super caput ejus** — thet is, "yef thi fa hungreth, fed him. To his thurst, yef him

long labor. **242–43 Alswa ure Laverd . . . to hure**, Just so our Lord for more than thirty-two years toiled for (or, strove after) their love, and for all His painful toil wanted nothing but love as pay. **243–45 Ah i the ende . . . bitter onde!** But in the end of His life, which was as if in (i.e., like) the evening-time when one pays workmen their day's wages, look how they repaid Him: for the spiced wine of honey love [they gave Him the] vinegar of sour spite and gall of bitter envy! **246 tha**, then. **247–48 ne sweameth . . . i-don habbe**, does not pain or trouble me at all in comparison to this — that I give away (i.e., am giving away) everything I have done in this way. **248 This eisil thet . . . mi pine**, This vinegar which you offer Me, this sour pay, completes (or, consummates) My pain. **249 thonc**, thought; **acwencheth**, quenches. **251 ha is Giwes make**, she is a Jew's equal (or, companion). **251–52 thurhfulleth onont hire**, fulfills as [it] regards her, (or, as far as she is concerned). **252–53 Me warpeth . . . overkimeth ham**, One throws Greek fire on his enemies (lit., foe-men) and so one overcomes them. **253–54 Ye schule don alswa . . . weorre**, You (pl.) must do likewise when God raises up for you any attack from any foe. **254 Hu ye hit schule warpen . . . teacheth**, How you should throw it Solomon teaches. **254–56** *Si esurierit inimicus tuus . . . caput ejus*, "If your enemy be hungry, feed him; if he be thirsty, give him drink. Thus you truly heap burning coals over his head" (Proverbs 25:21–22; see Romans 12:20).

drunch." Thet is to understonden, yef he efter thin hearm haveth hunger other thurst, yef him fode of thine beoden thet Godd do him are. Yef him drunch of teares. Wep for his sunnen. "Thus thu schalt," seith Salomon, "rukelin on his heaved bearninde gleden" — thet is to seggen, thus thu schalt ontenden his heorte for-te luvie the. For heorte is in Hali Writ bi heaved understonden. O thulli wise wule Godd seggen ed te dome: "Hwi luvedest tu the mon other the wummon?" "Sire, ha luveden me!" "Ye," he wule seggen, "thu yulde thet tu ahtest. Her nabbe ich the nawt muches to yelden." Yef thu maht ondswerien, "alle wa ha duden me, ne na luve ne ahte ich ham, ah, sire, ich luvede ham for thi luve" — thet luve he ah the, for hit wes i-yeven him ant he hit wule the yelden.

Migge — as ich seide — thet acwencheth Grickisch fur, is stinkinde flesches luve, the acwencheth gastelich luve, thet Grickisch fur bitacneth. Hweat flesch wes on eorthe se swete ant se hali as wes Jesu Cristes flesch? Ant thah he seide him-seolf to his deore deciples, **Nisi ego abiero, paraclitus non veniet ad vos.** Thet is, "Bute ich parti from ow, the Hali Gast — thet is, min ant mines feaderes luve — ne mei nawt cumen to ow. Ah hwen ich beo from ow, ich chulle senden him ow." Hwen Jesu Cristes ahne deciples, hwil thet ha fleschliche luveden him, neh ham foreoden the swetnesse of the Hali Gast, ne ne mahte nawt habben bathe

258 yef him fode of thine beoden . . . are, give him the food of your prayers that God may do (i.e., grant) him grace. **259–60 "rukelin . . . gleden,"** "pile up burning embers on his head." **260–61 thu schalt ontenden . . . luvie the,** you will ignite (or, set on fire) his heart to love you. **261–62 For heorte is . . . dome,** For the heart is to be understood in Holy Writ by "head." In such a way will God say at the Judgment. **263 ha luveden me!** they loved me! **263–64 "Ye . . . to yelden,"** "Indeed," He will say, "you repaid what you owed. Here I do not have anything much to repay to you." **264–66 Yef thu maht ondswerien . . . yelden,** If you could answer, "they did every misery to me, and I owed them no love, but, sir, I loved them for Your love" — [then] that love He owes you, for it was given to Him and He will repay it to you. **267 Migge,** Urine. **267–68 is stinkinde flesches luve . . . bitacneth,** is the stinking love of the flesh, which extinguishes spiritual love, which Greek fire symbolizes. **269 Ant thah,** And nevertheless. **270 *Nisi ego abiero . . . ad vos,*** "Unless I go away, the Paraclete (i.e., the Holy Spirit) will not come to you" (John 16:7). **271 Bute,** Unless. **272 ich chulle,** I will. **273–75 Hwen Jesu Cristes ahne deciples . . . bathe togederes,** When Jesus Christ's own disciples, while they loved Him bodily (or, in the body), near Him they went without (lit., forwent) the sweetness of the Holy Spirit, nor might they have both

275 togederes. Demeth ow-seolven: nis he wod, other heo, the luveth to swithe hire ahne flesch, other eani mon fleschliche swa thet ha yirne to swithe his sihthe other his speche? Ne thunche hire neaver wunder yef hire wonti the Hali Gastes frovre. Cheose nu euch-an of thes twa — eorthlich elne ant heovenlich — to hwether ha wule halden, for thet other ha mot leten. For i the tweire monglunge, ne mei ha

280 habben neaver mare schirnesse of heorte — thet is, as we seiden ear, thet god ant te strengthe of alle religiuns ant in euch ordre. Luve maketh hire schir, grithful ant cleane. Luve haveth a meistrie bivoren alle othre; for al thet ha rineth, al ha turneth to hire, ant maketh al hire ahne. **Quemcumque locum calcaverit pes vester — pes videlicet amoris — vester erit.** Deore walde moni mon buggen a swuch thing,

285 thet al thet he rine to, al were his ahne. Ant ne seide hit th'ruppe feor, ane thurh thet tu luvest thet god thet is in an-other, with the rinunge of thi luve thu makest withuten other swinc his god thin ahne god, as Sein Gregoire witneth? Lokith nu hu muchel god the ontfule leoseth. Streche thi luve to Jesu Crist, thu havest him i-wunnen. Rin him with ase muche luve as thu havest sum mon sum-chearre, he is

together. **275–77 Demeth ow-seolven ... his speche?** Judge for yourselves: is not he insane — or she — who loves too much her own body or [who loves] any man physically so that she [may] yearn too much for the sight of him or his talk (or, conversation)? **277 Ne thunche hire neaver wunder ... frovre,** [Let it] not seem strange to her if the Holy Ghost's comfort is lacking to her (i.e., if she lacks the comfort of the Holy Spirit). **278–79 Cheose nu ... mot leten,** [Let] each one now choose from (i.e., between) these two — earthly and heavenly strength — to which she will hold, for she must leave the other. **279–80 For i the tweire monglunge ... heorte,** For, in the mixture (or, contamination) of the two, she can nevermore have purity of heart. **281 grithful,** peaceful. **282–83 a meistrie bivoren alle othre ... ahne,** a power above all others; for everything that she touches, everything she turns to herself, and makes everything her own. **283–84 *Quemcumque locum ... vester erit,*** "Whatever place you set your foot on" — the foot, clearly, of love — "will be yours" (Deuteronomy 11:24, with gloss). **284–85 Deore walde moni ... his ahne,** Many a man would buy such a thing dearly (i.e., at a high price) [so] that everything he might touch against [it], everything would be his own. **285–87 Ant ne seide hit th'ruppe ... thin ahne god,** And [was] it not said far above (see 4.1271–74), simply by the fact that you love the good that is in another, with the [Midas] touch of your love, you make without [any] other work his good your own good. **288 the ontfule,** the envious; **Streche thi luve,** If you stretch (or, extend) your love. **289 Rin him,** Touch Him (imper.); **sum mon,** for some man (or, person). **289–90 sum-chearre ... wilnest,** sometime, He is yours to do everything with that you will.

290   thin to don with al thet tu wilnest. Ah hwa luveth thing thet leaveth hit for leasse
then hit is wurth? Nis Godd betere unevenlich then al thet is i the world? Chearite
is cherte of leof thing ant of deore. Undeore he maketh Godd ant to unwurth mid
alle, thet for ei worltlich thing of his luve leasketh, for na thing ne con luvien riht,
bute he ane. Swa overswithe he luveth luve, thet he maketh hire his evening. Yet

295   ich dear segge mare — he maketh hire his meistre ant deth al thet ha hat as thah he
moste nede. Mei ich pruvien this? Ye, witerliche ich, bi his ahne wordes, for thus
he speketh to Moyses the monne meast him luvede: **In Numeri: Dimisi juxta
verbum tuum, non dicit preces**. "Ich hefde," quoth he, "i-munt to wreoke mine
wreaththe i this folc. Ah thu seist I ne schal nawt. Thi word beo i-forthet." Me

300   seith thet luve bindeth; witerliche luve bint swa ure Laverd thet he ne mei na thing
don bute thurh luves leave. Nu preove her-of, for hit thuncheth wunder. **Ysaias:
Domine, non est qui consurgat et teneat te**. "Laverd, thu wult smiten," seith
Ysaie. "Wei-la-wei! Thu maht wel — nis nan thet te halde," as thah he seide, "yef

---

290–91 thet leaveth hit . . . is wurth? who leaves it (or, gives it up) for less than it is
worth (i.e., for something that is worth less)? **291 Nis Godd betere . . . the world?** Is God
not incomparably better than everything that is in the world? **291–92 Chearite is cherte
. . . deore,** Love (lit., charity) is the cherishing of a beloved and precious thing. **292–94
Undeore he maketh Godd . . . he ane,** He (i.e., that person) makes God cheap (lit., un-
dear) and too worthless by far, who for any worldly thing slackens in his love, for nothing
can be loved (passive inf.) rightly, but He alone (or, no creature can love rightly, except
He alone). **294–96 Swa overswithe . . . moste nede,** So excessively He loves love that He
makes her His equal. Yet I dare say more — He makes her His master and does all that she
commands as though He must needs [do it]. **296 Ye, witerliche ich,** Yes, certainly I [can
prove it]. **297 the monne meast him luvede,** who of [all] men loved Him most. **297–98** *In
Numeri . . . dicit preces,* In Numbers: "I have pardoned according to your word" (Numbers 14:20) — [note that He does not say "prayers."] **298–99 "Ich hefde . . . i-forthet,"**
[God to Moses:] "I had," He said, "resolved to wreak my anger on this people. But you say
I must not. Let your word be furthered (or, advanced)." **299–300 Me seith,** They say. **300–
01 witerliche luve bint . . . leave,** certainly, love binds (*bint* = reduced form of *bindeth*)
our Lord in such a way (lit., so) that He can do nothing except by love's permission. **301
Nu preove . . . wunder,** Now [here is] the proof for this, since it seems strange. **302
*Domine, non est . . . teneat te,*** "Lord, there is no one who rises up and lays hold of You
(i.e., prevents You)" (Isaiah 64:7). **303–04 "Wei-la-wei! . . . to smiten,"** "Alas! You might

ei luvede the riht, he mahte halden the ant wearnen the to smiten." **In Genesy, ad**
305 **Loth: festina, et cetera. Non potero ibi quicquam facere, donec egressus fueris**
illinc. Thet is, tha ure Laverd walde bisenchen Sodome ther Lot his freond wes
inne, "hihe the," quoth he, "ut-ward. For hwil thu art bimong ham, ne mei ich
nawt don ham." Nes thes with luve i-bunden? Hwet wult tu mare? Luve is his
chamberleng, his conseiler, his spuse, thet he ne mei nawt heole with, ah teleth al
310 thet he thencheth. **In Genesy: Num celare potero Abraham que gesturus sum?**
"Mei ich," quoth ure Laverd, "heolen Abraham thing thet ich thenche to donne?
Nai, o nane wise." Nu con thes luvien the thus speketh ant thus deth to alle the
him inwardliche leveth ant luvieth. The blisse thet he yarketh ham, as ha is
unevenlich to alle worldes blissen, *alswa* ha is untalelich to worldliche tungen.
315 **Ysaias: Oculus non vidit Deus absque te que preparasti diligentibus te.**
Apostolus: Oculus non vidit, nec auris audivit, et cetera. Ye habbeth of theos
blissen i-writen elles-hwer, mine leove sustren. This luve is the riwle the riwleth

well [do it] — there is no one who could hold (or, stop) You," as though he said, "if anyone
loved You rightly, he could hold you and prevent You from smiting (lit., to smite)." **304–06** *In*
Genesy, ad Loth . . . fueris illinc, In Genesis, [God] to Lot: "hurry, etc. I will not do anything
there until you will have left that place" (Genesis 19:22). **306–08 tha ure Laverd . . . don ham**,
when our Lord wanted to sink Sodom where Lot his friend was (lit., was in), "Rush yourself," he
said, "out from here (lit., outward). For while you are among them (i.e., the Sodomites), I
cannot do anything to them." **308 Nes thes . . . i-bunden?** Was He (lit., this one) not bound by
love?; **Hwet wult tu mare?** What more do you want? **309 chamberleng**, chamberlain; **thet he**
ne mei nawt heole with, whom He can hide nothing from. **310** *In Genesy . . . gesturus sum?*
In Genesis: "Can I conceal from Abraham what I am about to do?" (Genesis 18:17). **311 Mei**
ich . . . to donne? "Can I," says our Lord, "hide from Abraham the thing that I think to do?"
312–14 Nu con thes . . . worldliche tungen, Now this person can love (or, knows how to
love), who speaks this way and acts thus to all who trust and love Him inwardly (or, spiritually). The joy which He prepares (or, is preparing) for them, just as it is incomparable (i.e.,
cannot be compared) to all the world's joys, likewise it is indescribable to (i.e., cannot be
described by) worldly tongues. **315–16** *Ysaias: Oculus non vidit . . . audivit*, Isaiah: "The eye
has not seen O God except You, what You have prepared for those who love You" (Isaiah
64:4); The Apostle: "Eye has not seen, or ears heard [nor has it entered into the heart of man
what things God has prepared for those who love Him]" (1 Corinthians 2:9). **316–17 Ye habbeth**
. . . elles-hwer, You have, concerning these joys, [something] written elsewhere [in this book].

the heorte. **Confitebor tibi in directione — id est, in regulatione — cordis. Exprobatio malorum, generatio que non direxit cor suum**. This is the leafdi
320   riwle — alle the othre servith hire. Ant ane for hire sake me hat ham to luvien. Lutel strengthe ich do of ham, for-hwon thet theos beo deore-wurthliche i-halden. Habbeth ham thah scheortliche i the eahtuthe dale.

318–19 *Confitebor tibi . . . cor suum*, "I will confess to You in uprightness" — that is, the regulation — "of the heart" (Psalm 118:7). "Reproach of the wicked, a generation which did not regulate its heart" (Psalm 77:8). **319–20 leafdi riwle**, lady rule. **320–22 Ant ane for hire sake . . . eahtuthe dale**, And only for her sake it is commanded (lit., one commands) to love them (i.e., the other rules). I put little importance on them, as long as this one be reverently (lit., preciously) kept. You have them (i.e., will find them), though, briefly in the eighth part.

Part Eight

The Outer Rule

Bivoren, on earst, ich seide thet ye ne schulden na-wiht as i vu bihaten for-te halden nan of the uttre riwlen. Thet ilke ich segge yetten, ne nane ne write ich ham buten ow ane. Ich segge this for-thi thet othre ancren ne seggen nawt thet ich thurh mi meistrie makie ham neowe riwle. Ne bidde ich nawt thet ha halden ham. Ah ye yet moten changin hwen-se ye eaver wulleth theose for betere. Ayein thinges the beoth bivoren — of ham is lutel strengthe.

Of sihthe ant of speche ant of the othre wittes is inoh i-seid. Nu is this leaste dale, as ich bihet on earst, todealet ant i-sundret o lutle seove stucchen.

Me let leasse of the thing thet me haveth ofte. For-thi ne schule ye beon bute — as ure brethren beoth — i-huslet in-with tweolf-moneth fiftene sithen: (i) Mid-

1–2 **Bivoren, on earst . . . uttre riwlen**, Before, at first (or, at the beginning) I said that you should not in any way promise to keep any of the outer rules as if in a vow. 2–3 **Thet ilke ich segge . . . ow ane**, I say the same still, nor do I write them for any but you alone. 3–4 **Ich segge this . . . neowe riwle**, I say this so that other anchoresses may not say that I by my authority make them a new rule. 4–6 **Ne bidde ich nawt . . . for betere**, Nor do I ask that they keep them. But you must continually change these whenever you want for better ones. 6 **Ayein thinges . . . strengthe**, In comparison to the things which are [described] before — there is little importance for them (i.e., they have little importance). 7 **sihthe**, sight; **is inoh i-seid**, enough is said. 7–8 **Nu is this leaste dale . . . stucchen**, Now this last part is, as I promised at first, divided and separated into seven little pieces (or, sub-sections). 9–10 **Me let leasse . . . fiftene sithen**, One values (*let* = reduced form of *leoteth* — see glossary) less highly the thing which one has often. Therefore you should not receive the Eucharist (lit., be houseled) — except as our brothers do (lit., are) — fifteen times within a year. 10–16 **Midwinter Dei . . . Seint Andrews Dei**, Midwinter Day (December 21), Twelfth Day (January 6 — Epiphany, twelve days after Christmas), Candlemas Day

winter Dei, (ii) Tweofte Dei, (iii) Condelmeasse Dei, (iiii) a Sunnedei mid-wei bitweonen thet ant Easter, other Ure Leafdi Dei, yef he is neh the Sunnedei, for the hehnesse, (v) Easter Dei, (vi) the thridde Sunnedei th'refter, (vii) Hali Thursdei, (viii) Witsunne Dei, (ix) Midsumer Dei, (x) Seinte Marie Dei Magdaleine, (xi) the Assumptiun, (xii) the Nativite, (xiii) Seinte Mihales Dei, (xiii) Alle Halhene Dei, (xv), Seint Andrews Dei. Ayein alle theose beoth cleanliche i-schrivene, ant neometh disceplines, neaver thah of na-mon bute of ow-seolven, ant forgath an dei ower pitance. Yef ewt i-limpeth misliche thet ye ne beon nawt i-huslet i theose i-sette tearmes, beoth hit the neste Sunnedei, other yef the other terme is neh, abideth athet tenne.

15

20

Ye schulen eoten from Easter athet te Hali Rode Dei — the leatere, the is in hervest — euche dei twien bute the Fridahes, [other Umbri-dayes, Yong-dayes, vigilies. I theose dayes] ne i the Advent ne schule ye nawt eoten hwit bute neode

(February 2), a Sunday midway between that (i.e., Candlemas) and Easter (moveable), or Our Lady's Day (the Annunciation of the Virgin, March 25), if it is near the Sunday, because of its loftiness, Easter Day (moveable), the third Sunday after that, Holy Thursday (Christ's Ascension, fifth Thursday after Easter), Whitsunday (Pentecost, seventh Sunday after Easter), Midsummer's Day (June 24), St. Mary Magdalene's Day (July 22), the Assumption [of the Virgin] (August 15), the Nativity [of the Virgin] (September 8), St. Michael's Day (September 29), All Hallows Day (November 1), St. Andrew's Day (November 30). **16–18 Ayein alle theose . . . pitance,** In anticipation of all these, be (imper.) thoroughly confessed, and take on disciplines (i.e., a physical penance; for example, scourging), never though from anyone but yourself, and forgo for one day your ration of food. **18–20 Yef ewt i-limpeth . . . athet tenne,** If anything happens amiss (or, goes wrong) so that you are not houseled (i.e., given the Eucharist) in these set times, let it be the next Sunday, or if the other time is near, wait until then (*tenne* = reduced form of *thenne* after preceding *-t*). **21–24 Ye schulen eoten . . . makie,** You must eat twice each day from Easter until the Holy Rood Day (September 14, the Exaltation of the Cross) — the latter one, which is in the fall — except on the Fridays, or Ember-days (i.e., days of prayer and fasting, occurring on the Wednesday, Friday, and Saturday after certain feast days), Processional Days, and vigils (i.e., devotions the night before a holy day). In these days, nor during Advent you must not eat

hit makie. The other half yer feasten al, bute Sunnedahes ane, hwen ye beoth in
heale ant i ful strengthe — ah riwle ne tweast nawt seke ne blod-letene.

Ye ne schulen nawt eoten flesch ne seim, bute for muche secnesse other hwa-
se is over-feble. Potage eoteth blitheliche, ant wunieth ow to lutel drunch. No-
the-les, leove sustren, ower mete ant ower drunch haveth i-thuht me ofte leasse
then ich walde. Ne feaste ye na dei to bread ne to weattre, bute ye habben leave.

Sum ancre maketh hire bord with hire gest ute-with. Thet is to muche
freondschipe, for of alle ordres thenne is hit uncundelukest, ant meast ayein ancre
ordre, the is al dead to the world. Me haveth i-herd ofte thet deade speken with
cwike — ah thet ha eten with cwike ne fond ich yet neaver.

Ne makie ye nane gestnunges, ne ne tulle ye to the yete nane uncuthe hearloz;
thah ther nere nw uvel bute hare meadlese nurth, hit walde letten other-hwile
heovenliche thohtes. Ne limpeth nawt to ancre of other monnes ealmesse to makien
hire large. Nalde me lahhen a beggere lude to bismere the leathede men to feaste?

white food unless necessity force it. **24–25 The other half yer . . . blod-letene,** The entire
second half year fast (imper.), except Sundays alone, when you are in health and full
strength — but [this] rule does not bind the sick or those who have had blood let (lit., the
blood-let [ones]). **26 flesch ne seim,** meat nor fat. **26–27 other hwa-se is over-feble,** or
[when] someone (lit., whoever) is overly feeble. **27 Potage eoteth blitheliche . . . drunch,**
Eat (imper. pl.) vegetable dishes happily, and accustom you[rself] to little drink. **28 haveth
i-thuht me,** have seemed to me. **29 Ne feaste ye . . . leave,** Do not fast any day on bread or
on water unless you have permission. **30 Sum ancre maketh . . . ute-with,** Some anchoress
(i.e., sometimes an anchoress) will sit to dinner (lit., make her board) outside with her
guest. **30–31 to muche freondschipe,** too much friendship. **31–32 for of alle ordres . . .
to the world,** for in all orders then it is unnatural, and [it is] most contrary [to the] order of
the anchoress, who is completely dead to the world. **32–33 Me haveth i-herd . . . yet
neaver,** People have (lit., one has) heard often that the dead have spoken with the living
— but that they have eaten with the living I never yet discovered. **34–36 Ne makie ye
nane gestnunges . . . thohtes,** Do not give (lit., make) any entertainments (or, entertain
any guests), nor attract to the gate any unknown (i.e., strange) vagabonds; even though
there would be no other evil but their unbridled racket (or, noise), it would sometimes
hinder heavenly thoughts. **36–37 Ne limpeth nawt . . . to feaste?** It is not fitting for an
anchoress to make herself generous with another person's charity (or, donations). Would
not people (lit., one) laugh a beggar loudly to scorn who invited people to a feast?

Marie ant Marthe ba weren sustren, ah hare lif sundrede: ye ancren beoth i-numen
ow to Marie dale, the ure Laverd seolf herede: **Maria optimam partem elegit.**
40 "Marthe, Marthe," quoth he, "thu art [in] muche baret. Marie haveth i-core bet,
ant ne schal hire na thing reavin hire dale." Husewifschipe is Marthe dale; Marie
dale is stilnesse ant reste of alle worldes noise, thet na thing ne lette hire to heren
Godes stevene. Ant lokith hwet Godd seith, thet "na thing ne schal ow reavin this
dale." Mar*the* haveth hire meoster — leoteth hire i-wurthen. Ye sitten with Marie
45 stan-stille ed Godes fet ant hercnith him ane. Marthe meoster is to feden povre ant
schruden, as hus-leafdi. Marie ne ah nawt to entremeatin th'rof. Yef ei blameth
hire, Godd seolf i-hwer wereth hire, as Hali Writ witneth: **Contra Symonem:**
duo debitores, et cetera. Contra Martham: Maria optimam partem, et cetera.
Contra apostolos murmurantes, ut quid perditio hec? Bonum, inquit, opus,
50 **et cetera.** On other half, nan ancre ne ah to neomen bute meathfulliche thet hire to

38 ba, both. **38–39 ah hare lif sundrede . . . herede**, but their lives parted (i.e., differed): you
anchoresses have taken you[rselves] (i.e., given yourselves) to Mary's part (or, role), whom our
Lord Himself praised. **39–40** *Maria optimam partem elegit*, "Mary has chosen the better part"
(Luke 10:42). **40–41 "thu art [in] muche baret . . . hire dale,"** "you are in a great fuss (or,
commotion). Mary has chosen better, and nothing will steal her portion from her." **41–43**
Husewifschipe is Marthe dale . . . stevene, Managing a household (lit., housewifery) is Martha's
part; Mary's part is stillness and rest from all the world's noise, so that nothing may hinder her
from hearing (lit., to hear) God's voice. **43 lokith**, look (imper. pl.). **44 meoster**, job (or, occupation). **44–46 leoteth hire i-wurthen . . . hus-leafdi**, let her be. You should sit with Mary
stone-still at God's feet and listen to Him alone. Martha's job is to feed the poor and clothe
[them], like the lady of a house. **46–47 Marie ne ah . . . wereth hire**, Mary ought not to meddle
(or, busy herself) in that. If anyone blames her, God Himself defends her at all times. **47–50**
Contra Symonem . . . opus, et cetera, [Jesus] in response to Simon: "[A certain moneylender
had] two debtors. [The one owed five hundred denarii, the other fifty. As they had no means of
paying, he forgave them both. Which of them, therefore, will love him more?" Simon answered
and said, "He, I suppose, to whom he forgave more." "You have judged rightly" (Luke 7:36–
41).] [Jesus] in response to Martha: "Mary [has chosen] the better part," etc. (Luke 10:42). In
response to the apostles grumbling [about a woman pouring expensive oil on Christ's hair,
saying,] "To what purpose is this waste?" He said, "[She has done me] a good work," etc. (Matthew 26:8). **50–51 On other half . . . large?** At the same time (lit., on the other side), no anchoress
ought to take [anything] except what is necessary for her (i.e., what she requires) in moderation.

neodeth. Hwer-of thenne mei ha makien hire large? Ha schal libben bi ealmesse ase meathfulliche as ha eaver mei, ant nawt gederin for-te yeoven. Ha nis nawt huse-wif, ah is a chirch-ancre. Yef ha mei spearien eani povre schraden, sende ham al dearnliche ut of hire wanes. Under semblant of god is ofte i-hulet sunne.

55 Ant hu schulen theose *riche* ancres, the tilieth other habbeth rentes i-sette, don to povre nehburs dearnliche hare ealmesse? Ne wilni ha nawt to habbe word of a large ancre, ne for-te yeoven muchel, ne beo nan the gred[i]ure for-te habben mare. For-hwon thet gredinesse beo rote of thet gederunge, of hire bitternesse al beoth the bohes bittre, the of hire spruteth. Bidden hit for-te yeoven hit nis nawt

60 ancre rihte. Of ancre curteisie, of ancre largesce is i-cumen ofte sunne ant scheome on ende.

Wummen ant children ant nomeliche ancre meidnes the cumeth i-swenchet for ow — thah ye spearien hit on ow, other borhin other bidden hit — makieth ham to eotene with chearitable chere, ant leathieth to herbarhin.

65 Na mon ne eote bivoren ow bute bi ower meistres leave, general other spetial: [general] as of freres preachurs ant meonurs, spetial of alle othre. Ne leathie ye

With what then can she be generous (lit., make herself generous)? **51–52 Ha schal libben . . . yeoven**, She must live by donations as moderately as ever she can, and not accumulate (or, save) in order to give. **53–54 Yef ha mei spearien . . . sunne**, If she can spare any poor scraps, (let her) send them entirely secretly out of her rooms. Under the appearance of good, sin is often hidden. **55–56 the tilieth . . . hare ealmesse?** who till (i.e., have land in tillage) or have set incomes, give (lit., do) their donations to their poor neighbors secretly? **56–58 Ne wilni ha nawt . . . habben mare**, Let her not want to have the reputation of [being] a generous anchoress, or [the reputation] of giving (lit., to give) much, or of being (lit., to be) any the greedier to have more. **58–60 For-hwon thet gredinesse . . . rihte**, As long as greediness be the root of the gathering (or, collecting), all the branches which sprout from it (will) be bitter from its bitterness. To ask for it (i.e., something) in order to give it away is not right for an anchoress. **60–61 Of ancre curteisie . . . on ende**, From an anchoress' courtesy, from an anchoress' generosity, sin and shame have often come in the end. **62–64 ant nomeliche ancre meidnes . . . to herbarhin**, and especially anchoresses' maidens (i.e., servants) who are (lit., come) put to trouble for you — even if you must do without it for you[rself], or borrow or beg for it — have them eat with loving hospitality and invite (them) to lodge (or, stay) [with you]. **65–66 Na mon ne eote . . . alle othre**, Let no man eat in your presence except by your director's permission, [whether] general (i.e., blanket) or special [permission]: general for preaching friars (i.e., Dominicans) and friars minor (i.e., Franciscans), special for all others. **66 leathie**, invite.

nane othre to eoten ne to drinken bute alswa thurh his leave. Liht is, me seith, leave. Na-wiht ne yirne ich thet me for swucche boden telle ow hende ancren. I-hwear thah ant eaver yemeth ow thet nan from ow thurh ower untuhtle ne parti 70 with scandle.

Ed gode men neometh al thet ow to nedeth. Ah thet lokith ow wel, thet ye ne kecchen the nome of gederinde ancren. Of mon thet ye misleveth thurh his fol semblant other bi his wake wordes, nowther ne neome ye ne leasse ne mare. Neode schal driven ow for-te bidden ei thing; thah eadmodliche schawith to gode men 75 ant wummen ower meoseise.

Ye, mine leove sustren, bute yef neod ow drive ant ower meistre hit reade, ne schulen habbe na beast bute cat ane. Ancre the haveth ahte thuncheth bet huse-wif, ase Marthe wes — ne lihtliche ne mei ha nawt beo Marie, Marthe suster, with grithfullnesse of heorte. For thenne mot ha thenchen of the kues foddre, of heorde-80 monne hure, olhnin the hei-ward, wearien hwen he punt hire, ant yelden thah the hearmes. Ladlich thing is hit, wat Crist, hwen me maketh i tune man of ancre ahte.

67–68 Liht is . . . hende ancren, As they say, permission is easy. I do not at all desire that people consider you fashionable (or, courtly) anchoresses because of such precautions (lit., commands). **68–70 I-hwear thah . . . scandle**, Everywhere though and at all times be careful (reflex.) that no one part from you with scandal (i.e., scandalized) by your bad manners. **71–72 Ed gode men . . . gederinde ancren**, From good people take all that is necessary to you (i.e., all you need). But see to it well (reflex.) that you do not catch the name of acquisitive (lit., gathering) anchoresses. **72–73 Of mon thet ye misleveth . . . mare**, From a person (or, man) that you mistrust because of his foolish pretenses or by his weak words, neither take (imper.) less or more (i.e., anything). **73–75 Neode . . . meoseise**, Need (or, distress) must drive you to ask for anything; nevertheless show your hardship humbly to good men and women. **76–79 bute yef neod ow drive . . . of heorte**, unless distress drive you and your director advise it, you should have no animal but one cat only. An anchoress who has property (or, livestock) seems more (lit., better) a housewife, as Martha was — she cannot easily be Mary, Martha's sister, with [her] tranquillity of heart. **79–81 For thenne mot ha . . . the hearmes**, For then she must think about the cow's fodder, about the herdsman's wages, [she must think about] flattering (lit., to flatter) the hay-warden (see *hei-ward* in glossary), cursing [him] when he impounds her (i.e., the cow) (*punt* = reduced form of *pundeth*), and paying for the damages nevertheless. **81 Ladlich thing . . . ancre ahte**, It is a disgusting thing, Christ knows, when people in town complain (lit., make moan) about an anchoress' property (or, livestock).

Nu thenne yef eani mot nedlunge habben hit, loki thet hit na-mon ne eili ne ne hearmi, ne thet hire thoht ne beo na-wiht th'ron i-festnet. Ancre ne ah to habben na thing thet ut-ward drahe hire heorte.

85   Na chaffere ne drive ye. Ancre thet is chepilt — thet is, buth for-te sullen efter biyete — ha chepeth hire sawle the chap-mon of helle. Thing thah thet ha wurcheth ha mei, thurh hire meistres read, for hire neode sullen. Hali men sum-hwile liveden bi hare honden.

Nawt, deore dehtren, ne wite ye in ower hus of other monne thinges, ne ahte ne
90   clathes, ne boistes, ne chartres, scoren ne cyrograffes, ne the chirch vestemenz, ne the calices, bute neode other strengthe hit makie, other muchel eie. Of swuch witunge is muchel uvel i-lumpen ofte sithen.

In-with ower wanes ne leote ye na-mon slepen. Yef muchel neod mid alle maketh breoken ower hus, hwil hit eaver is i-broken habbeth th'rinne with ow a wummon
95   of cleane lif deies ant nihtes.

For-thi thet wepmen ne seoth ow, ne ye ham, wel mei don of ower clath, beo hit hwit, beo hit blac, bute hit beo unorne, warm ant wel i-wraht, felles wel i-tawet — ant habbeth ase monie as ow to neodeth to bedde ant to rugge.

82–83 yef eani mot nedlunge . . . i-festnet, if any[one] must necessarily have it (i.e., a cow), see that it not annoy or harm anyone, or that her thought not be at all fastened on it. **84 drahe,** may draw. **85–86 Na chaffere . . . of helle,** Do not engage in buying and selling. An anchoress who is a business-woman — that is, buys in order to sell for a profit — she sells her soul to the dealer of hell. **86–88 Thing thah thet ha . . . honden,** Nevertheless, things which she makes (lit., works) she can, by her director's advice, sell for her need[s]. Holy people sometimes lived by their hands. **89–92 Nawt, deore dehtren . . . ofte sithen,** Dear daughters, do not keep in your house anything of other people's things, neither property, nor clothes nor [medicine] chests, nor charters, tally sticks (see *scoren* in glossary), nor documents (see *cyrograffes* in glossary), nor the church vestments, nor the chalices, unless necessity or force compel it, or great fear. From such safekeeping much evil has happened oftentimes. **93 wanes,** rooms (or, apartments). **93–95 Yef muchel neod . . . deies ant nihtes,** If great emergency furthermore forces your house to be broken (passive inf.) open, while it is broken, have in it with you a woman of pure life day and night. **96–98 For-thi thet wepmen . . . to rugge,** Because men do not see you, nor you them, it makes little difference (lit., it may well be proper) concerning your clothing, if it be white, if it be black, except it be plain, warm and well made, skins well tanned — and have (imper.) as many as it is necessary for you (i.e., you need) for bed and for back (i.e., to wear).

100 Nest flesch ne schal nan werien linnene clath bute hit beo of hearde ant of greate heorden. Stamin habbe hwa-se wule, hwa-se wule beo buten.

Ye schulen in an hetter ant i-gurd liggen, swa leotheliche thah thet ye mahen honden putten ther-under. Nest lich nan ne gurde hire with na cunne gurdles, bute thurh schriftes leave, ne beore nan irn ne here, ne iles-piles felles, ne ne beate hire ther-with, ne with scurge i-leadet, with holin ne with breres, ne biblodgi hire-

105 seolf withute schriftes leave, no-hwer ne binetli hire, ne ne beate bivoren, ne na keorvunge ne keorve, ne ne neome ed eanes to luthere disceplines, temptatiuns for-te acwenchen. Ne for na bote ayein cundeliche secnesses, nan uncundelich lechecreft ne leve ye, ne ne fondin, withuten ower meistres read, leste ow stonde wurse.

110 Ower schon i winter beon meoke, greate ant warme. I sumer ye habbeth leave bear-vot gan, ant sitten, ant lihte scheos werien.

Hosen withute vampez ligge in hwa-se liketh. I-scheoed ne slepe ye nawt, ne no-hwer bute i bedde. Sum wummon inoh-reathe wereth the brech of here ful wel

99–100 **Nest flesch . . . buten**, Next to the body no one must wear linen cloth (or, clothing) unless it be [made] of rough and coarse flax. Whoever wants [may] have a stamin (i.e., a coarse undergarment worn by monks and ascetics), whoever wants [may] be without [it]. 101–02 **Ye schulen in an hetter . . . ther-under**, You should lie (i.e., sleep) in a robe and belted (i.e., with a belt), so loosely though that you can put [your] hands under it (i.e., the belt). 102–07 **Nest lich . . . acwenchen**, Next to the body let no one gird (or, belt) herself with any kind of belt, except by a confessor's permission, or [let anyone] wear any iron, or haircloth, or hedgehog's skins, or beat herself with them, or with a leaded scourge (i.e., a lead-tipped scourge), with holly or with briars, or bloody herself without [her] confessor's permission, in no place benettle herself (i.e., whip herself with nettles), or beat [herself] in front, or cut any slashes, or take at one time [any bodily] punishments too severe in order to quench temptations. 107–09 **Ne for na bote . . . wurse**, And do not believe in unnatural healing for a remedy against natural sicknesses, nor try [it], without your director's permission, lest (i.e., for fear that) it stand worse for you (i.e., lest you grow worse). 110 **Ower schon . . . warme**, Let your shoes in winter be soft, large and warm. 111 **bear-vot gan**, to go barefoot. 112–13 **Hosen withute vampez . . . i bedde**, Whoever likes may lie (i.e., sleep) in stockings without feet. Do not sleep with your shoes on (lit., shoed) or anywhere but in bed. 113–16 **Sum wummon . . . heard here**, Some women (lit., woman) readily enough wear breeches of haircloth very thoroughly knotted, the leggings down to the feet laced very firmly, but the sweet and gentle (lit., sweet)

404

115 i-cnottet, the streapeles dun to the vet i-lacet ful feaste, ah eaver is best the swete ant te swote heorte — me is leovere thet ye tholien wel an heard word, then an heard here.

120 Yef ye muhen beo wimpel-les ant ye wel wullen, beoth bi warme cappen ant ther-uppon hwite other blake veiles. Ancren summe sungith in hare wimplunge, na leasse then leafdis. Ah thah seith sum thet hit limpeth to euch wummon cundeliche for-te werien wimpel. — Nai. Wimpel ne heaved-clath nowther ne nempneth Hali Writ, ah wriheles ane: **Ad Corinthios: Mulier velet caput suum.** "Wummon," seith the Apostle, "schal wreon hire heaved." "Wrihen" he seith — nawt "wimplin." Wrihen ha schal hire scheome, as Eve sunfule dohter, i mungunge 125 of the sunne thet schende us on earst alle, ant nawt drahe the wriheles to tiffunge ant to prude. Eft wule the Apostle thet wummon wreo i chirche hire neb yetten, leste uvel thoht arise thurh hire on-sihthe. **Et hoc est propter angelos.** Hwi thenne, thu chirch-ancre, i-wimplet, openest thi neb to wepmonnes ehe? Toyeines [the] the sist men speketh the Apostle, yef thu the ne hudest. Ah yef thet ei thing wriheth

heart is always best — it is more preferable to me that you suffer a hard word well than a hard (or, coarse) haircloth. **117–19 Yef ye muhen . . . then leafdis,** If you (pl.) can be without wimples (see glossary) and you fully want to, be in (i.e., wear) warm caps and over them white or black veils. Some anchoresses sin in their wimpling, no less than ladies do. **119–21 Ah thah seith sum . . . wriheles ane,** But nevertheless someone will say that it is naturally fitting for each woman to wear a wimple. — No. Holy Writ does not mention either wimple or headcloth, but the veil (or, covering) only. **121** *Ad Corinthios . . . caput suum*, [Letter] to the Corinthians: "Let a woman cover her head" (1 Corinthians 11:6). **122 wreon (wrihen),** cover. **123 "wimplin,"** put on a wimple; **scheome,** shame. **123–25 i mungunge . . . to prude,** in memory of the sin that disgraced us all in the beginning, and she must not turn the veil (or, covering) to ornament and to ostentation (lit., pride). **125– 26 Eft wule the Apostle . . . on-sihthe,** Moreover the Apostle wishes that a woman [should] cover her face in church continually, lest (i.e., for fear that) evil thought arise through sight of her. **126** *Et hoc est propter angelos*, "And this is because of the angels" (based on 1 Corinthians 11:10). **126–28 Hwi thenne . . . ne hudest,** Why then, you church-anchoress, do you, wimpled, open your face to a man's eye? The Apostle speaks against you (sing.) who see men, if you do not hide you[rself]. **128–30 Ah yef thet ei thing . . . wimplunge,** But if anything [else] covers your face from man's eye, be it wall, be it a cloth in a well-

405

130 thi neb from monnes ehe, beo hit wah, beo hit clath i wel i-tund windowe, wel mei duhen ancre of other wimplunge. Toyeines the the thus ne dest speketh the Apostle, nawt toyeines othre, thet hare ahne wah wriheth with euch monnes sihthe, ther awakenith ofte wake thohtes of — ant werkes other-hwiles. Hwa-se wule beon i-sehen, thah ha atiffi hire nis nawt muche wunder. Ah to Godes ehnen ha is lufsumre, the is for the luve of him untiffet withuten.

135 Ring ne broche ne habbe ye, ne gurdel i-membret, ne gloven, ne nan swuch thing thet ow ne deh to habben. A meoke surpliz ye mahen in hat sumer werien.

Eaver me is leovere se ye doth greattre werkes.

Ne makie ye nane purses for-te freondin ow with, bute to theo thet ower meistre yeveth ow his leave, ne huve, ne blod-binde of seolc, ne laz, buten leave. Ah 140 schapieth ant seowith ant mendith chirche clathes ant povre monne hettren. Na swuch thing ne schule ye yeoven withuten schriftes leave, na-mare then neomen thet ye ne seggen him fore — as of othre thinges: kun other cuththe, hu ofte ye undervengen, hu longe ye edheolden. Tendre of cun ne limpeth nawt ancre beonne.

closed window, it may well serve an anchoress in place of other wimpling. **130–32 Toyeines the . . . other-hwiles,** Against you who do not do so the Apostle speaks, not against others, whom their own wall covers from each man's sight, from where (i.e., from which sight) weak (or, foolish) thoughts often arise — and deeds sometimes. **132–34 Hwa-se wule beon . . . withuten,** Whoever wants to be seen, if she beautify herself, [it] is not much wonder. But to God's eyes she is more lovely who is unadorned on the outside for love of Him. **135 broche,** brooch. **135–36 gurdel i-membret . . . werien,** a decorated belt (see *i-membret* in glossary), or gloves, or any such thing that is not fitting for you to have. You (pl.) may wear a modest gown in hot summer. **137 Eaver me is leovere . . . werkes,** It is always preferable to me that (lit., so) you make coarser (i.e., less fine) [handi]work. **138–40 Ne makie ye . . . monne hettren,** Do not make any purses to make friends for you[rself] with, except for those whom your director gives you his permission, or [do not make a] cap, or bandage (lit., blood-bandage) of silk, or silken cord, without permission. But fashion (or, cut out) and sew and mend church vestments and poor people's clothes. **140–43 Na swuch thing . . . edheolden,** You should not give any such things (i.e., this kind of handiwork) without [your] confessor's permission, any more than receive what you do not tell him about before (i.e., receive anything without telling him beforehand) — as with other things: family or friends, how often you might receive [them], how long you might keep [them]. **143 Tendre of cun . . . beonne,** It is not fitting for an anchoress to be [too] soft to kin (or, attached to her family).

A mon wes of religiun, ant com to him efter help his fleschliche brother, ant he
145 tahte him to his thridde brether, the wes dead biburiet — the ondswerede wundrinde:
"Nai," quoth he, "nis he dead?" "Ant ich," quoth the hali mon, "am dead gasteliche.
Na fleschlich freond ne easki me fleschlich frovre." Amites ant parures worldliche
leafdis mahen inoh wurchen. Ant yef ye ham makieth, ne makie ye th'rof na
mustreisun. Veine-gloire attreth alle gode theawes ant alle gode werkes. Criblin
150 ne schal nan of ow for luve ne for hure. Taveles ne forbeode ich nawt, yef sum
riveth surpliz other measse-kemese. Othre rivunges ne rive ha nawt, nomeliche
overegede, bute for muche neode.

Helpeth ow with ower ahne swinc se forth se ye eaver mahen to schruden ow-
seolven ant feden, yef neod is, ant theo the ow servith.

155 As Sein Jerome leareth, ne beo ye neaver longe ne lihtliche of sum thing allunges
idel, for anan-rihtes the feond beot hire his werc, the i Godes werc ne swinketh,
ant tuteleth anan toward hire, for hwil he sith hire bisi, he thencheth thus: "For
nawt ich schulde nu cume neh hire, ne mei ha nawt i-yemen to lustni mi lare." Of

---

144–45 A mon wes . . . wundrinde, There was a man of religion (i.e., in a religious order), and there came to him for help his bodily brother, and he directed him to his third brother, who was dead [and] buried — he (i.e., the bodily brother) answered amazed. **146 gasteliche,** spiritually. **147 Na fleschlich freond . . . frovre,** Let no bodily friend ask me for bodily comfort. **147–49 Amites ant parures . . . mustreisun,** Worldly ladies may well enough make scarves and their decorations. And if you make them, do not make any display of it. **149–50 Veine-gloire attreth . . . for hure,** Vainglory (i.e., vanity) poisons all good habits and all good works. None of you must make lace (see *criblin* in glossary) for love nor for money (lit., pay). **150–52 Taveles ne forbeode ich nawt . . . neode,** I do not forbid lace borders, if someone is trimming a surplice or mass-chemise (or, alb). Let her not trim other trimmings, especially overly elaborate ones, except for great necessity. **153–54 Helpeth ow . . . servith,** Help you[rselves] (imper.) with your own labor as far as ever you can to clothe and feed yourselves, if there is need, and those who serve you. **155–57 As Sein Jerome leareth . . . thus,** As St. Jerome teaches, you [should] never be completely idle for a long time or carelessly from some thing (i.e., kind of work), for immediately the devil offers (*beot* = reduced form of *beodeth*) his work to her who does not toil in God's work, and [the devil] whispers immediately to her, for while he sees her busy, he thinks the following. **157– 59 For nawt . . . fondunge,** "It is useless that (lit., for nothing) I should now come near her, nor can she pay attention to listen to my teaching." From idleness

idelnesse awakeneth muchel flesches fondunge. **Iniquitas Sodome saturitas panis**
160 **et ocium** — thet is, "Sodomes cwedschipe com of idelnesse ant of ful wombe."
Irn thet lith stille gedereth sone rust. Weater the ne stureth nawt readliche stinketh.

Ancre ne schal nawt forwurthe scol-meistre, ne turnen ancre-hus to childrene
scole. Hire meiden mei learen sum other meiden thet were pliht of to leornin among
wepmen other bimong gromes, ah ancre ne ah to yemen bute Godd ane, thah bi
165 hire meistres read ha mei sum rihten ant helpen to learen.

Ye ne schulen senden leattres, ne undervon leattres, ne writen bute leave.

Ye schulen beon i-doddet other, yef ye wulleth, i-schaven fowr sithen i the yer,
to lihtin ower heaved — beo bi the her i-eveset, hwa-se swa is leovere — ant as
ofte i-leten blod ant, yef neod is, oftre. The mei beo ther-buten, ich hit mei wel
170 tholien. Hwen ye beoth al greithe i-lete blod, ye ne schule don na thing the threo
dahes thet ow greveth, ah talkith to ower meidnes, ant with theawfule talen schurteth
ow togederes. Ye mahen swa don ofte hwen ow thuncheth hevie, other beoth for

great temptation of the body arises (lit., awakens). **159–60 *Iniquitas Sodome . . . ocium*,**
"The crime of Sodom was a fullness of bread (i.e., a full stomach) and idleness (or, leisure)" (condensed from Ezekiel 16:49). **160 cwedschipe,** wickedness; **wombe,** belly. **161
Irn thet lith stille,** Iron that lies still; **the ne stureth,** which does not move, stir. **162–63
Ancre ne schal nawt . . . scole,** An anchoress must not degenerate into a school-teacher or
turn an anchor-house into a children's school. **163–65 Hire meiden mei learen . . . to
learen,** Her maiden (or, servant) may teach some other maiden who would be in danger to
learn (i.e., if she learned) among men or among boys, but an anchoress ought not to pay
attention to anything but God alone, though by her director's permission she can guide
some and help [them] to teach (or, learn). **166 leattres, ne . . . ne writen,** letters, nor
receive letters, nor write [them]. **167–69 Ye schulen beon i-doddet . . . oftre,** You must
be shorn (i.e., have your hair cut) or, if you like, shaved four times in the year, to lighten
your head — be trimmed by the hair (i.e., have your hair [merely] trimmed) whoever
prefers [it] so — and [be] let blood as often and, if there is a need, more often. **169–70 The
mei beon . . . tholien,** Whoever can be (i.e., go) without it (lit., there-without), I can well
allow it. **170–72 Hwen ye beoth al greithe . . . togederes,** When you are completely ready
to have blood let, you must not do any thing for the three days which give you discomfort
but talk to your maidens and entertain you[rselves] (or, pass the time) together with virtuous tales. **172–74 ow thuncheth hevie . . . to ancre,** [things] seem heavy (or, oppressive)
to you, or you are sorry or sick for some worldly thing though each worldly comfort is

sum worltlich thing sare other seke, thah euch worltlich frovre is unwurthe to ancre.

175 Swa wisliche witeth ow in ower blod-letunge ant haldeth ow i swuch reste thet ye longe th'refter mahen i Godes servise the monluker swinken, ant alswa hwen ye feleth eani secnesse. Muchel sotschipe hit is leosen for an dei tene other tweolve.

Wesscheth ow, hwer-se neod is, as ofte as ye wulleth, ant ower othre thinges: nes neaver fulthe Godd leof, thah poverte ant unorneschipe beon him lic-wurthe.

180 Understondeth eaver of alle theose thinges, thet nan nis heast ne forbod thet beoth of the uttre riwle, thet is lute strengthe of, for-hwon thet te inre beo wel i-wist, as ich seide i the frumthe. Theos mei beon i-changet hwer-se eani neod other eani skile hit easketh, efter thet ha best mei the leafdi riwle servin as hire eadmode thuften. Ah sikerliche withuten hire, the leafdi feareth to wundre.

185 Ancre the naveth nawt neh honde hire fode beoth bisie twa wummen: an eaver the leave ed hame, an other the wende ut hwenne driveth neod, ant theo beo ful unorne, withuten euch tiffunge — other a lutel thuftene other of feier ealde. Bi the

---

unworthy of an anchoress. **175–77 Swa wisliche witeth . . . tweolve**, Thus protect (or, look after) you[rself] judiciously in your blood-letting and keep you[rself] in such rest that long after that you can work in God's service the more manfully (or, vigorously), and also [look after yourself] when you feel any sickness. It is great stupidity to lose for one day ten or twelve. **178–79 Wesscheth ow . . . lic-wurthe**, Wash you[rselves], wherever there is need, as often as you like, and [wash also] your other things: filth was never beloved to God, though poverty and plainness are pleasing to Him. **180–82 thet nan nis heast . . . the frumthe**, that none [of these things] is a command or prohibition which is (lit., are) in the outer rule, which is of little importance as long as the inner [rule] be well directed, as I said in the beginning. **182–84 Theos mei beon i-changet . . . thuften**, This [outer rule] can be changed wherever any need or logical reason requires (lit., asks) it, by which (or, according to which) she can best serve the lady rule as her humble handmaid. **184 Ah sikerliche . . . to wundre**, But to be sure without her, the lady fares (i.e., gets along) terribly. **185–87 Ancre the naveth . . . feier ealde**, For the anchoress who does not have her food near at hand two women are employed: one who always should stay at home, another who should go out when need forces, and let her be very plain, without any adornment — either a little servant girl (lit., handmaid) or of fair age. **187–90 Bi the wei . . . ham cume**, On the path, as she is walking (lit., goes), let her go singing her prayers, and

wei as ha geath, ga singinde hire beoden, ne ne halde na tale with mon ne with wummon, ne sitte, ne ne stonde, bute thet leaste thet ha eaver mei ear then ha ham

190 cume. No-hwider elles ne ga heo, bute thider as me send hire. Withute leave, ne ne eote ha, ne ne drinke ute. The other beo eaver inne, ne withute the yeten ne ga withute leave. Ba beon obedient to hare dame in alle thing, bute i sunne ane. Na thing nabben thet heo hit nute, ne undervo na thing, ne ne yeove nowther, withuten hire leave. Na mon ne leoten in, ne the yungre ne speoke with na-mon bute leave,

195 ne ga ha nawt ut of tune, withuten siker fere. Yef hit swa mei beon, ne ne ligge ute. Yef heo ne con o boke, segge bi **Pater nostres** ant bi **Avez** hire ures, ant wurche thet me hat hire withute gruchunge. Habbe eaver hire earen opene toward hire dame. Nowther of the wummen ne beore from hare dame, ne ne bringe to hire, nane idele talen, ne neowe tidinges, ne bitweonen ham-seolf ne singen, ne ne

200 speoken nane worldliche spechen, ne lahhen swa ne pleien, thet ei mon thet hit sehe mahte hit to uvel turnen.

let her not hold any tale with man or with woman, or sit, or stand around, provided that [she does this] the least that she ever can before she come[s] home. **190 No-hwider elles . . . send hire**, Let her go nowhere else but where she was sent (lit., one sent her). **190–91 ne ne eote ha . . . ute**, let her not eat or drink while out. **191–92 The other . . . i sunne ane**, Let the other [woman] always be inside, nor let her go outside the gates without permission. Let both be obedient to their lady in all things, except in sin alone. **192–93 Na thing nabben . . . yeove nowther**, Let them have nothing which she (i.e., the anchoress) does not know about, [let them] not receive anything or give [anything] either. **194–95 Na mon ne leoten in . . . siker fere**, They should let no man in, nor should the younger [one] speak with any man without permission, nor should she go out of town without a reliable companion. **195–96 Yef hit swa mei beon, ne ne ligge ute**, If it may so be (i.e., if possible), let her not lie (i.e., sleep) out. **196–97 Yef heo ne con o boke . . . gruchunge**, If she cannot [read] in a book, let her say her hours with "Our Fathers" and with "Hail Marys," and let her do what people tell her without complaining. **197 Habbe**, Let her have. **198 Nowther . . . ne beore**, Neither of the women should bear (or, carry). **199 nane idele talen**, no idle tales; **neowe tidinges**, news; **bitweonen ham-seolf**, amongst themselves. **200 spechen**, talk (lit., speeches). **200–01 ne lahhen . . . turnen**, nor laugh or play in such a way that any man who would see it might turn it to evil.

Over alle thinges, leasunges ant luthere wordes heatien. Hare her beo i-corven; hare heaved-clath sitte lahhe. Either ligge ane. Hare cop beo hehe i-sticchet ant bute broche. Na mon ne seo ham unleppet ne open-heaved. Lah locunge habben.

205 Heo ne schulen cussen na mon, ne cuthmon ne cunnesmon, ne for na cuththe cluppen ne weschen hare heaved, ne lokin feaste o na mon, ne toggin with ne pleien. Hare weden beon of swuch schape, ant al hare aturn swuch, thet hit beo edscene hwer-to ha beoth i-turnde. Hare lates lokin warliche, thet nan ne mahe edwiten ham in hus ne ut of hus. On alle wise forbeoren to wreathen hare dame,

210 ant as ofte as heo hit doth, ear ha drinken other eoten, makien hare **Venie**, o cneon dun bivoren hire, ant seggen, **Mea culpa**, ant undervon the penitence thet ha leith upon hire, lutinde hire lahe. The ancre th'refter neaver mare thet ilke gult ne upbreide for na wreaththe, bute yef ha eft sone falle i thet ilke, ah do hit allunge ut of hire heorte. Yef ei strif ariseth bitweone the wummen, the ancre makie either to

215 makien other **Venie** o cneon to ther eorthe, ant either rihte up other, ant cussen on

---

202–03 leasunges . . . sitte lahhe, let them hate lies and wicked words. Let their hair be cut [short]; their head-cloth sit low. **203–04 Either ligge ane . . . open-heaved**, Let each one sleep alone. Let their cape[s] be stitched (or, fastened) up high and without a brooch. Let no man (or, no one) see them unwrapped (i.e., without a cloak) or bare-headed. **204–07 Lah locunge habben . . . ne pleien**, Let them have a low gaze (i.e., keep their eyes low). They must not kiss any man, neither acquaintance nor kinsman, nor hug out of any friendship or wash their (i.e., the men's) head[s], nor look steadily at any man, nor tussle with nor play [with them]. **207–08 Hare weden . . . i-turnde**, Let their clothes be of such a fashion and all their attire such that it is evident in which direction (lit., to where) they are turned (i.e., on what they are intent). **208–09 Hare lates . . . hus**, They should look to their behavior carefully, so that none can upbraid them in the house or out of the house. **209–12 On alle wise . . . hire lahe**, In every way they should refrain from angering (lit., forbear to anger) their lady, and as often as they do it, before they drink or eat, [let them] make their "Pardon," down on [their] knees before her, and say "The fault is mine," and receive the penance which she (i.e., the anchoress) lays upon her, bowing (reflex.) low. **212–14 The ancre th'refter . . . hire heorte**, Let the anchoress thereafter nevermore upbraid that same fault out of any anger, unless she (i.e., the servant) soon fall into that same [fault], but let [the anchoress] put it completely out of her heart. **214–17 the ancre makie either to makien . . . gulte**, let the anchoress make each [of them] make to the other a "Pardon" on knees [bent] to the ground (*ther* = def. art.: see glossary), and let each raise up

ende, ant te ancre legge on either sum penitence, mare up-o the ilke the greatluker gulte. This is a thing — witen ha wel — thet is Gode leovest: sahtnesse ant some — ant te feond lathest. For-thi he is eaver umben to arearen sum leaththe. Nu sith the sweoke wel, thet hwen fur is wel o brune, ant me wule thet hit aga, me sundreth

220 the brondes, ant he deth [on] hond thet ilke. Luve is Jesu Cristes fur, thet he wule thet bleasie aa i thin heorte, ant te deovel blaweth for-te puffen hit ut. Hwen his blawunge ne geineth nawt, he bringeth up sum uvel word, other sum other nohtunge, hwer-thurh ha tohurten either frommard other — ant te Hali Gastes fur cwencheth hwen the brondes thurh wreaththe beoth i-sundret. For-thi halden ham

225 i luve feaste togederes. Ant ne beo ham nawt of, hwen the feond blawe, nomeliche yef monie beon i-veiet somet, ant wel with luve ontende. Thah the ancre on hire meidnes for openliche gultes legge penitence, to the preost no-the-leater schriven ham hwen neod is, ah eaver thah with leave.

Yef ha ne cunnen nawt the mete-graces, seggen in hare stude **Pater noster**

230 bivoren, ant **Ave Maria**, ant efter mete alswa, ant a **Credo** mare, ant segge thus

the other, and kiss finally, and let the anchoress lay on each some penance, more upon the one who more greatly misbehaved. **217–18 This is a thing . . . lathest**, This is a thing — let them know well — that is dearest to God: reconciliation and harmony — and most hateful to the fiend. **218–20 For-thi he is eaver umben . . . thet ilke**, Therefore he is always busy to stir up (lit., raise up) some hostility. Now the deceiver sees well that when a fire is well aflame, and one wishes that it die out, one separates the brands (or, logs), and he (i.e., the devil) does just the same. **220–21 thet he wule . . . heorte**, which He wishes that would blaze continually in your heart. **222 ne geineth nawt**, gains nothing (or, is of no use). **222–24 sum other nohtunge . . . i-sundret**, some other insult through which they recoil from each other (lit., knock each away from the other) — and the Holy Spirit's fire goes out when the brands are separated by anger. **224–25 For-thi halden ham . . . togederes**, Therefore let them keep themselves firmly together in love. **225–26 Ant ne beo ham nawt of . . . ontende**, And let it be nothing to them, when the fiend may blow, especially if many are joined together, and well set on fire (lit., ignited) with love. **226–28 Thah the ancre on hire meidnes . . . with leave**, Though the anchoress [herself] lay penance on her maidens for open offenses, nonetheless let them confess themselves to the priest when there is need, but always though with permission. **229–31 Yef ha ne cunnen . . . on ende**, If they do not know the meal graces (i.e., prayers), let them say in their place "Our Father" beforehand, along with "Hail Mary," and after the meal likewise, and one "I be-

412

on ende: "Feader, Sune, Hali Gast, [an] almihti Godd, yeove ure dame his grace, se lengre se mare, ant leve hire ant us ba neomen god ende. Foryelde alle the us god doth, ant milci hare sawle the us god i-don habbeth — hare sawle, ant alle Cristene sawles."

235   Bitweone mel ne gru*seli* nawt nowther frut ne other-hwet, ne drinken bute leave, ant te leave beo liht in al thet nis sunne. Ed te mete na word, other lut, ant teo stille. Alswa efter the ancre Complie, athet Prime, ne don na thing ne seggen, hwer-thurh hire silence mahe beon i-sturbet.

    Nan ancre servant ne ahte bi rihte to easkin i-set hure bute mete ant *clath* thet
240 ha mei flutte bi — ant Godes milce. Ne misleve nan Godd — hwet-se tide of the ancre — thet he hire trukie. The meidnes withuten, yef ha servith the ancre alswa as ha ahen, hare hure schal beon the hehe blisse of heovene. Hwa-se haveth ehe of hope toward se heh hure, gleadliche wule ha servin ant lihtliche alle wa ant alle teone tholien: with eise ant with este ne buth me nawt blisse.

245   Ye ancres ahen this leaste stucche reden to ower wummen euche wike eanes, athet ha hit cunnen. Ant muche neod is thet ye neomen to ham muche yeme, for ye

lieve" more. **232 se lengre se mare . . . ende**, "the longer the greater, and grant her and us both to have (lit., take) a good end." **232–34 Foryelde alle . . . sawles**, Reward all [those] who do us good, and have mercy on souls of those who have done us good — their souls, and all Christian souls. **235–36 Bitweone mel . . . nis sunne**, Between meals let them not snack (or, munch) on either fruit or anything else, or drink without permission, and let the permission be quick in everything that is not sin. **236–38 Ed te mete . . . i-sturbet**, At the meal (lit., food) let there be no words, or few, and those quiet. Also after the anchoress' Compline until Prime, let them not do anything or say [anything] by which her silence may be disturbed. **239–40 Nan ancre servant . . . milce**, No anchoress' servant ought by right to ask for fixed wages except [enough] food and clothing that she can live by (or, survive on) — and God's mercy. **240–41 Ne misleve nan . . . trukie**, Let no one mistrust God — whatso[ever may] happen to the anchoress — that He [might] fail her. **241 The meidnes withuten**, The maidens outside (i.e., who go outside). **241–42 alswa as ha ahen**, just as they ought. **242 hare hure**, their wages (or, pay); **ehe**, eye. **243 se heh hure**, such high wages. **243–44 wule ha servin . . . blisse**, will she serve and easily bear all woe (or, pain) and all hardship: one does not buy joy with comfort and with pleasure (*buth* = reduced form of *buggeth*). **245–47 ahen this leaste stucche . . . i-wurset**, ought to read this last section to your women once each week until they know it. And there is great need that you pay (lit., take) much attention to them, for you (pl.)

mahen muchel beon thurh ham i-godet, ant i-wurset. On other half, yef thet ha sungith thurh ower yemeles, ye schule beo bicleopet th'rof bivore the hehe deme, ant for-thi as ow is muche neod, ant ham yet mare, yeornliche leareth ham to

250 halden hare riwle, ba for ow ant for ham-seolf, litheliche ant luveliche, for swuch ah wummone lare to beonne, luvelich ant lithe, ant selt-hwenne sturne. Ba is riht thet ha ow dreden ant luvien, ant thah thet ter beo eaver mare of luve then of drede. Thenne schal hit wel fearen. Me schal healden eoli ant win ba i wunden efter Godes lare, ah mare of softe eoli then of bitinde win. Thet is, mare of lithe

255 wordes then of suhinde, for ther-of kimeth thinge best — thet is, luve eie. Lihtliche ant sweteliche foryeoveth ham hare gultes hwen ha ham i-cnaweth ant bihateth bote.

As forth as ye mahen, of mete ant of clathes, ant of othre thinges thet neode of flesch easketh, beoth large toward ham, thah ye nearowe beon ant hearde to ow-

260 seolven. Swa deth the wel blaweth: went te nearewe of the horn to his ahne muth, ant ut-ward thet wide. Ant ye don alswa as ye wulleth thet ower beoden bemin

can be greatly improved or diminished (lit., worsened) by them. **247–51 On other half . . . sturne**, At the same time (lit., on the other side), if they sin through your carelessness, you will be called before the high judge for it (lit., thereof), and therefore as it is very necessary (lit., there is great need) for you, and still more for them, eagerly teach them to keep their rule, both for you and for themselves, [teach them] mildly and lovingly, for so ought women's teaching to be, loving and mild, and seldom stern. **251–53 Ba is riht . . . fearen**, Both is (i.e., are) right, that they should fear and love you, and nevertheless [it is right] that there (*ter* = reduced form of *ther* after preceding -*t*) should be more of love than of fear. Then it will go (lit., fare) well. **253–55 Me schal healden . . . luve eie**, One must pour both oil and wine on wounds according to God's teaching, but more of soft oil than of biting wine. That is, more of mild words than of painful [ones], for from that comes the best of things — that is, love's fear (or, fear inspired by love). **255–57 Lihtliche ant sweteliche foryeoveth . . . bote**, Forgive them their faults easily (or, readily) and sweetly when they acknowledge them and promise repentance (or, a remedy). **258–60 As forth as ye mahen . . . ow-seolven**, As far as you (pl.) can, with food and with clothes, and with other things that the need[s] of the body demand, be generous towards them, even though you are sparing and severe to yourselves. **260–63 Swa deth . . . swa mote, amen**, [The person] who blows [a trumpet] well does so (or, like this): he turns (*went* = reduced form of *wendeth*) the narrow

414

wel ant dremen i Drihtines earen, nawt ane to ower ahnes, ah to alle folkes heale
— as ure Laverd leve thurh the grace of him-seolf thet hit swa mote, amen.

265 Hwen ower sustres meidnes cumeth to ow to frovre, cumeth to ham to the thurl
ear-under ant over-under eanes other twien, ant gath ayein sone to ower note
gastelich, ne bivore Complie ne sitte ye nawt for ham over riht time, swa thet hare
cume beo na lure of ower religiun, ah gastelich biyete. Yef ther is eani word i-seid
thet mahte hurten heorte, ne beo hit nawt i-boren ut, ne i-broht to other ancre thet
is eth-hurte. To him hit schal beon i-seid, the loketh ham alle. Twa niht is inoh
270 thet ei beo edhalden, ant thet beo ful seldene, ne for heom ne breoke silence ed te
wmete ne for blod-letunge, bute yef sum muche god other neod hit makie.

The ancre ne hire meiden ne plohien nane worldliche gomenes ed te thurle, ne
ne ticki togederes, for ase seith Seint Beornard, unwurthe thing is to euch gastelich
mon, ant nomeliche to ancre, euch swuch fleschlich frovre, ant hit binimeth
275 gastelich thet is withute met utnume murhthe — ant thet is uvel change, as is i-
seid th'ruppe.

[part] of the horn to his own mouth and [turns] the wide [part] outward. And you should do
likewise as (or, if) you want your prayers to trumpet well and make music in the Lord's
ears, not only for your own but for all people's salvation — as our Lord grant through the
grace of Himself that it might [be] so, amen. **264–67 to frovre . . . biyete,** for comfort,
come to them at the window in the late morning (or, perhaps, before noon) and early
afternoon once or twice, and go again immediately to your spiritual work, do not sit around
before Compline beyond the proper time, so that their coming may be no loss of your religion
(i.e., regulated life), but a spiritual benefit. **268 thet mahte hurten heorte,** which might hurt
the heart (i.e., someone's feelings). **268–69 ne beo hit nawt . . . eth-hurte,** let it not be carried
out, nor brought to another anchoress who is easily hurt. **269–71 To him . . . hit makie,** It must
be said (or, told) to him, who looks after them all. Two nights is enough for (lit., that) any
maiden to be kept [as a guest], and let that be very seldom, and do not break silence for them
at the meal (lit., the food) or for blood-letting, unless some great good or emergency force it.
272–76 The ancre ne hire meiden . . . th'ruppe, Let neither the anchoress or her maiden play
any worldly games at the window, nor tussle together, for as St. Bernard says, every such
bodily comfort is an unworthy thing for each spiritual person, and especially for an anchoress,
and it takes away the spiritual which is beyond measure the supreme happiness — and that is
a bad exchange, as is said above (see 4.137–41, 4.366–70).

Part Eight

280

Of this boc redeth hwen ye beoth eise euche dei leasse other mare. Ich hopie thet hit schal beon ow, yef ye hit redeth ofte, swithe biheve thurh Godes muchele grace, elles ich hefde uvele bitohe mi muchele hwile. Me were leovere, Godd hit wite, do me toward Rome, then for-te biginnen hit eft for-te donne. Yef ye findeth thet ye doth alswa as ye redeth, thonckith Godd yeorne; yef ye ne doth nawt, biddeth Godes are, ant beoth umben ther-onuven thet ye hit bet halden efter ower mihte.

285

Feader, Sune, Hali Gast — an almihti Godd wite ow in his warde. He gleadie ow ant frovri ow, mine leove sustren, ant for al thet ye for him dreheth ant dreaieth, ne yeove ow neaver leasse then al togedere him-seolven. Beo he aa i-heiet from world into world aa on ecnesse. AMEN.

Ase ofte as ye habbeth i-red ea-wiht her-on, greteth the Leafdi with an **Ave** for him thet swonc her-abuten. Inoh meathful ich am the bidde se lutel. **Explicit.**

290

I-thench on thi writere i thine beoden sum-chearre: ne beo hit ne se lutel, hit turneth the to gode, thet tu bidest for othre.

---

277 Of this boc, From this book; **hwen ye beoth eise**, when you are at ease. **278 swithe biheve**, very beneficial; **muchele**, great (or, abundant). **279–80 elles ich hefde . . . donne**, otherwise I would have wasted (lit., used badly) my great time (i.e., the great time it took to write the book). I would rather (lit., to me it would be preferable), God knows, put myself [on the road] towards Rome, (i.e., go to Rome) than to begin to do it again. **280–83 Yef ye findeth . . . ower mihte**, If you find that you do (i.e., behave) as you read (i.e., as the book advises), thank God earnestly; if you do not, ask for God's grace, and be busy afterwards that you keep it better according to your strength. **284–86 an almihti Godd . . . himseolven**, one almighty God protect you in His keeping. May He gladden you and comfort you, my dear sisters, and for everything that you suffer and endure for Him, may He never give you less than all of Himself together (or, at once). **286–87 Beo he aa i-heiet . . . ecnesse**, Let Him be exalted forever from world into world always in eternity. **288–89 Ase ofte as ye habbeth i-red . . . Explicit**, As often as you have read anything herein (i.e., in this book), greet the Lady with a "Hail Mary" for him that labored on it (lit., here-about). I am moderate enough who ask so little. The End. **290–91 I-thench on thi writere . . . othre**, Think about your writer (or, scribe) in your prayers sometime: be it ever so little, it will turn to good for you (i.e., do you good), that you pray for others.

Explanatory Notes

Abbreviations: **Caius**: Gonville & Caius MS 234/120; **Cleo.**: British Library Cotton MS Cleopatra C.vi; **Corpus**: MS Corpus Christi College, Cambridge 402; **Lat.**: Latin text of *Ancrene Riwle*; **MED**: *Middle English Dictionary*; **Nero**: British Library MS Cotton Nero A.xiv; **OED**: *Oxford English Dictionary*; **PG**: *Patrologia Graecae*; **PL**: *Patrologia Latina*; **Titus**: British Library MS Cotton Titus D.xviii; **Trinity**: Trinity College MS R 147 (French text); **Vernon**: Vernon MS (Oxford, Bodleian Eng. Poet a.1); **Vitellius**: British Library MS Cotton Vitellius F.vii (French text)

These notes focus on a) introducing and outlining each of the eight parts of *AW* (in headnotes for each section), b) explaining problematic words and passages, c) pointing the reader to relevant scholarship, d) tracing the most important sources and influences, and e) identifying allusions which might be difficult for a modern reader to interpret. These notes do not aim, however, at providing an exhaustive account of all known (or suspected) sources. Readers interested in a more detailed treatment should consult the excellent notes in Savage and Watson's *Anchoritic Spirituality*, as well as those in Bella Millett's full critical edition (forthcoming) and, for Parts Six and Seven, those in Geoffrey Shepherd's edition. Our understanding of the sources for *AW* have been greatly expanded by the unpublished work of Mary Baldwin ("*Ancrene Wisse* and its Background in the Christian Tradition of Religious Instruction and Spirituality") and Sister Ethelbert Cooper ("Latin Elements of the *Ancrene Riwle*") — see Savage and Watson's notes for the details of their findings.

Bibliographical references are listed here by author and, where helpful, an abbreviated title. See the Select Bibliography (pp. 45–58) for full references. See the Textual Notes (pp. 481–559) for a list of changes made to the original text either to correct errors in the MS or to restore missing text.

Author's Preface

The Preface or introduction to *AW* establishes one of the over-arching concepts of the work — the distinction between the inner (spiritual) and outer (bodily) orientation. The structure of the entire *AW* is built around the tension between these two, as Janet Grayson points out: "the collective inner Rule . . . undergoes conversion from concern with the physical world to the spiritual, from preoccupation with the means to achieve Love to the actual reception of Love. Just as the individual image-motifs and distinctions move inward towards a settling in Christ, so the inner Rule moves relentlessly inward toward the center: the heart, Love, grace, Christ" (*Structure and Imagery*, p.12). Grayson goes on to suggest that the Parts One and Eight, which are mainly concerned with the outer rule, are also appropriately made into the outer chapters — they encircle the inner rule "like a protective band of tougher fiber" (p. 15).

Dobson has probably given the closest attention to the Preface (see chapter 1 of *Origins*), using it to argue for the author's Augustinian affiliation on the basis of references to the "order of St. James" and to the habits of various religious orders (see Explanatory Notes to Pref.79, Pref.97, and Pref.110).

Outline

Inner versus Outer rule (Pref.2–53). The opening of the Preface sets out in very clear terms the division between the inner and outer rules (governing the heart and the body respectively), likening them to a lady and her handmaiden (Pref.2–29). The author stresses the superiority of inner rule, as well as the variability of the outer for women of various circumstances (Pref.30–53).

The Danger of Vows (Pref.54–77). This section outlines the dangers of vowing or promising anything pertaining to the outer rule. Anchoresses should vow three things only: obedience, chastity, and steadfastness of place (Pref.54 ff.). Other vows can lead to despair (Pref.71–77).

Religious Orders and the Outer Rule (Pref.78–129). Membership in a particular religious order is unimportant so long as the anchoresses belong to the "Order" of St. James: i.e., they keep themselves chaste and unstained by the world (Pref.78–129). Habits of the various orders signify unity, but for hermits and anchoresses habits are largely unimportant — inner unity is paramount (Pref.109–29).

Conclusion (Pref.130–51). The Preface concludes with a brief chapter outline of all eight parts of *AW*.

The distinction between the inner and outer rules seems to be borrowed from Aelred of Rievaulx's *De Institutione Inclusarum* ("On the Instruction of Recluses [lit., enclosed women]"), a guide he wrote for his sister between 1160–62. Several other details in the Preface, Part Six, and Part Eight also lean heavily on Aelred's treatise (see Savage and Watson, p. 339n1). Throughout these notes, I will refer to Sister Penelope's translation in *Aelred of Rievaulx: Treatises & Pastoral Prayer*. Dobson sees a number of parallels between the Preface and various documents associated with the Rule of Augustine (see *Origins*, chapter 1 in particular).

1 *Ancrene Wisse*. The title given here, "Anchoresses' Guide," is often used to distinguish the Corpus version (the *Ancrene Wisse* proper) from all other versions, traditionally referred to as the *Ancrene Riwle*. Francis P. Magoun, however, argues convincingly that *Ancren Riwle* (Morton's editorial title) has little authority and that all texts should be called "*Ancrene Wisse*" (pp. 112–13). *Wisse* is a rare word derived from the OE verb *wissian* "to direct, guide, show the way" and, more rarely, "to rule, govern." Although

it may merely be the English equivalent of French-derived *riwle* "rule," Dobson suggests that the author uses it here to avoid the implication that the text is an actual rule (i.e., the formal rule or *regula* of an established order) and that it may mean something more than "advice" but less than "command" (*Origins*, p. 53). Dobson's argument may be a bit tendentious, however, since he takes this position in order to bolster his claim that the *Ancrene Wisse/Riwle* was written by an Augustinian canon. The MED's translation of the title as "Rule for Nuns" is probably inaccurate on two counts — *wisse* probably does not mean "rule," and *ancrene* probably does not mean "nuns'" but rather "anchoresses'" (see Explanatory Note to Pref.30). See Yoko Wada's *"Temptations" from Ancrene Wisse* (pp. xiii–xviii) for an extensive discussion of the title.

2–6   *Recti diligunt te . . . Recti diligunt te.* The Latin opening, probably composed by the author, plays on various forms of the root *rectus* "straight, right" including *regula* "rule," *directionem* "regulation" and *rectificationem* (see Savage and Watson, pp. 339–40n2). In the body of *AW*, most Latin quotations are translated, sometimes quite loosely. It is notable that the long Latin passages on the first page of the Preface (lines 2–6, 15–23, and 25–26) go essentially untranslated. All are rhetorically charged in a way that most of the other quotations are not: the first relies on word play (*paronomasia*), while the second uses a rather technical rhetorical term (*antonomastice*, line 18). The discussion of right grammar, geometry, and theology (lines 2–5, 26) makes a clear reference to university subjects, and it seems possible that the author wished to open *AW* in an academic tone to establish his scholarly credentials to other religious who might scrutinize the treatise or act as spiritual directors (see Millett, "Women in No Man's Land," pp. 94–95). Shortly after this, the author settles into the more or less regular pattern of providing loose (and often expanded) translations, usually just after Latin citations.

8–9   *Ant ye, mine leove sustren, habbeth moni dei i-cravet on me efter riwle.* A very similar sentence appears in the opening of Aelred's preface: "For many years now, my sister, you have been asking me for a rule to guide you" (p. 43). The *AW* author lends a personal tone to the work by sprinkling direct address ("my dear sisters") throughout, occasionally dropping into the singular. Aelred also addresses his sister directly, usually simply as "sister." In *AW* the direct address at times seems suggestive of a homiletic style derived from vernacular preaching.

11   *withute cnost ant dolc of woh in-wit.* The meaning of *dolc* is debatable. The sense descended from OE *dolg* is "gash, scar," though Baldwin argues that the word really comes from the diminutive of OE *dæl* "valley" and means something like a "small hollow or cavity" ("Some Difficult Words," p. 274). In using these two words *cnost*

"swelling" and *dolc* "cavity," the author is attempting to show the hills and valleys of an uneven (*woh*) surface.

15–23 This passage combines Psalm texts with their explanatory glosses (taken from Peter Lombard's standard Psalm commentary) and is unique to Corpus; at the same point in the Cleo. version, scribe B (perhaps the *AW* author) has added an explanation of how a bad conscience makes the heart lumpy and knotty but how the rule smoothes and softens it, returning to the images in Pref.10–11.

18 *anto[no]masice*. A rhetorical term, antonomasia, which describes a kind of substitution: here, "the good" is substituted for the concept of "those who direct their wills by the rule of the divine will." This serves to unite Psalm 35:2 and Psalm 124:4 so that in the latter verse David is seen to use the term "good" as a substitute shorthand for the virtue described in Psalm 35:2.

20 The recto side of the first folio of Corpus contains the following text, written in at the bottom margin in a later hand: *Liber ecclesie sancti Jacobi de Wygemore, quem Johannes Purcel dedit eidem ecclesie ad instanciam fratris Walteri de Lodel' senioris tunc precentoris. Siquis dictum librum alienaverit a predicta ecclesia vel titulum hunc maliciose deleverit, anathema sit. Amen. Fiat, fiat, fiat. AMEN.* ["(This is) a book belonging to (lit., of) the church of St. James of Wigmore, which John Purcel gave to the same church at the request of brother Walter de Lodel, then senior precentor (i.e., director of singing). If anyone removes the said book from the aforementioned church, or defaces this title maliciously, let there be excommunication (i.e., let the culprit be excommunicated). Amen. Let it be so, let it be so, let it be so. Amen."]

Dobson uses this dedication to bolster his identification of the *AW* author as Brian of Lingen, an Augustinian canon of St. James, Wigmore (*Origins*, pp. 137–38), though it is equally plausible that the Corpus MS arrived at Wigmore through some other means, especially given the fact that John Purcell came from a south Shropshire family (to the north of Wigmore) and that the dedication is much later, sometime around 1300 (see *Origins*, pp. 16, 291). For an amusing history of book curses see Marc Drogin's *Anathema: Medieval Scribes and the History of Book Curses* (Montclair, NJ: Allanheld and Schram, 1983).

26 *geometri[c]o*. The fact that the scribe sometimes misspells technical terminology (see Textual Notes to this line and to Pref.18 and 2.361) might lead one to suspect that he or she was not university trained.

30   *ancren.* The term *ancre* (pl. *ancren*, gen. pl. *ancrene*) has a range of meanings from "recluse," "solitary," "hermit," perhaps to "monk" or "nun" (see MED). It is probably best rendered by "anchorite" since the word can refer either to men or women. The OED points out that the specifically female form *ancress* appeared first in the fourteenth century. However, since the *AW* assumes that an *ancre* is a woman, the word is translated here as "anchoress." In this assumption, the *AW* reverses the common pattern in English in which nouns describing the doer of an action designate both the generic and male. In *AW*, *ancre* seems to be both generic and female.

42   *quantum scilicet ad observantias corporales.* Baldwin, "Some Difficult Words," points out that Bernard uses a very similar phrase in his discussion of inner and outer rules in *On Rule and Dispensation* II.3–5 (see Savage and Watson, p. 341n9).

73–76   Aelred recommends that the anchoress not vow extra psalms or commemorations: "here again the number should not be determined by vow or obligation but inspired by devotion" (chapter 9, p. 56).

79   *of Sein James.* The "order" of St. James is in many ways a kind of "anti-order" which includes both secular priests — who visit widows and orphans — as well as recluses — who keep themselves pure (James 1:27). Dobson notes that Augustinian canons used this same verse to defend themselves against the supposedly superior claims of monks (*Origins*, pp. 32–33).

97   *hwit ne blac.* An apparent reference to the traditional colors of the Cistercians and the Benedictines, respectively, though Dobson thinks that black and white refer to two different sub-groups among the Augustinian canons: the Premonstratensians and the Victorines (*Origins*, p. 31). See Explanatory Note to Pref.110.

99–101 *Pawel . . . Antonie . . . Arsenie . . . Makarie . . . Sare . . . Sincletice.* As a group, these are desert saints, who appear in roughly this order in *The Lives of the Desert Fathers*, a work cited by title in *AW* (see Explanatory Note to 2.310). Much like the anchoresses themselves, these saints withdrew from society and took up solitary lives as hermits and recluses in the deserts of Egypt. Desert or "eremitic" spirituality viewed the body with disdain and sought to conquer it through a heavy regimen of physical tests and disciplines of sometimes incredible proportions: fasting for days before a plate of food, wearing shirts made of bristles, lashing the body with whips or nettles, sitting stationary, sometimes on the tops of poles, for months or even years on end, etc. For recent discussions of desert spirituality, see Peter Brown's *The World of Late Antiquity* and Phillip Rousseau's *Ascetics, Authority, and the Church in the Age of Jerome and*

Cassian. For a passionate appreciation of desert spirituality, see *The Wisdom of the Desert* by the poet Thomas Merton (New York: New Direction, 1970).

Paul (?229–342), called the "first hermit" to distinguish him from the Apostle Paul, fled the persecutions of the Emperor Decius and took up residence as a hermit in the Egyptian desert. St. Jerome visited him and wrote his life.

Anthony (251–356), the founder of western monasticism, abandoned a life of wealth and became a hermit in a cemetery near Memphis. He eventually wandered to a more desolate retreat, an abandoned fort on Mt. Pispir, and lived on whatever food was thrown to him over the walls. Later he organized a group of solitaries who had gathered around the mountain into a loose community with a rule. After battling the Arian heresy he returned to the solitary life in a cave on Mt. Kolzim. His life was written by St. Athanasius. See 4.1231–34 for an anecdote about him.

Arsenius "the Great" (?355–450) was a well-educated man who became the tutor of Emperor Theodosius' sons before renouncing the world to lead a solitary life in the desert of Scetis. Near the end of his life, he was driven from the desert by invading barbarians. See 3.496–99 for an anecdote about him.

Macarius (c. 300–90), called "the Elder" to distinguish him from Macarius "the Younger," another Egyptian hermit, was a camel herder as a young man but became a hermit of the most severe type. Later, falsely accused of impregnating a woman, he showed great patience during his trial and after his acquittal fled to the desert of Scetis.

Sarah (probably fourth century), called Amma ("mother"), was one of the desert mothers whose sayings are preserved in *The Lives of the Desert Fathers*. See 4.681–90 for an account of her austerity.

Syncletica (c. 316–400) was born of wealthy parents in Alexandria. She refused to marry and eventually became a recluse with her sister after giving her inheritance to the poor. She undertook austere fasting and other mortifications of the body.

110   *nawt i the wide hod, ne in the blake cape, ne i the hwite rochet, ne i the greie cuvel.* Continuing with the idea that the inner disposition of the heart is more important than the trappings of various external orders, the author says that religion "is not in the wide hood, nor in the black cope, nor in the white surplice, nor in the gray cowl." This list of ecclesiastical garb may describe several garments in the unique habit of the Augustinian canons (Dobson, *Origins*, p. 31). They may, however, point not to one order, but

several. The "wide hood" probably refers more generally to the hood of a priest or any member of a religious order (MED). Allen suggests that the black cope indicates the Benedictines, the white rochet the Cistercians, and the gray cowl the monks of Savigny ("The Origin," p. 423), though Baldwin ("Some Difficult Words," pp. 289–90) rejects this idea, pointing out that black, white, and gray cowls may very well stand for the orders Allen suggested, but that the specific words "cope" and "rochet" point to a more complicated interpretation. She suggests that the black cope may signify regular canons (often known as "black canons"), while the white rochet may indicate the Augustinian canons. Fletcher suggests different identifications: the black cope (Dominicans), the white rochet (regular canons), and the gray cowl (the Franciscans). See his "Black, White, and Grey in *Hali Meiðhad* and *Ancrene Wisse*" for details (pp. 74–75). For a further reference to ecclesiastical clothing, see 2.82–86.

111–16 Dobson points to a close parallel for this passage in the Statutes of Prémontré (c. 1174–90), a document which influenced both the Augustinian and Dominican rules (*Origins*, pp. 19–20), though his claim of direct dependence on the Premonstratensian institutes may be a bit exaggerated since the verbal parallels are not exact.

131 *destinctiuns*. This rather academic word is translated by the English *dalen* "parts." In Latin, *distinctio* could refer simply to a division or section of a learned treatise, but could also describe a kind of theological writing popular in the late twelfth and early thirteenth centuries. In collections called *Distinctiones*, individual entries would list a number of alternate meanings for biblical words or theological concepts, often with full allegorical treatment. Though the *AW* author does not apparently use the word in this technical sense, it probably had a learned, Latinate sound. See Richard H. and Mary H. Rouse's "Biblical *Distinctiones* in the Thirteenth Century" and Alexandra Barratt's "The Five Wits" (p. 13).

139 *Davith*. This spelling of David (MS: *Davið*) reflects the way the word was pronounced in medieval Latin (see Shepherd, p. 34).

Part One

The *AW* proper begins with a section devoted almost wholly to the outer rule — the description of the anchoress' hours. Part One sketches out in rough chronological order the daily prayers (with their accompanying antiphons, responses, versicles, hymns, psalms, etc.) from early morning to just before bedtime, with a scattering of votive prayers which could be recited during any spare moment. This is perhaps the most daunting part of *AW* for modern readers. As Dahood remarks in "Design in Part I of *Ancrene Riwle*," "The subject-matter is rather dry and, to many, alien: what prayers should be said and when, what gestures and postures should accompany the prayers, and what atonement should be made for errors of recitation. Many of the prayers, moreover, are not in Middle English but in Latin, and many are cited only by incipit. To modern readers Part I may seem curiously fragmented, a loose assemblage of incipits, prayers and instructions" (p. 1). However, Dahood shows, on the basis of manuscript divisions, that Part One has a tight structure consisting of four main parts, with heavy emphasis on the "normal routine," which was centered around the Little Office of the Virgin, a scaled back version of the divine office, with prescribed prayers for the seven canonical hours (matins/lauds, prime, terce, sext, nones, vespers, and compline). The Little Office formed the backbone of the anchoress' daily devotions.

The following outline of Part One has been adapted from Dahood's "Design in Part I of *Ancrene Riwle*," pp. 5–6.

Outline

I. *Normal Routine* (1.2–373)
    A. Principal devotions between arising and bedtime (1.2–73)
        1. Non-official devotions before matins
        2. The daily office (1.74–98)
            a) Gestures and postures, mainly accompanying the Little Office (1.82–84)
            b) Performance and scheduling of the Little Office and dependent activities (1.84–87)
            c) Performance and scheduling of the Office of the Dead (1.88–98)
        3. Non-official devotions after prime (1.99–337)
            a) At terce and between prime and terce (1.99–172)
                seven penitential psalms and the litany (1.99–113)
                prayer to the Trinity (1.114–26)
                prayer to the crucified Christ (1.127–33)
                prayer for the seven gifts of the Holy Spirit (1.134–40)
                prayer for forgiveness for broken ten commandments (1.141–49)
                prayer to favorite saints (1.150–56)
                prayer for the souls of the departed faithful (1.157–63)
                special prayers for the poor and wretched (1.164–72)
            b) During the mass (1.173–206)
                at the elevation of the Host (1.173–203)
                at the kiss of peace (1.203–06)
            c) At about midday or at some other time (1.207–337)
                special prayers to the Cross: the five greetings (1.207–31)

prayers based on the five joys of the Virgin (1.232–64)
Aves and hymns to the Virgin (1.264–337)

B. Lesser devotions and activities between arising and bedtime (1.338–53)
1. Recommended as defenses against idleness (1.338–45)
    a) Additional *Pater nosters, Aves*, psalms, and prayers (1.338–40)
    b) Singing from the Psalter (1.340)
    c) Reading of holy meditations in English or French (1.340–42)
    d) Work (1.343)
    e) Hours of the Holy Ghost before corresponding hours of the Little Office (1.344–45)
2. Required (1.346–53)
    a) Listening to the priest's hours as much as possible (1.346–47)
    b) Graces before and after meals and when drinking between meals (1.347–53)

C. Bedtime Prayers (1.354–73)
1. Prayer for forgiveness (1.354–59)
2. Prayers and hymns with signs of the Cross (1.359–73)

II. *Substitute Routine* (1.374–84)

III. *Penance for Errors of Recitation* (1.384–88)

IV. *A Short Formal Conclusion* (1.389–91)

As Ackerman and Dahood point out, "Even after making allowance for optional acts of worship, one must conclude that the anchoress' liturgical day was a crowded one" (p. 36). See the Introduction (pp. 8–9) for a reconstructed itinerary.

Many scholars have attempted to match the liturgical practices outlined here to those of a particular order and thus narrow the search for the author. See the Introduction (pp. 11 ff.) for a summary of the various theories.

The best guide to the details of Part One is Ackerman and Dahood's edition, *Ancrene Riwle: Introduction and Part I*, along with Dahood's later article "Design in Part I of *Ancrene Riwle*." For more information on the origin or use of particular prayers, hymns, psalms, etc. in Part One, see especially the former. Barbara Raw's article, "The Prayers and Devotions of the *Ancrene Wisse*," in *Chaucer and the Middle Ages: Studies in Honour of Rossell Hope Robbins*, ed. Beryl Rowland (London: Allen & Unwin, 1974), pp. 260–71, is also useful in that it reveals the influence of late Anglo-Saxon liturgical practice.

2–3   As Ackerman and Dahood note, making the sign of the Cross and invoking the Trinity after awaking was an "established monastic custom" (p. 92n1).

13   *hehe weoved*. The anchoress could see the high altar through her "church-window," that is the slit or "squint" pointed towards the altar in the church. See 2.259–61 for a reference to this window.

49   In "The Liturgical Day in *Ancrene Riwle*," Ackerman takes the scattered instructions about such things as kneelings as evidence that the anchoresses had not gone through a novitiate and thus were not nuns: "explicit directions about kneeling, beating the breast, signing oneself with the cross, and the like are the best evidence that the original anchoresses were without liturgical training" (p. 739).

74   *hire ures*. These "hours" refer to the Little Office of the Virgin and represent the core of the liturgical day (see the headnote to Part One).

88 ff.   This paragraph describes how the anchoresses are to say the Office of the Dead, which begins with the antiphon, *Placebo Domino in regione vivorum* ("I shall please the Lord in the land of the living").

95   *efter the suffragies of uht-song seggeth commendaciun*. Ackerman and Dahood explain: "Suffrages are prayers intercessory in nature and may include prayers for the souls of the dead. Commendations are prayers for the dead at burials and commemorative services which usually end *Tibi, Domine, commendamus*" (p. 96n41).

99   *letanie*. The Litany consists of a series of prayers and invocations to various saints. Though part of the public liturgy of the mass, it became very popular in private devotions as well.

127   *fif wunden*. The Five Wounds of Christ as well as the Five Joys of Mary (see Explanatory Note to 1.232) became stock motifs in literature and art by the late Middle Ages (see Ackerman and Dahood, p. 97n55).

134   *seove yiftes of the Hali Gast*. Ackerman points out that this series of prayers is "based on number symbolism" ("The Liturgical Day," p. 737): the *five* wounds of Christ, the *seven* gifts of the Holy Spirit, the prayer about the *ten* commandments, etc.

232   Here begin a series of five prayers based on the Five Joys of Mary, which describe the joy of the Virgin at five key events: 1) the Annunciation, 2) the Nativity, 3) the

426

Resurrection, 4) the Ascension, and 5) the Assumption (of the Virgin into heaven). The subject was often treated in English lyrics — see, for example, the six poems in the section entitled "The Joys of Mary" in Karen Saupe's edition *Middle English Marian Lyrics* (Kalamazoo, MI: Medieval Institute Publications, 1998), pp. 137–46. Ackerman and Dahood note that the "theme of five joys was especially popular in England in contrast to the seven joys figuring in works originating on the Continent. Later, fifteen and even twenty-five joys were distinguished" (p. 100n100). These prayers must have been well known to either the scribe or intended readers of the Corpus version since they are heavily abbreviated, often with a single letter standing for an entire word (a practice unusual for this scribe): for example, line 1.255 appears in the MS as "Leafdi seinte Ma. for þe il. m. b. þet tu h. þa þu sehe. . . . "

305–06 *the fif leattres of ure Leafdis nome*. A series of five biblical verses which spell out the name *M-A-R-I-A* with their first letters: the canticle *Magnificat* (from Luke 1:46–55), *Ad Dominum cum tribularer* (Psalm 119:1), *Retribuo servo tuo* (Psalm 118:17), *In convertendo* (Psalm 125:1), and *Ad te levavi* (Psalm 122:1) (Ackerman and Dahood, p. 102n120).

360 A "✚" appears in the MS where the anchoresses are to make the sign of the Cross.

Part Two

Part Two is in some ways the most complex section of *AW*: it moves by a logic that is not always obvious. In general, this section deals with the guarding of the five senses, each of which is treated in sequence, but this description alone is inadequate to understand some of its sharper twists and turns. In fact, Part Two conceives of the senses not only in terms of the traditional five (sight, hearing, smell, taste, and touch), but re-imagines them as sites on the body (eyes, ears, nose, mouth, and hands), and this can make for complications when, for example, the mouth is conceived of as the site not only of the sense of taste but also of speech. In "The Five Wits and Their Structural Significance in Part II of *Ancrene Wisse*," Alexandra Barratt links this tendency to mix the senses with the organs that produce them to penitential treatises and formulas of the late twelfth and early thirteenth centuries (pp. 19–20). It is almost as if the body parts associated with the five senses function as a sort of mnemonic device and organizing principle, in much the same way that the concept of the seven deadly sins helped the penitent to discover or remember sins in the confessional. Both act as a sort of heuristic device.

The controlling image established early on in Part Two by a complex series of comparisons is that of the leaping or escaping heart, and the organs associated with the five senses become dangerous sites because they are the portals through which the heart may leap out or evil leap in.

Much of Part Two is concerned with closing these windows (or at least restricting them as much as possible). Thus, in the midst of some reasonably complex theorizing about sin and how it begins come several practical pieces of advice about the anchoress' window which forms part of the outer rule (in fact, this section is mentioned in Part Eight as a kind of companion piece: see 8.7 ff.) — injunctions against touching hands at the window, for maintaining silence at meals, deciding when and to whom to talk, never talking at the altar window, not swearing, etc. On a deeper level, however, the anchoress' window begins to take on the metaphorical significance of an eye and comes to stand for the dangers of the senses in general. Thus, the practical advice gradually collects a deeper significance. In fact, Part Two touches on almost all the main themes of the entire *AW*, including the idea of the temptation of the senses (Part Four), the best way to make one's confession (Part Five), the value of suffering (Part Six), and Christ as lover (Part Seven).

The main sources for this section, as Savage and Watson point out (p. 347n1), are Gregory the Great's *Pastoral Care, Moral Discourses on Job,* and *Homilies on Ezechiel*, as well as Bernard's *The Steps of Humility and Pride*.

The following outline attempts to draw a reasonably clear picture of the complicated structure of Part Two. For a fuller analysis, the reader should consult the two best commentators on this section, Barratt ("The Five Wits") and Grayson (*Structure and Imagery*, chapter 2).

Outline

Introduction to the Five Senses (2.1–15). Part Two begins with a conventional list of the five senses (2.4–5) and then establishes a central image — that of the fleeing or leaping heart (2.7–15).

Sight/Eyes (2.16–199). Since David's heart leapt through his eye, sight is the first sense to be discussed, with the negative examples of Lucifer, Eve, Dinah, and Bathsheba, followed by advice about who may *see* an anchoress. Sight is dangerous in both the active and passive senses, both in looking and in being seen.

Taste/Mouth (2.200–392). A treatment of speech, not really one of the five senses, follows because it, like taste, is located in the mouth. This section begins with practical instructions about when the anchoress should talk and to whom (to which visitors or spiritual advisors, what to say at confession, etc.) and even when she should *not* talk.

Hearing/Ears (2.393–489). Hearing comes next and is colored by the preceding discussion of active speech. It is dominated by a discussion of evil speech which the anchoress might hear, and includes idle, poisonous (heretical, lying, flattering, and backbiting), and filthy speech.

Inner Senses: The First Three Senses/Organs Together (2.490–651). At this point, instead of proceeding to the next "sense," the author says that he wants to treat these first three (i.e., sight, speech, and hearing) together. The digression which follows is perhaps the most clearly mystical section of *AW*, where the author discusses how inner, spiritual senses compensate for the loss of the outer senses. Jesus appears first as a jealous lover *watching* his beloved (sight), and the section looks forward to Part Seven in that it paints a picture of a spiritual romance with Christ which the outer senses impair. To compensate for the loss of the physical senses, the anchoress receives spiritual sight, spiritual hearing, spiritual speech, and even spiritual taste, culminating in a mystical union with God.

Smell/Nose (2.652–71). Next, the text returns to its analysis of the senses with a discussion of smell, though still very much under the spell of the preceding digression on the spiritual senses: the main emphasis is on the heavenly smells which compensate the anchoress for all the evil smells she has in her anchorhold. Christ also suffered in His sense of smell, and this thought leads to another detour, an extensive discussion of how Christ suffered in the other four senses (2.672–743), though this section actually paints a detailed picture of how Christ suffered in the organs of the senses: His eyes, mouth, tongue, hands, ears. In the context of Christ's sufferings, the fleshly, grouchy, pleasure-loving anchoress seems almost a monstrous creature.

Feeling (2.744–825). Finally, the author comes to discuss the last sense, feeling, and how Christ suffered in this sense more than in the others and then turns with some disgust to abuses of the sense of touch, saying that he would rather see his three charges hung on a gallows than exchange a fleshly kiss with a man or touch a man's hands through her window, etc. (2.809–11). Instead, the anchoress should in a sense crucify her body with sufferings which mirror Christ's sufferings.

2   *Omni custodia serva cor tuum.* Bernard cites this verse at the beginning of his discussion of pride and the steps that lead up to it in *The Steps of Humility and Pride.* See Explanatory Note to 2.52.

7   *The heorte is a ful wilde beast.* Savage and Watson note that the "instability of the heart was a favorite theme with twelfth-century spiritual writers" and offer Baldwin of Ford's similar treatment of a slippery and greasy heart which eludes the grasp of its owner (p. 347n2).

        Seint Gregoire. Pope Gregory the Great (c. 540–604) is one of the most frequently cited authors in *AW*, which quotes extensively from his *Pastoral Care* (a handbook on the duties of bishops), *Moral Discourses on Job* (a running commentary on the book of Job), and *Dialogues* (a collection of miracles, anecdotes, and sayings of various Italian saints).

11   In some modern Bibles, the two books of Samuel are called I and II Kings, while I and II Kings become III and IV Kings.

16–17   *Alle beon ha lutle, the parlurs least ant nearewest.* It is not exactly clear what *parlur* means here and in 2.29. As the MED points out, the word can refer either to a separate room or to a simple grate set in a wall (see glossary) — both reserved for consultation and talking (see OF *parler* "to talk"). Though the MED suggests that *parlur* refers to a grate in *AW*, the syntax of this sentence, which describes the "parlor's window," makes sense only if the *parlur* is a separate chamber since the "grate's window" is difficult to understand. For a discussion of the architectural arrangements of the anchorhold, see the Introduction (pp. 9 ff.).

52   *Low, hu Hali Writ speketh.* As Savage and Watson explain, much of this section is based on Bernard's early work, *The Steps of Humility and Pride* (p. 349n8). Bernard imagines the ascent to pride as a ladder with a number of rungs or steps, the first being curiosity. Under this heading, he treats the sins of Satan, Eve, and Dinah, as well as those who follow after goats (see 2.601 ff.). For an English version of Bernard's text, see M. Ambrose Conway's translation. Barratt notes that Adam of Dryburgh (a Carthusian) has a similar treatment of Dinah ("Anchoritic Aspects," p. 43).

63 ff.   *Eve, thi moder, leop efter hire ehnen.* R. E. Kaske connects this series of leaps to the medieval exegesis of Song of Songs 2:8 (where the bridegroom leaps on mountains), a passage expounded on at some length in 6.392 ff. Kaske believes that the questionable humor and "surface inconsequentiality" (p. 23) of Eve's leaps are redeemed by the ironic reference to the Song of Songs. However, Eve's leaps seem to fit logically into a series of leaps or falls caused by sight (an important metaphor in Part Two).

67   *of lutel muchel waxeth.* Proverbial. See B. J. Whiting's *Proverbs, Sentences and Proverbial Phrases*, L402.

70 ff.   Elizabeth Robertson analyzes this interpretation of Dinah, observing that it tends to de-emphasize matters of theological theory and stress the practical ("The Rule of the Body," pp. 118 ff.).

97   *o wepmen, ah.* At this point, two leaves are missing from the Corpus MS. See the textual note to this line for a fuller explanation.

99 ff.   Concerning the interpretation of the pit (see Exodus 21:33–34), Savage and Watson observe that the infuriating sexism which modern readers may detect in this passage (that is, that sin is "always the woman's fault") is somewhat blunted by the fact that "male responsibility is mostly irrelevant here — though it is dealt with satirically in the next paragraph" (p. 349n13).

119–20 *Hund wule in bluthelich hwar-se he fint open.* Proverbial. See Whiting, H568.

128 ff. *lecheries prickes.* Millett (*Hali Meiðhad*, pp. 230–31) traces the imagery of lechery's arrows to Hugh of Folieto's *De Claustro Animae* ("On the Enclosed Spirit") I.4 (*PL* 176, cols. 1026–27). Savage and Watson believe that the rest of the paragraph may depend on Hugh as well (p. 350n17).

161 *Ore pur ceo.* See the Textual Note to this line.

178 ff. There are some general resemblances between *AW*'s warnings about seeing men and Aelred's discussion of whom an anchoress should or should not see — both, for example, refer to the anchoress who refused to allow St. Martin to see her. Aelred writes, "Let me now indicate the people to whom you may speak. Happy is the recluse who is unwilling to see or speak with a man, who has never admitted Martin. . . . Never must she let him touch or stroke her hand, for the evil within our bodies is always to be feared; it can so often arouse and unman even the oldest. Never must there be any reference to thinness of face and arms or roughness of skin, lest in seeking a remedy you run a greater risk. . . . Avoid all conversation with young men or with people of doubtful character; never permit them to speak to you unless there is a real need and then only in the presence of the priest who is acting as your spiritual father. And, without his permission and express command, you should not speak to chance comers except it be a bishop, abbot, or well-known prior" (chapters 6–7, p. 52). Savage and Watson (pp. 350–51n21) think that the more immediate source is Sulpicius Severus' *Dialogues* 2.12 (*PL* 22, cols. 209–10).

223–24 *cave deovel.* Literally, this phrase could either mean "impudent devil" or "crow-devil," or perhaps both by way of a pun on *cave* (from OE *caf* "bold") and *kaue* "crow, jackdaw" (from OF *cauwe*), a distinct possibility since the MS uses *u* for both *u* and *v* and so represents these words as *caue* and *kaue*. Diensberg ("*Ancrene Wisse/Riwle*," p. 80), arguing for "crow-devil," cites the later *dogge-deovel* (4.1385) as a parallel.

234 *Worltliche leveth lut.* Baldwin ("Some Difficult Words," p. 285) argues that the author is thinking not so much of worldly people in general as secular clergy — i.e., priests. Religious are monks or friars in orders.

236 The admiring mention of the Dominicans and Franciscans is an addition to the original text and strongly suggests that *AW* was written at some point not long after the arrival of the friars (the Dominicans arrived in England in 1221, the Franciscans in 1224). The enthusiasm for the friars, who took a leading role in the new penitential system as

confessors, gave way quickly to cynicism. See Penn Szittya's *The Antifraternal Tradition in Medieval Literature*. For another added reference to the friars, see 8.66.

237   *wende ehe towart te wude lehe*. See Explanatory Note to 2.569–70.

248 ff.   Aelred also recommends that interviews with men be witnessed by a third party: "If someone well-known and held in high esteem — an abbot perhaps or a prior — should wish to speak to you, he should only do so in the presence of a third person" (chapter 7, p. 52).

269   Aelred's guidelines for silence are considerably more strict: "From Easter until the Exaltation of the Holy Cross she should observe silence from compline until dawn. When the office of prime has been said she may speak with her attendant; if there are visitors with whom she should speak she may do so between none and vespers. After vespers she may again make whatever arrangements are necessary with her attendants until collation" (chapter 9, p. 54).

310   *Vitas Patrum. The Lives of the Desert Fathers* (see *PL* 73–74) was a very popular compilation of several originally separate texts (saints' lives, monastic histories, collections of sayings, etc.), almost all of which were translated from Greek into Latin. The *AW* author has a particular fondness for a section called the *Verba Seniorum* ("The Sayings of the Elders" — books 3–7 of the *Vitas Patrum*, *PL* 73, cols. 739 ff.) which is organized by theme in the Latin version though alphabetized by name of the speaker in the Greek. For a partial translation of the Latin text, see Helen Waddell's *The Desert Fathers* (London: Constable, 1960). Benedicta Ward's *The Sayings of the Desert Fathers* is a translation of the Greek text which served as the basis of the *Verba Seniorum*. Similarly, Norman Russell's *The Lives of the Desert Fathers* is a translation of the Greek text of the *History of the Monks in Egypt* (Book 2 of the Latin *Vitas Patrum* — see *PL* 73, cols. 707 ff.). In an important sense, the title *The Lives of the Desert Fathers* is misleading since the stories and sayings of the desert mothers are also recounted. Though the *Vitas Patrum* might seem to be particularly appropriate for recluses (and indeed it is), it is important to realize that the collection was known from Anglo-Saxon times and was used extensively in popular preaching. In fact, it served as an early exempla collection before the rapid multiplication of such reference works in the early thirteenth century. See J. Welter's *L'Exemplum dans la littérature religieuse et didactique du moyen âge* (pp. 14 ff.).

352 ff.   For an account of the birth of John the Baptist, see Luke 1:39 ff.

361   *Ypallage.* As noted in the gloss, *ypallage* refers to a kind of chiasmus in which two elements are reversed. In the following translation of this verse, the *AW* author exchanges "protect my ways" and "hold my tongue" so that in the next clause they read "hold my way" and "protect my tongue."

374   *hope is a swete spice.* Barratt thinks that there may be "a Latin pun on *spes* 'hope' and *species* 'spices': 'hope is a sweet spice' would be a fairly close translation of 'species, id est spes,' which might suggest the use of a *distinctio* collection" ("The Five Wits," p. 24n42). Barratt traces other motifs in this section of Part Two — see her careful notes in "The Five Wits." For more on *distinctiones*, see Explanatory Note to Pref.131.

403   *with scharpe sneateres.* See Cecily Clark's article, "'Wið Scharpe Sneateres': Some Aspects of Colloquialism in 'Ancrene Wisse,'" which argues that *AW* as well as medieval sermons may preserve something like real colloquial speech in simulated dialogues. It is in fact very difficult to give the full colloquial force of *sneateres*, translated in the bottom glosses as "sharp murmurings" (see the gloss as well as the glossary).

420 ff.   Barratt notes that in *De Naturis Rerum* Alexander Neckham describes how crows eat corpses, though the allegorical interpretation of this fact is different ("The Five Wits," p. 24n46). Interestingly, though, Neckham does devote two consecutive paragraphs to flatterers (*de adulatoribus*) and backbiters (*de detractoribus*) (Wright, pp. 111, 316–21).

430–33 *Ne videatur . . . tristis linguam detrahentem.* The author drops into Latin to describe a possibly distasteful interpretation (a practice followed well into the twentieth century by editors of the classics). This excerpt welds together biblical verses with glosses, probably from the *Glossa Ordinaria* (see Explanatory Note to 6.126) or Isidore's *Etymologies.* Savage and Watson note that the "method of interpretation here, which may seem strained, involves translating (often mistakenly) the Hebrew names in a passage and then building a tropological (moral) commentary on the result (in this case, loosely)" (p. 354n50).

464 ff.   *Bac-biteres, the biteth bihinde bac othre.* This passage, as Savage and Watson point out (p. 354n54), is based on Bernard's widely known *Sermons on the Song of Songs* 24 (*PL* 183, col. 869).

483 ff.   Compare Aelred: "They think it enough to confine the body behind walls; while the mind roams at random, grows dissolute and distracted by cares, disquieted by impure desires. The tongue too runs about all day through towns and villages, market-place and

square, prying into other people's lives and behavior and into such affairs as are not only idle but often shameful. How seldom nowadays will you find a recluse alone. At her window will be seated some garrulous old gossip pouring idle tales into her ears, feeding her with scandal and gossip" (chapter 2, p. 46). For a similar complaint, see Jerome's letter to Eustochius (chapter 2, p. 22).

485   *rikelot*. It seems easiest to derive this word from medieval Latin *rikelota* "magpie" (see R. E. Latham, ed., *Revised Medieval Latin Word-List from British and Irish Sources*). Zettersten discusses several possibilities for the word's origin but finally derives it from OF *rik-*, an imitative root for "chatter" and *-ote*, a double diminutive suffix, found also in *gigelot* (see glossary). This derivation, if correct, explains why *rikelota* could come to mean "magpie," a chattering bird. Zettersten would define *AW*'s *rikelot* as "a chattering woman," a translation of Aelred's *nugigerula mulier* "garrulous old gossip" (*Middle English Word Studies*, pp. 13–15). See Explanatory Note to 2.483 ff.

485–86 *"From mulne ant from chepinge, from smiththe ant from ancre-hus me tidinge bringeth."* Proverbial. See Whiting, M552.

520 ff. For further notes on the intellectual sources and background of the following passage, see Savage and Watson (pp. 355 ff.).

569–70 *"eaver is the ehe to the wude lehe."* Apparently a fragment of a popular song or poem which also occurs in 2.237 — the Latin version quotes the phrase in English: "Iuxta illud Anglice: Euere is þe eye to þe wode lye" (D'Evelyn, p. 28), and the Nero version adds a second verse: "þerinne is þet ich luuie" (wherein is what I love). In his collection of fables, Odo of Cheriton (d. 1247) cites a similar phrase to describe corrupt clergy — even though a wolf were hooded as a priest, "evere beth his geres to the grove-ward" (his inclinations are always [tending] toward the [wild] grove). See Whiting's review of Carleton Brown's *English Lyrics of the Thirteenth Century* (p. 219), Zettersten (*Studies*, p. 198), as well as Whiting, E207. There are some intriguing clues about this song in Cleo., where Scribe A has interlarded (at random intervals and apparently with no sense for the meaning of the existing text) several metrical snatches. A bit like Dr. Franken-stein, Dobson stitches these fragments together and animates them: "I incline to think that the three additions in C[leo.], and the Nero addition . . . are fragments of a humorous poem describing a woman thinking of an assignation in a woodland clearing (to which, perhaps, she had on a former occasion followed a lame he-goat and there met a lover, possibly an outlaw) while attempting to do household accounts; her excuse to get out of the house; and a discovery *in flagrante delicto*" (*Origins*, p. 77).

> Eauer is þe ehe to þe wudelehe,
> Ant þe halte bucke climbeð þeruppe
> Twa ant þreo, hu feole beoð þeo?
> Þreo halpenes makeð a peni — amen . . .
> Eauer is þe ehe to þe wudelehe,
> Þerinne is þet ich luuie.
>
> — — —
>
> Ant swa ich habbe a nede ernde
> Dun in þe tun; þah hit reine arewen,
> Ich habbe a nede ernde.
>
> — — —
>
> Lokede blind hors, ant wudemonnes ehe
> Orn al ut. (Dobson, *The English Text*, p. 77)

["The eye (i.e., my eye) always [glances] to the woodland clearing/ and the lame buck (i.e., he-goat) climbs up there./ Two and three, how many are they?/ Three ha'pennies make a penny — Amen . . . /My eye is always [glancing] at the woodland clearing/ wherein is what I love. . . . / And so I have an urgent errand/ Down in the town, though it rain arrows (i.e., even though there may be serious obstacles, I must go there),/ I have an urgent errand. . . . / A blind horse looked, and a woodman's eyes popped right out" (presumably as they catch the lovers in the act).]

It is difficult to know what to make of Dobson's perhaps overingenious reconstruction, but it does seem likely that the fragments in Cleo. are from some kind of poem or popular song, perhaps from several. All that can be said for certain is that the phrase cited in Corpus "The eye is always [glancing] to the woodland clearing" must mean something like "The eye always looks longingly towards forbidden pleasures."

599   The following interpretation of Song of Songs 1:7 is largely dependent on Bernard. See Explanatory Note to 2.52.

617   *totilde ancre*. Literally, this phrase translates as "peeperess anchorite" (i.e., a female peeper) since *totilde* comes from *totin* "to peep" and *-ild* (feminine doer).

691–94   *Muchel hofles hit is . . . the worlde*. The Corpus version adds this passage.

712 ff.   For sources and analogues to the images and comparisons within this passage, see Savage and Watson's helpful notes (pp. 358 ff.).

435

786   *blodletunge*. See 8.170–74, which describes how those who have had blood let should be treated.

801 ff. Dobson points out that the *Moralities on the Gospels* (pp. 131–32), in its discussion of Christ's sufferings, comments on the particular tenderness of Christ's flesh.

815 ff. *Ha schulden schrapien euche dei the eorthe up of hare put.* Savage and Watson comment, "The grave dug in the anchorhouse floor here is of course metaphorical, part of the complex of images in which the anchorhouse is itself seen as a grave. The ending of part II is harsh to an extent that has sometimes occasioned disapproving comment. But for the author of *Ancrene Wisse* the sins associated with touch, especially lechery, can only be dealt with in crude terms, sufficient to make the body flinch from them" (p. 359n89).

Part Three

This section likens the anchoress to various birds, as the author's outline states (Pref.139–40). Before Part Three progresses very far, however, it is easy to see that the comparison to birds is only part of a much more complex approach which deploys a variety of images (drawn broadly from the natural and human worlds) as well as a number of exempla (from the Old Testament in particular). Popular preaching often used bestiary lore, properly allegorized, to drive home a point, though the effect here is far from simple: it would be a mistake to reduce this section to a simple working out of the phrase "Of dumbe beastes leorne wisdom ant lare" (3.191). James Maybury ("On the Structure and Significance of Part III of the *Ancrene Riwle*") believes that Part Three is based on an extended exegesis of Psalm 101:7–8: "I am like the pelican of the desert [lit., solitary places], I am become like an owl in the midst of ruins. I lie awake and moan, like a bird [lit., sparrow] all alone on the housetop." Maybury's article gives a detailed picture of how Part Three agrees with or departs from the standard Psalm commentaries and the *Physiologus* and bestiary traditions. As Savage and Watson note (pp. 359–60n1) the principal sources for this section are Guigo's *Consuetudines*, Gregory's *Moral Discourses on Job* and *Homilies on the Gospels* as well as a number of allegorized bestiaries and books on nature, including Alexander Neckham's *On the Natures of Things*, perhaps Isidore of Seville's *Etymologies* and Hugh of Folieto's *On Birds* (see the notes below). Interested readers should refer to Savage and Watson's detailed source notes.

The main theme of Part Three centers on the necessity, theory, and practice of the inward, solitary life. Like Part Two, Part Three's structure is by and large associational and often driven by a complex web of images and comparisons, many drawn from the world of the bestiaries. Grayson believes that the main theme of Part Three is the "regulation of the inner feelings," complementing Part Two, which outlines the regulation of the outward senses (p. 57). Perhaps one could also say that Part Three shows the anchoress how to guard, hide, and enclose the inner life sketched out near the end of Part Two (2.490–651).

Outline

Wrath and its remedies (3.1–108). Part Three opens with a discussion of wrath and its remedies: the wrathful or petulant anchoress is like the pelican or she-wolf and can only cure her wrath by realizing that insulting words are mere puffs of wind. Thus, the beginning points back to Part Two's warnings about listening to hurtful speech (2.393–489) but ahead to Part Four's discussion of wrath and its remedies (4.847–969), where wrath is singled out as the main enemy of life in a religious community. On another level, wrath indicates that the anchoress' heart is pointed outwards, and the shape of Part Three, like that of Part Two, is to start with the outer and move ever deeper to the inner. Grayson notes that "Anger dominates the chapter because it is inimical to love," the key component of an anchoress' inner life (p. 57).

True and False Bodies (3.109–230). Next, the discussion turns to various types of false and true anchoresses based on their attitude towards the body and the anchorhold (as intertwined concepts): false anchoresses are like ravenous foxes, filthy Saul, over-fed ostriches, fat calves, etc., while good anchoresses are like lean birds in their upward flight and their pausing only briefly on the earth, their anchorholds like nests. The emphasis in this section is on bodies — how they should be kept disciplined and lean, not allowed to grow fat in pleasure.

Linking of Soul and Body (3.231–64). Now the discussion turns to what we might call the mystery of soul and body — why such an exalted thing as the soul is tied to the dead clump of the body.

Taming the Body (3.265–308). The anchoress must tame her body and chant through the night like the night bird since such discipline benefits the entire church through the efficacy of her prayers. Holding vigils and remaining vigilant (like both the nightbird and the sparrow) is another discipline, and eight reasons to stay awake follow (lines 290–308).

Hiding in the Anchorhold (3.309–83). Like Esther, the true anchoress remains hidden in the anchorhold (another characteristic of the night bird), and this section shows the danger of revealing an anchoress' inner life through a series of images (the fig tree, shouting peddlers, etc.) and exempla (Moses' hand).

The Importance of the Solitary Life (3.384–626). This core argument of Part Three is built carefully, starting with the idea of the solitary sparrow and moving on to a series of exempla from the Old and New Testaments, how figures like Isaac, Moses, Elijah, Jeremiah, John the Baptist, and even Christ himself sought solitude. After the exempla come eight reasons to pursue the solitary life (3.504–626): [1] safety, [2] preservation of virginity, [3] the reward of heaven, [4] proof of nobility, [5] proof of generosity, [6] intimacy with the Lord, [7] brightness of spirit, and

[8] swiftness of prayer. No anchoress should, like Shimei or the foolish thief, wish to venture out from her refuge (3.583–626).

The Falling Sickness — a Link to Part Four (3.627–40). This last section points out that besides living solitary lives, sparrows have the tendency to suffer from the falling sickness, and so the anchoress will suffer from various bodily illnesses and temptations which cause her to "fall" into humility. These tame her flesh and humble her, so that she will not fall further into pride.

5 ff. In the bestiaries and Psalm commentaries, the pelican usually stands for Christ, whose dead chicks (the lost) are revived by the blood of his crucifixion. Maybury, however, points out that at least two naturalist writers allegorize the pelican in a way similar to *AW*: Hugh of Folieto in his *De Avibus* ("On Birds," *PL* 177, cols. 29–30) and Alexander Neckham in *De Naturis Rerum* ("On the Natures of Things"). The latter parallel is close enough in wording, Maybury believes, to be a direct source for this passage in *AW*: "The nature (of the pelican) in these things represents a man who kills his good works through sins, who afterwards led to penance, rejects the adornment of clothing, and crucifying himself, expresses great inner sadness with sighs. His heart opens in confession, and by the heat of love the works which were done before in charity come back to life" (as cited by Wright, p. 119). See T. H. White's *A Book of Beasts* for an accessible translation of an important Latin bestiary produced in twelfth-century England.

32 *Ira furor brevis est.* As Savage and Watson note, the Latin version of *AW* adds a further quotation from Gregory's *Moral Discourses on Job*, both here and at 3.61–62 (p. 361nn9 and 13)

50 *hwet is word bute wind?* Dobson points to a similar passage in *Moralities on the Gospels* (p. 134): "For a word is nothing but a certain wind. Therefore whoever topples angry at any word shows himself (or, herself) to be very weak indeed."

55 *Seint Andrew.* The Apostle Andrew, son of a fisherman and brother to St. Peter, was, according to tradition, crucified on an x-shaped cross. Peter himself is said to have been crucified upside-down in Rome.

57 *Sein Lorenz.* St. Lawrence (d. 258) was one of the deacons of Rome during a time of terrible persecution under the emperor Decius. He was martyred on a red-hot griddle, but before he died, he answered the mockings of Decius with the famous phrase, "Look, wretch, you have me well done on one side, turn me over and eat!" (Ryan, *Golden Legend*, vol. 2, p. 67).

57–58 *Seinte Stefne.* Stephen (martyred c. 35), a charismatic preacher active in the earliest days of the church, was killed by stoning and thus became the first martyr of the Christian church. His story is told in Acts 6–7.

64 *the hali mon i Vitas Patrum.* See *The Lives of the Desert Fathers* 7.3 (*PL* 73, col. 1029).

78 *for thear as muche fur is, hit waxeth with winde.* Proverbial. See Whiting, F191.

101 *Eft upon other half, pellican . . . is aa leane.* Compare Alexander Neckham's description in *De Naturis Rerum* ("On the Natures of Things"): "Indeed this bird is lean; thus, the penitent person should vex (or, make lean) his or her body" (Wright, p. 119). See also Hugh of Folieto's *On Birds* (*PL* 177, col. 30).

111–12 *The foxes beoth false ancres, ase fox is beast falsest.* The following comparison of anchoresses to foxes relies on Hugh of Folieto's *On Beasts and Birds,* 2.7 (*PL* 177, col. 59).

122 *as dude Saul into hole.* As Savage and Watson (p. 362n20) explain, Saul is linked to the preceding account of foxes through the hole (which can be either a hole in the ground or a cave — see the glossary). This hole symbolizes the anchorhold.

150 *spreadeth hare wengen ant makieth creoiz of ham-seolf.* Dobson points to a similar passage in *Moralities on the Gospels* (p. 134).

153 *The strucion.* As Maybury points out, the ridiculous spectacle of the plump ostrich flapping its wings furiously, pretending to fly, may come from Gregory the Great's *Moral Discourses on Job* (39.13), where the ostrich becomes a symbol for the hypocrite (p. 98). But Alexander Neckham also uses the ostrich to symbolize the hypocrite: "This bird flies low and briefly although it is equipped with wings. To all appearances it is capable of high flight. [The ostrich], indeed, represents the hypocrite, who although he or she puts forward the face of a contemplative person, nevertheless refrains from spiritual flight" (Wright, p. 101). As Dobson points out, the ostrich is also a symbol for the hypocrite in *Moralities on the Gospels* (p. 135). See also Hugh of Folieto's *On Birds* 1.27 (*PL* 177, cols. 35–39).

178 *fortitudinem meam.* Savage and Watson note that this verse "is often cited as a proof of the need to exercise discretion in self-mortification" (p. 363n29).

192 ff.   *"achate" hatte.* In medieval lore, gemstones were thought to have a number of medicinal and quasi-magical properties. Information about such stones was collected in books called *lapidaries*. The agate in particular was thought to act as an antidote to snake venom. Dobson points to a passage in *Moralities on the Gospels* in which an eagle carries an agate stone for a similar purpose (p. 136). For a history of medieval lapidaries, see Joan Evans' *Magical Jewels of the Middle Ages and the Renaissance*.

225   *Salt bitacneth wisdom.* See Colossians 4:6.

256–57 *curre is kene on his ahne mixne.* Proverbial. See Whiting, H567.

265 ff.   *The niht-fuhel.* In bestiaries, the *nictorax* is usually, but not always, identified with the owl. Maybury thinks that its treatment here is "basically in accord with much traditional exegesis of Psalm ci.7" (pp. 98–99).

272 ff.   As Savage and Watson explain, "there is a dynamic opposition between two principles: while the holiness of anchoresses gives stability to the whole church, it is nonetheless of vital importance that it be concealed from everyone, or else it ceases to be holiness" (p. 364n39).

279–80 The characteristics of the sparrow are allegorized here as well as in 3.384–89 and 3.627 ff. See Explanatory Note to 3.627 ff.

290 ff.   Most of the eight reasons to stay awake are also treated in *Sawles Warde* (see Savage and Watson, p. 365n43).

296–97 The author of *AW* certainly knew Anselm's *Meditation* 1, a terrifying contemplation of hell and final judgment designed as Anselm says "to stir up fear." Further excerpts from this meditation appear in 5.70–73, 5.267–69, and 5.429 ff. For a full text in English, see *The Prayers and Meditations of Saint Anselm*, translated by Benedicta Ward, pp. 221–24.

330   *Moyseses hond.* Dobson points to a similar treatment in *Moralities on the Gospels* (p. 137).

340 ff.   The allegory of the fig tree is based in part on Joel 1:7, but also on Matthew 21:18–22, where Christ curses a fruitless fig tree and it withers on the spot. As Maybury suggests (p. 99), the specific application here may depend on Gregory the Great's *Moral Discourses on Job* (chapter 8).

371 *A sapere the ne bereth bute sape ant nelden yeiyeth hehe thet he bereth.* This comparison is based ultimately on a famous passage from the tenth satire of Juvenal (line 22), as Savage and Watson point out (p. 366n51).

391 ff. The following discussion on the importance of the solitary life seems to be freely adapted from Guigo's *Consuetudines* — see Barratt, "Anchoritic Aspects" (pp. 46–53) for a detailed comparison. Guigo's work (c. 1128) codifies the practices of the Carthusians, and may demonstrate how Carthusian customs influenced those of the Augustinians and, in turn, the Dominicans.

406 *Bi Moysen ant bi Helye.* For the stories of Moses, see Exodus chapters 3–4 and 19, and for Elijah see 1 Kings 19. Savage and Watson comment: "It is notable that [the author] assumes the anchoresses will 'hear' of these stories rather than reading them for themselves; they do not, in other words, have personal access to a Bible" (p. 367n58).

489–90 *Pawel ant Antonie, Hylariun ant Benedict, Sincletice ant Sare.* With the exception of Benedict, these saints were recluses and hermits of the Egyptian desert (see Explanatory Note to Pref.99–101).

Hilarion (c. 291–371), a Palestinian educated in Alexandria, became the companion of St. Anthony. Later he returned to Gaza and took up a hermitage near Majuma. Distracted by the admiring people clamoring to see him, Hilarion fled first to Egypt, then Sicily, Dalmatia, and Cyprus — each time he was found out and the faithful began to flock around him.

St. Benedict (c. 480–547), the founder of the Benedictine order, is included here because he lived for a time as a hermit in a cave near Subiaco. He emerged reluctantly from his solitude to become abbot of the monastery in Vicovaro, where his prescriptions were so strict that the monks there tried to poison him.

For the other saints listed here, see Explanatory Note to Pref.99–101.

496–99 The anecdote about St. Arsenius comes from a part of *The Lives of the Desert Fathers* known as *The Sayings of the Elders* 3.190 (*PL* 73, col. 801): "Having withdrawn to the solitary life he made the same prayer again and he heard a voice saying to him, 'Arsenius, flee, be silent, pray always, for these are the source of sinlessness'" (Ward, p. 9).

504–05 *Yef a wod liun urne yont te strete, nalde the wise bitunen hire sone?* Dobson points to a similar story about a dangerous lion in *Moralities on the Gospels* (pp. 139–40).

511–12 *The other reisun is . . . bute ha fol were?* Compare Aelred, "Bear in mind always what a precious treasure you bear in how fragile a vessel and what a reward, what glory, what a crown the preservation of your virginity will bring you" (chapter 14, p. 63).

524 *Virginem virgini commendavit.* See Bede's *Retractatio in actus apostolorum* ("Reconsideration of the Acts of the Apostles") 8.72, where this phrase applies to the entrusting of the Virgin to the virginal John.

546 ff. The word *relef* "donation" is understood here in its etymological sense as "something left behind."

566 *as is i-seid th'ruppe.* See 2.541–50.

601 *the ethele fif wittes.* Savage and Watson note, "As part III draws to a close, themes from part II, to which this part has been a companion-piece, are deliberately reintroduced" (p. 368n78).

627 ff. *Spearewe haveth yet a cunde.* Maybury writes, "The three symbolic characteristics of the sparrow discussed in the *Riwle* are its watchfulness, its solitariness, and its humility. The first two are considered to some extent in traditional interpretations of Psalm ci.8, but the third is not" (pp. 99–100). The general meaning of this third comparison, bizarre as it may be, is clear enough: the anchoress should be like the sparrow, which as people say, has the "falling sickness" (3.638–39) — that is, the anchoress should let herself fall into low humility in the same way that sparrows fall sick or dead to the ground. The "falling sickness," the medieval term for epilepsy, may refer to some actual disease of sparrows which caused them to drop from the sky. Alexander Neckham (*De Naturis Rerum*) says of the sparrow that "this bird is frequently vexed by epileptic sickness (*morbo epilemtico*)," and this may be a folk belief since he goes on to say "what is known to the common folk I do not blush to commit to writing, provided that I may guide the morals of my reader" (Wright, p. 109).

Part Four

The structure of Part Four, by far the longest section of *AW*, is much more straightforward than the preceding sections, however intricate the subdivisions may be. The author keeps the focus squarely on temptations, with the lion's share of the attention going to the inner temptations: the seven deadly sins, the comforts, and finally the remedies for them.

In his study of the seven deadly sins, Morton Bloomfield points out that *AW* follows the Gregorian order (with pride at the beginning and gluttony and lechery at the end) rather than the earlier monastic ordering (codified in Cassian's listing of the eight deadly sins): gluttony, fornication, greed, wrath, despair, sloth, vainglory, and finally pride (pp. 69, 72, 150). Cassian does exert some influence on Part Four, however: in the *Institutes*, he discusses the remedies for each of the deadly sins, and in the *Collationes* or "Conferences" (chapter 16), he traces the offspring or children of each sin. Cassian's writings exerted a strong influence throughout the Middle Ages, particularly on monastic writers. Bloomfield also identifies *AW* as the first text in English which portrays the sins as animals (p. 151). For an index of other associations between the sins and animals see Bloomfield's Appendix I (pp. 245–49). See also Siegfried Wenzel's "The Seven Deadly Sins: Some Problems of Research," *Speculum* 43 (1968), 1–22.

In some ways, Part Four hangs closely together with Parts Five and Six since the seven deadly sins were often used as a mnemonic device to organize confession (see 5.415–19 for an explicit statement of this idea) — in fact, Parts Four, Five, and Six might be said to form a miniature treatise on penance. J. H. Gray goes so far as to say that Parts Four and Five did not originally belong to *AW* but were excerpted from a separate treatise on penance, an idea that Linda Georgianna (*The Solitary Self*, p. 120) rightly rejects.

It may also be significant that late twelfth-century preachers' manuals often included an extensive treatment of the seven deadly sins. Alan of Lille's treatise on the art of preaching, the *Summa de arte praedicatoria* (*PL* 210, cols. 109–98), for example, contains a series of remedies for each of the seven deadly sins as well as a discussion of the cardinal virtues. The author of *Hali Meiðhad*, a text closely associated with *AW*, may have known and borrowed from Alan's work directly, according to Millett (*Hali Meiðhad*, p. xlvi). Much of the content and method of treatment in Part Four, then, has interesting points of contact with a variety of manuals and preachers' aids, suggesting that in this regard these sections of *AW* are best understood in the context of works like the *Manuel des Pechiez* and *Handlyng Synne*, rather than in the context of mystical writings written for or by women, such as Julian of Norwich's *Divine Showings* or *The Book of Margery Kempe*.

Outline

Introduction (4.1–199). The main division between outer and inner temptations appears here, with further subdivisions, including a brief discussion of how to handle outer temptations (4.55–164), already the subject of Part Two.

Inner Temptations: The Seven Deadly Sins (4.200–471). The rest of Part Four is dedicated to the inner sins, beginning with a detailed list of the seven deadly sins and their offspring

(4.200–401), followed by the comic set-piece of the seven deadly sinners as entertainers in the devil's court (4.402–71).

Theory of Inner Temptation (4.472–591). This section includes a discussion of when temptation is most likely to come (4.472–80), the reasons for and the good that comes from temptation (4.481–512), and goes on to divide temptations into four categories according to how strong and how obvious they are (4.513–81) and warn against their almost endless variations (4.582–91).

Comforts for Inner Temptations (4.592–740). This section lists nine comforts which compensate for the pain of inner temptation (4.592–717) and then describes the rewards for those who stand against the devil's assaults (4.718–40).

Remedies (or Medicines) for Inner Temptations (4.741–1455). Much of this vast section imagines the struggle against temptation as a kind of spiritual warfare, and each of the remedies becomes a weapon with which to fight the devil. The remedies are first listed in a loose outline form (4.741–46) and then discussed in turn: [1] holy meditations and other thoughts and images (4.747–85), [2] continual prayer (4.786–826), [3] hardy faith (or, right thinking) applied against each of the seven deadly sins in turn: pride, envy, wrath (with an extensive discussion of peace and the strength of community as a remedy against wrath), sloth, covetousness, gluttony, and lechery (4.827–1023), followed by a more general discussion of hardy belief as a weapon against the various subtle wiles of the devil, moving to a discussion of the seven deadly sins as serious wounds (4.1024–1191), [4] specific remedies for each of the seven deadly sins in turn: for pride (4.1192–1270), envy (4.1271–88), wrath (4.1289–1319), sloth (4.1320–29), covetousness (4.1330–32), lechery and gluttony (4.1333–57), [5] other weapons to use against the devil (the crucifix, the sign of the cross, devotion to the wounds of Christ, the shield of the passion, tears of penitence) (4.1358–1451), and [6] above all, confession — the subject of Part Five (4.1452–55).

4   *windes of fondunges*. For the idea of temptations as winds, see Gregory, *Moral Discourses on Job* 2.53.76 (*PL* 75, col. 592), etc.

75–76   The comparison of an enemy to a file is paralleled in Peter of Blois' *De XII Utilitatibus Tribulationis* ("On the Twelve Uses of Suffering") (*PL* 207, col. 994), according to Baldwin ("*Ancrene Wisse* and its Background," pp. 186–87).

92–93   *Thet deboneire child . . . cusseth the yerde*. Proverbial. See Whiting, Y3.

164   After *eche blisse*, Corpus omits a long paragraph, preserved in Nero, addressed apparently to the original audience of three sisters. In revising Corpus for a wider readership, the author probably deleted the section because of its personal references.

From it we learn that the sisters were of noble birth, were well provided for by a single male patron or family member, and that they entered their anchorholds at a young age:

> Ye, mine leove sustren, beoth theo ancren thet ich i-knowe thet habbeth lest neode to vrovre ayean theos temptaciuns, bute one of sicnesse. Vor mid more eise ne mid more men[s]ke not ich none ancre thet habbe al thet hire neod is, thene ye threo habbeth, ure Loverd beo hit i-thoncked. Vor ye ne thencheth nowiht of mete, ne of cloð, ne to ou ne to ouwer meidenes. Everich of ou haueth of one vreonde al thet hire is neod. ne therf thet meiden sechen nouther bread ne suvel fur þene et his halle. God hit wot moni other wot lutel of thisse eise, auh beoth ful ofte i-derved mid wone ant mid scheome, ant mid teone. In hire hond yif this cumeth, hit mei beon ham vrovre. Ye muwen more dreden þe nesche dole thene the herde of theos fondunges thet is uttre ihoten. Vor vein wolde þe hexte cwemen ou, yif he muhte mid oluhnunge makien ou ful-itowen, yif ye [MS. heo] nere the hendure. Muche word is of ou, hu gentile wummen ye beoth, for godleic ant for vreoliec i-yirned of monie, and sustren of one veder ant of one moder — ine blostme of ower yuwethe vorheten alle wor[l]des blissen, ant bicomen ancren. (Day, p. 85)

> [You, my dear sisters, are the anchoresses whom I know (i.e., of all those I know) who have the least need of comfort for these temptations, except only for sickness. For I know of no anchoress who may have with more comfort and more honor all that she might need than you three have, our Lord be thanked. For you do not worry (lit., think) about food or about clothing, either for you or for your maidens. Each one of you has all that she needs from one friend, nor does your servant (lit., maiden) need to seek either bread or food (see *suvel* in glossary) further than at his hall. God knows, many others know little of this kind of ease (or, abundance) but are often afflicted with want, with shame, and with hardship. If this [book] comes into their hands, it may be a comfort to them. You must fear the soft more than the hard portion (i.e., share) of these temptations which is called outer. For happily would the devil (lit., sorcerer) please you if he might with flattery make you badly behaved (or perverse), [and this might happen] if you were not cleverer (or, more gracious). There is much talk of you, what noble women you are, sought after for your goodness and generosity, and sisters of one father and one mother — in the blossom of your youth [you] forsook all the world's joys and became anchoresses.]

Another paragraph, also omitted in the Corpus MS but preserved in Nero, warns the anchoresses against those who would flatter them and then follow their flattery with the offer of a lecherous kiss. This paragraph ends with a more explicit link between outer and inner temptations: "hwat-se cume withuten to vonden ou mid licunge, other mid mislicunge, holdeth ever ower heorte in on withinnin, leste the uttre vondunge kundlie the inre" (Day, pp. 85–86) ["whatever may come from the outside to tempt [or, test] you with pleasure or displeasure, always keep your heart continuously within, for fear that external temptation may kindle inner temptation"]. Both these paragraphs may be based loosely on a passage in Aelred's *De Institutis Inclusarum* (see chapter 4, p. 48).

185–86 *Ure wither-iwines beoth threo: the feond, the worlt, ure ahne flesch.* This three-fold division probably comes from Bernard's *Sermon on Various Things* 23 (*PL* 183, col. 601) — see Siegfried Wenzel's "The Three Enemies of Man."

206 *Her beoth nu o rawe i-tald the seoven heaved sunnen.* Savage and Watson observe that the "order given here is not that given two paragraphs before, where the spiritual sins are given as pride, envy, anger and covetousness, the bodily sins as lechery, gluttony and sloth. The author prefers to end with lechery, which he tends to use as an image for sin in general, and to expatiate on at some length. The Corpus revision of *AW* adds a good deal of extra material to the already lengthy discussion of the sins in the original work" (p. 373n23).

230–52 *The teohethe is contentio . . . The ealleofte hwelp . . . of hali theawes.* As Savage and Watson point out, the tenth and eleventh whelps of pride, "which pointedly depict specially female vices," have been added in the Corpus version (p. 374n26).

242 ff. Bernard also describes the facial expressions and body language of the prideful — see *The Steps of Humility and Pride* 10.28 (Conway, pp. 57 ff.).

242 *supersticiuns.* The context makes it unlikely that this word takes its modern meaning, "an irrational belief based on fear." In medieval Latin, *superstitio* could mean "frivolity" and "wrongheadedness," while in classical Latin, it could refer (in a transferred sense) to excessive attention to detail, or punctilliousness. White is probably right in reading *supersticiuns* etymologically, "in a sense derived from its component elements 'above' and 'standing'" (p. 221). Here it is translated as "superior airs" — see the glossary for other meanings. The Latin version translates this word as *nutus superbie* "the nod of pride."

259 *The Neddre of attri onde haveth seove hwelpes.* There are actually ten offspring, not seven: the Corpus version adds three whelps.

283 ff. *The Unicorne of wreaththe.* In medieval bestiaries, the unicorn is not usually allegorized as wrath or ferocity. The more common treatment makes the unicorn out to be a small, wily creature which cannot be caught by hunters. It is attracted to the lap of a virgin who is the only one who can catch it. The unicorn, despite the sexual suggestiveness of this

story, was most often seen as a symbol of Christ who is "caught" in the womb of the Virgin. For a typical treatment, see the *Physiologus* (Curley, p. 51). Wrath is appropriate to the unicorn, however, if its horn is seen as a weapon, and it may be that the picture of the wrathful unicorn owes something to that of the charging rhinoceros. This is the case in Isidore's *Etymologies*, who calls the unicorn a *monoceros* (the description immediately follows that of the *rhinoceros*). He says that the horn of the unicorn is "sharp and powerful, so that whatever it attacks it either tosses or gores," and goes on to describe how the unicorn lays its head in a virgin's lap "having put aside all its ferocity" (Lindsay, Book XII, chapter 2, pp. 12–13).

287   *wel ut of hire witte.* See the opening section of Part Three (also about wrath) for the comparison of anger to madness (3.23).

289 ff. *The seovethe hwelp.* Another of Corpus' additions to the basic text.

294 ff. *The Beore of hevi slawthe.* Nancy Hunt traces the theme of sloth throughout the entire *AW* in "Sloth in a Guide for Contemplatives, *The Ancrene Riwle*," *Centerpoint* 1 (1974), 66–70.

322–36 For a similar division of gluttony into five parts, see Gregory's *Moral Discourses on Job* 30.18.60 (*PL* 76, cols. 556–57).

327   *The Scorpiun of leccherie.* Lucinda Rumsey's "The Scorpion of Lechery" provides useful background on this section by tracing lore about scorpions from naturalistic writers, the Bible, and surveying the allegorizations of the scorpion in various patristic and literary sources. According to Rumsey, the *AW* author knows and develops motifs from the traditional handling of the scorpion (p. 56).

341 ff. *Ich ne dear nempnin the uncundeliche cundles of this deofles scorpiun.* Savage and Watson remark that "Lechery cannot be anatomized like the other sins, since the very names of some of its offspring are corrupting. It nonetheless takes up more space than any of them, partly in exhortation, partly in this satirical portrait of the devil's beast, which acts as a transition to the next, predominantly satirical section. Here, as in part II . . . and several times later in this part, lechery appears to be operating as a symbol for all sin" (pp. 374–75n37).

376–77 *lefunge . . . o nore.* This phrase refers to the belief that sneezing could be used to foretell the future. J. A. W. Bennett cites a passage from an unpublished penitential handbook which condemns, among other superstitions and pagan beliefs, "divinatio sternutationibus, sompniis, et sortibus quas falso dicunt apostolorum" ("Lefunge O Swefne," p. 280) — that is, "divination by sneezes, dreams, and lots which they falsely say are of the apostles." As Joy Russell-Smith points out, the practice of divination by sneezing was condemned by various writers including Pseudo-Augustine, Ælfric, and Thomas de Chabham, an author nearly contemporary with the *Ancrene Wisse*. In his *Summa de Casibus* (dated to around 1217–22), Thomas mentions, among many other serious sins and superstitions, divination by sneezing: "Alii si surgentes sternutaverint bonum vel malum inde sibi credunt futurum" (p. 267) — that is, "Others, if they sneeze upon rising (i.e., standing up), believe that from that the future will be good or bad for them." Russell-Smith believes that references to such superstitions may "have been commonplace in penitential literature," especially since several are mentioned in Canon Law, including the belief that one ought "redire ad lectum, si quis, dum se calciat, sternutauerint" (p. 267) — that is, "to return to bed, if someone has sneezed while putting on one's shoes."

In his magisterial *A History of Magic and Experimental Science*, Lynn Thorndike summarizes a discussion of augury in Michael Scot's *Phisionomia*: "Michael also discusses the significance of sneezes. If anyone sneezes twice or four times while engaged in some business and immediately rises and moves about, he will prosper in his undertaking. If one sneezes twice in the course of the night for three successive nights, it is a sign of death or some catastrophe in the house. If after making a contract, one sneezes once, it is a sign that the agreement will be kept inviolate; but if one sneezes thrice, the pact will not be observed" (II, p. 330).

392 ff. As Georgianna points out, these lines look forward to Part Five: "the author indicates one purpose for the long section of the deadly sins: to teach the anchoress how to classify her own sins. This purpose looks forward to part V ("Confession"), where the sinful anchoress is instructed to examine her conscience according to the seven deadly sins" (*The Solitary Self*, p. 130).

400 ff. *servith him in his curt.* There is no known source for the seven deadly sinners as entertainers in the devil's court. See Savage and Watson's helpful note for a number of general references to similar satirical portraits (p. 375n39). Comedy of this sort abounded in popular preaching — see G. R. Owst's *Literature and Pulpit in Medieval England* (chapter seven).

413 ff. *Yef ei seith wel.* Compare Bernard's description of the person giddy with pride: "His eyes are closed to anything that shows his own vileness or the excellence of others, wide open to what flatters himself" (*The Steps of Humility and Pride* 12; Conway, p. 67).

448

438   *eskibah.* Though the second element in *eski-bah* has yet to be convincingly explained, it is clear that the entire word must refer to a hearth tender or ash stirrer, more than likely in a pejorative sense, since Vitellius translates *his eskibah* as *son despit enfant* "his contemptible child." For a full discussion of the *-bah* element, see Joan Turville-Petre's article, "Two Etymological Notes."

462 ff.   The exemplum of the stinking lecher comes from *The Lives of the Desert Fathers* 6.3 (*PL* 73, col. 1014).

481 ff.   *Sum weneth that ha schule stronglukest beon i-fondet.* This paragraph is based largely on Gregory's *Moral Discourses in Job* 24.11 (*PL* 76, cols. 302–03), as Savage and Watson point out (p. 376n45).

485 ff.   *Hwen a wis mon.* This exemplum about the husband who puts his wife through unreasonable tests has roots in medieval folklore. See the last tale of Boccaccio's *Decameron* as well as Chaucer's adaptation of the same story in The Clerk's Tale.

513 ff.   Savage and Watson cite a number of parallels to the interpretation of Psalm 90:5–6 given here (p. 376n48).

559–81   This series of exempla comes from *The Lives of the Desert Fathers* 6.4 (*PL* 73, col. 1022), 5.7 (*PL* 73, col. 899), and 7.16 (*PL* 73, col. 1039).

586   *He haveth se monie buistes ful of his letuaires.* Compare a story told of Macarius (see Explanatory Note to Pref.99–101) in the *Verba Seniorum* section of *The Lives of the Desert Fathers*: "The old man was surveying the road when he saw Satan drawing near in the likeness of a man and he passed by his dwelling. He seemed to be wearing some kind of cotton garment, full of holes, and a small flask hung at each hole. . . . The old man [i.e., Macarius] said, 'And what is the purpose of these small flasks?' He replied, 'I am taking food for the brethren to taste.' The old man said, 'All those kinds?' He replied, 'Yes, for if a brother does not like one sort of food, I offer him another, and if he does not like the second any better, I offer him a third; and of all these varieties he will like at least one'" (Ward, *The Sayings of the Desert Fathers*, p. 126).

593 ff.   Dobson sees the references to cement (ME *lime*) as a veiled reference to Limebrook Priory where he believes the original anchoresses lived (see *Origins*, pp. 274 ff.).

600 ff.   From this point on, there are a number of echoes and adaptations from Gregory's *Moral Discourses on Job*. See Savage and Watson's notes (pp. 377 ff.) for a fuller picture of the borrowings.

633–34   *he pleieth with us*. In *Jesus as Mother*, Caroline Walker Bynum lists several writers such as Hugh Lacerta, Bernard, Julian of Norwich, Mechthild of Hackeborn, and St. Bridget of Sweden who employ the theme of God as a loving and tender mother (p. 131n72). This passage, Savage and Watson argue, may have conceivably influenced Julian of Norwich (p. 378n61).

659–64   The story of the demon armies of the West comes from a section of *The Lives of the Desert Fathers* 5.7 known as the *Verba Seniorum* ("The Sayings of the Elders") — the story is told of Abba Moses and collected under the heading "On Foresight or Contemplation" (*PL* 73, col. 982). See Explanatory Note to 2.310 for more information about *The Lives of the Desert Fathers*.

681–89   The account of Sarah's thirteen-year temptation comes from *The Lives of the Desert Fathers* 5.10–11 (*PL* 73, col. 876; see Explanatory Note to 2.310): "It was related of Amma [i.e., Mother] Sarah that for thirteen years she waged warfare against the demon of fornication. She never prayed that the warfare should cease, but she said, 'O God, give me strength.' Once the same spirit of fornication attacked her more insistently, reminding her of the vanities of the world. But she gave herself up to the fear of God and to asceticism and went up to her little terrace to pray. The spirit of fornication appeared corporally to her and said, 'Sarah, you have overcome me.' But she said, 'It is not I who have overcome you, but my master, Christ'" (Ward, *The Sayings of the Desert Fathers*, pp. 229–30). This story occurs under the heading "On Fornication."

E. G. Stanley points out that Sarah's cursing of the demon, "thu lihest . . . ful thing!" (4.687) has a close parallel in *The Owl and the Nightingale* (line 1335; see "*The Owl and the Nightingale*," p. 152).

690   *Sein Beneit, Seint Antonie, ant te othre*. See Explanatory Notes to Pref.99–101 and 3.489–90.

741–46   This list of the remedies against temptation does not exactly mirror the structure of the following discussion (see the headnote to Part Four for an outline). The first three (meditation, prayer, and strong belief) are each treated in turn, but the list which follows (reading, fasting, holding vigils, physical disciplines, comfort from another person, humility, generosity of heart, unity) is a rather random collection of remedies from the two following sections: a) hardy faith applied to each of the seven deadly sins (see 4.839–1024) and b) the remedies against each of the seven deadly sins (see 4.1192–94). That is, reading, fasting, holding vigils, and physical disciplines are all remedies against sloth and lechery, while humility is a remedy for pride, generosity for covetousness, and unity for wrath. Savage and Watson note that the remedies "are not merely described; many of them are accompanied by meditations designed to help apply them. Hence this is one of the most important, as well as being one of the lengthiest, discussions in the course of *AW*" (p. 379n72).

749   *nota culpe*. The more literal translation of this phrase is "the mark of guilt"; Bennett and Smithers think that it may refer to the mark made on the forehead on Ash Wednesday (p. 404, note to line 11).

752 ff.   The first four lines of this metrical passage also occur in *St. Marherete* (Mack, *Seinte Marherete*, p. 34). In Corpus, at least two lines are metrically defective. "Thench ofte with sar of thine sunnen" should probably read "Thench ofte with sare of thine shome synne" (4.752), as Vernon reads. Line 755 mistakenly repeats *ofte* (Bennett and Smithers, p. 404).

759 ff.   Smithers sees the following discussion of earthly pain and joy (as mere shadows and paintings of hell and heaven) as an example of high medieval Platonism (the parable of the cave), transmitted through Hugh of St. Victor; he attempts to match the concepts to technical philosophical terms of substance and shadow ("Two Typological Terms," pp. 126–28). Millett, however, makes the convincing case that the treatment of shadow and painting probably comes from "practical pastoral writing" and cites a parallel from Alan of Lille's manual for preachers, the *Summa de arte praedicatoria* ("*Peintunge* and *Schadewe*," pp. 402–03).

785   *fleschliche sawlen*. Baldwin argues that the phrase "fleshly souls" is an unlikely paradox, suggesting that *sawlen* here must refer to "persons." She translates *fleschliche sawlen* as "carnal people" ("Some Difficult Words," p. 284).

791 ff.   This exemplum about the power of prayer is contained in *The Lives of the Desert Fathers* 6.2 (*PL* 73, col. 1003) as well as in some twelfth-century sermons (see Bennett and Smithers, pp. 405–06).

795–96   For the account of Ruffin the devil, who attacked St. Margaret, see *St. Marherete* (Mack, *Seinte Marherete*, pp. 28, 30). As Bennett and Smithers note, "The cryptic allusion of *AW* is clarified by the information in *St. Marherete*, and thus not only shows the latter to have been composed before *AW*, but constitutes the kind of link between the two that would support a case for common authorship" (p. 406). Savage and Watson remark that "though *Margaret* was written for public reading . . ., it is described here as 'your book,' i.e., one of which the anchoresses had a private copy" (p. 380n78).

796–98   This anecdote comes from the life of St. Bartholomew. See *The Golden Legend* (Ryan, vol. 2, p. 110) for an accessible account. Another version can be found in *The South English Legendary* (D'Evelyn and Mill, vol. 2, pp. 373–84).

798 ff.   The gift of tears figures largely in *The Book of Margery Kempe*. See Sandra McEntire's "The Doctrine of Compunction from Bede to Margery Kempe," in *The Medieval Mystical Tradition in England*, ed. Marion Glasscoe (Cambridge: D. S. Brewer, 1987), pp. 77–90, for more details.

814   *ant te sunne th'refter schineth the schenre.* Proverbial. See Whiting, C315 and R15.

839 ff.   The seven deadly sins appear in different guises at least three times in Part Four: the first in the discussion of inner temptations, the second (this one) in a discussion of how right thinking (lit., "hardy belief") can counter the seven deadly sins, and finally in an extensive explanation of the remedies for the seven deadly sins (see the headnote to Part Four).

892   *The seovethe forbisne.* As Bennett and Smithers point out (p. 408), this is apparently the fifth exemplum, not the seventh.

897   *Nu ye habbeth nihene.* There seem to be only seven examples illustrating the power of unity.

916 ff.   *Ye beoth the ancren of Englond.* The direct address occurs only in the Corpus version. By the time it was written, the audience of *AW* seems to have expanded from the original three sisters to a group of anchoresses numbering twenty or more. As sections in Parts Four and Eight indicate, individual anchoresses apparently were united in a kind of community via their maidens who carried messages between anchorholds (see 4.942–45 and 8.267 ff.). It is important to note that the author says that this group is *like* an order, implying that they are in fact not nuns. The "motherhouse" probably refers to the Cistercian organizational model in which daughter monasteries answered to the authority of their founding motherhouses. This schema exerted a strong influence on other orders, especially after the Fourth Lateran Council (1215). For a further discussion of this passage, see the Introduction, pp. 15 ff. Dobson argues that *Englondes ende*

(4.927) refers to the Welsh borders, not far from Limebrook Priory (*Origins*, pp. 284–86).

922   *an cuvent of Lundene ant of Oxnefort, of Schreobsburi, other of Chester.* If, as Dobson believes, *AW* was written by a canon near Wigmore, the exclusion of Worcester (the closest center of learning) is puzzling (*Origins*, p. 134). There seem to be at least two answers for this: Millett, arguing for a Dominican origin for *AW*, points out that all of these towns had significant Dominican foundations, Chester being the latest in 1236 ("The Origins," p. 219). On the other hand, Margaret Laing and Angus McIntosh, using dialectical features of Titus (containing the Katherine Group texts and a version of the *Ancrene Wisse*), place the scribal origin of this particular MS much further north from Wigmore in southern Cheshire, not very far from Chester. Though these conclusions are based on an analysis of Titus only, Laing and McIntosh make the case that the Titus scribe carries over dialectical features from the exemplar. The evidence is, however, incomplete at this stage (pp. 257–59).

942–45   *"Ure meistre haveth i-writen us . . . schule beon unblamet."* These lines were added in the Corpus version.

945–47   Part Eight also offers advice about messengers and how to prevent misunderstandings (see 8.267 ff.).

1007 ff.   The discussion of complaints to friends about a lack of food does not occur in Cleo., Nero, or Titus. It seems to have been added for the wider audience which *AW* was acquiring, since we know that the original anchoresses were well provided for (see Explanatory Note to 4.164).

1025 ff.   This passage plays on the etymological sense of *article*, which originally meant "a little joint" — see glossary.

1049–50 *"Afech" on Ebreisch spealeth "neowe wodschipe."* Savage and Watson refer to Pseudo-Jerome's *On Hebrew Names* (*PL* 23, col. 1314), where *Aphec* is etymologized as *furor novus* "new madness" (p. 383n100).

1079   *Incurvare ut transeamus.* "Bow down that we may go over" (Isaiah 51:23). The verse continues: "And you have laid down your body as if (it were) the ground, and a path to them that went over." See also 4.1082.

1133   *Recabes sunen, Remon ant Banaa.* The text mistakenly transposes *Recab* and *Remon*, as 2 Samuel 4:1 (in some Bibles, 2 Kings 4:1) makes clear. Rechab and Baana were the sons of Remon the Berothite.

1198   *I the licome is fulthe ant unstrengthe.* Savage and Watson (p. 384nn109–10) point out that the disgust with the human body in the following lines belongs to the *contemptus mundi* tradition, influenced by Pope Innocent III's *Misery of the Human Condition* (c. 1195). See also Chaucer's The Pardoner's Tale, especially *CT* VI(C)517–59, for similar rhetoric in popular preaching.

1218 ff.   This exemplum also appears in 4.576–81.

1231–35 The account of Anthony's vision of a world covered with snares and traps comes from *The Sayings of the Desert Fathers*, where Abba Anthony says, "I saw the snares that the enemy spreads out over the world and I said groaning, 'What can get through from such snares?' Then I heard a voice saying to me, 'Humility'" (Ward, p. 2).

1275 ff.   *Aliena bona si diligis, tua facis.* The following passage in *AW* is based on Gregory's discussion in the *Pastoral Care*.

1353 ff.   *Thenne is he kene, the wes ear curre.* Here *curre* must refer to a dog whose bark is worse than its bite — a growling but cowardly dog (see glossary). In fact, many of the other versions substitute a word meaning "coward" for *curre*. In Cleo., scribe D altered *curre* to read *cuard* "coward"; Nero has *eruh* (from OE *earg* "cowardly"); Vitellius *couard*; Trinity *porous* (OF for "fearful"); and Lat. *timidus*, while Caius, Titus and Vernon preserve *curre*.

1382–83 *the mei with toheoven up hire threo fingres overcumen hire fa.* Dobson points to a similar passage in *Moralities on the Gospels*: "Likewise, that person would be considered more wretched than the most miserable human being if he fell to the enemy in a battle which he could have won by the lifting up of three fingers" (p. 151).

1386 ff.   *his wunden.* This passage on the wounds of Christ is, according to Savage and Watson, one of the earliest treatments of this theme in English. The devotion to the wounds became very popular in the later Middle Ages and may have been inspired by medieval interpretations of the Song of Songs 2:14 (p. 385n127).

1415   *Sein Beneites salve.* St. Benedict's remedy is the scourge or whip, which (as Savage and Watson point out) was "used in all medieval monasteries, and by many secular and devout laypeople. When prayer, meditation and fantasy couched in the most forceful and physical language fails to work, the physical remedy is all that is left" (p. 386n130). In *The Golden Legend*'s version of his life, Benedict applies physical pain as a remedy for lust: "Soon the devil brought to the holy man's mind the image of a woman whom he had once seen, and he was so aroused by the memory of her that he was almost overcome with desire, and began to think of quitting the solitary way of life. But suddenly, touched by the grace of God, he came to himself, shed his garment, and rolled in the thorns and brambles which abounded thereabouts; and he emerged so scratched and torn over his whole body that the pain in his flesh cured the wound in his spirit. Thus he conquered sin by putting out the fire of lust, and from that time on he no longer felt the temptations of the flesh" (Ryan, vol. 1, p. 187).

1427–28 *ant tobreketh [to] the stan*. See Genesis 3:15 for this image, developed further by Cassian, Gregory, and Benedict (Savage and Watson, p. 386n133).

1434 *i the heaved feble*. In his *Etymologies*, Isidore says that "The head of bears is feeble (*invalidum*): their greatest power is their arms and loins" (Lindsay, Book XII, chap. ii, 22). Neckham reflects this tradition (Wright, pp. 212, 366).

1442 *muchel kimeth of lutel*. Proverbial, with reference to popular narrative. See Whiting, M783 and M776.

Part Five

The bulk of this section is taken up with a description of confession and its attributes. Confession, called "schrift" in *AW*, is one stage in a three-step system which includes 1) contrition of heart, 2) confession of mouth (to a priest), 3) restitution (or, penance — in the specific sense). The priest grants absolution with the formula, "I absolve thee." In *The Solitary Self*, Linda Georgianna sketches out the contemporary controversies surrounding this system and places *AW* in the middle of two extreme positions. The "contritionists" believed that private contrition alone could bring forgiveness, while the "post-contritionists" placed much more emphasis on confession of mouth to a priest, who alone could grant absolution (pp. 96–119). Georgianna points out that *AW*, on the one hand, stresses the importance of oral confession in its analysis of Judith and Holofernes (see 5.5 ff.), but on the other hand tends to de-emphasize the role of the priest in the anchoresses' confessions — he appears mainly as an observer rather than an active investigator, and he is not to lay any penance on the anchoresses beyond the daily penance of their austere lives (see 5.521 ff.). Furthermore, *AW* passes over the stages after confession, restitution and absolu-tion, only very briefly near the end of Part Five. As Georgianna notes, "By emphasizing both the self-reflection and oral confession, the *Wisse* author combines the most psychologically useful aspects of both contritionist and postcontritionist thought" (pp. 115).

AW's concern with confession fits in with its early thirteenth-century origin. In 1215, the Fourth Lateran Council made yearly confession mandatory (Canon 21): "Every Christian of either sex after reaching the years of discretion shall confess all his sins at least once a year privately to his own priest and try as hard as he can to perform the penance imposed on him" (Rothwell, pp. 654–55). Priests were enjoined to inquire "into the circumstances both of the sinner and of the sin, from which to choose intelligently what sort of advice he ought to give and what sort of remedy to apply" (Rothwell, p. 655). To meet the needs of confessors a new array of manuals and treatises on all aspects of the penitential system were produced (Georgianna, p. 99), and Parts Four and Five of *AW* have many points of contact with contemporary Latin handbooks. For a useful summary of current scholarship on confession before and after the Fourth Lateran Council, see Peter Biller's "Confession in the Middle Ages" in *Handling Sin: Confession in the Middle Ages*, ed. Peter Biller and A. J. Minnis (Woodbridge, Suffolk: York Medieval Press, 1998), pp. 1–33, and L. E. Boyle's "Summae confessorum."

After the sometimes hard-to-follow organization of Part Four, it comes as something of a relief that Part Five has such a simple structure.

Outline

Introduction (5.1–4). The introduction divides the section into two basic parts: 1) the power confession has, and 2) what confession should be (i.e., the attributes of proper confession).

Power of Confession (5.5–52). This section treats the six powers of confession: three against the devil: 1) it chops off his head, 2) puts his army to flight, 3) deprives him of his land, and three in the penitent: 1) it washes the filth of sin away, 2) restores what we lost through sin, and 3) makes us into God's children. Most of the powers are illustrated with Old Testament exempla suitably allegorized.

Sixteen Attributes of Confession (5.52–485). The sixteen traits are first outlined (5.54–57) and then dealt with in turn: confession should be accusing (5.58–112), bitter (5.113–74), complete (5.175–98), naked (5.199–273), made often (5.274–87), made in haste (5.288–332), humble (5.333–52), full of shame (5.353–68), made in fear (5.369–75), hopeful (5.376–414), wise and made to a wise man (5.415–19), true (5.420–37), willing (5.438–58), one's own (5.459–64), steadfast (5.465–72), and considered beforehand (5.473–78). The section concludes with a summary of the six powers of confession (5.483–85).

Notes on Confession Specifically for Anchoresses (5.486–533). Since the sixteen attributes of confession could apply to any believer, the author gives advice directed specifically toward anchoresses. After listing a number of lapses ranging from the seven deadly sins to practical problems such as letting food go moldy and clothes unrepaired (5.488–501), the author recommends that the anchoress confess at least once a week (5.498) and then suggests various ways to confess without revealing details to a priest who may himself be vulnerable to temptation (5.504–19). The priest should not lay much penance (i.e., restitution) on an anchoress, since her life alone is penance enough (5.520–33).

Transition to Part Six (5.532–33). The sixteen attributes of confession, in a different form, appear in a mnemonic verse found in several manuscripts, and are also treated similarly in the *Moralities on the Gospels* (see Explanatory Note to 5.54 ff.).

9 ff.   *i Judithe deden*. As Georgianna notes, in the allegory of Judith as confession, "Not only is the sequence of events muddled, but also the parallels between the events of the story and the acts of confession are unclear" (p. 106). First of all, the hacking off of Holofernes' head seems to represent contrition (see 5.13–14), while the showing of the head to the priests is confession itself, which puts the devil's army to flight. This sequence causes problems since contrition alone should not have the power to cut off the devil's head (see the headnote to Part Five), and a bit later, it seems that "the devil's head is only cut off and 'trampled on' *after* or *as* it is shown forth to the priest in confession" (p. 106). As Georgianna observes, "By continually rearranging the events of his story the author suggests that the drama of confession is not a linear story but a circular one. Each 'event' includes all the others. Confession is not several acts, but only one" (p. 107).

14   *schrift on heorte*. Baldwin suggests that "confession in heart" must refer to the intention of going to confession of mouth, since confession which takes place only in the heart is not complete ("Some Difficult Words," p. 278).

54 ff.   *Schrift schal beo*. The *Moralities on the Gospels* also assigns sixteen qualities to confession, as Dobson points out (pp. 152–65), though in a different order, quoting a mnemonic verse which appears in other manuscripts:

> Que [sc. Confessio] cuiusmodi debeat esse ex dicendis advertas. Versus:
> Integra, certa, frequens, humilis, cita, fusa rubore,
> Plena metus, discreta, volens, sua, nuda, morosa,
> Fidens, vera (prius totum, post singula signans),
> Accusans et amara rei confessio fiat.
> (Dobson, *Moralities*, p. 152)

> [Notice from (the following) sayings what confession of this kind must be. Verses:/ Whole, certain, frequent, humble, quick, spread over with blushing (or, shame),/ Full of fear, separate, willing, one's own, naked, fastidious,/Faithful, true (every [sin

committed] before, afterwards noting single [sins]),/Accusing and bitter let the confession of a thing be.]

Such mnemonic lists are commonplace in pastoral and confessional materials.

60   *Thus Eve ant Adam wereden ham.* See Genesis 3:12–13. For a number of specific source attributions in the following passages, see Savage and Watson's helpful notes (pp. 388 ff.).

70–73   *Hinc erunt accusancia peccata . . . se premet.* For further references to Anselm's terrifying *Meditation* 1, see Explanatory Note to 3.296–97.

117   *thet an mot cumen of the other.* Georgianna notes that the "Juda-Thamar marriage tie makes clear that neither sorrow nor confession is meaningful without the other" (p. 107).

169–70 *me nimeth ed uvel dettur aten for hweate.* Proverbial. See Whiting, D118.

172–74 *Vitas Patrum . . . in helle.* This anecdote comes from the *Verba Seniorum* section of *The Lives of the Desert Fathers* 5.3 (*PL* 73, col. 861) under the heading "On Compunction" and is told of Macarius (see Explanatory Note to Pref.99–101): "The old men asked him to say a word to the brothers. When [Macarius] heard this, he said, 'Let us weep, brothers, and let tears gush out of our eyes, before we go to that place where our tears shall burn our bodies'" (Ward, *The Sayings of the Desert Fathers*, p. 136).

175 ff. *The povre widewe.* The comparison between sweeping out dust and making a good confession was probably a commonplace of penitential literature and popular preaching. Dobson points to a loose parallel in *Moralities on the Gospels*: "And so conscience is like a material house. You know that if any head of the house would instruct his servant girl to clean his house with a broom, and afterwards to throw out even the smallest dust, if she did not obey his instructions, certainly he would beat her. The head of the house is the spirit, moreover this servant girl is flesh; thus, the spirit instructs the flesh to clean his house (that is the conscience) with a broom (that is the tongue) from the filth of sin. Afterwards she sprinkles water (that is penitential tears) over it, so that through penitential tears even the smallest circumstances (or, details) of sin are dissolved. . . . Thus by this said method, after the dirt of vices has been ejected from the floor of the conscience, and the dust of carnal desire has been removed, the conscience is restored to its pristine state" (p. 160).

182 ff.   Of this series of warnings, Savage and Watson observe, "*Exempla* such as these, warning of the dire consequences of failing to confess, or of failing to do so in the proper way, formed a vital part of the propaganda surrounding the institution of confession as a sacrament, and continued to be found useful in the literature of confession" (p. 389n25).

211   *Abute sunne liggeth six thing.* This phrase shows an etymological understanding of the word *circumstances* (line 212), which describes things "standing around" something else. The English translation of *circumstance* is *totagge* "something tagged or pinned on something else" — see the glossary. These circumstances (who, what, how, where, why, when, through whom, how often) are found in a number of manuals for confessors (see Savage and Watson, p. 390n27 for a list of analogues).

216 ff.   *Ich am "an ancre," "a nunne," "a wif i-weddet," "a meiden."* This "fill-in-the-blank" list implies that Part Five is intended for a general (female) audience. See Explanatory Note to 5.486.

220   *"a ladles thing," "a wummon as ich am."* Apparently a reference to homoeroticism. See Judith C. Brown, *Immodest Acts: The Life of a Lesbian Nun in Renaissance Italy* (New York: Oxford University Press, 1986).

224–25   *"hondlede him i swuch stude, other me-seolven."* The penitential handbooks assigned various penances for sexual sins such as masturbation. See Pierre Payer's *Sex and the Penitentials: The Development of a Sexual Code, 550–1150* (Toronto: University of Toronto Press, 1984).

251   *Yef eoile schet of a feat.* Dobson advances a parallel to this comparison from *Moralities on the Gospels*: "Again, therefore, Jeremiah teaches with these words how one should proceed with the flowing of penitential waters: 'Pour out your hearts like water in the sight of God.' By water the sinner or his sins are understood. . . . Afterwards, when water is poured out fully, no taste or smell of it remains. God wants sin to be poured out in confession in just this way, so that no taste or smell of it may remain" (pp. 161–62).

276 ff.   For these etymologies, see Pseudo-Jerome's *On Hebrew Names* (*PL* 23, col. 1218).

360 ff.   *Ant Sein Bernard seith.* Savage and Watson (p. 391n41) trace this thought to Bernard's *Sermons on the Octave of the Assumption of the Blessed Virgin Mary* 10 (*PL* 183, col. 435).

385 ff. *the deofles tristen.* See the glossary for an explanation of *tristen* "traps, hunting stations." The *AW* plays on the similarity between this word and various forms of *trust.*

391–92 The reference to Psalm 9 is particularly appropriate to this discussion since the image of hunting in 5.386–89 seems to be inspired by, or suggestive of Psalm 9:30: "He lies in ambush in dark places like a lion in his den; he lies in wait to catch the helpless man; he seizes and drags the helpless one into his net."

483–84 *haveth the ilke muchele mihten thet ich earst seide.* See 5.5 ff., though as Savage and Watson point out, the three powers of confession against the world have not been treated, "nor is it clear what they are" (p. 392n57).

486 *this fifte dale . . . limpeth to alle men i-liche.* Most of Part Five was written with a general audience in mind (see Explanatory Note to 5.216 ff.), and may indicate that the *AW* author expected his treatise to circulate more widely among laypeople or that confessors might use it in their pastoral work. Savage and Watson note that Part Five "would also have been useful for the anchoresses in directing the spiritual lives of their maids" (p. 392n58).

Part Six

Penance in Part Six is treated not as the next step in the penitential system after confession of mouth (Part Five), but as a more generalized kind of suffering. The main idea seems to be that penance in the technical sense (more narrowly understood as satisfaction or *deadbote*, lit. "deed-remedy") is not necessary since the anchoresses' difficult way of life is in itself penance enough. As Georgianna writes, "A marked change in the *Ancrene Wisse* author's attitude toward the anchoress occurs at the opening of part VI: while in part V he views her as a sinner who must confess, in part VI he views her as a saint whose life of penance imitates Christ's suffering" (p. 120).

Structurally, Part Six provides a steadily advancing transition between the penitential materials (Parts Four and Five) and the over-riding value of love (Part Seven). It begins with a description of penitential suffering, then describes the sweetness that arises from bitterness, and shows how this sweetness leads to love. And in fact, Part Six is filled with images of climbing from lower to higher (in symbolic terms: from penance to love).

Outline

Introduction (6.1–11). Here, the author announces that everything about an anchoress' life is penance and that she must share in the sufferings of the Cross. This will eventually lead to joy, a topic to which he will return.

Three Classes of Believers (6.12–85). The discussion now turns to three ascending ranks of God's chosen, each of which is described metaphorically: [1] pilgrims, the lowest, are in the world, but strangers to it and probably represent priests and those with secular ministries (6.16–44); [2] next come the dead — that is, the enclosed orders of monks and nuns who are dead to the world (6.44–59); and finally, [3] on the highest stair, those who willingly crucify themselves and who are dead not only to the world but to themselves — anchoresses (6.59–85).

Shame and Pain (6.86–198). Carrying over from the last section is the idea that anchoresses can expect to share in Christ's crucifixion, and specifically in its combined shame and physical pain. These two are imagined as the two uprights of a ladder (6.87) which will enable the anchoress to climb to heaven. Other images follow: Elijah's fiery wheels, the Cross itself, etc. Both have their rewards, however: honor compensates for shame and delight for pain (6.120–42). If anchoresses expect these rewards, though, they must be willing to suffer gladly alongside Christ and pay the price of martyrdom like the saints, offering up their bodies to be torn (6.143–98)

Is Pain Necessary? (6.199–301). In the style of contemporary theological writing, the author responds to a series of objections to the penitential life: [1] is it wise to torture oneself? (6.199–207); [2] will God punish sin so vengefully? (6.208–35); [3] how is God the better for my suffering? (6.236–46); [4] does God sell his grace? (6.252–301). Also included is a discussion of physical disciplines (fasting, holding vigils, self-flagellation, coarse clothing, etc.) and internal virtues (devotion, contrition, rightful love, and humility) which the anchoress should not spare herself (6.247–52). At the end of the section, this physical pain is now redefined as external bitterness, which leads to the next section on internal bitterness.

Internal Bitterness (6.302–32). Now the topic turns to three types of internal bitterness symbolized by the three Marys coming to anoint Christ's body and by the bittersweet spices they brought for that purpose: [1] contrition (306–12), [2] struggling against temptation (6.312–23), and [3] longing for heaven (6.324–32).

Sweetness after Bitterness (6.333–75). Sweetness, however is the reward for the anchoress' bitter life. The discussion is peppered with references to the "Love Book," the Song of Songs, as well as to the Wedding at Cana. Next comes a discussion of the special sufferings shared by Christ (imagined as an anchoress in Mary's womb and in his tight cradle) and the anchoresses: narrowness and bitterness (6.360–75).

Physical Suffering as Protection (6.376–410). Though the author does not encourage the anchoresses to apply physical disciplines to themselves (since their entire life is a kind of penance), he likens pain to thorns which enclose and protect young saplings (6.378 ff.). In an oblique transition, the anchoresses are called on to be like the thorns themselves: sharp (in the sharpness of their daily pain) and worthless (in their lowliness and humility). This will keep them safe from the devil. The section ends with a complex image drawn from the "sweet love book," the Song of Songs, where Christ as lover steps on his beloved, who is a high mountain. The imprint of his footstep on the anchoresses is like the imprint of Christ's suffering on the Cross.

Suffering Proves Love (6.411–33). Such suffering shows a sweet and deep love of God, deeper than that of man for woman. The section ends with an account of two people known to the writer (6.417–33). Both, a man and a woman, undergo heroic mortifications of the flesh, all for the sake of love. This provides a smooth transition to Part Seven.

1–3   *Al is penitence . . . derf ordre.* The series of clauses which begin with *al* seems to mirror the prayer of the priest from the end of Part Five (5.525–28).

10   *Ich chulle biginnin herre.* In this phrase, "higher" apparently refers to a passage which occurs earlier or "higher up" in Bernard's sermon (Savage and Watson, p. 393n3).

10 ff. The following section is based closely on Bernard's seventh Sermon for Lent, as Shepherd points out (p. 31). He provides a translation of the entire sermon in an appendix (pp. 71–72). See his excellent notes for a number of specific parallels between Part Six and this sermon.

12 ff. For an interesting rhetorical analysis of this passage, see Price (p. 203).

30   *Sein James other Sein Giles.* According to legend, the beheaded body of St. James (the Apostle) arrived in a rudderless boat near Santiago de Compostella in north-western Spain, and became the object of widespread veneration and pilgrimage.

        St. Giles (or, Aegidius, eighth century) was reportedly an Athenian who settled in France as a hermit and was befriended by Wamba, king of the Visigoths, or by some accounts Charlemagne. The town of St. Giles, near the mouth of the Rhône, grew up around the monastery which his patron built for him and was the object of pilgrimage. St. Giles was very popular in medieval England with at least 160 churches dedicated to him.

33   *Sein Julienes in.* St. Julian (the Hospitalier) is the patron saint of innkeepers, and to find "St. Julian's inn" means to find hospitable shelter. St. Julian's story has a heavy dose of folklore and romance elements. While out hunting, a hart tells him he will kill his father and mother. This prophecy comes to pass when his new wife welcomes his mother and father (on an unexpected visit). Julian, seeing a man and woman in bed,

suspects that his wife is romping with another man and he kills the two (his parents) in a rage. In remorse, he and his wife build an inn and hospital for the poor. He receives forgiveness when he puts a dying leper (really a divine messenger) into his own bed. This story is retold in *The Golden Legend* (Ryan, vol. 1, pp. 126–30), where the compiler Jacobus tries to sort out the legends of a plethora of Julians.

86 ff.   Shepherd traces the theme of shame and pain as the uprights of a ladder to *Declamations from St. Bernard's Sermons*, probably compiled by Geoffrey of Auxerre, and also notes that a ladder of humility appears in chapter 7 ("On Humility") of the *Benedictine Rule*. See Shepherd's note for other possible analogues (p. 34).

103   *Ah wel mei duhen.* Shepherd translates as "This (instead of something else which may come to mind) will serve the present purpose" (p. 35).

103–04   Note the wordplay between *hweol* "wheel" and *hwile* "while, period of time." As Shepherd points out, *hwilende* in OE means "passing, transitory."

110–116   Shepherd cites a passage from Adam the Scot's *On the Way of Life of the Praemonstratensian Canons* (*PL* 198, col. 591) which evidently served as the source for these lines (p. 35).

126   *Super epistolam Jacobi.* The sentence which follows this tag comes from the *Glossa Ordinaria*, the standard Bible commentary of the late Middle Ages, consisting of both interlinear and marginal glosses. It is essentially a massive compilation of extracts on particular biblical verses from important authorities. The *Glossa*'s commentary for each book of the Bible usually has a complicated history. See the *The Oxford Dictionary of the Christian Church* for further information (Cross and Livingstone, p. 572). Though Brepols is beginning to publish editions of the *Glossa* for individual books of the Bible, see the 1992 facsimile *Biblia Latina cum glossa ordinaria: Facsimile Reprint of the editio princeps Adolph Rusch of Strassburg 1480/81* for a text with both marginal and interlinear glosses. The version in *PL* 103–04 contains only the marginal gloss.

161   *Nis Godd ure heaved ant we his limen alle?* Shepherd (p. 38) cites a number of analogues to this topos, and notes that it is based on 1 Corinthians 6:15, 12:12–17, Ephesians 1:22–23, 4:15–16, and Colossians 2:19 ff.

175   *with liht leapes.* See the Textual Note for this line.

176–78   See the Explanatory Note to 3.55 for an account of Peter and Andrew's deaths, the Explanatory Note to 3.57 for St. Lawrence. St. Agatha (see the Explanatory Note to 6.265) had her breasts torn off, and St. Katherine was tortured on a wheel.

178   *heafdes bicorven.* Shepherd suggests that *heafdes* may be in the genitive singular. If so, this phrase would be translated as "cut off at the head" (p. 40).

179–94   For a detailed analysis of this passage, see Janet Grayson's "The Eschatalogical Adam's Kirtle."

209   *Ye, mon!* Though some translate *mon* loosely as "indeed," it seems clear from the other versions (Lat. *Ita, homo*, Vitellius *oil sire*, and Nero *Ye, mon, other woman*) that it does mean "man." The translation given here, "Yes, sir!" is an attempt to approximate the colloquial tone of the phrase.

215 ff.   Shepherd cites patristic discussions of the *umbra Christi*, Christ's flesh as a shadow (p. 42)

248–49   *as Seint Ailred the abbat wrat to his suster.* A reference to Aelred's *De Institutione Reclusarum* — see the outline of the Author's Preface (p. 418). From this point on, the author makes several references to Aelred (see notes below).

257 ff.   *Pot the walleth swithe.* See Job 41:11.

258   *nule he beon overleden, other cald weater i-warpe th'rin.* Shepherd reads this phrase as "won't it (i.e., the boiling pot) be overbrimmed (i.e., spill over) unless cold water be thrown in it?" (p. 44). It seems much more likely that the phrase should be translated, "will not it be ladled out or cold water thrown in it?" The Latin version reads, *Nonne oportet ollam multum bullientem exhaurire aliquantulum aut aquam frigidam inicere?* "Now then, is it not necessary to empty out a pot boiling greatly or to throw in either a little something or cold water?"

261–64   Compare a similar, though not identical passage in Aelred: "Now there are some who are impeded in the practice of virtue by a certain fear that overmuch fasting or undue lack of sleep may deprive them of vigor and so make them a burden to others" (chapter 21, pp. 68–69).

265   *Seinte Agace.* St. Agatha (dates unknown), a child of wealthy parents from Palermo or Sicily, was tortured by the lustful Quintian when she refused his advances. He sent her

to a bordello, had her breasts wrenched off, and finally had her rolled to death in hot coals. As John Delaney notes in his *Dictionary of Saints*, depictions of Agatha often show her "holding a pair of pincers or bearing her breasts on a plate" (p. 30). The incident referred to here takes place the night after her breasts have been torn off. An old man, who turns out to be the Apostle Peter, appears to her with medicine to heal her wounds, but she refuses to apply it. In the version contained in *The Golden Legend*, she says "I have never applied any material remedy to my body, and it would be shameful to lose now what I have preserved for so long" (Ryan, vol. 1, p. 155).

266   *Medicinam carnalem.* As Allen ("On the Author," pp. 660–61) and Shepherd (p. 44) note, this prayer was sung as an anthem on St. Agatha's feast day (5 February).

268   *the threo hali men.* The story of the man who coddles himself with medicine, Shepherd believes, is of Cistercian origin. He cites a number of analogues (p. 44).

279   *ancreful.* The word *ancreful* "anxious" (from ON *angr-fulr* "full of trouble") is not related to *ancre* "anchorite," though this passage probably plays on the similarity of the two words.

281   *Ypocras ant Galien.* The two most famous physicians known to the Middle Ages. Hippocrates (?460 B.C.–?377 B.C.), Greek physician and often called the "father of medicine," achieved fame through a number of texts gathered in the *Hippocratic Collection*. Most commentators believe that a good number of these texts were not written by Hippocrates himself but by a group of physicians and theorists who venerated him. Galen (c. 130–200) was also a Greek physician, born in Pergamum, who authored over 500 treatises in Greek, about a hundred of which survived. Galen's writings were lost after the disintegration of the Roman empire, but were reintroduced in the west through Latin translations of Arabic editions in the eleventh and twelfth centuries.

284 ff.   Aelred's discussion of sickness seems to lie behind this passage. He writes, "We sniff war from afar and are in such dread of bodily disease before it makes itself felt that we take no notice of spiritual sickness which is already troubling us — as if the flame of lust were easier to bear than the complaints of the stomach" (chapter 21, pp. 68–69).

288–89   *Ant this ne segge ich nawt . . . gode theawes.* Note the difficult double negative here. The sense is, "I say this so that prudence and moderation, which are the mother and nurse of all good virtues, will not be completely disregarded." The sentence comes from Aelred: "I do not say this in disparagement of discretion, the mother and nurse of all the virtues. But we must keep within due limits those things which provide material for vice (chapter 23, p. 70).

302 ff.   *Nichodemus brohte smirles.* Nicodemus is mentioned in John 19:39–42, while the story of the three Marys comes from Mark 16:1, Luke 24:1, and John 19:25–26. The interpretation of names probably comes from one of the many etymological handbooks of Hebrew names, inspired by and often drawing on the *Book of Hebrew Names*, wrongly attributed to St. Jerome (see Explanatory Note to 5.276 ff.). Shepherd points out that these texts were often the subjects of Easter sermons and goes on to cite some general analogues to the treatment of the three Marys in *AW* (p. 46).

322   *Inoh is i-seid th'ruppe.* See 4.1–22.

359–60   *non autem recedentes.* This phrase, added as a gloss to the quotation from Mark, goes untranslated in the text.

363 ff.   *nes he him-seolf reclus i Maries wombe?* Shepherd cites passages in Adam the Scot, *On the Way of Life of the Premonstratensian Canons* and Peter the Cantor for these images (p. 48), while Savage notes that in *AW* "the crucifixion is inverted into a feminine image: an enclosure, a prison, a narrow womb. . . . I believe these unusual interpretations are to some indefinable degree reflections of the writer's closeness to the women he wrote for, and they are in many ways fighting with the inherited literary tradition" ("The Translation of the Feminine," pp. 189–90).

376 ff.   Jocelyn Price notes that in the analogy of the sapling surrounded by thorns, *AW* forces readers to make a dramatic "conceptual reversal" by imagining the thorns pointed away from the body, to defend it, not pointed inward to inflict pain (p. 205). She sees this as the hallmark of *AW*'s goal of producing a sometimes violent redirection of thinking by pulling the audience through a rapidly shifting and unpredictable interior space (p. 204).

390   *Sluri the cokes cneave.* As Shepherd and Zettersten (*Studies*, p. 227) point out, *Sluri* is not a given name but instead a nickname which must mean something like "Lazybones" or "Slackard." Shepherd suggests "Sloppy" (p. 50n14) — see glossary.

392 ff.   *Mi leof kimeth leapinde.* Shepherd explains the difficulty of this complicated image: "The sense of this passage is involved because of the attempt to combine two mutually excluding metaphors: (i) that the beloved (Christ) leaps on and tramples the mountains, which signify those who lead the most arduous spiritual life; (ii) that Christ Himself is

the type of the highest life (and thus a mountain) who was shamefully trampled upon and abused by the world" (p. 50). See R. E. Kaske's "The Three Leaps of Eve" for an account of various medieval interpretations of this passage.

398   *munt of Muntgiw*. See the Textual Note to this line.

415 ff. For a discussion of self-flagellation and other mortifications of the flesh, see the Introduction (p. 4).

427–28 An alternate reading of these lines: "If any man suspects any such thing of Him (i.e., that God would throw this holy man into hell), he will be more confounded than a thief caught with his theft."

432   *as is i-seid th'ruppe*. See the discussion of remedies for envy (4.1271 ff.).

Part Seven

With Part Seven, *AW* reaches the core of the inner rule. As Shepherd shows, *AW*'s idea of love is very much influenced by Cistercian devotion and more particularly by Bernard's thinking (pp. xviii–li). Bernard's writings on divine love incorporate and develop a long tradition of commentary on the Song of Songs (see Ann Astell's *The Song of Songs in the Middle Ages*). The author employs a number of bizarre and audacious analogies — Christ as an abusive lover, God's love as spiritual napalm, etc. It is fair to say, though, that *AW* takes a less mystical approach to the love of God than later texts like *The Book of Margery Kempe* and the *Divine Showings* of Julian of Norwich. Although there are a few hints at mystical union with the divine, for the most part Christ delivers his embassy of love to an indifferent lady. In fact, Part Seven spends more time imagining what might harden an anchoress' heart to the lover-knight than in placing her in his arms and even imagines the rage which the reluctant beloved will endure for rejecting his love. Most scholarly work on this section has focused Christ as the lover-knight. Elizabeth Robertson argues that the romance elements imply a passive spirituality for women (*Early English Devotional Prose*, p. 72), an idea which Catherine Innes-Parker modifies by reading the parable of the lover-knight less in terms of medieval romance and more through the "affective mysticism of Bernard" ("The Lady and the King," p. 511). See also Woolf, "The Theme of Christ the Lover-Knight," and Rygiel, "The Allegory of Christ."

Outline

Introduction (7.1–41). The opening establishes forcefully the theme of Part Seven and the culmination of *AW*: the overriding importance of love, which brightens the heart.

God as Lover: How He Won Our Love (7.42–111). An account of how God won our love with noble gifts (7.42–53) leads naturally into the comparison of Christ to a human lover (7.53–58) who woos his beloved with letters and gifts. The attention turns next to the beloved herself, a lady besieged in the earthen castle (her body), but who is indifferent to the attentions of her lover (7.59–81). A full allegorical analysis follows (7.82–97) along with an answer to the question, "Could not He have saved us with less grief?" (7.98–111).

The Four Chief Loves (7.112–60). After outlining the four kinds of human love, this section shows how Christ's love surpasses them all: [1] love between friends (7.115–18), [2] love between man and woman (7.119–35), [3] love between mother and child (7.136–53), and [4] love between body and soul (7.154–57). Christ's love for his bride surpasses these (7.157–60).

The Wooing of Our Lord (7.161–209). Now Christ's love is revealed in a more dramatic mode — he woos his beloved in direct speech, sometimes offering the richest possible gifts (7.171–87), sometimes threatening force (7.188–94). This section ends with an account of Christ's fervent, burning love and why the anchoress should return this love with hot, not lukewarm love (7.195–209).

The Fire of Love (7.210–317). Picking up on the images of heat in the last section, the topic turns now to a comparison between God's love and fire, with a startling allegory of spiritual love as Greek fire (a kind of medieval napalm) and the ways it can be extinguished (7.223–68). The anchoress must choose between earthly and spiritual love — it is impossible to have both (7.268–82). Earthly love seems paltry compared to the unbelievable richness of spiritual love (7.282–95), and besides, God's love is so extreme that He cannot help doing anything his beloved asks (7.295–318).

Conclusion and Transition to Part Eight (7.317–22). Here the author reaffirms the sovereignty of the inner rule of love over the more or less inconsequential outer rule, which will be treated briefly in Part Eight.

For a slightly different outline of this section, see Rygiel's "Structure and Style in Part Seven of *Ancrene Wisse*."

1–2   *alle uttre heardschipes, alle . . . al*. Shepherd notes that this rhetorical repetition (as well as that in 7.11–12) echoes the repetition of *al* at the beginning of Part Six (p. 52).

11   *the hali abbat Moyses*. Not the Old Testament Moses, but one of the desert fathers. In *The Sayings of the Desert Fathers*, Ward provides this biography: "Moses, called the Robber or the Negro, was a released slave who lived as a robber in Nitria; late in life he became a monk and was trained by Isidore the priest and become one of the great fathers

of Scetis. On the advice of Macarius he retired to Petra; he was martyred with seven others by barbarian invaders" (p. 138). The title *abbat* "abbot" translates the Greek *abba* "father," often used for the desert fathers (*amma* "mother" was applied to holy women). Shepherd thinks that Abba Moses came to the attention of the *AW* author through Cassian's *Collations* (1 and 2), where he is the central figure, though it is also likely that the author knew of him from the *Verba Seniorum* ("The Sayings of the Elders") section of *The Lives of the Desert Fathers* (see Explanatory Note to 2.310). In *The Lives of the Desert Fathers*, the story of the holy man terrified of the demon army is told about Abba Moses (see 4.659–63).

20 ff.   *twa thinges*. Shepherd (p. 53) traces this idea to Bernard's *Tractate on the Office and Duty of Bishops*, chapter 3 (*PL* 182, col. 817).

25–26   *Augustinus: Habe caritatem . . . voluntate videlicet rationis.* Shepherd points out that a number of twelfth-century writers (including Aelred, Adam the Scot, and Peter of Blois) quote this phrase. Since a misinterpretation of the phrase is possible — the author adds an important condition (p. 53).

32–33   *Minus te amat qui preter te aliquid amat, quod non propter te amat.* This phrase from Augustine's *Confessions* appears in a number of medieval texts (Shepherd, p. 53).

34   *Schirnesse of heorte.* As Savage and Watson point out (p. 398n6), this is the first of several echoes from the Author's Preface (see Pref.33 ff.).

38   *Seinte Mihales weie.* St. Michael the archangel (mentioned in Daniel 10:13 ff., 12:1, Jude 9, Revelations 12:7–9) appeared in a number of apocryphal works in which he guided Moses and Isaiah to heaven. As *The Oxford Dictionary of the Christian Church* points out, "In connexion with the Scriptural and apocryphal passages he was early regarded in the Church as the helper of Christian armies against the heathen, and as a protector of individual Christians against the devil, esp[ecially] at the hour of death, when he conducts the souls to God" (Cross and Livingstone, p. 913).

42 ff.   *Godd haveth ofgan ure luve.* Shepherd traces a number of texts which treat this theme (why God is to be loved) similarly (p. 54). See in particular Alcher of Clairvaux's *On the Love of God* (*PL* 40, col. 861).

53 ff.   *as a mon the woheth.* The idea of Christ as lover comes ultimately from the Song of Songs and its medieval commentaries (including a famous one by Bernard — see Ann Astell's *The Song of Songs in the Middle Ages*). Shepherd traces a number of analogues

to *AW*'s treatment in various writers including Origen, Aelred, Anselm, and Hugh of St. Victor (p. 55), while Dobson points out some parallels in the *Moralities on the Gospels* (pp. 173 ff.) but thinks that many of the details are of the author's own invention. Savage and Watson note that the famous passage from *Piers Plowman* in which Christ jousts on the Cross is the climax of this tradition (p. 399n12).

55–56   *leattres i-sealet . . . leattres i-openet*. Letters sealed with wax, bearing the imprint of a signet ring were private communications, while letters patent (i.e., "opened letters"), as the OED explains, are "usually from a sovereign or person in authority, issued for various purposes, e.g., to put on record some agreement or contract, to authorize or command something to be done, to confer some right, privilege, title, property, or office; now, especially, to grant for a statutory term to a person or persons the sole right to make, use, or sell some invention." Letters patent proclaim a privilege publicly. Millett and Wogan-Browne point out that the Old Testament as a "sealed" letter is "an apt metaphorical expression of the idea that the Old Testament allegorically foreshadowed the New" (*Medieval English Prose*, p. 158).

60   *an eorthene castel*. The castle represents the body, also made of earth (see Genesis 2:7 and 1 Corinthians 4:7), while the lady symbolizes the soul (see 7.59 and 7.81).

73   *to scheome death*. Literally, to a death of shame — *scheome* is a possessive noun (see glossary).

86–89   Shepherd traces a similar image of Christ's crucified body as a shield (wide at the top and narrow at the bottom) to Bernard's Sermon 5 on Psalm 91 (see Saïd's translation, p. 141). Crucifixes with one nail through both feet seem to have become popular around the year 1200 — see Shepherd (p. 57). Savage and Watson point out that the "older images depict two nails in his feet, which are often also placed on a small stand, giving a sense of Christ's physical control and power at this critical moment in his battle with the devil. The newer ones depict Christ's feet crossed over on another and driven through with a single nail, so that his body seems twisted with suffering — and is also 'narrow beneath.' The new iconography evolved in parallel with a new focus, not on Christ's victory at the passion, but on his suffering" (p. 399n15). See *Moralities on the Gospels* (pp. 176–79) for further analogues.

105   *the thridde reisun*. Exactly what the first two reasons are is somewhat unclear. R. A. Waldron, analyzing the *AW* author's tendency to number his arguments, offers the following explanation: "The three answers which he gives to this question [see 7.98–99] are (i) to deprive us of all excuse for refusing Him our love . . . [7.99–100], (ii) to attract

our own love by the price He paid for it . . . [7.102], and (iii) to demonstrate His love openly [7.110]" ("Enumeration in *Ancrene Wisse*," p. 87).

108 ff. Both Anselm's *Meditation on Human Redemption* (see Ward's translation, pp. 230–37) and Bernard *Sermons on the Song of Songs* 11.7 (*PL* 183, col. 827) advance similar arguments for the necessity of the crucifixion (Savage and Watson, p. 399n17).

112 ff. *Fowr heaved luven.* Dobson points to a very close parallel between the four loves as described here in the *Moralities on the Gospels* (pp. 173 ff.), while Rouse and Wenzel (in their review of Dobson's *Moralities on the Gospels*) point to other analogues, among them in the *Summa brevis* of Richard Wetheringsette. Edward Wilson also identified a close parallel to the four loves in a sermon preserved in a late fifteenth-century manuscript (Lincoln Cathedral, MS 50). Shepherd lists a number of more general analogues (p. 59).

115 ff. Behind this story of the loyal friend lies the memory of the legendary friends Damon and Pythias. Shakespeare's *The Merchant of Venice* is a later handling of the same folkmotif. Though the antisemitism in this passage is drearily commonplace, there may be an echo of contemporary developments. As Shepherd writes, "The Jews in Henry II's reign had had a recognised place in the national economy and were much used by the king in the collection of money. From the beginning of Richard I's reign (1189), outrages directed against the financial monopoly of the Jews were numerous. Hatred was intensified by the fall of Jerusalem and during the preparation for the Third Crusade (1189–92)" (pp. 59–60). For more recent accounts of Christian-Jewish relations in this period, see Anna Sapir Abulafia's *Christians and Jews in the Twelfth Century Renaissance* and Andrew Colin Gow's *The Red Jews: Antisemitism in an Apocalyptic Age, 1200–1600*.

128–29 *"Yet he eorneth . . . swire."* The English translation is based not on the Latin paraphrase of Luke immediately preceding, but directly on the Vulgate text.

131 *as Seint Austin seith.* Though the exact reference to Augustine has not been identified, Millett and Wogan-Browne (*Medieval English Prose*, p. 159) point to a passage in *De symbolo* (*PL* 40, cols. 1191–92) and another in his *Sermon* 188 (*PL* 38, col. 1005).

136–37 *beath of blod.* The bath of blood seems to be a folktale motif. See Shepherd (p. 24) for analogues in secular literature.

157 ff. Cecily Clark detects a complex rhetorical pattern in the following passage, tracing its use of embedded parallelisms and to the style of St. Augustine in particular ("As Seint Austin Seith," pp. 212–13).

161 ff. Shepherd lists some parallels to this passage in the writings of Bernard (*On the Love of God*) and Gerard of Liège (p. 61). In some ways, the passage echoes the sentiments of *Þe Wohunge of Ure Lauerd* (see the edition by W. Meredith Thompson), where the soul sings a love song to Christ, cataloging His excellencies (see particularly lines 165 ff.). As Savage and Watson note, "The fierceness of Christ, especially in the threatening final sentences of his speech, is part of his knightly *persona* as well as being a feature of his divine authority, and is perhaps intended to produce a mixture of fear and awe, spiritual longing and erotic excitement" (p. 400n25).

161–62 *for-te yeoven . . . to sullen . . . to reavin . . . to neomen.* This series of verbs are passive infinitives — that is, they have a passive sense: "to be given, "to be sold," etc.

176 ff. *Wult tu castles.* Shepherd believes that a passage in Anselm's *Proslogion* (perhaps as adapted by Honorius of Autun) underlies this section on the gifts which the blessed will receive in heaven (pp. 62–63). For further details of Honorius' text, see Shepherd's article, "All the Wealth of Croesus . . . : A Topic in the 'Ancrene Riwle.'"

184–85 *Asaeles swiftschipe . . . of urn.* The word *of urn* may be a compound meaning "swift running," perhaps "greater speed in running" (Bennett and Smithers, p. 543) or a prepositional phrase *of urn* "in running." In the first case, the sentence would read "who strove with the swift running of the hart" (*heortes* must be genitive singular). The alternative, to take *of urn* as a prepositional phrase, would yield "who strove with harts in running."

189 *thurh nawt to leosen.* The meaning of *thurh* in this phrase is puzzling. Shepherd suggests that it blends two meanings, "in consequence of having nothing to lose" and "even though you have nothing to lose" (p. 63). The translation of this line in Vitellius, *pur nule rien perdre*, suggests that *thurh nawt to leosen* here might mean "in order to lose nothing," and may be an instance where French usage (*pur* as infinitive marker) has influenced the English syntax.

210 ff. Shepherd lists similar interpretations of the woman of Sarephta from Hugh of St. Victor, Augustine, Baldwin of Ford, and Peter Blois (p. 64).

218   *as to beoden cos*. Savage and Watson point out that the "kiss of Christ's mouth" is a motif which appears frequently in Bernard's *Sermons on the Song of Songs* (particularly sermons 1–8) (p. 401n32).

223   *Grickisch fur*. Greek fire was a kind of ancient napalm, a flaming liquid either sprayed onto enemy ships via hand-powered pumps or poured onto hostile armies from the battlements of a stronghold. This secret weapon of the Byzantine empire (hence the name "Greek" fire) was first employed in the seventh century against an invading Arab fleet. Medieval Europeans probably first heard about Greek fire from the reports of returning Crusaders, and relative to the date of *AW* perhaps from veterans of the sack of Constantinople in 1204. Recipes for Greek fire survive in Greek, Arabic, and Latin, but there is considerable scholarly debate about the original composition of Greek fire (Bert Hall's introduction to J. R. Partington's *A History of Greek Fire and Gunpowder* offers a good summary of this debate). Many of the recipes, however, call for some combination of sulphur, naptha, petroleum, as well as other ingredients, possibly saltpeter (linking Greek fire to the later invention of gunpowder).

Marcus Graecus' recipe in his *Liber Ignium ad Comburendos Hostes* (*The Book of Fires for Burning Enemies*) (see Partington, pp. 42–63) holds special interest for readers of *AW* since it mentions urine, vinegar, and sand as extinguishers of Greek fire: "You will make Greek fire in this way. Take live sulphur, tartar, sarcocolla and pitch, boiled salt, petroleum oil and common oil. Boil all these well together. Then immerse in it tow and set it on fire. If you like you can pour it out through a funnel as we said above. Then kindle the fire which is not extinguished except by urine, vinegar, or sand" (Partington, p. 50). Urine, vinegar, and sand may seem to be rather eccentric counter-agents for Greek fire, but as Partington points out, "Ancient fire extinguishers were water, sand, dry or moist earth, manure, urine (which contains phosphates), and especially vinegar, which was considered to be particularly cold. Plutarch said vinegar 'conquers every flame'" (p. 5).

AW's "recipe," unlike that in Marcus Graecus' handbook, is clearly not practical since it says rather mysteriously that Greek fire is made of the "blood of a red man," a jumping off point for the allegory, since Christ is the man made red by his bloody suffering. An odd passage in a thirteenth-century Latin romance, *De Ortu Waluuanii* (*On the Rise of Gawain*), also mentions the blood of a red man as an ingredient (one of many) in Greek fire. A long passage giving a recipe for Greek fire interrupts a description of a sea battle in which the Knight of the Surcoat uses Greek fire to destroy the remaining ships of a scattered enemy fleet. Bruce, the editor of the romance, calls this long digression an "outrageously burlesque receipt" (p. 384). And indeed, the list of ingredients does seem more than a little fanciful: toads fed on honey, dove's flesh, the milk of a freshly delivered cow, the venom of an asp, the hide and testicles of a wolf, the head, heart, and liver of a crow. The next ingredient is the blood of a red man, which is collected from a youth with a red beard and hair. He is fattened for a month and given women to gratify him sexually. Finally, he is stretched out on the floor, with food and drink unpurged from his body, surrounded by burning coals, and slowly bled (to death). His blood goes into the pot with the other ingredients. It seems likely that all these operations (digestion, sex, and fire) are intended to increase the heat of the blood. Next comes the blood of a red dragon, and then the known ingredients of Greek fire — sulphur, naptha, etc. It is difficult to know what to make of this recipe, but it may be that "red man" and "red dragon" are alchemical code words which here have been interpreted fancifully. In later alchemical writings, "red man" referred to sulphurized mercury (OED), and in his classic study (*Mysterium Conjunctionis*), Jung connects it to the production of the philosopher's stone itself (p. 492). For an accessible text of *On the Rise of Gawain*, see Mildred Leake Day's translation in Wilhelm's *The Romance of Arthur*, pp. 383–86.

The *Moralities on the Gospels* mentions Greek fire but uses it as a metaphor for lust, not divine love: "Exemplum concerning Greek fire and the sin of luxury (or, lust): Therefore, just as Greek fire is extinguished by vinegar, so also the flame of lust is extinguished by recollecting the blood of Jesus Christ" (Dobson, p. 182). Ian Bishop cites another analogue, a thirteenth-century love lyric, "De Ramis Cadunt Folia" (The Leaves Fall from the Boughs), whose last stanza uses Greek fire as a metaphor for the fire of love kindled by the eye and touch of a maiden: "Greek fire is extinguished/ right away with wine most sour;/ but that love (i.e., the love for a maiden) is not extinguished in the most wretched;/ rather, it is actually fed by abundant remedies" (p. 198).

238 ff.   This account of Christ's receiving vinegar to drink is also treated in 2.683 ff.

297–98   *In Numeri . . . dicit preces.* This added gloss on Numbers stresses that Moses *commanded* God with his word, not that he made a request through prayer, thus supporting the idea that God's love is so intense that He allows himself to be mastered by it.

319–21   *the leafdi riwle . . . i-halden.* See Pref.27–29.

Part Eight

With this section, *AW* returns to the subject of the outer rule with a series of prescriptions and suggestions about such things as food, clothing, servants and other practical arrangements. As in the Preface, the outer rule is treated as a variable and relatively unimportant aspect of the anchoritic life. Some of the prescriptions seem to be adapted from Aelred's *De Institutione Inclusarum* (see the headnote to the Author's Preface and the notes below) and perhaps also from other rules (see Barratt's "Anchoritic Aspects," pp. 37, 40–41 and Dobson's *Origins*, pp. 27 ff.). If the section has a leading theme, it is that the anchoress should choose the role of Mary (representing the contemplative life), not Martha (the active life) — see 8.38 ff.

Outline

Introduction (8.1–8). The introduction begins by stressing the variability and adaptability of the outer rule and that fact that unlike the previous three sections, this one is exclusively for anchoresses. The author announces that Part Eight is divided into seven sections — there is an outline of these divisions in Pref.147–51 — but does not number them here.

1. Food and Drink (8.9–70). This section begins with prescriptions about communion (8.9–20) and then moves on to discuss when and what the anchoress should eat (8.21–29), how she should treat guests at the table (8.30–33), why she should not hold parties or dinners — with a discussion of the roles of Mary and Martha, who symbolize the contemplative and active lives respectively (8.34–61) — and ends with advice about feeding servants and eating in the presence of men (8.62–70).

2. What an Anchoress Can Receive, Own, or Keep (8.71–95). Anchoresses should be careful about receiving things from men (8.71–75) and should keep only a cat, not livestock or goods to sell (8.76–88). Anchoresses should not store anything for safekeeping or allow any man to sleep in their apartments (8.89–95) — a lapse that could result from her agreeing to keep valuables.

3. Clothing (8.96–136). Amidst a number of prescriptions, the main theme is that an anchoress' clothing should be comfortable but plain.

4. Work (8.137–66). The author writes that he wishes the anchoresses would concentrate on making plain and useful kinds of cloth goods, not fine purses or lace (8.137–39), especially for men or relatives. Next follows a list of specific pieces of advice and prohibitions (8.139–61). Other kinds of work are also discussed: the anchoress is not to run a school (8.162–65) or send, receive, or write letters (8.166).

5. Care of the Body (8.167–84). In this section the author advises the anchoresses about the cutting of their hair (8.167–74), about bloodletting (8.175–77), and washing (8.178–79), reminding them that matters of the outer rule can be changed and adjusted (8.180–84).

6. Maidens' Rule (8.185–244). Here Part Eight discusses in depth the servants or maidens the anchoress is to keep — how many there should be, what their ideal qualities are, how they should behave (8.214–28), and what they should eat and wear (8.235–44).

7. Teaching of Maidens (8.245–76). The author suggests reading the preceding "rule" to the maidens once a week until they know it (8.245–47), then goes on to give advice about how to govern and provide for her own maidens (8.247–63), and how to treat the visiting maidens of her sisters (8.264–76).

Conclusion (8.277–91). Here the author gives recommendations for reading *AW* itself, offers a prayer for the anchoresses (8.284–87) and in turn asks for prayers on his behalf (8.288–91).

7   *Of sihthe ant of speche ant of the othre wittes is inoh i-seid.* This reference to the contents of Part Two is good evidence that the author considered it to be part of the outer rule.

10   *as ure brethren beoth.* In an attempt to identify the order of the author (referred to in this phrase), Dobson discusses at length how the Dominicans, Franciscans, and Augustinian canons took communion (the number of times and what dates). He concludes that the description here parallels Dominican practice (Dobson, *Origins*, p. 64).

21 ff.   See Aelred's more elaborate and restrictive advice about meals and fasting: "On vigils of feasts, on Ember Days and on the Wednesdays and Fridays out of Lent she should fast on a Lenten diet. In Lent one meal a day should suffice, and on Fridays, unless ill-health prevent her, she should fast on bread and water. From the Exaltation of the Holy Cross until Lent she should have one meal a day after none, while in Lent she should not break her fast until after vespers. From Easter to Pentecost, except for the Rogation Days and the vigil of Pentecost, she should take dinner after sext and supper in the evening; this should be the rule throughout the summer except for the Wednesdays and Fridays and solemn fasts. On these fast days in summer, she may, instead of taking a midday sleep, allow herself a short rest between lauds and prime" (chapter 12, p. 60).

23   *ne schule ye nawt eoten hwit.* White food contains milk.

26 ff.   As Savage and Watson note, the "French version of *AW* preserved in the Cotton Vitellius manuscript here adds a short passage offering a slightly less rigorous alternative, as followed by the Augustinian canons, in which meat can be eaten three times a week . . . . The passage also mentions that the more rigorous practice is that of the Augustinian friars and Benedictines" (p. 403n7).

38 ff.   For the account of Mary and Martha, see Luke 10:38–42. In the medieval exegesis, Mary and Martha stood for the contemplative and active lives, respectively. See Barratt's "Anchoritic Aspects" (pp. 38–40) for a review of the standard interpretations of Mary and Martha in medieval exegesis.

66   *freres preachurs ant meonurs*. This reference to the Dominicans and Franciscans is, as Millett and Wogan-Browne point out, a later addition (*Medieval English Prose*, p. 162). See Explanatory Note to 2.236.

71   *Ed gode men neometh al thet ow to nedeth*. See Explanatory Notes to 4.164 and 4.1007 ff. In *Anchorites and their Patrons*, Warren devotes considerable attention to anchoresses' sources of income, concluding that they had to show proof of private means or outside patronage before the bishop would approve their enclosure (see especially chapters 5–8).

71–95   This rather odd collection of advice about food, cats, cows, etc., is tied together by its interest in possessions — what an anchoress can receive, own, keep, etc. The last prohibition (8.92–95) imagines human guests as objects that should not be kept within the anchorhold.

79 ff.   Aelred also warns against the dangers of property: "Others . . . are yet so eager to make money or to increase the size of their flocks, are so painstaking about it and exert themselves so strenuously that they could well be mistaken for châtelaines rather than anchoresses. Finding pasture for their flocks and shepherds to tend them; demanding a statement of the numbers, weight, and value of the flock's yearly produce; following the fluctuations of the market. Their money attracts money, it accumulates and gives them a thirst for wealth" (chapter 3, p. 47). Savage and Watson observe that "Ownership of a cow involves the anchoress deeply in the local economy, land-rights and bylaws. It is interesting that the author still concedes that it may be necessary for some anchoresses (failing other means of livelihood) to own one anyway" (p. 404n14).

89   *Nawt . . . ne wite ye in ower hus of other monne thinges*. Anchorholds were often used as a kind of vault — see H. Mayr-Harting's "Functions of a Twelfth-Century Recluse," pp. 337–52, and Warren, pp. 111–12.

96 ff.   The advice about clothing shows a number of parallels to Aelred's, including the mention of coarse linen (chapter 13, p. 60).

117 ff.   The advice on wimples is greatly expanded in the Corpus version.

136 ff.   See Aelred: "It is a common custom now to send a young monk or priest a belt, a gaily embroidered purse, or some such thing, but this only fosters illicit affections and can cause great harm. Employ yourself rather with something necessary or serviceable; the proceeds can be used for your own needs, or if you have none, given, as I have already said, to the church or the poor" (chapter 8, p. 53).

144 ff.   *A mon wes of religiun.* This exemplum from *The Lives of the Desert Fathers*, Corpus' addition to the basic text, also appears the early thirteenth-century exempla collections of Odo of Cheriton and Jacques de Vitry, as Hall points out (*Selections*, p. 73), as well as in Cassian's *Collationes* 24.9 (*PL* 49, cols. 1297–98).

161   *Irn thet lith stille gedereth sone rust. Weater the ne stureth nawt readliche stinketh.* Both sentences are proverbial. See Whiting, I59 and W85.

162   This warning against running a school may be derived from Aelred, however much reshaped: "Never allow children access to your cell. It is not unknown for a recluse to take up teaching and turn her cell into a school. She sits at her window, the girls settle themselves in the porch . . . . Swayed by their childish dispositions, she is angry one minute and smiling the next, now threatening, now flattering, kissing one child and smacking another . . . . For yourself, be content with services and conversation of your two attendants" (chapter 4, pp. 49–50). See Warren (pp. 112–13) for similar warnings in other anchoritic rules.

166   Compare Aelred's warning: "Never allow messages to pass between you and any man, whatever the pretext, whether to show him kindness, to arouse his fervor, or to seek spiritual friendship and intimacy with him. Never accept letters or small gifts from a man, nor send them yourself" (chapter 7, pp. 52–53). Hall cites a similar passage in the Gilbertine Rule (p. 99).

167 ff.   Millett and Wogan-Browne point out that bloodletting was considered as a kind of vacation or recreation (*Medieval English Prose*, p. 162), hence the relaxing of normal discipline after bloodletting. Dobson (*Origins*, p. 33 ff.) attempts to match the number of bloodlettings to those prescribed in other rules, pointing out a number of parallels to the Prémontré statutes of 1236–38.

180 ff.   This paragraph is another expansion found only in the Corpus version.

185 ff.   Aelred gives similar though not identical advice about servants: "Choose for yourself some elderly woman, not someone who is quarrelsome or unsettled or given to idle

gossip; a good woman with a well-established reputation for virtue. She is to keep the door of your cell, and, as she thinks right, to admit or refuse visitors; and to receive and look after whatever provisions are needed. She should have under her a strong girl capable of heavy work, to fetch wood and water, cook vegetables, and when ill-health demands it, to prepare more nourishing food. She must be kept under strict discipline, lest, by her frivolous behavior she desecrate your holy dwelling-place" (chapter 4, p. 49). In *AW* maidens have a much more important role to play.

267 ff. See 4.944–46 for practical advice about sending messengers in a section devoted to peace and community (as a remedy for wrath).

273   *ne ticki togederes*. The word *ticki* may refer to a children's game (involving chasing) of the same name (see OED *tick* [v.]), a suggestion first made by Hall. See Millett and Wogan-Browne's discussion for further details (*Medieval English Prose*, p. 163).

       ase seith Seint Beornard. This sentiment has so far not been traced to any of Bernard's works, though Hall (p. 220) cites a loose parallel in a letter ascribed to Bernard.

277   *Of this boc redeth hwen ye beoth eise*. This advice may echo the ending of Augustine's *Letter* 211, incorporated into the Augustinian Rule, as Millett and Wogan-Browne point out (*Medieval English Prose*, p. 163).

289   *Inoh meathful ich am*. Dobson, attempting to identify the author of *AW*, detects an anagram in this line on the phrase, *Of Linthehum* "from *Lingen*," the birthplace of Brian of Lingen, whom Dobson advances as the likely author of *AW* (*Origins*, pp. 365–68). Though the suggestion is intriguing, Dobson makes his attribution on the basis of a series of inferences and educated guesses — in fact, *Linthehum* is a conjectural form which does not appear in any medieval text. No one inference seems completely unlikely, but when added together, they make Dobson's conclusion seem rather shaky.

290–91 This last sentence occurs only in the Corpus version and is probably the farewell of the scribe, as Millett and Wogan-Browne point out (*Medieval English Prose*, p. 163).

Textual Notes

In the following Textual Notes, "Tolkien," unless otherwise noted, refers to the emendations and notes of J. R. R. Tolkien's EETS edition of Corpus Christi College, Cambridge 402, while references to "Dobson," unless otherwise noted, point to comments in E. J. Dobson's edition of the Cleopatra MS of the *Ancrene Riwle*. In supplying the variants from the other versions, I have silently expanded the abbreviations, unless they are problematic in some way. In a few cases in which scribes or correctors have altered any of the texts, the revisions generally appear in pointed brackets < >, while a slash (/) indicates an original line break in the MS.

In order to allow readers to follow editorial decisions more easily, I have provided variants from the other MSS in full rather than condensed or schematic form, and have made an effort to write the notes in terms reasonably easy to understand. The variants, grouped into English, French, and Latin versions, appear in rough order of authority, based on their date and relationship to Corpus (see the Introduction for more details about the individual MSS). In the cases where a variant text omits the passage in question, "lacking" means that it was intentionally excluded or recast, while "lost" means that the text is missing due to lost leaves or damage to the MS. For some of the most obvious mistakes, no variants are listed, while those which involve questions of Middle English spelling or grammar often include the variants from the English texts only.

Since this edition aims to provide a working text of the Corpus version of the *Ancrene Wisse*, and not a full critical edition, I rarely emend the text merely to bring it into line with the other versions. Instead, the text is changed only when it is problematic on its own terms. Revisions and variations in Corpus are allowed to stand.

Abbreviations: **Bod.**: Bodleian Library; **BN**: Bibliothéque Nationale; **Caius**: Gonville & Caius MS 234/120; **Cleo.**: British Library Cotton MS Cleopatra C.vi; **Corpus**: MS Corpus Christi College, Cambridge 402; **Lan.**: Bodleian MS. Eng. th.c.70; **Lat.**: Latin Text of the *Ancrene Riwle*; **Nero**: British Library MS Cotton Nero A.xiv; **Pepys**: Magdalene College, Cambridge MS Pepys 2498; **Royal**: British Library MS Royal 8 C.i; **Titus**: British Library MS Cotton Titus D.xviii; **Trinity**: Trinity College MS R 147 (French text); **Vernon**: Vernon MS (Oxford, Bodleian Eng. Poet.a.1.); **Vitellius**: British Library MS Cotton Vitellius F.vii (French text)

Author's Preface

7   *deore-wurthe*. MS: *deorwerðe*. A later reader modernized some spellings in the first few folios. Tolkien remarks, "On this page an ungainly late 14th-century hand began an attempt to modernize the text, chiefly by erasing, here and there, obsolete *þ, ð* and substituting *ǽ* [runic wynn] for *w*; and incidentally altering dialectal *e, ea* to *a*. This 'emender' fortunately only looked at recto pages, and tired of the operation after disfiguring f. 3a" (p. 5, fol. 1a). Though the changes leave an interesting, though brief, record of a later engagement with the text, this edition will restore the original readings where possible, indicated in the text (though not in the notes) by italics. [Cleo.: *deorewurðe*; Titus (lost); Nero: *deorewurðe*; Vernon: *derworþe*; Pepys: *derworþe*; Caius (lacking).]

9   *efter*. The emender changed the original *a* to *e*, though the *e* is still partially visible.

12–13   *is eaver in-with*. MS: *is eauer inwið*. Although Tolkien believes that *inwið* (i.e., *inwith*) is a mistake for *inwit* (p. 5, fol. 1a, line 18), neither the sense of the phrase or the other readings bear out this suggestion. The form *inwið* appears frequently in Corpus as both a preposition and an adverb meaning "within." The MS form is retained here. [Cleo.: *is eauer Inwið*; Titus (lost); Nero: *is euerre wiðinnen*; Vernon: *is euer in wiþ*; Pepys: *is euere inwiþ*; Caius (lacking); Vitellius: *est touz(iours) dedenz*; Trinity: *est dedenz*; Lat.: *est semper interior*.]

18   *anto[no]masice*. MS: *an/tomasice*. Apparently a scribal error for *anto[no]masice* (Tolkien, p. 6, fol. 1b, lines 25–26). [Cleo. (lacking); Titus (lost); Nero: *antonomatice*; Vernon: *antomasice*; Pepys: *atthonomasice*; Caius (lacking), Vitellius (lacking); Trinity (lacking); Lat.: *anthonomatice*.]

25   *exercitio*. MS: *exerci<ta>tio*. As Tolkien notes, a faint hand has interlined *ta* after the *ci* of MS: *exercitio* (p. 6, fol. 1b, line 6). *Exercitio*, however, is a legitimate late Latin form (see the *Oxford Latin Dictionary*). See 7.3 for another occurrence of this spelling. [Cleo. (lacking); Titus (lost); Nero: *excercitio*; Vernon: *exercicio*; Pepys: *exercicio*; Caius (lacking); Vitellius: (lacking); Trinity: *exercitacio*; Lat.: *excercitatio*.]

26   *geometri[c]o*. MS: *geometrio*. Apparently a mistaken reading of *geometrico*, the standard form, though *geometria* is also possible. [Cleo. (lacking); Titus (lost);

Nero: *geometrico*; Vernon: *geometrico*; Pepys: *geometrio*; Vitellius (lacking); Trinity: *geometrico*; Lat.: *geometrico*.]

39   *god.* MS: *goð.* The scribe writes *ð* for *d*, a common mistake (see Tolkien, p. 7, fol. 1b, line 26). Here it is emended to *god* "good." [Cleo.: *god*; Titus (lost); Nero: *god*; Vernon: *goode*; Pepys: *goode*; Caius (lacking); Vitellius (lost); Trinity: *bonte*; Lat.: *perfectio*.]

48   *mot te mare wurchen.* MS: *moten mare wurchen.* Tolkien suggests that *moten mare wurchen* "[they] must work more" is a mistaken reading of *mot te mare wurchen* "[he/she] must work the more" (p. 7, fol. 2a, line 12), a suggestion adopted here, as it is supported by the other MSS, and since Corpus' reading seems grammatically difficult: *sum* is singular and *moten* plural. [Cleo.: *mot þe mare wurchen*; Titus (lost); Nero: *mot te more wurchen*; Vernon: *and mot þe more worchen*; Pepys: *hij moten þe more wirchen*; Caius (lacking); Vitellius: *couient le plus orer*; Trinity: *couient il le plus laborer e ourer*; Lat.: *quidam seruare possunt*.]

78   *as summe doth, ye telleth me.* MS: *as summe doð þe telleð me.* As it stands, the text "as some do who tell me" probably should read "as some do you tell me" or "as some do as you tell me," as Tolkien notes (p. 9, fol. 3a, line 1). Here, *þe* "who/which" is emended to *ye* "you," as the least intrusive and best supported of these two alternatives (see particularly Cleo., closely related to the exemplar for Corpus). [Cleo.: *ase summe doð ʒe telleð me*; Titus (lost); Nero: *alse sum deð alse ʒe telleð me*; Vernon: *as summe doþ ʒe telleþ me*; Pepys: *as mamy foles willen*; Caius (lacking); Vitellius: *sicome vous me contez*; Trinity: *si com aucune fols genz uolent fere*; Lat.: *sicut quidam faciunt*.]

82   *openluker descrivet ant i-sutelet then is i Sein James canonial epistel.* MS: *openlukest descriueþ ant isutelet þen is i sein iames canonial epistel.* There are two problems here. First, MS *þen* "than" seems to require the comparative *openluker* "more openly" rather than MS *openlukest* "most openly." Secondly, as Tolkien points out (p. 9, fol. 3r, line 6), the emender has mistaken *descriuet* "described," a past participle, for the third-person singular form *descriueþ* "describes" and has changed the likely original *-t* to *-þ*. The superlative form *openlukest* is here emended to *openluker*, and *descriueþ* is changed to *descrivet*. [Cleo.: *openlukest descriuet ant isutelet þet(/þus) is i(n) seint iames pistel*; Titus (lost); Nero: *openluker descriued and isuteled; þen is i sein iames canoniel epistle*; Vernon: *openlokest descriuet and isotelet. þet is in seynt James canonial*

epistel; Pepys (recast); Caius (lacking); Vitellius: *plus ouertement (descr)it. Cest en la epistre canonicale seint Jake*; Trinity: *plus ouertement e plus apertement descrit e mustre quei est ordre e religion. ke en le epistle canonies* (BN, Bod.: *canonciel*) *seint Iake*; Lat.: *apertius describitur quam in canonica Iacobi.*]

83   *hwet*. MS: *what*. Altered from the probable original form *hwet* by the emender. [Cleo.: *hwat*; Titus (lost); Nero: *hwuch*; Vernon: *wher*; Pepys (recast); Caius (lacking).]

86   *wydewen ant fe[der]lese children*. MS: *wydues ant fa/lese children*. Tolkien observes, "[E]mender omitted *der* [from *falese*]; original probably *widewen ant feder[lese]*, not room for *feader*" (p. 9, fol. 3a, line 11). Accordingly the text is emended to read *wydewen ant federlese children* "widows and fatherless children." [Cleo.: *widewen ant federlase children*; Titus (lost); Nero: *widewen ant federlease children*; Vernon: *widewen and faderes children*; Pepys: *faderles children ant widewen*; Caius (lacking).]

91   *wydewen ant feaderlese children*. MS: *wydewes ant faderlese*. The emender altered, among other things, the original plural *-n* of "widewen" to *-s*. Tolkien believes that the "space here suggests that original had *wi/dewen ant feaderlese*" (p. 10, fol. 3a, lines 19–20), a suggestion adopted here. [Cleo.: *widewen ant federlese children*; Titus (lost); Nero: *widewen ant federlease children*; Vernon: *widewen and faderles children*; Pepys (recast); Caius (lacking).]

92   *sawle*. MS: *sowle*. The last of the emender's alterations — changed here to the usual form, *sawle*. [Cleo.: *saule*; Titus (lost); Nero: *soule*; Vernon: *soule*; Pepys (lacking); Caius (lacking).]

101   *Sincletice*. MS: *Sicleclice*. The confused spelling here is probably owing to a mistake in the exemplar, also appearing in Cleo., where it was subsequently corrected by Scribe B (see Dobson, p. 10, note c). [Cleo. original *sinchete* corrected to *sincletece*; Nero: *sincletice*; Vernon: *sincletyse*; Pepys: *Sincletice*; Caius (lacking); Vitellius: *synclitice*; Trinity: *sincletice*; Lat.: *Sincletica.*]

106   *of ower ordre*. MS: *of ower ~~boc~~ ordre*. The scribe wrote and then canceled *boc* "book."

121   *god*. MS: *godd*. Very probably a mistaking of *godd* "God" for *god* "good," a spelling distinction consistently maintained in Corpus: probably influenced by the

appearance of *godd*, almost directly underneath. [Cleo.: *god*; Titus (lacking); Nero: *god*; Vernon: *God*; Pepys (recast); Caius (lacking).]

126   *spurcicia*. MS: *spursica*. A mistake for *spursicia* (See Tolkien, p. 11, fol. 4a, line 14). [Cleo. (lacking); Titus (lacking); Nero (lacking); Vernon: *spurcicia*; Pepys: *spurcicia*; Caius (lacking); Vitellius (lacking); Trinity: *spurcicia*; Lat.: *spurcicia.*]

137–38   *of euch wit*. MS: *of euch hwet*. Tolkien believes that *hwet* is a mistake for *wit* (p. 11, fol. 4a, line 28), though Dobson ("Affiliations") disagrees, arguing that Corpus has the correct reading *of euch hwet* "of each (of them)": "in the context, it is easy to understand how *hwet* could be corrupted into *wit*, but hardly conceivable that *wit* would be corrupted or revised to *hwet*" (p. 130). The OED (see the entry for "what") lists the use of "what" as a noun in such phrases as "all what," "anywhat," "otherwhat," though not "each what." Mistaking *wit* for *hwet* may not be entirely implausible as a copying error, given the presence of "hwer" in the previous line, which could have influenced the respelling of *wit* as *hwet*. In addition, all the other versions, both English and French have the *wit* reading. Thus, MS: *hwet* is here emended to *wit*. [Cleo.: *of vh an (wit)*, with *wit* erased but still visible; Titus (lacking); Nero: *of eueriche wit*; Vernon: *of uche a wit*; Pepys (lacking); Caius (lacking); Vitellius: *de chescun sen*; Trinity: *de checun sen*; Lat. (lacking).]

139   *of anes cunnes fuheles*. MS: *of anes cunnes fuheles*. Ackerman and Dahood defend Cleo.'s *fif cunnes fo[w]eles* "five kinds of birds" as follows: "Cleopatra seems occasionally, if in a minor way, to offer a better reading than Corpus, as in the rehearsal of the contents of *AR* at the end of the Introduction. The third 'distinction', or part, as [the] A [scribe of Cleopatra] accurately informs us (Cleopatra, fol. 8v), consists of likening the anchoress to five kinds of birds. But Corpus, in agreement with the other manuscripts of *AR*, speaks of *anes cunnes fuheles*, 'birds of one kind' to which David, as an anchorite, compared himself. In fact, Part III of the rule goes beyond the biblical basis for this comparison (Psalm 101:6–7), for in the Psalm only three different birds are mentioned. Moreover, the margins of Cleopatra contain emendations by B not carried over into Corpus which nonetheless improve the sense of the basic text" (pp. 5–6). In his translation, White provides a possible answer to the difficulty by rendering *anes cunnes fuheles* as "birds of a certain kind." Though it is tempting to follow Cleo. here, the MS reading is retained. [Cleo.: *of fif cunnes fo(w)eles*; Titus (lost); Nero: *of ones kunnes fuweles*; Vernon: *of one kunne foules*; Pepys (recast), Caius

(lacking); Vitellius: *dune maniere doyseaus*; Trinity: *de une manere de oiseaus*; Lat.: *de natura cuiusdam auis.*]

Part One

57–58   *buhinde sum-deal dune-ward seggeth Pasternoster.* MS: *buhinde sumdeal duneward seggeð. Pater noster.* Tolkien, with an eye on Nero, suggests that a *; 7* (that is, a mark of punctuation and the abbreviation for *ant*) has fallen out before *seggeð*. In Cleo., Scribe B writes an ampersand over an original point, though Dobson calls this a "[f]alse alteration . . . but superficially attractive and also found in Nero . . . ; cf. also [Vitellius'] more consistent *abaissez . . . et dites*, which shows what the corrector [in Cleo.] and the Nero scribe had in mind" (p. 18, note n). The Corpus reading is retained here. [Cleo.: *buʒinde sumdel duneward. (ant) segeð. Pater noster*, with an ampersand written over the point; Titus (lost); Nero: *buinde sumdel duneward. ant siggeð paternoster*; Vernon: *bouwynde sumdel dounward. sigge pater noster*; Pepys: *boweþ sumdel dounward wiþ þe. Pater noster*; Caius (lacking); Vitellius: *abaissez auq . . . vers val. et dites [Pater] noster*; Trinity (lacking); Lat. (lacking).]

62   *hit [is] hali-dei.* MS: *hit hali dei.* The missing *is* is restored here. [Cleo.: *hit is hali dai*; Titus (lost); Nero: *hit is halidei*; Vernon: *hit is haly day*; Pepys: *it is haliday*; Caius (lacking); Vitellius: *sil est iour ouerable*; Trinity (lacking); Lat. (lacking).]

86–87   *bivoren uht-song ant efter prime ant eft[er complie]; from ower complie athet.* MS: *biuoren uhtsong ant efter prime. ant eft from ower complie aþet . . .* Since the first part of the sentence stipulates *three* hours, the scribe probably omitted *efter complie* by eye-skip to the next phrase (*from complie athet efter pretiosa*), altering *efter* to *eft*. The text is restored on the model of Cleo. [Cleo.: *biforen vchtsong. ant et prime ant et compelin. From ouwer compelin oðet . . .* ; Titus (lost); Nero: *biuoren vhtsong ant efter prime. ant efter cumpelie vrom þet efter preciosa . . .* ; Vernon: *Bifore matyns and after prime and after cumplye. til that preciosa*; Caius (lacking); Pepys: *Att Matyns. Att Pryme. and att complyn. with þe Pater noster. and after Preciosa . . .* ; Vitellius: *Deua[nt] [matines et ap]res prime. et apres [com]pli. de vostre compli deskes [apres] . . .* ; Trinity (lacking); Lat. (lacking).]

124   *vere fidei eternae gloriam.* MS: *uere fidei eter. gloriam.* Tolkien notes that *trinitatis* has been omitted after *gloriam*. [Cleo. (lacking); Titus (lost); Nero: *uere*

fidei eterne trinitatis; Vernon (lacking); Pepys (lacking); Caius (lacking); Vitellius (lacking); Trinity (lacking); Lat. (lacking).] In general Nero provides longer versions of Latin quotations.

125–26   *hwa-se hit haveth, other [sum other] of the hali thrumnesse segge the wulle.* MS: *hwa se hit haueð. oðer of þe hali þrumnesse segge þe wulle.* The text in Corpus — which now reads "or whoever wants [may] say of the Holy Trinity" — seems corrupt, probably due to eye-skip from one *oþer* to the second, and here the missing phrase *sum oþer* is supplied from Nero (since Cleo.'s text is problematic), giving the reading "or whoever wants [may] say some other [prayer] of the Holy Trinity." See Dobson (p. 24n3) for an involved description of this line, much corrected and muddled, in Cleo. [Cleo.: *hwase hit haueð al <;> oðer sum. oðer of þe hali Trumnesse; segge wase wulle*; Titus (lost); Nero: *hwo se hit haueð oþer sum oþer of ðe holi þrumnesse sigge þe wulle*; Vernon: *hose hit haueþ oþer of þe holy trinite sigge þat wole.*; Pepys (lacking); Caius (lacking); Vitellius: *ke lad. ou auscun altre oroison de la seinte trinitee; die qe vult*; Trinity (lacking); Lat. (lacking).]

145   MS: *tweof apostles.* Tolkien believes that *tweof* is "probably a genuine form," (p. 18, fol. 7v, line 10), and does indeed appear again in 4.481; 8.11 reads *tweofte*, however. Thus, it seems best to allow the MS form to stand. [Cleo.: *tweolf apostles*; Titus (lost); Nero: *tweolf apostles*; Vernon: *twelue apostles*; Pepys: *alle þine Apostles*; Caius (lacking).]

150   *H[a]lhen.* MS: *Hlhen.* Omitted *a* restored. [Cleo.: *Haleȝen.*]

151   *[F]or alle.* MS: ¶*or alle.* Tolkien remarks, "a red paragraph [symbol], ornamented with blue, mistakenly substituted for *F*" (p. 19, fol. 7v, line 19). It is emended to *F* here. [Cleo.: *For alle.*]

158   *yeven.* A later reader or perhaps the emender has striken through *yeuen*, as Tolkien says, "with a bold stroke" (p. 19, fol. 7b, line 28), in the mistaken belief that *ȝeuen/ȝeoue* was a repetition of the same word. It clearly is not, however: *marhe-yeven* is a "morning gift" (or dowry) and the *yeove* (following at the top of the next folio) is the verb.

164   *other.* MS: *oder.* A clear mistake for *oðer.* [Cleo.: *oðer.*]

210–11   *cneolin to euch an ant blescin.* MS: *cneolin to euchan ant blescin.* Tolkien
suggests emending *cneolin* and *blescin* to their singular imperative forms since the
verbs before and after them are singular (p. 21, fol. 9a, line 1). However, it seems
likely that a variation between singular and plural imperatives is a matter not so
much of a copying error as an actual linguistic process. Thus, the plural forms are
retained here: *blescin* (pl.) occurs between two singular imperatives *segge* "say!"
and *beate* "beat!" [Cleo.: *cneoli to vhan. ant blescin*; Titus (lost); Nero: *kneolinde
to euerichon ant blesceð*; Vernon: *also knelen to uchon. and blessen*; Pepys:
kneleþ to vchone and blisseþ; Caius (lacking); Vitellius: *genoilliez a chescune. et
vous seignez*; Trinity (lacking); Lat. (lacking).]

212   *Tuam crucem. [Salve, crux sancta.] Salve, crux que.* MS: *Tuam crucem. Salue
crux que.* One of the five greetings listed here has fallen out between *Tuam
crucem* "your cross" and *Salue crux que* "Hail, cross which . . . ," namely *Salue
crux sancta* "Hail, Holy Cross," a phrase which appears in Cleo., Vitellius, and
(in expanded form) Nero as well. The omission is probably due to eye-skip from
one *Salue crux* to the next. The missing phrase is restored from Cleo. [Cleo.: *tuam
crucem. Salue crux sancta. salue crux que*; Titus (lost); Nero: *Adoramus te christe
et benedicimus tibi quia per sanctam crucem tuam redemisti Mundum. Tuam
crucem adoramus domine. tuam. gloriosam. recolimus passionem miserere
nostri. qui passus es pro nobis. Salue crux sancta abor digna que sola fuisti digna
portare regem celorum et dominum. Salue crux que in corpore O crux gloriosa
o crux adoranda o lignum preciosum et admirablie signum per quod et diabolus
ext uictus et mundus christi sanguine redemptus*; Vernon: *Adoramus te christe et
bn t. g. p. crucem t. r. mund. Quam crucem et c. Salue crux et cetera. Salue crux
que in corpore et cetera O crux lignum. et cetera*; Pepys: *Tuam crucem
adoramus. Salue crux sancta. O crux lignum*; Vitellius: *Tuam crucem. Salue crux
sancta. Salue crux que*; Trinity (lacking); Lat. (lacking).]

262–63   *cwene crune on heaved.* MS: *cwene crune of heaued.* Of "off" should probably
read *on*, as in the other versions. Perhaps the text was faulty in the exemplar,
reflected in the heavily reworked text in Cleo. (see Dobson, p. 33, notes g, h)
contributing to the confusion here. [Cleo.: ~~cuwene~~ <*cwenene*> *crune on heaued
<sette þé>*; Titus (lost); Nero: *quene crune on heaued*; Vernon: *qweene croune
on hed*; Pepys: *quenes croune vpon þine heued*; Caius (lacking); Vitellius: *corone
de royne sur ta teste*; Trinity (lacking); Lat. (lacking).]

270   MS: *salue radix sancta.* Although Tolkien sees an error here — "*porta* omitted
after *sancta*" (p. 24, fol. 10r, line 17) — the other versions do not bear this out.

488

[Cleo.: *Salue radix sancta exqua mundo*; Titus (lost); Nero: *salue radix sancta ex qua mundo*; Vernon: *Salue radix sancta. ex qua mundo*; Pepys (lacking); Caius (lacking); Vitellius (lacking); Trinity (lacking); Lat. (lacking).]

372   *On ende, [on] ow-seolf ant o the bedd bathe.* MS: *on ende ow seolf ant o þe bedd baðe.* The text reads, "in the end yourself and on the bed both." An *on* probably omitted before *ow* is restored here. [Cleo.: *On ende on ouself ant on oure bed baðe*; Titus: *On ende on owself ant o þe bed baðe*; Nero: *alast ou sulf ant ower bed boðe*; Vernon: *On ende. on ow self. and on the bed bothe*; Pepys: *on ȝoure self and on ȝoure bedde*; Caius (lacking); Vitellius: *A la fin sur vouis meismes et sur vostre lit ausi*; Trinity (lacking); Lat. (lacking).]

386   *owe[r] Venie.* MS: *owe venie.* As Tolkien notes (p. 29, fol. 12r, line 20), the MS form is a clear mistake for *ower.* [Cleo.: *ouwer venie*; Titus: *owre uenie*; Nero: *ower uenie*; Vernon: *ower venye*; Pepys (recast); Caius (lacking).]

Part Two

8   *etflith.* MS: *etflið.* In Tolkien this appears mistakenly as *etflid.*

20   *swa withuten.* MS: *swa wið<u>/ ten.* Missing *u* supplied by a different hand.

29   *te parlures [clath] beo.* MS: *te parlures beo.* As it stands, the sense of the text is, "the parlor's [gen.] is." Tolkien (p. 30, fol. 13r, lines 12–13) argues that a singular noun is understood or omitted, probably in the archetype. In Cleo. it is inserted by a corrector, while Corpus and Nero omit it, the latter attempting to make sense of the text by construing *parlurs* as a plural form rather than a singular possessive (see the pl. verb *beon*). Cleo.'s reading is adopted here. [Cleo.: *þe parlures <clað> beo*; Titus: *te parlurs cla ð beo*; Nero: *te parlurs beon*; Vernon: *þe parlors cloþ. euer ben*; Pepys: *scheteþ wel ȝoure wyndowes and ȝoure dores*; Caius (lacking); Vitellius: *louerture del parler soit*; Trinity: *le drap du parlour*; Lat. (lacking).]

48   *in hire sunne in-yong of hire eh-sihthe.* MS: *in hire sunne inȝong of hire ehsihðe.* Tolkien argues that a verb has fallen out between *sunne* "sin" and *inȝong* "entrance" (p. 31, fol. 13b, line 12), but it seems best, following the MED (see *inyongen*), to take *inȝong* as a past-tense verb: "sin entered into her through her eyesight." [Cleo.: *in hire sunne inȝeong*; Titus: *in hire sunne. inȝong*; Nero: *in*

hire neowe in ʒong; Vernon: *of hire synne in ʒong*; Pepys (recast); Caius (lacking); Vitellius: *lentree de son pecchee*; Trinity: *prist primes entre en soen pecchee*; Lat.: *peccatum in eam ingressum habuit*.]

53   *Thus eode sihthe bivoren*. MS: *þus eode sunne biuoren*. Tolkien points out that the scribe has inadvertently replaced *sihðe* "sight" with *sunne* "sin," mistakenly repeated from the previous line (p. 31, fol. 13v, line 19). This suggestion, fully supported by other MSS, is adopted here. [Cleo.: *Þus heode sichðe biuoren*; Titus: *Þus eode sihðe bifore*; Nero: *þus eode sihðe biuoren*; Vernon: *þus eode siht biforen*; Pepys (recast): *how first siʒth bigan . . . þus ʒede it first bifore*; Caius (lacking); Vitellius: *Issi ala vewe deuant*; Trinity: *Issi ala li regard deuant*; Lat. (recast): *ex aspectu sequebatur affectus*.]

55   *alle the thing thet lust falleth to*. MS: *al þe ~~wa~~ <þing> þet lust falleð to*. In the MS, *wa* is canceled, with *þing* written in the left margin to replace it, a correction borne out by the MS tradition, though the original reading makes perfectly good sense in its own right. [Cleo.: *alle þe þing þet lust falleð to*; Titus: *euch þing þet lust falles to*; Nero: *alle þe þing þet lust falleð to*; Vernon: *al þe þing þat lust falleþ to*; Pepys: *al þing þat lust falleþ to*; Caius (lacking); Vitellius: *toutes celes choses la ou chiet desir*; Trinity: *checune chose ou desir e delit est depecche*; Lat.: *omne delectabile in quo est peccatum*.]

97   *lokeden cangliche o wepmen, ah*. MS: *lokeden cangliche o wepmen; ah . . .* Two leaves are missing from the Corpus MS after the word *ah*. The lost text is supplied mainly from Cleo. (the version most closely related to Corpus), which was heavily edited and expanded by a second scribe (Scribe B), perhaps the *AW* author (see Dobson, pp. xciii ff.). Scribe B's corrections and expansions are silently accepted where they seem to represent the best readings, as corroborated by other versions. In cases where B's corrections or expansions seem themselves in error in some way, a note is supplied. See Dobson's edition of Cleo. for an exhaustive account of B's editorial activities. Nero, though an authoritative MS with a much cleaner text, tends to simplify difficult passages and thus is less useful than Cleo. for restoring Corpus.

104   *Al yet the feayeth hire, hwet-se hit eaver beo*. MS: *Al ~~ʒet~~ <B: þet> þe feaʒeð hire. hwt se hit eauer beo*. Dobson: Scribe B struck through the word *ʒet* "and wrote *þet* above it, to give the sense 'all that which makes her beautiful . . . '. This is a meaningful but unnecessary change (since [Scribe] A's text is supported by F, Nero, Vernon, and Titus and is presumably correct) . . . . it is therefore revision

490

rather than correction" (p. 48, fol. 24v, note c). [Titus: *al ӡet þet feahes ow*; Nero: *al ӡet þet falleð to hire*; Vernon: *Al ӡit þer feleþ hire*; Pepys: *al þat falleþ to hir*; Caius (lacking); Vitellius: *tout ceo ensement qe la . . .*; Trinity: *E quanke vus vus atiffez*; Lat. (recast).]

112   *Strong yeld is her.* MS: *strong ӡeld his her*. The *h* is canceled (according to Dobson, by Scribe A) to indicate a change from *his* to *is*: "here is a stiff payment!" [Titus: *strong ӡeld is her*; Nero: *strong ӡeld is her*; Vernon: *strong ӡeld is her*; Pepys: *stronge ӡelde is þis*; Caius (lacking); Vitellius: *Ici est tresforte soute*; Trinity: *fort guerdon cia*; Lat.: *Difficilis reddicio*.]

114–15   *Thu thet unwrisd this put, thu thet dest ani thing thurch hwet mon is of fleschliche i-fonded.* MS: *þu þet dest ani þing ~~þurch~~ þet mon is þorch ~~þe~~ fleschliche ifonded.* Scribe A muddled the text here and has attempted to patch it, causing a syntactical problem by canceling *þe* and thus recasting the sentence, though not the sense. Dobson comments, "[Scribe] A's exemplar . . . must have had the true text, which is *þurh hwet mon is of þe fleschliche ifondet* (so Titus, Vernon, F); but after writing *þurch*, A subpuncted it, to continue in the next line with his own modification of the text . . . . The *þe* erased, obviously by the same hand as made previous erasure, to give the sense 'which man is physically tempted by'" (Cleo., p. 49nn3 and 4). The text is restored according to Dobson's reconstruction. [Titus: *þu þet dest eni þing hwar of þet mon is fleschsliche ivonded of ðe*; Nero: *þu þet dos ani þing þurh hwat mon is of þe fleschliche ifondet*; Vernon: *þou þat deest eny þing. þorwh what mon is of þe. fleschliche i.fondet*; Pepys: *Þou þat vnhiles þe putt. and doos any þing whar þorouӡ þat man is any þing of þe atempted fleschlich*; Caius (lacking); Vitellius: *Vous qe fetes nule rien par quey nul homme est de vous charnelement tempte*; Trinity: *Vus ke fetes aucune chose par quei homme charnelement est temptez*; Lat.: *contra eum qui aliquid facit per quod alius carnaliter temptatur*.]

117–18   *the fondunge thet of the, thurch thi dede, awacnede.* MS: A: *þe fondunge hwer þurch þe dede awakenede*; with B's alterations: *þe fondunge þe þurch þe ant et þe awacnede*. Scribe B has again rewritten A's text, by means of several erasures and insertions, to make it more comprehensible. Dobson describes these as follows: "B strikes through *hwer* and writes *þe* above . . . . B strikes through *dede* and writes *ant et þe* above. He thus produces the text (words retained from A in brackets): . . . *{þe fondunge} þe {þurch þe} ant et þe {awacnede}*, which has the same sense and balance, but not the wording, of the original, which is *þe fondunge þe of þe, þurch þi dede, awacnede* (so F, Titus, Vernon). B has turned

491

A's definite article before *dede* into the pronoun 'thee'; he apparently did not notice . . . that A had originally written *þurch þi dede* . . . which in it itself was correct" (Cleo., p. 49, notes c and d). Here the text is restored according to Titus, perhaps the most comprehensible of the many versions. [Titus: *þe fondinge þet of þe þurh þi dede wacnede*; Nero: *þe vondunge of ðe þet þuruh þine dede is awakened*; Vernon: *þe fondynge. þat of þe. þorw þi dede awakenede*; Pepys (recast): *for þe fondynge aros first of þe þorouȝ þi dede*; Caius (lacking); Vitellius: *la temptacion qe de vous par vostre fait esueilla*; Trinity: *la temptacion ke par uostre ouere comenca*; Lat. (lacking).]

129   *with sweordes egge.* MS: *wið sweordes echȝe.* Dobson: "So MS., for *egge* 'edge'" (p. 50, fol. 25r, note 10). [Titus: *wið swordes egge*; Nero: *mid sweordes egge*; Vernon: *wiþ swerdes egge*; Pepys (recast): *wiþ sweerd*; Caius (lacking).]

130   *with spere [of] wundinde word.* MS: A: *wið spere wundunges word*; B: *wið spere wundinde word.* Scribe B has corrected A's *wundunges* "woundings" (a noun) to *wundinde* "wounding" (an adj.) but has not supplied the necessary *of* (which is restored here) before the corrected word. (See Dobson, p. 50, fol. 25r, note g.) [Titus: *wið spere of wundinde word*; Nero: *mid spere of wundinde word*; Vernon: *wiþ spere of woundynde word*; Pepys: *wiþ spere of woundynge woorde*; Caius (lacking); Vitellius: *od lance de parole naufrante*; Trinity: *ou gleiue de naufrant parole*; Lat. (recast): *verbo vibrante cor quasi lancea uulnerat.*]

135   *Sweordes dunt [is] dun-richt.* MS: *Sweordes dunt dun richt.* The verb *is*, necessary to complete the sense, is supplied here. [Titus: *Sweordes dunt is dunriht*; Nero: *sweordes dunt is adun riht*; Vernon: *Swerdes dunt doun riht*; Pepys: *þe swerd of dedlich hondelynge smyteþ deþes dynt*; Caius (lacking); Vitellius: *Cop despee dreit en valant cest la manere*; Trinity: *E en par coup del espee fiert dreit ius*; Lat.: *Ictus gladij est tactus quia gladius de prope ferit et ictum mortis infert.*]

145–46   *as men walden steoke feste uh thurl [of hire hus].* MS: *as vh mon walde steoke feste vh þurl.* As Dobson notes, the original reading here was probably plural (see the pl. verbs which follow). This suggestion is adopted by deleting *vh*, changing *mon* to *men*, and adding a plural *n* to *walde*, following Titus, Nero, and Vernon. Note B's clarifying addition *of his hus* inserted after *þurl*, which helps to make the comparison clearer. Here it is emended to its plural form [Royal: *of hire house*]. [Titus: *swa men walden steke faste euch þurl*; Nero: *ase men wolden steken veste euerich þurl*; Vernon: *as men wolden. steken faste uche þurl*; Pepys: *what vuche*

492

man wolde scheten fast her wyndewes; Caius (lacking); Vitellius: *come gent clorreient ferm chascune ouerture*; Trinity: *com lem uoudreit fermement ueroiller e barrer checun huis e checun fenestre*; Lat.: *Sed quam sedulo clauderet homo fenestram.*]

146   *heo machten bisteoken death th'rute.* MS: *heo machten bisteoken deað þrute.* Dobson: "Both minims of final *n* subpuncted [i.e., canceled] by B (certainly not by A himself). This accords with his evident intention to change to the singular throughout; but *heo* should also have been altered to *he*, and is not" (p. 52, fol. 26r, note e). [Titus: *þet he muhten steke deaþ þer ute*; Nero: *þet heo muhtten bisteken deað þer vte*; Vernon: *þat me mouȝte steken deþ ther oute*; Pepys: *and hij myȝtten scheten out deþ*; Caius (lacking); Vitellius: *issi qil puissent forclore la mort*; Trinity: *quei ke lem peust for clore la mort*; Lat.: *ut mortem excluderet.*]

148–49   *moni ancre.¶ [Al holi writ is ful of warningge of eie.] David: averte oculos meos.* MS: *moni ancre. Dauid auerte oculos meos.* A sentence which occurs in all of the other versions between *moni ancre* and *David* is supplied here. [Titus: *moni anker. Al hali writ is ful of warninge of ehe. Dauid. Auerte oculos meos*; Nero: *monion ancre. Al holi writ is ful of warningge of eie. Dauid seide. auerte oculos meos*; Vernon: *Al holy writ. is ful of wardynge of eiȝe. Dauid Auerte oculos meos*; Pepys (recast): *Þorouȝ al holy wrytt it is techynge and warnynge of kepynge of eiȝen Auerte oculos meos*; Caius (lacking); Vitellius: <text lost> *(p)leine de gard* <text lost>; Trinity: *meinte recluse . . . Tote seinte escripture en mouz de lius en parout. e nus en garnit des regarz de nos euz. kar daui li seint homme dit issint . . . Auerte oculos meos*; Lat.: *multis. Tota sacra scriptura custodiam suadet oculorum. Psalmista: Auerte oculos meos.*]

155   *Hwenne.* MS: *Wenne.* Apparently a mistake for *hwenne* (see Dobson, p. 52). [Titus: *Hwen*; Nero: *hwon*; Vernon: *Whon*; Pepys: *whan*; Caius (lacking).]

156   *beo i-cumen to moni mon ant [to moni wumman].* MS: *beo icumen to moni mon.* The following phrase *ant to moni wumman* "and to many [a] woman," seems to have dropped out after *to moni mon* "to many a man" and is supplied from Nero. [Titus: *is to moni mon and to moni wummon*; Nero: *is to moni mon. oþer to moni wummon icumen*; Vernon: *is to mony men i.comen. and to mony wommon*; Pepys (recast): *þan may a synful man make for his oiþer a womman*; Caius (lacking); Vitellius: *est avenue a meinte homme et a meinte femme*; Trinity: *deut meint homme e meinte femme fere*; Lat.: *prouenit hominibus seu mulieribus.*]

157   *The wise askith.* MS: *Þe hwise askið.* Apparently a mistake for *wise.* [Titus: *Þe wise askes*; Nero: *þe wise askeð*; Vernon: *þe wyse mon askeþ*; Pepys: *Þe wise man askeþ*; Caius (lacking); Vitellius: *Li sage demande*; Trinity: *li sages hom en eclesiastice en quiert e demande*; Lat.: *queritur.*]

158   *Oculo quid nequius.* MS: *Oculo quid nequicius.* MS: *nequicius* (a non-existent word) should read *nequius*, as Dobson points out (p. 53, fol. 26v, note 1). [Titus: *Oculo quid nequius*; Nero: *oculo quid nequius*; Vernon: *Oculo quid nequius*; Pepys: *Oculo quid nequius*; Caius (lacking); Vitellius: *Oculo quid nequius*; Trinity: *oculo inquid quid nequius*; Lat.: *Nequius oculo quid creatum est.*]

159   *teres.* MS: *terres.* On the form *terres*, Dobson comments: "Abbreviated *t'res*, with mark for *er* above *t*; doubling of *r* probably not consciously intended" (Cleo., p. 53n2). [Titus: *teares*; Nero: *teares*; Vernon: *teres*; Pepys: *þe teres*; Caius (lacking).]

159   *for the ehe-sichthe.* MS: *for <þe ehe>/þech3e sichðe.* Dobson: "At the end of line B adds *þe ehe* (correct form of AB language), but omits to delete *þech3e* at beginning of next line" (p. 53, fol. 26v, note b).

160   MS: *to warni þe seli.* After this sentence, most of the other versions add a further comment which may be authorial, though it does not appear in Cleo. [Titus: *to werne þe seli. we schulen þah sone her after speke mare her of*; Nero: *to warnie þeo selie. we schulen þauh sone her efter speken herof more*; Vernon: *to warne þe sely ¶ We schulle þei3 sone herafter speken her of more*; Pepys (recast): *now we haue spoken of þe ei3en. speke we now of þe oþer wyttes*; Caius (lacking); Vitellius: *pur garnir li benure. Ci en apres tost parlerum de ceo plus.*]

161 ff.   At this point, the French version of the *AR* contained in the damaged Vitellius preserves an authorial addition, not found in any other version, and clearly part of the lost portion of Corpus. The text is supplied from Vitellius — see the glosses for a translation. Ellipsis marks indicate that the damaged text is unreadable at that point.

         Note also that after this sentence in Cleo., Scribe B ends his or her regular emendation of the text until fol. 124v, and has noted in the margin, *Hider to is amendet* "corrected up to this point."

185   *bisch[o]p.* MS: *bischp.* As Tolkien notes (p. 34, fol. 15r, line 20), an *o* has inadvertently dropped out of this form.

204   *essinien.* MS: *essinieien.* Tolkien notes, "sic clearly; probably *essinien* written for *essuinien/essunien* (the forms natural to this text) with dittography [i.e., accidental repetition] of *ie*" (p. 35, fol. 15v, line 21). The word, derived from French *essoinier* "to excuse," is typically spelled with *a-* in earlier texts, while the spelling with *e-* is first attested (MED) in 1464. Nevertheless, the best course seems to accept the first part of Tolkien's suggestion, that *ie* has been inadvertently repeated. Thus, the word is emended to *essinien.* The MED represents the word in Corpus as *essunien* without comment. [Cleo.: *asonien*; Titus: *aseinen*; Nero: *asunien*; Vernon: *asoynen*; Pepys (lacking); Caius (lacking).]

269   *ant al the swiing-wike athet non on Easter even.* MS: *al þe swiing wike aðet non <on easter> ant̶f̶r̶o̶m̶ ̶n̶o̶n̶ ̶e̶f̶t̶e̶r̶ ̶m̶e̶t̶e̶ ̶a̶ð̶e̶t̶ euen.* The original text was muddled here, and a scribe has attempted to correct it. Tolkien describes the problem: "In pencil, *from* to *aðet* expuncted, and in right margin, rubbed, *on easter*, joined by line to first *non*. MS. error apparently due to reading *aðet non on e(a)ster euen* as *aðet non . . . efter euen*, and supplying *ant from* and *mete aðet* in attempt to make sense" (p. 38, fol. 17v, lines 7–8). Before being corrected, the text read, "[Hold silence] all Holy Week until None and from None after the meal until evening." The text as it appears in this edition incorporates the scribe's corrections, but (following Cleo.) omits the *ant* after *easter*. [Cleo.: *þe swi<ȝen> wike. oðet non an ester euen*; Titus: *al þe swihende wike. ai til non of ester euen*; Nero: *al þe swiðwike uort non; of ester euen*; Vernon: *and al þe passion wike. riht to noon of after euen*; Pepys: *And in al þe sueiȝeng week. And on Ester Euen to ȝoure seruaunt ȝe may speke*; Caius (lacking); Vitellius: *et toute la symeyne penouse. et deske. noune de la veille de paske*; Trinity: *e tote la semeine penuse deske la ueille de paske*; Lat. (lacking).]

277   *ower eh-thur[l] sperreth to.* MS: *ower ehþurhsperreð to.* Tolkien: "*ehþurhsperreð* for *ehþurl sperreð*" (p. 3, fol. 17v, line 20). The missing *l* is supplied. Given the variety of readings here, it seems likely that there was a problem early on in the textual transmission. [Cleo.: *spareð ower ech þurles*; Titus: *owre eheþurl sperres*; Nero: *ower eie þurles tuneð*; Vernon: *ac oure eȝe siht .i.sperret to*; Pepys (lacking); Caius (lacking); Vitellius: *[le]s ouertures de voz oilz cloez*; Trinity: *le oil du pertuis de uostre fenestre enserrez*; Lat.: *nec solum claudende sunt aures sed et fenestre.*]

285–86   *Ancre naveth for-te loken bute hire ant hire meidnes.* MS: *Ancre naueð forte <loken>/<bute> hire ̶a̶n̶e̶ ant hire meidnes.* The text has been heavily corrected: Tolkien explains the mistakes and insertions: "the MS. now reads *naueð forte* *loken bute hire*; in a different, slightly larger, hand *loken* added at the end of [line] 4 . . . , *bute* at the beginning of 5 . . . ; *ane* expuncted. The main hand probably wrote *forte/wite hire ane*, mistakenly omitting *bute* after *wite*" (p. 39, fol. 18r, lines 4–5). The scribe's corrected text is reproduced here. [Cleo.: *Ancre naueð to lokin buten hire seluen ant hire meiden*; Titus (lacking); Nero: *ancre naueð to witene buten hire ant hire meidenes*; Vernon: *Ancre ne haueþ to loken; but hire. and hire maydens*; Pepys (lacking); Caius (lacking).]

329   MS: *longinqum*. As Tolkien points out (p. 41, fol. 19r, line 15), *longinquum* is the standard form, though the spelling with one *u* seems to have been acceptable to other scribes, and thus it is allowed to stand. [Cleo.: *longinquum*; Titus: *longinqum*; Nero: *longius*; Vernon: *longinquum*; Pepys: *longinqum*; Caius (lacking); Vitellius: *longinqum*; Trinity: *longinqum*; Lat.: *longinquum*.]

353   *The thridde time*. MS: *þet þridde time*. Tolkien argues that *þet* ("that third time") should be *Þe* ("the third time") (p. 42, fol. 19v, line 22). [Cleo.: *hire oðere wordes* (a later scribe added the number *3* in the margin); Titus: *Þe þridde time*; Nero: *þe þridde time*; Vernon: *þe þridde tyme*; Pepys: *Þe þridde word*; Caius (lacking); Vitellius: *La tierce foiz*; Trinity: *La quinte foiz*; Lat.: *Tercium verbum*.]

353–54   *thet ha spec, thet wes ed te neoces*. MS: *þet ha spec þet ha spec wes ed te neoces*. The scribe inadvertently repeated *ha spec* (see Tolkien, p. 42, fol. 19v, line 23). This edition differs from Tolkien in retaining the second *þet* (attested in a number of the other versions). [Cleo.: *þet ha spec þoa ha wes ed þe neoces*; Titus: *þet ha spek þet was ad te neoces*; Nero: *þet heo spec; þet was ette neoces*; Vernon: *þat heo spek; þat was atte neoces*; Pepys (recast); Caius (lacking); Vitellius: *qele parla ceo fut a les noeces*; Trinity: *ke ele parla; ceo fu as noces*; Lat.: *fuit in nupcijs*.]

361   *Ypallage*. MS: *ywallage*. As Tolkien points out (p. 42, fol. 20r, line 6), the scribe has confused runic wynn (the normal way of representing *w* in Corpus) with a *p* — an easy mistake since the letters are very similar. The scribe seems to have particular problems with rhetorical terminology — see Textual Note to Pref.18. [Cleo.: *Ypallage*; Titus: *Ypallage*; Nero (lacking); Vernon: *I.pallage*; Pepys (lacking); Caius (lacking); Vitellius: *ypallage*; Trinity (lacking); Lat. (lacking).]

372–73   *schal beon ure strengthe i Godes servise*. MS: *schal beon ure strengðe in godes strengðe*. The second occurrence of *strengðe* is apparently a mistaken repetition replacing the original *seruise*. [Cleo.: *in godes servise*; Titus: *schal beon owre* strengðe i godes seruise; Nero: *schal beon vre strencðe ine godes seruise*; Vernon: *schal ben ure strengþe in godes seruice*; Pepys (recast); Caius (lacking); Vitellius: *serra nostre force en la seruise dieu*; Trinity: *esterra nostre force en seruice deu*; Lat. (recast).]

393 MS: *For al uuel speche mine leoue sustren stoppið ower earen.* Though other versions read *From* at the beginning of this sentence, it seems likely on the evidence of Cleo. (where the insertions were added much later by Scribe D) and Vitellius that the original reading was *For*, which makes sense if it means "before, in the presence of." Thus it is retained here. [Cleo.: *F<r>or<m> al uuele speche*; Titus: *For alle uuele speches*; Nero: *Vrom al vuel speche*; Vernon: *From alle vuel speche*; Pepys (lacking); Caius (lacking); Vitellius: *Pur toutes males paroles*; Trinity: *pur totes mauueises paroles*; Lat.: *Ab omni auditu malo.*]

402–03 *dutten his muth.* MS: *dutten his mud.* As Tolkien points out (p. 44, fol. 21r, line 8), *mud* is a clear mistake for *muð.*

431 MS: *corus domino.* This phrase, "north-west wind of (lit., to) the Lord," seems to be acceptable, though Tolkien, in an attempt to regularize the Latin, marks it down as a mistake (p. 45, fol. 21v, line 24), presumably for *Chorus.* [Cleo. (lacking); Titus: *corus domino*; Nero (lacking); Vernon: *coram domino*; Pepys: *chorus domino*; Caius (lacking); Vitellius (lacking); Trinity: *thorus domino*; Lat. (lacking).]

451 *Nart tu nawt i this thing the forme ne the leaste.* MS: *nart tu nawt te ane i þis þis þing þe forme ne þe leaste.* As Tolkien indicates (p. 46, fol. 22r, lines 24–25), there seem to be two copying errors here. The scribe has mistakenly supplied *te ane* from the following line (*ne geast tu nawt te ane*) and has inadvertently repeated the word *þis.* [Cleo.: *nart þu naut þe forme ne þe leste*; Titus: *Art tu nawt i þis þing þe forme ne þe laste*; Nero: *nert tu nout i þisse þinge; þe uorme ne þe laste*; Vernon: *Nart þu nouȝt in þis þing; þe furste ne þe laste*; Pepys: *ne artou nouȝth in þis þe first. ne þou ne schalt nouȝth be þe last*; Caius (lacking); Vitellius: *Vous nestes pas en ceste chose le primers. ne le derain ne serrez*; Trinity: *Vus ne estes le primers; ne li dereins ne serrez*; Lat.: *Non es tu primus qui sic egit nec eris vltimus.*]

458 *her[c]nith.* MS: *her/nið.* The scribe has dropped a *c* at the end of the line, as Tolkien notes (p. 46, fol. 22v, line 6). The word should read *hercnið.* [Cleo.:

hercnið; Titus: *hercnen*; Nero: *hercneð*; Vernon: *herkneþ*; Pepys (lacking); Caius (lacking); Vitellius: *esco[utent]*; Trinity: *escoutont*; Lat. (lacking).]

484   *to feden hire earen*. MS: *to feden hire ~~ehnen~~ earen*. The scribe first wrote *ehnen* "eyes" and then canceled it with a stroke through the word.

556–57   MS: *toward te þurl clað*. Though Tolkien (p. 51, fol. 25r, line 12) favors Cleo.'s reading ("toward you through the cloth"), Corpus' *toward te þurl-clað* ("toward the window-cloth") makes good sense and is supported by Vitellius, Vernon, Titus, and Nero. Thus, we retain the MS reading here. [Cleo.: *towart þe þurch þe clað*; Titus: *toward te þurl clað*; Nero: *touward ðe þurl cloð*; Vernon: *to þe þurl cloþ*; Pepys (lacking); Caius (lacking); Vitellius: *vers le drap de la fenestre*; Trinity: *uers le drapel du pertuis de uostre fenestre ou uers vus*; Lat.: *manum porrigat*.]

608   *ant telest her[-of] to lutel*. MS: *ant telest her to lutel*. It seems likely that this phrase as it stands ("you care here too little") is corrupt in some way and that it was an early mistake since most of the versions find different alternatives. The simplest solution is to emend the text to *telest her[-of] to lutel* "if you care for this too little." [Cleo.: *ant tellest þer/ of lutel*; Titus: *ant tellest her to lutel*; Nero: *ant tellest herto lutel*; Vernon: *and tellest herto luytel*; Pepys: *and litel letest þere of*; Caius: *and tellest herto lutel*; Vitellius: *et poi en tenez*; Trinity: *e pou de force en facez*; Lat. (lacking).]

612   *thet is, as he seide*. MS: *þet is as ich seide*. Tolkien suggests that this phrase should read *þet is as þah he seide* "that is as though he said . . ." (p. 54, fol. 26v, line 10), although the other MSS (with the exception of Caius) do not support *þah*. This edition emends the phrase to read *þet is as he seide*. [Cleo.: *þet is as he seide*; Titus: *þet is. as he seide*; Nero: *þet is ase he seide*; Vernon: *þat is as he seyde*; Pepys: *he seiþ*; Caius: *as þah he seide*; Vitellius: *ceo est ausi come il deist*; Trinity: *Cest ausi com il deist*; Lat. (recast).]

617   MS: *stincinde lust*. Tolkien (p. 54, fol. 26v, line 17) apparently objects to the spelling of *stincinde* "stinking" with a *c* instead of a *k*, the usual spelling in Corpus. The original spelling is retained here on the chance that it may represent an OE spelling. [Cleo.: *stinkinde lust*; Titus: *stinkende lust*; Nero: *stinkinde lust*; Vernon: *a stynkynde lust*; Pepys: *stynkande likyng*; Caius: *stinkinde lust*.]

619   MS: *lahte wið his cleaures hire heorte heved.* Tolkien (p. 54, fol. 26v, line 20) claims that *hire heorte heved* "her heart's head" is a mistake, but Dobson refers to a gaffe in Cleo. which is *right* in Vitellius which has *le chief de son queor* "the head of her heart." It seems best to retain the MS reading here (on the authority of Vitellius, Nero, and Titus) and to translate "and snatched with sharp claws her heart's head." [Cleo.: *lahte eauer hire wið his cleaures hire heorte he haueð*; Titus: *lahte wið his clokes hire herte heaued*; Nero: *cauhte mid his cleafres hire heorte heaued*; Pepys: *lauȝt hym in her cloches*; Vernon: *cauhte hire with his claures. hire herte heued*; Caius: *clachte eauer toward hire heorte heaued*; Vitellius: *hapa od ses vngles le chief de son queor*; Trinity: *en lassasf . . . le cheitif quer de son uentre.* Lat.: *vngulis capud cordis sic rostrantis aliquociens apprehendit.*]

623–24   MS: *to himmere heile. hire to wraðer heale.* All other MSS except Cleo. lack the phrase *to himmere heile,* which Tolkien thinks is a mistaken form (p. 54, fol. 26v, line 26). Salu notes that the "meaning of *himmere* is unknown" (p. 44). It seems likely that the form *himmere* is muddled in some way. The MED makes a brave attempt to understand it: "?Error for *unmere*; c.p. OE *unmære.* Excrescent initial *h* is rare in *Ancr.*, rare in the pref[ix] *un-* in ME generally. Inglorious, miserable." Dobson thinks that *to himmere heile* might represent a place name, Dinah's destination, *Salem Sichimorum* (Genesis 33:18), while Morton suggests emending *himmere* to *grimmere* "with bad (or, worse) luck" (for these last two possibilities, see Zettersten, pp. 97–98). The phrase is allowed to stand here (especially since it is corroborated by Cleo.). What does seem clear, however, is that the *-ere* of *himmere* is an old adjectival ending (see *to wrather heale*) and that the *heile* may come from or have been influenced by ON *heill* "luck." The phrase should be considered doubtful, though; perhaps it is a confused anticipation of *hire to wraðer heale.* [Cleo.: *Iacobes dochter to himmereheale. þet is . . .* ; Titus: *Iacobes dohter. to wraðerheale þet is . . .* ; Nero: *iacobes douhter. to wroðere hele. þet is . . .* ; Vernon: *to wroþehele*; Pepys (recast); Caius: *Iacobes dochter to uwelleer hele. þat is . . .* ; Vitellius: *la fille iacob a malhoure de soen. cest . . .* ; Trinity: *la filie iacob; sei a male eure. Cest . . .* ; Lat. (lacking).]

694   *i-haved i the worlde.* MS: *ihaued i / i þe worlde.* The scribe has inadvertently repeated the preposition *i* due to the line break (Tolkien, p. 57, fol. 28v, lines 16–17).

697   *Sein Jeremie.* MS: *sein ierome.* As Tolkien points out, *ierome* should read *ieremie* (p. 57, fol. 28v, line 21), since the quotation comes from Lamentations 4:1. [Vernon: *O. seiþ Ieremye*; Vitellius: *Dit li prophete Jeremie.*]

697   Only two other versions (Vernon and Vitellius) contain the addition beginning with *Quomodo obscuratum* and continuing to 2.737, and each places it differently (Vernon at the end of the entire text, as an addendum [fol. 392r]; Vitellius, much earlier in Part Two [at 2.198]). It seems likely that the addition appeared at one time on a separate leaf inserted at the appropriate place and that it subsequently became detached.

702–03   MS: *beoð bicumene al fleschliche. al fleschliche iwurðen lahinde.* There seems to be an inadvertent repetition here of the same thought. But it is retained on the chance (perhaps rather slim) that it may represent a rhetorical repetition. [Vernon: *Beoþ bicomen al fleschlich¶ lauӡwhinge;* Vitellius: *estes deuenues toutes charneles riantes.*]

708–09   *Yef ha maketh hire wrath ayeines gult of sunne, ha [shulde] setten hire wordes.* MS: *ӡef ha makeð hire wrað aӡeines gult of sunne. ӡef ha setteð hire wordes swa efne.* This sentence seems to be incomplete or faulty as it stands since it consists of two *if* clauses with no main clause. The second *ӡef* may be a mistaken repetition. Removing it and altering the verb in the second clause (following Vernon) gives a sentence which reads, "If she makes her[self] angry against the guilt of sin, she should set (or, arrange) her words so evenly . . . " [Vernon: *yif heo make hire wroþ aӡeynes gult of sunne; heo schal setten hir wordes so euene*; Vitellius: *Si ele se fet corouce encontre trespas de pecche ele deit asseer ses paroles si owelement quele napierge trop moeuee*; others lack this section.]

714   *gasteliche earmes.* MS: *gasteliche earmðes.* This phrase should probably read *gasteliche earmes* "spiritual arms" rather than *gasteliche earmðes* "spiritual miseries" (see Tolkien, p. 58, fol. 29r, line 18). [Vernon: *gostliche armes*; Vitellius: *les braz espiritals*; other versions lack this section.]

744   *of Godes fowre.* MS: *of godes froure.* Tolkien suggests emending *froure* "comfort" to *fowre* "four," and indeed the immediate context (the four ways in which Christ suffered in His senses) as well as the readings in Nero, Vernon, and Vitellius support the change. The current reading was probably influenced by the presence of "froureð" in the next line. [Cleo.: *godes froure*; Titus: *Godes fowere*; Nero: *godes foure*; Vernon: *Godes foure*; Pepys (lacking); Caius (lacking); Vitellius: *des quatre sens nostre seignour*; Trinity: *du confort dampne . . .* ; Lat. (recast).]

765   *ful of angoisse.* MS: *ful of angosse. Angosse* is apparently a misspelling of *angoisse* "anguish," the usual spelling in Corpus (see Tolkien, p. 60, fol. 30v, line 6). [Cleo.: *ful of anguise*; Titus: *ful of angoisse*; Nero: *ful of anguise*; Vernon: *ful of anguysse*; Pepys: *his Anguisch*; Caius (lacking); Vitellius: *plein dangois*; Trinity: *pleine de angoisse*; Lat.: *anxius*.]

787   MS: *<ne> brohten <ha> him to present. ne win*, with *na* and *ha* inserted. The text reads slightly differently in some versions, though it seems best to retain the corrected MS reading here. [Cleo.: *ne brochten ha him to Present ne win* (with *to* altered to *no* by Scribe D); Titus: *ne brohten him na present. ne win*; Nero: *ne brouhten heo him to presente ne win*; Vernon: *ne brouȝten heo him no present. nouþer wyn*; Pepys (recast); Caius (lacking); Vitellius: *ne li porterent pas present ne de vin*; Trinity: *ne lui apporterent point de present ne vin*; Lat.: *non optulerunt vinum.*]

815–16   *ha schulen rotien in.* MS: *ha schulien rotien in. Schulien* may be a confused spelling of the the usual form *schulen*. Tolkien sees the mistake as an inadvertent anticipation of the *-ien* in *rotien* (p. 62, fol. 31v, line 24). Many of the other versions have the past subjunctive form *schulden*, but here Cleo.'s reading is preferable. [Cleo.: *ha schule rotien inne*; Titus: *ho schulden rotien inne*; Nero: *heo schulden rotien in*; Vernon: *þat heo schulden roten in*; Pepys (recast); Caius (lacking); Vitellius: *eles punirunt* (sic, for *purri-* or *puru-?*) *dedenz*; Trinity: *eles purrirunt*; Lat.: *putrescent.*]

826   *up-o the thridde.* MS: *o þe þe þridde*. The inadvertent repetition of *þe* (see Tolkien, p. 63, fol. 32r, line 11) is removed here.

Part Three

57–58   *Seinte Stefne tholede the stanes thet me sende him.* MS: *Seinte Stefne þet te stanes þet me sende him*. The text is corrupt, with no verb in the main clause. Dobson remarks, "*þolede* is required; author's MS must have used an *ad hoc* abbreviation (probably *þ.*; cf. *m.b.* for *muchele blisse*), miscopied from the start as *þet*. Otherwise Scribe A's text is correct; Corpus goes wrong here" (Cleo., pp. 99–100n19). This edition substitutes *þolede* for the *þet* after *Stefne* and emends the definite article *te* to *þe* (since no dental immediately precedes it). Corpus substitutes *sende* "to direct at, hurl" (see *senden* in the MED, def. 8e), for Cleo.'s *steanede* "stoned," and though this is less vivid, it probably represents a genuine revision, especially since Corpus omits *wið*. [Cleo.: *Seinte stefne þet þe stanes þet me steanede him wið*; Titus: *Saint Steuene þet te stanes. þet mon stanede him wið*; Nero: *ðet te stones þet me stenede him mide*; Vernon: *Saint steuene. þat þe stones. þat me stenede him wiþ*; Pepys: *seint Steuene whan men stoneden hym in þe mouþe and oueral*; Caius: *Seinte steuene þat þe stanes þat me stenede him vid*; Vitellius: *Seint esteuene qi les pieres dunt len li lapida*; Trinity: *Seinte estefne au-sint soffri ke les peres dont lem le la-pidout le sus leuerent en haut au ciel*; Lat.: *Beatus Stephanus, quod lapides quibus lapidatus est.*]

58–59   MS: *bed for ham þe ham senden him*. Though other versions have various readings here, it is possible to make sense of Corpus: "prayed for them who sent (or, hurled — see glossary) them (i.e., the stones) at him." The reading in Cleo. is clearer, though itself probably an *ad hoc* attempt to revise a very early corruption in the text: *ant bed for ham þe schenden him* ("and pray for those who dishonored him"). [Cleo.: *bed for ham þe schenden him*; Titus: *bed for ham þat ham senden him*; Nero (lacking); Vernon: *beed for hem. þet þren3 on him. so fele stones*; Pepys: *badd wiþ folden honden for her enemyes*; Caius (lacking); Vitellius: *pria pur ceaux qi les li enueierent*; Trinity: *pria pur ceus ke le lapiderunt*; Lat.: *pro lapidantibus orauit.*]

87   *ure rancun*. MS: *ura rancun*. The clearly mistaken *ura* is emended to *ure* "our" (see Tolkien, p. 67, fol. 34r, line 28). [Cleo.: *ure ranceun*; Titus: *vre rauncun*; Nero: *ure raunsun*; Vernon: *ure ransum*; Pepys (lacking); Caius (lacking).]

153, 159   *strucion(s)*. MS: *strucoin(s)*. Both Tolkien (p. 70, fol. 35v, lines 12, 20) and the MED think that this spelling is a mistake for *strucion(s)* (from OF *estrucion*) and accordingly it is so emended here. The word must have been obscure to the scribes, prompting some of them to grope for substitutes. [Cleo.: *strucion(es)*; Titus: *ostrice(s)*; Nero: *steorc, strorkes*; Vernon: *storken, storkens*; Pepys (lacking); Caius (lacking); Vitellius: *estruction.*]

160   *i-lich*. MS: *ilihc*. A clear mistake for *ilich* "like" (Tolkien, p. 70, fol. 35v, line 21).

216   *Mi leof is i-featted*. MS: *Mi leof is ifeatteð*. The scribe has mistakenly substituted an *ð* for a *d*, a common mistake. [Cleo.: *Mi leof is ifatted*; Titus: *Mi leof ifatted*; Nero: *Mi leof is ivetted*; Vernon: *3if my leof is i fattet seiþ ur lord*; Pepys (lacking); Caius (lacking); Vitellius: *Mon ami est engressi*; Trinity (recast); Lat.: *Dilectus meus est inpinguatus.*]

218　MS: *Þis featte kealf haueð þe feond strengðe.* The inverted word order of this sentence "This fat calf (obj.) has the fiend (subj.) the power to weaken," confused scribes in the other versions. Perhaps an attempt at correction was underway in Cleo. before it went horribly wrong and was scrapped. Dobson comments: "The *es* subpuncted by A himself. It is not clear what was happening; he omits here *þe feond*" (Dobson, p. 109n3). [Cleo.: *þis fatte calf haueð es strengðe*; Titus: *Þis calf haues te feond vn-strengðet*; Nero: *þis fette kelf haueð ðe ueondes strencðe*; Vernon: *þis fatte calf. hath the fendes strengthe*; Pepys (recast); Caius (lacking); Vitellius: *Cest graas veel ad lenemi poer*; Trinity: *Sour ceo cras ueel si en ad li maufez force*; Lat.: *Hostis habet potestatem infirmandi istum crassum vitulum.*]

254–55　*ne hwuch ha schal thunche yet in hire ahne riche.* MS: *ne hwuch / ha schal þunche ȝet in hire ahne cunde riche.* The scribe first wrote *cunde* "nature, kind" but canceled it with a stroke through the word.

286　MS: *wakieð ant ibiddeð ow þet schal don ow stonden.* Tolkien believes that an *ant* has fallen out between *ibiddeð ow* and *þet*, due to unusual crowding on this folio (p. 75, fol. 39r, line 26). The MS reading is retained, however, since the *ant* is not necessary for sense. If any word were to be restored, the better candidate might be *for* (see Cleo.). [Cleo.: *wakieð ant biddeð ou for þet schal don ou stonden*; Titus (folio lost); Nero: *wakieð and ibiddeð ou; and tet schal makien ou stonden*; Vernon: *wakeþ and bidde ou. þet schal don ou stonden*; Pepys (recast); Caius (lacking); Vitellius: *veillez et priez ceo qe vous fra esteer*; Trinity: *ueilliez. e orrez. e ceo vus fera resteer*; Lat.: *sic vigilate et orate; hoc faciet vos stare.*]

318　*thet tu hefdest i-don privement.* MS: *þet tu hefdest idon priuement darnliche.* A later reader has canceled *priuement* "secretly" (from OF) and substituted the apparently more comprehensible English equivalent *darnliche* above the canceled word.

324　MS: *magna uerecundia est.* Tolkien thinks that: *uerecundia* is a mistake for *uecordia* (p. 77, fol. 40r, line 20). However, the MS form is retained since it is a legitimate word and not a copying error. [Cleo.: *uecordia*; Titus: *uecoardia*; Nero: *uerecundia*; Vernon: *uerecundia*; Pepys: *verecundia*; Caius (lacking); Vitellius: *uecordia*; Trinity: *uerecundia*; Lat.: *verecundia.*]

347　*ne nowther ne bereth hit frut.* MS: *no nowðer ne bereð hit frut.* Tolkien rightly points out that *no* should read *ne* "not" (p. 78, fol. 40v, line 23). [Cleo.: *Ne nouðer hit ne bereð frut*; Titus: *ne nowðer hit ne beoreð fruit*; Nero: *ne nouðer hit ne bereð frut*; Vernon: *ne nouþer ne bereþ hit frut*; Pepys: *noiþer it ne bereþ fruyt*; Caius: *ne nouþer. ne beret hit na frut*; Vitellius: *ne nuldur ne porte ele fruit*; Trinity: *e si ne porte point de fruit*; Lat.: *nec fert postea fructum.*]

364   *as Sein Gregoire seith.* MS: *as sein geegoire seið.* A clear mistake for *gregoire.*

417   MS: *Vt lugeant.* Tolkien: "sic for *lugeam*" (p. 81, fol. 42v, line 2). The MS reading is retained here since it is grammatically sound, though not in agreement with the Vulgate. Tolkien often cites as mistakes any deviations from the Vulgate, even though slight adaptations in biblical citations are common in *AW*. [Cleo.: *ut lugeam*; Titus: *V<t> lugeam*; Nero: *ut lugeam*; Vernon: *Ut lugeam*; Pepys: *Vt lugeam*; Caius (lacking); Vitellius (lacking); Trinity: *ut lugeam*; Lat. (lacking).]

431   MS: *percuscienti.* Tolkien: "sic (*sc* for *c/t* = *ts* as in vernacular spelling)" (p. 82, fol. 42v, line 22). Since this spelling reflects a native orthographic convention, the MS reading is allowed to stand instead of emending to *percucienti.* [Cleo.: *percucienti*; Titus: *percutienti*; Nero: *percucienti*; Vernon: *percucienti*; Pepys: *percucienti*; Caius (lacking); Vitellius: *percucienti*; Trinity: *percucienti*; Lat.: *percucienti.*]

441   *bathe siker ant biheve.* MS: *bathe 7 siker 7 biheve.* The first *ant* is a mistaken addition. [Cleo.: *is baðe siker 7 biheue.*]

443   *al were he thurh miracle of baraigne i-boren.* MS: *al were he þurh miracle of bereget iboren.* The form *bereget* is difficult to understand as a mistake, though it must be related to the OF *baraigne* "barren" in some way. If we could assume that the *-et* of *bereget* is a mistake for *-n* (both with two minims), we would have the form *beregn* which is much closer to the attested English forms *barain* and *baraigne.* It seems likely that the form as it appeared in the ancestor of Cleo. must have been puzzling enough for Scribe A to omit it altogether in that MS. Perhaps the best remedy here would be to supply the word in a form which preserves MS: *g.: baraigne.* Diensberg tries to make sense of MS *bereget* by deriving it from OF *bereing* "barren" + *-et* (a derivational suffix seen in words like *baret* and *verset*). He suspects that a macron (the abbreviation for a nasal) over the second *e* has unintentionally fallen out, and so would restore the word to *berenget.* The difficulty here is that this word would mean something like "barrenness," a reading which would go against the extant English versions, as well as the French and Latin versions which translate "a barren woman." [Cleo.: *al were þurch Miracle iboren*; Titus: *Al were he þurh miracle iborn of barain ȝe*; Nero: *al were*

he þuruh miracle of barain iboren; Vernon: *Al Were he þorw miracle. of Bareyne iboren*; Pepys: *þei3 al were he þorou3 myracle bi3eten*; Caius (lacking); Vitellius: *tout fust il par miracle conceu de femme baraigne*; Trinity: *e tot nasquist il par miracle de femme baraigne*; Lat.: *licet fuisset miraculose ex sterili natus.*]

446–47   MS: *leste he wið speche sulde his cleane lif.* Tolkien: "blending of *fulen, sulien* (probably linguistic)" (p. 83, fol. 43r, line 13). The MS reading makes sense and is well supported by other authoritative versions. [Cleo.: *leoste he wið speche schulde cle his cleane lif for fulen*; Titus: *leste he wið speche schulde his cleane lif fuilen*; Nero: *leste he mid speche fulde his clene lif*; Vernon: *leste he wiþ speche foulede his clene lyf*; Pepys: *lest he schulde haue filed his lippes þorou3 foule speche*; Caius (lacking); Vitellius: *qil par parole ne soillast sa nette vie*; Trinity: *ke il par orde parole ne soillast sa nette uie*; Lat. (lacking).]

466   MS: *preminences.* Tolkien: "for *preeminences*" (p. 83, fol. 43v, line 6). To judge from the other versions, the *prem-* spelling (for *pre-em-*) seems to have caused little difficulty and hence the MS reading is allowed to stand. [Cleo.: *pre eminences*; Titus: *preminences*; Nero: *be3eaten*; Vernon: *preminences*; Pepys (recast); Caius (lacking); Vitellius: *preminentes*; Trinity: *preminences*; Lat.: *preeminencias.*]

485   *ne desturbin his god, he thah.* MS: *ne desturbin his goddhe þah.* As Tolkien points out, the scribe has canceled the second *d* of *goddhe*, though has not added a point to indicate the syntactical break (p. 84, fol. 44r, line 4). [Cleo.: *ne his good to sturben. he þach*; Titus: *ne desturben his god; he þah*; Nero: *ne desturben him of his god. he þauh*; Vernon: *ne distorben his god*; Pepys (lacking); Caius (lacking); Vitellius: *ne desturber son bien. il nepurquant*; Trinity: *ne puet son bien amenuser ne de ses prieres tant ne quant destou<r>ber*; Lat.: *nec suum bonum perturbare.*]

489   *Hylariun.* MS: *hy/larium.* Tolkien: "sic for *hilariun*" (p. 84, fol. 44r, lines 9–10). Again, though we usually resist Tolkien's tendency to standardize an eccentric spelling which may be a legitimate variant, mistaking a final *m* for an *n* after a series of three minims (*iu*) seems paleographically plausible, though there is no need to change *y* to *i*. [Cleo.: *yllarium*; Titus: *hylarun* <Zetterseten: sic "for *hylariun*">; Nero: *hilariun*; Vernon: *Hillarii*; Pepys (lacking); Caius (lacking); Vitellius: *hyllarion*; Trinity: *Hyllarion*; Lat.: *Hillarius.*]

499   MS: *i sum stude ut of monne.* Tolkien: "omission, if any, probably early; the versions vary" (p. 85, fol. 44r, line 22). [Cleo.: *in sum stude <from monne>*; Titus: *isum stude ut of monnes floc*; Nero: *in sume stude; ut of monne sihðe*; Vernon: *in sume stude out of peple*; Pepys: *in o stede stedfastlich out of Men*; Caius (lacking); Vitellius: *en ascun lieu hors des gent*; Trinity: *en aucun liu hors de la compaignie. e hors de la presse de genz*; Lat.: *in aliquo loco extra tumultum hominum.*]

515   *other eft[er] meith-lure.* MS: *oðer eft meiðlure.* *Eft* "again" is apparently a mistake for *efter* (Tolkien, p. 86, fol. 44v, line 13). [Cleo.: *oðer efter meidene lure*; Titus: *oðer after meidenlure*; Nero: *oðer efter meidelure*; Vernon: *after maydenhodes lure*; Pepys (recast); Caius: *oðer efter maidlure*; Vitellius: *ou apres del pucellage*; Trinity: *ou apres le despuceler*; Lat. (recast).]

515–16   *[is] bruchel as is eani gles.* MS: *bruchel as is eani gles.* Though Tolkien (p. 86, fol. 44v, line 14) suggests that *as* and *is* have been transposed here, Cleo., Nero, and Vitellius indicate that an *is* had dropped out of Corpus before *bruchel*. [Cleo.: *is bruchel as is ani gles*; Titus: *bruchel as ani glas*; Nero: *is bruchelure þene beo eni gles*; Vernon: *bruchel as eny glas*; Pepys: *wel brotiler þan þe glas*; Caius: *bruchel as is eni gles*; Vitellius: *est freignant ausi come vn verre*; Trinity: *si en est plus frelle e plus brisable. ke ne soit nul uerre du siecle*; Lat.: *fragile est ut vitrum.*]

540   *mid te sothe sunne.* MS: *mið te soðe Sunne.* Tolkien: "sic (*mid* half altered to *wið*)" (p. 87, fol. 45r, line 18). It is perhaps easier to explain this form, though, not as an incomplete correction to *wið* but as a mistake of *ð* for *d*, a common mistake — it is so emended here. [Cleo.: *mid þe soðe sunne*; Titus: *mid te sunne*; Nero: *mid te soðe sunne*; Vernon: *wiþ þe soþe sonne*; Pepys: *in soþe. Sunne þat is ihesus crist*; Caius: *mið þe seoðe sunne*; Vitellius (lacking); Trinity: *du uerrai soillel*; Lat.: *vero sole.*]

541–42   *ne beoreth nane packes.* MS: *ne beoreð nanes packes.* The *-s* at the end of *nane* "none" is grammatically impossible and probably a mistaken anticipation of the *-es* of *packes*. Thus it is emended to *nane*. [Cleo.: *ne beoreð nane packes*; Titus: *ne beoreð na<ne> bagges*; Nero: *ne bereð nout packes*; Vernon: *ne bereþ nout* (last word smudged); Pepys: *bere none purses ne bagges*; Caius: *ne beored none packes*; Vitellius (lacking); Trinity: *nen a portent point de fardeus*; Lat.: *non ferunt sarcinas.*]

549   *kinge[s] ant keisers habbeth.* MS: *kinge ant keisers habbeð.* As Tolkien points
        out (p. 87, fol. 45v, line 1), *kinge* should appear as a plural, an emendation
        adopted here. [Cleo.: *kinges ant caisers habbeð*; Titus (lacking); Nero: *kinges and
        kaisers*; Vernon: *kynges and Caysers. habbeþ*; Pepys (lacking); Caius: *kinges and
        kaisers. habbeð*; Vitellius (lacking); Trinity (lacking); Lat.: *reges et principes
        victum habent*]

554   *for-te folhi [the] ec into the blisse of heovene.* MS: *forte folhi ec in to þe blisse of
        heouene.* Tolkien: "*þe* probably omitted between *folhi* [and] *ec*" (p. 87, fol. 45v,
        line 8). The context as well as the other MSS bear out this reading, which we
        adopt. [Cleo.: *forto foleʒe þe ec into þe blisse of heouene*; Titus: *for to folhi þe ec
        ito þe blisse of heuene*; Nero: *uor te uoluwen ðe ec; into ðe blisse of heouene*;
        Vernon: *forte folwen þe ek. in to þe blss* (sic) *of heuene*; Pepys (lacking); Caius:
        forte folihi þe ec into þe blisse of heuene; Vitellius (lacking); Trinity: *e iloc
        unkore vus suieroms*; Lat.: *ut sequamur te in gaudium celeste.*]

558–59 MS: *famíliarite. muche cunredden.* The MED suggests that *cun-redden* "kindred"
        may be a mistake for *cuð-reden* "familiarity, acquaintance." Though this seems
        at first a plausible suggestion, confirmed by Titus and Caius, it is likely that the
        early meaning of *familiarite* was still very much dependent on Latin *familia*
        "household, family." It could very well be that *cun-redden* is the intended form,
        despite the *cuð-reden* reading in Titus and Caius (for which, see the glossary).
        The *AW* author often glosses French-derived words such as *familiarite* with their
        native English equivalents, but the absence of the English explanation in Cleo.
        and Nero may indicate that it was originally an interlinear or marginal gloss.
        [Cleo.: *familiarite. þet is to beo priuee*; Titus: *Familiarite. Muche cuðredne. for
        to be priue*; Nero: *familiaritate. þet is. forte beon priue*; Vernon: *ffamiliarite.
        muche felaweschupe*; Pepys (lacking); Caius: *familiarite. Muchel cudþradden.
        forte beon priue*; Vitellius (lacking); Trinity: *la grant familiarite de deu e la tres
        grant drurerie pur estre priuez*; Lat.: *desiderium familiaritatis cum Deo.*]

569   *ha wes the King Assuer over al i-cweme.* MS: *ha wes þe ~~cwen~~ <king> assuer ouer
        al icweme.* The scribe first mistakenly wrote *cwen* "queen" but canceled this word
        and inserted *king* above as an interlinear correction.

578   *totreode ham.* MS: *totreoden ham.* Tolkien thinks that this phrase "(to) trample
        them" should be singular (p. 89, fol. 46r, line 12). Though Cleo.'s reading solves
        the problem of the infinitive *totreoden*, it is probably best to follow Tolkien here
        in emending *totreoden* to the singular subjunctive (parallel to the preceding

"breoke") *totreode.* [Cleo.: *ha ach to treoden ham*; Titus: *to treoden ham*; Nero: *to trede ham*; Vernon: *to treden þe schomelese*; Pepys (recast): *totreden þe schemeful*; Caius: *tetroden ham*; Vitellius (lacking); Trinity: *e les despisent tantost e reuillent*; Lat.: *ipsum contempnendo.*]

588   *he folhede ham ant wende ut efter ham.* MS: *he folhede ham ant brec <wende> ut efter ham.* The scribe has written *wende* directly above *brec*, but without canceling *brec.* By itself, *brec* makes sense: "he followed them and broke out after them," though *wende* was probably the reading in the exemplar and *brec* an inadvertent repetition of *brec* from the previous line. [Cleo.: *he foleȝede ham. wende ut ham efter.*]

615–16   *For nis ower nan thet nere.* MS: *for nes ower nan þet nere. Nes* "was not" is probably a mistake for *nis* "is not," as the other versions suggest. [Cleo.: *nis ower nan þet nes*; Titus: *for nis owre nan þet nere*; Nero: *nis non of ou þet nes*; Vernon: *ffor ther nis non that nis otherwhile godes thef*; Pepys (lacking); Caius (lacking).]

623–24   *as spearewe deth [thet is] ane.* MS: *as spearewe deð ane.* Tolkien: "before *ane* is omitted *þet is*" (p. 91, fol. 46v, line 19). This is a plausible suggestion since Cleo. is slightly muddled, and *deð* and *ðet*, with the sequence of *d*'s and *ð*'s, appear to have confused the scribe of Nero. [Cleo.: *as þe sparewe þe deað ane*; Titus: *As sparewe þet is ane*; Nero: *as speruwe ðeð ðet is one*; Vernon: *as sparwe doþ one*; Pepys (lacking); Caius (lacking); Vitellius (lacking); Trinity: *si com li m̄ moisson <fet ki est seul>*; Lat.: *sicut passer solitarius.*]

631   *to wel leoten of [hire-seolven].* MS: *to wel leoten of.* Tolkien: "*hire seoluen* omitted after *leo/ten of*" (p. 91, fol. 47v, lines 1–2). Though Dobson doubts that *hire seluin* was the original reading (it was inserted much later into Cleo. by Scribe D), it does complete the sense which otherwise may be lacking. [Cleo.: *to wel leten of <hire seluin>*; Titus: *to wel leten of*; Nero: *leten to wel; of hire suluen*; Vernon: *to wel leten of*; Pepys: *leten to wel of oure seluen*; Caius (lacking); Vitellius (lacking); Trinity: *eles trop . . . grant pris de eus memes ou de eles*; Lat.: *de se nimium reputaret.*]

Part Four

18   *ha mahe ant schule.* MS: *ha mahen ant schulen.* Tolkien notes that these plural forms are a misreading for the singular (p. 93, fol. 48r, line 16), and thus they are emended to the singular forms. [Cleo.: *ha muhte ant schulde*; Titus: *ho muhe*; Nero: *þet heo muwe ant schule*; Vernon: *þat heo mowe and schulle*; Pepys: *þat he may for hem þe better ben yholpen*; Caius (lacking); Vitellius (lacking); Trinity: *ke il ou ele puisse le mieuz estre par icels temptacions sauuez*; Lat.: *quod possit et debeat per temptationes melius saluari.*]

27   MS: *þet te flesch eileð. wiðinnen; heorte sar.* Tolkien: "*mislicunge* omitted before *wiðinnen*" (p. 93, fol. 48r, line 26). The textual evidence for this emendation is slim, especially since Cleo., Titus, and Lat. apparently assume that *mislicunge* carries over from the previous sentence. [Cleo.: *eileð. Wið innen; heorte sare*; Titus: *eiles. Wið innen; heorte sar*; Nero *ðet eileð þe vlesche. Mislikunge wiðinnen; ase heorte sor*; Vernon (lacking); Pepys: *þat þe flessche feleþ. wiþinnen hert sore*; Caius (lacking); Vitellius (lacking); Trinity: *ke ala char nuist. Desplesance par de denz si est; doel de quer*; Lat.: *quodlibet nocumentum corporale carni nocens. Interior, dolor cordis.*]

27–28   *grome — ant wreaththe alswa, onont thet ha is pine. Licunge withuten.* MS: *grome. ant wreaððe. Alswa onont þet ha is pine. licunge wiðuten.* Tolkien makes the plausible case that the capital *A* in *Alswa* is a mistake since this entire phrase belongs together. Tolkien also believes that there is a problem with the word *pine* "pain": "*pine*, sic for *i pine* or *ipinet*" and that the mistake must have come early in the textual transmission since each version attempts to solve the problem differently (p. 93, fol. 48r, line 27). It is possible to make good sense of the MS reading *onont þet ha is pine* "in the sense that she (i.e., wrath) is pain" since it explains why wrath, which does not at first seem to be an internal displeasure, really is one. [Cleo. (lacking); Titus: *grome wraððe. Alswa onont þet he is ipinet likinge wið uten*; Nero: *grome. ant wreððe. also onont ðet heo is likunge wiðuten*; Vernon: *Grome. and. Wraþþe. ¶ Also anont þat heo is pyne. þat is sunnes ernynge ¶ Likynge wiþouten*; Pepys: *greme oiþer tene oiþer wraþþe for þat he is pyned in his body*; Caius (lacking); Vitellius (lacking); Trinity: *corouz. e ire. ausint en droit de ceo ke il est penez*; Lat.: *ira, iracundia. Similiter placencia seu delectatio exterior.*]

42   *the thuncheth thah gode.* MS: *þe þencheð þah god.* Tolkien: "*þencheð*, sic for *þuncheð*" (p. 94, fol. 48v, line 17). [Cleo.: *þet þuncheð þach gode*; Titus: *þet*

semen þah gode; Nero: ðet þuncheð þauh gode; Vernon: þat þuncheþ þauh gode; Pepys: þat men þenchen þat hij ben good; Caius (lacking); Vitellius (lacking); Trinity: *e si resemblent nekedent bones*; Lat.: *apparentes tamen bone.*]

49   *for hwen ha is i-pruvet.* MS: *for hwen ha is ipruet.* Tolkien: "*ipruet*, sic" (p. 94, fol. 48v, line 26). [Cleo.: *for þenne he bið ipreoued*; Titus: *Hwen he is ipreouet*; Nero: *vor hwon heo is ipreoued*; Vernon: *ffor whon he is i.preuet*; Pepys: *for what he is yproued*; Caius (lacking); Vitellius (lacking); Trinity: *quant il auera este temptez*; Lat.: *cum probatus fuerit.*]

58   *mede, [vi].* MS: *mede.* The scribe has numbered each of the six benefits of sickness by placing a Roman numeral above the first word of each. The number six, which does not appear, is supplied.

72   *thet ageath, thurh ei uvel.* MS: *þet agead þurh ei uuel.* Tolkien: "*agead*, sic" (p. 95, fol. 49r, line 27). A common exchange of *d* for *ð*, which also occurs in Cleo. [Cleo.: *þet aged þurh ani uuel*; Titus: *þet ouergas. þurh ani uuel*; Nero: *þet ageð; þuruh eni vuel*; Vernon: *þat ageþ ffor eni euel*; Pepys: *He þat may þan atstirten þat ilche griselich wo*; Caius (lacking); Vitellius (lacking); Trinity: *par aucun mal corporel ke isci tost passe*; Lat.: *per transitoriam infirmitatem, per aliquid malum.*]

88   MS: *Michi uindictam.* Tolkien: "*uindictam*, sic" (p. 96, fol. 49v, line 19). Another instance of Tolkien regularizing quotations from the Vulgate. [Cleo.: *Michi vindictam*; Titus: *Michi uindictam*; Nero: *michi uindictam*; Vernon: *michi vindictam*; Pepys: *Michi vindictam*; Caius (lacking); Vitellius (lacking); Trinity: *Michi uindictam*; Lat.: *Michi vindictam.*]

94   *thet ye cussen nawt with muth.* MS: *þet ȝe cussen nawd wið muð.* As Tolkien points out, *nawd* should read *nawt* "not" (p. 96, fol. 49v, line 27). [Cleo.: *þe ȝe cussen naut Mid muð*; Titus: *þet ȝe cussen. nawt wið muð*; Nero: *þet ȝe cussen. nout mid muðe*; Vernon: *þat ȝe cussen not wiþ mouþ*; Pepys: *ne kisse nouȝth wiþ mouþ*; Caius (lacking); Vitellius (lacking); Trinity: *ne ou bouche corporele les acolez e beisez*; Lat.: *non osculari ore eos.*]

103   *other-h[w]ile.* MS: *o/þerhile.* The missing *ƿ* (wynn) is restored. [Cleo.: *oðerhwile*; Titus: *oðerhwile*; Nero: *oþerhwule*; Vernon: *oþerwhile*; Pepys: *oiþer while*; Caius (lacking).]

152   *nawt withuten hurt felen.* MS: *nawt wið uter hurt felen.* Clearly, *wið uter* should read *withuten*. [Cleo.: *ne machten hit for uten hurt felen*; Titus: *hwas schadewe ʒe ne mihten naht for grislich bihalden*; Nero: *nout for grislich biholden*; Vernon: *not. wiþ oute hurt felen*; Pepys: *nouʒth with outen hirt it þolien*; Caius (lacking); Vitellius (lacking); Trinity: *la puissez sanz blesceure sentir*; Lat.: *pre (pro?) horrore conspicere non possetis.*]

165–67   *For the uttre is [adversite ant prosperte ant theos cundleth the inre: mislicunge] in adversite ant i prosperite licunge the limpeth to sunne.* MS: *for þe uttre / is in aduersite ant i prosperite licunge þe limpeth to sunne.* Several words have apparently dropped out of Corpus due to eye-skip from *is aduersite* to *in aduersite*. The missing words are restored here from Cleo. [Cleo.: *for þe uttere is ~~asper~~ aduersite ant prosperte ant þeos cundleð þe inre. Aduersite Mislicunge. per<s>perite. licunge þe limpeth to sunne*; Nero: *uor þe uttre uondunge is mislicunge in aduersite; ant ine prosperite. and þeos foundunge kundleð þe inre uondunge. þet is. in aduesite; mislikunge*; Titus: *for þe uttre is in aduersite and in prosperite. and teose cundlen þen inre. Aduersite; mislikinge. prosperite; likinge þet limpes to sunne*; Vernon: *ffor the uttere is in aduersite. and prosperite. and þeos cundeleth the innore. aduersite. myslykynge. prosperite. lykinge that toucheth to synne*; Pepys (recast): *þe vtter in aduersite and prosperite. þat is in wele and in wo. and boþe þise kyndelen þe inner fondynge. Aduersite is miyslikynge. And prosperite is lykyng that likeneþ to synne*; Caius (lacking); Vitellius (lacking); Trinity: *Car la foreine temptacion si est; en aduersitez en prosperitez e icestes si conceiuent en lui. Aduersite; desplesance. prosperite; plesance. dont pecche en auient*; Lat.: *Exterior enim est in aduersitate et prosperitate. Est igitur, ut dixi, temptatio interior.*]

188   *proprement.* MS: ~~*proprement*~~ *<ouneliche>*. A later hand (in darker ink and with a different script) crossed out the original *proprement* "naturally" (from OF) and substituted the presumably native form *ouneliche* just above the deleted word. Tolkien comments, "The emendation . . . had the same motive as that seen in *darnliche* [3.318]; but if due to the same purist, he took more care here to imitate the main hand. The natural native word here is *cundeliche* and may have suggested it" (p. 100, note to fol. 52a, lines 2, 4). The MED dates the addition to 1300 apparently on paleographical grounds and derives it from OE *agen* "own." Since these changes represent a later intervention in the text, the original readings are restored.

199   *flesch.* MS: *fleschs.* A clear mistake for *flesch*, probably influenced by the plural form a few words before: *fles/ches.*

219–20   *nawt ane the ne buheth, [ah the] other grucchinde deth, other targeth to longe.* MS: *nawt ane þe ne buheð. oðer grucchinde deð. oðer targeð to longe.* An *ah þe* ("but [also] the person who") is necessary here to complete the phrase which began with *nawt ane* ("not only"), as Tolkien notes: "*ah þe* probably omitted after *buheð*" (p. 102, fol. 52v, line 15). [Cleo. (lacking); Titus (lacking); Nero (lacking); Vernon: *Oþer gricchinde idon. oþer tarende*; Pepys (lacking); Caius (lacking); Vitellius (lacking); Trinity (lacking); Lat.: *factum cum murmure seu tarditate.*]

247   *to ove[r]gart acemunge.* MS: *to ouegart acemunge.* Tolkien rightly points out that an *r* is missing from *ove[r]-gart* "excessive" (p. 103, fol. 53r, line 22). [Cleo. (lacking); Titus (lacking); Nero (lacking); Vernon: *ouergart semynge*; Pepys: *to ouer girt as meninge. oiþer hei3einge*; Caius (lacking); Vitellius (lacking); Trinity (lacking); Lat.: *subtilitas in gestu.*]

251–52   *Of heh lif waxeth prude.* MS: *Of heh cun waxeð prude.* The other versions bear out Tolkien's observation that *heh cun* "high kin" (repeated from the previous line) has inadvertently replaced *heh lif* "high (or, holy) life" (p. 103, fol. 53r, line 28). [Cleo.: *of hech lif of strengðe þet waxeð of Prude*; Titus: *of heh lif waxen prude*; Nero: *of heie liue waxeð prude*; Vernon: *of hei3 lyf. waxeþ pruyde*; Pepys: *of holy þewes comeþ pride*; Caius: *of heh lif waxed prude*; Vitellius (lacking); Trinity (lacking); Lat.: *ex sublimi vita pululat superbia.*]

259   *haveth seove hwelpes.* MS: *haueð seoue hwelpes.* The expanded text in Corpus in fact goes on to include ten whelps. [Cleo.: *haueð seoue cundles*; Titus: *haues seouen cundles*; Nero: *haueð seoue kundles*; Vernon: *haþ þeos whelpes cundles*; Pepys: *haþ þise kyndlen*; Caius: *haued seoue cundles*; Vitellius (lacking); Trinity (lacking); Lat.: *habet hos catulos.*]

261   *mon.* MS: ~~godd~~ <*mon*>. The scribe has marked *godd* for deletion and inserted *mon* just above it. This appears to be a correct emendation since the scribe seems originally to have skipped ahead to the next phrase *ah þet godd deð him.* The uncorrected text reads, "I do not say only that God does it, but the God does it." The scribe's corrected text is retained. [Cleo.: *Ich segge naut ane þet mon deð him, ach þet god deð him.*]

263   *me nimeth to lutel yeme.* MS: *me nimeð to ~~muche~~ <lutel> ȝeme.* The scribe has canceled *muche* with a vertical stroke and inserted *lutel* just above. The uncorrected text reads, "too much attention is paid [to this sin]." The scribe's emendation is preferable to make sense of the phrase and is thus reproduced here. [Cleo.: *Me nimeð tolute ȝeme.*]

271   *thide[r]-ward.* MS: *þideward.* The missing *r* is restored. [Cleo. (lacking); Titus (lacking); Nero (lacking); Vernon: *þiderward*; Pepys (lacking); Caius (lacking).]

283   MS: *bereð on his nease þe þorn.* Tolkien thinks that *þorn* "spine, thorn" is a mistake for *horn* (p. 104, fol. 54r, line 14). Though a significant number of versions have *horn* where Cleo. and Corpus have *thorn*, the MS form is retained since it does make sense as "spine." [Cleo.: *bereð on his nase þe þorn*; Titus: *beres on his nase þe horn*; Nero: *bereð on his neose þene horn*; Vernon: *bereþ horn on his neose*; Pepys: *þat haþ þe horne in þe heued*; Caius: *bered on his n<e>ase þe horn*; Vitellius (lacking); Trinity (lacking); Lat.: *fert cornu seu spinam super nasum.*]

308   MS: *prinschipe of ȝeoue.* The MED believes *prinschipe* "parsimony" to be a mistake for *privschipe* "deprivation, robbery" from OF *priver* "to deprive, rob," though Dobson claims that Cleo.'s *Principe* is a mistake for the correct form *prinschipe* in Corpus. Both Titus and Caius preserve the spelling of Corpus, and thus it seems best to treat it as a genuine form. Zettersten (1969, p. 244) derives the word from OF *prin* — see MED *prinnen* "to take, acquire." [Cleo.: *Principe of ȝeoue*; Titus: *prinschipe of ȝeoue*; Nero: *uestschipe of ȝeoue*; Vernon: *Prinue-schupe of gift*; Pepys: *Pinching*; Caius: *prinshipe. of ȝeoue*; Vitellius (lacking); Trinity (lacking); Lat.: *au[g]mentum vltra donum uel comodatum.*]

340   *incolumis.* MS: *incolimis.* This seems to be a mistake for *incolumis* (see Tolkien, p. 106, fol. 55v, line 4). [Cleo.: *incolumis*; Titus: *incolumis*; Nero: *incolumis*; Vernon: *incolumis*; Pepys: *incolumis*; Caius: *incolums*; Vitellius (lacking); Trinity (lacking); Lat.: *incolumis.*]

351   *ant slea with deadbote.* MS: *ant wið deadbote slea.* Tolkien: "*wið deadbote* and *slea* marked for transposition with "above *de* and *sl*" (p. 107, fol. 55v, line 20). [Cleo.: *ant slea wið dedbote*; Titus: *ant swa* (sic?) *wið deaðbote* (sic); Nero: *ant slea hit mid dedbote*; Vernon: *and sle hit wiþ dedbote*; Pepys (lacking); Caius: *and slea wid deatbote*; Vitellius (lacking); Trinity (lacking); Lat.: *et satisfactione interficiat.*]

359   *fiketh mid te heaved.* MS: *fikeð mid te heaueð.* A common mistake here of *ð* for *d* in *heaueð* is corrected. [Cleo.: *sikeð wið þe heaued*; Titus: *fikeð mid te heaued*; Nero: *fikeð mid te heaued*; Vernon: *fekeþ myd þe hed*; Pepys: *fikeleþ wiþ þe heued*; Caius: *fiked mid þet heaued*; Vitellius (lacking); Trinity: *de la teste blandist*; Lat.: *blanditur cum capite.*]

396   *alle the for[th]-fearinde.* MS: *alle þe forfearinde.* Tolkien: "*forfearinde*, sic, probably for *forð-*" (p. 109, fol. 56v, line 24). ME *forfearen* usually means "to perish" while *forðfearen* would mean "to travel forth, pass along," a meaning more appropriate for this context. [Cleo.: *alle þe forð farinde*; Titus: *alle þe forð farinde*; Nero: *alle ðe uorðfarinde*; Vernon: *alle þe forþfarynde*; Pepys (lacking); Caius: *alle þe forfarinde*; Vitellius: *touz les passanz*; Trinity (lacking); Lat. (lacking).]

409–10 *Of the wind "drahinde in for luve of here-word," seith [Jeremie] as ich seide.* MS: *Of þe wind drahinde in for luue of hereword seið as ich seide.* Tolkien's suggestion, corroborated by Nero and Vitellius and adopted here, is to supply *Ieremie* between *seið* and *as*. [Cleo.: *Of þe wind draȝinde for luue of hereword seið as ich seide*; Titus: *Of þe prud drahinge in for luue of hereword seið as ich seide*; Nero: *of þeo ðet draweð wind inward uor luue of hereword, seið Ieremie ase ich er seide*; Vernon: *Of þe wynt drawinde in . for loue of preysinge. seiþas i seyde*; Pepys: *Of þe wynde draweyinge in for þe loue of weredelich ernynge. summe þere ben . . .* (*Ieremias* in margin); Caius: *Of þe wind drahinde in for luue of hereword; seid as ich seide*; Vitellius: *Del vent tra . . . z pur amour de renoun dit [Jerem]i come ieo dis*; Trinity (lacking); Lat. (lacking).]

416   *thider-ward schuleth mid either.* MS: *þiderward schuleð mið eiðer.* The scribe writes *mið* for *mid*, a common mistake. [Cleo.: *þiderwart schuleð wið eiðer*; Titus: *þiderward. sculeð mid eiðer*; Nero: *þiderward heo schuleð mid eiðer eien*; Vernon: *þiderward. stareþ mid eiþer*; Pepys (lacking); Caius: *þiderward shuled mid eiþer*; Vitellius: *regardent en esclench dambe parz*; Trinity: *garde del un e del autre oil*; Lat. (lacking).]

417   *ah the lust ayein thet uvel is eaver wid open.* MS: *ah the luft ayein thet uvel is eaver wid open.* Following Dobson ("Affiliations," p. 134n1), Zettersten (p. 150) suggests that in this phrase, *luft* ("left"), is a mistake for *lust* ("hearing") and would translate "but the hearing is always wide open for evil" as opposed to the current reading, which translates, "but the left [ear] is always wide open for evil." The two forms *lust/luft* would be easy to confuse, since *f* and long *s* are very

similar. In fact, it is difficult to decide which form was intended in Vernon, where the cross-bar of the following *t* touches the vertical stroke of *s* or *f* without continuing through it. Since the envious have clapped down *both* ears, it makes less sense that the left is open. Though Vitellius was able to make sense of *luft* as "left," it seems best to emend to *lust* ("hearing"). [Cleo.: *Ach þe luft aȝein þe uuel is eauer wid opene*; Titus: *Ah þe luf aȝein þet uuel is eauer wið opene earen*; Nero: *auh þet lust aȝean þet vuel; is eauer wid open*; Vernon: *Ac þe luft (lust?) aȝeyn þe euel; is euer wyd opene*; Pepys: *ac þe loue aȝein þat yuel is euere yopened redy*; Caius: *Ah þe lust agein þet uuel is eawid (*sic for *eauer wid) opene*; Vitellius: *Mez la senestre enqore al mal est touz iours ouerte*; Trinity: *en contre mal ad il tot dis les oreilles ouertes*; Lat.: *sed auditus contra malum est sempter apertus.*]

443   *nis bute eorthe ant esken.* MS: *nis bute eorðe ant ahte esken.* An apparent dittography (i.e., unintentional repetition): the scribe, seeing the preceding phrase *eorðlich/ahte* (line 443), mistakenly inserts *ahte* after the second *eorðe*-form (Tolkien, p. 111, fol. 58r, line 2). [Cleo.: *nis buten eorðe ant esken*; Titus: *nis bute eorðe ant askes*; Nero: *nis buten eorðe ant asken*; Vernon: *nis bote eorþe and asken*; Pepys: *nys bot askes*; Caius: *nis buten eorðe and esken*; Vitellius: *nest fors terre et ceindre*; Trinity: *ne est fors terre e cendre*; Lat.: *non sunt nisi terra et cineres.*]

456–57   *ant ye schule beon feo[ndes fod]e.* MS: *ant ȝe schule beon feorle.* The text is muddled here. Tolkien notes that MS *feorle* (misprinted in Tolkien's text as *feode*) must stand for *feo[ndes fo]de* (p. 111, fol. 58r, line 19), a reading supported by the other versions. The scribe apparently blended the two words, imperfectly, into one. [Cleo.: *ant ȝe schule beon feondes fode*; Titus: *and ȝe schulen beo feondes fode*; Nero: *ant ȝe schulen beon ueondes fode*; Vernon: *And ȝe schul beon. feondes foode*; Pepys: *and ȝe schullen ben þe fendes fode*; Caius: *and ge shulen beon feondes fode*; Vitellius: *et vous serrez la pouture del enemy*; Trinity (lacking); Lat. (lacking).]

481   MS: *tweof-moneð.* The form without *l* seems to be genuine (see 1.145 above). [Cleo.: *tweolf moneð*; Titus: *twelf / moneð*; Nero: *tweolf moneð*; Vernon: *twelfmoneþ*; Pepys: *in þe first ȝere*; Caius (lacking).]

519   *alluvione.* MS: *alliuione.* Tolkien: "*alliuio/ne,* sic for *alluuione*" (p. 114, fol. 59v, lines 22–23). [Cleo.: *alluuione*; Titus: *aluuione*; Nero: *alluuione*; Vernon:

alluuione; Pepys: *allimone*; Caius (lacking); Vitellius: *aluu(i)one*; Trinity (lacking); Lat.: *alluuione*.]

546   *se reowthful is hire heorte.* MS: *se reowðful is heorte. hire.* Tolkien: "*heorte. hire* marked for transposition with two strokes above each *h*" (p. 115, fol. 60v, line 3). [Cleo.: *se rewful is hire heorte*; Titus: *se rewful is hire herte*; Nero: *se reouðful is hire heorte*; Vernon: *so reuþful is hire herte*; Pepys: *haþ a rewful hert and a sorouȝful*; Caius (lacking); Vitellius: *son queor qest si plein damour et de pitee*; Trinity (lacking); Lat.: *cor caritatiuu*m *et misericorde*m *habentem*.]

564   *wes i-gan o dweole, [ant weop] as meoseise thing.* MS: *wes igan o dweole as meoseise þing.* Corpus seems to have omitted the necessary verb *weop* "wept," which is restored here, so that the sentence reads "she said she had gone astray, [and wept] as an unfortunate creature for lodging." [Cleo.: *wes igan adweoleð. ant weop ~~efter~~ <as> meoseise þing*; Titus: *was iGan o dweole. ant wep as mesaise þing*; Nero: *was igon a dweoleð. ant weop ase meoseise þing*; Vernon: *was i.gon a dwelet. and weop as meseise þin*; Pepys (recast): *a Man com to hym and wepe as mysaise vpon hym*; Caius (lacking); Vitellius (recast): *fut fornee et plorrout sicome chose meseisee querant herberge*; Trinity (lacking); Lat.: *quod oberrauerat, fleuit tanquam misera ut haberet hospicium.*]

583–84   MS: *Ne mahte ich wene ham namon nomeliche nempnin.* Discussing the corresponding passage in Cleo., Dobson suggests that the "text which underlies the scribe's was probably *ne muchte ich wene ham nan muð nomeliche nempnin* (cf. [Vitellius], Corpus, Titus, Nero; but even Corpus has *namon* for *nan muð*)" (p. 167n5). However, the wording in Corpus makes good sense and probably represents a minor revision; thus, *namon* "no one" is not emended to *nan muð* "no mouth" here. [Cleo.: *ne muchte ich wið muðe nomeliche nempnen*; Titus: *ne muhte ic wene muð nomeliche nempni ham*; Nero: *nene muhte ase ich wene mid none muðe; nomeliche nemmen ham*; Vernon: *Ne mouȝte ich wene no mouþ nomeliche nempnen*; Pepys: *Ac þat alle þat Men wiþ ytempted ne may ich nouȝth nempny hem*; Caius (lacking); Vitellius: *ne les porreit ceo quid nule boche par noun nomer*; Trinity (lacking); Lat.: *Dictum est . . . non de millesima parte temptationum.*]

661   *athet te othre seide him.* MS: *aþet te oðre seiden him.* Tolkien rightly points out that *seiden* "said" should be singular *seide* (p. 120, fol. 63r, lines 16–17). [Cleo.: *oðet þe oðer seide him*; Titus: *Aðet oðer seide him*; Nero: *uort tet þe oðer holi mon seide to him*; Vernon: *On þat oþer syde*; Pepys: *and his felawe seide vn to*

hym; Caius (lacking); Vitellius: *desqatant qi laltre li dit*; Trinity (lacking); Lat. (lacking).]

710   MS: *þis ilke niht ofsaruet*. Tolkien thinks that *of-saruet* is a mistake for *of-earnet* "earned, deserved," and indeed Cleo. and Nero have this form. However, the word *ofseruet* occurs later in the account (see 4.717) and is a genuine form, attested in *St. Katherine* and *St. Juliene* and other early texts. According to the MED, *-sarven* is a Northern and early Southwest Midlands form of *-serven*. [Cleo.: *þis ilke nicht of earned*; Titus: *þis ilke niht ofearned*; Nero: *þeos ilke niht of earned*; Vernon: *þis niht i ernet*; Pepys: *erned while þat þou slepe*; Caius (lacking); Vitellius: *en cest nuit deseruies*; Trinity (lacking); Lat.: *tuus meruit discipulus hac nocte.*]

713   *ne mah[te] ich for reowthe*. MS: *ne mah / ich for reowðe*. The scribe, coming to the end of the line, has inadvertently failed to finish the word *mahte*. [Cleo.: *ne machte ich for reuðe*; Titus: *ne mihte ich for reowðe*; Nero: *ich ne muhte uor reouðe*; Vernon: *ne mouht ich for rouþe*; Pepys: *I ne miȝth nouȝth for rewþe*; Caius (lacking); Vitellius: *ieo nen poiei pur pitee*; Trinity (lacking); Lat.: *misertus non potui.*]

736–37   *ah to leate thenne [naut-for-thi! For efter uvel, god is penitence. Thet is the best thenne.] Speowen hit anan ut*. MS: *ah to leate þenne. Speowen hit anan ut*. Corpus omits a sentence after *þenne* which appears in Cleo. (somewhat altered), Nero, and Vitellius. The omission seems to be inadvertent (due to eye-skip from *þenne* to *þenne*) and is restored from Cleo. — however, omitting the apparently false repetition of *for*. [Cleo.: *to late þenne. naut for þi. for efter uuel god is penitence þet is þe best þenne*; Titus: *ah to late þenne. Spewe hit anan ut*; Nero: *nout for þi; efter vuel; god is penitence. þet is ðet beste þeonne*; Vernon: *Ac to late þenne. not forþi. aftur euel. good is penitence. þis is þe beste þenne. Scheuh hit anon riht to þe prest; out wiþ schrift*; Pepys: *for þan better is late þan neuere. After yuel þan is goode penaunce spewe out þat venym*; Caius (lacking); Vitellius: *Nepu(rquant) ceo; apres le mal. bon est penitence. Cest dunque le mielz le vomir*; Trinity (lacking); Lat.: *sed tunc tarde. Nichilominus post peccatum bona est penitencia. Tunc melius est statim vomere, hoc est, in confessione sacerdoti expuere.*]

755   *munneth ofte i mode*. MS: *munneð ofte / ofte i mode*. As Tolkien notes (p. 123, fol. 65r, lines 21–22), there is an unintentional repetition of *ofte* in this passage.

765 MS: *nawt þe hors eschif iliche. Hors eschif* "horse skittish" is a French construction (with a French-derived adjective following the noun it modifies) not shared by Cleo. and Nero, but very similar to Vitellius. [Cleo.: *lokeð þet ȝe ne beon naut ilich þe scheunchinde hors þet scheuncheð for an shadewe*; Titus: *Lokes þet ȝe ne beo nawt þe skerre hors iliche þet schuntes for a schadwe*; Nero: *lokeð þet ȝe ne beon nout i liche ðe horse þet is scheouh. ant blencheð uor one sheadewe*; Vernon: *Lokeþ þat ȝe beo not þe hors. restif iliche. þat schuncheþ for a schadewe*; Pepys: *Be we nouȝth eschu of þe schadewe. Þe hors þat stondeþ opon þe brynk ant is eschu for þe schadewe*; Caius (lacking); Vitellius: *Veez qe vous ne resemblez le chiual eschieu. qi se eschieu pur vne vmbre*; Trinity (lacking); Lat.: *Videatis ne sitis tanquam equus vmbratilis qui dum timet vmbram.*]

778–79 MS: *ant þine leoueste freond.* Tolkien observes that in this sentence *freond* must stand for the genitive "friend's" (p. 124, fol. 65v, line 24), "your and your dearest friend's salvation." [Cleo.: *ant of þine leoueste freont*; Titus: *and tine leueste frendes*; Nero: *ant þine leoueste ureond*; Vernon: *and þine leoueste frend*; Pepys (recast); Caius (lacking); Vitellius: *apres vostre saluacion et de voz chers amis*; Trinity: *apres uostre sauacion a vus e a vostre plus cher ami*; Lat.: *tuam et amicorum tuorum saluationem.*]

803 *Hwen me asa[i]leth burhes.* MS: *hwen me asaleð burhes.* As Tolkien points out, the form *asaleð* is apparently a mistake for *asaileð* (p. 125, fol. 66v, line 1). [Cleo.: *me asaileð burchȝes*; Titus: *mon assailȝes burhes*; Nero: *me asaileð buruhwes*; Vernon: *Whon me sayleþ citees*; Pepys (recast): *Whan þe deuel assaileþ ȝou*; Caius (lacking).]

807 *te drake heaved.* MS: *te drake heaueð.* As frequently elsewhere, the scribe writes here an *ð* for *d*. [Cleo.: *þe drake heaued*; Titus: *þe drake heaued*; Nero: *þe drake heaued*; Vernon: *þe drake heued*; Pepys (recast); Caius (lacking); Vitellius: *la teste del dragon*; Trinity: *la teste au dragoun*; Lat.: *capita draconum.*]

816 *ant [te] sothe sunne schineth.* MS: *ant soðe sunne schineð.* A *te* (the reduced form of *þe* after a preceding dental) has apparently fallen out between *ant* and *soðe*, as Tolkien points out (p. 126, fol. 66v, line 18). [Cleo.: *ant þe soðe sune schineð*; Titus: *ant te soðe sunne schines*; Nero: *ant te soðe sunne þet is iesu crist schineð*; Vernon: *And þe soþe sonne schyneþ*; Pepys: *And so doþe þe soþ sunne*; Caius (lacking); Vitellius: *et le verrai solailz lust*; Trinity: *e li uerai solail lust*; Lat.: *et verus sol postmodum clarius splendet.*]

819   *toward h[e]ovene.* MS: *toward houene.* A clear mistake for *heouene.* [Cleo.: *towart heouene;* Titus: *toward heuene;* Nero: *touward heouene;* Vernon: *touward heuene;* Pepys (recast): *perceþ heuen;* Caius (lacking).]

835   *the hali halhen alle overcomen.* MS: *þe hali halhen al/hen alle ouercomen.* As Tolkien notes, and the other versions confirm, *halhen alhen alle* is most likely a copying error for *halhen alle* (p. 126, fol. 67r, lines 16–17). [Cleo.: *þe hali haleȝen alle ouercomen;* Titus: *Þe hali halhes alle ouercomen;* Nero: *alle ðe holie haluwen ouercomen;* Vernon: *þe holy halewen. alle ouercomen;* Pepys: *Þise holy halewen ouercomen;* Caius (lacking); Vitellius: *les seinz touz venqirent;* Trinity: *les seinz hommes uenquirent;* Lat. (lacking).]

846   *f[e]or ha hefde heone-ward hire bileave ehe.* MS: *for ha hefde heoneward hire bileaue ehe.* Tolkien suggests that *for* reads better as *feor* "far" (p. 127, fol. 167v, line 3), a reading corroborated by Cleo., Nero, and Vitellius. [Cleo.: *feor ha hefde heoneward hire bileaue echȝe;* Titus: *for he hafde heoðenward hire bileaue ehe;* Nero: *ful ueor heo hefde heoneward hire eien of bileaue;* Vernon: *for heo hedde heneward hire bileeue eiȝe;* Pepys (recast): *an ancre had almest lorne þe eiȝe of hir bileue for a quayer þat on of hire susters wolde haue borowed at hir and sche nolde nouȝth lene it hir;* Caius: *feor he haued heneward his bi leaue ehe;* Vitellius: *il auoit loinz deci loil de sa creance;* Trinity: *il ne ad pas regard asez nostre seignur par le oil de fei;* Lat. (lacking).]

847   *thr[e]o-fald.* MS: *þrofald.* A mistake for *þreofald.* [Cleo.: *þreofald;* Titus: *þreo fald;* Nero: *þreo uold;* Vernon: *þreofold;* Pepys: *þrefold;* Caius: *þreofold.*]

856   *In hoc cognoscetis quod dicipuli mei sitis.* MS: *In hoc cognoscetis quoð discipuli mei sitis.* Though the Vulgate reads *quia* where Corpus has the clearly mistaken *quoð* ("said" in ME), the form is emended to *quod* here and in 4.859 where it appears again. [Cleo: *In hoc cognoscitis quod dicipuli mei sitis;* Titus: *In hoc cognoscetis quod discipuli mei sitis;* Nero: *In hoc cognoscetis quia discipuli mei sitis;* Vernon: *In hoc cognoscetis quod discipuli mei estis;* Pepys: *In hoc cognoscetis si discipuli mei sitis;* Caius: *In hoc cognoscetis quod discipuli mei sitis;* Vitellius: *In hoc cognoscetis; quod discipuli mei sitis;* Trinity: *In hoc inquit cognoscent omnes homines quod uere mei discipuli estis;* Lat.: *In hoc cognoscent homines quod discipuli mei estis.*]

882   *the beoth i-nempnet th'ruppe.* MS: *þe beoð itemptet þruppe.* As Tolkien points out and the other versions confirm, *itemptet* "tempted" is a clear mistake for

inempnet "named." [Cleo.: *þe beoð inempned þeruppe*; Titus: *þet arn inempnet þruppe*; Nero: *ðet beoð inemmed þer uppe*; Vernon: *þat beoþ inempnet þeruppe*; Pepys (lacking); Caius: *þat beod inemned þer uppe*; Vitellius: *qe sunt auant nomez la sus*; Trinity (lacking); Lat.: *supra sub accidia nominata.*]

917–18   MS: *god ow mutli*. It is tempting, with Tolkien (p. 130, fol. 69r, line 15) to emend *mutli* to the more standard form *mucli* "to increase," since it seems to contain a plausible error: *c* and *t* have very similar forms in Corpus. However, Bennett and Smithers think the spelling is the result of a phonological process — see Textual Note to 4.1445–46 below [all other versions lack this section].

945   *Euch, no-the-le[s], warni*. MS: *Euch noðele warni*. The scribe failed to complete *noðele[s]*. [Cleo.: *euchan noðeles warne*; Titus: *Euchan naðeles warni*; Nero: *euerich noðeleas warnie*; Vernon: *Uche noþeles warne oþer*; Pepys (recast); Caius: *Euch noþeles warni.*]

957   MS: *þet euch of ow luuie oþer*. As Tolkien indicates, other authoritative versions have *leve* "trust" where Corpus has *luuie* "love." However, since the text makes good sense, *luuie* may well represent a revision and thus is retained (p. 132, fol. 70r, line 12). [Cleo.: *þet euch of ow luuie oþer*; Titus (lacking); Nero: *ðet euerich of ou i leue oðer*; Vernon: *þet uche of ow. leeue oþer; as hire owne seluen*; Pepys (lacking); Caius: *and luuie as him seoluen*; Vitellius: *qe chescune de vous creie altre*; Trinity: *e lui autre creit alui si come a lui memes*; Lat.: *quod quelibet alteri credat tanquam sibi.*]

999–1000   *ne moste he habben a grot for-te deien upon*. MS: *ne moste he habben a greot forte deien up on*. The word *greot* "sand" is most likely a mistake for *grot* "fragment, particle" (Tolkien, p. 133, fol. 71r, line 14). [Cleo.: *ne moste he habben agrot forto dei3en upon*; Titus: *ne moste he habben a grot for to deien upon*; Nero: *ne moste he habben agrot forte deien uppon*; Vernon: *ne moste he habben a greot forte dyen onne*; Pepys: *of nou3th ne hadde bot a fote of erþe to dyen opon*; Caius: *ne moste he habben agrot forte deien up on*; Vitellius: *ne poeit il auer vne bleste pur morir sure*; Trinity: *ne poeit li sire de totes terres point auer amorir sure*; Lat.: *non habuit aliquid in quo moreretur.*]

1023   *ich habbe i-herd of swuch*. MS: *ich habbe iherd þetof swuch*. As Tolkien points out, the abbreviation for *þet* which immediately precedes *of* must be a mistaken addition (p. 134, fol. 71v, line 18). The concordance (p. xiii) reads *þet of* as *þer of*, though this compound is unnecessary given the following object, *swuch* "such a one" [all other versions lack this section].

1031   *non fatiget[is]*. MS: *non fatiget*. Although the Vulgate has *fatigemini* "you (pl.) will grow weary," it seems best to read MS *fatiget* as an incomplete form of *fatiget[is]* "you (sing.) will grow weary" (Tolkien, p. 135, fol. 72r, line 1). [Cleo.: *non fatigemini*; Titus: *non fatigemini*; Nero: *non fatigetis*; Vernon: *non fatigetis*; Pepys: *non fatiget*; Caius: *non fatigemini*; Vitellius: *fatigemini*; Trinity: *non fatigemini*; Lat.: *non fatigaremini (*Magdalen 67*: fatigemini)*.]

1034–36   *athet te schedunge of ower blod," [as he dude of his for ow — ayeines him-seolven, anont he mon wes of ure cunde. Yet ye habbeth thet ilke blod], the[t] ilke blisfule bodi*. MS: *aþet te schedunge of ower blod. þe ilke blisfule bodi*. As Tolkien notes, Corpus omits part of a sentence here, skipping from one *blod* to the next and leaving out the text in between (p. 135, fol. 72r, line 5). The missing text (necessary to complete the sense) is supplied from Cleo. and MS *the* is emended to *thet*. [Cleo.: *oðet schedunge of ower blod. as he dude of his for ow aȝeines him seoluen anont þet he mon wes of ure cunde ȝet ȝe habbeð þet ilke blod þet ilke blisfule bodi*; Titus: *aðat te scheadinge of ower blod as he dude of his for ow aȝaines himseluen onont þet he mon was of ure cunde. ȝet ȝe ha<bben> þet ilke blod. þet ilke blisfule bodi*; Nero: *ðet þe schedunge of ower blode. ase he dude of his for ou; aȝeines him suluen. ononte ðet he was mon of ure kunde. and ȝet ȝe habbeð þet ilke blod. ant tet ilke blisfule bodi*; Vernon: *anont þe scheding of oure blood. as he dude of his for ow. aȝeynes him seluen. anont þet he mon was. of ure kuynde ¶ ȝit ȝe habbeþ. þat ilke blod. þat ilke blisfole bodi*; Pepys: *tyl schedyng of ȝoure blode. as he dude for vs. wil we clepe hym to help he is euer redy biforne vs atte Messe and scheweþ hym as þeiȝ he seide*; Caius: *aþet þe shedunge of ower blod. as he dude of his for ow. ageines him seoluen onont þat he mon wes of ure cunde. get ge habbeð þat ilke bloð. þat ilke blisfule bodi*; Vitellius: *desqe al espandre de vostre sang sicome il fist del seon pur vous (encontre) sei meismes endroit de c(eo qil) fut homme de nostre nature. Vnquore auez vous cel mei(s)me sang cel meisme gloriouse corps*; Trinity: *deske al espandre de uostre sanc. ausi com il espandi soen sanc pur nus . . . Oncore aues vus en le sacrement del auter soen precious sanc e soen beneit cors*; Lat.: *v[sque] ad sanguinis effusionem, sicut ipse fecit pro uobis quatenus homo erat. Ad huc habetis eundem sanguinem, idem gloriosum corpus*.]

1039–40   MS: *on oþres lite under breades furme*. Though Tolkien thinks *lite* "color" a mistake for *liche* "likeness, appearance" (p. 135, fol. 72r, line 9), the word *lite* can be traced to ON *litr* "color," and is a legitimate word (see also *litunge* ["painting, coloring"]). It may be that *lite* has been influenced by its cognate form *wlite* (see glossary) which can mean both "color" and "appearance, form." [Cleo.: *on oðeres liche under breades furme*; Titus: *on oðres liche vnder breades furme*; Nero: *in oðres like; under breades heowe*; Vernon: *bitornd þauh also under bredes foorme*; Pepys (lacking); Caius: *an oþer liche under breades furme;* Vitellius: *en altrui colour desouz la especie de pain*; Trinity: *nekedent de sur la forme de pain;* Lat.: *tectum et velatum sub forma panis.*]

1051   *beginneth the deovel to weden.* MS: *biginneð þe deovel to ~~lihen~~ weden.* The scribe first wrote *lihen* ("to lie or deceive") but crossed it out and wrote *weden.* This change brings Corpus into line with the other manuscripts: "the devil begins to rage." [Cleo.: *bigineð þe deoflen to weden.]*

1057   *In Paralipomenis.* MS: *IN parabolis.* Tolkien: "wrongly for *paralipomenon,* or *-is*" (p. 136, fol. 72v, line 1). [Cleo.: *Inparalipomenon*; Titus: *In paralipomenon*; Nero: *In parabolis*; Vernon: *In parabolis*; Pepys (lacking); Caius: *In parabolis*; Vitellius: *In parabolis*; Trinity: *In libro enim paralipomenon*; Lat.: *Paralipomenorum.*]

1075–76   *ye schulen [seon] mi sucurs.* MS: *ȝe schulen ~~stonden sikerliche~~ mi sucurs.* The scribe has canceled *stonden sikerliche* ("stand confidently") which seems to be repeated from the previous phrase. As Tolkien points out (p. 137, fol. 72v, line 24), the word *seon* ("to see") has been replaced by this mistaken repetition and is restored here. [Cleo.: *ȝe schule seon mi sucurs*; Titus: *and ȝe schulen seo mi sucurs*; Nero: *ȝe schulen haben mi sukurs*; Vernon: *ȝe schulen ise myne socours*; Pepys (lacking); Caius: *ge schulen seon mi sucurs.*]

1090   *ha dude a sunne i the il[ke] niht.* MS: *ha dude a sunne in þe il/ niht.* The scribe has apparently failed to complete the last word in the line: *il[ke]* (Tolkien, p. 137, fol. 73r, lines 14–15). [Cleo.: *ha dude an sunne in þe nicht*; Titus (lacking); Nero: *heo dude one swuche sunne i ðet ilke niht*; Vernon: *he dude a sunne iþe niht*; Pepys (lacking); Caius: *ha dude a sunne iþe nicht*; Vitellius: *ele fist vn pecche en la nuit*; Trinity (lacking); Lat.: *vna nocte per temptationem peccatum commisit.*]

1099–1100   MS: *þe wið swilli gest hardiliche ne fehteð.* Though Tolkien thinks that the form *swilli* is a mistake for the more usual *þulli* or *swuch,* both meaning "such" (p. 138, fol. 73r, line 26), Zettersten makes the plausible case that *swilli* is probably a blending of OE forms of these two words: *þyllic* and *swilc* (p. 106). [Cleo.

(lacking); Titus: *þet wið þulli Gast hardiliche ne fihteð*; Nero: *ðet wið swuche gost herdeliche ne uihteh*; Vernon: *þet wiþ such a blessed gost. hardiliche ne fihteþ*; Pepys (lacking); Caius: *wid þulli gest herdiliche ne fechteð*; Vitellius: *qi od . . . hardiement ne combatent;* Trinity: *ke ne combatent hardiement en contre le maligne spirit*; Lat.: *qui cum adiutorio talis hospitis audacter non pugnant.*]

1105 *as thah hit were o Godes half.* MS: *ah þah hit were o godes half.* As Tolkien points out and the other versions confirm, *ah* should probably read *as* (p. 138, fol. 73v, line 5). [Cleo.: *as þach hit were on godes half*; Titus: *as þah were o godes half*; Nero: *ase þauh hit were a godes halue*; Vernon: *As þauȝ hit weore a godes halue*; Pepys (lacking); Caius: *As þat hit were o godes half*; Vitellius: *ausi come (s)il fust de part dieu*; Trinity: *de par deu*; Lat.: *tanquam essent ex parte Dei.*]

1107 *thet haveth moni hali mon grimliche biyulet.* MS: *þet he haueð moni hali mon grimliche biȝulet.* The readings in Cleo., Vitellius, and Lat., which omit Corpus' apparently mistaken *he*, make better sense (Tolkien, p. 138, 73v, line 7) than Corpus, and thus *he* is omitted here. [Cleo.: *þet haueð Moni halimon grimliche biȝeuled*; Titus: *þet he haueð wið. moni hali mon grimliche biGulet*; Nero: *þet he haueð monie holie men grimliche biȝuleð*; Vernon: *þat he haþ mony holy men. gimliche* (sic) *bigiled*; Pepys: *For þe fende haþ many bigiled þere þorouȝ*; Caius: *þat he haued moni hali men grimliche ibuled*; Vitellius: *qad meinte seint hom horriblement deceu*; Trinity: *par ont il li ad meint seint homme e femme greuousement deceu*; Lat.: *per quam multos sanctos decepit.*]

1119 *yef thet [tu] maht wakien wel.* MS: *ȝef þet maht wakien wel.* Tolkien's suggestion (that the abbreviation for *þet* should read *þu* or, more likely, *þet tu* — p. 139, fol. 73v, line 23) is supported by Cleo. and Nero and thus adopted here. Though the other readings include the personal ending for the second-person singular, *maht* is the usual form in Corpus' language — in fact, *mahtest* occurs only once, and only when separated from the pronoun (see 5.67). [Cleo.: *ȝef þet þu machtest wakien wel*; Titus: *ȝif þu mihtes waken wel*; Nero: *ȝif þet tu muhtest wel wakien*; Vernon: *ȝif þu mouhtest waken wel*; Pepys (lacking); Caius: *gif þat þu mahtest wakien wel*; Vitellius: *si vous pensez bien veiller*; Trinity: *se il uout ke vus poez bien uelier*; Lat.: *Si bene poteris vigilare.*]

1133 *ant comen Recabes sunen.* MS: *ant comer recabes sunen.* As Tolkien points out, *comer* is a clear mistake for *comen* (p. 139, fol. 74r, line 12). [Cleo.: *ant Comen Re<cabes> sune<n>*; Titus: *and comen Recabes sunes*; Nero: *ant comen recabes sunen*; Vernon: *And coomen Recabus sones*; Pepys: *And þan com recasbesones* (sic); Caius: *and comen racabes sunes*; Vitellius: *et vindrent les fiz Rechabee*; Trinity: *e vindrunt les fiz recab*; Lat.: *Venerunt filij Rechabes.*]

1138–39   *schaden the eilen ant te chef.* MS: *schaden þe eilen ant te ant te chef.* The scribe inadvertently repeats *ant te*, a repetition which is removed here. [Cleo.: *schade þe eilen ant þe chef*; Titus: *Scheaden þe eiles ant te chaf*; Nero: *scheaden ðe eilen ant tet chef*; Vernon: *scheden þe eilen from þe chaf*; Pepys: *departen þe whete fram þe chaf*; Caius: *Sheaden þe eilen and þe chef*; Vitellius: *seuerir les arestes et la paille*; Trinity: *seuerir e de partir la uaspail du net ble*; Lat.: *separare granum a palea.*]

1147   *unwaker, ant swa nesche yete-ward.* MS: *unwaker. ant swa nesfhe ȝeteward.* Tolkien: "*nesfhe*, sic, but *f* is probably alteration of tall *s* to *c*, without erasure of top" (p. 140, fol. 74v, line 2). [Cleo.: *unwaker ant swa nesche ȝetewart*; Titus: *vnwaker. ant se nesch ȝateward*; Nero: *unwaker ant so nesche ȝeteward*; Vernon: *so unwakere. and so nessche ȝateward*; Pepys (lacking); Caius: *unwaker and se neshe geteward.*]

1150   *In i[n]guine.* MS: *In iguine.* A mistake for *in inguine* (Tolkien, p. 140, fol. 74v, line 6). [Cleo.: *In ingwine*; Titus: *In inguine*; Nero: *Ininguine*; Vernon: *In ing<i>ne*; Pepys: *Igniuie*; Caius: *In inguine*; Vitellius: *In inguine*; Trinity: *In inguine*; Lat.: *In ynguine.*]

1186–87   MS: *þench o þe attri pine þet godd dronc o þe rode.* Tolkien apparently follows Nero here in suggesting that Corpus' *dronc* is a mistake for *droh* "suffered" (p. 142, fol. 75r, line 21). However, every version except Cleo. and Nero supports Corpus' *dronc* — the witness of Vernon and Vitellius carry particular weight. Though *droh* would make better literal sense, the meaning here is figurative. [Cleo.: *þench on þe attri pine þe god drong on þe rode*; Titus (lacking); Nero: *þench o þe attrie pinen ðet god suffrede o ðe rode*; Vernon: *þench on þe attri pynen þat God dronk o þe roode*; Pepys: *þench on attry pyne þat Ihesus drank opon þe rode*; Caius: *þench o þe eattri pinen þat god dronc o þe rode*; Vitellius: *pensez de la venimouse peine dunt nostre seignour beut en la croiz*; Trinity: *pensez enterinement tantost de la grant peine ke deu soffri pur vus en la seinte croiz*; Lat.: *cogita de amaris penis Christi quas bibit in cruce.*]

1194   MS: *freo heorte. þet is to seggen. Nu of þe earste.* The phrase *þet is to seggen* ("that is to say") occurs in no other version. Generally, this phrase introduces a subsequent explanation or clarification which is lacking here. Though it might be that the phrase is a mistaken addition, from eye-skip back to *heorte* in fol. 75r, line 20, *frommard te heorte. þet is to seggen. þench o þe attri pine* (line 1186), it is possible to make reasonably good sense of the phrase: "It [i.e., the following] is to be said [passive inf.] now first of all concerning the first [of these remedies]." [Cleo.: *freo heorte. Nu of þe earste*; Titus (lacking); Nero: *ureo heorte. nu of ðe uorme*; Vernon: *freo herte Now aller furst. at þe bigynninge*; Pepys (recast); Caius: *freo heorte. Nu of þe eareste on alre earest*; Vitellius: *franc queor. Ore de la primere tout al comencement*; Trinity (lacking); Lat.: *cor liberale. Nunc de primo.*]

1203–04   MS: *nart tu fulðe fette.* Tolkien would bring Corpus into agreement with the other versions by emending *fette* ("vat") to *fetles* ("vessel") (p. 142, fol. 75v, line 14). Dobson describes the reading in Cleo.: "Between lines, beginning over *l* of *fulðe*, B writes *oðer vetles* (alternative, or gloss, to *vette*)" (p. 203, note a). There seems to be no reason to emend, however, since *fette*, derived from OE *fæt* "vat, vessel," makes perfectly good sense. [Cleo.: *Nart þu nu fulðe vette <oðer vetles>*; Titus (lacking); Nero: *nert tu mid fulðe al i fulled*; Vernon: *Nartou fulþe uessel*; Pepys (lacking); Caius: *Nartu fulþe fette*; Vitellius: *Nestes vous ore vessel dordure*; Trinity: *ne estes vus uessel de soilleure e de feens*; Lat.: *Nonne es vas sordium.*]

1216–17   *For ofte thet tu wenest god.* MS: *for ofte þet tu wenest godd.* As Tolkien suggests, *godd* (the usual form of "God") is emended to *god* "good" (p. 143, fol. 76r, line 2). [Cleo.: *for ofte þet þu wenest good*; Titus: *for ofte þet tu wenes God*; Nero: *vor ofte ðet tu wenest þet beo god*; Vernon: *ffor ofte þat þu wenest beo good*; Pepys (lacking); Caius: *for ofte þat þu wenest god*; Vitellius: *kar souent ceo qe vous quidez qe soit bien*; Trinity: *kar souent ceo ke vus quidez ke est bien*; Lat.: *quia sepe quod putas bonum.*]

1226   *thet [is], "Alswa as prude is wilnunge.* MS: *þet alswa as prude is wilnunge.* An *is* is supplied after *þet* to complete the sense — no other version contains a *þet*, and it is possible that it is a mistaken or incomplete addition. [Cleo.: *Alswa as prude is wilnunge*; Titus: *Al swa se prude is wilninge*; Nero: *also ase prude is wilnunge of wurðschipe*; Vernon: *Also as prude. is wilnynge of worþschupe*; Pepys: *Also as pride is willyng of worschipp*; Caius: *Alswa as prude is winunge of wurdshipe*; Vitellius: *Ausi come orgoil est desir*; Trinity: *ausi com orgoil est vn amur de sa propre hautesce*; Lat. (lacking).]

1237–38   *Seint Cassiodre hit witneth.* MS: *Seint Cassi/oðre hit witneð.* Tolkien: "not [a] normal *ð*" (p. 144, fol. 76r, line 28). [Cleo.: *Seint Cassiodre hit witneð*; Titus:

Sein Cassiodre; Nero: *Seint cassiodere*; Vernon: *Seint Cassiodre*; Pepys: *cassiodorus*; Caius: *Seint cassiodere*; Vitellius: *Seint cassiodre*; Trinity: *cassiodre*; Lat.: *Cassiodorus*.]

1239   *Ubi humilitas, ibi sapientia.* MS: *Vbi humilitas; ibi humilitas; ibi sapientia.* The phrase *ibi humilitas* is a false repetition, as Tolkien observes (p. 144, fol. 76v, lines 1–2) — it is removed here. [Cleo.: *vbi humilitas ibi sapiencia*; Titus: *Vbi humiltas; ibi sapientia*; Nero: *vbi humilitas ibi sapiencia*; Vernon: *Ubi humilitas ibi sapiencia*; Pepys: *Vbi humilitas. ibi sapiencia*; Caius: *Vbi humilitas ibi sapiencia*; Vitellius: *Vbi humilitas; ibi sapiencia*; Trinity: *Vbi humilitas. ibi sapiencia*; Lat.: *Vbi humilitas, ibi sapiencia*.]

1264–65 MS: *ah flowinde ʒeotteð weallen of his graces.* Tolkien, with an eye on Nero, thinks that the double *t* of *ʒeotteð* is a mistake (p. 145, fol. 77r, line 4). Since it corroborated by Cleo., however, the spelling of *ʒeotteð* with two *t*'s is retained. [Cleo.: *Ach flowinde ʒeotteð wellen of his graces*; Titus: *ah flowinde wattres walles of his grace*; Nero: *auh ʒeoteð vlowinde wellen of his grace*; Vernon: *ac flowynde stremed wellen of his grace*; Pepys: *ac foloweand he heldeþ in hem his grace*; Caius: *Ah flowinde geoted wellen of his grace*; Vitellius: *mes espand par grant cours les fontaignes de sa grace*; Trinity: *mes fet par funteines decorans*; Lat.: *sed habundanter influit fontes suarum graciarum*.]

1273–74 *Sulement luve [h]is god.* MS: *Sulement luue is god.* Though it might be possible to make sense of *is* here, the following *þrof* suggests that the best reading, following Cleo., Vitellius, Lat., and Titus, is *his*. Since Corpus does not use *is* for "his," the spelling is emended here. [Cleo.: *Sulement luue his god*; Titus: *Sulement luue his god*; Nero: *Sulement luue is god*; Vernon: *Outerliche loue is good*; Pepys: *Loue oþere Mennes gode*; Caius: *Sulement luue is god*; Vitellius: *Soulement amez son bien*; Trinity: *Amez donc autri bien*; Lat.: *Solum ama bonum eius*.]

1309   MS: *wrekeð him. o þe oðer on him seoluen.* Tolkien: "*on*: false addition" (p. 147, fol. 78r, line 1). Following Tolkien and on the authority of Cleo. and Vitellius, it seems attractive to remove the *on* before *him seoluen*, but it is possible to make good, though slightly difficult, sense of the Corpus reading, and thus it is retained here, and can be translated as "avenges himself on the other by himself." [Cleo.: *wrekeð him o þe oðer him seoluen*; Titus: *wrekes him o þe oðer on him seluen*; Nero: *ant awrekeð him of þe. oðer of him suluen*; Vernon: *and awrekeþ him. or þet day come*; Pepys: *þat demes þe or þat day come*; Caius: *awreked him oþe oþer on him seoluen*; Vitellius: *se venge sur laltre. il meismes*; Trinity: *euenge sei memes del autre*; Lat.: *se de alio vindicat.*]

1312–13   *hwet woh se me deth the: [the richtwise deme haveth i-set te dei to loki richt bitwenen ow.] Ne do thu nawt him scheome*. MS: *hwet woh se me deð þe. ne do þu nawt him scheome*. Tolkien: "after *deð þe* twelve words referring to Judge (*him*) omitted" (p. 147, fol. 78r, line 4). The text is restored, with one emendation, from Cleo. [Cleo.: *hwet woch seme doð þe. Þe richtwise deme haueð iset todei to loki richt bitwenen ow. no do þu naut him scheome*; Titus: *hwat who se mon dos te. þe rihtwise deme haues iset te dai to don riht bitwenen ow. Ne do þu him nawt schome*; Nero: *hwat wouh so me euer doð þe. þe rihtwise demare haueð iset enne dei uorte loken riht bitweonen ou. ne do ðu nout him scheome*; Vernon: *What harm so me doþ þe. þe riȝtwyse demere. haþ i.set þulke day; to loken riht bitwenen ou. Ne do þu not him schome*; Pepys (lacking); Caius: *hwet woh þat me ded þe, þe rihtwise demere haued iset þene dai to lokin riht bitweonen ow. Ne do þu him nawt shome*; Vitellius: *qel tort qe len vous face. li droiturel iuge ad assis le iour de esgardier droit entre vous. Ne li fetes pas honte*; Trinity: *ke lem vus mes face ore en ceo secle isci. kar li dreiturel iuge ad assis le iour a fere dreit entre vus e uostre mesfesour. Ne lui facet point de hontage*; Lat.: *quecumque tibi fiat iniuria. Justus et sapiens iudex diem prefixit ad ius discernendum inter vos. Non iniurieris ei desperando.*]

1333   *for as Sein Gregoire seith*. MS: *for as as sein Gregoire seið*. The scribe mistakenly repeats *as* (Tolkien, p. 148, fol. 78r, line 28).

1388–89   *with his deore-wurthe blod biblodge thin heorte*. MS: *wið his deorewurðe blod biblod/de þin heorte*. Tolkien is probably right in observing that *biblodde* should read *biblodge* (p. 151, fol. 79v, lines 13–14), an idea supported by Zettersten (p. 215) and suggested by OE *blodegian* "to make bloody." [Cleo.: *biblodgede*; Titus: *biblodeke*; Nero: *biblodege*; Vernon: *biblodgi*; Pepys (recast); Caius: *biblodege*.]

1390   *hud te i the dolven eorthe*. MS: *hud te i þe deoluen eorðe*. The context requires *dolven* "hollowed out," the past participle (acting as an adj.), rather than the *deolven* "to dig out," the infinitive (see Tolkien, p. 151, fol. 79v, line 15). [Cleo.: *hud þe in þe doluen eorðe*; Titus: *huid te þu* (sic) *doluen i þe eorðe*; Nero: *hud þe i ðe doluene eorðe*; Vernon: *huid þe in þe doluen eorþe*; Pepys: *crepe in to þe doluen erþe*; Caius: *hud þe iþe doluen eorðe*; Vitellius: *muscez vous en la terre foue*; Trinity: *muscez vus en la terre fuie*; Lat.: *abscondere fossa humo.*]

1418–19   *Yef thu thus ne dest nawt, [ah] slepinde werest te.* MS: *ȝef þu þus ne dest nawt;* / *slepinde werest te.* Almost certainly an *ah* has been inadvertently dropped before *slepinde*, probably because of the line break (Tolkien, p. 152, fol. 80r, line 25) — it is restored here. [Cleo.: *ȝef þu þus ne dest naut. Ach slepinde werest þe*; Titus: *ȝif þu þus ne dost nawt. ah slepende wereste*; Nero: *ant ȝif þu þus ne dest nout. auh slepinde werest ðe*; Vernon: *ȝif þu þus ne dest not. ac slepynge werest þe*; Pepys: *ȝif þou werest þe slepeande he wil come vpe þe for delytt*; Caius: *gif þu þus ne dest nawt. Ah slepinde werest þe*; Vitellius: *Si vous issi ne fetes; mes en dormant vous defendez*; Trinity: *Si vus issi nel facet; mes ausi com en dormant us defendez*; Lat.: *Si sic non facis, si quasi dormiens te defendis.*]

1427–28   *the withhalt hire on earst, ant tobreketh [to] the stan the earste sturunges, hwen the flesch ariseth, hwil thet ha beoth.* MS: *þe wið* / *halt hire on earst. ant tobrekeð þe stan. þe earste sturunges beoð.* The text as it stands reads, "and breaks the stone, which are the first stirrings." Apparently the scribe, after leaving out a *to* after *tobrekeð*, reinterpreted the following phrase as a relative clause and inserted *beoth* to complete it. Most other versions read "and shatter the first stirrings on the stone." Tolkien: "*to* omitted after *tobrekeð*; *beoð* falsely inserted after *sturunges*" (p. 152, fol. 80v, lines 7–9). The most authoritative versions follow Tolkien's reading, and thus it is restored here, especially since *beoth* (pl.) refers only awkwardly to *stan* (sing.). [Cleo.: *þe wið halt hire on earst. ant to brekeð to þe stan þe earste sturunges*; Titus: *þet wið haldes him on earst. ant to breokes to þe stan þe earste sturinges*; Nero: *ðet wiðhalt hire on erest and tobrekeð to ðe stone ðe ereste sturunges*; Vernon: *þat wiþ stont hire atte biginninge. and to brekeþ to þe ston þe furste sturynges*; Pepys: *þat brekeþ to þe ston atte first skirminge*; Caius: *þe wid halt him anerest. and to breked to þe stan; þe eareste surunge*; Vitellius: *se tient al comencemen<t et . . . > pesce a la piere les primers moeuementz*; Trinity: *se detient au comencement; e depiece alapiere les premers pointures*; Lat.: *ab incio abstinet et primos motus carnis insurgentes allidit ad petram.*]

1445–46   MS: *ant mutleð his beali bleas.* Though Tolkien thinks that *mutleð* a mistake (p. 153, fol. 81r, line 4 — see also Textual Note to 4.917–18), it appears to be a genuine spelling, and so is retained here. Of the form "mutli," Bennett and Smithers comment, "examples of this form are restricted to the 'Katherine Group'. Cf. *mutleð* in *Ancrene Wisse* f. 81a.4; *mutli* in *St. Juliene* 174; and *muclin* in *St. Marherete* 34.28 . . . . It is evidently a form of *mucli, much(e)lin*. However, it is probably not the product of the standard palæographical error of writing *t* for *c* (or vice versa), but a phonetically significant spelling and an early example of the tendency for [k] to become [t] before *l* or *n* (for which see E. J. Dobson, *English Pronunciation*, ii, § 378)" (p. 409n223). [Cleo.: *Mudleð his bali bles*; Titus: *muccles his balies*; Nero: *mucheleð his beli bles*; Vernon: *and mucheleþ his baly bles*; Pepys (lacking); Caius: *and mucheled his bali bles*; Vitellius: *li diable soefle del houre quil primes nest. de ses fols et apres toutz iours sicome il crest*; Trinity: *li dyable la soffle. e la norist e le crest plus e plus e enflamme tot le cors*; Lat.: *et flatum suum auget.*]

Part Five

1   *Twa thinges neometh yeme.* MS: *Twa þinges neomed ʒeme.* The scribe writes *neomed* for *neomeð*, a common mistake. [Cleo.: *Twa þinges neomeð ʒeme*; Titus: *Twa þinges nimes ʒeme*; Nero: *Of two þinges nimeð ʒeme*; Vernon: *Two þinges nymeþ ʒeme*; Pepys: *two þinges nymeþ ʒeme of schrift*; Caius: *<T>wa þinges nimeð geme* (initial missing).]

8   *Either haveth hise threo.* MS: *Eider haueð hise þreo.* Again, the scribe writes a *d* for a *ð*. [Cleo.: *Eiðer haueð his þreo*; Titus: *And eiðer haueð his þreo*; Nero: *Aiðer haues his þreo*; Vernon: *Eiþer haueþ his þreo*; Pepys (lacking); Caius: *Eyþer haued his þreo.*]

18–19   *Thenne fli[t]h his ferd anan as dude Olofernes: his wiheles.* MS: *þenne flih his ferd anan as dude olofernes his wiheles.* The text now reads, "then flee his army at once as Holofernes did his wiles" — a confused sentence. Tolkien sensibly suggests, on the basis of Cleo. and Vernon, that the scribe has omitted an *ð* after *flih*, as well as a punctuation mark after *olofernes* (p. 154, fol. 81v, line 15). With these changes, the text reads, "then his army flees at once just as Holofernes did; his wiles. . . ." Corpus' text falters unless the following phrase is altered (as it is in Nero), to make Judith the subject of *dude*. [Cleo.: *þenne flið his ferd anan as dude olofernes. his wiʒeles*; Titus: *þenne fleos his ferd anan as did olofernes. His wrenches*; Nero: *þeonne vlih his ferde anon; ase dude iudit olofernes. and his wiʒeles*; Vernon: *þenne flihþ his feerde anon as dude Oloferne. his wiles and his wrenches*; Pepys (recast): *þan he fleiʒeþ and alle his wrenches and alle his wiles as Iudif* (sic) *dude Oloferne*; Caius: *þenne flið is ferde anam as dude olofernes. his wiheles*; Vitellius: *Dunqe senfuit son host sicome fist lost holoferne. Ces sunt ses engins*; Trinity (recast): *E en apres est li host au diable destruit e destret par confession*; Lat.: *Tunc statim fugi eius excercitus sicut Olofernis.*]

30   *the sunfule mon.* MS: *þe sunfule ~~lond~~ mon.* The scribe first wrote and then canceled *lond* ("land"), a mistaken insertion from the previous passage which describes how confession takes away the devil's land.

31–33   *This beoth nuthe threo thing [thet schrift deth o the deovel. The other threo thing] thet hit deth us-seolven — thet beoth theose her-efter.* MS: *þis beoð nuðe þreo þring þet hit deð us seoluen. þet beoð þeose her efter.* As Tolkien observes, *þring* is a clear mistake for *þing* (p. 155, fol. 82r, line 5), but Corpus also omits a phrase (probably due to eye-skip from the first *þreo þing* to the second) contained in the other versions. The missing phrase is necessary for the sense and is restored here from Cleo. [Cleo.: *þis beoð nu þreo þing þet schrift deð o þe deouel. þe oðere þreo þing þet hit deð us seoluen. beoð þeose þerefter*; Titus: *Þise beon þre þinges. þet schrift dos o þe deouel. Þe oðer þreo þinges þet hit dos un us self arn her iwriten after*; Nero: *þis beoð nu þreo þinges þet schrift deð oþe deouel. þe oðer þreo þinges ðet hit ðeð on us seoluen; beoð þeos her efter*; Vernon: *þis beoþ nou þreo þinges; þat schrift deeþ o þe deuel. þe oþer þre þinges þat hit deeþ us seluen; beoþ þeos heer aftur*; Pepys (lacking); Caius: *þis beod nu þreo þing. þat shritft ded oþe deoule. þe oðre treo þing þat hit ded us seoluen beod her efter*; Vitellius: *Ces sunt ore trois choses qe confession fet al diable. les altres trois choses qele fait a vous meismes; sunt cestes ici apres*; Trinity: *Ore vus ai ieo dit les treis uertuz ke confession fet encontre le diable. les autres treis choses ke confession fet e countre nos meimes sunt cestes. ke ioe uus dirrai ore*; Lat.: *Premissa tria facit confessio contra diabolum. Alia tria que facit in nobis sunt hec.*]

37–38   *et exuit se vestimentis sue viduitatis.* MS: *et exuit se uestimentis sue uidue/tatis.* As Tolkien notes, "*uidue/tatis,* sic (but *e* altered from *i*)" (p. 155, fol. 82r, line 11). [Cleo.: *et exuit se uestimentis uiduitatis*; Titus: *et exuit se uestimentis sue uiduitatis*; Nero: *et exuit se uestimentis uiduitatis*; Vernon: *et exuit se uestimentis sue iocunditatis!*; Pepys: *et exuit se vestimentis viduitatis*; Caius: *et exuit se uestimentis viduitatis*; Vitellius: *et exuit se de uestimentis sue viduetatis*; Trinity: *Exuit se inquit iudith uestimentis uiduitatis sue*; Lat.: *depositis vestibus viduitatis.*]

40   *This wes bitacnet thurh thet Judith schrudde hire.* MS: *þis wes bitacnet þurh þet dauið schrudde hire.* The scribe or a reader noted the mistake here by putting a faint squiggle over *dau.* The correct reading is *Judith,* as the context bears out.

48–49   MS: *ba ha spealieð an; on ebreische ledene.* Tolkien suggests lacking sense here: "sic; the 'interpretation' *bitternesse* omitted or replaced by *an*" (p. 159, fol. 84r, lines 7–8), a notion supported by the other MSS. However, the passage makes sense if *an* is interpreted as "one and the same thing," and thus may be a legitimate revision. [Cleo.: *ba ha speleð bitternesse on ebreisse ledene*; Titus: *baðe ha spelen bitternesse on ebreische leodene*; Nero: *boð heo spelieð bitternesse; o ebreu*; Vernon: *merariht and Thamar. boþe heo spelen bitternesse. on Ebrewes speche*; Pepys (lacking); Caius: *ha spelied bitternesse on ebreisse leodene*; Vitellius: *ambedous dient atant come amertume en ebreu*; Trinity: *E merai e thamar dient au tant com amertune*; Lat.: *Ambo autem Merari et Thamar in Hebreo interpretantur 'amaritudo.'*]

54–55   *eadmod, scheomeful, [dredful], hopeful.* MS: *Eadmod. Scheomeful. Ho/peful.* Tolkien correctly notes that *dredful* has been omitted after *scheomeful* (p. 156, fol. 82v, lines 7–8). [Cleo.: *Edmod. Scheomeful. Dredful ant hopeful*; Titus: *Eadmod. Schomeful. dredful. Hopeful*; Nero: *edmod. scheomeful. dredful. and hopeful*; Vernon: *meokeful. schomeful. Dredeful. and hopeful*; Pepys (lacking); Caius: *Eadmod. Shemeful. Dredful. and hopeful*; Vitellius: *humble. hountouse. pourouse. et esperante*; Trinity: *Li setime est; ke ele seit umble. Li oitime est; ke ele seit hontouse. Li nouime est; ke ele seit pourouse. Le dime est ke ele soit oue ferme esperance de auoir pardon*; Lat.: *humilis, pudorosa, timorosa, spe subnixa.*]

57   *ant we [schulen] of euch-an sum word sunderliche seggen.* MS: *ant we of euchan sum word sunderliche seggen.* Tolkien: "*wule* omitted after *word*" (p. 156, fol. 82v, line 10). Dobson, after noting how the other versions supply various modal verbs, comments, "But [Cleo.'s] text agrees with Corpus and Vernon. Probably error in archetype, independently corrected by various scribes; Caius is best correction" (p. 224n5). However, Corpus normally prefers the construction *we schulen* for such forecasting statements (see 2.5, 2.199, 4.44, etc.), and so *schulen* is supplied here. [Cleo.: *ant we of euch an sum word sunderliche seggen*; Titus: *we schulen of euchan sum word sunderlich seien*; Nero: *we schulen siggen of euerichon sum word sunderliche areawe*; Vernon: *And we of uchon sum word. sunderliche siggen*; Pepys (lacking); Caius: *An we of uchan sum word wule seggen*; Vitellius: *et nous de chescune ascun mot seuralment dirrom*; Trinity (recast); Lat.: *De hijs singillatim aliquid est dicendum.*]

70–71   *illinc, ter[r]ens justicia; supra, iratus judex; subtra, patens horridum chaos inferni.* MS: *Illinc terens iusticia. Supra; iratus iudex. Subtra patens horridum chaos inferni.* The word *terens* should probably read *terrens.* Further, both Tolkien (p. 157, fol. 83r, lines 2–3) and Zettersten (p. 130, line 30) think that *subtra,* an apparently non-existent word, is a mistake for *subtus.* Dobson, though, makes a convincing case for allowing *subtra*: "So MS., written in full; not a scribal error due to misreading of an abbreviation, as assumed by Herbert (cf. Tolkien in his edition of Corpus), but an obvious analogical form modelled on *supra* (and *infra*); *subtra* is the reading of Cleopatra, Corpus, Caius, Vernon, Titus, Pepys, and the Latin version, *subtus* only of F, Nero, and the Trinity French version, each of which is contradicted by the most closely related MS. or MSS. (F by C, Nero by Vernon, Trinity by Latin version, Titus and Pepys)" (p. 225n12). [Cleo.: *Illinc terrens iusticia supra. iratus iudex. subtra patens orridum chaos inferni*; Titus: *Illinc terrens iustitia. Supra; iratus iudens. Subtra; patens horridum chaos inferni*; Nero: *inde terrens iusticia. subtus patens horridum chaos inferni. desuper iratus iudex*; Vernon: *Illinc terrens iusticia. Supra iratus iudex. Subtra patens horridum chaos inferni*; Pepys: *Hinc erunt accusancia terrens supra iratus iudex. subtra patrinus horrendum chaos inferni*; Caius: *illinc terrens iusticia. supra iratus Iudex. subtra patens horridum chaos inferni*; Vitellius: *Illinc terrenis <sic for terrens> iusticia. supra; iratus iudex. subtus; patens horridum cahos inferni*; Trinity: *illinc terrens iusticia supra; iratus iudex. subtus; patens horridum chaos inferni*; Lat.: *illinc terret iusticia; supra iratus Iudex, subtra patens horridum chaos inferni.*]

73–74   *o Domes[-dei] schulen ure swarte sunnen strongliche bicleopien us.* MS: *o domes schulen ure swarte sunnen strongliche bicleopien us.* Tolkien rightly points out that *domes* should read *domes-dei* (p. 157, fol. 83r, line 5). [Cleo.: *o demesdei schulen vre swarte sunnen strongliche bicleopen us*; Titus: *o domes dai schulen ure swarte sunnes strongluche bicalle us*; Nero: *adomesdei schulen ure swarte sunnen bicleopien us stroncliche*; Vernon: *o domes day. schullen ur swarte sunnen. strongliche biclepen us*; Pepys: *On domesday schal þe deuel of helle stonde on þi riȝth half þine blake synnes on þi left half and biclepe þe*; Caius: *a domes dai shulen ure swarte sunnen strongliche biclepien us*; Vitellius: *al iour de iuise; noz veirs <sic, for uous> pecchez forment nous accuserunt*; Trinity (recast); Lat.: *Accusabunt enim nos pecat de mordra anime.*]

105–06   *pini the flesch ute-with mid feasten.* MS: *pini þe flesch utewið mið feasten.* Here *mið* seems to be a mistake for *mid*.

125   *weren astorven ferliche.* MS: *weren asteoruen ferliche.* Tolkien detects an error with *asteoruen* here: it appears in its infinitive form but, as the context shows, a past participle is required. Accordingly, *asteoruen* is emended to *astoruen*, the past participle (p. 159, fol. 84r, line 21). [Cleo.: *weren astoruen feorliche*; Titus: *weren istoruen ferliche*; Nero: *weren i storuen uerliche*; Vernon: *weoren istoruen ferliche*; Pepys (recast); Caius: *weren istorwen ferlich*; Vitellius: *fuissent touz*

morz merueillousement; Trinity: *fussent touz meintenant subitement morz*; Lat.: *subito fuissent mortui*.]

144   MS: *o bearninde wearitre*. Tolkien thinks the spelling of *wearitre* faulty, and that it presumably should read *-treo* (p. 160, fol. 84v, line 21), but the Corpus spelling is allowed to stand here on the chance that the loss of final *o* may represent a phonological process. Dobson: "D writes *galwis* above" (p. 230n9). [Cleo.: *on berninde wari/treo*; Titus: *o bearninde waritreos*; Nero: *o berninde waritreo*; Vernon: *on bernynde wartreo*; Pepys: *opon þe galewes*; Caius: *o berninde waritre*.]

163–64   *Wat Crist*. MS: *wac crist*. A clear mistake for *wat crist* (Tolkien, p. 161, fol. 85r, line 20). [Cleo.: *wat crist*; Titus: *Wat crist*; Nero: *wat crist*; Vernon: *wot crist*; Pepys (lacking); Caius: *wat crist*; Vitellius: *Dieu le siet*; Trinity: *E ceo sache deu omnipotent*; Lat.: *Nouit Christus*.]

164   *to se g[ent]il wardein*. MS: *to segil wardein*. As Tolkien observes, *segil* is a compressed version of the two words *se gentil* "so gentle" (p. 161, fol. 85r, line 21). [Cleo.: *to swa gentil wardein*; Titus: *to swa gentil wardein*; Nero: *to so gentil wardein*; Vernon: *to so gentil wardeyn*; Pepys: *to swich a gentil wardeyn*; Caius: *to so gentil wardein*; Vitellius: *si gentil gardein*; Trinity: *si tres gentil gardein*; Lat.: *tam nobili custodi*.]

182–83   *ah is i-lich the mon*. MS: *as is ilich þe mon*. It seems likely that *as* should be *ah* "but" (see Tolkien, p. 162, fol. 85v, line 19). [Cleo.: *A<c> is ilich þe mon*; Titus: *Ah is ilich þe mon*; Nero: *auh is i liche þen monne*; Vernon: *Ak he is lyk þe mon*; Pepys (recast); Caius: *As is ilich þe mon*.]

188–89   *he wes lute child tha he hit wrahte*. MS: *he wes lute child þa he hit / hit wrahte*. The scribe accidentally repeated the last word of the previous folio (see Tolkien, p. 162, fols. 85v–86r, lines 28–29).

189   MS: *þurh þe abbates ropunge þet he hit seide*. The syntax of this sentence suggests that the MS *þet*, though attested in other authoritative versions, does not belong here. The reading is allowed to stand on the perhaps dubious assumption that an understood "it was" may lie underneath the *þet*. [Cleo.: *þurch þe abbedes roping þet hit seide*; Titus: *þurh þe abbotes ropinge þet he hit seide*; Nero: *þuruh þen abbodes gropunge; he hit seide*; Vernon: *þorwȝ þe abbotes tysinge*; Pepys (recast); Caius: *þurh þe abbodes ropunge; þat he hit seiede*; Vitellius: *par le*

monestement labbe. qil le dit; Trinity: *par le cri ke lui abbe cria*; Lat.: *per abbatis hortatum illud dixit.*]

198   MS: *yef he cuthe seggen.* Most of the other versions include a Latin quotation at the end of this paragraph, a sentence lacking in Corpus: *Augustinus: Si conscientia desit, pena satisfacit.* ("If knowledge fails, penance makes amends"). [Cleo.: *Augustinus. Si consciencia desit pena satisfacit*; Titus: *Augustinus. Si conscientia desit pena satisfacit*; Nero: *Si conscientia desit; pena satisfacit. augustinus*; Vernon: *Aug[ustinus]. si consciencia desit pena satisfacit*; Pepys: *Si consciencia desit pena satisfacit*; Caius: *Augustinus. Si consciencia desit; pena satisfacit*; Vitellius (lacking); Trinity: *Quia ut dicit augustinus. aut deus pie ignoscet aut ad memoriam reducet*; Lat.: *Augustinus: Si consciencia desit, pena satisfacit.*]

200   MS: *ah schulen þe wordes beon ischawet efter þe werkes.* Tolkien makes a case for rejecting the MS reading *i-schawet* ("shown, revealed") in favor of *i-schapet* ("shaped, formed"), on the basis of Vitellius but reflected in Cleo. (p. 162, fol. 86r, line 17). However, Dobson believes that Cleo.'s form *ischape<n>* is itself a mistake: "[Scribe] A first wrote *ischaped* but subpuncted *d* and added abbreviation-mark for *n* over *e*; this may suggest that his exemplar had the true reading *ischawed* (cf. Corpus) and that his initial error was misreading *wynn* as *þ*, the change from weak to strong conjugation being a necessary consequence" (p. 235n15). Since it is possible to make very good sense of the MS reading, and since other versions (Nero, Caius, Lat.) also read *i-schawet*, the MS reading is retained. [Cleo.: *Ach schule þe wordes beon ischape<n> efter þe werkes*; Titus: *Ah schulden wordes beo iset and iseid ischrift after þe wo<e>rkes*; Nero: *auh ðe wordes schulen beon i scheawede efter ðe werkes*; Vernon: *Ac schulle þe wordes ben ischewet. aftur þe werkes*; Pepys (recast): *Ac saie þe wordes after þe werkes*; Caius: *þe wordes beon iswawed <sic, for ischawed> after þe werkes*; Vitellius: *Mes deiuent les paroles estre tailleez apres les oeures*; Trinity: *Nuement donc deiuent les paroleS estre asises e dites en confession solonc les oueres du pecche*; Lat.: *sed debent sermones exponi secundum opera.*]

221   *eode o ring.* MS: *Eede o Ring. Eede* is most likely a mistake for *Eode* "went" (see Tolkien: "*Eede* sic, for *Eode*; the last *e* is altered from *o*," p. 163, fol. 86v, line 19). [Cleo.: *eode on ring*; Titus: *Eode in Ring*; Nero: *eode oðe pleouwe*; Vernon: *Eode on Daunse in chircheȝard*; Pepys (lacking); Caius: *Eode o ringe.*]

235–36   *Tale is the fifte totagge.* MS: *Tale is þe feorðe totagge.* As Tolkien points out, the
          scribe should have written *fifte* instead of *feorthe* (p. 164, fol. 87r, line 10). [Cleo.:
          Tale is þe fifte totagge; Titus: *Tale is te fifte totagge*; Nero: *tale; is ðe vifte
          totagge*; Vernon: *Tale; is þe ffyfþe braunche*; Pepys: *Tale is anoþer*; Caius: *Tale
          is þe fifte totag*; Vitellius: *Numbre est la quinte circumstance*; Trinity: *Nombre est
          la quinte circumstance*; Lat.: *Numerus est quinta circumstancia.*]

235–42   *Tale is the fifte totagge — [hu ofte hit is i-don.] Cause is hwi thu hit dudest.* MS:
          feorðe totagge. Cause is hwi þu hit dudest. Tolkien: "passage dealing with *Tale
          . . .* omitted, between *. . . totagge* and *. . . Cause is*" (p. 164, fol. 87r, line 11). This
          is a clear case of eye-skip from one *totagge* to the second. The passage is restored
          from Cleo. Note that near the end of the passage, other authoritative versions
          provide slightly different readings of Cleo.'s *to þus feole.ant þus feole siðen.*
          [Cleo.: *hu ofte hit is idon tellen al. Sire ich habbe þis þus ofte idon. iwonet for to
          speoke þus hercni þullich speche. þenchen hwiche þochtes. for ʒeme þing ant for
          ʒeoten. lachʒen eoten drinken lasse oðer mare þenne neode askeð. Ich habbe
          ibeon þusofte wrað seoððen ich wes ischriuen nest ant for þulli þing ant þus longe
          hit leste Þus ofte iseid les. þus ofte þis ant þis. ich habbe idon þis to þus feole. ant
          þus feole siðen. Cause is þe seste totagge. Cause is hwi þu hit dudest*;
          Titus: *hu ofte hit is idon tellen al. Sire i haue þis tus ofte idon. wunet for to speken
          þus. hercne þulli speche. þenchen þulli þohtes for ʒeme þing and for ʒeten.
          lahhen. Eten. Drinken. lesse oðer mare þen ned asked. I haue beon þus ofte wrað
          siðen iwas last schriuen. and for þis þing. and tus longe hit laste. þus ofte iseid
          leas. þus ofte þis and tis. Ich haue idon þis to þus feole. and oþus fele wisen.
          Cause is te Sixte totagge. Cause is hwi þu hit dides*;
          Nero: *tellen al hu ofte hit is idon. Sire ich habbe þis. þus ofte i don. iwuned forto
          speken þus. ant hercnen swuche spechen. ant þenchen swuche þouhtes. vor ʒemed
          þinges: ant for ʒiten. lauhwen. eten. drinken. lesse oðer more; þen neod were. Ich
          habbe ibeon þus ofte wroð; seoððen ich was i schriuen nexst. ant for swuche
          þinge. ant þus longe hit ileste. þus ofte i seide leas. þus ofte þis ant tis. Ich habbe
          i don þis; þus feole siðen. ant o þus feole wisen. ant to þus feole. Cause: is þe sixte
          totagge. cause is; hwi ðu hit dudest*;
          Vernon: *Now ofte hit is idon. so tellen al. Sire ichabbe þis. þus ofte idon. iwont
          forte speken þus. herkenen such speche. þenken such þouhtes. ffor ʒeme þing. and
          for ʒeten. Lauʒwhen. eten. drinken. Lasse. oþer more; þen neod askeþ. Ichabbe
          iben þus ofte wroþ. seþþen ich was ischriuen last. and for such þing. And þus
          longe hit laste. þus ofte iseid fals. þus ofte þis and þis. Ichabbe ido þis; þus ofte.
          to þus feole. and o þus feole wysen. Cause; is þe sixte braunche. Cause is; whi þu
          hit dedest*;

Pepys: *tellen hou oft þus oft yspoken yseide les. Þou3th þus fele þou3tte. for3emed þing þat my3th haue holpen man oiþer for3eten þing. lau3en eten dronken lesse oiþer more þan hij hadden nede to þus ofte in wraþþe siþþen i was last schriuen. Cause whi þou dedest it;*

Caius: *hu ofte hit is idon. tellen al. Sire ich habbe þis þus ofte idon. iwuned forte speke<n> þus Hercni swulli speche. þenche swuche þochtes. forgemen þing. and feorgeten. lahhen. eoten. drinken. les oþer mare þen neod eskede. Ich habbe þus ofte ibeon wrað seoðþen ich wes ischrwen nest. and for þulli þing. and þus longe hit laste. þus ofte iseide les. þus ofte þis and þis. Ich habbe idon þis þus ofte to þus feole. and o þus feole wise. Cause is hwi þu hit dudest;*

Vitellius: *come souent cest fet tout countier. Sire iai cest si souent fet ieo acustome. de issi parler. tiele parole escoutier. pensir tiels pensirs. Malgarder chose; et oblier. Rire. mangier. boire . . . plus qe bosoigne ne de . . . e. Jai estee si souent corou(cee) puis qe ieo fu dereinement con(f)essee et pur tiele chose. et issi longement dura. Issi souent ai dit faus. Issi souent cest et cest. Jai fet cest a tantz et en tantes manieres. Cause est la sixte circumstance. cause est pur quai vous le feites;*

Trinity: *ke doit estre nomee en confession. ceo est. homme deit dire quante foiz il ad fet le pecche si il en soueigne en iceste manere. Sire ieo ai fet cest pecche tantes foiz. e dire quantes foiz si il set. Sire ieo ai este acostoume de parler en tiele maniere. e issint escuter teles paroles e teus penseres penser e en teu pensers <mout men ai delitez e longement. Sire ieo ai mange e beu meintes fez plus ke mester ne me fust. Ieo ai este tantes foiz corucez pus ke-ioe fu de reine>ment confes. e pur ceste chose tant longement me durra il coruz. Tantes foiz ai ieo dit faus ou menti ascient. Tantes foiz ai ieo fet cest chose. ieo ai fet teu pecche oue tants ou oue tanz e en tant maniers. Cause; est la sime circumstance de ki homme deit fere mencion en sa confession;*

Lat.: *dicere totum quociens factum est. 'Assuetus sum sic loqui, talia audire, talia cogitare, negligere, obliuisci, ridere, commedere, bibere plus aut minus quam oporteret. Sic sepius iratus sum postquam proximo confitebar et pro tali re et tam diu durauit ira; tam frequenter dixi falsum, tociens hoc et illud feci et hoc tot et tot modis.' Causa est sexta circumstancia, videlicet, quare illud fecisti.*]

261 *shalt trusse ant al torplin into helle.* Diensberg thinks that *trusse* is a French-derived past participle meaning "packed up" and would emend the text to *ant swa with al the schendlac thu schalt trusse(e) in to helle.* His translation: "and thus with all that shame all packed up you shall fall into hell" ("*Ancrene Wisse/ Riwle,*" p. 81). However, it seems more likely that *trusse* is an infinitive parallel to *torplin.*

292   MS: *ȝef he lið biþencheð him hwenne he wule arisen.* Tolkien: "*biþencheð*, sic: probably for *biþenched* (F *gist sei purpensant*); cf. *biswenchet*, f. 112b. 7" (p. 166, fol. 88r, line 24). Dobson comments, "The collation shows that Corpus and Cleopatra correctly reproduce the archetype, and makes improbable Tolkien's suggestion that the Corpus reading is an error for *biþenched* (unless we assume error in the archetype); rather this is an idiom involving the early ME verbal noun in *-eð*, for which the participial ending *-ed* was substituted (cf. Chaucer's *was go walked* etc.). F's [i.e., Vitellius'] translation is in either case correct" (Dobson, p. 241n21). It seems simpler and less intrusive, though, to take the form as a present tense verb parallel to *lið* and to assume a lost point after *lið*. [Cleo.: *ȝef he lið biþencheð him*; Titus: *ȝif ho lið ant biþencheð hire*; Nero: *ȝif he lið ant biþencheð*; Vernon: *ȝif he liþ biþenkeþ him. whonne he wole arysen*; Pepys (lacking); Caius: *gif he lid and biþenched him þenne he wule arisen*; Vitellius: *sil gist sei purpensant*; Trinity: *si il gise en pes en feu. e se purpense quant il ueut leuer*; Lat.: *si iaceat et deliberet quando surgere voluerit.*]

295   *thet ahten hihin to schrift.* MS: *þet ahten hihin <þe> to schrift.* Tolkien rejects the addition of *þe* (p. 166, fol. 88v, line 1), and indeed no other version contains it. In Cleo., Scribe D translates this phrase into Latin: *debent accelerare confessionem* "(which) ought to hurry confession" (Dobson, p. 241n32). [Cleo.: *þet achten hiȝe to schrift*; Titus: *þet ahten hihen to schrift*; Nero: *ðet ouhten hien touward schrifte*; Vernon: *þat ouȝte hiȝen to schrift*; Pepys: *whi a Man auȝt go sone to schrift*; Caius: *þat ahten hihen schrift*; Vitellius: *qe duissent hastier confession*; Trinity: *ke nus deusunt par reson haster a confession*; Lat.: *que festinare debent confessionem.*]

305–06   *Principiis obsta. [Sero] medicina paratur cum mala per longas.* MS: *Principiis obsta. Medicina paratur cum mala perlongas.* Tolkien: "*sero* omitted before *Medicina*; *perlongas*, sic, for *per longas [conualuere moras]*" (p. 167, fol. 88v, line 15). A quote from Ovid's *Remedia Amoris*, lines 91–92. In full this line reads "Principiis obsta; sero medicina paratur, / Cum mala per longas convaluere moras." [Cleo.: *<Sero. med.>*; Titus: *Principiis obsta sero medicina paratur*; Nero: *principiis obsta sero medicina paratur*; Vernon: *Principium obsta. sero. medicina*; Pepys: *Principi constalere medicina paratur*; Caius: *principiis obsta sero medicina paratur*; Vitellius (lacking); Trinity: *principiis obsta. sero medicina paratur*; Lat.: *Principijs obsta; sero medicina paratur.*]

313–25   *Circumdederunt me canes multi . . . swuch beatunge.* Tolkien: "*Circumdederunt me canes multi* to *swuch beatunge* is placed later" (p. 166, fol. 88r, line 28).

Dobson comments, "The preceding sentence, *se me deoppere . . . latere*, is similarly placed in Nero, Titus, Pepys, Latin version, and Trinity version (i.e. the MSS. which give the *Circumdederunt* passage at the earlier point, with the exception of F), but immediately before *Þe achtuðe þing* (and therefore immediately after the *Circumdederunt* passage) in Corpus, Caius, and Vernon; it is entirely omitted by F. Probably another early addition to the basic text, which seems to me to belong immediately after *haueð ilein longe* (l. 12), since it continues the thought of the Augustinian citation, i.e. Corpus etc. place it essentially rightly but spoil the sequence of thought by bringing in the *Circumdederent* passage before it" (p. 243n15).

320   *other awuri[e]th ahte.* MS: *oðer awurið ahte.* Tolkien: "*awurið*, sic" (p. 167, fol. 89r, line 5). An *e* seems to have dropped out of *awurið*, which as it stands is a plural form. It is emended to the singular *awurieth*. [Cleo. (lacking);Titus: *oðer wuries ahte*; Nero: *oðer awurieð eihte*; Vernon: *oþer aworieþ auӡte*; Pepys (lacking); Caius: *oþer awuried eahte*.]

322   *mid ti tunge [i] schrift.* MS: *mid ti tunge schrift.* Tolkien correctly points out that the preposition *i* ("in") has been omitted after *tunge* (p. 167, fol. 89r, line 7). [Cleo. (lacking); Titus: *wið þi tunge i schrift*; Nero: *mid þine tunge ine schrifte*; Vernon: *mid þi tonge in schrift*; Pepys (recast); Caius: *wid þi tunge i schrift*; Vitellius: *od vostre lange en confession*; Trinity: *par uostre lange en confession*; Lat.: *cum lingua in confessione*.]

334–35   *he schulde habben unw[r]ihen hise wunden.* MS: *he schulde habben unwihen hise wunden.* As Tolkien notes, the scribe has mistakenly left the *r* out of *unw[r]ihen* (p. 168, fol. 89r, line 24). The common ancestor of Corpus and Cleo. must have contained the same mistake: Dobson comments on Cleo.'s text, "[Scribe] D adds insertion-mark after *wynn* and writes *r* above. But [Scribe] A's form agrees with Corpus *unwihen* against *unwrihen* Titus, Caius, Nero (with variations of spelling); the coincidence in error is very odd. Perhaps the archetype was itself faulty" (p. 243n5). [Cleo.: *he schulde habben unwiӡen hise wunden*; Titus: *he schulde hauen unwrihen hise wundes*; Nero: *he schulde habben unwrien his wunden*; Vernon: *he schulde habben unhuled his wounden*; Pepys (recast); Caius: *he schulde habben unwhrihen hise wunden*; Vitellius: *il deust auer descouert ses plaies*; Trinity: *il le deust auoir moustre ses plaies*; Lat.: *debuit sua wlnera reuelasse.*]

336   *hare flowinde cweise.* MS: *hare flowinde gi cweise.* The scribe first wrote *gi* but canceled it. Tolkien thinks that it was "probably [the] beginning of erroneous repetition of *gute*" (p. 168, fol. 89r, line 27).

340   *eadmodnesse eadmodliche bigileth ure Laverd.* MS: *eadmodnesse ead/modliche bigileð ure lauerd.* Tolkien: "*ead/modliche* for *eadiliche*" (p. 168, fol. 89v, line 4). The Corpus reading is grammatically sound, and thus is retained, though it is possible (judging by the other versions) that it represents a mistaken repetition (dittography). [Cleo.: *edmodnesse eadiliche bigileð ure lauerd*; Titus: *eadmodnesse eadiliche bigles ure lauerd*; Nero: *edmodnesse. eadiliche bigileð ure louerd ant edmodliche*; Vernon: *mekenesse eþelyche bigyleþ ur lord*; Pepys (recast): *Þus þe lowe Man of hert bigileþ god*; Caius: *eadmodnesse eadiliche bigiled ure lauerd*; Vitellius: *humilite seintement degile nostre seignour*; Trinity: *ele de gile e de ceit e engingne quenses nostre seignur sutilment*; Lat.: *Sic humilitas feliciter Dominum decipit.*]

382   *Theos twa na-mon ne parti from other, for as Sein Gregoire seith.* MS: *Þeos twa namon ne parti from <oðer>. for as sein gregoire seið.* A later scribe or reader has inserted the word *oþer* between *from* and *for*, rightly correcting the faulty sentence. [Cleo.: *Þeos twa na mon ne parti from oðer. for as seint greg*ori *seið*; Titus: *Þeose twa mon ne schal ne twinne. ne parti fram oðer for as Seint Gregorie seis*; Nero: *þeos two. no mon ne to dele urom oðer. vor ase seint gregorie seið*; Vernon: *þeos two; no mon ne parte from oþer. ffor as seint Gregorius. seiþ*; Pepys: *Þise two noman ne parte hem asundre*; Caius: *þeos twa namon ne parti from oþer. for as seint gregorie seið*; Vitellius: *Ces dous nul hom ne departe. lun de laltre*; Trinity: *Cestes deus choses ne deit nul homme <desseurer ne la une> del autre de partir*; Lat.: *Has duas molas nemo separet ab iuicem quia sicut dicit Gregorius.*]

411   *thet for a cwene word.* MS: *þet for a cwene worð.* The scribe mistakenly wrote a *ð* instead of a *d*, a common mistake. [Cleo.: *þet for acwene word*; Titus: *and tat for a cwene word*; Nero: *and tet for ane cwene worde*; Vernon: *for a cwene word*; Pepys (lacking); Caius: *þat for a cwene word*; Vitellius: *par le mot dune baisse*; Trinity: *pur la parole de une ueilie*; Lat.: *pro uoce ancille.*]

412   *hu the theof o rode.* MS: *O<f> þe þeof o rode.* A scribe or reader tried to make sense of this odd error by changing *O* to *Of*. The other versions make it clear, however, that *O* mistakenly replaces *Hu* "how" (see Tolkien, p. 171, fol. 91r, line 16). [Cleo.: *hu þe þeof o rode*; Titus: *Hu þe þeof o rode*; Nero: *and hwu þe þeof*

oþe rode; Vernon: *Hou þe þeof on Roode*; Pepys: *and þe þef also*; Caius: *Hu þe þeof on rode*; Vitellius: *comment li larron en la croiz*; Trinity: *comment li laron*; Lat.: *quomodo latro in cruce.*]

417   *as ha beoth th'ruppe i-writene.* MS: *as ha ~~weren~~ beoð þruppe iwrite/ne.* The scribe first wrote *weren*, but canceled it and wrote *beoth* instead, most likely bringing the text into agreement with the exemplar (see Tolkien, p. 172, fol. 91r, lines 22–23). [Cleo.: *as ha beoð þruppe iwritene*; Titus: *as ho arn þruppe iwriten*; Nero: *as heo beoð þer uppe i writene*; Vernon: *as heo beoþ þroppe iwriten*; Pepys (lacking); Caius: *as ha beod þeruppe iwriten*; Vitellius: *sicome il sunt la sus escrites*; Trinity (lacking); Lat.: *sicut supra libro iiij° scribuntur.*]

455–56   MS: *swote i godes nease smeallinde flures.* It seems likely that an *ase* has dropped out after *nease* very early on in the textual transmission, probably due to eye-skip (*nease ase*). The MS reading is retained, however, since an *as* (*come*) appears only in Trinity, and is most likely an *ad hoc* revision. Other scribes were able to make sense of the phrase as it stands, though Nero's revision simplifies the syntax. [Cleo.: *swote in godes nase smellinde flures*; Nero: *swote smellinde flures ine godes neose*; Titus: *swete i godes nase smellinde flures*; Vernon: *swote in godes neose. smullinde floures*; Pepys (lacking); Caius: *swote i godes nase. smellinde flures*; Vitellius: *flurs al nes dieu doucement fleirantes*; Trinity: *mout doucement <flerent> en nes nostre seignur come flours odouranz*; Lat.: *suaues in eius naribus.*]

461   *ha ne mei nawt fulleliche wreien hire-seolven.* MS: *ha ne mei nawt fulleliche wreien ~~hire~~ / hire seoluen.* The scribe corrects the erroneous repetition of *hire* by striking through the first one (Tolkien, p. 174, fol. 9r, line 26).

Part Six

26–27   *ah we secheth other.* MS: *ah we sech./eð oþer.* Tolkien is justified in rejecting the intrusive point after *sech*, especially since it occurs in the middle of a word (p. 178, fol. 94r, lines 17–18).

29–30   *for other pilegrimes gath [i] muche swinc.* MS: *for oðer pilegrimes gað muche swinc.* A preposition seems to missing here: "pilgrims go great travail." Though Shepherd suggests a *wið* "pilgrims go with great travail," Tolkien's solution (to insert an *i* "in"— p. 178, fol. 94v, line 21) is less intrusive and better supported (see Cleo. and Vitellius), and thus is adopted here. [Cleo.: *gað in muche swinc*; Titus: *gan wið muche swinke*; Nero: *goð mid swinke*; Vernon: *ffor oþer pilgrimes. goþ mid muche swynk*; Pepys: *goþ wiþ mychel trauaile*; Caius: *for oþere pilegrims. gad mid muchele swinc*; Vitellius: *vount en grant trauail*; Trinity: *kar autres pelerins uont ou grant trauail*; Lat.: *alij peregrini cum multo labore tendunt.*]

47   MS: *eadeaweð ant springeð as þe dahunge efter nihtes þeosternesse*. Tolkien believes that spelling of *eadeaweð* is faulty and that it should appear as *ed-*, since it derives from OE *ætawan* "to appear, reveal" (p. 179, fol. 95r, line 14). The word was apparently obscure to several scribes. However, it seems to represent a genuine spelling since OE *æ* is sometimes rendered as *ea* in Corpus (see Zettersten, p. 243), and thus the MS form is retained here. [Cleo.: *edeawet ant springeð as þe daȝunge efter nichtes þeosternesse*; Titus: *adaies and springes as te dahing after nihtes þeosternesse*; Nero: *daweð and springeð ase þe dawunge efter nihtes þeosternesse*; Vernon: *deweþ and springeþ. As þe dewynge aftur nihtes þesternesse*; Pepys: *schal springen after þe daweyng after niȝttes þesternes*; Caius: *deweð and springeð. as dahunge efter nihtes þeosternesse.*]

68   *i the wor[l]des wei*. MS: *i þe wordes wei*. The clearly mistaken *wordes* is emended to *worldes* here following Tolkien's suggestion (p. 180, fol. 95v, line 11), one fully supported by the MS evidence. [Cleo.: *in worl/des wei*; Titus: *i þe worldes wei*; Nero: *i ðe worldes weie*; Vernon: *in worldes wei*; Pepys: *in þe werlde*; Caius: *i þe worlddes wei*; Vitellius: *en la voie del siecle*; Trinity: *en chemin du siecle*; Lat.: *in via mundi.*]

69   MS: *wreaðeð him for weohes*. Tolkien would emend *weohes* "injuries," to *wohes*, the standard spelling of the word in Corpus (p. 180, fol. 95v, line 13), but the MS reading may well represent a genuine form — both Zettersten and Shepherd accept it, and thus it is allowed to stand. [Cleo.: *wreðceð him for woȝes*; Titus: *wraðdes him for wohe*; Nero: *wreðdet him uor wowes*; Vernon: *wraþþeþ him for wowes*; Pepys (lacking); Caius: *wredded him for wohes.*]

80   *Hwet-se beo of othre*. MS: *hwet se beo of ordre*. Though MS *ordre* makes grammatical sense here, it is unlikely, as Shepherd points out, that the author intends a "censure of other religious ways of life" (p. 34n6/4). Both Shepherd and Tolkien (p. 180, fol. 95v, line 27) emend to *oðre*, the form attested in the other authoritative versions, an emendation which is adopted here. [Cleo.: *hwet se beo of oðre*; Titus: *Hwat se beo of oðre*; Nero: *hwat se beo of oþre*; Vernon: *What so*

541

ben of oþere; Pepys (lacking); Caius: *hwet se beo of oþre*; Vitellius: *queiqe soit dautres*; Trinity: *Quei ke seit de autres*; Lat.: *Quicquid sit de allijs*.]

110   *Nis hit i-writen bi him*. MS: *Nis hit iwriten bi him* <*seolf*>. The interlinear addition of *seolf* above *him* does not seem to be necessary for sense, though it does bring Corpus into line with Nero and Pepys. [Cleo.: *nis hit iwriten bi him*; Titus: *Nis hit writen bi him*; Nero: *nis hit iwriten bi him sulf*; Vernon: *Nis hit iwriten bi him*; Pepys: *nys it writen by hum seluen*; Caius: *Nis hit iwriten of him*; Vitellius: *Nest il escrit de lui*; Trinity: *ne est il issi escrit de lui*; Lat.: *Nonne de eo scriptum est*.]

122   *Ysa[ias]*. MS: *ysa*. Tolkien: "sic for *ysaie*" (p. 182, fol. 96v, line 23); Shepherd emends to *Ysaias*. We follow Shepherd here because the Latin form *Ysaias* rather than the English *Ysaie* is called for by the context of the Latin quotation; Corpus distinguishes rather carefully between forms in this regard. Rather than a mistake, *ysa* may be an accepted or slightly altered abbreviation for *Ysaias* or *Ysaie*. [Cleo.: *ysaye*; Titus: *Ysaias*; Nero: *Isaie*; Vernon: *Isaias*; Pepys: *ysayas*; Caius: *ysayas*; Vitellius: *Ysaias*; Trinity: *Ysaias*; Lat.: *Ysaie*.]

125   *ne the gode nabbeth*. MS: *ne þe / þe gode nabbeð*. The accidental repetition of *þe* is removed, as both Tolkien (p. 182, fol. 96v, lines 26–27) and Shepherd suggest.

175–76 MS: *weneð wið lihtleapes buggen eche blisse*. The phrase *wið liht leapes* is difficult to understand. One should probably hesitate to translate it simply as "with light leaps" because *liht* lacks the expected plural ending *-e* — that is, *liht-leapes* may well be a compound. If so, it probably follows the pattern of *sunder-lepes* "separately" and *an-lepi* "single" in which *-lepes*, an adverbial genitive (from OE *hliep* ["leap"]), seems to carry little meaning other than marking the word as an adverb or adjective. If this is the case, then the word could mean "easily, cheaply" (see *liht* [adj.]). But the preposition *wið* seems awkward since it takes *lihtleapes* as an object. Shepherd speculates that *wið lihtleapes* means "with easy steps," while Day would read *liht cheapes* "with cheap bargains" (see Titus and Pepys). As Shepherd points out, the spelling *leapes* is unusual for the AB dialect, where *lupe* "leap" is the common form. It is possible that *leapes* comes from OE *leap* "basket, measure" and means in this phrase "with light measures." There is sufficient evidence from the other versions that *lihtleapes* is the original reading, especially since both French versions translate with *a/de legier marche* "with light step." The form, though, seems to have confused some of the scribes. It is retained here. [Cleo.: *weneð wið licht lepes buggen eche blisse*;

Titus: *wenen wið lihte scheapes buien eche blisse*; Nero: *weneð mid liht-leapes buggen eche blisse*; Vernon (lost); Pepys: *wenen wiþ liȝth chep bugge so heiȝe blis*; Caius: *wened wid lichteleapes to buggen eche blisse*; Vitellius: *a legier marchee achatier pardurable ioie*; Trinity: *de legier marche la uie parduarable achater*; Lat.: *putantes vili precio sublimem emere gloriam*.]

179–80   *riche feaderes.* MS: *ȝape feaderes.* Both Tolkien and Shepherd emend *ȝape* ("sly, clever") to *riche*, a clearly necessary emendation which is also adopted here, since the fathers are anything but clever in giving in to their spoiled offspring. Tolkien: "*ȝape* false repetition for *riche*" (p. 185, fol. 98r, line 13). [Cleo.: *riche fadres*; Titus: *riche faderes*; Nero: *riche uederes*; Vernon (lost); Pepys: *riche faders*; Caius: *riche faderes*; Vitellius: *riches pieres*; Trinity: *riches peres*; Lat.: *patres . . . diuites*.]

188   *he cleopeth "folc fearlich."* MS: *he cleopeð folc fearlac.* Tolkien's suggestion (p. 185, fol. 98r, line 24) that *fearlac* "fear" is a mistake for *fearlich* "fearful" is fully supported by other MSS and is adopted here. [Cleo.: *he cleopeð folc feorlich*; Titus: *he cleopes folc fear-lich*; Nero: *he cleopeð folk ferlich*; Vernon (lost); Pepys: *he clepeþ hem wonderful folk*; Caius: *he cloped foelc ferlich*; Vitellius: *Il le apeele poeple hydous*; Trinity: *apele il pople espontable*; Lat:. *Populum . . . vocat terribilem*.]

189–90   *Pellem pro pelle et uni[versa], et cetera.* MS: *Pellem pro pelle et uni et cetera.* Though Tolkien thinks that *uni* is a mistake for *universa* (p. 185, fol. 98r, line 26), it seems more likely that it is an *ad hoc* abbreviation. Note the close relationship between Corpus and Cleo. [Cleo.: *Pellem pro pelle et uni et cetera*; Titus: *Pellem pro pelle. et cetera*; Nero: *pellem pro pelle et uniuersa et cetera*; Vernon (lost); Pepys: *PELLem pro pelle et cetera*; Caius: *Pellem pro pelle et uniuersa que habet et cetera*; Vitellius: *Pellem pro pelle et uniuersa que habet homo dabit pro anima sua*; Trinity: *Pellem inquid pro pelle. et omnia que habet homo dabit pro anima sua*; Lat.: *Pellem pro pelle et, et cetera*.]

202   *fortheth his lustes.* MS: *forðeð his lustes.* As Tolkien points out, *forðeð* ("de-stroys") is unsatisfactory since it gives a sense opposite to the one demanded by the context (p. 186, fol. 98v, line 14). As the other MSS show, the better reading is *forðeð* "furthers, encourages," though Shepherd, following Mack, defends *forðeð* as a possible assimilated form of *forðeð*, while admitting that the *d/ð* confusion is common. On Cleo.'s *for-* Dobson comments, "Erased; surviving traces faint but sufficient to show A's text was as Corpus." On *deð*, "The loop of

the *ð* erased to make *d*, doubtless by [Scribe] D" (p. 268, fol. 168v, nn10 and 11). [Cleo.: *(for)de(ð) his lustes*; Titus: *forðes hise lustes*; Nero: *fedeð his lustes*; Vernon (lost); Pepys (recast): *takeþ al þat his hert stondeþ*; Caius: *forþed his lustes*; Vitellius: *parfet ses desirs*; Trinity: *e par emplit ses desirs*; Lat.: *vitam cito amittit.*]

265–66   *seide to ure Laverdes sonde the brohte salve.* MS: *seide to ure lauerdes sonde. þe brohte* ~~sonde~~ *<salve>*. The scribe first wrote *sonde* "message" (apparently a mistaken repetition of the word from the previous phrase) but canceled it and wrote *salve* "medicine, remedy" above it. [Cleo.: *seide to ure lauerdes sonde. þe bochte salue.*]

270   *the tweien othre [the], thah ha weren seke.* MS: *þe tweien oþre þah he weren seke.* A relative pronoun has apparently fallen out between *oþre* and *þah* (see Tolkien, p. 188, fol. 100r, line 14). The *þe* "who" is necessary to establish the relative clause and thus is supplied. [Cleo.: *þe twa oðre. þe þach ha weren seke*; Titus: *þe twa oðre. þah ho weren seke*; Nero: *þe twei oþre. þeo þauh heo weren seke*; Vernon (lost); Pepys: *þe oþer to þeiȝ hij weren seek*; Caius: *þe twa oþere. þah ha weren seke*; Vitellius: *les dous altres les queus tout fuissent il malades*; Trinity: *les esu autres. kar ia seit i ceo ke eus fusent malades*; Lat. (recast).]

279   *he hit mei wel notien.* MS: *he hit mei wel* ~~him~~ *notien.* Correct emendation by the scribe.

315   *for the[o] yet i fondunges.* MS: *For þe ȝet i fondunges.* As Tolkien notes, *þe* "who" must stand for *þeo* "those" (p. 190, fol. 101r, line 17). [Cleo.: *for þeo ȝet in fondunges*; Titus: *for þa ȝet te fondinges*; Nero: *for ðe ȝet foundunges*; Vernon (lost); Pepys (recast); Caius: *for þe fondunges*; Vitellius: *Kar ceaux vnquore par temptacions*; Trinity: *kar adonc onkore temptacions*; Lat.: *quia illi adhuc in temptationibus.*]

318   *Pharones hond.* MS: *hParones hond.* A clear mistake for *Pharones*. Shepherd refers to D'Ardenne, who in her edition of the Katherine Group from Oxford, Bodleian Library, MS Bodley 34 (p. 201) comments on "the occasional uncertainty of KG scribes with *h*" (p. 47n14/29), though Tolkien's conjecture that the scribe inadvertently skipped *Pharones* and began to copy the next word, *hond*, seems more plausible (p. 190, fol. 101r, line 21). [Cleo.: *pharaones hond*; Titus: *pharaones hond*; Nero: *pharaones hond*; Pepys: *pharaoos honde*; Caius:

pharaones hond; Vitellius: *le main pharaon* <MS: *ph'on*>; Trinity: *le mein pharaon*; Lat.: *manu Pharaonis*.]

346   *i-blescet beo thu, Laverd*. MS: *iblescet ibeo þu lauerd*. As Tolkien points out, there is an inadvertent repetition of *i* before *beo*, probably because of the presence of *iblescet* immediately before (p. 191, fol. 102r, line 2). [Cleo.: *iblescet beo þu lauerd*; Titus: *Iblesced be þu lauerd*; Nero: *iblesced beo þu louerd*; Vernon (lost); Pepys: *blissed be þou lorde*; Caius: *Iblessed beo þu lauerd*.]

370   *ah [wes] as ut of the world*. MS: *ah as ut of þe world*. It seems likely that a *wes* has fallen out between *ah* and *as*. Cleo.'s text, without the *as*, reads more cleanly, but in view of Titus, Nero, Vitellius, Trinity, and Lat., the *as* is retained. [Cleo.: *ach wes ut of world*; Titus: *ah was as ut of worlde*; Nero: *ah was ase ut of ðe worlde*; Vernon (lost); Pepys (recast); Caius (lacking); Vitellius: *mes fut ausi come hors del siecle*; Trinity: *mes fu ausi com hors du siecle*; Lat.: *sed fuit quasi extra mundum*.]

381   *ow is neod*. MS: *ow is neoð*. Shepherd (p. 49n17/2) suggests that the form *neoð*, where we would normally expect *neod* ("needful, necessary"), may represent a form of assimilation with following *þet* and that it may be influenced by the ON form *nauð*. The common interchanging of *ð* and *d* seems much more likely here, however, and thus this edition follows Tolkien in emending to *neod* (p. 193, fol. 102v, line 19), the usual spelling in Corpus. [Cleo.: *ow is neod*; Titus: *ow is ned*; Nero: *ou is neod*; Vernon (lost); Pepys (recast): *And so it is good*; Caius (lacking).]

389   *na mare then of deade*. MS: *ne mare þen of deade*. *Ne* "not" is probably a mistake for *na* "no." Both *na* and *ne* occur in the previous clause and may have confused the scribe. [Cleo.: *na mare þenne of dede*; Titus: *na mare þen of deade*; Nero: *na more þen of deade*; Vernon (lost); Pepys (recast); Caius (lacking); Vitellius: *nient plus qe del mort*; Trinity: *plus ke de homme mort*; Lat.: *magis verbum quam de mortuo*.]

393–95   *leapinde," ha seith, "o the dunes, [overleapinde hulles." . . . leapeth o the dunes] — thet is*. MS: *leapinde ha seið o þe dunes. þet is*. Corpus drops two lines here due to eye-skip between two appearances of the phrase *leapinde/-eð o þe dunes*. The missing text is restored from Cleo. [Cleo.: *ha seið leapinde o þe dunes ouer leapinde hulles. dunes bitacneð þeo þe leadeð hech3est lif hulles beoð þe lach3ere. Nu seið ha þet hire leof leapeð o þe dunes. þet is*; Titus: *ho seis leapinde o þe dunes ouerleapende hulles. Dunes bitacnen þa þet leaden hehest lif. Hulles arn þe lahre Nu seis ho þet hire leof leapes i þ dunes. þet is*; Nero: *heo seið leapinde oðe dunes. ouerleapinde hulles. Dunes bitocneð þeo þet ledeð hexst lif. hulles beoð ðe lowure. nu seið heo ðet hire leof. leapeð o ðe hulles þet is*; Vernon (lost); Pepys: *sche seiþ comeþ lepeande ouer þe dounes and ouerlepeþ þe hilles. By dounes is bitokned hij þat leden heiȝest lyf. And hylles ben hij þat ben in lower lyf. Now sche seiþ þat hir lef comeþ lepeande ouer þe dounes. þat ben*; Caius (lacking); Vitellius: *dit ele saillantz sur les montz tressaillanz les huterels. Montz signefient ceaux qe meinent plus haute vie. huterels sunt les plus basses. Ore dit ele qe son amy saut sur les montz. Cest il*; Trinity: *Des queus montaignes <oez coment la dame parout en le liuere de amurs a soen ami. Mon ami veent fet ele sailant es montaignes.> tressaillant les tertres. Montaignes signefient ceus; ke meinent plus haute uie. tertres ceus ke plus basse. Ore dit ele; ke soen ami saut en les montaignes. Ceo est*; Lat. (recast).]

397   *i-finde hu he wes totreden.* MS: *ifinden hu he wes totreden.* Tolkien suggests that *ifinden* should read *ifinde*, to make it parallel to the preceding subjunctive form *trude* (p. 194, fol. 103r, line 10): "that they might tread in them [the tracks]; [that they might] find how he was trodden down." Shepherd (p. 50n17/22), on the other hand, believes that *ifinden* is an infinitive dependent on *trude*: "that they might tread in them (the tracks), to find how he was trodden down." In truth, there is little semantic difference between the two, though the MS evidence favors Tolkien. [Cleo.: *ant finde hu he wes totreden*; Titus: *ant finde hu he was totreden*; Nero: *ant iuinde hwu he was totreden*; Vernon (lost); Pepys (lacking); Caius (lacking); Vitellius: *et croisse coment il fut defolee* (Herbert thinks *croisse* a mistake for *trouue*); Trinity: *e penser coment il sunt defulez*; Lat. (recast).]

398   *munt of Muntgiw, dunes of Armenie.* MS: *munt of muntgiw. Dunes of armenie.* Tolkien thinks *munt* should appear as plural *mun(t)z* (p. 194, fol. 103r, line 11), though the MS evidence is mixed. Shepherd (p. 50n17/23) points out that in OE *Muntgiw* referred generally to the Alps, though it can refer to a specific peak, St. Gotthard. The strange reading in Cleo. may indicate an early error patched differently by various hands. In view of the confusion, this edition retains the MS reading which, though not parallel, seems to represent an authentic reading. [Cleo.: *ase munt þemungyu*; Titus: *As munz of muntgiw*; Nero: *ase þe munt of mungiwe*; Vernon (lost); Pepys (lacking); Caius (lacking); Vitellius: *les montz de mongiu. les montaignes de armeine*; Trinity: *li mont de monieu e les monz de ermenie*; Lat. (lacking).]

399 MS: *as þe leafdi seið hire seolf. he ouerleapeð*. Tolkien would emend *seolf* to *leof* ("beloved"), following the reading in Cleo. (p. 194, fol. 103r, line 13), though the Corpus text makes good sense. Dobson comments, "C[leo.] is supported by both French versions, the Latin version, and Pepys, against Corpus (*hire seolf he*), Nero (*hire sulf*), and Titus (*hire self*). But Corpus may be right, and *hire leof* an early corruption due to omission of *he* in [the beta branch of MSS] and influence from [*venit dilectus meus saliens in montibus*]" (p. 279n3). Thus, the Corpus reading is retained since it makes sense and may be original. [Cleo.: *as þe lafdi seið hire leof ouerleapeð*; Titus: *as te lafdi seis hire self. ouerleapes*; Nero: *ase ðe lefdi seið. hire sulf ouerleapeð*; Vernon (lost); Pepys (lacking); Caius (lacking); Vitellius: *sicome la dit la (dame) passe son ami*; Trinity: *com la dame dit; soen ami tresaut*; Lat.: *Salit dilectus in montibus*.]

399–400 *for hare feblesce ne mahte nawt tholien*. MS: *for hare feblesce. ne ne mahte nawt þolien*. Tolkien points out that the doubling of *ne* here as well as the point after *feblesce* must be mistakes (p. 194, fol. 103r, line 14). [Cleo.: *for hare feblesce. ne muchte naut þolien*; Titus: *for hore feblesce ne mihte nawt þolien*; Nero: *uor hore febblesce. uor ne muhte heo nout iþolien*; Vernon (lost); Pepys: *for he* (Zettersten: sic for *her*) *feblesse ne may nouȝth þolen*; Caius (lacking).]

404 *Ah the dunes undervoth the troden of him-seolven*. MS: *ah þe* ~~troden~~ *<dunes> undervoð þe troden of him seolven*. In its corrected form, the text reads, "the hills receive his tracks." The scribe first mistakenly wrote *troden* "tracks" (anticipating the appearance of this word after the verb) and then canceled it, writing *dunes* "hills," above it.

423 *he wepeth to me, [as] wivene sarest*. MS: *he wepeð to me wiuene sarest*. The text as it stands is clearly faulty. Dobson suggests emending to *wiuene sune sarest* "most grief-stricken of the sons of women," while Shepherd proposes *wið euene sarest* "in the bitterest fashion." Both stress that *wiuene* must be part of the original reading since it is contained in both Corpus and Titus, which otherwise "do not share inherited errors" (Dobson, p. 280n3). Another solution, which preserves more of the original reading, would be to insert an *as* before *wiuene* to give *he wepeð to me ase wiuene sarest* ("he weeps to me as [or, like] the most sorrowful of women"). Given the complexity of issues, we quote Dobson and Shepherd's notes in full. Dobson: "So also Nero, but probably by independent emendation of the reading *wiuene* (Corpus, Titus). Corpus and Titus do not share inherited errors, and independent substitution of *wiuene* for *monne* is in the context almost unthinkable; moreover the other texts running seem to be avoiding

a difficulty, since neither French version has a word corresponding to *wiuene* (or *monne*) and the Latin version and Pepys omit the whole phrase *wiuene* (or *monne*) *sarest*. Probably the author intended the phrase *wiuene sune sarest* 'most grief-stricken of the sons of women'; cf. Corpus f. 43a, l. 4 *wiues sunen* (Nero *wiuene sunes*)" (p. 280n3). Shepherd: "MS. *wiuene sarest* 'sorest of women' (so Tolkien) has no relevance in this context. The scribes of N and C attempting apparently a correction of the same reading *wiuene sarest*, wrote *monne sarest*, which improved nothing but the gender. The emendation proposed implies at some earlier stage of transcription the omission of *ðe*, which is readily understandable. *euene* . . . is in common use in KG texts (see MED's *evene*), deriving from ON *efni*, 'material', 'means', 'state'. The nuances of meaning in ON are various; so too in ME, where there were apparently associations added from adj. *even* (see MED's *even*, adj. 12.(e)), and also from OE *hæfen*, (cp. *MED*'s *having*, n.3). Within the range of EME usage, a meaning of 'in bitterest fashion' for *wið euene sarest* here is acceptable" (p. 51n18/19). Zettersten would retain as is: "I think it is possible to accept *wiuene sarest* as a kind of quasi-predicative with the meaning 'as the saddest of women'" (p. 211). [Cleo.: *he wepeð to me monne sarest*; Titus: *he wepes to me wiuene sarest*; Nero: *he weopð on me monne sorest*; Vernon (lost); Pepys (recast): *wepe to his schrift fader*; Caius (lacking); Vitellius: *se pleint il a mei plorant angoissousement*; Trinity: *plora il sur lui mout tendrement*; Lat.: *Adhuc flendo dicit* . . .]

Part Seven

3   MS: *Exercitio*. Tolkien would emend to *Exercitatio* (p. 195, fol. 104r, line 5), as a corrector did at p. 25, but the form appears to be a legitimate one for late Latin. [Cleo.: *exercicio*; Titus: *Excercitatio*; Nero: *excercitio*; Vernon (lost); Pepys: *Exercitacio*; Caius (lacking); Vitellius: *Exercitacio*; Trinity: *Exercitacio*; Lat.: *Excercitatio*.]

17   *loki mid his grace ant makie the heorte schir*. MS: *loki mid his grace ant maketh the heorte schir*. As Millett and Wogan-Browne point out, *maketh* should probably read *makie* (the subj. form) to make it parallel to *loki*. As it stands, the text reads, "no suffering of the flesh is to be loved except for the reason that God may look the more readily in that direction with His grace and may make (MS: makes) the heart pure." The only other version which unambiguously corroborates Corpus is Nero, though in Cleo. *lokeð* and *makeð* are expanded from abbreviations. [Cleo.: *lokeð mid his grace ant makeð þe heorte schir*; Titus: *loke wið his*

grace. ant make þe herte schir; Nero: *loke þideward mid his grace. and makie ðe heorte schir*; Vernon (lost); Pepys: *lokeþ þiderward wiþ his grace and makeþ þe hert schire*; Caius (lacking); Vitellius: *regarde od sa grace. et fet le queor pur*; Trinity: *gardereit landreit par sa grace. e par ceo fereit le quor tut cler*; Lat.: *per graciam suam respicit et facit cor serenum*.]

38   MS: *seinte Mihales weie*. Tolkien would regularize to *Mi[c]hales* (p. 197, fol. 104v, line 20), but since the form without *c* was acceptable to at least two scribes — those of Titus and Nero — it seems to represent a legitimate spelling, and thus we retain it. [Cleo.: *seinte Michales weie*; Titus: *seinte mihales weie*; Nero: *seinte miheles weie*; Vernon (lost); Pepys: *seint Miȝels weiȝe*; Caius (lacking); Vitellius: *la balance seint michel*; Trinity: *en balance seint michel*; Lat.: *beati Michaelis libra*.]

50   *wrecches*. MS: *wrecch/ces*. As Tolkien points out, this inadvertent misspelling for *wrecches* "wretches" was probably encouraged by the line break (p. 198, fol. 105r, lines 7–8).

55   *proph[et]es*. MS: *prophes*. An *-et-* is missing from this word. Tolkien prints the corrected form *prophetes* in the text, putting the mistaken MS form, *prophes*, in the note (p. 200, fol. 105r, line 14) — as Käsmann points out. Here it is emended to *proph[et]es*.

113   *bi[tweone] wif ant hire child*. MS: *bi / wif ant hir child*. As Tolkien (p. 200, fol. 106v, line 3) and Millett and Wogan-Browne (p. 116) point out, the scribe fails to copy the rest of *bitweone* ("between") after the line break.

117   MS: *swuch fordede*. Tolkien's note: "for or derived from *forðdede* (OE. *forðdæd*)" (p. 201, fol. 106v, line 9). The MS reading, *fordede* "service, or deed of assistance," however, is most probably correct since both Nero and Titus (which often recast difficult passages) retain the form. The prefix here is presumably not the pejorative *for-* as in *for-don* "to destroy," but a prefix meaning "in behalf of." The MED thinks the word was formed on the basis of MLat. *profecti*. [Cleo.: *swich forðdede*; Titus: *swuch fordede*; Nero: *swuch fordede*; Vernon (lost); Pepys: *swich a fordede*; Caius: *swuch fordede*.]

132   *swa muchel is bitweonen Godes neoleachunge*. MS: *Swa muchel is bitweonen. bituhhen godes neoleachunge*. Shepherd notes that "*bitweone(n)* is the usual form in *AW*; *bituhhen* occurs occasionally. The double writing is probably a scribal

slip" (p. 60n23/36). A sensible emendation adopted here, though Millett and Wogan-Browne make sense of the repetition by bracketing the phrase with dashes: "Swa muchel is bit-weonen — bituhhen Godes neoleachunge ant monnes to wommon — thet . . ." (p.118). [Cleo.: *Swa muchel is bitwenen. bituchȝe godes neolechunge*; Titus: *Swa muchel is bitwene godes neohleachinge*; Nero: *So muchel is bitweonen godes neihlechunge*; Vernon (lost); Pepys: *so Michel Departyng is bitwene knowleching of Man and womman. and god and his lemman*; Caius: *Swa muche is bitwenen godes nehunge and mones to wummon*; Vitellius: *Tant i ad de difference entre la renouelure de dieu*; Trinity: *Tant est entre la conisance deu e homme e femme*; Lat.: *Tanta est dif<f>erencia inter coniugium Dei.*]

141   *weschen hire.* MS: *weschen him <re>.* The scribe first wrote *him* but canceled the *m* and interlined *re* above it to give *hire* "her."

149   MS: *resun.* Tolkien believes this a mistake (p. 202, fol. 107r, line 19), and indeed the word *reisun* "reason" is spelled very consistently with *ei* in Corpus. However, on the chance that the form represents a phonological or orthographical phenomenon and not a copying error, it is retained here. [Cleo.: *reisun*; Titus: *reisun*; Nero: *reisun*; Vernon (lost); Pepys: *resoun*; Caius: *reisun*; Vitellius: *reisone*; Trinity: *resoen.*]

164   MS: *nam ich weolie wisest.* Tolkien believes that *weolie* is a mistaken form: "*weolie,* sic; original word probably *weore* 'of men' (as Tolkien). L *peritorum* suggests intermediate stage *weote, weotie*" (p. 202, fol. 107r, line 9). Thus Tolkien believes that an intermediate adaptation of *weore* was *weote* "witty or expert," the translation of Latin *peritorum.* Shepherd retains the MS reading and defines *weolie* as "of rich men," taking the word as plural adjective (in the genitive) functioning as a noun, the best, least intrusive course. [Cleo.: *nam ich weolie wisest*; Titus: *Nam i weore wisest*; Nero: *nam ich weolie wisest*; Vernon (lost); Pepys: *ne am ich wisest*; Caius: *Nam ich weolie wisest*; Vitellius: *Ne sui ieo de touz le plus sage*; Trinity: *e li plus sages*; Lat.: *Num peritorum sapientissimus.*]

170–71   *buggen hire? [Hu?] Other with other luve.* MS: *bugge hire; bugge hire? oðer wið oðer luue.* Though it may be possible to accept the MS reading (as Shepherd does), it seems best to follow Millett and Wogan-Browne (p. 120) who show that text is muddled here by the omission of a *hu* "how" after the second *bugge hire* "buy her!" — an emendation supported by Cleo. and Vitellius in particular. [Cleo.: *bugge hire. buggen hire. hu; oðer wið oðer luue*; Titus: *buggen hire. hu oðer wið oðer luue*; Nero: *bugge hire; do seie hwu; oðer mid oþer luue*; Vernon (lost); Pepys: *buggen it ჳif it schal be selde it owe forto be bouჳth wiþ loue*; Caius: *bugge hire. buggen hire; hu? oþer wið ower luue*; Vitellius: *len achate. achatez le. comment. ou od altre amour*; Trinity: *lem achate; dites coment vus la uoleez doner. Cest adire ou par amurs*; Lat.: *ematur, quomodo potest emi? aut alio amore.*]

171–72   *Me suleth wel luve [for luve] ant swa.* MS: *Me suleð wel luue; ant swa.* As Tolkien (p. 203, fol. 107v, lines 18–19) and Millett and Wogan-Browne (p. 120) point out, the scribe has inadvertently dropped two words, *for luue*, after *wel luue*. [Cleo.: *Me sulleð wel luue for luue. ant swa*; Titus: *Mon selles wel luue for luue. And swa*; Nero: *Me sulleð wel luue uor luue. and so*; Vernon (lost); Pepys: *Men sellen wel loue for loue and so*; Caius: *Men sulled wel luue for luue*; Vitellius: *Len vent bien amour pur amour. et issi*; Trinity: *Lem uent amur pur amur*; Lat.: *Amor venditur pro amore et sic.*]

180–81   MS: *Ne schal neauer heorte þenchen hwuch selhðe.* Millett and Wogan-Browne emend *hwuch* ("whatever, any") to *swuch* ("such"), the reading in all the other versions. It seems possible, though, to accept *hwuch* as a minor variation which changes the meaning of the sentence only slightly. [Cleo.: *Ne schal neauer heorte þenche swich selchðe*; Titus: *Ne schal neauer heorte þenche swuch selhðe*; Nero: *ne schal neuer heorte þenchen swuch seluhðe*; Vernon (lost); Pepys: *ne schal neuer þink so mychel*; Caius: *Ne schal neauer heorte þenchen swuch selehþe*; Vitellius: *Ja ne pensera queor tiele beneurte*; Trinity: *Ia quer ne purra penser nule si ouruse chose*; Lat.: *Non poterit cor cogitare tantam felicitatem.*]

190–91   MS: *todealen lif ant sawle. ant bisenchen ham ba.* It is difficult to tell whether *to* is an infinitive marker (*to dealen lif ant sawle* "to separate life and soul") or a verb prefix (*todealen lif ant sawle*) — if it is a prefix, there seems to be a missing infinitive marker. Tolkien would emend as follows: *[to] todealen lif ant sawle*, and assumes that a *to* dropped out at a very early stage in the MS transmission (p. 204, fol. 108r, line 15), but other versions must interpret *to* as an infinitive marker since the following parallel phrase also begins with a *to* (as inf. marker). It seems best then to allow the MS reading to stand. [Cleo.: *to deale lif ant saule ant to bisenchen ham boa*; Titus: *to deale lif ant sawle. ant to bisenchen ham baðe*; Nero: *to dealen lif ant soule. and to bisenchen botwo*; Vernon (lost); Pepys: *to todelen lyf and soule and caste hem boþe*; Caius: *to dealen (inf.) lif and saule. and bisenchen ham ba*; Vitellius: *pur seuerir vie et alme et pur tresbucher ces dous*;

Trinity: *a de partir uostre alme de uostre cors. e a engeter amedeus dekes en feu de enfern*; Lat.: *ad separandum vitam et animam et ad vtraque submergendum*.]

191   MS: *to beon deofles hore*. Millett and Wogan-Browne point out (p. 120), that most of the other versions insert the adverb *þer* ("there") between *beon* and *deofles*, but since the sense of the passage is not affected, the Corpus text is reproduced unchanged. [Cleo.: *to beo þer deofles hore*; Titus: *to beo þer deoueles hores*; Nero: *uorto beon þer deofles hore*; Vernon (lost); Pepys: *to be þe deuels hore*; Vitellius: *pur estre la puteine al diable*; Trinity: *pur estre illoc la uoutre le diable*; Lat.: *vt ibi sis meretrix diaboli*.]

201   *ontenden his luve i his leoves heorte*. MS: *ontenden his luue. ant his leoues heorte*. Although Corpus' reading "ignite his love and his beloved's heart" makes a certain amount of sense on its own, the other versions show that *ant* must originally have read *i* or *in* ("ignite his love *in* his beloved's heart"). The text here is restored to *i* because it seems to be a spelling more easily confused with the abbreviation (7) for *ant*. [Cleo.: *ontenden his luue in his leoues heorte*; Titus: *entenden his luue in his leoues heorte*; Nero: *ontenden his luue in his leoues heorte*; Vernon (lost); Pepys (recast); Caius: *tenden his luue in his leoues heorte*; Vitellius: *alumer et esprendre samour en le queor samie*; Trinity: *pur enbracer sa amur en quer de sa amie*; Lat.: *amorem suum accendat in corde sue dilecte*.]

238–39   MS: *Consumatum est*. The spelling should be *consummatum* "finished, completed," with two *m*'s, to avoid confusion with the verb *consumatum* "consumed, eaten up." Though the other versions all have the correct spelling, the Corpus scribe repeats the spelling in line 246, making it unlikely that the spelling is an inadvertent mistake. It may be that in the exemplar for Corpus *consum-matum* was written with an abbreviation in place of one of the *m*'s, an abbreviation easily overlooked. [Cleo.: *Consummatum est*; Titus: *Consummatum est*; Nero: *consummatum*; Vernon (lost); Pepys: *Consummatum est*; Caius (lacking); Vitellius: *Consummatum est*; Trinity: *Consumatum inquit est* and *Consummatum est*; Lat.: *Consummatum est* and *Consummatum est*.]

252   *Jesues pine o rode*. MS: *iesues pine o rode*. Though it looks a bit strange, *iesues* "Jesus'" probably should stand as is, especially since it occurs with this spelling in Cleo. Tolkien, though, thinks it is an error (p. 206, fol. 109v, line 7). See the similar form *iesuse* (6.14). [Cleo.: *Iesues pine on rode*; Titus: *iesues pine o rode*; Nero: *godes pine o rode*; Vernon (lost); Pepys (recast): *al my pyne on rode*; Caius

(lacking); Vitellius: *la peine ihesu en la croiz*; Trinity: *la peine iesu crist*; Lat.: *eius penam in cruce*.]

278   *Cheose nu euch-an of thes twa.* MS: *Cheose euchan of/ <thes twa>*. A scribe or reader has added *thes twa* "these two" in the margin after *of*. Tolkien rightly points out that the addition of "these two" in a smaller script running into the margin is an unnecessary later addition, since *euchan* "each one" is an adequate subject for *Cheose* and the other MSS lack it (p. 208, fol. 110r, line 10). However, since it is an early scribal addition which sharpens the tone of the passage, it is retained here. Shepherd separates *euchan* into two words: *Cheose euch an of thes twa* "[Let] each choose one of these two," though this reading goes against the orthography of the MS which clearly shows *euchan* as one word. [Cleo.: *Cheose nu euch an of eorðlich elne*; Titus: *Cheose nu euch an of earðlich elne*; Nero: *cheose nu euerichon of eorðlich elne*; Vernon (lost); Pepys (lacking); Caius (lacking); Vitellius: *Eslise ore chescune de terreine confort*; Trinity: *Ore donc elise checun de terrien confort*; Lat.: *Eligat nunc quilibet de terestri solatio*.]

285   MS: *al þet he rine to.* Both Tolkien (p. 208, fol. 110r, line 19) and Millett and Wogan-Browne (p. 126) detect a missing adverb, *þerwið*, after *rine*. If restored, the text would read "everything that he touched against with it." Though this suggestion would bring Corpus into line with the other MSS, it seems that the reading here, *al þet he rine to* "everything that he touches against," is perfectly understandable in its own right. A similar construction occurs in another AB text, *Seinte Juliene*, where the blades on the wheel of torture are "kene to keoruen al þet ha rinen to" (Bodley version, lines 547–48) — that is, "sharp to cut everything that they touch against." And thus, *rine to* probably represents a revision or valid variation rather than an error. The MS reading is retained here. [Cleo.: *al þet he rine þer wið*; Titus: *al þet he roan þer wið*; Nero: *al ðet he arinede þere mide*; Vernon (lost); Pepys (lacking); Caius (lacking); Vitellius: *tout ceo qil en adessast*; Trinity: *//* (p. 159); Lat. (recast): *per quam quicquid optarent*.]

314   *alswa ha is untalelich.* MS: *alswa as ha is untalelich.* Millett and Wogan-Browne detect a problem with *alswa as* which is the second part of a comparison. Unemended, the text would read, "as the joy of heaven is incomparable to all the world's joys, just as [*alswa as*] it is indescribable." *Alswa as* usually functions as the first part of a comparison: "Just as . . . so." As Millett and Wogan-Browne point out, all the other versions omit the *as* after *alswa*. And indeed *alswa* ("likewise, so") makes much better sense of the phrase. Perhaps the scribe mistakenly construed this clause as the first rather than the second part of a

comparison. [Cleo. (lost); Titus: *Alswa ho is untaleliche*; Nero: *Also heo is untalelich*; Vernon (lost); Pepys (lacking); Vitellius: *ausi est ele nient contable*; Trinity: *ausi est ele non contable*; Lat.: *ita est inenarrabile*.]

320   *me hat ham to luvien*. MS: *me hat ham to luuien*. Tolkien: "*hat*, sic for *ah*" (p. 209, fol. 11r, line 7). The Corpus reading seems to represent a legitimate revision or variation of *hat* "commands" for *ah* "ought" rather than a mistake. [Cleo. (lost); Titus: *man ah ham to luuien*; Nero: *me ham ouh forto luuien*; Vernon (lost); Pepys (lacking); Caius (lacking); Vitellius: *dut lem les altres amer*; Trinity (lacking); Lat. (recast).]

Part Eight

11   MS: *Tweofte dei*. Tolkien, somewhat paradoxically, thinks that this is both a mistake and a genuine form (p. 210, fol. 111r, line 25). Probably he means that it is a deviation from the original reading but legitimate in its own right (see note to 1.145). [Cleo. (lost); Titus: *twelfte dai*; Nero: *tweolfte dei*; Vernon (lost); Pepys: *þe xij day*; Caius (lacking).]

22–23   *bute the Fridahes [other Umbri-dayes, Yong-dayes, vigilies. I theose dayes] ne i the Advent*. MS: *bute þe fridahes. ne i þe aduent*. It is difficult to decide whether the omission of several words before *ne* is the result of scribal error or conscious revision, but since a legitimate case can be made for eye-skip between the two *dahes* and since the omitted passage occurs in most of the other versions, it is restored here from Cleo. [Cleo.: *bute fridaȝes oðer umbridaȝes. ȝeoncdaȝes. vigilies. i þeose daȝes ne i þe aduenz*; Titus: *bute fridaies ant imbringdahes. ȝong dahes ant vigiles in þose sahes. ni i þe advenz*; Nero: *bute uridawes and umbridawes and ȝoingdawes. and uigiles. i þeos dawes*; Vernon (lost); Pepys: *bot friday one and ymbryng dayes. and vigiles. Þe goyng dayees ne in þe aduent*; Caius (lacking); Vitellius: *les vendredies et quatuor tempres rouoisons et veilles en ces iours ne les aduentz*; Trinity (lacking); Lat.: *Rogacionum et vigiliis Sanctorum dum taxat ex ceptis. et in hiis diebus nec in Aduentu*.]

40   *thu art [in] muche baret*. MS: *þu art muche baret*. Tolkien's observation (p. 211, fol. 112r, line 6), accepted by Millett and Wogan-Browne (p. 132), that a preposition has been dropped before *muche* is fully supported by the other MSS, and thus we insert an *in*, which was probably lost due to eye-skip since its three minims would have looked like an *m*. [Cleo.: *þu art in muche baret*; Titus: *þu art*

in muche baret; Nero: *þu ert ine muche baret*; Vernon (lost); Pepys (lacking); Caius (lacking); Vitellius: *vous estes en grant barat*; Trinity (lacking); Lat.: *so[lici]ta es.*]

44   *Marthe haveth hire meoster*. MS: *Marie haueð hire meoster*. As Tolkien (p. 212, fol. 112r, line 11) and Millett and Wogan-Browne (p. 132) point out and the context confirms, the scribe has inadvertently substituted Mary for Martha, and thus *Marthe* is restored here. [Cleo.: *Marthe haueð hire mester*; Titus: *Marthe haues hire mester*; Nero: *Marthe haueð hire mester*; Vernon (lost); Pepys (lacking); Caius (lacking); Vitellius: *marthe ad son mester*; Trinity (lacking); Lat.: *Opus Marthe est.*]

55   *theose riche ancres*. MS: *þeose chirch ancres*. The scribe's eye has apparently skipped back to MS lines 22–23, *ah is a chirch ancre* (line 53), leading her or him to substitute *chirch* for the correct reading *riche*, demanded by the context. This edition follows Tolkien (p. 212, fol. 112r, lines 25–26) and Millett and Wogan-Browne (p. 132) in emending to *riche*. [Cleo.: *þeos riche ancres*; Titus: *þise riche ancres*; Nero: *þeos riche ancren*; Vernon (lost); Pepys (lacking); Caius (lacking); Vitellius: *ces riches recluses*; Trinity (lacking); Lat. (lacking).]

55–56   MS: *to poure nehburs*. Tolkien finds the spelling of *nehburs* faulty (p. 212, fol. 112r, line 27), and indeed the other versions all have an *e* before the *b*. The missing *e* would correctly represent the *ge-* prefix in OE *neah-gebur* "near dweller," but it seems possible that the form without -*e*- results from linguistic processes, not error. [Cleo.: *to poure necheburs*; Titus: *to poure nehhebures*; Nero: *to poure neihebures*; Vernon (lost); Pepys (lacking); Caius (lacking).]

57   *ne beo nan the gred[i]ure*. MS: *ne beo nan þe gnedure*. The word *gnedure* seems to be a mistake for *grediure* "greedier," and thus it is emended here, following Tolkien (p. 212, fol. 112v, line 1), Zettersten (p. 200), and Millett and Wogan-Browne (p. 132). It is just possible that the word represents a legitimate revision in Corpus, since *gnedure* could mean "more frugally" (see OE *gnead* "frugal"). The MS text would then read: "let no one be the more frugal to have more." [Cleo.: *ne beo nan þe gredure*; Titus: *ne beo nan þe gredire*; Nero: *ne beo non þe grediure*; Vernon (lost); Pepys (lacking); Caius (lacking); Vitellius: *ne soit nule plus coueitouse*; Trinity (lacking); Lat. (recast).]

65–66   *general other spetial: [general] as of freres preachurs ant meonurs, spetial of alle othre*. MS: *general oðer spetial. as of freres preachurs. ant meonurs. spetial;*

of alle oþre. Salu conjectures that the "word *general* seems to have been omitted between *spetial* and *as*" (p. 184n3). This suggestion makes good sense, and it is adopted here. [All other versions lack this addition.]

73–74   MS: *ne leasse ne mare. neode schal driuen ow*. Corpus omits a phrase between *mare* and *neode* which survives in most of the other MSS: *Naut swa muche þet beo an rote of ginguire* ("not so much as (lit., that is) a root of ginger") The fact that it is canceled in Cleo. must be related to its exclusion from Corpus, though it is difficult to know why the cancellation in Cleo. was made. [Cleo.: *lesse ne mare. ~~Naut swa muche þet beo an rote of ginguire.~~ Muche neode schal driuen ow*; Titus: *lasse ne mare. nawt swa muchel þet beo a rote of ginguire. Muchel ned schal driuen ow*; Nero: *lesse ne more. nout so muche ðet beo a rote of gingiure. Muchel neode schal driuen ou*; Vernon (lost); Pepys (lacking); Caius (lacking); Vitellius: *ne plus ne meins ne tant soulement qe soit une racine de zinzeure. Grant bosoig vous deit chacer*; Trinity (lacking); Lat. (recast).]

123   MS: *as eue sunfule dohter*. Tolkien argues that *sunfule* "sinful" should come before *eue* "Eve's" (p. 215, fol. 113v, line 26) and Millett and Wogan-Browne agree (p. 138), though of course the phrase makes perfect sense as "Eve's sinful daughter" (i.e., womankind) and is thus retained. [Cleo. (marginal addition): *as sunful eue dohte<r>*; Titus (lacking); Nero (lacking); Vernon: *as sunful Eue douhter*; Pepys (lacking); Caius (lacking); Vitellius (lacking); Trinity (lacking); Lat. (lacking).]

127–28   *Toyeines [the] the sist men*. MS: *toȝeines þe sist men*. As it stands, the text reads, "Against who see (pres. 2. sg.) men the Apostle speaks." As Tolkien notes (p. 215, fol. 114r, line 4), in order to make sense of this phrase, another *þe* must be provided: "Against you who see men . . . ," A suggestion supported by Cleo. [Cleo.: *Teȝeines þe. þe isist men*; Titus (lacking); Nero (lacking); Vernon (lacking); Pepys (lacking); Caius (lacking); Vitellius (lacking); Trinity (lacking); Lat. (lacking).]

194   *Na mon ne leoten in, ne the yungre ne speoke with na-mon*. MS: *Na mon ne leote ȝe in. ne þe ȝungre ne speoke wið namon*. On its face, this sentence makes perfect sense "Let no man in" — a command in the imperative. Tolkien suspects a mistake here, "sic, for *leoten ha*" (p. 218, fol. 115v, line 6) because the passage is instructing the anchoress on the behavior of her maidens and thus the context demands third-person pl., "they are to let no man in," instead of the second in both the verb ending and the pronoun. Millett and Wogan-Browne, with an eye

on Cleo., Titus, and Vitellius emend to *ne leoten in* (p. 142), the correction adopted here. [Cleo.: *Nanmon ne leten in ne ne speoken wið ute leaue*; Titus: *Na mon ne letin in. ni þi ʒungre ne speke wið na wepmon*; Nero: *nenne mon ne leten heo in. ne ðe ʒungre ne speke mid none monne*; Vernon (lacking); Pepys (lacking); Caius (lacking); Vitellius: *Nul hom ne lessent entrer ne la plus joefne ne parole od nul hom*; Trinity (lacking); Lat. (lacking).]

220   *he deth [on] hond thet ilke.* MS: *he deð hond þet ilke.* At first glance, the MS text makes little sense. Tolkien suggests a missing *on* before *hond* to yield *he deð [on] hond þet ilke* ("he does in time the same") (p. 219, fol. 116r, line 14) — *on hond* is an idiom meaning "in time, as time goes by" (see 5.306 for another example in Corpus). Millett and Wogan-Browne (p. 144 and glossary) attempt to keep the MS reading by interpreting *hond* as a free-standing adverb meaning "just, exactly." See Zettersten (p. 41) for a summary of earlier, less likely solutions. Since *hond* as an adverb in English is doubtful, this edition follows Tolkien here. [Cleo.: *he deð þet ilke*; Titus: *and he dos hond to þet ilke*; Nero: *he deð onond þet ilke*; Vernon (lacking); Pepys (lacking); Caius (lacking); Vitellius: *il fet meismes ceste chose*; Trinity (lacking); Lat. (lacking).]

231   *Hali Gast, [an] almihti Godd.* MS: *hali gast al mihti godd.* Millett and Wogan-Browne rightly note that *an* has fallen out between *gast* and *mihti.* [Cleo.: *haligast an almichtin god*; Titus: *hali gast. an al mihti godd*; Nero: *holi gost. ant on almihti god*; Vernon (lacking); Pepys (lacking); Caius (lacking); Vitellius: *seint esperit vn dieu*; Trinity (lacking); Lat. (lacking).]

235   *ne gruseli nawt.* MS: *ne gruchesi ʒe nawt.* There are two problems here. The word *gruchesi* has been altered by a later hand, and though it is difficult to detect the original reading, it was most likely *grulesi* (Tolkien, p. 220, fol. 116v, line 4) — the emender altered the *l*, inserting *ch.* The original *grulesi* was itself apparently an mistake for *gruseli* — though it is possible that the original reading was *gruseli* and the emender changed the final *l* to a long *s.* The reading in Cleo. argues against this idea. The second problem has to do with a shift in persons as above (8.194): "*ʒe* is, as context shows, an error for *ha* or *heo*." The best course seems to be to follow Cleo., which has no pronoun and to see *ʒe* as a natural slip into the imperative. [Cleo.: *ne gruuesi naut*; Titus: *ne gruse ʒe nawt*; Nero: *ne gruselie ʒe nout*; Vernon (lacking); Pepys (lacking); Caius (lacking); Vitellius: *ne manguent*; Trinity (lacking); Lat. (lacking).]

239   *i-set hure bute mete ant clath*. MS: *iset hure. bute mete ant hure*. Tolkien rightly points out that the second *hure* is an "erroneous repetition replacing *hetter* or *claŏ*" (p. 220, fol. 116v, line 9). Millett and Wogan-Browne also endorse this solution (p. 146). [Cleo.: *iset hure bute mete ant claŏ*; Titus: *iset hure. bute mete and claŏ*; Nero: *i sette huire; bute mete and cloŏ*; Vernon (lacking); Pepys (lacking); Caius (lacking); Vitellius: *louer fors le mangier et a uestir*; Trinity (lacking); Lat. (lacking).]

245   *ahen this leaste stucche reden*. MS: *ahen þis leaste stucche reden*. Millett and Wogan-Browne would emend *þis leaste stucche* "this last part" to bring it in line with the other MSS: *þis leaste lutle stucche* ("this last little part") (p. 146). Though this is an attractive addition, one might argue that Part Eight of Corpus, which is much fuller and longer than any of the other versions (especially since several marginal additions were made in Cleo. and further additions made in Corpus) the word *lutle* no longer seemed appropriate. The MS reading is retained here on this possibility. [Cleo.: *achȝe þis laste lutle stuche reden*; Titus: *ahen þis laste lutle stucche rede*; Nero: *owen þis lutle laste stucchen reden*; Vernon (lacking); Vitellius: *deuez ceste dereine petite parcel lire*; Trinity (lacking); Lat. (lacking).]

Appendix One

Motif and Exempla Index
(Index of Similitudes, Exempla, Etymologies, etc.)

The following index focuses on similitudes (i.e., comparisons) and exempla, though it also includes some references to saints and Biblical figures. Etymologies appear without further explanation between quotation marks. The references are to part and line numbers: thus 7.183 refers to Part Seven, line 183. Readers interested in finding a particular proper name should consult the Proper Names Index (pp. 573–80).

559

branches see *boughs*

bread (simple instruction as broken) 5.481–83

bride (the anchoress as Christ's) 2.507, 2.742–43, 3.37–38, 3.45, 3.543–44, 4.1381, 5.282–83; (the soul as a reluctant) 7.195 ff.

bridle (restraint of the tongue as a) 2.317 ff.

brothers (exemplum: how a man seeks out his brother, a monk, who directs him to the third brother, now dead, to show that monks are dead to the world) 8.144–47

bundles see *luggage*

burial (the anchorhold as a) 2.707–08

buying (choosing heaven or hell as) 4.137; (lechery as deceptive market goods) 4.360–71; (redemption as) 7.100–02, 7.170 ff., 7.284

cackling (idle talk as) 2.223 ff., 2.485

Caesar (example of his generosity) 7.186

cage see *birdcage*

calf (the flesh as a fattened) 3.213–19

cancer (evil speech as a) 2.576

carrion (the backbiter's prey as) 2.421 ff.

castle (the anchorhold as a) 2.141–42; (the overly talkative person as a defenseless) 2.308; (the soul as a) 4.805, 6.194; (a good man as a) 4.809–12; (Christ's strength as a) 4.1047; (the body as a) 7.59 ff.

cat (the devil as a) 2.618

cave (the anchorhold as a) 3.130

cement (steadfast love as) 4.594– 99, 4.914, 4.937

chaff (idle speech as) 2.274 ff.; (evil as the devil's) 4.1140

chalice (the good anchoress as a carefully worked) 4.1300–03

chamberlain (love as God's) 7.308–09

chess (fighting the devil as a game of) 5.504

chest see *bosom*

chest wound (serious temptations as a) 4.174

chewing (chattering or silence as) 2.383 ff.

child (the anchoress as a beaten) 4.92–95, 6.225–29; (the anchoress as a stumbling) 4.109–11; (inexperienced believer as a) 5.480; (good works as children) 5.134–36; (exemplum: how a child is turned against his father by a negligent foster father) 5.155 ff.; (anchoresses as shrewd children who tear their clothes) 6.178 ff.; (the soul as a diseased) 7.136

Christ (as lover) see *lover*

clapper (the tongue as a mill) 2.275

claws (temptations as cat's) 2.621

cloak (the flesh as a torn) 6.179 ff.

clod of earth see *dust*

cloister (heaven as a) 4.935

clothing see *festive clothing* and *widow's clothing*

Core (God's wrath revealed in the fate of) 5.408

cottage (even a trivial thing is like building a) 6.174

counselor (love as God's) 7.308–09

cow (the soul as) 3.246

coward (the devil as a cowardly fighter) 4.1178–80

falling down (the incarnation as) 4.1249– 50; (humility as) 4.1258–59

father (exemplum: a father, after beating his child to correct it, throws the rod into the fire) 4.83–95; (God as a) 5.160 ff.; (God as father who beats his child) 6.225–29

feast (heaven as a) 4.133

feet (of an ostrich, pleasures as) 3.158– 59; (desires of the flesh as) 4.1180–82

festive clothing (joy as) 5.41

fig (a good deed as a) 3.358

fig tree (good deeds, disclosed, as a stripped) 3.341–60

file (slanderers and attackers as an anchoress') 4.76–78, 4.1296–99

filth (or **muck**) (sin as) 2.459, 5.34

finger (as an unsympathetic limb of God's body) 6.167–68

fire (love as a) 3.77–78, 7.201 ff., 8.218–24; (testing sickness as) 4.53–54; (lecherous lust as a burning) 4.349; (temptation as a cleansing) 4.609, 4.1298–303; (shame and pain as a cleansing) 4.1306, 6.102–03; (sin as a) 4.1441 ff., 5.82–83; (the genitals as a) 6.260; see also *Greek fire*

flaming sword of the cherubim (Genesis 3:24) (shame and suffering as the) 6.104 ff.

flight (the humble anchoress' life compared to a bird's) 3.142–44

flock (unity of love as a protective) 4.875–78, 4.930 ff.

flood (many words as a) 2.327

floodgates (the mouth as a set of) 2.302–03

flowers (willing confession as blooming) 5.451–53

foot see *feet*

footprint (Christ-like suffering as a) 6.404 ff.

footstool (the world, when despised, as a) 3.533–34

foot wound (fleshly temptations as a) 4.172–73, 4.1180 ff.

foreign land (the world as a) 6.127–30

fox (the false anchoress as a) 3.111 ff.; (the hypocrite as a) 3.117; (covetousness as a) 4.306–21; (disunited anchoresses as Samson's foxes) 4.902–11; (the first inklings of sin as young foxes) 4.1429–33

friend (Christ as a man willing to incur his friend's debts) 7.115–18

fruit (a good deed as a sweet) 3.358

Galilee ("wheel") 5.277

gallows (hell as) 5.143–44

gate (the mouth as a) 2.310

gatekeeper (reason as) 4.1138

glass vessel (the body as a brittle) 3.511–21, 3.524–30

goats (desire of the flesh as stinking) 2.609 ff., 2.642 ff.

gold (the anchoress as fire-tested) 4.51–54

gold-hoard (what one desires as a buried) 2.719–24; (the kingdom of heaven as a) 3.361–62; (a good deed as a) 3.362 ff.

goldsmith (God as a) 4.52; (sickness as a) 4.62–63

grafted branch (the believer as a) 6.149– 50

grave (the anchorhold as a) 2.707, 3.565, 6.369

Greek fire (God's love as) 7.223 ff.

plum: how a man and woman torture their bodies for the love of God) 6.417–28

homeland (heaven as a) 6.134

hood (purity as a white) 4.1345

horse (the tongue as a runaway) 2.320–21; (the foolish anchoress like a horse on a bridge, afraid of its own shadow) 4.765–66; (the weak anchoress as the devil's) 4.1080 ff.

house fire (sin as a) 4.1441 ff.

hung to death (the anchoresses as those) 6.13–14, 6.61 ff.

hunt (temptation as the devil's) 5.385 ff.

husband (exemplum: Christ as the wise husband who waits to test and correct his wife until they have been married for a while) 4.485–99; (exemplum: Christ as the husband who is pleased that his wife mourns his absence, or displeased that she is enjoying herself) 6.238–46

incense (the sweetness which follows bitterness as) 6.351 ff.

infection (or **inflammation**) (lust as an) 4.1184 ff.

ink (Christ's blood as) 7.57

insanity (anger/wrath as) 3.32

iron (idleness as rusty) 8.161

Isaac (exemplum: how Issac sought out a solitary place) 3.399–401

Isboseth (exemplum: how Isboseth slept and set a woman to guard his house. The woman fell asleep, and enemies came and killed Isboseth) 4.1132 ff.; ("a confused man") 4.1136; (the confused and sleepy soul as) 4.1147–48

Jacob (exemplum: how Jacob, in a solitary place, saw God) 3.403–05; (exemplum: how Judah won Benjamin away from Jacob) 5.46 ff.

jailor (fear as a) 5.99–106

Jehoshaphat (prayer as) 4.1055, 4.1068 ff.

Jeremiah (exemplum: why he sat alone and wept) 3.410 ff.

Jerusalem ("sight of peace") 3.594; (the anchorhold as) 3.594, 3.615

John the Baptist (exemplum: as great as he was, he dwelt alone) 3.439–69

John the Evangelist (exemplum: how his virginity was restored) 3.521–24

Joshua ("salvation") 5.25

Judah (confession symbolized by) 5.23 ff., 5.114 ff.; (exemplum: how Judah won Benjamin away from Jacob) 5.46 ff.

Judas Maccabeus (confession symbolized by) 5.21 ff.; ("confession") 5.25

Judea ("confession") 5.276

judge (reason as an enthroned) 5.95 ff.

Judith (the enclosed anchoress as) 3.104, 3.135; (confession as) 3.205 ff., 5.9 ff., 5.35 ff., 5.113 ff., 5.276; (exemplum: how Judith struck off Holofernes' head) 5.9 ff.; (exemplum: how she put off her widow's weeds and dressed in festive clothes) 5.35 ff.

jugglers (the envious as the devil's) 4.411–23

kids (the five senses as) 2.614

king (exemplum: a king entrusted his son to a negligent foster father who let the child be kidnapped by foreigners and who then turns against his own father)

Mary Salome ("bitterness" and "peace") 6.326–32

meat (the flesh as rotting) 3.229–30

medicine (spiritual sight as) 2.534; (heaven as) 2.800; (help against temptation as) 4.12–13, 4.45–46, 4.177–79; (sickness or suffering as the soul's) 4.59–61, 6.263 ff., 6.281 ff.; (temptation as the devil's) 4.586–91; (envy as detrimental) 4.1275–76

Merari (Judith's father) ("bitterness") 5.115–16, 6.305

merchant (the silent anchoress like a rich) 2.226–27; (the secretive anchoress as a rich) 3.372; (the devil as a deceptive) 4.367–71

messenger (suffering as God's) 4.145–58; (discord as the devil's) 4.940; (the Old Testament patriarchs as Christ's love-) 7.54–55

mill (the mouth as a) 2.274 ff.

millpond (the mouth as a) 2.292 ff.

minion (the slothful as the devil's favorite) 4.431–37

mirror (the faithful anchoress as a) 2.503; (a spiritual vision as a) 2.528

moat (humility as a tear-filled) 4.811–12

moon (the foolish anchoress as the) 2.712; (the unstable world as the) 3.536–40

Mordecai ("bitterly trampling the shameless") 3.575–76

Moses (as a solitary) 3.406; (his vigor) 7.186

mother (God as a playful, hiding) 4.634–40; (God as) 4.666; (Jesus as a self-sacrificing) 6.227–31, 7.136 ff.

mountains (spiritual people as) 6.393 ff.

muck (the flesh as) 3.238

murder (sin as) 5.142–44

murderer (a sinner as a) 5.142 ff.

myrrh (bitterness as) 6.351 ff.

needle prick (earthly pain as a mere) 4.67–68

nest (the anchoress as a) 3.175 ff.; (the anchorhold as a) 3.186–90, 3.203; (the heart as God's) 3.199–200

Nichodemus (example of Nicodemus, who brought bitter spices to anoint Christ's body) 6.292 ff.

night (secrecy as) 3.379

night-bird (in the eaves, the recluse as a) 3.265; (gathering its food by night, the vigilant anchoress as a) 3.276–79, 3.307–08, 3.387–90

noble men and women (exemplum: how noble people do not carry their own luggage) 3.541–45; (exemplum: how noble people give generous donations) 3.546–55

noise (worldliness as) 2.509 ff.

nurse or foster mother (a liar as the devil's) 2.409–10; (swearers as a) 4.224–26

offspring or brood (the branches of the seven deadly sins as) 4.172; (of the serpent of envy) 4.259–82; (of the scorpion of lechery) 4.327–54

oil (reconciliation as) 8.253–55

ostrich (the carnal anchoress as an) 3.155 ff.

packs see *luggage*

paddle see *rod*

paint (Christ's blood as) 7.104–05

painting (earthly pain and joy like a mere) 4.767–69

root (greed as the tree-) 8.58–59

rowing against the stream (the virtuous life as) 2.714

rubbing with spices see *anointing*

Ruffin the demon (exemplum from the Life of St. Margaret: how he was overcome by prayer) 4.795–96

rust (sin as) 4.77

saints (example of their solitary lives) 3.489–92

salt (wisdom as preserving) 3.225–30

Samson (example of his strength) 7.185

Samson's foxes see *fox*

sanctuary (the anchorhold as criminal's) 3.615–23

sand (idleness as) 7.232 ff.

saplings (anchoresses as God's) 6.378–83

Sarah (example of her solitary life) 3.490; (exemplum: how the saint withstood thirteen years of physical temptation) 4.681–90

Sarephta (the example of the poor woman of) 7.211 ff.

Saul (relieving himself, the bad anchoress as) 3.122 ff., 3.133 (as the devil) 3.129

scalding water (prayers as) 4.804 ff.

scorpion (lechery as a) 4.327–71; (the pleasant beginning of sin as the head of the) 4.362–63; (the bitter penitence as the tail of the) 4.363–67

scraper (confession as a scraper to erase sins listed in the devil's roll) 5.499 ff.

scribe (the devil as a recording) 5.498 ff.

seed (discord as the devil's) 4.277

selling see *bargain* and *buying*

sepulcher see *grave*

servant (the outer rule as a) Pref.27–28, 8.182–84

shadow (earthly pain and joy compared to that of hell and heaven — a mere) 4.762 ff.; (the flesh of Jesus as a) 6.209 ff.; (the likeness of Christ as a) 6.401 ff.

sheep (the anchoress as a wandering) 4.930–32

shield (the crucifix as a) 4.1404–08; (Christ's body as a battle) 7.86 ff.; (allegory of the shield) 7.103–05

Shimei (exemplum: how Shimei foolishly broke house arrest) 3.583–606; (the outward looking anchoress as) 3.590; ("hearing") 3.591

ship (the church as an anchored) 3.268–71; (sinful man as a ship with many holes) 5.185–87

shoes (a trivial thing as laced) 6.174–75

sick man (the unwary or terrified anchoress as a) 4.7–22; (the parable of the two sick men) 6.200–05

slaves (the five senses as) 3.600–06

slippery (the tongue as) 2.323

slipping and sliding (temptation as) 4.881

smacking see *beating*

smithy (the world as God's) 4.1305 ff.

snake (the backbiter as a stinging) 2.418; (the vindictive anchoress as a stinging) 3.45; (the devil as) 3.201; (poisonous envy as a) 4.259–82

snare (the window of the anchorhold as a) 2.194–97; (the devil's temptation as a) 3.173–74, 4.1231 ff., 5.385 ff.

soap-seller (the noisy anchoress like a) 2.226; (whoever reveals a good deed as a) 3.371

tournament (the crucifixion as a) 7.83 ff.

tower (the good anchoress as a high) 4.592–95; (Christ's help as a) 4.1045–47

trampling (despising evil as) 3.576–80, 4.1425; (the devil's temptations as) 4.1080; (the mark of Christ's sufferings as) 6.404 ff.

trap see *snare*

tree see *root*

tree-bark (hiding a good deed as) 3.340–60

trimmings (circumstances of sin as) 5.206 ff.

trumpeters (the proud as the devil's) 4.402–10

unicorn (angry man as a) 3.29; (wrath or anger as a) 4.283–93

urine (the love of the body as) 7.232 ff., 7.267 ff.

vagabond (the mendicant anchoress as a) 6.117

venom (hurtful speech as) 2.418, 2.466; (evil as) 3.194 ff.

vessel (the body as a pungent) 4.1198–204; (exemplum: how the smell of any fluid but water stays in the vessel even after the fluid is poured out — confession should be like water) 5.251–53

vials (temptations as a plethora of medicine-filled) 4.586–90

vinegar (a sour heart as) 7.236 ff.

Virgin see *Mary (the Virgin)*

vomiting (confession as) 2.461, 4.348, 4.737, 5.516

warfare (spiritual struggle as) 4.827 ff., 4.1046 ff., 4.1404 ff.

warrior (the devil as) 2.141, 2.309 ff., 4.601 ff., 4.805–10, 4.812–13, 4.1405 ff.

washing (confession as) 5.34 ff.; (exemplum: in the same way that fabric or cloth, washed only once, may not be white, a soul must be washed several times by confession) 5.280–84

watchmen or guards (the five senses as) 2.4, 2.648, 2.822–23

water (the insensitive heart as) 6.338 ff.; (tribulation as extinguishing) 7.229; (idleness as stagnant) 8.161

wedding gifts (swiftness and light as) 2.542 ff.

wheat (holy speech as) 2.273

wheels see *Elijah*

whelps (**cubs** or **pups**) (of pride) 4.207–258; (of wrath) 4.283–93; (of sloth) 4.294–305; (of covetousness) 4.306–21

whore (the lecherous anchoress as the devil's) 4.1381; (the sinful anchoress as a) 5.207; (the sinful soul as a) 7.130–31, 7.191

widow (exemplum: how the poor widow swept out her room — a symbol of confession) 5.175 ff.

widow's clothing (sorrow as) 5.36

wife see *bride*

wild animals (the anchoresses as) 4.195–99; (the seven deadly sins as) 4.200–05

wilderness (the anchorhold as a) 4.194–95

wind see *puff of wind*

windows (the eyes as) 2.145

Appendix Two

Proper Names Index

The following index lists all proper names in *AW*, providing a complete list of occurrences (by part and line number) along with a brief biographical identification. Readers should also consult the Explanatory Notes which provide more detailed information in some cases.

Abraham (7.311–12) Old Testament patriarch (see Genesis 11:26–17:5)

Absalones (7.183) Absolon, the rebellious son of King David, renowned in the Middle Ages mainly for his beauty (see 2 Kings 13–18)

Abyron (5.410) a rebel, along with Core and Dathan, Abiron against the leadership of Moses and Aaron (see Numbers 16)

Adam (2.216, 5.60, 5.270, 5.404, 6.181, 7.43) the first man (see Genesis 1:26–5:5)

Afech (4.1045–49) the site where the Philistines attacked Israel (see 1 Kings 4)

Ailred (6.248–49) Aelred of Rievaulx (1109–67), an abbot and important Cistercian writer, author of a guide on the anchoritic life for his sister

Alixandres (7.186) Alexander the Great (356–23 B.C.), the famous Macedonian king and conqueror

Andrew (3.55, 6.176; *Andrews* 8.16) the Apostle Andrew, brother of Peter (see Mark 1:16–20 ff.)

Anna (6.344) the wife of Tobias the elder (see Tobias 1:1–9), though the speech ascribed to her in *AW* really belongs to Sarah, the wife of Tobias the younger

Anselme (2.274, 5.70) St. Anselm of Bec (1033–1109), Archbishop of Canterbury, philosopher and theologian whose *Meditations* exerted widespread influence on popular piety

Antonie (Pref.99, 3.489, 4.690) founder of western monasticism and most famous of the desert saints

Armenie (6.398) Armenia, an ancient country located in what is now northeastern Turkey, the former Soviet Union, and Iranian Azerbaijan; Noah's ark came to rest in the mountains of Armenia (see Genesis 8:4)

Arseni, Arsenie (Pref.99, 3.497–99) St. Arsenius the Great (?355–450) a prominent desert saint (see Explanatory Note to Pref.99–101 for a fuller biography)

Asaeles (7.184) Asael, the brother of Joab, David's military commander, was slain by Abner, the ally of Saul;

Asael was known for his swiftness (see 2 Kings 2:18 ff.)

Assuer (3.309–12) Ahasuerus, king of Persia, and husband of Hester (or, Esther)

Austin, **Awstin** (2.125, 2.406, 2.652, 2.762, 3.237, 3.242–43, 4.338, 4.649, 4.821, 5.91, 5.312, 5.359, 5.371, 5.420, 5.447, 6.317, 7.31, 7.131) St. Augustine of Hippo (354–430), theologian and church father

Banaa (4.1133) Baana, son of Remon, and a general for Isboseth, the son of Saul (see 2 Kings 4:1 and Explanatory Note to 4.1133)

Bartholomew (4.797–98) the Apostle Bartholomew (see Matthew 10:3) who according to tradition traveled to India and was martyred in Armenia

Belial (5.154; *Beliales* 4.795) a demon mentioned in 2 Corinthians 6:15

Benedict, **Beneit** (3.490, 4.690; *Beneites* 4.1415) St. Benedict of Nursia (c. 480–c. 550), founder of the Benedictine order

Benjamin (5.47) son of Jacob and brother to Joseph (see Genesis 35 ff.)

Beornard, **Bernard** (2.143–44, 2.343, 2.763, 3.75, 4.703, 4.825, 4.1084, 4.1224, 4.1337, 4.1339, 5.261, 5.263, 5.270, 5.360, 6.87, 6.136, 7.20, 8.273; *Beornardes* 6.11) St. Bernard of Clairvaux (1090–1153) prominent Cistercian theologian

Bersabee (2.81; *Bersabees* 2.91) Bathsheba (or Bethsabee), the object of David's lust (see 2 Kings 11 ff.)

Bethanie (4.994) Bethany, a village near Jerusalem and the home of Mary, Martha and Lazarus

Calvaire, **Calvarie** (2.669, 4.974) the mount of Calvary, scene of the crucifixion [OF]

Cassiodre (4.1237) St. Cassiodorus (c. 490–c. 583) Roman theologian known for his Psalm commentary

Caymes (5.390), Cain, son of Adam and Eve, slayer of Abel (see Genesis 4)

Cesares (7.186) Julius Caesar (100–44 B.C.) Roman emperor and historian

Chanaan (5.30) Canaan (or, Chanaan), the promised land (see Exodus 6:4)

Chester (4.922) a town in Cheshire, sixteen miles south of Liverpool

Chore (5.408) a rebel, along with Dathan and Abiron, against the leadership of Moses and Aaron (see Numbers 16)

Creasuse (7.182) Croesus (died 546 B.C.), king of Lydia, renowned for his wealth

Dathan (5.408) a rebel, along with Core and Abiron, against the leadership of Moses and Aaron (see Numbers 16)

Davith (Pref.139, 1.363, 2.9, 2.14, 2.30, 2.86, 2.149, 3.4, 3.98, 3.102, 3.122–23, 3.127, 3.131, 3.133, 3.262, 3.280, 3.313, 3.386, 3.626, 4.559, 4.641, 4.806, 4.1427, 5.314, 5.393, 5.450, 6.89, 6.93, 6.96, 7.95; *Davithes* 2.81) David, king of Israel, author of the Psalms

Dina, **Dyna** (2.70–71, 2.78, 2.96) Dinah, daughter of Leah and Jacob, violated by Sichem (see Genesis 34)

Ebreisch(e) (3.133–34, 3.208, 3.213, 3.310, 3.312, 4.1050, 5.48, 5.116) Hebrew

Ebrew (4.1136) Hebrew

Egypte (4.501, 6.318) Egypt

Elyzabeth (2.351) Elizabeth, the mother of John the Baptist and cousin of the Virgin Mary (see Luke 1:36)

Emores (2.78) Hemor, father of Sichem (see Genesis 34)

Englelond, Englond (2.405, 4.917; *Englondes* 4.927) England

Englisc, Englisch(e) (adj. & n. 1.340, 3.134, 3.208, 3.310, 3.312, 3.465, 3.568, 4.796, 4.1063, 4.1136, 4.1158) English

Eve (2.47, 2.50, 2.56–57, 2.60–61, 2.63, 2.215, 2.220, 2.235, 5.60, 5.271, 8.123) the first woman (see Genesis 2:21 ff.)

Exode (2.496, 4.200) the Biblical book of Exodus

Ezechie (3.372) Hezikiah (or, Ezechias) king of Judah (see 4 Kings 18 ff.)

Ezechiel (6.321) the prophet Ezekiel, taken captive to Babylon (for his story, see Ezechiel 1 ff.)

Frensch (adj. 1.340, 4.1297) French

Gabriel (1.298, 2.347, 3.442; *Gabrieles* 2.236) the archangel Gabriel

Galien (6.281) Galen (c. 130–c. 201), Greek physician and author

Galilee (5.277) Galilee, where Jesus' ministry began (see Matthew 5:23)

Genesy, Genesys (2.71, 2.252, 3.401, 5.47, 7.304, 7.310) the Biblical book of Genesis

Giles (6.30) St. Giles (eighth century) a Greek hermit living in France (see Explanatory Note to 6.30)

Giw (*Giwes* 2.794, 2.797, 7.251; *Giws* 1.256, 2.681, 2.794, 7.117, 7.237; *Giwene*) a Jew, a member of the Jewish faith [OF *Giu*]

Giwerie (7.115–16) Jewry; *in Giwerie* = in pawn to Jewish money-lenders [OF *Giu-* + suffix; see AN *Juerie*]

Gommorre (5.404) Gomorrah, city destroyed by God because of its wickedness (see Genesis 10)

Gregoire (2.7, 2.294–95, 2.419, 2.515, 2.550, 3.323, 3.364, 4.6, 4.645, 4.649, 4.882, 4.1150, 4.1153, 4.1170, 4.1229, 4.1275, 4.1333, 5.327, 5.382, 5.423, 6.412, 6.431, 7.37, 7.288; *Gregoires* 2.331) St. Gregory the Great (540–604), pope and church father, author of several influential commentaries

Grickisch (adj. 7.223–24, 7.228, 7.249, 7.252, 7.267–68) *Grickisch fur* = "Greek fire" or burning pitch used as a weapon (see Explanatory Note to 7.223)

Helye, Helie (3.406, 7.213, 7.219–20; *Helyes* 6.100, 6.107) the prophet Elijah (see 3 Kings 17 ff.) [based on the Greek form, *Elias*]

Hester (3.309–10, 3.568, 3.571–72, 3.575, 3.579, 3.583, 3.591, 3.607–08, 3.610–11, 3.625; *Hesteres* 3.309, 3.574, 3.614) Hester (or Esther) Queen of Persia and wife of King Ahasuerus; her story is told in the Biblical book of Esther

Hylariun (3.489) St. Hilarion (291–371), a desert saint (see Explanatory Note to 3.489–90)

Isaac (3.399–401) son of Absalom (see Genesis 21–28; 35)

Israel (4.1048, 4.1052, 5.353, 5.407; *Israeles* 6.318) the Hebrew nation, named after Israel, whose twelve sons gave their names to the tribes of Israel

Jacob (2.70, 2.520, 3.403, 5.47, 5.49, 6.126, 6.314; *Jacobes* 2.71, 2.623) Jacob, Old Testament patriarch, son of Isaac (see Genesis 25–50)

Jame (Pref.79, Pref.87, Pref.91, Pref.95, Pref.97, 2.315, 4.158, 4.827; *James* Pref.82, Pref.100, Pref.108, 6.30) St. James "the Great" (to distinguish him from James, the brother of Jesus), one of the sons of Zebedee and brother to the Apostle John; his relics were venerated at a popular shrine in Compostella, Spain

Jeremie (2.154, 2.697, 3.410, 3.423, 3.431, 4.182, 4.408, 4.410, 4.1401, 5.128, 5.132, 5.250, 7.92, 7.124) Jeremiah (seventh century B.C.) prophet of Judah (see the Biblical books of Jeremiah and Lamentations)

Jerome (2.386, 3.492, 4.1324, 5.369, 8.155) St. Jerome (c. 342–420) church father, Biblical scholar, translator of the Vulgate

Jerusalem (3.585, 3.593–94, 3.596, 3.600, 3.615, 4.201–02, 4.991, 5.171; *Jerusalemes* 4.373) Jerusalem

Jesu (1.7, 1.127, 1.132, 1.145, 1.218, 1.233, 1.291, 1.314, 2.381, 2.591, 2.593, 2.597, 2.736, 2.785, 2.801, 2.820, 3.37, 3.193, 3.375, 3.565, 4.21, 4.496, 4.688, 4.725, 4.777–78, 4.841, 4.862, 4.900, 5.282–83, 5.518, 5.526, 6.7–8, 6.60, 6.62, 6.75, 6.78, 6.81–82, 6.212, 6.282, 6.359, 6.40–08, 6.410, 7.82, 7.108, 7.114, 7.144, 7.157, 7.225, 7.270, 7.274, 7.289, 8.220; *Jesues, Jesuse* 6.14, 7.252) Jesus Christ

Job (2.15–52, 2.719, 3.186, 3.247, 3.333, 4.518, 4.523, 4.528, 4.626, 4.1252, 6.132, 6.189, 6.283, 7.134; *Jobes* 2.293) Job, the symbol of patient suffering (see the Biblical book of Job)

Johel (3.339) the prophet Joel (see the Biblical book of Joel)

Josaphath (4.1055, 4.1068, 4.1072) Jehoshaphat, king of Judah (see 3 Kings 15 ff.)

Josep, Joseph (2.252, 2.356, 4.983) Joseph, son of Rachel and Jacob (see Genesis 30, 37, and 39)

Josue (5.25; *Josues* 5.22) Joshua, successor to Moses (see Exodus 17)

Judas (5.21, 5.23, 5.25, 5.47–49, 5.114, 5.118–19; *Judase* 5.27) Judah, a son of Jacob (see Genesis 29, 35)

Judas (4.1294; *Judase, Judasen* 4.1293, 5.390) disciple and betrayer of Christ

Judas (Macabeu) (5.21, 5.23, 5.30; *Judase* 5.27) Judas Maccabeus (died 161 B.C.), leader of the Jews against the Syrians (see the four books of Maccabees)

Judee (5.275–76) Judea, a province of Palestine

Judith (3.104–07, 3.205, 3.208–210, 3.219–20, 5.9, 5.15, 5.25, 5.36, 5.40, 5.48, 5.113, 5.117; *Judithe* 5.9) Judith, slayer of Holofernes (see the Biblical book of Judith)

Juhan (2.352, 2.533, 3.439, 3.459, 3.468, 3.521, 7.144, 7.205; *Juhanes* 2.673, 3.535, 4.80) the Apostle John

Julienes (4.793) Emperor Julian the Apostate (331–63)

Julienes (6.33) St. Julian, patron saint of hospitality (see Explanatory Note to 6.33)

Latin (adj. 5.212) Latin

Lazre (5.171, 5.307, 5.310) Lazarus, raised from the dead by Christ (see John 11)

Lorenz (3.57, 6.177) St. Lawrence (died 258), a Roman martyr roasted to death

Lot (7.305–07) Lot, nephew of Abraham (see Genesis 13–18)

Lucifer (2.46, 3.245) the devil (as an angel of light)

Lundene (4.922) London

Macabeu see *Judas (Macabeu)*

Makarie (Pref.100) Macarius "the Elder" (c. 300–90), a desert saint (see Explanatory Note to Pref.99–101)

Mardoche (3.575; *Mardochees* 3.575, 3.579) Mordecai, the uncle of Hester (see Esther 2 ff.)

Margarete (4.796) St. Margaret of Antioch, a saint reportedly martyred in the Diocletian persecutions; her life forms part of the "Katherine Group"

Marie (1.64, 1.73, 1.85, 1.232, 1.239–41, 1.246, 1.248, 1.253, 1.255, 1.259, 1.261, 1.264, 1.285, 1.288, 1.292, 1.312, 1.316, 1.327, 1.334, 1.375, 2.218, 2.341, 2.344, 2.356, 4.549,

4.624, 4.994, 4.1372, 5.128, 5.310, 5.436, 6.170, 6.305, 6.337, 6.356, 6.365, 6.367, 8.14; *Maries* 1.64, 6.363, 6.367, 6.369) the Virgin Mary

Marie (of Bethany) (8.38, 8.40–41, 8.44, 8.46, 8.48, 8.78) sister of Martha and Lazarus and representative of the contemplative life (see Luke 10:38–42, John 11:1)

Marie Jacobi (6.313) Mary, mother of James the Less and Joseph (see Mark 15:40), who was present at the crucifixion

Marie Magdaleine (6.308, 6.310, 8.14) a follower of Christ (see Luke 8:2–3) from whom seven devils were cast (see Mark 16:9), and who was present at the crucifixion (see Matthew 27:56)

Marie Salomee (6.327) Mark 15:40 and 16:1 name her simply as Salome, a follower of Christ who was present at the crucifixion

Maries (pl. 2.673, 2.756, 6.303–04, 6.334, 6.336, 6.338, 6.359–60) referring to the three Marys who visited Christ's tomb: Mary Magdalene, Mary (mother of James the Less), and Mary Salome

Marthe (8.38, 8.40–41, 8.44–45, 8.48, 8.78; *Marthen* 4.995) sister of Mary of Bethany and Lazarus and a representative of the active life (see Luke 10:38–42, John 11:1)

Martin (2.189) St. Martin (died 397), bishop of Tours and promoter of monasticism; his life was written by Sulpicius Severus

Meraht (6.305) apparently referring to the bitter fountain at Mara (see Exodus 15:23)

Merariht (5.115, 5.117, 6.305; *Merarihtes* 5.114) Merari, father of Judith (see Judith 16:8)

Michee (Pref.118, Pref.120) the prophet Micah (or Micheas) or the Biblical book written by him

Mihales (7.38, 8.15) the archangel Michael (see Revelations 12:7)

Moyses (7.11) the abbot Moses, a desert saint (see Explanatory Note to 7.11)

Moyses (7.297; *Moysen* 3.406; *Moyseses* 3.330; *Moysese* 7.186) Moses, the Old Testament patriarch

Muntgiw (6.398) Mount of Jove, (specifically) the St. Gotthard mountains of the Lepontine Alps in central Switzerland; the Alps (in general)

Naum (5.255) the Old Testament prophet Nahum

Nichodemus (6.292, 6.302) Nicodemus, a Jewish leader and follower of Jesus (see John 3:1 and 19:39)

Noes (5.406) Noah, builder of the ark (see Genesis 6:9 ff.)

Oloferne (3.208, 3.211, 3.214, 3.219–20, 5.10; *Olofernes* 3.12, 5.19) Holofernes, Assyrian general beheaded by Judith (see Judith 2:4 ff.)

Origene (4.697) Origen (c. 185–c. 254), born in Alexandria, controversial church father and Biblical scholar

Osee (3.559, 4.535) the Old Testament prophet Osee (or, Hosea)

Oxnefort (4.922) Oxford

Pawel (1.147, 2.281, 4.161, 4.559–60, 4.611–12, 4.676, 4.720, 4.1030, 4.1032, 5.67, 5.358, 6.4, 6.6, 6.152–53, 6.406, 7.1, 7.36, 7.51; *Paweles* 6.149) the Apostle Paul

Pawel (Pref.99, 3.489) Paul, the first hermit (see Explanatory Note to Pref.99–101)

Peter (3.505, 3.547, 3.550, 4.673, 4.829, 4.1028, 5.411, 6.16, 6.176; *Petres* 3.508) the Apostle Peter

Pharaon (4.503, 6.317; *Pharaon* 6.320; *Pharaones* 4.501) Pharoah, leader of Egypt (see the Biblical book of Exodus)

Phares (5.119–20) Phares, son of Judah and Thamar (see Genesis 38: 27–30, Matthew 1:3)

Philistews (pl. 4.1049) the Philistines, the enemies of the Israelites (see 1 Kings 4 ff.)

Publius (4.791) a holy man mentioned in *The Lives of the Desert Fathers* (see Explanatory Note to 4.791)

Rebecca (3.401–02) wife of Issac and mother of Jacob and Esau (see Genesis 24:15 ff.)

Recabes (4.1133, 4.1146) Rechab, son of Remon, and a general for Isboseth, the son of Saul (see 2 Kings 4:1 and Explanatory Note to 4.1133)

Remon (4.1133) Remon the Berothite, father of Rechab and Baana

Ruben (4.1347) Reuben, son of Jacob (see Genesis 29:32)

Ruffin (4.795) a devil

Salome(e) see *Marie Salome*

Salomon (2.2, 2.305, 2.308, 2.324, 2.365, 2.414–15, 2.417, 2.422, 2.477, 2.500,

2.645, 2.824, 3.584, 3.589, 3.596–97, 3.606, 4.136, 4.648, 4.819, 4.889, 4.953, 4.1238, 6.347, 7.228, 7.254, 7.259; *Salomones* 2.6, 2.711) Solomon, Old Testament patriarch, son of King David

Samsones (4.902, 4.911, 7.185) Samson, champion of the Israelites (see Judges 13 ff.)

Sare (Pref.100, 3.490, 4.681, 4.686) Sarah (flourished fourth century), desert saint (see Explanatory Note to Pref.99–101)

Sarepte (7.212, 7.222) Sarephta, a Sidonian city and home to the widow of Sareptha (see 3 Kings 17:9 ff.)

Sareptiens (pl. 7.228) Sarephtans (i.e., like the widow of Sarephta)

Sathan (4.673–74) Satan

Saul (3.122–23, 3.127–29, 3.133–34) Saul, king of Israel and enemy of David

Schreobsburi (4.922) Shrewsbury (Shropshire) located on the English-Welsh border

Semei, Semey (3.583, 3.590–91, 3.595, 3.600, 3.606–07; *Semeis* 3.593) Shimei, an ally of Saul and enemy to David (see 2 Kings 19:16 ff.)

Seneke (2.291–92) Lucius Annaeus Seneca, or Seneca the Younger (c. 4 B.C.–65 A.D.), Roman statesman, philosopher, and playwright

Sichen (2.78) Sichem, violator of Dinah (see Genesis 34)

Sincletice (Pref.101, 3.490) St. Syncletica (c. 316–400), an early ascetic (see Explanatory Note to Pref.99–101)

Sluri (6.390) Slurry, the cook's boy (see entry in glossary)

Sodome (5.404, 7.306, 8.159; *Sodomes* 8.160) Sodom, city destroyed by God because of its wickedness (see Genesis 10)

Stefne (3.58) St. Stephen, the first martyr of the Christian Church (see Acts 7:54 ff.)

Syon (2.495, 2.498, 2.502) Zion, one of the high places on which Jerusalem is built; in the New Testament the name sometimes refers metaphorically to the Church

Thamar (5.115, 5.118–19) Thamar, mother (by Judah) of Phares and Zara (see Genesis 38:12 ff.)

Tobie (2.520, 6.344) probably the blind prophet Tobias, who was led into captivity but lived an exemplary life of patience (see the Biblical book of Tobias)

Urie (2.92) Uriah, husband of Bathsheba (Bersabee) and slain by David (see 2 Kings 11)

Ynde (5.485) India

Ypocras (6.281) Hippocrates (c. 460–c. 377 B.C.), Greek physician and author

Ysaac (3.399–400) Isaac, son of Abraham

Ysaie (2.336, 2.363, 2.366, 2.371, 2.655, 3.452, 4.446, 4.455, 4.1079, 5.145, 6.122–23, 6.184, 6.198, 6.226, 7.146, 7.304) the prophet Isaiah

Ysboset (4.1132, 4.1135–36, 4.1141, 4.1147, 4.1170, 4.1178) Isboseth, the youngest of Saul's four sons (see 2 Kings 4)

Zacharie (2.495, 5.42) the prophet Zacharia (or Zacharias) or the Biblical book written by him

Zaram (5.119–20) Zara, son of Judah and Thamar (see Genesis 38:27–30, Matthew 1:3)

Glossary

The following glossary provides entries for all but the most recognizable words in the *AW*. Entries generally contain the following: 1) the base form in boldface, 2) its part of speech, 3) definition, 4) breakdown of inflected forms, and 5) etymology (in square brackets [ ]), sometimes with a bibliographical reference.

To help readers understand these often very difficult words, I have followed what seems to me a very useful practice of Friedrich Klaeber's in the glossary of his edition of *Beowulf* (Boston: Heath, 1950), whereby a word in ALL CAPS represents the modern descendant of the ME word. In a text as difficult as this one, any hints of the familiar should be very welcome indeed. To help make the vocabulary more transparent, cognates in other languages, particularly German, are provided. If the development of a word is unproblematic, its etymology appears as a simple abbreviation of its source language (for example, OE, OF, ON, etc.), though in the case of more difficult or interesting words, fuller etymologies appear, sometimes with bibliographic references, where appropriate. For words of Old English origin, OE means that the ME word has descended regularly from a known OE word; *OE that the ME word goes back to an OE word which does not appear in the corpus of OE texts but which is theoretically reconstructable; "from OE," that the word is based on a new combination or development of OE elements.

Outside the OED and MED, the leading authority on the vocabulary of the *AW* is Zettersten, whose *Studies in the Dialect and Vocabulary of the Ancrene Riwle* (covering mainly native forms) and "French Loan-Words in the *Ancrene Riwle* and Their Frequency" manage between them to treat almost every word in the *AW*.

Though there is unfortunately no cross-referencing to line numbers in the text, to find specific words or word-forms readers may consult either the concordance to the *AW* (Potts et al.) or the on-line version of this text on the TEAMS Middle English Texts website: http://www.lib.rochester.edu/Camelot/TEAMS/tmsmenu.htm.

Abbreviations

1	first person	adv.	adverb
2	second person	AF	Anglo-French
3	third person	AN	Anglo-Norman
adj.	adjective	art.	article

compar.	comparative
conj.	conjunction
def.	definite
demons.	demonstrative
F.	French
fem.	feminine
fig.	figuratively
gen.	genitive, possessive
Ger.	German
imper.	imperative
impers.	impersonal construction
indef.	indefinite
inf.	infinitive
interj.	interjection, exclamation
interrog.	interrogative, question word
Lat.	Latin
lit.	literally
masc.	masculine
MDu	Middle Dutch
ME	Middle English
MED	Middle English Dictionary
med.	medieval
MFlem	Middle Flemish
MLG	Middle Low German
MWelsh	Middle Welsh
ModE	Modern English
n.	noun
neut.	neuter
num.	number
obj.	objective
OE	Old English
OED	Oxford English Dictionary
OF	Old French
ONF	Old Norman French
orig.	originally
pl.	plural
past part.	past participle
prep.	preposition
pres.	present tense

pres. part.	present participle
prob.	probably
pron.	pronoun
reflex.	reflexive
sing.	singular
subj.	subjunctive
superlat.	superlative
v.	verb

a- (prefix) forth, away; (a general intensifier) [OE]

a, an (adj.) ONE; first (in a series); single; (indef. art., & pron.) A, AN; one [OE]

aa (adv.) always, ever, continuously; at all [OE]

abbat (n.) ABBOT (gen. sing. *abbates*) [OE, from Lat.]

a-beate (v., pres. subj. sing.) BEAT down, strike [OE]

a-bereth (v., pres. 3 sing.) BEARS, endures [OE]

a-biden (v.) to wait, delay; to wait for, expect (imper. sing. *abid*; imper. pl. *abideth*; pres. subj. sing. *abide*; pres. 3 sing. *abit* [= *abideth*]) [OE]

a-blende (v.) to take away sight, to blind; dazzle, confuse the senses (pres. 3 sing. *ablendeth*) [from OE]

a-blindeth (v., pres. 3 sing.) goes or becomes BLIND [from OE]

a-breiden (v.) to start (out of one's sleep), awake suddenly (past 3 sing. *abreaid*) [from OE; see *breiden* (v.)]

absolutiun (n.) ABSOLUTION, the remission of sin (one of the stages in the sacrament of penance) [OF, from Lat.]

a-buggen (v.) to pay for, atone for, suffer for; pay back, avenge (subj. 3 sing. *abugge*) [OE; ModE *buy*]

a-bute(n) (adv.) around, on every side; near, in the neighborhood; (prep.) around, ABOUT; near [OE]

a-buten (prep.) forever without [see *aa* (adv.) + *buten* (prep.)]

a-buve(n) (prep.) ABOVE [OE]

accidie(s) (n.) sloth (one of the seven deadly sins), torpor [AF, from Lat.]

acemin (v.) to adorn, decorate [OF]

acemunge (n.) adornment, decoration

ach (conj.) see *ah* (conj.)

achate (n.) agate, eagle-stone (with special powers) [Lat.]

achiesun (n.) reason, cause, motive; *withuten achiesun* = in vain (pl. *achiesuns*) [AF]

acointance (n.) ACQUAINTANCE (referring to the special treatment one might get through knowing someone with influence) [OF]

acointet (adj. & v., past part.) ACQUAINTED, familiar, informed, knowledgeable [OF]

a-colin (v.) to COOL down [OE]

a-corien (v.) to suffer, be punished; to pay for, pay the penalty for [*OE]

a-covrin (v.) to recover, regain (one's health) [OE, related ultimately to ModE *recover*]

a-cursede, a-curset (adj. & v., past part.) ACCURSED; worthy of a curse, detestable, execrable [from OE]

a-cwellen (v.) to kill, destroy [OE]

a-cwenchen (v.) to QUENCH, extinguish, put an end to; satisfy (pres. 3 sing. *acwenct*) [OE]

a-cwikien (v.) to QUICKEN, come to life; revive, bring back to life (pres. 3 sing. *acwiketh*) [OE]

a-cwiti(n) (v.) to ACQUIT, release, settle (a debt) [OF]

a-deadin (v.) to die; to mortify, kill (pres. 3 sing. *adeadeth*; past sing. *adeadede*) [OE]

a-dotede (adj. & v., past part.,) silly, foolish [*OE; ModE *dote* "to grow silly"]

a-drenchen (v.) to drown, be drowned (pres. 3 sing. *adrencheth*; past sing. *adrencte*; past part. *adrenct*) [OE]

a-drong (v., past sing.) drowned; was swallowed up (in hell, filth) [OE; related to *adrenchen* (v.)]

a-druhien (v.) to become DRY, dry up; perish (pres. 3 sing. *adruheth*; past sing. *adruhede*; past part. *adruhet*) [OE; see *drue* (adj.)]

a-dun (adv.) DOWN, downward [from OE]

Advent, Advenz (n.) ADVENT, the penitential season before Christmas, four Sundays beginning with the Sunday falling closest to St. Andrew's Day (November 30) [OF]

a-fealleth (v., pres. 3 sing.) FALLS down, dies down [OE]

a-feitet (v., past part.) disposed, inclined; trained, subdued [OF]

a-fellen (v.) to lay low, FELL, kill; overthrow, overcome [OE]

affectiun (n.) emotion, feeling; a moving of the mind; AFFECTION [OF]

a-flieth (v., pres. 3 sing.) puts to FLIGHT, drives out; dispels, thwarts (past part. *afleiet*) [OE]

a-gan (v.) to GO, depart; vanish; escape; go to ruin; die (fig., pass away); *ben agan* = to be lost (pres. subj. sing. *aga*; pres. 3 sing. *ageath*; pres. pl. *agath*) [OE]

a-geasten (v.) to terrify, make AGHAST; be frightened, terrified; to deter [from OE]

a-grisen (v.) to quake, shudder, tremble (in fear); be afraid, terrified (past sing. *agras*) [OE; see ModE *grisly*]

a-gulte (v., past sing.) was GUILTY (of sin); did wrong, sin [OE]

ah (conj.) but, and [OE]

ahelich (adj.) inspiring AWE or respect; considerable, impressive [ON]

ahen (v.) to OWE; should, OUGHT (pres. 2 sing. *ahest*; pres. 3 sing. *ahe*; pres. pl. *ahen, ahe (ye)*; past sing. *ahte*; past pl. *ahten*) [OE]

a-hon, a-honget (v., past part.) HANGED [from OE]

ahte (n., sing./pl.) possessions, property; ownership; cattle, livestock [OE]

ake (v., pres. subj. sing.) ACHE, feel pain (pres. part. *akinde*) [OE]

a-keast (v., past part.) CAST, knocked down, thrown over [ON]

a-keldeth (v., pres. 3 sing.) COOLS down, makes cold [from OE]

al (adj. & n.) ALL, every; everyone (pl. *alle*; gen. pl. *alre*) [OE]; (adv.) ALL, completely, entirely; exactly; right; (conj.) even though (usually with reversal of subject and verb) *al gan ha* = even though they go; *al meast* = mostly all; very nearly [OE]

alas (interj.) ALAS! [OF]

ald(e) (adj.) OLD; primeval, original [OE]

ale (n.) ALE, a fermented drink [OE]

a-le(a)st (adv.) at LAST, finally [from OE]

a-lith (v., pres. 3 sing.) subsides, LIES down [OE; see *liggen* (v.)]

alle-gate (adv.) in all ways, in every way; entirely; continual; in any event; nevertheless [OE + ON]

alles (adv.) completely, totally; in some way, at all; all told, in all

allunge(s) (adv.) in every way, wholly, entirely; in any way, at ALL; after all [OE]

al-mihti (adj.) ALMIGHTY, all powerful [OE]

aloes (n. pl.) ALOES, a bitter drug derived from the East Indian *Aloexylon* or *Aquilaria* genus [OE, from Lat.]

al-swa (conj.) ALSO, likewise; *alswa as* = just as, in the same way that [OE]

al-swuch (conj.) just as, just SUCH [OE]

a-mainet (adj. & v., past part.) MAIMED, crippled; (fig.) helpless [OE + OF]

a-mansede (v., past sing.) cursed, swore; excommunicated (past part. *amanset*) [OE]

ame (interj.) Here! Hey! "addressed to a dog . . . app[arently] an invented gesture-word" (Bennett & Smithers, p. 436)

a-mead (adj.) demented; MAD, crazy [from OE]

a-measet (adj. & v., past part.) stunned, AMAZED; stupefied, dazed [OE]

a-mendement (n.) correction, improvement [OF]

a-mendin (v.) to correct, reform, MEND; remedy (past part. *amendet*) [OF]

ami (n.) friend; *beal ami* = (my) fine friend (a form of address) [OF]

a-mid, a-midde(n) (prep.) AMIDST, in the middle of [OE]

amites (n. pl.) handkerchiefs, scarves; (later) albs [OF]

ampoiles (n. pl.) AMPOULES, vials, flasks [OF]

an (adj. & n.) ONE, first (in a series) (gen. sing. *anes*) [OE]

anan (adv.) immediately, ANON, at once; in one direction, straight on, even [OE]

anan-riht, -rihtes (adv.) at once, immediately

ancre (n.) anchorite (man or woman); anchoress (pl. *ancres, ancren*; gen. sing. *ancre*; gen. pl. *ancrene*) [OE]

ancreful(e) (adj.) anxious; careful, devoted [ON *angr-fullr* "full of trouble"]

ancre-hus (n.) ANCHOR-HOUSE [from OE]

ancre-wahe (n.) ANCHOR-wall, wall of an anchorhold (pl. *ancre-wahes*)

ancrin (v.) to ANCHOR, secure with an anchor (past part. *i-ancret*) [OF, perhaps via OE]

ane (adj.) alone; (adv.) only [OE]

anes-weis (adv.) ONE WAY, in one direction (adverbial gen.)

ane-wil(e) (adj.) stubborn, obstinate; persistent, single-minded [OE *an-wille* "ONE-WILL(ed), single minded"]

an-ful (adj.) singular, individual

angoise (n.) ANGUISH, agony, intense physical pain [OF]

angoisuse (adj.) ANGUISHED, excruciating [OF]

aniversaries (n. pl.) ANNIVERSARIES, commemorations of the dead on the anniversary of their deaths [Lat.]

an-lepi (adj.) single, individual, solitary [OE]

anli, anlich (adj.) solitary; lonely (superlat. *anlukest*) [OE; ModE *only*]

an-nesse (n.) ONE-NESS, unity [OE]

anont (prep.) see *onont* (prep.)

an-red (adj.) resolute, persistent; reliable, sure [see *an* (adj.) + *read* (n.)]

an-rednesse (n.) constancy, resolve, single-mindedness; reliability

ant (conj.) AND; but [OE]

antefne (n.) ANTIPHON; OED: "A versicle or sentence sung by one choir in response to another" (pl. *antefnes*) [OE, from Lat.]

are (n.) grace; mercy [OE]

a-reache(n) (v.) to succeed in REACHING; get hold of; to obtain; get at (an enemy), attack; strike (pres. 3 sing. *areacheth*) [OE]

a-rearen (v.) to REAR up, raise, erect (pres. subj. sing. *areare*; pres. 3 sing. *areareth*; past sing. *arearde*; past part. *arearet*) [OE]

a-reowen (v.) to pity, feel compassion for, feel sorry about; to regret, repent [OE; see ModE *ruth*]

a-reownesse (n.) pity, compassion; repentance, regret

arewen (n. pl.) ARROWS [OE]

a-risen (v.) to ARISE, rise (imper. pl. *ariseth*; pres. subj. sing. *arise*; pres. 1 sing. *arise*; pres. 3 sing. *ariseth*; past sing. *aras*; pres. part. *arisinde*) [OE]

ariste (n.) ARISING, resurrection [OE]

aromaz (n. pl.) (AROMATIC) spices; perfume [OF, from Lat.]

article (n.) separate clause or statement (in the Creed or a rule); provision; ARTICLE (of faith) (pl. *articles*) [OF, from Lat. *articulus* "little joint"]

a-rudde (v., past sing.) saved, rescued; RID (someone of danger); freed, liberated (past part. *arud*) [OE]

as(e) (conj.) AS; when; where, whither; such as, for example; as though, as if [OE]

asailin (v.) to ASSAIL, attack, assault (pres. 3 sing. *asaileth*; pres. pl. *asailith*; past part. *asailet*) [OF]

asawz (n. pl.) ASSAULTS [OF]

asketh (v., pres. 3 sing.) ASKS, requires (pres. pl. *askith*) [OE]

a-skur (v., imper. sing.) chase, drive away [?MDu, perhaps related to ModE *scour*]

a-sneasen (v.) to gore, pierce; hit, strike against (pres. 3 sing. *asneaseth*) [OE]

asprete (n.) severity, harshness, roughness [OF, from Lat.; ModE *asperity*]

Assumptiun (n.) the Assumption of the Virgin into heaven (feast celebrated on August 15) [Lat.]

asswa (conj.) see *al-swa* (conj.)

a-steorven (v.) to kill, destroy (pres. subj. sing. *asteorve*; pres. 3 sing. *asteorveth*; past part. *astorven*) [OE; see Ger. *sterben* "to die"]

a-stihen (v., imper. pl.) climb up [OE]

aten (n. pl.) OATS [OE]

at-foren (adv.) in front of, in the presence of, BEFORE [OE]

ath (n.) OATH (pl. *athes*) [OE]

athet (conj. & prep.) until [OE *oþ þæt* "until"]

a-thrusmin (v.) to suffocate, choke; "to imprison" (Zettersten [1965], p. 154) [OE]

a-tiffi (v., pres. subj. sing.) to adorn, deck out, beautify [OF]

atter (n.) poison, venom; bile, bitter substance; moral corruption; death [OE]

atter-lathe (n.) antidote (to a poison) [OE; see *atter* (n.) + *lath* (adj.)]

atternesse (n.) corruptness, sinful conduct; malice, maliciousness

attreth (v., pres. 3 sing.) poisons, envenoms, embitters (pres. pl. *attrith*; past part. *i-attret*)

attri(e) (adj.) poisonous, venemous; bitter (superlat. *attrest*)

a-turn (n.) attire, clothing [OF, related to ModE *attire*]

a-turnet (v., past part.) transformed, changed, TURNED; (legal) transferred [OF]

auctorite (n.) AUTHORITY, authoritative author or book [OF]

augrim (n.) reckoning with Arabic numbers; calculating, accounting [OF *augorisme*, med. Lat. *algorismus*, from Arabic *Al-Khowarazm*, surname of the mathematician Abu Ja'far Mohammed Ben Musa]

aventure (n.) chance, accident [OF]

aves (n.) AVES, Hail Marys [Lat.]

a-wakenin, a-wacnin (v.) to AWAKE, arise, spring from (pres. 3 sing. *awakeneth*; pres. pl. *awakenith*; past sing. *awaknede, awacnede, awakede*; past part. *awakenet*) [OE]

a-warpen (v.) to throw away; cast down, aside [OE]

a-wealdeth (v., pres. 3 sing.) takes control of, subdues [from OE; see ModE *wield*]

a-wearien (v.) to curse; (past part. as adj.) *aweariede* = accursed [OE; see *wearien* (v.)]

a-wed (adj. & v., past part.) mad, insane [OE; see *wod* (adj.)]

awei-ward (adv.) AWAY [from OE]

a-wildgeth (v., pres. 3 sing.) see *a-wilgin* (v.)

a-wilgin (v.) to grow WILD, unruly; dazzle (the eyes) (pres. 3 sing. *awildgeth, awilgeth*) [OE]

a-wrec (v., past sing.) avenged [OE]

a-wurieth (v., pres. 3 sing.) strangles (to death), kills (by strangulation); WORRIES, tears the throat (pres. pl. *awurith*; past part. *awuriet*) [OE]

ayein (prep.) AGAINST, as a defense against, in response to, in compensation for, in spite of, despite; (adv.) back, in the opposite direction; in return [OE]

ayein-ward(es) (adv.) back, away; in the opposite direction

ba (pron.) both [OE]

baban (n.) BABY [perhaps from MWelsh *baban*, though perhaps imitative; see Breeze (1993), pp.12–13]

babanliche (adv.) in a BABYISH way, childishly [MWelsh; Diensberg (1978), pp. 81–82 derives the word from OF *boban* "pride" and defines it as "haughtily, arrogantly"]

bac (n.) the BACK (of the human torso) [OE]

bac-bitere (n.) BACKBITER, (secret) slanderer (pl. *bac-biteres*)

bac-bitunge (n.) BACKBITING, slander

bagge (n.) BAG, small pouch (pl. *baggen*) [ON]

bald (adj.) BOLD, brave [OE]

baldeliche, baltliche (adv.) BOLDLY, bravely, fearlessly

baleful (adj.) BALEFUL, harmful; deadly [OE]

bal-plohe (n.) BALLPLAY; (fig.) something easy and pleasant

ban (n.) BONE (pl. *banes*) [OE]

bandun (n.) jurisdiction, dominion, control; *beon in bandon* = be in someone's control, at someone's disposal [OF]

banere (n.) BANNER, standard, flag (pl. *baneres*) [OF]

bar (n.) BEAR [OE]

baraigne (adj. as n.) BARREN [OF; the MS reading, *bereget*, is problematic — see Textual Note to 3.443)

baret (n.) strife, conflict; combat, battle; trouble, commotion; bargaining, argument; deception, fraud [OF]

basme (n.) aromatic resin, BALM, fragrant oil [OF]

bat (n.) BOAT [OE]

bathe (adj.) BOTH [ON]; (adv. & conj.) BOTH

bead (v., past sing.) see *beoden* (v.)

beah (v., past sing.) see *buhen* (v.)

beaketh (v.) pecks; pushes the BEAK out, peeps out (pres. subj. sing. *beaki*; pres. 3 sing. *beaketh*; past sing. *beakede*) [OF]

beal (adj.) fine, fair; *beal ami* = (my) fine friend (a form of address) [OF]

bealdeth (v., pres. 3 sing.) EMBOLDENS, makes brave, encourages [OE]

beali(e) (n.) BELLOWS (pl. *bealies*) [OE; related to ModE *belly*]

bearm (n.) lap; embrace [OE]

bearn (n.) child, offspring, BAIRN (gen. *bearnes*; pl. *bearnes*) [OE]

bearne (v.) to BURN, be burned (pres. 3 sing. *bearneth*; past sing. *bearnde*; pres. part. *bearninde*; past part. *i-bearnd*) [OE]

bear-vot (adj.) BAREFOOT [OE]

beaten (v.) to BEAT, hit (pres. 3 sing. *beat*, *beateth*, past sing. *beot*, past part. *i-beate*, *i-beaten*) [OE]

beath (n.) BATH (pl. *beathes*) [OE]

beawbelez (n. pl.) jewels [med. Lat. *baubellus* "jewel"; probably not from OF *baubel* "toy, plaything"]

bed(e) (v.) see *bidden* (v.)

bedd(e) (n.) BED [OE]

beggilde (n.) a female beggar, beggar-woman [see *beggin* (v.) and *-ild* (suffix)]

beggin (v.) to BEG [origin obscure]

beie (v., pres. 3 subj. sing.) (might) bend [OE, related to *buhen* (v.)]

beme (n.) trumpet (for warfare, hunting) (pl. *bemen*) [OE]

bemere (n.) trumpeter (pl. *bemeres*)

bemin (v.) to blow, blast (on a trumpet); resound (like a trumpet), to trumpet

bench (n.) BENCH, pew [OE]

bencin (v.) to BEND or arch (the eye-brows) [*OE; see Zettersten (1965), p. 71]

benen (n. pl.) prayers; requests [OE]

beo(n) (v.) to BE (imper. sing./pl. *beo*; pres. subj. sing. *beo*; past subj. sing. *were*; pres. 3 sing. *is, bith*; pres. pl. *beoth*; past sing. *wes*; past pl. *weren*; inflected inf. *to beonne*; past part. *i-beon*; negative forms: pres. subj. sing. *nere*; pres. 1 sing. *nam*; pres. 2 sing. *nart*; pres. 3 sing. *nis*; past sing. *nes*; past pl. *neren*) [OE]

beode (n.) prayer (pl. *beoden*) [OE; see Ger. *gebet* "prayer"]

beoden (v.) to offer; command, bid, urge (pres. subj. sing. *beode*, pres. 3 sing. *beot*, *beodeth*; pres. pl. *beodeth*; past sing. *bead*; past part. *i-bote*) [OE; see Ger. *bieten*]

beodes-mon (n.) prayer-MAN, one who prays for the souls of others; an almsman, one paid to pray for others in return for lodging in an almshouse [see *beode* (n.) + *mon* (n.)]

beore (n.) BEAR (the animal representing sloth) [OE]

beoren (v.) to BEAR, carry; give birth to; endure, preserve; (reflex.) to behave oneself, act *bereth ow/hire on heorte* = (it) weighs on your/her heart (imper. sing. *ber*; imper. pl. *beoreth*; pres. subj. sing. *bere*; pres. 2 sing. *berest*; pres. 3 sing. *bereth*; pres. pl. *beoreth*; past pl. *beren*; past part. *i-boren*) [OE]

beot(e) (v.) see *beaten* (v.) or *beoden* (v.)

beoth (v., pres. 3 sing.) see *beon* (v.)

beowiste (n.) dwelling, living; abode, home; living, life; way or condition of life [OE]

berkest (v., pres. 2 sing.) BARK [OE]

bersten (v.) to BURST, break (pres. subj. sing. *berste*; pres. 3 sing. *bersteth*) [OE]

bet (adv.) BETTER (compar. of *god* [adj.]) [OE]

beten (v.) to amend, restore; pay for, compensate; atone, make restitution for (a sin) (imper. pl. *beteth*; past part. *i-bet, i-bette*) [OE; early ModE *boot* "remedy"]

betles (n. pl.) mallet, sledgehammer; OED: "An implement consisting of a heavy weight or 'head,' usually of wood, with a handle or stock, used for driving wedges or pegs, ramming down paving stones, or for crushing, bruising, beating, flattening, or smoothing, in various industrial and domestic operations, and having various shapes according to the purpose for which it is used" [OE; see *beaten* (v.) + -*(e)les* (suffix)]

bi (prep.) BY, close to, near; concerning, about [OE]

bi-barret (v., past part.) enclosed, confined securely (with a BAR or bolt) [OF]

bi-blodge (v., imper. sing.) BLOODY, make bloody (pres. subj. sing. *biblodgi*; past part. *bibled*) [OE]

bi-burien (v.) to BURY, inter (a corpse) (past part. *biburiet*) [OE]

bi-chearren (v.) to lead astray, mislead; to seduce, deceive (pres. subj. sing. *bichearre*; past part. *bichearret*) [OE; see Ger. *bekehren* "to convert"]

bi-cleopien (v.) to cry out against, accuse (legal) (pres. subj. sing. *bicleopie*; past part. *bicleopet*) [OE; see *cleopien* (v.)]

bi-cluppeth (v., imper. pl.) embrace (affectionately); surround, envelop; contain, confine (pres. subj. sing.

bicluppe; past sing. *biclupte*; past part. *bicluppet*) [OE; see *cluppen* (v.)]

bi-cluset (v., past part.) ENCLOSED [OE]

bi-clusunge (n.) ENCLOSURE [OE]

bi-clute (v., imper. sing.) mend with a patch or CLOUT, cover with a cloth; (fig.) dress up, prettify [from OE]

bi-corven (v., past part.) cut off, CARVED off [see *keorve* (v.)]

bi-cumen (v.) to BECOME, turn into; be suitable, becoming (pres. 3 sing. *bikimeth*; past sing. *bicom*; past part. *bicumene*) [OE]

bidden (v.) to ask, request, beg; pray, say a prayer (for); command, BID, order, direct (imper. sing. *bide*; imper. pl. *biddeth*; pres. 1 sing. *bide*; pres. 2 sing. *bidest*; pres. 3 sing. *bit, bid, biddeth*; pres. pl. *biddeth*; past sing. *bede, bed*) [OE]

biddunge (n.) BIDDING, request; prayer [see *bidden* (v.)]

biden (v.) to remain, stay, live; wait for, expect; endure, experience [OE; ModE *bide*]

bi-don (v.) to befoul (a place), defile, beshit (oneself); (lit.,) BE-DO (pres. 3 pl. *bidoth*) [OE]

bi-dweolieth (v., pres. pl.) mislead; delude, trick [from OE]

bi-falleth (v., pres. pl.) BEFALL, happen to; belong to [OE]

bi-fon (v.) to grasp, seize [OE]

bi-fule(n) (v.) to BEFOUL, make filthy (in a physical or moral sense); defile (pres. 3 sing. *bifuleth*) [from OE]

bi-gileth (v., pres. 3 sing.) BEGUILES, tricks, deceives (past part. *bigilet*) [OF]

bi-ginnin (v.) to BEGIN (imper. sing. *bigin*; imper. pl. *biginneth*; pres. subj.

sing. *biginne*; pres. 3 sing. *biginneth*; past
sing. *bigon*; past part. *bigunnen*) [OE]

bi-gurd (v., pres. 3 sing. [= *bigurdeth*])
encircles, encloses (with something);
besieges (past part. *bigurde*) [from OE;
see *gurdel* (n.)]

bi-gurdel (n.) purse, moneybag (hanging
from a belt or GIRDLE) [OE]

bi-halde(n) (v.) to hold, keep, observe; to
pertain, relate to; signify, mean; to
BEHOLD, keep in view; consider, think
about (imper. sing. *bihald*; imper. pl.
bihaldeth; pres. 2 sing. *bihaldest*; pres. 3
sing. *bihalt*; pres. pl. *bihaldeth*; past sing.
biheold) [OE]

bi-haldunge (n.) a BEHOLDING, sight
[see *bi-halden* (v.)]

bi-haten (v.) to promise, vow (pres. 3 sing.
bihat; pres. pl. *bihateth*; past sing. *bihet*)
[OE; see *hate* (v.)]

bi-heafdunge (n.) a BEHEADING [OE;
see *heaved* (n.)]

bi-heve (adj.) profitable, useful, necessary,
BEHOOVEFUL (superlat. *biheveste*)
[OE]; (n.) profit, advantage, benefit,
BEHOOVE [OE]

bi-hinde (prep.) BEHIND, at the back [OE]

bi-hinden (adj.) at the rear; earlier, past;
later; *beon bihinden* = to be at a
disadvantage, be badly off (or, inferior),
be backward, slow, tardy [OE]

bi-hofde (v., past sing.) had need of,
required; (impers.) it was necessary, it
BEHOOVED [OE]

bi-hove (n.) profit, need, BEHOOF [OE]

bi-kimeth (v., pres. 3 sing.) see *bi-cumen*
(v.)

bi-leasunges (n.) lies, falsehoods;
fabrications, slanders [from OE]

bi-leave (n.) BELIEF, faith [from OE]

bi-leppet (v., past part.) clothed or
enveloped; (fig.) surrounded [from OE
læppa "loose garment"]

bi-limeth (v., pres. 3 sing.) cuts off a
LIMB, mutilates (reflex.) [from OE]

bi-limpeth (v., pres. pl.) befit, belong to
[OE]

bi-lohen (v., past part.) lied about,
slandered [OE]

bi-loken (v.) to shut; enclose, LOCK; (past
part. as adj.) *bilokene* = contained [OE]

bi-lokin (v.) to see, LOOK at; examine
(pres. 3 sing. *biloketh*) [from OE]

bi-lurd (v., past sing.) LURED (orig. a
hawking term), enticed; set a trap for,
tricked [*OE or OF]

bi-malscret (v., past part.) bewildered,
confused; bewitched [OE *malscrung*
"charm, enchantment"; see ModE
maskering]

bi-measet, bi-measede (adj. & v., past
part.) stupefied, confused, bewildered
[*OE; see ModE *amazed*]

bi-mong (prep.) AMONG [OE]

binde(n) (v.) to BIND, fasten, tie (up)
(imper. sing. *bind*; pres. 3 sing. *bindeth*,
bint; pres. pl. *bindeth*; past part. *i-
bunden*) [OE]

bi-neomen (v.) to take away (something),
do away with, destroy; to deprive,
despoil; take, take hold of (pres. 3 sing.
binimeth; pres. pl. *bineometh*) [OE; see
Ger. *benehmen* "to deprive of"]

bi-neothen (adv. & prep.) BENEATH [OE]

bi-netli (v.) to NETTLE, whip with nettles
[from OE]

bi-pilet (v., past part.) stripped (bare),
PILLAGED [see *pilewin* (v.)]

bi-pilunge (n.) a stripping, plundering

bi-pinnet (adj. & v., past part.) PENNED in, confined [from OE]

bi-reafde (v., past sing.) BEREAVED, deprived, robbed [OE]

bi-reinet (adj. & v., past part.) RAINED on [from OE]

bi-reowsunge (n.) repentance, remorse, contrition, RUE [OE]

birlen (v.) to serve, ply with (a drink), pour out; serve (pres. 3 sing. *birleth*) [from OE *byrele* "cup-bearer"; ultimately related to *beoren* (v.) "to carry"]

bi-sahe (n.) proverb, saying [on the model of Lat. *pro-verbium*]

bi-sampleth (v., pres. 3 sing.) explains, explains away; offers excuses, rationalizes (past part. *bisamplet*) [OF]

bi-seche(n) (v.) to BESEECH, beg; to ask, supplicate; seek after, search for (imper. sing. *bisech*; imper. pl. *bisecheth*; pres. 3 pl. *bisecheth*; past pl. *bisohten*; past part. *bisoht*) [OE]

bi-semde (v., past sing.) SEEMED to be (in a certain state) [from ON]

bi-senchen (v.) to SINK, plunge (something into fire or water), submerge (past sing. *bisencte*) [OE]

bi-seo(n) (v.) to consider; to SEE to, look after; to provide, arrange (imper. pl. *biseoth*) [OE]

bi-set (v., past part.) surrounded; besieged, BESET [OE]

bisi (adj.) BUSY, occupied; diligent (pl. *bisie*; compar. *bisgre*) [OE]

bisiliche (adv.) BUSILY; carefully, attentively

bisischipe (n.) BUSINESS, activity

bismere (n.) ridicule, mockery; scorn, contempt; *lahhen to bismere* = laugh to scorn [OE]

bi-smuddet (adj. & v., past part.) BESMUTTED, dirty, stained [from OE]

bi-smulret (adj. & v., past part.) besmeared, beslobbered, filthy [see *smirles* (n.)]

bi-socne (n.) request, entreaty [from OE]

bi-sperret (v., past part.) shut in, locked up [see *sperreth* (v.)]

bi-spit (v., pres. 3 sing.) SPITS on [OE]

bi-spottith (v., pres. pl.) sullies, BESPOTS, splatters [Ger., though precise origin is obscure]

bist (v., pres. 2 sing.) see *beon* (v.)

bi-steathet (v., past part.) placed; beset (by enemies), hard pressed [from ON]

bi-steoken (v.) to confine, shut up; to lock, bar [from ME *steken* "bar, lock"; see *steoke* (v.)]

bi-stonden (v., past part.) harassed, attacked; surrounded [OE]

bi-swiken (v.) to deceive, cheat, betray (pres. subj. sing. *biswike*; pres. 3 sing. *biswiketh*) [OE]

bit (v., pres. 3 sing.) see *bidden* (v.)

bi-tacnin (v.) to BETOKEN, symbolize; mean (pres. subj. sing. *bitacni*; pres. 3 sing. *bitacneth*; pres. pl. *bitacnith*; past sing. *bitacnede*; past part. *bitacnet, bitacned*) [OE; see *tacne* (n.)]

bi-tacnunge (n.) symbol, sign; meaning, significance; BETOKENING

bi-teachen (v.) to hand over, deliver; entrust, commit (past part. *bitaht*) [OE]

bi-tellunge (n.) excuse, justification [from OE]

biten (v.) to BITE; taste, drink (a liquid) (pres. 3 sing. *biteth*; pres. pl. *biteth*; pres. part. *bitinde*) [OE]

bi-teon (v.) to bestow, spend, give away; (past part. as adj.) *uvele bitohe* = misspent, wasted (pres. 1 sing. *biteo*; past part. *bitohe*) [OE]

bith (v., pres. 3 sing.) see *beon* (v.)

bi-thencheth (v., pres. 3 sing.) considers, THINKS about; remembers (past subj. sing. *bithohte*; pres. pl. *bithencheth*; past part. *bithoht*) [OE]

bi-thoht(e) (v., past sing., past part.) see *bithencheth* (v.)

bi-tiden (v.) to happen, befall, BETIDE [OE]

bi-timeth (v., pres. 3 sing.) happens, comes about [from OE]

bi-tohe (v., past part.) see *bi-teon* (v.)

bi-trept (v., past part.) TRAPPED, ensnared [OE]

bi-truileth (v., pres. 3 sing.) dupes, tricks, deceives [from OF, see *truiles* (n.)]

bitter, bittre (adj.) BITTER; sour, morose; harsh, severe (gen. sing. *bittres*; compar. *bittrure*) [OE]

bitterliche (adv.) BITTERLY; harshly, sharply (compar. *bitterluker*) [OE]

bittrin (v.) to EMBITTER, make bitter [OE]

bittrure (adv., compar.) BITTERER [OE]

bi-tuhe(n), bi-tuhhen (prep.) between, among [from OE]

bi-tunen (v.) to enclose, confine, shut in; entomb (past sing. *bitunde*; past part. *bitund(e)*) [OE]

bi-turn (v., imper. sing.) to TURN, direct towards; (of colors) to change (past part. *biturnd*) [OE]

bi-twe(o)nen (prep.) BETWEEN, among, with; (adv.) between, in the midst [OE]

bivoren-hand (adv.) BEFOREHAND, ahead, in advance, in anticipation

bi-wenden (v.) to turn oneself around (reflex.) (pres. 3 sing. *biwent*) [OE]

bi-wepe(n) (v.) to BEWEEP, cry for (imper. pl. *biwepen*; past sing. *biweop*) [OE]

bi-winneth (v., pres. pl.) obtain, gain, WIN (past sing. *biwon*) [from OE]

bi-wrabbet (v., past part.) wrapped, enveloped [prob. Ger., specific origin obscure]

bi-wrencheth (v., pres. 3 sing.) cheats, tricks [OE]

bi-wrixlet (v., past part.) changed, transformed [from OE]

bi-wunnen (v., past part.) overcome, defeated [OE]

bi-yeote(n) (v.) to acquire, GET, obtain (by effort); receive (pres. 3 sing. *biyeoteth, biyet*; past sing. *biyet*; past part. *biyete*; inflected inf. *to biyeotene*) [OE]

bi-yete (n.) acquisition, property, possession; gain, profit, benefit, advantage; spoils, booty; prey [see *bi-yeoten* (v.)]

bi-yulet (v., past part.) deceived, bewitched [see *yulunges* (n.)]

bla (adj.) black, dark; pale, gray, ashen [ON]

blac, blake (adj.) BLACK; (as n.) blackness [OE]

blameth (v., pres. 3 sing.) BLAMES (past part. *i-blamet*) [OF]

bla-mon (n.) black-MAN, African, Moor [see *bla* (adj.)]

blawen (v.) to BLOW (pres. subj. sing. *blawe*; pres. 3 sing. *blaweth*) [OE]

blawunge (n.) BLOWING [see *blawen* (v.)]

bleachen (v.) to whiten, clean, BLEACH (past part. *i-bleachet*) [OE]

bleas (n.) a blowing, gust; blowing (of horns), BLAST [OE]

blease (n.) torch, firebrand (pl. *bleasen*) [OE; ModE *blaze*]

bleasie (v., pres. subj. sing.) BLAZE, burst out in flame [see *blease* (n.)]

bleddest (v., past 2 sing.) BLED (past sing. *bledde*; past pl. *bledden*) [OE]

bleddre (n.) BLADDER, a bag made from an animal bladder [OE]

blenchen (v.) to flinch, twitch, start; swerve aside [OE *blencan*]

blenden (v.) to BLEND, mix, stir [OE *blendian*]

blent (v., pres. 3 sing.) BLINDS, bedazzles; confuses, misleads; grows (spiritually) blind (a reduced form of *blendeth*) [OE *blendan*]

blescin (v.) to BLESS, consecrate; make the sign of the cross (imper. sing. *blesce*; imper. pl. *blescith*; pres. pl. *blescith*; past sing. *blescede*; past part. *i-blescet*) [OE]

blikien (v.) to shine [OE]

blind(e) (adj.) BLIND [OE]

blind-feallunge (n.) a BLINDFOLDING [see *blint-fealli* (v.)]

blint-fealli (v., pres. subj. sing.) BLINDFOLD (someone) (past sing. *blindfeallede*; past part. *i-blintfeallet*) [from OE]

blisful(e) (adj.) happy, BLISSFUL; blessed, glorified [OE]

blisfulliche (adv.) joyously, happily BLISSFULLY

blisse (n.) BLISS, joy, happiness (pl. *blissen*, *blisses*) [OE]

blissin (v.) to rejoice, be happy (reflex.); to gladden, make happy (imper. pl. *blissith*; pres. 1 sing. *blissi*; past part. *i-blisset*) [OE]

blithe (adj.) happy, joyful, BLITHE; (adv.) happily, joyfully [OE]

blitheliche, bluthelich (adv.) BLITHELY, joyfully, happily [OE]

blod(e) (n.) BLOOD (gen. sing. *blodes*) [OE]

blod-binde (n.) bandage (for stopping BLOOD) [from OE]

blodi (adj.) BLOODY [OE]

blod-leten(e) (adj. & v., past part.) BLOODLET (person), a person who has had blood let [from OE]

blod-letunge (n.) BLOODLETTING, phlebotomy, a medical procedure

blostmen (n. pl.) BLOSSOMS [OE]

bloweth (v., pres. pl.) to bloom, blossom [OE]

boc (n.) BOOK (pl. *bokes*) [OE]

bode (n.) command, behest; news, messages (pl. *boden*) [OE *bod*]

bodeth (v., pres. 3 sing.) preaches; proclaims, announces; foretells, prophesies (pres. pl. *bodieth*) [OE *bodian*]

boh (n.) BOUGH, branch (pl. *bohes*) [OE]

bohte(n) (v., past) see *buggen* (v.)

boistes, buistes (n. pl.) jars, boxes, or chests (for medicines or cosmetics) [OF]

boke(s) (n.) see *boc* (n.)

bolheth (v., pres. 3 sing.) swells, puffs up (with air or pride); (past part. as adj.) *i-bollen* = swollen, puffed up, inflated [OE]

bollen (adj. & v., past part.) swollen (with pride), puffed up, inflated [see *bolheth* (v.)]

bone (n. 1) prayer; request (pl. *bonen*) [ON; ModE *boon*] (n. 2) slayer, murderer, BANE [OE]

bord (n.) BOARD, plank; (dining) table, (fig.) meals; ship, side of a ship [OE]

borhi (n., pres. subj. sing.) BORROW (pres. subj. pl. *borhin*) [OE]

bosum (n.) BOSOM, chest, embrace; (fig.) heart, inward thoughts [OE]

bote (n.) good, benefit; remedy, cure; repentance, restitution (pl. *boten*) [OE]

botte (n.) cudgel; OED: "The thicker end of anything, esp. a tool or weapon" [OE *bott*, related to OE *batt* "bat, cudgel"]

brad(e) (adj.) BROAD, wide [OE]

bread, brede (n.) BREAD (gen. sing. *breades*) [OE]

breade (n.) breadth, extent [OE; see *brad* (adj.)]

breath (n.) BREATH; evil, stinking breath, halitosis; odor, smell, stench [OE]

brech (n.) BREECHES, short trousers, covering the body from the lower waist to the knee [OE]

breden (v.) to BREED, engender; to cherish, foster, nourish (pres. 3 sing. *bret* [= *bredeth*]; past sing. *bredde*) [OE]

breide(n) (v.) to dart, dash, jump; twist, turn, draw; brandish; seize, grasp, attack; fling, toss; weave, BRAID (imper. sing. *breid*; pres. 3 sing. *breideth, breid*; past sing. *breid*) [OE]

breoke(n) (v.) to BREAK, tear; crush, defeat; break into, open; violate; escape (imper. sing. *breoke*; past subj. pl. *breken*; pres. 3 sing. *breketh, breoketh*; past sing. *brec*; past pl. *breken*; pres. part. *breokinde*; past part. *i-broke, i-broken, i-brokene*) [OE *brecan*]

breord (n.) brim, brink, margin [OE *brerd* "margin"]

breost-wunde (n.) chest WOUND [from OE]

breres (n. pl.) BRIARS, thorns; bramble-bushes [OE]

bres (n.) BRASS [OE]

bret (v., pres. 3 sing.) see *breden* (v.)

brid (n.) BIRD of any kind; young of a bird, fledgling, nestling, chick (this meaning current throughout ME period) (pl. *briddes*) [OE]

bridli (v., pres. subj. sing.) BRIDLE, restrain (pres. 3 sing. *bridleth*; past part. *i-bridlet*) [OE]

briht(e) (adj.) BRIGHT (compar. *brihtre*) [OE]

brihte (adv.) BRIGHTLY, brilliantly; (see, understand) clearly, distinctly; loudly (compar. *brihtluker*) [OE]

brihtin (v.) to BRIGHTEN make bright; illuminate, explain (pres. 3 sing. *brihteth*) [OE]

bringe(n) (v.) to BRING; lead, convey; carry (pres. 3 sing. *bringeth*; pres. pl. *bringeth*; past sing. *brohte*; past pl. *brohten*; past part. *i-broht*) [OE]

broche (n.) BROOCH, ornamental clasp or pin [OF]

brokes (n.1 pl.) streams, torrents; tributaries; (fig.) branches, offshoots [OE; see ModE *brook*]; (n. 2 pl.) afflictions, miseries [OE *broc* "affliction"]

brondes (n. pl.) BRANDS, fires, flames; OED: "a piece of wood that is or has been burning on the hearth" [OE]

brother (n.) BROTHER, fellow member of an order; *ane brethren* = a group, collection of brothers (obj. sing. *brether*; pl. *brethren*) [OE]

bruche (n.) BREACH, rift, fracture; violation, breaking (of a command) (pl. *bruchen*) [OE; related to *breoken* (v.)]

bruchel(e) (adj.) easily broken, brittle; transitory, vain; morally weak (compar. *bruchelure*) [from OE]

brud (n.) BRIDE [OE]

brugge (n.) BRIDGE [OE]

bruhen (n. pl.) BROWS, eyebrows [OE]

bruken (v.) to enjoy, take one's pleasure in; to possess, get, take, keep; employ, use; consume, eat or drink [OE; see ModE *to brook*]

brune (n.) fire, flame; BURNING heat, burning; *o brune* = aflame, burning [OE]

brunie (n.) BYRNIE, heavy body-armor, a coat of mail [ON]

buc (n.) belly; trunk (of the body); corpse, body [OE]

bucke (n.) BUCK, the male of a variety of animals [OE]

buffet (n.) BUFFET, blow (pl. *buffez*) [OF]

buffeteden (v., past 3 pl.) BUFFETED, pummeled [OF]

buggen (v.) to BUY, pay for; (fig.) pay for (in suffering) (pres. subj. sing. *bugge*; pres. 3 sing. *buth*, *buggeth*; pres. pl. *buggeth*; past sing. *bohte*; past pl. *bohten*; past part. *i-boht*) [OE]

buhen (v.) to BOW, bend; kneel; be submissive; submit to, obey (imper. sing. *buh*; imper. pl. *buhen*; pres. 3 sing. *buheth*; past sing. *beah*; pres. part. *buhinde*) [OE]

buhsum (adj.) pliant; obedient [from *buhen* (v.) + OE suffix *-sum*; ModE *buxom*]

buistes (n. pl.) see *boistes* (n. pl.)

bulten (v.) to rebound, BOLT back, recoil; reverberate (pres. 3 sing. *bulteth*) [from OE]

bultunge (n.) recoil, rebounding; reverberation

bune (n.) a purchase, buying [OE]

bunkin (v.) to beat, pound, bonk [prob. imitative; see OF *bonge*]

bur (n.) BOWER, chamber, bedroom [OE]

burde (n.) birth [from OE]

burgeise (n.) BURGESS, a full (and prosperous) citizen of a borough; an official of a borough [OF]

burgurs (n. pl.) BURGLARS, pillagers [OF]

burh (n.) castle, stronghold; tower; city, town (pl. *burhes*) [OE; see ModE *burg*]

burhen (v.) to save, rescue [OE; see *i-borhen* (v.)]

burh-men (n. pl.) citizens, town-men [from OE]

burinesse (n.) BURIAL place; a burying [OE]

burtherne (n.) BURDEN; anything that is hard to endure; suffering, penance; feudal obligation; importance, significance [OE]

bute(n) (conj.) except (that), unless, only; (prep.) except; (adv.) *bute the an, buten an* = only the one [OE]

buth (v., pres. 3 sing.) see *buggen* (v.)

buve(n) (prep. & adv.) ABOVE [from OE]

cader (n.) cradle [MWelsh *cader* "cradle"; compare F. *cadre* "frame"]

cage (n.) CAGE [OF]

cahte (v., past sing.) see *kecchen* (v.)

cakele (adj. & n.) CACKLING, chattering; cackler, chatterer [see *cakelin* (v.)]

cakelin (v.) to CACKLE, to cluck like a laying hen or other bird (pres. 3 sing.

cakeleth; pres. part. *cakelinde*; past part. *i-cakelet*) [imitative, prob. from Ger.]

cald(e) (adj.) COLD [OE]

calices (n. pl.) see *chaliz* (n.)

cancre (n.) spreading sore, ulcer, CANKER [ONF]

cang (n.) fool (gen. sing. *canges*) [prob. ON; see *cang* (adj.)]

cang, chang (adj.) foolish; lewd, wicked, lustful [prob. ON, see *kangin-yrði* "jeering words," perhaps via OF (note *c/ch* interchange)]

cangen (v.) to fool, trick; make a fool of

cangliche (adv.) foolishly; lewdly, wickedly

cangschipe (n.) foolishness, stupidity

cangun (n.) fool; (or, perhaps) changeling, a fickle or inconstant person [either from *cang* (n.) or OF *cangoun* "changeling"]

canonial (adj.) CANONICAL, in the biblical canon [OF]

cape (n.) COPE, an ecclesiastical garment with a hood [ONF]

capitale (adj.) of the head [OF]

cappen (n. pl.) CAPS, head-coverings [OE]

carien (v.) to be concerned, CARE about; be troubled, anxious about, to worry about [OE]

carles (adj.) free from CARE, worry; (hence) safe [from OE; see ModE *careless*]

carnel (n.) battlement, CRENELATION; OED: "One of the open spaces or indentations alternating with the merlons or cops of an embattled parapet, used for shooting or launching projectiles upon the enemy" (pl. *carneus*) [ONF]

castel (n.) fort, fortification; CASTLE (pl. *castles*) [ONF]

cave, kave (adj.) bold, eager, courageous; quick; impudent [OE]

celer (n.) pantry, storeroom, CELLAR [OF]

celles (n. pl.) store-rooms, store-closets [OF, from Lat.]

chaf(f)le (n.) jabber, gossip, jawing [OE *ceafl* "the jaw"]

chaffere (n.) dealing, buying and selling, trading; bargain [*OE; related to *chap* (n.) + *fearen* (v.)]

chafleth (v., pres. 3 sing.) chatters, jabbers, jaws (pres. pl. *chafflith*) [see *chaffle* (n.)]

chaflunge (n.) chattering, jabbering, jawing

chalengest (v., pres. 2 sing.) accuse, arraign; find fault with, CHALLENGE (past part. *i-calenget*) [OF]

chaliz (n.) drinking cup, goblet; CHALICE, cup from which sacramental wine is served in the Eucharist (pl. *calices*) [OF, from Lat.]

chamberleng (n.) CHAMBERLAIN [OF]

chambre (n.) CHAMBER, (private) room [OF]

champiun (n.) fighter, combatant; CHAMPION (pl. *champiuns*) [OF]

chang (adj.) see *cang* (adj.)

change (n.) EXCHANGE, trade [OF]

changin (v.) to CHANGE, alter (imper. pl. *changeth*; pres. 3 sing. *changeth*; past part. *i-changet*) [OF]

changunge (n.) CHANGING, alteration

chap (n.) bargain, trade; price [OE; ModE *cheap*]

chapeth (v.) bargains (for); trades, buys (past sing. *chapede*) [OE]

chapitres (n. pl.) sections or divisions of a book; CHAPTERS [OF]

chap-mon (n.) merchant, trader, dealer; bargainer; buyer, customer [see *chap* (n.)]

charge (n.) cargo, freight, action of loading; burden; encumbrance; hardship, harm, trouble; duty, responsibility; importance [OF]

charoines (n. pl.) carcasses, corpses, CARRIONS [OF]

chartres (n. pl.) legal documents or deeds [OF]

chast (n.) fighting, strife; quarreling, bickering, dispute [OE]

chaste (adj.) CHASTE, pure [OF]

chastete (n.) CHASTITY [OF]

chastiement (n.) CHASTISEMENT, reprimand [OF]

chastien (v.) to CHASTISE; to correct, reprove (imper. pl. *chastie*) [OF]

chearitable (adj.) loving, CHARITABLE [OF]

chearite (n.) CHARITY, love [OF]

chearre (n.) time, occasion [OE]

chef (n.) CHAFF [OE]

cheke (n.) CHEEK (pl. *cheken*) [OE]

cheorl (n.) peasant, serf [OE]

cheosen (v.) to CHOOSE (imper. sing. *cheos*; imper. pl. *cheose*; pres. 3 sing. *cheoseth*; past part. *i-core, i-coren[e]*) [OE]

cheoweth (v., pres. 3 sing.) CHEWS [OE]

chepeth (v., pres. 3 sing.) see *chapeth* (v.)

chepilt (n.) business woman, woman merchant [see *chap* (n.) and *-ild* (suffix)]

chepinge (n.) trade marketing, bargaining, buying and selling; (a) market [see *chapeth* (v.)]

chere (n.) human face; facial expression, grimace; outward appearance, show of emotion; bearing, manner, mood; friendliness, hospitality; *maken (someone) chere* = to welcome, entertain

(someone), treat (someone) well (pl. *cheres*) [OF; ModE *cheer*]

cherte (n.) dearness, fondness, cherishing [OF; related to *chearite* (n.)]

cherubines (n., gen. sing.) CHERUBIM'S, the angel's (sword) [from Lat.]

chideth (v., pres. 3 sing.) CHIDES, scolds [OE]

chidildes (n. pl.) CHIDING, quarrelsome women [see *chideth* (v.) and *-ild* (suffix)]

childene (adj.) CHILDISH [from OE]

childhad(e) (n.) CHILDHOOD [OE]

chirch(e) (n.) CHURCH [OE]

chirche-thurl (n.) CHURCH-window; the window in an anchorhold facing inward to the church's altar

chirmin (v.) to chirp, warble, CHIRM (pres. 3 sing. *chirmeth*) [OE]

chiterin (v.) to chatter, twitter (imper. pl. *chiterith*; pres. 3 sing. *chitereth*; pres. part. *chiterinde*) [imitative]

chulle (v.) see *wullen* (v.)

cite (n.) CITY [OF]

clane (adv.) see *clene* (adv.)

clath (n.) CLOTH; clothing (pl. *clathes*) [OE]

clathinde (v., pres. part.) CLOTHING, dressing [OE]

clauses (n. pl.) (short) sentences, phrases [OF]

cleane (adj.) pure, CLEAN, chaste [OE]

cleanliche (adv.) completely, thoroughly, CLEANLY [OE]

cleannesse (n.) purity, chastity [OE]

cleansin (v.) to CLEANSE, clean; purify (imper. sing. *clense*; pres. 3 sing. *cleanseth, clenseth*; pres. pl. *cleansith*; pres. part. *cleansing*) [OE]

cleap(pe) (n.) CLAP, stroke; CLAPPER, OED: "The contrivance in a mill for striking or shaking the hopper so as to make the grain move down to the mill-stones"; (fig.) the tongue; *ed an cleap* = at one stroke, at once [from OE]

clearc (n.) CLERK, cleric, scholar, student (pl. *clearkes*) [OE or OF, from Lat.]

cleavers (n. pl.) claws [OE]

cleches (n. pl.) clutches [from OE]

clene (adv.) CLEANLY; clean, completely [OE]

cleopien (v.) to speak, call (for), shout; to name, give a name, call; to greet; invite (imper. sing. *cleope*; pres. subj. sing. *cleopie*; pres. 3 sing. *cleopeth*; pres. pl. *cleopieth*; past sing. *cleopede*; past part. *i-cleopet, i-cleopede*) [OE]

clergesse (n.) a female scholar, a learned woman; female member of a religious order [OF, fem. form of *clerc*; see *clearc* (n.)]

climben (v.) to CLIMB (pres. 3 sing. *climbeth*; pres. 1, 3 pl. *climben*; past sing. *clomb*; past pl. *clumben*; past part. *i-clumben*) [OE]

cloistre (n.) CLOISTER, convent [OF]

clokes (n. pl.) claws, CLUTCHES; (fig.) control [*OE]

clomb, clumben (v.) see *climben* (v.)

clot (n.) lump, CLOD (of earth); (fig.) the human body [OE]

clowes de gilofre (n. pl.) CLOVE-GILLY flower, the spice clove [OF *clou de gilofre*]

cluppen (v.) to CLIP, hug, embrace; envelop, surround (pres. 3 sing. *cluppeth*) [OE]

cluppunge (n.) embracing, embrace, clasping (pl. *cluppunges*)

clut (n.) a piece of cloth used as a patch or rag (pl. *clutes*) [OE; ModE *clout*]

cluti (v., pres. subj. sing.) patch up, add (to), embellish (with) [see *clut* (n.)]

cnawen (v.) to KNOW, understand, have (full) knowledge of (pres. 2 sing. *cnawest*; pres. 3 sing. *cnaweth*; pres. pl. *cnawen*) [OE]

cnawle(a)chunge (n.) KNOWLEDGE, understanding, recognition [from OE]

cnawunge (n.) a KNOWING, understanding, recognition

cneave (n.) boy; servant or menial [OE; see ModE *knave*, Ger. *knabe* "boy"]

cneo (n.) KNEE (pl. *cneon*) [OE]

cneolin (v.) to KNEEL (imper. pl. *cneolith*; pres. part. *cneolinde*) [OE]

cneolunges (n.) KNEELINGS

cnif (n.) KNIFE (pl. *cnives*) [OE]

cnif-warpere (n.) KNIFE thrower [see *cnif* (n.) and *warpen* (v.)]

cniht (n.) KNIGHT (pl. *cnihtes*) [OE]

cnihtschipe (n.) KNIGHTLY behavior; chivalry, valor

cnost (n.) swelling, lump, tumor [*OE]

cnut (v., pres. 3 sing. [= *cnutteth*]) KNOTS, puts a knot in [OE]

cogitatiun (n.) COGITATION, consideration, thinking (pl. *cogitatiuns*) [OF]

cointe (adj.) clever, wise, prudent; crafty, wily, cunning; famous, notorious; fashionable; proud, vain [OF; ModE *quaint*]

cokes (n., gen. sing.) COOK'S [OE]

collecte (n.) a COLLECT, a short liturgical prayer [OF, from late Lat.]

com, comen (v., past) see *cumen* (v.)

commendaciun (n.) COMMENDATION; OED: "an office originally ending with the prayer *Tibi, Domine, commendamus* [to you, Lord, we commit (their spirits)], in which the souls of the dead were commended to God; said before their burial, and in anniversary or comme- morative services" [OF, from Lat.]

complie (n.) COMPLINE, the last liturgical hour of the day [OF]

con (v., pres. 1, 3 sing.) see *cunnen* (v.)

Condelmeasse (n.) CANDLEMAS (Feb- ruary 2); OED: "The feast of the puri- fication of the Virgin Mary (or present- ation of Christ in the Temple) celebrated with a great display of candles"[OE]

confort, cunfort (n.) COMFORT; strengthening, encouragement (pl. *cunforz*) [OF]

conseiler (n.) COUNSELOR, adviser [OF]

consens (n.) consent, permission [OF]

consenti (v.) to CONSENT, agree [OF]

const (v., pres. 2 sing.) see *cunnen* (v.)

contenemenz (n.) behavior [OF]

continuelement (adv.) CONTINUALLY [OF]

contumace (n.) CONTUMACY, stubbornness, rebelliousness [OF]

cop (n.) summit, crown, top [OE; see Ger. *kopf* "head"]

cop, cape (n.) CAPE, cloak; habit (of a monk or friar), COPE [ON or Lat.]

corbin (n.) a raven, CORBIE [OF]

cornes (n. pl.) grains [OE]

cos (n.) KISS (pl. *cosses*) [OE]

costnede (v., past sing.) COST, was expensive or costly [OF]

cote (n.) COTE, cottage, hovel [OE]

countenance (n.) bearing, behavior; appearance, facial expression; face [OF]

cover (adj.) villainous, vile [OF, from late Lat. *co-libertus* "freeman, serf"]

coverschipe (n.) villainy, treachery [OF + OE]

cradel (n.) CRADLE [OE]

cravant (adj.) defeated, vanquished; *yeien cravant* = to cry "(I am) defeated!," "I give up!"; to surrender [from OF; see Diensberg (1978), pp. 80–81]

craven (v.) to ask for earnestly, beg for, CRAVE (something) (past part. *i-cravet*) [OE]

crecche (n.) manger [OF]

crenge (v.) to strut, swagger; condescend; bend haughtily, *crenge with swire* = to arch the neck (proudly) (pres. subj. sing. *crenge*) [*OE; related to ModE *cringe*]

creoiz (n.) CROSS [OF]

creop (v., imper. sing.) CREEP, crawl (imper. pl. *creopen*) [OE]

criblin (v.) to make fine lace or embroidery (whose intricate design resembles the pattern of holes in a sieve) [from OF *crible* "sieve"]

crie(th) (v., imper. pl.) CRY, weep (pres. subj. sing. *crie*; past sing. *criede*) [OF]

Cristene (n. pl.) CHRISTIANS

crohhe (n.) pot, CROCK, jug [OE]

crokede (adj.) false, treacherous, CROOKED [OE]

crokes (n.) CROOKED behaviors, tricks, deceptions [ON];(n. pl.) clutches, claws [*OE, perhaps ON]

crome (n.) CRUMB, scrap (pl. *cromen*) [OE]

croppeth (v., pres. 3 sing.) CROPS, trims [from OE]

cros (n.) CROSS (pl. *crosses*) [ON form; see OF derived *creoiz* (n.)]

crossith (n., imper. pl.) CROSS, make the sign of the cross [from *cros* (n.)]

cruchen (v.) to make the sign of the cross; cross (oneself) (past part. *i-cruchet*) [OE blended with OF]

cruelte (n.) CRUELTY [OF]

crune (n.) CROWN; (fig.) head; highest, topmost person (pl. *crunen*) [AN]

crunen (v.) to CROWN (pres. 3 sing. *cruneth*; past part. *i-crunet*) [AN]

crununge (n.) CROWNING

cubbel (n.) hobble, a block of wood or clog used to hobble livestock [*OE]

cuchene (n.) KITCHEN [OE]

cudde (v., past sing.) see *cuthen* (v.)

cuggel (n.) CUDGEL [OE]

cul (n.) a blow, stroke [see *culle* (v.)]

culchen (v.) see *gulchen* (v.)

culle (v., pres. subj. sing.) strike, hit; to clear out, empty (a pot) [OE; see ModE *kill*]

culvert (adj.) see *cover* (adj.)

culvre (n.) dove (gen. sing. *culvres*) [OE *culfre* from Lat. *columba*]

cume (n.) COMING, arrival [OE]

cumen (v.) to COME; *kimeth up* = arises, develops (imper. sing. *cum*; imper. pl. *cumeth*; pres. subj. sing. *cume*; pres. 3 sing./pl. *cumeth, kimeth*; pres. pl. *cumen*; past sing. *com, come*; past pl. *comen*; pres. part. *cuminde*; past part. *i-cumen*) [OE]

cumplie (n.) see *complie* (n.)

cun(ne) (n.) KIN, race, family; pedigree; kind, sort (gen. sing. *cunnes*; pl. *cunnes, cunes*) [OE]

cunde (n.) nature; characteristic(s), temperament; instincts; class of creatures; tribe, family, clan; parentage, lineage [OE]

cundel (n.) brood, litter; offspring, young of any animal (pl. *cundles*) [from OE]

cundelich(e) (adj.) natural, innate; (adv.) naturally, innately, by nature [OE]

cundleth (v. 1, pres. 3 sing./pl.) gives birth to, breeds, brings forth [see *cundel* (n.)]; (v. 2, pres. 3 sing.) KINDLES, ignites; inflames, excites [ON]

cunfort, cunforz (n.) see *confort* (n.)

cunnen (v.) CAN, be able, capable; to have mastery, skill; to know, know how to do; *connen thank* = to be grateful (imper. pl. *cunneth*; pres. subj. sing. *kunne*; pres. 1, 3 sing. *con*; past sing. *cuthe*; past pl. *cuthen*) [OE]

cunnes-mon (n.) KINSMAN, relative

cun-redden (n.) family, KINDRED, relative(s); kinship, intimacy (of a household or family) (error for *cuth-reden*? — see Textual Note to 3.558–59) [late OE]

cunsail (n.) COUNSEL, advice; secret, confidence [OF]

cunsense (n.) CONSENT [OF]

cuple (n.) COUPLE, pair; combination [OF]

cupleth (v., pres. 3 sing.) COUPLES, links, joins (past part. *i-cuplet*) [OF]

cur(re) (n.) a CUR, OED: "a worthless, low-bred, or snappish dog"; (perhaps) a cowardly dog who only growls but does not bite (?); (adj.) currish, craven [related to ON *kurra* "to snarl"]

curnles (n. pl.) KERNELS [OE]

cursild (n. pl.) woman given to cursing [see *-ild* (suffix)] [from OE]

curt, curz (n.) COURT [OF]

curteisie (n.) COURTESY; generosity, nobility [OF]

curtel (n.) tunic, coat, KIRTLE, gown (pl. *curtles*) [OE *cyrtel* "tunic"]

cussen (v.) to KISS (pres. subj. sing. *cusse*; pres. subj. pl. *cussen*; pres. 3 sing. *cusseth*; past sing. *custe*; pres. part. *cussinde*) [OE]

custe (v., past sing.) see *cussen* (v.)

cuth(e) (adj.) known, familiar; well-known, famous [OE]

cuthe(n) (v., past) see *cunnen* (v.)

cuthen (v.) to make known, reveal; show, demonstrate (imper. sing. *cuth*; pres. 2 sing. *cuthest*; past 1, 3 sing. *cudde*; past part. *i-cud, i-cuththet*) [OE]

cuth-mon (n.) acquaintance, friend [OE; see *cuth* (adj.)]

cuth-redden (n.) acquaintance, familiarity [*cuth* (adj.) + OE *ræden* "state"]

cuththe (n.) knowledge, acquaintance; (collective) acquaintances, friends [OE; ModE *kith*]

cuththunge (n.) friendship, intimacy; acquaintance [see *cuth* (adj.)]

cuvel (n.) COWL, hooded garment [OE *cufle*, from Lat.]

cuvent (n.) CONVENT, community (of monks, nuns, or friars) [AF]

cuvertur (n.) blanket, coverlet [OF]

cwaer (n.) a small book (usually unbound); a gathering of sheets of parchment (for a book) [OF; ModE *quire*]

cwakien (v.) to QUAKE, tremble (with fear) [OE]

cwalm-hus (n.) house of death [from OE]

cwalm-stowe (n.) place of execution; (lit.) "death-place" [OE]

cweade (adv.) wickedly, evilly [see OE *cwead* "filth"]

cwe(a)dschipe (n.) wickedness, wicked deed (pl. *cweadschipes*)

cweise (n.) boil, sore [ON]

cweme(n) (v.) to please, gratify (pres. 3 sing. *cwemeth*) [OE]

cwen (n.) QUEEN [OE]

cwenchen (v.) to QUENCH, extinguish, put out (a fire); to be extinguished, go out; satisfy, slake (imper. sing. *cwench*; pres. 3 sing. *cwencheth*; past part. *i-cwenct*) [OE]

cwene (n.) lowborn woman, QUEAN; old woman, crone; harlot [OE]

cweth (v., past sing.) spoke [OE; see *quoth* (v.), the usual form]

cwic, cwike (adj.) alive; lively, QUICK (gen. sing. *cwikes*; compar. *cwikcre*) [OE; see ModE phrase *the quick and the dead*]

cwich (v., tense uncertain) flinch(ed), tremble(d), QUAKED [OE]

cwicliche (adv.) in a lively way, vigorously; rapidly, QUICKLY (compar. *cwicluker*) [OE]

cwicnesse (n.) vitality, life, quality of being alive

cwiddeth (v., pres. 3 sing.) says [OE]

cwide (n.) legacy, inheritance; promise [OE]

cwitance (n.) freeing, release [OF]

cwite (adj.) free, clear; released, excused [OF]

cwitin (v.) to pay, repay, settle (a debt) [OF]

cyrograffes (n. pl.) (formal) documents; deeds [OF, from Greek *chirograph* "hand-written"]

dahes (n. pl.) see *dei* (n.)

dahunge (n.) dawn, DAWNING, daybreak [OE]

dale (n.) part, subdivision, branch; share, (one's due) portion; *muche deale* = a great deal (adv.) (pl. *dalen*) [OE; see ModE *dole*, Ger. *teil* "part"]

dame (n.) lady (of rank), a professed nun; a mother [OF]

dameiseles (n., gen. sing.) young lady's, of a young, unmarried lady (of rank) [OF]

danger (n.) dominion, subjugation, domineering; power (of a master); power to injure; reluctance, grudging, standoffishness; bad mood, grumpiness; arrogance [OF]

dangerus (adj.) difficult, arrogant, severe; reluctant, standoffish

dayes (n. pl.) see *dei* (n.)

dead(e) (adj.) DEAD; unfeeling, numb (compar. *deaddre*) [OE]

dead-bote (n.) amends for an evil DEED; penance, repentance; *don deadbote* = to do penance [OE; see *dede* (n.) + *bote* (n.)]

deade (adj.) DEAD, not living [OE]

deadlich(e) (adv.) DEADLY, mortal [OE]

deadlicnesse (n.) DEADLINESS; mortality

deal (n.) see *dale* (n.)

deale (interj.) see *dele* (interj.)

deale(n) (v.) to separate, distinguish; divide, cut up; give away, DEAL or DOLE out, distribute; share, participate in (pres. 1 sing./pl. *deale*; pres. 3 sing. *dealeth*; past sing. *dealde*; past part. *i-dealet*) [OE; see Ger. *teilen* "to divide"]

dealen (n. pl.) DALES, valleys [OE]

dear (v.) see *durren* (v.)

dearne (adj.) secret, hidden [OE]

dearnliche (adv.) in a hidden, unnoticed way; privately, secretly; inwardly, deeply (compar. *dearnluker*) [OE]

death-uvel (n.) mortal illness, deadly disease

deatte (n.) DEBT (pl. *deattes*) [OF]

deattur (n.) DEBTOR, a person in debt [OF]

deawes (n., gen. sing.) DEW'S [OE]

deboneire (adj.) meek, gentle; gracious, courteous, well-behaved [OF, from the phrase *de bonne aire* "of good disposition"]

deboneirte (n.) graciousness, gentleness, courteousness [OF]

deciple (n.) DISCIPLE, pupil (pl. *deciples, desciples*) [OF]

dede (n.) DEED, action (pl. *deden*) [OE]

degre (n.) step, a support to kneel on during prayers; (fig.) stage (in a process), step (pl. *degrez*) [OF, from Lat. *de-* "down" + *gradus* "step"]

deh (v.) see *duhen* (v.)

dehtren (n. pl.) see *dohter* (n.)

dei (n.) DAY; *from deie to deie* = from day to day (gen. sing. *deies*; obj. sing. *deie*; pl. *dahes, dayes*) [OE]

deien (v.) to DIE (pres. 3 sing. *deieth*; past sing. *deide*; past pl. *deiden*) [OE]

dei-hwamliche (adj.) DAILY [OE]

dele (interj.) what! (an expression of surprise); Look! See! (used to call attention to something) [origin obscure]

delices (n. pl.) (with sing. meaning) joy, delight, pleasure; sensual pleasure, lust [OF]

delitin (v.) to DELIGHT, take great pleasure in; to please, give pleasure [OF]

delivrede (v., past sing.) DELIVERED, set free (past part. *delifret*) [OF]

delven (v.) to dig; bury; to gouge by digging; (past part. as adj.) *dolven* = dug, hollowed out (pres. 3 sing. *delveth*; past subj. sing. *dulve*; past pl. *dulven*; past part. *[i-]dolven*) [OE]

delvunge (n.) digging, DELVING

deme (n.) judge [OE]

demen (v.) to judge; condemn (imper. sing. *dem*; imper. pl. *demeth*; pres. 1 pl. *demeth*; past sing. *demde*; past part. *i-demet*) [OE; ModE *deem*]

demeori (v., imper. pl.) delay, loiter, pause [OF; ModE *demur*]

deop(e) (adj.) DEEP; profound [OE]

deopeth (v., pres. 3 sing.) goes DEEP, penetrates [OE]

deopliche (adv.) DEEPLY, profoundly (compar. *deopluker*) [OE]

deoppre (adv., compar.) DEEPER

deor(e) (adj.) DEAR, beloved; expensive (compar. *deorre*) [OE]

deore (adv.) DEARLY; expensively, at a high price (compar. *deorre*)

deores (n., gen. sing.) animal's [OE; see Ger. *tier* "animal"]

deore-wurthe, deore-werthe (adj.) precious [from OE]

deore-wurthliche (adv.) honorably; precisely

deovel (n.) DEVIL (gen. sing. *deofles*; pl. *deoflen*) [OE]

depeint (v., past part.) depicted, PAINTED, portrayed [OF]

derf (n.) trouble, suffering; torture [OE]; (adj.) see *derve* (adj.)

derfliche (adv.) cruelly, painfully

derve (adj.) bold, daring; audacious, impatient; wicked; powerful; fierce, cruel; difficult, hard to do [OE, prob. influenced by ON]

derven (v.) to afflict, torment, torture; damage, hurt; *ben i-dervet* = to be distressed (pres. 3 sing./pl. *derveth*; past part. *i-dervet*) [OE]

descorde (n.) DISCORD [OF]

descriveth (v., pres. 3 sing.) DESCRIBES, records in writing [OF]

descumfit (v., past part.) defeated, routed, undone [OF]

deseosperance (n.) despair, wanhope [OF]

despuilen (v.) to DESPOIL, rob, strip (of clothes) (imper. sing. *despoile*; past sing. *despulede*; past part. *despuilet*) [OF]

dest, deth (v., pres. sing.) see *don* (v.)

destinctiun (n.) division, section (pl. *destinctiuns*) [OF]

destruet (v., past part.) ravaged, laid waste, DESTROYED [OF]

desturbin (v.) to DISTURB; destroy, deprive of [OF]

dettur (n.) see *deattur* (n.)

deu-le-set (interj.) God knows [OF *dieu le set* "God knows it"]

deveth (v., pres. 3 sing.) plunges or submerges (in water); DIVES [OE]

devot (adj.) DEVOUT, reverent [OF]

devotiun (n.) DEVOTION; feeling of (religious) awe, devotion [OF]

dich (n.) DITCH [OE]

diete (n.) DIET, food; way of life [OF]

diggin (v.) to DIG [OF]

dignete (n.) DIGNITY, nobility, worth [OF]

dimluker (adv., compar.) more faintly, indistinctly [OE]

discepline (n.) DISCIPLINE, correction; self-flagellation; OED: "in religious use, the mortification of the flesh by penance;

603

also, in a more general sense, a beating or other infliction . . . assumed to be salutary to the recipient" (pl. *disceplines*) [OF, from Lat.]

doddunge (n.) cutting, clipping, trimming (of the hair); tonsuring [see *i-doddet* (adj.)]

dogge (n.) DOG [OE]

dohter (n.) DAUGHTER (pl. *dehtren*) [OE]

dolc (n.) wound, scar, gash; hollow or cavity [OE *dolg* "wound" or ME *dalk* "hollow"; see Baldwin (1976), p. 274]

dolven(e) (adj. & v., past part.) see *delven* (v.)

dom (n.) judgment, sentence, condemnation; Last Judgment (obj. sing. *dome*; pl. *domes*) [OE; ModE *doom*]

Domes-dei (n.) DOOMSDAY, Day of Judgment [OE]

domes-mon (n.) a judge [from OE]

dom-seotel (n.) judgment SEAT [from OE]

don (v.) to DO, perform, behave; finish; make, construct; to cause, make (something happen); to place, put, send (pres. subj. sing. *do*; pres. 3 sing. *dest*, *deth*; past 2 sing. *dudest*; past 3 sing. *dude*; past pl. *duden*; past part. *i-do, i-don*; inflected inf. *to donne*) [OE]

dosc (adj.) dark, dim, dull, DUSKY; (fig.) obscure [OE]

dotie (v., pres. subj. sing.) might behave foolishly, become silly, rave, lose one's wits [prob. OE]

dragse (v., imper. sing.) DRAG along [ON; see d'Ardenne (1983), p. 21]

drahe(n) (v.) to DRAW, drag, pull; gather, collect (pres. subj. sing. *drahe*; pres. 2 sing. *drahest*; pres. 3 sing. *draheth*; pres. pl. *drah (we)*; past sing. *droh*; past pl.

drohen; pres. part. *drahinde*; past part. *i-drahe[n]*) [OE]

drake (n.) dragon, DRAKE [OE, from Lat.]

dreaieth (v. 1, pres. 2 pl.) see *drehen* (v.); (v. 2, pres. 3 sing., pres. pl.) pulls, tends (toward); suffers, endures [OE, close relative of *drahen* (v.), perhaps confused with *drehen* (v.)]

dream (n.) sound (of a bell or trumpet); voice, speaking; noise, din [OE]

dred (n.) DREAD, fear [see *dreden* (v.)]

dreden (v.) to fear, DREAD, be afraid of (pres. subj. sing. *drede*; pres. subj. pl. *dreden*; pres. pl. *dredeth*; past sing. *dredde*) [OE]

drehe(n) (v.) to suffer, endure; experience, feel; tolerate (pres. subj. sing. *drehe*; pres. 3 sing. *dreheth*; pres. 2, 3 pl. *dreheth*; past sing. *droh*) [OE]

dremen (v.) to make a joyful noise, make music [OE]

dreori (adj.) miserable, DREARY; cruel; bloody (? — OE meaning) [OE]

dreori (n.) experience; suffering, misery

drif (v., imper. sing.) see *driven* (v.)

drihtines (n., gen. sing.) the Lord's [OE]

driven (v.) to DRIVE, force, compel (imper. sing. *drif*; imper. pl. *drive (ye)*; pres. subj. sing. *drive*; pres. 2 sing. *drivest*; pres. 3 sing. *driveth*; pres. part. *drivinde*) [OE]

droh(en) (v., past) see *drehen* (v.) or *drahen* (v.)

dronc (n.) DRINK [OE]

drope (n.) DROP (pl. *dropen*) [OE]

drope-mel (n.) DROP by drop, in drops [OE; see ModE *piece-meal*]

dross (n.) DROSS, impurities [OE]

drue (adj.) DRY [OE]

druerie (n.) love, romantic affection; flirtation, dalliance; love-token, gift [OF]

dru-fot (adj.) DRY-FOOTED, with dry feet [from OE]

druhieth (v., pres. pl.) DRY (something); become dry (past sing. *druhede*) [from OE]

drunch (n.) DRINK (pl. *drunches*) [OE]

druncni (v., pres. subj. sing.) drown (pres. pl. *druncnith*) [*OE]

drunc-wile (adj.) desirous of drink; (n.) drunkard [OE]

drupi (adj.) DROOPY, downcast, sad [ON *draupr*]

duble (adj.) DOUBLE [OF]

dude(n) (v., past) see *don* (v.)

dug (n.) DUKE, leader; commander [OF]

duhen (v.) to be good for, serve, be proper, fitting; to thrive (pres. 3 sing. *deh*) [OE]

dulle (adj.) blunt, DULL [*OE]

dulve(n) (v., past) see *delven* (v.)

dun (adv.) DOWN [OE]

dun (n.) hill, mountain; -DOWN (in place-names) (pl. *dunes*) [OE; related to ModE *dune*]

dune-ward(es), dune-wart (adv.) DOWNWARD; down

dunge (n.) DUNG, manure, filth [OE]

dun-riht (adj.) directly descending; direct, plain, definite, blunt; absolute, thorough, out and out [OE; ModE *downright*]

dunt(e) (n.) blow, strike; stroke (of a sword), blow (of a hammer) (pl. *duntes*) [OE]

durren (v., pres. pl.) DARE, are so bold as to (do something) (pres. 1, 3 sing. *dear*; past sing. *durste*) [OE]

durste (v.) see *durren* (v.)

dusi(e) (adj.) foolish, stupid (superlat. *dusegest*) [OE; ModE *dizzy*]

dusischipe (n.) stupidity, ignorance, folly [see *dusi* (adj.)]

dust (n.) DUST [OE]

dusten (v.) to fling, throw, toss, cast; plunge, crash, fall (past subj. sing. *duste*) [*OE; see d'Ardenne (1961), p. 149]

dusteth (v., pres. 3 sing.) is DUSTY [OE]

dute (n.) DOUBT; fear, apprehension [OF]

duteth (v., pres. 3 sing.) is anxious, afraid; fears, DOUBTS [OF]

dutten (v.) to shut, close; to stop up, plug (a hole) (pres. pl. *dutteth*; past pl. *dutten*) [OE]

dweole (n.) deception, trickery; error, wrong-doing; stupor, trance [OE]

dyaloge (n.) dialogues of St. Gregory the Great [OF]

ead-eaweth (v., pres. 3 sing.) appears, reveals (oneself); shows, reveals (past sing. *eadewede*, *edeawde*) [OE]

eadi(e) (adj.) blessed, favored (by God); rich, wealthy [OE]

eadiliche (adv.) fortunately, blessedly [see *eadi* (adj.)]

eadinesse (n.) blessing, happiness (pl. *eadinesses*) [see *eadi* (adj.)]

ead-mod(e) (adj.) humble, gentle, meek (gen. sing. *eadmodies*) [OE; related to *eth* (adj.) + *mode* (n.)]

ead-modieth (v., imper. pl.) humble [see *ead-mod* (adj.)]

ead-modliche (adv.) humbly

ead-modnesse (n.) humility [OE]

eahte (num.) EIGHT [OE]

eahtuthe (adj.) EIGHTH

eairen (n. pl.) eggs [OE]

eal (n.) AWL, shoemaker's tool for punching holes in leather (pl. *eawles*) [OE]

ealde (n.) age, stage of life (pl. *ealdes*) [OE]

ealdren (n. pl., orig. compar.) ELDERS [OE]

ealleofte (num.) ELEVENTH [OE]

ealmesse (n.) ALMS, charitable gift; deed of mercy [OE, from Lat.]

eanes (adv.) ONCE [OE]

eani(e) (adj.) ANY; (pron.) any person [OE]

eape (n.) APE [OE]

eape-ware (n.) APE-WARE, counterfeit ware(s)

eappel (n.) APPLE [OE]

ear (adv.) early, soon; before, at an earlier time; rather; (conj. & prep.) before, ERE [OE]

eard (n.) homeland, native place [OE]

eare (n.) EAR (pl. *earen*) [OE]

eares (n. pl.) EARS (of grain) [OE]

earh (adj.) cowardly, craven; vile, wretched; slothful, sluggish [OE]

earliche (adj. & adv.) EARLY [OE]

earm (adj.) miserable, poor [OE]; (n.) ARM (pl. *earmes*) [OE]

earmite (n.) HERMIT [OF]

earmliche (adv.) miserably [see *earm* (adj.)]

earmthes (n. pl.) miseries [OE]

earn (n.) eagle (pl. *earnes*) [OE]

earowen (n. pl.) see *arewen* (n.)

earre (adj., compar.) EARLIER, previous, aforementioned; the former (as opposed to the latter) [see *ear* (adv.)]

earst(e), earest (superlat.) (adj.) first; (adv.) first, at first; *on alre earst* = first of all [OE; see *ear* (adv.)]

ear-under (adv.) EARLY in the morning; (perhaps) before tierce, the third liturgical hour [see *under* (n.)]

earveth (adj.) difficult, hard [OE]

easkeres (n. pl.) ASKERS, questioners (i.e., those who ask or question) [OE]

easki(n) (v.) to ASK, require, demand (pres. subj. sing./pl. *easki*; imper. pl. *easketh*; pres. 3 sing. *easketh*; pres. pl. *easkith*; past sing. *easkede*) [OE]

easkunge (n.) ASKING, questioning; request (pl. *easkunges*)

eatelich(e) (adj.) hideous, repulsive (compar. *eateluker*) [OE]

eathe (adv.) easily, without difficulty; readily [OE; see *eth* (adj.)]

eaver, eavre (adv.) EVER, always, constantly [OE]

eaver-euch (adj.) EACH and EVERY, every [OE]

eaw-bruche (n.) adultery; BREACH of marriage [OE *æw* "law, marriage" + *bruche* (n.)]

ea-wiht (adv.) at all, to any extent; (pron.) anything [OE]

eawles (n. pl.) see *eal* (n.)

eawt (adv.) at all, in any way; (pron.) anything, AUGHT [from OE]

ec (adv.) also, as well [OE]

eche (adj.) eternal, everlasting [OE]; (n.) ACHE, pain [see *ake* (v.)]

eche, echnen, echye (n.) see *ehe* (n.)

echeliche (adv.) eternally, forever [OE]

echen (v.) to increase, add to (pres. subj. sing. *echi*; pres. 3 sing. *echeth*) [OE; related to *ec* (adv.)]

ec(h)nesse (n.) eternity, eternal nature [OE]

ed- (prefix 1) (with verbs of motion) away, away from; (with verbs of position) at, against [OE]; (prefix 2) see *eth-* (prefix)

ed (prep.) AT; from, at the hands of [OE]

ed-brec (v., past sing.) BROKE away from, escaped (past pl. *edbreken*) [from OE]

ed-eawde (v., past sing.) see *ead-eaweth* (v.)

ed-fallen (v., past part.) fallen (away), dropped [OE]

ed-fleon, et-fleon (v.) to FLEE away, escape from (pres. subj. sing. *edfleo*; pres. 3 sing. *etflith*; past pl. *edfluhen*; past part. *edflohe*) [OE]

ed-halden (v.) to keep, detain, HOLD back; keep, fix something in mind, understand (pres. 3 sing. *edhalt, ethalt* [= *edhaldeth*]; past pl. *edheolden*) [OE]

ed-lutien (v.) to lurk, hide (from); escape notice (pres. 3 sing. *edluteth*) [OE]

ed-scene, et-scene (adj.) easily SEEN, plain, clear [OE]

ed-slopen (v., past part.) SLIPPED away (from), vanished [OE]

ed-stearten (v.) to START, get away from, escape (pres. 3 sing. *edstearteth*; past part. *etsteart*) [OE]

ed-stonden (v.) to stand firm; resist, withstand (something) (imper. sing. *edstont, edstond*; pres. 2 sing. *edstondest*, pres. 3 sing. *edstont*) [OE]

ed-stuteth (v., pres. pl.) to stop (at), linger [see *ed-* (prefix 1) and *stutten* (v.)]

ed-witen (v.) to blame, censure, reproach, criticize (pres. 3 sing. *edwit* [= *edwiteth*]) [OE; see *witest* (v.), ModE *twit*]

ed-witunge (n.) reproach, blame

efficacies (n. pl.) powers (to effect something); effects [OF]

efne (adj.) even, flat, steady; (adv.) EVEN; evenly, steadily; exactly [OE]

eft (adv.) again, second time; back, back again, in turn; afterwards, then; likewise, moreover; in return, in reply; conversely [OE]

efter (prep.) AFTER; accord-ing to; in imitation of; (adv.) afterwards [OE]

efterward(e), efterwart (adv.) AFTER-WARDS

egede (adj.) foolish, absurd [OE; see MED *egede* (n. & adj.)]

egge (n.) EDGE, sharp side of a sword-blade [OE]

eggin (v.) to give an EDGE to; to entice, tempt, incite, EGG on (pres. subj. sing. *eggi*; pres. 3 sing. *eggeth*; past sing. *egede*) [ON]

eggunge (n.) urging, inciting, tempting, EGGING on

ehe (n.) EYE (pl. *ehnen, echnen*) [OE]

eh-sihthe, ech-sihthe, echye-sihthe (n.) EYESIGHT

eh-thurl (n.) the window of the EYE; eye (pl. *ech-thurles*) [see *ehe* (n.) + *thurl* (n.)]

ei (adj. & pron.) any; any (person) [OE]

eie (n.) fear, awe; anger [OE; ModE *awe* from ON cognate]

eil (n.) harm, trouble; AILMENT [from OE]

eile (n.) the bristly beard (awn) of barley or other grain [OE]

eilen, eili (v.) to annoy, afflict, trouble (mentally or physically), AIL (pres. subj. sing. *eili*; pres. 3 sing. *eileth*) [OE]

eil-thurl (n.) window of pain (with pun on *eh-thurl* [n.]) (pl. *eil-thurles*)

eir (n.) AIR [OF]

eise (adj.) at ease, at leisure; able, having opportunity; comfort, having no discomfort [OF]; (n.) EASE, physical comfort, leisure; tranquillity, peace of mind; pleasure, enjoyment; desire, gratification of the flesh; profit, benefit; means, opportunity, ability (to do something) [OF]

eisfule (adj.) horrific, terrifying, frightful [OE; related to *eie* (n.)]

eisil (n.) vinegar [OF]

either (adj. & pron.) each of two, one or the other (of two), both [OE; ModE *either*]

either (adv.) also, as well; both [OE]

ek (adv.) see *ec* (adv.)

el- (prefix) foreign, strange [OE; related ultimately to ModE *alien*]

elbohen (n. pl.) ELBOWS [OE]

el-heowet (adj.) pale [see *el-* (prefix) + *heowin* (v.)]

-(e)les (suffix) a suffix for making nouns out of verbs, or causative nouns from other nouns [OE]

elles (adv.) ELSE, otherwise [OE]

elne (n.) strength, vigor; comfort (in biblical sense) [OE]

elnin (v.) to strengthen, hearten [OE; see *elne* (n.)]

el-theodie (adj.) foreign (person); (n.) foreigner [OE; see *el-* (prefix) + *theode* (n.)]

enbrevet (v., past part.) recorded, inscribed, enrolled [OF]

en-chearre (adv.) once, one time [see *sum-chearre* (adv.)]

ende (n.) END; *toward Englondes ende* = toward the end (border) of England [OE]

endeattet (v., past part.) INDEBTED, in debt [OF]

endeles (adj.) ENDLESS, without end [OE]

endin (v.) to END, bring to an end, finish; complete (imper. pl. *endith*; pres. subj. sing. *endi*; pres. 3 sing. *endeth*) [OE]

engel (n.) ANGEL (gen. sing. *engles*; gen. pl. *englene*) [OE]

engoni (v., pres. 1 sing.) ENJOIN, impose [OF]

eni (adj. & pron.) see *eani* (adj. & pron.)

ennu (n.) discomfort, aggravation, vexation [OF; see ModE *annoy, ennui*]

entente (n.) INTENT, intention; goal (pl. *ententes*) [OF]

entre-meatin (v.) to busy oneself (reflex.); meddle, INTERFERE (pres. 3 sing. *entreme[a]teth*) [OF]

eode(n) (v., past) see *gan* (v.)

eoil(e) (n.) OIL [?blending of OE and OF]

eornen (v.) to RUN (past subj. sing. *urne*; pres. 3 sing./pl. *eorneth*; past pl. *urnen*) [OE]

eorre (adj.) angry, IREFUL; (n.) anger, ire [OE]

eorth(e) (n.) EARTH, ground; dirt [OE]

eorthene (adj.) EARTHEN [*OE]

eorthlich(e) (adj.) EARTHLY, worldly, having to do with worldly (rather than spiritual) matters

eote(n) (v.) to EAT (imper. pl. *eoteth*; pres. subj. sing. *eote*; pres. 2 pl. *eoteth*; past sing. *et*; past pl. *eten*; inflected inf. *to eotene*) [OE]

erede (v., past subj. sing.) plough, would plough [OE; see ModE *arable*]

erende-beorere (n.) ERRAND-BEARER, messenger

eritage (n.) inheritance, legacy; HERITAGE [OF]

ernde (n.) message, ERRAND; petition [OE]; (v., imper. sing.) obtain (by intercession), grant [OE]

erveth (adj.) see *earveth* (adj.)

eschif (adj.) skittish, easily startled, frightened [OF; ModE *eschew* (adj.)]

esken (n. pl.) ASHES [ON]

eski-bah (n.) ASH-stirrer, hearth-tender, (perhaps with an insulting overtone) lackey [origin of -*bah* is obscure; see MED, Zettersten (1965), pp. 28–29, Turville-Petre (1969), pp. 156–58]

essample (n.) EXAMPLE, exemplum, illustrative story [OF]

essinien (v.) to excuse (reflex.); avoid, withdraw from [OF; MED *essoinen*]

est (n.) the EAST [from OE]

estat (n.) ESTATE, status, (social) position; state, condition (pl. *estaz*) [OF]

este (n.) delight, pleasure, indulging, gratification; favor, grace [OE]

esteliche (adv.) luxuriously, indulgently [see *este* (n.)]

esten (adv.) EASTERLY; *bi esten* = to the east

est-ful(e) (adj.) pleasure-seeking, picky, fastidious with food; delicate, delectable (compar. *estfulre*) [OE]

estoires (n. pl.) stories, narratives, HISTORIES [OF]

et- (prefix) see *ed-* (prefix 1)

et (prep.) see *ed* (prep.)

eth- (prefix) easy, easily [OE]

eth (adj.) comforting, agreeable; easy, not difficult; (adv.) easily, readily [OE]

et-halt (v., pres. 3 sg.) see *ed-halden* (v.)

ethele (adj.) noble, excellent, famous; innate, natural [OE]

ethelich (adj.) insignificant, slight; weak, frail, humble [OE]

etheliche (adv.) easily, readily [OE]

eth-fele (adj.) easy to feel [see *eth-* (prefix) and *felen* (v.)]

eth-hurte (adj.) EASILY hurt, sensitive, thin-skinned [see *eth-* (prefix.) and *hurten* (v.)]

ethre (n.) blood-vessel, vein (pl. *ethren*) [OE; see Ger. *ader*]

eth-warpe (adj.) easy to overthrow, tottering [see *eth-* (prefix) + *warpen* (v.)]

et-steart (v., past part.) see *ed-stearten* (v.)

euch(e), euc (adj. & pron.) EACH (gen. sing. *euches*) [OE]

euch-an (pron.) EACH ONE (gen. sing. *euchanes*) [from OE]

even (n.) EVENING [OE]

evene (n.) nature, character, kind; ability, capacity, resources; occasion, cause [OE, from ON *efni* "material"]

eveneth (v., imper. pl.) compare, liken; makes level, smooth; moderate; make equal, treat as equal (pres. 3 sing. *eveneth*; pres. pl. *evenith*; past part. *i-evenet*) [OE]

even-song (n.) EVENSONG, Vespers (one of the canonical hours) [OE]

even-tid (n.) EVENINGTIDE, evening time [OE]

evenunge, evening (n.) comparison; alignment, adjustment; equal, peer [see *eveneth* (v.)]

evesede (v., past sing.) trimmed, clipped the hair (of a person) (past part. *i-eveset*) [OE]

evesunge (n.) roof edge or EAVES of a building; trimming or clipping (of the hair); clippings [OE; ModE *fringe* can also mean a border or "bangs" of hair]

Ewangeliste (n.) the Evangelist, one of the Gospel writers [OF]

ewt (adv. & pron.) see *eawt* (adv. & pron.)

fa (n.) FOE, enemy (gen. sing. *faes*; pl. *fan, van*) [OE]

fahenunge (n.) FAWNING, servile flattery; OED: "Of an animal, especially a dog: To show delight or fondness (by wagging the tail, whining, etc.) as a dog does" [from OE]

failede (v., past sing.) FAILED, lost power or strength; fell short of, did not obtain [OF]

fal (n.) FALL, downfall [OE]

faleweth (v., pres. 3 sing.) loses color, turns yellow or brown; fades or withers [OE]

fallen (v.) to FALL (down); fall spiritually; to die; to fall upon (someone, as a responsibility); to start, enter upon; to be comprised (of), pertain to; to be necessary, fitting; to fall to, come to (imper. pl. *falleth*; pres. subj. sing. *falle*; past subj. sing. *feolle*; pres. 3 sing./pl. *falleth*; past sing. *feol*; pres. part. *fallinde*; past part. *i-fallen*) [OE]

fallunge (n.) FALLING, a falling down

falsi (v., pres. subj. sing.) may deceive, pretend; cause to fail, break down; fail, give way, show weakness (pres. pl. *falsith*; pres. part. *falsinde*) [OF]

falsliche (adv.) FALSELY, dishonestly

fame (n.) (good) reputation, FAME [OF]

fa-men, va-men (n. pl.) FOE-MEN, enemies [OE]

familiarite (n.) intimacy, fellowship, closeness; faithful service, fidelity to a superior [OF, from Lat. *familia* "household, family"]

fawtes (n. pl.) FAULTS, imperfections [OF]

feahede (v., past sing.) adorned [ON *fægja* "to polish, cleanse"]

fealh (v., past sing.) see *feleth* (v.)

fearen (v.) to FARE, get along, live; travel, go, proceed; depart, escape (pres. 3 sing./pl. *feareth*; past part. *i-fearen*) [OE]

fearlac (n.) FEAR, terror [from OE]

fearlich (adj.) FEARFUL, dreadful, terrifying

fearliche (adv.) suddenly, unexpectedly; astoundingly, wonderfully [OE]

feaste (n. 1) feasting, entertainment; FEAST, celebration; a saint's feast day or church holiday; re-joicing, joy, *maken feaste* = to make merry [OE]; (n. 2) FAST, an act of fasting, going without food (pl. *feasten*) [prob. ON]; (adv.) FAST, firmly; steadily, diligently; quickly (compar. *feastluker*) [OE]

feasten (v. 1) to FAST, go without food; to fast on bread and water or a restricted diet of some kind (imper. pl. *feaste (ye)*; pres. 2 pl. *veasteth*; past pl. *feasten*) [OE]; (v. 2) to make FAST, bind; settle, conclude (past part. *i-feast*) [OE]

feastre (n.) ulcer, sore [OF; ModE *fester*]

feat, fette (n.) VAT, cask [OE]

featte (adj.) FATTENED [OE]

feattin (v.) to FATTEN, make fat, grow fat (pres. 3 sing. *featteth*; past part. *i-featted*) [OE]

feayeth (v., pres. 3 sing.) see *feieth* (v.)

feblesce (n.) FEEBLENESS, weakness, infirmity [OF]

febli (v., pres. subj. sing.) to grow FEEBLE, to weaken

fecchen (v.) to FETCH, bring [OE]

fede(n) (v.) to FEED, serve food to; suckle, nurse; sustain, support; nurture, rear, bring up (imper. sing. *fed*; pres. 3 sing. *fedeth, fet*; past sing. *fedde*; past part. *i-fed*) [OE]

feh (n.) property, possessions, wealth; livestock [OE; ModE *fee*]

feherest(e) (adj.) see *feier* (adj.)

feht (n.) FIGHT, warfare, battle (obj. sing. *fehte*) [OE]

fehten (v.) to FIGHT, do battle; strive (pres. 3 sing./pl. *fehteth*; past pl. *fuhten*) [OE]

fehtunge (n.) FIGHTING

feier(e), feir(e) (adj.) FAIR, beautiful; pleasant; proper (superlat. *feherest[e]*) [OE]

feiernesse (n.) FAIRNESS, beauty, attractiveness

feieth (v., pres. 3 sing.) joins, binds together; links, associates, allies (past part. *i-feiet, i-veiet*) [OE]

fein (adv.) gladly, willingly, FAIN [OE]

feire (adv.) beautifully, pleasantly; clearly, properly, completely [OE]

fel (n.) FELL, skin, hide (pl. *felles*) [OE]

feld (n.) FIELD, meadow, pasture [OE]

felde (v., past sing.) see *felen* (v.)

felen (v.) to FEEL, experience; detect (pres. 2 sing. *felest*; pres. 3 sing. *feleth, veleth*; past sing. *felde*; past part. *i-felet*) [OE]

feleth (v., pres. 3 sing.) gets, enters into (pres. 3 sing. *feleth*; past sing. *fealh*) [OE]

fen (n.) mud, muck; FEN [OE]

fenniliche (adv.) muckily, muddily; (fig.) vilely, sinfully, miserably [OE; see *fen* (n.)]

feol (adj.) cruel, fierce, FELL [OF, related to ModE *felon*]; (v., past sing.) see *fallen* (v.)

feolahe (n.) FELLOW, companion, friend, equal; (in a negative sense) accomplice (pl. *feolahes*) [late OE, from ON]

feolahlich (adj.) companionable, friendly; "brotherly"

feolahliche (adv.) companionably, in a friendly way

feolah-re(a)dden (n.) fellowship, companionship, company [from *feolahe* (n.) + OE *ræden* "condition"]

feolahschipe (n.) FELLOWSHIP, companionship, society

feole (adj.) many, much; (adv.) to a great extent, much; (n.) many [OE; see Ger. *viel* "much"]

feole-valde (adj.) various, manifold [from OE]

feole-weis (adv.) in many WAYS

feolle (v.) see *fallen* (v.)

feond (n.) enemy; the devil, the FIEND (gen. sing. *feondes*) [OE]

feondschipe (n.) enmity, hostility [OE]

feor (n.) price [OF]

feor (adj.) FAR, distant; (adv.) FAR, afar; *of feor* = some distance away, apart [OE]

feorli(ch) (adj.) strange, marvelous, astounding; (n.) something astounding, a wonder, marvel [OE]

feorren (adv.) from AFAR, from a distance; far away [OE]

feorrene (adj.) FAR away, distant

feorthe (adj. & n.) FOURTH [OE]

ferd(e) (n.) army; company, troop, multitude (pl. *ferdes*) [OE]

fere (adj.) sound, strong [ON]; (n.) companion, friend, partner, comrade (pl. *feren*) [OE]

ferhen (v.) to FARROW, give birth (to piglets) (past part. *i-ferhet*) [from OE]

ferien (v.) to FERRY, transport, convey; (in a boat) [OE]

ferliche (adv.) see *fearliche* (adv.)

fer-redden (n.) companionship, fellowship [see *fere* (n.) + *ræden* "condition"]

fersch (adj.) fresh, eager [OE]

feste (adv.) see *feaste* (adv.)

festnith (v., imper. pl.) FASTEN, make firm; bind; settle, conclude, make (an agreement) (past part. *i-festned, -et*) [OE]

festschipe (n.) parsimony, stinginess (gen. sing. *festschipes*) [from OE]

feth (v., pres. 3 sing.) begins, starts to (often with *on*); seizes, takes (pres. pl. *foth*) [OE; see Ger. *anfangen*]

fetherin (v.) to load, weigh down, burden; charge (with meaning) (pres. 1 sing. *fetheri*; past part. *i-fetheret*) [see *fother* (n.)]

fetles (n.) vessel, container [OE]

fette (n.) see *feat* (n.)

fevre (n.) FEVER [prob. OF]

fier (n.) fig tree, tree of genus *ficus* [OF]

fif (adj. & num.) FIVE [OE]

fifte (adj.) FIFTH [OE]

fiftene (adj.) FIFTEEN

fifti (num.) FIFTY

figures (n. pl.) forms, shapes, FIGURES [OF]

fikele (adj.) treacherous, deceitful [OE]

fikelere (n.) flatter; traitor, deceiver (gen. sing. *fikeleres*) [OE]

fikeleth (v., pres. 3 sing.) flatters, deceives, beguiles [OE]

fikelunge (n.) flattery, (pleasing) deception

fiketh (v., pres. 3 sing.) flatters, deceives; fawns (on) (pres. part. *fikiende*) [from OE]

file (n.) FILE [OE]

fileth (v., pres. 3 sing.) FILES, scrapes away, smoothes (past part. *i-filet*) [from OE]

finden (v.) to FIND, discover (past subj. sing. *funde*; pres. 3 sing. *fint*; pres. 1 pl. *finde [we]*, *findeth*; pres. pl. *findeth*; past sing. *fond*; past pl. *funden*; past part. *i-funde[n]*) [OE]

firsi (v., pres. subj. sing.) forsake, distance one's self from, flee, stay away; remove (pres. 3 sing. *firseth*) [OE; related to ModE *far*]

fisistien (n.) PHYSICIAN (pl. *fisistiens*) [OF, from Lat.]

fite-rokes (n. pl.) ragged upper garments [from ME *fittered* "ragged" + OE *rocc* "over-garment"]

fitheren (n. pl.) FEATHERS [blend of two OE words]

five (adj. & num.) see *fif* (adj. & num.)

flaa (n.) arrow [OE]

flaski (v., pres. subj. sing.) splash, sprinkle (pres. 3 sing. *flasketh*) [OF]

fleah (v., past sing.) see *fleon* (v. 2)

fleaw (v., past sing.) see *floyen* (v.)

flehe (n.) FLY (the insect); perhaps also FLEA [OE *fleah*] (pl. *flehen*) [OE]

fleon (v. 1) to FLY; fly (from), flee (imper. sing. *flih*; past subj. sing. *fluhe*; pres. 3 sing. *flith*; past sing. *fleh*; past pl. *fluhen*; pres. part. *fleonninde*) [OE; forms confused with *fleon* (v. 2)]; (v. 2) to FLEE; escape (imper. sing. *fleo*; pres. 3 sing. *fleoth*; past sing. *fleah*; past pl. *fluhen*; past part. *i-flohe[n]*) [OE]

fleos (n.) FLEECE [OE]

fleotinde (v., pres. part. as adj.) floating, wandering; flowing, in constant motion [OE; ModE *fleet*]

fles(ch) (n.) FLESH, the body; the carnal (as opposed to the spiritual) (gen. sing. *flesches*) [OE]

fleschlich(e), flesliche (adj.) FLESHLY, carnal, bodily

fleschliche (adv.) carnally, bodily, in the flesh

flesch-wise (adj.) FLESHly, carnal, concerned with the body

flih, flith (v.) see *fleon* (v. 1)

flikereth (v., pres. 3 sing.) trifles, toys (with); flutters, behaves frivolously [OE *flicorian* "to flutter"]

flint (n.) FLINT, a very hard stone [OE]

floc (n.) FLOCK, herd; group of people; host, squadron; gang (of evil spirits) [OE]

flow- (v.) see *floyen* (v.)

floyen (v.) to flow (with liquid); proceed (pres. 3 sing. *floweth*; past sing. *fleaw*; past pl. *flowen*; pres. part. *flowinde*) [OE]

fluht (n.) FLIGHT, escape, fleeing (obj. sing. *[on] fluhte*) [OE]

flures (n. pl.) FLOWERS, blossoms [OF]

fluthrunges (n. pl.) flirtings; flutterings, "unseemly movements" [perhaps imitative] (Zettersten [1965], p. 134)

flutrunge (n.) unseemly movement, flirting (?); FLITTING about [ON]

flutte(n) (v.) to live by, survive on (usually with *bi* "BY, on") [ON]

foddre (n.) FODDER, food for livestock [OE]

fode (n.) FOOD, sustenance [OE]

fol (adj.) sinful, evil; foolish [OF]; (n.) simpleton, silly person, FOOL (pl. *foles*) [OF]

fol-hardi (adj.) FOOLHARDY

folhere (n.) FOLLOWER

folhi(n) (v.) to FOLLOW, imitate; pursue (imper. sing. *folhe*; pres. 3 sing. *folheth*; pres. pl. *folhith*; past sing. *folhede, fulede*) [OE]

folliche (adv.) foolishly [see *fol* (adj.)]

fond (v., past sing.) see *finden* (v.)

fondin (v.) to test, try; tempt, test; find out, discover, experience; to concern, busy oneself about (imper. pl. *fondin*; pres. 1 sing. *fondi*; pres. 3 sing. *fondeth*; pres. pl. *fondith*; past sing. *fondede*; past pl. *fondeden*; past part. *i-fondet, -ed*) [OE]

fondunge (n.) temptation; testing, trying (pl. *fondunges*)

for- (prefix) adds 1) a pejorative emphasis to a word, often implying destruction or fragmentation, or 2) the sense of forward movement or advancing, 3) the idea of being ahead of or BEFORE something, 4) a general intensifying effect, like the adv. *very*

for (adv.) BEFOREHAND, previously; forward (in space or time) [OE]

for-bearneth (v., pres. 3 sing.) BURNS up, is consumed by fire (past part. *forbearnd[e]*) [OE]

for-beode (v., pres. subj. sing.) FORBID, prohibit, make impossible (pres. 1 sing. *forbeode*; past sing. *forbeot*; past part. *forbode*) [OE]

for-beoren (v.) to be patient, FORBEAR, put up with; to avoid, shun (pres. subj. pl. *forbeoren*; pres. 3 sing. *forbereth*; past sing. *forber*) [OE]

for-bisne (n.) example, pattern; precedent; parable, lesson, exemplum; symbol, omen (pl. *forbisne*) [OE]

for-bod (n.) prohibition, a FORBIDDING [OE]

for-bode(n) (adj., orig. past part.) FORBIDDEN [see *for-beode* (v.)]

for-buhen (v.) to escape; stop, refrain from; shun, avoid, disobey (pres. 3 sing. *forbuheth*; past pl. *[ye] forbuhe*) [OE]

for-culiende (v., pres. part.) charring, blackening (by heat) (past part. *forculet*) [origin obscure]

for-dede (n.) service, favor; DEED done FOR someone [OE; MED *for(e)-dede*]

for-demet (v., past part.) condemned, judged, DOOMED [OE]

for-don (v.) to destroy, undo, do away with (inflected inf. *to fordonne*)

for-druhede (adj. & v., past part.) DRIED up, withered [see *druhieth* (v.)]

for-drunke (adj. & v., past part.) very drunk, addicted to drink [OE]

fore (adv.) beforehand [OE]

fore-cwiddre (n.) prophet, foreteller [from OE; see *fore* (adv.) + *cwiddeth* (v.)]

for-eoden (v., past pl.) see *for-gan* (v.)

fore-ridles (n. pl.) FORE-RIDER, one who rides ahead, messenger; forerunner, precursor; preliminary [from OE]

foreward (n.) agreement, pact [OE]

for-feareth (v.) perishes, is destroyed; goes to waste; goes astray, is mislead (past pl. *forferden*; pres. part. *forfearinde*) [OE]

for-fret (v., pres. 3 sing. [= *forfreteth*]) devours, gobbles up (past pl. *forfreten*) [from OE]

for-gan (v.) to FORGO, go without, omit; refuse, avoid (imper. pl. *forgath*; pres. 3 sing. *forgeath*; pres. pl. *forgath*; past pl. *foreoden*) [OE]

for-gneaieth (v., pres. 3 sing.) GNAWS up, away [OE]

for-gult(e) (adj., orig. past part.) (made) GUILTY, convicted with sin [OE]

for-hate (v.) to renounce [OE]

for-heaved (n.) FOREHEAD [OE]

for-hohien (v.) to neglect, disregard; despise, scorn, reject (imper. sing. *forhohie*; pres. 3 sing. *forhoheth*) [OE]

for-horin (v.) to WHORE around, prostitute (oneself); commit adultery (pres. subj. sing. *forhori*; past part. *forhoret*) [from OE]

for-hwi (adv.) WHY, for what reason, for which cause; (conj.) because, provided that [OE]

for-hwon (conj.) why, for what reason; *forhwon thet* = provided that, as long as [see *hwon* (conj.)]

for-idelet (adj., orig. past part.) ruined by idleness [from OE]

for-keastunge (n.) rejection, casting away [OE + ON]

for-keorven (v.) to cut out, CARVE away (pres. subj. sing. *forkeorve*) [OE]

for-leavet (v., past part.) LEFT behind, abandoned [OE]

for-leosen (v.) to LOSE; destroy; (past part. as adj.) *forloren* = lost, damned (imper. sing. *forleosen*; pres. 3 sing./pl. *forleoseth*; past 2 sing. *forlure*; past 3 sing. *forleas*; past part. *forloren[e]*) [OE]

for-leten (v.) to abandon, forsake, give up [OE]

for-lorenesse (n.) perdition, destruction

forme (adj.) first [OE]

for-roteth (v., pres. 3 sing.) ROTS away, putrefies, goes bad [OE]

for-saken (v.) to renounce, refuse; FORSAKE, abandon (pres. subj. sing. *forseke*; past 2 subj. sing. *forsoke*; pres. 2 sing. *forsakest*; pres. 3 sing. *forsaketh*; past part. *forsaken*) [OE]

for-scaldet (v., past part.) SCALDED severely, or to death; destroyed by scorching [OF; see *scaldinde* (adj.)]

for-schuppeth (v., pres. 3 sing.) MISSHAPES, transforms; degrades, perverts (past part. *for-schuppet*) [OE]

for-schuppilt (n.) sorceress, one who transforms or deforms [see *forschuppeth* (v.) and *-ild* (suffix)]

for-seothen (v., pres. subj. pl.) scald, boil to death [OE; ModE *seethe*]

for-stoppith (v., imper. pl.) STOP, block up [*OE]

for-swolhen (v.) to devour, SWALLOW up (pres. 3 sing. *forswolheth*) [OE]

for-te, for-to (inf. marker) TO, in order to; (lit.) FOR TO

forth (adv.) forward (in time, place, or sequence); further; out (into view), away, out of doors; to an advanced point, far in (compar. *forthluker*) [OE]

forthe (adj.) away, gone [OE]

fortheth (v., pres. 3 sing.) FURTHERS, encourages, advances (past part. *i-forthet*; *i-vorthet*) [OE]

forth-fearen (v., past part.) FARED FORTH, passed on, departed; (fig.) dead [OE]

for-thi (adv. & conj.) therefore, for this reason; *for-thi thet* = (conj.) because; to the end that

forth-marhen (n.) late morning, i.e., advanced time in the morning [OE elements]

forthre (compar.) (adj.) before someone/something in rank, position; more extended, advanced, FURTHER along; (adv.) to a greater extent, more; (of time) later; moreover [compar. of *forth* (adv.)]

forth-riht (adv.) immediately, straight away; directly forward [from OE]

forth-ward (adv.) from then on, from that time FORWARD; continually [OE]

forth-yong (n.) progress, advance, course; a GOING FORTH [OE]

for-warpe (v.) to throw off, cast off, reject (pres. 3 sing. *forwarpeth*; past part. *forwarpe[n]*) [OE]

for-weolewet (v., past part.) faded, withered [from OE]

for-wreiet (v., past part.) accused, charged (with a crime); handed over [OE]

for-wurthe(n) (v.) to degenerate into (something); to perish, die, be destroyed; become feeble, useless (pres. 3 sing./pl. *forwurtheth*; past part. *forwurthen*) [OE]

for-yef (v., imper. sing.) FORGIVE (pres. 3 sing. *foryeveth*)

for-yelde (v., pres. subj. sing.) repay, recompense [OE]

for-yeme (v.) to disregard, neglect (pres. 3 sing. *foryemeth*) [OE]

for-yeoten (v.) to FORGET (pres. 3 sing. *foryeoteth, foryeteth, foryet*; past pl. *foryeten*; past part. *foryete[n]*) [OE]

for-yevelich (adj.) FORGIVABLE

for-yevenesse (n.) FORGIVENESS [OE]

for-yeveth (v., pres. 3 sing.) see *for-yef* (v.)

fostreth (v., pres. 3 sing.) FOSTERS, nourishes, supports (past sing. *fostrede*) [OE]

fostrilt (n.) nurse, fosteress [see *fostreth* (v.) and *-ild* (suffix)]

fot (n.) FOOT (gen. sing. *fotes*; pl. *fet, vet*) [OE]

foth (v., pres. pl.) see *feth* (v.)

fother (n.) a cart-load; fig., a large amount; heavy weight, burden; crowd [OE]

fot-wunde (n.) FOOT WOUND (pl. *fot-wunden*)

fowr (adj.) FOUR [OE]

fowre (num.) FOUR

frakel(e) (adj.) vile, foul, wretched, worthless [OE]

freame (n.) benefit, profit, advantage; *don freame* = to do good (to someone) [OE]

freamien (v.) to help, aid, advance (someone); strengthen (someone) (pres. 3 sing. *freameth*) [OE]

frech (adj.) bold, impudent [OE]

frechliche (adv.) greedily; eagerly; boldly, fiercely [OE]

freini (v., pres. subj. sing.) make an inquiry; ask, request (imper. pl. *freinith*; pres. 3 sing. *freineth*) [OE; see Ger. *fragen*]

fremede (adj.) strange, unfamiliar [OE; see Ger. *fremd* "strange"]

freo (adj.) FREE; noble, generous (superlat. *freoest*) [OE]

freolec (n.) freedom (from servitude); nobility of character: kindness, generosity [OE]

freond (n.) FRIEND (gen. sing. *freondes*; pl. *freond*) [OE]

freondin (v.) to gain friends, befriend (someone) [from *freond* (n.)]

freoten (v., pres. subj. pl.) to eat, gobble up, devour (used mainly for animals); chew up, gnaw (pres. 3 sing. *fret* [= *freteth*]) [OE; see Ger. *fressen*]

freote-wil (adj.) ravenous, desirous of devouring

freres (n. pl.) FRIARS, brothers [OF]

Fridei (n.) FRIDAY (pl. *Fridahes*) [OE]

Fri-niht (n.) the NIGHT before Good FRIDAY; the night of Good Friday [OE]

from (adv.) away, apart [OE]

frommard (adj.) contrary, different (to, from = obj.) [OE]; (adv.) opposite; (of location) away to, away from; away at a distance, turned away; (of time) onward; (prep.) away from, out of, from; different from, contrary to [OE]

frommardschipe (n.) difference, contrariness, willfulness [see *frommard* (adj.)]

frotunge (n.) rubbing, polishing; working (of a metal by rubbing) [from OF *froter* "to rub"]

frovre (n.) comfort, encouragement (pl. *frovren*) [OE]

frovrin (v.) to comfort, encourage, cheer, help (imper. pl. *frovrith*; pres. subj. sing. *frovri*; pres. 3 sing. *frovreth*) [OE]

frumthe (n.) beginning, start; beginning (of the world), creation; early times [OE]

frut (n.) FRUIT [OF]

fuhel (n.) FOWL, bird (pl. *fuheles*; gen. pl. *fuhelene*) [OE]

fuhten (v., past pl.) see *fehten* (v.)

ful(e) (adj.) FOUL, dirty, nasty; wicked, evil, guilty; dishonest; convicted (compar. *fulre*; superlat. *fuleste*) [OE]

ful (adv.) fully, completely; very, quite; (with numbers) exactly [OE]

fulde (v., past sing.) FILLED [OE]

fule (v., imper. sing.) BEFOUL, besmirch, make dirty, filthy (pres. 3 sing. *fuleth*; past pl. *fuleden*; past part. *i-fulet*) [OE]

fule, fulle (adv.) FOULLY, disgustingly; badly; disgracefully, obscenely; insultingly [OE] **ful-itohe(n)** (adj., orig. past part.) badly disciplined, instructed, brought up; ill-mannered; careless, badly executed (pl. *ful-itohene*) [see *fule* (adv.) and *teoth* (v.)]

ful-itoheliche (adv.) ill-mannerly, in an undisciplined way

fulle (adv.) see *fule* (adv.)

fulle(n) (v.) to FILL, satisfy; fulfill, accomplish, complete (pres. 3 sing. *fulleth*; past sing. *fulde*; past part. *i-fullet*) [OE]

fulleliche (adv.) FULLY, completely [OE]

fulliche (adv.) FOULLY, in a dirty, nasty way

fulluht (n.) baptism [OE]

fulthe (n.) FILTH, filthiness, impurity, nastiness, vileness, corruption (pl. *fulthen*) [OE]

funde(n) (v.) see *finden* (v.)

fundles (n.) discovery; invention, innovation; windfall, treasure trove; (pl.) deeds, devices invented by the mind [OE; see *finden* (v.) + *-(e)les* (suffix)]

fur (n.) FIRE; *Grickish fur* = "Greek fire," burning liquid used as a military weapon (obj. sing. *fure*; gen. sing. *fures*) [OE]

furene (adj.) FIERY, burning [OE]

furme (adj. & adv.) first, earliest [OE]; (n.) FORM, shape, likeness, image [OF]

furthreth (v., pres. 3 sing.) FURTHERS, encourages [OE]

fustes (n. pl.) FISTS [OE]

gabbeth (v., pres. 3 sing.) mocks, scoffs [OF]

gal(e) (adj.) bitter, filled with GALL or bile [OE]

galle (n.) GALL; intensely bitter substance; (fig.) bitterness [OE]

galnesse (n.) lasciviousness, lust, lechery (gen. sing. *galnesses*) [OE]

gan (v.) to GO, walk (imper. sing. *ga*; imper. 2 sing. *geast [tu]*; imper. pl. *gath*; pres. subj. sing. *ga*; pres. 1 sing. *ga*; pres. 3 sing. *geath*; pres. pl. *gath*; past sing. *eode*; past pl. *eoden*; past part. *i-gan*) [OE]

garces (n. pl.) cuts, gashes [OF]

gast, geast (n.) spirit, soul (as opposed to the body); *Hali Gast* = the Holy Spirit, third person of the Trinity (gen. sing. *gastes*; pl. *gastes*) [OE]

gastelich(e) (adj.) spiritual, (GHOSTLY) [OE]

gat (n.) GOAT (pl. *geat*) [OE]

gate (n.) GATE, entryway to a house [OE]

gate-heorden (n. pl.) GOATHERDS

gavel (n.) usury, lending at interest; accrued interest; rent, payment; tribute, tax [OE *gafol* "tribute"]

geal-forke (n.) GALLOWS-FORK, a fork-shaped stake used as a gallows [from OE]

gealstrith (v., pres. pl.) barks, yelps; (MED mistakenly defines as "stinks"; see its entry for *gelstren*) [related to OE *galan* "to sing, cry out"]

gealunge (n.) pleasure [*OE]

gederin (v.) to join, unite; GATHER, collect; accumulate, acquire; *gederinde* (pres. part. as adj.) = acquisitive, grasping (imper. sing. *gedere*; pres. 1 sing. *gederi*; pres. 2 sing. *gederest*; pres. 3 sing. *gedereth*; pres. pl. *gederith*; past pl. *gedereden*; pres. part. *gederinde*; past part. *i-gederet*) [OE]

gederunge (n.) acquisition, accumulating (of wealth); GATHERING

gcineth (v., pres. 3 sing.) GAINS; is of use, help [ON]

gelus(e) (adj.) JEALOUS; vigilant in guarding [OF]

gelusie (n.) JEALOUSY; zeal, vigilance in guarding (something) [OF]

general (adj.) GENERAL, not specific or limited, blanket [OF]

genterise (n.) nobility; graciousness, generosity; courtesy [OF]

gentil(e) (adj.) GENTLE, noble, of high birth; generous, kind [OF]

gentilliche (adv.) nobly, delicately, elegantly, exquisitely

gersum (n.) treasure, (valued) possessions or gift [OE, from ON]

gestnin (v.) to lodge, be a GUEST, stay as a guest (past sing. *gestnede*) [OE influenced by ON]

gestnunges (n. pl.) banquets, feasts; entertainments, lodging of guests, hospitalities [ON]

gigge (n.) a flighty, giddy girl (or boy); a coquette, flirt [imitative: *gigge* "something that whirls"; perhaps related to F. *gigue* "gawky young woman"]

gile (n.) GUILE, deceit [OF]

gingivre (n.) GINGER [OE *gingifer*, from Lat.]

giste (n.) lodging(s); guest [OE]

give-gaven (n. pl.) playthings, toys; GEWGAWS; fig., something trivial, worthless [a reduplication, orig. obscure]

Giwerie (n.) JEWISH quarter or district [OF]

glead(e) (adj.) GLAD, happy [OE]

gleadful(e) (adj.) GLAD, joyful (compar. *gleadfulre*)

gleadien (v.) to gladden, make glad, happy (imper. pl. *gleadieth*; pres. subj. sing. *gleadie*)

gleadliche (adv.) GLADLY, happily; willingly; *gleadluker* = more gladly, willingly, happily, etc. (compar. *gleadluker*)

gleadluker (adv.) see *gleadliche* (adv.)

gleadschipe (n.) gladness

gleadunge (n.) GLADDENING, joy

gleam (n.) brilliant light, GLEAM, flash, ray (pl. *gleames*) [OE]

gleden (n. pl.) live coals, embers [OE]

gleo (n.) entertainment, sport; mirth, joy; mockery, jest [OE; ModE *glee*]

gleowde (v., past sing.) made merry, enjoyed oneself; played (music), sang [OE; see *gleo* (n.)]

gles (n.) GLASS [OE]

gloire (n.) GLORY; (fig.) heaven [OF]

gloven (n. pl.) GLOVES [OE]

gluccheth (v., pres. 3 sing.) gulps down [*OE]

gluffeth (v., pres. 2 pl.) skip over, say wrongly [origin obscure — see MED *gliffen* (v.)]

gneat (n.) GNAT [OE]

gnedeliche (adv.) barely, frugally; miserly [*OE]

gnedure (adj., compar.) more frugal, more sparing [see *gnedeliche* (adv.)]

gnuddin (v.) to rub, scratch; crush, bruise (past pl. *gnuddeden*) [OE, from ON]

god (n.) GOOD, benefit; goods, wealth [OE]

god(e) (adj.) GOOD (old fem. obj. sing. *goder* — see *heale* [n.]) [OE]

Godd (n.) GOD (gen. sing. *Godes*) [OE]

god-dede (n.) a GOOD DEED (pl. *god-deden*) [OE; see Shepherd, p. 56n22/6]

Godd-head (n.) GODHEAD, divinity [OE]

godin (v.) to make GOOD, improve, better; to do good to, to benefit (a person) (past part. *i-godet*) [from *god* (adj.)]

godlec (n.) GOODNESS, kindness [ON]

Godspell (n.) GOSPEL, one of the four New Testament gospels (pl. *Goddspelles*) [OE]

gold-hord, golt-hord (n.) HOARD of GOLD, treasure (gen. sing. *golt-hortes*) [OE]

gold-smith, golt-smith (n.) GOLDSMITH [OE]

gomen (n.) joy, happiness; entertainment, revelry, music; athletic contest, GAME, bout (pl. *gomenes*) [OE]

gomnede (v., past sing.) played, sported, amused oneself (sometimes in a sexual sense) [from OE; see *gomen* (n.)]

gong-hus (n.) going-HOUSE, outhouse, toilet [from OE]

gong-men (n. pl.) toilet attendants

gong-thurl (n.) going-hole, toilet hole

granin (v.) to GROAN (pres. part. *graninde*) [OE]

grant (n.) GRANTING, consent; admission [OF]

grapi (v., pres. subj. sing.) feel, touch; handle, treat; probe, examine (pres. 3 sing. *grapeth*) [OE; ModE *grope*]

grapunge (n.) touching, feeling; caressing, fondling; questioning, probing [OE]

grea-hunz (n. pl.) GREYHOUNDS [OE]

greaste (adj.) see *great* (adj.)

great(e) (adj.) GREAT, large; coarse, rough (i.e., not fine); (pejorative) disgraceful, wicked; dangerous; haughty, insolent; (superlat.) *greaste* = GREATEST (compar. *greattre, greatluker*; superlat. *greaste*) [OE]

greatin (v.) to make GREAT, enlarge [OE]

greatluker (adj., compar.) see *great* (adj.)

greden (v.) to cry out, shout; wail; announce, publish (with a loud voice) (imper. sing. *gred*; pres. subj. sing. *grede*; pres. 3 sing. *gredeth*; past sing. *gredde*; past pl. *gredden*) [OE]

gredi (adj.) voracious, gluttonous, ravenous; GREEDY (for money) (compar. *grediure?*) [OE influenced by ON]

gref (n.) suffering, hardship, GRIEF [OF]

greie (adj.) GRAY [OE]

greithe (adj.) ready, prepared, willing; dressed, attired; skilled, informed; plain, direct; wealthy, powerful [ON]

greithede (v., past sing.) prepared, made ready (past part. *i-greithet*) [ON]

gremien (v.) to enrage, provoke (pres. 3 sing. *gremeth*) [OE]

grene (adj.) GREEN [OE]; (n.) GREEN foliage [OE]

greneth (v., pres. 3 sing.) GREENS, grows green [OE]

grennin (v.) to gnash the teeth, grimace; GRIN [OE]

grennunge (n.) grimacing, GRINNING [OE]

greot (n.) sand, gravel, small stones [OE; ModE *grit*]

grete(n) (v.) to GREET, welcome, say hello to; salute, hail (imper. pl. *greteth*; past sing. *grette*) [OE]

gretunge (n.) GREETING, salute (pl. *gretunges*)

grevi (v., pres. subj. sing.) oppress, harm; give pain, GRIEVE; cause grief, sorrow (pres. 2 sing. *grevest*; pres. 3 sing. *greveth*) [OF]

gridil (n.) GRIDDLE, the means of St. Lawrence's martyrdom [OF]

grim, grimme (adj.) GRIM, fierce, cruel, harsh (superlat. *grimmest*) [OE]

grimliche (adv.) GRIMLY, cruelly, fiercely; frightfully, terribly, horribly [OE]

grindel-stanes (n. pl.) GRIND-STONES [*OE]

grinden (v.) to GRIND (pres. 3 sing. *grint* [= *grindeth*]) [OE]

grinnen (v.) to grimace, snarl, growl; gape; to sneer, laugh unpleasantly [OE; see ModE *grin*]

gris (n.) piglet, young pig [ON]

grise (v., pres. subj. sing.) shudder, tremble (with fear, horror); be afraid (pres. 3 sing. *griseth*) [*OE]

grislich(e) (adj.) GRISLY, terrifying, horrific

grith (n.) peace, law and order; protection, shelter, refuge; sanctuary, haven; mercy, pardon, clemency [late OE, from ON]

grithful (adj.) peaceful, tranquil

grithful(l)nesse (n.) peacefulness, tranquillity

grome (n.) rage, anger, hostility; dispute; grief, sorrow, remorse; harm, injury; punishment [OE]

gromes (n. pl.) boys [origin obscure; see ModE *groom*]

grot (n.) a fragment, particle [OE; ModE *groats* "crushed grain"]

grucchi (v., imper. pl.) complain, grumble (pres. subj. sing. *grucchi*; past sing. *gruchede*; pres. part. *grucchinde*) [OF; related to ModE *grouch*]

grucchilt (n.) complaining woman (pl. *grucchildes*) [see *grucchi* (v.) and *-ild* (suffix)]

grucchunge, gruchunge (n.) grumbling, GROUCHING, complaining

grulleth (v., pres. 3 sing., impers.) trembles (with fear), is afraid) [*OE]

grunde (n.) bottom, depth; GROUND, earth; *bringen to grunde* = bring down, destroy [OE]

grune (n.) snare, trap; OED: "snare for catching birds or animals, made of cord, hair, wire, or the like, with a running noose" (pl. *grunen*) [OE]

grure (n.) horror, terror; pain, suffering [OE]

grureful(e) (adj.) terrifying, horrific

grurefulliche (adv.) horrifically, frighteningly

gruselin (v.) to munch, snack on

gruttene (adj.) bran, made of bran; coarse [from OE]

gulchen (v.) to drink greedily; to spew, spit, vomit; (fig.) to utter plainly and fully (pres. subj. sing. *culche*; pres. 3 sing. *culcheth*) [OE]

guldene (adj.) GOLDEN [OE]

gult (n.) fault, offense, sin, crime; GUILT (pl. *gultes*) [OE]

gulte (v., pres. subj. sing.) do wrong, misbehave, commit a crime; sin (pres. 1 sing. *gulte*; pres. 3 sing. *gulteth*; past sing. *gulte*; past pl. *gulten*) [OE]

gunfanuner (n.) standard bearer [derived in some obscure way from OF *gunfalon*; from Ger. **gunþ* "war" + **fano* "banner"]

gurde (v., past sing. & v., pres. subj. sing.) struck, rained blows on [OE]; (v., pres. subj. sing.) cinch, belt, GIRD (past part. *i-gurd*) [OE]

gurdel (n.) belt (pl. *gurdles*) [OE; ModE *girdle*]

gurdunge (n.) belting, the GIRDING of the body with a belt

gure-blode (n.) gushing, flowing BLOOD [from OE; see Zettersten (1965), p. 149]

gute-feastre (n.) flowing, running sore [see *yeotteth* (v.) + *feastre* (n.)]

ha (personal pron., 3 fem. sing. or 3 pl.) she; they [OE; see d'Ardenne (1961), p. 156]

habben (v.) to HAVE, possess; experience (a feeling); (a helping verb) (imper. sing. *have*; imper. pl. *habbeth*; pres. subj. sing. *habbe, have*; pres. subj. pl. *habben*; pres. 1 sing. *habbe*; pres. 2 sing. *havest*; pres. 3 sing. *habbeth, haveth*; pres. pl. *habbeth*; past 2 sing. *hefdest*; past 3 sing. *hefde*; past pl. *hefden*; past part. *i-haved*) [OE]

habit (n.) dress, clothing; HABIT, clothing signifying membership in a religious order [OF]

hacketh (v., pres. 3 sing.) HACKS, chops (past sing. *hackede*; past part. *i-hacket*) [*OE]

hades (n. pl.) offices, functions, persons [OE]

haggen (n. pl.) HAGS, harpies [*OE]

haher (adj.) skillful, clever [ON]

hal(e) (adj.) HEALTHY, healed, wholesome; intact, not damaged, whole, undivided (superlat. *halest*) [OE]

hald (n.) restraint, HOLD [OE]

halde(n) (v.) to HOLD, keep, protect; avail, do good, be of use (imper. sing. *halde*; imper. pl. *haldeth*; pres. subj. sing. *halde*; past subj. sing. *heolde*; pres. 2 sing. *haldest*; pres. 3 sing. *halt, haldeth*; pres. pl. *haldeth*; past sing. *heold*; past pl. *heolden*; past part. *i-halden*) [OE]

haldunge (n.) HOLDING, keeping

half (n.) part, side, direction; *on Godes half* = for God's sake, in God's name; *on other half* = on the other hand, at the same time (pl. *halves*) [OE]

halflunge (adv.) HALFWAY, partially; imperfectly [OE]

halhen (n. pl.) saints (gen. pl. *halhene*) [OE]

halheth (v., pres. 3 sing.) HALLOWS, sanctifies, purifies, make holy; *halwende* = purifying, hallowing (pres. part. *halwende*; past part. *i-halhet*) [OE]

hali (adj.) HOLY (pl. *halie*) [OE]

hali-dahne (adj.) HOLIDAY

halinesse (n.) HOLINESS [OE]

Hali-rode (n.) *Hali-rode dei* = Feast of the Holy Cross [from OE]

halle (n.) a HALL or residence [OE]

halnesse (n.) WHOLENESS, intactness, state of being intact

halse (v., imper. sing.) beseech, beg, entreat, plead (imper. pl. *halseth*; pres. 1 sing. *halsi*; pres. 3 sing. *halseth*; pres. part. *halsinde*; past part. *i-halset*) [OE]

halt (v., pres. 3 sing.) see *halden* (v.)

halve (n.) see *half* (n.)

halven-dal (n.) the HALF-part, a half; (adj.) half [see *half* (n.) + *dale* (n.)]

halwende (adj., pres. part.) HEALING [OE]

ham (adv.) HOMEWARDS

ham (e) (n.) HOME (pl. *hames*) [OE]

ham (personal pron., 3 pl., obj. form) them; (reflex.) themselves

ham-seolf, hamseolven (pron., reflex.) THEMSELVES

hanche-turn (n.) hip-move [AF + OF; see ModE *haunch*]

hardi (adj.) strong, stout, HARDY; secure, sure; bold, courageous; audacious, FOOLHARDY [OF, from Ger.]

hardiliche (adv.) HARDILY; forcefully, vigorously, violently; boldly, daringly; firmly

hare, heore (pron. pl., possessive) their

hat(e) (adj.) HOT (compar. *hattre*) [OE]

hate (v., pres. subj. sing.) order, command; call, name (imper. sing. *hat*; pres. 3 sing. *hat* [= *hateth*]; past part. *i-haten*) [OE]

hate, heate (n.) HEAT [OE]

hatte (v., pres. 3 sing.) is called, named (past part. *het*) [passive form of *hate* (v.)]

have (v.) see *habben* (v.)

haved-sunne (n.) see *heaved-sunne* (n.)

heafde, heafdes (n.) see *heaved* (n.)

healden (v.) to pour, throw out [OE *hyldan*]

heale (n.) HEALTH, benefit, healing, cure; state of happiness, prosperity; protection, help; salvation; *to goder heale* = to one's GOOD health, to one's benefit; *to wrather heale* = to one's destruction (lit.) to one's bad health [OE]

heale(n) (v.) to HEAL, cure (imper. sing. *heal*; pres. subj. sing. *heale*; pres. 3 sing. *healeth*; past sing. *healde*; past part. *i-healet*) [OE]

Healent (n.) Savior, HEALER [OE; see Ger. *Heiland*]

healewi (n.) sweet, HEALING liquid, syrup, or lotion; medical balm; antidote; (white) linctus [OE]

heap (n.) HEAP, pile [OE]

heard(e) (adj.) HARD, strong; heavy, difficult, severe; coarse, rough (compar. *heardre*; superlat. *heardest*) [OE]

hearde (adv.) HARD, heavily; harshly, cruelly [OE; see *heard* (adj.)]; (n.) coarse part of flax or wool, HARDS; rough garment, hair shirt (pl. *heorden*) [OE]

heardin (v.) to HARDEN, become tough [OE]

heare (n.) HARE [OE]

hearlot (n.) vagabond, beggar, layabout; scoundrel (pl. *hearloz*) [OF]

hearm (n.) HARM, injury, damage; trouble, distress (pl. *hearmes*) [OE]

hearmin (v.) to HARM, injure (pres. subj. sing. *hearmi*; pres. 2 sing. *hearmest*; pres. 3 sing. *hearmeth*; past part. *i-hearmet*) [OE]

hearmite (n.) HERMIT [OF]

heast(e) (n.) command, order, instruction; promise, vow, agreement (pl. *heastes*) [OE]

heatel (adj.) cruel, fierce, hostile [OE]

heaten (v.) to HEAT, make hot [OE]

heathenesse (n.) heathendom, heathen lands [OE]

heatien (v.) to HATE (pres. subj. sing. *heatie*; pres. subj. pl. *heatien*; pres. 2 sing. *heatest*; pres. 3 sing. *heateth*; pres. pl. *heatieth*; past sing. *heatede*) [OE]

heatunge (n.) HATE, hatred

heaved (n.) HEAD; (fig.) source, origin; leader; (quasi-adj.) chief, principal (pl. *heafdes*) [OE]

heaved-eche (n.) HEADACHE [see *heaved* (n.) + *eche* (n.)]

heaved-sunne (n.) capital SIN, deadly sin [see *heaved* (n.) + *sunne* (n.)]

heavie (adj.) HEAVY, weighty, profound; oppressive, hard to bear; (adv.) HEAVILY [OE]

hechhest (adj., superlat.) see *heh* (adj.)

hef (v.) see *heoven* (v.)

heh(e) (adj.) HIGH; exalted, lofty; arrogant, proud; noble, splendid; main, chief; (compar.) *herre, herrure* = higher; further above (in the text); *sum-hwet herres* = something higher (with old neuter *-es*) (compar. *herre, herrure, herres*; superlat. *hehest, hechhest, hest*) [OE]

hehi (v.) to raise, lift up; to rise, go up; worship, esteem (pres. subj. pl. *hehin*; past part. *i-hehet, i-heiet*) [from OE]

hehliche (adv.) HIGHLY, lavishly, in a noble way

hehnesse (n.) HIGHNESS, tallness, loftiness (of height, rank, or spirit) [OE]

hehschipe (n.) honor, place of honor, exultation; majesty, power; nobility, excellence; height, loftiness; loudness of voice (?)

hehunge (n.) raising, exaltation

heile (n.) health; state of happiness or prosperity; fortune, good luck, profit [OE]

hei-ward (n.) HAYWARDEN; OED: "An officer of a manor, township, or parish, having charge of the fences and enclosures, esp. to keep cattle from breaking through from the common into enclosed fields; sometimes, the herdsman of the cattle feeding on the common"

hel, heleth (v.) see *heolen* (v.)

hele (n.) HEEL [OE]

hellene (adj.) HELLISH, infernal [from OE]

helpe(n) (v.) to HELP (imper. pl. *helpeth*; past subj. sing. *hulpe*; pres. 3 sing. *helpeth*; past 2 sing. *hulpe*; past 3 sing. *healp*; past part. *i-holpen*) [OE]

hen (n.) HEN (gen. sing. *henne*; pl. *hennen*) [OE]

hende (adj.) courteous, fashionable, polite, gracious (superlat. *hendest*) [from OE]

hendeliche (adv.) courteously, politely; graciously

heo (personal pron.) see *ha* (personal pron.)

heole(n) (v.) to hide, conceal; cover (imper. sing. *hel*; pres. 1 sing. *heole*; pres. 3 sing. *heleth*; past part. *i-hole[n]*) [OE]

heom (personal pron., 3 pl.) see *ham* (personal pron.)

heonne (adv.) HENCE, away from here [OE]

heonne-ward, -wart (adv.) away from here, there [OE]

heorde (n.) HERD [OE]

heorde-monne (n., gen. sing.) HERD-MAN'S, herder's (gen. pl. *heorde-menne*) [from OE]

heorden (n. pl.) see *hearde* (n.)

heoren (pron. pl., possessive) theirs [see *hare* (pron. pl.)]

heorte (n.) HEART; chest, breast (gen. sing. *heortes*; pl. *heorten*) [OE]

heorteliche (adv.) HEARTILY; gladly

heoven (v.) to lift, raise up; exalt (in pride) (imper. sing. *hef*; past subj. sing. *heve*; pres. 3 sing. *heveth*; pres. pl. *heoveth*; past sing. *hef*; past part. *i-hoven*) [OE; ModE *heave*]

heovenliche (adv.) HEAVENLY, celestial

heove-riche (n.) HEAVEN-kingdom, kingdom of heaven (gen. sing. *heove-riches*) [OE; see *riche* (n.)]

heow (n.) form, shape, appearance; complexion; color, HUE (pl. *heowes*) [OE]

heowin (v.) to color; stain (lit. or fig.); to ornament; (past part. as adj.) *i-heowet* = colored (past sing. *heowede*; past part. *i-heowet*) [OE]

heowunge (n.) coloring, dyeing

her (adv.) HERE [OE]; (n.) HAIR [OE]

her-abuten (adv.) ABOUT or concerning this [from OE]

her-ayeines (adv.) AGAINST this, in contrast, distinction to this, in comparison with this

herbarhin (v.) to shelter, lodge, provide lodging (past sing. *herbearede*) [OE]

herbearhe (n.) lodging, shelter [see *herbarhin* (v.)]

her-bi (adv.) HEREBY; as a result of this, by this means [from OE]

her-bivoren (adv.) BEFORE this, earlier (in this text) [OE]

hercni (v.) to HEARKEN, listen to; attend to, pay attention to (imper. sing. *hercne*; imper. pl. *hercnith*; pres. 3 sing. *hercneth*;

pres. pl. *hercnith*; pres. part. *hercninde*) [OE]

hercnunge (n.) hearing, the sense of hearing; listening

herc-wile (adj.) desirous of listening, eager to listen or HEARKEN [from OE]

here (n.) HAIR-cloth, hairshirt (pl. *heren*) [OE]

here(n) (v.) to HEAR, listen to; pay attention to (imper. pl. *hereth*; pres. subj. sing. *here*; pres. 2 sing. *herest, herst*; pres. 3 sing. *hereth*; past 2 sing. *herdest*; past sing. *herde*; pres. part. *herinde*; past part. *i-herd*) [OE]

her-efter (adv.) AFTER this

here-vore (adv.) for this reason, therefore; instead of, in consideration of this

here-word (n.) PRAISE-WORD, praise, glory; reputation [OE; see *herien* (v.)]

herie(n) (v.) to praise, laud (pres. 1 sing. *herie*; pres. pl. *herieth*; past sing. *herede*) [OE]

her-of (adv.) OF this, about this

herre (n.) superior, master [either from OE *herra* "master" (see Ger. *Herr*) or from *herre* (adj.), the compar. of *heh* "high"]

herre, herrure (adj., compar.) see *heh* (adj.)

her-towart (adv.) towards this, to this end

her-toyeines (adv.) in comparison to this, against this

herunge (n. 1) HEARING, sense of hearing; listening [see *heren* (v.)]; (n. 2) praise, worship; song of praise [see *herien* (v.)]

hervest (n.) fall, autumn; August [OE; see ModE *harvest*, Ger. *herbst*]

hest (n.) promise, vow [OE; see ModE *behest*]

hest(e) (adj., superlat.) see *heh* (adj.)

heste (n.) see *heast* (n.)

het (v., past part.) see *hatte* (v.)

hete-feste (adv.) see *hete-veste* (adv.)

heterliche (adv.) sternly, violently [from OE; related to ModE *hate*]

hete-veste, hete-feste (adv.) cruelly, hatefully, relentlessly; firmly, tightly, securely; (Bennett & Smithers) "with relentless firmness" [from OE]

hetter (n.) clothing; a garment, robe (pl. *hettren*) [OE]

heve, heveth (v.) see *heoven* (v.)

heved (n.) see *heaved* (n.)

hevi(e) (adj.) HEAVY, weighty; serious; sluggish, slow; sad [OE]

hevie (adv.) HEAVILY, with great weight [OE]

hevinesse (n.) HEAVINESS; sluggishness

hexte (n.) sorcerer; the devil [OE *hægtes* "fury, witch, pythoness"; related to ModE *hag*]

hider (adv.) HITHER, towards this place; *hider ne thider* = here nor there, anywhere [OE]

hider-to (adv.) HITHERTO, up to this point [from OE]

hihful (adj.) speedy, prompt; hasty

hihin (v.) to hasten, hurry, rush, HIE (imper. sing. *hihe*; imper. pl. *hihith*; pres. subj. sing. *hihe, hihi*; pres. 1 sing. *hihi*; pres. 3 sing. *hiheth*) [OE]

hihthe (n.) haste, speed; exertion, impetuosity [OE]

himmere (adj.) inglorious, miserable (?) [see Textual Note to 2.623; MED: "?Error for *unmere; cp.* OE *unmære*. Excrescent initial *h* is rare in *Ancr.*, rare in the pref. *un-* in ME generally"]

hind-ward (adv.) BACKWARDS [OE]

hine (personal pron., 3 masc. sing., obj. form) him [OE *hine*]

hird (n.) household, family; company of servants, members of court; (fig.) heavenly retinue [OE]

hire, hiren (personal pron., 3 fem. sing., possessive) HER; (reflex.) herself; *hiren* = hers

hit (pron., 3 neut./masc. sing.) IT, his

hod (n.) HOOD, cowl (of a habit) [OE]

hofles (adj.) immoderate, excessive; unreasonable, senseless [ON]

hoker (n.) contempt, scorn, disdain; mockery, derision (obj. sing. *hokere*; pl. *hokeres*) [OE]

hokerin (v.) to scorn, mock, spite [from *hoker* (n.)]

hokerlich (adj.) scornful, spiteful, mocking

hokerunge (n.) scorn, mockery, spite, derision

hole (n.) hollow space; cave, den; HOLE (pl. *holen*) [OE]

holieth (v., pres. sing./pl.) makes HOLES, burrows, digs [OE]

holin (n.) HOLLY [OE]

homeres (n. pl.) HAMMERS [OE]

homicide (n.) murder [OF]

hommen (n.) the knee joint or back of the knee; *with hommen i-falden* = kneeling (lit., with folded knee-joints) [OE]

hond (n.) HAND; (fig.) control, power; *on hond* = as time goes by (see OED, *hand*, 32f); *honde* = to hand, handy (obj. sing. *honde*; pl. *honden*) [OE]

honde (adv.) to HAND, handy

hond-hwile (n.) instant, moment; (lit.) HAND time [OE]

hondlin (v.) to HANDLE, touch; treat (pres. subj. sing. *hondli*; past sing. *hondlede*) [OE]

hondlunge (n.) touching

hongin (v., passive inf.) to HANG; be hung (pres. 3 sing. *hongeth*; past sing. *hongede*; pres. part. *honginde*; past part. *i-hongede*) [OE]

hopien (v.) to HOPE; look for, expect; to trust, have confidence in; to think, suppose (pres. 1 sing. *hopie*; pres. pl. *hopieth*) [OE]

hord (n.) HOARD, cache [OE]

hore (n.) WHORE, prostitute; lewd woman; *hore ehe* = a whore's eye, "immodest looks" (Zettersten [1965], p. 218) (gen. sing. *hore*) [OE]

horedom (n.) prostitution, fornication, adultery; illicit sex; WHOREDOM

hosen (n. pl.) stockings [OE]

hu (adv.) HOW; in what way, in the way, as; (interj.) hey!, HO! (interjection used to call attention to something) [OE]

huckel (n.) cloak, cover; (fig.) pretense [OF]

hude (n.) skin, HIDE [OE]

hudeles, hudles (n.) a secret place, HIDING place; refuge [OE; related to *huden* (v.)]

huden (v.) to HIDE, conceal; (fig.) protect, preserve; (past part. as adj.) *i-hudde* = hidden, concealed (imper. sing. *hud*; pres. 1 sing. *hude*; pres. 2 sing. *hudest*; pres. 3 sing./pl. *hudeth*; past sing. *hudde*; past. part. *i-hud*) [OE]

hudunge (n.) HIDING

hukel (n.) cloak, mantle [OF, see Zettersten (1970), p. 241]

hul (n.) HILL (pl. *hulles*) [OE]

hulen (n. pl.) shelters, huts, tents (pl. *hulen*) [OE; related to *hulien* (v.)]

hulie(n) (v.) to hide, conceal (pres. 3 sing. *huleth*; pres. pl. *hulieth*; past part. *i-hulet*) [*OE or ON]

hulpe (v., past) see *helpen* (v.)

hulunge (n.) covering, concealing

hund (n.) dog, HOUND (gen. sing. *hundes*; pl. *hundes*) [OE]

hungri (adj.) HUNGRY [OE]

hungrin (v.) to HUNGER, to feel or grow hungry (pres. 3 sing. *hungreth*; past sing. *hungrede*) [OE]

huni (n. as adj.) HONEY [OE]

hunti (v.) to HUNT, chase after; seek eagerly (pres. 3 sing. *hunteth*; past sing. *huntede*) [OE]

hupe (n.) HIP [OE]

hurd (n.) see *hurt* (n.)

hure (adv.) at least, least of all, at any rate; especially, particularly; (sometimes doubled with same meaning) *hure ant hure* [OE *huru* "at least, indeed"]

hure (n.) HIRE, wages, pay; reward [OE]

hure (v.) to HIRE, pay someone, to reward; to bribe [OE]

huriunge (n.) HEARING [OE]

hurlith (v., pres. pl.) to rush; jostle, collide [imitative; ModE *hurl*]

hurlunge (n.) jostling, collision; tumult, uproar

hurnen (n. pl.) corners, nooks; hiding-places [OE]

hurt, hurd (n.) a knock, blow, (physical) injury; HURT, injury (pl. *hurtes*) [see *hurten* (v.)]

hurten (v.) to knock, strike (against); to wound, inflict pain, HURT (pres. subj.

sing. *hurte*; pres. 3 sing. *hurteth*; past sing. *hurte*; past part. *i-hurt*) [OF]

hurtunge (n.) HURTING, injury; hitting

hus (n.) HOUSE (often used to indicate the anchorhold) (obj. sing. *huse*; pl. *huses*) [OE]

husel (n.) the Eucharist, HOUSEL [OE]

huse-wif (n.) HOUSEWIFE, woman in charge of a household [OE]

husewifschipe (n.) managing a household, HOUSEWIFERY [see *huse-wif* (n.)]

hus-leafdi (n.) HOUSE-LADY, lady or mistress of the house [from OE]

hus-thurles (n. pl.) HOUSE-WINDOWS, openings [see *thurl* (n.)]

hut (pres. 3 sing.) see *huden* (v.)

huve (n.) cap, turban [OE]

hwa (pron.) WHO (obj. form: *hwam* "whom"; gen. *hwas* "whose") [OE]

hwar-se (adv.) see *hwer-se* (adv.)

hwa-se (pron.) WHOSOEVER, whoever [from OE]

hweat (pron.) see *hwet* (pron.)

hweate (n.) WHEAT [OE]

hwelp (n.) WHELP, pup; young of various wild animals; (the pejorative meaning, offspring of a noxious creature, first appears in the fourteenth century according to the MED) (gen. sing. *hwelpes*; pl. *hwelpes*) [OE]

hwen, hwenne, hweonne (adv. & conj.) WHEN [OE]

hwen-se (adv.) whenever; (with a following *eaver*) WHENSOEVER

hweol (n.) WHEEL, circle; wheel (as instrument of torture) (pl. *hweoles*) [OE]

hweolinde (adj., pres. part.) revolving, turning, WHEELING [from *hweol* (n.)]

hwer (adv. & conj.) WHERE [OE]

hwer-of (adv.) from WHERE, from which

hwer-se (adv.) WHERESOEVER, wherever

hwer-thurh, hwar-thurch (adv.) THROUGH what, through which, by what, by which

hwer-to (adv. & interrog.) to what; to what end, for what purpose, why

hwer-vore (adv.) WHEREFORE, for what reason, why

hwet, hwat (pron.) WHAT

hwet (pron. & interrog.) WHAT [OE]

hwether (conj.) WHETHER; (pron.) which (of two); *hwetheres* = whose (of two); (interrog.) WHETHER, (particle marking a general question, usually not translated) (gen. sing. *hwetheres*) [OE]

hwet-se (pron.) WHATSOEVER, whatever [OE]

hwi (adv. & interrog.) WHY [OE]

hwic, hwiche (adj.) see *hwuc* (adj.)

hwider (adv.) WHITHER, to where, to what place [OE]

hwider-ward (adv.) TOWARDS what place

hwil(e) (conj.) WHILE, during the time that; (n.) time, WHILE; hard-spent time, effort; *the hwile* = in the meantime, for the time being; *ane hwile* = for while [OE]

hwile (adv.) at times; *hwile . . . hwile* = at one time . . . at another time [OE]

hwiles (adv.) *the hwiles* = for, until that time [OE; ModE *while*]

hwilinde (adj., pres. part.) temporary, passing [OE]

hwit (n.) WHITE food, food made from milk [OE]

hwit(e) (adj.) WHITE (compar. *hwittre*) [OE]

hwitel (n.) bed cover, sheet [from *hwit(e)* (adj.)]

hwiteth (v., pres. 3 sing.) WHITENS, grows white [OE]

hwon (conj.) *for hwon* = as long as, provided that [OE]

hwuc(h), hwucche (adj.) what, WHICH; what kind of [OE]

i- (prefix) the *i-* prefix usually marks the past participle of verbs: for these, see the base form (without *i-*), if it exists; in a few cases, the *i-* prefix appears as part of the main verb, where it adds a general sense of completion to the meaning of the stem. These forms are listed here, along with any original past participles which had become frozen adjectives.

i, in(e) (prep.) IN, on; into, onto [OE]

i-biddeth (v., imper. pl.) pray (reflex.) [OE]

i-bocket (v., past part.) BOOKED, recorded (in a book); prophesied [OE]

i-boht (v., past part.) see *buggen* (v.)

i-bollen (v., past part.) see *bolheth* (v.)

i-boren (v., past part.) see *beoren* (v.)

i-borenesse (n.) birth [from past part. *i-boren* "born"]

i-borhen (v., past part.) (only in past part.) saved, rescued; granted salvation [OE]

i-broht (v., past part.) see *bringen* (v.)

i-broke, i-broken, i-brokene (v., past part.) see *breoken* (v.)

i-bunden (v., past part.) see *binden* (v.)

i-caht (v., past part.) see *kecchen* (v.)

i-calenget (v., past part.) see *chalengest* (v.)

ich (pron. 1 sing.) I [OE]

i-cluht (adj. & v., past part.) clenched, grasping, tight-fisted; (lit.) CLUTCHED [OE]

i-clumben (v., past part.) see *climben* (v.)

i-cnawen (v.) to identify, recognize, distinguish; KNOW, perceive; acknowledge, admit, confess; (past part. as adj.) *i-cnawen* = well known, famous; *i-cnawen is* = confesses, admits; *beo i-cnawes* = confess, admit (*-es* = old adj. ending) (pres. subj. sing. *i-cnawe*; pres. 3 sing. *i-cnaweth*; past part. *i-cnawen*) [OE]

i-cnottet (adj. & v., past part.) KNOTTED [OE]

i-colet (v., past part.) COOLED [OE]

i-corene (adj. & v., past part.) chosen (ones) [see *cheosen* (v.)]

i-corven (v., past part.) see *keorve* (v.)

i-cravet (v., past part.) CRAVED, asked earnestly, begged [OE]

i-cruchet (adj. & v., past part.) see *cruchen* (v.)

i-cud (v., past part.) see *cuthen* (v.)

i-cunnet (adj. & v., past part.) born, of family or KIN [from *cunne* (n.), fashioned into a past part.-like word]

i-curet (v., past part.) chosen [related to *cheosen* (v.)]

i-cweme (adj.) pleasing, agreeable, acceptable [OE]

idel(e) (adj.) IDLE, empty, vain; (n.) idle person; idleness [OE]

idelnesse (n.) vanity; IDLENESS, avoidance of work (pl. *idelnesses*)

i-demet (v., past part.) see *demen* (v.)

i-doddet (adj. & v., past part.) shorn (used of the hair) [from ME *dodden*]

i-dolven (v., past part.) see *delven* (v.)

i-don (v.) to DO, perform [OE]

i-evenet (v., past part.) see *eveneth* (v.)

i-falden (v., past part.) FOLDED, bent [OE]

i-feiet (v., past part.) see *feieth* (v.)

i-fele (v., pres. subj. sing.) FEEL, touch (pres. 3 sing. *i-feleth*; past part. *i-felet*) [OE; see *felen* (v.)]

i-fere (n.) companion, mate, comrade (pl. *i-feren*) [OE; related to *fearen* (v.)]

i-ferhet (v., past part.) see *ferhen* (v.)

i-finde(n) (v.) to FIND out, discover (past subj. sing. *i-funde*; pres. 3 sing. *i-fint, i-find, i-findeth*; pres. pl. *i-findeth*; past sing. *i-fond*; past part. *i-funde[n]*) [OE]

i-fluret (v., past part.) FLOWERED; flourished; (helping verb *is* = has) [see *flures* (n.)]

i-fole(n) (adj. & v., past part.) (lit.) entered, begun; about (to do something), on the point (of); *i-fole o slepe* = fallen asleep, or, on the point of sleep [see *feleth* (v.); related to and often confused with *fallen* (v.); see Shepherd, p. 45]

i-fond (v., past sing.) see *i-finden* (v.)

i-gracet (v., past part.) thanked, blessed [OF]

i-hal(e) (adj.) WHOLE, intact, undamaged [see *hal(e)* (adj.)]

i-haten (v., past part.) see *hate* (v.)

i-heafdet (adj. & v., past part.) HEADED; *hal i-heafdet* = clear headed [see *heafde* (n.)]

i-heiet (v., past part.) see *hehi* (v.)

i-heortet (adj., orig. past part.) HEARTED, with the heart disposed in a certain way [from OE]

i-heren (v.) to HEAR, listen to (pres. pl. *i-hereth*) [OE]

i-heveget (v., past part.) made HEAVY, weighed down; oppressed [OE]

i-holpen (v., past part.) see *helpen* (v.)

i-hongede (adj. as n., orig. past part.) HUNG, people who have been hung [from *hongin* (v.)]

i-hoven (v., past part.) see *heoven* (v.)

i-hudde (adj., orig. past part.) HIDDEN [see *huden* (v.)]

i-huslet (v., past part.) given the Eucharist, HOUSELED [OE]

i-hwer, i-hwear (adv.) everywhere; at all times [OE]

i-impet (v., past part.) (of trees) grafted, inserted [OE; see *impe* (n. pl.)]

i-kepen (v.) to take (something on oneself), receive; to expect, anticipate (pres. subj. sing. *i-kepe*; pres. 3 sing. *i-kepeth*; past sing. *i-kepte*) [late OE; see *kepe* (v.)]

i-lacet (v., past part.) LACED [OF]

i-laht (v., past part.) see *lecche* (v.)

i-latet (adj., orig. past part.) behaved, having a certain kind of attitude or behavior [see *lates* (n.)]

-ild, -ilt (suffix) (a n. ending which indicates a female doer) *-ess* [origin obscure]

i-leadet (adj.) LEADED, with lead tips attached [OE]

i-leanet (adj., orig. past part.) LOANED [OE; see *lane* (n.)]

i-lecchet (v., past part.) caught, captured [OE; related to *lecche* (v.)]

i-leid (v., past part.) see *leggen* (v.)

iles-piles (n., gen. sing.) hedgehog's [from OE: *il* "hedgehog" + *pil* "prickle"]

i-leven (v.) to believe firmly (imper. pl. *i-leveth*) [OE]

i-lich(e) (adj.) like, similar to (often with obj.); (adv.) equally, similarly; (conj.) LIKE

i-liche (n.) LIKE, equal, equivalent [see *i-lich(e)* (adj., etc.)]

i-licnesse (n.) LIKENESS, image [OE]

i-limet (v., past part.) stuck (together), cemented, adhered; joined, united [OE; see *lim* (n. 2)]

i-limpen (v.) to happen, occur (pres. 3 sing. *i-limpeth*; past sing. *i-lomp*; past part. *i-lumpen*) [see *limpe* (v.)]

ilke (adj.) previously mentioned, the same, the very (one, thing); (pron.) that same one, very person or thing [OE]

i-lome (adv.) often, frequently [OE]

i-lomp, i-lumpen (v.) see *i-limpen* (v.)

i-meane (adj.) shared, common; held in common, together [OE; see Ger. *gemein* "common"]

i-membret (adj.) MEMBERED, having members; divided into links (or, perhaps, decorative panels) [from OF]

i-mene (adv.) together, jointly, in common; in a body [OE]

i-mengt (v., past part.) see *mengde* (v.)

i-mette (v., past sing.) MET, came together with [OE]

i-mid (prep.) AMID, in the middle, midst of [OE]

i-mist (v., past part.) MISSED, noticed the loss of [OE]

i-mong (prep.) among, in, amidst [OE]

impe (n. pl.) young shoots or saplings; grafted branches [OE]

i-munt (v., past part.) see *munten* (v.) or *i-munten* (v.)

i-munten (v.) to intend, resolve (to do something) (past part. *i-munt*) [OE]

in (n.) INN, lodging, dwelling [OE]

-inde (pres. part. ending) = ModE *-ing*

i-neilet (v., past part.) NAILED [OE]

inne (adv.) IN, inside

in-obedience (n.) DISOBEDIENCE [OF]

i-noh(e), i-noch (adj.) ENOUGH; (adv.) enough, sufficiently [OE]

inoh-reathe (adv.) readily ENOUGH, quickly, eagerly; very rashly [see *i-noh* (adj.) + *reathere* (adv.)]

inre (adj.) INNER [OE]

in-read (adj.) very RED, ruddy [*in-* here is an intensifier]

in-turn (n.) coming, visit; a "TURNING IN" [OE + OF]

i-nume, inumen(e) (v., past part.) see *neomen* (v.)

in-ward(e) (adj.) INWARD, profound, deep; earnest, deeply felt [OE]

in-wardliche (adv.) INWARDLY; intimately, thoroughly, fervently, profoundly; secretly, silently, to oneself (compar. *inwardluker*; superlat. *inwardlukest*) [OE]

in-wit (n.) conscience [a ME word, formed from *in-* "interior" + *wit* "knowledge," not related to OE *inwit* "deceit"]

in-with (adv.) WITHIN, on the inside; (prep.) within, inside of

in-wuniende (adj., pres. part.) in-dwelling [see *wunien* (v.), based on Lat. *inhabitare*]

in-yong (n.) entrance; (fig.) entry, beginning, opportunity; permission [OE; see Ger. *eingang*]

i-paiet (v., past part.) see *paien* (v.)

i-pliht (v., past part.) see *plihten* (v.)

i-readet (v., past part.) REDDENED, made red [OE]

i-rend (v., past part.) RENT, torn, stripped [OE; ModE *rend*]

irene (adj.) IRON, made of iron

i-riht (v., past part.) see *rihten* (v.)

irn (n.) IRON; mail-shirt made of iron (used to mortify the flesh); iron bit of a bridle (gen. sing. *irnes*) [OE]

i-rotet (v., past part.) ROOTED, established [late OE, from ON]

i-rudet (v., past part.) reddened, made RUDDY [from OE]

i-sahtnet (v., past part.) see *sahtni* (v.)

i-scandlet (adj. & v., past part.) SCANDALIZED, shocked; injured by evil example, led astray [later occurrences preserve the etymological sense of "stumble, cause to stumble"; see *scandle* (n.)]

i-schake (adj., orig. past part.) violent, SHAKEN [see *schaken* (v.)]

i-schaven (v., past part.) SHAVEN [OE]

i-scheod (adj. & v., past part.) SHOD, with shoes on [from OE]

i-schriven, i-scrive (v., past part.) see *schriven* (v.)

i-schrud (v., past part.) see *schruden* (v.)

i-sealet (adj., orig. past part.) SEALED; OED: "Bearing the impression of a signet in wax (or other material), as evidence or guarantee of authenticity" [OF]

i-seo(n) (v.) to SEE, look on; observe, perceive; visit (pres. subj. sing. *i-sehe*; pres. 1 sing. *i-seo*; past sing. *i-seh* [OE]

i-slein(e) (v., past part.) see *slean* (v.)

i-smaket (v., past part.) adorned (Vitellius translates *acemee* "adorned") [OE *smacian* "to allure, seduce"]

i-soht (v., past part.) see *sechen* (v.)

i-sompnet (v., past part.) joined, gathered [OE; see Ger. *sammeln* "to collect"]

i-sontet (v., past part.) SAINTED, made saints [OE, from Lat.]

i-spearet (v., past part.) see *spearien* (v.)

i-spenet (v., past part.) SPENT [*OE]

i-staket (v., past part.) STAKED, tied to a stake [from OE]

i-sticchet (adj. & v., past part.) STITCHED, fastened, sewn up [from OE]

i-straht(e) (v., past part.) see *streche* (v.)

i-stunt (v., past part.) stopped, ceased; stupefied, exhausted [OE]

i-sturbet (v., past part.) DISTURBED, upset [OF; clipped form of *disturb*]

i-sutelet (v., past part.) see *suteli* (v.)

i-swipt (v., past part.) SWEPT (away) [*OE]

i-sworen (v., past part.) see *swerien* (v.)

i-swunken (v., past part.) see *swinken* (v.)

i-tachet (v., past part.) ATTACHED, fastened [OF]

i-taht (v., past part.) see *teachen* (v.)

i-tald (v., past part.) see *tellen* (v.)

i-tawet (adj. & v., past part.) (of leather) tanned; softened, broken-in [OE]

i-techen (v.) to deliver, bestow; TEACH, instruct [OE]

i-teiet (v., past part.) see *teith* (v.)

i-teilet (adj.) TAILED, having a certain kind of tail [OE; from *teil* (n.)]

i-thench (v., imper. pl.) THINK, think about [OE]

i-thoht (v., past part.) see *thenchen* (v.)

i-thoncket (adj. & v., past part.) thoughted, minded [from OE *ge-þanc* "thought"]; see *thonkin* (v.)

i-thorschen (v., past part.) see *thersche* (v.)

i-thuht (v., past part.) see *thunchen* (v.)

i-toh, i-tohene (v., past part. as adj.) see *teoth* (v.)

i-toren (v., past part.) see *tereth* (v.)

i-trusset (adj. & v., past part.) see *trusse* (v.)

i-tuht (v., past part.) taught, instructed, disciplined [OE; see ModE *tighten*]

i-turplet (v., past part.) see *torplin* (v.)

i-uppet (v., past part.) see *uppin* (v.)

i-veiet (v., past part.) see *feieth* (v.)

i-vithered (v., past part.) FEATHERED, equipped with a feather [OE]

i-vorthet (v., past part.) see *fortheth* (v.)

i-warth (v., past sing.) see *i-wurthen* (v.)

i-weallet (v., past part.) boiled [OE]

i-weddet (v., past part.) married, WED [OE; see *wed* (n.)]

i-weiet (v., past part.) see *weien* (v.)

i-wis, i-wiss (adv.) certainly, assuredly; indeed [OE]

i-wist (v., past part.) see *witen* (v. 1)

i-wite (v., past part.) see *witen* (v. 2)

i-wonet (v., past part.) see *wunien* (v.)

i-wordet (adj.) WORDED [from *word* (n.)]

i-wraht(e) (v., past part.) see *wurchen* (v.)

i-wriyen (v., past part.) see *wrihen* (v.)

i-wunnen (v., past part.) WON, gained [OE]

i-wurthe(n) (v.) to happen, occur; to become, be; *let i-wurthen* = to let (something) be, leave alone (pres. subj. sing. *i-wurthe*; pres. 3 sing. *i-wurtheth, i-wurth*; past sing. *i-warth*; past part. *i-worthen*) [OE; see *wurthen* (v.)]

i-yemen (v.) to pay attention (to), care about, attend to [see *yemen* (v.)]

i-yeve(n) (v., past part.) see *yeoven* (v.)

juggi (v.) to JUDGE [OF]

juglurs (n. pl.) minstrel, singer; entertainer (usually itinerant); JUGGLER, dancer; (pejorative) enchanter, deceiver (pl. *juglurs*) [OF]

jurnee (n.) (a day's) JOURNEY [OF]

kaue (n.) one of several birds of the crow family: crow; jackdaw, jay [OF, imitative; see ModE *caw*]

kealch-cuppe (n.) tosspot, drunkard [*kealch-* perhaps related to *gulchen* (v.) "to vomit"]

keast (n.) see *chast* (n.)

keaste(n) (v.) to CAST, throw, toss; set (past part. *i-keast*) [ON; see d'Ardenne (1961), pp. 159–61]

kecchen (v.) to hunt for, chase; CATCH, capture; seize, lay hold of (imper. sing. *keche*; pres. subj. sing. *kecche*; pres. 3 sing. *kecheth*, past sing. *cahte*; past part. *i-caht*) [ONF, related to ModE *chase*]

keiser (n.) emperor (pl. *keisers*) [ON, from Lat. *Caesar*]

kempe (n.) fighter, warrior (gen. pl. *kempene*) [OE]

kempe-ifere (n.) fellow fighter [see *kempe* (n.) + *i-fere* (n.)]

kene (adj.) bold, brave; eager, ready, daring; fierce, savage, cruel; sharp, KEEN, pointed; pungent; shrewd, observant [OE]

kenneth (v., pres. 3 sing.) declares, makes known [OE, related to *cunnen* (v.); see ModE phrase *beyond our ken*]

keorfunge (n.) see *keorvunge* (n.)

keorve (v., pres. subj. sing.) cut; slash, injure by cutting; *keorvinde* (pres. part. as adj.) = cutting, sharp (past subj. sing. *kurve*; past sing. *kearf*; pres. part. *keorvinde*; past part. *i-corven*) [OE; ModE *carve*]

keorvunge (n.) cutting; cut, gash

kepe (v.) to KEEP, hold; care (for), desire; to notice, regard; try to catch, wait for; greet (past subj. sing. *kepte*; pres. 1 sing.

kepe; pres. 3 sing. *kepeth*; past sing. *kepte*; past part. *i-kepte*) [late OE; see also *i-kepen* (v.)]

kimeth (v.) see *cumen* (v.)

kinedom (n.) KINGDOM (pl. *kinedomes*) [OE]

ku (n.) COW (gen. sing. *kues*) [OE]

kun (n.) see *cun* (n.)

kunne(n) (v.) see *cunnen* (v.)

kurve (v.) see *keorve* (v.)

lachhere (adj.) see *lah* (adj.)

lachyen (v.) see *lahhen* (v.)

lade (n.) LOAD, burden [OE]

ladlechin (v.) to disfigure, spoil, render LOATHsome [from *ladlich* (adj.)]

ladles (adj.) see *lathles* (adj.)

ladlich(e) (adj.) hateful, disgusting, horrible, LOATHLY (superlat. *ladlukeste*) [OE]

ladliche (adv.) fiercely, angrily; harshly, seriously; in a cowardly way, basely; disgustingly, in a LOATHSOME way; wickedly

lah(e) (adj.) LOW; humble, brought low; base, contemptible (compar. *lahre, lachhere*; compar. gen. sing. *lahres*) [ON]

lahe (n.) LAW [OE]

lahe, lahhe (adv.) LOW, in a low position; humbly [ON]

lahedest (v., past 2 sing.) humbled, brought LOW [see *lah* (adj.)]

lahhen (v.) to LAUGH (imper. pl. *lahheth*; pres. 3 sing. *laheth, lahheth*; pres. part. *lah(h)inde*) [OE]

lahnesse (n.) LOWLINESS, humility

lahschipe (n.) LOWLINESS, humility

lahte (v., past sing.) see *lecche* (v.)

lahter (n.) LAUGHTER (pl. *lahtren*) [OE]

lahtre(n) (n.) see *lahter* (n.)

lakes (n. pl.) gifts, offerings [OE]

land-uvel (n.) LAND disease; epidemic, pestilence

lane (n.) LOAN; *to lane* = as a loan [OE]

lanhure (adv.) at least [from OE]

lare (n.) teaching, LORE [OE; see *learen* (v.)]

larewes (n. pl.) teachers [OE; see *lare* (n.)]

large (adj.) generous, bountiful; ample, abundant; wide, LARGE (compar. *largere*) [OF]

largeliche (adv.) freely, copiously

largesce (n.) generosity, LARGESSE [see *large* (adj.)]

lastin (v.) to blame, find fault with (imper. sing. *laste*) [ON]

lastunge (n.) blame, detraction

lates (n. pl.) gestures, expressions; bearing, behavior, way; facial expression, aspect; appearance; pretense, false seeming [ON]

lath (adj.) hostile, spiteful; LOATHSOME, repulsive, hateful (compar. *lathre*, superlat. *lathest*) [OE]

lathi (v., pres. subj. sing.) be hateful, unpleasant; (impers.) *thet him lathi* = so that (it) may be hateful to him

lathles (adj.) innocent, harmless [from *lath* (adj.) + *-les* "LESS"]

lave (n.) remnant, legacy, what is LEFT [OE]

laverd (n.) LORD: a human lord, or God (gen. sing. *laverdes*) [OE]

laz (n.) a silken cord, cord of braided silk [OF; ModE *lace*]

leaddre (n.) LADDER [OE]

leaddre-steolen (n. pl.) LADDER-uprights, sides (of a ladder) [from OE]

leade(n) (v.) to LEAD, bring; conduct (one's life) (imper. sing. *lead*; pres. subj. sing. *leade*; pres. 3 sing. *leadeth, leat*; pres. 2 pl. *leadeth*; past sing. *leadde*; past part. *i-lead*) [OE]

leaf, leafde (v.) see *leaven* (v.)

leafdi (n.) LADY, either a woman of the nobility or the Virgin (pl. *leafdis*) [OE]

leafdiluker (adj., compar.) more LADYLIKE, more like a noble woman

leafdischipe (n.) LADYSHIP; standing, rank as a lady

leane (adj.) LEAN, emaciated [OE]

leapen (v.) to LEAP, jump; leap upon; dance; run; (pres. part.) *leapinde* = leaping (pres. subj. sing. *leape*; pres. 3 sing. *leapeth*; past sing. *leop*; pres. part. *leapinde*) [OE]

leapes (n. pl.) LEAPS; baskets, measures (?) [related either to *leapen* (v.) or to OE *hleap* "measure"]

learen (v.) to teach, instruct; to learn (pres. 3 sing. *leareth*; past sing. *learde*; past part. *i-learet*) [OE; see Ger. *lehren* "to teach"]

leas(e) (adj.) false, lying, untruthful; faithless; LOOSE, immoral [see *leas* (n.)]

leas, les (n.) falsehood, lie [OE]

leasketh (v., pres. 3 sing.) weakens, lowers in quality, loosens, slackens [OF, from Lat. *laxare* "to loosen"]

leasse, lasse (adj. & adv.) LESS (compar. of *lut* [adj.]) [OE]

least (adj.) LEAST, least substantial, important; (adv.) least, in the least way, at all (superlat. of *lut* [adj.])

leaste (adj.) LAST, previously mentioned (superlat. of *lut* [adj.]) [OE]

leasten (v.) to LAST, continue; stop, pause (pres. 3 sing. *least, leasteth*; pres. pl. *leasteth*) [OE]

leasunge (n.) lie, lying tale, falsehood (pl. *leasunges*) [OE]

leat (v., pres. 3 sing.) see *leaden* (v.)

leate (adv.) slowly, reluctantly; LATE, after a long time; much later; recently, lately (compar. *leatere*) [OE]

leate-meste (adj.) final, LATEMOST, latest, last; lowest in rank, humblest [OE]

leathie (v., imper. pl.) to invite, call, summon (pres. 3 sing. *leathieth*; past sing. *leathede*) [OE; see Ger. *einladen* "to invite"]

leaththe (n.) hostility, ill-will [OE, from *lath* (adj.)]

leattre (n.) LETTER; literal meaning (pl. *leattres*) [OF]

leave (n.) permission, LEAVE [OE]

leaveden (v., past pl.) washed, flowed [OE, from Lat.; see ModE *lavatory*]

leaven (v.) to LEAVE; abandon, desert, give up; stop, omit; to depart; persist, endure; stay, remain, linger; leave (as an inheritance) (imper. sing. *leaf*; imper. pl. *leaveth*; pres. subj. sing. *leave*; pres. 1 sing. *leave*; pres. 3 sing. *leaveth*; past 2 sing. *leafdest*; past sing. *leafde*; past pl. *leafden*; past part. *i-leavet*) [OE]

lecche (v., pres. subj. sing.) catch, snatch, seize, LATCH onto; trap, snare; take, receive, get; catch (a sickness) (pres. 3 sing. *lecheth*; past sing. *lahte*; past part. *i-laht*) [OE]

leccherie (n.) LECHERY, sinful lust (pl. *leccheries*) [OF]

lecchur (n.) LECHER; person debauched by lust (pl. *lecchurs*) [OF]

leche (n.) doctor, LEECH [OE]

leche-creft (n.) medicine, physic, art of healing [OE; see early ModE *leechcraft*]

lechni(n) (v.) to cure, heal; administer medicine [OE; from *leche* (n.)]

ledene (n.) language, tongue [OE]

lef, lefde (v.) see *leven* (v. 2)

leflich (adj.) attractive, LOVELY; lovable [OE]

lefunge (n.) BELIEF [OE]

leggen (v.) to LAY, place, put; to lay (an egg); set on (imper. sing. *lei*; pres. subj. sing. *legge*; pres. 1 sing. *legge*; pres. 3 sing. *leith*; past sing. *leide*; past pl. *leiden*; past part. *i-leid*) [OE]

lehe (n.) field, meadow, glade, clearing; *wenden eie towarde the wode lehe* = "to turn the eye to the woodland glade," (MED) i.e., have an interest in wild or forbidden pleasures [OE; ModE *lea*]

lei(e) (n.) flame, fire, blaze [OE]

lei(e), leien (v., past) see *liggen* (v.)

leide(n) (v., past) see *leggen* (v.)

leith (v., pres. 3 sing.) see *leggen* (v.)

leitin (v.) to flash, glow, blaze (pres. 3 sing. *leiteth*; pres. pl. *leitinde*) [*OE; related to *leie* (n.)]

lei-ven (n.) lake-FEN, swamp [from OE]

lenden (n. pl.) loins [*OE]

lengre, lengrest (adv.) see *longe* (adv.)

lenten (n.) LENT; spring [OE]

leof (adj.) see *leove* (adj.)

leoflich(e) (adj.) lovable, LOVELY; attractive

leofliche (adv.) LOVINGLY, pleasantly, graciously; beautifully [OE]

leof-mon (n.) beloved, sweetheart, lover (gen. sing. *leof-monnes*) [OE]

leohe (n.) shelter [OE; ModE *lee*]

leome (n.) light, brightness; flash, gleam [OE]

leonie (v., pres. subj. sing.) LEAN, support (oneself) [OE]

leop (v., past sing.) see *leapen* (v.)

leor (n.) the cheek; face [OE]

leorni(n) (v.) to LEARN (imper. sing. *leorne*; imper. pl. *leornith*; pres. subj. sing. *leorni*; past sing. *leornede*; past pl. *leorneden*; pres. pl. *leornith*) [OE]

leosen (v.) to LOSE; misplace (pres. 3 sing./pl. *leoseth*; past part. *i-losed*) [OE]

l(e)oten (v.) to LET, leave; allow, to have (something done); omit, leave out; shed, LET (blood); *leoten of* = to look upon, regard; pretend, let on; *leoten wel of* = to think highly of, esteem (something) (imper. sing. *leote*; imper. pl. *leoteth*; pres. 3 sing. *let, leoteth*; past sing. *lette*; past part. *i-let, i-lete, i-lete[n]*) [OE]

leotheliche (adv.) loosely [from OE]

leove (adj.) beloved, dear, pleasing; (compar.) *leov(e)re* = more pleasing, preferable (superlat. *leovest[e]*) [OE]

leovest (adj., superlat.) see *leove* (adj.)

lepruse (adj.) LEPROUS [OF]

-les(e) (suffix) -LESS, without [OE]

lesceune (n.) reading; lecture; LESSON (pl. *lesceunes, lesceuns*) [OF]

lesen (v.) to release, set LOOSE [OE]

lesewe (n.) pasture, field (pl. *lesewen*) [OE]

leste (conj.) LEST, for fear that [from OE]

letanie (n.) LITANY; a prayer taking the form of a series of petitions, often to various saints [OF, from Lat.]

lete(n) (v.) see *leoten* (v.)

lette (v., past sing.) see *leoten* (v.)

letten (v.) to hinder, delay; to stop (pres. subj. sing. *lette*; past part. *i-lette*) [OE]

letuaire (n.) medicine (usually in syrup form) (pl. *letuaires*) [OF, from Lat.]

leve (n.) see *leave* (n.)

leven (v. 1) to allow, grant, give LEAVE [OE]; (v. 2) to BELIEVE, trust, have faith in (imper. sing. *lef*; imper. pl. *leveth, leve (ye)*; pres. subj. sing. *leve*; pres. 1 sing. *leve*; pres. 3 sing. *leveth*; past sing. *lefde*; past pl. *lefden*; past part. *i-levet*) [OE]

levunge (n.) BELIEVING, trust, faith [OE]

li (v., imper. sing.) see *liggen* (v.)

libben, libbeth (v.) see *livien* (v.)

lich (n.) (living) body; corpse [OE; see ModE *lichgate*, Ger. *leiche* "corpse"]

liche (n.) LIKENESS, similitude [OE]

lichomliche (adj.) bodily, physically; carnally [OE; see *lich* (n.)]

lickre (adj., compar.) more LIKE, more similar [see *i-lich* (adj.)]

licnesse (n.) LIKENESS, similarity, resemblance [OE]

licome (n.) (living) body, flesh; (dead) body, corpse; life, existence (gen. sing. *licomes*; pl. *licomes*) [OE]

licomlich(e) (adj.) bodily, physical

licomliche (adv.) physically, bodily

licunge (n.) pleasure, delight; lust, (illicit) desire; gratification [OE]

licur (n.) LIQUID, fluid [OF]

lic-wurthe (adj.) LIKE-WORTHY, pleasing, agreeable; acceptable [OE]

lideth (v., pres. 3 sing.) covers, puts a LID on (past part. *i-lided*) [OE]

lif (n.) LIFE; (adj.) *lives* = alive (gen. sing. *lives*) [OE]

lif-hali (adj.) LIFE-HOLY, holy of life

lif-lade (n.) food, provisions; conduct, behavior, way of life [OE]

liggen (v.) to LIE, recline; *liggen on, under* = to suffer from (imper. sing. *li*; pres. subj. sing. *ligge*; pres. 3 sing. *lith*; pres.

pl. *liggeth*; past sing. *lei[e]*; past pl. *leien*; past part. *i-lein*) [OE]

liggunge (n.) LYING, reclining; sleeping

lihen (v.) to LIE, not tell the truth; speak falsely; to trick, deceive; *lihen on* = to tell lies about (someone) (imper. sing. *lih*; pres. subj. sing. *lihe*; pres. 2 sing. *lihest*; pres. 3 sing. *liheth*) [OE]

liht (n.) LIGHT [OE]

liht(e) (adj.) LIGHT, not heavy; trivial, frivolous; of little value, cheap; easy, not difficult; quick (compar. *lihtre*) [OE]

lihte (adv.) LIGHTLY, easily

lihten, lihtin (v.) to lighten, become LIGHT, lose heaviness; become clear, evident; to arrive, come; to descend, ALIGHT, drop down (pres. 3 sing. *lihteth*; past sing. *lihte*; past part. *i-liht, i-lihtet*) [OE]

lihtliche (adv.) LIGHTLY, easily; cheaply; carelessly, irresponsibly [see *liht* (adj.)]

likin (v.) to please (impers.), be pleased; to LIKE, wish, want, choose; *(hit) liketh hire* = she is pleased, glad (pres. subj. sing. *liki*; pres. 3 sing. *liketh*) [OE]

lim (n. 1) LIMB, member (gen. sing. *limes*; pl. *limen*) [OE]; (n. 2) LIME, mortar, cement [OE]

lime (n.) file [OF]

limpe (v., pres. subj. sing.) befall, happen (to); be proper, suitable; belong, apply, pertain (to) (pres. 3 sing. *limpeth*; past part. *i-lumpen*) [OE]

limunge (n.) a joining or cementing (of one thing to another), uniting [OE]

linnene (adj.) LINEN, made from linen [OE]

lippen (n. pl.) LIPS [OE]

liste (n.) dexterity; ability, skill, art; cunning trick, stratagem; *with liste* =

deftly, cunningly, wisely [OE; see Ger. *list* "cunning"]

listen (v.) to desire, wish; (impers.) *hire list* = she desires, wishes [OE]

lite (n.) color; appearance [ON]

lith (n.) limb, member; joint (pl. *lithes*) [OE]; (v., pres. 3 sing.) see *liggen* (v.)

lithe (adj.) gentle, meek, mild [OE]

litheliche (adv.) mildly, gently, meekly

lithere (v., imper. sing.) sling, hurl, let loose [from OE]

litien (v.) to dye, color; paint (the face); (fig.) give the appearance (of something else), color (pres. 3 sing. *liteth*) [ON]

litunge (n.) coloring, painting

live (n.) see *lif* (n.)

liveneth (n.) provision, food, sustenance; livelihood; spiritual food [ON]

lives (adj.) see *lif* (n.)

livien (v.) to LIVE, exist (pres. 1 sing. *livie*; pres. 3 sing. *liveth*; pres. pl. *libbeth, livieth*; past sing. *livede*; past pl. *liveden*; pres. part. *liviende*; past part. *i-lived*) [OE]

lo, low (exclamation) oh!; see! (an expression used to direct attention to something) [OE]

locunge (n.) LOOKING, gaze; look, expression; observation, observance (pl. *locunges*) [see *lokin* (v.)]

lof (n.) a spar holding out and down the windward tack of a square sail; *wenden lof* = to change course [Ger., exact origin obscure]

loft-song (n.) song of praise, hymn, psalm [from OE; see MED *loft* (n. 2)]

logeth (v., pres. 3 sing.) LODGES; encamps, takes up a position (past sing. *logede*; past part. *i-loget*) [OF]

loke (adj., orig. past part.) LOCKED, fastened [see *loken* (v.)]

loken (v.) to LOCK, shut securely (past part. *i-lokene*) [OE]

loki(n) (v.) to LOOK; make sure, see too it that; have the appearance of being, seem; to consider, regard, look to (something) (imper. sing. *loke*; imper. pl. *lokith*; pres. subj. sing. *loki*; pres. 1 sing. *loki*; pres. 2 sing. *lokest*; pres. 3 sing. *loketh*; pres. pl. *lokith*; past sing. *lokede*; past pl. *lokeden*; past part. *i-loket*) [OE]

lome (n.) tool, implement; weapon (pl. *lomen*) [OE; ModE *loom*]

lond(e) (n.) country, LAND, nation (pl. *londes*) [OE]

lond-uvel (n.) LAND-EVIL, disease that engulfs an entire land; plague, epidemic [see *uvel* (n.)]

longe (adv.) LONG, for a long time (compar. *lengre*; superlat. *lengest*) [OE]

longeth (v., pres. 3 sing.) LONGS for; (impers.) *thet longeth ham to* = which they long for [OE]

longunge (n.) desire, wish, LONGING; sexual desire; distress, anxiety, weariness [OE]

loquacite (n.) LOQUACITY, talkativeness [OF]

lorimers (n. pl.) workers in small ironware (for example, bits, harnesses, spurs, etc.), ironworkers [OF]

lot (n.) share, LOT, part [OE *hlott* "lot" as in "to cast lots"]

lowr (interj.) look!, look where!, lo! [contraction of *lo hwer*]

lowse (adj.) LOOSE [ON]

lowsith (v., imper. pl.) LOOSEN, let loose, release [ON]

lud(e) (adj. & adv.) LOUD (compar. *luddre*) [OE]

lufsum(e) (adj.) LOVESOME, lovable; lovely (compar. *lufsumre*; superlat. *lufsumest*) [OE]

luft (n. & adj.) LEFT; (with pejorative implications) left as a "sinister" side [OE]; (n. 2) the air, atmosphere; sky [OE; see Ger. *luft*]

lufte (n.) air, sky [OE]

lupe (n.) a LEAP, jump [OE]

lure (n.) loss; hurt, damage (pl. *luren*) [OE; related to *leosen* (v.)]

lust (n.) pleasure, delight; desire, appetite (pl. *lustes*) [OE; ModE *lust*]

luste (v., pres. 3 sing.) (impers.) (it) pleases; *him luste* = (it) pleases him, he desires (past sing. *luste*) [OE; see Jack (1977), pp. 24–26]

lusti (adj.) joyful; vigorous, LUSTY [OE]

lustni (v.) to LISTEN to, hear; pay attention to; obey (past: *lustnede*) [*OE]

lut (pron.) few [from *lut* (adj.)]

lut(e) (adj.) LITTLE, small; (adv.) little, not very much [OE]

lute (v., imper. sing.) bow, stoop (in submission) (imper. pl. *luteth*; pres. part. *lutinde*) [OE]

lutel, lutle (adj. & adv.) LITTLE (gen. sing. *lutles*) [OE]

lutes-ihweat (n.) trifle, LITTLE-WHAT, a little something

luther(e) (adj.) deceitful, treacherous, wicked; hurtful, severe [OE]

luthere (adv.) wickedly, treacherously [see *luther* (adj.)]

lutherliche (adv.) wickedly, viciously [OE]

lutles-ihweat (n.) a LITTLE something

luve (n.) LOVE (gen. sing. *luves*; pl. *luven*) [OE]

luve-gleames (n. pl.) LOVE-GLEAMS, love-rays

luve-lates (n. pl.) LOVE-LOOKS, -gestures [see *lates* (n. pl.)]

luvelich (adj.) LOVING, kind [OE]

luveliche (adv.) LOVINGLY, kindly [OE]

luve-lokin (v.) to cast LOVE-LOOKS, (lit.) to LOVE-LOOK

luve-salve (n.) LOVE cure [see *salve* (n.)]

luve-wurthe (adj.) LOVEWORTHY

luvie(n) (v.) to LOVE (imper. pl. *luvieth*; pres. subj. sing./pl. *luvie*; pres. 2 sing. *luvest*; pres. 3 sing. *luveth*; pres. pl. *luvieth*; past 2 sing. *luvedest*; past sing. *luvede*; past pl. *luveden*; past part. *i-luvet*) [OE]

ma (adj., adv., & n.) MORE [OE]

mahe (n.) stomach [OE; see Ger. *magen* "stomach"]

mahe, mahen, maht, mahte, mahten (v.) see *mei* (v.)

make (n.) lover, mate, partner; equal, companion [OE]

makie(n) (v.) to MAKE, put, do; cause (to do something) (imper. sing. *make*; imper. pl. *makieth, makie (ye)*; pres. subj. sing. *makie*; pres. 1 sing. *makie*; past 2 sing. *makedest*; pres. 3 sing. *maketh*; pres. pl. *makieth*; past sing. *makede*; past pl. *makeden*; past part. *i-maket, i-makede*) [OE]

man (n.) MOAN, complaint; sorrow [*OE]

manciple (n.) supplier, purchaser of food and provisions [OF]

manere (n.) MANNER, way; way of life; usage, practice, custom (pl. *maneres*) [OF]

mare (adj. & adv.) see *ma* (adj. & adv.)

marhen (n.) MORN, morning [OE]

marhe-yeove (n). MORROW-GIFT: a gift presented to the bride on the morning (morrow) after the wedding; a dowry (pl. *marhe-yeoven, -yeven*) [OE]

mat (adj.) check-MATED; conquered, beaten, overcome [OF]

maten, matin (v.) to conquer, beat, overcome; to check-MATE [OF]

materie (n.) MATTER, subject, topic [OF]

matten (n. pl.) MATS, beds [OE]

me (adv. & interj.) but, on the contrary; moreover [OE; perhaps modeled after OF *mais*]

me (indef. pron.) one, someone, a person; they, people (indef.); (constructions with *me* can often be translated as passive) [a further reduction of unstressed ME *men* from OE *man* "one"]

meadles(e) (adj.) without restraint or moderation, unbridled; continuous, persistent [OE]

meadlesliche (adv.) without moderation or restraint; continuously, without limit (compar. *meadlesluker*)

meadluker (adj., compar.) MADDER, more insane; more furious, violent [from OE]

meadschipe (n.) MADNESS, insanity; absurdity in thought, foolishness; audacity, rashness [from OE]

mealteth (v., pres. 3 sing.) MELTS, dissolves, dwindles (past part. *i-mealt*) [OE]

meane (v., pres. 1 sing.) MEAN, intend [OE]

meanen (v.) to complain; MOAN, wail; cry to; (reflex.) to make a complaint; bewail, mourn for (past sing. *meande*) [OE]

meanildes (n.) women given to complaining [from OE; see *meanen* (v.) and *-ild* (suffix)]

meapeth (v., pres. 3 sing.) wanders aimlessly, strays (reflex.); MOPES [origin obscure; see Bennett & Smithers, pp. 409–10]

mearciable (adj.) MERCIFUL [OF]

meare (n.) MARE, female horse [OE]

mearewe (adj.) tender, delicate [OE]

mearke (n.) MARK, sign; boundary, limit; district, province (pl. *mearken*, *merken*) [OE]

mearken (n.) to MARK, brand; describe, designate (past part. *i-mearket*) [OE]

measeliche (adv.) confusedly, in a dazed, bewildered way [related to *a-measet* (v.)]

measse, messe (n.) MASS, service of the Eucharist (pl. *meassen*) [OE, from Lat.]

measse-cos (n.) MASS-KISS, kiss of peace in the mass [from OE]

measse-kemese (n.) MASS-CHEMISE, alb (a church vestment: a long, white tunic) [from OE, both elements ultimately from Lat. sources]

measseth (v., pres. 3 sing.) says or celebrates MASS [OE]

meast(e) (superlat.) (adj.) MOST, greatest; (adv.) most, to the greatest extent; mostly [OE; see *ma* (adj. & adv.)]

meatheleth (v., pres. 3 sing.) talks, speaks; tells; chatters, prates (pres. part. *meathelinde*) [OE *maðelian* "to speak formally"]

meathelilt (n.) a gossip, a woman given to talking or chattering [from OE; see *meatheleth* (v.) and *-ild* (suffix)]

meathelunge (n.) talk, chatter

meathful (adj.) moderate, modest [OE]

meathfulliche (adv.) modestly, moderately

mede (n.) reward, merit; payment (pl. *meden*) [OE]

medeles (adj.) lit. MEEDLESS, without reward or merit, undeserving, unworthy [OE; see *mede* (n.) + *-les(e)* (suffix)]

mehe (n.) kinswoman [OE]

mei (v., pres. sing.) MAY, be able (pres. subj. sing. *mahe, muhe*; pres. subj. pl. *muhe(n)*; past subj. sing. *muhte*; pres. 2 sing. *maht;* pres. pl. *mahen;* past 2 sing. *mahtest*; past sing. *mahte*; past pl. *mahten*) [OE]

meiden-had (n.) MAIDENHEAD, virginity [OE]

meister, meistre (n.) MASTER; teacher, spiritual director (gen. sing. *meistres*; pl. *meistres*) [probably OF rather than OE]

meistrie (n.) great, MASTERFUL deed, feat, triumph; force, power; authority (pl. *meistries*) [OF]

meistrin (v.) to MASTER [OF]

meith-had see *meiden-had* (n.)

meith-lure (n.) loss of virginity; fornication [OE; see *lure* (n.)]

mel (n.) MEAL, food taken at a customary time (for example, breakfast, supper) [OE]

men (n. pl.) see *mon* (pron.)

mendith (v., imper. pl.) MEND, repair [OF]

menestraws (n. pl.) servants, MINISTERS; MINSTRELS, jugglers, entertainers [OF]

mengde (v., past sing.) mixed, blended; united, brought together; stirred up, confused; MINGLED with (in conversation, intercourse, or marriage) (past part. *i-mengt*) [OE]

menske (n.) honor, repute; kindness, humanity; beauty, fairness (pl. *mensken*) [ON]

menskeliche (adv.) courteously, reverently; honorably [see *menske* (n.)]

meoke (adj.) soft, MEEK, humble; modest [ON]

meokin (v.) to humble, soften, make MEEK; abase (oneself) (imper. pl. *meokith*) [ON]

meonurs (n. pl.) *freres meonurs* = "lesser brothers"; (i.e.,) the Franciscans [OF; translation of Lat. *fratres minores*]

meoseise (adj.) miserable, wretched; poor, destitute, hungry; infirm, feeble [OF];(n.) physical, mental discomfort; need, hardship, poverty (pl. *meoseises*) [OF]

meoster (n.) employment, position; job, occupation; function, task; skill, art (pl. *meosters*) [OF; ModE *mystery* "profession"]

meosure (n.) MEASURE; moderation, due proportion [OF]

mercer (n.) cloth merchant, merchant [OF]

merite (n.) MERIT, reward [OF]

merke(n) (n.) see *mearke* (n.)

mest (adv.) MOST, to the greatest extent (superlat. of *ma* [adj.]) [OE]

met(e) (n. 1) measure, proportion; moderation [OE]; (n. 2) food (in general); meal (pl. *metes*) [OE; ModE *meat*]

mete-graces (n. pl) FOOD-GRACES, prayers of thanks for food or at meals [see *mete* (n. 1) + OF *grace* "thanks," from Lat. *gratia*]

meteth (v., pres. 3 sing.) measures [OE]

mid (prep.) with; among; *mid al(le)* = withal; in addition, besides, at the same time; further, moreover; perhaps; entirely, completely, at all [OE]

mid-dei (n.) MID-DAY

middel (adj.) MIDDLE (superlat. *midleste*) [OE]; (n.) MIDDLE (part); waist; intermediate cause, means; agent [OE]

mid-marhen (n.) MID-MORROW, mid-morning

mid-wei (adv.) MIDWAY, in between

migge (n.) urine [OE, perhaps related to ModE *micturate*]

mihte (n.) MIGHT, power; ability (pl. *mihten, mihtes*) [OE]

milce (n.) mercy, forgiveness; pity, compassion; grace [OE]

milci (v., pres. subj. sing.) have mercy on, show mercy to [OE]

milde (adj.) MILD, kind, gentle (compar. *mildre*) [OE]

mild-heortnesse (n.) MILD-HEARTED-NESS, kindness [from OE]

milzfule (adj.) gracious, merciful [see *milce* (n.)]

mirre (n.) MYRRH, a rare, expensive, fragrant resin used in perfumes and incense [OE, from Semitic]

mis (adv.) sinfully, wickedly; erroneously, inadequately, improperly; AMISS, awry; (n.) offense, sin, guilt; *seien mis* = to lie

mis-do (v., pres. subj. sing.) do wrong, wrong; harm, injure (pres. 3 sing. *misdeth*; past sing. *misdude*) [OE, with close relatives in ON and OF]]

misericorde (n.) mercy [OF]

mis-fearen (v.) to do wrong, go wrong [OE]

mis-hapnunge (n.) MISHAP, accident [from OE, perhaps modeled on OF *mescheance*]

mis-herest (v., pres. 2 sing.) MISHEAR, hear wrongly, incorrectly [OE]

640

mis-leve (v., pres. subj. sing.) MISTRUST, fail to believe (pres. 3 sing. *misleveth*) [from OE]

mislich(e) (adj.) various, diverse; (of two things) unlike; variable, not always the same [OE]

misliche (adv.) in various ways; amiss, wrongly; *i-limpeth misliche* = to go amiss, go wrong [see *mislich* (adj.)]

mis-licunge (n.) displeasure, discomfort, unhappiness [see *licunge* (n.)]

mis-likin (v.) to displease, offend [OE]

mis-neome (v., pres. subj. sing.) mistake, make a mistake or error (pres. 2 pl. *mis-neometh*; pres. 3 sing. *misnimeth*; past part. *misnumene*) [from OE; see *neomen* (v.)]

mis-neomunge (n.) mistake, error

mis-nimeth (v., pres. 3 sing.) see *mis-neome* (v.)

mis-noteth (v., pres. 3 sing.) abuses, mis-uses [from OE]

mis-notunge (n.) abuse, misuse

mis-numene (v., past part.) see *mis-neome* (v.)

mis-ortrowunge (n.) false suspicion [from OE]

mis-paieth (v., pres. 3 sing.) mispleases, displeases; angers, annoys (past part. *mispaiet*) [OF]

mis-segge (v., pres. subj. sing.) to slander, speak evil of; MISSAY, say something wrong; blaspheme (pres. 3 sing. *misseith*; pres. pl. *misseggeth*; past sing. *misseide*) [from OE]

mis-thenche (v., pres. subj. sing.) MISTHINK, think wrongly [see *mis* (adv.) + *thenchen* (v.)

mis-thoht (n.) MISTHOUGHT, mistake; evil or bad thought [from OE]

mis-tohe (adj.) mistrained, unruly; dis-ordered [see *teoth* (v.)]

mis-trowet (adj. & v., past part.) MIS-TRUSTED, not believed [ON]

mis-trum (adj.) poor, weak [see *mis* (adv.) + OE *trum* "firm, strong"]

mis-witen (v.) to neglect, watch badly [from OE; see *witen* (v. 2)]

mis-word (n.) insult, angry WORD [from OE]

mixne (n.) dung hill, pile of refuse; (in proverbs, a term of abuse) filthy creature [OE]

mode (n.) mind, spirit, heart [OE; ModE *mood*]

moder (n.) MOTHER (gen. sing. *modres*) [OE]

moder-hus (n.) MOTHER-HOUSE; the founding house of a religious order

moder-sunnen (n. pl.) MOTHER-SINS; sins which give birth to others

molden (n. pl.) MOLD, pattern; type, nature [OF]

mon (pron., n.) MAN; (indef.) one, a person; sir (gen. sing. *monnes*; pl. *men*; gen. pl. *monne*) [OE]

mon-cun (n.) MANKIND (gen. sing. *mon-cunne*) [OE]

mone (n.) MOON [OE]

mong (n.) mixture, MINGLING; traffic, intercourse; contamination, adulteration [OE]

monglin (v.) to mix; MINGLE, intertwine (hands) (pres. 3 sing. *mongleth*) [from OE]

monglunge (n.) mixing, MINGLING; admixture; contamination [from *mong* "mixture"]

mon-head (n.) MAN-HEAD, manhood, humanity [from OE]

moni (adj.) MANY, a great number of; (n.) many, many (a person or thing) (pl. *monie*; gen. pl. *monies*) [OE]

moni-falde (adj.) MANIFOLD, numerous; varied [OE]

moni-falden (v.) to multiply, make MANIFOLD [OE]

moni-hwet (pron.) many a thing; (MANY WHAT)

moni-valde (adj.) see *moni-falde* (adj.)

monlich(e) (adj.) human; MANLY, virile [OE]

monluker (adv., compar.) more MANLY

monne (n., gen. pl.) see *mon* (n.)

mon-slaht (n.) MANSLAUGHTER, killing; murder [OE]

morthre (n.) MURDER; crime; injury, torment [OE]

most (v.) see *moten* (v.)

mot (n.) MEETING, assembly; debate, argument; clash [OE]

moten (v.) MUST; to require (pres. subj. sing./pl. *mote*; past subj. sing. *moste*; pres. 2 sing. *most*; pres. 3 sing. *mot*; pres. pl. *moten*; past sing. *moste*) [OE]

muche (adj.) great, MUCH, a lot; (adv.) greatly, MUCH (gen. sing. *muches*) [OE]

muchel (adv.) greatly; (gen. sing. as adv.) *mucheles* = MUCH, by far [OE]

muchel(e) (adj.) MUCH; great, powerful [OE]

mucheres (n. pl.) secret, petty thieves, pilferers [prob. OE]

muchleth (v., pres. 3 sing.) increases, multiplies [OE; see *mutli* (v.)]

muhe(n) (v.) see *mei* (v.)

muhelin (v.) to molder, grow moldy (pres. part. *muhelinde*) [?ON]

mulne (n.) MILL, a flour or grist mill, usually powered by water [OE]

mun(e)gunge (n.) memory; reminder [OE *mynegung*]

munegin (v.) to remind; mention; warn, exhort; to remember (pres. 3 sing. *munegeth*) [OE]

munegunge, mungunge (n.) memory, remembrance; reminder, warning [OE]

munek, munk (n.) MONK [OE]

munneth (v., imper. pl.) recall, remind, consider [OE; related closely to *munegin* (v.)]

munt (n.) mountain, MOUNT [OF]

munten (v.) to rise up, ascend, MOUNT; promote; be worth (past part. *i-munt*) [OF]

murhthe (n.) MIRTH, (religious) ecstasy, happiness (pl. *murhthen, murhthes*) [OE]

murie (adj.) MERRY, pleasant, delightful; (adv.) merrily, festively, pleasantly [OE]

murnin (v.) to MOURN, be sorry for, regret (pres. 3 sing. *murneth*; past sing. *murnede*) [OE]

murnunge (n.) MOURNING, sorrow, regret

murthredest (v., past 2 sing.) MURDERED, killed (past part. *i-murthret*) [OE]

mustreisun (n.) show, display; boasting [OF, see ModE phrase *to pass muster*]

muth (n.) MOUTH (gen. sing. *muthes*; obj. sing. *muthe*; gen. pl. *muthene*) [OE]

mutli (v., pres. subj. sing.) increase, multiply (pres. 3 sing. *mutleth*; pres. pl. *mutlith*) [related to *muchel* (adj.)]

myrre (n.) see *mirre* (n.)

na (adj.) NO [OE]

nabbe (v., pres. subj. sing.) the negated form of *habben* (= *ne habben*), not HAVE, do not have (pres. subj. pl. *nabben*; pres. 1 sing. *nabbe*; pres. 2 sing. *nast, navest*; pres. 3 sing. *nabbeth, naveth*; pres. pl. *nabbeth, nabbe [we, ye]*); past sing. *nefde*) [see *habben* (v.)]

nahhi(n) (v.) to near or NIGH, come near, approach (pres. subj. pl. *nahi*; pres. 3 sing. *nahheth*; pres. pl. *nahhith*; past sing. *nahhede*) [ON]

nahunge (n.) an approach; sexual intimacy [see *nahhin* (v.)]

naket (adj.) NAKED; candid, plain, unadorned; unconcealed [OE]

naketliche (adv.) NAKEDLY, candidly, in an open way [OE]

nalde, nalden, naldest (v., past) see *wullen* (v.)

na-mon (pron.) NO one, nobody; (*na mon* = no man)

nan(e) (adj. & n.) NONE [OE]

nanes (n.) NONCE, present time, occasion, purpose; *for then anes = for the nanes* [from OE, related to ModE *once*]

nanes-weis (adv.) in NO WAY, not by any means [from OE; orig. a n. phrase in the gen.]

nart (v., pres. 2 sing.) see *beon* (v.)

nast (v., pres. 2 sing.) see *nabbe* (v.); see *witen* (v. 1)

nat (v., pres. sing.) see *witen* (v. 1)

naut-for-thi (adv.) nevertheless

navest, naveth (v.) see *nabbe* (v.)

na-wiht (adv.) not a WHIT, not at all; (n.) nothing, NAUGHT [OE]

nawt-for-thi (conj.) nevertheless

ne (adv.) not [OE]

neappith (v., pres. pl.) NAP, take a nap [OE]

nearewe, nearow(e) (adj.) NARROW, small; constricting, strait; strict, sparing; stern, harsh; oppressive; (n.) *nearewe* = the narrow part (superlat. *nearewest*) [OE]

nearowe, nearowliche (adv.) NARROW-LY; sparingly, strictly; harshly

nearowthe (n.) NARROWNESS, confinement; distress [see *nearewe* (adj.)]

nease (n.) NOSE (gen. sing. *neases*) [OE]

neb (n.) the human face (or nose); bill or beak of a bird (gen. sing. *nebbes*) [OE]

nebscheft (n.) countenance, face; likeness, image [from OE]

ned(e) (n.) see *neod* (n.)

neddre (n.) serpent, snake; (ADDER) (pl. *neddren*) [OE]

nede (adv.) NEEDS, by necessity; *mot nede* = must needs, must by necessity [OE]

neden (v.) to force, compel (with violence); NEED, require (pres. 3 sing. *nedeth*; past part. *i-ned, i-nedd[e]*) [OE]

nedlunge (adv.) by necessity, by force [see *neod* (n.)]

ned-swat (n.) sweat of anguish, bloody sweat, lit., agony-sweat [see *neod* (n.) + *swat* (n.)]

nefde (v., past sing.) see *nabbe* (v.)

neh (adj.) near, close, nearby, NIGH; (superlat.) *nehhest*: next in a series; *for neh* = nearly (adv.) (compar. *neorre*; superlat. *nehhest, nest*) [OE]

nehbur (n.) NEIGHBOR (pl. *nehburs*) [OE *neah-gebur* "near dweller"]

nehhest (adv.) closest, most immediate; immediately preceding or following (superlat. of *neh* [adv.]) [see *neh* (adj.)]

nelde (n.) NEEDLE; (fig.) something of little value (gen. sing. *nelde*; pl. *nelden*) [OE; ME form reverses *l* and *d* (metathesis)]

nempni(n) (v.) to NAME, call (imper. sing. *nempne*; pres. 3 sing. *nempneth*; past sing. *nempnede*; past part. *i-nempnet*)

nempnunge (n.) NAMING, calling

neoces (n. pl.) nuptials, wedding [OF]

neod (adj.) necessary

neod(e) (n.) NEED, necessity; force, compulsion; distress, emergency, difficulty (pl. *neoden*) [OE]

neodeluker (adv., compar.) more NEED-FUL; more forcefully, more urgently

neoden (v.) to be necessary (to someone) (impers.); to force, compel (pres. 3 sing. *neodeth, nedeth*) [OE]

neodful (adj.) NEEDY, destitute; eager [OE]

neoleachunge (n.) approach, a drawing near or NIGH [OE]

neolechede (v., past sing.) approached, neared, drew near (past sing. *neolechede*) [OE; see *neh* (adj.)]

neome(n) (v.) to take; grasp, understand; to catch (imper. sing. *nim*; imper. pl. *neometh*; pres. subj. sing. *neome*; pres. 1 sing. *neome*; pres. 2 sing. *nimest*; pres. 3 sing. *nimeth*; past sing. *nom*; past pl. *nomen*; past part. *i-nume, i-numen[e]*) [OE; see Ger. *nehmen* "to take"]

neomunge (n.) taking, receiving

neorre (adj.) see *neh* (adj.)

neothere (adj., compar.) lower, under, NETHER [OE]

neowliche (adv.) NEWLY, recently [OE]

nep (n.) drinking cup, bowl; chalice (pl. *neppes*) [OE]

nesche, nessche (adj.) soft, tender; slack, negligent, made soft by vice; effeminate [OE]

nest (adv., superlat. of *neh* [adj.]) recently, just, immediately following or preceding; nearest, closest (see *neh* [adj.]) [OE]

nicketh (v., pres. 3 sing.) denies, makes a denial [OE, from the phrase *ne ich* "not I!"]

nihe (adj.) NINE [OE]

nihene (num.) NINE [OE]

nihethe (adj.) NINTH [OE *nigoða*]

niht (n.) NIGHT; (gen. sing. as adv.) *deies ant nihtes* = day and night (gen. sing. *nihtes*) [OE]

niht-fuhel (n.) NIGHT-bird

nim, nimest, nimeth (v.) see *neomen* (v.)

nis (v., pres. 3 sing.) see *beon* (v.)

nisteth (v., pres. pl.) NEST, make a nest [OE]

nith (n.) strife, violence; hatred, evil, spite [OE]

nithfule (adj.) envious, quarrelsome, evil

nivelin (v.) to snivel; wrinkle, turn up the nose; make a face, grimace [from OE *hnifol* "forehead"]

noblesce (n.) nobility [OF]

noht (n.) NAUGHT, nothing [OE]

nohtunge (n.) scorn, insult, disparagement [from *noht* (n.)]

no-hwer (adv.) NOWHERE, in no place

no-hwider (adv.) nowhere, to no other place

nome (n.) NAME; reputation; fame (pl. *nomen*) [OE]

nome-cuthe (n.) known by NAME, famous [from OE]

nomeliche (adj.) special, particular, singular, individual [from *nome* (n.)];

(adv.) especially, chiefly, NAMELY, particularly, specifically; that is to say; at least, at any rate [from *nome* (n.)]

non (n.) the canonical hour of prayer originally recited at the ninth hour (approx. 3 p.m.) [Lat.]

nore (n.) sneezing [OE]

note (n.) use, utility; benefit, good; occupation, work, employment [OE]

no-the-leater(e) (adv.) nevertheless, none the LATER; (lit., not-the-later)

no-the-les (adv.) NONETHELESS, not withstanding

notien (v.) to use, make use of, put to good use; partake of, eat or drink; to need, require (pres. subj. sing. *notie*; pres. 3 sing. *noteth*; pres. pl. *notieth*) [OE]

notith (v., imper. pl.) NOTE, pay attention to, observe carefully [OF]

nowther (adj., adv., conj., pron.) NEITHER; (conj.) *nowther . . . ne* = neither . . . nor [from OE, on analogy to *either*]

nu (adv.) NOW [OE]

nulle, nulleth, nult (v.) see *wullen* (v.)

nunan (adv.) NOW, just now; already [ON]

nunne (n.) NUN, a woman in a religious order (pl. *nunnen*) [OE]

nurrice (n.) NURSE, fosterer, a woman who nurses a baby [OF]

nurth (n.) noise, din, racket [occurs only in *AW* and Katherine Group texts] [*OE, or perhaps MDu]

nuste, nute, nuten (v.) see *witen* (v. 1)

nuthe (adv.) NOW [from OE]

nutten (v.) to take, use, make use of; eat [OE; see Ger. *nutzen* "use"]

of- (prefix) away, OFF, for [OE]

of (adv.) OFF, away [OE *of*]; (prep.) OF; OFF, from; by [OE]

of-drahen (v.) to DRAW out, attract, win (pres. 3 sing. *ofdraheth*) [from OE]

of-dred (adj.) afraid, frightened [OE]

of-earneth (v., pres. 3 sing.) EARNS, deserves (past sing. *ofearnede*; past part. *ofearnet*) [from OE]

offe (adv.) OFF [OE]

of-fearen (v.) to frighten, make FEARFUL, terrify; (past part. as adj.) *offearet* = terrified, frightened (past sing. *offearede*; past part. *offearet*) [from OE]

of-fearunges (n. pl.) terrors, frights

offrin (v.) to OFFER, present, give (imper. pl: *offrith*; pres. 3 sing. *offreth*; past pl. *offreden* [OE, from Lat.]

of-fruht (adj. & v., past part.) FRIGHTENED, afraid [from OE]

of-gan (v. 1) to gain, win (pres. 3 sing. *ofgeath*) [OE]; (v. 2) to get, gain; require, demand [OE]

of-hungret (adj. & v., past part.) famished, HUNGRY [OE]

of-sarvet (v., past part.) see *of-serveden* (v.)

of-secheth (v., pres. 3 sing.) SEEKS out, searches for [from OE]

of-serveden (v., past pl.) earned, deserved, merited (past part. *ofservet*, *ofsarvet*) [OE + OF; *of-* a translation of *de* in OF *deservir*]

ofte (adv.) OFTEN, frequently (compar. *oftre*; superlat. *oftest*) [OE]

of-thenchen (v.) to THINK of [OE]

of-thunche (v., pres. subj. sing.) grieve over, regret; repent (of something) [OE]

of-thunchunge (n.) grief, displeasure; repentance, regret

of-thurst (adj.) very thirsty, overcome with thirst [OE]

of-token (v., past part.) over-TOOK [OE, from ON]

o-hwider (adv.) anywhere, to any place [OE]

oker(e) (n.) the loan of money at interest, usury; interest (on a loan); ill-gotten gains [ON]

okereth (v., pres. 3 sing.) accrues interest [see *oker* (n.)]

olhnin (v.) to flatter; cajole, blandish [from OE]

olhnunge (n.) flattery; cajoling, blandishment, persuasion; "courtship" (MED)

onde (n.) envy (as one of the seven deadly sins); spite, hatred (gen. sing. *ondes*) [OE]

ondfule (adj.) envious, spiteful

ondswere (n.) ANSWER, reply (pl. *ondsweres*) [OE]

ondswerien, ondsweren (v.) to ANSWER, reply; compensate for, correspond to (imper. sing. *ondswere*; imper. pl. *ondswerieth*; pres. subj. sing. *ondswerie*; pres. 2 sing. *ondswerest*; pres. pl. *ondswerieth*; past sing. *ondswerede*) [OE]

on-licnesse (n.) LIKENESS, similarity, resemblance [OE]

onont, onond (prep.) next to, close to, near; across from, facing, toward; according to; concerning, as regards, with respect to; in the sense that [from OE]

on-sihthe (n.) SIGHT, a looking on (something) [see *sihthe* (n.)]

on-tenden (v.) to ignite, set on fire, kindle [OE]

on-tendunge (n.) (an) igniting, kindling

ontful(e) (adj.) see *ondfule* (adj.)

on-ward (prep.) toward, against [OE]

open(e) (adj.) OPEN; clear, obvious; receptive [OE]

open-heaved (adj. & adv.) BAREHEAD, bareheaded, with an uncovered head

openin (v.) to OPEN; reveal; (of trees and flowers) to bloom (imper. pl. *openith*; pres. 3 sing. *openeth*; pres. pl. *openith*) [OE]

openlich(e) (adj.) OPEN; clear, obvious; (adv.) OPENLY, clearly, without concealment (compar. *openluker*; superlat. *openlukest*) [OE]

or (n.) ORE, metal; brass [OE]

ord (n.) point, tip [OE]

ordre (n.) ORDER, religious community (pl. *ordres*) [OF]

orhel (n.) pride, haughtiness [OE; OF *orgueil* prob. from Ger.]

ornre (adj., compar.) more particular, picky [OE; see *unorne* (adj.)]

ortrowi (v.) to despair (of), doubt [OE]

other (adj.) OTHER; second (in a series) (pl. *othre*); (conj.) or, and; unless; *other . . . other* = either . . . or [OE]

other-hwet (pron.) something else; something different, additional; anything else; other things

other-hwile (adv.) sometimes, at times

other-hwiles (adv.) sometimes, occasionally, at times; *other-hwiles . . . other-hwiles* = at times . . . at other times [OE]

other-weies (adv.) in ANOTHER WAY, otherwise; *nan other-weies* = in no other way [OE]

over- (prefix) excessively, too much; entirely, thoroughly

over (adv.) OVER; above; excessively

over-al (adv.) everywhere, all through, in every part

over-cumen (v.) to OVERCOME, conquer, prevail; master (past 2 sing. *overcome*; past 3 sing. *overcom*; past pl. *overcomen*) [OE]

over-cuthre (adj., compar.) entirely more familiar [see *over-* (prefix) and *cuth* (adj.)]

over-don (v.) to OVERDO, do too much [OE]

over-egede (adj.) OVERLY elaborate, foolishly excessive [see *egede* (adj.)]

over-feble (adv.) excessively FEEBLE, too weak [OE + OF]

over-forth (adv.) very far forward [OE]

over-fullet (adj. & v., past part.) abundant, overflowing; (OVERFILLED) [OE]

over-gan (v.) to GO away, pass over; GO OVER, surpass (pres. 2 sing. *overkimest*; pres. 3 sing. *overkimeth*) [OE]

over-gart (adj.) excessive, given to excess; presumptuous [OE + ON]

over-guldeth (v., pres. 3 sing.) GILDS OVER, covers in gold [OE]

over-herunge (n.) excessive praise [see *herien* (v.)]

over-hohe (n.) contempt, disdain; arrogance; *over-hohe i-heortet* = with a disdainful heart [from OE]

over-keasten (v.) to overthrow, CAST down; (fig.) defeat [OE + ON]

over-kimeth (v., pres. 3 sing.) see *over-gan* (v.)

over-leapeth (v., pres. 3 sing.) LEAPS OVER, jumps over (pres. part. *overleapinde*) [OE]

over-leden (v., past part.) drawn or ladled out (OVER the side of); (Shepherd, p. 103) "to spill over" [OE *ofer* + *hladen*, past part. of *hladan* "to draw (water), load"; related to ModE *ladle*]

over-muchel (adv.) OVER MUCH, too much

over-strong (adj.) very severe, OVERLY harsh

over-sturet (adj. & v., past part.) OVERLY STIRRED up, excessively emotional [from OE; see *sturien* (v.)]

over-swithe (adv.) OVER much, too greatly, excessively, exceedingly [from OE; see *swithe* (adv.)]

over-trust (n.) excessive confidence, OVER-TRUST, presumption [see *trust* (v.)]

over-trusten (v.) to TRUST too much, be overconfident [see *trust* (v.)]

over-trusti (adj.) too TRUSTING; OVERCONFIDENT

over-turnen (v.) to revolve, spin, TURN OVER (pres. pl. *overturneth*) [see *turnen* (v.)]

over-under (adv.) (lit.) after morning, perhaps after Tierce (9:00, the third canonical hour); afternoon [see *under* (n.)]

over-uvel (adj.) OVERLY evil, excessively bad

over-waden (v.) to WADE through or across [OE]

over-warpen (v.) to overthrow, turn over [OE]

over-weieth (v., pres. 3 sing.) out-WEIGHS, weighs more, is more important [from OE]

ow (personal pron., 2 pl., obj. form) YOU [see *ye* (personal pron.)]

ower (adj.) YOUR (pl.) [OE]

ow-seolf, -seolven (pron., reflex.)
YOURSELF, -SELVES

owther (pron.) EITHER

packes (n. pl.) bundles, PACKS [MDu]

pagine (n.) PAGE [Lat. *pagina* "page"]

pagne (n.) PAGE [OF]

paie(n) (v.) to please, satisfy; PAY, pay for
(pres. 3 sing. *paieth*; past part. *i-paiet*)
[OF]

Pape (n.) POPE [OE or OF, from Lat.]

parais (n.) PARADISE; garden of Eden;
heavenly paradise (gen. sing. *paraise*)
[OF, ultimately from Old Persian]

parlur (n.) PARLOR, room for talking;
MED: "(a) A chamber in a religious
house used for consultation or
conversation, esp. for conversation with
persons outside the monastic community;
(b) a grate or window through which the
enclosed religious can make confession
or communicate with persons outside the
cloister" (gen. sing. *parlurs, parlures*)
[OF; from *parler* "to talk"]

paroschien (n.) PARISHIONER, lay
member of a parish [OF]

parti (v., pres. subj. sing.) PART, separate;
DEPART, go away from (pres. 1 sing.
parti; pres. 3 sing. *parteth*) [OF; see F.
partir "to leave"]

parures (n. pl.) ornaments (for an *amite*);
"an ornamental part of an alb or other
vestment" (MED) [OF; see ModE *pare*
"to peel or shave"]

passin (v.) to PASS, proceed; to SUR-
PASS, exceed (pres. 3 sing. *passeth*) [OF]

passiun (n.) suffering, pain; Christ's
PASSION, his sufferings on the cross

(gen. sing. *passiunes*; pl. *passiuns*) [OF,
from Lat. *passio* "suffering"]

pater nostres (n. pl.) Lord's Prayers,
PATERNOSTERS [OF, from Lat.]

peathereth (v., pres. 3 sing.) stirs, pokes
(ashes) [?OE; see ModE *pother*, *powder*;
MED *patheren*; Zettersten (1965), p. 237]

pece (n.) PIECE, part, fragment; piece of
cloth [OF]

peinture (n.) a PAINTING, picture [OF]

peis (n.) PEACE [OF]

penitence (n.) PENITENCE; the sacrament
of penance; penance or restitution, the
third step in the penitential system;
penitential suffering [OF]

peoddere (n.) PEDDLER, a traveling seller
of small wares [*OE]

peolkin (v.) to pick clean, peck (used of
birds); rob [ON]

peonehes (n. pl.) PENNIES, coins [OE]

peonsin (v.) to consider, study, think over;
complain, be fretful or anxious [OE, from
Lat. *pensare* "think, consider"]

peril (n.) danger, risk [OF]

pes (n.) see *peis* (n.)

phariseus (n. pl.) PHARISEES; hypocrites
[OE, from Lat.]

pilche (n.) fur or leather garment, robe [OE,
from Lat.; see ModE *pelt*]

pilche-clut (n.) a ragged garment (made
from animal skin or fur); tattered cloak
[OE *pilece* "fur garment" + OE *clut*
"patch, rag"]

piler (n.) PILLAR, post [OF]

pilewin, pilien (v.) to rob, PILLAGE,
plunder; to strip, PEEL [OE, from Lat.]

piment (n.) spiced, sweetened wine [OF]

pinchen (v.) to PINCH, pluck (the
eyebrows) [ONF]

pinchunge (n.) PINCHING, plucking (of eyebrows)

pine (n.) punishment; suffering, PAIN, torment (pl. *pinen*) [OE, from Lat.]

pinful (adj.) PAINFUL, full of suffering

pinin (v.) to inflict PAIN, suffering; to torment, torture, trouble, distress (pres. subj. sing. *pini*; pres. 1 sing. *pini*; pres. pl. *pinith*; past part. *i-pinet, pinet)* [OE, from Lat.]

pinsunge (n.) pain, torture; mortification, subduing (of the flesh) (pl. *pinsunges*) [origin obscure; related to *pinin* (v.), perhaps as ModE *cleanse* relates to *clean*]

pitance (n.) donation, bequest to a religious house of food and drink; allowance of food; ration; a poor ration, PITTANCE [OF]

place (n.) PLACE (of battle), field [OF]

pleanin (v.) to COMPLAIN (reflex.) [OF]

pleien (v.) to PLAY; frisk, dance, dart around quickly; perform; have fun; (*plohian* is the northern form) (pres. 3 sing. *pleieth*; past sing. *pleide*) [OE]

pleinte (n.) COMPLAINT [OF]

pliht (n.) danger, risk [OE; ModE *plight*]

plihten (v.) to pledge, promise (past part. *i-pliht*) [OE; see ModE phrase *plight one's troth*, Ger. *pflichten* "to obligate"]

plohe (n.) PLAY; frisking [see *pleien* (v.)]

plohien (v.) see *pleien* (v.)

point (n.) POINT; situation, case, state of being; clause; opportunity [OF]

potage (n.) vegetable broth or soup; dish of vegetables (usually boiled in a POT) [OF]

poverte (n.) POVERTY, destitution [OF]

povre (adj.) POOR, humble [OF]

povreliche (adv.) POORLY, badly

preachin (v.) to PREACH (imper. pl. *preachi (ye)*; past part. *i-preachet*) [OF]

preasse (n.) crowd, PRESS, throng [OF]

preisin (v.) to PRIZE, set a high value on; PRAISE (imper. sing. *preise*; pres. 3 sing. *preiseth*; past sing. *preisede*; past part. *i-preiset, preiset*) [OF]

prelat, prelaz (n.) PRELATE, ecclesiastic of high rank: archbishop, bishop, pope, abbot, prior; a superior [OF]

preminences (n. pl.) a distinction, distinctive privilege [OF]

preon (n.) pin, clasp, brooch; nail, spike [OE]

preove (n.) PROOF, evidence, demonstration; testing, trial [OF]

present (n.) something PRESENTED or given; offering, present, gift (pl. *presenz*) [OF]

pric(c)hunge, pricunge (n.) PRICKING; goading [OE]

pricke (n.) PRICK, jot (i.e., a tiny distance) [OE]

prikieth (v., pres. pl.) PRICK, goad, spur on (pres. part. *prikiende, prikinde*) [OE]

prime (n.) PRIME, the first liturgical hour of the day, around 6 a.m. [OE]

prinschipe (n.) tightness, stinginess; reluctance [from OF *prin* "avaricious"; Zettersten (1964), pp. 30–32]

pris (n.) PRICE, value [OF]

prisun (n.) PRISON; imprisonment; prisoner, captive (pl. *prisuns*) [OF]

priur (n.) PRIOR, leader of a religious house [OE, from Lat.]

prive(e) (adj.) secret, concealed; private, personal; peculiar, special; intimate, friendly; mysterious, mystical [OF]

priveiliche (adv.) PRIVATELY, confidentially [OF]

privement (adv.) privately, secretly; alone, in solitude [OF]

privilegie (n.) special right or advantage; immunity [Lat.]

privite (n.) secret, divine secret, revelation (pl. *privitez*) [OF]

procunge (n.) poking, prodding, goading; (fig.) instigation (pl. *procunges*) [see *prokie* (v.)]

professiun (n.) PROFESSION, religious vow [OF]

prokie (v., pres. subj. sing.) poke; stir, goad, incite [origin obscure]

proprement (adv.) characteristically, by nature [OF]

prosperte (n.) PROSPERITY [OF]

prud(e) (adj.) PROUD; (superlat. *prudest*) [late OE]

prude (n.) PRIDE, ostentation

pruden (v.) to be, become PROUD, act proudly (pres. subj. pl. *pruden*)

prufunge (n.) PROOF, evidence [see *pruvien* (v.)]

pruvien (v.) to make trial of, test; go through, experience; treat, deal with; demonstrate (pres. 3 sing. *pruveth*; pres. pl. *pruvieth*) [OF; ModE *prove*]

Psalm-wruhte (n.) PSALM-WRIGHT, Psalmist [OE]

puffen (v.) to PUFF, blow (in short bursts) (pres. 3 sing. *puffeth*; past sing. *pufte*) [OE]

puint (n.) see *point* (n.)

pundeth, punt (v., pres. 3 sing.) encloses, pens (livestock); confines, IMPOUNDS; dams or stops up; restrains (past part. *i-pund*) [*OE]

puplicanes (n., gen. sing.) PUBLICAN'S (see Matthew 18:17); belonging to a worldly or sinful person [OF]

purs (n.) bag, pouch, PURSE; treasury (pl. *purses*) [OE, from Lat.]

purte (n.) PURITY, pureness [OF]

put (n.) PIT, cave, ditch, hole [OE]

putten (v.) to place, set, PUT (pres. subj. sing. *putte*; pres. 3 sing. *putteth*; past sing. *put*; pres. part. *puttinde*; past part. *i-put*) [late OE]

quarreus (n. pl.) bolts; OED: "A short, heavy, square-headed arrow or bolt, formerly used in shooting with the cross-bow" [OF]

quene (n.) QUEEN; QUEAN, hussy [OE]

quite (adj.) free, clear, rid (of something); QUIT [OF]

quoth (v., past sing.) spoke; SAID, mentioned [OE, always abbreviated as *qð* in Corpus]

rad (v., past sing.) see *riden* (v.)

rancun (n.) RANSOM, payment to release a prisoner [OF]

rawe (n.) ROW, line; order, succession; company, group; *on rawe* = completely, altogether; *(rawe) bi rawe* = in order, one by one [OE]

reacheth (v., pres. 3 sing.) stretches out, extends; REACHES, goes as far as (imper. sing. *reach*) [OE]

read (n.) counsel, advice, piece of advice; decision, plan, strategy, course of action; help, remedy (pl. *reades*) [OE]

read(e) (adj.) RED [OE]

reades-mon (n.) advisor, counselor

readeth (v., imper. pl.) advise, give counsel (pres. subj. sing. *reade*) [OE]

readliche (adv.) READILY, quickly [OE]

reaflac (n.) theft, pillaging, plundering [OE; see ModE *bereft*]

reathere (adv., compar.) earlier, quicker, sooner [OE]

reavenes (n., gen. sing.) see *reven* (n.)

reaveres (n. pl.) robbers, plunderers [OE]

reavi(n) (v.) to rob, plunder, pillage, steal; REAVE (pres. subj. sing. *reavi*; pres. 3 sing. *reaveth*) [OE]

reawe (n.) see *rawe* (n.)

recche (v., pres. subj. sing.) care, be concerned; matter, be important; (impers.) *me ne recche* = (it) does not matter to me (past sing. *rochte*) [OE]

reccheth (v., pres. 3 sing.) goes, wanders, strays; *recchinde* (pres. part. as adj.) going, wandering [OE]

recchinde (adj., pres. part.) see *reccheth* (v.)

rech(e)les (n.) incense; smoke, aroma of incense (gen. sing. *rech[e]leses*) [OE; see ModE *reek* + *-(e)les* (suffix)]

recordin (v.) to memorize, commit to memory; to repeat, recite [OF]

reculin (v.) to beat back, drive back; cause to retreat [OF, from Lat. *culus* "posterior"]

rede(n) (v.) to READ, recite; interpret, declare (imper. pl. *redeth*; pres. subj. pl. *reden*; pres. 3 sing. *redeth, red, ret*; pres. pl. *redeth*; past part. *i-red*) [OE]

redunge (n.) READING, (devotional) reading

regibeth (v., pres. 3 sing.) kicks [OF]

reimin (v.) to ransom (someone), redeem (also reflex.); to plunder, rob, fleece; to gain control of [OF]

reisun (n.) REASON, argument; reasoning faculty, ability to think (pl. *reisuns*) [OF]

relef (n.) remains, remnants, residue [OF]

religiun (n.) religious profession; OED: "condition of one who is a member of a religious order" (pl. *religiuns*) [AN]

religius(e) (adj.) RELIGIOUS, living under a religious rule

remissiun (n.) REMISSION, forgiveness of sin [OF]

rengeth (v., pres. 3 sing.) roams, RANGES about (pres. part. *renginde*) [OF]

renginde (adj. & v., past part.) see *rengeth* (v.)

rentes (n. pl.) RENTS, income [OF]

reopen (v.) to seize, catch; touch [OE]

reopunge (n.) touching, sense of touch, sensation [OE]

reowfule (adj.) RUEFUL, deserving pity [OE]

reowfulnesse (n.) compassion, sympathy; RUEFULNESS [OE]

reowthe (n.) pity, compassion, mercy, RUTH; sorrow, grief [OE + *-th* from ON]

reowtheful (adj.) sorrowful, pitiful; compassionate; RUEFUL, piteous [see *reowthe* (n.)]

reowthful (adj.) compassionate, FULL of pity or RUTH

resun (n.) see *reisun* (n.)

reven (n.) RAVEN (gen. sing. *reavenes*) [OE]

riche (adj.) powerful, great; RICH (superlat. *richest*) [OE]; (n.) kingdom, realm [OE; see Ger. *Reich*]

richesces (n. pl.) RICHES [OF]

richt (adj.) see *riht* (adj.)

ride(n) (v.) to RIDE (past sing. *rad*; pres. part. *ridinde*) [OE]

ridli (v.) to put through a sieve, sift [from OE *hriddel* "sieve"]

riht (adv.) directly, in a straight way; immediately; exactly, just, quite

riht(e) (adj.) RIGHT, upright, righteous, proper; straight; (n.) right, just cause [OE]

rihten (v.) to straighten, make RIGHT; direct; establish, set up; raise, rear; bring to an upright position (pres. subj. sing. *rihte*; past part. *i-riht*) [OE]

riht-hondes (adj.) RIGHT-HAND, favorite

rihtliche (adv.) justly, correctly; (Shepherd, p. 104) "justifiably" [OE]

riht-wis(e) (adj.) righteous, just, upright [OE]

riht-wisnesse (n.) righteousness, justice, integrity [OE]

rikelot (n.) magpie; (fig.), chattering woman, gossip [Lat. *rikelota* "magpie"]

rikeneres (n. pl.) auditors, account keepers, RECKONERS [see *rikenin* (v.)]

rikenin (v.) to count, RECKON, calculate; tell, narrate (past part. *i-rikenet*) [OE]

rin (v., imper. sing.) touch; strike; pertain to, concern (pres. subj. sing. *rine*; pres. 3 sing. *rineth*) [OE]

ring (n.) RING; ring dance, dance in a round [OE]

rinnen (v.) to seize, take [OE]

rinunge (n.) touching, touch [see *rin* (v.)]

riote (n.) RIOT, debauchery, extravagance; (prob. not a hunting term designating the scent of the wrong animal, as Salu and Zettersten suggest — see Dolan [1979], pp. 189–200) [OF]

ris (n.) (living) twig, branch, bough [OE]

risede (v., past sing.) trembled, shuddered [OE; MED *resen*]

rive (v., pres. subj. sing.) edge, trim, put a trim on (pres. 3 sing. *riveth*) [ON *rifa* "to sew up loosely"; see ModE *reef*]

rivunges (n. pl.) trimmings, borders (?); sewn garments

riwle (n.) RULE, code of conduct; a religious rule (pl. *riwlen*) [OF]

riwlin (v.) to RULE, govern, regulate (pres. 3 sing. *riwleth*; pres. pl. *riwleth*) [OF]

riwlunge (n.) governance, RULING, management

rixleth (v., pres. 3 sing.) rules, reigns; holds sway, prevails [from OE; see Lat. *rex* "king"]

rixlunge (n.) rule, sway, dominance

robbeth (v., pres. 3 sing.) ROBS, plunders, steals from (pres. pl. *robbith*; past part. *i-robbed, i-robbet*) [OF]

rochet (n.) an church vestment, a surplice (worn by bishops or abbots) [OF]

rochte (v., past subj. sing.) see *recche* (v.)

rode (n.) ROOD, cross [OE]

rode-scheld (n.) ROOD-SHIELD, the cross as a protecting shield

rode-steaf (n.) ROOD-STAFF, the cross as a weapon

rode-taken (n.) sign (TOKEN) of the cross; a crucifix; a vision of Christ's cross [OE]

rolle (n.) ROLL, scroll; official or legal document [OF]

ron (v., past sing.) see *runnen* (v.)

rondes (n. pl.) logs or stripped branches [OF; ModE *round*]

ropunge (n.) crying, shouting; loud insistence [OE]

rote (n.) ROOT, cause [OE]

rotet, rotede (adj. & v., past part.) ROTTED, decayed [see *rotien* (v.)]

rotien (v.) to ROT (pres. subj. sing. *rotie*; pres. 3 sing. *roteth*; pres. pl. *rotieth*; past sing. *rotede*; past part. *i-rotet*) [OE]

rude (n.) RUDDINESS, red; complexion [OE]

rudi (adj.) RUDDY, red (used of a healthy complexion); red-faced [OE]

rug(ge) (n.) (the) back; *wenden rug* = to turn one's back [OE; ModE *ridge*]

ruhe (adj.) ROUGH (compar. *ruhre*) [OE]; (n.) roughness; something rough, rough garment, rough surface [OE]

rukelin (v.) to heap up, pile up; amass, assemble (something) (pres. 3 sing. *rukeleth*) [see *ruken* (n.)]

ruken (n. pl.) piles, heaps [ON]

rukin (v.) to squat, crouch [?ON]

rune (n.) RUNNING [OE]

runes (n.) secrets, mysteries [OE; see ModE *rune*]

rungen (v.) to rise, get up (imper. pl. *rung*) [origin obscure]

rungi (v.) to WRING, squeeze out [OE]

runnen (v.) to RUN (past sing. *ron*) [OE]

rustin (v.) to RUST, tarnish (pres. 3 sing. *rusteth*; past part. *i-rustet*) [from OE]

rute (n.) ROUTE, course, way, path [OF]

sabraz (n.) elixir, potion, medicine [OF]

sacles (adj.) GUILTLESS, innocent [OE, perhaps influenced by ON]

sacreth (v., pres. 3 sing.) CONSE-CRATES, blesses [OF, from Lat.]

sahe (n.) saying, speech, SAW [OE]

sahte (n.) reconciliation, agreement; peace [OE]

sahtnesse (n.) reconciliation, peace, accord [OE]

sahtni (v.) to reconcile, make peace with (pres. 3 sing. *sahtneth*; past part. *i-sahtnet*) [see *sahte* (n.)]

salde (v., past sing.) see *sullen* (v.)

salm (n.) PSALM (pl. *salmes*) [OF]

Salmiste (n.) PSALMIST; David, as author of the PSALMS [OF]

Salm-wruhte (n.) see *Psalm-Wruhte* (n.)

saluz (n.) greeting, salutation [OF]

salve (n.) SALVE, healing ointment, medicine; remedy, cure [OE]

salvith (v., pres. pl.) rub with a SALVE or ointment; heal, remedy, treat (past part. *i-salvet*) [OE]

sape (n.) SOAP [OE]

sapere (n.) SOAP maker, seller; SOAPER

sar(e) (adj.) SORE, painful; sad, sorrowful (compar. *sarre, sarure*; superlat. *sarest*) [OE]

sar (n.) pain, wound; disease, sickness; SORROW, suffering, hardship, misfortune (pl. *sares*) [OE]

sarcurne (adj.) querulous, complaining (about a wound); touchy, sensitive [OE; see *sar* (n.) + OE *crene* "tender"]

sare (adv.) SORELY, heavily, intensely; painfully, bitterly (compar: *sarre*) [OE]

sari(e) (adj.) sad, sorrowful; SORRY, regretful; causing pain or sorrow; painful (compar. *sarure*) [OE]

sariliche (adv.) SORRILY, sorrowfully, sadly; painfully [see *sari* (adj.)]

sarmun (n.) speech, words; SERMON [OF]

savur (n.) SAVOR, taste; relish, delight [OF]

saweth (v., pres. 3 sing.) SOWS, scatters (seed); (fig.) scatter, disperse [OE]

sawle (n.) SOUL (gen. sing. *sawle, sawles*; pl. *sawles, sawlen*; gen. pl. *sawlene*) [OE]

sawter (n.) PSALTER, the book of Psalms, often arranged for liturgical use [OF]

sawunge (n.) SOWING; spreading

sawvin (v.) to SAVE, rescue; save (in a theological sense) (pres. 3 sing. *sawveth*) [OF]

scaldinde (adj., pres. part.) SCALDING [ONF]

scale (n.) drinking cup, bowl [ON]

scandle (n.) cause of offense or stumbling; MED: "discredit to religion resulting from the misbehavior of a religious person"; "also, perplexity of conscience occasioned by the conduct of one who is looked up to as an example" (The OED notes that before the sixteenth century, this word occurs only in *AW/AR*) [AF *scandle*, from Lat. *scandalum* "stumbling, offense"]

scarn(e) (n.) SCORN, contempt, mockery [OF]

scarnith (v., imper. pl.) SCORN, mock, deride (pres. 3 sing. *scarneth*) [OF]

schaden (v.) to separate [OE; see Ger. *scheiden* "to separate"]

schakeles (n. pl.) fetters, bonds, SHACKLES; hobble [OE]

schaken (v.) to SHAKE, shake off; brandish; rush, go quickly; (pres. part. as adj.) *schakinde* = rash, quick; brandishing, threatening (?); (past part. as adj.) *i-schake* = violent (in that it has shaken the entire body?) (imper. sing. *schake, schec*; pres. 3 sing. *schaketh*; pres. part. *schakinde*; past part. *i-schake*) [OE]

schal (v., pres. sing.) SHALL, will (as marker of the future tense); (past tense forms) should, ought (pres. subj. sing. *schule*; pres. 2 sing. *schalt*; pres. pl. *schulen, shule (we)*; past 2 sing. *schuldest*; past sing. *schulde*; past pl. *schulden*) [OE]

schape (n.) SHAPE; cut [OE]

schapieth (v., imper. pl.) SHAPE, fashion; cut out (clothing) (past part. *i-schapet*) [OE]

scharpschipe (n.) sharpness; hardship [from OE]

schawere (n.) mirror; (SHOWER) [OE]

schawi(n) (v.) to see, view; be seen, visible; to appear (to be); reveal, SHOW; to treat, behave (imper. sing. *schaw*; imper. pl. *schawith*; pres. 3 sing. *schaweth*; past sing. *schawde*; past part. *i-schawde, i-schawet*) [OE]

schawunges (n. pl.) SHOWINGS, visions, revelations

schec (v., imper. sing.) see *schaken* (v.)

scheden (v.) to divide; SHED (blood), pour (out), be poured out; spill (a liquid); waste, destroy; (past part. as adj.) *schede* = spilled (imper. sing. *sched*; pres. 3 sing. *sched, schet*; pres. pl. *schedeth*; past sing. *schedde*; past part. *i-sched, schede*) [OE]

schedunge (n.) SHEDDING (of blood)

scheld (n.) SHIELD [OE]

schench (n.) leg [?OE; related to *schonke* (n.)]

schende (v.) to shame, disgrace; confuse, destroy (pres. 3 sing. *schent*; past sing. *schende*; past part. *i-schent, i-schend*) [OE]

schendfule (adj.) humiliating; shameful, disgraceful [from OE]

schendfulliche, schentfulliche (adv.) disgracefully, shamefully; with disgrace, shame

schendfulnesse (n.) wickedness, vileness

schendlac (n.) shame, disgrace; humiliation (pl. *schendlakes*) [from OE]

schene (adj.) beautiful; bright (compar. *schenre*) [OE; ModE *sheen*]

schentful(e) (adj.) see *schendfule* (adj.)

scheoiende (pres. part.) SHOEING, putting on shoes [from OE]

scheome (n.) SHAME, humiliation, disgrace, insult [OE *sceamu*]

scheomel (n.) footstool, (according to the MED, can also refer to the "raised section of floor on which the altar stands") [OE, from Lat.]

scheomeliche (adv.) disgracefully, shamefully [OE]

scheomien (v.) to be ashamed, blush (pres. subj. sing. *scheomie*; pres. 3 sing. *scheometh*) [OE]

scheon (n. pl.) see *scheos* (n. pl.)

scheop (v., past sing.) created, formed, SHAPED [OE]

scheortliche (adv.) SHORTLY, briefly; soon [OE]

scheos (n. pl.) SHOES [OE]

scheot (v., pres. 3 sing. [= *scheoteth*]: SHOOTS [OE]

schere (n.) groin [OE]

schet see *scheden* (v.)

schilde(n) (v.) to SHIELD, protect, shelter (pres. subj. sing. *schilde*; pres. 3 sing. *schilt*) [OE]

schine (v.) to SHINE (pres. 3 sing. *schineth*; pres. part. *schininde*)

schir(e) (adj.) pure, bright [OE; ModE *sheer*]

schireth (v., pres. 3 sing.) purifies, brightens; makes clear, says [OE]

schirliche (adv.) clearly, brightly

schirnesse (n.) brightness, purity

schonke (n.) leg, SHANK (pl. *schonken*) [OE]

schraden (n. pl.) scraps, SHREDS [OE]

schraf (v. past sing.) see *schriven* (v.)

schrapien (v.) to scrape, dig; erase (the method of erasing letters from parchment) (pres. 3 sing. *schrapeth*; past part. *i-schrapede*) [OE; ModE *scrape* from ON cognate]

schrif (v., imper. sing.) see *schriven* (v.)

schrift(e) (n.) confession, penance; confessor (gen. sing. *schriftes*) [OE, from Lat.]

schrift-feader (n.) confessor, confession-FATHER (pl. *schrift-feaderes*) [from OE, influenced by ON]

schrive(n) (v.) to confess (reflex.) (imper. sing. *schrif*; pres. subj. sing. *schrive*; pres. subj. pl. *schriven*; pres. 1 sing. *schrive*; pres. 2 sing. *schrivest*; pres. 3 sing. *schriveth*; past sing. *schraf*; past part. *i-schriven[e]*, *i-scrive*) [OE]

schrud (n.) clothing, garment (pl. *schrudes*) [OE; ModE *shroud*]

schruden (v.) to dress, clothe (oneself); be dressed; to adorn; (past part. as adj.) *i-schrud* = veiled, hidden, enveloped (pres. 3 sing. *schrudeth*; past sing. *schrudde*; past part. *i-schrud*) [OE; see *schrud* (n.)]

schucke (n.) demon, fiend; the devil [OE]

schuhteth (v., pres. 1 pl.) drive away, repel [OE]

schulde, schulden, schuldest (v.) see *schal* (v.)

schuldi (adj.) guilty, culpable, sinful [OE; see Ger. *schuldig* "guilty"]

schuleth (v., pres. 3 sing.) looks askance, squints [OE *sceol* "awry, squinting"]

schunche (v., imper. sing.) frighten, scare; be terrified, frightened (pres. 3 sing. *schuncheth*) [OE]

schunien (v.) to SHUN, avoid, reject (pres. subj. sing. *schunie*; past pl. *schuneden*) [OE]

Schuppent (n.) Creator, SHAPER [OE]

Schuppere (n.) Creator, SHAPER

schurteth (v., imper. pl.) SHORTEN, pass (the time); (reflex.) entertain yourself [OE]

schutteth (v., imper. pl.) SHUT [OE]

schuveth (v., pres. 3 sing.) SHOVES, thrusts, sweeps (past part. *i-schuven*) [OE]

scleaterunge (n.) daubing, plastering [OE]

scole (n.) SCHOOL [OE]

scol-meistre (n.) SCHOOL-MASTER, school teacher

scoren (n. pl.) tally sticks; sticks with notches SCORED into them to keep track of accounts [ON]

scotti(n) (v.) to share, participate (in) (pres. 2 pl. *scottith*) [OE, perhaps influenced by ON]

scratleth (v., pres. 3 sing.) scratches, scrapes [probably imitative]

scrowe (n.) scroll [OF]

scureth (v., pres. 3 sing.) SCOURS, polishes [from OF or MDu]

scuter (adj.) derisive, taunting [ON]

se (adv.) SO, as [OE]

seac (v., past sing.) see *siken* (v.)

sec, seke (adj.) SICK, ill; (n.) sick (person); sickness, disease (compar. *seccre*) [OE]

seccli (v., pres. subj. sing.) SICKEN, grow weak or ill (pres. 3 sing. *secleth*) [OE]

sechen (v.) to SEEK; attempt, try; pursue, attack; aim (imper. sing. *sech*; imper. pl. *secheth*; pres. subj. sing. *seche*; pres. 1 sing. *seche*; pres. 3 sing. *secheth*; pres. pl. *secheth*; past 2 sing. *sohtest*; past sing. *sohte*; pres. part. *sechinde*; past part. *i-soht*) [OE]

secnesse (n.) SICKNESS, illness (pl. *secnesses*) [OE]

sed (n.) SEED; granule, particle (pl. *sedes*) [OE]

seel (n.) SEAL (usually of wax and which closes a document to keep it private); (fig.) secrecy, confidentiality [OF]

sege (n.) seat (for a person of status or authority) [OE; ModE *siege*]

segge(n) (v.) to SAY, speak; declare (imper. sing. *sei*; imper. pl. *seggeth*; pres. subj. sing. *segge*; pres. 1 sing. *segge*; pres. 2 sing. *seist*; pres. 3 sing. *seggeth*, *seith*; pres. pl. *seggeth*; past 2 sing. *seidest*; past sing. *seide*; past pl. *seiden*; past part. *i-seid*) [OE]

seide, seiden, seidest (v., past) see *seggen* (v.)

seim (n.) fat, lard [OF]

Sein, Seint, Seinte (n.) SAINT (usually part of a name) [OF]

seke (adj.) see *sec* (adj. & n.)

sel-cuth (adj. or n.) wonder, unusual, unfamiliar (thing) [OE *seld* "SELDOM, little" + *cuth* (adj.)]

seldene (adj.) infrequent, rare; (adv.) SELDOM, not often [OE]

selhthe (n.) happiness; good fortune, luck, prosperity [OE]

seli(e) (adj.) blessed, favored, holy; excellent; innocent, harmless; weak, wretched, unfortunate [OE]

seliliche (adv.) happily

selt (adj.) SELDOM, infrequent [OE]

selt-hwenne (adv.) SELDOM, rarely, not often [from OE]

selt-sene (adj.) SELDOM SEEN, rare [OE]

semblant (n.) appearance, shape, form, expression; outward show, deception, pretense; *don semblant* = to make a pretense, pretend, give an impression that something is so (pl. *semblanz*) [OF]

semlich (adj.) SEEMLY, fitting [ON]

senden (v.) to SEND; direct (at), throw, hurl (imper. sing. *sende*; imper. pl. *sendeth*; pres. subj. sing. *sende*; pres. 3 sing. *send, sent*; past sing. *sende*; past pl. *senden*) [OE]

senre (adj., compar.) more visible, easy to see or be SEEN [from OE]

sentence (n.) opinion, judgment, meaning; aphorism [OF]

seo(n) (v.) to SEE, look; see (something) (imper. sing. *sih*; pres. subj. sing. *seo*; past subj. sing. *sehe*; pres. 1 sing. *seo*; pres. 2 sing. *sist*; pres. 3 sing. *sith*; pres. pl. *seoth*; past sing. *seh*; past pl. *sehen*; past part. *i-sehen[e]*; inflected inf. *to seonne*) [OE]

seode (n.) a purse; *binden seode mid the muth* = to purse the lips, pucker [OE]

seolc (n.) SILK [OE]

seolf (pron. & adj.) SELF (objective form: *seolve, seolven*)

seoththen (adv.) afterwards, since, later; (conj.) as soon as, when, since, after that, inasmuch as [OE]

seove, seoven(e) (adj. & n.) SEVEN [OE]

seove-niht (n.) a week; SENNIGHT [from OE]

seovethe (adj.) SEVENTH [OE]

seove-vald, seve-vald (adv.) SEVENFOLD, seven times [OE]

seowith (v., imper. pl.) SEW [OE]

servi(n) (v.) to SERVE, render service to; perform (pres. 3 sing. *serveth*; pres. pl. *servith*) [OF]

servise (n.) SERVICE, liturgical duties (pl. *servises*) [OF]

seste (adj.) SIXTH [OE]

set, seten (v., past) see *sitten* (v.)

sete (n.) SEAT [OE]

setten (v.) to SET, place, put; dispose, arrange, establish, fix (a date or deadline); to settle, subside (imper. sing. *sete*; pres. 3 sing. *set, setteth*; past sing. *sette*; past part. *i-set, i-sette*) [OE]

shute (n.) SHOT, volley [OE]

sibbe (adj.) related (by family); related to, pertaining (to); (n.) peace, friendship, kinship; freedom, harmony; kin, family, relatives [OE; see ModE *sibling*]

sicles (n. pl.) SHEKELS [OF from Hebrew]

side (n.) SIDE; side of the body; *o siden* = to the side, askance (pl. *siden*) [OE]

signe (n.) SIGN; SIGNAL, gesture (pl. *sines*) [OF]

siheth (v., pres. 3 sing.) strains (out), separates with great care (pres. pl. *siheth*) [OE]

sihthe (n.) SIGHT; marvel, vision (pl. *sihthen*) [OE]

sike(n) (v.) to sigh, moan (imper. pl. *siketh*; past sing. *seac*) [OE]

siker(e) (adj.) sure, safe; reliable, trustworthy (compar. *sikerure*) [OE; see Ger. *sicher* "safe"]

sikerliche (adv.) with conviction, certainty; without doubt, hesitation; confidently; firmly [late OE]

657

sikernesse (n.) certainty; assurance; pledge, security (for the performance of an agreement) [OE]

sikes (n. pl.) sighs [see *siken* (v.)]

simple (adj.) SIMPLE, honest, innocent [OF]

sines (n. pl.) see *signe* (n.)

sinetin (v.) (lit.) to stamp with a SIGNET ring; (fig.) to confirm, emphasize (words) with a gesture [OF]

singularite (n.) SINGULARITY, individual difference or peculiarity [OF]

sire (n.) SIR (form of address) [OF]

sith (n.) time, occasion (pl. *sithen*, *sithe*) [OE]

sithe, sithen (n. pl.) times, occasions [OE]

sitten (v.) to SIT, crouch; sit around; prevail; to be suitable, fitting, becoming, to suit (imper. sing. *site*; imper. pl. *sitteth, sitte ye*; pres. subj. sing. *sitte*; pres. 3 sing. *sit, sitteth*; pres. pl. *sitteth*; past sing. *set*; past pl. *seten*; pres. part. *sittinde*) [OE]

sittunge (n.) SITTING

sker (adj.) pure, cleansed, innocent; free, safe; clear, bright (compar. *skerre*) [ON]

skerin (v.) to acquit, clear (a person of a charge) [see *sker* (adj.)]

skile (n.) reason, reasonableness, discretion; what is reasonable, right; explanation, logical argument (gen. sing. *skiles*) [ON]

skirmi (v.) to fight (with a weapon); thrust, fence (pres. 3 sing. *skirmeth*) [OF]

skiwes (n. pl.) skies, heavens [prob. ON, related to ModE *sky*]

skleatteth (v., pres. pl.) flap or slam down [?OE; origin obscure, perhaps related to ModE *slat*]

slakien (v.) to STOP; SLACK [OE]

slaw(e) (adj.) SLOW, sluggish, lethargic [OE]

slawthe (n.) SLOTH (as one of the deadly sins); laziness [from OE]

slean (v.) to strike powerfully; to SLAY, kill with a blow (imper. sing. *slea*; pres. 3 sing. *sleath*; pres. pl. *sleath*; past sing. *sloh*; past pl. *slohen*; past part. *i-slein[e]*; inflected inf. *to sleanne*) [OE]

sleateth (v., pres. 3 sing.) drives, bates (with dogs); hunts (after) [OE; see MED *sleten* (v.)]

slei (adj. & v., past part.) SLAIN, dead [see *slean* (v.)]

slep (n.) SLEEP (obj. sing. *slepe*) [OE]

slepen (v.) to SLEEP (imper. sing. *slep*; imper. pl. *slepe (ye)*; pres. subj. sing. *slepe*; pres. 3 sing. *slepeth*; pres. pl. *slepeth*; past 2 sing. *sleptest*; past sing. *slepte*; pres. part. *slepinde*) [OE]

slepi (adj.) SLEEPY, drowsy [OE *slæpig*, see *unslæpig*]

sleven (n.) SLEEVES, a distinctive part of a religious habit [OE]

sliddrunge (n.) SLIDING, slipping [from OE]

sliden (v.) to SLIDE, slip (pres. 3 sing. *slit*) [OE]

sloggi (adj.) SLUGGISH [ON or imitative]

sloh, slohen (v., past) see *slean* (v.)

slubbri (adj.) slippery [prob. OE, not MFlem—see Zettersten (1965), p. 137]

slummi (adj.) drowsy, sleepy, SLUMBERFUL [prob. OE]

Sluri (n.) SLURRY (not a given name, but a nickname); Lazy, Slacker [Ger., perhaps OE; see MLG *sluren* "to be lazy"; see Zettersten (1964), p. 35]

smahte (v., past sing.) tasted, experienced by tasting (past part. *i-smaht*, *i-smecchet*) [OE; see Ger. *schmechen* "to taste"]

smeal (n.) SMELL (either pleasant or unpleasant) (pl. *smealles*) [OE]

smeal(e) (adj.) SMALL; light, slight, insubstantial (compar. *smealre*) [OE]

smeallen (v.) to SMELL (pres. part. *smeallinde*; past part. *i-smeallet*) [OE]

smeallunge (n.) sense of SMELL [OE]

smech (n.) taste, savor, good taste [see *smahte* (v.), Ger. *geschmeck* "taste"]

smechles (adj.) TASTELESS, bland

smechunge (n.) (the sense of) taste; tasting [see *smahte* (v.)]

smeort (adj.) SMART, vigorous; sharp, painful [OE]

smeorten (v.) to SMART, be sharply painful; to give (someone/something) a sharp pain (pres. 3 sing. *smeorteth*) [OE]

smeortliche (adv.) quickly, sharply; painfully

smeortunge (n.) SMARTING, pain (from a wound or injury)

smeothien (v.) to forge, fashion, shape (something metal); to SMITH (pres. 3 sing. *smeotheth*) [OE; see ModE *blacksmith*]

smethe (adj.) SMOOTH [OE]

smethin (v.) to SMOOTH, make even (pres. 3 sing. *smetheth*) [OE]

smirien (v.) to SMEAR, anoint, rub in (an ointment or balm); *smiret* (past part. as adj.) = anointed (pres. pl. *smirieth*; past part. *i-smired*, *smiret*) [OE]

smirles (n.) ointment, salve [OE; see *smirien* (v.) + *-(e)les* (suffix)]

smiten (v.) to SMITE, hit, beat; pierce (pres. 3 sing. *smit*; past sing. *smat*) [OE]

smitere (n.) SMITER, one who hits or strikes, attacker

smith (n.) BLACKSMITH, metal worker [OE]

smiththe (n.) SMITHY, workshop [OE]

smothre (n.) dense, stifling smoke, [from OE *smorian* "to smother, choke"]

smuhel (adj.) stealthy, slippery; "soft in movement, lithe, creeping" (Zettersten [1965], p. 144) [perhaps related to OE *smugan* "to creep"]

snakereth (v., pres. 3 sing.) sneaks, creeps, SNAKES around, approaches stealthily (pres. 3 sing. *snakereth*; pres. part. *snakerinde*) [*OE]

sneateres (n. pl.) SNATTERINGS, babblings; (hence) mere verbal reprimands [*OE; see MDu, MLG *snateren* "to babble, talk"; see Zettersten (1964), pp. 11–12]

snecchen (v.) to snap, bite [origin obscure, perhaps related to ModE *snatch*]

softe (adv.) SOFTLY, gingerly; compliantly [OE]

softeth (v., pres. 3 sing.) SOFTENS, mollifies (pres. 3 sing. *softeth*) [from OE]

sol (adj.) SOILED, dirty [from OE]

some (n.) peace, harmony [OE; related to ModE *same*]

somet (adv.) together; at the same time, in the same direction [OE]

somet-readnesse (n.) concord, agreement [see *somet* (adv.) + *read* (n.)]

sond (n.) SAND [OE]

sonde (n.) errand, embassy, a SENDING; message, communication; messenger, envoy (pl. *sonden*) [OE *sand*, *sond*, influenced by *sende*]

sondes-mon (n.) messenger, (lit. message man) [from OE]

sone (adv.) SOON; quickly, straight away (compar. *sonre*; superlat. *sonest*) [OE]

sontes (n. pl.) SAINTS [OE, from Lat., as opposed to the OF form *seint*]

sorege (n.) see *sar* (n.)

sorhe (n.) SORROW, suffering, misery; pain [OE]

sorhful(e) (adj.) SORROWFUL (compar. *sorhfulre*)

sorhfulliche (adv.) SORROWFULLY

sorhin (v.) to grieve, SORROW for [OE]

sot, sotte (adj) foolish, stupid; (n.) a fool, SOT) [OE; also see OF *sot* and med. Lat. *sottus*]

soth(e) (adj.) true, genuine; (n.) truth [OE; see ModE *soothsayer*]

sothes (adv.) in truth, truthfully

sothfestliche (adv.) truly, truthfully

sothliche (adv.) truly, truthfully

sotschipe (n.) stupidity, foolishness [see *sot* (adj.)]

spatlunge (n.) spitting [OE; see ModE *spittle*]

spealeth (v., pres. 3 sing.) means, signifies; interprets (pres. pl. *spealieth*; past part. *i-spealet*) [OF]

spearewe (n.) SPARROW; *spearewe uvel* = sparrow's disease [OE]

spearien (v.) to SPARE; to leave unhurt, unpunished; do without, dispense with (imper. sing. *speare*; pres. subj. pl. *spearien*; pres. 3 sing. *speareth*; past part. *i-spearet*) [OE]

spearren (v., pres. subj. pl.) see *sperreth* (v.)

spece (n.) type, kind, SPECIES; branch, subclass [OF, from Lat.]

speces (n. pl.) SPICES [OF]

speche (n.) talk, SPEECH (pl. *sprechen*) [OE]

speken (v.) to SPEAK, say (pres. 1 sing. *speoke*; pres. 3 sing. *speketh*; past sing. *spec*; past part. *i-speken*) [OE]

spelles (n. pl.) stories, tales [OE]

spellunge (n.) speaking, an act of speaking, utterance; tale [OE]

speoke(n) (v.) to SPEAK, say, talk (imper. pl. *speoke (ye)*; pres. subj. sing. *speoke*; past subj. sing. *speke*; pres. 1 sing. *speoke*; pres. 2 sing. *spekest*; pres. 3 sing. *speketh*: pres. pl. *speoketh*; past sing. *spec*; past pl. *speken*; past part. *i-speken*; inflected inf. *to speokene*) [OE]

speokele (adj.) talkative, loquacious [OE]

speonse (n.) EXPENSE, money for expenses [OF]

speowen (v.) to SPEW, vomit (pres. subj. sing. *speowe*; pres. 3 sing. *speoweth*) [OE]

sperclinde (adj., pres. part.) SPARKLING, bright [OE]

speren (n. pl.) SPEARS (gen. sing. *speres*) [OE]

sperreth (v., imper. pl.) close, shut; fasten (with a bar) (pres. subj. pl. *spearren*) [prob. from MDu]

spi (interj.) (an expression of disgust) fie! or shame! [probably from MDu]

spieden (v., past pl.) SPIED; plotted, lay in wait [OF]

spillen (v.) to kill brutally; lay waste, devastate, destroy; ruin, damn (pres. pl. *spilleth*; past part. *i-spillet*) [OE]

spit (v., pres. 3 sing. [= *spiteth*]) SPITS (imper. *spite*; past sing. *spitte*) [OE]

spital-uvel (n.) leprosy; *spital* = shortened form of HOSPITAL, a quarantine for lepers, institution sheltering the poor or infirm [see *uvel* (n.)]

spitel-steaf (n.) spade, shovel [OE *spitel* "small spade" + OE *stæf* "staff"]

spreaden (v.) to SPREAD, stretch; expand, open (pres. 3 sing. *spreat* [= *spreadeth*]; pres. pl. *spreadeth*; past part. *i-spread*, *spredde*) [OE]

spredde (adj. & v., past part.) SPREAD, open [see *spreaden* (v.)]

sprengeth (v., imper. pl.) sprinkle; scatter, disperse (past part. *i-sprengde*) [OE]

spreove (n.) trial, testing; PROOF [from OF *esprover*; *es-* from Lat. *ex-*]

springen (v.) to SPRING; rise, rise up (pres. 3 sing. *springeth*) [OE]

spritlen (n. pl.) young twigs, shoots [OE]

spruteth (v., pres. pl.) SPROUT, grow [OE]

spurnen (v.) to stumble, trip over, bump into; kick; reject, SPURN (pres. 3 sing. *spurneth*) [OE]

spus(e) (n.) SPOUSE, marriage partner; bride or bridegroom (respectively) [OF]

spus-bruche (n.) adultery; (lit. SPOUSE-BREACH) [from OE]

spus-had (n.) marriage [OF + OE; see ModE *spousehood*]

sput (v., pres. 3 sing. [= *sputteth*]) urges, incite [*OE]

stalde (v., past sing.) set, placed; established (past part. *i-stald*) [OE]

stamin (n.) a rough undergarment worn by monks and ascetics [OF]

stanene (adj.) STONE, made of stone [OE]

stant (v., pres. 3 sing.) see *stonden* (v.)

stat (n.) ESTATE, condition, standing [OF]

steah (v., past sing.) see *stihen* (v.)

steale-wurthliche (adv.) STALWARTLY, stoutly, bravely

steal-wurthe (adj.) STALWART, brave, courageous; sturdy, stout [OE]

stearf (v., past sing.) died [OE; see ModE *starve*, Ger. *sterben* "to die"]

steathel-vestnesse (n.) STEAD-FASTNESS, firmness [OE]

steire (n.) STAIR, step (pl. *steiren*) [OE; related to *stihen* (v.)]

steoke (v.) to close up, shut [OE, related to ModE *stuck*]

steolen (n. pl.) uprights, the two vertical boards (of a ladder) [OE; see ModE *stile*]

steort-naket (adj.) stark-NAKED; (lit. "tail-naked") [from OE]

sterke (adj.) stern, strict, STARK [OE]

stert-hwile (n.) a twinkling, rapid moment [from ME *stert* "a leap, start" + OE *hwile* "time"]

stevene (n.) voice, sound; summons, call [OE; see Ger. *stimme* "voice"]

sti (n.) STY, pig pen [OE]

sticcke, sticke (n.) STICK; spoon [OE]

stiche (n.) puncture, prick; STITCH, sudden pain (pl. *stichen*) [OE]

stihe(n) (v.) to climb, ascend (pres. subj. sing. *stihe*; pres. 3 sing. *stiheth*; past sing. *steah*; past part. *i-stihen*) [OE; see Ger. *steigen* "to climb"]

stiketh (v., pres. 3 sing.) stays put, hangs around, STICKS to [OE]

stille (adj.) STILL, unmoving, quiet; (adv.) quietly, silently [OE]

stilthe (n.) silence, STILLNESS [from *stille* (adj.)]

stinken (v.) to STINK, emit a smell; to smell (something); (fig.) to be offensive (pres. subj. sing. *stinke*; past subj. pl.

stunken; pres. 3 sing./pl. *stinketh*; past sing. *stonc*; pres. part. *stincinde, stinkinde*) [OE]

stiward (n.) STEWARD, manager [OE]

stod, stode (v.) see *stonden* (v.)

stod-meare (n.) a STUD-MARE, a mare (a female horse or ass) reserved for breeding; a breeder; (fig.) a lascivious woman [OE elements]

stonc (v., past sing.) see *stinken* (v.)

stonde(n) (v.) to STAND, stand firm, resist; endure; (impers.) *hu hire stonde* = how (it) may stand with her, how it is with her (imper. pl. *stondeth*; pres. subj. sing. *stonde*; pres. subj. pl. *stonden*; past subj. sing. *stode*; pres. 2 sing. *stondest*; pres. 3 sing. *stont*; pres. pl. *stondeth*; pres. part. *stondinde*; past sing. *stod*) [OE]

stondinge (n.) STANDING

stoppeth (v., pres. 3 sing.) STOPS, stops up, dams, shuts [*OE]

straf (v., past sing.) see *striveth* (v.)

strahte (v., past sing.) see *streche* (v.)

strea (n.) STRAW [OE]

streapeles (n. pl.) leggings, worn from the knee to the feet; breeches [OE]; see Zettersten (1965), p. 237]

streche (v., imper. sing.) prostrate (one's body), STRETCH out; extend, stretch (pres. 3 sing. *strecheth*; past sing. *strahte*; past part. *i-straht[e]*) [OE]

strenge (n.) STRENGTH [OE]

strengeth (v., pres. 3 sing.) prevails; STRENGTHENS; makes strong (past pl. *strengden*; past part. *i-strengthet*) [OE]

strengthe (n.) STRENGTH, power; violence, force; health, vigor; influence, import, importance [OE]

streon (n.) gain, acquisition; sex, begetting; offspring, progeny; kin, family [OE; see ModE *strain* (n.)]

streoneth (v., pres.3 sing.) to beget, give birth to, conceive, breed (pres. pl. *streonith*; past sing. *streonede*; past part. *i-streonet, i-streonede*) [OE; related to ModE *strain*]

strif (n.) STRIFE, conflict; striving, contending [OE]

striken (v., past pl.) STRUCK; (of a liquid) flowed, ran [OE]

striveth (v., pres. 3 sing.) contends, STRIVES with; competes with (past sing. *straf*) [OF]

strong(e) (adj.) STRONG, powerful; imposing, formidable; severe, heavy, difficult; adverse, dangerous; flagrant, blatant; amazing, marvelous (compar. *strengre*; superlat. *strengest*) [OE]

stronge (adv.) STRONGLY, powerfully; severely, violently (superlat. *strongest*) [OE]

strongliche (adv.) STRONGLY, severely (superlat. *stronglukest*) [OE]

strucion (n.) ostrich (*struthio camelus*), sometimes confused with the stork; (The MS spelling, apparently mistaken, is *strucoin*) (pl. *strucions*) [AF *estrucion*]

strueth (v., pres. pl.) DESTROY [OF]

strunden, strundes (n. pl.) streams, rivulets [*OE]

stucche (n.) fragment, piece; *ane hwile stucche* = for a short time (pl. *stucchen, stuchen*) [OE; see Ger. *stück* "piece"]

stude (n.) place, location (pl. *studen*) [OE; ModE *stead*]

stude-festliche, -vestliche (adv.) STEAD-FASTLY, steadily, constantly

stude-vest (adj.) STEADFAST, firm, reliable [OE]

stunde (n.) time, period (of time); moment, a brief space of time; *umbe stunde* = at times [OE; see Ger. *stunde* "hour"]

stunken (v., past subj. pl.) see *stinken* (v.)

sturbunge (n.) tumult, DISTURBANCE, trouble [from OF]

sturie(n) (v.) to STIR, move; (reflex.) to be active or busy, bestir (oneself); to stir up (in an emotional sense), affect (imper. sing. *sture*; imper. pl. *sturieth*; past sing. *sturede*; pres. part. *sturiende*) [OE]

sturne (adj.) STERN, strict, severe [OE]

sturunge (n. pl.) shaking, wagging (in derision or mockery); (pl.) STIRRINGS, first beginnings

stutten (v.) to stop, pause; put an end to; remain, stay (pres. 3 sing. *stut* [= *stutteth*]) [ON; d'Ardenne (1961), p. 166]

sucurs (n.) help, assistance, SUCCOR; reinforcements (sometimes understood as plural) [AF]

suffragies (n. pl.) SUFFRAGES, intercessory prayers [OF, from Lat.]

suffrin (v.) to allow, SUFFER (imper. sing. *suffre*) [AF]

suhe (n.) SOW [OE]

suheth (v., pres. 3 sing.) feels sorrow or pain; inflicts suffering, distress; *suhinde* (pres. part. as adj.) = painful (pres. subj. sing. *suhie*; pres. part. *suhinde*) [*OE; related to ModE *sigh*]

sulement (adv.) solely, only [AF]

sulen (v.) to dirty, SOIL, sully, make filthy; (past part. as adj.) *sulede* = SULLIED, unclean (pres. 3 sing. *suleth*; past sing. *sulde*; past part. *i-sulet, sulede*) [OE]

sulh (n.) plow [OE]

sulle(n) (v.) to SELL; give (imper. sing. *sule*; pres. 3 sing. *suleth*; past sing. *salde*) [OE]

sulli, sullich (adj.) strange, curious, marvelous [OE *sellich*]

sum (adj.) SOME; one, (a) certain; (n.) some(one) or some(thing) (gen. sing. *sumes*; pl. *summe*) [OE]; (pron.) SOME, a certain; (n.) someone, some person; *sum . . . sum* = one . . . another [OE]

sum-chearre, cheare (adv.) once, formerly; sometimes [from OE; see *chearre* (n.)]

sum-deal, -del (adv.) a bit, somewhat, SOME DEAL [from OE; see *sum* (adj.) + *dale* (n.)]

sum-hwet (pron.) something, a certain amount

sum-hwile (adv.) in a former time, SOME WHILE ago; once; at some time (or another [see *sum* (adj.) and *hwile* (n.)]

sum-wis (adv.) SOME WISE, in some way [from OE]

sunder-lepes (adv.) separately, individually; specially; (adj.) distinct, separate [OE; see ModE *asunder*]

sunderliche (adv.) separately [OE]

sundri (adj.) SUNDRY, various; distinct, individual [OE]

sundri (adv.) separately, individually; (v.) to part, divide, separate; to distinguish (pres. 3 sing. *sundreth*; past sing. *sundrede*; past part. *i-sundret, i-sundrede*) [OE]

sunegin, sungin, sungi (v.) to SIN, commit a sin (pres. subj. sing. *sunege*; pres. 1 sing. *sunegi*; pres. 2 sing. *sunegest*; pres. 3 sing. *sungeth*; pres. pl. *sungith*; past sing. *sunegede*, past part. *i-suneget, i-sunget*) [OE; see Ger. *sündigen* "to sin," d'Ardenne (1961), pp.166–67]

sunne (n. 1) SIN (pl. *sunnen*) [OE]; (n. 2) SUN [OE]

sunne-gleam (n.) a GLEAM of SUN-shine [from OE]

Sunne-niht (n.) the NIGHT before sunday, (i.e.,) Saturday night [OE]

supersticiuns (n. pl.) SUPERSTITIONS; superior airs (?), frivolities; wrong-headedness [OF; see Explanatory Note to 4.242]

sur(e) (adj.) SOUR (compar. *surre*) [OE]

surpliz (n.) SURPLICE, gown (usually worn over other clothes) [AF, from Lat. *super-* "over" + *pellicia* "fur"]

surquide (adj.) proud, presumptuous [AF; see Diensberg (1978), p. 79]

suster (n.) SISTER (gen. sing. *sustres*; pl. *sustren*) [OE]

sutel (adj.) clear, evident; easily understandable, unambiguous [OE]

suteli (v., pres. subj. sing.) make clear or manifest, reveal; become evident (past part. *i-sutelet*) [OE]

sutelliche (adv.) clearly

sutere (n.) shoemaker; cobbler, mender of shoes [OE, from Lat.; related to ModE *sew*]

suti (adj.) dirty, filthy [*OE; ModE *sooty*]

sutil (adj.) thin, fine, delicate; rarefied, ethereal, elusive, not easily grasped; refined, cunningly crafted; clever, cunning [OF; ModE *subtle*]

suvel (n.) food (such as meat or cheese) eaten with bread [OE]

swa (adv.) SO; thus, in such a way [OE]

swa-liches (adv.) in such a way

sware (n.) answer, reply; speech, talk; promise; swearing, cursing, blaspheming [from OE]

swart(e) (adj.) dark, SWARTHY, black (compar. *swartre*) [OE]

swat (n.) SWEAT; liquid [OE]

swati (adj.) SWEATY

swealm (n.) heat, inflammation; burning of lust, anger, etc. [*OE]

sweamen (v.) to afflict, cause pain, grieve (pres. 3 sing. *sweameth*) [*OE]

sweaten (v.) to SWEAT, exude (liquid) (pres. subj. sing. *sweat*; pres. 3 sing. *swet, sweat* [= *sweateth*]; past sing. *sweatte*) [OE]

swefne (n.) sleep; dream, vision (pl. *swefnes*) [OE]

swelte (pres. subj. sing.) die, expire [OE; see ModE *swelter*]

swenche(n) (v.) to put to work or trouble; afflict, harass; mortify (past part. *i-swenchet*) [OE; see *swinc* (n.)]

sweng (n.) SWING, stroke, blow (with a weapon); throw (in wrestling) (pl. *swenges*) [OE]

swengen (v.) to fling, dash [OE]

sweoke (n.) traitor, deceiver [OE]

sweokele (adj.) see *swikele* (adj.)

swerien (v.) to SWEAR (past part. *i-sworen*)

swet (v., pres. subj. sing.) see *sweaten* (v.)

swete (adj.) SWEET (superlat. *swetest*) [OE]

sweteliche (adv.) SWEETLY

sweteth (v., pres. 3 sing.) SWEETENS, make sweet [OE]

swiftschipe (n.) speed [from OE]

swiing-wike (n.) silence week, (i.e.,) Holy Week, during which silence was observed [*swiing* from OE *swigian* "to be silent"; see Ger. *schweigen* "to be quiet"]

swikele (adj.) deceitful, treacherous, lying (compar. *swikelure*) [OE]

swilli (adj.) SUCH; MED: "of the sort previously mentioned, described" [from *swich* (adj.), perhaps blended with OE *þullich* (adj.)]

swinc (n.) work, labor; travail, toil, struggle; trouble, difficulty; fruits of labor (pl. *swinkes*) [OE]

swincful(e) (adj.) laborious, full of toil, toilsome; hardworking, diligent

swingen (v.) to beat, whip; fling, hurl; SWING back and forth (past sing. *swong*) [OE]

swinken (v.) to toil, labor, work (hard) (pres. 3 sing. *swinketh*; pres. part. *swinkinde*; past sing. *swonc, swong*; past part. *i-swunken*) [OE; see *swinc* (n.)]

swinkes (n. pl.) see *swinc* (n.)

swire (n.) neck [OE]

swithe (adj.) strong, great, immense (compar. *swithre)*; (adv.) strongly, greatly; severely; quickly; (modifying an adj. or adv.) very (compar. *swithere, swithre*; superlat. *swithest*) [OE]

swohinde (adj., pres. part.) SWOONING, fainting [OE]

swolhen (v.) to SWALLOW (pres. 3 sing. *swolheth*) [OE]

swong (v., past 3 sing.) see *swinken* (v.)

swopeth (v., pres. 3 sing.) sweeps [ON; related to ModE *sweep*]

swote (adj.) sweet, gentle; (adv.) sweetly, gently (superlat. *swotest*) [OE]

swotliche (adv.) sweetly

swuch (adj.) SUCH (a); (pron.) such a one, such things; *swucches* = such things (pl. *swucche*) [OE]

sygaldren (n. pl.) incantations, (magical) charms [OE *sige-* "victory" + *gealdor* "enchantment, spell"]

symonie (n.) SIMONY, the practice of selling ecclesiastical offices or benefits [OF]

ta (adv.) see *tha* (adv.)

tac (v., imper. sing.) TAKE (pres. 3 sing. *taketh*; past sing. *toc*) [late OE, from ON]

tacne (n.) TOKEN, sign, symbol; evidence [OE]

tacunge (n.) TAKING

tadden (n. pl.) TOADS, often imagined as malevolent creatures of hell [OE]

tah (conj.) see *thah* (conj.)

talde, talie (v.) see *tellen* (v.)

tale (n.) story, TALE; conversation; trifle, lie; claim, assertion; number, (full) count; value, account (pl. *talen*) [OE]

targeth (v., pres. 3 sing.) delays, is delayed; tarries, is slow [OF]

taveles (n. pl.) narrow lace borders [OF]

te (def. art.) see *the* (def. art.)

te (relative or personal pron.) see *the* (relative pron.) or *thu* (pron., 2 sing.)

teache(n) (v.) to TEACH, instruct; direct, refer (pres. subj. sing. *teache*; pres. 3 sing. *teacheth*; past sing. *tahte*; past part. *i-taht*) [OE]

team (n.) brood (litter, flock, etc.); family, line (pl. *teames*) [OE; see ModE *teem*]

tearme (n.) TERM, limit, deadline; (set) time (pl. *tearmes*) [OF]

teieth (v., pres. 3 sing.) TIES, fastens, binds; restrains, restricts (past sing. *teide*; past part. *i-teiet*) [OE]

teil(e) (n.) TAIL (pl. *teiles*) [OE]

teilac (n.) entanglement [from *teieth* (v.) + OE *-lac* "play, strife"]

teke (adv.) moreover, in addition, besides, eke; (prep.) in addition to, besides [from OE]

tellen (v.) to TELL, reckon; count, count up; consider, account (imper. sing. *tele*; pres. subj. sing. *telle*; pres. 1 sing. *talie*; pres. 2 sing. *telest*; pres. 3 sing. *teleth*; pres. 2 pl. *telleth*; past sing. *talde*; past part. *i-tald*) [OE]

tellunge (n.) counting, considering

temeth (v., pres. 3 sing.) brings forth, gives birth to; has offspring (pres. pl. *temith*) [OE; see *team* (n.)]

temie (v.) to TAME, subdue (pres. 3 sing. *temeth*; past sing. *temede*) [OE]

temptin (v.) to TEMPT, test (imper. sing. *tempte*; pres. subj. sing. *tempti*)

tendre (adj.) TENDER, loving; yielding (to); soft, weak, fragile [OF, from Lat. *tenerum* "delicate"]

tenne (adv.) see *thenne* (adv.)

teo (pron.) see *the* (relative pron.)

teohethi (v.) to TITHE, give a tenth part of one's income (past part. *i-teohethet*) [OE]

teohthe (adj.) TENTH [OE]

teolunges (n. pl.) reproof, rebuke, blaming; sorcery, witchcraft [OE *tælan* "to speak evil of, mistreat" perhaps blended with ON *tæla* "to betray"]

teone (n.) injury, harm; pain, physical suffering; misfortune, hardship; aggravation, chagrin, anger [OE]

teose (adj.) see *this* (adj. & demons. pron.)

teoth (v., pres. pl.) draw, pull; raise, train, educate; (past part. as adj.) *i-tohe(ne)* = trained [OE; see Ger. *ziehen* "to pull"]

teowi (adj.) exhausted, restless; erring [origin obscure — see Zettersten (1965), p. 259]

tep (v., imper. sing.) TAP, strike lightly; rap [ME, echoic]

tereth (v., pres. 3 sing.) TEARS, rips (past part. *i-toren*) [OE]

terme (n.) see *tearme* (n.)

ter-teken (adv.) see *ther-teken* (adv.)

tes (pron.) see *this* (adj. & demons. pron.)

tet (conj.) see *thet* (conj.)

teth (n. pl.) see *toth* (n.)

tha (adv.) then; (conj.) when; *tha . . . tha* = when . . . then [OE]

thah, thach, thauh (conj.) THOUGH, although [OE]

the (def. art.) THE (remains of the OE inflected forms: 3 fem. sing objective/gen. *ther*; 3 masc. sing. objective *then*; 3 masc./neut. gen. sing. *thes*; reduced form after preceding -*d* or -*t*: *te*); (relative & demons. pron.) which, who; this (3 fem. sing./pl. *theo*; reduced form: *teo*) [OE]

theafunge (n.) consent, permission

thear (adv.) see *ther* (adv.)

thearf (v., pres. sing.) need; be forced or obligated to (do something); (impers.) there is a need, it is necessary (pres. pl. *thurve*; past sing. *thurfte*) [OE]

theaw (n.) custom, habit, practice; trait, characteristic; good quality, virtue (pl. *theawes*; gen. pl. *theawene*) [OE; see ModE *thew*]

theawfule (adj.) virtuous, of good morals or habits

theh (n.) THIGH [OE]

then (def. art.) see *the* (def. art.)

then, thene (conj.) THAN [OE]; (def. art.) see *the* (def. art.)

thenche(n) (v.) to THINK, think of; consider, plan; to be reminded (imper.

sing. *thenc, thench*; imper. pl. *thencheth*; pres. subj. sing. *thenche*; past subj. sing. *thochte*; pres. 2 sing. *thenchest*; pres. 3 sing. *thencheth, thenchet*; pres. pl. *thench-eth*; past 2 sing. *thohtest*; past sing. *thohte*; past pl. *thohten*; past part. *i-thoht*) [OE]

thenne (adv.) THEN [OE]

theode (n.) nation, people; land [OE]

theof (n.) THIEF (pl. *theoves*) [OE]

theofthe (n.) stolen goods, loot [OE; see ModE *theft*]

theone-ward (adv.) away from there, from that direction, THENCEWARD

theonne (adv.) THENCE, from there, from that place [OE]

theonne-vorth (adv.) THENCEFORTH, from that time forward

theos, theose (adj. & pron.) see *this* (adj. & demons. pron.)

theosternesse (n.) darkness, gloom [OE]

theostre (n.) darkness, gloom [OE; see Ger. *düster* "gloomy"]

theostrith (v., pres. pl.) darken (past part. *i-theostret*) [OE]

theoteth (v., pres. 3 sing.) howls, screeches [OE]

theowdom (n.) servitude, thralldom, slavery [OE]

theowe (n.) servant, slave, thrall [OE]

ther (def. art.) see *the* (def. art.); (adv.) THERE; *ther . . . ther* = on one side . . . on the other side [OE]

ther-abuten (adv.) about that, concerning that, THEREABOUT

ther-ayein (adv.) in return for that; AGAINST that

there-with (adv.) WITH that; in opposition to, in response to that

ther-frommard (adv.) away from there

ther-onont (adv.) about, concerning, in reference to that [see *onont* (prep.)]

ther-onuven (adv.) thereafter, after that; on top of that, above that

thersche (v.) to THRASH, beat, flog, batter (past part. *i-thorschen*) [OE]

ther-teken (adv.) (lit.) there-besides; besides that, in addition to that [see *teke* (adv. & prep.)]

ther-toyeines (adv.) by contrast, in opposition to that

ther-with (adv.) by means of that, on that account

thes (adj. & pron.) see *this* (adj. & pron.)

thet (conj. & relative pron.) (conj.) THAT; (relative pron.) what, which

thi, thin(e) (adj.) THY, THINE (note reduced forms after preceding -*d* or -*t*: *ti, tin, tine*) [OE]

thicke (adj.) THICK, dense (compar. *thiccre*) [OE]

thider (adv.) THITHER, to that, towards that [OE]

thider-ward (adv.) in that direction

thilke (adj.) the same, aforementioned (person, thing) [prob. from *the* (def. art.) + *ilke* (adj.)]

thing (n.) THING; creature (pl. *thing, thinges*) [OE]

this (adj. & demons. pron.) THIS; this one (sing. *this, thisse*; gen. sing. *thisses*; 3 masc. sing. *thes*; 3 fem. sing. *theos*; pl. *theos, theose*; note reduced forms after preceding -*d* or -*t*: *tis, tes, teose*, etc.) [OE]

thither (adv.) in that direction, THITHER [OE]

thither-ward (adv.) towards that place, in that direction [OE]

thoht, thocht (n.) THOUGHT; study, reverie (pl. *thohtes, thochtes*) [OE]

thohte, thohtest (v., past) see *thenchen* (v.)

thole-mod(e) (adj.) patient, meek, submissive [OE; see *mode* (n.) + *tholien* (v.)]

thole-modliche (adv.) patiently

thole-modnesse (n.) patience; meekness, humility [OE]

tholie(n) (v.) to suffer (pain); allow, permit; experience (something painful); be patient, forbear, put up with; endure, survive (pres. subj. sing. *tholie*; pres. 1 sing. *tholie*; pres. 2 sing. *tholest*; pres. 3 sing. *tholeth*; pres. pl. *tholieth*; past sing. *tholede*; past pl. *tholeden*) [OE]

thon (inflected form of def. art.) *with thon thet* = provided that; in order that, for the reason that, to the end that

thonc (n.) thought; THANKS (originally, a favorable thought); *cunne him thonc* = to acknowledge or express gratitude to him, to give thanks [OE; related to *thenchen* (v.)]

thoncki(n) (v.) to THANK, show gratitude towards (pres. 3 sing. *thonckith*; past sing. *thonckede*; past part. *i-thoncket*) [OE]

thonkin (v.) to THANK; think (imper. sing. *thonke*; imper. pl. *thonkith, thonckith*; pres. subj. sing. *thonki, thoncki*; past subj. sing. *thonckede*; past part. *i-thoncket, i-thonket*)

thorn (n.) THORN; sharp, prickly bramble; a spine; OED: "A spine or spiny process in an animal"; *thornene crune* = crown of thorns (pl. *thornes*; gen. pl. *thornene*) [OE]

thorni (adj.) THORNY

threal (n.) THRALL, slave, underling; servant (pl. *threalles*) [OE, from ON]

threasten (v.) to crowd, throng, jostle; (of water) to rush, pour in (pres. 3 sing. *threasteth*) [OE]

threatin (v.) to urge, press, induce (esp. by force or THREAT of force); threaten; rebuke, reprove (imper. pl. *threatith*; pres. 3 sing. *threateth, threatith*; past sing. *threatte* [= *threatede*]) [OE]

threatunge (n.) THREAT, menace; threatening, menacing; ambush, attack; reproof, correction

th'refter (adv.) THERE-AFTER, after that; afterwards

threo-fald, -vald (adj.) THREEFOLD, triple, consisting of three parts [OE]

threottene (adj.) THIRTEEN [OE]

thridde (adj.) THIRD [OE]

thrien (adv.) three times, THRICE

thrile (adj.) threefold [OE; see ModE *twill*]

th'rin (adv.) THERE-IN, in that

th'rinne (adv.) inside

thritti (adj.) THIRTY [OE]

thriveth (v., pres. 3 sing.) THRIVES; grows; is successful [ON]

throwunge (n.) suffering; martyrdom [OE]

thruh (n.) coffin, tomb [OE]

thrumnesse (n.) Trinity [OE]

thrung (n.) crowd, THRONG; tumult; distress, anxiety, trouble [*OE]

thrungeth (v., pres. pl.) THRONG, crowd, band (together)

th'ruppe (adv.) UP THERE, earlier (in the text)

thu (personal pron., 2 nom. sing.) THOU, you (obj. sing. *the*) [OE]

668

thucke (n.) blow, thwack; injury; malicious, mischievous trick [*OE]

thuften(e) (n.) servant, handmaid [OE]

thuldeliche (adv.) patiently [from OE; see Ger. *geduld* "patience"]

thulli, thulliche (adj.) such, of such a kind, suchlike [OE]

thume (n.) THUMB [OE]

thunchen (v.) to seem, appear; (impers.) *us thuncheth* = (it) seems to us (pres. subj. sing. *thunche*; pres. 3 sing. *thuncheth*; past sing. *thuhte*; past part. *i-thuht*) [OE]

thunne (adj.) THIN, narrow; scanty, scarce [OE]

thurfte (v., past sing.) see *thearf* (v.)

thurh, thurch (prep.) THROUGH; *thurh thet* = (conj.) because [OE]

thurh-fulleth (v., pres. 3 sing.) completes, FULFILLS (past part. *thurhfullet*) [from OE]

thurh-sticheth (v., pres. 3 sing.) STICKS THROUGH, pierces, punctures (past pl. *thurh-stichden*) [from OE]

thurh-wuniende (adj., pres. part.) perpetual, abiding; (through-dwelling) [orig. pres. part. of OE *þurh-wunian* "to remain"]

thurl(e) (n.) window; hole, opening, piercing (pl. *thurles*) [OE]

thurlin (v.) to pierce, bore (a hole in), perforate; pass through (pres. 3 sing. *thurleth*; pres. pl. *thurlith*; past pl. *thurleden*; past part. *i-thurlet*) [OE]

thurlunge (n.) piercing

thurs (n.) demon, devil; giant (from Ger. mythology) [OE *ðyrs* "giant"; see also ON *þurs*]

thurve (v., pres. pl.) see *thearf* (v.)

thwe(a)rt-over (adv.) cross-wise, transversely; over across, horizontally; (prep.) across, from one side to the other of, crosswise to [ON + OE]

thweart-over (adj.) perverse, antagonistic; something that obstructs or THWARTS

thwongede (adj. & v., past part.) THONGED, laced, (provided) with straps [from OE]

ti (adj.) see *thi* (adj.)

ticchen (n.) young goat, kid (pl. *tichnes*) [OE]

ticki (pres. subj. sing.) tussle, dally, play [*OE or imitative]

tide (n.) time; period, season, hour; (canonical) hour, one of the hours of the divine office (pl. *tiden*) [OE]

tiden (v.) to BETIDE, happen to, occur, befall (pres. subj. sing. *tide*; past subj. sing. *tidde*; pres. 3 sing. *tit* [= *tideth*]; past sing. *i-tidde*) [OE]

tidinge (n.) TIDING, piece of news (pl. *tidinges*) [late OE, influenced by ON]

tidliche (adv.) quickly, in a timely way; soon; immediately

tiffunge (n.) (personal) adornment, ornament [OF]

tildeth (v., pres. 3 sing.) spreads (a net), sets (a trap) (past part. *i-tild*) [OE; related to Ger. *zelt* "tent"]

tildunge (n.) spreading (of a net), setting (of a trap)

tilie(n) (v.) to TILL, have land in tillage; to cultivate; work, labor; strive for (pres. 3 sing. *tileth*; pres. pl. *tilieth*; past sing. *tilede*; past part. *i-tilet*) [OE]

tilunge (n.) cultivation, tending, care; TILLING

timbri(n) (v.) to build, construct, make (from wood: TIMBER); (fig.) to form; cause, bring about (past part. *i-timbret*) [OE]

timbrunge (n.) edification; building

timeth (v., pres. 3 sing.) happens, occurs, befalls [OE]

tin, tine (adj.) see *thi* (adj.)

tindes (n. pl.) rung (of a ladder); TINE [OE]

tippe (v., pres. subj. sing.) strike, hit [prob. *OE, not MDu]

tis (demons. pron.) see *this* (pron.)

tit (v., pres. 3 sing.) see *tiden* (v.)

tittes (n. pl.) breasts, TEATS [OE]

to- (prefix) away, apart, in pieces; excessively, up (as in *puff up*); towards; in addition to [OE]

to (adv. & prep.) off, away, out; towards; TO, into, towards; near, close, up, at [OE]

to-beot (v., past sing.) BEAT severely, thrash [OE]

to-blaweth (v., pres. 3 sing.) BLOWS away, scatters; puffs up, inflates; (past part. as adj.) *toblowen* = inflated, swollen [OE]

to-bollen (adj. & v., past part.) severely swollen or puffed up (with pride or anger, etc.) [OE; see *bolheth* (v.)]

to-breken (v.) to BREAK, break up, shatter (pres. 3 sing. *tobreketh*; past pl. *tobreken*; past part. *tobroken[e]*) [OE]

toc (v., past sing.) see *tac* (v.)

to-cheoweth (v., pres. 3 sing.) CHEWS up, gnaw [OE; see *to-* (prefix) + *cheoweth* (v.)]

to-dealen (v.) to divide, separate (pres. subj. sing. *todeale*; pres. 1 sing. *todeale*; past part. *todealet* [OE]

to-dreaven (v.) to drive apart, scatter (imper. sing. *todreaf*) [OE; closely related to *todriveth* (v.)]

to-driveth (v.) to DRIVE apart, scatter; destroy [OE]

to-fallen (v.) to crumble, collapse; FALL apart, go to ruin, be destroyed [OE]

to-fleoten (v.) to FLOAT away, disperse (pres. 3 sing. *tofleoteth*) [OE]

to-fleoten (v., pres. subj. pl.) FLOAT away [OE]

to-fret (v., pres. 3 sing. [= *tofreteth*]) gnaws up or apart [OE; see *freoten* (v.)]

to-fuleth (v., pres. 3 sing.) dirties or BEFOULS thoroughly, besmirches, sullies [OE; see apparently unrelated OF *defouler* "to trample down"]

togederes, -gedere (adv.) TOGETHER, in a unified way [OE]

toggin (v.) to pull, TUG; tussle, touch in a playful or sexual way [OE]

toggunge (n.) TUGGING, scuffling, playful or erotic tussling or touching [OE]

to-hurten (v.) to dash apart, knock in pieces [see *hurten* (v.)]

to-hwitheret (v., past part.) whirled apart, into pieces (?) [origin obscure]

tole (n.) TOOL, instrument [OE]

to-limeth (v., pres. 3 sing.) dismembers, tears LIMB from limb (past part. *tolaimet*) [from OE]

tolleth (v., pres. 3 sing.) attracts, lures (a term from falconry), decoys, entices; instigates; (pres. part. as adj.) *tollinde* = enticing, flirtatious [*OE]

tollunge (n.) act of enticing, provoking, inciting; pulling, tugging, horseplay

to-luketh (v., pres. 3 sing.) rips, tears, plucks apart [OE]

to-marhen (n. & adv.) TOMORROW [OE]

tomre (adj., compar.) TAMER, more subdued or under control [OE; see *temie* (v.)]

to-rendeth (v., pres. 3 sing.) RENDS, rips to pieces [OE]

torplin (v.) to tumble, fall, topple (pres. pl. *torplith*; past part. *i-turplet*) [OF]

to-spreat (v., pres. 3 sing. [= *tospreadeth*]) SPREADS out, opens [OE]

to-tagge (n.) something added or TAGGED on; trimming, trapping, embellishment (orig. of clothing?); a circumstance, OED: "something tagged or attached to a fact" (pl. *totagges*) [see *to-* (prefix) + *OE *tag* "something hanging or attached to something else, usually by way of ornament," origin obscure — see MED *totagge* (n.)]

to-teoren (v.) to TEAR apart, to pieces (pres. pl. *toteoreth*; past part. *totore, totoren[e]*) [OE]

toth (n.) TOOTH; *went te grimme toth to* = make a face or grimace at; *unthonc hise teth* = damn his teeth, against his will [OE]

totilde (n.) peering, prying woman [see *totin* (v.) + *-ild* (fem. suffix)]

totin (v.) to look, gaze, peek, peer, peep, spy; (pres. part. as adj.) *totinde* = spying, peering, i.e., too observant of the outside world (pres. 3 sing. *toteth*; pres. part. *totinde*) [OE *totian* "to stick or peep out, protrude"]

to-treoden (v.) to TREAD down, stomp on, trample (to pieces) (imper. sing. *totred*; pres. subj. sing. *totreode*; pres. 3 sing. *totret* [= *totredeth*]; pres. part. *totreodinde*; past part. *totreden*) [OE]

to-treodunge (n.) a TREADING or trampling down (on something)

totunge (n.) peering, peeping, staring (in a curious way) [OE; see *totin* (v.)]

to-tweamde (v., past sing.) separated, divided in TWO [OE]

to-warpeth (v., pres. 3 sing.) throws down, breaks into pieces, destroys [OE; see Ger. *werfen* "to throw"]

to-warplet (adj. & v., past part.) thrown, pulled down [related to *to-warpeth* (v.)]

to-weavet (v., past part.) WAFTED away, dispersed [OE]

to-went (v., pres. 3 sing. [= *towendeth*]) turns over [see *wenden* (v.)]

to wundre (adv.) see *wunder* (n.)

toyein, toyeines (prep.) against, in opposition to; next to; in comparison to [OE]

to-yeves (adv.) freely [OE; related to *yeove* (n.)]

treo (n.) TREE; piece of wood (gen. sing. *treoes*; pl. *treon*) [OE]

treowe (adj.) TRUE, loyal; not false, genuine [OE]

treoweliche (adv.) TRULY, faithfully, steadfastly, securely

treoweschipe (n.) faithfulness, reliability, fidelity [from OE]

treownesse (n.) faithfulness, loyalty

treowthe (n.) see *trowthe* (n.)

trichunge (n.) betrayal, TREACHERY, cheating [OF]

triste (n.) hunting station, i.e., trap (pl. *tristen*) [OF; see ModE *tryst*, orig. "a place to rendezvous"]

triws (n. pl.) TRUCE [OE, related to *treowe* (adj.)]

trochith (v., pres. pl.) fail, are insufficient, fall short [OE]

trode (n.) TREAD, footprint, track (pl. *troden*) [OE]

trone (n.) THRONE [OF]

trowth (n.) trust, faith, faithfulness, fidelity [OE]

trowthe (n.) TROTH, promise, oath; trust, fidelity, faithfulness (pl. *trowthen*) [OE]

truandise (n.) dishonest begging, swindling, vagabond-like behavior, loitering; knavery [OF, from *truant* "vagabond"]

trubli (v.) TROUBLE, disturb, agitate [OF]

trude (v., imper. sing.) TREAD, walk; trample, set foot on; (fig.) seek out, track down, investigate; to overcome (pres. subj. sing. *trudde*; pres. 3 sing. *truddeth*) [OE]

truiles (n. pl.) a trick, deception [OF]

trukie (v., pres. subj. sing.) fail, be lacking; deceive; abandon (pres. 3 sing. *truketh*; past sing. *trukede*) [OE]

trusse, trussin (v.) to bundle, pack; to load (with a bundle), weigh down; to pack off, depart (past part. *i-trusset*) [OF]

trussen (n. pl.) parcel, traveler's pack, bundle [OF; see ModE phrase *truss up*]

trussews (n. pl.) bundles, packs, bags [prob. AF]

trust (v., imper. sing.) TRUST, have faith, confidence in [*OE or ON]

trusti (adj.) faithful, loyal, TRUSTY; safe, secure; full of religious faith, trusting; *beon trusti (up)on* = to trust in

tu (personal pron.) see *thu* (personal pron.)

tuhte (v., past sing.) taught, trained (past part. *i-tuht*) [OE; related to *teoth* (v.)]

tuk (v., imper. sing.) mistreat, abuse (verbally or physically), torment; scorn, upbraid (pres. subj. sing. *tuki*; pres. 3

sing. *tuketh*; past part. *i-tuket*) [OE; see ModE *tuck* (v.) in various senses]

tulle (v., imper. pl.) attract, allure; pull, drag (past pl. *tulden*) [related to *tolleth* (v.)]

tune (n.) TOWN, enclosed or walled settlement [OE]

tunen (v.) to enclose, shut, stop up (imper. sing. *tun*; pres. subj. pl. *tunen*; past part. *i-tunet*) [OE; related to *tune* (n.)]

tunne (n.) TUN, beer barrel, wine cask [OE]

tur (n.) TOWER; stronghold, fortress (gen. sing. *tures*) [OF]

turn (n.) TURN; cycle, sequence; throw, move, OED: "a device, or trick, by which a wrestler attempts to throw his antagonist"; stratagem, wile [AF]

turneiment (n.) TOURNAMENT; chivalric contest [OF]

turnen (v.) to TURN, change; change the course of (something), direct; revolve; convert, transform (imper. sing. *turn*; imper. pl. *turneth*; pres. subj. sing. *turne*; pres. 2 sing. *turnest*; pres. 3 sing. *turneth*; past sing. *turnde*; pres. part. *turninde*; past part. *i-turnd[e], i-turnt*) [OE, from Lat., probably reinforced by OF]

turpelnesse (n.) tumultuousness, turmoil [see *torplin* (v.)]

tutel (n.) the mouth (with the lips protruded in the act of whispering), chops (pl. *tuteles*) [*OE]

tuteleth (v., pres. 3 sing.) whispers; suggests (used of the devil's temptations); jabbers, jaws (pres. part. *tutelinde*) [see *tutel* (n.)]

twa (adj. & n.) TWO (gen. *tweire*) [OE]

twa-fald, -vald, -valt (adj.) TWOFOLD, consisting of two parts or kinds; double [OE]

tweamen (v.) to divide (in TWO), separate (imper. sing. *tweam*; past part. *i-tweamet*) [OE]

tweamunge (n.) separation

tweast (v., pres. 3 sing. [= *tweasteth*]) binds, constrains, obligates [*OE; related to ModE *twist*]

tweie (adj. & pron.) TWO (pl. *tweien*) [OE]

tweire (pron.) see *twa* (adj. & n.)

tweof (adj. & n.) TWELVE [apparently a reduced form of *tweolf*]

tweof-moneth (n.) TWELVE-MONTH, a year [from OE, influenced by ON]

tweolf, tweolve (adj. & n.) TWELVE [OE]

twien (adv.) TWICE, two times [OE]

twi-mel-dei (n.) TWO MEAL DAY; a day on which two meals are prescribed

twinnin (v.) to separate (two things), sever, part [from OE]

twinnunge (n.) separation, parting

uggi (v.) to terrify, horrify; (impers.) *ow uggi with* = [it] may horrify you with [ON, related to ModE *awe*]

uht-song (n.) Matins (canonical hour celebrated before daybreak); (lit.) dawn SONG [OE]

umbe(n) (prep.) around, about; concerning; busied with, seeking after, aiming for; after (someone to do something); (adv.) around, about [OE influenced by ON]

umbe-hwile (adv.) at times, sometimes

umbe-stunde (adv.) at times, sometimes

Umbri-dayes (n. pl.) EMBER-DAYS, [see *Umbri-wiken* (n.)]

Umbri-wiken (n. pl.) EMBER-WEEKS, i.e., a week in which special fasting was prescribed. EMBER days consisted of four groups of three days in the church calendar during which fasting was observed [*OE]

un- (prefix.) (negation) not, lacking; (intensification) very, excessively; (pejoration) bad, wrong; foreign [OE]

un-bileave (n.) disbelief, lack of belief

un-bilevet (adj. & v., past part.) UNBELIEVING

un-bischpet (adj., past part.) unsaved, unconfirmed (in the church, by the BISHOP) [from OE]

un-bisehnesse (n.) inattention, negligence [see *bi-seon* (v.)]

un-cleannesse (n.) moral impurity, lack of chastity

un-cumelich (adj.) UNCOMELY, unbecoming, improper

un-cundelich(e) (adj.) unnatural, improper (superlat. *uncundelukest*) [OE]

un-cundeliche (adv.) unnaturally; with unnatural morality, with unnatural cruelty; contrary to right feeling [OE]

un-cuth(e) (adj.) unknown, uncertain; strange; unknowing, ignorant [OE; see *cuth* (adj.), ModE *uncouth*]

un-cuththe (n.) unknown (person), stranger; things not commonly known; strange land [from OE]

un-deadlich (adj.) immortal, not subject to DEATH [OE]

un-deore (adj.) unvalued, cheap, worthless [OE]

under (n.) morning; Tierce, third liturgical hour (approx. 9 a.m.); noon (?) [OE *undern*]

under-fon (v.) to receive, accept; take (pres. 3 sing. *underveth*; pres. pl. *undervoth*; past sing. *underfeng, underveng*; past pl. *undervengen*) [OE]

673

under-neomen (v.) to undertake (past part. *undernume*) [see *neomen* (v.)]

under-sete (v., imper. sing.) SET UNDER, support [from OE]

under-stiprin (v.) to prop up, support [see OE *stipere* (n.) "post, prop"]

under-stonde(n) (v.) to UNDERSTAND; (passive sense) to be understood (imper. sing. *understond, understont*; imper. pl. *understondeth*; pres. subj. sing. *understonde*; pres. 1 sing. *understonde*; pres. 3 sing. *understondeth, understont*; pres. pl. *understondeth*; past sing. *understod*; past part. *understonden*) [OE]

under-tid (n.) (lit.) morningtide; Tierce, the third canonical hour (approx. 9 a.m.) [OE; see ModE *undern*]

under-venge (v., past) see *under-fon* (v.)

under-veth, -voth, -vo(n) (v.) see *under-fon* (v.)

under-yeoten (v.) to become aware of, perceive, observe; learn, understand (pres. 2 sing. *underyetest*; pres. pl. *underyeoteth*; past pl. *underyeten*) [OE]

un-duden (v., past pl.) undid, unwrapped, opened [see *don* (v.)]

un-efne (adj.) UNEVEN, unequal; unfair [see *efne* (adj.)]

un-endeliche (adv.) infinitely, UNENDINGLY [OE]

un-evenlich (adj.) incomparable, not comparable, unlike [OE]; (adv.) incomparably, beyond comparison [OE]

un-festnin (v.) to UNFASTEN, untie [see *festnith* (v.)]

un-fondet (adj. & v., past part.) untested, untried; not tempted [see *fondin* (v.)]

un-freinet (adj. & v., past part.) unasked, unrequested [see *freini* (v.)]

un-graciuse (adj. pl. as n.) UNGRACIOUS (people) [OF]

un-hal(e) (adj.) unhealthy, unwholesome; incomplete, not whole (compar. *unhalre*) [see *hal* (adj.)]

un-hap (n.) misfortune, mishap [OE + ON]

un-heite (adj.) UNWELL, unfit, infirm [from AF *heit* "pleased"]

un-hende (adj.) impolite, rude, rough; unfitting, improper [see *hende* (adj.)]

un-holde (adj. pl. as n.) disloyal, false (people); enemies [OE]

un-hope (n.) lack of hope, hopelessness, despair

un-huleth (v., pres. 3 sing.) uncovers, makes visible (past part. *unhulet*) [see *hulien* (v.)]

un-imete (adj.) inordinate, immoderate, exceeding; immeasurable; (adv.) inordinately, immoderately, exceedingly; immeasurably [OE; see *mete* (n. 2)]

un-lathnesse (n.) un-hatefulness, peace-fulness; harmlessness, friendliness [see *lath* (adj.)]

un-leppet (adj. & v., past part.) uncovered; not covered by a cloak, veil, or headdress [from OE; see ModE *overlap*]

un-lideth (v., pres. 3 sing.) uncovers, takes the LID from (past sing. *unlidede*) [see *lideth* (v.)]

un-limin (v.) to UNLIME, unglue; detach, sever (pres. 3 sing. *unlimeth*) [see *i-limet* (v.)]

un-limp (n.) misfortune, calamity, catastrophe [from OE; see *limpe* (v.)]

un-lust (n.) evil desire; disinclination, laziness, lack of desire [OE; see *lust* (n.)]

un-meath (adv.) exceedingly, extremely; (lit.) immoderately [OE]

un-meteliche (adv.) immeasurably [OE]

un-mundlunge (adv.) unexpectedly; unawares [OE; see ModE *unmindful*]

un-neathe (adv.) with difficulty, not easily; scarcely, barely [OE; see *eathe* (adv.)]

unnen (v.) to wish, desire; to grant, allow, permit (pres. 2 sing. *unnest*; past part. *i-unnen*) [OE]

un-net (adj.) unforced, uncompelled [from *neoden* (v.) "to compel"]; (n.) idleness, vanity, that which is useless or worthless [see *un-nete* (adj.)]

un-net(e) (adj.) useless, worthless, unprofitable [OE; see *nutten* (v.), Ger. *unnütz* "useless"]

unnunge (n.) granting, permission; desiring, wish [see *unnen* (v.)]

un-orne (adj.) plain, simple, humble; mean, wretched; (of food) poor, inferior [*un-* "not" + OE *orne* "unusual, excessive"]

un-orneschipe (n.) plainness, simplicity

un-recheles (adj.) thoughtless, indifferent; *on unrecheles* = an indifferent, thoughtless (person) [from OE]

un-schriven (adj.) unconfessed [see *schriven* (v.)]

un-selhthe (n.) unhappiness, misery, wretchedness; misfortune [OE; see *seli* (adj.)]

un-seli (adj.) unhappy, unfortunate, wretched, pitiful; unlucky; wicked, evil-doing; *unselies sahe* = the saying of an wicked (person) (gen.sing. *unselies*) [OE; see *seli* (adj.)]

un-seowet (v., past part.) UNSEWN

un-seowlich (adj.) unseemly, ugly, not beautiful [OE]

un-sibsumnesse (n.) strife, trouble; (lit.) unpeacefulness [OE; see *sibbe* (n.)]

un-siker (adj.) unsure, uncertain [see *siker* (adj.)]

un-spende (v., past sing.) unclasped, unlocked, released [OE + ON]

un-sperren (v.) to unfasten, unblock, open [see *sperreth* (v.)]

un-steathelvest (adj.) unsteadfast; weak [OE]

un-strengen (v.) to weaken, deprive of STRENGTH (pres. 3 sing. *unstrengeth*; pres. pl. *unstrengeth*)

un-strong (adj.) not STRONG, lacking strength (compar. *unstrengre*)

un-talelich(e) (adj.) indescribable; uncountable, innumerable [see *tale* (n.)]

un-theaw (n.) vice, (lit., unvirtue); a bad habit; fault (pl. *untheawes*) [OE; see *theaw* (n.)]

un-theode (n.) a foreign, alien people (or, nation) [see *un-* (prefix) + *theode* (n.)]

un-thonc (n.) annoyance, offense, injury; ingratitude, ill will [OE]

un-thonckes, un-thonkes (semi-adv.) (usually with possessive) unwillingly, against a person's will, without one's consent; *sare hire unthonkes* = very much against her will [OE]

un-tiffet (adj. & v., past part.) unadorned [see *a-tiffi* (v.)]

un-time (n.) the wrong, improper, unsuitable TIME [OE]

un-tohe, un-tohen(e) (adj. & v., past part.) untrained, undisciplined; unruly [see *teoth* (v.)]

un-trusset (adj. & v., past part.) unburdened, unloaded [see *trusse* (v.)]

un-trust (n.) lack of trust, confidence; despair, insecurity [see *trust* (v.)]

un-trusten (v.) to despair, lose confidence [see *trust* (v.)]

un-tu (n.) an ill-mannered, wanton thing [see *un-tohe* (adj.)]

un-tuhtle (n.) bad manners, misbehavior [see *tuhte* (v.)]

un-valden (v.) to UNFOLD, uncover; reveal [OE]

un-waker (adj.) unwatchful, unawake, not vigilant [OE; see *waker* (adj.)]

un-warre (adj., compar.) more unprepared, less WARY [see *war* (adj.)]

un-wemmet (adj. & v., past part.) un-blemished, unstained; pure [see *wem* (n.)]

un-wen(e)liche (adv.) unseemly, in an ugly way, repulsively; unworthily [OE *wenlich* "beautiful, excellent"]

un-weote (n.) ignorant person [OE; related to ModE *wit*]

un-weoteness (n.) ignorance, unawareness

un-wiht (n.) monster; evil spirit, devil; an alien WIGHT or creature (gen. sing. *unwihtes*; pl. *unwihtes*) [OE; see *un-* (prefix) + *wiht* (n.)]

un-wine (n.) enemy, foe; the devil (pl. *unwines*) [OE *unwine* "un-friend"]

un-wreast(e), un-wrest(e) (adj.) poor, vile, paltry, pitiful; evil, wicked, vicious; (lit.) unstrong [OE]

un-wreaste (adv.) weakly, feebly, poorly; wickedly

un-wreastlec (n.) wickedness, evil

un-wrench (n.) an evil design, base trick [OE; see *un-* (prefix) + *wrench* (n.)]

un-wreo(n) (v.) to uncover; reveal, strip away (imper. sing. *unwreo, unwrih*; pres. 2 sing. *unwrisd*; pres. 3 sing. *unwreoth, unwrith*; past sing. *unwreah*; past pl. *unwriyen*; past part. *unwrihen, unwriyen*) [OE; see *wrihen* (v.)]

un-wrestlec (n.) wickedness, sinfulness

un-wrisd (v., pres. 3 sing.) see *un-wreon* (v.)

un-wurth(e) (adj.) WORTH-less, without value, of no account; (n.) worthlessness, unworthiness (superlat. *unwurthest*) [OE]

up-breide (v., pres. subj. sing.) UPBRAID, reprimand, scold (pres. 3 sing. *upbreideth*) [OE]

up-brud (n.) scorn, UPBRAIDING [from OE]

uppard, uppardes, uppart (adv.) UPWARD [OE]

uppin (v.) to bring UP, raise, mention, disclose, reveal: (past part. as adj.) *i-uppet* = mentioned, revealed (pres. 3 sing. *uppeth*; past part. *i-uppet*) [*OE]

uppinge (n.) mention; revealing

up-rowunge (n.) (the act of) ROWING upwards

ure (adj.) OUR [OE]

ureisun (n.) prayer (pl. *ureisuns*) [OF]

ures (n. pl.) HOURS, the seven canonical hours of the divine office; a specific liturgical office [OF, from Lat. *hora*]

uri (v.) to pray [OF, from Lat. *orare* "to pray"]

urn (n.) (a) gallop, RUN; rush; *on urn* = in a hurry, in passing; *an urn* = violently [see *eornen* (v.)]

urne, urnen (v.) see *eornen* (v.)

us (n.) USE, application [OF]

ut-cume (n.) escape, a COMING OUT [from OE]

ute (adv.) outside, away from home [OE]

ute-with (adv.) outside, on the outside [from OE]

uthe (n.) wave (of the sea) (pl. *uthen*) [OE]

ut-lahen (n. pl.) OUTLAWS, criminals [late OE, from ON]

ut-nume (adj.) exceptional, supreme, extreme; (adv.) exceptionally, especially [from OE; see *ute* (adv.) + *neomen* (v.), Ger. *ausnahme* "exception"; see d'Ardenne (1982), p. 3]

ut-runes (n. pl.) news, gossip, whisperings; things whispered out [from OE; see ModE *rune*]

utterliche (adv.) UTTERLY, completely; sincerely, truly, plainly, straight out [see *ute* (adv.)]

ut-totunge (n.) a peeping, gazing OUT [see *totin* (v.)]

uttre (adj.) OUTER [OE]

ut-ward, -warde, -wart (adv.) OUTWARD, towards the outside [OE]

uvel(e) (adj.) EVIL, bad; miserable; difficult [OE]; (n.) EVIL, wrongdoing; trouble, misfortune, harm; sickness, disease; *fallinde uvel* = the falling disease (i.e., epilepsy) (pl. *uveles*) [OE]

uvele (adv.) badly, miserably, poorly; in an EVIL way [OE]

uve-mest (adj., superlat.) outermost, top-most [OE]

uvere (adj.) OVER, top; (superlat.) *uvemest* = topmost, outermost [OE]; (compar.) upper, top [OE]

va, van (n.) see *fa* (n.)

val (n.) see *fal* (n.)

vampez (n. pl.) feet (of a pair of stockings) [AF; from *avan(t)* "before" + *pi* "foot"]

veaste (n.) see *feaste* (n. 2)

veasten, veasteth (v.) see *feasten* (v. 1)

veieth (v., pres. 3 sing.) see *feieth* (v.)

veine-glorie (n.) VAINGLORY, empty glory, vanity [OF]

veiunge (n.) joining, linking, association [see *feieith* (v.)]

veleth (v., pres. 3 sing.) see *felen* (v.)

venies (n. pl.) pardon, forgiveness; kneelings or prostrations (as a sign of desire for forgiveness) [AF, from Lat. *venia* "pardon"]

verseilin, versaili (v.) to recite or sing (versicles or psalms) [OF]

verseilunge (n.) (the) singing or recitation (of versicles or psalms)

verset (n.) versicle, a short verse, often taken from the Psalms, said or sung in worship and usually accompanied by a response [OF]

vertu (n.) VIRTUE (pl. *vertuz*) [OF]

vet (n. pl.) see *fot* (n.)

vetles (n.) see *fetles* (n.)

vigilies (n. pl.) VIGILS, watches [Lat.]

vilainie (n.) VILLAINY, wrongdoing, wickedness [AF]

vile (n.) see *file* (n.)

vilte (n.) VILENESS, meanness; something morally or physically repulsive [OF]

vore, vorth (adv.) see *fore* (adv.), *forth* (adv.)

vox (n.) FOX (pl. *voxes*) [OE; see ModE *vixen*]

vrovre (n.) see *frovre* (n.)

vu (n.) VOW [OF]

wa (n.) WOE, misery, suffering, distress; (physical) pain, harm; *don the/hire/him wa* = to inflict distress on, or harm you/her/him (pl. *weohes*) [OE]

wac (adj.) WEAK (physically or morally); foolish [OE]

wacliche (adv.) WEAKLY, feebly [OE]

wacnesse (n.) WEAKNESS

waden (v.) to WADE; proceed, go (pres. 3 sing. *wadeth*) [OE]

waggith (v., pres. pl.) stir, move; stagger, totter; shake, tremble [OE]

wah (n.) wall (of a house), partition (pl. *wahes*) [OE]

wake (adj.) see *wac* (adj.)

wake (n.) vigil, watch, state of WAKE-FULNESS (usually for devotional purposes); celebration, OED: "The local annual festival of an English parish, observed (originally on the feast of the patron saint of the church, but now usually on some particular Sunday and the two or three days following) as an occasion for making holiday, entertainment of friends, and often for village sports, dancing, and other amusements" (pl. *waken*) [OE]

wake-men (n.) WATCHMEN

waker(e) (adj.) unsleeping; watchful, vigilant [OE]

wakien (v.) to stay AWAKE, to go without sleep (often for devotional purposes) (imper. pl. *wakieth*; pres. subj. sing. *wakie*; pres. 3 sing. *waketh*; past sing. *wakede*; past pl. *wakeden*; pres. part. *wakiende, wakinde*; past part. *i-waket*) [OE]

walde (n.) power, control [OE; see ModE *wield*, Ger. *gewalt* "power"]

walde, walden, waldest (v.) see *wullen* (v.)

waldes (adv.) intentionally, purposefully; *willes ant waldes* = willing and ready, willingly and intentionally [OE]

walewunge (n.) a rolling, thrashing, tumbling; WALLOWING [from OE]

walleth (v., pres. 3 sing.) rages, boils, seethes; (pres. part. as adj.) *wallinde* = boiling, raging; (fig.) fervent [OE]

wallinde (adj., pres. part.) see *walleth* (v.)

wanes (n. pl.) dwellings, houses; rooms, apartments [prob. ON]

war (adj.) AWARE, informed; prepared, watchful, vigilant, WARY; prudent, wise [OE]

warde (n.) GUARD, watchfulness, vigilance; guardian, protector; guardian-ship, control [OE; modern forms with *gu*- represent the F. development of the word; the native forms begin with *w*-]

wardein (n.) GUARDIAN, protector, WARDEN (pl. *wardeins*) [OE blended with OF form]

wardi (v., pres. subj. sing.) GUARD, protect (pres. 3 sing. *wardeth*) [OE, influenced by OF]

ware (n. 1) WARES, merchandise [OE]; (n. 2) population, inhabitants [OE]

warinesses (n. pl.) cursings; profane, impious talk [see *wearien* (v.)]

wariunge (n.) cursing, profane talk, blas-phemy (pl. *weariunges*) [see *wearien* (v.)]

warliche (adv.) WARILY, cautiously, carefully [OE]

warne (n.) refusal, denial [OE; see *wearnen* (v.)]

warni(n) (v.) to caution, put on guard, WARN (pres. subj. sing. *warni*; pres. 3 sing. *warneth*; past part. *i-warnet*) [OE]

warningge (n.) WARNING

warpe(n) (v.) to throw, cast down, drive away (imper. sing. *warp*; imper. pl. *warpeth*; pres. subj. sing. *warpe*; past subj. sing. *wurpe*; pres. 2 sing. *warpest*; pres. 3 sing. *warpeth*; past sing. *weorp*;

past part. *i-warp[e], i-warpen*) [OE; see Ger. *werfen* "to throw"]

warpere (n.) thrower, one who throws (something)

warre (adj.) see *war* (adj.)

warschipe (n.) wariness, caution, vigilance [OE; see *war* (adj.)]

warth (v., past sing.) see *wurthen* (v.)

wast, wat (v., pres.) see *witen* (v. 1)

Water (n.) WALTER [like *Wilyam* (n.)]

waxen (v.) to grow, grow stronger, develop; (of the moon) to WAX (pres. subj. sing. *waxe*; pres. subj. pl. *waxen*; past subj. sing. *weoxe*; pres. 3 sing. *waxeth*; past sing. *weox*) [OE; see Ger. *wachsen* "to grow"]

we (personal pron., 1 pl.) WE (objective form: *us*; reflex. *us-seolf, us-seolven*) [OE]

wealden (v.) WIELD, rule; have at one's disposal, possess [OE]

wealdent (n.) WIELDING (one), ruler [orig. pres. part. of *wealden* (v.)]

wealle (n.) WELL, wellspring; stream (from a well) (pl. *weallen*) [OE]

wea-mod(e) (adj.) petulant, angry; passionate [see *wa* (n.) and *mode* (n.)]

weane (n.) misery, woe [related to *wa* (n.)]

weari (n.) outlaw, criminal; cursed one [OE; see *wearien* (v.)]

wearien (v.) to curse [OE]

weari-tre, -treo (n.) gallows, gibbet [OE; see *weari* (n.) + *treo* (n.)]

weariunges (n. pl.) see *wariunge* (n.)

wearliche (adv.) WARILY, carefully, vigilantly [from OE]

wearnen (v.) to refuse, deny (a request); to prevent (a thing) (past sing. *wearnde*) [OE]

weater (n.) WATER; washing (pl. *weattres*) [OE]

weattri (adj.) WATERY [see *weater* (n.)]

web (n.) WOVEN fabric [OE]

wecche (n.) vigil, WATCH, staying AWAKE (pl. *wecchen*) [OE]

wed (n.) pledge; OED: "something deposited as a security for a payment or the fulfillment of an obligation" [OE]

wed(de) (adj.) maddened, mad, demented; (of dogs) rabid [orig. past part. of *weden* (v.); see Ger. *wut* "rage"]

weddet (adj. & v., past part.) WED, married [see *i-weddet* (v.)]

weden (n. pl.) clothes, WEEDS [OE]; (v.) to be, go mad; to rage, be furious; go wild (pres. subj. sing. *wede*; past sing. *wedde*) [OE; see *wod* (adj.)]

wedlac (n.) WEDLOCK, marriage [see *weddet* (adj.)]

wefdes (n. pl.) see *weoved* (n.)

wei (n.) WAY; path, road, route; manner; *summes weies* (adverbial gen.) = to some extent, in some way; *thisses weis* (adverbial gen.) = in this way (obj. *weie*; gen. sing. as adv. *weies, weis*; pl. *weies*) [OE]

weie (n.) a WEIGHT, (standard) measure; scales (pl. *weien*) [OE]

weie(n) (v.) to WEIGH; estimate, consider, judge (pres. subj. sing. *weie*; pres. 3 sing. *weieth*; past part. *i-weiet*) [OE]

wei-la, wei-la-wei (interj.) alas! (an exclamation of sorrow or regret) [OE, influenced by ON; see Ger. *O weh!*, Yiddish *Oi vay!*]

weiti (v., pres. subj. sing.) WAIT, lie in wait; plot, scheme (pres. 3 sing. *weiteth*; pres. pl. *weitith*) [OF]

wel (adv.) WELL; fittingly; really, entirely [OE]

wem (n.) spot, blemish, defect; scar; injury [OE]

wenchel (n.) child [OE, related to OE *wancol* "weak, tottering"]

wende, wenden (v., past) see *wenen* (v.)

wenden (v.) to turn, alter, change; turn over; direct (oneself); depart, go away; proceed, travel, WEND; happen (imper. sing. *wend, went*; imper. pl. *wendeth*; pres. subj. sing. *wende*; pres. 2 sing. *wendest*; pres. 3 sing. *went, wendeth*; past sing. *wende*; past pl. *wenden*; past part. *i-wend, i-went*) [OE]

wene (n.) expectation, hope; opinion, judgment [OE; see *wenen* (v.)]

wenen (v.) to consider, expect, WEEN; hope (pres. subj. sing. *wene*; pres. subj. pl. *wenen*; pres. 2 sing. *wenest*; pres. 3 sing. *weneth*; past sing. *wende*; past pl. *wenden*) [OE; see ModE *overweening*]

went (v.) see *wenden* (v.)

weohes (n. pl.) see *wa* (n.)

weolcne (n., obj. form) WELKIN, sky, clouds [OE; see Ger. *wolken* "clouds"]

weole (n.) WEALTH, riches; prosperity, happiness (pl. *weolen*) [OE]

weolie (adj., gen. pl.) of rich, WEALTHY (men) [OE]

weoret (n.) company, troop, host (pl. *weoredes*) [OE]

weorp (v., past sing.) see *warpen* (v.)

weorre (n.) WAR, conflict; attack (pl. *weorren*) [late OE, from OF]

weorreth (v., pres. 3 sing.) makes WAR on, attacks (pres. pl. *weorrith, worreth*; past sing. *weorrede*) [see *weorre* (n.)]

weote (n.) witness; consciousness [OE *wita* "wise person"]

weote (n.) see *wite* (n.)

weoved(e) (n.) altar (pl. *wefdes*) [OE]

wepen (v.) to WEEP, cry; complain, lament (imper. sing. *wep*; pres. subj. sing./pl. *wepe*; pres. 3 sing. *wepeth*; pres. pl. *wepeth*; past sing. *weop*; pres. pl. *wepinde*) [OE]

wep-man (n.) male, man (gen. sing. *wep-monnes, -mones*; pl. *wepmen*) [OE *wæp-ned-man* "BEWEAPENED person, male"]

wepne (n.) WEAPON (pl. *wepnen, wepnes*) [OE]

wergith (v., pres. pl.) grow WEARY, tire [OE]

wergunge (n.) WEARINESS, exhaustion [see *wergith* (v.)]

werie(n) (v.) to protect, defend (pres. 2 sing. *werest*; pres. 3 sing. *wereth*; pres. pl. *werieth*; past pl. *wereden*) [OE; Ger. *wehren*]

werien (v.) to WEAR, be dressed in; to wear away, waste, damage, destroy by use (pres. 3 sing. *wereth*; past sing. *werede*) [OE]

werreth (v., pres. 3 sing.) see *weorreth* (v.)

werunge (n.) something for WEARING: clothing, a garment [see *werien* (v.)]

weschen, wesschen (v.) to WASH (imper. pl. *wesscheth*; pres. 2 sing. *weschest*; pres. 3 sing. *wescheth*; past: *wesch*; past part. *i-weschen, i-wesschen*) [OE]

wesschunge (n.) WASHING

wet(e) (adj.) WET, moist; (n.) fluid, moisture [OE]

wicce-creftes (n. pl.) WITCHCRAFTS, demonic powers, sorceries [OE]

wid(e) (adj.) WIDE, broad; (adv.) widely, far and wide [OE]

widewe (n.) WIDOW (pl. *widewen, wydewen*; gen. pl. *widwene*) [OE]

widewe-had (n.) WIDOWHOOD [OE]

wif (n.) woman; WIFE (gen. sing. *wives*; gen. pl. *wivene*) [OE]

wigleth (v., pres. 3 sing.) staggers, WIGGLES [*OE]

wiheleare (n.) sorcerer, magician; deceiver [see *wiheles* (n.)]

wiheles (n. pl.) sorceries; deceptions, wiles [from OE *wiglian* "to perform divination," perhaps influenced by OF *wile*]

wiht (adj.) at all, a WHIT [OE]; (n.) creature, being [OE]

wike (n.) WEEK [OE]

wil (n.) WILL, desire, wish [OE]

wil-cweme (adj.) satisfied, pleased; well-disposed, gracious [OE; see *wil* (n.) + *cwemen* (v.)]

willeliche (adv.) WILLINGLY [OE]

willes (adj.) willing, voluntary; (adv.) willingly, voluntarily; *willes ant waldes* = willing and ready, willingly and intentionally [OE]

wilni(n) (v.) to wish, desire (pres. subj. sing./pl. *wilni*; pres. 2 sing. *wilnest*; pres. 3 sing. *wilneth*; past sing. *wilnede*; past part. *i-wilned*) [related to *wil* (n.)]

wilnunge (n.) desire

wil-schrift (n.) WILLING, voluntary confession

wilt (n.) WILE, guile [from OE]

wiltes (n. pl.) wiles; crafts, cunning [origin obscure]

wiltfule (adj.) wily

Wilyam (n.) WILLIAM; a generic name for a male, as in "Tom, Dick, or Harry"

wil-yeove (n.) a WILLING, voluntary, or free GIFT [see *wil* (n.) and *yeove* (n.)]

wimpel (n.) a (fashionable) head dress made of linen or silk [late OE]

wimpelles (adj.) WIMPLELESS, without a wimple

wimplin (v.) to WIMPLE, put on a wimple (past part. *i-wimplet*)

wimplunge (n.) WIMPLING, the way or style in which a wimple is worn

win-berien (n. pl.) WINE-BERRIES, grapes

winche (v.) to start back, recoil, flinch [AF; ModE *wince*]

windeth (v., pres. 3 sing.) flies up [OE; related to *wenden* (v.)]

wind-feallet (adj. & v., past part.) FELLED or toppled by the WIND

windwin (v.) to WINNOW, separate wheat from the chaff by tossing in the air (past: *windwede*) [OE]

windwunge (n.) WINNOWING

winkin (v.) to close or shut the eyes (pres. pl. *winkith*) [OE; ModE *wink*]

wint (v., pres. 3 sing.) see *windeth* (v.)

win-yardes (n. pl.) VINEYARDS [OE]

wipen (v.) to WIPE, dry (pres. 3 sing. *wipeth*)

wis (adv.) surely, certainly

wis(e) (adj.) WISE (compar. *wisre, wisure*; superlat. *wisest*) [OE]

wise (n.) manner, WISE (pl. *wisen*) [OE]

wisliche (adv.) WISELY (compar. *wisluker*)

wisse (n.) guide, advisor, rule [from OE; see Ger. *weisen* "to direct, guide"; see explanatory note to Pref.1]

wit (n.) WIT, faculty (of the mind), sense (as in the five bodily senses); mind, reason; wisdom (obj. form: *witte*; pl. *wittes*) [OE]

wite, weote (n.) blame, accusation, reproach; offense, wrongdoing; penalty, fining, extortion (by threatening a penalty) [OE]

witen (v. 1) to know, be familiar with (imper. pl. *wite (ye), witeth*; pres. subj. sing. *wite*; pres. sing. *wat*; pres. 2 sing. *wast*; pres. pl. *witen*; past sing. *wiste*; past part. *i-wist*; negative forms: pres. subj. sing. *nute*; pres. 2 sing. *nast*; pres.1, 3sing. *nat*; pres. pl. *nute(n)*; past sing. *nuste, nute*; past pl. *nuten*) [OE]; (v. 2) to protect, defend; keep safe, preserve, guard (imper. sing. *wite*; imper. pl. *witeth*; pres. 3 sing. *wit, witeth*; past part. *i-wite*; inflected inf. *to witene*) [OE]

witer (adj.) sure, certain; clear, evident [see *witerliche* (adv.)]

witerliche (adv.) clearly, plainly, certainly (compar. *witerluker*) [ON; but see d'Ardenne (1961), p. 172]

witest (v., pres. 2 sing.) blame, find fault with [OE; see *wite* (n.), *ed-witen* (v.)]

with- (prep.) WITH, along with; against, in opposition to [OE]

with-al (adv.) along with the rest, in addition; besides, moreover, likewise

with-buhe (v.) to escape, avoid (pres. 3 sing. *withbuheth*) [OE]

with-drahen (v.) to WITHDRAW, take back; keep back, restrain (pres. subj. sing. *withdrahe*; pres. 3 sing. *withdraheth*; past sing. *withdroh*; past part. *withdrahene*) [from OE, modeled on Lat.]

wither-iwines (n. pl.) enemies, adversaries [OE *wiþer-winna* "against-fighter"]

with-halden (v.) to hold back, restrain; (reflex.) to restrain oneself (pres. 3 sing. *withhalt* [= *withhaldeth*]) [OE]

within (n.) pliant twig or bough (of willow) [OE]

with-saken (v.) to fight against [OE; see Ger. *widersacher* "adversary"]

with-seggen (v.) to GAINSAY, contradict, deny; oppose, resist (imper. pl. *withseggeth*; pres. pl. *withseggeth*; past sing. *withseide*) [OE]

with-seggunge (n.) denial, refusal

with-stonde(n) (v.) to WITHSTAND, stand against, resist (imper. pl. *withstondeth*; past subj. sing. *withstode*; past part. *withstonden*) [OE]

with-ward (prep.) together with [from OE]

witi (adj.) guilty; blameworthy [OE *wite*]

witles (adj.) WITLESS; foolish, reckless [OE]

witneth (v., pres. 3 sing.) bears WITNESS, testifies, attests [ON]

witunge (n.) guarding, safekeeping [see *witen* (v. 2)]

wivede (v., past sing.) married, got married, took a WIFE; had sex with (past part. *i-wivet*) [OE]

wivene, wives (n.) see *wif* (n.)

wleatie(n) (v.) to disgust, nauseate; feel disgust, gag; (impers.) *ham walde wleatie* = (it) would nauseate them [OE]

wleatunge (n.) disgust; nausea

wlech, wlecche (adj.) lukewarm, tepid [OE]

wlispin (v.) to LISP, imitate a child's speech [OE]

wlite (n.) beauty, splendor; face, countenance; form, appearance [OE]

682

wod(e) (adj.) mad, raging, insane (compar. *woddre*) [OE; see Ger. *wut* "rage"]

wodeliche (adv.) furiously, ferociously; madly [from *wode* (adj.)]

wodschipe (n.) madness, insanity; fury

woh (adj.) crooked, twisted; wrong; (n.) wrong, injury, harm, evil; mistake; *habben woh* = to be in the wrong (pl. *wohes*) [OE; see Baldwin (1976), pp. 275–77]

wohere (n.) WOOER, suitor [OE]

wohin (v.) to WOO, court (pres. 3 sing. *woheth*; past sing. *wohede*) [OE]

wohlech (n.) wooing, courting [from OE]

wohunge (n.) WOOING, courting

wombe (n.) belly, stomach [OE; ModE *womb*]

wombe-pot (n.) BELLY-POT, cauldron of the stomach [see *wombe* (n.) + OE *pott*]

wone (n.) want, lack, shortage; need, poverty [OE]

woneth (v., pres. 3 sing.) (of the moon) WANES, diminishes; *woniende* = waning, lacking (pres. part. *woniende*) [see *wone* (n.)]

wonte (n.) WANT, need [ON]

wonti(n) (v.) to be lacking, missing (+ obj. of person) (pres. subj. sing. *wonti*; pres. 3 sing. *wonteth*) [prob. ON]

wont-re(a)the (n.) misery, distress; hardship, poverty [ON, first element related to *wonte* (n.), the second to *read* (n.)]

wonunge (n.) WANING, diminishing [see *woneth* (v.)]

wop (n.) WEEPING, crying [OE]

wopi (adj.) WEEPY, tearful

word (n.) WORD; news; speech; common report praising a person or his/her accom-plishments; repute, fame (obj. form: *worde*; pl. *word, wordes*) [OE]

woreth (v., pres. 3 sing.) falters, dries up; troubles, confuses, disturbs (trans.) (pres. pl. *worith*) [*OE]

wori (adj.) troubled, confused [see *woreth* (v.)]

worldlich(e), worltlich(e) (adj.) WORLD-LY, of this world; not spiritual [OE]

worreth (v., pres. pl.) see *weorreth* (v.)

wracfulliche (adv.) vengefully, angrily [see *wrake* (n.)]

wrag(e)lunge (n.) struggling, striving, resisting [*OE; prob. related to ModE *wriggle*]

wrahte (v.) see *wurchen* (v.)

wrake (n.) vengeance, revenge; punishment [OE; see ModE *wrack* and *wreak*]

wrat (v., past sing.) see *writen* (v.)

wrath(e) (adj.) WROTH, angry, enraged; bad, evil (old fem. obj. sing. *wrather* — see *heale* [n.]) [OE]

wrathen (v.) to be, become angry; rage; to irritate, enrage (someone) [from OE; see *wreaththe* (n.)]

wreah (v.) see *wrihen* (v.)

wreastle(a)re (n.) WRESTLER [see *wreastlin* (v.)]

wreastli(n) (v.) to WRESTLE (pres. 3 sing. *wreastleth*) [OE]

wreastlunge (n.) WRESTLING

wreathen (v.) to become angry, WROTH; to anger, enrage (someone); provoke, incite (pres. subj. sing. *wreathe*; pres. 3 sing. *wreatheth*; pres. pl. *wreatheth*; past part. *i-wreathet*) [from OE; see *wrath* (adj.)]

wreathful(e) (adj.) WRATHFUL, filled with anger [from OE]

wre(a)ththe (n.) WRATH, anger (as one of the seven deadly sins) (gen. sing. *wreaththes*) [OE]

wrecche (adj.) poor, miserable, WRETCHED; despicable, vile; (n.) WRETCH, wretched person (pl. *wrecchces*) [OE]

wreien (v.) to accuse, arraign (imper. pl. *wreie (we)*; pres. subj. sing. *wreie*; pres. 2 sing. *wreieth*; pres. pl. *wreieth*, past sing. *wreide*; pres. pl. *wreiyende*) [OE; early ModE *bewray*]

wreiful (adj.) accusing, full of accusation

wreiunge (n.) blame, denunciation, accusation [see *wreien* (v.)]

wrench (n.) trick, deceit, crooked action (pl. *wrenches*) [OE; ModE *wrench* "to twist"]

wrenche(n) (v.) to twist, WRENCH, pull; to draw out, expel; divert, deflect (pres. 2 sing. *wrenchest*; pres. 3 sing. *wrencheth*; pres. pl. *wrencheth*) [OE]

wrenchfule (adj.) tricky, crafty, deceitful [see *wrench* (n.)]

wreo, wreon (v.) see *wrihen* (v.)

wreoke(n) (v.) to vent (an emotion); WREAK revenge, avenge; punish (imper. pl. *wreoke (ye)*; pres. 3 sing. *wreketh*; past sing. *wrec*) [OE]

wreothie (v., pres. subj. sing.) lean on; prop, hold up, support (oneself) [OE]

wrihe (adj. & v., past part.) see *wrihen* (v.)

wriheles (n.) : covering, veil; garment, clothes [OE; see *wrihen* (v.) + *-(e)les* (suffix)]

wrihen (v.) to cover, conceal; protect, disguise; *wrihe* (past part. as adj.) hidden, concealed, with hidden meaning (pres. subj. sing. *wreo*; pres. 3 sing. *writh*, *wriheth*; pres. pl. *wriheth, wreoth*; past sing. *wreah*; past part. *wrihe, i-wriyen*) [OE]

wrinnith (v., pres. pl.) struggle against, fight [*OE]

writ (n.) a WRIT, something written; *Hali Writ* = the Holy Scriptures [OE]

writen (v.) to WRITE, copy down in writing (pres. 1 sing. *write*; pres. 3 sing. *writeth*; past sing. *wrat*; past part. *i-writen*) [OE]

writere (n.) WRITER, scribe, copyist [OE]

writh (v.) see *wrihen* (v.)

wrong-wende (adj. & v., past part.) turned awry or aside, distorted [ON + OE; see *wenden* (v.)]

wruhte (n., gen. sing.) maker's, WRIGHT'S, fashioner's [OE; see *wurchen* (v.)]

wude (n.) WOOD [OE]

wullen (v.) to wish, WILL, want (+ inf.); (also a marker of the future tense, as in ModE, sometimes with subj.) (past subj. sing. *walde*; pres. 1 sing. *wule, wulle, (ich) chulle*; pres. 2 sing. *wult*; pres. 3 sing. *wule, wulle*; pres. pl. *wulle (ye), wulleth*; past sing. *walde*; past pl. *walden*; negative forms: pres. 1 sing. *nulle*; pres. 2 sing. *nult*; pres. 3 sing. *nule*; pres. pl. *nulleth, nulle (ye)*; past 1 sing. *nalde*; past 2 sing. *naldest*; past sing. *nalde*; past pl. *nalden*) [OE]

wulvene (n.) SHE-WOLF [OE]

wumme (interj.) alas! WOE is ME! [from OE]

wummon, wumman (n.) WOMAN (pl. *wummen*; gen. pl. *wummone*) [OE]

wummonlich (adj.) WOMANLY, not manly [from OE]

wunde (n.) WOUND, injury (pl. *wunden*) [OE]

wunder (adj.) WONDROUS, strange; monstrous, shockingly evil [see *wunder* (n.)]; (n.) WONDER, cause for amazement; miracle, marvel; a shocking evil or monstrosity; (adverbial phrase) *to wundre* = dreadfully, horribly, terribly; marvelously (pl. *wundres*) [OE]

wunderfule (adj.) WONDERFUL, full of wonder; marvelous

wunderlich (adj.) wonderful, remarkable, strange [OE]

wunde-studen (n. pl.) WOUND-places, places where Christ was wounded in the crucifixion [see *wunde* (n.) + *stude* (n.)]

wundi (v., pres. subj. sing.) WOUND, injure (pres. 2 sing. *wundest*; pres. 3 sing. *wundeth*; pres. part. *wundinde*; past part. *i-wundet*) [OE]

wundre (n.) see *wunder* (n.)

wundrin (v.) to WONDER, marvel, be amazed; (reflex.) be surprised; (pres. part. as adj.) *wundrinde* = wondering, amazed (imper. pl. *wundri (ye)*; pres. 3 sing. *wundreth*; pres. part. *wundrinde*) [OE]

wune (n.) habit, custom [OE; see *wunien* (v.), Ger. *gewohnheit* "habit"]

wunie(n) (v.) to dwell, live, inhabit; remain, stay; to accustom (oneself to), be WONT to (imper. sing. *wune*; imper. pl. *wunieth*; pres. 1 sing. *wunie*; pres. 2 sing. *wunest*; pres. 3 sing. *wuneth*; pres. pl. *wunieth*; past 2 sing. *wunedest*; past sing. *wunede*; pres. part. *wuniende*; past part. *i-wunet, i-wonet*) [OE]

wunne (n.) joy (pl. *wunnen*) [OE]

wununge (n.) dwelling, abode, house [OE; see Ger. *wohnung* "apartment"]

wurchen (v.) to make, form, build, WORK (something); do, perform (pres. subj. sing. *wurche*; pres. subj. pl. *wurchen*; pres. 1 sing. *wurche*; pres. 3 sing. *wurcheth*; pres. pl. *wurcheth*; past sing. *wraht[e]*; pres. part. *wurchinde*; past part. *i-wraht*) [OE]

wurpe (v., pres. subj. sing.) see *warpen* (v.)

wurse (adj., compar.) WORSE, more harmful, more painful; harder, more difficult; (adv., compar.) WORSE, in a more careless, reprehensible, sinful way [OE]; (n.) a person or thing that is WORSE [OE]

wursi (v., pres. subj. sing.) WORSEN, deteriorate, grow worse (pres. 3 sing. *wurseth*; past part. *i-wurset*) [OE]

wurst(e) (adj. & n., superlat.) WORST [OE]

wursum (n.) pus, corruption [OE, related ModE *worm*]

wurth (n.) price, value [OE]

wurth(e) (adj.) WORTH, equal in value, valuable; worthy, honorable, deserving [OE]

wurthen (v.) to become, be; happen (pres. subj. sing. *wurthe*; past sing. *warth*; past part. *i-wurthe[n]*) [OE; see Ger. *werden* "to become"]

wurthfule (adj.) WORTHFUL, valuable; worthy [OE]

wurthgunge (n.) honor, respect [see *wurth* (n.)]

wurthli (adj.) WORTHY, excellent, of great value [OE]

wurthliche (adv.) WORTHILY, with dignity, splendor [OE]

wurthmunt (n.) honor, worship [OE]

wurthschipe (n.) WORSHIP, honor, recognition [OE]

wydewen (n. pl.) see *widewe* (n.)

yape (adj.) clever, shrewd; nimble, active [OE]

yare (adv.) a long time ago, in time past, formerly [OE; ModE *yore*]

yarketh (v., pres. 3 sing.) prepares, makes ready for (past part. *i-yarket*) [OE]

yarow (adj.) ready, prepared [OE]

ydelnesse (n.) see *idelnesse* (n.)

ye (interj.) YEAH, yes; indeed [OE]; (person pron., 2 pl., nominative form) you, you all [OE]

yeddeth (v., pres. 3 sing.) says, speaks [OE]

yef (conj.) IF; to see if [OE]; (v., imper.) see *yeoven* (v.)

yeien, yeiyen (v.) to cry out, shout (imper. pl. *yeieth*; pres. subj. sing. *yeie*; pres. 3 sing. *yeieth*; past subj. sing. *yeide*; past sing. *yeide*; past part. *i-yeiet*) [*OE; d'Ardenne (1961), p. 155]

yein-cume (n.) return, a COMING AGAIN [OE]

yeld (n.) payment [OE; see Ger. *geld* "money"]

yelde(n) (v.) to pay, repay; give, render; restore, compensate for; take vengeance on; YIELD up, give up (imper. sing. *yeld*; imper. pl. *yeldeth, yelde (ye)*; pres. subj. sing. *yelde*; pres. 2 sing. *yeldest*; pres. 3 sing. *yelt, yeldeth*; past: *yulde*; past pl. *yulden*) [OE]

yelp (n.) boasting; glory [OE]

yelpen (v.) to boast, speak vaingloriously; cry aloud, sing aloud; utter a YELP [OE]

yeme (n.) attention, care, heed, caution; *neomen yeme* = to pay attention [OE]

yemeles (adj.) careless, heedless, negligent; (n.) negligence, carelessness

yemelesliche (adv.) carelessly, negligently, inattentively

yemelesschipe (n.) carelessness, inattentiveness, negligence

yemen (v.) to care about, pay attention to, attend to, look after; control, take charge of (pres. 3 sing. *yemeth*) [OE; see *yeme* (n.)]

yeoc (n.) YOKE; (fig.) service [OE]

yeoi (interj.) yes! indeed! [OE]

yeolow (adj.) YELLOW [OE]

yeoniende (adj., pres. part.) gaping (in order to swallow or devour something) [OE; ModE *yawn*]

yeorne (adv.) eagerly, earnestly, diligently, carefully; willingly, gladly; quickly; longingly, YEARNFULLY [OE]

yeornful (adj.) eager, diligent [OE]

yeornfulliche (adv.) eagerly, diligently

yeornliche (adv.) eagerly, earnestly, zealously, diligently (compar. *yeornluker*) [OE]

yeotteth (v., pres. 3 sing.) pours; gushes forth (imper. sing. *yeot*) [OE; see Ger. *giessen*]

yeove (n.) GIFT; grace [OE]

yeove(n) (v.) to GIVE, grant (imper. sing. *yef*; imper. pl. *yeoveth*; pres. subj. sing. *yeove, yeve*; pres. subj. pl. *yeoven*; pres. 2 sing. *yevest*; pres. 3 sing. *yeveth*; pres. pl. *yeoveth*; past part. *i-yeve, i-yeven*; inflected inf. *to yeovene*)

yer (n.) YEAR (pl. *yeres*) [OE]

yerde (n.) rod (for administering punishment), cudgel, stick (pl. *yerden*) [OE]

yet(e) (adv.) YET, still; besides, even; up to now; once, before; at length, ultimately; even now, to this day [OE]

yete (n.) GATE (pl. *yeten*) [OE]

yete-ward (n.) GATE-WARDEN, gatekeeper, porter (gen. sing. *yete-wardes*) [from OE]

yette (v., imper. sing.) grant, allow; bestow, concede; acknowledge, confess (pres. subj. sing. *yetti*; pres. 3 sing. *yetteth*; past sing. *yettede*) [OE influenced by ON; see ModE *yea* "yes"]

yette(n) (adv.) continually, YET, still, further [from OE]

yettunge (n.) permission, consent, granting [see *yette* (v.)]

yicchinde (adj., pres. part.) ITCHING [OE]

yicchunge (n.) itching

yiftes (n. pl.) GIFTS [OE]

yimmes (n. pl.) GEMS [OE]

yim-stan (n.) GEMSTONE, precious gem (pl. *yim-stanes*) [OE]

yirni (v.) to YEARN for, long for; to express a desire for, request (pres. 1 sing. *yirne*; past part. *i-yirned*) [OE]

yirnunge (n.) YEARNING, desire

yiscere (n.) a covetous person, one who longs enviously for something [see *yiscin* (v.)]

yisc(e)unge (n.) covetousness, avarice, lust (to have something) (gen. sing. *yisceunges*)

yiscin (v.) to covet, lust for (pres. 3 sing. *yisceth*) [OE]

yiver(e) (adj.) greedy, gluttonous; avaricious [OE]

yiverliche (adv.) voraciously, gluttonously, ravenously; greedily

yivernesse (n.) greediness, avarice; voracity, gluttony [OE]

ymagnes (n. pl.) IMAGES, devotional images of saints [OF]

ymne (n.) HYMN [OF, from Lat.]

yond, yont (prep.) over, throughout [OE; ModE *beyond*]

Yong-dayes (n. pl.) processional days, days on which processions take place [for first element, see *gan* (v.)]

ypallage (n.) HYPALLAGE, a rhetorical figure; OED: "A figure of speech in which there is an interchange of two elements of a proposition, the natural relations of these being reversed" [OF or Lat.]

ypocresie (n.) HYPOCRISY [OF]

ypocrite (n.) HYPOCRITE [OF]

yuhethe (n.) YOUTH, time of youth or childhood [OE]

yuhethehad (n.) YOUTHHOOD, youth [OE]

yulunges (n. pl.) deceptions, ruses; bewitchings [?related to OE *geog(e)lere* "magician"]

yung(e) (adj.) YOUNG (compar. *yungre*) [OE]

yur (n.) howl, roaring [OE, probably imitative, like ModE *grrr*!]

zedual (n.) SETWALL, a medicinal herb native to India [AF]

Volumes in the Middle English Texts Series

The Floure and the Leafe, *The Assembly of Ladies*, and *The Isle of Ladies*, ed. Derek Pearsall (1990)

Three Middle English Charlemagne Romances, ed. Alan Lupack (1990)

Six Ecclesiastical Satires, ed. James M. Dean (1991)

Heroic Women from the Old Testament in Middle English Verse, ed. Russell A. Peck (1991)

The Canterbury Tales: Fifteenth-Century Continuations and Additions, ed. John M. Bowers (1992)

Gavin Douglas, *The Palis of Honoure*, ed. David Parkinson (1992)

Wynnere and Wastoure and The Parlement of the Thre Ages, ed. Warren Ginsberg (1992)

The Shewings of Julian of Norwich, ed. Georgia Ronan Crampton (1993)

King Arthur's Death: The Middle English Stanzaic Morte Arthur and Alliterative Morte Arthure, ed. Larry D. Benson and Edward E. Foster (1994)

Lancelot of the Laik and Sir Tristrem, ed. Alan Lupack (1994)

Sir Gawain: Eleven Romances and Tales, ed. Thomas Hahn (1995)

The Middle English Breton Lays, ed. Anne Laskaya and Eve Salisbury (1995)

Sir Perceval of Galles and Ywain and Gawain, ed. Mary Flowers Braswell (1995)

Four Middle English Romances: Sir Isumbras, Octavian, Sir Eglamour of Artois, Sir Tryamour, ed. Harriet Hudson (1996)

The Poems of Laurence Minot (1333–1352), ed. Richard H. Osberg (1996)

Medieval English Political Writings, ed. James M. Dean (1996)

The Book of Margery Kempe, ed. Lynn Staley (1996)

Amis and Amiloun, Robert of Cisyle, and Sir Amadace, ed. Edward E. Foster (1997)

The Cloud of Unknowing, ed. Patrick J. Gallacher (1997)

Robin Hood and Other Outlaw Tales, ed. Stephen Knight and Thomas Ohlgren (1997)

The Poems of Robert Henryson, ed. Robert L. Kindrick (1997)

Moral Love Songs and Laments, ed. Susanna Greer Fein (1998)

John Lydgate, *Troy Book: Selections*, ed. Robert R. Edwards (1998)

Thomas Usk, *The Testament of Love*, ed. R. Allen Shoaf (1998)

Prose Merlin, ed. John Conlee (1998)

Middle English Marian Lyrics, ed. Karen Saupe (1998)

John Metham, *Amoryus and Cleopes*, ed. Stephen F. Page (1999)

Four Romances of England: King Horn, Havelok the Dane, Bevis of Hampton, Athelston, ed. Ronald B. Herzman, Graham Drake, Eve Salisbury (1999)

The Assembly of Gods: Le Assemble de Dyeus, or Banquet of Gods and Goddesses, with the Discourse of Reason and Sensuality, ed. Jane Chance (1999)

Thomas Hoccleve, *The Regiment of Princes*, ed. Charles R. Blyth (1999)

John Capgrave, *The Life of St. Katherine*, ed. Karen Winstead (1999)

John Gower, *Confessio Amantis*, Vol. 1, ed. Russell A. Peck (2000)

Richard the Redeless and *Mum and the Sothsegger*, ed. James Dean (2000)

Walter Hilton, *Scale of Perfection*, ed. Thomas Bestul (2000)

Other TEAMS Publications

Documents of Practice Series:

Love and Marriage in Late Medieval London, by Shannon McSheffrey (1995)

A Slice of Life: Selected Documents of Medieval English Peasant Experience, edited, translated, and with an introduction by Edwin Brezette DeWindt (1996)

Sources for the History of Medicine in Late Medieval England, by Carole Rawcliffe (1996)

Regular Life: Monastic, Canonical, and Mendicant Rules, selected with an introduction by Douglas J. McMillan and Kathryn Smith Fladenmuller (1997)

Commentary Series:

Commentary and Notes on the Book of Jonah, Haimo of Auxerre, translated with an introduction by Deborah Everhart (1993)

Medieval Exegesis in Translation: Commentaries on the Book of Ruth, translated with an introduction by Lesley Smith (1996)

Nicholas of Lyra's Apocalypse Commentary, translated with an introduction and notes by Philip D. W. Krey (1997)

Rabbi Ezra Ben Solomon of Gerona: Commentary on the Song of Songs and Other Kabbalistic Commentaries, selected, translated, and annotated by Seth Brody (1998)

To order please contact:

MEDIEVAL INSTITUTE PUBLICATIONS
Western Michigan University
Kalamazoo, MI 49008–5432
Phone (616) 387–8755
FAX (616) 387–8750

http://www.wmich.edu/medieval/mip/index.html